# Medicine in the Twentieth Century

# Medicine in the Twentieth Century

Edited by

**Roger Cooter**

*Wellcome Unit for the History of Medicine*
*University of East Anglia, UK*

and

**John Pickstone**

*Wellcome Unit for the History of Medicine*
*University of Manchester, UK*

**harwood academic publishers**
Australia • Canada • France • Germany • India • Japan • Luxembourg • Malaysia
The Netherlands • Russia • Singapore • Switzerland

Amsteldijk 166
1st Floor
1079 LH Amsterdam
The Netherlands

British Library Cataloguing in Publication Data
ISBN 90-5702-479-9

# Contents

# LIST OF CONTRIBUTORS

OLGA AMSTERDAMSKA
Department of Science Dynamics, University of Amsterdam, Amsterdam,
The Netherlands

WARWICK ANDERSON
Department of History of Science, Melbourne University, Melbourne, Australia

DAVID ARMSTRONG
Department of General Practice and Primary Care, Guy's Hospital, London, UK

BRIAN BALMER
Department of Science and Technology Studies, University College London, UK

VIRGINIA BERRIDGE
London School of Hygiene and Tropical Medicine, London, UK

STUART BLUME
Department of Science Dynamics, University of Amsterdam, Amsterdam,
The Netherlands

JOANNA BOURKE
School of History, Classics and Archaeology, Birkbeck College, London, UK

ALLAN M. BRANDT
Department of History of Science, University of Harvard, Massachusetts, USA

FRANCESCA BRAY
Department of Anthropology, University of California, Santa Barbara, USA

JOAN BUSFIELD
Department of Sociology, University of Essex, Colchester, UK

DAVID CANTOR
National Institute of Health, Bethesda, Maryland, USA

ROGER COOTER
Wellcome Unit for the History of Medicine, School of History, University of East
Anglia, Norwich, UK

MARK G. FIELD
Davis Center for Russian Studies, Harvard University, Massachusetts, USA

MARTHA GARDNER
Department of History of Science, Harvard University, Massachusetts, USA

JANET GOLDEN
Department of History, Rutgers University – Camden, Camden, New Jersey, USA

JORDAN GOODMAN
Manchester School of Management, UMIST, Manchester, UK

LESLEY A. HALL
The Wellcome Trust Centre, London, UK

JULIAN TUDOR HART
Welsh Institute for Health and Social Care, University of Glamorgan, Pontypridd, UK

ANJA HIDDINGA
Department of Science Dynamics, University of Amsterdam, Amsterdam,
The Netherlands

JOEL D. HOWELL
Clinical Scholars Program, University of Michigan, Ann Arbor, USA

MARK S.R. JENNER
Department of History, University of York, York, UK

RUDOLF KLEIN
King's Fund, London

GERRY LARKIN
School of Social Science and Law, Sheffield Hallam University, Sheffield, UK

CHRISTOPHER LAWRENCE
: The Wellcome Trust Centre, London, UK

SUSAN E. LEDERER
: Department of History of Medicine, Yale University, USA

JANE LEWIS
: Department of Sociology and Social Policy, University of Oxford, UK

ILANA LÖWY
: Centre de Recherche Medicine, Maladie et Sciences Sociales, Paris, France

HILARY MARLAND
: Department of History, University of Warwick, Coventry, UK

MARK S. MICALE
: Department of History, University of Illinois at Urbana – Champaign, USA

ANNE-MARIE MOULIN
: Institut Recherche Pour le Developpment, Paris, France

RANDALL M. PACKARD
: Department of History, Emory University, Georgia, USA

NAOMI PFEFFER
: School of Community Health, University of North London, London, UK

JOHN PICKSTONE
: Centre for the History of Science, Technology and Medicine, University of Manchester, Manchester, UK

PATRICE PINELL
: CSE, IRESCO, Paris, France

DOROTHY PORTER
: School of History, Classics and Archaeology, Birkbeck College, London, UK

ANNE MARIE RAFFERTY
: London School of Hygiene and Tropical Medicine, London, UK

NAOMI ROGERS
: Women and Gender Studies Program, Yale University, USA

MIKE SAKS
: Faculty of Health and Community Studies, De Montfort University, Leicester, UK

LYN SCHUMAKER
: Centre for the History of Science, Technology and Medicine, University of Manchester, Manchester, UK

SONU SHAMDASANI
: The Wellcome Trust Centre, London, UK

JENNIFER STANTON
: London School of Hygiene and Tropical Medicine, London, UK

STEVE STURDY
: Science Studies Unit, University of Edinburgh, Edinbugh, UK

PAT THANE
: School of Social Science, University of Sussex, Brighton, UK

BERTRAND O. TAITHE
: Department of History, University of Manchester, Manchester, UK

MATHEW THOMSON
: Department of History, University of Warwick, Coventry, UK

TOM TREASURE
: Consultant Cardiothoracic Surgeon, St. George's Hospital, London, UK

JON TURNEY
: Department of Science and Technology Studies, University College London, London, UK

RUSSELL VINER
   Paediatric Services Department, Middlesex Hospital, London, UK

CHARLES WEBSTER
   All Souls College, University of Oxford, Oxford, UK

PAUL WEINDLING
   School of Humanities, Oxford Brookes University, Oxford, UK

MICHAEL WORBOYS
   Cultural Research Institute, Sheffield Hallam University, Sheffield, UK

# Introduction

ROGER COOTER AND JOHN PICKSTONE

I n many ways the history of medicine in the twentieth century is the history of the twentieth century. Through the century, medicine became increasingly central to changing expectations of life and death and to institutions of welfare and education. It pervasively and profoundly influenced the ways in which people came to maintain their bodies, to mind their minds and to interact with the world around them. The 'proper' food to be eaten, air to be breathed, 'dirt' to be avoided, thoughts to be thought, and dispositions to be analyzed, were strongly determined by bio-medical and psycho-medical knowledge and practices. Materially, conceptually, intellectually, socially and culturally, medicine in the twentieth century affected the human condition in unprecedented ways. Although the power of doctors was often contested by politicians and publics, and their social authority frequently challenged, has any other profession acquired such far-reaching influence in the governance of human life?

Nor can this be the only reason for considering the history of medicine as integral to the history of the century. With as much as sixteen percent of some countries' GNP expended on health care (US, 1990s), medicine over the twentieth century became crucial to the political economy of modern nations; politicians and publics alike were 'taxed' by the increasing costs of medical care, disability welfare, and malpractice suits. And through the growth of the medical insurance and pharmaceutical industries — to say nothing of the gene business, the test-tube baby industry, and the trade in body parts — medicine became entwined with global capitalism. (In turn, the profits of the insurance and pharmaceutical industries fed the academic history of medicine: The Burroughs-Wellcome Foundation, The Lilly Foundation, The Hannah Foundation and, above all, The Wellcome Trust being among its generous patrons.)

Not surprisingly then, innovations in medicine and medical science have frequently been regarded as measures of the century. High on the list is chemotherapy — from Paul Ehrlich's 'magic bullet' for syphilis in 1917, to antibiotics, beta blockers and psychoactive drugs. 'Revolutionary' achievements in diagnostic technology cascaded from the discovery of X-rays at the end of the nineteenth century, through ECGs and fetal monitors, to CAT and MRI scans; and from Wassermann tests to diagnostic breathalyzers. Transplant surgery, sensationalized through the first successful heart transplant in 1967, became as memorable as the first men to land on the moon (1969) or the assassination of Kennedy (1963). As marvelous for an interwar generation was the isolation of insulin (1926), the discovery of vitamins around the same time, and the identification of the sex hormones in the 1930s (their later synthesis leading ultimately to the marketing of the birth-control pill in the early 1960s). From the modeling of DNA (1953) to the human genome project, molecular genetics is hailed as the major scientific and technological achievement of recent times.

But the record is not all rosy: eugenics, thalidomide and lobotomies cast long shadows. And rather more memorable than the worldwide eradication of smallpox is the barbarism committed by Nazi and Japanese doctors during the Second World War. Appalling discrepancies in the care of patients — depending usually on their incomes, class, color, and religions, or on the region, country and continent of their abode — were all-too-common a feature of the twentieth century. A catalogue of unnecessary and harmful drugs, bogus conditions, worse-than-useless therapies and less-than-competent practices provided rich pickings for the critics of medicine, from George Bernard Shaw to Ivan Illich.

Indeed, by the last decades of the century, many of the criticisms of modern western medicine were accepted by the profession itself. Within medical journalism at least, the high-cost of medical technology came to be seen not as the solution to a problem, but as "the problem that needs a solution."[1] Others in the profession went some way to "share the blame for playing to the gallery of public opinion in promoting medical advance as a series of breakthroughs."[2] And when the profession announced its attachment to 'evidenced-based medicine' as new, it invited concern — at least about the basis of its previous practice.

'Medicine' seems so all-permeating, in part because its meanings are so protean. 'Modern medicine' can refer to that which we take or receive 'for our own good' from a bottle, a package of pills, or a hypodermic syringe; or to the multi-national industries that produce such products. Commonly it is equated with the professional practice of healers (licensed or unlicensed) in their various economic, political, and social settings. But it can also refer to the institutions of research, education and healing — whether in the form of journals, societies, hospitals, or the premises of individual practitioners. And 'medicine' is also the provision made by nation states for the well-being and surveillance of their populations — in the furtherance of labor-power, war or life-styles; through compulsory insurance schemes or nationalized health services.

Much of 'medicine' is knowledge about the body in sickness and health, but medical knowledge does not exist independently of the social, political and cultural contexts in which it is produced and used. All knowledge involves assumptions and implicit power-relations, but medical knowledge — especially in the twentieth century — may be unique in the extent and depth of its social penetration.

Whereas much 'natural science' is remote from everyday life, most medical science is intimate, whether we experience it as healthy citizens or sick persons. Knowledge about the causes of cancer or of AIDS, for example, alters consciousness and behavior in ways that discoveries of new galaxies do not. Germ theory, commercially exploited early in the twentieth century, not only altered conceptions of dirt and attitudes to putative agents of infection such as flies, but also rendered arbitrary the Victorian moral universe which had linked social class and disease causation — infections might now be picked up anywhere, not only in the miasmatic confines of the poor.[3] Likewise, with the science of nutrition that emerged towards the end of the nineteenth century, traditional discourses about good food gave way to thermodynamic understandings of calorific intakes — so helping position the laboring body as a mechanical, calculable economic unit of production. And at the dawn of the twenty-first century, the language of information technology has become common in biomedicine,[4] when for most of the twentieth century the dominant metaphors were drawn from engineering and warfare.

Although mid-twentieth century sociological polemics against the 'medicalization' of social life may have exaggerated the power of the medical profession over 'docile bodies', and although late twentieth-century laities were often sufficiently empowered to stand as jury for medicine on trial, yet even so, Western bio-medicine remains a pervasive secular force, shaping and shaped by modern culture and cosmology. It cannot be treated simply as the sum of its technical achievements, nor merely as knowledge for the purposes of healing and caring. As for other historical periods, twentieth-century medicine has to be seen as part and parcel of its times, not above or outside them.

To put it another way, the history of medicine in the twentieth century is about the history of power: not just the power of knowledge in the abstract, but power in the hands of doctors and (increasingly) patients; in the hands of institutions such as churches, charities, insurance companies, and pharmaceutical manufacturers, and, not least, in the hands of industrialists, economists and governments in peacetime and war. So, too, the writing of medical history, inevitably, was bound up with the complex, ever-changing politics of medicine.

The profession of medical history expanded rapidly from the 1960s, and much of the new intellectual impetus came from the anti-authoritarian 'cultural revolution' of the 1960s and 1970s. Histories of medical progress — of the growth of science, professions and welfare — were challenged by histories of surveillance, of social control, and the de-skilling of patients. But that moment proved fraught with contradictions: the anti-professionalism of radical critics and feminists was also to fuel the 'free' market ideologues and anti-abortionists of the 1980s and 90s. By the end of the century, attitudes to medical science were ambivalent and complex, and debates over services seemed ever more multi-focal and multi-vocal. Current historiography of medicine is correspondingly varied, complex and multi-layered.

As is evident in the chapters that follow, historians now stress local and regional phenomenon as well as the national and global, and they attend to the complex interactions. The historiography recognizes major hinges, not least in the politics of health-care delivery; but it also attends to subtle shifts of power and discourse, the analysis of which can neither be easy nor simple. Were it easy, there would be little need for the efforts of historians; the polemical, commercial, and political self-servings of others within and without medicine would suffice.

Three factors compound the difficulty of analyzing twentieth century medicine. The first is the paucity of historical studies upon which one can build. Those that exist refer primarily to the first half of the century. As in historical studies generally, the Second World War is still often taken as a cut-off date — a telling reminder of the way in which wars continue to structure historical imagination; in British health studies the usual marker is 1948 with the post-war implementation of the National Health Service.[5] We have a few 'triumphs-and-failures' historical overviews of post-war medicine written by doctors,[6] and a number of surveys of national medical politics that include later periods;[7] otherwise we must rely largely on monographs on a few particular issues, such as abortion and birth control.[8]

The sheer novelty of some of the subject matters of late twentieth-century medicine is a second challenge. Many of the contributors to this volume have had to cut interpretive pathways across rapidly changing fields. Indeed, to greater or lesser degrees this has been the intellectual challenge for all our contributors, and we trust it will be so for our readers as well. In the absence of secondary literatures to synthesize, our contributors were encouraged to surf the primary literature, speculate, hypothesize and innovate.

A third problem is periodization. We are only beginning to exercise our medico-historical imaginations on the century as a whole. The twentieth century has already been characterized as that of 'total war', an 'age of extremes', and 'the century of Freud'. Medicine in the twentieth century could easily be squared with each of these depictions, yet, obviously, all such characterizations are very partial. Centuries are arbitrary and misleading blocks of time; the unity is deceptive. From the point of view of welfare ideologies, and possibly 'new age' healing movements too,[9] the twentieth-century's end and its beginning might be regarded as having more in common with each other than with the middle decades. For medical science, we might date the century from the conceptual revolution around bacteriology some two decades before 1900. The present 'new challenges' — genetics, new reproductive technologies and informatics — often appear as the creation of the last quarter century; perhaps medical historians will come to write of a 'long twenty-first century', dated from c1975.

For many commentators on medicine, especially those concerned with science and with the scale of organization, the century hinged around the Second World War. Medical research, medical education, medical industries (and in the UK, medical services) were transformed by massive public investment, carried forward from the war effort and reinforced by the cold war. With that investment came new forms of structuring and new relations between professions and governments. From the inside, it seemed to some that medicine became far more politicized during the second half of the century. "Looking back," reflected an eminent American surgeon in 1995,

> it seems that 50 years ago all this government consulting was somehow more leisurely and joyous than it is today. Less hassle and less political. More the feeling of a community of scientists joining in patriotic service. Under President Nixon, even appointments to NHI advisory councils became politicized for the first time. Some of the joy of public service disappeared.[10]

From a very different perspective, Pickstone, in his introductory essay, also makes a hinge at mid century. Behind the continued growth of welfare and science, he notes a major shift in the focus of the 'political economy' of medicine — the rapid, silent fading of western governments' preoccupations with the health and strength of working men, soldiers and mothers that had been so prominent in the first half of the century. But for many of our contributors, the mid-century was more a change of gear than of direction. Many see the decades from *c*1880 to *c*1970 as marked by the increasing authority of medicine — the rate of change may have varied with economic conditions, but the direction was clear and fairly constant. With regard to the last quarter of the century, perhaps paradoxically, there is considerable unanimity among historians. Almost all our authors detect a loss of confidence in science, the professions, and state welfare from about 1970. Was it easier for us to get a perspective on the times we lived through, than on the times of our parents and grandparents? Or will a more distant view of our *fin de siecle* reveal a different, more varied picture? Time may tell.

ORGANIZATION

As all of this suggests, there are very many ways in which a history of twentieth-century medicine could be organized, and as many good reasons for not choosing our way! Indeed, were we to begin again, we would doubtless make different choices. In order to be as inclusive as possible in our coverage of the different kinds of contexts and social relations that have borne upon medicine in the twentieth century, we chose to structure its history according to a tripartite division of *Power*, *Bodies* and *Experiences*.

By *Power* we mean both the general political-economic systems under which medicine has been organized by nation states, and the different kind of agencies and brokers involved in the structuring of health care. We have not sought to cover the medical politics of every nation state; most of our contributors focused on Britain, western Europe and the US, but we have also included a chapter on the former Soviet Union and some discussion of the third world. Nor did we try to cover all the agencies of medicine; rather, we focused on the dominant forms of expression of medical power over the century. Thus in this section of the book, after two contrasting interpretative survey chapters, the organization is largely epochal. It runs from the medicine of the Progressive Era at the beginning of the century, through to that associated with the counter culture of the 1960s and 1970s, to that following the 'crisis' of welfare states towards the end of the century. Interspersed are chapters on colonial and post-colonial medicine, the pharmaceutical industry, and on medicine in relation to technology and industry.

Our second section, *Bodies,* is concerned more with the changing concepts, representations, and discursive frameworks of medicine in the twentieth century. Although 'the body' now features prominently in the titles of hundreds of social, historical, and anthropological studies of medicine and culture ('embodiment' and 'the politics of the body' being favored tropes), we use it here to include not only the corporeal/material entity that has long been at the center of the medical gaze, but also the lay and professional packages (and packers) of knowledge that have contributed to the making of the human body over the course of the century. Thus the ordering of this section is thematic, from the 'Healthy Body' through to the 'Dead Body', and the perspective is unashamedly Western. Chapters explore how various configurations of the body (including body history) have been fashioned and utilized by practitioners and publics. They reveal that different constructions/reductions of the healthy/diseased body have different histories, each being bound to political, social and cultural forces as well as, in most cases, to scientific and technological ones. "Bodies embody", as one historian recently put it; they are "the business of medicine, but they are also the matrix in which are written the rights a society allots to people of various genders, races, and classes."[11]

The final section, *Experiences,* engages with some of the major sites where medicine has been encountered in the twentieth century. One of these is the media, with which the section opens; its representations of doctors, patients and medical institutions have become for many people (perhaps now the majority) the principal point of entry into modern medicine. Other sites include those of patients and patient groups, such as sick children, the aged, those with cancer or with AIDS, and those in mental asylums. So far as it is possible for the historian to do so, this section views medicine from the 'bottom up', in contrast to section one's 'power down' orientation, or section two's conceptual approach to bodies of knowledge and practice.

But not all of the perspectives gathered in this third section are those of patients. Included are chapters on institutions, such as hospitals and the military, and types of health-care workers, such as nurses, general practitioners and surgeons. This section also contains a chapter on China, as a geo-political site where medical encounters differ from those common to the West. Last, but not least, we include a chapter on malaria, in part to construct a twentieth-century perspective on medicine from the point of view of an agent of infection, the mosquito.

Even so, our coverage is limited. As within each of the chapters, much of the history of twentieth-century medicine has had to be radically compressed. The medical experience of different ethnic, racial and religious groups, for example, does not here receive the focused attention it deserves. Conspicuously absent from the section on power are the chapters we failed to secure on philanthropy and on the insurance industry; and among the 'missing bodies', as it were, are chapters drawn from anthropology, linguistics, discourse analysis, and political theory. Some of these omissions and silences can be blamed on the limits of space, and on our failure to locate the appropriate historical expertise. Nevertheless, we trust that our selection and its organization is sufficiently broad and ingenious to provide more than a predictable introduction to the last 100 years of medicine. We also hope that the interpretations offered will stimulate and provoke discussion and debate.

Of course, in the final analysis there can be no 'final analysis' of medicine in the twentieth century, not now, not ever. History may be about the past, but its interpretations are driven by the conceptual frameworks and political agendas of the present. Through history we render explicit some of what may be implicit in the conceptual world we have inherited, and hence clarify what may be clouded in myth. To do so for medicine in the twentieth century is to expose, comprehend, and invite for transformation, some of the constraints and possibilities under which we continue to live in the twenty-first century.

### ACKNOWLEDGEMENTS

Both editors would like to thank the contributors for their forbearance, and Joan Mottram for her editorial assistance.

### REFERENCES

1.  Chris McManus, 'The physician-as-scientist; the physician-as-shaman', *Lancet* (25 Oct. 1997), p. 1257.
2.  Mac Armstrong (BMA secretary), 'We must not let science bind us', *British Medical Journal, News Review* (March 1995).
3.  Nancy Tomes, *The Gospel of Germs: Men, Women, and the Microbe in American Life.* (Cambridge, MA: Harvard University Press, 1998).
4.  Scott Montgomery, 'Codes and Combat in Biomedical Discourse', *Science as Culture* (1991), **12**: 341–90. See also Susan Sontag, *Illness as Metaphor and AIDS and its Metaphors* (Penguin, 1991), pp. 65–72, 177–80.
5.  Rudolf Klein, *The Politics of the National Health Service.* (2nd edn., London: Longman, 1989), and Charles Webster, *The Health Services Since the War.* 2 vols (London: HMSO, 1988, 1996).
6.  Stephen Lock, 'Medicine in the Second Half of the Twentieth Century' in Irvine Loudon (ed.), *An Illustrated History of Western Medicine.* (Oxford University Press, 1997), 123–44.
7.  See, for example, Helen Jones, *Health and Society in Twentieth Century Britain.* (London: Longman, 1994); and Virginia Berridge, *Health and Society in Britain Since 1939.* (Cambridge University Press, 1999).
8.  Linda Gordon, *Woman's Body, Woman's Right: a social history of birth control in America.* (Harmondsworth: Penguin, 1976), Kristin Luker, *Abortion and the Politics of Motherhood.* (Berkeley: University of California Press, 1984) and Leslie J. Reagan, *When Abortion was a Crime: Women, Medicine and Law in the United States, 1867–1973.* (Berkeley: University of California Press, 1997).
9.  James Beckford, 'The World Images of New Religious and Healing Movements' in R. Kenneth Jones (ed.), *Sickness and Sectarianism.* (Aldershot: Gower, 1985), 72–112.
10. Francis D. Moore, *A Miracle and a Privilege: recounting a half century of surgical advance.* (Washington, D.C.: Joseph Henry Press, 1995), p. 281.
11. Christopher Hamlin, *Public Health and Social Justice in the Age of Chadwick.* (Cambridge University Press, 1998), p. 17.

## CHAPTER 1

# Production, Community and Consumption: The Political Economy of Twentieth-Century Medicine

### JOHN PICKSTONE

There are two complementary questions to be asked of twentieth–century medicine. What are its major features within a longer history of medicine? And, what features does twentieth-century medicine share with the wider political economy of that century? This chapter is focused on the latter question, but first I introduce the former.

Until the 1960s the answer to the first question would have seemed indisputable. In the history of medicine, the twentieth century (especially if it could begin about 1880) was the century of medical *science*, of the undisputed authority of the medical *profession*, and of the extensive involvement of *governments* in the support of clinical medicine as well as of public health. This great troika of progress — science, profession, state — has been the basis of many histories of medicine, whichever element they stressed.

Since the 1960s more critical attitudes have spread among the public (and among historians). Medical science now seems a worry as well as a resource, and the authority of doctors has diminished under criticism from left-wing sociologists and from right-wing free-marketeers and proponents of management. Throughout much of the world there has been a 'rolling back' of welfare, not necessarily in terms of total expenditure, but in the transfer of some functions to the private sector and a general pessimism about the possibility of maintaining comprehensive medical services through *public* funding. In some countries the 'rolling back' has been a result of political conviction, e.g. Thatcherite Britain; in most countries there is a fear of exponential cost increases; and in Eastern Europe and much of Africa, state services have partially collapsed, forcing patients into such private provision as they can find and afford. So histories of the 'rise' in status of science, professions or welfare, are now also histories of 'falls' — albeit relatively small falls. That might be said to be the profile of several of the following articles, including the chapter by Allan Brandt and Martha Gardner which is placed as a second introduction. But 'rise' and 'fall' still suggests a linear history, albeit no longer unidirectional, whilst one aim of this book is to anatomize continuing, contested dynamics.

For example, I would wish to point to the proliferation of medical professionals — within and outwith the institutions of orthodox medicine. In this respect the historiography of twentieth-century medicine echoes that of the early modern period which has stressed the variety of practitioners, especially in the 'informal sector'. Such historiography combines with medical anthropology to remind us that even in the 1950s, medicine was not just a matter of medical authority and wonder drugs — it has always been intricately intertwined with personal belief, family life and neighborhood support systems. And to discuss medical 'consumerism,' so evident at the end of the twentieth century, is to recall the long history of medical commerce, so well illuminated by historians of the eighteenth century and by those who have studied patent medicines in and beyond the nineteenth.

Another theme now coming to the fore is medicine in the third world. Some decades after decolonization, we are able to place imperialism and its medical branch — tropical medicine — within a historical perspective, and to ask how this episode in the history of non-Western countries corresponded to the contemporary metropolitan histories. For this reason, I would have liked this chapter to be more international, but, like most of our contributors, I have neither the range of knowledge required nor the resources to conduct the necessary explorations in a complex, patchy and ill-coordinated literature. Like most of them, I concentrate on what I know best — Britain, and I gesture towards other countries — Western and non-Western. Given the scholarly investment in history of medicine over recent decades, this collective lack of international accounts is properly a matter for apology. (Historians are so good at miniatures, so timid in attempting larger pictures.) But in compensation, I have tried to focus this essay on themes that might provide a basis for truly comparative history.

I will deal but lightly with medical science (the focus of the following chapter), concentrating instead on the political economy of medicine — the politics of medical services and the 'purposes' of medicine as they appeared in public discussions over the century. My themes are those of my title — *production, community* and *consumption,* which I see as central not just to modern medicine but to the political economy of the century, and thus as answering my *second* opening question.

## MODELLING PUBLIC MEDICINE

This chapter explores the historical dynamics of three 'types' of medicine — productionist, communitarian and consumerist — which might be said to be *successively* characteristic of the political economy of medicine during the twentieth century.

I use the term *'productionist medicine'* to refer to the concern with the health and strength of workforces and armed forces and with their reproduction, that was central to so much discussion of medicine in the first half of the century. I choose the term *'communitarian medicine'* for medicine as expressing and developing a sense of social solidarity, either by charity or by statutory means; public-service medicine, not least the mid-century National Health Service, seems to me one of the *moral* achievements of this century. By *'consumerist medicine'* I point to medicine(s) as a commodity, chosen by individuals, usually in free markets (though I will argue that 'consumerist' attitudes are now widespread in the public sector also).

I use these terms to link medicine to wider economic and political histories. They seem to me useful partly because they cut across the usual divisions between public and private, welfare services and markets. Thus, though states were chiefly responsible for productionist medicine, industrial companies and trades unions sometimes shared the same interests, hoping to maximize the productivity of their workplaces as well as the national work-force. Communitarian medicine can be found both in state-services and in medical charities. 'Consumerism' suggests individual choices by patients/consumers (as opposed to choices by governments or professionals): but we should also recall the 'patients' associations' (groupings of sufferers from particular diseases), some of which have developed as 'group consumers' to lobby or pay for the services and research which they as a collective deem important.

I deploy these 'kinds of medicines' as ideal types in the Weberian sense, and with the usual warnings. Most specimens of medicine-in-action will approximate to one type more than to the others, but all specimens may include all my types (*and* others). Thus a baby-welfare clinic may have been set-up to create a stronger population, but it may also help build a community, and/or sell orange juice. For such reasons it is hard to quantify the balance between the types and the changes over time; one service may have multiple meanings. Even so, one may venture a narrative for twentieth-century Britain, not as a simple *sequence*, but in terms of shifting emphases within a dynamic system.

My story features *consumption* throughout, but more obviously at the beginning and end of our century. Consumerist medicine is prominent at the start because public-medicine was then relatively small, and at the end because the century has seen a massive growth of medical industries and the spread of consumer attitudes to many areas once immune (universities, public services, etc).

*Communitarianism* was perhaps most obvious at mid-century when for the first time Britain had a universal, state-provided health-care system — a model for much of the West. But the NHS, in this aspect, was built on nineteenth-century foundations — on local medical charities and friendly societies, as well as on the statutory arrangements for National Health Insurance which bound workers into the existing system of national politics. Towards the end of the essay I consider the present and future of 'communitarianism' in the face of globalization of consumerism.

But *'productionism'* has the most remarkable profile. Though historians know the lineament of its rise, they have generally failed to note its silent diminution in the West, from around the mid-century. Whilst consumers and communities have always been major aspects of medicine, evident in Victorian Britain and throughout our century, productionist medicine rose to prominence in the early twentieth-century and then so faded that we need reminding of its prior importance. By focusing on *absence* we enhance our understanding of the specificity of our own times.

These three types, then, are the elements of my twentieth-century. But they are not the whole story by any means. I have played down two types of medicine which are central for European states in the *nineteenth century* (and in so doing I fear I may have reduced the applicability of my twentieth-century model for non-Western countries). Here I am thinking of the two linked aspects of 'state medicine' in nineteenth-century liberal states — the medical care of the *destitute,* and that *protection* of the public against hazards which came to be know as 'public-health.'

In a sense, both were about *margins*— about the medical management of people at the margins of the economy, and about protecting living spaces from contamination, contagion, poisons, adulterated food etc. These activities continued to be important in the twentieth-century, but were to some extent subsumed under the 'types' I have already discussed. In advanced societies the 'destitute' came to be treated, more or less, as citizens with special needs (rather than as peculiar objects of welfare); protection from hazard came to be linked to the promotion of public health by *positive* means, often for productionist reasons.

Britain is a good model for political analysis of modern medicine — not because it is typical, but because of the significant discontinuities. At the start of the twentieth-century, Britain was a 'follower' nation in terms of welfare — national health insurance was German, demographic concerns often French. But at mid-century, Britain's NHS was a model for the West, and in the 1980s, Thatcherite Britain became a model for privatization. Arguably these shifts are illuminating even for more continuous medical polities, whether mostly private, e.g. the US, insurance based, e.g. France and Germany, or state provided, e.g. Scandinavia.

To set the scene for these discussions of the twentieth century, we turn now to the dynamics of public medicine in the nineteenth. Again, I focus on Britain, noting that in Continental Europe, the late–century enlargements of state and professional functions were built upon a longer tradition of governmental medicine. In the US, the same trends were superimposed on a larger and stronger medical market than in Britain.

## THE NINETEENTH-CENTURY BACKGROUND

In accounting for the growth of state medicine in the nineteenth century, we may distinguish six areas: the care of the destitute, protection against hazard, the state's own (military) interests, the promotion of medical science, the care of the deserving, and the care of the 'political collective' (the voting classes).

At the start of the nineteenth century, the direct responsibilities of the British state included little besides foreign and military interests. But because of the changes associated with industrialization and urbanization, even liberal states became ever more involved in medicine for civilians, notably with the *institutional care of the destitute* and with the *protection of public health*.

By the late-nineteenth century, in most European countries, institutional accommodation for the poor was supervized by resident doctors and, in some countries, by professional nurses. In continental Europe, many of the big-city poorhouses were centers for medical teaching. In Britain and the USA poorhouses were rarely so used; medical schools used charity hospitals which catered primarily for the deserving poor rather than the destitute.

We can stress here that these services for the destitute were marginal to the economy. They were not *productionist*, not intended to increase the size or strength of the labor force — rather to meet the basic needs of those who by infirmity or incapacity were excluded from the economy of work (and family support). For the working classes, medicine, like the other necessities of life, was meant to be a responsibility of individual families, and usually a function of the medical 'marketplace.'

From around the mid-nineteenth century, however, most European states took some responsibility for supplying clean water and adequate sanitation, usually through the agency of local government. Such measures were prompted by 'revelations' of insanitary conditions, by fear of epidemic diseases crossing social boundaries, and by recognition that huge numbers of 'preventable deaths' among the urban poor were a threat to good order and to the self-image of a Christian nation. In so far as the danger seemed to lie in environmental conditions, rather than individual behavior, the state assumed some responsibility for the protection of the working classes against undue hazard.

The state was *productionist* chiefly for its own armed forces. The maintenance of a standing army and navy involved some investment in medicine and especially hygiene, and the lessons of enlightenment hygienists were here reinforced by nineteenth-century sanitarians. Military authorities took note. The deaths from disease which afflicted armies in peace as in war, were substantially reduced by systematic public health measures applied to readily disciplined populations.

By the 1880s, elite military sanitarians were influential within British public health and more so in Germany, where Koch's bacteriology was strongly identified with military and imperial interests (sometimes in opposition to the more liberal regimes of some German states and free cities). Government use of medical authority in the armed forces was one reason for their support of medical licensing and the privileging of regularly trained medical practitioners (as opposed to fringe practitioners).

In much of continental Europe, the military played a central role in medicine — witness the role of military hospitals in Paris or Berlin. In Britain and America the impact on civilian medicine was probably more limited and more restricted to times of war. The Crimean War and the American Civil War had significant effects on nursing, hospital administration and civilian emergency services.

It was largely in connection with public health — civilian, military and imperial — that states began to sponsor *medico-scientific investigations.* Government commissions in the early-nineteenth century interviewed witnesses or elicited reports on local conditions. In the latter half of the century, the state's medical officers also commissioned laboratory investigations, and by the early-twentieth century substantial programs of laboratory work were undertaken for public inquiries, e.g. on tuberculosis. By this time most regions had public health laboratories which undertook routine bacteriological testing.

The *promotion of medical science* was also central to reforms of medical education, advocated chiefly by medical school staff who wanted salaries for research and teaching (without relying on clinical practices). Such reformers modeled themselves on the 'scientists,' especially chemists, then gaining salaried posts in reformed universities. The claim to support for science was based on the improvement of diagnosis (e.g. by biochemical or histological analysis), and on the supposed ability of laboratory work to turn medical students into 'scientific' clinicians.

Though the state's support of medical science in public health and education was expected in the long-term to reduce mortality and perhaps morbidity, only at the end of the century was it presumed to increase 'national efficiency.' Before then, when 'public health' extended into factories, it was primarily to reduce the scandal of preventable deaths rather than to increase the efficiency of the work force.

If Victorian medicine had a role in 'maintaining' the work-force (other than protection from hazard), it was mostly exercised through the charity sector — *the care of the deserving.* Voluntary hospitals were meant as evidence of Christian benificence on the part of the upper classes, though they were also directly useful to such classes for the care of servants (and by extension, for the care of employees). By the last third of the century, especially in smaller towns, charity hospitals — mostly new — were major foci of civic pride and inter-class solidarity. British hospitals, perhaps more than American, were strongly identified with *place* (rather than religious or racial groupings, or the market interests of doctors). Hospitals rarely competed with each other; they were seen as quasi-civic institutions to which all classes could contribute, and from which the deserving poor could benefit (with no demeaning resort to statutory aid for paupers).

Though some working-class radicals 'saw through' a system in which their financial contributions secured little power (or convenience), most seem to have accepted hospitals as objects of pride. In the early-twentieth century, especially in industrial areas, workers' donations tended to be replaced by contributory schemes, providing the upper-working-classes with insurance for hospital care. Though governors of big city hospitals and many county hospitals were still remote from the working classes, by the inter-war years the facilities in many small industrial towns (or city districts) were seen as peoples' hospitals, an attitude that carried over into the National Health Service after World War Two (WWII).

In some senses, the major extensions of *statutory welfare benefits* introduced between 1900 and 1914 could be seen as state substitutions (or reinforcements) for functions previously thought appropriate only for charity, or for workers' mutual support schemes such as the Friendly Societies which supplied sickness and unemployment benefit. Some of the reforms were modeled on Germany, where after 1870 health insurance had been made compulsory, explicitly to secure the loyalty of the working classes and to prevent their attachment to socialist parties representative of labor. Similarly in Britain, such benefits, along with old-age pensions, were meant to convince working-class (male) voters that 'welfare' was a sound alternative to socialism. Workers were not to be excluded from the citizenry as a result of unemployment, sickness or age.

It was not just in Britain that governments in the new century began to secure 'positive' freedoms for workers, rather than merely providing protection and care 'at the margins.' Most Western states show similar patterns, which can in part be read as responses to the increasing *political* power of the working classes. There is a trajectory here — of increasing franchise and increasing welfare — which was to be played out for much of the twentieth century (and to which we shall return in our discussions of individuals and communities).

But by the opening of the new century, major new factors were in play, strengthening the political-response arguments for welfare, but also stimulating and facilitating a range of new measures for working men and families — the interventions characteristic of 'productionist states' during the first half of the new century.

## THE PRODUCTIONIST STATE

It is hard, *c*2000, to imagine a western state for which the health and strength of the population was a central concern. The productive power of the economy depended on a large, able-bodied (mostly male) work-force. The military forces and the improvement of empire depended on a rich supply of strong young men, and were compromised by the sickly recruits from industrial cities. Future work-forces and armed-forces depended on a good supply of healthy babies and children. So childbirth was to be protected, infants and school children were to be supervised and measured (and sometimes fed). After the Great War, antenatal care was extended and the government supported maternity hospitals. *Families* were one strong focus of welfare policies.

The other focus was *working men*. From 1911 they were granted compulsory medical insurance — extending schemes organized by Friendly Societies. Many doctors resented this intrusion of the state into 'the market,' but many also welcomed the protection from the negotiating powers of the Friendly Societies, and most found the new financial arrangements greatly to their advantage. Chronic diseases, and especially tuberculosis, attracted more attention — partly because death rates for acute infectious diseases were now declining, partly because they were seen as major hindrances to the economy. Especially after the Great War, occupational medicine, physical medicine and rehabilitation came to the fore as means of boosting productive power.

The reasons for the new concern with production and reproduction are not hard to find. By 1900 the major Western nations saw themselves in competition for industrial and imperial advantage. Even liberal states that had benefited from promoting free trade across the globe, began to think in terms of national interest and national efficiency. *Population* seemed central to national efficiency and success, for several, cumulative reasons. Whereas for most of the nineteenth century Britain had seemed to have too many people (and emigration was encouraged), now the population problem was reversed. Even when there was unemployment at home, the colonies (and the armed forces) needed good strong men to bolster Britain's imperial power; but supply was decreasing in quantity and quality. Birth rates were falling (though not so far as in France); the health of the social body was threatened both by middle-class constraints on their own birth rates, and by the 'feckless reproduction' of the lowest classes — the 'social residuum.'

The 'organicism' of social thought in this period echoed the 'biologism' in the understanding of individuals and their connections across generations. In its most conspicuous formulation this was eugenics — the science and art of better breeding. The better classes were to be encouraged to breed more, the social residuum was to be controlled so that poor constitutions, mental defect, and tendencies to crime, alcoholism and prostitution would not be passed on. Some of the leaders of the eugenics movement supposed these characteristics to be inherited in the simple patterns unveiled in pea-plants by the horticultural monk, Gregor Mendel. This strand of human genetics became notorious because of its association with euthanasia and the genocide programs of Nazi Germany.

But belief in heredity was not always negative. A general belief in the inheritance of 'constitutions' was entirely compatible with positive welfare measures, especially for those who did not draw a line between inherited characters and such modifications to individual lives as could not be transmitted. Part of the enthusiasm for state (and voluntary) programs for infants and mothers came from the belief that more was at stake than the well-being of the individual child. If the health of babies could be increased, they would in turn have healthier babies, and so the population could be advanced (by welfare rather than merely by selection). And if potential parents were free of diseases, these would be less likely to affect their children. The application to venereal disease was obvious (and France had compulsory medical examination of intending parents), but the same ideas applied more generally to tuberculosis (and could be extended to mental problems).

Campaigners for health had much evidence on their side. Throughout the first half of the century the curves of mortality against age were shifting downwards while retaining much the same shape (except for infants); each generation seemed healthier than the last. (Only after WWII did these patterns change — partly because of smoking and cancer. Epidemiologists then became so focused on 'presently-acting' factors as to be surprised by studies in the 1980s pointing to the long-term effects of peri-natal deprivation.)[1]

## PRO-NATALISM AND PRODUCTION, 1914–1950

Though WWI has sometimes been presented as the birthplace of modern medical organizations, it might better be seen as a flowering of 'progressive' schemes in a theater of carnage and improvisation. In Britain, the elite of medical science was organized by the new Medical Research Committee (later Council) to research immediate, novel, problems — how best to heal huge and filthy wounds; or what to do about 'shell-shock' or 'disorderly action of the heart.' Clinical specialists, e.g. the nascent orthopedists, were encouraged to set up special services — behind the battlefields and 'at home,' often in association with American teams. Generally, the war involved doctors in organization and bureaucracy of unprecedented vastness; the goals were clearly 'productionist,' returning men to the fight. Though most of the organization vanished at the end of the war as people and institutions reverted to their former functions, some institutions emerged much stronger, and many would-be organizers had tasted the possibilities.

In many European countries, at the end of the war, new Ministries of Health were set up to improve the health of populations, but hopes were often betrayed. For medicine as for higher education, the inter-war decades generally saw consolidations of pre-war initiatives, now beset by economic difficulties. In the UK, the new Ministry changed little in the short-term, partly because of economic recession. In the US the pre-war 'progressive' momentum was lost (though regained in the 'New Deal'). In France, employers and doctors frustrated attempts to extend to the whole country the social-insurance which Alsace-Lorraine enjoyed as a former German region. In Germany, the near revolution and the short-lived left-wing government of Weimar certainly changed the balance of medical politics; in as much as most of the doctors were politically conservative, their opposition to state and insurance medicine deepened.

But, of course, the greatest effects were in the new Soviet Union, where medicine was socialized by the Bolsheviks. They developed a system of hospitals and clinics which greatly impressed visiting Western reformers (not least in the orientation towards industrial production), thus tending to align medical politics with the more general political divides of the 1920s and 1930s. In reaction, the League of Nations and the big American foundations promoted public health measures in Central Europe, supporting the elite doctors who shared their attachment to medical science. The Rockefeller foundation was also very active in Latin America, as informal, scientific, US imperialism increasingly replaced European agencies. In the British Empire, science was supported as a means of 'development' and labor-enhancement. Nutritional researchers (who had previously worked on cattle) applied international standards for diets and so began to suggest that 'malnutrition' was characteristic of Africa.

Population remained a central concern. The loss of actual and potential fathers, 'the best of a generation,' and the continuance of imperial rivalries together underpinned the continuance of pro-natalist policies. Feminist reformers, who in some countries has achieved female suffrage, now campaigned for child-benefit and better maternity services; in the US their successes were a major component of inter-war welfare. New institutions were devised for mothers, adolescents, problem families, etc., and immunization was extended; demography emerged as an academic/policy discipline to address worries about falling birth rates.

But the Great War also had major effects on welfare services for British workers, who were now patients of state-funded medical practice. Questions of organizational efficiency and patterns of work had been much to the fore in armament factories (staffed largely by women), and governments had employed physiologists to investigate fatigue. Such concerns persisted after the War, interwoven with labor-protection legislation, scientific management (Taylorism), and industrial welfare schemes which had roots among Victorian philanthropists, but which in the inter-war years often seemed a 'middle-way' between capitalism and the growing power of labor unions. 'Physiological medicine' was applied to workforces as to fighting forces — the goals were the better 'functioning' of individuals and teams. Models of social organizations as coordinated teams resonated with similar models of biological organisms, and with schemes for the better organization of medicine, e.g. for integrated TB services, or fracture clinics (that would reduce time away from work).

From 1912, workers in Britain received primary medical care paid for partly by employers and the state; the resulting bureaucracy could calculate the costs of illness, not in medicines, but in the loss to industry from absences, sickness payments and impaired efficiency. Health services had the potential to reduce the costs to industry and to the exchequer, partly because preventive measures and timely diagnosis might reduce the need for later treatment.

Nineteenth-century British governments had invested in public health measures; in the new century the productionist state also set up clinics; and between the wars hospital treatments joined the agenda. In Britain, hospitals that had served welfare recipients were upgraded for 'citizens,' isolation hospitals were further medicalized, and doctors in mental asylums tried to find curative routines (e.g. shock therapies) which looked 'medical.' TB services became models of scientific integration between community services, clinics, sanatoria and specialist hospitals. As infectious diseases declined further and people lived longer, cancer emerged as a major public health problem of the 1930s; the solution in the UK (and France) included specialist regional centers for radiotherapy, fed by peripheral clinics — an early model of 'big medicine.' Characteristically, this 'high tech' medicine was often a part of 'public health' programs — an extension of the services developed for acute infectious diseases (with TB as an intermediary). Cancer was a public disease, a disease of the economy, a threat to the population as well as to individuals.

## What Happened to 'Productionist' Medicine?

Historians have been slow to note the eclipse of productionist medicine, for disappearances are less obvious than appearances. Historians working on limited time-scales can share too easily the languages of their periods, forgetting to note the *differences* between periods: similarly, historians working on restricted topics can miss the *generality* of the changes they minutely anatomize. Though historians of reproduction and 'the population question' have noted the post-war demise of

### Table 1: Overall Contrasts in the Public-Medicine of the West (Especially Britain)

|  | *c.* 1870 | early 20th century | late 20th century |
|---|---|---|---|
| **Healthy-labor demand** | | | |
| industry | x | ✓ | x |
| military | x | ✓ | x |
| empire | ? | ✓ | x |
| **Demography** | | | |
| pro-natalism | x | ✓ | x |
| emigration | ✓ | x | x |
| immigration | x | x | ✓ |
| **Birth rate worries** | | | |
| metropolitan | x | too low | x |
| colonies | ? | too low | too high |
| retired population | lowest | low | high |
| % of children. | high | low | lowest |
| women seen as | mothers | mothers | women |
| contraception | little | more | much |
| motherhood concern is | philanthropic | productionist | individual |
| children as | family resource | family & state | commodity |
| **Medicine/Public health (PH)** | | | |
| concern re infections | ✓✓ | ✓ | re-emergent |
| defence is | PH | PH | drugs |
| science for PH | ✓ | ✓✓ | ? |
| medical charity for | Care | Care & Research | Research especially |

pro-natalism in the West and the shift of 'populationist' concerns to third-world 'excesses,' this phenomenon has not been linked to concurrent changes in the economy, demography and politics of the West (see Table 1).

With awful exceptions, including the Jews and Soviet Russia, population losses in the Second World War were considerably less than in the Great War. Indeed, the health of civilian populations in Britain was maintained at a high level (with the exception of groups displaced from long-term hospitals). Pregnant women, babies and children were well-nourished on milk, orange juice, cod-liver oil and malt, variously supplied by public clinics. School children were offered treatments for teeth and eyes, with sun-rays for the puny. These services built on inter-war developments but were now more or less universal.

After the war came a baby boom, so that when the Royal Commission on Population reported in 1949,[2] the usual inter-war fears of impending population decline were disappearing. But the change was more than local and temporary — the context of calculation had also changed. It was clear by the 1950s that the Empire would be dismantled as colonies gained independence. Emigration to Australia and New Zealand was encouraged by Commonwealth governments pursuing 'whites only' policies; but though there were many in Britain who looked to the development of the white Commonwealth, populating it was no longer an aim of the British state. Nor did manpower seem important to the military, who were increasingly focused on strategy for nuclear wars that were expected to be brief.

The '50s in Britain were times of high employment, but there were few calls for more babies. If workers were needed, they could be imported from the 'New Commonwealth,' especially the West Indies, and later from South Asia. Indeed, non-white immigration had become a political issue by the 1960s; though public services, including the NHS, now depended heavily on 'colored' immigrants, the continued flow was seen as threatening the job supply for natives. And the nature of work was also changing. As heavy industry such as ship-building declined, the future appeared to lie with the 'new' industries developed in southern England between the wars, relying more on skill than brawn.

The changes in the health service reinforced the wider changes in economy and society. Maternity homes, which had been part of 'public health,' were transferred in 1948 to a national hospital service, led by hospital consultants. Pressure for more maternity beds persisted, not least from women's groups, but was not expressed in populationist terms. Rather, demand was for services that were better technically, though still also countering the effects of poor home-environments. And if obstetrics had become one among several hospital specialisms, occupational medicine had fallen outside the new NHS. Paradoxically, when a Labour government and its advisors planned a service based on hospital disciplines, they marginalized such traditional 'labor' interests as local government in the cities, public health, worker-run health schemes, and occupational medicine.

'Public health' remained in the hands of local government; but without the hospitals they had built-up between the wars most Medical Officers of Health (MOsH) felt their roles much reduced. Infectious diseases had been their historic stronghold, but infectious disease hospital services were now concentrated and controlled by the hospital boards. As with maternity services, MOsH were left with 'surveillance' and clinics 'in the community.'

Anyway, as antibiotics grew in the post-war consciousness, infectious diseases looked set to disappear. Though TB sanatoria had been a priority at the end of the war, by the late 50s TB was being cured and sanatoria were turned over to other uses. The public–health doctors did not even get the credit for the change. Antibiotics were products of laboratories and thereby associated with hospital medicine and with the rising profile of the pharmaceutical companies. It became a medical commonplace that infectious diseases and poverty had been conquered — the new frontiers were chronic conditions, including those caused by bad genes or bad life-styles. For all these reasons, attention shifted from production and reproduction towards the triumphs of 'scientific medicine,' the need for more hospital services, and the cost thereof.

In the 1960s a new generation emerged which took for granted both good health and medical services, and which sought to exercise choice in matters of life-style, especially sexual behavior and reproduction. By now neither pro-natalism nor traditional religion were substantial barriers to contraception. So when oral contraceptives were developed to help stem population-growth in the third world, they were rapidly taken-up by young women in the West, as a form of contraception which they could control. As we shall discuss below, medicine for women was being redefined — away from motherhood, towards the autonomy of individual women exercising choice in matters of reproduction.

By the 1960s, the 'population problem' had moved abroad and reversed. The spread of public health measures, vaccines and antibiotics, and initially effective campaigns against malaria had lowered the death rates throughout much of the third world, without corresponding falls in birth rates. Western governments feared that 'excess' population growth would produce political instability — doubly dangerous when the Soviet Union was competing with the West for influence. It was in this context that research on oral contraceptives had begun to attract substantial support. But whether from illiteracy, poverty, or traditional commitments to large families, few women in the third world could use 'the pill' in the Western way.

## PROFESSIONS AND COMMUNITIES

I have argued that the state's involvement with clinical medicine had been in part a response to 'pressures from below,' in part a matter of productionist medicine. What then happened to the public purposes of medicine as productionist medicine largely disappeared from the West, (though remaining central in the USSR, not least because of WWII losses)?

I will argue below that Western medicine has become increasingly approximated to the consumerism now general in western societies. This would seem particularly true in the US. But in Western Europe, and especially in Britain, in the decades from 1948 to 1968, neither productionism *nor* consumerism were particularly prominent. The values then promoted were social inclusion and professional progress. For this social-democratic modernism the usual foreign models, for medicine as for furniture, were Swedish.

We have already stressed the roots of medical communitarianism in local charity hospitals and in workers' mutualism. The statutory services, associated with relief for the destitute and with confinement for epidemic disease (or madness), were less loved. Though it is hard to recover public attitudes to baby clinics in the Edwardian period, we do know that 'health visitors' were often resented as 'nosy-parkers,' prying into the homes of the poor. But by the 1930s, statutory services seem to have been more accepted as community facilities. After 1929 many of the workhouse hospitals became part of the municipal services — for all citizens, not just the destitute. The involvement of women and of working-class men in the governance of the destitute had helped 'soften' institutions, and between the wars, improvement of welfare services was a favorite object of feminist politics. Pro-natalism also had its communitarian aspects — maternity-homes were valued by mothers, not least for the break they offered from family duties. Though private medical insurance increased in the UK as in the US, the inter-war decades also witnessed a greater 'inclusiveness'; increasingly, both municipal and charity health services were 'for the citizens.'

The WWII plans for a new health service built on this communitarianism, even though they came to undermine 'local government' in the sense of multi-function local-authorities. Indeed the special conditions of the war strengthened this atti-tude, as it also strengthened the involvement of the central state with both municipal and charity hospitals. War-time morale was maintained by talk of a better world thereafter. There was enormous popular support for universal social security and for the introduction of the NHS in 1948, not least for the provision of such neglected services as dentistry and spectacles.

In most areas of medicine there was little debate as to the *direction* which services should take. Doctors, especially in hospitals, knew what needed to be done; and progressive taxation and equitable distribution of benefit seemed the obvious, fair and efficient mechanism. Whereas the 'medical market' had generally proved insufficient to support consultants outside the major cities, the NHS paid salaries and could distribute consultants according to need. Hospitals in minor towns received their first consultant physicians, surgeons and obstetricians; and ne-glected patient groups gained their own specialists (e.g. geriatricians for the 'wards of old ladies', and psychiatrists for the 'mild mental cases' in workhouses around Manchester).[3] Specialisms with small private markets e.g. rheumatology, were able to take root in medical schools (sometimes promoted by research charities). Thus the needs of would-be specialists met the needs of the patients hitherto neglected. Though many doctors had opposed the NHS as 'state-regulation,' they were to look back on the post-WWII decades as a high point of professional autonomy and public appreciation. In most Western countries the 1950s and 1960s saw steady expansion of health services.

## CRITIQUES AND CONSUMPTION

The very success of medicine in apparently removing the scourge of infectious disease, meant that the post-war generation assumed a right to be healthy. In most of the West, the economy was buoyant, unemployment low and consumer expectations high. It was in this context that young people, women, and racial minorities, first in the USA, became increasingly assertive against the paternalism, racism and homophobia which they saw in the post-WWII consensus. Organized medicine seemed to be allied with states and churches in prescribing behavior as well as potions. Policy on abortion had emerged post-WWII as a question for doctors — most births were now in hospitals and termination was therefore less 'private;' but by the 1970s, abortion along with contraception, had become a woman's right in most non-Catholic countries. Medicine was for women, not just for 'mothers.'

The meaning of 'public' was also changing by the late 1960s. In the formal politics of British hospitals, representation of the public as 'owners' gave way to representation of the public as patients. 'Disease charities' moved from elite philanthropy to mass participation and to patient (or family) involvement. 'Disability,' first in the US and then in Europe, became a question of minority rights and of access to leisure activities as well as to work. By 1970, people with physical and mental disabilities were increasingly 'in the community,' their standard of life judged by consumption rather than production in special workshops or asylum farms. As life expectancies increased, a higher proportion of the population was beyond working age, but still consuming — especially medicines. As ambitions for personal health and fertility increased, articulate consumers demanded more of medicine.

By the 1970s, as Western economic growth flattened or reversed, the ever-rising cost of health-care consumption became more and more worrying, not least to business interests and the rightist governments common by the 1980s. Again Britain is a key example. For Thatcherites the NHS was a cause of excessive taxation, a bastion of professional power, and a source of endless labor disputes. It was also popular, a representation of community, and remarkably efficient, especially compared to the excesses of the American market. Nonetheless, government prescriptions for the British system were often American (and copied in other European countries). In general, health-services were to become more 'business-like.'

One answer was more accountants and professional managers. In Britain around 1974, a NHS restructuring led by management consultants placed *teams* of managers, nurses, doctors etc. at various levels in the hierarchy. Though much of that reform soon needed reforming, the managers remained and increased their influence, especially after 1990.

Another solution was to transfer some costs to the private market. In an insurance system this could be done by insisting on some payment from the individual, or by limiting the range of services covered by the insurance. In Britain, it was done at the margins of the NHS. By the 1990s, dentistry and opticians were largely 'private', except for the very poor; and the vast majority of beds for old people who needed nursing were in privately-run homes for which patients paid if they owned significant capital or a house.

Consumerism was also encouraged by popular medical journalism, by private health-care companies and by high profile pharmaceutical companies seeking markets. From the 1970s, 'fitness' became a cult and a business, part of the private market in leisure. Female and then male bodies became sexual commodities for individual investment. Where employers now invest in 'fitness' or medical services for employees, it is less to ensure efficiency than to encourage corporate loyalty. The growth of private medicine in Britain since the 1970s has been fueled by employment 'packages' for the better paid.

At the end of the century, health and work-performance seem linked chiefly by the concept of 'stress' — a late flowering, perhaps, of the 'functional disorders' of WWI. But stress is for white-collar workers more than laborers (though it is also recognized amongst the unemployed); the solutions sought by individuals and/ or firms now lie as much in psychology or fringe-medicine as in medical orthodoxy. Indeed, so powerful was the spread of medical consumerism, that by the late 1990s orthodox practitioners had much reduced their previous hostility to 'complementary' medicine.

If 'global competition' re-emerged in the 1990s as a reason for governments to encourage 'national efficiency,' the remedies advocated are very different from those of 1900. In economies built on technology and consumption rather than muscular production, more *education* rather than medical care is said to hold the key. Medical care is supported by Western governments, not to increase the strength of populations, but to meet the demands of potential consumers in ways not so unequal as to provoke effective political resentment.

In the 1980s, the Conservative government in Britain considered a wholesale shift to an insurance system on the American model; but the plan aroused furious opposition, and American models were not reassuring for cost-controllers. Instead, on the advice of an American health economist, they introduced 'internal markets' into the NHS. All procedures were to be costed; hospitals would run as independent trusts and charge for their services, competing with each other where possible; payments would be made by local health authorities, or by general practitioners who had chosen to be 'fund-holders.' As of 1999, the 'internal market' is set to be reduced by a centrist government with more faith in planning and cooperation.

The reforms highlighted questions of rationing which are now high-profile in many countries. The advance of technology and the aging of the population are presented as inevitably increasing demands on state medical services, whether state-managed or insurance-based. But as Rudolph Klein argues below, most systems, certainly the NHS, are managing by reducing marginal expenses, even when they are frightened to increase taxation. We are already seeing serious attempts to move treatments outside hospitals; in that respect general medicine is now following mental health services. One may foresee a substantial 'de-hospitalization' of medicine, though this is unlikely to remove hospitals from the center of medical power.

Nor is it certain that technologies *must* increase costs; there are counter-examples, especially the antibiotic treatment of TB which emptied the sanatoria. And because so much of the cost of medicine is incurred for people near to death, future patterns of expenditure could change with public expectations. A postwar generation which has watched so many of its parents live-out their slow and sad declines, may learn to protect themselves from such fates. Choices, both private and public, will be made about the ending of life and the distribution of resources.

The rapid advance of a new empiricism — evidence based medicine (EBM), is further evidence of a political economy of medicine focused on the cost-effectiveness of services rather than directly on the heath of the population, as was once the case. It also contrasts strongly with a second feature of the earlier twentieth-century — the faith in laboratory training, rather than mere statistics, as the basis of good medicine. Perhaps there is a connection between the rise of EBM and the move to 'problem-based learning' in 'reformed' medical schools, where laboratory training has declined markedly, along with dissections and the use of live animals — all of which were once emblematic of the claim to 'science.' Perhaps clinical 'problems' are to be solved from computerized 'manuals' of 'best-practice'?

The science that matters now around medical schools, is not for students but for the researchers who staff the end-of-century boom in bio-medicine — in universities, research institutes, pharmaceutical companies, and in all the hybrid forms now woven into the medico-industrial complex. The international market in medical commodities is now so large that the production of drugs and technologies is seen as a major growth area of the national economy, and a major reason for public investment in medical research. Biological entities — organisms, cells and genes are being commoditized in ways which would have appalled the medical scientists of the early twentieth-century who saw themselves as uncovering nature for the public good. Indeed, the very notion of expertise in the service of the public is jeopardized by the growing interdependence of public, charitable and for-profit institutions.

If from 1900 the focus of the political economy of medicine was industrial production by mass body-power; from 2000 it may be the high-tech production of medical commodities, as ends rather than means. The interactions of the medico-industrial complex with consumers, public associations and governments will be a major theme in the Western political economy of the twenty-first century. The interactions in the presently-declining economies of Eastern Europe and of Africa will be even more fraught.

## PROSPECT FROM 2000

*Re/productionist* medicine seems unlikely to return to the West, though recent concerns about negative population growth are interesting. The involvement of international capitalism in health care, as well as pharmaceuticals, equipment and other medical commodities, seems unlikely to decrease. (One recalls the health care schemes provided for families who give blood to companies producing blood products — enlightened business or farmed humans?). The cultivation of health and beauty is now so central to Western consumerism, that medicine, in a general sense, will thrive in private markets.

And yet, national health services, via insurance or direct state provision, seem reasonably secure in Western Europe for the mass provision of expensive services. They are more efficient than markets, considered over the whole population, and much more effective politically. In some ways the 'left' agenda has returned from state socialism to the once-New Liberalism of 'positive freedoms,' national (educational) efficiency, and local action. Public health may not be required for populations, but as environmentalism gains strength, governments may be pushed to more careful regulation, both local and global; and audits of health-factors may steer governmental and corporate actions to increase freedom for 'the pursuit of health.' Public demand for information, and the technologies to distribute it, may extend the power of (some) medical consumers, at the expense of (some) professionals; and there are possibilities here for the extension of newer forms of public participation — for more effective patients' lobbies, for better public assessment of medicines, for better *local information*, and for better quantification of standards of life, so that public and private commodity choices can be placed in wider perspectives. Patients will be less passive, but not necessarily more individualist.

But what of the non-West? In America, AIDS is a disease of leisure, or a by-product of medical technology; in Africa it is a threat to production, to the economy of innumerable communities. In Europe contraceptives are sexual liberators; in India a means to reduce family size and the threat of over-population. In the West, sanitation is taken for granted; in many non-Western states it is minimal, even in cities, and the consequences are death-rates far higher than could be achieved at comparable economic levels. But Western governments now have little need to cultivate the populations of third-world states; we do not depend on their commodities, nor vie with each other for territorial possessions. Since the end of the Cold War, medicine no longer benefits from competition for political influence.

Though sanitation and basic medical treatments are not expensive by Western standards, they are beyond the means of most individuals and governments in the third world. If they are to be achieved, it will not be by productionism nor individual consumption. It will require global political mechanisms for articulating demands from the poor and prudence from the rich in such ways as created the health services of twentieth-century Europe. We need a sense of *global community*, extending that which carried forward the medical benefits of productionism and which now moderates the excesses of medical consumption.

## REFERENCES

Grateful acknowledgements (and absolution) to the authors of the following chapters and to the friends and colleagues who helped, especially David Cantor, David Edgerton, Jonathan Harwood, Jenny Stanton, Naomi Pfeffer, Charles Webster and Michael Worboys.

1. Diana Kuh and George Davey Smith, 'When is mortality risk determined? Historical insights into a current debate,' *Social History of Medicine* (1993), **6**: 101–23.
2. Naomi Pfeffer, *The Stork and the Syringe. A Political History of Reproductive Medicine.* (Cambridge: Polity Press, 1993), esp pp. 19–20, 109.
3. J.V. Pickstone, 'Psychiatry in district general hospitals,' in Pickstone (ed.), *Medical Innovations in Historical Perspective.* (Basingstoke: Macmillan, 1992).

## FURTHER READINGS

Berridge, Virginia, *Health and Society in Britain since 1939.* (Cambridge: Cambridge University Press, 1999).

Fox, Daniel, *Health Policies, Health Economics: The British and American Experiences, 1911–1965.* (Princeton: Princeton University Press, 1986).

Fox, Daniel, *Power and Illness. The Failure and Future of American Health Policy.* (Berkeley: University of California Press, 1993).

Hollingsworth, J. Rogers, *A Political Economy of Medicine: Great Britain and the United States.* (Baltimore: Johns Hopkins University Press, 1986).

Hollingsworth, J. Rogers, Haget, Jerald and Hanneman, Robert A., *State Intervention in Medical Care: Consequences for Britain, France, Sweden and the United States, 1890–1970.* (Ithaca: Cornell University Press, 1986).

Klein, Rudolf, *The Politics of the NHS.* (London: Longman, 1983).

Porter, R. (ed.), *The Cambridge Illustrated History of Medicine.* (Cambridge: Cambridge University Press, 1996).

Rosen, George, *A History of Public Health.* (New York: MD Publications, 1986).

Rosenberg, Charles E., *The Care of Strangers: The Rise of America's Hospital System.* (New York: Basic Books, 1987).

Starr, Paul, *The Social Transformation of American Medicine: The Rise of a Sovereign Profession and the Making of a Vast Industry.* (New York: Basic Books, 1982).

Stevens, Rosemary, *Medical Practice in Modern England: The Impact of Specialization and State Medicine.* (New Haven: Yale University Press, 1966).

Stevens, Rosemary, *In Sickness and in Wealth: American Hospitals in the Twentieth Century.* (New York: Basic Books, 1989).

Webster, Charles, *The National Health Service. A Political History.* (Oxford: Oxford University Press, 1998).

# CHAPTER 2

# The Golden Age of Medicine?

ALLAN M. BRANDT AND MARTHA GARDNER

In the last years of the nineteenth century and the first of the twentieth, medical knowledge, practice, and policy were radically transformed. Medicine and a new science became powerfully interconnected during this period, and many invoked the phrase 'golden age of medicine' to describe this transformation. This 'golden age' has no distinct moment of inception. Usually the term is used by historians, medical professionals, and others to signify the period in which they see medicine — utilizing a range of new scientific knowledge, practices, and technical apparatus — coming to have a dramatic impact on patterns of disease and human longevity. Also characteristic of this so-called 'golden age' was a sharp rise in the confidence of both physicians and the public in the efficacy of medical science. Basic questions about both medical and popular perceptions of efficacy are implicit in the discussion and debates about the 'golden age of medicine,' as are questions about the underlying causes of epidemiological change and issues of confidence in the medical institutions and practices that have dominated twentieth-century scientific medicine.

There are several key features to what came to be called the 'golden age of medicine.' Conceptually, the rise of the 'golden age' is associated with the dramatic new medical knowledge and practices of late nineteenth and early twentieth centuries. During this period, researchers identified microbes as the specific cause of many diseases and went on to develop therapeutic measures to destroy them in those who were infected. The 'golden age of medicine' is typically associated with the 'conquest' of epidemic infectious disease.[1]

The ability to identify the causes of disease and offer incisive remedies led to a remarkable rise in prestige and stature for members of the medical profession throughout the Western world. In order to achieve and maintain such status, the medical profession had to develop effective social and bureaucratic mechanisms for differentiating themselves from the long train of 'pretenders' to healing authority: quacks, alternative healers, and those poorly or inadequately trained. Prior to the twentieth century, drawing firm boundaries around the profession in many industrialized countries had proven difficult if not impossible. After centuries of contested authority and often low status, physicians emerged in the first decades of the twentieth century as powerful and respected representatives of a new bio-medical science. In particular, the 'golden age of medicine' is typically associated with high esteem for the medical profession and high expectations of their ability to treat disease effectively through powerful new techniques and technologies.

A further characteristic of the 'golden age of medicine' is the substantial invest-ment made on the part of both governments and philanthropies which created the dramatic expansion of medical institutions for education, research, and patient care. Beginning in the early twentieth century, unprecedented resources flowed to medicine. This both assured the growth and power of medical institutions among developed nations, and it enhanced public expectations in medical knowl-edge and care.

An additional central element of the 'golden age of medicine' is the dramatic improvement in standards of health during the first half of the twentieth century. This period witnessed steep declines in infant mortality and other deaths from infectious agents, as well as a remarkable rise in life expectancies in the West. Overall, these improvements were typically ascribed to the efficacy of the new scientific medicine. Not only did public confidence in medicine grow substantially, medical researchers and practitioners came to celebrate its effectiveness and power to identify and cure diseases which had perplexed humankind for centuries.

After briefly tracing the rise of the 'golden age of medicine,' this essay will also evaluate a series of critiques of medicine that arose in the second half of the twentieth century, challenging medicine's power and effectiveness from various directions. Finally, it will assess the persistence of notions of a 'golden age' in the face of criticism. To an impressive degree, the status and authority of the biomedi-cal ideals which created the 'golden age of medicine' remained transcendent as the twentieth century came to an end.

## Microbe Hunters

Crucial to an understanding of the 'golden age of medicine' is the rise of the germ theory of disease in the last years of the nineteenth century. After generations of dispute about the nature of contagion and epidemic disease, a series of pathbreaking discoveries, mostly in French and German laboratories, seemed to settle the central debate over disease causality. Between 1880 and 1900, investigators identified more than twenty micro-organisms, each which they associated with a *specific* disease.

Identifying these microbes, as well as devising the process for their isolation and growth in laboratories, had obvious implications for the practice of medicine and public health. Applications of the germ theory ranged from stronger justifications for antisepsis and asepsis in hospital and surgical practices, to new demands for public and personal hygiene, to new approaches to inoculation and vaccination. Ultimately, research focused on the introduction of anti-microbial treatments that could destroy the specific organisms *in vivo*.

By early in the twentieth century, scientists laboring in laboratories, inveterately seeking to isolate and identify disease-causing organisms, had come to be known as 'microbe hunters.' This image, of scientists searching far and wide across the microscopic 'field,' inspired a new generation of physicians and researchers eager to apply this new technique.[2]

The search for therapeutic measures to destroy or incapacitate disease-causing microbes came to preoccupy twentieth-century medicine. An important step was taken when researchers first went beyond isolation of harmful microbes to effecting their destruction. The 'golden age of medicine,' some historians would suggest, was actually born in immunologist Paul Ehrlich's laboratory in 1909, when he and Japanese bacteriologist Sahachiro Hata identified an arsenic compound that could destroy the syphilis-causing *treponema* through an intramuscular injection, returning infected patients to health.

Ehrlich painstakingly experimented with chemical compounds that, like the dyes he had used so successfully to stain microbes for microscopic viewing, would attach themselves to particular microbes and destroy them. Seeking a germicide for the syphilitic spirochete, Ehrlich's trials ended on the 606th attempt when his arsenic concoction destroyed the disease-causing treponema.

Ehrlich called the discovery of 606, soon commercially renamed Salvarsan, a 'magic bullet,' a new therapeutic weapon which could *specifically* locate and destroy those organisms causing disease. This notion of specificity — 'magic bullets' drawn to specific targets — while obviously most applicable to the treatment of certain bacterial infections, had a powerful impact on the organization and practice of biomedicine overall. Ehrlich's powerful metaphor became a central organizing feature of twentieth-century medicine and the widespread image of the 'golden age.' The 'magic bullet' imagery depicted the institution of medicine and its practitioners as able to control and vanquish disease. The new biomedical paradigm of specific cause and cure, with its strong ties to laboratory science and new technological apparatus, also was central to the rising status of medicine so characteristic of the 'golden age.'

Although Ehrlich's discovery of a chemotherapy for syphilis was not followed quickly by other anti-microbials, by the 1930s the development of sulfa drugs marked the continued promise of 'magic bullet' medicine. In the early 1930s, German biochemist Gerhard Domagk, following Ehrlich's approach of applying specific dyes, demonstrated that Prontosil, a red dye, cured streptococcal infections in laboratory animals. Soon the medication, whose active component was sulfanilamide, was used with dramatic success to treat streptococcal infections in children as well as puerperal sepsis. A number of other sulfa-based drugs followed to treat a wide range of bacterial infections. While these drugs sometimes did not cure, they did significantly reduce the morbidity and mortality associated with many bacterial infections.

The next 'magic bullet' was found in the early 1940s. E.B. Chain and H.W. Florey of Oxford seized on Alexander Fleming's 1928 discovery of penicillin, demonstrating its ability to successfully treat infections in humans. Their recognition that microorganisms themselves produce anti-bacterial substances marked a critical finding in the battle against germs. This research prompted American laboratories to begin full-scale production of the antibiotic. Penicillin proved effective against many organisms resistant to sulfa drugs; as production improved and the development of oral antibiotics was perfected, the full benefits of penicillin came to be recognized.

Writing in 1954, Boris Sokoloff described penicillin as "a weapon of such magnitude and power that it may yet fulfill the dreams of generations of scientists."[3] Penicillin sharply reduced mortality from many bacterial infections including pneumoccocal pneumonia, otitis media, bacterial meningitis and puerperal sepsis. Further, it made possible significant advances in surgery by lowering the incidence of infections often associated with invasive procedures.

Soon after scientists came to appreciate penicillin, soil biologist Selman Waksman and his colleagues identified another fungal agent, streptomycin, in 1943. This substance was demonstrated to be effective against tuberculosis first in animals, then in humans. Despite the dramatic success of streptomycin in many cases, some infections proved recalcitrant, and patients relapsed. The addition of new agents such as para-aminosalicylic acid (PAS) and isoniazid by the late 1940s offered the possibility of combination therapies which proved to be remarkably successful in treating tuberculosis. Antibiotic treatments for tuberculosis marked one of the great triumphs of twentieth-century medicine; tuberculosis, perhaps the most significant infection in world history, could now be decisively treated. Five years after the discovery of antibiotic therapy, many tuberculosis hospitals and sanatoria had closed; these structures now stood as historical monuments to the 'golden age of medicine.'

The discoveries of penicillin, streptomycin and other antibiotics marked the fulfillment of 'magic bullet' medicine — the therapeutic cornerstone of the 'golden age.' With these powerful drugs, traditional fears of disease-causing microbes receded. The development of anti-microbial drugs seemed to close the gap — once and for all — between understanding the causes of disease and finding the mechanisms for their effective treatment.

Notions of microbial specificity also found applications beyond antibiotics; effective vaccines also marked the success of the 'golden age of medicine'. The discovery and deployment of polio vaccines at mid-century quickly became yet another embodiment of new scientific medicine. A crippling scourge, especially in Western nations, was virtually eliminated. Unable to visualize viruses just a short time ago, now determined medical researchers isolated polio virus and moved decisively to develop effective immunizations. The development of the polio vaccines in the 1950s by Jonas Salk and Albert Sabin served as a powerful example of the promise of biomedicine. The impressive and sophisticated skills brought to bear to isolate and cultivate polio virus in the 1930s and the 1940s and the subsequent development of effective vaccines in the 1950s demonstrated the emergence of modern microbiology and virology. Although policy approaches and resources to assure access to the vaccine lagged, such shortcomings rarely tarnished the image of a biomedical enterprise typically viewed as above the fray of ideology and politics.

Smallpox and its vaccine provided another especially powerful symbol of biomedicine's potential. An acute viral disease responsible for 10 to 15 percent of deaths in Europe through the eighteenth century, smallpox was first successfully treated by Edward Jenner in 1798, using 'cowpox' which proved safer than earlier inoculations with smallpox itself. European and American governments disseminated Jenner's vaccine widely throughout the nineteenth and the first half of the twentieth century, by which time developed countries had the disease in hand. Around 1966, the World Health Organization began a campaign to eradicate the disease altogether across the globe, a goal fully realized by 1979 when the Global Commission for the Certification of Smallpox Eradication released its official report.

The ideal of the 'magic bullet' ultimately came to extend beyond infectious disease into other areas. An early and notable example of this extension was in combating diabetes. Building on late-nineteenth century research connecting pancreatic function to diabetes, Canadian researchers just after World War I isolated particular secretions from the pancreas. They then generated insulin which was very effective in combating the symptoms of diabetes. While not a cure for the condition, since diabetics became dependent on insulin and also had to monitor their diet, its effects were striking. Many diabetics who had been wasting away gained weight back and began to lead ordinary lives.

All the various triumphs of medical science in the first half of the twentieth century seemed confirmed by a dramatic epidemiologic transition. Simultaneous to the rise of a biomedicine were impressive improvements in the patterns of disease, rates of morbidity and mortality, and substantial increases in life expectancy. In particular, most Western nations experienced a substantial decline in acute infectious diseases as a cause of death between 1870–1950. Rates of tuberculosis, pneumonia and diarrhea enteritis, among the most prominent killers, declined sharply. By mid-century, systemic, chronic, diseases of later life — especially heart disease, cancer and stroke — became more prominent as causes of death. With this change, life expectancies rose precipitously; in the US for example, in 1900, life expectancy at birth for men was approximately 48 years, by 1970, it neared 70, and continued to climb for the remainder of the century. Other developed countries enjoyed similar increases in life expectancy during the twentieth century: in France, life expectancy for men improved from 45 years in 1900 to 69 in 1972, in England and Wales from 52 years in 1910 to 69 in 1970.[4] As epidemic diseases receded to be replaced by chronic, degenerative diseases, the power of the new biomedical paradigm seemed confirmed. Inevitably, in both medical and public discourse these empirical changes were associated with the rise of Western scientific biomedicine, its technology, and its institutions.

"What is the goal toward which medical bacteriology is heading?" asked one observer of medicine at mid-century. The answer seemed clear:

> It sounds like a dream or a fairy tale, this goal towards which medical science is moving, as though propelled by Destiny: the goal is simply *to live in a world without menacing microbes*, to have all disease-producing microbes rendered harmless and domesticated; to see infectious diseases vanish from the earth, or at least be easily controlled, to make this planet free from the dangers of death from infectious diseases, so that the common cold, pneumonia, plague, meningitis, tuberculosis, and other dread ailments may be as rare phenomena as dangerous wild beasts are... Will such a world exist? We believe so.[5]

This optimism and confidence stood as a bulwark of the 'golden age;' certainty in the progressive and triumphal march of rational investigation and its humane benefits created an aura around medicine that seemed inviolable. By mid-century, the potential of medicine appeared boundless, and expectations and public confidence in biomedical science reached new heights.

## INSTITUTIONS

The great triumphs of twentieth-century bioscience did not, of course, occur outside of specific institutional and social contexts. The 'golden age of medicine' can only be assessed by also examining those settings for research and patient care that served to make cutting-edge discoveries possible and to translate them to the bedside. During the course of the twentieth century, research, educational, and patient care institutions were critically linked and dramatically expanded. Among industrialized nations, new resources — both public and private — flowed to medical education, research, and patient care. These funds served to secure prestige for the medical profession as they enhanced confidence in biomedical knowledge and intervention.

Germany was where the emphasis on research and basic science commenced. With strong support from the government as early as the 1860s, Germany could boast numerous universities with impressive laboratories and research programs. By 1891, Germany already had 300 scientists focusing on medical research at a time when the UK had only 50 and the US very few. Physicians from other countries came to visit German universities to supplement their training. Prominent Johns Hopkins researcher William H. Welch for one was duly impressed when he visited Germany in the 1870s. Private philanthropies such as the Koch Institute in Germany, the Pasteur Institute in France, the Rockefeller Foundation in the US and the Wellcome Trust in the UK also began to make substantial contributions to the growing biomedical infrastructure for education and research.

In the US, significant private funding preceded governmental backing. Donations to universities in the late nineteenth century was the first step taken. By the early twentieth century, the 'era of private support' had begun in earnest.[6] John D. Rockefeller spearheaded philanthropic efforts and established the Rockefeller Institute for Medical Research in 1902. The Institute housed the first independent research laboratories in the United States as well as providing key funding to medical schools just beginning to emphasize basic sciences in their teaching. And Rockefeller was not alone in adopting the cause. By 1930, 40 foundations were funding American medical research, education and public health work. In contrast, research funding in the UK was at first primarily governmental. The Medical Research Council, set up in 1913, was the first force behind biomedical research there. Private funders, most notably the Wellcome Trust, did not get involved until the 1930s, and it was not until the 1960s that the Trust became a dominant force in biomedical research.

By the early twentieth century, laboratory science had transformed medical education in most Western nations. These institutions, whether state-run or private, soon became fully committed to the new science and its clinical applications. Medical education became increasingly standardized, with students rotating through both laboratories and wards in university-based programs. While considerable differences in medical education persisted across western nations, more impressive still was the 'universalization' of medical knowledge and practices. Attention to basic scientific knowledge and laboratory research, first used in nineteenth-century Germany, came to be the model throughout Western medical education.

In the course of the twentieth century, access to medical education became increasingly restricted to candidates with intensive and costly preparation, further encouraging the rise in status of the profession. Professional boundaries and credentials came to be sharply drawn by the 'privileged' knowledge of biomedicine and its techniques. By the time of the 1910 Flexner survey of American medical schools (funded by the Carnegie Foundation), laboratory research had become an integral and respected part of medical education across Europe and North America.

The emphasis on biomedicine in education and practice was firmly established by the mid-twentieth century. The Second World War, in particular, heightened national commitments to biomedical research programs, as budgets for basic science research swelled. The increases in funding for research in this period was marked. In the US, concern that Germany could no longer provide the basic research other countries had relied on in the past provided impetus for the expansion. The national shift from primarily philanthropic to governmental funding took place as the National Institutes of Health (NIH) became the main vehicle for research. Established in 1930, the NIH became dominant in the 1940s and 1950s. Its budget doubled between 1950 and 1955 (from 28 to 60 million dollars), with funds allocated to both independent laboratories and universities. Funding continued to increase at an even more rapid pace after 1955. Other countries also followed this path of medicalization.

With this infusion of resources and the rise of powerful institutions of research, medical teaching and patient care, the stature of medicine rose precipitously. Access to medicine was increasingly viewed by the general public and policy makers as a social and political good. In Western Europe, the US and other developed nations, political pressure increased to assure that individuals had access to medical treatment and care. Although programs to provide this varied structurally and politically, by mid-century most industrialized nations had committed substantial resources to purchasing health care.

Between 1900 and 1971, not just research but overall health expenditures increased sharply, especially between 1945 and 1970. France increased its expenditures for personal medical services ninefold between 1891 and 1971, while the US did so fourteen times.[7] While the specifics in each country vary, the trend of expanding resources devoted to medicine continued in the last quarter century throughout Europe and North America (and nowhere more exponentially than the US). By 1996, the US devoted 14.2 per cent of its Gross Domestic Product to health (though the rate of increase has slowed down a great deal in recent years), Germany 10.5 per cent, France 8.9 per cent and the UK 6.9 per cent.[8]

The hospital, perhaps more than any other single institution, became the structural emblem of the 'golden age.' In Western developed societies, hospitals became increasingly central and salient cultural institutions during the twentieth century, often housing both births and deaths, as well as serving the widest range of social welfare functions. In many instances, the modern hospital brought together the widest array of technologies so characteristic of the 'golden age.' Here the esoterica of the laboratory was brought to the public. Following the paradigm of biomedicine, problems of disease would be brought to the hospital to be isolated, identified, and when possible treated. With only 178 hospitals in the US in 1873, the number had increased to 1500 by 1904, 4,445 in 1944 and 5,736 in 1960.[9] While the US holds the place as most technologically-oriented and specialized in medical care, other developed countries followed a similar trend. For example, in England, hospital beds per 100,000 rose from 628 in 1890 to 1,335 in 1970, in France from 588 to 1,582 in those same years.[10]

The many new hospitals of the early to mid-twentieth century contained a range of new scientific machinery which had particular appeal to patients seeking the advantages of the 'new' medicine. The hospital became the principal institution in which the general public would come in contact with cutting edge science and technology such as X-rays, IV treatments, and sophisticated new technical monitoring. The modern surgical theater marked the capabilities of medicine to radically alter pathologies of the body through complex combinations of skill, technique and technology. The exigencies of the machine increasingly dictated the organization and structure of the hospital.

The expanded resources devoted to medicine illustrated by its institutions — hospitals, medical schools and research laboratories — confirmed the high value society placed on medicine. The new science, as well as powerful social and cultural trends emphasizing expertise and instrumental approaches to problems of health or disease, encouraged the consolidation of the medical profession in most Western cultures. Physicians possessed considerable authority, for example, in determining access to medical care, technology, and oversight. Medical training, whether regulated by state certification or voluntary organizations, was seen as an important social good, guaranteeing access to new and valuable medical knowledge. Although the precise legal and regulatory mechanisms that supported professional sovereignty in various nations were distinctive, common to these industrialized Western societies were medical professions of high stature and significant autonomy.

## CHALLENGES TO THE GOLDEN AGE

By mid-century the dramatic successes of the biomedical paradigm had created great prestige for medical researchers and practitioners, public adulation for the profession, and heightened expectations of new triumphs. At the very moment in which prospects soared, however, some observers began to question the salience of biomedicine. A series of sharp critiques of its reductionist qualities began to come forth. After a half century of rising status for medicine, these attacks marked a new skepticism about the efficacy, power, and ethics of modern medical theory, practice, and institutions.

Critics suggested that the anticipated utopia, free of disease, was but an illusion. A central voice was that of René Dubos of the Rockefeller Institute. Himself a preeminent microbiologist who in 1939 discovered gramicide, an early antibiotic used to combat pneumonia, by the 1950s Dubos came to seriously question the structure and outlook of modern medicine. He had begun to focus his research on tuberculosis, looking beyond examination of bacilli in the laboratory to transmission in the larger environment. He challenged utopian predictions. "The Golden Age means different things to different men, but the very belief in its existence implies the conviction that perfect health and happiness are birthrights of men," explained Dubos. "Yet, in reality, complete freedom from disease and from struggle is almost incompatible with the process of living."[11] According to critics like Dubos, the very success of twentieth-century bioscience exposed its limitations. He warned of the inappropriate and dangerous expectations of "medical utopias" and the "mirage of health." According to Dubos, success in battling diseases often exposed new problems. "My personal view," he wrote, "is that the burden of disease is not likely to decrease in the future, whatever the progress of medical research and whatever the skill of social organizations in applying new discoveries… Threats to health are inescapable accompaniments of life."[12]

Taking a broadly ecological and evolutionary view of the relationships between humans and the microbial world, critics like Dubos suggested that social and political factors might be even more significant in effecting these fine balances than new scientific advances. Dubos pointed out that social and environmental variables often determined whether omnipresent microbes wreaked disease; small changes in the balance between host and agent significantly affected patterns of sickness and death.

Moreover, the microbes would not stand still in the face of human efforts to destroy them. Faced with powerful anti-microbial agents, these micro-organisms would inevitably adjust, becoming *resistant*. Even before penicillin became widely available in 1946, Alexander Fleming (who had discovered penicillin in 1928) warned that microbes would rapidly learn to resist penicillin if the drug was misused. By the late 1950s, it was already becoming clear that some antibiotic successes would be short-lived, as problems of drug resistance developed. And indeed, widespread and sometimes inappropriate use of antibiotics often encouraged the development of additional resistant strains. 'Magic bullets,' it seemed, had vulnerabilities.

Other critics followed Dubos, emphasizing the limited impact of the new scientific medicine on patterns of disease. Among the most searching attacks was that offered by British epidemiologist Thomas McKeown, professor in the Department of Social Medicine at the University of Birmingham, UK, McKeown emphasized the need to consider population-based data when assessing improvements in health and the effectiveness of biomedicine. By reviewing a wide range of demographic and epidemiologic data, McKeown and his colleagues suggested that the impressive rises in life expectancy for most Western nations were not the result of the application of biomedical interventions, as many had assumed. Rather, they showed, the longer and healthier lives characteristic of industrialized (and medicalized) countries resulted principally from higher standards of living, better housing, nutrition, and emerging patterns of family limitation.

McKeown used tuberculosis as a central example. He showed that this most prominent killer of peoples across the globe was in sharp decline in many Western countries before its elucidation by the germ theory of disease. And, perhaps most tellingly, rates had fallen significantly before the modern biomedical paradigm produced any decisive therapeutic intervention. He questioned the relative contribution of biomedicine to improvements in health during the twentieth century.

Implicit in this critique was the notion that modern medicine had accrued undeserved accolades for improvements in health generated outside of medicine. In the process, according to McKeown, biomedicine had directed attention and resources away from a crucial set of social variables that had a powerful impact on patterns of disease. He attacked basic assumptions about what medicine should be, arguing,

> Medical sciences and services are misdirected, and society's investment in health is not well used, because they rest on an erroneous assumption about the basis for human health. It is assumed that the body can be regarded as a machine whose protection from disease and its effects depends primarily on internal intervention. The approach has led

to indifference to the external influences and personal behaviour which are the predominant determinants of health.[13]

One particularly impressive example of the effectiveness of existing biomedicine, the vaccination for smallpox, was in fact a deceptively exceptional case. McKeown admitted that smallpox did represent an instance in which a medical intervention reduced disease, but he insisted that smallpox was in a class of its own historically. Since unlike so many other epidemic diseases it was an airborne disease, only transmitted through human contact (rather than through animals, insects, food or water), smallpox had a particularly unique potential for eradication. Prospects for other medical cures to live up to the optimistic story presented by the elimination of smallpox were very slim, argued McKeown and his followers.

Others, following McKeown, began to ask systematic questions about the relative effectiveness of biomedicine to address persistent patterns of disease, especially as epidemiologic patterns shifted impressively away from the predominance of infection as a cause of morbidity and mortality to chronic diseases like cancer, stroke, and heart disease. Indeed, the dramatic decline of infectious, epidemic disease revealed a substrate of systemic, degenerative diseases difficult to address within the paradigm of 'magic bullet' medicine. In its emphasis on the treatment of acute disease, approaches to prevention and modifying the environment had often received short shrift.

The prime early example in which a 'magic bullet' did have a discernable effect on a chronic disease only proved the need to expand beyond the model, some argued. The discovery and dissemination of insulin, while highly beneficial to those with diabetes, did not by any means eliminate the underlying disease. Insulin's ability to cover over the symptoms of diabetes without eradicating it created only an imperfect solution. Along with taking insulin, diabetics had to eat very balanced diets, and many complications from diabetes still arose. Also, their life expectancy, while much better than before insulin came into use, was significantly lower than that of the general population. Critics suggested that even dramatic discoveries like insulin proved to be 'half-way' technologies, transforming acute disease into chronic conditions requiring intensive medical oversight and management.

Further, critics also argued that 'diseases of civilization' and modernity were unlikely to be successfully addressed through the development of new, more powerful biomedical interventions. Heart disease, for example, a prominent cause of death in affluent nations, could be modified through diet, exercise, and smoking cessation. Yet, the biomedical paradigm offered few insights into prevention, behavior modification, and the reduction of environmental and social risks. The rise of modern quantitative epidemiology in the years after the Second World War directed attention to powerful causes of morbidity and mortality relating to health behavior, accidents, and socioeconomic status, yet efforts to establish comprehensive health promotion and disease prevention programs lagged behind the lure of a biotechnical fix.

But even in the areas where biomedicine had proved efficacious, medical treatments did not reach a large portion of those with curable diseases. One of the most powerful ironies of the 'golden age of medicine' was how inconsistently its benefits were spread throughout the world. Profound disparities in both rates of disease and life expectancy persisted in the face of new and sometimes life-saving interventions. Further, considerable social, political, and economic obstacles to the delivery of effective medical interventions existed not only in the developing world, but in the developed world as well. Critics often recognized the power of medical intervention at the same time decrying the problems of equitable access.

Challenges to the 'golden age of medicine' also arose among those who did have access to medical care. The very successes of medicine led to substantial questions about its power, its efficacy, and its costs. By the 1960s and 1970s, a series of focused critiques of medicine came to be sharply articulated. In spite of the many successes of the biomedical paradigm, some critics began to cast serious doubts upon its essential orientations, values, and approaches to problems of disease. The bioethics and patients' rights movements were the form these new critiques took. With the dramatic advances of medical science and the rise of a powerful medical profession, the patient had become fundamentally disempowered, they typically argued.

According to many medical ethicists, paternalistic doctors ignored the wishes of their patients; the rise of medical sovereignty so characteristic of the 'golden age' had led to arrogance and abuses of individual rights in both the clinic and in human experimentation. In the shadow of Nazi experimentation, failures to obtain informed consent and other egregious violations of human rights in research with human subjects drew further attention to the unchecked power of medical science, encouraging new forms of regulation and codes of ethics. With the rise of the ability to cure, medicine had lost its capacity to care, some suggested. The very bureaucratic and instrumental institutions that had become emblematic of the 'golden age' were now often identified as alienating; care of patients was reported to be fragmented with the increase in technical diagnostics and procedures, and the increase in professional specialization.

By the 1970s and 1980s, many had identified a crisis in trust and authority in doctor-patient relationships. Doctors and patients had become 'strangers' in highly bureaucratized and impersonal institutions. The very technologies celebrated at the height of the 'golden age' now became symbolic of the sterile, technocentric nature of modern health care. Indeed, the paradox that life-saving technologies could also extend life indeterminately led to fears of comatose and vegetative patients being tethered to machines sometimes only for the purpose of having organs harvested for transplantation. Intensive Care Units with monitors beeping and respirators whirring became symbols of a technological medicine deeply alienating to patients' interests. By the 1980s the 'right to die' had become a prominent hallmark in the critiques of the excesses of modern medicine.

Not only were doctor-patient relationships examined critically, some observers also proposed that the overall structure of medicine had notable flaws. Three related criticisms suggested that the intensive commitment to acute, tertiary, technologically-intensive medicine — so characteristic of the 'golden age' — failed to address the underlying causes of disease, contributing to the misallocation of resources. Firstly, some observers suggested that these technologies were enormously expensive, often prolonging life with little attention to the quality of that life. Aggressive resuscitation and artificial respiration of the very old adult or the very premature infant were typically invoked as examples of the biotechnical feats of medicine that disregarded the social and economic implications of intervention.

Secondly, the heavy emphasis on specialization, technology, and hospital care was seen as overshadowing the particular medical needs of those with chronic illness, now often the most prevalent category of disease. And finally, the very articulation of 'magic bullet' medicine, with its emphasis on basic science and specificity, directed resources away from social, behavioral, and preventive measures more likely to benefit populations at risk for disease. According to these critiques, the elegance of bioscience and its impressive technology had misdirected medicine, creating powerful professional interests that now worked against alternative visions of health care and public health.

Even in the most established realm of success for biomedical research — that of infectious disease — a new disease brought a serious challenge to the model in the 1980s. The emergence of the AIDS pandemic was viewed by many as a powerful indicator of the end of the 'golden age of medicine.' Hopes for a world free of infectious epidemics had been dashed; the AIDS pandemic, for some, represented the limits of biomedicine to effectively control the dangers of the microbial world. The fact that HIV had such devastating impacts in Western nations was a powerful reminder that infectious threats were not limited to the developing world where resources were severely limited. AIDS opened up transcultural anxieties of emerging new diseases which was compounded by the resurgence of older, known infections, such as tuberculosis and malaria. Perhaps, some observers of world epidemiological patterns reasoned, half a century of freedom from major disease outbreaks was coming to an end; that biomedicine would have little to offer when confronted by 'new' pathogens — especially viruses unresponsive to traditional antibiotics and inoculations.

If the 'golden age of medicine' was characterized by the successful development of 'magic bullets,' specific treatments for specific diseases, those treatments could prove elusive, especially as patterns of disease shifted. The burden of disease proved to be a moving target. The very successes of the 'golden age', the scientific and technical breakthroughs in the ability to identify and treat previously catastrophic diseases, ironically also demonstrated some of the important limitations of biomedicine. The biomedical model was threatened both from within and from without, with challenges on theoretical, policy, and practical levels.

CONCLUSION

As these challenges to modern medicine have arisen, has the 'golden age' come to an end? Did these critiques effectively reveal the ephemeral nature of medical effectiveness and prestige? At the end of the twentieth century, it seems that in spite of all these limitations and critiques, biomedical institutions remain powerful. The health-care professions — for all the controversy they have weathered — remain generally respected and of high stature.

Even if the AIDS epidemic and growing concern about 'emerging new diseases' such as ebola and handovers created anxiety about the ability of medical science and institutions to meet new and often unforeseen threats, nonetheless, confidence in a transnational medical establishment remained high. In many respects the ability to utilize scientific investigation to at least ameliorate and control the AIDS epidemic came to be seen as impressive. In fact, the rise of new scientific knowledge in the course of the twentieth century made it possible to identify and *detect* the organism that causes HIV disease. The 1983 identification in French and American laboratories of a human retro virus (given the name Human Immunodeficiency Virus) and, especially, the development of serological tests to discern evidence of the virus in blood were sophisticated achievements of elite biomedicine. These findings were crucial discoveries providing a modicum of control over the epidemic around the world, drastically reducing blood-borne transmission.

Another recent indicator of the continuing success of biomedicine has been the rise in authority and significance of medical genetics. The discoveries related to HIV, and many others, rested fundamentally on the revolution in molecular biology that had transformed the biological sciences since the middle of the century. With the untangling of the structure of DNA and the rise of recombinant genetic research, the potential for new biomedical interventions at the genetic level has been viewed with great promise. Genetic diseases once deemed beyond the reach of the biomedical paradigm are now often seen as the next challenge. The establishment of the international human genome project in 1990 marked the rise in stature of molecular medicine. Gene therapy, promised its proponents, would become "a major part of our lives in the new millennium."[14] Extensive new resources have flowed to basic sciences research and genetic research, and a new multinational biotechnology industry has arisen to market medical interventions arising from genomic science, although few applications have yet to prove efficacious.

As the twenty-first century dawns, whether or not the promise of the new molecular medicine and the biomedical paradigm it represents will be fulfilled remains an open question. The 'magic bullet' approach has expanded far beyond infectious and viral disease. Many diseases once deemed outside the reach of reductionist biomedical intervention — congenital, hereditary, psychiatric, and behavioral — are all now targets of new research to identify and modify the 'flaws' causing disease at the chromosomal level.

Therefore, despite the chorus of criticism, the biomedical paradigm has not come crashing down. Indeed, many have suggested that the 'golden age of medicine' and the particular forms of medical theory and practice that it represents remains in full force. Rather than soberly noting the demise of 'magic bullet' medicine and its limitations, they celebrate its tenacity and growing efficacy. Throughout the world, powerful economic and political interests underscore an intensive commitment to biomedicine.

The resilience of the biomedical model emphasizing individual clinical interventions *over* social and behavioral change has been an impressive aspect of late twentieth-century approaches to persistent problems of health and disease. Further, in spite of critiques that present the importance of social conditions and their amelioration as the key to good health, science-based technocentric medicine continues to be a goal for most developed and developing societies. In the US for example, funding for basic medical research (which had stagnated somewhat in the early 1990s) now appears to be expanding rapidly. Recent indications are that federal funding for the National Institutes of Health may increase by 50 per cent between 1998 and 2003.[15]

Historians, physicians, and scientists will no doubt continue to debate the parameters of the 'golden age of medicine.' Deeply embedded in discussions of the 'golden age,' its character and longevity, are essential perspectives on the nature and meaning of medical knowledge and practice in the twentieth century. Rather than asking when the 'golden age' began and ended, it may well be more productive to investigate the authority, legitimacy, and status of the biomedical paradigm and its impact on human health. Any assessment of the 'golden age of medicine,' its dramatic accomplishments and its impressive limitations, ultimately affects how we regard the character of medical science and practice in the twentieth century.

## REFERENCES

1.  Charles-Edward Amory Winslow, *The Conquest of Epidemic Disease*. (Madison, Wis.: University of Wisconsin Press, 1980, *c*1943).

2.  Paul De Kruif, *Microbe Hunters*. (New York: Blue Ribbon Books, 1926).

3.  Boris Sokoloff, *The Miracle Drugs*. (Chicago: Ziff-Davis Pub. Co., 1949), p. 94.

4.  *Statistical Yearbook 1948*. (New York: UN Statistical Office. 1949), pp. 52–60 and *Statistical Yearbook 1973*. (New York: UN Publications, 1974), pp. 80–85.

5.  Sokoloff, p. 254, *op.cit.*

6.  Richard H. Shryock, *American Medical Research*. (New York: The Commonwealth Fund, 1947), pp. 39–173.

7.  J. Rogers Hollingsworth, Jerald Hage and Robert Hanneman, *State Intervention in Medical Care: Consequences for Britain, France, Sweden, and the United States, 1890–1970*. (Ithaca: Cornell University Press, 1990), p. 64.

8.  'In Search of Value: An International Comparison of Cost, Access, and Outcomes,' by Gerard F. Anderson, *Health Affairs*, November/December 1997, exhibit one and Chart D-6, in Leon Wyszewianski et al. (eds), *Medical Care Chartbook*, 9th Edition. (Ann Arbor, Mich: Health Administration Press, 1991), p. 116.

9.  Rosemary Stevens, *In Sickness and in Wealth: American Hospitals in the Twentieth Century*. (New York: Basic Books, 1989), pp. 27 and 229.
10. Hollingsworth, p. 43, *op.cit.*
11. Rene Dubos, *Mirage of Health: Utopias, Progress and Biological Chance*. (New York: Harper & Brothers, 1959), p. 1.
12. Rene Dubos, *Medical Utopias*. (New York: Rockefeller Institute Press, 1959), p. 59.
13. Thomas McKeown, *The Role of Medicine: Dream, Mirage, or Nemesis?* (Princeton, N.J.: Princeton University Press, 1979), pp. xv–xvi.
14. William R. Clark, *The New Healers: The Promise and Problems of Molecular Medicine in the Twenty-First Century*. (New York: Oxford University Press, 1997), p. viii.
15. Aaron Zitner, 'Boston Medical Work May Get Boost,' *Boston Globe* (February 25, 1998), p. 1.

## FURTHER READING

Austoker, Joan and Bryder, Linda, *Historical Perspectives on the Role of the MRC: Essays in the History of the Medical Research Council of the United Kingdom and Its Predecessor, the Medical Research Committee, 1913–1953*. (Oxford, New York: Oxford University Press, 1989).

Bliss, Michael, *The Discovery of Insulin*. (Chicago: University of Chicago Press, 1982).

Bonner, Thomas Neville, *Becoming a Physician: Medical Education in Britain, France, Germany, and the United States*. (New York: Oxford University Press, 1995).

Brandt, Allan M., *No Magic Bullet: A Social History of Venereal Disease in the United States since 1880*. (New York: Oxford University Press, 1985).

Brown, Richard E., *Rockefeller Medicine Men: Medicine and Capitalism in America*. (Berkeley: University of California Press, 1979).

Burnham, John C., 'American Medicine's Golden Age: What's Happened to It?', *Science* (March 19, 1982), **215**: 1474–1479.

Callahan, Daniel, *False Hopes: Why America's Quest for Perfect Health Is a Recipe for Disaster*. (New York: Simon & Schuster, 1998).

Chesnais, Jean-Claude (translated by Elizabeth and Philip Kreager), *The Demographic Transition: Stages, Patterns, and Economic Implications*. (Oxford: Clarendon Press, 1992).

De Kruif, Paul, *Microbe Hunters*. (New York: Blue Ribbon Books, 1926).

Dubos, Rene J., *Mirage of Health: Utopias, Progress and Biological Chance*. (New York: Harper & Brothers, 1959).

Dubos, Rene J. and Dubos, Jean, *The White Plague; Tuberculosis, Man and Society*. (Boston: Little, Brown, 1952).

Feudtner, Chris, 'A Disease in Motion: Diabetes History and the new Paradigm of Transmuted Disease,' *Perspectives in Biology and Medicine*. (Winter, 1996), **39**: 158–170.

Fox, Daniel M., *Health Policies, Health Politics: The British and American Experience, 1911–1965*. (Princeton, N.J.: Princeton University Press, 1986).

Fox, Daniel M., *Power and Illness: The Failure and Future of American Health Policy*. (Berkeley: University of California Press, 1993).

Hall, A. Rupert and Bembridge, B.A., *Physic and Philanthropy: A History of the Wellcome Trust, 1936–1986*. (Cambridge [Cambridgeshire]; New York: Cambridge University Press, 1986).

Harden, Victoria Angela, *Inventing the NIH: Federal Biomedical Research Policy, 1887–1937*. (Baltimore, Md.: Johns Hopkins University Press, 1986).

Hobby, Gladys L., *Penicillin: Meeting the Challenge*. (New Haven: Yale University Press, 1985).

Hollingsworth, Rogers J., Hage, Jerald and Hanneman, Robert, *State Intervention in Medical Care: Consequences for Britain, France, Sweden, and the United States, 1890–1970*. (Ithaca: Cornell University Press, 1990).

Kiple, Kenneth F., *The Cambridge World History of Human Disease*. (New York: Cambridge University Press, 1993).

Knowles, John H., *Doing Better and Feeling Worse: Health in the United States*. (New York: W.W. Norton & Company, 1977).

Lederberg, Joshua, Shope, Robert E. and Oaks, Stanley C., Jr. (eds), *Emerging Infections: Microbial Threats to Health in the United States.* (Washington D.C.: National Academy Press, 1992).

McKeown, Thomas, *The Origins of Human Disease.* (Oxford, UK and New York: B. Blackwell, 1988).

McKeown, Thomas, *The Role of Medicine: Dream, Mirage, or Nemesis?* (Princeton, N.J.: Princeton University Press, 1979).

Omran, Abdel R., 'The Epidemiological Transition: A Theory of the Epidemiology of Population Change', *Milbank Memorial Fund Quarterly* (October 1971), **49**: 509–538.

Paul, John R., *A History of Poliomyelitis.* (New Haven and London: Yale University Press, 1971).

Rosenberg, Charles E., *The Care of Strangers: The Rise of America's Hospital System.* (New York: Basic Books, 1987).

Rothman, David J., *Strangers at the Bedside: a History of How Law and Bioethics Transformed Medical Decision Making.* (New York: Basic Books, 1991).

Shryock, Richard H., *American Medical Research.* (New York: The Commonwealth Fund, 1947).

Sokoloff, Boris, *The Miracle Drugs.* (Chicago: Ziff-Davis Pub. Co., 1949).

Starr, Paul, *The Social Transformation of American Medicine.* (New York: Basic Books, 1982).

Stevens, Rosemary, *In Sickness and in Wealth: American Hospitals in the Twentieth Century.* (New York: Basic Books, 1989).

Taylor, F. Sherwood, *The Conquest of Bacteria, from Salvarsan to Sulphapyridine.* (New York: Philosophical Library, 1942).

Tesh, Sylvia Noble, *Hidden Arguments: Political Ideology and Disease Prevention Policy.* (New Brunswick: Rutgers University Press, 1988).

Wainwright, Milton, *Miracle Cure: The Story of Penicillin and the Golden Age of Antibiotics.* (Oxford, UK; Cambridge, Mass., USA: Blackwell, 1990).

Waksman, Selman A., *The Antibiotic Era: A History of the Antibiotics and of their Role in the Conquest of Infectious Diseases and in other Fields of Human Endeavor.* (Tokyo: Waksman Foundation of Japan, 1975).

Warner, John Harley, 'From Specificity to Universalism in Medical Therapeutics: Transformation in the Nineteenth-Century United States', in Judith W. Leavitt and Ronald L. Numbers (eds), *Sickness and Health in America.* (Madison: University of Wisconsin Press, 1997), 3rd edn, pp. 87–101.

Winslow, Charles-Edward Amory, *The Conquest of Epidemic Disease: A Chapter in the History of Ideas.* (Madison, Wis.: University of Wisconsin Press, 1980, c1943).

## CHAPTER 3

# Health and Medicine in Interwar Europe

### PAUL WEINDLING

In recent years health care and the interwar welfare state have been analyzed from the perspectives of gender, eugenics, professionalisation, and the modernization of the voluntary sector. The findings represent a departure from long-held assumptions that health and welfare reforms arose from pressure from left-wing political movements. Such new approaches — assisted by accounts which one might loosely associate with Foucault's analysis of how biopolitics pervaded institutional and theoretical power structures — have brought fresh perspectives on total institutions and the establishing of networks of care as if society was itself a total institution. The persistence of social inequalities and ill-health has formed a recurrent area of debate, for example, on whether health deteriorated during the Depression. The organization of health services and their finances offer insight into the politics of public finances as well as into social conditions of 'recipients' — for example, industrial workers, families, and a range of so-called deviant groups like vagrants and mental defectives. Seen from such perspectives, the new welfare states, kitted out with modernistic hospitals, clinics, sanitary and preventive systems, seem rather less than altruistic and rather more authoritarian.

Between the wars European welfare states took on a range of common features as international organizations promoted international interaction and transfer of welfare systems. One historical approach to this phenomenon makes comparisons between national welfare states; there are numerous such comparisons of public health and welfare in anything from two to a dozen countries. But this genre is generally unhelpful in stressing monolithic and unitary states, generally beginning with a misunderstanding of Bismarck's decentralized schemes, ignoring the quite different systems for sickness insurance, pensions and accident insurance. For however authoritarian the political regime — ranging from Stalin's Soviet Union to Hitler's racial state, health and welfare systems have usually been administratively divided, localized, and fragmented. While schemes for a single national ministry of health, social security and food — often to be headed by a doctor or technical expert — have recurred in various countries since the revolutions of 1848, no such mega-ministry has ever lasted long. Divisions between voluntary and state systems have ebbed and flowed, and the tiers of the state — municipalities, provincial, federal state and central government — have contained an array of departments and authorities. Moreover — and this is difficult to grasp for anyone associating insurance solely with the commercial sector — an array of public but autonomous insurance agencies have thrived: mutual societies, friendly societies, or Genossenschaften have been a feature of the European welfare landscape throughout the nineteenth and twentieth centuries, and their administration, regulation and activities are complex. They are difficult to penetrate historically as their records may not be held by state archives, yet when appropriate sources are found, they often provide rich insight into such issues as accidents and sickness.

## MINISTRIES OF HEALTH AND NATIONAL SYSTEMS

The makers of the new European order in 1918 certainly had health and welfare in mind: equitable provision of health and welfare was intended to reduce internal social conflicts and, consequently, international tensions. Yet the strengthening of state administrations meant restricting population movements and disadvantaged ethnic minorities. Hopes arose that ministries of public health would — as the Polish Minister of Public Health wrote to the US President — produce "a new breed of men" and promote "health in the widest sense of the word".[1] In the new European welfare states it was not enough to contain the spread of infections: positively healthy social arrangements were required.

The First World War saw a range of countries, including Germany, accept welfare as a direct responsibility of the state, and such recognition was by no means a prerogative of the political left. Britain and France were both influenced by the Rockefeller Foundation.

But which country had the first dedicated ministry of health? Austria established separate ministries for social welfare and public health in June 1917, replaced in March 1919 by a single authority for welfare, food and health. Poland came next: the Ministry of Public Health, Welfare and Labor Protection established in April 1918 under the Austrian and German occupying authorities marked the beginning of a Polish medical system, and Public Health was allocated to a separate ministry under Ignacy Paderewski, Poland's first president. In the Balkans a Ministry of Public Health was founded in 1918 when the Serbian, Croat and Slovene Kingdom was proclaimed, and in July 1919 it established a Social Hygiene Division. In Czechoslovakia a Ministry of Public Health and Physical Education was inherited from Austria-Hungary. Throughout central and eastern Europe, the model of a centralized state hygiene administration predominated — a legacy of the Austro-Hungarian Empire, coordinating the production of vaccines and a range of scientific and primary health measures.

Public health was intended to take a central role under communism: in January 1918 the Bolshevik government established 'Collegeia' to direct health activities, leading in July 1918 to a Commissariat of Public Health to centralize health care at a time of epidemics and civil war. Although Soviet social medicine — often referred to as 'Red Medicine' — enjoyed an ultra-radical reputation, the first Commissar for Health, Semashko, favored diverse technocratic approaches. Feminist reforms like free abortion on demand were only fleetingly granted, and rapidly retracted. Many elements of Soviet social medicine were transplanted from German models, which conceptualized society as a biological organism. Thus during the 1920s a number of eugenics societies flourished in the Soviet Union. Despite socialization of medical services, experts wielded considerable power, and would have gone on doing so had it not been for the vagaries of Stalin's regime of terror.

Social welfare programs were designed to remove the causes of poverty and persecution that had spurred the mass emigration out of Europe prior to the First World War. The containment of populations in new nation states went with elaborate welfare programs. The tightening of border controls and immigration quotas meant that the United States received diminished numbers from Eastern Europe, while supporting medical reconstruction programs in the Central European successor states, which it hoped would be model democracies. The Western allies supported specialized ministries, which were symptomatic of a new professionalism: a Ministry of Health was established in Great Britain in 1919; in France a National Office of Social Hygiene was organized in 1924 in the Ministry of Labor, Hygiene and Public Welfare. Although in Germany aspirations for a central ministry of health, welfare and social security were not realized, certain *Länder* promoted integration of health and social services: the Prussian Ministry of Welfare combined responsibilities for health and housing.

The question arises to what extent medical reforms were internally generated by distinctive domestic political issues and agendas, and to what extent expert groups were able to transfer innovative forms of welfare provision from one country to another? It is a question which undermines the prevailing single-country approach to the politics of welfare, as the interwar period marked the transition from treaties and conventions between nation states to the establishment of a brave new world of international organizations, designed to promote health and welfare. How health conditions were shaped by what might be construed as autonomous, transnational scientific and professional factors suggest an intriguing and under researched problem. The realities of health — however measured — need to be set against such new priorities as women's employment, eugenics and pronatalism, as maternal and child health became dominant themes in the galaxy of interwar welfare measures.

Aggregate national disease statistics could mask considerable social, regional and occupational differentials. International organizations not only provided assistance, particularly to remedy the widespread starvation and epidemics after WWI, they then took a role in establishing biological standards — by the 1930s such standard-setting activities were extended to diet, housing, and revealed

considerable national disparities. International organizations undertook comparative evaluations, both quantitative — with a range of statistical data presented so
as to facilitate international comparisons — and qualitative, particularly dealing
with organizational structures, service provision and social conditions. Such surveys could be politically problematic because member states feared the violation
of their national sovereignty, and it was sometimes difficult to arrange programs
including, for example, both German and Soviet experts. But that such programs
were possible is important testimony to the effectiveness of the international ideal
— at least at a professional and scientific level.

### RELIEF AGENCIES

Alongside the operation of their new national medical bureaucracies one must
place the emergent international relief programs — including food aid, emergency
hygiene measures and the distribution of clothing etc. Here the famine relief
measures in the Soviet Union between 1921–23 are instructive — one of the first
instances of modern disaster relief. Fridtjof Nansen, the Arctic explorer and
naturalist, took a leading role in mobilizing international support and in coordinating relief programs. The most ambitious international aid agency, the American
Relief Administration, was directed by the former mining engineer and later US
President, Herbert Hoover. Such relief was not disinterested, given the fears that
migrants 'carrying' cholera and typhus, amounted to a 'new black death' that
could overwhelm Western European civilization.

Relief programs remained necessary to cope with the refugees resulting from
the redrawing of frontiers; during the 1930s fascist and kindred regimes produced
a new generation of displaced persons to be cared for. Scrutiny of relief work
during the Depression shows novel scientific concerns, as with the testing of new
diets and therapies. Moreover, the whole concept of relief in situ contrasted sharply
with the freedom of movement allowed to refugees during the nineteenth century.
Migration had been a safety valve in the event of poverty and persecution: the new
spirit of national self-determination had its reverse side with restrictive policies on
migration necessitating largescale international assistance and welfare programs.

### THE MODERN MEDICAL SERVICES

The interwar decades saw a first shift in the ethos of public health and medicine,
away from charity and towards a scientific understanding of the causes of poverty
and disease. The Weimar constitution proclaimed family welfare as a fundamental
state responsibility, whereas it had previously been a task for the voluntary sector.
Poor law systems involving the deprivation of civil rights and much stigma were
being replaced. Public health systems were expansive: including new model health
centers which angered medical professions, in that they undertook comprehensive
services. German doctors organized strikes and boycotts against the socialist-sup-
ported *Ambulatorien*, Policlinics or health centers. (The term Policlinic had a

double meaning: the provision of a multiplicity of services, and medical care on a free and universal basis.) Berlin saw pioneering experiments such as a cosmetic clinic (for persons disfigured after operations for cancer or from accidents), baby gymnastics and birth control. London also supported pioneering experiments ranging from the holistic ethos of the Peckam Health Centre to the public health oriented Finsbury Health Centre.

Mental hygiene and mental deficiency, child guidance, and school health services seem to typify the services available for hitherto neglected groups of children and adolescents. Yet when the quality of provision is scrutinized, we are often left with some highly idiosyncratic experiments such as open air schools for children with respiratory problems, and encouragement to exercise. Air and light, and physical exertion were all low cost commodities and moreover, many such facilities had strong eugenic overtones. A war was waged between birth control campaigners wanting to provide sexual advice and contraception clinics for adolescents, and eugenicists demanding marriage advice clinics whereby potential for marriage and having high quality children could be ascertained and a certificate of suitability issued.

For all that the services were fragmenting, the political right launched a bitter onslaught against the cost of public medical services and insurance. The physician-author Céline debunked the system by arguing that a patient wanted nothing more than to have himself declared tuberculous so that a lifelong pension could be paid. As such arguments came to a high point during the Depression, one solution was sterilization for persons held in mental institutions. Positive health gave way to negative eugenic measures, not only in Germany but also in France and Scandinavia. Sterilization of the mentally ill became a favored cost-cutting measure allowing release into the community.

The more that corporate medical organizations developed (e.g., sickness insurance,) the more entrenched became the medical opposition: a medical version of class conflict emerged with doctors' representative bodies demanding freedom from the scientised and bureaucratized state and from corporate insurances. Bureaucratic medicine came under attack both from left and right, and both sets of critics included advocates of 'natural healing' and 'alternative' therapies. Many rank and file physicians saw state medicine as reductive and as neglecting the whole person: in mid-1920s Germany, Erwin Lick exemplified this right-wing practitioner backlash against scientific medicine.

## PUBLIC HEALTH

The increasingly internationalist outlook of public health elites was encouraged by public health interchange schemes, massively funded by the Rockefeller Foundation through the League of Nations Health Organization (LNHO). The League of Nations provided a framework of collective security and regulation, and a health organization was among its technical agencies intended to promote social stability.

Article 23 (f) of the Treaty of Versailles stated that "The members of the League will endeavor to make international arrangements to the end of preventing or combating disease", while being vague about the means of achieving these ends. Positive policies were formulated to promote health and welfare on a wide range of issues. However, resentment by national governments and competition from the voluntary sector and from the International Office of Public Hygiene in Paris meant that the LNHO itself became a battleground for conflicting strategies of international health work.

Although the interwar medical researchers enjoyed increasing prestige, their discoveries were slow to benefit populations. Tuberculosis prevention is a case in point. Though the theoretical underpinnings for the BCG vaccine were developed before WWI, by scientists associated with the Pasteur Institutes, the French government was slow to act. Even in terms of public education, the Rockefeller Foundation's Sanitary Commission found the French situation highly frustrating. German distrust of the BCG culminated in a disastrous use of a contaminated batch of vaccine at Lübeck in 1930.

Despite intensive research into bacteriology there were few practical outcomes after the Great War: influenza swept the world and doctors could do nothing. Improvements to diphtheria serum therapy meant that anatoxin serum was available for preventive immunization, but this was only very partially used. For typhus, and many other infectious diseases, vaccines were difficult to produce and only partially effective, and there was no chemotherapy; typhus remained endemic in eastern Poland and Russia. A similar situation pertained to malaria in Southern Europe which was more amenable to destroying the mosquito habitats than to vaccines or anything other than the traditional quinine therapy. Some drug-based therapies continued to be highly toxic, e.g., salvarsan therapy for syphilis — public campaigns were waged against its compulsory use. Cancer became an increasing but intractable problem. Heroic surgical treatments were attempted for TB, e.g., the use of collapsed lung therapy. Generally this was an age of severe medical interventions — of malaria therapy for syphilis, or insulin coma shock therapy for mental illness. The techniques were dramatic although the outcomes were highly dubious. Eugenic sterilization fitted well with such draconian remedies, and its use became routine not only in Nazi Germany from July 1933 but also in Scandinavia.

It is difficult to assess the overall impact of medicine and hygiene on levels of health care. On the whole, life expectancy was improving in Western Europe, although not in the East. Infants, who had proved resilient in the postwar turmoils of influenza and inflation continued to show a decline in mortality. Only the Depression and conditions in Nazi Germany saw a rise in children's diseases.

## ROCKEFELLER MEDICINE AND INTERNATIONAL PUBLIC HEALTH

Like the state medical services, the voluntary sector, was also undergoing a process of modernization linked to professionalisation of social and public health work, as is well exemplified by the controversial history of the Rockefeller Foundation (RF), the most powerful and tenacious of the US agencies offering medical assistance. The international role of the RF — and other kindred corporate philanthropies like the Carnegie, Milbank Memorial Fund and Commonwealth Fund substantially qualified the impression of US withdrawal from the world stage.

Whilst British experts often favored quasi-military solutions to Europe's health problems, using quarantine and disinfection stations to establish sanitary cordons, the Rockefeller favored programs of *positive* preventative measures. Hygiene institutes were to be bulwarks against epidemics by acting as centers of a new infrastructure of clinics and health centers staffed by doctors and nurses trained in modern public health methods. Improved nutrition and personal hygiene would promote the body's physical resistance to infections. Moreover, the broad agenda of social and preventive medicine would reinforce political stability by building up internal administrative structures.

The RF's policy tried to avoid local political complications. It was keen that French microbiology and German bacteriology should be supplanted by American-style public health, which emphasized the sanitary infrastructure. 'Central Europe' (a term used in preference to the marginalizing concept of Eastern Europe) became a strategically important area of intervention with policies designed to promote a combination of scientific and social values, rather than simply to contain epidemics from the East. RF officers worked on a country by country basis, making visits, keeping meticulous diaries and compiling reports. Within each country, the RF sought to locate the scientifically innovative elite institutions and above all dynamic and far-sighted "men" — and in certain spheres like public health nursing, women — who would take a leadership role in research, teaching and the implementation of American-style thinking. A report on Poland commented that even though there was no true political consciousness, "if the unusual individuals get a chance at control the country will forge ahead rapidly."[2] Ethnic and national conflicts were simply ignored as irrational features of a past imperial order.

American training systems replaced the previous dependence in Central Europe on German and Austrian medical education and public health — even independent Serbia had relied on Vienna for medical training. RF policy was to transplant American models of public health — in the belief that European institutions were rendered backward by the war, and that the old guard of university professors were militaristic nationalists. By November 1920 Czech medical officers were inspecting the Johns Hopkins School of Hygiene in Baltimore which was advertised as a model for a central state hygiene institute: this visit began a process of study visits by Eastern European public health officials to the USA. Clinics and health centers promoted primary health care. The strategy was supported by grants, fellowships, and lavish contributions towards the building and running of palatial new institutes of hygiene. The Foundation provided full time public health advisors to the new health ministries, and RF fellows on their return to their home countries were expected to take over public health administration. Yet the RF did not wish to promote a two class system of medicine with scientific medicine only available for the wealthy. In identifying modern systems of preventive medicine and positive health with policies of collectivization, the RF was to encounter increasing difficulties.

The RF praised the reconstruction programs for war-ravaged Yugoslavia as "an outstanding achievement." In 1923 an institute of social medicine was established in Belgrade, along with ambitious plans for thirty health centers. The RF identified Andrija Stampar, the chief medical officer, as "a man of energy and wonderful enthusiasm," his vision of a collectivized primary health care infrastructure coincided with the RF's opposition to private medical practice and faith in a scientifically based system of public health.[3] Doctors were to be "social workers" rather than fruitlessly confined to hospitals and surgeries. Although Stampar believed in a unitary national administration, the federalist tide was recognized with his scheme for a new school of public health, epidemiological institute, and a central health office for Croatia and Slovenia, located at Zagreb.

The emergence of a belt of central state hygiene institutes between the Baltic and the Black Sea was to be completed by new institutes and dispensary clinics in Bulgaria and Roumania. The rationale for the massive injection of funds in Central Europe becomes apparent once it is appreciated that were no public health fellowships either for Germany or the Soviet Union. Although the Foundation claimed its philanthropy was devoid of political calculation, the contrast was stark between lavish funding in Eastern Europe and the refusal of appeals from individual Russian institutions like the Bacteriological Institute of the Moscow School of Medicine. The Foundation denied the Soviets aid for typhus and famine relief during 1921, and rejected requests for a RF "Plenipotentiary" to develop social hygiene early in 1923. However, the RF did not rule out sending medical literature and making small grants and traveling fellowships available to Soviet scientists, even as its officers emphasized the antithesis between communism and the RF's ideal of a "liberal and benevolent society".[4] The RF supplemented the League of Nations anti-malaria program in Russia and South East Europe, but not its scheme of 1923 for an LN-supported school of malaria in Soviet Georgia.

The RF did much to create an international community of medical researchers. Its renowned Fellowships enabled much cross-fertilization to take place between researchers from different laboratories. Yet its record in helping medical refugees from Nazism was limited to an elite of top flight researchers and the most outstanding of the younger generation. The Society for the Protection of Science and Learning, in which the British Nobel-prize winners Henry Dale and A.V. Hill were active, was more catholic and generous, partly from humanity, partly in the hope that well-qualified continental researchers could raise the standards of British science and medicine.

## FROM POSITIVE HEALTH TO TOTAL SURVEYS

The interwar period was marked by a decline in the birth rate offset by continuing improvements of infant mortality. Infectious diseases were on the wane, being replaced by chronic degenerative diseases, notably heart disease and cancers. Although in the long-term one can argue for convergence of European health trends, there were considerable class, regional and international differentials. The declining birthrate and declining mortality were most pronounced in Western and Northern Europe (Sweden's birth rate fell from 23.6 births per 1000 of the population in 1920 to 15.4 in 1939) infant mortality fell from 63 deaths per 1000 live births in 1920 to 40 in 1939). Infant mortality remained high in Eastern European countries like Roumania (at 221 per thousand live births in 1921 and 176 in 1939) and Yugoslavia (at 143 deaths per 1000 live births in 1925 and 140 in 1938).[5] Despite the innovative, and often inspirational health planning in the Soviet Union, health conditions remained atrocious, due to postwar famine exacerbated by the upheavals of collectivization.

For all the monitoring of health conditions, sanitary measures were driven more by ideology than by need. The Leitmotiv of the interwar measures was welfare for the 'coming generation' — a favored phrase among German advocates of social medicine — and positive health, the creed of the Belgian, René Sand. Turn of the century concerns with infant welfare and maternal advice gained widespread currency. By contrast, there was far less concern for the problems of old age, apart from patent methods such as Sergei Voronoff's rejuvenation by grafting of monkey glands. Muriel Paget's maternal and child health clinics, using a model from London's East End, were transplanted to areas of White Russian control in the East. In fascist Italy, Countess Daisy de Montherlant's infant welfare organization, ONMI, urged Italian mothers to breast feed as a patriotic duty. Ideas of puericulture attracted support in France, Italy and Spain.

Child welfare gained new intensity with school health services taking a prominent role in tackling problems of infestation (notably with head lice) and infection. This went with prescriptions for exercise, as well as exposure to air, sun and light as part of measures to promote "positive health" — all conveniently inexpensive. Open air schools were a favored innovation. Child and adolescent mental health became a preoccupation to stem the tides of dissipated youth. Clinics for 'psychopaths', and for child guidance were a new feature of the medical map.

Preventive medicine gained widespread currency. Although measures to combat sexually transmitted diseases date from the turn of the century, there was a rash of special clinics and hospital departments. These increasingly tolerated the use of condoms as a prophylactic against infections, and encouraged mass health education campaigns. Mass radiography was used from the early 1930s to screen for tuberculosis. Vaccination became routine, notably against smallpox, diphtheria, tetanus and typhoid. Some vaccines remained experimental: the BCG vaccine against tuberculosis encountered excessive suspicion, and the Polish government encouraged a new vaccine against typhus, laboriously produced from louse-guts. Those seeing food as the key to health were enthusiastic about the discovery of "vitamins" (a term coined by Casimir Funk, originally from what became Poland). These "accessory food factors" aroused much hope among environmentally-oriented medical researchers.

There were increasing expectations of curative medicine. New drugs like insulin for diabetes, and the sulfonamide drugs increased possibilities of maintenance or cure. Municipalities modernized hospital provision, ensuring that the burgeoning populations on the peripheries of cities were provided with district and specialized hospitals. The London County Council illustrates such efforts in the 1930s, as it strove to develop world class hospitals for research, teaching and therapy, such as the Maudsley for psychiatry and the Brompton Hospital for internal medicine. New operations like collapsed lung therapy for tuberculosis, malaria therapy for syphilis, or insulin coma therapy were hazardous, but commanded immense respect.

At a more mundane level there was a proliferation of clinics, sponsored by local government, insurance agencies or charities. Most controversial were birth control clinics; opinions differed as to whether these should be only for the married, offer advice (and a Wassermann test) on the medical suitability of an intended spouse, or offer assistance to all-comers. The wave of new specialized clinics led to some multifunctional clinics covering all aspects of primary health. Shortly after the war, there were innovative schemes for 'health centres' in Britain, for *Ambulatorien* in Germany, and for Policlinics in the Soviet Union. There was also new enthusiasm for industrial medicine to ensure that the factory was an efficient and healthy environment with the provision of medical screening, aptitude tests, sanitary facilities, canteens, leisure facilities and housing. New model communities surrounded large factories, as Siemensstadt near Berlin-Spandau, or Port Sunlight sponsored by Lever Brothers near Birkenhead.

Health became a value instilled in mass propaganda campaigns. The German Hygiene Museum in Dresden, having developed a technique of rendering anatomical preparations visible, created a sensation with its 'Visible Man' and 'Visible Woman' exhibitions. Mothers Days, Health Weeks, mass exhibitions, films and radio talks were all part of the arsenal of health propaganda.

Left and right supported welfare to ensure an economically and militarily fit future generation, but the reverse side of the coin was surveys to weed out social undesirables. Weimar Germany saw criminal-biological databanks identifying the 'anti-social'; the eugenicists involved correlated a range of police, economic and other social data with medical records. Similarly, Alexis Carrel, transplanted the Rockefeller Foundation scheme for a National Institute of Health into Vichy France. There his Institute sponsored medical and demographic schemes like the *carnet de santé*: continuous health checks on children were to draw on the co-operation between school medical officers, teachers, psychologists and the clergy.

The Vichy schemes found a parallel in Nazi health surveys, correlating medical and demographic data. Joachim Mrugowsky, from 1939 head of the hygiene institute of the Waffen-SS, applied botanical studies of the ecology and sociology of plant communities to teaching racial hygiene. He argued that hygiene involved study of the interactions of the living with their environment or *Umwelt*. His biogeographical approach to the social problems of the Mansfeld miners who lived in villages near the Harz mountains was geared to the Nazi policy of moving industry to rural areas. In line with Nazi views of dynamic and holistic science, he constantly criticized Koch's bacteriology as narrow in its concern with infections rather than with the totality of physical, social, cultural, historical and geographical factors shaping health.

Although in reality quite sporadic, the new 'comprehensive' medical services encountered savage opposition, as noted above. Disgruntled physicians equated socialization of health care with socialism and conservatives attacked expenditure on medical institutions as a burden on the economically productive. The argument for eugenics and for economy converged in the Nazi attack on mental hospitals and institutions for the disabled: killing the mentally ill to improve the race cost but little — in financial terms.

The new welfare measures were often opposed by feminists and radical socialists, who disliked the prescriptive medical controls over birth control and abortion. Such opposition was intense among German radical feminists, who campaigned for the woman's rights over her body as sovereign. There was rapid disillusionment with the Soviet system of abortion as excessively dependent on medical controls. A campaign was waged in Germany to remove the criminal penalties against abortion, and radical campaigners for birth control attacked Weimar social hygiene advocates as excessively medical in their stress on the eugenically fit. This was part of a thoroughly radical critique of professional powers over health, welfare and medical knowledge.

### CONCLUSION

Health care, of its nature, depends on local contingiencies within the family, on housing, occupation and the environment, as well as on practitioner-patient interactions. Neither welfare states nor international bureaucracies were able to achieve massive health improvements, and to overcome the disruptions of politics, economic crises and ultimately a second world war. The verdict on the interwar public health has to be ambivalent. The short time span, the lack of resources and the numerous political obstacles must be taken into account in making the achievements of welfare states and international health organizations all the more remarkable. Yet the health and humanitarian work should not be viewed uncritically. The spirit of the brave new world of interwar public health and welfare was not without its more sinister aspects, and such agencies as the International Committee of the Red Cross proved unable to protect the victims of military oppression and racial ideologies of the Axis powers during the Second World War.

REFERENCES

1.  T. Janiszewski, 'The Versailles Treaty and the Question of Public Health', *International Journal of Public Health* (1921), **2**: 140–51.
2.  P.J. Weindling, 'Public Health and Political Stabilisation: the Rockefeller Foundation in Central and Eastern Europe Between the Two World Wars', *Minerva* (1993), **21**: 253–67, and RAC RF 1.1/789/2/13 R.M. Pearce, 'Poland, report on Medical Education' ca 1920.
3.  Rockefeller Archive Center (hereafter RAC) RF 6.1/1.3/46/524 report by Gunn, 5 September 1924.
4.  RAC RG5 S.1.2B148 folder 1958 Sissin to RF letter of December 1922, folder 2272 letters of Rose to Sissin 19.2.1923 and Sissin to Rose 3.4.1923.
5.  B.R. Mitchell, *European Historical Statistics 1750–1975*. (London, 1981), p. 141.

FURTHER READING

Alter, P. (ed.), *Im Banne der Metropolen. Berlin und London in den zwanziger Jahren*. (Göttingen, 1993), pp. 174–187.

Baldwin, N., *The Society for the Protection of Science and Learning Archive*. (Oxford, 1988).

Baldwin, P., *The Politics of Social Solidarity. Class Bases of the European Welfare State*. (Cambridge, 1990).

Brown, E.R., 'Public Health in Imperialism,' *American Journal of Public Health* (1976), **66**: 897–903.

Céline, *Voyage au bout de la nuit*. (Paris, 1932).

de Swaan, A., *In the Care of the State: Health Care, Education and Welfare in Europe and the USA in the Modern Era*. (New York, 1988).

Fisher, H.H., *The Famine in Soviet Russia 1919–1923*. (New York, 1927).

Grmek, M. (ed.), *Serving the Cause of Public Health. Selected Papers of Andrija Stampar*. (Zagreb, 1966).

Kamminga, A. and Cunningham, A. (eds), *The Science and Culture of Nutrition*. (Amsterdam, 1995).

Lang, Slobodan 'A Corner of History. Andrija Stampar, 1888–1958' *Preventive Medicine* (1975), **4**: 591–5.

Marrus, M., *The Unwanted. European Refugees in the Twentieth Century*. (New York and Oxford, 1985).

Quine, M.S., *Population Politics in Twentieth-century Europe. Fascist Dictatorships and Liberal Democracies*. (London, 1996).

Rose, K.W. (ed.), *The Availability of Foundation Records: A Guide for Researchers*. (Pocantico Hills, 1990).

Sablik, K., *Julius Tandler. Mediziner und Sozialreformer*. (Vienna, 1983), pp. 140–51.

Semashko, N.A., *Health Protection in the USSR*. (London, 1934).

Solomon, S.G., 'Social Hygiene in Soviet Medical Education, 1922–30', *Journal of the History of Medicine and Allied Sciences* (1990), **45**: 607–43.

Solomon, S.G. and Hutchinson, J.F. (eds), *Health and Society in Revolutionary Russia*. (Bloomington and Indianapolis, 1990).

Stampar, A., 'The Public Health Program of Yugoslavia', *International Journal of Public Health* (1921), **2**: 384–7.

Voronoff, S., *Rejuvenation by Grafting*. (London, 1925).

Weindling, P.J., 'Population Policies under Fascism: Germany, Italy and Spain Compared' in Teitelbaum, M.S. and Winter, J. (eds), *Population, and Resources in Western Intellectual Traditions*. (Cambridge University Press, 1989); also in *Population and Development Review* (1988), **14** *Supplement*: pp. 102–121.

Weindling, P.J., *Epidemics and Genocide in Eastern Europe 1890–1945*. (Oxford, 2000).

Weindling, P.J. (ed.), *International Health Organisations and Movements 1918–1939*. (Cambridge, 1995).

Weindling, P.J., 'The Rockefeller Foundation and German Biomedical Sciences, 1920–1940: from Educational Philanthropy to International Science Policy' in Rupke, N. (ed.), *Science, Politics and the Public Good*. (Basingstoke, 1988), pp. 36–62.

Weissman, B.M., *Herbert Hoover and Famine Relief to Soviet Russia 1921–23*. (Stanford, 1974).

# CHAPTER 4

# Soviet Medicine

## MARK G. FIELD

Soviet socialized medicine (SSM) was a distinct product of the Soviet system, shaped by its ideology, functional requirements and the vicissitudes of historical circumstances. It is indissolubly associated with the Soviet regime and lasted as long as the Soviet Union, for a period of about 70 years. After the collapse of the Union of Soviet Socialist Republics at the end of 1991, it too began to disintegrate, to be slowly replaced by a confused amalgam of reforms and of measures intended both to align SSM with the new ideological, economic and political realities and to remove some of the major problems that had characterized it during the Soviet period. This chapter will deal primarily with the Russian Federation, the largest of the successor states, with a population about half of the Soviet Union; the situation is not radically different in the other states that inherited the Soviet legacy. The health care system that has emerged in the first five years of the post-Soviet period bears, as might well be expected, many of the hallmarks or stigmata of SSM, and will do for many years to come. Indeed, most aspects of SSM now co-exist with new types of medical organization, management and financing which are oriented towards market decentralization, insurance, privatization and to a search for the efficiency and the efficacy that had been missing in the Soviet Union. Health care reform in the post-communist phase is hampered by political instability, faltering governmental structures, economic stagnation and a general lack of direction. In health care, as for other components of the safety-net system, there is policy inaction or what could be called "state desertion."[1]

SSM, in the past, had often provided an essential counter-argument to any negative appraisal of the Soviet regime. It was considered by many as the crown-jewel of the Soviet welfare state, its most important *redemptive* feature, the equivalent perhaps of the claim that Mussolini had made the trains run on time which was used to justify the excesses of Italian Fascism. And yet the co-existence of a welfare system, including universal health care, inside a totalitarian envelope presents us with an uncomfortable paradox: images of concentration camps clash with those of clinics, hospitals and personnel in white gowns; the wanton disregard of human life sits side by side with the struggle to protect and prolong it. Even seasoned dialecticians, accustomed to view social reality as a never-ending confrontation of the positive and the negative leading inexorably to a higher synthesis, find this reconciliation difficult to achieve. But a resolution of sorts can perhaps be attempted by looking at health as a 'natural resource,' a source of labor and fighting capacity.

The Soviet Union was the first country in the world to provide health services to the entire population as a public service paid from the state treasury. SSM was used by the regime's propaganda apparatus, at home and abroad, as evidence of the regime's 'concern for the people' and its overall superiority to capitalism's disregard for the welfare of the workers. Particularly before World War II, SSM often served as a model for other nations to emulate in the provision of health care. Indeed, the association of socialized medicine with the Soviet regime was such that Western advocates of national and universal health security were sometimes accused of wanting to use socialized medicine as a first wedge for the introduction of socialism, and eventually communism — a charge that had as much logic as arguing that firehouses cause fires.

SSM was born in the cauldron of the Bolshevik Revolution, when the new regime came to power toward the end of 1917, after three years of a devastating war. It faced a particularly difficult problem with epidemics that took a heavy toll from a population that was undernourished and lacked such common disinfectants as soap. "Typhus," Lenin declared shortly after the revolution, "among a population [already] weakened by hunger without bread, soap, fuel, may become such a scourge as not to give us an opportunity to undertake socialist construction. This [must] be our first step in our struggle for culture and for [our] existence."[2] And in 1919, at the height of the epidemic, he faced the Congress of the Soviets with the blunt choice "either the louse [carrier of typhus] conquers socialism or socialism conquers the louse."[3] Stemming the impact of epidemics on the civilian and military population had priority, but those in the regime who were concerned with health and medical matters had well-defined views on the nature of medicine, health services and public health. From the time of the Bolshevik Revolution of October 1917 to the end of the 1920s, Soviet medicine was dominated by the ideas of social hygienists (inspired by their German colleagues) and by Marxist ideology.

This ideology saw illness and (premature) mortality as primarily the product of a sick or pathological society, i.e. capitalism, to be brought under control first by socialism, and then by communism. This would usher in a new period for mankind that would eventually be free of the socially produced ills of the former structure. The social hygienists, in particular, felt that the causes of most illnesses and early deaths lay in social habits and institutions. The solution was to be the transformation of society and the re-education of the population. Clinical medicine (the treatment of illness after it occurred) was relegated to a secondary position; its usefulness would gradually dwindle and it would be replaced by a more 'sociological' approach. Thus the orientation of the Commissariat of Health Protection, founded by a decree signed by Lenin in 1918, was to be preventive and social rather than clinical or remedial. And the curriculum in medical schools reflected this orientation. The term Health Protection (*zdravookhranenie* in Russian) conveys a sense that is broader than both medicine and public health. In its ideal form it means a comprehensive approach to the preservation of health in which the distinction between clinical medicine and public health is blurred. The pathologies that were to be addressed were more social than biological: alcoholism, sexually transmitted illnesses and prostitution, drug abuse, industrial hygiene, occupational diseases, and so on. To this general orientation one must add the tradition of *Zemstvo* or 'land' medicine which had arisen in Russia in the second half of the nineteenth century, as part of a general movement among certain groups of the Russian intelligentsia to 'go the people' in the countryside, and to bring them the benefits of education and health care. Physicians who had volunteered to serve as *Zemstvo* physicians forsook the advantages, comforts and financial rewards of the cities to bring a modicum of medical attention to the peasantry which made up the vast majority of the population. They were paid a small salary by land assemblies, and were generally regarded as cultural heroes who sacrificed themselves to benefit 'the people.' The Soviet regime was to invoke this tradition, particularly as it turned medical professionals into state employees and replaced the voluntary aspects of medicine with a more coercive approach, posting physicians and other health personnel to the countryside. At the same time, the regime destroyed the associational bases of the medical profession and the limited autonomy it had enjoyed even under the repressive Tsarist autocracy. This was in line with the new regime's unwillingness to countenance independent sources of power.

That first period in the history of SSM embraced the turbulent years of War Communism (1918–1921) and the period of the New Economic Policy (1921–1928) which permitted a limited amount of capitalistic free enterprise, giving the Soviet regime a much needed breathing spell after the traumas of War Communism. The NEP came to an end when Stalin was able to establish his undisputed sway over Soviet society. This meant a return to Bolshevik principles, the abandonment (at least temporarily) of attempts to foment world-wide revolutions, and the decision to establish socialism in one country, i.e., Soviet Russia. This translated into ambitious programs for the collectivization of agriculture and the rapid industrialization and militarization of the country, so as to protect it from an expected onslaught by a hostile 'capitalist world.' These programs were to be financed primarily from enforced savings at home, rather than by borrowing capital from abroad. The succession of Five Year Plans from 1928 to 1941 led not only to rapid industrialization and urbanization, but to a considerable deterioration in an already low standard of living, and to massive coercion at all levels. From 1941–1945 the Soviet Union fought Germany. It emerged victorious but economically and demographically devastated. Stalin's reign came to an end in 1953, and was followed by the regimes of Khrushchev, Brezhnev, Andropov and Chernenko, and finally Gorbachev, who introduced the reforms known under *perestroika* from 1985 to the dissolution of the Soviet Union in 1991.

In health care, the period from 1918 to 1928 can be called 'idealistic': the following period (1928–1991) might be called 'practical.' Health policies changed radically from the ideologically driven sociological schemes to more conventional remedial and clinical approaches. In fact the industrialization drive created (or re-created) the very same conditions that social hygienists and especially Marxists had excoriated as associated with the early stages of capitalism and the merciless exploitation of workers. In this second period, the major purpose of the health care system became 'functional' — to maintain and repair the working and fighting capacity of the population. As the social and preventive approach was downgraded, the medical curriculum reverted to a more traditional form, re-emphasizing the clinical medicine which had been so downplayed in the earlier phase as to produce doctors with limited capacity to meet the immediate problems and needs of patients. It was during these years that what became known as SSM took its shape; after Stalin's death there were attempts to tinker with it at the margins, but there were no fundamental changes in the philosophy and the structure of the health care system. It was also during these years of construction, political purges, war devastation and totalitarian controls that the health care system expanded at an explosive rate, both in terms of the number of health personnel (particularly doctors) and hospital beds. This quantitative growth, however, was not paralleled by qualitative improvements.

## SOCIALIZED MEDICINE SOVIET-STYLE

Perhaps the most striking aspect of SSM was the official commitment, backed by constitutional provisions, to free and universal (though not necessarily equal) access to qualified medical care as a public service at the expense of the state treasury, i.e., paid from taxes, and at no direct cost to the patient. This was a 'first' in history, and although SSM has now more or less collapsed, its basic ideological and organizational blueprint continues to deserve attention as one possible variant in the provision of health services to the population of an industrializing and urbanizing society. The Soviet experiment is suggestive and its failings may be partly attributable to the soil in which it was implanted and which, for a variety of reasons could not sustain it.

The constitutional promise of universal health care at the expense of society varied, in its formulation, from constitution to constitution but the basic provisions of the idea of 'entitlement' remained more or less the same. The last Soviet Constitution, adopted in 1977 and in force at the time of the collapse, stated:

> Citizens of the USSR have the right to health protection. This right is insured by the development and improvement of safety and hygiene in industry, in carrying broad prophylactic measures; by measures to improve the environment; by special care for the health of the youth including the prohibition of child labor, excluding the work done by children as part of the school curriculum; and by developing research to prevent and reduce the incidence of disease and ensure citizens a long and active life.[4]

The above formulation, which can be interpreted as the fundamental law of SSM was put into practice through a series of principles or by-laws, listed below not necessarily in their order of importance. Some of these, as will be noted, were observed more in the breach than in reality.

1. *Health care is a public or governmental responsibility.* Public health and clinical medicine (a distinction between the two, as noted earlier, was not very marked) were a responsibility of the state implemented by the government as a public service. This left no room for the private sector (with one major exception, see 4 below) nor for charity, voluntary activities or the market.

2. *The planned nature of the health system.* Like the rest of the Soviet system, the unfolding of health care policy and services was not a spontaneous process, the result of a myriad decisions, but was closely integrated with the development of the economy, particularly its drive toward industrialization, urbanization and militarization. Planning had been part of Soviet policy ever since Stalin launched the Five Year Plans at the end of the 1920s. Because health care was a government responsibility and financed almost entirely by the state, there was real control over the health system.

3. *Administrative and bureaucratic centralization.* The general management of the health system was vested, at the highest national level, into one central authority, the Ministry (formerly Commissariat) of Health Protection of the USSR. The Minister was thus the Chief Medical Officer of the entire Soviet Union, a member of the cabinet (the Council of Ministers of the USSR) and always a doctor. The Ministry operated directly in matters of national significance, or through counterpart ministries of the constituent republics, and all the way down through health protection departments at every administrative level, including the localities. As such the Ministry controlled about 90% of all medical facilities, the exception being the facilities of special departments or other ministries (such as the armed forces, the railroads or the security organs) to which we shall refer later.

4. *Free services.* One of the basic aspects of SSM, and the one that has attracted most attention, was the fact that the services were free. There was no provision for a financial transaction between the patient and the doctor or the clinic or the hospital. The financing of health care was assumed by the state, and was paid from the state budgets at the different administrative levels. These funds were raised from taxes, most of which were invisible to the consumer, i.e., they were included in the price of most goods and commodities. Most of the population received relatively small incomes, including health personnel, who earned about 70% of the average national income. In essence, the system spread the costs of health care and allied services to the entire population, providing a sense of psychological assurance or reassurance that illness would not be an economic catastrophe and that no one would be deprived of medical

care. Indeed, most persons who left the Soviet Union, presumably because they were dissatisfied with life and opportunities there, reported that the provision of free health services (although the quality was often poor) was one of the more positive aspects of the Soviet system, and one of the few aspects worth preserving.

There were, however, some officially sanctioned exceptions. For example, there were state operated polyclinics where, for a modest fee, one could see a more qualified and experienced physician than at the free clinic and where the waiting time was considerably less. Pharmaceuticals, prescribed for out-patient use, also had to be paid for by patients, although those suffering from chronic conditions (such as diabetes) were usually exempted. But perhaps most interesting was the fact that the private practice of medicine was never illegal in the Soviet Union, although it was heavily taxed and in fact restricted to a small number of physicians who had enough room in their apartments. The official explanation was that there were still some problems in medical care but that once these had been ironed out, people would stop going to physicians privately when they could get the same level of care free of charge. There were no officially sanctioned private medical facilities, such as hospitals, although there were equivalents, to be described below. More disturbing, particularly in the years preceding the collapse, was the increasing tendency of doctors and other health personnel to exact 'money under the table' for services that were supposed to be free. This custom, sometimes known as 'envelope passing medicine' could make a sick joke of the vaunted gratuity of health services; it was also a heavy burden on patients with low incomes.

5. *Prevention as the official cornerstone of socialized medicine.* One of the fundamental tenets of Soviet medicine was its preventive orientation. This often translated into ambitious programs such as mass screenings of population groups deemed to be particularly at risk (adolescents, women, coal miners, and so on); such programs, called *dispensarizatsia*, were destined eventually to cover the entire population. Screenings, which in the West have not proven cost effective, were often performed perfunctorily. As mentioned earlier, the preventive orienta-tion that was so prevalent in the first phase of SSM became increasingly marginal in later years, when the system was increasingly directed to the treatment of disease and trauma.

6. *Unity of theory and practice.* The official stand of SSM, given the symbolic importance of ideology in the USSR, was the close connection between theory (the Soviet interpretation of Marxism or Marxism-Leninism) and practice. This meant that research was to be oriented primarily toward the solution of practical problems, for example the impact of a flu epidemic on labor pro-ductivity, rather than to basic or esoteric research that had no immediate results. Given its limited resources, Soviet medicine relied to a great extent

on foreign medical research. There have been no Nobel Prizes in Medicine or Physiology awarded to Soviet researchers.

7. *Role of the people.* Ideologically, and in official theory, the health system belonged to the people, and could not operate without their support. In fact the lay population had very little role in assisting or supporting the health system. In most cases, their support was limited to relatives bringing food to hospitalized patients.

8. *Priority.* As long as health care was regarded as a scarce resource, access and quality were determined, to a large extent, by the patient's position, occupation or rank in a society that had become highly stratified. The elites received the best that was available, as did members of their immediate families. For the peasants, care was often Spartan and dispensed in most instances by *feldshers* (physician assistants) rather than medical practitioners.

## THE STRUCTURE OF SOVIET SOCIALIZED MEDICINE

A fundamental characteristic of Soviet socialized medicine was its position as a governmental department, subordinate to the state and particularly to the Communist Party, the real ruler of Soviet society. It was thus an integral instrument of the polity. The apex of the Soviet system of socialized medicine was the Ministry of Health Protection of the USSR, of which the responsibilities were enormous, including the provision of medical and preventive services, the education and training of health personnel (which it shared with the Ministry of Education), the financing and supervision of medical research, the procurement (and sometimes the manufacturing) of medical equipment and pharmaceuticals. As noted earlier, the Ministry was responsible for matters of national (or federal relevance), and operated through subordinate republican health ministries, and health departments. Each administrative unit of the Ministry (except the national one) was simultaneously part of the governmental unit to which it was attached and to the next higher unit of the Ministry from which it received both mandate and some logistic support. The Ministry became a large, unwieldy, bureaucratic organization, slow to respond to emergencies and new situations, as was the case, for example, in the Chernobyl catastrophe, and often more prone to brush problems under the rug than to face them squarely.

Doctors worked as state employees (some would call them medical bureaucrats) trained, assigned and remunerated (poorly) by the state, and devoid of most of the attributes that generally characterize a professional occupation, such as an autonomous professional association that could defend their interests. articulate their views and raise their incomes.

The low point in the history of the Soviet medicine was, perhaps, the infamous Doctors' Case. Early in 1953 the press announced that a group of highly regarded physicians, most of whom were Jews, catering to the highest elites, had conspired to murder or hasten the death of their patients with contra-indicated treatment.

The charge was anti-Semitic, patently absurd, and later revealed as a complete fabrication, but not a single voice, medical or non-medical, was or could have been raised to protest the accusation. After Stalin's death, which providentially happened three months after the charges, the physicians were released (some had died during interrogations) and such flagrant abuses did not occur again, though physicians remained politically powerless until the end of the regime. The abuse of psychiatry to repress dissidents between 1960 and 1990 was also indicative of the subordinate status of physicians.

## ACCESS TO CARE

One of the distinctive aspects of SSM was that, in theory, everyone was assigned to a medical facility, not as a result of personal choice, but as a function of residence, occupation or rank. Organizationally, the population was served by two networks of medical facilities: the territorial or residential network and the closed or departmental network.

1.  In the Territorial or Residential Network, which served the great majority of the population, residential address determined the outpatient polyclinic to which the individual (or the family) was assigned. For this purpose the population was divided into catchment areas known as medical districts of about 40,000 persons (about 10,000 children and 30,000 adults), though the numbers could vary. The physical size of the districts depended on population density, being quite small in the cities, and very large in the countryside. The district was thus *not* a geographical area but an administrative-medical one. It was in turn sub-divided into micro-districts of about 4,000 persons, each of which was served by two or three physicians, *terapevti*, preferably including a pediatrician, plus a nurse and other supportive personnel. A polyclinic served a district, i.e., about 40,000 persons and was a primary care, out-patient facility, though in the countryside where distances were great and the roads often impassable, it might have a small (less than 10 beds) in-patient unit. The district polyclinic served as the gateway into the medical care system. Each one had a complement of specialists, who covered more than one micro-district and each was affiliated with hospitals (again serving several medical districts) to which patients could be referred for in-patient care. There were, in addition, specialized out-patient dispensaries for specific conditions or population groups (pre-natal care, tuberculosis, cancer, nervous diseases and so on). The territorial or residential principle (which had been in part inspired by certain aspects of pre-Revolutionary *Zemstvo* medicine) meant that each inhabitant knew where to turn for medical attention. And in that scheme of automatic assignment a mutual choice of patient and doctor was not practical. Physicians saw patients at the polyclinic for about half of their working day, and made home-visits for the other half. Clinic consultations were usually limited to a

few minutes (often less than ten), and half of the time was consumed by paper work. Dr G Ivanov, in a letter to Izvestiia in 1986, complained that he was so pressed for time that he had to make diagnoses and prescribe treatment as speedily as a "jet pilot in aerial combat."[5] Another doctor reported that she went through her appointments without looking up at her patients. Her load was 36 patients in four hours, thus 7 minutes per patient, with more than half of that time consumed by paper work[6].

2. The Closed or Departmental Network encompassed a variety of medical systems, access to which was determined by occupation or rank rather than residence. Departmental health care systems were reserved for the members of certain administrations or ministries, as well as a number of organizations such as the Academy of Sciences or even the employees of large department stores. They were not available to the general population, hence the title 'closed.' In addition, industrial enterprises had their own medical hospitals and clinics, the larger the enterprise the more comprehensive these facilities. In factories and plants, the factory doctor in charge of the health of the workers in that unit was the functional equivalent of the micro-district physician. There were, in addition, a whole range of closed facilities reserved for the members of the different elites, culminating in the hospitals, clinics and rest-homes of the Kremlin (called the *Kremlinovka*) where the highest officials (and their families) had access to the best medical care, equipment and buildings available in the country. In some instances patients could also be sent abroad for treatment. These palatial facilities, the equivalent of private hospitals and clinics in the West, were considered as perquisites of rank and part of 'socialized medicine'; and as far as we know, they were financed from the budgetary allocations to health protection.

Thus medical care reflected the highly stratified nature of Soviet society, and promotion or demotion changed one's medical category. The closed facility meant higher status, and the health care was better than in the territorial network used by ordinary people. The lavish elite and specialized medical institutions employed a disproportionate amount of the financial and personnel resources available for health care; the territorial network suffered shortages of all sorts. In a country that boasted more doctors and hospital beds per capita than anywhere else in the world, ordinary people received minimal assistance, with long waits and poorly equipped hospitals. In 1987, for example, about half of all doctors in Moscow worked in special or closed polyclinics or hospitals.[7] It has been estimated by Christopher Davis[8] that about one tenth of one percent of the population received superlative care (in Soviet terms); 25% received relatively high quality care in departmental and capital cities facilities. Another 24% received acceptable services in medium city and industrial subsystems. And about half of the population received poor or substandard care in the countryside and low density areas. As seems to be the case universally, the elites knew how to take care of themselves and displayed a Marie Antoinettish insouciance for the others.

## PREVENTION

Although, as mentioned earlier, prevention was supposed to be central to Soviet socialized medicine, relatively few resources were devoted to it. One of the keystones of prevention was the Sanitary-Epidemic Station, usually with its own laboratories, that was to monitor both the quality of the environment, such as water purity and air pollution, and the levels of morbidity and mortality. As mentioned earlier toward the end of the Soviet regime, there was a campaign to screen the entire population.

## EDUCATION AND TRAINING OF PERSONNEL

The training of physicians began at the age of 18, following the European model, at the completion of secondary education. The medical curriculum lasted six years, except in dentistry (considered as a sub-specialty of medicine) and in pharmacology where it was shorter by about one year. Upon completion of formal medical studies, the graduate received the diploma of *vrach*. He or she (the majority of medical students and practitioners were women) followed an internship program, and was assigned to work in the countryside, a fate that many managed to escape through bureaucratic manipulations or getting married. The idealism of *Zemstvo* medicine was seemingly lacking among young Soviet physicians. Work in the countryside was generally disliked not only because of the primitive living conditions and lack of 'culture,' but because inexperienced doctors were afraid of taking responsibility for the health of patients when they had so little practical experience. Another feature of the medical educational system was the existence of refresher institutes where courses were available to doctors who had been in practice for several years, and where they could be brought up to speed on medical advances and new treatment procedures. Indeed, practitioners were obliged to go on such courses at regular intervals, provided some arrangement be made for their replacement while away. Practitioners desirous to pursue a career in academic medicine or in research usually followed a course of post-graduate studies. These led first to the degree of Candidate of Medical Sciences (the equivalent of a degree between a Masters and a PhD in the West) and eventually a Doctor of Medical Sciences. This was usually achieved in mid-career and the doctoral thesis was expected to be an important contribution to medical science. It opened the path to a Professorship. Additional recognition, and particularly prestigious, was the appointment first as a Corresponding, then a Full Member of the Academy of Medical Sciences (distinct from the Academy of Sciences – the highest accolade reserved for those making advances on the frontiers of knowledge).

Access to training for positions in the category of semi-professional personnel was open after seven years of secondary education, and lasted two to three years depending upon the specialty. These included, among other, *feldshers* (physician-assistants in several sub-specialties), nurses, midwives, laboratory, x-ray, dental and other technicians.

## MEDICAL RESEARCH

As already mentioned, medical research was not a high priority in Soviet socialized medicine. It was the responsibility primarily of the Academy of Medical Sciences, and to some degree of the Academy of Sciences, and their affiliated institutes. The Academy of Medical Sciences was financed by the Ministry of Health which was in a position to direct and control the activities of the Academy. Though Soviet medicine had certain technical advances to its credit (in the application of lasers, for instance), the major concern was the application of medical knowledge produced elsewhere.

## ACHIEVEMENTS

The Soviet regime, in the course of its 70-year history, created a very large health care system almost *de novo* although it did inherit certain important elements from its Tsarist past, such as the concept of *Zemstvo* medicine (and the territorial principle mentioned earlier) and a tradition of state services for the poorer members of the population. It built a huge network of health care facilities, and it trained large numbers of physicians (more than 60% of whom were women.) These quantitative accomplishments were not, however, matched by high quality, whether in the training of physicians or in the medical establishments, excepting those reserved for the higher orders of Soviet society. During the period of *glasnost* the Health Protection Minister of the USSR appointed by Gorbachev pointed out in some detail the flaws of Soviet health care and bore down hard on the quality of physicians, declaring that about 10% were incompetent and should either be re-trained, demoted to *feldshers* or drummed out of medicine. Many of the hospitals had unsuitable buildings and often, particularly in the countryside and the periphery, devoid of such necessities as hot and cold water, running water and a sewerage system. The equipment was often primitive, pharmaceutical supplies limited, and the clinical care mediocre — probably about 20 years behind the West. Because they were kept isolated from foreign contacts, even the doctors were often ignorant of advances in other countries.

But whatever the shortcomings of clinical care, as judged by current Western standards, health indices, except for periods of stress and demographic trauma such as the Second World War, improved substantially during the Soviet years, a tribute both to economic development and medical care. The conventional wisdom is that only about 10% of the variance in morbidity and mortality is due to the efforts of medical personnel; more significant are living conditions (50%), the environment (20%) and genetics (20%).[9] But toward the late 60s the health indices began to show a reversal of the trend. This may have been the result of the inability of SSM to recognize and cope with the shift from infectious diseases to non-infectious and degenerative conditions. It may also have reflected the decision taken by Soviet leaders after the Cuban episode, to devote all their energies and resources to building a defense establishment to match that of NATO, and this with a Gross National Product considerably smaller than that of the West. When Gorbachev came to power he was shocked to find that military expenditures were not 16% of the national budget but 40%, and that this amounted not to 6% of the GNP but to 20%;[10] more than three times the corresponding figure for the United States. The result was a further decrease in the standard of living and the relegation of health care (and other safety-nets) to a marginal, or as Dr E.I. Chazov, called it, a 'residual',[11] priority — after all other expenses had been met, the leftovers would go to health protection. It can be estimated that in the 60s the Soviet Union spent about 6 to 6.5% of its GNP on health, a respectable figure in line with Western European countries. The figure fell to 4.1% in 1970 and 3% in 1980. In 1988, Health Protection Minister Chazov complained that, on an international scale, the Soviet allocation to health as a proportion of the GNP ranked about 75th among 126 countries.[12] At the time of the demise of the regime, this figure had dwindled to probably less than 3%.[13]

The collapse of the Soviet Union at the end of 1991 only served to exacerbate the health care crisis. Five years later the situation had become critical, with a very significant increase in mortality (particularly adult male) and a decrease in natality accompanied by an increase in abortions, the traditional means of birth control in the USSR. By 1996 the net result, especially in the Russian Federation, was a natural decrease of the population, i.e., more people died than were being born, a shortfall of about 0.4 to 0.6% per annum.[14] In the rush to dismantle the socialized medicine associated with the ancien regime, the post-communist world had neither the time nor the financial resources to build a replacement. There have been endless discussions about health care reform, and about market-oriented insurance, competition, and efficiency (if not effectiveness), but the results have been very uneven, and often dismal. In the absence of a viable alternative, the remnants of the old state-system continue to provide mediocre care. Medical practitioners and other health personnel are, for the most part, still poorly paid (as before earning about 70% of the average income of the working population), and doctors have gone on strike complaining they were being paid less than veterinarians and bus drivers, and warning that a 'hungry surgeon (or physician) was dangerous to your health.' Attempts are being made to reestablish professional associations and a professional ethic, but these are hampered by the lack of experience, and particularly by the shortage of economic means.

## DISCUSSION AND CONCLUSIONS

A central element in socialized medicine is the principle of entitlement, of a citizens' right to a service — a claim, backed by a constitution. Socialized medicine provides an element of psychological assurance that the state not only has the duty to take care of the health of its citizens, but that it has assumed this obligation in earnest. The Soviet regime provided this assurance as part of a basket of safety-nets which the population accepted as its due.

A health care system, however, does not exist in a vacuum but is part of the social and of the cultural milieu of the society which it serves. It partakes of the characteristics of that socio-cultural structure from which it must derive its sustenance — a variety of general resources which it metabolizes into specialized services aimed at the health problems it has decided to address. Thus the Soviet state, having assumed the responsibility for health services, had to implement it within a bureaucratic administration and an economy which from the 1960s was falling behind those of the West.

More recently, the inability of the post-communist government to collect more than a fraction of taxes has rendered it incapable of performing its assigned functions, and led to the perception of 'state desertion' mentioned earlier.

The noble purpose that socialized medicine was to serve led to a grand design, but also to a flawed execution and mixed results.[15] Of the many causes for these problems the following must be listed, not necessarily in the order of their importance.

1. *Bureaucratization and statization*: one of the major characteristics of the Soviet system of socialized medicine was its bureaucratization, and the nature of that administration seeped into the work, attitudes and behaviors of the physicians, often fostering a '9 to 5' mentality. This 'segmental' approach, however, is not unique to the Soviet system of socialized medicine, but is now becoming characteristic of medical practice the world over, and particularly in industrialized societies, with their advanced division of labor. The Soviet system seems to have been a harbinger of such trends, because of the extent of its reach (the entire population), and because of its official status as a governmental organization. It was the first national 'health maintenance organization'. The bureaucratic/statist nature of the physician's position was revealed, with great clarity, when physicians (mostly psychiatrists) were asked or ordered to diagnose political or ideological dissidents as suffering from a mental disorder.

2. *Loss of professional autonomy and corporate existence*: from the early days of the regime, physicians were deprived of their position as members of a medical/corporate entity capable of taking a stand against the polity and enjoying the degree of the autonomy that is an important mark of the professional in contemporary society. Doctors did join a Union of Medical Workers, which was in essence a company union (the company being the state), which also included all other personnel in the health field, and which functioned to maintain labor discipline, and to take care of certain administrative functions such as determining the level of pensions. There were, it is true, associations of

physicians and scientific societies, but they were not 'political' in any sense.

3. *Decreased economic support*: whereas in most developed countries the proportion of the GNP spent in health increased from World War II, often reaching critical levels (as is the case in the United States where it was about 14% in 1995), in the Soviet Union it began to decline in the 60s. It may now, (1996), be as low as 1.4%, although this figure is an estimate and does not include 'under the table payments.'

4. *General corruption*: this penetrated the medical care system in many of its aspects. Students were sometimes admitted to medical schools through bribery, and often received their diplomas without being capable of the simplest medical procedures. The low incomes received by health personnel may, to some extent, explain the asking and taking of bribes.

5. *The cumbersome nature of the Health Protection Ministry*: this made it difficult for the Minister to react to problems or conditions, and also to shift its efforts from the control of infectious and communicable diseases to chronic conditions. In addition, the secretive nature of the communist regime made it possible to hide the true nature of the situation either by not publishing statistical data, or by manipulating such data. In a way, health and demographic data were considered by the regime as strategic information that often could not be divulged in case it should give aid and comfort to the enemy (the West).

6. *Low priority of the health care sector*: this affected the whole health care field and especially the development and the production of medical equipment and pharmaceuticals. To a high degree, the Soviet Union became 'addicted' to the supply of pharmaceuticals from Eastern Europe, and neglected its own pharmaceutical industry. Before the collapse of the Soviet regime, these drugs were paid in rubles or non-convertible currencies. After the collapse, the producers demanded to be paid in hard currency, which was in very short supply, thus creating serious shortages.

7. *Stratification*: Soviet society was far from egalitarian but the perception of a universal right to health-care may have helped assuage the resentment of those in the lower orders; it might be easier to accept differences of housing or income than in health care which is often a question of life and death. We may note here that many of the lavish health facilities which once served the Soviet elite have now been privatized and are catering to the newly affluent members of Russian society.

8. *Isolation*: the Soviet regime kept the population isolated from the rest of the world, which it depicted as hostile to the Soviet Union. This isolation fostered xenophobia; it also kept physicians and medical scientists from close contacts with foreign colleagues and foreign developments.

We may conclude that the principles of SSM were laudable, but the environment in which these principles were put into practice was not propitious for the healthy growth of socialized medicine. In some sense, all industrial nations are now moving in the direction of universally available medical care as a right of citizenship, though they are using diverse modes of finance and administration. The history of the Soviet experiment with socialized medicine will remain an illustration of the complexity of the problem and the fragility of good intentions.

## REFERENCES

1. Abel and J. Bonin, 'State desertion and convertibility: the case of Hungary,' in I.P. Székely and D. Newberry (eds), *Hungary: An Economy in Transition.* (Cambridge: Cambridge University Press, 1993), cited in Michael Ellman's 'The increase in death and disease under 'katastroika',' *Cambridge Journal of Economics* (August 1994), vol. 18, **4**: 329–355.
2. Quoted in A.F. Tretyakov, *The Protection of the Peoples' Health in the RSFSR* (in Russian). (Moscow: Gospolitizdat, 1944), p. 12.
3. N.A. Vinogradov and I.D. Strashun, *Health Protection of the Workers in the Soviet Union* (in Russian), Moscow 1947, p. 6.
4. Article 42 in R. Sharlet, *The New Soviet Constitution of 1977.* (Brunswick, Ohio: King's Court Communication Inc, 1978).
5. G. Ivanov, 'Frankly,' (in Russian) *Izvestiia,* (7 February 1986).
6. A. Paikin and G. Silina, 'The district physician,' (in Russian) *Lituraturnaia gazeta,* (27 September 1978), and Iu. Tomashevskii, 'Paper fever,' (in Russian) *Izvestiia,* (7 January 1986).
7. T. Borich, 'For a limited circle-polemical remarks on special polyclinics and special hospitals,' in *Current Digest of the Soviet Press* (1987), no. 21, **39**: 2.
8. Christopher M. Davis, 'The Economics of the Soviet Health System: An Analytical and Historical Study, 1921–1978,' Ph.D. diss. Economics. (Cambridge University, 1979).
9. Natalia Rimashevskaia, 'The individual's health is the health of society,' *Sociological Research* (May–June 1993), p. 22.
10. Cited by Marshall I. Goldman, 'From Russia with scorn,' *Economic Newsletter,* Davis Center for Russian Studies, Harvard University, 22/3, (November 18, 1996), p. 3.
11. Evgenii I. Chazov, *Health and Power: The Reminiscences of a 'Kremlin' Physician* (in Russian). (Moscow: Novosti Press Agency, 1992), p. 10.
12. Evgenii I. Chazov, 'In search of the new, obstacles on the way,' *Meditsinskaia gazeta* (in Russian) (16 February 1990).
13. Mark G. Field, 'The health crisis in the former Soviet Union: a report from the 'post-war zone',' *Social Science and Medicine* (1995), **41**: 1469–1478.
14. *Ibid.*
15. Mark G. Field, 'Noble purpose, grand design, flawed execution, mixed results,' *American Journal of Public Health* (1990), **80**: 144–145.

## FURTHER READING

*Bol'shaia Meditsinskaia Entsiklopedia* Large Medical Encyclopedia (Moscow: State Publisher of Medical Literature, 1956–1964) in 36 volumes.

Davis, Christopher M., 'Developments in the health sector of the Soviet economy, 1970–1990' in US Congress Joint Economic Committee, *Gorbachev's Economic Plans.* (Washington: USGPO, 1987).

Davis, Christopher M., 'The Soviet health system: a national health service in a Socialist society,' in Mark G. Field, (ed.), *Success and Crisis in National Health Systems: A Comparative Approach.* (London: Routledge, 1989).

Feshbach, Murray, editor-in chief, *Environmental and Health Atlas of Russia.* (Moscow: PAIMS, 1995).

Field, Mark G., *Soviet Socialized Medicine: An Introduction.* (New York: Free Press, 1967)

Field, Mark G., *Doctor and Patient in Soviet Russia.* (Cambridge, MA: Harvard University Press, 1957).

Field, Mark G., 'Post-Communist medicine: morbidity, mortality and the deteriorating health situation,' in James R. Millar and Sharon L. Wolchik (eds), *The Social Legacy of Communism.* (Washington: Woodrow Wilson Center Press and Cambridge University Press, 1994).

Frieden, Nancy M., *Russian Physicians in an Era of Reform and Revolution, 1856–1905.* (Princeton: Princeton University Press, 1981).

Gantt, Horsley W., *A Medical Review of Soviet Russia.* (London: British Medical Association, 1928).

Haines, Anna J., *Health Work in Soviet Russia.* (New York: Vanguard Press, 1928).

Kaser, Michael, *Health Care in the Soviet Union and Eastern Europe.* (London: Croom Helm, 1976).

Knaus, William A., *Inside Russian Medicine.* (New York: Everest House, 1981).

Newsholme, Sir Arthur and John Adams Kingsbury, *Red Medicine: Socialized Health in Soviet Russia.* (Garden City, NY: Doubleday, 1933).

Ryan, Michael, *Doctors and the State in the Soviet Union.* (New York: St. Martin's Press, 1990).

Sigerist, Henry E., *Medicine and Health in the Soviet Union.* (New York: Citadel Press, 1947).

Solomon, Susan G. and John F. Hutchinson, (eds), *Health and Society in Revolutionary Russia.* (Bloomington: Indiana University Press, 1990).

# CHAPTER 5

# Colonial Medicine

## MICHAEL WORBOYS

In the twentieth century, the term 'colonial medicine' was primarily associated with the institutions established by European imperial powers to manage the health problems of their dependent territories in Africa, Asia and Latin America. However, if the term 'colonial' is taken to refer to relations of power and dependence between industrialized countries of the North and non-industrialized societies in the South in the context of imperialism, then 'colonial medical relations' can be seen analytically in four settings. Firstly in the colonies of European settlement, for example Australia and Canada, where medical relations largely mirrored political ones — in other words, European-style institutions and practices were copied and were expected to remain subordinate to established medical centers. However, as these colonies gained greater political autonomy through the century, they also struggled to establish less dependent medical cultures. In the second type of colony, where a small European army and administration governed developed cultures, as in India, Vietnam (Indo-China), North Africa and the Middle East, medical services directly supported imperial economic and political aims. In these orientalist colonies a continuing supply of European-trained doctors, often military medical men, worked in difficult climatic and cultural conditions to promote the health of Europeans and control the epidemics that threatened trade and social order. Medicine also helped legitimate the 'civilizing mission,' an increasing part of which was the training of local people in Western medicine and the censuring of indigenous medical systems. A third type of relations was evident in the newly annexed colonies of Africa and the older colonies in the West and East Indies. In these mostly tropical colonies a relatively small European military and administrative establishment ruled often sparsely populated regions, with cultures that varied from the 'primitive' to the highly developed. A major problem for imperial powers was the high rates of death and invalidism amongst the European military, administrative and commercial population due to the effects of so-called tropical diseases and lack of an effective sanitary infrastructure. As part of the policy to accelerate the material development of these territories, European doctors developed new specialisms and preventive technologies to protect colonists and their interests. Missionaries took Western clinical medicine to the local population, while state services focused on public health in urban areas and controlling epidemics. Western medicine remained an exotic import as only limited steps were taken to train local people or to foster the development of primary care. The fourth instance of medical dependency was in those formally independent countries in which European powers, and increasingly America and Japan, were major economic and cultural influences. The so-called 'informal' empires of the major powers included former Spanish colonies in South America, such as Argentina and Brazil where Britain and Germany had major financial interests, and China and Japan where Western economic and cultural power, including medicine, went hand-in-hand. American medical influence was felt in Latin America and the Pacific, not least through the health and medical education programs of the Rockefeller Foundation.

The history of colonial medicine in the twentieth century can be divided into three phases:

- Imperial medicine, 1900–1920;
- Colonial health and welfare, 1920–1950;
- Welfare and internationalism, 1945–1975.

In the first phase European and North American dominance was taken for granted, as imperial governments and medical agencies assumed that colonial peripheries of all types would continue to be dependent on Northern centers for many decades, if not centuries. Explicit medical policies for dependent colonial territories were mostly developed in Europe and North America, and were promoted around the power of doctors to wield new 'tools of empire.' Medical hegemony elsewhere followed from the size and depth of the medical cultures in the North and the networks of dependence that had been constructed over many centuries.

After 1920, medical institutions in both formal and informal colonies began to seek greater autonomy, though the power of the North was hard to break down. However, medical policies in the South increasingly showed adaptations to local conditions and there were attempts to establish new medical centers.

After 1945 almost all colonies gained formal political independence, though economic and cultural independence proved more elusive. None the less, international agencies such as the World Health Organization (WHO) played an increasing role as medical policies attempted to link economic development and welfare in new ways. Paradoxically, as colonial medical institutions gained greater formal autonomy they were drawn into international medical and science networks which meant that rather than setting their own priorities, they were drawn to the priorities of the North and its approach to disease control. Due to its association with development and welfare, along with the seemingly ever increasing ability of Western medicine to prevent and cure disease, colonial medicine has been seen as one of the few positive benefits of colonialism. Sanitary measures, vaccinations, antibiotics, insecticides, surgery, etc., undoubtedly saved the lives of many thousands of indigenes. However, any audit of colonial medicine would have to be based around assessments of what could have been achieved if alternative policies had been pursued, and of the legacy left to post-colonial medicine.

The periodization outlined does not apply to all colonies as twentieth-century imperialism was anything but uniform. Different imperial powers operated distinct regimes, from the centralized French at one extreme to the devolved British Empire at the other. Colonies varied enormously in size, geography, social structure, ethnic diversity, level and type of economic development, medical systems and other cultural variables. India was so large that it was often spoken of as an empire in its own right, whereas many island colonies had tiny populations. Numerically, the most common type of colony was the African and Eastern territories of Britain and France, but such was the variety that a new recruit in the French colonial service could find themselves on a Caribbean or Pacific island, in the desert of northern Africa, in tropical Madagascar, or a city in Indo-China. There was also variation within a single region. For example, in sub-Saharan Africa, Zimbabwe (then Southern Rhodesia) had a developed economy and a large settler population, while in Zaire (the Belgian Congo) a minimal European military administration ran one of the most oppressive of colonial regimes.

## IMPERIAL MEDICINE, 1900–1920

In 1900 medicine in British settler colonies remained a modest and dependent enterprise, though the model of the United States suggested that a high degree of self-sufficiency was obtainable in the long-term. Settler colonies had their own national professional organizations, including medical schools, and many of these were of quite long-standing. Most institutions were imitative of those in Europe and it was assumed that new knowledge and techniques would continue to be imported. The British Medical Association's first overseas annual meeting in Canada in 1897 testified to its expected continuing role as the dominant professional organization in what was called 'Greater Britain.' In settler colonies the actual number of doctors was quite small though the doctor-patient ratio for settlers in towns was often higher than in Britain. The weaknesses of private and philanthropic practice meant that medicine was more dependent upon the state than in Europe and North America. Scarce resources and relative isolation led to some adaptation of medical ideas, practices and institutions to local circumstances. However, the expediency of many such innovations was seen as confirming the subordination of colonial medicine rather than celebrating its vitality. Distance from European centers was experienced as a problem, not least as many students travelled abroad to gain qualifications from more prestigious institutions. Many such graduates chose not to return but those who did, and those who remained at home to receive their medical training, still looked to Europe and North

America as exemplars against which colonial practice was seen to be inferior. The 'centers' for emulation and association were not fixed. In Latin America the initial influence of Spain gave way in this century, first to France and then to the United States. Calls for greater political and economic autonomy found echoes amongst the professions, including medicine, and this process was accelerated by the disjuncture of the First World War.

Colonial medicine, in the sense of specific named institutions to support imperial policies, was created at the turn of the twentieth century. However, while states created colonial medical services, doctors established the less politically charged specialism of 'tropical medicine and hygiene.' This enterprise was a product of two developments: (i) the new imperialism associated with the annexation of new colonies in Africa and the consolidation of possessions elsewhere; and (ii) the medical developments associated with the identification of specific bacterial pathogens as the causes of epidemic and infectious diseases. The key moment in this new medical enterprise was the identification of the role of the mosquito in spreading the malaria parasite, and the hopes this raised that such knowledge could be applied to reduce European mortality and morbidity. Supporters claimed that investment in the specialism would improve the health of colonizers and that this would encourage investment, trade, and settlement, as well as aiding those pursuing the 'civilizing mission.' With powerful political backing and a high professional profile, tropical medicine soon acquired all the features of a successful, modern, medical specialism — journals, research programs, institutions, education courses, and qualifications. Britain led the development of the new specialism when the Liverpool School of Tropical Medicine, funded largely by merchants with West African interests, opened in 1897. Similar institutions followed in London (1898), Harvard (1900), Hamburg (1901), Paris (1901), New Orleans (1902), Berlin (1905), Brussels (1906) and Amsterdam (1912). Although designed to provide special training for medical practitioners embarking on colonial service and as the vehicle for research into the health problems of expatriates and their communities, 'tropical medicine' was presented as a category defined by nature rather than late nineteenth-century colonial imperialism. However, in its earliest forms it had little or nothing to say on the health of 'tropical people.'

Tropical medical experts followed trade and the flag. The early research and sanitary expeditions from metropolitan institutions concentrated on economically important colonial towns and ports. The most famous colonial medical institutions created after 1900 were the chain of Pasteur Institutes that spanned France itself, the French colonial empire, and countries beyond. Founded with a mixture of voluntary, private and state support in different locations, the Institutes were established to diffuse anti-rabies measures and other vaccinations. However, staff worked on other methods of disease prevention and took advantage of the opportunities for research into the local health problems. The policies and work of the Pasteur Institutes, as direct offshoots of European medicine, illustrate several important issues in colonial medicine. How different were the disease problems of colonies from those of Europe? To what extent were differences due to physical conditions of climate and geography, or to human factors such as race, culture, and socio-economic conditions? How appropriate were the medical ideas and practices developed in Europe for physical and social environments in the colonies? How best could Western medicine, appropriately reshaped, be diffused to the colonies? The traffic in ideas and techniques was assumed to be one-way, as doctors dismissed indigenous medical systems as superstitious, backward and ineffective, with nothing to teach European medicine.

Different answers to these questions were developed in different colonies and for particular health problems. The French and German empires tended to favor the direct transfer of the programs of laboratory medicine to the colonies, essentially exporting the schools of Louis Pasteur and Robert Koch. Indeed, Koch had worked on cholera in Egypt and India in the 1880s and in the 1900s returned to Africa several times to study relapsing fever, sleeping sickness, malaria, and red water fever in cattle. However, in Britain and the United States tropical medicine and hygiene developed distinct interests and approaches, focusing on a small group of vector-borne parasitic diseases said to be unique to tropical-colonial conditions. Malaria remained the most significant disease both practically and symbolically, with conditions such as sleeping sickness, schistosomiasis, Leishmaniasis, and leprosy reinforcing the notion that the tropical disease environment was one of parasites and vectors, and quite different to temperate climes. How important these diseases were to the health and well being of indigenes was unknown, though it was assumed they enjoyed some racial and adaptive immunity. The medical specialisms and their technologies showed the power of the colonial state at the periphery and of imperial states in the North. Considerable scientific prestige was attached to finding a new pathogen and inter-imperial rivalry over priority and recognition was rife. This was most apparent when Ronald Ross was awarded the second Nobel Prize for Medicine and Physiology in 1901. Italian malariologists were outraged that the claims of Giovanni Battista Grassi had been overlooked, and French sensibilities were only assuaged in 1907 when, almost thirty years after the event, Alphonse Laveran received the Nobel Prize for his identification of the malaria parasite.

In many of the orientalist colonies medical services had developed from military services and these were influenced by the initiatives developed for tropical colonies. Western medical and sanitary services had long served commerce and the state in orientalist colonies, being the dominant players in a mixed economy with missionary practice, voluntary organizations and private practice. In these cultures indigenous medical systems and beliefs were officially condemned, though in practice they were tolerated, not least because they continued to provide care to the great mass of the population. Medical colleges had been established in India in the mid-nineteenth century and provided training for both British and Indian students. These graduates, together with the men of the military Indian Medical Service (IMS), formed an Anglo-Indian medical community which, while dependent on Britain, had its own style and ideologies. Anglo-Indian medical institutions provided very limited opportunities for Indians to train as doctors but did offer many more openings for them to train and serve in assistant and supporting roles. In 1905, due to pressure from the Indian National Congress, the IMS was opened up to Western-trained Indian doctors and by 1914 they constituted a quarter of new recruits to the IMS.

In the early decades of the century almost all colonial territories developed state medical services alongside other government welfare and technical departments. In Dutch, German and Belgian colonies, as in British India, medical services continued to be based on the military. While few doctors saw any conflict over their dual identity of state official and medical professional, indigenes tended to see medical officers as agents of the colonising state, much like administrators collecting taxes or the police. That said, Western medicine was welcomed and used by many indigenes who were quite pluralist in their choice of medical care. Some colonial medical departments built and ran hospitals for their European communities and some state officers had private practices. As in orientalist colonies, state medical services became concerned about the indigenous population when epidemics threatened social dislocation, as with sleeping sickness in central Africa in the 1900s. The vector-borne infection model was interpreted to support the view that the best means of prevention and control was to eradicate the insect and other species that carried the infection. Thus, 'species sanitation' promised the permanent elimination of diseases and had the advantage of allowing medical experts to concentrate on the natural environment and avoid the political problems of working with the local people. A first step in many campaigns was to improve the sanitation of European settlements, often by importing the latest sanitary thinking and technologies. Such approaches also supported the emerging policy of segregating European enclaves at some distance from the local population, beyond the flight range of insects and apart from possible disease-carrying indigenes. This disregard for the health of indigenous peoples, and the failure to provide them with health services, was also evident in settler colonies. Indeed, the poor health and depletion of the Aborigine and Maori peoples of Australasia was sometimes regarded as an indication that these 'races' were beyond the help of medicine — they had run out of 'vigor' and were dying out naturally. Knowledge of the health status of indigenes remained poor, apart from the fragmentary data from missionary medical work, the army, and jails. Missionary hospitals and dispensaries provided curative services and although numbers were small, they had a symbolic importance. It was ironic that as Western medicine became ever more secular, colonial peoples first encountered its potent curative form in a religious context.

The Western medical institutions that emerged in China and Japan in the early years of this century were derived from models, personnel and knowledge from

Europe and North America. In Japan, medical schools had tried to follow German exemplars and though these links remained strong in this century, US influence grew rapidly. The spread of Western medicine in China followed a similar pattern to that in Japan, except that medical missionaries played a larger role, especially in medical education. In China the decision to adopt and develop Western medical training and institutions was a political one. It followed various crises and wars in the 1900s, the plague epidemic in 1911, and the establishment of the national government in the same year. The greater openness of the new regime allowed the building of close links with the United States. For example, Harvard University joined a co-operative venture in medical education in Beijing in 1912 and the Rockefeller Foundation played a leading role in the development of the Union Medical College from 1914. However, in 1915 the role of the Christian Medical Missionary Association as the leading professional agency promoting the adoption and spread of Western medicine was taken over by the newly formed National Medical Association of China. Such a change was repeated many times over the next half century, as colonial institutions became 'national' ones.

## COLONIAL HEALTH AND WELFARE, 1920–1950

Both contemporaries and historians speak of a watershed in colonial medicine in the 1920s and 1930s as colonial peoples and their institutions gained greater autonomy. In settler and orientalist colonies the influence of imperial agencies was increasingly resented and attempts were made to develop self-sufficiency in education and to create research institutions. As British settler colonies became centers in their own right, they broke historical ties and began to look to the United States. In orientalist colonies, the political demands of indigenous peoples for self-determination and then independence found echoes in medicine, and this led to the opening of state medical positions to local people with Western medical training. However, in tropical colonies the character of medical personnel changed little. There was less political pressure for change and medical education was both unaffordable and unobtainable by all but a tiny number of students sponsored by missionary societies or their families. Medical colleges began to open in sub-Saharan Africa, Latin America and the Far East, but these concentrated on the training of assistants, nurses and other support staff. The best a qualified African doctor could hope for was a precarious existence in private practice or a subordinate position in the state service, most of which continued to operate 'color bars.'

In tropical colonies medical policy remained closely linked to wider economic development objectives. In the late 1920s colonial development was given renewed impetus and this led to an expansion of medical services. The aim of the new policy was to develop colonial economies to supply raw materials and tropical products for the North, while in return serving as soft and captive markets for industrial goods and financial services — what development economists now term classic 'underdevelopment.' By 1920, certain British and Dutch Far Eastern colonies had emerged as models: their plantations supplied rubber and other commodities, and their peoples promised to be growing markets for manufactures. In most tropical colonies, significant 'development' initiatives were state-led as neither companies from Europe nor local entrepreneurs could raise the capital to operate on the scale required. Tropical latitudes proved not to be rich in easily mined raw materials, and tropical agriculture, particularly the favored forms of monoculture, proved to be ecologically precarious and at the mercy of swings in commodity markets. The services dedicated to support 'colonial (male) labor' in plantations, mines and towns were expanded but development was now cast within the framework of the 'dual mandate' — to develop and protect. Hence, medical and welfare services were also spread to towns and rural areas, and — really for the first time — to women and children. One reason for the new policy was that improved sanitation and drainage, segregated housing, mosquito nets, quinine, and greater medical understanding had reduced European mortality to tolerable levels. Ex-patriates still suffered high morbidity rates and avoided the midday sun, but conditions had improved sufficiently for medical officers to take their families with them, and for women to be appointed to state and missionary medical services.

The system created in most tropical colonies was of a central department, usually in the capital or largest port, with a hospital, laboratory, and perhaps research facilities. The colony was usually divided into districts or departments, with each having at least one medical officer whose role was to oversee all health matters. Working from the administrative center, district medical officers toured regularly, advising on sanitation, reporting on epidemics and offering some clinical services. Colonial medical departments expanded rapidly in the 1920s, but numbers fell back in the economic recession of the 1930s. For example, in Ghana the strength of the medical department rose from 46 in 1918 to a maximum of 81 in 1928, reducing to 71 in 1938. However, by the end of the 1930s there were ten Ghanaians in the special, though subordinate, grade of African Medical Officer. One response to the shortages of doctors was to make greater use of nurses, dressers and other assistants to tour villages offering limited clinical services, vaccinations and sanitary advice, as well as to act as gatekeepers to hospital services. The success of such systems fueled calls for colonial peoples to be given more opportunities to train for the full range of medical qualifications, and for wider fairer access to health care. Indeed, the limitations of colonial medical services were seized on by nationalists as one of the major reasons for throwing off colonial rule.

During the inter-war years, overseas Pasteur Institutes reduced their ambitions from the Pasteurization of the world and settled for the role of supporting the medical services in the French Empire. However, this more limited role did not prevent certain institutes at the periphery developing research profiles stronger than the central institute in Paris. For example, in Tunis, Charles Nicolle completed research on typhus that won him the Nobel Prize in 1928 and, unusually for a colonial appointee, was able to return to a senior post in France. In the 1920s the role of dominant international agency for colonial medical research was assumed by the International Health Board (IHB) of the Rockefeller Foundation. Operating from its New York office, the Foundation had first become interested in health in the 1900s through its support of programs to eliminate hookworm disease from the southern states of the US. The IHB then spread its remit to control hookworm disease elsewhere in the world, mostly in tropical colonies. At the same time, Rockefeller policy expanded from supporting disease-control measures to embrace tropical medical research, especially laboratory-based work. The extent to which Rockefeller Foundation health programs were examples of informal US imperialism can be gauged from two examples of their activities in the British colony of Sri Lanka (Ceylon) and in Latin America as described below. These activities also demonstrate another defining feature of colonial medicine in this period, the emphasis placed on campaigns to control single diseases. They typified what Farley has termed 'imperial tropical medicine': the successive elimination, one-by-one, of the major tropical diseases, as problems and solutions were "defined and imposed by practitioners of Western-style medicine without involving the indigenous populations."[1] However, the IHB work in Sri Lanka shows that colonial medical was not monolithic and that at the periphery there was considerable scope for innovation.

The IHB approached the Sri Lankan government and planters' associations in the early 1910s offering advice and support on the control of hookworm disease. Infection rates amongst plantation workers were over 95%, so given IHB successes in hookworm control in the US and Latin America, it was expected that 'Yankee know how' would produce spectacular results in Asia. The program was based on treating infected workers with two doses of the drug chenopodium which, as expected, rapidly reduced the incidence of the disease and absenteeism rates. Yet success was short-lived. Those who had been cured soon became re-infected as medical measures had not been backed up by improved sanitation, either on the plantations or in towns. In 1921, a plan was developed to control the parasite in towns, but survey work soon revealed that hookworm was one of many endemic disease problems and that tackling a single disease was unlikely to meet the overall objectives of reducing the economic losses caused by illness. In 1926, the IHB and colonial government combined to launch a new policy which aimed to establish 'health units' in each district, offering a full range of preventive services from health education and child welfare through to the control of infectious diseases. This was one of the earliest examples of what was to become known as 'horizontal' approaches to health, i.e., to develop primary and secondary care to deal with all health problems as opposed to 'vertical' approaches that targeted the control of single diseases.

The Rockefeller Foundation was also active in Latin America, with a major program for the control of yellow fever, and in the development of medical education. Yellow fever was a priority because of the threat it posed to the southern states of the US, and because it seemed susceptible to the kind of mosquito control measures that had worked elsewhere. IHB initiatives were acceptable to Latin American governments as they offered to kick-start public health provision and help emergent states meet international obligations for disease control. The project began with attempts to control yellow fever in urban areas, with the intention to extend them to rural areas. However, it soon became clear that the eradication of the disease in urban areas alone would be impossible, as they were continuously re-infected by 'jungle yellow fever' brought in by mosquitoes as well as by human and animal carriers. The disease had to be tackled in both places, or an alternative approach developed, such as vaccination. In the event, the latter course proved effective and followed a change in the overall policy of the Foundation towards the support of laboratory research and training in advanced, scientific medicine. By the mid-1930s the Foundation had produced a vaccine against yellow fever, though it did not prove easy to ensure mass vaccination in towns let alone rural areas.

The growth in medical services, the development of research and the perceived successes of specific disease-control projects led both colonial agencies and medical personnel to reflect positively on their contributions to the 'civilizing mission.' Louis Pasteur's grandson, Pasteur Vaillery-Radot explained the role of medicine in French colonies as follows in 1938:

> If French peace reigns over the boundless regions, if epidemics are prevented or thwarted, if sanitary reforms can be undertaken, cities built up, and harbours opened to trade, if Europeans can live safely in hostile Africa and the Far East, if morbidity and mortality decrease in a striking way in native populations, all the transformations must be attributed to colonial medicine.[2]

Alas, Vaillery-Radot was somewhat out of touch with events in the colonies. From the early 1930s there was a growing awareness that the health of the indigenes of many colonies was poor and a growing conviction that it was deteriorating as a result of colonialism. Surveys showed that indigenes did not enjoy racial or adaptive immunities to tropical diseases and suffered greatly from diseases such as tuberculosis and measles. There was also evidence that the nutritional status of colonial populations was poor and compromising their health — some doctors asked about the value of medical and disease prevention programs in malnourished communities. In debates mirroring those in Europe and North America, the extent to which malnutrition was due to ignorance or material poverty was a key issue, but growing social unrest and political moves, at both the center and periphery, ensured that health became linked with welfare in the growing crisis of colonialism.

The Health Organization of the League of Nations pursued issues of malnutrition and poor health in Europe and independent states in the northern hemisphere, but it largely ignored colonial territories as they were the responsibility of imperial governments. In the 1930s the world recession and the crisis in Europe forced colonial policy down the metropolitan political agenda, yet this relative neglect facilitated much greater innovation at the periphery. In medicine and public health there was a re-examination of existing policies and alternatives were proposed. The major options were to continue with the existing policy of 'vertical' disease-control programs along with the gradual replication of a doctor-hospital dominated medical system from Europe, or to invent something more appropriate to colonial conditions which was able to reach colonial peoples more quickly. One alternative model was the system developed in French African colonies where central hospitals and facilities were the bases from which medical personnel — doctors and para-professional — went out into the 'field' to advise and treat people. By contrast, in many British colonies, centralized facilities attracted patients and health workers to what became medical centers. One implication of the French approach was that medical education in the colonies should not try to replicate European standards, but instead concentrate on intermediate and lower level training to provide assistants and nurses. Needless to say, amongst the elites of colonial peoples, as well as their emergent professional bodies, there were complaints that such developments merely ensured the persistence of inferior services.

## INTERNATIONAL AND INDEPENDENT MEDICINE, 1945–1960

After 1945, settler colonies continued to enjoy greater autonomy and they, together with many orientalist colonies, had medical cultures that were as robust and self-reliant as many in the smaller states of Europe. Indian independence in 1947 and the wars in Indo-China that led to the French departure in early 1950s, brought medical as well as political independence, at least in the sense of national medical organizations. However, dependence on, and integration into, international research networks also worked to reduce autonomy, as did their growing reliance on the products of pharmaceutical companies and the advice of technical assistance agencies. In orientalist colonies, both Western doctors and medically trained indigenes began to question the superiority of Western medicine and to explore the value of indigenous medical systems. However, this was only the case with developed systems such as acupuncture and the Indian system of Ayurvedic medicine.

In the last bastions of colonial medicine in the tropics, imperial governments initiated new programs of medical service expansion, disease control and education. These initiatives were linked, as they had been in the 1930s, to economic development and welfare. The new initiatives were in part a response to attacks on colonial rule and the growth of nationalism, and in part the beginnings of preparations for independence. In fact, independence arrived much more rapidly than expected, with most countries in Africa, the Far East and the West Indies becoming sovereign States by the mid-1960s. In this context, international agencies, most notably the WHO, and the technical aid agencies of the US and the USSR, came to play important roles in both health care planning and disease-control strategies. Pharmaceutical, petrochemical and other medical companies also became major players in these areas, which were increasingly known as 'developing countries.'

A common assumption in the post-war era was that poor health was a major cause of economic 'backwardness' and that attacking disease, with advanced Western medical ideas and technologies such as synthetic insecticides and antibiotic drugs, would be a first step to 'development.' The impact of colonialism on health was difficult to measure as there were no reliable long-run statistics, but it was clear that there had been improvements for urban elites and those most closely associated with the colonial state or colonial companies — with some notable exceptions, for example, miners in south and central Africa. The general picture in urban areas was mixed and complicated by migration and rapidly changing economic fortunes. However, the health of many people had clearly deteriorated: for example, irrigation schemes had facilitated the spread of the Bilharzia parasite, urbanization had helped spread tuberculosis and other respiratory infections, and the arrival of milk powder as a substitute for breast feeding had raised the incidence of infant diarrhea.

In the 1950s many British colonies adopted Ten Year National Health Development Plans. In Ghana, even before independence, the colonial medical department became the Ministry of Health. The main priority of the Ministry became the creation of Medical Field Units to facilitate the spread of health care to rural areas, many of which remained untouched even after over half a century of colonial medicine. Hospital care was given a low priority; between 1950 and 1960 only two new government hospitals were opened, while the number of health centers rose from three to 23 with another 23 under construction. Against these initiatives, the power of Western hospital based medicine continued to shape the training of doctors and the expectations of urban elites. One irony in British territories was that locally trained doctors still had to go to metropolitan schools for advanced training in tropical medicine. In policy circles there was a rerun of the pre-war debate over whether colonies needed institutions as good as those in Europe or ones appropriate to their needs; though a key issue remained the power to define those needs. More often than not the answer was dictated by resources, which remained meagre, or by the growing power of advanced expert opinion. As colonial and post-independence medical institutions were drawn into international medical and scientific networks they were drawn into adopting their priorities, in part because of poor linkages to local medical schools and rural health services. Not all imperial powers took steps to encourage a degree of self-reliance to prepare for independence. When the Belgian government withdrew rapidly from Zaire in 1960, the absence of trained Zairian doctors precipitated a 'world emergency,' with the WHO bringing in doctors from all over the world to take over hospitals and other services until local people could be trained.

During decolonization the WHO and the technical aid programs of the superpowers played an increasingly pivotal role in colonial medicine. WHO activity was largely orchestrated through the work of expert committees and this meant that its initiatives were primarily medical in approach. Whether it had any alternative to developing 'technical' approaches is doubtful, as the organization had neither the power nor the resources to initiate broader schemes; it tacitly defined health as the absence of disease and its programs were devised to prevent, control and treat specific diseases, mostly infections. Armed with new research-based products such as DDT, penicillin and streptomycin, Western experts approached colonial health problems with renewed optimism and with an outlook that remained that of 'imperial tropical medicine.' The paradigmatic 'vertical' campaign was that against malaria, which promised the eradication of the disease. The program was based largely on spraying homes and surrounding areas with insecticides to eliminate malaria-carrying mosquitoes. Teams of Northern experts moved through towns and the countryside, assisted by local assistants, while also relying on air and road transportation and other imported technologies. One effect, for this disease and for this style of disease-control campaign, was to increase the dependence of colonial territories on external medical expertise and resources. That said, the initiative did see the incidence of malaria fall and for the first time there was at last unambiguous evidence of colonial medicine improving the health of indigenes. Perhaps for the first time, colonial medical services began to reach the whole population in certain regions of orientalist and tropical colonies. Unfortunately we now know the gains barely outlasted the colonial era and malaria returned, often in a less tractable form as mosquitoes developed resistance to insecticides and the parasite gained some immunity to prophylactic drugs.

## CONCLUSION

Colonial medicine in the twentieth century followed closely the contours of the economic and political history of North-South relations. In settler and informal colonies, national medical organizations developed rapidly as part of the drive for greater autonomy from imperial powers. However, the influence and pull of Western centers remained, and in some ways grew, as the strength of a national medical community came to be measured by their participation in international networks. Relations of power and dependence remain a feature of international medical relations, and it is worth noting on a longer timescale that a former imperial power like Britain is subordinate in many areas of medical research to its former colony the United States. In Oriental and tropical colonies, medicine was a 'tool of empire,' especially in the priorities of the advocates of 'tropical medicine' and the 'vertical' disease control programs that were a feature of every phase of twentieth century colonialism. However, there was more to colonial medicine than 'imperial tropical medicine,' or the importation of Western 'bio-medicine.' Missionary doctors took clinical care to the indigenous population, while colonial states ran hospitals in urban areas and established, albeit unevenly, public health services which provided limited sanitation and vaccination. In the

1930s and 1950s, 'horizontal' programs were implemented in some colonies which aimed to provide basic health services. Even in those colonies in which these policies were followed they proved inadequate, with improved services barely being able to keep up with population growth, migration and burgeoning demand.

REFERENCES

1. J. Farley, *Bilharzia: A History of Imperial Tropical Medicine*. (Cambridge: Cambridge University Press, 1991), p. 293.
2. P. Vallery-Radot, *Mémoires d'un non-conformiste, 1886–1966*. (Paris: 1966), p. 251.

FURTHER READING

Addae, Stephen, *The Evolution of Modern Medicine in a Developing Country: Ghana, 1880–1960*. (Durham: Durham Academic Press, 1997).

Arnold, David (ed.), *Imperial Medicine and Indigenous Societies*. (Manchester: Manchester University Press, 1988).

Cueto, Marcus (ed.), *Missionaries of Science: The Rockefeller Foundation and Latin America*. (Bloomington: Indiana University Press, 1994).

Cunningham, Andrew and Andrews, Bridie (eds), *Western Knowledge as Contested Knowledge*. (Manchester: Manchester University Press, 1997).

Denoon, Donald, *Public Health in Papua New Guinea: Medical Possibility and Social Constraint, 1884–1984*. (Cambridge: Cambridge University Press, 1989).

Farley, John, *Bilharzia: A History of Imperial Tropical Medicine*. (Cambridge: Cambridge University Press, 1991).

Harrison, Mark, *Public Health in British India: Anglo-Indian Preventive Medicine, 1859–1914*. (Cambridge: Cambridge University Press, 1994).

Hewa, Soma, *Colonialism, Tropical Disease and Imperial Medicine: Rockefeller Philanthropy in Sri Lanka*. (Lanham, MD.: University Press of America, 1995).

Kleinman, Arthur, *Patients and Healers in the Context of Culture: An Exploration of the Borderland between Anthropology, Medicine and Psychiatry*. (Berkeley: University of California Press, 1980).

Lyons, Maryinez, *The Colonial Disease: A Social History of Sleeping Sickness in Northern Zaire, 1900–1940*. (Cambridge: Cambridge University Press, 1992).

MacLeod, Roy and Lewis, Milton (eds), *Disease, Medicine and Empire: Perspectives on Western Medicine and the Experience of European Expansion*. (London: Routledge, 1988).

Manderson, Lenore, *Sickness and the State: Health and Illness in Colonial Malaysia, 1870–1940*. (Cambridge: Cambridge University Press, 1996).

Vaughan, Megan, *Curing their Ills: Colonial Power and African Illness*. (Cambridge: Polity Press, 1991).

CHAPTER 6

# Health and Health Care in the Progressive Era

JANE LEWIS

## HEALTH ISSUES AT THE TURN OF THE CENTURY

The term 'Progressive Era' is commonly used only of the United States between 1890 and 1920, but historians have recognized the existence of a progressive alliance in Edwardian Britain too. The years at the beginning of the century are associated with large scale efforts at social reform, focused in the United States on the welfare of mothers and children and on conditions of employment, and in many European countries additionally on what are often regarded as the building blocks of modern welfare states: social insurance provision for times of sickness and unemployment and old age pensions. Such reforms required active intervention on the part of the state, something that had been abhorred by nineteenth-century classical liberalism. It was justified in terms of ensuring a 'positive liberty' for individuals — enabling them to fulfill their potentials — but also in terms of what was considered to be beneficial for the nation as a whole. Most historians would argue that the social reforms of the Progressive period, health included, had as much to do with furthering the nation's health and welfare as they did with securing individual rights. In a country like Britain, the rhetoric often revolved around the need to improve the welfare of an imperial nation.

Significant improvements in age specific mortality rates occurred during the second half of the nineteenth century. In Britain, the death rate of children and young women under 25 declined in the 1870s. The most sensitive indicator, the infant mortality rate remained high throughout the nineteenth century, peaking in Britain at 163 per 1000 in 1899 before falling rapidly after 1902. These aggregate data mask wide variations in life chances between rural and town dwellers, between social classes and occupational groups, and, in the United States in particular, between blacks, aboriginal peoples and whites. The contrast between rich and poor was concentrated in infancy and old age. In Britain, the death rate of middle-class women in childbirth was higher than that for poor women, probably because the former were more exposed to infection at the hands of medical men in nursing homes rather than at the hands of midwives in their own dwellings.

Since Thomas Mckeown argued in the 1970s that the main reason for the decline in nineteenth-century mortality rates was a rise in living standards, with public health interventions running a poor second and the contribution of personal health care services figuring hardly at all, a lively debate has ensued. Harris is surely right in her recent review of this debate that mortality rates were the product of many socio-economic and cultural factors, including not merely real income, medicine, and sanitation, but conditions at work, levels of alcohol consumption, local access to medical care and the strength or weakness of familial and community support.

The determinants of health status are known now to be notoriously complex, but during the late nineteenth century there was considerable optimism about the possibility of social progress. This was fed by the impact of evolutionary ideas, which entailed a firm notion of linear development and had a strong effect on social thought, economic growth and a shift in economic ideas from the rather dismal laws and predictions of the classicists towards the more expansive possibilities held out by the neo-classicists. In this intellectual and economic environment the issue became what to do about the poverty and disease that remained in the midst of burgeoning plenty.

Significant strands of 'progressive' thought were extremely widespread. After 1900, ideas about eugenics and social hygiene, for example, spread from Britain and America to Sweden, Norway, Russia, Switzerland, Germany, Poland, France and Italy. Such a widespread dispersal must be explained in part by the promise these ideas held out of understanding and coming to terms with social change. Progressive Era governments are generally understood to have been more interventionist, but this does not mean that there was unanimity in promoting state intervention. Eugenicists, for example, could believe in the idea of nature taking its course, which meant a minimalist role for the state, or could contemplate 'eugenically-friendly' legislation to promote more childbearing by those considered 'fit' and less by those deemed 'unfit.'

Countries differed widely in the nature of and their commitment to intervention. In Britain and the United States, the voluntary sector was extremely important in the delivery of social welfare. In Britain as late as 1911, the gross annual receipts of registered charities exceeded public expenditure on the poor law and this sum excluded the money tied up in mutual aid, as well as in unregistered charities. Nor were voluntary institutions 'the fortuitous corollary of the limited state,'[1] but were rather understood to be part of the very fabric of the state. Nineteenth-century Britain had effective central government institutions, but a small central bureaucracy and a strong desire to limit the activities of central government. Political ideas, especially ideas about liberalism, changed significantly at the turn-of-the-century, making it possible to conceive of enabling legislation, but Britain did not share Germany's conviction as to the "civilizing mission" of the organic state.[2] However, both Britain and Germany had introduced social insurance programs before the First World War. Thus the patterning of similarities and differences between countries is complicated in terms of both the framework of ideas and the balance within 'the mixed economy of welfare' (that is between the state, the voluntary sector, the market and the family).

In regard to health and health care issues, the late-nineteenth and early-twentieth centuries saw the end of public health as a prism for all sorts of social reform, although the strong link made between health and welfare, and between health and morality continued to exercise a powerful effect on particular campaigns for social reform, for example in respect of protective labor legislation and a minimum wage for women workers in Europe and the United States. While the era of classic public health reform in terms of clean water, sewerage and the rest was far from over (in England infant morality rates were shown to be highest in towns such as Hull, where in 1914 54 per cent of households were without 'water closets,' relying instead on ash privies or middens), with the dissemination of germ theory the attention of public health reformers focused more on the individual. Thus the welfare of mothers and children, which exercised such concern during the period, became primarily a matter for personal preventive clinical medicine. This kind of care was undertaken in most western countries by a combination of voluntary organizations and local government authorities. But care of the predominantly male workforce, which was subjected to increasing pressure as industrial competition grew fiercer, became the subject of central government intervention in the form of health insurance schemes in some Western European countries. Health reform thus became more compartmentalized during the Progressive Era and the kind of intervention undertaken by the state was profoundly gendered.

## WOMEN AND CHILDREN FIRST?

The impetus to improve the health of mothers and children was strong in virtually all Western European countries and in North America during this period. Anxiety about competitiveness and relative military strength keyed into concern about high levels of infant mortality and class and race differentials in birth rates. In brief, concern about the quantity and quality of population led directly to motherhood and mothering.

Most prominent among the propagandists for maternal and child welfare cross nationally were the eugenicists, who drew members from all points of the political spectrum, bound together by a set of ideologies about social health. Soloway has argued persuasively that it was:

> demographic change and post-Malthusian ideas of population control that were of central importance in the transformation of eugenics from an unfocused, comparatively unknown set of late Victorian ideas about heredity into an organized movement and, increasingly, an important facet of biological thinking prominent in educated middle- and upper-class circles.[3]

Thus concern about demographic trends, and in particular the differential birth rate, made eugenics a popular movement, which in turn proved far more influential than its rather limited formal organizational base would suggest.

Heredity was defined by eugenicists as a physiological connection between generations that was open to research and measurement. It was believed to determine not just physical characteristics but temperament and behavior as well. Richard Dugdale's famous study of the American Jukes family, published in 1877, in which he traced seven generations of social misfits, was cited to show the importance of heredity, even though Dugdale himself had attributed the family's position in significant part to environmental conditions.[4] Karl Pearson, who from 1911 held the Galton Professorship of Eugenics at University College, London, argued in the Chadwick Lecture of 1913 that the health and habits of parents were fifteen times as influential as any other factor causing infant death. The possession of good or bad habits was linked primarily to the health of the mother and were, like health itself, considered to be hereditary characteristics.[5] Ethel Elderton, a researcher in Pearson's Biometric Laboratory, summed up the importance of heredity for eugenicists:

> Improvement in social conditions will not compensate for a bad hereditary influence...
> The only way to keep a nation strong mentally and physically is to see to it that each new
> generation is derived chiefly from the fitter members of the generation before.[6]

This meant as Havelock Ellis, the radical British sexologist, recognized in 1912 that marriage and what we would today call family policy became central to the agenda of eugenics.

Tackling the crucial question of encouraging the 'fit' — always defined in terms of high levels of income, wealth and education — to have more children and discouraging the 'unfit' from so doing led to a distinction between positive and negative eugenics. Marriage permits and eugenic certificates would allow only the fit to reproduce, while segregation and sterilization would stop the unfit from doing so. By 1914, thirty US states had new marriage laws and the first law permitting sterilization of the unfit was passed in 1907 in Indiana. In this respect, the United States, which is usually portrayed as the least inclined to state intervention and a 'welfare lagard' was the most active. While the Eugenics Education Society took credit for the passing of the Mental Deficiency Act in Britain in 1913, this legislation did not impose mandatory segregation or mention sterilization.

But eugenics encompassed a much more complicated set of ideas and positions than those usually associated with later developments in Nazi Germany. As Paul Weindling has observed, social hygiene in pre-World War I Germany was authoritarian but it did not necessarily point the way towards Nazi racism. Eugenics gave priority to nature over nurture, but, as in other countries, eugenicists made common cause with social hygienists to offer solutions to the social problems that were manifest in TB, VD, alcoholism and the like. Eugenic ideas were used by public health doctors, feminists and socialists, as well as more conservative members of the educated, Protestant, white elite to legitimate social reform. Advances in a field such as the study of child development in the 1890s by pioneers such as G. Stanley Hall in the USA, swiftly focused in the next generation on intelligence testing, which became linked to fears that the differential decline in fertility was producing a decline in the 'national intelligence.'

Public health doctors could agree that 'maternal efficiency' was the most important variable affecting infant welfare. However, they did not necessarily believe that this was determined by heredity. Rather, in common with many other reformers, they sought greater equality in environmental conditions in order to allow 'heredity' to develop. Eugenic ideas merged with concerns about 'national efficiency,' and national deterioration or degeneration (terms that were often used interchangeably). In Britain, much publicity was attached to the poor quality of army recruits during the Boer War; 40% were rejected as unfit in the industrial towns. As a result an Inter-Departmental Committee on Physical Deterioration was set up which concluded in 1904 that most children were born healthy, but deteriorated due to a number of factors including ignorance, neglect, malnutrition, poor housing, excessive drinking, polluted water and inadequate medical care. Two pieces of legislation followed, making it possible for local government to provide meals for school children and to undertake school medical inspections.

Thus the early-twentieth century saw a particularly strong exchange in the long-running debate over nature versus nurture. But the debate was far from clear cut. Those favoring social reform, and on the whole this included public health doctors and other elements of the medical establishment, were likely to use the fear of physical deterioration that had been whipped up by the popularizers of eugenics as part of their arguments for more social provision. The main problem was that demands for social reform couched in the language of eugenics and social hygiene were likely to be narrow in scope.

This was particularly true of the measures taken to improve the health of mothers and children through both protective labor legislation designed chiefly to limit women's hours of work and to control their conditions of labor — for example by providing maternity leaves — and the efforts to set up clinics, milk depots, schools for mothers and like institutions intended chiefly to educate mothers in the care of their infants. Much of the recent history of social welfare provision has stressed the importance of 'maternalism' in securing social reform on behalf of mothers and children in the Progressive period. Maternalist discourses flowered in most Western countries at the turn-of-the-century. Broadly speaking they centered on the importance of women's roles as mothers and were propounded by women speaking as feminists and philanthropists as well as by male doctors, imperialists, eugenicists, socialists, and politicians. French pronatalism, which had been primarily directed towards increasing population since the Napoleonic years, gave rise to some of the earliest infant welfare clinics — the Gouttes de Lait — which in the years before the First World War promoted breastfeeding, provided pure, modified cows' milk and weighed babies. In Austria, the Catholic church directed maternalist energies towards promoting explicit demands for married women to stay out of the workforce in order to pay attention to their families. In Britain, public health officials, eugenicists and imperialists joined with women philanthropists concerned to reduce infant mortality to launch a major educational campaign that culminated in a network of voluntary 'schools for mothers' in the 1900s. In the USA, it has been argued that the efforts of women philanthropists secured extensive health provision in the form of the Children's Bureau, set up in 1912, and welfare benefits in the form of mothers' pensions, which were the most extensively provided benefits prior to the New Deal.

While the emphasis on motherhood brought many measures from which women and children derived considerable benefit, the narrow focus of maternalism on what constituted good motherhood meant that many of the real needs of mothers went unmet. As Michel has shown, maternalism proved to be a self-limiting and self-defeating discourse for the US day nursery movement, even while it achieved success in respect of mothers' pensions.[7] Maternalism often benefited women and children while controlling their behavior in a manner befitting the aims of social hygienists. In France, where the voice of pronatalism far outweighed any contribution from the women's movement, maternalism delivered some of the most generous services and benefits to mothers and children. However, allied to Catholicism, it became explicitly anti-feminist in the inter-war years, denouncing all female employment. Nor did all women benefit equally. In the United States the efforts at enhancing child care were largely directed at white urban immigrant populations in the early 1900s and later at rural white women to the neglect of African-American women.

The alliance between feminism and other strands in the maternalist discourse was inevitably uneasy. Many feminists were keen eugenicists when it came to those areas on the borderland between social and moral reform: curbing male lust and VD rates, and campaigning against alcohol abuse, as well as helping women as mothers. Radical feminists such as the Swedish writer Ellen Key, who achieved acclaim in both England and the United States, or the League for the Protection of Mothers (Bund für Mutterschutz) in Germany used the language of social hygiene to claim the right of women to motherhood without marriage. However, feminists did not go along with the "sexual science"[8] of the period that made motherhood incompatible with other activities, including higher education. The idea that there was a 'natural' basis for sexual difference, as opposed to patently artificial class differences, was powerful and long-lived. As the eminent British physician Henry Maudsley put it in 1874, "sex is fundamental, lies deeper than culture, [and] cannot be ignored or defied with impunity."[9] Otto Weininger, gynecologist and polemicist, wrote in 1906 that "man possesses sexual organs; her sexual organs possess woman."[10] Two British biologists, Patrick Geddes and

J. Arthur Thompson believed that sexual differences were physiologically based and lauded women as "eupsychic inspirer and eugenic mother."[11] The corollary of all this as far as middle-class women were concerned was that their access to higher education was often blocked (much more successfully in Britain than in America) in the name of conserving their energies for reproduction, while in the case of working-class women, it was their right to participate in the labor market that was questioned.

Protective labor legislation, which sought to set limits on women's hours and conditions of work, was opposed by most late nineteenth-century European feminists. However, after 1900 the appeal to 'sacred motherhood' in the British and American campaigns against 'sweated' women's labor, which involved long hours of work at home and in small workshops for very small wages, attracted the support of feminists as well as other maternalists. Laws prohibiting women's work at night were common all over Europe by the 1870s. After 1890, in the wake of a series of international congresses and several national investigations of the situations of women and children in the labor force, the employment of women as actual and potential mothers became the principal subject for debate. Concern about the infant mortality rate and the conviction on the part of many public health doctors that going out to work prevented women from breastfeeding, and that carrying infants to nurse in the early morning exposed them to the dangers of respiratory infections, led to demands for maternity leave. The 1890 Berlin Conference on protective legislation recommended a four-week leave. Britain adopted a four-week limit in 1891, the same year that Germany expanded its three-week minimum to six weeks. The power of the international maternalist discourse is manifest in the way in which leading male politicians felt pressured to adopt protective labor legislation for fear of appearing uncivilized in the face of national pressure to improve the 'race' and international concern for humane conditions. Thus Greece, though relatively rural, passed legislation granting maternity leaves in 1912.

The campaign against sweated labor (classically in the tailoring trades, but also in occupations as various as paper flower making and the covering of tennis balls) in both Britain and the United States appealed to the need to improve both health and morality. One of the major preoccupations of the promoters of the 1909 British Trade Boards Act, which laid down minimum male and female rates in particularly low paid trades, was the perceived link between low wages and prostitution on the one hand, and impoverished mothers and high infant mortality on the other. In the state of Illinois, women campaigners used a smallpox outbreak in 1894 to raise the spectre of transmission to the better-off. Just as no provision for wage replacement was made when maternity leaves were legislated, so little attention was paid to the often desperate financial need that drove poor women to engage in sweated labor. Maternalist legislation tended to meet only part of women's needs as mothers.

In fact in most countries the main source of help for mothers and children was not legislative action by the state, but the voluntary and informal sectors. Marks' study of the welfare of Jewish mothers and children in London's East End during this period has also demonstrated the importance of familial and community sources of support in securing low infant and maternal mortality rates. Mothers were generally recognized to be of crucial importance to the welfare of families, particularly in terms of their capacities to budget and run a household on small, irregular incomes. However, most maternalists also believed them to be lacking in knowledge about mothercraft. Diarrheal diseases, which were the main cause of infant mortality in the late nineteenth and early twentieth centuries, were believed to be due to contamination in the home from dirty feeding bottles, dummies and the like. In line with the shift towards personal preventive medicine, public health doctors put less emphasis on the need to improve sanitation and attend to unpaved streets and yards. Rather, mothers were to be made aware of their responsibilities for personal hygiene and the control of domestic dirt. Inefficient motherhood was attributed either to ignorance or carelessness, although no hard and fast line was drawn between the two. The fatalism of working-class mothers was generally deplored by contemporary reformers and has been interpreted by some historians as indicating that women in the past did not love their children. However, as Ross has commented, working women's devotion to their children's health and welfare was at odds with their "linguistic frugality" on the subject.[12] The idea that babies did not necessarily 'come to stay' can be interpreted as part of the distancing necessary in a period of high infant mortality.

In France, women philanthropists in the form of 'lady visitors' were central in the maternal and child welfare movement. Beginning in 1908, the French government expanded its subsidies to the charities undertaking this work, however, French women made their mark on maternity and child welfare programs by volunteering to assist in a national cause, rather than as advocates of a distinctive program of their own making, as was the case in the US. In Germany and Britain both local authorities and voluntary organizations were important in the provision of care for mothers and children, although legislative and administrative reform was always more important in the German context. The 'Elberfield' system of visiting those drawing poor relief relied on volunteers and was much admired in Britain and Japan, but in the last instance anyone refusing to perform voluntary service as a visitor of the poor could be forced to do so by the state, something that would have been anathema in the turn-of-the-century British state. Thus the precise nature of the relationship between the statutory and voluntary sectors varied considerably between countries during this period.

Volunteer visitors and early infant welfare clinics in all countries focused on education rather than treatment. Typically early clinics weighed babies and advised mothers on feeding, sleeping arrangements for the child and the frequency of outings and baths. Mothers were often also encouraged to participate in cookery demonstrations and become members of savings clubs. Considerable weight was attached to the importance of home visiting by the British, where the visitor was supposed to counter the influences of old-fashioned grandmothers and interfering neighbors. Given that in the early part of the century most women visitors were untrained, it is likely that many were relatively insensitive to the different concerns and cultural practices of poor mothers. In Britain, in 1907 visitors were being advised that they should knock before entering a working-class home. Somerset Maugham's portrayal of home visiting in *Of Human Bondage*, published in 1915, might have been somewhat exaggerated, but it nevertheless captured the element of control that accompanied so much of maternalism:

> the district visitor excited their bitter hatred. She came in without so much as a "by your leave" or a "with your leave"... she pushed her nose into corners, and if she didn't say the place was dirty you could see what she thought right enough.[13]

It seems that the American child welfare movement did rather better in this respect. Staffed by trained women from the outset, the extensive records of the Children's Bureau have revealed very few instances of discontent among the mothers served. The United States was more prepared to countenance state intervention in respect of some aspects of maternal and child welfare than was Britain. American women philanthropists often pressed for legislative intervention to accompany voluntary action (albeit not in respect of maternity leave because it was assumed that mothers with children should not work for wages). Thus Mary Richmond, the founder of modern American social work, spoke of the importance of both 'retail' work with individual mothers and families and 'wholesale' reform in the form of government legislation on behalf of vulnerable groups. As a result of the lobbying by the women at the Children's Bureau, the US Federal Government passed the Sheppard-Towner Act in 1921, which was intended to provide women with advice and nursing care. As Dwork has noted, war has often proved 'good' for babies and young children in that it increases awareness of the importance of the next generation.[14] This was true in Britain during the First World War, as well as America. The American legislation entitled all women to services and was not restricted to the poor. It was in fact the only piece of state provided health care legislation passed in the USA, but the funds for even this limited measure were withdrawn in 1929 chiefly because of the intense lobbying against 'state medicine' by the American Medical Association. In Britain too, general practitioners lobbied hard against the infant welfare clinics provided by local authorities during the 1920s, but to no avail.

US maternalism was also successful in securing cash benefits for mothers in the form of mothers' pensions, which were legislated in forty states by 1920. This has led Skocpol to suggest that women in the USA 'came close' to forging a maternalist welfare state, while Koven and Michel have written of American women's social action constructing 'a kind of shadow welfare state' during the Progressive period.[15] Skocpol and Ritter have argued that compared to the USA, early twentieth century British welfare legislation was 'paternalist' because its major achievements centered on the introduction of national health and unemployment insurance, which mainly benefited male workers. It was possible for women workers to be insured in their own right, but only 10 per cent of married British women were in insurable employment in 1911, when social insurance was introduced. Women also gained entitlements to maternity benefits as the dependants of men, but this came slowly and remained discretionary under early German social insurance. Widows pensions were long delayed in Germany and the mortality rate among widows and divorcees in the early part of the century was 27.7 per cent higher than for married women. The importance of the role played by women maternalists has been a matter of some debate, but gender was certainly the main fault-line in terms of the nature of social provision during the period. At the end of the day, France could be said to have constructed the most maternalist welfare state, building an extensive system of benefits for families with children, but as a result of pronatalism rather than women's action.

The patterning of the extensive Progressive reform on behalf of women and children remains intriguing. In many ways the reforms were as paternalist as maternalist in the sense that they sought to control women's behavior, whether in terms of prohibiting labor market participation or seeking to change the child care practices of poor mothers. Reform was perhaps strongest in legislative terms in the USA, the country in which other forms of welfare provision remained conspicuously absent. Everywhere voluntary action was important in securing services for mothers and children and remained so for as long as women and children were excluded from the health insurance schemes that began to come into being in many western European states.

## THE HEALTH AND WELFARE OF MALE WORKERS

The debate about the health and welfare of male workers was carried on separately from that about women and children. This was because in the United States, adult male labor was not considered a legitimate target of government legislation at all. In Europe during the Progressive period, the health of increasing numbers of European male workers was protected by social insurance, which provided income maintenance during periods of sickness and unemployment, and, in the case of health insurance, some access to medical care. In the United States, where some of the most draconian legislation was introduced in respect of matters of concern to eugenicists and social hygienists, such as sterilization, opposition to state intervention in the form of social insurance was entirely successful.

Social insurance operated via the labor market, which made the position of those marginal to it, such as women, precarious. Until cover was extended to women and children as the dependants of men, they remained untouched by this major development in social provision, notwithstanding the concern about their health. When Britain introduced national insurance in 1911, legislators also hesitated to provide for women and children dependants for fear of undermining men's incentive to provide for them. As was later made explicit, married women were considered too great an insurable risk if they were not themselves employed. In any case, married women were always treated as a class apart for insurance purposes and during the Great Depression they found their health insurance benefits cut because of their high risk of sickness, even though no other group with excessive claims (for example, miners) was singled out for similar treatment.

In the main, early twentieth century health insurance was about income stabilization rather than the financing of medical care. It aimed to prevent destitution due to sickness rather than to meet need grudgingly in the manner of a poor law system. In Germany social insurance was pursued as part of the idea of a Kulturstaat, that is, as part of the civilizing mission of the organic state. In Britain, the scheme was envisaged more as part of a 'national minimum' level of provision to be secured by a range of measures that included school meals and medical inspection for children and state pensions for the elderly. In the United States, there was no unified political authority to push through health insurance in the face of strong opposition by the American Federation of Labor, although not, initially, from the medical profession itself. The weak central state that permitted women's voluntary action to flourish in the USA also proved incapable of enacting collectivist health care arrangements.

The treatment offered under health insurance was limited, although Germany was more generous than Britain and included hospital care. In Britain the insured got access to a 'panel doctor' (a general practitioner), whose standards of practice varied considerably. Both Britain and Germany also provided access to TB sanatoria. In Britain this happened more because of anxieties about national efficiency than because of medical advances, although confidence in institutional cures had increased substantially by 1900. TB was also known to be a fundamental cause of pauperization and the British move towards social insurance had a lot to do with the desire to take particular groups who were deemed to be deserving outside the ambit of the poor law. In Germany too existing social provision under the poor law was under strain, whereas in France, where no insurance schemes were developed until the inter-war years, there was no national system of poor relief. Publicly both British and German officials argued that social insurance would increase economic efficiency. In Britain, Lloyd George remarked that a 'C3' population would not do for an 'A1' empire.

The legislation nevertheless offered an entering wedge for the direct provision of health care by the state and the question of who was to be covered for which medical services was hard fought by the medical profession. By offering a relatively high capitation fee to those prepared to participate in the panel doctor scheme the British Government was in the end able to detach the often rather hard pressed general practitioners from their much better off consultant colleagues to gain their acceptance of the reform. In fact, British general practitioners found the idea of control by a national insurance scheme a somewhat lesser evil than control by mutual aid societies, such as friendly societies and trades unions, who had operated their own medical insurance schemes prior to 1911 and who had exerted considerable control over the doctors they employed. In Germany there was no active professional association of doctors when the health insurance legislation was passed in 1883 and hence Bismarck did not have to contend with the interest group politics that beset Lloyd George almost thirty years later. Employees exerted considerably more control over insurance funds in Germany than was the case in Britain. In Denmark, medical insurance remained voluntary until the Second World War and yet achieved greater coverage than either the British or German schemes during the inter-war years.

The patterning of social insurance legislation during the period is complicated and as difficult to explain as patterns of provision for mothers and children. States moved first to support medical care for workers and veterans via insurance programs. As these programs were extended to dependants, which was only beginning in the Progressive period, so states became increasingly involved in funding medical care and, slowly, in controlling prices and medical personnel. But this does not explain the choice of insurance as the system for health care delivery. In Britain, for example, the Fabian socialist strand of opinion favored building upon the services of the local public health departments who were involved in clinic work among mothers and children to promote hygienic habits among the poor. Fabian socialists were as concerned about national efficiency as the Liberal Government, but their choice of system for additional health care provision was dictated by their wider aim to build a preventive public health service. The Liberal Government of the period 1906–1914 preferred to take specific action on behalf of particular groups; it was in the national interest to guarantee the health and efficiency of regularly employed male workers. This example shows the importance of understanding the historical specificity of each national case.

Nevertheless, it is possible to suggest some key variables in determining the development of health insurance. Hollingsworth et al. have suggested that where the central state was strong, where the working class was mobilized, and where the medical profession was weakly organized, then state intervention came early. They suggest that this model fits the experience of Sweden and Germany, whereas the USA and France tended in the opposite direction. There are inevitably problems with models of this kind. In Britain, where intervention came relatively early, working-class organization in trade unions was strong, but while unions tended to support the idea of old age pensions, they opposed the introduction of social insurance because it threatened the kind of mutual aid already operated by unions and friendly societies, and threatened to interpose the state between these organizations and their members. Nor was the medical profession especially weak, which resulted in a prolonged set of negotiations before health insurance was passed. Kuhnle has suggested that the introduction of compulsory insurance was likely when classical economic liberalism was weak and/or when voluntary insurance funds were also weak. As in the case of Hollingsworth et al.'s model, these factors are certainly an important part, if not the whole, of the story. In Germany, classical liberalism was weak. In Denmark, the position in respect of the voluntary sickness insurance funds was similar to Germany, but liberalism was strong and state compulsion was long delayed. In Britain, the mutual aid societies may not have welcomed the advent of state intervention, but the increasing call on their funds by members who were elderly and sick was a source of concern as early as the 1880s.

Despite the fears of the medical profession, the introduction of health insurance gave registered practitioners a monopoly over practice at the expense of alternative practitioners, such as homeopaths. In Britain general practitioners made significant advances in terms of pay under the state insurance system. While in the long run, doctors were materially best off in the United States where health care delivery was left substantially to the private sector, differences in the development of health care systems did not impact on the growing power of, and faith in, the medical profession and the hospital.

## CONCLUSION

It is extremely difficult to gauge the effects of increased state intervention on behalf of mothers, children and male workers on the people themselves. The effects of medical advances, for example, must also be considered. Thus the advent of serum therapy in the 1890s coincided with intensified measures to improve housing and environmental conditions, while the origins of antiseptic surgery during the 1860s (albeit not applied systematically in obstetrics until much later) and of bacteriology during the 1870s also coincided with more general attempts to clean up the urban environment and with improvements in diet, housing and income.

The growth of modern systems of medical care certainly increased the power and prestige of doctors, but historians have been more skeptical about their benefits for patients. Nevertheless, Cronje has been much more inclined to a positive view of the therapies introduced for TB sufferers during the period than others,[16] while Dwork has been more inclined to give credit to public health doctors for their work in respect of maternal and child welfare than have Davin or Lewis.[17] Regardless of the precise effect of infant welfare clinics and schools for mothers on the infant mortality rate, such evidence as is available from sources such as the autobiographies of working people suggests that women welcomed more information regarding their children's and their own health. As George Orwell noted in regard to middle and working-class food habits in *The Road to Wigan Pier*, the knowledge possessed by educated middle-class people was usually valuable, but it depended how it was passed along.[18]

One of the chief characteristics of life in the twentieth century has been the emergence of certainty in respect of the life cycle. The confidence that one is highly likely to live to an old age, will receive a prescribed number of years of education and entitlements to health care, be employed to the age of retirement, and get a pension in old age have been significant elements constructing the new certainty. Some elements have been considerably weaker in some countries than in others, for example, entitlements to health care in the USA, and some have again become weaker at the end of the twentieth century, particularly expectations regarding employment. The importance of social insurance in securing greater certainty regarding both income and access to basic medical care is manifest. The measures taken in the Progressive period in respect of mothers and children were more equivocal because maternalism was defined so narrowly, with the result that mothers could be deprived of access to waged work without any compensation in the name of improving standards of motherhood. However, the advice and limited amounts of care that were offered often served to increase confidence. The motivation behind much of the legislation of the Progressive period, tied as it was to the desire to improve national efficiency and racial hygiene, often made programs self-limiting, but the benefits to the population were nonetheless tangible.

## REFERENCES

1. P. Thane, 'Women in the British Labour Party and the construction of State Welfare, 1906–1939,' in S. Koven and S. Michel (eds), *Mothers of a New World. Maternalist Politics and the Origins of Welfare States.* (London: Routledge, 1993), pp. 358–9.
2. G.A. Ritter, *Social Welfare in Germany and Britain.* (Leamington Spa: Berg, 1986), p. 8.
3. R. Soloway, *Demography and Degeneration. Eugenics and the Declining Birth Rate in Twentieth Century Britain.* (Chapel Hill: University of North Carolina Press, 1990), p. xvii.
4. D.J. Kevles, *In the Name of Eugenics. Genetics and the Uses of Human Heredity.* (Harmondsworth: Penguin, 1985), p. 71.
5. J. Lewis, *The Politics of Motherhood. Child and Maternal Welfare in England, 1900–1939.* (London: Croom Helm, 1980).
6. Kevles, *op. cit.*, p. 40.
7. S. Michel, 'The Limits to Maternalism: Policies towards American Wage-Earning Mothers during the Progressive Era,' in Koven and Michel (eds), *Mothers of a New World*, pp. 277–320.
8. C. Eagle Russett, *Sexual Science. The Victorian Construction of Womanhood.* (Cambridge, Mass.: Harvard University Press, 1989).
9. H. Maudsley, 'Sex in Mind and in Education,' *Fortnightly Review* (1874), **XV**: p. 477.
10. V. Skultans, *Madness and Morals. Ideas on Insanity in the Nineteenth Century.* (London: Routledge and Kegan Paul, 1975), p. 74.
11. P. Geddes and J.A. Thompson, *Sex.* (London: Williams and Norgate, 1914), p. 244.
12. E. Ross, *Love and Toil. Motherhood in Outcast London 1870–1918.* (Oxford: Oxford University Press, 1993), p. 167.
13. S. Maugham, *Of Human Bondage.* (London: Heinemann, 1915), p. 560.
14. D. Dwork, *War is Good for Babies and Other Young Children. A History of the Infant Welfare Movement in England, 1898–1918.* (London: Routledge, 1987).
15. T. Skocpol, *Protecting Soldiers and Mothers.* (Cambridge, MA and London: Harvard University Press, 1992), Seth Koven and Sonya Michel, 'Womanly Duties: Maternalist Politics and the Origins of Welfare States in France, Germany, Great Britain and the United States, 1880–1920,' *American Historical Review* (1990), **XCV**: 1076–1108.
16. G.C. Cronje, 'Pulmonary Tuberculosis in England and Wales, 1851–1910,' unpublished PhD thesis, University of London, 1990; Smith, *The Retreat of Tuberculosis 1850–1950.* (London and New York: Croom Helm, 1988).
17. Dwork, *op.cit.*, Lewis, *op.cit.*
18. George Orwell, *The Road to Wigan Pier.* (Harmondsworth: Penguin, 1970), first edition 1937.

## FURTHER READING

Flora, P. and Heidenheimer, J. (eds), *The Development of Welfare States in Europe and America*. (New York: Transaction Pubs., 1995).

Harris, J., *Private Lives, Public Spirit. A Social History of Britain, 1880–1914*. (Oxford: Oxford University Press).

Hollingsworth, J.R., Hage, J. and Hanneman, R.A., *State Intervention in Medical Care. Consequences for Britain, France, Sweden and the United States, 1890–1970*. (Ithaca: Cornell Press, 1990).

Kevles, D., *In the Name of Eugenics. Genetics and the Uses of Human Heredity*. (Harmondsworth: Penguin, 1985).

Koven, S. and Michel, S. (eds), *Mothers of a New World. Maternalist Politics and the Origins of Welfare States*. (London: Routledge, 1993).

Lewis, J., *The Politics of Motherhood. Child and Maternal Welfare in England, 1900–1939*. (London: Croom Helm, 1980).

Pedersen, S., *Family Dependence and the Origins of the Welfare State, 1914–1945*. (Cambridge: Cambridge University Press, 1993).

Ritter, G.A., *Social Welfare in Germany and Britain*. (Leamington Spa: Berg, 1986).

Starr, P., *The Social Transformation of American Medicine*. (New York: Basic Books, 1982).

Wikander, U., Kessler-Harris, A. and Lewis, J. (eds), *Protecting Women. Labor Legislation in Europe, the United States and Australia, 1880–1920*. (Urbana: University of Illinois Press, 1995).

# CHAPTER 7

# Post-Colonial Medicine

RANDALL M. PACKARD

The term 'post-colonial' has come to signify more than a period of time that post-dates the period of European and American domination of non-Western peoples. Thanks largely to the recent work of literary scholars and subaltern historians, the post-colonial moment has come to represent a rejection of scholarly oppression. It is also marked by a breaking free from the influences of Western epistemologies that defined how the arts, sciences, literature, and history defined the experiences of people living within the colonial world. The post-colonial moment is about attempts to resurrect indigenous modes of thought and representation, not as pristine entities, but as forms of knowledge that are shaped by, and reflective of, the legacy of the colonial era. It is about raising up and empowering alternative visions of modernity. Finally, and perhaps most critically, the post-colonial moment represents the persistence of powerful colonial forms of knowledge and representation and the tension between these forms and those which are struggling to emerge from under the shadow of colonialism.

Post-colonial scholarship raises important questions for the history of medicine in the post-colonial era. Most centrally, what is the meaning of post in post-colonial medicine, or put more directly, have post-colonial medical systems broken free from colonial forms of knowledge, practice, and representation? If so, where has this occurred and under which circumstances? If not, why has post-colonial medicine been resistant to such challenges?

Of all the bodies of colonial knowledge, medicine has been perhaps the least challenged by post-colonial questioning. Wherever one turns, one is struck by the continuities rather than by the re-workings. The relative absence of serious challenges to the hegemony of Western biomedicine is not for a lack of trying. There certainly have been efforts to liberate medical systems from a narrow adherence to Western biomedical models and to make them both more responsive to local cultural and social realities. Yet whether one looks at the struggles of indigenous healers to gain official recognition in Zaire or Zimbabwe, or the integration of Ayurvedic medicine in south Asia, one is inevitably confronted by the continued hegemony of Western biomedical knowledge and practice and its resistance to innovation. If anything, the power of biomedical models has expanded as a result of the growing dependence of developing nations on Western aid and the parallel growth of international health and development agencies, such as the World Health Organization and UNICEF, which work within a Western biomedical paradigm.

None of this should be read to indicate that medical systems within developing countries remained unchanged following the end of colonialism. Changes certainly did occur. Yet these changes were initiated in most cases prior to the end of colonialism. Moreover, they represent the results of advances in biomedical knowledge and technology; they occurred within a Western biomedical paradigm.

The purpose of this chapter is to examine the development of post-colonial medical systems, the forces that have shaped them, and to present some explanations for their relative resistance to change. While it will examine how traditional healing has intersected with post-colonial medical systems, it will not attempt to explore the significant transformations that have occurred independently within these indigenous systems. This is an important subject, which deserves more exploration than is possible here. Throughout the period covered in this chapter, local populations frequently employed indigenous healing methods alongside, or in preference to, Western biomedical services. The failure of post-colonial governments to effectively integrate indigenous healing methods into their health systems is reflective of the broader failure of these systems to make a decisive break from the legacy of colonial medical systems.

## COLONIAL MEDICINE

In order to understand the extent to which post-colonial medical systems have reproduced forms of knowledge and practice which developed during the colonial era, it is necessary to begin by outlining essential characteristics of colonial medicine. A more extensive discussion of these characteristics occurs in the chapter by Worboys.

Western efforts to deal with the health of developing regions of the globe from the end of the nineteenth century to the late 1920s shared certain characteristics. First they were closely linked to the economic interests of colonizers. Health was not an end in itself, but rather a pre-requisite for development. Colonial or tropical medicine was concerned, primarily, with maintaining the health of Europeans living in the tropics, since these imperial agents were viewed as essential to the success of the colonial project. Tropical medicine was only concerned with the health of colonized subjects to the extent that their ill health threatened colonial economic enterprises or the health of Europeans. This concern had two consequences. First, the success or failure of health interventions was measured in terms of their ability to maintain or increase levels of production rather than in terms of levels of health among the native population. Production losses, defined in terms of days or shifts lost, served as a surrogate measure for the health of the native work force. Secondly, health services for native populations were located near areas of European settlement and sites of production, and thus primarily in or near urban centers. Colonial governments did little to build rural health services for the general native populations. Rural health services, which served the needs of local populations, were run by missionaries and focused primarily on maternal and child health. For most rural inhabitants contact with Western medical services was limited to occasional medical campaigns.

The second characteristic of colonial medical services was that they tended to be narrowly technical in their design and implementation. Health was defined as the absence of disease and could be achieved by understanding and developing methods for attacking diseases, one at a time. This preoccupation with disease and particularly parasitic diseases was shaped by the emergence of the sub-field of tropical medicine at the end of the nineteenth century and by the research interests of colonial medical practitioners. It was also driven by a faith in the ability of Western science to overcome the health problems of colonized subjects. Finally, a narrow disease approach to health pleased colonial administrators, for it appeared to be cheaper and more manageable than efforts to improve the general health and well being of colonial subjects through social and economic development. Colonial authorities viewed both the provision of broad based health care and efforts to deal with the underlying social and economic determinants of illness as both impractical and unnecessary.

Faith in the ability of Western medicine to cure the ills of colonial subjects discouraged colonial medical authorities from learning much about the colonized. As John Farley noted in his study of Bilharzia:

> The link between parasitology and tropical medicine also led to the belief that parasitic diseases could be prevented without the involvement of the people with the diseases... This technical view of prevention was as attractive to the British medical officer in the 1920s as it was to the WHO official in the 1960s. For success it merely required suitable chemicals to kill mosquitoes and snails, and scientifically trained experts to administer them. The population at risk could be ignored.[1]

More subtly, colonial medical systems generally posited ideas and images about the physical, behavioral and mental characteristics of colonized subjects which often served to reinforce the assumptions upon which colonial rule was predicated. This was particularly true in colonial Africa.

Colonial medical authorities generally discounted the medical knowledge of local populations, and at times persecuted indigenous health practitioners. There were, however, important exceptions to this pattern. In colonial India, British doctors drew on the knowledge of Indian medical practice to assist them in the identification of local illnesses. They also expanded their pharmaceutical knowledge by incorporating local plants and herbs.

Some of these characteristics of colonial medicine were challenged at various points during the colonial era, and particularly during the late twenties and thirties, when efforts to examine the social and economic basis of ill health infused discussions of malaria and malnutrition. Yet, they remained the central principles upon which colonial medical services were maintained prior to WWII.

## POST–WAR VISIONS OF HEALTH AND DEVELOPMENT

The post-war period brought about significant changes in the practice of colonial medicine. However, these changes did not lay the groundwork for a re-localization of health systems, the reassertion of indigenous models, or even the development of a more effective integration of Western biomedical models with local knowledge and conditions. Nor did these changes lead to fundamental shifts in the ideas and images of colonized peoples that permeated Western biomedical thinking about colonial subjects. Instead the immediate post-war period laid the foundation for the internationalization of health and a reaffirmation of Western biomedical models. Moreover in a number of fields, such as in efforts to control malaria and smallpox, this internationalization of health moved the control and practice of health care even further from local settings.

The post-war vision of the link between health and development differed in significant ways from that which had existed before the war. To begin with it was much more pervasive and encompassing. Health policies, as well as rhetoric, reflected a new realization of the need to extend the provision of health care to entire populations, not just select communities of productive workers and Europeans. This shift in vision reflected a more fundamental re-conceptualization of development and its goals following the war, as well as technological developments which for the first time made the extension of certain types of health intervention affordable on a broad scale.

Discussions on the health of peoples living in underdeveloped areas of the globe (a phrase which increasingly replaced 'the colonies,' as colonial empires began to be dismantled in the post-war era) emerged from a growing awareness on the part of Western industrial nations that their economic future depended on increasing the production of raw materials as well as markets for manufactured goods. The period saw an increased interest by colonial powers in the development of their tropical dependencies and a realization that increases in the productivity of tropical labor would require investments in social and economic infrastructure including greater investments in public health. This enlightened self-interest was reflected in a series of post–war development and welfare acts.

Within the United States as well, there was a growing awareness that the development of the so-called underdeveloped world was critical for the economic health of the industrialized world. The US needed to expand overseas markets for US manufactured goods. They needed a form of development that would lead to broad-based increases in consumption, not just production, in the developing world. The fear of post-war recession resulting from an inability to support the country's greatly increased wartime manufacturing capacity, placed a high premium on increasing the overseas consumption of US manufactured goods. The control of tropical diseases was a necessary prerequisite for tropical development.

In addition to its economic benefits, tropical disease control quickly became viewed as a critical weapon in the war against international Communism. By the late 1940s Communism was viewed as a major obstacle to the goal of a revitalized global economy, envisioned by Western economic and political leaders. With time, of course, defeating Communism became a goal in and of itself. In his welcoming address to the conference on "Health Problems of Industries Operating in Tropical Countries," Dr. James S. Simmons, Dean of the Harvard School of Public Health observed:

> In these days of mounting international crisis, this conference takes on significance far beyond the mere improvement of the health of industrial workers as a means to increase production. The health and manpower of the free nations of the world are now the most vital resources in our fight against Communism. They are part and parcel of the defense program of the democratic countries.[2]

Simmons' statement contrasted the broader health agenda, which the war against Communism required, with the narrow economic interest, which US industries operating overseas had in the health of its workers.

Harry Cleaver has argued that concern for combating Communism was the primary motivating factor behind the Eisenhower administration's support for the World Health Organization's Malaria Eradication Program in 1957. United States Operations Mission (USOM) records from Vietnam and Thailand show that in the early fifties, malaria control programs were very much part of the US war against Communism. The apparent speed with which malaria could be brought under control with DDT, together with its short term effects on other household pests, made malaria control particularly attractive for those who saw tropical disease control as an instrument for 'winning hearts and minds' in the war against Communist expansion. Malaria control programs were defined by the US Special Technical and Economic Missions to Vietnam and Thailand as 'impact programs.' These were programs that were designed to have a rapid positive effect on local populations in order to build support for local governments and their US supporters. In short, within the context of the war against Communism, health interventions needed to be broad based. Protecting the health of a few thousand plantation workers would be of little help in winning support of local villagers subjected to Communist propaganda. Local governments also perceived disease control as a means to gain popular political support. As A. Viswanathan, the distinguished Indian malariologist, pointed out, "No service establishes contact with every individual home at least twice a year as the DDT service does unless it be the collection of taxes."[3]

The expansion of health services within newly emerging developing countries in the post-war period was also linked to the development of new technologies which made possible relatively inexpensive methods of disease control. The most important of these was DDT. Developed just before the war by German scientists, DDT was employed during the war with great effect in combating typhus and malaria. Sprayed on the walls of huts once every six months, DDT could control or even eliminate the transmission of malaria for a small fraction of the cost involved in the use of earlier forms of insecticide, which required much more frequent applications, or costly drainage work.

Streptomycin and Isoniazid (INH), developed during the 1940s, provided an effective cure for tuberculosis and thus the technical basis for a greatly expanded campaign against this deadly disease. The development of miniature x-ray equipment furthered the attack. The 1950s saw mass X-ray campaigns and treatment programs established throughout many developing countries. Similarly, the development after the war of an effective freeze dried vaccine for smallpox, eliminating the need for expensive refrigeration and the maintenance of a cold-chain, made it possible to attack smallpox on a broad scale in the tropics. It thus raised the possibility of a global campaign to eradicate smallpox.

## THE INTERNATIONALIZATION OF HEALTH

Paralleling the expanding vision of international health in the post-war era, and contributing to it, was the growing internationalization of health and the relocation of health decision making from local governments and colonial metropoles, to new centers of international health and development in Geneva, New York, Washington, and Atlanta. This relocation played a significant role in defining the nature of post-colonial medical systems and in insuring the continued hegemony of Western biomedicine.

International organizations dedicated to the improvement of global health first emerged during the inter-war period. The Rockefeller Foundation's International Health Board, established in 1914, and its successor organization, the International Health Division, supported the development of disease control campaigns and the training of doctors and public health officials in Latin America, Asia, Africa, and the Middle East. Similarly, the League of Nations, established immediately after World War I, created Commissions dedicated to the control of malaria and rural sanitation and, through the International Labor Organization, struggled to improve international occupational health standards. Although these organizations were influential in shaping international health ideas and practices, their direct impact on the health of peoples living within European colonies was limited. Decisions concerning the nature and extent of health services remained firmly in the hands of European colonial officials. The Rockefeller Foundation's primary contribution to the practice of colonial medicine was through its funding of the London School of Tropical Medicine and Hygiene.

The influence of international health organizations on the health of colonized peoples increased substantially after World War II. The gradual dismantling of colonial control in Asia and Africa relaxed restrictions that had limited the activities of international health organizations. At the same time, de-colonization produced a demand in newly independent countries for a new cadre of health experts who were at least nominally independent of former colonial rulers. Within this changing political environment the newly formed United Nations, which replaced the League of Nations, gave birth to a series of new international organizations. In the field of health the World Health Organization (WHO) and to a somewhat lesser extent the United Nations International Children's Emergency Fund (UNICEF) emerged as powerful centers for the production and distribution of expert knowledge on health and nutrition. In addition to the United Nations' organizations, new players in the field of international health emerged within the politically dominant post-war nations.

The process which led to the creation of the WHO and UNICEF shaped the subsequent activities of both agencies and in turn the development of postcolonial medical systems in two distinct ways. The United Nations system emerged during a period in which Europe and America maintained their imperial control over large areas of the globe. Consequently both commissions created to design the United Nations' system, and the resulting agencies, contained few representatives from the developing world. During the late forties and fifties the World Health Assembly, the executive committees of WHO, and the so-called 'expert committees,' which reviewed and made recommendations about a range of health problems, were all dominated by representatives of Western Europe, the US, the Soviet Union and British Commonwealth countries. Only a handful of non-Western countries were included in these bodies. Only one sub-Saharan African country, Liberia, had a representative on the World Health Assembly. As a result, there were few if any voices to express concern about the continued narrow application of Western biomedical models to the health problems of colonial peoples. Nor were there advocates for a more effective integration of biomedical and indigenous health systems, or to assert the importance of broad based approaches to health which addressed the very real social and economic determinants of ill-health that existed in developing countries.

Secondly, as Socrates Litsios has recently shown, the creation of the United Nations system of agencies produced a division of labor, through which various agencies took on responsibilities for specific functions. While there was some overlap in these responsibilities, and consequently some competition among agencies, especially between WHO and UNICEF, the development agendas and activities of each agency tended to be narrowly defined. This resulted in a separation of health from broader social and economic development initiatives. Despite the rhetoric of health as a pre-requisite for development, there was little if any cooperation between WHO or UNICEF on the one hand, and agencies such as FAO and UNDP which were charged with developing programs for social and economic advancement, on the other. Litsios sees this separation as being in large measure a product of the political environment of the post-war period. He argues that Western governments wished to avoid the creation of statist patterns of multi-sector development which were associated with both Fascist and Communist systems of government. Attacks by conservative legislators in the US Congress on broad-based multi-sector development projects, such as the Tennessee Valley Association, were a warning to the architects of the UN system. Cooperation among the resulting agencies proved difficult given their varied responsibilities and interests, as well as interagency competition for funds.

The separation of agency responsibility within the UN system meant that the activities of WHO and UNICEF, like the activities of colonial governments, became defined along narrow biomedical lines and seldom addressed the links between health and social and economic development. This narrow definition of health countered the spirit of the original declaration of health by the WHO, which defined health in very broad terms.

The absence of colonial voices within the emerging international health and development organizations following World War II and the separation of health from broader social and economic concerns within the UN system of agencies produced models of health care which shared many of the characteristics of colonial medical systems.

First, health continued to be viewed as a vehicle for social and economic development, rather than an end in itself. This remained so despite the lack of coordination between health and development activities within international agencies. The scale of health interventions increased but the goals remained the same.

Secondly, health interventions were driven by a continued faith in the ability of Western biomedical technology, and those who wielded it, to overcome the health problems of peoples living in developing countries. This faith had been reinforced by the technological developments, which came out of the war. Characteristic of this confidence was the following reference to US sponsored malaria control programs from a 1950 Department of State report on the Point Four Program:

> The most dramatic results from the employment of *a very small number of skilled men and very small quantities of scientifically designed materials* have been achieved in the field of medicine. In many areas of the world one trained public-health doctor or a group of two or three working with local people able to follow their guidance have been able to rout one of man's oldest and deadliest enemies (emphasis added).[4]

Thirdly, post-war health planning and implementation continued to view local populations as inherently unhealthy and incapable of caring for their own health needs. In fact, one can discern an even greater tendency in this direction among Western health authorities working in India in the post-war period than had occurred during the colonial era. Local medical knowledge continued to be undervalued and little effort was made to incorporate indigenous notions of health and healing into post-colonial health systems until the late 1970s. Faith in Western biomedical technology and disregard for local abilities or knowledge led to the creation of vertical medical programs designed by committees of Western health authorities and implemented from the top down with little local participation.

Conversely, little attention, and even fewer resources, went to the development of local health services. The expansion of health services to local populations in reality meant expansion of health campaigns rather than the development of health infrastructure. The scale and frequency of these campaigns increased but the colonial pattern of locating health services in urban and industrial sites and serving rural populations through campaigns continued.

The great disease eradication campaigns against malaria and later smallpox were characteristic of the narrowly defined vertical approach to health which emerged within international health agencies during the post-war years. While the failure of malaria eradication to achieve its goals undermined faith in this approach, the subsequent success of smallpox eradication reaffirmed it. Moreover, despite the movement toward Primary Health Care in the late 1970s, with its affirmation of the need for popular participation in health planning and implementation, international health practice retained many of the characteristics of the narrowly defined top down biomedical approach that characterized eradication efforts in the 1950s and 1960s.

## INDEPENDENCE, HEALTH, AND DEPENDENCY

The centrality of international health agencies in defining the health agendas of developing countries was directly linked to patterns of political and economic dependency within newly independent countries. This dependency was in turn a legacy of colonialism.

The process of de-colonization began in the late 1940s in Asia and the late 1950s in Africa. By the mid-1960s nearly all European colonies had achieved some form of independence, with the exception of white settler dominated colonies in southern Africa. The leaders of newly independent countries were faced with a broad range of development needs, including better and more pervasive health care for their citizens. At the same time, they possessed very limited financial and human resources with which to fulfill these needs. Colonial development policies had restricted local accumulation of capital, preferring to export the capital earned from various economic enterprises to metropolitan treasuries and private corporations. Similarly, colonial education policies had limited the training of persons with advanced technical skills. This was especially true in the health sector. Together these economic and educational policies produced a heavy dependence on external human and financial resources. Foreign advisors, primarily from Western industrial countries, flocked to newly independent countries, replacing or working along side former colonial administrators. These advisors brought with them plans for development that originated in Western drawing rooms and reflected Western interests and goals for development. Financial resources in the form of grants and aid funds also flowed into the newly independent countries. This aid, like the foreign advisors, came with implicit or explicit expectations about what constituted 'development.' These expectations limited the extent to which local leaders could develop models of development which deviated from those projected by Western development agencies. Leslie Doyal has noted in particular the link between British advice and financial assistance in the health field and the financial interests of British manufacturing firms. She argues that British aid agencies advocated the strengthening of tertiary care facilities in its former colonies, as opposed to investments in primary health care, because this policy created more sales opportunities for British health equipment manufacturers. This form of self-interested aid was not unique to Britain. Dinham and Hines have estimated that nine out of every ten dollars given by USAID to African countries, came back to the US in the form of orders for US manufactured equipment and supplies.

The very process of de-colonization also created limitations on local innovation. The procedure by which colonial authorities turned over the control of their former possessions all but insured that political leadership would be assumed by a cadre of local elites who had been inculcated with the value of Western models of development. While this effort to reproduce existing patterns of development was not completely successful, it did produce a first generation of political leaders who tended to fall in line with the development agendas of the West.

In addition, the class interests of these leaders contributed to a continuation of colonial patterns of development, particularly in the health sector. Local elites, who lived primarily in national capitals and other large metropolitan areas, demanded access to the best medical care that their governments could provide. This demand led governments to make heavy investments in large urban hospitals. Given limits in overall health budgets, the build up of tertiary care facilities prevented governments from making investments in much needed rural health facilities. Thus inequalities in the distribution of health services continued and in some cases grew larger.

The vertical programs focusing on single health problems which characterized international health activities during the 1950s, 1960s and 1970s reinforced these inequalities in the distribution of health services. Programs in disease eradication and family planning supplemented national health services and permitted national governments, with limited resources, to claim that they were providing health benefits to the masses, at the same time that they sustained a class based system of health care.

Among the local elites most resistant to transforming local health systems were the physicians themselves. Efforts to transform medical school curricula to better serve local health needs were met with resistance by students who feared that these changes would limit the value of their medical degrees and ultimately their ability to find employment overseas. Having received their degrees, newly trained physicians often resisted assignment to rural areas and became lobbyists for the development of tertiary care centers. Consequently, the professional health practitioners in charge of health ministries had little direct knowledge of local rural health conditions. These conditions consequently played little role in national health policy decision making. While not all local physicians shared these characteristics, there were enough to inhibit efforts to transform local medical systems.

Local political leaders tended to share these Western biomedical perspectives. As a result of their shared vision of development and class based interests few leaders of newly independent countries espoused alternative visions of health development. Julius Nyerere of Tanzania was one of the few independence leaders to successfully pursue an alternative model of health care as part of his broader effort to develop a system of African Socialism. Nyerere's vision of health was influenced by the People's Republic of China's successful effort to spread health resources away from urban areas and develop a system of primary health care based on a cadre of grass roots paramedics or barefoot doctors. Tanzania's adoption of this model led to a significant improvement in the country's infant mortality rate during the 1960s and 1970s.

## PRIMARY HEALTH CARE

By the late 1960s, the limitations and failures of post-war efforts to improve the health of peoples living in developing countries produced a growing critique of existing strategies, and calls for new approaches. This critique was part of a broader reexamination of development strategies, emanating both from the Western development community and the developing world.

Development agencies, particularly in the US, began to question whether development could be achieved by simply increasing the ability of developing economies to export raw materials. This strategy had led to investments in export industries, the transfer of technology, and the funding of large-scale development projects, particularly in agriculture. Critics of this approach argued that it had produced growth without development and that the majority of local populations benefited little from the growth that occurred. They called for a new emphasis on providing for the basic needs of a country's entire population through policies that focused on reducing poverty and encouraging small-scale local projects. As Martha Finnemore has shown, this shift was particularly marked in the World Bank under Robert McNamarra in the early 1970s.

Paralleling this shift in Western development thinking, and in some ways influencing it, was a growing critique of underdevelopment among scholars located in developing countries. This attack had its origins in the work of structural economists in Latin America during the 1940s. These economists questioned the progressive integration of national economies into world markets, warning that global markets posed dangers as well as opportunities to primary-product producers. They called instead for the development of local economies through investments in import substitution industries. Their calls for national economic planning and industrialization provided a starting point for more radical departures leading to dependency theory and a wider critique of Western driven development agendas that produced underdevelopment rather than development.

This growing critique of development can be seen as well in the field of international health. During the early 1970s a chorus of academics and health practitioners began to criticize capital intensive strategies based on the transfer of health technologies, such as had been employed in WHO's failed global malaria eradication campaign. This approach was seen as having only a limited impact on health. At the same time, there was a growing appreciation of the potential of more grassroots efforts based on disease prevention strategies, popular participation, and self-reliance as had been demonstrated by the successes of China, Cuba and Tanzania. A major proponent of this alternative health strategy was Dr Halfdan Mahler, who was elected Director General of WHO in 1973.

Mahler had spent most of his medical career working in developing countries. This experience had made him critical of technological solutions to deep-seated health problems. While he appreciated the successes that had been achieved through immunization campaigns and especially the attack on smallpox, he believed strongly in the need to develop broad-based health services at the grassroots level. Under Mahler's leadership, and after much discussion and resistance, the WHO shifted its direction and adopted the strategy of Primary Health Care (PHC) at the World Health Assembly meeting in Alma Ata, Russia in 1978. PHC called for investments in basic health infrastructure at the local level. It also highlighted the need for local participation in health planning and implementation. Disease prevention as well as curative medicine should be encouraged. Finally, PHC recognized the need to attack the social and economic root causes of ill health.

Without going into the history of primary health care, its success and failings, it is important to note that as the central movement within the field of international health, Primary Health Care, as originally proposed in 1978, was short lived. The rhetoric of primary health care continued, and in fact continues to the present and projects persist. Yet their character has changed in significant ways. Attention to the broader social and economic determinants of sickness and health was never taken seriously in terms of the funding of international health initiatives. Financial constraints and political sensitivities made such an emphasis impossible. This became particularly true within US development agencies during the 1980s. The growing global recession, combined with the fiscal and political conservatism of the Reagan and Bush administrations, put a damper on efforts to cope with the underlying causes of ill health or to invest in health infrastructure. Developing countries wedded to the PHC concept found little financial support for the concept coming from the aid and development community.

At the same time, the successes of smallpox eradication led to a renewed faith in technological approaches to health. The WHO expanded immunization programs, and UNICEF's global immunization campaigns took center stage in international health programs.

Primary health care was replaced by selective primary health care, in which vertically organized health programs were piggy-backed on to local health infra-structures. Local health promotion became narrowly focused on particular health problems rather than on the broad based health and well being of the populations at risk. This shift away from broad-based primary health care has been justified in terms of cost effectiveness. Selective primary health care, Combatting Child-hood Communicable Diseases (CCCD) or Child Survival programs, requires lim-ited investments in health infrastructure. However, like the campaigns of the 1950s and 1960s, selective primary health care pays little or no attention to the underlying causes of ill health. Moreover, it defines health as the absence of disease and ignores a broad range of health problems. The emphasis that PHC placed on popular participation has been all but abandoned in favor of a hierarchical struc-ture in which health knowledge trickles down. The abandonment of efforts to insure popular participation in the development of health systems has prevented further localization of post-colonial health systems.

The history of efforts to incorporate indigenous forms of healing into primary health care is symptomatic of the general failure of primary health care to create a significant break from Western biomedical models of health care. During the 1970s, in association with the move to primary health, efforts were made to integrate indigenous healers into national health services in Africa and Asia. These efforts promoted by the World Health Organization's 1978 Report on *The Promotion and Development of Traditional Medicine*, involved the organization and recognition of traditional healer associations, such as Zimbabwe's National Traditional Healers' Association (ZINATHA), and efforts to incorporate traditional healers and mid-wives into the system of primary health care. In Africa, healers, bonesetters, midwives and herbalists were identified and given elementary training in Western biomedical skills. Research by medical anthropologists into indigenous medical systems supported calls for integration. Similarly, in parts of south Asia, efforts were made to selectively employ healers and midwives as providers of primary health care. While these efforts represented an advance over earlier patterns of segrega-tion and the overt denigration of indigenous medical systems, they fell short of achieving an effective integration which would have contributed to the localization of medical knowledge and practice. This is primarily because the Western biomedi-cal community dictated the terms of integration. Local healers and midwives had little say in the shaping of integration. Integration was limited to those practices and skills that corresponded to Western biomedical conceptions of medicine. Much of what healers did remained unacceptable. The wider cultural context within which healing practices occurred, the vast compendium of cultural knowl-edge and practice which gave meaning to local medicine, continued to be ignored and in some cases actively suppressed. The end result was the creation of a cadre of so called indigenous healers and midwives whose role within the Primary Health Care system often bore little resemblance to their former identity. Stacy Pigg's work on efforts by international development organizations to integrate traditional medical practitioners and midwives into the primary health care system of Nepal under the banner of popular participation clearly shows how the role of traditional medical practitioners, *dhamis*, was transformed by the process of integration. She concludes that "… the universalizing principles inherent in development discourse systematically dismantle and decontextualize different socio-cultural realities in the course of taking them into account."[5] Indigenous healing systems have continued to thrive alongside those provided by Western biomedicine. Patients navigate their way through the various therapeutic options, but there remains only limited communication between Western and non-Western medical settings.

## CONCLUSION

Western biomedicine has achieved a great deal in relieving health problems in developing nations. Yet the health of local populations in many former colonies continues to lag far behind that of the majority of peoples living in former colonizing countries. The World Bank's measures the cost of ill health on human populations in terms of Disability Adjusted Life Years Lost (DALYS). The Bank's calculation of the DALYS per 1000 population in various regions of the world gives a crude indication of the gap that exists between the health of people living in developing countries and those in more developed economies [Table 1].[6]

TABLE 1: DISABILITY ADJUSTED LIFE YEARS BY REGION PER 1000 POPULATION

Many factors account for this gap. One of these is the failure of post-colonial health systems operating within developing countries to meet the needs of local populations. Local populations need to be participants in the development of their own health services. Indigenous medical knowledge, together with local social, cultural, and economic realities, need to be integrated into health planning and in the training of health workers at all levels. With few exceptions, this type of reorientation has not occurred, despite the rhetoric of international health agencies in the post-Alma-Ata era. This chapter has attempted to identify various conditions operating within individual countries, in international health and development agencies, and ultimately in the wider international political and economic order, which have prevented the effective development of truly post-colonial health systems.

## REFERENCES

1. John Farley, *Bilharzia: A History of Imperial Tropical Medicine*. (Cambridge, 1991).
2. James Steven Simmons, "Welcoming Address,' Conference on Industry and Tropical Health', *Industry and Tropical Health* (1950), **vol 1**: 12.
3. Randall M. Packard, 'Postwar Visions of Postwar Health and Development and their Impact Public Health Interventions in the Developing World,' in F. Cooper and R. Packard (eds), *International Development and the Social Sciences: Essays in the Politics and History of Knowledge*. (Berkeley, 1997).
4. Department of State, *Point Four: Cooperative Program for AID in the Development of Underdeveloped Areas*, Department of State Pub. 3719, Economic Cooperation Series 24. (Washington, 1950), p. 150.
5. Stacy Pigg, 'Acronyms and Effacement-Traditional Medical Practitioners (TMP) in International Health Development,' *Social Science and Medicine* (1995), **41, 1**: 47–68.
6. World Bank, *World Development Report 1993: Investing in Health*. (Oxford University Press, 1993), p. 215.

## FURTHER READINGS

Arnold, David, *Colonizing the Body: State Medicine and Epidemic Disease in Nineteenth Century India*. (Berkeley, 1993).

Dinham, Barbara and Hines, Colin, *Agribusiness in Africa*. (Trenton, 1991).

Doyal, Leslie, *The Political Economy of Health*. (Boston, 1971).

Cooper, Frederick and Randall M. Packard (eds), *International Development and the Social Sciences: Essays in the Politics and History of Knowledge*. (Berkeley, 1997).

Courtright, P., Lewallan, S. and Kanjaloti, S., 'Changing Patterns of Corneal Disease and Associated Vision Loss at a Rural African Hospital following a Training Program for Traditional Healers,' *British Journal of Opthalmology* (1996), **80**: 8.

Cleaver, Harry, (1977) 'Malaria and the Political Economy of Public Health', *International Journal of Health Services*, **7(4)**: 557–579.

Finnemore, Martha, 'Redefining Development at the World Bank,' in Cooper and Packard, *International Development and the Social Sciences: Essays in the Politics and History of Knowledge*. (Berkeley, 1997), 203–227.

George, Susan, *How the Other Half Dies*. (New York, 1976).

Goodfield, June, *A Chance to Live*. (New York, 1991).

Greenhough, Paul, 'Intimidation, Coercion and Resistance in the Final Stages of the South Asian Smallpox Eradication Campaign, 1973–1975,' *Social Science and Medicine* (1995), **41, 5**: 633–655.

Justice, Judith, *Policies, Plans and People: Foreign Aid and Health Development* (Berkeley, 1988).

Litsios, Socrates, 'Malaria Control, Rural Development and the Post-War Re-ordering of International Organizations,' in *Malaria and Development*, special issues of *Medical Anthropology* (1997), **14, 2**: 255–278.

MacCormack, Carol, 'Healthcare and the Concept of Legitimacy in Sierra Leone,' *Social Science and Medicine* (1981), **15B**: 423–428.

MacLeod, Roy and Lewis, Milton (eds), *Disease Medicine and Empire: Perspectives on Western Medicine and the Experience of European Expansion.* (New York, 1988).

Navarro, Vincent, *Medicine under Capitalism.* (Croom Helm, 1976).

Oshiname, F.O. and Brieger, W.R., 'Primary Care Training for Patent Medicine Vendors in Rural Nigeria,' *Social Science & Medicine* (1992), **35, 12**: 1477–1484.

Packard, Randall M. and Brown, Peter (eds), *Malaria and Development,* special issues of *Medical Anthropology* (1997), **14, 2**.

Packard, Randall M., 'The Invention of the "Tropical Worker": Medical Research and the Quest for Central African Labor on the South African Gold Mines, 1903–1936,' *Journal of African History* (1993), 34.

Pigg, Stacy Leigh, 'Found in most Traditional Societies: Traditional Practitioners between Culture and Development,' in Cooper and Packard *International Development and the Social Sciences: Essays in the Politics and History of Knowledge.* (Berkeley, 1997), 259–290.

Segal, Malcolm, 'The Politics of Primary Healthcare,' *Bulletin of the Institute of Development Studies* (1983), **14, 4**: 27–37.

Sidel, Victor and Ruth Sidel, *Serve the People-Observations on Medicine in the People's Republic of China.* (Boston, 1973).

Stone, Linda, 'Primary Health Care for Whom: Village Perspectives from Nepal,' *Social Science and Medicine* (1986), **22(3)**: 293–302.

Turshen, Merideth, *The Political Ecology of Disease in Tanzania.* (New Brunswick, 1984).

Vaughan, Megan, *Curing their Ills: Colonial Power and African Illness.* (Stanford, 1991).

Worboys, Michael, 'Manson, Ross and Colonial Medical Policy: Tropical Medicine in London and Liverpool, 1899–1914' in Roy MacLeod and Milton Lewis (eds), *Disease Medicine and Empire: Perspectives on Western Medicine and the Experience of European Expansion.* (New York, 1988).

# CHAPTER 8

# Medicine and the Counter Culture

MIKE SAKS

This chapter is centered on the challenge posed to orthodox medicine in the Western world in the twentieth century, of which Britain and the United States are taken as the primary examples. Modern medicine is seen as based on a biomedical approach which is focused on the body rather than the mind, and in which the body appears as divisible into parts that can be repaired on breakdown. The 'counter culture,' for this purpose, is conceived as a subculture established in opposition to the dominant prevailing culture of medicine. In an international and historical perspective, the attributions 'orthodox' and 'countercultural' are relative to place and time. In some current Third World societies, biomedicine may be seen as part of a counter culture in relation to more traditional types of folk medicine. And an existing counter culture might become the mainstream medical culture of the future, whether in the developing or developed world.

The chapter starts by outlining the nature of 'orthodox medicine' in modern Western societies. Whilst there are obvious differences between, say, Britain and the United States, their dominant medical cultures are similarly based on the biomedical frame of reference. This has been in the ascendance, as far as the medical profession is concerned, since the start of the twentieth century. Medical counter cultures were relatively weak in the first half of this century. This is not to say that the therapeutic pluralism that prevailed in the early nineteenth century had completely waned, nor to deny the persistence of widespread public scepticism about biomedicine. Nor, indeed, should it be thought that there was a total consensus at this time even amongst orthodox doctors — some of them employed unorthodox remedies in their practice, even in the bureaucratised medical settings which were developing in the first part of the twentieth century.

However, in the second half of the twentieth century, to which this chapter gives particular emphasis, medicine has come under increasing challenge and a more substantial counter culture has blossomed, especially from the 1960s. The growth of this counter culture will be documented here, including trends in litigation and self-help, and rising public interest in alternative medicine and holistic health care in an increasingly open, market-centered, context. Continuities with the past are highlighted as well as novel dimensions of the emergent counter culture. We should not assume, even today, that unorthodox practitioners have a monopoly on holistic practice or that all alternative therapists necessarily have a holistic orientation. In this context, this chapter assesses how deeply developments outside medicine have challenged the prevailing biomedical orthodoxy, given the strategic choices available to both orthodox and unorthodox practitioners.

## THE DOMINANCE OF MEDICINE UP TO THE 1950S

By the beginning of the twentieth century, the medical profession had established a formidable power base. In Britain, in the wake of the 1858 Medical Registration Act, the newly forged, self-regulating profession, with its monopoly of title, was increasingly able to establish its control over the process of diagnosis and treatment, following a highly charged war of words with rival practitioners. Similar patterns were in evidence in the United States where the dominant position of medicine is of more recent origin and underpinned on different grounds; there, a more formally restrictive and nationally fragmented system of state licensing of medicine covered much of the country by the turn of the century. The power of the profession on both sides of the Atlantic, moreover, was intensified as the twentieth century unfolded, reinforced, amongst other things, by the introduction of National Health Insurance legislation in Britain and the spread of state licensure and educational reform in the United States — as well as by the incorporation and subordination of a number of other health occupations.

In both countries, as the dominance of the medical profession was further underwritten in the first half of the twentieth century, so the intellectual framework of orthodox biomedicine was reinforced — based on the separation of the mind and body, the subordination of the patient to the (typically male) medical practitioner, and the centrality of clinical examination and laboratory tests. This framework had developed from the nineteenth-century concern to classify disease on the basis of the examination of patients in hospitals; it was elaborated by laboratory tests and experimentation from the mid-nineteenth century, and dominated the teaching hospitals. Though some public-health doctors pointed to wider social and environmental determinants of health, the medical schools were primarily oriented to recognizing diseases in the individual in a depersonalized manner, especially in the (poor) patients on the hospital wards. It was partly in opposition to these developments in medical orthodoxy that alternative medical subcultures took shape in the nineteenth century. Healers outside the medical profession organized movements to popularize their methods and attract adherents — whether for medical botany, osteopathy or chiropractic. Homeopathy, we should note, always attracted some practitioners with orthodox training.

In early twentieth-century Britain, several groups lobbied to expand state health care beyond that supported by the medical profession. The development of this counter culture was especially apparent in relation to women and childbirth, to which little attention had previously been paid by doctors acting within the framework of the state. Even when the official provision was enhanced — as in the case of the development of state midwifery services under medical auspices — this did not eliminate oppositional forms. Reform still allowed a substantial role for non-registered abortionists, since this area was not adequately covered by legislation, and there were large gaps in what medicine offered in relation to birth control. This left the field open for campaigners such as Marie Stopes, and for advice from relatives, friends and neighbors in a lay subculture which also served to shape broader interpretations of health and illness.

In the United States, self-diagnosis and self-treatment of a wide range of health problems were part of a tradition that continued into the first half of the twentieth century, not least because doctors were expensive and not always available. The use of patent medicines and home-spun remedies for ailments such as influenza and rheumatism was also significant in early twentieth-century Britain. That this was in part a countercultural phenomenon is suggested by evidence that the upper classes, as well as lower- and middle-class families, often rejected medical advice, in an era in which George Bernard Shaw had seen doctors and other professional groups as conspiracies against the laity. Ethnic minority groups, such as the Jewish community in Britain, often made their own provision for health care because their needs were not always catered for within the sometimes hostile, wider society. In this case, however, the medical aspect of the facilities rarely differed much from those serving the wider community.

The starkest manifestation of counter culture in this era in Britain was the continued popularity of various forms of alternative therapy, even though the number of alternative medical practitioners seems to have decreased substantially between $c$1850 and $c$1910. (The downward trends in the United States seem to have been later and less steep, given its more populist traditions). The therapies in question ranged from herbalism and water cure, which were seen as representing a return to nature, to such all-encompassing religious systems as Christian Science, which was founded in the second half of the nineteenth century and offered a framework for understanding health and illness vastly different from that of orthodox medicine.

The counter cultural aspects of these therapeutic movements are underlined by the sporadic attacks launched by organized medicine against the fringe, mostly through the pages of the leading medical journals. This was particularly evident where the medical establishment perceived its wealth, status and power to be under direct threat — as in the 1920s when the medical profession and the British Ministry of Health rebuffed the osteopaths who sought official parity with conventional medicine; and when American chiropractors, in challenging attempts by the medical profession to marginalize their practice, found themselves faced with arrest and imprisonment. But alternative subcultures existed even among doctors with orthodox qualifications and state registration. Some such doctors converted to homeopathy in spite of the efforts of the medical elite to contain potential subversion by controlling entry to the profession and medical career prospects.

In spite of, or perhaps because of, such challenges, the power of orthodoxy continued to increase. By the middle of the century, its dominance was shored up by ever greater levels of state support, not least through the consolidation of the medical licensing system in the United States and the development of the National Health Service in Britain, which further underwrote the medical monopoly. Such dominance was critically underpinned by the pharmacological revolution and the advent of such miracle drugs as penicillin and antibiotics in the 1940s. The promised cures for all ailments, and new forms of physical diagnosis, increased the legitimacy of medicine by the 1950s as it pursued its mission under the banner of scientific progress. This scientific edifice, however, came under challenge in the 1960s, as part of a wider critique of medicine that spawned a much more robust counter culture in the closing decades of the century, albeit one that had at least some continuities with the earlier development of alternative approaches.

## THE DEVELOPMENT OF THE COUNTER CULTURE FROM THE 1960S

The emergence of such a medical counter culture cannot be seen in abstraction from the broader call for change which swept the Western world in the 1960s, challenging mainstream materialistic values and technocratic conceptions of human problems. This demythologising of the 'progress' implicit in the scientific world view involved a refusal to defer to existing authority and the exploration of alternative lifestyles aimed at transcending the perceived spiritual bankruptcy of the existing order. New styles in clothing, hair, and drug-use manifested the desire for a more 'natural' existence, in an age that also saw the revival of interest in meditation and mysticism. In the years that followed, adherents of the counter culture came to question the authority of professional experts in general and doctors in particular.

This challenge went hand in hand with other attacks on high technology medicine, as dehumanizing the patient, for being less technically effective than commonly supposed, and for creating iatrogenic illnesses. Key issues included the damage resulting from thalidomide, and the questionable results of radical surgical procedures for diseases such as breast cancer. Indeed, from the mid-1970s, critics began to draw attention to the fact that epidemiological analyses of the Western population indicated that more of the improvement in health over the past century had arisen from factors such as enhanced food supplies and better sanitation than from interventions by orthodox biomedicine. This critique of modern medical advance had initially been directed at the softer target of institutional psychiatry, which was viewed by its critics not so much as an instrument of liberation as one of therapeutic oppression. But it was not long before leading countercultural figures like Ivan Illich had defined the whole of orthodox Western medicine as counterproductive.

In the wake of this critique, two central aspects of consumer power have emerged in the health field, with the active support of politicians. The first is growing pressure from patients wanting more responsibility for themselves and more accountability from professionals. In this respect, the growth of self-help groups has created significant lobbies, as well as providing health care and advice in a number of fields. The second is the growth of consumer interest in alternative medicine and holistic health, which has presented a real threat to orthodox biomedicine. Both of these facets of the medical counter culture have their roots earlier in the century, but both have been taken to new heights in the more challenging climate of the late twentieth century. We shall consider each of these in turn.

## CONSUMER POWER AND SELF-HELP

In the United States, a number of authors have drawn attention to a recent decrease in professional power in medicine. Their claims have largely revolved around the increasing impact of multinational corporations, rather than the growing influence of patients in their own right. It could, however, be argued that the power of American patients over their physicians has expanded with attempts to contain rising medical expenditure — as, for example, through Health Maintenance Organizations acting on behalf of consumers. Litigation has also provided an important point of leverage in the United States, with the challenge to professional expertise from the new health rights movement that has developed since the late 1960s. This has focused on obtaining rights to health care as well as rights in health care — including the right to informed consent, to refuse treatment and to see personal medical records. As such, it has been a pivotal part of lay resistance to medical decision making.

In Britain too, on a lesser scale, patients have challenged medicine through the courts, especially from the early 1970s when active consumerism gathered momentum. At this time Community Health Councils were formed to represent the public in the National Health Service and lay membership was strengthened on a number of medical committees, including those of the General Medical Council itself. This consumer lobby has helped to ensure that greater amounts of data about options and standards in the health service are now available to inform patient choice. However, the business model of management that has recently been introduced into the running of the National Health Service could be seen to have limited, rather than expanded, the extent to which consumers can directly influence medical care. Serious questions in this respect can be raised about how far the ideology of patient power has truly been transferred into practice — despite the advent of the Patients Charter — when services are bought by general practitioners and purchasing authorities on behalf of consumers, rather than by consumers themselves. Nonetheless, in both Britain and the United States there has been more empowerment of the consumer in the health sector than in the first half of the twentieth century, and this has crucially underpinned the development of the modern medical counter culture.

Within this counter culture overt criticism has been commonest in specific fields where medicine has relatively little to offer, as in the management of reproduction, chronic conditions and disability and in areas of experimentation such as organ transplantation that give rise to fundamental social concerns. Older, popular lay subcultures also remain in existence, even though they do not map directly on to biomedical belief systems — e.g., the idea that the common cold is related to personal responsibility for dressing inadequately in damp weather. Indeed, such subcultures still sustain a heavy reliance on self-prescribed medicines, the supply of which rivals those obtained through more conventional medical channels on both sides of the Atlantic. This highlights that the public continue to be locked into informal social networks through which consultation about the signs and symptoms of illness occurs outside of orthodox medicine. These shape not only referral patterns to physicians and compliance with medical advice, but also the paths that consumers follow in relation to self-care.

This reference to self-care suggests that self-help groups can sometimes be seen as an important part of the lay resistance to orthodox medical dominance in the latter decades of the twentieth century. The number of visible and active campaigning self-help groups has increased in the Anglo-American context in recent times, covering areas as diverse as black health and HIV/AIDS. They range from the Patients Association and the Association of Victims of Medical Accidents in Britain, to the National Women's Health Network in the United States. Interestingly, the counter culture of self-help and environmentalism has also begun to challenge medical definitions of public and environmental health, through legal disputes over scientific evidence and the interpretation of risks in the generation of conditions such as leukemia. At another level, the animal rights movement has been involved in Britain and the United States since the mid-1970s in endeavoring to stop medical scientists from using animals in research on the basis of moral arguments against vivisection. In general terms, the more the self-help group in question engages in radical protest against mainstream values and institutions in health care, the more it can be seen to be part of the new counter culture.

The women's movement has certainly been a central focus in this sense, by lobbying strongly for health services for women while attacking orthodox biomedicine for helping to maintain a patriarchal, gender-based society. The initial thrust of the attack in the Anglo-American context in the 1960s and 1970s was to criticise sexism towards women as consumers of medical services; the low proportion of women admitted to medical schools was also condemned. The focus of the feminist critique in Britain has now shifted towards defending and, where possible, expanding facilities such as Well Women's Clinics within the National Health Service, and endeavoring to enhance the wider living and working conditions of women. In the more privatized American health system — building on the underground abortion referral service offered by the Chicago Women's Liberation Union in the late 1960s — the women's movement has increasingly sought to establish alternative provision to meet the needs of women, with limited involvement from health professionals. It is here that feminist ideals and self-help most clearly come together, as illustrated by the work of the Boston Women's Health Collective, which has tried to demedicalize women's lives and demystify modern medicine through information dissemination and lobbying around issues such as home births.

### ALTERNATIVE MEDICINE AND HOLISTIC HEALTH CARE

The growing emphasis on self-help and consumer rights, including that engendered by the women's movement, has also been associated with the late twentieth-century expansion of alternative medicine. The escalation of consumer demand for consultations with alternative practitioners — prompted by, amongst other things, the striving for more 'natural' forms of health care — has focused on established unorthodox therapies such as homeopathy, faith healing and acupuncture. There are, however, national variations: e.g., osteopathy is more popular in Britain than the United States, whereas the reverse is true for chiropractic. But within this counter culture, consumers are now also turning to highly marginal practices such as aromatherapy, reflexology, biofeedback and crystal therapy — often on a self-help basis, as well as purchasing ever more health foods and related products.

The challenge thus posed to orthodox medicine derives not just from self-help or the use of alternative practitioners, but from the holistic approach which underlies many, if not all, of the therapies concerned, so providing a basis for the development of a coherent oppositional subculture. This approach gives greater significance to the whole being and the inter-relationship between mind and body in diagnosis and treatment. Despite moves in this direction by general practitioners, such an approach can be seen to conflict philosophically with the mind-body dualism underpinning much of contemporary biomedicine and with its concern to rectify malfunctions primarily through surgical intervention and drug regimes. The 'alternative' emphasis on consumer 'engagement,' as opposed to patient passivity, is also more appealing in a 'new age' context, especially when combined with the attention characteristically given to prevention. In this light, it should not be surprising that the development of more holistic forms of alternative medicine has placed the medical profession on the defensive.

In Britain the scale of the challenge is underscored by the fact that, while there is legislation variously limiting the therapeutic claims that can be made by alternative practitioners, therapists like herbalists and naturopaths are free to practise under the common law, even though they cannot yet operate independently in their own right within the National Health Service. In the United States too, the challenge is not insubstantial, despite the existence of more formally restrictive methods of regulation. Chiropractors have now generally gained state licensure and reimbursement rights within the Medicare and Medicaid schemes, as well as being the beneficiaries of the late 1980s court ruling that the American Medical

Association must end its boycott of their services — which has helped to provide them with open access to diagnostic facilities in hospitals and consultation rights with physicians. When such moves are placed in the context of the tens of thousands of practitioners of an ever widening range of alternative therapies, it is not difficult to appreciate the significance of this element of the medical counter culture.

The challenge that such practitioners present is sharpened by the association of alternative medicine with the wider holistic health movement which has mushroomed since the 1960s in Britain as well as the United States. This has involved not only the therapeutic belief that the whole is more than the sum of the parts, but also an emphasis on other aspects of holistic health — such as the need to consider clients in the context of their wider social and physical environment and to ensure a cooperative approach amongst the range of health personnel involved, based on interprofessional and multidisciplinary working. Such philosophies broaden the challenge to orthodox biomedicine, especially in the acute sector. In general practice and in 'public health,' doctors have themselves pressed for holistic approaches, e.g., for personal preventive measures and environmental changes, and for social interventions across a wider span of public-policy areas.

The challenge that this poses to reductive biomedicine may also help to explain why the medical establishment in both the countries under consideration here has engaged in such vociferous campaigns against alternative practitioners, particularly when their philosophy is explicitly holistic. This is illustrated by the 1986 report of the British Medical Association on alternative therapies, which was scathing about their safety, research base and lack of scientific credentials compared to the tangible benefits of progressive and rational orthodox medicine. The threat to the medical elite — as current guardians of the legacy of biomedicine — has also increased as primary-care doctors have proved increasingly ready to employ certain kinds of unorthodox therapy, either directly or through sub-contracting arrangements with other practitioners. Ironically, this latest development may call in question the extent to which consumer interest in alternative therapies is indeed 'countercultural.'

COUNTER CULTURE: FROM CHALLENGE TO MEDICAL INCORPORATION?

In this regard, there is evidence to suggest that many consumers who use alternative therapies do not turn their backs on orthodox health care; rather, alternative remedies are most frequently sought for a restricted range of conditions and used in a complementary manner to biomedicine. Within medicine itself, alternative therapies have also been employed primarily on a restricted basis by doctors, who have tended to incorporate them into their own biomedical repertoires. This is well exemplified by the case of acupuncture, which has usually been adopted on the basis of a neurophysiological rather than classical Oriental explanation of its *modus operandi*, and employed mainly as an analgesic as opposed to a general panacea. Such moves lessen the challenge to the medical profession and may help to explain the growing willingness of doctors, especially those in general practice, to utilize such techniques in limited fashion, particularly for chronic illness where orthodox medicine is arguably less effective.

Such trends have been mirrored at a macro-level in Britain where the 1993 report of the British Medical Association on alternative medicine does not castigate such therapies, but rather acknowledges their popularity — arguing for the need for improved knowledge of them and for collaborative links with non-conventional practitioners within a framework of enhanced professional regulation. This can be viewed as an attempt to extend the terrain of medical dominance in the increasing market-based conditions within the National Health Service. The report goes on to call for orthodox doctors to maintain responsibility for the patient, for the medicalization of the curriculum of courses for alternative practitioners, and for the primacy of the randomized controlled trial, even in the evaluation of alternative therapies. Similar processes of incorporation by the medical profession are in evidence in the United States, where the trend began sooner. In the case of osteopathy, the osteopathic curriculum first started to mirror that of medical schools over sixty years ago.

As mentioned earlier, some orthodox practitioners have also tried to develop models that incorporate other disciplinary perspectives into a biomedical approach. The psychosocial model of Engel is based on an holistic frame of reference encompassing the family, community and national contexts, amongst others, along with the more scientific aspects of biomedicine; however, the model clearly remains rooted in a restrictive positivistic medical tradition. Against this, it should be stressed that alternative practitioners themselves are not always very faithful to the ideology of holistic health care they so characteristically espouse. Collaboration with other health professionals and sensitivity to the broader socio-political environment are not always in evidence and the demands of private practice can lead — just as in conventional medicine — to an excessively individualistic approach to health care. Caution is therefore needed in assessing not only how far the contemporary counter culture has become absorbed into orthodoxy, but how far there is real evidence of a counter culture in the first place.

This is also true of the critique of the high technology pharmaceutical-based medicine that is often taken to underpin the development of an oppositional subculture. The critics typically view such preparations as unnatural in contrast to alternative therapies — even though it is difficult to see why, say, inserting needles into the skin with acupuncture is any more 'natural' than taking antibiotics. It should be noted too that a sceptical view of drugs may be perfectly compatible with drawing on and using other forms of biomedical advice. Self-prescription may also be complementary to more conventional forms of health care, particularly when employed as a precursor to such treatment or as a back up if it does not work. Similarly, the growth of self-help groups cannot necessarily be taken as a sign of consumer resistance to domination by medical experts. Some have been set up at the instigation of health professionals to fill gaps in official provision, as illustrated by the Ileostomy Association and the Society for Skin Camouflage in Britain which provide services that resonate with orthodox medicine. Indeed, even those self-help groups which are formed to meet needs that are not currently being institutionally met can be hijacked by professionals for their own ends.

The notion of a sweeping backlash against orthodox medicine based on a 'new age' consciousness therefore requires considerable qualification: both 'camps' are heterogeneous, in principles and practices, and there is increasing overlap between them. As consumer choice and private markets expand, so alternative practitioners and the use of alternative approaches multiply; many patients, and some doctors, however, are coming to see them as part of a spectrum of health care, which is complementary rather than oppositional. In this light, they may be viewed as being less of a challenge to orthodox medicine and more as aspects of health care that have been subject to medical incorporation in the contemporary context.

CONCLUSION

There has nonetheless been a substantial shift over the twentieth century in the degree to which there can be said to be a medical counter culture in Western countries like Britain and the United States. Opposition to medicine did exist in the first half of the century, but was easily portrayed as continuing devotion to medical sects formed in the nineteenth century when orthodox medicine was relatively powerless. It was believed that the growth of scientific medicine, from germ theory to antibiotics, would outshine the alternatives, and that the power of orthodoxy would continue to marginalize them. However, that was not the outcome: rather the 1960s acted as a critical watershed, serving as a platform for the development of the modern concept of counter culture in health care, paralleling other sectors of everyday life. This counter culture has attained higher public visibility — not least through reporting in the mass media which has helped to shape consumer perceptions. Journalists, who previously deferred to the achievements of scientific medicine, have become more willing to challenge orthodoxy by contesting medical decisions and adopting lay perspectives.

While the current establishment of a medical counter culture on both sides of the Atlantic is a significant phenomenon in its own right, the response of the medical profession is no less important. As has been seen, there has been a limited incorporation of oppositional subcultures into orthodox medicine, which retains a good deal of its dominance in this field — despite claims by some social scientists about the increasing proletarianization or deprofessionalization of medicine in capitalist societies. This highlights that the medical profession is proving more adaptable than is often supposed and that today's counter culture may ultimately become part of tomorrow's mainstream medicine, albeit through a process of incrementalism rather than revolution.

## FURTHER READING

Alster, Kristine, *The Holistic Health Movement.* (Tuscaloosa: University of Alabama Press, 1989).

Bruce, Debra Fulgham and McIlwain, Harris, *The Unofficial Guide to Alternative Medicine.* (New York: Macmillan, 1998).

Coward, Rosalind, *The Whole Truth: The Myth of Alternative Health.* (London: Faber and Faber, 1989).

Fulder, Stephen, *The Handbook of Alternative and Complementary Medicine,* 3rd edition. (Oxford: Oxford University Press, 1996).

Gabe, John, Kelleher, David and Williams, Gareth (eds), *Challenging Medicine.* (London: Routledge, 1994).

Gevitz, Norman (ed.), *Other Healers: Unorthodox Medicine in America.* (Baltimore: Johns Hopkins University Press, 1988).

Gordon, James, *Holistic Medicine.* (New York: Chelsea House Publishers, 1988).

Illich, Ivan, *Limits to Medicine.* (Harmondsworth: Penguin, 1976).

Jones, Helen, *Health and Society in Twentieth-century Britain.* (Harlow: Longman, 1994).

Lyng, Stephen, *Holistic Health and Biomedical Medicine: A Countersystem Analysis.* (New York: SUNY Press, 1990).

Phillips, Angela and Rakusen, Jill (eds), *Our Bodies Ourselves: A Health Book by and for Women,* 3rd edition. (Harmondsworth: Penguin, 1996).

Porter, Roy (ed.), *Medicine: A History of Healing.* (London: Ivy Press, 1997).

Roszak, Theodore, *The Making of a Counter Culture.* (London: Faber & Faber, 1970).

Saks, Mike (ed.), *Alternative Medicine in Britain.* (Oxford: Clarendon Press, 1992).

Saks, Mike, *Professions and the Public Interest: Medical Power, Altruism and Alternative Medicine.* (London: Routledge, 1995).

Sharma, Ursula, *Complementary Medicine Today: Practitioners and Patients,* revised edition. (London: Routledge, 1995).

Starr, Paul, *The Social Transformation of American Medicine.* (New York: Basic Books, 1982).

CHAPTER 9

# Medicine and the Welfare State 1930–1970

CHARLES WEBSTER

The emergence, consolidation and growth of the Welfare State has had profound implications for the practice of medicine and the structure of health care. Indeed, from the outset, health was one of the main preoccupations of welfare state policies and most of the measures undertaken impacted on health. The famous *Kaiserliche Botschaft* of Bismarck in 1881 announced his intention to embark on a program of insurance covering sickness, industrial accidents, old age and invalidity. The German sickness insurance legislation dated from 1883, after which fresh welfare legislation proceeded at regular intervals. By a process of diffusion or autonomous response to economic and political circumstances, the German example was replicated throughout Europe, with sickness insurance always high on the social welfare agenda.

In Germany social expenditures reached 3 per cent of GDP in 1900, and 5 per cent in 1915. The UK and Sweden were just five years behind Germany in this social welfare procession, and similarly France, but this was just a little slower to reach 5 per cent. This marked the beginning of an inexorable process, which took social expenditures in the major OECD countries to an average of 12 per cent of GDP in 1960, and 22 per cent in 1970.

By this date health expenditures commonly accounted for about one-quarter of this amount. Taking the twentieth century as a whole, health expenditures started at levels below 1 per cent of GDP, but then steadily increased their share of the social welfare budget to reach between 6 and 10 per cent of GDP in the major European economies by 1970.[1]

This short essay is concerned with health services during the phase of optimum growth of the welfare state, which is conventionally taken as the period from 1930 to 1970. As already noted, this is not to deny the existence of a lengthy period of gestation, extending back into the previous century. However, the term 'welfare state' seems not to have been used until the 1930s, and it was only then that major political groups in western economies embraced the full concept of state welfare in a relatively non-restrictive sense as a tenet of policy. From this point onwards all the advanced economies were challenged to realize the entire welfare program in a coordinated manner through the agency of the state. This inevitably raised the profile of the state in the protection of health of its citizens. The state had of course long been concerned with questions of public health and poor law; the former involved measures to protect health of the entire community; the latter was restricted to health maintenance among paupers. By the 1930s, in advanced economies, the state moved towards recognizing a wider obligation, either on the basis of compulsory insurance or direct taxation, taking wider responsibilities for preventive, promotive and curative health services for the entire population.

## Appearance of Convergence

At a superficial level, the history of state intervention in health care seems remarkably similar throughout the advanced capitalist economies. With minor differences of chronology and emphasis, a similar evolutionary path seems to be followed everywhere. States built on their historical, sometimes ancient, public health and poor law foundations. In the later nineteenth century they regulated the professions involved in medicine and also laid down legislation to control the mutual aid societies, friendly societies or sickness funds. As a next stage in this apparently logical progression, the Bismarckian pattern of sickness insurance was applied on a compulsory basis for selected groups of employees. From relatively small beginnings, compulsory sickness insurance was extended to wider groups of workers, and also to their dependents; in addition the scope of services covered by insurance was increased. In a handful of cases, epitomized by the United Kingdom, the state assumed a more direct role, by establishing a 'national health service', using resources from taxation for comprehensive health care provided in public hospitals and predominantly by publicly employed personnel. The superior resources provided by payroll deductions and other forms of taxation provided one of the most ready means by which the benefits of high technology medicine and modern hospital facilities could be made available to the entire population. However, these developments produced an escalation of costs way beyond the expectations of the original architects of the welfare state. Indeed, health care was the part of the welfare system most prone to escalating costs and most resistant to cost containment.

By the above sequential process the state came to supervise a large scale and complex industrial organization employing a vast workforce. This 'health industry' resembled other parts of the corporate empire, for instance high technology industries, retail stores, or hotel chains: an industrial style of management and organization was imposed to benefit from economies of scale, maximize the use of scarce skills, or meet the growing demand for expensive services. The health services seemed therefore to replicate the evolutionary stages of large corporations; better than other sectors of the welfare state, the health services seem to be controlled by the same unseen hand guiding the progression of the entire economic system. This phenomenon of convergence has rendered the health services attractive to theorists subscribing to the logic of industrialism or moderni-

TABLE 1: MEDICAL EXPENDITURES PER CAPITA (1938 CONSTANT US DOLLARS), AND PERCENTAGE OF PUBLIC FUNDING, 1890–1970

| Year | United States | Great Britain | France | Sweden |
|------|---------------|---------------|--------|--------|
| 1890 | 8.41 (0.9)    | 8.35 (3.0)    | 5.61 (7.1)   | 1.51 (21.0)  |
| 1900 | 10.76 (8.5)   | 8.37 (6.0)    | 4.99 (10.8)  | 2.71 (23.0)  |
| 1910 | 14.31 (6.4)   | 8.39 (11.2)   | 4.43 (16.9)  | 3.93 (25.0)  |
| 1920 | 15.55 (10.4)  | 6.71 (16.9)   | 3.08 (33.5)  | 5.59 (27.7)  |
| 1930 | 25.21 (9.1)   | 9.63 (16.3)   | 3.63 (33.5)  | 7.58 (29.1)  |
| 1940 | 29.55 (12.8)  | 20.37 (20.0)  | 6.63 (44.7)  | 14.94 (35.8) |
| 1950 | 43.37 (18.5)  | 28.24 (81.8)  | 14.14 (54.1) | 17.44 (51.9) |
| 1960 | 61.21 (17.6)  | 36.23 (78.2)  | 28.85 (52.8) | 31.31 (57.9) |
| 1970 | 119.45 (31.4) | 56.87 (85.7)  | 51.92 (63.6) | 69.72.(57.1) |

Percentage public funding in brackets.[2]

zation perspective. Hence there is a widespread tendency to explain change within health care systems with reference to technical considerations and in consensual terms, thereby greatly reducing the importance of shifts in political influence, class confrontations, or modifications in state or institutional structures.

### EVIDENCE OF DIVERGENCE

But, as the divergence between states opting for national health insurance and those choosing a national health service indicates, it is in practice difficult to reduce developments in health services to a common pattern required by the logic of industrialism or modernization hypotheses. Any move beyond superficial inspection reveals substantial and by no means inessential differences between the courses of policy followed in the advanced economies. Even if it is granted that there has occurred a substantial degree of convergence in the field of biomedical science, medical technology, or in the education of health professions, it is by no means axiomatic that a similar degree of parallelism will be detected in the development of the health care systems of the advanced western economies.

Examination of the total physical resources allocated to health care suggests that there are substantial underlying differences between the developed economies. As indicated by Table 1, summarizing the health spending record for the United States, Great Britain, France and Sweden, there was in each case a substantial rise in spending on health during the development of the welfare state. However, the extent of the expansion, the role of public funding, and the pattern of change were very different. In each state the pattern reflected the impact of political initiatives. For instance, in the US, the most dramatic increase in spending occurred during the 1960s, and can be attributed to the introduction of federal government Medicaid and Medicare systems. In the UK the increase can be attributed to the growth of the state sector taking place in stages from 1930 onwards, but with acceleration in the 1960s owing to relaxation of restraints in public spending. In France the relative stagnancy until after the Second World War is attributable to economic depression and political instability; the slow and uneven rise in health spending is attributable to the additive effect of a series of modest changes thereafter. In Sweden, after a gradual increase in spending owing to political initiatives of the 1930s, a major increase in spending took place in the 1950s, attributable to the greater reliance on taxation for funding health services. Examination of other indicators reflecting the character of the health care system also suggests little uniformity between the western states. Throughout the first seventy years of the century, the four above economies therefore showed striking differences in their percentages of qualified medical practitioners to population, percentages of specialists among qualified medical practitioners, and in total or general hospital beds per 100,000 population.

Even the standard indices are sufficient to suggest that substantial differences exist between the health care arrangements adopted in the western economies. Further attention to detail, with particular reference to the US, the UK, France and Sweden will throw light on the sources of these differences.

This exercise will confirm that the pattern of development in each case was often related to shifts in the balance of political power and nature of constitutional arrangements.

DOCTORS VERSUS THE STATE

Extending the health rights of the population was never straightforward. While there was always agreement in principle to the desirability of providing health care to all sections of the community, every step towards realization of this objective was plagued by disagreement and was bitterly contested. The stages by which health care arrangements were extended through such avenues as compulsory insurance and state provision tended therefore to be subjected to long drawn out delays not ascribable to economic barriers.

The main difficulty was in reaching a formula for collectivization and modernization of services that would satisfy the medical profession. From the outset bodies representing the profession were suspicious that changes would operate against their interests. The medical profession, as an entrenched and articulate vested interest, was often able to exercise a veto over new arrangements. When unable to achieve this objective single-handed, the profession could team-up with powerful corporate allies, for instance from the drug industry or the insurance world. Governments have rarely been willing to impose medical arrangements unacceptable to the profession. In return for some concessions on the part of doctors, governments have modified their schemes to guarantee professional compliance, or indeed remitted matters of contention to adjudication by bodies responsive to professional opinion. Therefore, although the medical avant-garde was often at the forefront of planning, the profession as a whole inclined to obstruct change, an important qualification of any idea that the professional elite was necessarily in the vanguard of modernization.

Since their basic interests were sharply at variance, it was inevitable that government and the medical profession would collide. Steeped in their experience of providing medical assistance through the agency of poor law, it was inevitable that governments should be anxious about the cost of expanded services. They were particularly afraid that doctors would employ resources extravagantly, especially when this was in their own economic interests. Governments were therefore inclined to impose controls on doctors, sometimes favoring their direct employment as civil servants.

On their side, doctors were vigilant to protect their traditional freedoms, financial independence, and especially the right for patients to select their own medical advice, and doctors to charge patients directly. Such principles were not only adopted as preferences by the medical profession, they were granted the status of a code of ethics, the protection of which was elevated into a fundamental professional duty. Examples of the use of such codes to protect their traditional rights are the Medical Charter, embodying the idea of 'médecine libérale' adopted by the Confédération des Syndicats Médicaux in 1928, the 'Ten Principles' of the American Medical Association (AMA) dating from 1934, or the Seven Principles and Family Doctor's Charter introduced by the British Medical Association (BMA) in 1945 and 1965 respectively. Although financial interest was central to such initiatives, the employment of ethical codes was politically invaluable in the efforts of doctors to claim the moral high ground.

## CONSOLIDATION OF WELFARE

The first stage of the contest between governments and the medical profession related to the effort to implement the Bismarckian program. By 1930, most European states had set in place most elements of the German welfare program. In the field of health care this involved a shift from the regulation of mutual sickness funds to the introduction of compulsory health insurance. Also by this date, some of these insurance schemes had been extended in scope to cover dependents and some forms of hospital treatment. However, as indicated by the low levels of expenditure involved, the state sickness insurance schemes tended to be limited in scale. As state interventions in health care they were commonly less important than public health and poor law medical services, or aid to particular groups such as mothers, infants, or schoolchildren. As illustrated by Table 1, the period between 1930 and 1945 was characterized by greater expansion in health expenditure than might have been anticipated given the troubled circumstances of the Depression and Second World War. Only in France was there little forward movement.

Obstacles to the drift towards national health insurance should not be overlooked. Sometimes the opponents exercised definitive influence, as in the case of Switzerland, which had led the way in advocacy of national health insurance. An ambitious scheme was adopted by the governing Radical-Democratic Party and this passed into law in 1899, but the coalition of diverse interests, including a sizable element of the medical profession, existing sickness funds, employers, and even trade unionists wanting a more radical scheme, were sufficient to defeat the 1899 law in a referendum. Similar moves towards national health insurance were again blocked by referendum after the Second World War, again in 1974, and the issue continues unresolved to the present day. Switzerland preserves its antediluvian system of state regulated mutual aid societies, albeit by 1974 involving a high degree of state subsidy, amounting to about one-third the cost of health care.

The power of the medical profession to veto moves towards national health insurance is demonstrated in its classic form in France, where the profession was united in its opposition, and increasingly well organized. More than in most European countries, doctors were active in parliamentary politics and commonly occupied ministerial office during the Third Republic. Little progress was made with national health insurance until after the First World War, when the reintegration of Alsace-Lorraine raised the question of depriving this region of its national health insurance rights established during the period of German administration. The government opted to apply national health insurance to the whole of France, but this objective was thwarted. The Social Insurance Law of 1928 contained this provision, but it was diluted by the more conservative Social Insurance Law of 1930, which represented an important victory for employers and the medical profession, led by the recently reorganized Confédération des Syndicats Médicaux. The 1930 law was an important victory because it secured the independence of the medical profession from the sickness fund administration and enabled the doctors to exercise greater control in establishing their fees. In general the 1930 Social Insurance Law is seen as excessively provider-orientated and weak in its redistributional benefits.

In the UK, the contest over national health insurance went against the doctors. The national health insurance legislation of 1911 appeared to humiliate the BMA, but the scheme was relatively generous in protecting the autonomy of doctors; also the capitation fees, as implemented, were higher than originally proposed. Above all, National Health Insurance constituted an obstacle against extension of local government health services, the alternative favored by the Labour Party. During the Depression National Health Insurance proved its economic value to general practitioners and the profession tempered its original hostility. Indeed, in 1930 and 1938 the BMA proposed further extension of this scheme as the basis for a future national health service. The government was wary of change in this direction; a wide range of inter-war legislation for publicly funded health services favored local government rather than health insurance.

That British public health expenditure doubled in the course of the 1930s (in Table 1) is the product of two distinct trends: firstly, the ossified system of national health insurance, and secondly a shift of balance in favor of local government health services and expansion of public spending on these services. This gave local government its first opportunity for major investment in acute hospital services. By 1939 some of the leading local authorities, such as the London County Council, were embryonic regional health authorities, supplying a virtually comprehensive health service for their areas.

But these incremental changes lacked an overall sense of direction. An ambitious and complete development plan, embodied in the Dawson Report of 1920, advocated an elaborate primary care system, based on groups of general medical practitioners working from publicly provided health centers, but Dawson's scheme raised suspicions on the part of all the major vested interests. It was unceremoniously buried and planning activity in this controversial sphere was suspended.

As indicated by Table 1, despite its advantages of centralized administration and a long tradition of public welfare, Sweden was behind the UK in the extension of its public provision for health care. Until 1932, developments largely followed the Swiss pattern of public regulation of mutual sickness funds. Although national health insurance had been a live issue since before the turn of the century, in the context of a series of weak governments of the right, a coalition of doctors, sickness funds and business interests was sufficient to protect the status quo. The doctors gained strength through the reorganization of their professional bodies in 1919 to form the Swedish Medical Association. High unemployment and industrial unrest, unalleviated by welfare provision, contributed to a more conciliatory social policy and then ultimately in 1932 resulted in a Social Democratic government reliant on coalition with the Agrarian Party. This administration negotiated a compromise in which the economy remained on a capitalist basis, but full employment, progressive taxation and active welfare policies were adopted. Changes in health care were the mirror image of developments in the UK, and in both cases there was a doubling of health expenditures in the course of the 1930s.

The Sickness Fund Law of 1931 was a product of the transition period during which the main political parties were attempting to secure their position in conditions of economic crisis. In these circumstances political prudence caused the melting away of opposition to the long-gestated Sickness Fund Law; and even the Swedish Medical Association was ineffective in its opposition owing to internal divisions between a leadership that advocated cooperation and a rank and file that pushed for outright opposition. As a consequence of the Sickness Fund Law the administrative system of sickness funds was unified and regulated on a scale much greater than had proved possible in France. Medical benefits were extended in stages until they reached approximately 50 per cent of the population by 1945, which was slightly above the level of coverage of the UK NHI system. The level of state subsidy of health insurance was much higher than in the case of the UK.

In comparative studies, the USA is usually contrasted with Europe for its consistent resistance to national health insurance, and the continuing dominance of occupational or corporate welfare provisions. However, developments during the

New Deal period demonstrated certain parallels with Europe, and especially with social democratic Sweden. The Social Security Act of 1935 was the analogue of social democratic aspirations in Europe, and provided a platform for later attempts to extend Federal involvement in welfare.

Though its practical effects were limited with respect to health, the federal schemes for unemployment and old age insurance helped services to specified groups such as the elderly, disabled, and mothers and infants. (As a measure of redistribution the effects of these subsidies were limited by the wide element of discretion allowed to the states over implementation). The 1935 Act was planned as a first step towards more ambitious health and welfare measures, although a national scheme of health insurance was not envisaged at this stage, partly because it was thought to be unconstitutional. Further plans were included in the National Health Program of July 1938, but by that stage the momentum of New Deal had been lost and foreign affairs were assuming center stage.

## PLANNING FOR THE GOLDEN AGE OF WELFARE

The period between 1945 and 1975, customarily regarded as the golden age of the welfare state, was rudely ended by the economic downturn following the oil crisis of 1973. In this phase of rapid economic growth, as already noted, the share of GDP absorbed by social expenditures rapidly increased. In West Germany this reached almost 30 per cent of GDP by 1975. On average in the leading OECD economies public spending on health increased from about 3 per cent to 6 per cent of GDP over the period 1950 to 1975. As indicated by Table 1, both health expenditure and the public share of health spending increased at an accelerating rate during this period. However the pattern was not uniform. Both with respect to the welfare state in general, and health services in particular, it is possible to isolate three distinct phases: first a stage of legislative activity and reconstruction after the Second World War, secondly a phase of modest expansion lasting until about 1960, and thirdly, a stage of rapid increase in expenditure combined with further substantial legislative activity.

The Second World War shaped post-war changes for a number of reasons. First, German welfare arrangements were introduced into occupied countries such as Belgium and the Netherlands; Spain and Italy also extended their systems of national health insurance during the war. (These changes are reminiscent of the rationalization of institutions that took place over exactly the same territory during the ascendancy of Napoleon.) Secondly, at least in the UK, the increased state intervention in health care necessitated by the war introduced changes that were impossible to reverse in conditions of peace. Among other things, the war exposed the weaknesses of the acute hospital services, and suggested that the voluntary sector was no longer capable of shouldering responsibility for this key health function. Finally, for the purpose of maintaining the morale of both civilian and fighting forces in the hugely stressful conditions of total war, governments throughout the western world were forced to commit themselves to ambitious schemes of peacetime reconstruction; indeed their legitimacy depended on these schemes carrying a high degree of veracity.

In these circumstances, governments became more receptive than ever before to idealistic planning initiatives, and were prepared to abandon the painfully slow and ineffective piecemeal approach to social reform that had characterized the earlier part of the century. These circumstances account for the first free-flowering of the idea of a welfare state. In retrospect, friends and enemies alike have commented on the 'messianic', 'utopian', or 'new Jerusalem' flavor of the schemes that emanated from the planning documents of this period. Under the banner of peacetime reconstruction, these planning efforts related to every aspect of economic, social and cultural affairs.

The best known of the planning documents was the Beveridge Report of 1942, written by William Beveridge, who was an independent expert on social security, and also had long-standing experience of practical affairs. Although the Beveridge Report was not directly concerned with health, one of the two main assumptions in his report was that a future comprehensive social security scheme would be supported by a "national health service for prevention and comprehensive treatment available to all members of the community."[3] Beveridge also assumed that this national health service would be financed mainly by central taxation and, like education or the police, be provided free at point of delivery. By the political standards of the time in the UK, the Beveridge approach was indeed bold, but in practice he was voicing an approach to social policy consistent with Keynesian economics, and reflecting policy in Sweden and the US during the New Deal.

Indeed, though Beveridge was far ahead of much political thinking in the UK, he was more conventional in his outlook than the standing Socialvårdskommitté that deliberated on social policy in Sweden, or indeed the Fabian Society in the UK, which devised a scheme for the reform of social security and health care that had much in common with the approach of Beveridge. Nevertheless, his report captured the limelight and has stayed there ever since. Perhaps because it echoed the spirit of the growing Keynesian ascendancy, the Beveridge Report exerted a global impact, endowing Beveridge with some of the same significance as Bismarck some fifty years previously. The report was particularly influential in the British Dominions, where similar documents, such as the Gluckman Report on the health services of South Africa, advocated health centers, and were in advance of any health-planning document produced for the UK.

In the UK, there was no medical equivalent to the Beveridge Report. The planning documents emanating from government sources showed all the defects of political horsetrading, and comprised schemes of such massive complexity that they were regarded as unworkable, even by their bureaucrat authors. The only major planning document to reflect the earnest idealism of Beveridge was the Interim Report of the Medical Planning Commission of 1942, which was produced by a large group of medical experts, but was disowned by the bodies representing the medical profession. Its emphasis on a primary care led health service, conducted by groups of general medical practitioners and other professionals working in large publicly-provided health centers derived from the Dawson Report; it was also influenced by the famous medical experiment at the Peckham Health Centre, and it was also arguably influenced by propaganda about health services in the Soviet Union.

The French analogue of the Medical Planning Commission was the report produced by Robert Debré for the Medical Committee of the Resistance in 1944, which also proposed a national health service based on a system of health centers. In Sweden, the first obvious analogue to the Beveridge Report was the twenty seven point Labour Movement Postwar Programme issued by the Trade Union confederation and Social Democratic Party in 1944. Also relevant, although not published until 1948, was the Report of the Höjer Commission, established in 1943 to resolve long-standing disagreements between county councils and general medical practitioners over the role of hospital outpatient clinics. The Commission in practice adopted a wider remit, and its recommendations closely echoed the policies advocated during the Second World War by the Labour Party in the UK. It proposed extending direct public provision of health services: the already established municipal hospital sector would be complemented by a new system of primary care, also administered by county councils, and conducted by full-time salaried personnel, including doctors, working from publicly-provided health centers. In the US an echo of Beveridge was provided by the Wagner-Murray-Dingell Bill of 1943 and its related planning documents, which reviewed the National Health Program, but also reflected the expansionism of the time by including a conclusive commitment to national health insurance.

In effect, the Second World War reconstruction planners returned to the ideas of Dawson in advocating a primary-care led health service operated from health centers by full-time salaried personnel. Besides its intrinsic rationality, a strong primary care system of this type seemed essential for preventing escalation of costs in the uncertain economy of the post-war period.

## CONTINUING DIVERSITY

Of all the advanced economies, the UK was particularly well placed to undertake rationalization and extension of its health services. On the basis of bipartisan political support for the Beveridge Report, in 1944 the Coalition government developed an enormously detailed plan for establishing a national health service. The appearance of consensus was deceptive. Within the Coalition, the Conservatives favored a modest extension of the existing system, whereas the Labour Party wanted a complete local government health service, involving public ownership of all hospitals, and general practitioners employed on a full-time salaried basis, working from publicly-provided health centers. The medical profession, led by the

BMA, attacked the government's schemes from the outset. In the effort to gain accord, the 1944 White Paper embodied major concessions, and afterwards the Conservatives within the Coalition agreed to further retreats.

Taking advantage of the large Labour majority in the 1945 general election, Aneurin Bevan, the new Minister of Health, took a political gamble by selecting a hitherto little considered and radical option: nationalization and regional administration of the entire municipal and voluntary hospital system. In order to avoid fighting on too many fronts, general practitioners were allowed to continue with terms of employment only slightly modified from the previous national health insurance regime, but this retreat from Labour's long-standing policy for full-time salaried service in health centers did not pacify the BMA, which exploited minor grievances to attack Bevan personally and spread alarm about Labour's totalitarian intentions.

Compromise with the medical profession was reached only shortly before the National Health Service was launched in July 1948. The government did however succeed in some of its policy objectives: the service was universal in its coverage, comprehensive in its range, and funded largely from central taxation. On the other hand, the suppliers, especially hospital doctors and general practitioners, gained substantial concessions protecting their independence and economic interest. In many ways these were prejudicial to the efficient use of scarce resources, and also to the effective planning and modernization of the service, as well as obstructing egalitarian objectives.

In practice, the NHS worked remarkably well in the short term and political opposition to the service melted away. The medical profession appreciated that the new service endowed them with many benefits and few losses; success in battles with the government over remuneration demonstrated that the NHS could be made to work in their favor. Although there were serious shortcomings in the service from the point of view of the consumer, especially vulnerable groups and the poor, these defects were stoically tolerated, partly on account of expectations of future improvement, but by the 1960s there was general agreement that greater rationalization and administrative unification was needed. However, the profession vetoed the most obvious route to this objective, which was return to administration by local government, the alternative favored by the Royal Commission on Local Government in England in 1968. The Labour government abandoned this option, but was unable to locate an alternative arrangement capable of commanding support. Preparations for reorganisation dragged on until 1974. The final reform was a compromise, attempting to reconcile all the vested interests. This resulted in a system conferring few advantages, but importing many fresh administrative anomalies. Consequently the measure designed to definitively strengthen the NHS had precisely the opposite effect.

During the Second World War France looked likely to undertake a reform in its health care arrangements quite as radical as those planned for the UK; this link was not surprising in view of the UK associations of the National Council for the Resistance. Immediately after the liberation, the Provisional Government featured health among its pledges to establish a new social order. Free from the constraints affecting the weak governments of the Third Republic, it instituted fresh Social Security Ordinances in October 1945, precisely the date that Bevan was presenting his ideas to the Cabinet in London. But the new ordinances were largely a consolidation of previous legislation; they were especially cautious with respect to health care, rationalizing and extending the coverage of the existing system and improving central control of the local arrangements for determining doctors' fees. Notwithstanding the limited nature of the intended reform, it provoked hostility from the Confédération des Syndicats Médicaux, which effectively vetoed the scheme during the entire life of the Fourth Republic. Although the post-war changes increased coverage of the compulsory insurance scheme to 65 per cent of the population, the health service as a whole remained in its pre-war state.[4]

The opportunity for substantial reform was deferred until the collapse of the Fourth Republic. By this stage, the adverse position of the French health care system was a matter of acute concern, and its reform was granted high priority under General de Gaulle, creating opportunities for intervention by Robert Debré. The resulting decrees and ordinances of December 1958 and May 1960 were reinforced by a further consolidation of legislation in 1967. These measures allowed a renewed attempt to impose greater central control and rationalization on the fee system for non-hospital doctors. The scheme was more radical than that attempted in 1945, and it was therefore the subject of a vigorous campaign by the Confédération des Syndicats Médicaux, further demonizing Robert Debré.

However, on this occasion, splits within the profession between rural and urban practitioners, younger and older doctors, hospital and non-hospital personnel, weakened the force of opposition. The introduction of these changes and incremental extension of the insurance system resulted in almost complete coverage of the insurance arrangements by 1967. The new ordinances also laid the foundations for substantial reform in the hospital sector, based on a structure of regional teaching and research centers, and a move towards full-time service of hospital medical personnel. These changes were only slowly implemented, but they were broadly supported within the hospital service. By 1970 the health service in France had achieved the basic objectives of the Second World War planning exercise.

Sweden provided a rare instance of settled Social Democratic government and the privilege of non-combatant status during the Second World War. As already noted, the war was taken as an opportunity to plan a comprehensive overhaul of the welfare system. In the field of health, as in France, the government adopted a cautious approach. The National Health Insurance law of 1947 allowed for the consolidation of voluntary sickness funds into public sickness funds, a modest change that was implemented after some delay. This proposal evoked opposition from the usual quarters, including the Swedish Medical Association, but the grounds for complaint were too weak to justify more than token resistance. A more serious cause for confrontation occurred in 1948 when the Höjer Commission's Report proposed a total overhaul of the health service, based on local government. The Höjer Commission was unfortunate to report at a moment of temporary weakness of the Social Democratic government, and even on the Social Democratic side, especially among the county councils, there was fear that the medical profession would be able to sabotage the reforms. The Swedish Medical Association and its allies rose to the occasion by vilifying Höjer in a manner evocative of the attacks on Bevan and Debré. The government jettisoned the Höjer Report, which was an unusual indignity for a Swedish Royal Commission Report, providing a parallel with the demise of the Dawson Report in 1920.

However, the Höjer Report provided the intellectual guidelines for future policy, and its aims were pursued incrementally over the next two decades. As a prudent step, the intake into medical schools was increased, in order to reduce the capacity of hospital doctors to sabotage moves towards full-time service. As a result of changes instituted in 1959 and 1969, the key Höjer proposal to eliminate private practice from hospitals was achieved, thereby removing barriers to rationalization of hospital services and hospital planning on a regional basis. Hence by 1969 Sweden had achieved by degrees a national health service not dissimilar to the UK system. In the course of the next two decades, Italy and Spain also opted to move from national health insurance to a national health service.

In the US an important breakthrough occurred in 1943 with the Wagner-Murray-Dingell Bill, which for the first time placed a proposal for national health insurance at the center of its package of reforms. Naturally a radical proposal of this kind required a further period of consultation and political lobbying. The proponents of national health insurance coopted support from President Roosevelt, and then his successor, President Truman. The opponents of enhanced state intervention also gathered their forces. As usual, the seasoned AMA was their coryphaeus, but the insurance and private health care interests, who had by the end of the war become a powerful corporate interest, also contributed some useful muscle. The opponents were also assisted by support from the Republicans, who detected electoral benefit in this issue. Almost regardless of these pressure group factors, national health insurance was killed by an ideological shift, which identified state intervention of this kind as sign of softness towards 'socialized medicine' and thereby evidence of the penetration of international communism.

The humiliating defeat inflicted on national health insurance in 1948 effectively ruled this option out of court permanently. The recent abortive Clinton health reforms provide a reminder of the unacceptability of anything akin to national health insurance to American corporate interests. In general, since 1948, the health field has been dominated by corporate insurance bodies, which evolved a range of alluring mixtures of service and indemnity benefits to suit a wide section of the community. The service providers have remained predominantly private and have benefited from the generous resources available from private and public schemes alike.

Table 1, which also indicates the serious nature of cost inflation within the system, confirms the buoyancy of the American medical market. By 1950, per capita spending was running at twice the average for the other three western economies, and that differential persisted. By 1960, the excessive cost of the American health system was causing concern to economists, employers and the middle classes.

Rediscovery of the problem of poverty also underlined the failure of the system to address the problem of equity. The 1960s were characterized by a revival of many of the New Deal ideas about addressing the problems of access through a variety of public initiatives, under the banners of community care, community medicine, and Medicare. Collectively these contributed to the sharp rise in public spending on health indicated in Table 1. Most of the federal-state schemes were on a relatively small and experimental scale, but Medicare (the federal program providing health benefits for the elderly), and Medicaid (the federal-state revenue-sharing program for providing services to the poor), were larger. These ambitious schemes were products of the Kennedy era, but passed into law under President Johnson in July 1965. Although linked in their origins, the two schemes were very different in character. Medicare was an extension of social security, and embodied national standards of eligibility and benefits. Medicaid carried the stigma of public assistance; the level and character of its implementation was at the discretion of the individual state. Medicare was more attractive to the doctors because, like the pre-1967 French system, it permitted the charging of fees above the level of the public subsidies. Although public funds fueled the system, the services were conducted by private providers in contract with private fiscal intermediaries or insurance carriers. Although nominally a move in the direction of state involvement, in reality Medicare operated as a huge subsidy to the private sector, with regulations even entailing generous subsidies for private hospital redevelopment. Once this lax regime was established, it was extremely difficult to control, with the result that this well-intentioned effort at assisting the needy contributed further to the problem of cost control, without increasing equality. The shortcomings of Medicare and Medicaid contributed to the gathering sense of crisis that overtook the American health care system in the 1970s.

## CONCLUSIONS

The four illustrative examples selected for this essay demonstrate the persisting diversity in the health care arrangements adopted in the advanced western economies. In the period under consideration, there certainly existed pressures towards a convergence of the kind that were prevalent in other sectors of the economy. Indeed, some convergence did take place in the biomedical sciences, in the practice of medicine, and in professional training. But it is striking that these unifying factors failed to carry over into health care structures. This diversity persisted in the face of planning initiatives designed to import greater uniformity into the system. Consequently, although state involvement increased greatly, the policies adopted, the chronology of change, forms of regulation and the intervention adopted, still vary enormously from place to place. The role of the medical profession in this process is striking. On the one hand, in the interests of improving care, the medical profession represented the interests of technological advance and innovation. On the other hand, as a professional lobby, doctors opposed virtually every specific health care reform required to achieve reasonably efficient and egalitarian application of medical advance. Health services were the most contentious province of the welfare state empire, and implementation of the Second World War policies for universal and comprehensive health care was pitifully slow. Even in 1970, the conditions imposed by powerful vested interests had resulted in systems that were seriously dysfunctional and riddled with perverse incentives. None of the formulae adopted in western economies was sufficiently credible to prevent erosion of confidence. As the economic downturn would show, the system of mutual aid, national insurance, or national health service systems, (or their hybrids), carried only poor immunity to the virus of crisis that overtook all the rival systems of health care in the 1970s.

## REFERENCES

1. P. Flora (ed.), *Growth to Limits*, volume 1. (Berlin: De Gruyter, 1986); OECD, *Social Expenditure 1960–90: Problems of Growth and Control*. (Paris: OECD, 1985).
2. J. Rogers Hollingsworth, J. Hage and R.A. Hanneman, *State Intervention in Medical Care*. (Ithaca: Cornell University Press, 1990), Tables 2.1 and 2.4. As the authors concede in their Appendix pp. 211–4, this tabulation was notoriously difficult to compile. Among the notes of reservation, my own collation of sources relating to spending in Great Britain in 1939, indicates that four separate estimates suggest that public spending accounted for about 60 per cent of total health spending.
3. *Social Insurance and Allied Services*, Report by Sir William Beveridge. (HMSO, 1942), para 427.
4. E.M. Immergut, *Health Politics: Interests and Institutions in Western Europe*. (Cambridge: Cambridge University Press, 1992), p. 124.

## FURTHER READING

Anderson, O.W., *Health Services in the United States: A Growth Enterprise since 1875*. (Ann Arbour, MI: Health Administration Press, 1985).

Freddi, G. and Björkman, J.W., *Controlling Medical Professionals. The Comparative Politics of Health Governance*. (London: Sage, 1989).

Glaser, W.A., *Paying the Doctor. Systems of Remuneration and their Effects*. (Baltimore: Johns Hopkins University Press, 1970).

Gilbert, B.B., *The Evolution of National Insurance in Great Britain. The Origins of the Welfare State*. (London: Michael Joseph, 1966).

Hatzfeld, H., *Le Grand Tournant de la Médecine Libérale*. (Paris: Editions Ouvières, 1963).

Heclo, H., *Modern Social Politics in Britain and Sweden*. (New Haven: Yale University Press, 1974).

Heidenheimer, A.J. and Elvander, N. (eds), *The Shaping of the Swedish Health System*. (London: Croom Helm, 1980).

Herzlich, C., 'The evolution of relations between French physicians and the state from 1880 to 1980', *Sociology of Health and Illness* (1982), 4: 241–52.

Hirschfield, D.S., *The Lost Reform. The Campaign for Compulsory Health Insurance in the United States from 1932 to 1943.* (Cambridge, Mass.: Harvard University Press, 1970).

Immergut, E.M., *Health Politics. Interests and Institutions in Western Europe.* (Cambridge: Cambridge University Press, 1992).

Klein, R., *The New Politics of the National Health Service*, 3rd edn. (London: Longman, 1995).

Marmor, T.R., *The Politics of Medicare.* (London: Routledge, 1970).

Hollingsworth, J. Rogers, Hage, J. and Hanneman, R.A., *State Intervention in Medical Care. Consequences for Britain, France, Sweden, and the United States 1890–1970.* (Ithaca: Cornell University Press, 1990).

Starr, P., *The Social Transformation of American Medicine.* (New York: Basic Books, 1982).

Steffen, M., 'The medical profession and the State in France', *Journal of Public Policy* (1987), **7**: 189–208.

Stevens, R. and Stevens, R., *Welfare Medicine in America: A Case Study of Medicaid.* (New York: Free Press, 1974).

Webster, C., *The National Health Service: A Political History.* (Oxford: Oxford University Press, 1998).

## CHAPTER 10

# Pharmaceutical Industry

### JORDAN GOODMAN

During the twentieth century, the pharmaceutical industry has undergone profound change. At the turn of the century, most pharmaceutical companies were very small, did little or no research and development, prepared bulk therapeutics based largely on botanicals and were marginal to society's health concerns. Scarcely half a century later, pharmaceutical companies, whether in Europe or in the United States, were totally different. They were now devoting substantial funds to the discovery of new drugs and employing sophisticated marketing, legal and commercial techniques to get their products to patients. No longer dependent on natural products, pharmaceutical companies concentrated on synthetic approaches through organic chemistry to develop drugs that could be protected by patents. Associations between academic institutions, the state and the pharmaceutical industry became more complex and more controversial. As the thalidomide case revealed, the regulatory system of approving drugs proved not to protect the public. In recent years, the pharmaceutical industry has come under increasingly close public scrutiny. Issues of health, of bioethics, and of the north-south divide have vexed both national governments and international organizations. No longer at the margin of society, the pharmaceutical industry has itself become a site where many public issues surrounding life and death are debated.

Modern pharmaceutical investigation and manufacture began in Paris during the first half of the nineteenth century when pharmacists at the Ecole Superieure de Pharmacie isolated the active ingredients of some of the most significant parts of the materia medica, including quinine, strychnine, emetine and caffeine. German pharmacists were responsible for discovering morphine, veratrine and nicotine. By 1840 practically all the important active plant principles were isolated. Natural product extracts accounted for the bulk of nineteenth-century European and American pharmaceutical output. Pharmacists believed that the natural world contained pharmaceutical principles, which they would uncover, identify, and isolate, and then manufacture into standardized bulk extracts to be made into preparations by other pharmacists. The substances with the greatest commercial potential were codeine, morphine and quinine, within the broad classification of antipyretics and analgesics.

Just as pharmacists were reaping the rewards of their enterprise, their central position in supplying pharmaceuticals came under threat from an unexpected source. During the 1830s and 1840s, chemists managed to fractionate carbolic acid from coal-tar, thereby revealing the possibility that pharmaceutical potential lay hidden in this waste industrial by-product. August Hoffmann's work on the chemistry of coal-tar in the 1840s together with Charles Mansfield's techniques of fractional distillation and freezing clearly indicated that coal-tar was a mother substance, an insight thoroughly underscored by William Perkin's discovery of a seemingly inexhaustible source of synthetic dyestuffs. In 1856 Perkin accidentally found that one of the derivatives of coal-tar, which he hoped would be a synthetic version of quinine, dyed silk the color of mauve. Not surprisingly, given the overwhelming importance of the textile industry to the world's economy, many chemists and chemical companies, especially in Germany, Switzerland and France, became attracted to a potential synthetic dyestuff bonanza. Before too long, the chemical insight and engineering practice of dyestuffs spilled back into pharmaceuticals. In 1883, the board of management of Hoechst, one of Germany's leading synthetic dyestuff makers, decided to establish a separate scientific laboratory to investigate the possible link between synthetic dyes and biologically-active substances. In this they were following Paul Ehrlich's insight that dyes might act as selective histological stains in the same manner as they colored fibers.

Not surprisingly, the first pharmaceuticals to emerge from the dyestuff companies in Germany were antipyretics and analgesics. In 1883, Hoechst placed its first synthetic antipyretic on to the market followed, a few years later, by the more successful Antipyrin and Pyramidon. Aspirin, or acetylsalicylic acid, a derivative of salicylic acid, introduced into clinical medicine in 1899 and produced and marketed by Bayer, became the flagship of the firm's pharmaceutical business and eclipsed the sales of any other drug at the time.

The early antipyretics and analgesics were examples of what is termed 'economies of scope'; synthetic dyestuffs and synthetic pharmaceuticals shared common knowledges and practices. Firms could therefore economize on their inputs in research, development, production, standardization and even testing procedures. This program of integrated and strategic practices was eloquently described in 1913 by Carl Duisberg, the then director of Bayer.

> What an organization, what boundless intelligence is necessary, and what immense energy has to be expended in order to discover a new synthetic remedy and to smooth its path through the obstacles of commerce! First, we need a fully equipped chemical laboratory, then a pharmacological institute with a staff of men trained in medicine and chemistry, an abundance of animals to experiment upon, and finally...a chemotherapeutic and bacteriological department. Whatever has been...selected as useful, finds its way into the manufacturing department (then) the scientific department. Next, a host of clinicians and practitioners...And, finally, it is the calculating salesman's turn. If...a great hit is made...then the envious, the patent-and-trademark violator and even the smuggler cling to our heels.[1]

The German chemical firms were even more innovative than their exploitation of economies of scope might suggest. One of the first new ventures was the production of antitoxins for diphtheria and tetanus. Not only did they pursue new practices — they had to gain expertise in using animals as biological inputs — but they also entered into new networks of relationships including the state and research institutes. With antitoxin manufacture successfully underway, chemical companies, especially Hoechst and Bayer, turned their attention to diseases as targets of industrial innovation. In this they were particularly motivated by Ehrlich's development of the side-chain theory, receptors and the promise of experimental chemotherapy. Salvarsan, an arsenical compound for the treatment of syphilis, was the major preparation to come out of this practice before 1914.

The development of antitoxins had other far-reaching effects on pharmaceutical manufacture and the objectives of pharmaceutical firms. For one, companies established protocols of biological standardization — Ehrlich was instrumental here as well — in much the same way as they had done for synthetic dyestuffs. Antitoxins also forced pharmaceutical companies into the realm of public health and its politics. In the United States in particular, antitoxin research and manufacture was initially undertaken by public health laboratories but a few pharmaceutical companies, realizing the commercial possibilities, became directly involved in this new activity. Because biological formulations and preparations were administered directly into the bloodstream, antitoxin suppliers were the first to be subjected to strict regulatory regimes.

By the 1920s, the appearance of synthetic antipyretics, analgesics and biologicals reflected fundamental changes in the nature of pharmaceutical research, development and manufacture. From the perspective of the consumer, however, little seemed to have changed. The bulk of pharmaceuticals were still derived from natural sources. Ehrlich's great insights into the mechanism of action of pharmaceuticals, the elucidation of the structure and practice of experimental chemotherapy and his discovery of Salvarsan as an antibacterial synthetic did not constitute a practical paradigm. It is well to remember that Salvarsan was also known as '606,' that is the 606th preparation to be tested for specific activity. Given this meager hit rate, it is not surprising that most pharmaceutical manufacturers were not attracted to the experimental chemotherapy of infectious diseases, the great killers of the time, as a commercial proposition. Theirs was a cautious, conservative path, relying on well-established antipyretics and analgesics.

The Bayer firm was different. Belief in the biological potential of synthetic dyestuffs remained central to their strategy in pharmaceutical research and development but it was only a beginning. Heinrich Hörlein, the director of pharmaceutical research at Bayer in the late 1920s and 1930s articulated the key functions and possibilities of pharmaceutical chemistry. According to Hörlein, the pharmaceutical chemist could range over a potentially infinite range of compounds, both final and intermediate, searching for pharmacological activity within a paradigm of synthetic chemistry. This link between industry and science was critical and, in Hörlein's view, placed the industrial firm in a position superior to the university research institute. The research program was based on the practice of experimental chemotherapy; that is a research program where medical researchers and chemists worked as an integral unit, rather than in sequential fashion, to pursue specific goals. All biologically active compounds, not just classes of synthetic dyestuffs, were, in his opinion, the proper research interest of pharmaceutical chemistry and subject to manufacture through chemical engineering.

In the 1920s, Bayer made several breakthroughs in the treatment of parasitic diseases typically found in tropical countries. Then in 1932, just as Hörlein was pronouncing on research organization, and without any breakthrough in the therapy of infectious diseases, researchers in Bayer's medicinal laboratory, particularly Gerhard Domagk and Fritz Mietzsch, discovered that a red azo dye, synthesized at the Bayer works several years earlier and later named Prontosil, had a deadly effect on streptococcal infections, a class of disease previously untreatable. Ehrlich's vision of an experimental chemotherapy, Duisberg's construction of a research organization, and Hörlein's integrative medicinal chemistry had now come together.

Domagk's results were not published until 1935. Just one year later, a group of researchers at the Pasteur Institute in Paris demonstrated that Prontosil was cleaved in the body to form another compound, subsequently called sulfanilamide. The discovery by the Pasteur Institute that it was not the dye itself, but rather a molecular component of it that possessed biological activity, was even more profound than Bayer's achievement. The existence of sulfanilamide undermined the dominance of the dyestuff paradigm. It opened the chemotherapeutic market to other enterprises who were not educated in this paradigm and who did not have the resources of the dyestuff firms.

While Protonsil could not be patented because it was a well-known substance, sulfanilamide and all compounds chemically revealed from the new 'mother substance' could be. Thus May and Baker, an English pharmaceutical company, introduced their sulfa drug, sulfapyridine, more commonly known as M&B 693, in 1938 after two years research and development. It had a wider range of activity than sulfanilamide, extending to staphylococci, streptococci and pneumococci. Burroughs Wellcome in England, Merck, Sharp & Dohme, Squibb and Lederle, in the United States and Ciba in Switzerland turned their attention to this new field and within time developed, patented and manufactured their own sulfa drugs.

The inter-war period re-established the promise of the chemotherapy of infectious disease. The inter-war period was also important in drawing attention to so-called deficiency diseases, where no pathogen vector could be found (though many believed in this etiology). During the first 3 decades of the twentieth century, various laboratories in Europe and the United States demonstrated that several diseases — beri-beri, scurvy, pellagra and rickets — were caused by a deficiency in diet. Successive work revealed that certain trace elements, later called vitamins, constituted the deficiencies. Many of these, Vitamin A, $B_1$ and D in particular, became widely available during the 1930s either on their own or in mixtures. Vitamin sales boomed and became one of the most important sources of finance for many pharmaceutical firms. In the United States, for example, vitamins accounted for as much as 25% of total sales for Abbott Laboratories, one of the country's foremost pharmaceutical companies. Few companies could ignore the trend. In the United States, the wholesale vitamin market grew from less than $.5 million in 1925 to just under $100 million on the eve of the Second World War — by that time, vitamins claimed over 10% of the country's entire wholesale drug market. The situation was not that different in Europe where many pharmaceutical companies entered this lucrative field, prominent among them being Glaxo in Britain, Merck in Germany and Hoffmann-La Roche in Switzerland.

Vitamins were a world apart from the dyestuff paradigm version of pharmaceutical production. Unlike other preparations that were used to alleviate symptoms or to destroy disease vectors, vitamins were used to make up for diet deficiencies. Insights and practices were, therefore, not drawn from organic chemistry and the textile industry. Vitamins forged alliances in fields associated with nutrition and the food industry. The ensuing conflicts over the definition or classification of vitamin — drugs or food? — had profound impacts on the nature of these associations and on the definition of a pharmaceutical company.

Much the same was true of hormones. Scientific investigations in the late nineteenth and early twentieth century had established that glands secreted substances into the bloodstream that had direct and specific effects on physiological functions elsewhere in the body. During this period, hormones such as adrenaline, thyroxin, insulin and the sex hormones, estrogen and testosterone were isolated. Research on hormones was carried on at many sites and a few pharmaceutical companies quickly established a dominance in this field of endocrinology. Organon in Holland, Eli Lilly in the United States and Schering in Germany were the most important. New associations sprung up: with farmers and slaughter-houses for the supply of raw materials; with gynecologists, eugenicists and social engineers in their demands for sex hormones. Research into hormones indirectly influenced the discovery of the cause of diabetes mellitus when researchers in Toronto isolated a substance extracted by the pancreatic duct and named insulin. The pharmaceutical firm of Eli Lilly made an agreement with the University of Toronto trading manufacturing rights for royalties, an association rare at the time but foreshadowing many such relationships in the future.

Vitamins, hormones, insulin and the sulfa drugs were the great therapeutic successes of the inter-war period — and changed the nature of the pharmaceutical industry. The historically short but powerful domination of pharmaceutical research, development and manufacture by the synthetic dyestuff paradigm and the giant German chemical companies was being undermined. There were many niches in the new marketplace. Hörlein's vision of industrializing the therapeutic fields of endocrinology and nutrition was only one among many ways of providing material for the market. Specialist companies such as Organon in Holland, Schering in Germany and Miles Laboratories in the United States had other methods. Not only did the marketplace become more complex but it also became more populous. Pharmaceutical companies began to spring up in many countries previously reliant on others for supplies. Besides Holland one can point particularly to Switzerland where the city of Basle with its highly developed synthetic dyestuff industry came to be a major player in pharmaceutical activity — Ciba, Geigy, Sandoz and Hoffmann-La Roche would soon become internationally powerful companies.

## WORLD WAR II AND AFTER

A watershed in many areas, World War II helped usher in an entirely new era in the history of the pharmaceutical industry. Many associations and relationships previously formed on a piecemeal basis for specific, targeted activities became permanent. Whereas in the past, pharmaceutical companies sought out academic consultants for specific, targeted activities — insulin being a case in point — in the immediate post-war years, such associations became more permanent. Resistance to biomedical collaboration between academe and industry, already weakening during the inter-war period, quickly gave way to long-term research agreements with huge budgets. The same was true of the relationship between the pharmaceutical industry and the state. In the United States especially, the government targeted specific disease entities for national crusades, cancer being the most prominent. Eradication was seen as a federal responsibility and central funds were made available on a enormous scale for research and development, financing both public (government and universities) and private (pharmaceutical companies) sectors. Though such a relationship was signalled by the passage of the National Cancer Institute Act in 1937, it was not until after World War II and the demonstration of the potential of the chemotherapy of cancer that funds began to flow in enormous volume. One of the most important reasons for the acceleration of inter-war developments was the success of government-sponsored research and development programs during the war. The United States led in this area with its most spectacular successes in the medical field being the penicillin and the anti-malaria program.

The war did not change the belief that new pharmaceuticals could be discovered through screening and chemical alteration. Insights from basic science, however elegant, rarely seemed to pay industrial dividends. The discovery of the mechanism of action of sulfanilamide, the theory of competitive antagonism articulated in 1940, was greeted with applause by biomedical researchers but had no impact on the industrial model of research and development.

The same was true of antibiotics, the antibacterial compounds produced by micro-organisms, of which penicillin and streptomycin are the most famous. Antibiosis became an industrial heuristic in the immediate post-war era. The mechanism of action, once again, did not matter — indeed for penicillin, this was not revealed until more than 20 years after the drug became widely available. Pharmaceutical companies began screening as many micro-organisms in as little time as possible.

Penicillin was developed during the Second World War as a collaborative effort involving the American government, several agencies of state, universities and pharmaceutical companies in and from both the United States and Britain. For the pharmaceutical industry, the penicillin program demonstrated and reinforced the observation that what counted as corporate competence and competitive edge in one field and/or period, could change very quickly in another. A company such as Pfizer whose expertise resided in manufacturing citric acid by using moulds and microbiology moved rapidly into this new field while others remained on the side lines. What counted as a front-line science could also change abruptly. The success of penicillin and streptomycin moved the hitherto marginal disciplines of micro-biology, mycology and soil microbiology into the limelight and attracted financial support from pharmaceutical companies. Selman Waksman's association with Merck through streptomycin, the creation of the Waksman Institute of Microbiology and the global screening of soil samples was a particularly effective example of this new association.

Antibiotics were revolutionary therapies. By the early 1950s, penicillin was the single most important prescription pharmaceutical: in the United States, its sales alone accounted for 10% of the industry's total. The antibiotic bandwagon began to roll. Streptomycin and the broad-spectrum antibiotics — various tetracyclines and chloramphenicol — were introduced during the 1950s in the United States, Europe and Japan. Diseases such as tuberculosis, typhus and diphtheria, frightening and previously untreatable came under control. In the industrialized countries, death rates from these diseases fell so dramatically through the 1950s and 1960s that they ceased to command attention.

Pharmaceutical companies seized upon this much publicized change and trumpeted their successes. Antibiotics were powerful objects. Pharmaceutical companies were the capitalist vanguard of the war on microbes. But the history of antibiotics also revealed something about the pharmaceutical industry that was more unsavoury and would cause public concern in the future; namely that development and marketing, rather than research, were critical aspects of firm success.

This emerged clearly from court cases, acquisitions, private agreements and licensing arrangements concerning the broad-spectrum antibiotic tetracycline. Tetracycline was produced in the laboratories of Pfizer by chemically manipulating another antibiotic called Aureomycin, manufactured by a rival concern, Lederle. Pfizer's announcement of the discovery of tetracycline and its subsequent patent application was met by similar claims by Lederle and 3 other firms. In the resulting maneuvers, the Patent Office, which had the authority and responsibility to sort out the various competing and complicated claims, was side-stepped and the problems resolved in backrooms, boardrooms and courtrooms. An agreement was reached that five firms should manufacture and market tetracycline.

The product, tetracycline, was, of course, indistinguishable from one company to the other. Research could do nothing about this, but marketing could. Sharing access to tetracycline was only part of the story. The more significant part concerned market share, how to increase (or at least maintain) it. Each of the tetracycline producers increased their advertizing costs — including the budgets set aside for representatives — innovating in the style and nature of marketing their product and especially how they contacted and convinced physicians to prescribe their version of the drug. In addition, development work went into other, less fundamental ways of differentiating one company's product from another. Referring to his company's work on tetracycline and its new product forms, the president of Bristol Laboratories put the matter in the following words:

> None of these would qualify as a major scientific advance, but they were practical and useful improvements. They lay in such areas as making liquid suspensions more stable, making liquid forms simpler and more pleasant for the patient to take, combining injectable forms with a superior local anesthetic, and the like.

Antibiotics, especially penicillin and streptomycin, were immensely important developments. Three other pharmaceutical research and development areas became very important in the decades following World War II. The first was psychoactive preparations, compounds that mostly acted on the mind. Chlorpromazine, used for the control of psychotic patients, was one of the first and most successful psychoactive pharmaceuticals to be developed. This was followed by other preparations designed to treat less specific conditions, such as mood changes and depression. The benzodiazepines — Librium and Valium supplied by Hoffmann-La Roche in the late 1950s and early 1960s — had important consequences outside their medical uses. They challenged the definition of therapeutic class, dominated until now by infectious diseases of the body; and they showed that a single drug could make a fortune. By 1970, Valium sales in the United States were earning Hoffmann-La Roche $200 million — the biggest-selling and most profitable drug until then — and, in terms of overall sales, the company was now the largest in the world.

The other therapeutic class that became extremely important after World War II and especially from the 1960s was cardiovascular diseases. After the decline in infectious disease in Western industrialized countries, heart disease emerged as the single greatest killer, particularly of American males. The first drugs capable of lowering blood pressure, the β-blockers, were introduced during the 1960s and were soon joined by other preparations.

Finally there was the substantial research on steroids and their chemistry. Cortisone was the main achievement in this area immediately after World War II. It was used for the treatment of rheumatoid arthritis and generally as an anti-inflammatory agent and marketed by Merck. The other steroidal preparation to come out of the 1950s was the contraceptive pill marketed initially by Searle and Syntex.

All of these developments profoundly affected the range and distribution of pharmaceuticals. The contrast between the inter-war and post-war period is sharp. As late as the 1930s most medicines were natural product preparations, the alkaloids that were first extracted in the nineteenth century; pharmaceutical manufacturers during the 1930s could not afford to ignore this market. Tonics, potions, nostrums, vitamin-enhanced or not, were still the common perception of pharmaceuticals: in some societies, the idea that one would take a single preparation for a single ailment was preposterous. Proprietary drugs still dominated. In the United States, in 1939, proprietary preparations were, in value terms, more important than were prescription drugs. The situation in Britain and France was similar. By 1947, however, prescription preparations were already selling at a value 50% above those of proprietary ones: by 1954, the sales of the former outstripped those of the latter by a factor of three. Patients were increasingly introduced to medicines not through the traditional sources — pharmacists, advertisements, word-of-mouth — but rather through a consultation with the physician and the delivery of a prescription.

Advertizing and other more direct forms of marketing were now directed at the medical profession and financial outlays on marketing began to outstrip those on research and development. During the Kefauver hearings in the US Senate in the late 1950s, many of the largest American pharmaceutical producers reported that their outlay on marketing was well above 20% of sales and 4 times as much as they spent on research and development. In the mid-1970s, it was estimated that the marketing costs to sales ratio for the industry as a whole was around 20% and rising. One often quoted estimate is that the industry as a whole invests up to 40% of its revenue in promotional efforts. This expenditure has accounted for an increasing proportion of financial commitments over the last three decades, while that for research and development has remained relatively static. Pharmaceutical sales representatives (detailmen in the United States) represent the largest single outlay: in Western countries, there are as many as 1 sales representative for every 8 general practitioners (in the United States pharmaceutical companies spend $7000 per physician in promoting their products).

The importance of marketing to the pharmaceutical industry cannot be overstated. Neither can its devotion to developing congener, or me-too, drugs — compounds that are molecularly distinct but have identical therapeutic indications. During the 1950s, in the United States, there were twice as many duplicate products as single chemical entities on the market. In Britain in the early 1970s, more than 80% of newly patented pharmaceuticals were congener drugs.

The post-war era has seen immense structural change in the industry against the background of unprecedented growth in sales and in the total number of new drugs. Though the industry traditionally consisted of a myriad number of small and middle-size firms, the post-war era has witnessed the increasing power and dominance of a handful of giant multinational enterprises located primarily in the United States, Germany, Switzerland, France and Britain. At the same time, pharmaceutical companies have immensely increased their influence within the biomedical community and their public presence. With this have also come striking and damaging controversies.

## SCALE AND STRUCTURES

Before World War II, the world market for pharmaceuticals stood at $600 million. Thanks largely to the successes of the antibiotics, the global market reached $4000 million in the mid-1950s and $7000 million by the end of the decade. By 1975 the market was worth $38,500 million and in 1990 it had reached a staggering $180,000 million. It is estimated that in 2000, the corresponding figure will be $330,000 million. The industrialized countries in Europe, Asia and the United States account for over 80% of the world market, a ratio which has changed little over the last thirty years.

Notwithstanding the enormity of the market, pharmaceutical companies since 1945 have tended to concentrate their efforts on a small number of therapeutic classes. In the early 1960s, 44% of world drug sales were accounted for by anti-infectives and central nervous system therapies. These figures reflected the successful inroads into infectious diseases — the antibiotics — and mental disorders — the sedatives and antidepressants. Other therapeutic classes were poorly covered, particularly cancer and gastrointestinal conditions. Since then, cardiovascular diseases have become the principal target of pharmaceutical companies. In 1993, cardiovascular drugs were the most important source of revenue globally, accounting for about 22% of total sales: within Europe, cardiovascular drugs were even more important, accounting for 26% of sales. These figures compare to 4% for cancer.

Since World War II, many of the pharmaceutical companies have depended on a few leading drugs. In the 1960s, this was certainly the pattern among American pharmaceutical companies: Pfizer, Parke-Davis, Lederle, Upjohn and Merck, Sharp and Dohme each earned one-third of their revenue from just one drug. This has become more marked in recent years. In 1991, the figures were as follows: Glaxo's top 2 selling drugs accounted for 53% of total sales; for Merck, the corresponding figure was 40%; for Ciba-Geigy and Bristol-Myers Squibb, both 26%; and for Bayer, 47%. In 1993, each of the top 20 pharmaceutical compounds earned for their respective companies more than $1 billion in sales world-wide.

Another tendency that has become especially clear in recent years is the separation of pharmaceuticals from the chemical industry throughout the world. This deepening rift results from various restructuring programs initiated during the

TABLE 1: PHARMACEUTICAL COMPANIES WORLDWIDE 1976–1994

Pharmaceutical sales as % of total sales

| Company | 1976 | 1994 |
|---|---|---|
| Glaxo (UK) | 100 | 100 |
| SmithKline Beecham (UK) | 39 | 58 |
| Merck (USA) | 84 | 84 |
| Bristol-Myers Squibb (USA) | 54 | 57 |
| Pfizer (USA) | 50 | 69 |
| Hoechst (Germany) | 16 | 22 |
| Bayer (Germany) | 13 | 19 |
| Roche (Switzerland) | 51 | 55 |
| Ciba (Switzerland) | 28 | 33 |

Sources: M.L. Burstall, J.H. Dunning and A. Lake, *Multinational enterprises, governments and technology in the pharmaceutical industry* (Paris: OECD, 1981), **74**, SCRIP Yearbook (1995), **77**.

1970s, and from mergers and acquisitions which in recent years have been particularly brisk. Table 1 provides an illustration of this trend for a selected group of companies and in addition also shows that Bayer, Hoechst and Ciba continue to have a much wider range of activities than their American and British counterparts, reflecting in large part their late-nineteenth century origins.

The world's pharmaceutical market is structured in a peculiar way. On the one hand, it is dominated by a group of very large companies: in 1993/94, the top fifteen companies had pharmaceutical sales exceeding $4 billion dollars; they were to be found in the United States, Britain, Germany, Switzerland and Japan; and their combined sales accounted for just under 50% of total world sales of pharmaceuticals. On the other hand, no single company has a very large market share: Merck, the largest company in terms of sales, had a market share of only 5% in 1993. The corresponding share for Takeda, the 15th ranking company in this group, was 2.3%. In other words, the gap in sales between the largest and smallest company in this dominant group is not very large. The entire sector is composed of a very large number of very small companies. Research and development is concentrated in the largest companies who, on average, invest 20% of their sales in this activity.

PROBLEMS AND CRITICISMS

The success of the pharmaceutical industry ultimately depends on therapeutic success. But the pursuit has been both uncertain and controversial. The thalidomide tragedy in the 1960s showed up one fatal flaw in the governance of the pharmaceutical industry. The regulatory measures then in existence were simply too ineffective to guarantee protection to consumers. Though the industry had acknowledged that all pharmaceutical preparations had some side-effects, these were typically considered unavoidable nuisances. The problem of the toxicity of chemicals was far too narrowly investigated. Since the thalidomide case, the regulatory measures have been substantially tightened, especially in the United States and Europe, though as the OPREN case of the late 1970s and early 1980s shows, they are not as foolproof as they are often portrayed. Recent relaxation of some regulatory measures, especially in the United States, aimed at quicker approval of new drugs, may reintroduce unacceptable levels of risk.

Criticism against the pharmaceutical industry has also arisen in other quarters. One of these concerns the relationship between the pharmaceutical industry, located in the advanced industrialized countries, and the health market in the developing nations. Though the developing world contains most of the world's population, it accounts for 20% of the world pharmaceutical market. Targeting this market is and has been a strategic move for most pharmaceutical companies, and it is here that they have run into controversy. Criticisms have come from a variety of sources, accusing the pharmaceutical industry of such misdemeanors as: dumping drugs that either could not or did not pass the strict regulatory mechanisms in the developed world; overselling and over-promoting drugs; and promoting powerful drugs to treat conditions that are amenable to effective, safe and extremely inexpensive treatments.

In recent years, the pharmaceutical industry has also faced criticisms about its handling of intellectual property rights in drugs based upon plants and forest products, often from developing countries. After virtually abandoning interest in natural products in the late 1950s and 1960s, many pharmaceutical companies have returned to this area of research, partly because of several success stories and partly because of their own fear of diminishing returns from current practice. Critics of 'chemical or ethnobotanical prospecting' have called into question the terms of agreements pharmaceutical companies have entered into with national governments.

Another area of controversy concerns the relationships between the pharmaceutical industry and the medical community. Issues such as drug promotion to physicians; the possible influence of pharmaceutical companies on basic research either through the allocation of grants or through editorial influence; bias in company-funded clinical trials and the contributions to the finance of medical education; conflicts of interest in matters of technology transfer; the public worries that doctors have become corrupted by their peculiar relationship with pharmaceutical companies.

Finally, there are issues of health economics: the rising prices of drugs — legitimated by pharmaceutical company executives as a response to the huge and growing research and development costs (now put at $230 million per drug); the growing share of pharmaceutical sales in total health care costs in both developed and developing nations; the continuing marginal status of alternative therapies that promise effective and cheap results; and the political role of drugs as exemplified by the abortifacient RU-486 and the abortion debates in the United States and in the developing world.

Many of the criticisms and critiques of the pharmaceutical industry in the last 30 years will continue to be aired. They focus mostly on the industry's public presence. What has not been subjected to public scrutiny has been the nature of the research process itself. The reason for this is simple: from the late nineteenth century until the 1970s, pharmaceutical research rested on the premise that biologically-active natural and synthetic compounds could be found and made into safe and useful drugs.

During the 1970s and early 1980s, however, and within the context of a significant and seemingly relentless fall in the number of new drugs placed on the market — the number of new single entity drugs introduced to the American market between 1970 and 1985 was 40% down on the previous fifteen years — pharmaceutical research began to look for new search techniques. Rather than focusing on the chemical, research turned to the target, particularly to receptor geometry and biophysics. With the insight of molecular biology and computer technology, model compounds could be designed to block the receptors and thereby stem the natural history of the specific condition. This rational approach, as it has been called, is also designed to take the chanciness out of drug discovery.

Together with rapidly changing techniques of genetic engineering, pharmaceutical companies, with their massive financial resources, are set to incorporate a variety of state-of-the-art techniques both through well-established methods and more recent ones. In their desire to keep a tight grip over pharmaceutical manufacture, most large pharmaceutical companies in the United States and Europe are now collaborating with smaller biotechnology firms, under new alliances or through mergers. Many of these large companies have as much as 40% of their pipeline drugs in collaborative schemes. What the public will get remains to be seen.

## REFERENCES

1. Jonathan Liebenau, 'Industrial R & D in pharmaceutical firms in the early twentieth century', *Business History* (1984), **26**: 333.
2. Peter Temin, 'Technology, regulation, and market structure in the modern pharmaceutical industry', *Bell Journal of Economics* (1979), **10**: 441.

## FURTHER READING

Abraham, John, *Science, Politics and the Pharmaceutical Industry: Controversy and Bias in Drug Regulation.* (London: UCL Press, 1995).

Apple, Rima, *Vitamania: Vitamins in American Culture.* (New Brunswick, NJ: Rutgers University Press, 1996).

Chadwick, D.J. and Marsh, J., *Ethnobotany and the Search for New Drugs.* (Chichester: John Wiley & Sons, 1994).

Davenport-Hines, R. and Slinn, J.A., *Glaxo: A History to 1962.* (Cambridge: Cambridge University Press, 1992).

Joyce, Christopher, *Earthly Medicines: Medicine-Hunting in the Rainforest.* (Boston: Little, Brown, 1995).

Lader, Lawrence, *RU486.* (Reading, MA: Addison-Wesley, 1991).

Lesch, John, 'Chemistry and biomedicine in an industrial setting: the invention of the sulfa drugs', in Mauskopf, S.H. (ed.), *Chemical Sciences in the Modern World.* (Philadelphia: University of Pennsylvania Press, 1995).

Mann, Charles C. and Plummer, Mark L., *The Aspirin Wars: Money, Medicine, and 100 Years of Rampant Competition.* (Cambridge, MA: Harvard Business School Press, 1991).

Oudshoorn, Nelly, *Beyond the Natural Body: An Archeology of Sex Hormones.* (London: Routledge, 1994).

Parascandola, John (ed.), *The History of Antibiotics.* (Madison, WI: American Institute of the History of Pharmacy, 1980).

Silverman, M., *The Drugging of the Americas.* (Berkeley, CA: University of California Press, 1976).

Silverman, M., Lydecker, M. and Lee, P.R., *Bad Medicine: The Prescription Drug Industry in the Third World.* (Stanford, CA: Stanford University Press, 1992).

Swann, John P., *Academic Scientists and the Pharmaceutical Industry.* (Baltimore, MD: The Johns Hopkins University Press, 1988).

Temin, Peter, *Taking your Medicine: Drug Regulation in the United States.* (Cambridge, MA: Harvard University Press, 1980).

Weatherall, M., *In Search of a Cure: A History of Pharmaceutical Discovery.* (Oxford: Oxford University Press, 1990).

# CHAPTER 11

# The Crises of the Welfare States

RUDOLF KLEIN

This chapter analyses the successive 'crises' of the Welfare States since 1973; a useful starting point, since it was the sudden rise in oil prices of that year which plunged the world into economic turmoil and inaugurated a period in which most of the certainties that had shaped developments since the end of World War ll have come under increasing challenge. But the plural is the key to understanding. The concept of crisis is a tool of academic and political rhetoric that, on closer inspection, shatters into multiple meanings and can be used to convey a variety of messages. The concept of the Welfare State, similarly, is a hold-all notion which, when unpackaged, turns out to cover a wide spectrum of social and institutional arrangements: differences between nations are the norm. Before embarking on an account of the institutional, intellectual and ideological changes that have taken place in this 25 year period, it is therefore essential to clear the ground by hacking through the definitional jungle.

In medical usage, crisis is the point in the progress of a disease when a change takes place which is decisive of recovery or death. And if this strict definition were used, then the only question at issue in this analysis would be whether or not Welfare States have succumbed to the disease that afflicted them — which begs the question of whether they were so afflicted in the first place and, if so, what the nature of the disease was (both highly contentious issues) — or whether they have returned to health (however that may be defined).The longest death-bed scene in history, which still leaves the future of the patient uncertain, does not fit the medical definition. But, of course, in practice the word is used more loosely. In common usage, crisis is used to suggest a turning point in affairs. In political usage, the term is often invoked to imply impending catastrophe in the absence of drastic action to avert it. In academic usage, it has been used — particularly by Marxist analysts — to convey an unsustainable strain or contradiction that threatens societal stability.

None of these usages seem appropriate when tracing the evolution of policies over a quarter of a century. To anticipate our analysis, it has been a history of adaptation and incremental change that leaves open the question of whether, in the process, the defining characteristics of the 'Welfare State' (whatever they may be) will be transformed. The language of 'crisis' — although frequently and indiscriminately invoked — is consequently as apt to confuse as to illuminate: if it illuminates anything, it is the way words are mobilized in the service of political expediency and ideological conflict.

The 'Welfare State' is another protean notion. Welfare States come in many different shapes, and much academic energy has been devoted to arranging them into neat typologies. For the purpose of this chapter, the crucial point to stress is simply that differences in national welfare institutions reflect different historical paths, involving different political coalitions, constitutional arrangements and ideologies. Insofar as these differences persist, so we may expect reactions to challenges to differ.

In analyzing the 'crises' of Welfare States we are therefore dealing with slippery concepts on both sides of the equation. Welfare States have adopted many differing institutional strategies in pursuit of a variety of objectives, ranging from buying off working-class opposition (Bismarckian Germany) to creating a more equal society (post-1945 Sweden). Some Welfare States provide benefits on the basis of insurance: notionally at least, the benefits are 'earned' by contributions. Others distribute benefits on the basis of citizenship: the very fact of being a citizen brings an entitlement to benefits. And so on.

If we want to search for the lowest common denominator that defines all Welfare States, it is that they use public power to 1) modify the distribution of income produced by the operations of the market, 2) turn individual risks into collective risk and 3) establish some kind of minimum standard below which no member of the population will be allowed to fall. But even this modest definitional net allows quite a few countries which might claim to have Welfare States to slip through. It captures the advanced industrialized countries — which are the main focus of this chapter — but excludes many Latin American and Asian countries, which do not meet the third criterion (indeed many advanced industrialized countries did not meet it until the relatively recent past, since progress towards universal coverage tended to be a step-by-step process, with the self-employed and agricultural workers left to the last).

This minimalist definition, be it noted, does not include any question-begging reference to social justice or the promotion of welfare. To invoke the promotion of social justice or of welfare — both contested notions — as the defining characteristics of Welfare States is simply to invite a second-order inquiry into national differences in the way these concepts are interpreted. In particular, the evolution of Welfare States cannot be seen as a crusade for equality — although prescriptively, if ahistorically, their performance may well be judged on this criterion — but rather as the product of shifting coalitions of trade-unions and middle-class interest groups who shared a common purpose in promoting insurance schemes of various types that would protect them from the risks of ill health, old age and unemployment.

The emphasis in this discussion of the characteristics of Welfare States has deliberately been on the use of public *power* rather than public *funds*. The measure of Welfare State 'effort' employed in most comparative analyses — both as between different countries and different time periods — is the proportion of the Gross Domestic Product (GDP) that is spent by the State or by statutory insurance schemes on health care and social security, using the data produced by international organizations. This chapter follows this convention, which indeed captures a crucial — and increasingly controversial — dimension of Welfare States: the 'burden' placed on the population by taxation and insurance contributions. But it is, at best, only a partial measure. It is possible to conceive of a Welfare State which mandates responsibility for social protection to others, notably employers, and thus has near zero spending levels. The Regulatory State can, in effect, substitute for the Welfare State. Similarly, the tax system may — by offering incentives to personal spending on welfare provision — be used in part at least as a substitute for public expenditure. So, for example, private health care insurance or pension plans can be made compulsory, and contributions may be tax exempt. When account is taken of tax spending and mandatory welfare, the result is to shrink the differences between countries that appear when only public expenditure is considered.

In this chapter, however, the focus is on public expenditure. For it is the level of public expenditure — the fiscal burden imposed on governments — which provides the main theme running through the 25 year debate about Welfare States analyzed in subsequent sections. Similarly, and for the same reason, the focus is on total public expenditure on welfare, rather than on health care spending. This apparent neglect of health care funding as an issue in its own right in a book dedicated to medicine may appear perverse. But the reason is simple. Health care funding has only become an issue because it is part of a wider swell of concern about the increasing cost of Welfare States. Accordingly, the case of health care is only discussed in the final section as a coda to the general exposition in order to identify those dimensions of 'crisis' that are special to this policy area.

## SHATTERING THE POST-WAR DREAM

In the quarter of a century that followed the end of World War II the Welfare States of the advanced industrialized countries — here defined as the original 18 members of the Organization for Economic Co-operation and Development (OECD) — prospered on the dividends of the Growth State. Full employment, the condition stipulated by Beveridge as the foundation of his design for the UK Welfare State, was achieved everywhere. The countries concerned recorded steady, if variable, rates of economic growth. National wealth and standards of living rose. So, too, did public spending on social security and health care, as programs were expanded in scope and benefits were made more generous.

Indeed, spending by the Welfare States rose at a faster rate than the growth in national incomes. In the early sixties average spending in the OECD group of countries was respectively 7.3% and 2.7% of GDP for social security and health care. By the mid-seventies, the equivalent figures were 9.5% and 4.9%.[1] There were

TABLE 1: PUBLIC WELFARE EXPENDITURE IN SELECTED OECD COUNTRIES AS % OF GROSS DOMESTIC PRODUCT

| | Early 1960s | | | Mid-1970s | | |
|---|---|---|---|---|---|---|
| | Income mainenance | Health care | Total | Income maintenance | Health care | Total |
| Australia | 4.7 | 2.5 | 7.2 | 4.0 | 5.0 | 9.0 |
| Canada | 5.4 | 2.5 | 7.9 | 7.3 | 5.1 | 12.4 |
| France | 11.8 | 3.1 | 14.9 | 12.4 | 5.3 | 17.7 |
| Germany | 11.9 | 2.5 | 14.4 | 12.4 | 5.2 | 17.6 |
| Italy | 7.5 | 2.9 | 10.4 | 10.4 | 5.2 | 15.6 |
| Japan | 2.1 | 1.9 | 4.0 | 2.8 | 3.5 | 6.3 |
| Netherlands | 8.6 | 2.8 | 11.4 | 19.1 | 5.1 | 24.2 |
| Sweden | 6.0 | 3.6 | 9.6 | 9.3 | 6.7 | 16.0 |
| United Kingdom | 4.4 | 3.2 | 7.6 | 7.7 | 4.6 | 12.3 |
| United States | 5.5 | 1.2 | 6.7 | 7.4 | 3.0 | 10.4 |

considerable variations between countries, as Table 1 shows. But the trend everywhere was the same. Welfare State spending was absorbing an ever larger share of the national income while, conversely, the share of private consumption was falling as the taxes needed to finance the former ate into the take-home pay of the population. Nevertheless economic growth meant that this was not a zero sum game: even though the *share* of private consumption in GDP fell, *absolute* incomes continued to rise. It appeared to be the best of worlds for everyone.

The global economic turmoil precipitated by the 1973 rise in oil prices — the years of stagflation — put a question mark against the assumptions underlying the expansion of the Welfare States. No longer could sustained, steady economic growth be taken for granted. Nor, for that matter, could full employment. Whereas national income had grown at an average rate of 4.9% a year across the OECD countries in the years between 1960 and 1973 and the average rate of unemployment had been 3.2%, the equivalent figures in the following eight years were 2.4% and 5.5%.[2] The Growth State could no longer pay its dividends to the Welfare States. The post-war era of optimism was over.

The implications for spending on Welfare State programs were profound. The commitments made in the years of optimism — to higher pensions, better health care systems and so on — implied a steadily rising trajectory of public spending premised on continuing economic growth. If the rate of growth fell below the rate predicted when the plans for continued expansion were made, meeting the commitments would mean increasing taxation and effectively cutting private consumption: which is indeed what happened in some countries in the years after 1973. Moreover, the dilemmas of policy were compounded by the fact that the pressures on Welfare States were increasing just as the fiscal capacities of the countries concerned were reduced: national budgets were swollen by the measures taken to deal with unemployment and subsidies designed to soften the impact of rising prices.

Fiscal stress translated, in turn, into political alarm as taxation rose, thus giving greater visibility to the costs of the Welfare States. The post-1973 years were the period of tax backlash. In 1978 voters in California passed Proposition 13, effectively freezing property taxes in the State. In Denmark, the new Glistrup party soared into prominence on an anti-tax platform. In the UK, Margaret Thatcher's Conservative Government was elected to office in 1979 with a manifesto of commitments to reducing the State's share of the nation's income and cutting income tax. Interestingly the degree of the backlash did not appear to be closely correlated with the actual level of spending. Some countries with a high level of social spending, like Germany, seemed to be relatively immune; others with a low level of social spending, like the United States, appeared to be highly susceptible. Instead the reactions of different countries reflected both the structure of taxation, the mix of direct and indirect taxes, and the structure of the individual political systems, notably the degree of corporatism. It was not necessarily an anti-welfare backlash: support for the main programs of the Welfare States continued to be high. But the new economic pessimism called into question the future ability of governments to project the spending patterns of the past into the future: it was not difficult to demonstrate that the rates of growth in spending that had characterized the previous decades were no longer sustainable.

Did all this represent a crisis for Welfare States? In one sense, it indisputably did: it marked a turning point in the nature of much academic and political discourse. Before 1973 Welfare States were seen, and celebrated, as a solution to society's ills: as a way of promoting social cohesion, softening class conflicts and protecting people from catastrophic threats to their well-being. After 1973, however, the Welfare State increasingly came to be represented as the cause of at least some of society's ills: threatening the very prosperity which had allowed it to grow. But in another sense the notion of crisis, as we shall show, was misleading: when we come to trace the evolution of Welfare States in the decade after the promulgation of the 'crisis,' we shall find little evidence of fundamental change. Despite the widespread perception of impending catastrophe in the absence of radical action, the story in most countries is one of reasonably successful adaptation to a new economic environment as a result of fine-tuning at the margins. The next section explores the puzzle of the contrast between discourse and reality in more detail.

FISCAL STRESS, IDEOLOGICAL OPPORTUNITY

The stagflation of the mid-seventies — marked by soaring inflation, economic stagnation and rising unemployment — signaled the beginning of a Counter-Reformation in political and ideological discourse: a backlash against the bundle of ideas that had provided the intellectual underpinning of the notion of the 'Welfare State.' The ideas of John Maynard Keynes — the Luther of economics — appeared to be discredited. No longer could it be assumed that governments could guarantee full employment and continued growth. Instead, the doctrines of classical economics appeared to have been vindicated. The laws of the market confounded, it seemed, governmental attempts to modify them. The economic foundations of the Welfare States, it was tempting to conclude, had been based on an illusion.

This is, of course, to over-simply a complex debate. There were significant differences between countries. The Counter-Reformation was strongest in the Anglophone countries, especially the United States and the United Kingdom. It was less forceful in other countries, especially those — like Germany — where Keynesianism had never been fully embraced. But the main point remains. Economic turmoil provided the opportunity for an intellectual counter-revolution, giving the discipline of economics a new prominence in the debate about Welfare States. A new and threatening economic environment gave seeming credibility to the revival of old arguments about the viability and desirability of Welfare States.

The "rhetoric of reaction"[3] had a number of components. Most conspicuously it produced a curious alliance between the New Right and the Old Marxists who both argued that there was a fundamental incompatibility, indeed contradiction, between Welfare State spending and economic prosperity. Such spending, it was asserted, sapped capital investment, undermined incentives and fueled inflation. The paradox, it seemed, was that Welfare States were destroying the machine of economic growth which had made their development possible in the first place. Economic and social policies appeared to be set on a collision path.

The evidence for many of the assertions was ambiguous at best. So, for example, much ingenuity was devoted by economists and others in attempts to demonstrate that high public spending was associated with poor economic performance. But regression analysis refused to give a clear answer, although it did hint (no more) that higher spending nations tended to devote fewer resources to capital invest-ment. Ironically, the countries where the arguments of the Counter-Reformation took firmest hold — the United States and the United Kingdom — were countries also with relatively low levels of Welfare State spending: which, in turn, suggests that the appeal of the new faith had little to do with evidence and much to do with the ideological predelictions through which the evidence was filtered.

However, the critiques of the Welfare State that emerged during the seventies were not just the product of economic panic. The economic turmoil helped to crystallize — and to bring into prominence — other strands of dissatisfaction. For the New Right, Welfare States represented the triumph of self-seeking bureauc-racies intent on maximizing their budgets rather than serving the needs of their clients. For those on the Left, Welfare States were increasingly seen as instruments of social control, whether by doctors or social workers, paternalistically imposing professional values on the populations served. If the New Right saw Welfare States as robbing people of choice, the Left and the libertarian center increasingly saw them as robbing people of autonomy.

The preoccupation with these issues was international during the late seventies and early eighties. The stage seemed to be set for a dramatic transformation — a radical re-assessment — of Welfare States. It was a transformation destined not to happen. The eighties ended with the existing Welfare States of the advanced

TABLE 2: GROWTH RATES IN PUBLIC WELFARE EXPENDITURE IN SELECTED OECD
COUNTRIES

| | Annual growth rate % (real terms) | | | |
| --- | --- | --- | --- | --- |
| | 1960–1975 | | 1975–1981 | |
| | Income maintenance* | Health care | Income maintenance | Health care |
| Australia | 8.5 | 9.1 | 4.0 | –0.5 |
| Canada | 8.3 | 13.0 | 6.8 | 3.0 |
| France | 7.7 | 10.9 | 8.7 | 6.3 |
| Germany | 6.3 | 6.6 | 2.1 | 2.1 |
| Italy | 9.6 | 6.7 | 7.7 | 0.1 |
| Japan | 12.7 | 12.2 | 13.7 | 6.6 |
| Netherlands | 10.3 | 11.4 | 5.2 | 4.4 |
| Sweden | 8.7 | 11.3 | 6.9 | 3.4 |
| United Kingdom | 5.9 | 3.4 | 4.5 | 2.0 |
| United States | 7.2 | 10.3 | 4.4 | 3.8 |

*Pensions only

industrialized countries looking remarkably unchanged, their institutional framework intact. The reason was simple. Governments succeeded in restraining the
growth of welfare spending in line with lowered economic expectations. To the
extent that the post-1973 period represented a 'turning point' in social policy it
was in the micro-management of existing programs. The design of Welfare States
did not change. The supposed contradictions of the Welfare State — suggesting
an inherent lack of viability — proved capable of resolution by tinkering at the
edges. Even those governments most committed to the rhetoric of rolling back the
frontiers of the State — those of Ronald Reagan and Margaret Thatcher — stopped
well short of radical retrenchment or redesign.

One set of figures illustrates the success of the governments in the OECD
countries in bringing the apparently run-away growth of spending on their Welfare
States under control. Whereas the annual growth rate of deflated social expenditure (i.e., after ironing out the effects of inflation) was 8.4% between 1960 and
1975, the equivalent figure was 4.8% between 1975 and 1981:[4] the gap between
the growth of Welfare State spending and that of GDP had been narrowed though
still not closed. The severity of the cut-back varied from country to country, as
Table 2 shows, partly because of differences in the performance of their economies
and partly because of differences in the reaction of their governments. But the
trend everywhere was the same.

One reason for this deceleration was, of course, that by the end of the seventies
most Welfare States had achieved maturity. In the sixties and early seventies many
Welfare States were still expanding the coverage of their programs. Once near-
universal coverage had been achieved in most countries — with the United States
a notable exception — the dynamics of growth changed: the main impetus now
came from improvements in the level of benefits such as pensions and services
such as health care. Governments could therefore adjust to a new economic

environment by reining back increases in the level of benefits. For example, the Thatcher government changed the method for calculating the annual increment in pension levels: whereas previously they had been indexed to changes in the level of both prices and earnings, they were now linked only to the former. It was a strategy that had low political visibility — since the impact in any one year was small — but produced substantial savings over time. Other countries adopted similar strategies.

Much the same pattern characterized the rest of the eighties. Welfare States in the advanced industrialized States at the end of the decade were recognizably the same institutions that they had been before 1973. They had become somewhat more parsimonious — particularly in their treatment of vulnerable social groups with little political clout — but in no sense could it be said that they had been dismantled. Even in the UK, despite much alarm about cut-backs, spending on most programs (including the National Health Service) continued to increase if at a slower rate than in previous decades.

The resilience of the Welfare States of the advanced industrialized nations can be credited to two main causes. First, they created constituencies for their own survival. Those employed in Welfare States programs such as health care had a strong self-interest in maintaining the status quo. Second, Welfare States had satisfied the hopes of the various coalitions which had originally sought collective protection against individual risks. Whatever their other weaknesses, they were a success story in this respect. And success, in turn, brought them popular support. Cross-nationally, support for the heartlands of the Welfare States — notably pensions and health care — remained strong, though attitudes towards programs designed for groups perceived to be undeserving or deviant were more ambivalent. The support tended to cut across party allegiance and class. Ultimately, the political strength of Welfare States derived from the fact — often raised as a criticism — that they had only a limited redistributive impact and that the middle classes were among their chief beneficiaries. Individual welfare programs, ironically, were most vulnerable to the extent that they were targeted on the poorest, most marginal or (in the case of the United States) ethnic minority sections of the population.

However, the debate about Welfare States did not end with the achievement of modest retrenchment and seeming institutional stability by the end of the eighties. It was to continue, with some significant variations and some new themes, in the nineties: the subject of the next section.

## NEW TENSIONS AND STRESSES

If the prophesied death of Welfare States did not happen in the eighties, if the radical surgery on offer did not turn out to be required, the nineties proved a period of watchful waiting. There remained disquieting symptoms of stress and strain; there was chronic anxiety about the long-term sustainability of existing institutions. But it was far from self-evident what the diagnosis should be or what remedies were required, although plenty were on offer: an uncertainty which has been carried into the new millenium.

The reasons for continued debate and anxiety about Welfare States fall into two categories: those exogenous to the institutions concerned and those endogenous to them. Exogenous to them are the continued economic troubles of the global economy. Confidence in the capacity of the Western economies to resume a steady growth rate has not returned and their performance looks extremely sluggish when compared to the Asian 'tigers.' Unemployment has, if to varying degrees, continued at a high rate. Above all, two linked new themes have emerged. First, there is the theme of globalization: the extent to which, with the deregulation of markets and the mobility of capital, national governments are losing control over their own economies and investment searches out the cheapest sources of labor. Second, there is the related fear that Western economies are losing their competitive edge in the global struggle for markets.

Welfare States are implicated on both counts. To the extent that national governments can no longer — if they ever could — insulate their economies from global pressures, so keeping taxes and social insurance contributions down has become an even greater imperative than before. For social insurance contributions in particular are an important element in labor costs. And, so continues the argument, to the extent that paying for Welfare States raises labor costs, so competitiveness is imperiled. Further, high taxes may deter entry into the labor market; generous unemployment or sickness benefits may encourage people to stay away from work longer than they otherwise would; high pensions, particularly if early retirement is on offer, may give people an incentive to exit from the labor force. Labor is therefore in shorter supply (and more expensive) than it would otherwise be.

Once again, the evidence is far from clear cut. Globalization is a word that trips easily off the tongue but its effects can be exaggerated: national governments still have considerable autonomy in policy making. And contradictory findings have emerged from the many studies that have attempted to link evidence about the competitiveness of different economies to the configuration of their Welfare States. The main conclusion that can be drawn with any confidence is that any adverse effects of Welfare State expenditure on economic performance are contingent on the structure of benefits, and the political and social environment of individual countries, rather than on the level of spending or the generosity of provision.

However, other factors are exerting pressure on governments to cut public spending. In the case of the members of the European Union, the conditions for entry into the Single Currency bloc are forcing governments to retrench, persuading hitherto reluctant retrenchers like France, Italy and Germany to attempt to reduce social spending. In the case of other nations, particularly in Latin America and the former Communist bloc, the requirements of the International Monetary Fund and the World Bank as a condition for aid are having a similar effect.

Turning to the pressures endogenous to Welfare States, these can be divided into two categories: age and sex. The aging of the population, a phenomenon common to all countries if in varying degrees, raises the specter that ever fewer people of working age will have to support an ever larger number of pensioners: that the commitments made by Welfare States to their pensioners would, if met, mean unacceptably high taxes or social insurance contributions. Similarly, an aging population implies higher health care spending. The other source of tension is that most Welfare States were designed on the twin-assumptions that they were providing for a standard family and that the main purpose should be to ensure that the male bread-winner should have sufficient resources to meet his responsibilities at times of illness or unemployment. Neither assumption now holds. There has been a sharp increase in one-parent families everywhere — generating new demands on Welfare States — and in the participation of women in the labor force.

The change in the structure of families, and the relative roles of men and women, clearly demands radical adaptation by Welfare States in the structure of benefits systems. The case of the 'demographic time-bomb' — the emotive phrase often used to describe the aging of populations — is, however, more complex. The average OECD ratio between the working population aged between 15 and 64 and the over-65s will undoubtedly deteriorate sharply over the next 20 years: from 5:4 to 3:8, dropping further to 2:5 in 2040.[5] But taking such figures at face value leaves two crucial qualifications out of account. First, older populations have fewer dependent children: the overall ratio between the working population and all dependants (young and old) will therefore deteriorate at a much slower rate. Second, both numerators are elastic when it comes to calculating the economic impact of demographic change. The size of the effective working population will depend on the proportion of women taking part in the labor market; the number of pensioners and young dependants will depend on the public policies that determine retirement age, continued working after 65 and participation in education.

In short, the 'demographic time-bomb' emerges — on closer inspection — not to be a doomsday-machine, signaling inevitable disaster for Welfare States, but as a something that can be defused by appropriate policy response. For example, in the United States — though elsewhere as well — the specter of an unaffordable pensions burden has been much invoked to argue for abandoning social in favor of private insurance. Yet it has been convincingly argued[6] that the US social security scheme can be made financially viable by making relatively small changes in the level of contributions now that will have a large impact over time.

Overall then, the conclusion would seem to be that Welfare States everywhere are under stress, facing a variety of challenges, but that there is little evidence that the policies they embody are somehow "unsustainable."[7] Adaptation of existing commitments and policies rather than abandonment is, in practice, the norm in most advanced industrialized countries. Some indeed have even expanded the scope of welfare: thus Germany introduced a new scheme of insurance for the elderly in residential care. Generally, the trends of the eighties have continued into the nineties and a variety of adaptive measures have been taken. In many European countries, the age of retirement has been raised and the methods for calculating the value of pensions have been made more stringent; similarly access to unem-

TABLE 3: PUBLIC WELFARE EXPENDITURE IN SELECTED OECD COUNTRIES AS % OF
GROSS DOMESTIC PRODUCT

| | 1980 | | 1993# | |
|---|---|---|---|---|
| | Total social expenditure* | Of which health care | Total social expenditure | Of which health care |
| Australia | 11.7 | 4.6 | 16.4 | 5.7 |
| Canada | 13.3 | 5.3 | 19.8 | 7.2 |
| France | 23.5 | 6.0 | 28.7 | 7.3 |
| Germany (West only) | 25.0 | 6.3 | 24.7 | 6.0 |
| Italy | 18.2 | 5.6 | 25.0 | 6.3 |
| Japan | 11.0 | 5.0 | 12.5 | 5.3 |
| Netherlands | 28.7 | 5.9 | 30.3 | 6.7 |
| Sweden | 30.4 | 8.7 | 38.0 | 6.2 |
| United Kingdom | 18.3 | 4.9 | 23.4 | 5.8 |
| United States | 12.4 | 3.6 | 15.6 | 5.9 |

*This includes spending on all forms of income maintenance plus labour market
policies
#Where 1993 figures are unavailable, those for 1992 have been used   Source: OECD 1996

ployment benefits has been restricted and there has been an increasing emphasis
on 'targeting' benefits to those most in need. Even Sweden, a country long held
out as a model of how to reconcile high welfare spending with growth, has recently
been forced by economic pressures to adopt a policy of incremental retrenchment.

The overall effect can be seen in Table 3. This shows, for a selection of OECD
countries, that spending on social security and health care continued to rise into
the nineties, if to varying degrees. It also demonstrates the importance of unemployment as a factor driving up spending, which accounts for a large proportion
of the increase in Welfare States budgets, and helps to explain the re-orientation
of social policy towards labor market issues: a point explored in more detail below.

So fiscal stress remains an important factor in determining the terms of the
debate about Welfare States. It helps to explain continued interest in alternative
models of financing welfare: specifically the privatization of insurance against risk,
whether for health care or old age. But two other lines of argument have also
become more salient. The first is the assertion that Welfare States perversely
aggravate the social problems they are meant to solve. The second is, to return
to one of the themes of the seventies, that public provision of services is inherently
inefficient and overly-paternalistic, denying choice to consumers.

The argument about the perversity of social policies has a number of dimensions. The American version puts particular emphasis on the claim that welfare
benefits encourage illegitimate births and break up families: a claim which, like
so many of the perversity arguments, seems to rest on myths rather evidence. A
more plausible argument is that unemployment benefits may blunt incentives to
seek work. Here there is more substantial evidence, although much depends on
the way in which unemployment benefits fit into the wider structure of social
protection. Hence the widespread trend across countries — endorsed by both Left

and Right — towards replacing unemployment benefits by various versions of 'workfare': i.e., offering opportunities for work or training instead of cash.

Overall then, the institutions of the Welfare States survived the nineties, just as they survived the eighties and for much the same reasons. They have proved a successful constituency for their own survival and public support remains strong. The changes that have taken place are in the small-print of program administration and in the micro-management of service delivery, leaving the institutional framework intact. Incremental change over time may, of course, have a profound impact, particularly on specific sub-groups of the population. And there is some evidence that, certainly in the UK and the US, marginal groups at the edge of society have suffered. But it is as yet premature to attempt anything like a final evaluation, for the adaptive changes analyzed in this section — like those described in the previous ones — represent an unfinished story. If the first 25 years after World War II were a period in which Welfare States everywhere appeared to be converging towards a shared, ideal model of universal social protection, the subsequent 25 years have been a period in which they have been searching experimentally and diversely for adaptive strategies capable of dealing with a changed, less predictable, social and economic environment. The next section briefly sketches some of the characteristics of this new era.

New Concerns, New Perspectives

Perhaps the most notable change of the nineties was a shift in the language and agenda of discourse about Welfare States. The twin-imperatives of economic competition and high unemployment have led to a redefinition of the central concerns of social policy. There has been increasing recognition that labor market policies have an important impact on welfare, while conversely social policies have significant effects on the labor market. On the one hand, legislation regulating the labor market — such as provision for minimum wages or protection against dismissal — clearly affect the distribution of income and risk. On the other hand, welfare provision may — as previously noted — affect the workings of the labor market.

Given this inter-relationship, it is not surprising that the focus of attention in the debate about Welfare States has increasingly shifted to labor market concerns. The point emerges clearly in the policy agenda set by the Commission of the European Community[8] for the future directions of social policy. The emphasis of this document is very much on creating a more flexible, better trained workforce, albeit with a nod also towards relieving policy and integrating the socially excluded. Similar concerns emerge from the report of the Commission on Social Justice[9] set by the late John Smith, the then leader of the Labour Party, to revise a new program of action for the Left. Here the theme, shaping the detailed recommendations, is that the Welfare State should be seen as an investment in national prosperity: only by investing in training and education and by offering opportunities to all, will it be possible to create the conditions necessary for growth — a well-equipped labor force and social cohesion.

In summary, then, it is clear that the currency of discourse about Welfare States has changed in important respects. The Redistributive State has increasingly come to be seen as the Investment State. The emphasis has switched to do-it-youself social policies, which allow individual citizens greater scope for putting together their own packages of welfare. If Welfare States have not been transformed by crisis, they are certainly in the process of mutation under the pressure of new challenges. In important respects stability in the grand design of Welfare States conceals a multitude of adaptive changes which could either strengthen the institutions concerned or undermine them: on that, the jury will still be out for some decades to come.

## What's Special About Health Care?

Health care is neither the largest nor fastest growing component of public spending on welfare. The pattern of its evolution over time follows closely that of the major income maintenance programs. The 15 year period up to 1975 saw a rapid rate of growth in public expenditure on health and in the proportion of national incomes devoted to it, as Tables 1 and 2 show. Two factors explain most of this upward surge. First, spending went up as countries expanded the coverage of their national health care systems to the whole population: a self-limiting cause of growth, since it ceased to operate once 100% coverage had been achieved. Second, the cost of providing health care was becoming more expensive relative to the cost of producing other goods in the economies concerned: a trend which has continued to exert upward pressure on budgets. Subsequent to the mid-seventies, the rate of increase slowed down, although the proportion of the national income absorbed by public expenditure on health care continued to rise albeit more slowly. Indeed in some countries, as Table 3 shows, the proportion of the Gross Domestic Product devoted to it actually fell.

It is tempting, therefore, to see concern about the 'health care cost explosion' — the phrase that launched a thousand conferences and studies from the mid-seventies onward — as merely one item on the international agenda of concern about the Welfare State: one facet of the larger picture. But this would be a mistake. The continuing, unresolved debate about the organization and financing of health care systems that has characterized the past 25 years is more than a by-product of the general rhetoric of crisis. It also reflects the special features of health care.

The income maintenance programs that constitute the heartland of Welfare States involve shuffling money according to rules of entitlement laid down by central governments. If governments seek to retrench, they can change the rules of entitlement: a politically difficult and sensitive task but one which, as we have seen, has been carried out successfully in many countries. Health care is different in that, like education, it is a service-delivery program where public policy determines access to services but professionals decide what treatment will be delivered. Moreover, it is also a program — unlike education — where technology creates new demands rather than cutting costs: hence the tendency, noted above, for health care productivity to lag behind productivity in the economy at large, inflating unit costs as the intensity of treatment increases. Lastly, it is a program where supply tends to create demand. Even countries like Britain — the paradigm example of a country which controlled the budget so successfully that the NHS was frequently alleged to be suffering from a crisis of under-funding — therefore worried about the efficiency with which health care resources were being used.

These special characteristics of health care have shaped the international debate and the policies of individual countries. The crisis of health care — to the extent that there is one — has been seen as a crisis of control: a challenge to governments to impose fiscal discipline on the professionals delivering the service and on the pharmaceutical companies producing drugs. The efficiency and effectiveness with which resources were being used, as much as the total expenditure, became the focus of concern. In other words, while the upwards surge of income maintenance programs could be restrained by the incremental fine-tuning of entitlements, checking the momentum of health care spending required politically more visible interventions by governments that threatened the strongly organized interest groups — professional and others — created by the health care systems themselves. The clashes often precipitated by these interventions fed, in turn, the sense of crisis.

The effects of fiscal stress were compounded by the intellectual re-assessment of health care that also characterized the period. The arguments mirrored those deployed in the wider Welfare State debate: the effects of public provision of health care, it was asserted, were either perverse or futile (and often both). On the one hand, medical intervention might damage its supposed beneficiaries, just as income support created dependence. Self-interest rather than science drove medical practice, it was argued. On the other hand, medical intervention appeared to have only a tenuous relationship with the health of the population. If the aim of public policy was to improve a nation's health, then there were better ways of achieving this than by spending money on health care systems. In short, increasing intellectual skepticism about health care appeared to provide legitimacy for governmental policies of seeking greater control over the delivery of health care.

It is beyond the scope of this chapter to review in detail the various policies, bearing on both the supply of and demand for health care, adopted in different countries. But, oversimplifying only a little, it is possible to distinguish between two phases. The first, lasting until the late eighties, took the form of change within existing institutional frameworks. The measures ranged from controlling the price of drugs to restricting the freedom of doctors to prescribe; from imposing higher user charges to limiting the number of hospital beds and new technologies. The second, which is still unfolding, took the form of institutional reform. The emphasis switched from strengthening the direct capacity of central governments to control and plan the delivery of health care to re-designing health care systems so that the forces of competition would bring about the gains in efficiency that direct intervention had seemingly failed to deliver.

The shift from the language of planning to that of the market marked a transformation of the intellectual landscape. And it points to a curious paradox. This is that the international debate about health care has increasingly been shaped by ideas drawn from the country which has been least successful in controlling costs: the United States. Among advanced industrialized countries, the US is unique in that it both spends a higher proportion of the GDP (though not of public expenditure) on health care than any other nation but has failed to provide universal coverage for its population. The political failure to devise a comprehensive health care system where effective central budgetary control is possible has, in turn, lead to a reliance on market forces to do the work that government cannot. In a sense, the vocabulary of the market is an admission of the limits of government power in shaping the delivery of health care.

But the paradox — of American ideas being exported to countries which, in comparison, have been successful in both providing comprehensive services and restraining the rise in spending — is more apparent than real. For health care, to reiterate, is different from other Welfare State programs in that the international concern is as much with improving efficiency and effectiveness as with controlling the upward rise in spending. And it is the United States which, given its failure in the macro-management of the health care budget, has of necessity developed most experience in the micro-management of resources. It is also the United States which provides the outstanding example of scarcity amidst profligacy — inadequacies in both access and treatment despite a soaring budget — so allowing the prophets of scarcity, the economists, to take the lead in shaping the health care debate: again an international phenomenon.

Although the language of competition has become international, the use of a shared vocabulary disguises wide variations in the policies actually pursued in different countries. There are common themes. One such is competition between both purchasers and providers of health care, so introducing incentives for sensitivity to both prices and quality. Another is the concept of managed care which is all the more seductive for being capable of many interpretations, but essentially revolves around the notion of a single agent being responsible for the use of a fixed budget for the treatment of patients and therefore having an incentive to ensure that the resources are used efficiently and effectively. But despite rhetorical convergence on such themes — in New Zealand, Britain, Sweden and the Netherlands, as well as the United States — there is as yet little evidence of convergence in the policies adopted. International ideas are adapted to national circumstances, incrementally introduced and often transformed in the process.

Most fundamentally, however, there is no evidence that the countries involved in such experiments are weakening in their commitment to universal health care systems financed out of taxation or by comprehensive national insurance schemes. In common with the wider Welfare State, there have been significant changes in perceptions and the currency of discourse. In health care, however, the emphasis so far has been on changing the dynamics of the systems of health care provision rather than redirecting the welfare effort. Whether or not these adaptive changes lead to more fundamental transformations is, once again, an open question. And uncertainty is compounded in the case of health care because — in contrast to income maintenance programs — change is often driven from the bottom upward by developments in medical technology and organization. Not only may governments modify the behavior of health care providers but the providers may themselves modify the policy options available to governments.

## REFERENCES

1.   OECD, *Public Expenditure Trends.* (Paris: OECD, 1978).
2.   Paul Pierson, *Dismantling the Welfare State?* (Cambridge: Cambridge University Press, 1994).
3.   Albert Hirschman, *The Rhetoric of Reaction.* (Cambridge, Mass.: Harvard University Press, 1991).
4.   OECD, *Social Expenditure Statistics of OECD Member Countries.* (Paris: OECD, 1996).
5.   OECD, *New Orientations for Social Policy.* (Paris: OECD, 1994a).
6.   Marmor, Theodore, Mashaw, Jerry and Harvey, Philip, *America's Misunderstood Welfare State.* (New York: Basic Books, 1990).
7.   McLaughlin, Eithne, *Mortgaging the Future? The problem of developing sustainable social policies. Inaugural Lecture.* (Belfast: The Queen's University Mimeo, 1996).
8.   Commission of the European Communities, *European Social Policy: Options for the Union.* (Luxembourg: Office for Official Publications of the European Communities, 1993).
9.   Commission on Social Justice, *Social Justice: Strategies for National Renewal.* (London: Vintage, 1994).

## FUTURE READING

Adema, Willem, *et al., Net Public Social Expenditures. Labour Market and Social Policy Occasional Papers No. 19.* (Paris: Organization for Economic Co-operation and Development, 1996).

Atkinson, A.B., *The Welfare State and Economic Performance.* (London: Suntory-Toyota International Centre for Economics and Related Disciplines, London School of Economics, 1995).

Baldwin, Peter, *The Politics of Social Solidarity.* (Cambridge: Cambridge University Press, 1990).

Coughlin, Richard, *Ideology, Public Opinion & Welfare Policy.* (Berkeley: Institute of International Studies, University of California, 1980).

Esping-Andersen, Gosta, *Welfare States in Transition.* (London: Sage, 1996).

Fox, Daniel, *Economists and Health Care.* (New York: Prodist, 1974).

Goodin, Robert and Le Grand, Julian, *Not Only the Poor.* (London: Allen & Unwin, 1987).

Ham, Chris (ed.), *Health Care Reform: Learning from the International Experience.* (Buckingham: Open University Press, 1997).

Hirst, Paul and Thompson, Grahame, *Globalization in Question.* (Cambridge: Polity Press, 1996).

Jones, Catherine (ed.), *New Perspectives on the Welfare State in Europe.* (London: Routledge, 1993).

Klein, Rudolf and O'Higgins, Michael (eds), *the Future of Welfare.* (Oxford: Basil Blackwell, 1985).

Lalonde, Marc, *A New Perspective on the Health of Canadians.* (Ottawa: Information Canada, 1974).

Le Grand, Julian, *The Strategy of Equality.* (London: Allen & Unwin, 1982).

Lindberg, Leon and Maier, Charles S. (eds), *The Politics of Inflation and Economic Stagnation.* (Washington: The Brookings Institution, 1985).

Maxwell, Robert, *Health and Wealth.* (Lexington, Mass.: Lexington Books, 1981).

Millar, Jane and Bradshaw, Jonathan (eds), *Social Welfare Systems: Towards a Research Agenda.* (Bath: Centre for the Analysis of Social Policy, University of Bath, 1996).

OECD, *Public Expenditure on Health.* (Paris: OECD, 1977).

OECD, *The Welfare State in Crisis.* (Paris: OECD, 1981).

OECD, *Social Expenditures, 1960–1985.* (Paris: OECD, 1985).

OECD, *Health Care Systems in Transition: The Search for Efficiency.* (Paris: OECD, 1990).

OECD, *The Reform of Health Care: A Comparative Analysis of Seven OECD Countries.* (Paris: OECD, 1992).

OECD, *The Reform of Health Care Systems: A Review of Seventeen OECD Countries.* (Paris: OECD, 1994b).

Pierson, C., *Beyond the Welfare State?* (Cambridge: Polity Press, 1991).

Rose, Richard and Peters, Guy, *Can Government Go Bankrupt?* (London: Macmillan, 1979).

Saltman, Richad B. and Figueras, Josep (eds), *European Health Care Reform.* (Copenhagen: World Health Organization, Regional Office for Europe, 1997).

Wilensky, Harold, *The 'New Corporatism', Centralization and the Welfare State.* (London and Beverley Hills: Sage, 1976).

World Health Organization, *European Health Care Reforms: Analysis of Current Strategies.* (Copenhagen: WHO Regional Office for Europe, 1996).

# CHAPTER 12

# Medicine, Technology and Industry

## STUART BLUME

One of the most striking changes which medicine has undergone in the course of the twentieth century is in its technologies. Hospitals have been literally filled with instruments. Not that the notion of instruments as aids to the senses was new a century ago. The late-nineteenth century physician could make use of, for example, the stethoscope or the ophthalmoscope in his diagnostic work, whilst the thermometer enabled him to generate a much more precise and apparently objective record of a patient's temperature. But gradually, as medical technology (the term 'instrument' becomes less appropriate) became a key determinant of the structure of medical work, it became something more than the accoutrements of individual practice. Hospitals began to invest in devices which took more and more space, required specialized technicians to keep them in working order, and began to constrain the very architecture of the hospital. Think of today's instrument-filled intensive care unit, or the PET scanner with its dedicated cyclotron, or the computer systems on which both depend. But think too of the quite different kinds of technologies which microelectronics and the development of new materials have brought with them: artificial substitutes for internal organs for example, or myoelectric prostheses. The locus operandi of medical technology is no longer the hospital alone. For some, 'bionic man' is a walking testament to the achievements of science based medicine. For others, as we shall see, he is the source of a profound disquiet.

There is no simple answer to why all this has occurred, not only because many factors are involved, but also because the dynamics of the process have changed. From the perceptual level to the economic, the significance of technology has changed so dramatically that both profession and industry respond very differently to novelty than once they did. Perhaps X-ray (or roentgen) technology was a turning point. One historian has suggested that the cultural impact of this device was such as to bring about a shift from hygiene and social improvement to "miracle technology" as the basis of hope in a healthier future.[1] For Howell the importance of this technology lies in the reorganization of hospital work, and the increasing identification of professional interests with technology which it presaged. These changes, cultural and organizational, lie at the heart of technological medicine, emerging in the first third of the twentieth century. The trauma of World War II, wartime experience in applying science, the emergence of antibiotics: all enhanced faith in the benefits of science-based technology still further. The end of hostilities provoked a search for new applications (and markets) for technical and scientific skills developed in the war. Growing in scale, hospital medicine became an increasing focus for entrepreneurial activity. Government policies, committed to enhancing the quality of health care, typically took for granted that the more sophisticated the technology the better the care. In the 1970s this boundless technological optimism came to be questioned. Expenditures on health care were rising dramatically, with technical change apparently a major culprit. Is more technology necessarily reflected in better outcomes? Concerned by uncontrollably rising costs, governments began to search for ways of 'rationalizing' the introduction of new devices through regulation and financial restraints. At the same time new and critical voices began to make themselves heard: patient groups, feminists and sociologists all began to ask new kinds of questions about the impact of technological change both on the quality and the very aspirations of health care. Finally, the rising costs of bringing a new device on to the market, combined with the more complex political environment, were gradually forcing manufacturers to reconsider their strategies for the development of new medical technologies.

## The Rise of Technological Medicine

Howell has argued that the careers of two devices — X-ray technology and the electrocardiograph (ECG) — exemplify the changing position of technology within the practice of medical care. Both show with what difficulty the organization and practice of early-twentieth century medicine accommodated radically new ways of representing disease. Analysis of their uses and the testimonies of those who used them show that, however sophisticated the research, the routine practice of medicine was slow to change. Here, as in so much of European life, World War I shattered many old certainties. Industrial growth, and economic and social transformation more generally, were posing new questions of the medical profession. Such questions concerned less the precise interpretation of perceptible signs than the health assessment of individuals showing no signs of apparent ill-health. How fitted for work, or for military service, was a given category of men? Who would be offered health insurance, and at what price? A new realm of medical practice was opening, and it implied a need for large scale, and supposedly objective, methods of determining the health status of populations. As markets became ever larger, and with growing specialization, the manufacture of medical technologies changed too. More subtly, clinical experience became a formative influence upon the process of technological innovation itself.

In January 1896 Wilhelm Roentgen, Professor of Physics at the University of Würtzburg, published a paper with the title 'Uber eine Neue Art von Strahlen.' With its accompanying X-ray 'photograph' of his wife's hand, showing bones and ring, the paper attracted attention far beyond the scientific community. The story spread through the world's newspapers like wildfire, and the idea that it must now be possible to view the inner structures of the human body captured the world's imagination.

What was the fascination of the new technology? The X-ray was only one of a variety of new modes of visualization emerging at that time. The distinction between 'medical' techniques like X-ray and those of popular entertainment like the moving picture was far less clear cut than it seems to us now. Arguing against historians who have seen turn-of-the-century imaging techniques as a further extension of the clinician's visual senses, Cartwright argues for "a radically new visual sensibility" manifest as much in cinematography as in X-ray.[2] Industrialization, the desire to make optimum use of the physical powers of the working man, was provoking new approaches to understanding the working of the 'human motor.' Photography and the moving picture were pressed into the service of a new industrially-oriented physiology by EJ Marey and his followers, thus paving the way for a medicine still further dependent on new technologies of representation. But the path was to prove a stony one.

Anyone with access to a physics laboratory could try Roentgen's experiment, and many did. The remarkable powers of the rays became a source of popular entertainment, and an X-ray photograph something to be prized by the woman of fashion. Physicists, engineers and physicians were no less fascinated, and their investigations were pursued widely and with enthusiasm. Surgeons in particular, practical men more oriented to tools than their physician-colleagues, were rapidly convinced of the value of the new device. Often, a "local doctor or surgeon with a suitable case, usually a needle lodged in the patient's finger or foot, would seek the help of a science professor in the local college or university, and together they would produce a radiograph."[3]

Roentgen refused many financial incentives to patent his discovery, so that the apparatus could be freely produced. With remarkable speed, a thriving and dynamic X-ray industry came into being. Many early X-ray manufacturers were small, long-established makers of scientific instruments. One which was not was the General Electric Company already a very large corporation into which, in 1892, Thomas Edison's manufacturing interests had been merged. E.W. Rice, a GE Vice-President, was soon convinced that a market for X-ray tubes and apparatus existed. In March 1896 he asked Elihu Thomson to design an X-ray apparatus (tube plus high frequency coil to power it) suitable for commercial sale. Within a month GE "began to place large advertisements in electrical trade journals."[4] By August 1896 the firm's catalogue listed a full range of X-ray products: the new tube, excitation apparatus, interrupters, and other accessories. There was confidence that with their existing network of salesmen they would be able to reach the market among doctors, hospitals and scientific laboratories which they envisaged.

Early instruments were highly unreliable ("globes of glass surrounded by zones of profanity," one early practitioner called them),[5] and manufacturers with the necessary resources put considerable effort into improving their durability, quality and performance. This was the case with General Electric, where Thomson continued to work on improving the firm's X-ray products. Significantly, in the light of later developments, Thomson's work was inspired less by others' experience in using the device in a clinical setting (of which Thomson was aware) than by his own knowledge of the relevant physics.

The customers for this equipment were not only physicians, but physicists, engineers, electricians and photographers too. As hospitals gradually began to acquire X-ray equipment, it was not always a physician who was appointed to use it (in so far as it was used at all). The first medically qualified roentgenologists were very well aware both of the way in which physicians and surgeons viewed their place in the medical scheme of things and of the problem posed by the medically unqualified. The attempt to establish their own specialized medical role would have to be fought on two fronts. Even where, as in the larger British hospitals, a medical man was in charge of X-ray work, he was generally regarded as a technician. As AE Barclay (who started his practice in Manchester in 1906) recalled "It was only slowly that his colleagues came to recognize that the radiologist's constant experience in interpretation made his opinion on X-ray plates of real value", yet by 1914 there were still very few who had attained anything approximating to consultant relations with their colleagues.[6] Whilst in practice the roentgenologist might only be consulted where a foreign body had to be located, his research interest was extending far beyond this: seeking to translate existing symptoms of pathology into the terms of his new technology. As Barclay's recollections attest, clinicians, especially the elite of the medical profession with a vested interest in the status quo, reacted sceptically or hostilely. Perhaps, as Lawrence has suggested, new technologies seemed to symbolize a science-based form of medical practice which threatened the authority of their clinical judgement and as a consequence their status.

A struggle between competing intellectual approaches more obviously affected the reception of the electrocardiograph, developed by Dutch physiologist Willem van Einthoven at the turn of the century. The attempt to graphically represent the dynamic function of the heart was not original to Einthoven. Marey had invented a 'sphygmograph' to record pressure changes in the heart in 1860. Produced by one of France's leading precision watch-makers, the sphygmograph was widely known. What Einthoven did was to develop a much more sensitive galvanometer for recording the heart's electrical activity. Unlike the Roentgen apparatus Einthoven's instrument was very difficult indeed to build. And unlike Roentgen, Einthoven took a keen interest in its production. When other physiologists wanted him to build similar instruments for them Einthoven, who did not wish to see his workshop become a manufactory, sought a company to manufacture the instrument. After an approach to Siemens and Halske proved abortive, Einthoven reached agreement with Munich instrument maker Max Edelmann in 1903. Edelmann would manufacture and market the galvanometer and would pay Einthoven a royalty for each one sold. When, in early 1907, Edelmann found that he could improve on Einthoven's design he stopped paying the royalty. Disturbed and upset, Einthoven refused to have anything more to do with Edelmann, and approached Horace Darwin, youngest son of Charles and a director of the Cambridge Scientific Instrument Company (CSIC).

Looking to improve Einthoven's rather fragile and easily disturbed instrument, in 1907 the CSIC produced its 'Einthoven String Galvanometer.' The Company's catalogue pointed out that whilst the instrument had been developed for physiological work, it might be used wherever records of small alternating or pulsed currents were required. A long paper published by Einthoven in 1908 is said to have persuaded the Company of the utility of the device for diagnostic medicine. Further design work began, and the string galvanometer was incorporated into a complete electrocardiograph, the first of which was sold in 1908. The instrument was still cumbersome and could not be moved to the bedside, although further development work led to a 'table model' electrocardiograph in 1911, a prototype of which was loaned to (Sir) Thomas Lewis at University College Hospital, London. The eminent cardiologist played a central role in establishing the diagnostic utility of the device and in advising CSIC on its further improvement. Between 1911 and the outbreak of war in 1914 some 35 electrocardiographs were sold, of which ten went to the US. Although by this time other companies were also manufacturing electrocardiographs, production was still on a very small scale. The instrument was still seen principally as something for physiological research, rather than clinical practice.

Resistance to the introduction of the electrocardiograph derived not only from a general antipathy towards new technology, but also from specific and conflicting approaches to heart pathology. Use of an instrument like Einthoven's, which had its origins in physiological investigation, went hand in hand with a functional approach to heart disease: a 'New Cardiology,' beginning to develop in the 1880s. By contrast the dominant view was based in morbid anatomy, with heart pathologies distinguished in structural rather than functional terms. Emphasis on physiological functioning of the heart, associated with the 'New Cardiology,' was not universally welcomed:

> When the first ECG machine was installed at St Bartholomew's Hospital, it was placed in the physiology department, so as not, it was said, to 'offend too brusquely the susceptibilities of more conservative colleagues.' Sir Ian Hill remembered that "Those who, like myself, experimented with this instrument were thought to be rather dangerous backroom boys, unfit to be trusted with the welfare of patients."[7]

As far as roentgenology in particular was concerned, World War I was a watershed. The technology proved itself on the battlefield, and inummerable physicians returned home convinced of the value of the device. Industrialists had also been impressed by the military demand for X-ray equipment, so that General Electric for example, which stopped production of X-ray equipment around 1905, decided after the war that they should become a "full line X-ray equipment supplier."[8] Philips, the Dutch manufacturer of light bulbs, drew on its expertise with this technology first to repair and subsequently to produce X-ray tubes. Subsequently an X-ray research laboratory was established, and contact made with the Hamburg manufacturer CHF Müller (which Philips subsequently took over as part of its move into X-ray supply).

Competition between a large number of manufacturers, combined with the heterogeneity of their customers, gave rise to practices which were seen as inhibiting efforts at creating a clinical speciality. Thus Dr AU Desjardins, from the Mayo Clinic, argued that

> The trend of development in the technic of roentgenography has been marked chiefly by the constant endeavour of manufacturers to produce generators the operation of which would be so simple that an increasing number of physicians would be impelled to purchase them, regardless of their lack of that extensive body of special medical and physical knowledge necessary to take full and intelligent advantage of the possibilities of roentgenography...[9]

The inter-war years were essentially a period of consolidation. Radiological devices were gradually adapted to the exigencies of specialist practice and were also becoming routine features of hospital medicine. Specialization — seen by some authors as an important stimulus to innovation — was proceeding apace, though more rapidly in some countries than others. As specialist radiologists succeeded in taking control of diagnostic imaging (both in the hospital and, subsequently, in community and works-based screening programs), manufacturers began to attune product-improvement to the needs of this more homogeneous body of users. It is by virtue of these changes that we can talk of an inter-organizational field coming into being: a field of shared interest in technological advance in which manufacturers and their professional clients made common cause. Technological innovation was to their mutual advantage: attesting and adding to the status and the profits of each. This symbiosis of interests was markedly to influence the development of new imaging technologies decades later.

## THE MEDICAL INDUSTRIAL COMPLEX

Inspired by the technological successes of the Second World War — the atomic bomb of course, but also radar and computing — in the 1950s visions of a healthier future became increasingly technological. At a time of shortage and of reconstruction, of war-weary populations, and of the beginnings of the cold-war, technology seemed to promise so much. The field of health was no exception. David Sarnoff, chairman of Radio Corporation of America (RCA) pictured a future in which "miniaturized electronic substitutes will be developed to serve as long-term replacements for organs that have become defective through injury or age …. It is not too far-fetched to imagine a man leading a normal life with one or more vital organs replaced by the refined substitutes of the future."[10]

Many elements combined to reshape the relations between medicine and technology. Visions such as Sarnoff's were one. The search for new uses for skills and knowledge acquired during the war was another. Governments' determination to extend access to high quality health care was a third. From the late 1940s high quality health care was becoming available to millions who, before the war, would not have had access to it. Where neither the provider of care nor the recipient had to worry about the costs (increasingly covered by the health service or insurer) ready recourse to the most sophisticated treatments seemed unproblematic. Driven both by idealism and by the search for profits, entrepreneurial activity was increasingly addressed to the health care system. Much of what subsequently occurred can be viewed as the systematic attempt to redeploy skills, technologies, and knowledge developed in the war into medicine. But the changing scale of hospital work, the need to organize it more effectively, was a different but no less important stimulus to innovation, as illustrated by the development of the 'Autoanalyzer.'

Analysis of body fluids for diagnostic purposes had been a standard feature of hopital work for decades, but the instrumentation used had invariably been developed for other analytical chemical purposes. Only in the 1950s, with the growing demand for an increasing range of tests, did the field seem ripe for entrepreneurial activity.

Leonard Skeggs, a Cleveland (Ohio) biochemist who also ran the local VA hospital's chemistry laboratory, faced with an increasing work load and inadequate staffing, set about trying to develop an instrument that could analyse blood on a continuous flow basis. Between 1951 and 1954 Dr Skeggs showed his prototype to four companies, all of which turned him down. In the early 1940s industry could not yet conceive of hospitals investing in such expensive instrumentation for the laboratory. Finally, in February 1954, a small company named Technicon, which had been in the health field since 1939, purchased the technology and went on to develop the 'Autoanalyzer' commercially. It remained the only automated blood chemistry analyzer on the market until 1963.

Throughout this time clinical laboratory testing, and its costs, rose inexorably. Numbers of tests (for example in the area of prenatal care) were rising rapidly, and the market for clinical chemistry equipment was beginning to look attractive. Within five years some thirty automatic or semi-automatic systems were developed worldwide. Of these, Union Carbide's 'Centrifichem' system (based on technology developed at the Oak Ridge National Laboratory, which was managed by Union Carbide) was Technicon's major competitor. Dow Corning and DuPont were two other major corporations which entered this field. The industry had grown and become intensely competitive. Technicon, which had grown from a small family business into a multimillion dollar corporation, was subsequently taken over by a still larger firm (Revlon).

Other examples suggest the search for medical applications of a technology, rather than an operational problem, as the initial stimulus. But as we follow the innovation process the differences become less clear-cut. Whatever the initial stimulus, in both cases we find attempts being made to marry perceptions of technological possibilities with clinical needs. Let us look at two intriguing examples of this interplay between the technically-driven search for clinical applications on the one hand, and clinical priorities and concerns on the other.

The influence of wartime experience on the development of diagnostic ultrasound was profound. Sonar and radar, as new technologies, had proven remarkably effective means of spatial localization, so it is perhaps not surprising that analogies with mapping the human body were drawn. Both skills and components were available. Clinical pioneers who, in the 1950s, began to interest themselves in the diagnostic possibilities of very high frequency sound beams had quite different conceptions of what the medical uses of ultrasound might be, depending on their specific clinical specialty. Research on diagnostic ultrasound proceeded in parallel in radiology, neurology, ophthalmology, cardiology, and obstetrics, but it is in obstetrics and gynecology that the technology has become particularly familiar. In the mid-1950s Ian Donald at the University of Glasgow started to explore gynecological applications of ultrasound. By 1956, working together with Tom Brown, an engineer employed by Kelvin Hughes, a device had been developed which appeared to provide new and useful information on the female abdomen. Given concerns of the time with the dangers of obstetric radiography, ultrasound (which did not make use of ionizing radiation) seemed to offer attractive possibilities for obstetric use. Despite an early order from the British Ministry of Health for 5 prototypes there was still a long road ahead before this work would lead to a commercially available echoscope for obstetrics. The reasons had to do both with industrial rationalization, then proceeding apace, and with developments in electronics. Corporate rationalization led Smiths Industries, which had taken over Kelvin Hughes, to sell off its ultrasound work to a Scottish based firm, Nuclear Enterprises. The new owners held back on commercial production largely because of uncertainties in the face of the development of new electronics. It was only in 1972 that the device which had been developed from Brown and Donald's work — who had begun to work together 16 years earlier — finally reached the market (as the Diasonograph). By this time many obstetricians were claiming that all pregnant women should be given an ultrasonic scan, and use of the technique was rising rapidly.

Medical lasers, slightly later, also show the importance of experience built up during the war. When the first working laser was built in 1960 it was expected to have many applications: an explosion of interest, both academic and industrial, led to commercial lasers becoming available by 1961. At this time ophthalmologists began to investigate its possibilities for treating detachment of the retina. (The use of an intense light source for 'photocoagulation' had been tried in the 1950s, and in 1959 Zeiss developed and marketed a 'photocoagulator' using a xenon lamp.) Two groups began to work with the laser as a therapeutic device: one at Columbia-Presbyterian Medical Center in collaboration with the American Optical Corporation, and one involving Stanford University clinicians and Dr Narinder Kapany, a physicist who founded the company Optics Technology in 1960. At an AMA meeting of June 1964 the Stanford researchers presented work on 25 patients who had been treated with the laser. Despite the fact that almost no one had ever heard of a laser, physicians were impressed: 'It went like wildfire.' Although it was recognized that much more research on safety was needed, by 1963 both American Optical and Optics Technology were marketing ophthalmic lasers. The future, however, was to lie not with the ruby laser which these companies were making, but with the argon laser, which produces laser light of a different frequency, and which was developed initially by Bell Labs. In 1969 Coherent Incorporated started to produce and market ophthalmic argon lasers according to the Bell designs. Neither American Optical nor Optics Technology moved into argon lasers. From the late 1960s, surgical lasers were tried out in one speciality after another, and although applications of the laser were found in otolaryngology, gastroenterology, and many other specialities, it is in opthalmology that it continued to find most widespread use.

Through the 1940s, '50s and '60s the medical technology industry had not only grown but also changed dramatically in its structure. The manufacture of X-ray imaging equipment, by now the most important market segment, had become highly concentrated by the 1950s, as small producers had merged or been taken over. Growth and concentration continued. The US market for X-ray equipment was of the order of $500 million in 1978, with five firms having 96% of sales. Additionally, there were many small firms either making less technology-intensive products (for example disposables), or using highly specialized expertize to create new markets. Technicare and Optics Technology are examples of the latter process.

The power of the X-ray industry, able to capitalize on substantial resources as well as on its longstanding and mutually rewarding relationships with the radiological profession, shows itself nowhere more clearly than in regard to yet another important breakthrough: what became the CT scanner. This device was born of the idea of marrying X-ray technology with information–processing technology. Computer reconstruction of the data generated by X-ray images should provide clinicians with far more detailed morphological information without dangerously increasing dosage. At the end of the 1960s, when this work began, the idea of using computer technology to improve the quality of health care was very much in the air.

CT scanning was initially conceived and developed by (Sir) Godfrey Hounsfield in the central research laboratory of EMI: a British company which had made enormous profits from the sales of Beatles records and was in search of new markets. EMI had no experience of the market for medical equipment. In contrast to ultrasound, where development had proceeded in parallel in a number of specialities, here the objective was to develop an instrument for (neuro)radiological imaging. The CT scanner was destined for success even before it became available on the market in 1973. Agreement was rapidly reached regarding the relevance of the new technology for radiological practice, as well as over improvement to the first prototype. The enthusiasm of radiologists, the rapid volume of sales, provoked two important responses. On the one hand the established suppliers of radiological equipment tried to gain control of the new technology: they used their vast resources and clinical connections to increase the rate of innovation to far beyond what EMI (or other smaller and early entrants to the market) could afford. After head scanners, whole body scanners were developed and the speed of imaging was constantly increased. Smaller firms (including EMI) were forced to quit the market. Whereas in 1973–4 some 5 instruments per month were being installed in American hospitals, by 1975–6 this had increased to 19 per month, each costing of the order of $500,000. Governments, initially in the US, began to express concern at the cost implications of this new, promising — but as yet far from proven — technology.

Despite the differences to which I have alluded, these developments have one thing in common. Each in one way or another led to an innovation in hospital practice: a new mode of diagnosis, a new form of surgery, a more efficient way of providing large numbers of chemical analyses. With the emergence of micro-electronics, and of new (biocompatible) materials, what would subsequently appear as a quite different area of innovation also emerged. When the cardiac 'pacemaker' was first developed it too was viewed as yet another piece of hospital equipment: the notion of implant technology, whatever the dreams of visionaries like Sarnoff, was as yet unfamiliar. In the late 1950s surgeons asked Earl Bakken, an engineer who repaired electronic equipment at the Minnesota medical school, if he could make a small battery-powered pulse generator, for temporary use with children who had had open-heart surgery. Bakken and his brother set up a small firm, Medtronic Inc, which soon became the world's largest manufacturer of pacemakers. But because the pacemaker was principally seen as useful in relation to a rare heart disease or postsurgical heart block, that is for use in hospitals, large firms left the market to small speciality firms, such as Electrodyne and Medtronic, that already had relationships with medical research teams. Later, when the notion of the pacemaker as we know it today emerged — a totally implanted device intended permanently to supplement the heart — these firms were able to take advantage of the new conditions. Sales of cardiac pacemakers in the United States rose from 2–3,000 in 1965 to around 75,000 a decade later. Novelty emerged, as it were, later, as the pacemaker came to be viewed as a permanent part of the patient's body. Sarnoff's dream was becoming reality, and a whole new area of implants was emerging. The notion of the 'semi-artificial man' was upon us.

Whatever the subsequent cultural resonances of 'bionic man,' it was not the pacemaker but the CT scanner which initially provoked reconsideration of medicine's growing reliance on technology. A paper published in 1977 argued that acquisition of CT scanners was running far ahead of real proof of their clinical benefits. Did acquisition of such devices reflect principally user-enthusiasm, and perhaps research opportunities, rather than clinical advantage? Exemplifying an increasingly sceptical attitude to new technology, medical sociologist John McKinlay offered an only slightly ironic picture of the way in which new medical technologies entered practice. McKinlay painted a picture of vaguely grounded enthusiasm, based principally on initially promising reports, media exaggeration, and the gradual aggregation of professional and commercial interests around the new device. Formal evaluation of what the technology actually did, if ever carried out, was generally too late to impact on its diffusion. The CT scanner, with it enormous costs, was a case in point.

## New Complexity

By the mid-late 1970s health care costs were rising alarmingly, with the attempt to control them a major preoccupation of policy makers. Medical computing precisely exemplifies the shift in concerns. Where in the 1960s the principal concern had been with enhancing the quality of diagnosis, of clinical decision-making, by the mid-seventies computer systems were being promoted "for their ability to lower costs, to coordinate services on a broader institutional and inter-institutional level, and to allocate and reorganize medical services."[11] Rationalization of resource use was the key question.

Health economists were consistently arguing that new technology was responsible for a good deal of the cost inflation. If this were so, and if new devices were really being accepted and introduced for reasons which had more to do with technological enthusiasm than proven benefit, there seemed to be scope for rationalization. These considerations, sparked in particular by the rapid diffusion of expensive CT scanners, provided one stimulus to government rethinking. A second, more political, was public controversy over the possible danger of devices which had already entered widespread use. Politicians are particularly sensitive to possible risks to healthy populations of biological and pharmaceutical products. The 1970s had seen rapid expansion in the market for 'home-use' technologies, such as pregnancy tests and new contraceptive devices. It was one of these latter, the Dalkon Shield, which provoked particular controversy when its dangers became apparent. Politicians felt that action was required, and the United States Congress moved to extend the regulatory powers of the FDA from drugs to medical devices. The Medical Device Amendments of 1976 gave the FDA responsibility for evaluating new devices during all phases of development, testing and use. For one of the three classes of devices defined by law reviews similar to those traditionally applied to drugs would be obligatory: manufacturers would have to supply comprehensive information regarding the safety and efficacy of the new device at substantial cost in terms of time and money.

The general opinion, both among industrialists and policy analysts, is that this legislation did not greatly affect either the market or the innovation process. Indeed, since considerable data were needed in order to make a convincing case to the FDA, manufacturers were obliged to cooperate, perhaps still more urgently than before, with clinicians who could gather the data from patients. It has been suggested that this need to collaborate, and the incentives offered by manufacturers, might even have enhanced diffusion.

In addition, many governments sought means of rationalizing the distribution and use of expensive medical technologies. In a state health system such as in Britain this could be done by restricting the resources available for investment in new equipment. Other countries introduced other kinds of controls. In the United States from the early 1970s, individual states were required to introduce 'Certificate of Need' (CoN) laws in order to be eligible for certain Federal subsidies. In the Netherlands, legislation was also introduced in the early 1970s, obliging hospitals to seek permission from the Minister of Health if they planned to provide any one of a published list of expensive technologies (including CT scanners and dialysis machines). In France a still more complex and comprehensive set of controls were introduced in 1970, with national 'maps' showing the planned regional distribution of each of a list of expensive technologies.

Policy analysts soon began to discover that these regulatory measures were not having much effect. The desire of hospitals and doctors to improve their services, and competitive position, were far greater than the disincentives. Where major economic interests were at stake, ways of circumventing legislation were sought — and generally found. In the USA, since CoN controls only applied to hospital inpatient-settings, one approach was to move the facility in question out of the hospital. In the diagnostic imaging field, for example, American physicians started to set up independent 'imaging centers' to provide imaging facilities for hospitals and private physicians. Other services too, including clinical laboratory testing and hemodialysis, both with substantial profit potential, began to be provided outside their traditional hospital base, often on a commercial basis. Manufacturers would sometimes join with their clinical customer-colleagues in seeking ways around legal constraints. Bos suggests that Philips (one of the Netherlands' largest corporations) joined with clinicians in avoiding having magnetic resonance imaging limited by legislation.

If the incentives for manufacturers to innovate were little affected by FDA legislation and CoN, payment systems were to be another matter. In 1983 the US moved to a Medicare payment system in which hospitals would only be reimbursed a predetermined sum for a particular type of procedure. Using an expensive alternative to a cheaper existing form of treatment would no longer generate extra revenue for a hospital. From an industry standpoint, it seems that device R&D is responding to a situation in which hospitals are now greatly concerned with efficiency and (cost)effectiveness:

> incentives have increased for manufacturers to develop technologies that enable care to be moved to alternative, lower cost outpatient settings. Innovative developments such as cathetarization labs, angioplasty, and intraocular lens implants are driven to a great degree by the payment system, as is the production of imaging devices that can be moved about in a mobile van.[12]

Government policies of the late 1970s and early 1980s had begun to problematize medicine's reliance on new technologies and (less explicitly) the nature of those technologies. At the same time a different and more radical questioning of medicine's attachment to technology was emerging. Mounted both from within the medical profession itself (largely from the nonclinical fields of social medicine and public health) as well as by critical observers, this radical discourse has come to draw on a variety of scholarly and social resources. New theoretical perspectives on the 'social construction' of technology, showing the resources, interests and power involved in their making, played a part. Recent research has made disquietingly clear how powerful are the professional and economic interests involved, and how weak the mechanisms of (self) regulation. A growing concern with the rights of patients, viewed increasingly as 'consumers' of health services, added another dimension. So too did critical assessments from the standpoint of traditionally major consumers of medical care: women, for example, the elderly, and disabled persons. Here, technology typically becomes an instrument of professional control: a means of deauthenticating the normal lived experience of giving birth or growing old, or a barrier to the acceptance of physical difference.

Viewing innovation in medical technology not in terms of improved provision of service but of the exercise of professional power is a theme of the past two decades. It is one which has given rise to a substantial and dramatic literature, to which feminist scholars have made major contributions, for example through their analyses of technology in the birth process. The introduction of the fetal monitor, or routine obstetric ultrasound, whatever their contribution to the management of (high risk) labor, can also be read, and experienced, as a violation of something deeply personal and private. At a cultural, rather than psychological, level the routine use of obstetrical ultrasound has been associated with the 'construction' of the fetus as an independent being: letting a woman 'see' her unborn child should encourage bonding and discourage a woman from seeking an abortion. There are other examples of specific medical technologies being criticized by the group which they are intended to help. Deaf communities, for example, have seen the cochlear implant in these terms: as a medical counter attack in the face of deaf people's attempts to have themselves recognized as a distinctive community of sign language users (rather than simply having defective hearing).

We cannot easily say what the effects of these new critical perspectives may be. Although their political significance in some countries may be sufficient to influence use of a technology, their influence on industry, on technological development, is not yet clear. It is claimed that manufacturers are attaching new importance to patient preferences in developing new technologies: but who speaks for the 'patients'? Whatever the practical consequences, it is apparent that both the significance of technology for medical practice, and the relations between clinicians and industry, have been subject to a new problematization. Some clinicians have defended technological medicine by pointing to its many achievements. Others within the medical profession, such as Cassell, have taken a different view:

> Technology holds sway over medicine and its public because of its self-perpetuating character and its enhancement of power, as well as its capacity to induce wonder, root us in the immediate, remove ambiguity, and increase certainty. Since this is not well understood, it is hardly surprising that technology... should be blamed for the troubles it brings. The real culprits, however, are the doctors who use it, the public that loves it, and the narrow knowledge on which it is based. Medical technology's form and character arise from medicine's focus on disease and pathophysiology as the arena in which the origins and solutions to human sickness are to be found.[13]

Neither view has a monopoly on the truth. Medical technology is both effective and problematic. What is surely also true is that in the course of the past century the expectations and the interests associated with medical technologies have changed dramatically. New discourses have emerged. A tale of Willem Kolff, emigrating to the United States just after World War II with the prototype artificial kidney he had put together in German-occupied Holland is a tale for the 1960s. Plough's analysis of kidney dialysis in the United States, showing the influence of commercial interests and the mass media both on practice and on his own attempt at a critical analysis, is a tale for today.

REFERENCES

The author would like to thank Kick Wahlers for his help in the preparation of this chapter.

1. Nancy Knight, '"The new light": X-rays and medical futurism,' in J.J. Corn (ed.), *Imagining Tomorrow*. (Cambridge Mass: MIT Press, 1986), pp. 10–34.

2. L. Cartwright, 'Experiment of destruction: Cinematic inscriptions of physiology,' *Representations* (1992), **40**: 129.

3. E.H. Burrows, *Pioneers and the Early Years: A History of British Radiology*. (Alderney, C.I.: Colophon, 1986), p. 20.

4. B. Carlson, *Innovation as a Social Process*. (Cambridge: Cambridge University Press, 1991), p. 320.

5. Cuthbert Andrews, cited in A.E. Barclay, 'The old order changes,' *British Journal of Radiology* (1949), **22**: 302.

6. Burrows, *op. cit*, p. 179.

7. C. Lawrence 'Moderns and ancients: the "new cardiology" in Britain 1880–1930', *Medical History* (1986), **Supplement No. 5**: 10.

8. L.S. Reich, *The Making of American Industrial Research: Science and Business at GE and Bell, 1876–1926*. (Cambridge: Cambridge University Press, 1985).

9. A.U. Desjardins, 'The low status of radiology in America,' *Journal of the American Medical Asociation* (1929), **92**: 1035.

10. Quoted in K. Jeffrey, 'Pacing the heart: Growth and redefinition of a medical technology, 1952–1975,' *Technology and Culture* (1995), **36**: 595.

11. B. Kaplan, 'The computer prescription: medical computing, public policy, and views of history,' *Science Technology and Human Values* (1995), **20**: 5.

12. B.L. Holmes, 'Current strategies for the development of medical devices' in A.C. Gelijns (ed.), *Technology and Health Care in an Era of Limits* (Volume 3 of *Medical Innovation at the Crossroads*). (Washington DC: National Academy of Sciences Press, 1992), 219–230.

13. E.J. Cassell 'The sorcerer's broom: medicine's rampant technology,' *Hastings Center Report* (1993), p. 23.

## FURTHER READING

Banta, H.D., Behney, C.J. and Willems, J.S., *Toward Rational Technology in Medicine*. (New York: Springer, 1981).

Blume, S.S., *Insight and Industry: the Dynamics of Technological Change in Medicine*. (Cambridge Mass and London: MIT Press, 1992).

Burch, G.E. and DePasquale, N.P., *A History of Electrocardiography*. (San Francisco: Norman Publishing, reprint 1990).

Davis, Audrey D., 'Life insurance and the physical examination: a chapter in the rise of American medical technology,' *Bulletin of the History of Medicine* (1981), **55**: 392.

Foote, S.D., *Managing the Medical Arms Race: Innovation and Public Policy in the Medical Device Industry*. (Berkeley and Los Angeles: California University Press, 1992).

Fox, R.C. and Swazey, J.P., *Spare Parts. Organ Replacement in American Society*. (Oxford: Oxford University Press, 1992).

Hillman, B.J., 'Physicians' acquisition and use of new technology in an era of economic constraints,' in A.C. Gelijns (ed.), *Technology and Health Care in an Era of Limits* (Volume 3 of *Medical Innovation at the Crossroads*). (Washington DC: National Academy of Sciences Press, 1992), 133–151.

Howell, J.D., *Technology in Hospitals*. (Baltimore: Johns Hopkins University Press, 1995).

Lawrence, C., 'Incommunicable knowledge: science, technology and the clinical art in Britain, 1850–1914,' *Journal of Contemporary History* (1985), **20**: 503–520.

Pollack, Petchesky, R., 'Foetal images: the power of visual culture in the politics of reproduction,' in M. Stanworth (ed.), *Reproductive Technologies: Gender, Motherhood and Medicine*. (Cambridge: Polity Press, 1987), 57–80.

Pickstone, J.V. (ed.), *Medical Innovations in Historical Perspective*. (London: Macmillan, 1992).

Plough, A., *Borrowed Time: Artificial Organs and the Politics of Extending Lives*. (Philadelphia: Temple University Press, 1986).

Reiser, S.J., *Medicine and the Reign of Technology*. (Cambridge: Cambridge University Press, 1978).

Spetz, Joanne, 'Physicians and physicists: the interdisciplinary introduction of the laser into medicine,' in N. Rosenberg, A.C. Gelijns and H. Dawkins (eds), *Sources of Medical Technology: Universities and Industry* (Volume 5 of *Medical Innovation at the Crossroads*). (Washington DC: National Academy of Sciences Press, 1995), 41–66.

# CHAPTER 13

# The Historiographical Body

MARK S.R. JENNER AND BERTRAND O. TAITHE

In the last fifteen years 'the history of the body' has become fashionable to the point of ubiquity. Recent studies include titles as various as *Body Politics, Body Criticism, Body Work, The Body Emblazoned, The Body Social,* and *The Body and Samuel Johnson.* This chapter will not and cannot summarize all this diverse literature; rather, it provides a critical review of some of the cultural and intellectual developments which have made the body an important subject for historical inquiry and a central analytical category within research.

Despite its importance as a topic for research, the physical body remains largely absent from the mainstream of historical representation. Professional historians are deeply suspicious of modes of representation based upon bodily practices such as those followed by reenactment societies and sponsored by institutions such as English Heritage or the Museum of Colonial Life at Williamsburg in the United States. Even though such pedagogic techniques are commonplace and greatly valued in primary and secondary education, wielding a sixteenth-century scalpel, or dressing up as Louis Pasteur, is unlikely to enhance your academic reputation within most university departments, no matter how well it might go down with students. Unlike historians of music interested in performance, historians of medicine rarely seek theatrically to recapture and master the manipulative techniques, the precision of hand, and other *non-verbal* embodied skills which were and are at the core of much medical practice, and which, as the French anthropologist Pierre Bourdieu has emphasized, constitute a fundamentally different semiotic register from language. Although, as the seventeenth-century English doctor, Thomas Sydenham, argued, many patients prefer practitioners who cure them by *doing* something, rather than discoursing eruditely and eloquently about their condition, academic history (including the history of medicine) remains, as the historian and literary critic, Hayden White, has emphasized, a *literary* genre largely modelled on nineteenth-century novels.

From where has this sudden surge of interest in the body originated? It is worth stressing at the outset that history did not suddenly turn somatic in a road-to-Paris vision of the French philosopher Michel Foucault. In the standard accounts of this historiographical turn, sociologist, Bryan Turner, and historian, Roy Porter, have presented this new interest in the body on the part of the Western European and American historical professions (it is not noticeably shared by non-Western scholars) as one facet of a generalized narrative of emancipation. In such accounts the history of the body represents a belated recognition of the implications of feminism, the sixties and the death of Victorian sexual hypocrisy, recently tempered by the advent of AIDS. However, these claims to novelty are greatly exaggerated and to a significant extent misplaced.

Firstly, the history of medicine has almost always been concerned with the interpretation of sick bodies. As Georges Canguilhem pointed out, it has been predicated upon the shifting definitions of normativity and normality, the history of the normal and the pathological. Most nineteenth-century historians of medicine, like modern historical epidemiologists, not to mention medical archaeologists studying excavated human remains, emphasize the essential existence of their medical nosology throughout history; they have sought to perform the 'correct' retrospective diagnosis. In the 1890s, for instance, the French doctor and historian of medicine, François Buret, reinterpreted medieval leprosy as syphilis, while in the early 1980s Graham Twigg's *The Black Death* controversially argued that the epidemic was 'really' anthrax. There has thus long been a history of the pathological body. As we explore below, the history of the normal and normative body has by contrast only self-consciously been attempted since Michel Foucault.

The history of manners or *moeurs* (a fashionable topic for research after the translation of Norbert Elias' *The Civilizing Process*) was often the central theme of eighteenth- and nineteenth-century mainstream history writing. Manners, in the work of the Enlightenment philosopher Montesquieu, or the Victorian historian Henry Thomas Buckle, were an all-encompassing category of civilization. Their history concerned itself with bodily comportment as well social and political structures. In Britain, bodily themes such as costume or marital practices were only banished from academic history to become the preserve of the antiquarian or amateur enthusiast in the late-nineteenth and early-twentieth centuries when the discipline became entrenched in the universities and sought to achieve intellectual respectability to rival the allegedly more cerebral faculties of law or theology.

The first generation of the *Annales* school of French historians writing between the two world wars were strikingly preoccupied by bodies. You will find few finer examples of 'body history' than Marc Bloch's discussion of medieval and early modern monarchs' claims to heal scrophula by touching the afflicted, or Lucien Febvre's evocations of the sensory world of the sixteenth century. In Britain popular history writing such as *The Antiquary* series of the early-twentieth century continued this interest in bodily themes; while since the late-nineteenth century collectors and museums of folklife, such as the Castle Museum in York or the *Musée des Arts et Métiers* in Paris have preserved and displayed artefacts relating to the bodily practices of the past and the 'lower orders'.

Museums of ethnography established during the colonial period also stressed the different bodily practices of native populations; more generally colonial exhibitions, medical theories such as physiognomy and the wide distribution of colonialist images sought to ground white European superiority with reference to alleged bodily differences. This condescension of well–fed people to other cultures still permeates many modern views of the past.

The discipline of anthropology emerged hand-in-hand with the colonial enterprise; indeed, physical anthropology provided much of the data which sustained claims to racial superiority. However, from the early twentieth century cultural and social anthropologists, not least Bronislaw Malinowski, Marcel Mauss and, slightly later, Margaret Mead, broke away from some aspects of such unsavory ideologies. Nevertheless their work retained a pronounced focus upon bodies. Righthandedness, culinary habits, forms of bodily adornment and the social practices surrounding birth and sex were seen as expressing wider truths about social organization. This anthropological interest in what Mauss termed "the techniques of the body" has continued throughout the twentieth century,[1] and has had perhaps its greatest impact upon historians, and historians of medicine in particular, through the work of Mary Douglas and Victor Turner, notably *Purity and Danger* (1966) and *The Ritual Process* (1969) respectively.

Moreover, such concerns were not the exclusive domain of anthropologists. Throughout the nineteenth century strands of what are now described as psychology and sociology addressed similar themes. From Henry Mayhew (1856) to Havelock Ellis in *The Criminal* (1891) early sociologists and psychologists drew links between signs on the body and patterns of behaviour, between what they termed 'moral and physical deformities'. Early economic writing was similarly somatic. Political economy, notably the work of Malthus and Ricardo, not to mention Marx, was centrally concerned with the productive and reproductive capacity of human beings, developing the Enlightenment's intense interest in the statistical enumeration and surveying of bodies within particular places. Max Weber's interest in work discipline and in the redirection of asceticism towards production and profit emphasized its physical manifestations.

Unsurprisingly, therefore, the work of many economic historians and historical demographers over the last twenty-five years has paid a great deal of attention to the physical condition of past populations. Some scholars have used height and weight records of military recruits and schoolchildren to examine nutritional standards over time, while the monumental work of the Cambridge Group for the History of Population and Social Structure and other demographers has been centrally concerned with the interaction of the *biological* and physiological characteristics of human beings with changing cultural, ecological and economic circumstances. They have, for instance, argued over the influence of nutritional levels, breast-feeding on women's fertility, and on the susceptibility of populations to infectious diseases.

Moreover, one finds a striking preoccupation with the corporeal in the exciting syntheses of history, anthropology and social theory which characterized the emergence of social history and 'history from below' between the late 1960s and early 1980s. Peter Burke's *Popular Culture in Early Modern Europe* (1978), for instance, was structured around the Carnivalesque figures of Carnival and Lent to be found in *Rabelais and his World* (Eng. trans., 1968), the highly influential study of the Humanist and peasant culture written in the 1930s by the formalist literary critic, Mikhail Bahktin, and the paintings of Breughel. Natalie Zemon Davis influentially explored sixteenth- and seventeenth-century gender norms through a study of transvesticism and the inversion of bodily norms.

While many historians of the medieval and early-modern periods borrowed freely from social anthropology, the new social history of the nineteenth century and early-twentieth century was more influenced by the materialist claims of Marxism. Yet, as Eric Hobsbawn's article on the male and female figure within socialist iconography suggested nearly twenty years ago, the writing of many middle-class Marxist historians was suffused with an intellectualized desire for the beautiful and hard-(working) body of the proletarian. This is perhaps most fully articulated in the autobiography of the French Marxist philosopher, Louis Althusser, when he noted his sense that "I had no body" and yet simultaneously recorded the deep attraction he felt for Marxist theory because "I subscribed to it with my body" and because in it "I discovered a system of thought which acknowledged the primacy ... of ... bodily activity ...."[2]

Although somatic concerns are apparent within the pioneering work of Karl Sudhoff (1853–1938), Henry Sigerist (1891–1957) and Oswei Temkin (b.1902) in the history of (especially ancient and medieval) medicine, the first wave of professional social historians of medicine emerged alongside and in dialogue with the new social history. Charles Rosenberg thus emphasized the body of the patient in a series of studies leading up to *The Care of Strangers*, while the early issues of *Social History* contained a significant number of articles on medical themes such as chlorosis. There are clear parallels between the efforts of social historians to rescue women and the poor from what E.P. Thompson termed the "condescension of posterity"[3] and the critical stance taken towards professional medicine in the historical work of the anti-psychiatric movement of the 1960s and 1970s — notably that of Thomas Szasz and Andrew Scull — and in feminist critiques of medical knowledge by authors as diverse as Barbara Ehrenreich and Dierdre English, Mary Daly and Germaine Greer. Furthermore, many postcolonial historians such as the Subaltern Studies school in India and South East Asia (often directly inspired by Thompson) have denounced the ideological uses of science and medicine in the Imperial context.

Yet none of this work cared to style itself 'the history of the body'. The first question we should ask, therefore, is not why has 'the body' become fashionable, but why has a diverse range of historical and literary inquiry rallied behind this label rather than, say, the history of 'ordinary people', 'women' or the 'working class'?

The best explanation might be that in a post-Marxist and post-structuralist world such appeals to the body provide a more effective rhetorical rallying point than invocations of common class or gender experience. Historians working today often emphasize the role of body as the primary locus upon which power has been and is inscribed. Many contemporary black American poets and novelists as well as historians of slavery have thus foregrounded the whipped and branded body of the slave, while one of the most eloquent and ambitious general statements of this approach is Dorinda Outram's introduction to *The Body and the French Revolution*, where she seeks to make a phenomenology of pain the basis of political action and analysis. "[B]odies", she writes, "are important because the only experiences which cannot be co-opted by political systems are the inevitably personal bodily experiences of individuals."[4]

No matter how great one's sympathy is with this emphasis on the need historically to consider suffering and the ethical implications of the study of the body, many historians in the field would strongly disagree with Outram's contention that the body is a transhistorical category. Such scholars stress that the body is apprehended in radically different ways in different historical contexts and is consequently experienced and treated in wildly varying ways. Outram's own work on how French revolutionaries identified with Stoicism to the point of suicide, not to mention the Christian discourses of martyrdom, indicate that many ideologies are built upon the suffering bodies of their progenitors, and that many people will embrace and act out such agonies. Indeed, what were Freud's reinterpretation of Dora's 'seduction', or hagiographers' rewriting of St. Francis and his stigmata, but effective cooptions of terrible personal and bodily experiences?

This culturalist approach often points to a diversity of anthropological and historical work which has destabilized our understandings of biological 'knowledge'. Anthropologists have demonstrated that beliefs about physiology, let alone the maintenance of health, are widely variable. Contemporary understandings of sexual difference and of the link between sex and reproduction are not cultural universals. Barbara Duden has shown how early-modern women interpreted the internal workings of their bodies as an unpredictable system of flows. While in *Making Sex* (1990), perhaps the most influential work of medical history published in the last two decades, Thomas Laqueur argued that until the late-eighteenth century people interpreted human beings as having one sex but two genders. Mutual orgasm was thus necessary for conception. Contrary to the title of the feminist classic, then, our bodies are not unproblematically our own; for many historians they are only apprehended through culture and above all through discourse.

The body, we might conclude from the juxtaposition of these diametrically opposed approaches, is both supremely real and not real at all, a confusion often compounded in its historiography. 'Body history' has gained its considerable currency in part precisely because of this polyvalency and ambiguity. It appeals because it offers the seductive possibility that we might be able to have our deconstructive cake and eat it too. Histories of the body, or aspects thereof — childbirth, civility, corseting — derive much of their rhetorical purchase by implicating the body of the reader or auditor. The historian can see students wriggle as they somatically register the description of an early modern lithotomy or public execution, and yet his or her argument can also maintain the intellectual terrorism in which everything solid melts into the mist of discourse.

For one important factor in the growth of 'body history' has been the influence of aspects of literary studies and a wider concern with the notion of representation. Indeed overt historical interest in the body has grown in conjunction with a preoccupation with the determining role of discourse in society and/or a stress on the extreme difficulty of establishing a clear or stable link between language and 'social reality'. The body has thus offered a seductively productive site for interdisciplinary work in the humanities, and it was surely no accident that the seminal collection, *The Making of the Modern Body*, first appeared as a special number of the journal *Representations* in 1986.

Many literary critics interested in historical rather than formal or purely aesthetic evaluation of texts are now juxtaposing medical authors and the canon where once they might have traced levels of irony. Michel Foucault's bleakly compelling evocation of the panopticon in *Discipline and Punish* and the same book's powerful opening scene describing the horrible execution of the eighteenth-century regicide, Damiens, have served as the starting point for a succession of cultural historical works preoccupied with tracing the disciplinary workings of power within literary texts. Indeed, as Terry Eagleton sardonically noted, "few literary texts are likely to make it nowadays into the new historicist canon unless they contain at least one mutilated body."[5]

While these somatic concerns are linked to the omnipresent use of the (disproportionally white, young and semi-clothed) human form in the mass media and advertizing, they can also be seen as an extension of late nineteenth- and early twentieth-century attempts to transform cultures through physical practices, which were as various as military drill, organized sport or the mass rallies of Stalinism and Nazism. Indeed, it is striking how often we seem to be discovering or rediscovering authors of the 1920s and 1930s such as Battaille, Benjamin and Elias who were responding to the body culture of Fascism or Stalinism and/or were the exemplars of the international modernist avant garde. It is as if the history of the body exemplifies the argument of the Marxist political theorist, Alex Callinicos, that post-modernity is the irruption of bastardized high modernist esthetics into the genres of mass culture.

A further inspiration for this invocation of the body within cultural analysis has been the elaboration of a corporeal esthetic within certain strands of French feminism, building upon the work of the French psychoanalyst Jacques Lacan. Helène Cixous, Luce Irigaray and Julia Kristeva have influentially linked textuality and writing with sexuality. All three have argued that there is a particular affinity between the feminine and the body — both silenced by the patriarchal order of the Word. The convulsions of the hysteric or the witch at the Sabbath, the 'feminine' movement of fluids, and the pre-linguistic bond between lactating mother and infant are offered as points of departure for the construction of female desire and of *écriture féminine* — feminine writing — which (and this is crucial) transcends any form of biological essentialism. The implications of this work have perhaps been most fully developed by the American feminist philosopher, Judith Butler, who in *Gender Trouble* and *Bodies that Matter* argued that gender is something that is performed within a heterosexual matrix and is *not* simply overlaid upon an extracultural sexed body.

Although a number of historians have begun to refer to Butler's work, more influential within the historical mainstream have been the broadly Foucauldian and/or social constructivist traditions which maintain that bodies are ideologically or discursively produced. Since the late 1970s myriad books have argued that the factory, the prison, the hospital, the school and the army required and produced particular disciplined bodies. Yet ironically the old grand narratives of history — the Industrial Revolution, Romanticism, Professionalization — have generally been transposed onto the body and in these accounts have remained essentially the same. In striking contrast to historical uses of gender, for instance, writing the history of the body does not seem to have obliged most historians to reconsider periodization or the relative importance of causal factors.

Furthermore, crude Foucauldian accounts such as L. Murard and P. Zilmermann's *Le Petit Travailleur Infatigable*, transpose dystopias of class control into narratives of master-servant relations. In the work of David Armstrong and Michael Ignatieff the prison, the panopticon and the dispensary become fantastic Piranesi-like constructions of control, far more perfect than any regulatory system within the practice of everyday life. Such historical works revel in an almost masochistic celebration of human powerlessness; the post-Foucauldian clinical gaze is given the petrifying qualities of Medusa's. In such accounts (which sometimes smack of Maoist notions of false consciousness) we are all self-policing subjects, though no-one has yet produced an example of that creature caught in the act.

There is a disturbingly idealist, not to say inquisitorial, strand to much of this kind of scholarship. It often reduces the history of the body to the recitation of elite or literary discourses about the body. At times, the history of the body becomes synonymous with the history of medicine; the pronouncements of doctors about physical conditions are quite ludicrously treated as if university-educated medical practitioners have been uniquely authoritative and respected founts of knowledge about health and the body throughout Western history. Laqueur's *Making Sex* is a case in point. As a number of reviewers have pointed out, he not only provided an over-schematic and over-simplified account of changes in medical theory, but also largely ignored non-medical evidence about non-professional understandings of conception and sexual difference.

In such accounts early-modern, modern, or indeed post-industrial 'bodies' are reduced to their representations within particular genres or discourses, above all, disciplinary codes and prescriptive texts. From Galen to Samuel Smiles or Dr Spock, these genres often provide lessons through idealized portraiture. They center on the individual's use of their own physical and ethical resources in order to obtain the optimum results. This idealism of body and soul figured within Greek statues and sustained Foucault's account of desire and sexuality. There is a strong parallel between these histories of the body and Nikolas Rose's work on the construction of the self in twentieth-century psychiatry, for this too treats selfhood and the figuration of the self within educational texts as synonymous. Such claims are clearly fallacious: how many ordinary people when looking into *Gray's Anatomy* feel a thrill of self-recognition? The history of bodily representations, or discourses about the body, is a valid, important and exciting strand of scholarship, but to suggest that this is *the* history of *the* body is misguided.

Furthermore, historians' avowedly Foucauldian analyses of discourse upon the body all too often ironically end up being completely disincarnated and reifying. This is an almost inevitable consequence of the fundamental problems of translating Foucault's work from a philosophical to an historical context. Foucault often repeated that he was not a real historian, despite those sections of his work which invited such a reading. He was a philosopher developing the Nietzschean anti-humanist tradition in political and epistemological opposition to the Hegelian tradition underpinning the diverse strands of Marxism, existentialism and phenomenology which dominated French post-war intellectual culture. Foucault did not analyse discourse as if it were symptomatic of the 'speaking subject'; in his work discourse plays an autonomous role through which power operates. He was thus developing the Nietzschean intellectual heritage of Georges Bataille and Maurice Blanchot that denied the primacy of the subject as the origin of discourse.

As became readily apparent in his discussions with historians (published in *L'impossible Prison*), Foucault's work functioned within an entirely different discursive universe from that of empiricist historians; indeed his work undermined most of the tenets of history. The notions of historical identity, the subject, and individuality used by historians to write biographies or narrative history predicated upon simple notions of human agency are tied to phenomenological ideas of the individual. Foucault appears to have recognized the limitations of his own genealogical methodology. When he came to write the later and more substantive volumes of his *History of Sexuality* (his only avowed work of *history*), he felt the need to denounce his programmatic first volume and to abandon his initial project in favor of an exploration of the notion of the self within the hermeneutics of ethics and desire. The complexity of those volumes and their lack of a clearly transposable narrative meant that of all his work they remain the least used.

As a result of reifying tendencies which reduce bodies to their representations and which are to found in many accounts of social transformation such as those of Marx, Weber and Elias as well as in the work of Foucault, histories of the body all too often overlook differences of class, race and sex or reduce them to banal invocations of the 'other'. Many works have in one form or another traced the making of the modern body. But what is this uniform entity, the modern body? As the medical anthropologist Cecil G. Helman stressed, patients arrive in a practitioner's office with very different notions of the functioning of their bodies than those instilled in medical schools. Similarly the French anthropologist Jeanne Favret-Saada discovered when she lived in the Bocage region of France in the 1950s that magical understandings of the origin of disease were commonplace among *some* of the local inhabitants, and indeed they resorted to her as someone who could supposedly provide counter-magic. The cosmological understandings of the body provided by exorcism, crystal therapy and acupuncture are every bit as part of modernity (or post-modernity) as HRT and virtual sex.

Furthermore, most historical discussions of the operation of power on the body are strikingly non-somatic. Bodily activities shape individual histories. Eugenicists, medics, nutritionists and Lambrosian criminologists exercised power and shaped bodies through praxis as well as through discourse. But the nature and consequences of bodily practice are rarely discussed. One does not have to fall into the biological reductionism of the medical historian Edward Shorter, to agree that it is inherently likely that lobotomy or female circumcision will have some influence upon an individual's being and experience of the world. However, as was implied by ethnomethodological studies of non-verbal communication, popular in the 1970s, the exercise of a person's physical capacities using tools, clothes and space (the exercise of power *through* the body, if you like) shapes *and* expresses that person and their body. To take the example of one physical type — the Forest of Dean miner described by Dennis Potter in the 1960s (*The Changing Forest*, 1962): the miner is made in the active dialectic between himself and the coalface as well as in the dialectic between him and the bosses, and also in the interaction between him and his fellow workers, family and neighbors.

Another problem is that histories of the body generally either ignore subjectivity and the psychic process by which conceptual 'bodies' are allegedly instilled, or 'explain' them by invoking that black box of 'body history', the panopticon, which functions as the infernal dream machine of Dr Foucault. Most historians have been notoriously coy about deaing with the psyche, particularly after some alarmingly crude and reductive examples of psychohistory. Yet the one area of history-writing which really gives an active role to the body are authors working within the psychoanalytic tradition. Lyndal Roper, for instance, has suggested links between the deeply buried history of individual emotions and the social organization of infant care in order to interpret aspects of witch trials in early-modern Germany.

Meanwhile Klaus Theweleit has controversially argued that the *physical* experience of military service and military discipline combined with the experience of defeat in World War I produced a particular psychic formation which was articulated in the violence, misogogny and social imagery that surrounded the Freikorps. We are not saying that historians interested in the body should adopt a particular psycho-analytical approach. Rather, we would argue that if historians are to acknowledge the varying and on occasions individual understandings of the body, its workings and its illnesses, it is essential for them to go beyond abstract discussions of the body and to begin to discuss subjectivity and the self within history.

Operating alongside the essentialist and constructivist approaches within con-temporary writing on the history of the body is the long tradition that explores the ways in which the body has served as an source of social imagery. Although predominantly working on European history these authors have generally drawn their inspiration from the anthropological tradition which we outlined above. Phrases such as 'the body politic', an author's *'corpus'* and *'le corps médical'* indicate just how widespread such somatic images are within European languages. One does not have to think very hard for more elaborate examples of such metaphors. Aesop's fable of the revolt of the belly, for instance, has repeatedly been retold in discussions of the appropriate functioning of society, not least in Shakespeare's *Coriolanus*. The Pauline conception of the mystical body of the church, not to mention the corporeal imagery of the mass have been central to Christian history. Unsurprisingly, therefore, much scholarship has explored the role of the corporeal in the corporation. In his recent book, *Flesh and Stone*, for instance, Richard Sennett has sought to trace "the master images of the body" in the form and the organi-zation of western cities from the Greeks through the Venetian Ghetto to the present day, arguing for a fundamental transformation in the conceptualization of urban space with William Harvey's discovery of circulation.[6]

Foucault's *Discipline and Punish* artfully alludes to this tradition of scholarship as well as to the essentialist and constructivist strands described above without disentangling them. It paints a picture of Western society moving from one in which particular human bodies functioned as its organic embodiment, to an account of the discursive and disciplinary production of modern bodies. As he put it in an interview with the journal, *Quel Corps*, "In a society like that of the seventeenth century, the King's body wasn't a metaphor, but a political reality", while the nineteenth-century notion of the social body "never operated in the same manner."[7]

For once, the account of the history of the body politic which Foucault outlined was quite conventional and is shared by most historians who have discussed this theme. But there are problems with this standard account of the history of the body as symbol. Firstly, it assumes that the symbolic body is always human. Even within Christian and post-Christian societies (and thus leaving aside the anthro-pology of sacrifice) this is an erroneous assumption. One has only to think of the many animal images within political caricature — the Gallic cockrel, the bulldog, the bald eagle — to recognize that to this day the body politic is often endowed with some other bodily form from the natural world. More fundamentally this historiography tends to present 'primitive' or pre-modern societies as blissfully integrated, free from the alienation of symbol from actuality. It therefore unquestioningly reproduces a Protestant, rationalist and *philosophe* historical narrative which represents Roman Catholic sacramental theology and symbolic practice as crude and literal, as opposed to the supposedly more sophisticated sense of ritual in the modern world.

Lastly, there can be an unacknowledged circularity in this writing about the symbolic status of the body. Although many historians of the body cite Mary Douglas's contention "that the human body is always treated as image of society",[8] few acknowledge that in many contexts the body's workings are understood through social imagery and society through corporeal analogy. For example, although Sennett is unaware of it, if one examines William Harvey's anatomy lectures of 1616–18 or Vesalius's *De Fabrica Humani Corporis* (1543), one finds the anatomists comparing various sections of the intestinal tract with streets in London and Paris. For them the human body was a city as much as the city a body. Similar problems arise if one reconsiders the body/machine metaphor which the historian, Anson Rabinbach, has shown to have been extremely influential in nineteenth- and twentieth-century discussions of industrial workers and industrial efficiency and which the cultural historian, Daniel Pick, invested with apocalyptical meanings in his discussion of war and technology in the late-nineteenth and early-twentieth centuries. The machine was understood in terms of organic metaphors as often as the body was rendered a post-Cartesian machine. As Edmund Leach observed in a review of *Natural Symbols* in 1970, all Mary Douglas did was to turn Freud on his head. Whereas for the anthropologist the body symbolized the cosmos, for the analyst the house inevitably symbolized the body. We are in a classic chicken and egg situation which provides little analytical or political purchase.

There are perhaps three ways out of this conundrum. The first resolution would be to return to an image of society akin to that which the Shakespearean critic, E.M.W. Tillyard, outlined for sixteenth- and seventeenth-century societies — a culture structured by a system of correspondences. However, not only is this an empirically highly questionable description of early modern culture, but it is also in its presentation of a hermeneutic system a deeply conservative view of the world which not only fails to account for change but renders it well nigh unthinkable. A second way of avoiding the question would be to follow the new historicist literary critic, Stephen Greenblatt's embracing of one somatic metaphor already discussed; he has influentially written of the circulation of social energy and imagery without actually defining the arteries through which this cultural vital spirit flows or the historical determinants of its passage. Neither approach seems particularly satisfactory.

One possible way forward might be to abandon attempts to identify and thus reify a single source of somatic metaphor and turn our attention to the body-in-society, not the body and society. In an attempt to escape from the nature/culture dichotomy perhaps we should be examining a number of verbs, dynamic processes, actions — flow, degeneration, resistance — which can be observed in the natural world, or (more precisely) are terms which were and are applied both to give an account of bodily functions and to describe phenomena in the world at large. Examples of this methodology can, for instance, be found in the work of two historians of religion, Piero Camporesi and Caroline Walker Bynum. In their very different styles they have mapped the meanings of food and of physical corruption across Baroque and Renaissance and medieval culture respectively, exploring amongst other things the ways in which the bodies of saints could resist the process of decay. Similarly Roger Smith has recently traced the various uses of the notion of inhibition across Victorian culture, while in the 1970s historians of science such as Barbara Haines, Karl Figlio, Ludmilla Jordanova and John Pickstone explored the significance of the notion of organization within political economy and the life sciences.

This kind of analysis would necessarily lead us to look not just at the body-in-culture, but also require us to try to comprehend a society's understandings of metaphor. Ultimately it would lead us to the history of meaning and of signification. It is not surprising, therefore, that many of the best histories of the body have been written not by historians of medicine, but by historians of religion more used to analyzing the astonishing symbolic density of the techniques of the body within liturgy and religious ritual.

Indeed the soul, material and immaterial, has been inextricably entwined with understandings of the body and of subjectivity for most of the last two thousand years. Yet it is all too frequently omitted from somatic investigations, a criticism which is as true for many of the grand theorists — Foucault or Elias — as it is for more recent scholars. Nor should we assume in the aggressively secularist manner of Richard Dawkins, that such theological questions have no place in the late-twentieth century or in the modern biomedical sciences. For as Caroline Walker Bynum has provocatively argued, modern medicine, philosophy and mass culture continue to debate precisely the concerns of many Christian thinkers in the early middle ages — the boundaries of life, the individual and the ontological status of flesh.

However, the current generally secular historiography seems by contrast to have stripped the body of many of its meanings and ignored the ethical issues raised by the representations of other peoples' bodies. By focusing on the body *tout court* within literary, prescriptive, medical or other texts, one runs the serious risk of fetishizing the body, of ripping it from the cosmology of which it was a part. The beautiful Greek body taken from its original context becomes purely aesthetic — a kitsch garden ornament or a model for *Boyzz*. Furthermore, there is a revealing assumption that the history of the body can be collapsed to the history of sexuality and of sexual difference. It is astonishing how much of the history of the body presents the history of the naked body rather than the clothed body. At best such works present us with a Maurice Zapp-style strip show in which a variety of human forms twirl before our eyes clad in tantalizing but often obscurantist discourse. At worst we are presented with a variety of academic pornography which offers up to the reader or listener a succession of mute representations of nakedness and violence, thoroughly complicit in what the feminist art historian, Suzanne Kappeler, has termed the pornography of representation. Yet the best historical writing on the body recovers the diverse meanings of the carnal, meanings which go far beyond what the literary critic, Stephen Heath has termed the sexual fix. As historian, Carolyn Steedman, recently demonstrated, there is a conceptual and subjective history of the body in the nineteenth and twentieth century which is structured around notions of growth. There are surely equally important books to be written on the body and appetite and on the history of the aging and gradually failing body.

One of the things which the social history of medicine has accomplished in the last decade or so has been to focus attention on the care for the sick, weak, aged or infirm whether in institutions, the family or neighborhood. It is sad but revealing that so little of the new history of the body has turned to such themes. We have next to no historical discussions of the body of the loved one — parent, child or partner — (as opposed to the sexual body). This is all too often a historiography largely devoid of tenderness, of affect and indeed of respect.

## REFERENCES

We would like to thank Fay Bound, Mary Heiman, Ludmilla Jordanova, Dave Peacock, Edward Reiss, Frank Romany, Susan Vincent, Adrian Wilson and the participants at the Manchester workshop on 'The Body in Twentieth-Century Medicine' for discussions, suggestions, ideas and references which contributed to this chapter. We are particularly grateful to Patricia Greene who not only discussed these arguments but also read a draft of this chapter; her perceptive and supportive comments improved it immensely.

1.  M. Mauss, 'The techniques of the body' in M. Mauss (ed.), *Sociology and Psychology: Essays*, tr. Ben Brewster. (London: Routledge, 1979).
2.  L. Althusser, *The Future Lasts a Long Time*, tr. Richard Veasey. (London: Chatto and Windus, 1993), pp. 213–215.
3.  E.P. Thompson, *The Making of the English Working Class.* (London, 1968), p. 13.
4.  D. Outram, *The Body and the French Revolution.* (New Haven, London: Yale University Press, 1989), p. 5.
5.  T. Eagleton, *The Ideology of the Aethetic.* (Oxford: Blackwell, 1990), p. 7.
6.  R. Sennett, *Flesh and Stone.* (London: Faber and Faber, 1994), p. 23.
7.  *Power/Knowledge.* (1980), p. 55.
8.  M. Douglas, *Natural Symbols.* (London: Barrie and Rockliff, 1970), p. 98.

## FURTHER READING

Armstrong, D., *The Political Anatomy of the Body.* (Cambridge University Press, 1983).
Barnes, B. and Shapin, S. (eds), *Natural Order.* (London: Sage Publications, 1979).

Berger, J., *Ways of Seeing*. (London: British Broadcasting Corporation and Penguin, 1972).

Blacking, J., (ed.), *Anthropology of the Body*. (London: Academic Press, 1977).

Bloch, M., *The Royal Touch*. (London: Routledge, 1923, 1973).

Brown, P., *The Body and Society: Men, Women and Sexual Renunciation in Early Christianity*. (New York: Columbia University Press, 1988).

Bynum, C.W., *Holy Fast and Holy Feast*. (Berkeley: University of California Press, 1987).

Camporesi, P., *The Incorruptible Body*, tr. Tania Croft-Murray. (Cambridge University Press, 1988).

Canguilhem, G., *The Normal and the Pathological*, tr. Carolyn R. Fawcett. (New York: Zone Books, 1989).

Davis, N.Z., *Society and Culture in Early Modern France*. (London: Duckworth, 1975).

Deleuze, G. and Guattari, F., *Capitalism and Schizophrenia*, tr. Robert Hurley *et al.* (London: Athlone, 1984).

Duden, B., *The Woman Beneath the Skin*, tr. Thomas Dunlap. (London: Harvard University Press, 1991).

Elias, N., *The Civilizing Process*, tr. Edmund Jephcott. (Oxford: Blackwell, 1994).

Favret-Saada, J., *Deadly Words*, tr. Catherine Cullen. (Cambridge University Press, 1980).

Febvre, L., *The Problem of Unbelief in the Sixteenth Century*, tr. Beatrice Gottlieb. (Cambridge, Mass.: Harvard University Press, 1982).

Feher, M. *et al.* (ed.), *Fragments for a History of the Human Body*. (3 vols., New York: Urzone, Inc., 1989).

Foucault, M., *Discipline and Punish*, tr. Alan Sheridan. (Harmondsworth: Penguin Books, 1979).

Gates, H.L. (ed.), *Race, Writing and Difference*. (University of Chicago Press, 1986).

Gilman, S.L., *The Jew's Body*. (New York: Routledge, 1991).

Helman, C.G., 'Feed a cold, starve a fever', *Culture, Medicine and Psychiatry* (1978), **2**.

Ignatieff, M., *A Just Measure of Pain*. (Harmondsworth: Penguin, 1978).

Jordanova, L., *Sexual Visions: Images of Gender in Science and Medicine between the Eighteenth and Twentieth Centuries*. (New York: Harvester Wheatsheaf, 1989).

Kantorowicz, E., *The King's Two Bodies: A Study in Medieval Political Theory*. (Princeton University Press, 1997).

Mauss, M., *Sociology and Psychology: Essays*, tr. Ben Brewster. (London: Routledge, 1979).

Needham, R. (ed.), *Right and Left*. (University of Chicago Press, 1973).

Pick, D., *War Machine*. (New Haven, Conn.: Yale University Press, 1993).

Rabinbach, A., *The Human Motor: Energy, Fatigue, and the Origins of Modernity*. (Berkeley: University of California Press, 1990).

Richardson, R., *Death, Dissection and the Destitute*. (London: Routledge, 1988).

Roper, L., *Oedipus and the Devil*. (London: Routledge, 1994).

Said, E.W., *Orientalism*. (London: Routledge, 1978).

Shorter, E., *History of Women's Bodies*. (London: Allen Lane, 1983).

Sontag, S., *Illness as Metaphor*. (New York: Farrar, Straus and Giroux, 1978).

Strathern, M., *After Nature: English Kinship in the Late Twentieth Century*. (Cambridge University Press, 1992).

Temkin, O., *Galenism*. (Ithaca N.Y.: Cornell University Press, 1973).

Theweleit, K., *Male Fantasies*, tr. Chris Turner *et al.* (2 vols., Cambridge: Polity, 1988).

Thomas, K., *Religion and the Decline of Magic*. (London: Weidenfeld and Nicolson, 1997).

Tillyard, E.M.W., *The Elizabethan World Picture*. (Harmondsworth: Penguin Books, 1963).

Turner, B., 'Recent Developments in the Theory of the Body', in M. Featherstone *et al.* (eds), *The Body: Social Process and Cultural Theory*. (London: Sage, 1990).

# CHAPTER 14

# The Healthy Body

## DOROTHY PORTER

From the time that the physician and iconoclast, Bernard de Mandeville satirized the rise of hypochondriacal society in 1711 to the time that Jane Austen illustrated it in *Sanditon* in 1817, the eighteenth century invented a culture of sensibility which invited one to be sick to get ahead. At the century's end the Bristol doctor who invented a pneumatic institute, Thomas Beddoes, despised the way in which life in the fast lane in the *fin de siècle* involved flaunting an array of fashionable diseases of civilization. Two hundred years later, fashionable society is obsessed not with disease but with health. Diseased bodies now belong to the socially dysfunctional and economically inadequate. The beautiful people at the cosmopolitan heart of affluent society strive to have low heartbeat rates and toned muscles, abstain from degenerate poisons like tobacco and fill their bodies with 'health foods' which are organically grown, humanely killed and naturally processed without chemical additives. The macrobiotic muscle-bound revolution has taken off amongst the healthy, wealthy chattering classes. Bran sales are up, cigarettes are sold cheap to the Third World, business in the gymnasium is booming and citizens of the twenty-first century are jogging in Central Park because health has become a duty as much as a right of citizenship.

Health obsessed society did not happen overnight. Health has become a priority for the cosmopolitan citizen of the affluent society over a period of time. This chapter explores twentieth-century strategies for creating healthy populations in two of the most affluent societies in history, Britain and the United States. I start by investigating the various somatic discourses exploited by the state in its campaigns to build healthy citizens. At the beginning of the century, state concerns with health were driven by the goals of building economic strength and military might. These goals stimulated a new interrogation of the effects of social conditions and social behavior upon physical deterioration. They also resulted in a range of social policies to provide personal health services for the most vulnerable in order to alleviate the effects of structural deprivation. Public policy designed to improve social welfare had numerous other goals besides the construction of health, although these are not dealt with in this chapter. Instead, I focus on a second strategy employed by the state and targeted at the procurement of health: health campaigning to influence social behavior and educate people into adopting healthy life-styles. The alliance between medicine, social science and public policy in trying to modify social behavior altered the social contract of health between the modern state and its citizens. Moreover, the emphasis between the obligations of the state and the obligations of the individual in democratic societies changed throughout the course of the twentieth century as a number of the goals which had driven early twentieth-century state-health strategies proved to be chimerical. By the end of the century post-industrial, affluent societies had modified their aims, turning the promotion of the healthy body into a rearguard action to reduce the exponentially increasing costs of redeeming chronically broken bodies in an ever-ageing demographic structure.

State-organized health education did not have a monopoly on teaching the twentieth-century body how to shape up. Other architects competed to design a healthy body for the affluent society. A mass health culture has been promoted by voluntary associations and a range of commercial interests from the late nineteenth century which turned the construction of the healthy body into a moral crusade and a vastly profitable industry. Non-state health promotion has employed a variety of cultural discourses which have also changed their rhetorical focus since the beginning of the twentieth century. In this chapter I focus especially upon the way in which philosophies of diet and exercise, which were developed within the context of education in the nineteenth century, became ethics-for-sale in the twentieth century. The task of creating a mass health culture was taken up vigorously by private enterprise. John Harvey Kellogg viewed his breakfast cereals not just as a tasty option, but as part of a mission to bring sufficient roughage to the diet of the American nation. Industrial capitalism replaced idealized healthy agricultural laborers and the 'huntin' and fishin'' land owners with a sickly urban proletariat, sedentary office workers and neurotically stressed executive-entrepreneurs. However, you did not have to go on being a seven-stone, shivering weakling getting sand kicked in your face; commercial help was at hand. Charles Atlas and his contemporary, Bernarr Macfadden, had muscle-building programs and exercise philosophies to bring out the superman that was living inside you — at a price. From these early beginnings healthy living, eating and exercise became an industrial complex servicing Western society with a new moral code: be well or go to the wall at your own hand. Unhealthyness became inexcusable. Strive or take a dive in your social mobility; shape up or ship out of the affluent society.

As Sander Gilman has recently pointed out, the social construction of health has been historically bound to normative representations of beauty.[1] The healthy body is represented in a culturally defined form — a bodily shape, size, proportion and, sinisterly, skin tone. In the twentieth century, the competition to be healthy and the competition to be beautiful have escalated. The twentieth-century ideal of the beautiful and healthy body can trace its heritage back to eugenically inspired pre-Second World War movements promoting nude sun-bathing, social hygiene and the production of a blond-haired blue-eyed race. Ironically, however, as I will illustrate later, the contradictions of late twentieth-century health-obsessed culture are reflected in the representation of bodily distortion. Muscle-bound man does not have the perfectly proportioned muscular system of a Vesalius drawing, but is an 'Incredible Hulk' of testosterone treated flesh. Equally paradoxical, elite health-culture has come to embrace the self-defeating consumption both of health foods to prevent physiological degeneration, and designer narcotics — either on prescription or from the illegal market — to relieve the stress of modern life. The downside to health obsession and the fetishization of beauty is that gain often does require pain. Business-executives are giving themselves heart attacks on the squash courts and women are dying from silicone leaking from their breast implants. How did procuring health and beauty become such a dangerous pursuit?

This chapter follows the journey of state-medicine and commercial culture, largely within the Anglo-American context, as they succeeded in fetishizing health and comodifying sexuality in the construction of a reified healthy body in the twentieth century. This journey is also an heuristic device for investigating the cultural significance of somatic obsession, asking how our bodies function as tools of social, economic and political differentiation. Most of all, I want to ask, how do elite bodies — whether fashionably diseased at the end of the eighteenth century or fashionably health-obsessed at the end of the twentieth — help to sustain existing ruling orders?

## PROCURING HEALTH

Let us begin our journey by discussing the development of a type of medicine which focused on health — as opposed to disease — in the early twentieth century and the way it was employed by the British state to combat the physical deterioration of national stock.

The shocking state of recruits for the British Imperial Army as it prepared to fight South African farmers at the turn of the twentieth century raised a political furore about health. The Interdepartmental Committee set up in 1903 to investigate 'physical deterioration' was an expression of a desperate quest to pursue national efficiency through the reduction of ill-health and the prevention of imperial decline. The Committee's report of 1904 prompted the development of new legislation to introduce health inspection in schools along with free school dinners for poor children. The Committee's revelations of widespread malnutrition and ill-health amongst the poor all looked bad for the British public health service who had been charged with bringing about improvement from the late nineteenth century. Edwardian eugenists blamed the public health service and preventive medicine for committing 'race suicide' by saving the weakly and the robust indiscriminately and thereby contravening the Darwinian law of natural selection. Public health specialists hit back by citing insufficient political support for comprehensive health measures which would facilitate not only the prevention of disease but the procurement of national health. In order to justify their argument, leading members of the British public health service expanded their concept of the environment to include the social behavior of individuals and groups in order to influence that behavior for the benefit of obtaining health. Comprehensive health environmentalism, medicine from 'the social standpoint,' increased the social and political role of medicine in Britain as the state enacted more and more health legislation, eventually culminating in the creation of the National Health Service in 1948.

Making health a priority of a modern lifestyle was a central goal of Arthur Newsholme, England's Chief Medical Officer of the Local Government Board before the First World War. He suggested that a new type of medicine from "the social standpoint" should take-over the corporate management of communal life.[2] Newsholme and his contemporaries believed that one way to achieve this goal was by changing social behavior through the education of the ignorant masses, teaching them how to maximize their health status in order to reduce the chances of contracting disease. It was an idea which became institutionalized by the middle of the twentieth century in Britain, Europe and the United States in a new academic discipline called social medicine. Social medicine aimed to replace the public health officer with a new type of general practitioner, a social physician whose primary goal was the prevention of sickness through the management of the socio-biological relations of health. The social physician who practised medicine as a social science would manage health by becoming an advocate, a teacher, educating individuals and society how to maximize health and minimize infections and chronic illness. Proselytizing preventive medicine and health education became the primary focus of the social science of health in the twentieth century.

Managing health by educating individual behavior extended the concept of health as a right of citizenship which was created by the French and American Revolutionaries in the eighteenth century. Thomas Jefferson announced that despotism produced diseased populations and democracy would generate health amongst its free citizens. In 1791 the Constituent Assembly of the French Revolution declared health, along with work, as one of the rights of man. However, if health citizenship was a right it was also an obligation. As Ludmilla Jordanova has pointed out, the *idéologue*, Constantine Volney, reminded citizens of the new republic that his body was an economic unit belonging to the community and he had a social-political duty to lead a healthful, temperate existence in order to ensure his value for the commonwealth. Democratic states in the twentieth century have re-asserted this feature of the social contract of health by making it an individual responsibility. From the time that the medical profession and policy makers became aware of it, the epidemiological transition from infectious to chronic diseases in twentieth-century affluent societies has dominated public health policy-making. From the mid-twentieth century social medicine offered the state a new strategy for reducing chronic disease which used public information to persuade individuals to take up prescribed 'healthy' life-styles. A vast array of expertise was employed in state action to prevent chronic disease through public propaganda, most notably epidemiologists and public relations — advertising — agencies. Such an approach was employed in a variety of fields, including the prevention of cardio-vascular disease, digestive disorders and above all the prevention of lung cancer and related diseases from smoking.

Although smoking has been considered a habit rather than a dependency in the strict psychological definition of addiction since the Second World War, it has been represented as an individual responsibility. The post-war anti-smoking campaign spread the message that the key to the social management of chronic illnesses, such as lung cancer, was individual prevention by raising health consciousness and promoting self-health care. The model of prevention through the education of individuals gathered momentum in the wake of the anti-smoking campaign. Subsequent post-war campaigns offered 'life-style methods' for preventing heart disease, various forms of cancer, liver disease, digestive disorders, venereal disease and obesity. Self-screening has been the main strategy employed to prevent breast cancer, which has been the greatest cause of mortality amongst women since the Second World War. Technical and laboratory screening have been reduced in recent years to cut costs.

The anti-smoking campaign began to take on the character of a nineteenth-century campaign to prevent infectious disease once T. Hirayama published the results of a study, in 1981, which demonstrated that non-smoking wives of heavy smokers had a higher risk of contracting lung cancer than the wives of non-smokers. In Britain and the United States campaigns to prevent 'passive smoking' attacked the civil liberties of smokers in an attempt to reduce its effects upon the community. State action penalized and stigmatized cigarette smokers as social pariahs, failures, moral inferiors, reprobates and inadequates.

The prevention of substance abuse in Britain and the United States has been represented as a 'war' against degenerate behavior. The success of the Anglo-American state in its ongoing 'battles' is, however, mixed. Smoking has been reduced in both national contexts but alcohol consumption remains high. The consumption of narcotics grows despite the heavy international legal sanctions against their production, sale, distribution and consumption. The state has employed punitive actions to prevent smoking, such as banning cigarette advertising from television, placing compulsory health warnings on cigarette-packets and extracting high levels of indirect taxation on the sale of tobacco. But there has been no legal prohibition of tobacco consumption. In Britain and America the state has not yet risked completely opposing market demand. The last time the state took on consumers by instituting alcohol prohibition in the United States it was defeated. Thus expert administrators seek to reduce the costs of tobacco-related diseases upon the community but the state does not risk challenging the right to consume cigarettes. It is interesting to note that the force of consumer demand, even in the case of narcotics, may possibly reverse existing state policy in the future. Leading advocates for the legalization of narcotics in the United States are represented in both the Republican and the Democratic Parties. The individualistic emphasis of the new social contract of health between the modern state and its citizens allows the right to consume to remain a priority. The obligation to be healthy continues to be a subordinate value to the right of every citizen in a free-market democracy to be a consumer. The lack of legal prohibition upon the sale of tobacco serves the state's claim that ill-health is an individual responsibility which the state interferes with less and less in order to reduce the costs of state-intervention. As a result, those who choose ill-health face the consequences with less and less state assistance. Private health insurance for cigarette smokers has high premiums, but is increasingly necessary because smokers find it harder and harder to be treated by state-provided services. The first heavy smokers who were refused treatment in the British National Health Service made headline news; now such practices are becoming standard.

The mixed messages involved in the prevention of substance 'abuse', including tobacco consumption, have been reproduced in the health education campaigns that tried to prevent the spread of a new lethal virus which began to appear in the early 1980s, Human Immune-Deficiency Virus. Victims of the disease caused by the virus, AIDS, have suffered legal and social discrimination within popular culture and by official agencies. Even taking an HIV test can result in the subsequent failure to obtain personal insurance. The public knowledge of its acquisition can mean that the individual sufferer fails to continue to gain employment or shelter. Its association with sexual activity has re-created the representations of degeneracy which were made of syphilitics and other venereal disease victims since the fifteenth century. The implication of bodily and spiritual corruption has persisted as a powerful contemporary trope. HIV's association with the consumption of illegal substances has equally resulted in the characterization of disease victims as self-destructive degenerates. Even victims characterized as 'innocent,' such as children and hemophiliacs, who contracted the disease through heredity or blood transfusions experienced as much hostile discrimination as popular sympathy. The author and political campaigner for gay rights, Simon Watney, has argued that AIDS has promoted a cultural erotisization of the diseased body. Others have suggested that media health campaigns in a variety of national contexts which represented homosexuality as a legitimate sexual preference assisted in emancipating the social status of this group which historically has been discriminated against relentlessly.

From anti-smoking to the control of AIDS, post-war health campaigns have redrawn the parameters of the social contract of health in liberal democracies. Social medicine promoted a new model of prevention which emphasized the responsibility of individuals for their own health behavior. It is a model which utilized medical and social scientific analysis of health and illness to provide education aimed at maximizing the health chances of the individual by the adoption of prescribed life-styles, in short, the individual managerialism of health.

## PHYSICAL-CULTURE AND RACIAL SUPREMACY

The creation of a healthy citizenry in the twentieth century has not been limited to government action. The commercial potential of the commodification of the healthy body was taken up by enterprizing entrepreneurs in Europe and the United States. But the commercialization of health utilized moral narratives which had been established by the state and voluntary health education movements. Both states and voluntary/charitable organizations engaged in intellectual discourses surrounding health at the beginning of the twentieth-century. These discourses adopted their own moral plot imbued with cultural anxieties about imperial strength and weakness which were linked to beliefs about the biological determinants of social progress and regression. The moral value of biological progress was also vividly expressed in the commercial promotion of physical-culture.

The commercial promotion of physical-culture in the early twentieth century adopted the mores of an education service to society, mimicking Victorian movements which attempted to establish muscular Christianity through the institution of games and athletics in British and American public schools. Regulated games were co-opted into the creation of strong character within Thomas Arnold's educational system at Rugby School in the early nineteenth century. Subsequent Victorian teachers, curates and social reformers looked to organized games and sports such as football, cricket and fencing as means of indoctrinating English upper-class schoolboys into a culture of 'muscular Christianity' wherein Godliness was equated with manliness. Reformers such as Charles Kingsley believed that on the playing fields of Eton, Westminster, Harrow, Charterhouse, etc., the English upper class would be socialized into an authoritarian, disciplined social order which would prepare them for their role as rulers of an imperial nation. In America the development of physical education in schools was heavily influenced by the British example, but continental European gymnastics were also taken up. Before the Civil War the Swedish system of gymnastics founded by Henrik Peter Ling had been popularized as a method of indoor training especially appropriate for women. The German gymnastic system of *Turnen* was imported into the United States along with the expansion of German immigration after the Civil War. Both the German and Swedish gymnastic and athletic systems which were promoted by nineteenth-century physical-education reformers were successfully exploited for commercial gain by enterprizing entrepreneurs at the beginning of the twentieth century. The commercialization of exercise was represented as also servicing health-educational reform which would bring about as much moral as physical improvement amongst increasingly degenerate populations corrupted by civilization.

One of the many spectacular attractions at the World Trade Fair in 1893 was Eugene Sandow's displays of physical strength. Sandow had become an international showman through his world tours in which he demonstrated extra-ordinary physical feats. He represented the new distinctive American Herculean body, the physical superiority of which was demonstrated by American athletes the following year at the first Olympiad staged in Athens. By the time the second Olympic Games were held at St Louis in 1904, the association of physical, economic and industrial strength had been reinforced from the very top of the American political structure when President Teddy Roosevelt popularized his 'strenuous life' philosophy for invigorating the nation. Roosevelt, a folk hero of the sporting life, created the idea that a somatic map of national progress was to be found in the vigor of the new American male. The Olympian examples of American muscle and brawn began to redefine the image of the well-developed male body. The American sportsmen who triumphed in the early Olympiads were athletes of bulk after the Sandow fashion and contrasted sharply with the sinewy athletic sportsmen on the playing field in the early Victorian era. The image of the svelte Greek athlete which had characterized the somatic ideal from antiquity through the Renaissance up to the early nineteenth century was challenged by this late nineteenth-century representation of muscular mass and power.

Sandow was a strong-man in the tradition of the fun-fair freak, but he became an extravagantly successful health enterprise between 1890–97. After he settled in England in 1897, he began to commercialize his system of physical training through the establishment of an Institute of Physical-culture. He founded *Sandow's Magazine* in 1899 and published numerous volumes which he considered to be text-books for a new life-style. In large tomes such as *Strength and How to Obtain it* (1899) and *Life is Movement* (1919), Sandow represented himself primarily as an educator and savior-by-example of the deteriorating stock of the industrial nations. He advocated the elimination of disease through muscle-building. He aspired to play a direct political role in the development of physical education in schools in England, lobbying George Newman at the Education Department, and giving evidence to the Interdepartmental Committee on Physical Deterioration in order to have the 1907 Education Act advocate his system of physical training. But he was outflanked; by then the Ling method of gymnastic training had powerful advocates amongst female teachers in women's physical training colleges and high schools, and amongst army drills sergeants who had been sent to study the value of the Swedish system for military training. Sandow nevertheless continued to proselytize the importance of muscular development for the prevention of disease and physical deterioration. As he explained in *Life is Movement,* muscles could make a disease-proof body through the invigoration of the what he called the 'Alpha of life' the living cell:

> Through the cell we can reach, cultivate, train, develop and reconstruct every part and organ of the human body and every cell of the body is dependent on, kept alive and maintained in health and power by the movement of the voluntary muscles... *To keep all these cells in perfectly balanced strength is the true secret of health, vitality and resistant power to*

*disease...* This I contend we can only do by the balanced physical movement of the voluntary muscles.[3]

Civilization had created an artificial sedentary human existence which was responsible for the creation of disease. The only way to redeem human health was by counteracting this process with vigorous exercise that would build muscular strength.

Sandow was not alone in his avocation of muscle-building for the prevention of disease and the acquisition of perfect health. An even more adept entrepreneur emerged from the United States in the self-styled professor of 'kinesitherapy,' Bernarr Macfadden. Macfadden, the son of an alcoholic father and tubercular mother in the mid-west became one of the most notorious entrepreneurial crusaders for fitness, clean living and sexual efficiency of the early twentieth century. According to his biographers it was his attendance at the Chicago World Fair in 1893 that convinced him of his mission to develop and spread the gospel of physical culture. He emulated the muscle-building program of Sandow but commercialized his own system with extravagant financial success. A brilliant self-publicist he advertised his philosophical brand of physical-culture through his own magazine, *Physical-culture,* which he founded in 1899. He began his own 'healthatoriums,' founded the first physical-culture competitions in the late 1890s, and published many volumes on physical training, eating for fitness and, above all, on how to achieve sexual efficiency. In this Macfadden allied himself with the Progressivist philosophy of health, fitness and the war against prudery as the basis for building a revitalized society. The abolition of the wall of silence on sexuality and the encouragement of sexually fulfilling marriage to produce healthy offspring were the linchpins of Macfadden's physical-culture philosophy. Building physical strength and beauty was the route to achieving what he referred to as the 'well-sexed' man and woman who would, through their uninhibited and loving union in marriage, produce the children on which the nation could build its future. Macfadden was a eugenic advocate of national racism, supported immigration restriction, and promoted Nordic superiority.

But his radical, almost reckless, commercial exploitation of his own brand of physical-culture reform broke with and offended convention. His advertisements of the ideal feminine physique and sexuality caused the offices of his New York publishing company to be raided by Anthony Comstock and the Society for the Suppression of Vice in 1905. Comstock confiscated posters which advertised the 'Mammoth Physical-culture Exhibition' to be held at Madison Square Garden that year which depicted the winners of physique competitions dressed in union-suits and leopard-skin loin cloths. Later publications on health, beauty and sexual advice for women which displayed images of bare breasts were also prosecuted for obscenity. The mixture of exercise and dietary pedagogy and visual erotica, however, made Macfadden a fortune. The distribution of *Physical-culture* escalated to over 100,000 within its first year of publication. He combined this with the invention of gadgets and gimmicks for physical training, dieting and weight-gain to create a highly profitable commercial enterprise. In the process Macfadden contributed to revolutionizing the social profile of the female form from the fainting, corseted, distortedly wasp-waisted Victorian beauty to the robust, fully-figured, physical-culture girl of the twentieth century. The robust Rubenesque was physically enhanced in order to fulfil her primary — and supremely significant — social biological role of healthy motherhood. Virulently opposed to allopathic medicine, Macfadden sold an encyclopaedia of self-help health advice for achieving virile manhood and supreme motherhood which a nation could build its future upon, even if he had to break the obscenity laws to do so.

Before the Second World War the promotion of muscular strength, physical fitness, dietary and sexual reform remained linked in physical-culture philosophies. This philosophy of somatic reform was exploited by voluntary associations and groups interested in alternative healing, dress-reform, nudism, sun-bathing, hiking and mountain climbing, etc. Various physical-culture reformers all embraced this agenda emphasizing their own particular programs such as Mary Wood-Allen's concern with fiber consumption, Horace Fletcher's obsession with mastication and advocates of what James Whorton has described as "Muscular Vegetarianism."[4] Some reformers, like Bernarr Macfadden and Kellogg, turned the new physical-culture philosophy into highly successful commercial enterprises. The commercial exploitation of erotica was also legitimated within the language of progressive sexual reform and health commodification was justified as an educative necessity for the prevention of disease, race survival and nationbuilding.

National and personal health were bound within physical-culture patriotism in the years before the Second World War. In Britain and America the world of commerce no less than the dictates of the state told the man in the street that it was his duty to make sure that the Anglo-Saxon, English-speaking nations did not become or remain seven-stone weaklings. The self-styled 'Founder of the Fastest Health Strength and Physique Building System,' Charles Atlas, goaded his potential clientele into taking up his "dynamic-tension" system of muscle-building by shaming them for only being "half-alive," flat-chested and enfeebled, unable to deliver a "knockout defense" when insulted. The rhetoric of his advertisement campaigns echoed the concerns of the physical-culture movement with race-suicide and fears of imperial decline. Physical-culture movements in Britain and the United States had, however, strong competitors for creating Charles Atlas's "lion in the jungle" who made "every other animal sit up and take notice as soon as he lets out a roar."[5] Physical-culture movements in continental Europe appealed equally to the identity between the vigorously healthy body of the individual and the vigorous strength of the nation. The most resounding expression of the equation between bodily and national-racial strength was voiced in pre-war Germany. In this respect the healthy-body became reified into a metonymcal trope for the international culture of racial and national competition before the Second World War.

### The Fetishism of Commodities and the Reification of the Fit Body

Commercialized physical-culture expanded slowly after the Second World War up to the late 1970s and then made an exponential leap. As organized sports and competitive games became an ever greater mass-spectator form of leisure, so the culture of getting fit took off in the 1980s. Sports clothes manufacturers expanded their markets to provide casual attire which provided both comfort and an athletic fashion. The fashionability of track suits and running shoes reached murderous proportions in the 1990s when American teenagers occasionally killed each other in order to steal a pair of Nike pumps from their peers. A commercialized fitness-culture made athleticism fashionable creating entrepreneurial opportunities by popularizing new leisure activities such as jogging and weight-training. But the 'fitness culture' built upon the body-building cults of the pre-war era and set up new images of the ideal bodily shape and appearance.

The representation of racial supremacy through muscular strength and physical fitness declined in post-war cults of the healthy body but the links between fitness-building and life-style reform persisted. Like Sandow, Jo Weider, the entrepreneurial giant who created body-building as a professional sport in the post-war period promoted his system of muscle-building as a mission to create a new life-style. The Weider international commercial empire now dominates the market in body-building gym-clubs, sports-wear and equipment, food supplements and vitamin products and produces its own library of magazines and training manuals. The empire also controls the international professional competitions which include the 'Mr Olympia,' 'Ms Olympia' and the new 'Ms Fitness' titles. When describing his magazine, *Muscle and Fitness,* Weider suggested that:

> I think of *Muscle and Fitness* as more than a magazine. I think of it as a text-book — a text-book about the Weider Bodybuilding Lifestyle.[6]

Parts of his mission echo some of the themes of an earlier era, such as Macfadden's insistence that building muscular strength was the cure for impotence. Macfadden, Kellogg and Atlas had all suggested that what the world needed was "virile men," "Real Men" and "he-men" and suggested how their own particular brand of fitness fetishism would achieve it.[7] In the 1980s Armand Tanny — a one time Mr USA — wrote in Weider's magazine about counteracting the effects modern life-styles, including the gender revolution — on male potency:

> Men are particularly apprehensive when it comes to sex... Inhibited sexual desire may result from marital problems, a deteriorating relationship, depression, stress, major life changes and the sexual revolution... [because]... new female freedom in the sexual revolution has created pressures that have caused some males to retreat from sex.[8]

Tanny, like his predecessor Macfadden, brought the reassuring message to his reader that the situation could be rectified through bodybuilding — especially with your partner. But unlike Macfadden or Sandow, who were restricted to vague references about the effects of movement on cellular metabolism, Tanny was able to incorporate bits of the modern science of endocrinology into his discussion:

> Bodybuilding like many forms of vigorous exercise, is an aphrodiziac. Certainly the lean
> shapely muscular look of the bodybuilder's body is a psychological turn-on. But there is
> more to it than that. At the physiological level, scientists have found that vigorous exercise
> stimulates the production of the hormone responsible for the sex drive in both men and
> women — testosterone… When you are bodybuilding at an optimum level of exertion,
> you are likely to have the most testosterone at your disposal for both exercise and sex.[9]

Like every other modern competitive bodybuilder, Tanny should know, because
endocrinology has become central to the construction of the muscularly extraordinary. Ever since Soviet weightlifters, such as Vasily Stepanov, began using anabolic
steroids to build strength in the early 1950s testosterone has been a crucial weapon
in the cold war of hard flesh.

The physiological consequences of taking testosterone are not yet fully known.
Apart from distorting normal human muscle proportions, the short term effects
have a number of pathological results ranging from acne to liver damage. The aim
of the contemporary bodybuilding cult is not, however, to produce the perfectly
healthy human form or even a human form at all. The current criteria for achieving the most highly prised body-building title, Mr Olympia, is body-bulk which is
also 'cut.' The current title holder, Dorian Yates, is the perfect example of the
current body-building ideal weighing in at over 250lbs with a body-fat ratio of 2%.
A qualified doctor, Yates presumably has worked out how to keep the human body
functioning on such an abnormally imbalanced proportion of lean to fat tissue.
Arnold Schwarzenegger, who won the Mr Olympia title several times in the 1980s,
would not even come close to achieving it now.

The goals of body-building have changed since Schwarzenegger's day, taking on
a new post-modernist, 'post-human,' tonality. As illustrated by one of the currently
most popular bodybuilding magazines, *Ironman*, the desire of the contemporary
competitive-bodybuilder is to look 'alien' — or in the lingo of the locker-room to
look 'freaky.' As T.C. Louoma, writing in the first edition of the British publication
of *Ironman* in 1992 highlights, the competition between bodybuilders is to look
"out of this world." Louoma tells us that:

> On a recent episode of 'Star Trek, the Next Generation' Worf the Klingon had to have
> back surgery. When the cameras zoomed in on his weird, reptilian-looking back, however,
> I was disappointed. Oh, Worf's back had its share of bumps, lumps and bony protuberances,
> all right, but it looked a lot less alien than, say, Lee Haney's or Vince Taylor's back… Of
> all the hypertrophied bodyparts on a bodybuilder's physique, it is, perhaps, the back that
> looks the freakiest, the most alien… It's tough to acquire that freaky look from the rear
> because this bodypart is just plain hard to work.[10]

It is perhaps ironic that the contemporary bodybuilding cult which could trace
its heritage back to the role of the 'freak' strongman in the nineteenth-century
fun fair chooses to revive this particular Victorian value. The success of *Ironman*

depends, as its British editor and publisher Dave McInerney points out, upon its ability to deliver the freakiest show in town. McInerney recalls the moment he decided to take on the British publication of *Ironman* which had been published in the United States since 1936:

> The day after the British Grand Prix, John Balik [one of *Ironman*'s photographers] took a train from Nottingham to Birmingham to meet up with me, prior to his departure back to L.A. Sitting alongside John on the train were a group of bodybuilders, all with their noses stuck in one bodybuilding magazine. That magazine was *Ironman*. When John asked them what they liked about the mag, they echoed the opinions that both John and myself had about the attraction of the magazine. They loved the large, often freaky images and the hard-core training articles. They had only one complaint; namely that they had difficulty obtaining it at newstands in the U.K. John informed them, to their delight, that soon all that would be changing; and how right he was![11]

The alien look of professional bodybuilders can not be achieved without the illegal use of growth hormones. The use of male sex hormones in building bodies that look like tower blocks expresses the contradictions of contemporary somatic obsession in bodily distortion. This contradiction results from the way in which the fetishization of health has become a commodification of the erotic body. The relationship between health and human reproduction has been a persistent and central theme of the social construction of the healthy body expressed most vividly in a discourse of soft pornographic erotica. Prior to the Second World War the physical-culture movement recruited erotica into the race for national-racial su-premacy. In the post-war period the erotization of health has become an objective in its own right. One of the central goals of the healthy body was, from the beginning of the twentieth century, to become sexually attractive and supremely reproductively efficient. In the late twentieth century the sexually desirable body *defines* elite health status.

The body-building cult begat an offspring in the 1980s which has secured a massively larger market. 'Fitness Training' is a muscle-toning and aerobic exercise system which is not just the pre-occupation of the alienated who want to look like aliens. Its goal is the construction of a designer body whose defining characteristic is sexual desirability. The world of Fitness Training has its own commercialized regimen and dietetics, literature and specialized knowledge for sale to all who wish to turn their dreams of looking like a 'Hollywood Babe' or 'Himbo' into a reality. Magazines such as *Fit Body* advertise a commercially driven culture which is bring-ing the fashionable elite into the expensive health club dressed in their designer kits in order to acquire a designer-desirable body. The designer-desirable body is not constructed through anabolic steroids and does not aim to build bulk. By contrast its goal is the reduction of fat and the construction of 'shape' and the way to achieve it is through work — working out in the gym, in the aerobic class, the swimming-pool club, the squash court, etc. The designer-body aims for toned muscles which have a clear definition. The desirable body of our times is a designer commodity, which can be purchased by those with sufficient resources by employing a personal nutritionist, a personal trainer, an aromatherapeutic masseur and the best plastic surgeon in town. It is also a moral achievement because you have to purchase it with your own labor. You have to work and work-out to achieve the sensual ideal.

The defining characteristic of the designer-body is sexual attractiveness. This is the official criteria on which the recently established 'Ms Fitness' competitions are judged. And while its social construction is commercially driven, the designer-body obeys all the laws of health which are promoted by medical and state health education. Acquiring the designer-body requires low-fat, organically purified dietary regimes, strictly controlled vigorous exercise plans, extremely temperate designer-drug abuse — of alcohol, cocaine, dope, etc., — safe-tanning and safe-sex. It is disease-free and socially emancipating. 'Feminist' articles in fitness magazines tell their readers that the first step for women wishing to take control over their female destiny begins with learning to become physically powerful and stretching their physical endurance. Thus, the fetishization of health has become inherently bound to the reification of sexuality in the designer-body commodity which is desirable but not desiring. It is an ultimately narcissistic expression.

The designer-body also bears the social and economic relations of power. A range of social and economic groups including a high proportion of working class men and women pursue competitive bodybuilding. The gay community is also strongly represented within the bodybuilding world. But the distorted structures of the bodybuilt-body represent the contradictions of a sub-culture of somatic obsession. By contrast, the designer-toned body idealized by the leisure, fitness and entertainment industry is one of the new qualifications for membership to the cosmopolitan social and economic elite and you have to at least strive to achieve it even to apply. Elite social and status in late twentieth-century society requires your body, your economic activity and your life-style to be sexually attractive. For example, merchant banking has been one of the worlds most boring occupations for centuries but its elite economic power is now reaffirmed in the capacity it gives to its practitioners for purchasing sexy tropes such as a Porsche, a mews in Chelsea or Manhattan, Chanel suits and membership in the most expensive health club closest to the financial trading center. The latter is essential, because amongst other things crucial business deals are frequently negotiated on the squash court or in the bar afterwards. However, while your lifestyle and body have to be sexy in order to qualify for cosmopolitan elite social and economic status, your sex-life may be a complete contradiction to the appearance. Therein lies the reification of sexuality from sexual activity; i.e., the fetishization of sexuality in a commodity — the designer-body.

The designer form of the healthy body is a social map of economic power in late twentieth-century society. It serves as a moral instruction to the powerless masses and economically disadvantaged because it carries the same message which is forcefully promoted by the state promotion of health. The message of both the state and the commercial health-promotion industries is that achieving health, beauty and desirability is your own responsibility *and* your social duty. The economic elite and their political servants insist that society can or, at least, will no longer pay to provide health for all. With ever larger numbers of longer-living unproductive proportions of the population the modern state is redrawing the boundaries of its obligations to provide health as a right of citizenship especially to the most economically vulnerable. 'Be well or go to the wall' is relentlessly communicated through the political scaling down of public health care and service provision. It is a message which is re-enforced by the moral disgust which is bestowed upon the diseased, broken, abused, self-indulged, or neglected body. A recent survey quoted in the British *Independent* newspaper showed that 90% of a sample of women selected in the United States count a previous rape conviction in a prospective partner as being less unattractive than obesity.

Striving for health and perfect bodily desirability seems destined to be a moral qualification for elite citizenship in the affluent society of the twenty-first century. The comodified healthy body is a somatic trope of economic and political power in post-industrial society. It is a model representation of what Karl Marx identified as the personal and social alienation induced by the fetishism of commodities in a capitalist economic order.

## REFERENCES

I would like to thank all the people who read and commentated upon this paper. Joanna Bourke, Brian Dolan and Roy Porter. I would especially like to thank Roger Cooter.

1. Sander Gilman, *Health and Illness. Images of Difference.* (London: Reaktion Books, 1995), p. 51.
2. Quoted by Dorothy Porter, "'Enemies of the Race': Biologism, Environmentalism and the Public Health in Edwardian England", *Victorian Studies* (1991), **34(2)**: 159–178 at p. 170.
3. Eugene Sandow, *Life is Movement. The Physical Reconstruction and Regeneration of the People. (A Diseaseless World).* (London: The Family Encyclopaedia of Health, 1922), p. 151.
4. James Whorton, *Crusaders for Fitness. The History of American Health Reformers.* (Princeton: Princeton University Press, 1982), pp. 201–238.
5. Charles Atlas, *Charles Atlas, Founder of the Fastest Health, Strength and Physique Building System.* (London: Charles Atlas Ltd, 1930), p. 3.
6. Jo Weider, 'Editorial,' *Muscle and Fitness* (July, 1988), p. 7.
7. Bernarr A. Macfadden, *The Virile Powers of Superb Manhood. Ho Developed, How Lost: How Regained* (New York: The Physical Culture Publishing Company, 1900), 6; J.H. Kellogg, *Man The Masterpiece or, Plain Truths Plainly Told, Boyhood, Youth, and Manhood.* (London: International Tract Society, 1894), p. v; Atlas, *op.cit.*, p. 2.
8. Armand Tanny, 'Sex and Fitness. How Bodybuilding Cures Impotence,' *Muscle and Fitness* (July, 1988), p. 81.
9. *Ibid.*
10. T.C. Luoumo, 'Alien Back Attack,' *Ironman. For Ultimate Fitness* (November, 1992), **32–39**: at p. 33.
11. Dave McInerney, 'Editorial,' *Ironman. For Ultimate Fitness* (November, 1992), p. 5.

## FURTHER READING

Berryman, Jack, W. and Park, Roberta, J. (eds), *Sport and Exercise Science. Essays in the History of Sports Medicine.* (Urbana and Chicago: University of Illinois Press, 1992).

Chapman, David, L., *Sandow the Magnificent.* (Urbana and Chicago: University of Illinois Press, 1994).

Department of Health and Social Security, *Prevention and Health: Everybody's Business.* (London: H.M.S.O., 1976).

Goodman, J., *Tobacco in History. The Cultures of Dependence.* (London: Routledge, 1993).

Haley, Bruce, *The Healthy Body in Victorian Culture.* (Cambridge, Mass.: Harvard University Press, 1978).

Lock, Stephen and E.M. Tansey (eds), *Ashes to Ashes. A Wellcome Symposium on the History of Tobacco-smoking.* (Amsterdam and Atlanta: Rodopi, 1998).

McIntosh, Peter, C., *Physical Education in England Since 1800.* (London: Bell, 1981).

Mangan, J.A., *Athleticism in the Victorian and Edwardian Public School. The Emergence and consolidation of an Educational Ideology.* (Cambridge: Cambridge University Press, 1981).

Means, Richard, K. *A History of Health Education in the United States.* (London: Henry Kimpton, 1962).

Porter, Dorothy, *Health, Civilization and the State. The History of Public Health From Ancient to Modern Times.* (London, Routledge, 1998).

Ryle, John A., *Changing Disciplines.* (Reprinted New Brunswick: Transaction Publishers, 1994. 1st edition Oxford: Oxford University Press, 1948).

Smith, David, W., *Stretching Their Bodies. The History of Physical Education.* (London and Vancouver: Newton Abbot, 1974).

Walvin, James, *Leisure and Society, 1830–1950.* (London: Longman, 1978).

Whorton, James, C., *Crusaders for Fitness. The History of American Health Reformers.* (Princeton: Princeton University Press, 1982).

# CHAPTER 15

# The Industrial Body

## STEVE STURDY

Industrial work was a defining experience of twentieth-century life for increasingly large sections of the world's population. Industrial employment serves to locate individuals within the social institutions of class, wealth and prestige. And this social experience is intimately bound up with the bodily experiences associated with industrial work — experiences of physical labor, the exercise of manual skill and dexterity, bodily fatigue and work-related injury and illness. Such experiences are collectively realised in the shared language of work and labor itself, while their outward signs are often clearly legible in the bodies of industrial workers. Meanwhile, the physical capabilities and disabilities of workers' bodies have been objectified in the managerial and administrative structures that have served to order and organize industrial life. Bodily experience has thus been an important element in the differentiation and structuring of industrial society, and in the changing social relations that have characterized that society.

We do not, as yet, have any detailed historical ethnography of how industrial workers themselves have experienced and lived through their bodies. What we do have is a considerable body of research into the ways that managers, administrators and others in positions of power and authority have thought about and engaged with workers' bodies. This managerial and administrative interest has often involved the generation of detailed biological and medical knowledge about the bodily aspects of industrial life. One of the characteristic products of industrial culture has thus been the articulation of highly refined and detailed descriptions of workers' bodies and their role in industrial production. And as we shall see, such descriptions have been deeply implicated in mediating the political conflicts, negotiations and accommodations that have shaped the development of industrial society. Consequently, there is much to be gained by looking at the ways in which workers' bodies have been understood and described. Not least, it can throw light on some of the larger shifts in the formulation of social power that have taken place within industrial society over the past hundred years.

In the following pages, I will describe some of these shifts and the implications they have had for the ways in which workers' bodies are understood. However, interest in workers' bodies is not a phenomenon solely of the twentieth century.

Rather, its origins lie further back in time, in that period of social and technical transformation that we commonly call the industrial revolution. If we are to understand the peculiarities of twentieth-century understandings of the industrial body, it is worth outlining briefly some of the developments that took place in this earlier period.

## WORKERS' BODIES IN THE NINETEENTH CENTURY

Workers' bodies first crystallized as objects of public debate in the industrializing West during the late eighteenth and early nineteenth centuries, at a time when the nature and organization of large areas of industrial work were undergoing rapid changes. In part, such changes were precipitated by the mechanization of important areas of industrial production, and by the evolution of the factory system in order to make the most efficient use of such machinery. But these technical and managerial innovations were only part of a more generalized and more explicitly political assault on older forms of work organization and practice. Home working, workshop production, and the institutions of trade and guild all demarcated social spaces in which workers could exert control over the exercise and disposal of their own labor. From the late eighteenth century, these structures all came under concerted attack, both legally, with the banning of workers' organizations and the undermining of such practices as apprenticeship, and informally, as the new factories began to absorb significant sections of the labor force. Increasingly, older collective forms of work organization were being displaced by contract labor — a move that was sanctified by the new science of political economy, which privileged the contract between employer and employee as the defining relationship of industrial work.

This privileging of the law of contract over other forms of social relations was justified on the grounds that it offered the best means of ensuring a fair distribution of goods within an industrial economy. In order to back this claim up with formal arguments, political economists adopted a particular theoretical conception of workers' bodies and their role in industrial production. The body — along with any special skills it possessed — was to be regarded, in effect, as a form of property or capital that workers could invest in industrial production and realize in the wages they received for their labor. The market price of labor, it was argued, provided an objective valuation of the worth of such capital, and hence a fair return for the worker's bodily investment. That the labor market did in fact work in this beneficial manner was held to be evident in the way that the wage bargain tended to reflect any dangers that employees might face in the workplace. Thus, it was widely recognized that certain occupations were attended by unusually high rates of injury or work-related illness. But it was argued that workers in such occupations were able to demand a price for their labor which adequately recompensed any potential loss or depreciation of their bodily capital.

Workers themselves were rarely impressed by such economic reassurances, however. Rather, they were outraged by the massive disruption of social and economic relations that characterized the industrial revolution, and frequently reacted with outspoken and often violent opposition, in particular to the growth of mechanization and of the factory system. Increasingly, employers and their representatives in government came to accept that they must be seen to offer adjustments in the terms of industrial work if they were to appease their employees and take the steam out of political protest. They tended to do so, however, not by interfering in the organization of the labor market as a whole, but rather by imposing restrictions on the hours and conditions of employment of specific groups of workers — notably women and children — whom they deemed to be particularly vulnerable to exploitation and to other risks associated with industrial work.

Such measures tapped a deep vein of patriarchal values that ran through industrial as much as pre-industrial culture. Not least, they played to working- as well as middle-class assumptions about men's role as the principle breadwinners within the domestic economy. There is evidence to suggest that many working-class men worked within the same gendered economic assumptions as were adopted by their employers; some groups of workers, at least, clearly traded off earnings against health in choosing particular occupations or places of work, and even took pride in the risks that they ran to provide, as they saw it, for their families. By thus distinguishing between the economic roles of adult males on the one hand, and women and child workers on the other, early industrial health legislation served, in effect, to make the emerging economy of contract labor seem more natural and acceptable, at least to those sections of the working population who were left to participate freely in that economy. In effect, the free market in adult male labor was made socially viable by hedging it around with statutory restrictions on the employment of women and children.

Such restrictions were also legitimized, at least in part, by the development of expert medical knowledge about workers' bodies, and about the conditions under which the capital represented by those bodies might best be managed. This managerial knowledge would become increasingly refined and reoriented as economic assumptions about the organization of industrial society, and about the role of workers' bodies within it, were redefined during the later nineteenth and early twentieth centuries. By the mid-nineteenth century, Western industry was growing rapidly, not just in overall capacity, but also in the size and complexity of individual enterprises. Particular industries, and even particular firms, were now coming to dominate large sections of the economy, and hence the lives of large sections of the working population. At the same time, the nation state was emerging as a crucial unit of competition within the world economy. Increasingly, the pursuit of industrial productivity and wealth came to be identified, not just with the interests of private capital, but with corporate and national interests. Meanwhile, labor was emerging as an increasingly effective political force, organized into unions to demand better terms and conditions of employment, and increasingly capable of disrupting production to secure those ends. Consequently, the supply and management of labor came to be seen as one of the main factors limiting industrial productivity and the growth of national economies, and industrial managers and government administrators began to ask how to make the most efficient use of industrial labor.

These developments found expression in a reorientation of economic theory, and in the kinds of social policies that such theory legitimized. From the 1870s onwards, in Britain, continental Europe and America, successive generations of economic thinkers rejected the individualistic presuppositions of classical economic liberalism, and highlighted instead the need for more active management of the industrial economy and of industrial society as a whole. Among other things, they argued that far more could be done to husband and manage the productive power of labor. Their arguments were taken up by the medical profession, who by this time possessed a growing body of knowledge of health conditions in industry from which to argue that work-related illness and debility in the labor force were seriously undermining productivity. In effect, doctors argued, this ill health represented a depreciation not just of the bodily capital that individual workers were able to invest in industrial production, but of the national fund of productive labor. Consequently, if international competitiveness was to be maintained and improved, efforts needed to be made to protect that bodily capital from at least some of the dangers it faced at work.

Particular attention was paid to the workplace environment, with the passage of legislation requiring the fencing of machinery, the regulation of unhealthy industrial processes, and the observance of minimum standards of ventilation in factories and mines. In large part, such environmental measures were carried forward from earlier paternalistic efforts to protect the health of women and children. But significantly, later nineteenth-century legislation extended such measures to include adult male workers. What was now at issue was not just the smooth working of the labor market, but the health and efficiency of the entire working population. Increasingly, during the late nineteenth and early twentieth century, governments and industry came to share the view that the regulation of the working environment offered an important means of husbanding the bodily resources of the working population.

Nor was interest in the preservation of bodily capital confined to industrialists and their representatives in government. Workers, too, called for improvements in their working environment as part of their own efforts to improve the terms and conditions of industrial employment, not least with the aim of protecting their own earning power. Increasingly, workers' bodies were becoming objects of crucial importance, both in the management of the industrial economy and in the working out of industrial politics more generally. On the whole, however, the terms in which industrial bodies and their environmental relations were characterized and defined were not determined by workers themselves. Rather, they were articulated primarily within the discourses of medical and administrative science, and as such were commonly shaped more by managerial interests than by workers' own concerns. This is particularly clear in the way that the techniques and theories of experimental physiology — the most prestigious of the biomedical sciences for much of the first half of the twentieth century — were brought to bear on the study of workers' bodies.

## FATIGUE AND THE PHYSIOLOGICAL ECONOMY

Early twentieth-century medical and managerial interest in workers' bodies did not focus solely on the environmental determinants of industrial health and productivity. At the same time, medical experts also began to argue that significant improvements in the efficiency of industrial production could be made if closer attention was paid to the management and regulation of the working body itself. This interest in managing the productive capacity of industrial bodies was reinforced and focused by developments in the technical understanding of the human body. From the mid-nineteenth century, workers in the new laboratory-based biomedical discipline of experimental physiology had been developing techniques for defining and measuring the capacity of the living body to generate energy and perform physical work. Using such techniques, medical scientists in Germany, Britain, France and the United States were able to formulate a highly sophisticated account of the body as an energetic system. Researchers elucidated the energetic aspects of the processes of metabolism, the laws that governed the transformation of chemical energy into physical work in the muscles, and the control of such processes through the ordered distribution of electrical energy in nerve impulses.

This energetic understanding of the human body resonated with a similarly energeticist strand of thinking about the working of the industrial economy. The body itself was now commonly described as, in effect, an energetic economy, characterized by the regulation and integration of a host of physiological processes that together made possible the performance of physical work. If the body was the worker's capital, so energy was "the capital of the body,"[1] which, if invested wisely, would provide returns in the form of further bodily growth, production and reproduction. Such physiological production was also often conceived in explicitly industrial terms. Popular science books of the early twentieth century abound with images of the human body as a factory, in which complex machinery, a sophisticated division of labor, and the generation of physical energy are so organized as to create a unique capacity for performing productive work. But the flow of ideas between economic and physiological theory did not take place in one direction only. Conversely, physiological ideas about the management and regulation of the bodily economy were imported into the science of economics proper. It became something of a commonplace to argue that society could be understood as a living organism, analogous to a biological organism in the way that the different parts and processes of the social body needed to be integrated into a functional and self-regulating whole. Such views also found formal expression in the work of economic theorists, who likewise conceived of the industrial economy as a system of production and consumption analogous to the living body. From *The Physiology of Industry*, published by the British economist J.A. Hobson in 1889, to the physiologically informed economic speculations of the Harvard 'Pareto Circle' in the 1920s and 1930s, scientific ideas about the regulation, integration and coordination of the living body were incorporated into debates about how best to manage the body economic.

Energetic ideas about the industrial body also provided a language in which to articulate very general fears about the health of industrial society. Most notably, during the late nineteenth and early twentieth century, fatigue of one sort or another was commonly held to be responsible for a wide range of social problems. It was widely assumed that the accelerating pace of industrial life — not just the speed-up of industrial work, but also the excitements and distractions of life in the expanding industrial cities — exacted an increasingly severe toll upon the human organism. Fatigue was evident in the worn out bodies of the working poor. But it was also seen to have less material manifestations: in the emergence of new neurological diseases such as railway spine, hysteria and neurasthenia; in the nervousness and irritability that medical observers discerned in the social as much as the individual constitution; and in the increasingly ill-tempered and confrontational mood that now characterized labor relations. Fatigue was at once a somatic, psychological and social pathology. As such, it provided a powerful and resonant language for talking about the problems of maintaining social order and industrial competitiveness in increasingly industrialized Western societies.

But fatigue was also a measurable physiological phenomenon, observable in the laboratory as a decline in the rate at which a muscle could perform physical work, or as a reduction in the speed and accuracy of mental functioning. As such, the concept of fatigue provided a way of integrating a physiological understanding of the body into wider debates about the management of industrial society. In particular, it enabled medical scientists to claim special insight into the problems of managing the productive power of labor. Through the late nineteenth and early twentieth century, physiologists developed a battery of techniques and methodologies for measuring fatigue, not just in the laboratory, but also in the industrial workplace. And they used their findings to argue that appropriate managerial innovations would make it possible to make more efficient use of the productive capacity of workers' bodies.

One place where such claims found a political purchase was in renewed debates over the restriction of hours of work. From the 1880s, workers began to call for further legislation to restrict the length of the working day, not just for women and children, but also for men. These demands were backed up by physiological evidence that muscular and mental efficiency declined rapidly if specifiable limits on the duration and intensity of labor were exceeded, and that economic efficiency was consequently being compromised as a result of the excessive hours that were still commonly worked in many industries. Such arguments proved compelling. Since the mid-nineteenth century, a handful of employers in Britain, Belgium and Germany had been experimenting with shorter working hours, with favorable results. Subsequently, state legislatures also became involved, mobilizing physiological research both to defend existing restrictions on the working hours of women and children and to legitimize new controls on men's hours. The notion of fatigue also quickly became incorporated into calls for improvements in the environmental conditions of industrial work. Environmental regulation was no longer conceived simply as a way of protecting the body from work-related injury and illness — though this remained important — but also as a means of optimising the mechanical and mental efficiency of the working body and minimizing fatigue, for instance through the provision of adequate ventilation and the control of air temperature.

It was during the First World War, however, that the physiological approach to the management of workers' bodies became most deeply implicated in industrial practice. In the context of total war, governments were concerned that the energies of the entire non-combatant population should be employed as efficiently as possible in the work of war-related production. To this end, large sectors of industry, and of the industrial economy more generally, were brought under direct state control. At the same time, government administrators turned increasingly to medical scientists to provide them with technical criteria for defining the most efficient conditions of industrial work. Physiologists were drafted into various official committees on the regulation of working conditions; hours of work in government-run industries were reduced in line with the recommendations of fatigue researchers; scientifically ratified measures were implemented to improve environmental conditions in the workplace; and national food policies were formulated in keeping with physiological accounts of the kind and quantity of nutrition necessary to sustain the productive power of the workforce.

To an extent, such intervention may have been facilitated by residual paternalistic assumptions. During the war, unprecedented numbers of women found employment in munitions factories and other industries, and it may be that governments were at least partly motivated by a continuing belief that women were particularly vulnerable to the risks of industrial work. But efforts to protect the health and efficiency of women workers were only one facet of the more general extension of administrative and managerial control over industrial production and other aspects of the industrial economy during the war. Moreover, such measures were legitimized primarily in the universalistic language of physiological energetics, rather than in terms of the moral need to protect the health of a particular section of the working population. What took place during the war was the extension of an ideology of technical and managerial control into increasingly large areas of

industrial society — an extension that was underpinned by an energeticist understanding of the physiological economy.

Various government and philanthropic bodies continued to support research
into industrial fatigue and the physiological aspects of industrial efficiency in the
years that followed the First World War. But the relevance of such research to
managerial practice was now rapidly waning. With the inter-war economy spiraling
into recession and unemployment mounting, industrial production ceased to
depend primarily upon the efficient utilization of workers' bodies. At the same
time, labor asserted itself once more as a political as much as a productive force;
of use to industry, to be sure, but restive and capable of wrecking the delicate
system of checks and balances on which industrialists and government administrators increasingly supposed the industrial economy to depend. In this setting,
the physiological economics of labor power were seen to be an inadequate guide
to the complexities of industrial politics. The efficient management of the laboring
body was of decreasing importance. Far more pressing was the effective management of labor relations, in which area industrialists, managers and politicians
already possessed considerable skills without needing to listen to the advice of
fatigue researchers and other medical scientists.

After the war most governments were keen to withdraw from the fractious arena
of labor relations. Politicians had learned that, even when nations were unified
by the common enterprise of war, labor relations could be a fraught and difficult
matter. In the difficult political and economic circumstances of the 1920s and
1930s, they were largely happy to leave such matters in the experienced hands of
employers themselves. Consequently, while some government administrators continued to harbor a belief that physiological science offered important insights into
the efficient ordering of industrial society, they saw little immediate prospect of
being able to impose such order. Increasingly, work on fatigue and other physiological aspects of industry gave way to less technically focused and more
managerially useful research into the 'human factor' in industry, or was diverted
into the formulation of psychometric tests for use in selecting the most suitable
workers from a pool of excess labor. Consequently, while shorter working hours
became common during the inter-war years, this was largely as a result of negotiations with labor rather than pressure from fatigue scientists. By the time of the
Second World War, and the renewal of efforts to harness the productive energies
of the population to the national effort, the lessons of the previous war had been
forgotten, and the same problems of over-work were once again allowed to occur.

## INDUSTRIAL WELFARE AND WORKMEN'S COMPENSATION

With the decline in interest in physiological management during the inter-war
period, a rather different view of workers' bodies took precedence. Like the
physiological paradigm that it replaced, this new approach to the industrial body
had its roots in late nineteenth-century efforts to strengthen the industrial economy.

But unlike the physiological approach, it did not treat the worker's body primarily as a means of industrial production, and was not concerned with imposing direct managerial control on that body. Rather, it approached the body as a site around which to articulate a more conciliatory politics of labor relations. By the end of the nineteenth century, many businessmen and politicians were coming to the view that workers might be more willing to grant their trust and cooperation, and less keen to resort to industrial action, if they could be persuaded that their needs and concerns were being attended to, both in the workplace and elsewhere. Within this conceptual framework, the worker's body was regarded primarily as an object of welfare policy. One element in welfare thinking from the late nineteenth century onwards was the provision of various forms of health care, and of care for bodily needs more generally. From the 1890s, some companies began to provide a growing range of facilities for their employees, including canteens, baths, recreational facilities and workplace doctors. A similar approach was adopted by government agencies, and state-assisted medical insurance and the provision of medical care played an increasingly important role in government welfare policies from the 1870s until the mid-twentieth century.

Initially, at least, this concern with bodily welfare was closely bound up with an interest in physiological productivity. Throughout the first half of the twentieth century, the proponents of state medical care commonly equated health with the ability to perform industrial work, and argued that appropriate forms of medical provision were necessary to maintain a healthy and productive workforce. But the growth of medical welfare was not informed solely by a concern to promote efficient production. From the late nineteenth century onwards, economic thinkers came instead to privilege consumption as the key to a healthy industrial economy. By the mid-twentieth century, this view had come to dominate economic theory, most influentially in the doctrines of Keynesian economics. Consequently, many of the welfare measures adopted by the governments of industrial countries in this period — including unemployment insurance, old age pensions, wage legislation and 'social credit' — were at least partly justified on the grounds that they would help to reinforce consumption among the working class. To a considerable extent, the provision of medical care came to be understood in the same light, particularly during the period of labor surplus that followed the First World War. Thus, while health continued to be identified with the ability to perform industrial work, work itself now tended to be regarded, not so much as the driving force of production, but rather as the worker's means of earning a wage. In this context, state medical provision came to be regarded primarily as a way of insuring against the invalidity and loss of personal income that resulted from ill health, and thereby of addressing one of the most serious causes of poverty and financial insecurity among the working population. As such, medical welfare was expected to exert a beneficial effect on the industrial economy, not so much by boosting production as by shoring up consumption.

This becomes evident when we recognize how little attention was paid, within government medical policy, to specifically work-related medical care. Even in Britain, where an exceptionally comprehensive system of public medical care was established with the creation of the National Health Service in 1948, industrial medicine was expressly excluded from such provision. Insofar as medical surveillance and treatment were seen as ways of managing the productive energies of the workforce, it was expected that such measures could safely be left to the Ministry of Labour and to industry itself. By contrast, the role of the state medical services was simply to provide, as part of the welfare state, the same kind of general health care as consumers would otherwise have had to provide for themselves. A similar shift from a productivist to a welfare perspective on workers' bodies can be discerned in the way that nutritional standards were defined and debated during the first half of the twentieth century. During the First World War, physiologists had sought to determine the calorific intake necessary to maintain productive labor. But between the wars, against a backdrop of labor surplus, agitation over the minimum wage and concern at the condition of the under- and unemployed, such research generally gave way to more pragmatic efforts to define politically acceptable standards of nutrition and the minimum levels of income necessary to maintain subsistence.

The same economic and political priorities can be identified in what would become, in effect, the main legislative means of responding to the problems of specifically work-related ill health during the twentieth century, namely the growth of workmen's compensation. Within the contractual framework of mid-nineteenth-century employment law it was generally assumed, as we have seen, that workers — or at least adult male workers — were capable of assessing any bodily risks to which they might be exposed in the normal course of their work, and of ensuring that such risks were reflected in the price of their labor. In other words, injury and illness were natural or at least normal consequences of industrial work, and as such could readily be evaluated by any morally competent worker. Consequently, employers should only be held liable for such accidents as could be shown to have resulted from their neglect of what might reasonably be considered their contractual responsibilities towards their workers. But with the growth of organized labor, workers' representatives began to challenge these assumptions, calling for an extension of the legal definition of employers' liability to include not just those exceptional incidents that could be identified as a breach of contract on the part of the employer, but also many of the injuries that were seen to arise as a normal consequence of industrial work. The workmen's compensation schemes enacted from the later nineteenth century onwards went some way to meet these demands. Such schemes acknowledged, in effect, that the wage bargain alone did not adequately recompense workers for the dangers they faced at work. Consequently, employers were required to pay compensation for a growing list of industrial injuries and work-related illnesses.

Workmen's compensation generally fell far short of what workers had initially hoped for, however. In pressing for an extension of employer's liability, workers had hoped to be able to sue for any loss of earnings that might result from injury or illness. Implicit in this aim was the view that workers' bodies were, in effect, their capital, to be realized in the wages they earned over their working life. Compensation payments should therefore be set at such a level as to make good any loss or depreciation of this bodily capital. As actually enacted by government legislation, however, workmen's compensation, did little more than provide a minimum level of subsistence for those deprived of the ability to earn a living. Nor did workmen's compensation do much to protect the productive power of workers' bodies. Workers and medical policy makers had initially hoped that the expense of compensation would stimulate employers to take steps to preserve health and safety in the workplace. But in practice, employers generally found it easier simply to pay the requisite compensation than to tackle the managerially more demanding task of making work safer.

Indeed, the very fact that injury and illness occurred routinely and predictably in the course of industrial work meant that compensation could be administered on a straightforwardly actuarial basis. Workmen's compensation thus did little more than transfer the subsistence costs of those impoverished by industrial injury and illness onto employers, who simply absorbed them into the costs of production. In effect, bodily injury and incapacity continued to be regarded as a normal consequence of industrial work, to be managed within the framework of a welfare settlement that included not just routine compensation, but also such measures as unemployment insurance and public health care provision.

In general, then, within the political and economic framework of welfare thinking, workers' bodies ceased to be regarded as the motors of industrial production. Rather, they were simply the means by which individual workers could earn a living, and a site for the consumption of the fruits of their labors. Insofar as industry and the industrial state had a responsibility towards those bodies, it consisted chiefly in ensuring that their minimum needs were met in times of unemployment and sickness. It was left to workers themselves, and to their representatives in government, to press for further legislative measures to protect the working body from the risks it encountered in the workplace. Such pressure was to an extent successful. New occupational diseases continued to be recognized for compensation purposes and preventive intervention. But such measures did not result from any consensus that industrial societies had an intrinsic interest in protecting the productive power of workers' bodies. Rather, they were the outcome of negotiations between workers, employers and the state, conducted within the political framework of labor relations. Workers' bodies no longer constituted a key site around which to articulate managerial and administrative solutions to the political and economic problems of industrial society. Rather, they were just one among a number of sites where the politics of labor relations and welfare could be worked out.

## LATE INDUSTRIAL PRODUCTION AND FLEXIBLE BODIES

Since the Second World War, industrial society has undergone a series of remarkably rapid transformations, not always tending in the same direction. The years
immediately following the War marked the high point in the development of the
managed economy in the most developed industrial nations. The politics of post-
war reconstruction, combined with a period of relative labor shortage in the
advanced industrial economies, served to place a renewed value on the management and husbanding of the workforce and of workers' bodies in particular. Even
in the United States, where opposition to government intervention in the market
economy was more deeply entrenched than in other industrial nations, public
funding and organization of health care expanded rapidly up to the establishment
of Medicare and Medicaid in the 1960s. The bodily welfare of the working population was one of the priorities of the post-war state. At the same time, organized
labor found itself in a strong position to press for the introduction of new measures
to prevent work-related illness and injury, and for the establishment of increasingly
effective government agencies to enforce those measures.

It was not long, however, before the high tide of interest in industrial health
and safety began to ebb. From the 1960s, industries of mass employment relocated
with increasing rapidity from areas of established industrial production to developing countries or to less developed regions of the Western World, where plentiful
supplies of cheap and unorganized labor could be exploited with little concern
for workers' welfare. At the same time, such industries and businesses as retained
their base in the older industrial economies began to argue for a return to free-
market economics and a withdrawal of government regulation, in order to maintain competitiveness in the expanding global economy. Organized labor found
itself increasingly powerless to resist such changes, in part through the decline in
mass employment and the casualization of work, but also through deliberate
political attacks on the powers of trade unions. By the 1970s, the politics of
industrial health and welfare were in decline in the industrial West, while their
development in the new industrial economies was at best piecemeal. To an extent,
this was offset by an increase in litigation against companies who were judged to
have violated what were now widely accepted standards of care for the health of
their workers. But as we have seen, the pursuit of compensation is generally an
ineffective method of promoting health and safety at work. Moreover, such gains
tended to be restricted to that diminishing sector of the industrial economy in
which labor remained powerful and well organized. Overall, workers' bodies were
ceasing to occupy a significant role in the articulation and negotiation of industrial
politics and economics.

That said, in certain areas of industry, greater attention than ever before was
now being paid to the management of workers' bodies. Many of the industries that
retained a producer base in the developed world now looked increasingly to the
introduction of new technologies to maintain a competitive advantage within the

global economy. This was not simply a matter of improving the efficiency of production; it also had an important political dimension. In some sections of manufacturing industry, new technologies — for instance the development of numerical control machine tools — made it possible to appropriate workers' manual skills into machines themselves. This mechanization of skill not only helped to increase productivity by surpassing the physical capabilities of the human body; it also served the interests of manufacturers and their shareholders by minimizing the involvement of labor in the production process, and by imposing new forms of managerial control on those workers who remained. In effect, the introduction of new production technologies made possible a shift from labor-intensive to capital-intensive forms of industrial production.

Even in those industries in which bodily involvement in the work of production could be reduced to a series of stereotyped movements, however, it was rarely possible to remove workers from the production process entirely. Moreover, in many other areas of high-technology industry — particularly in those industries where production involved a degree of human judgement, for instance in business or the media — workers' embodied skills remained crucial in determining productivity, no matter how sophisticated the technologies they had at their disposal. Consequently, managers began to look for new ways of ensuring that the most effective use could be made of workers' skills. One site where they perceived that improvements in efficiency could be secured was in the interaction between workers and machines.

The science of ergonomics had its roots in the physiological research into industrial work that was conducted in the years around the First World War. Such work was revived with the resurgence of productivist politics during the Second World War. But in the more technologically sophisticated military setting of the early 1940s, a reductively physiological and energeticist approach to the performance of bodily work proved inadequate. Research tended to focus primarily on the performance of complex technical tasks, for instance the piloting of aircraft, and on ways in which technical processes could be so organized as to allow the most efficient operation of the human component of the human-machine ensemble. A more holistic approach, rooted primarily in a psychological rather than a physiological understanding of the ways that humans interacted with machines, and of the mental as well as physical skill that they brought to their work, was now adopted. After the War, this new-found ergonomic expertise found a place in the growth of industrial design, and particularly in the design of new technologies. Crucially, it lent itself to the problem of engineering the processes of industrial production so as to make the most efficient use of workers' bodies and skills.

Subsequently, and especially since the 1970s, this concern with engineering the performance of skilled work has developed far beyond the simply ergonomic, to incorporate a much wider repertoire of managerial techniques and methodologies. Increasingly tight competition in the technically more advanced industries has placed a premium on the adoption of ever more efficient production methods. Meanwhile, many industries have come to depend not just on efficiency, but also on rapid innovation both in the kinds of goods produced and in the methods of their production. The pursuit of such strategies of so-called 'flexible' production, with its emphasis on highly adaptable and responsive methods of skilled and often highly technical work, has led to an enormous growth of managerial involvement in the day-to-day work of industrial production through the adoption of such perspectives as 'total quality management.'

Managerial and economic conceptions of the identity and role of workers in the production process have also changed accordingly. Rather than simply being regarded as a source of motive power or the possessors of specific skills, workers themselves are now expected to display the same kind of flexibility as is required of production as a whole. For one thing, the liberalization of the labor market and the growth of structural unemployment have made it far easier to hire and fire workers as and when they are needed. Compared with older forms of industrial production, workers now have to cope with greater job insecurity and greater mobility between jobs. But even within jobs, workers are often expected to be able to adapt to, and indeed to help implement, rapid changes in production goals and methods. This has often involved delegating to workers a significant measure of responsibility for managing their own work, in the expectation that their knowl- edge and skills can thus be put to use in meeting the demands of flexible pro- duction. However, this delegation of managerial responsibility should not be mistaken for a return to the kind of autonomy that workers had sought to defend in the early days of industrialization. On the contrary, it represents an increasingly pervasive infiltration of managerial aims and interests into every level of productive work. Workers are rarely free to decide on the rate of production or the kinds of product they can turn out, but only on how they are to meet the stringent demands imposed on them by higher levels of management.

Such managerial innovations are not reducible to the management of workers' bodies. But they do have their bodily corollaries. This is particularly evident in the attention paid to a new class of what might best be termed psychosomatic pathologies of work, including stress, chronic fatigue syndrome or ME, and, most recently, 'information sickness.' Again, these conditions are not usually defined by physical disability alone — though such disability is often present — but rather by a more diffuse collection of functional symptoms including fatigue, anxiety and depres- sion. Medical scientists have tended to disagree over whether such conditions have a somatic seat, or whether they should be attributed solely to psychogenic causes. But insofar as they are understood to affect or reside in the body, this is commonly identified with some kind of dysfunction of the immune system, be it an immune deficiency or a form of auto-immunity. Whether or not there is any scientific consensus on such issues, this interest in the immune system has proved remarkably resonant in lay concepts of illness, including not just illnesses of work, but also many other problems of health in the late twentieth century. In particular, it pervades much popular thinking about the relationship between work and illness, and is deployed in managerial discussions of how to make the best use of the industrial workforce. This constant referral to modern conceptions of immunity is highly revealing of how workers' bodies are conceived within industry.

Early theories of immunity, as developed in the late nineteenth and early twentieth century, conceived of the body as a self-contained entity under threat of invasion and disruption by malign environmental agencies, in particular the microbial agents of disease. The immune system constituted a form of bodily defense against such invasion. More recent theories of immunity, developed from about the 1950s, conceive of it rather as a system of adaptive mediation, enabling the body to maintain a coherent and flexible self-hood, not just within a changing environment, but also through its own developmental and degenerative changes. This new understanding of immunity does not theorize the defense of the body from a threatening environment, so much as the active exchange of information between the world and the body, and its role in the maintenance of a dynamic and contingent bodily integrity. According to this view the immune system is an informational system which enables the body to redefine and, in effect, to re-imagine itself in response to changes both in its environment and in itself.

This understanding of the immune body reflects prevailing concerns about how best to manage workers within the new forms of flexible production. The characterization of the body as an adaptive information-based system provides a somatic focus for managerial efforts to promote and regulate the adaptive behavior of their employees. Most notably, the description of stress and other pathologies of advanced industry as dysfunctions of the immune system identifies them, in effect, as bodily expressions of the difficulties of adapting to the demands of flexibility, self-management and occupational identity that beset the new industries. Workers themselves commonly experience such stress as a problem. But it should not be supposed that managers see it in the same unequivocally negative light. On the contrary, ideas about stress increasingly play a positive role in management theory and practice. For one thing, stress effectively serves to mark the limits of the managerial demands that can be imposed on workers. In this respect, it provides a useful means of monitoring workers' performance and flexibility, not least with a view to identifying those individuals who are less able to cope with the demands of the job, and who can therefore be singled out for retraining or dismissal. But equally, the presence of a certain level of stress serves to indicate that managers are pushing workers to their limits, and are thus making the most effective use of their productive capacities. Understood in this way, as a somatic response to demands for adaptation and flexibility at work, stress is an important element in recent managerial theory and practice, to the extent that some critics have dubbed this body of practice "management by stress."[2]

Among the methods of "management by stress" may be included various techniques of 'stress management,' which have been widely adopted within industry under the guise of welfare services for employees. Such techniques commonly have a strong somatic component, ranging from meditation and breathing exercises, through massage to various forms of physical recreation. Significantly, the beneficial effects of such practices are commonly supposed to be mediated by a strengthening of the immune system. Similar ideas about bodily adaptability are also applied in a wide range of managerial training programs, most notably in the various forms of 'experiential learning' that are increasingly being used to promote teamwork and flexible working practices. Such programs start from the supposition that stress is an important and inevitable component of learning and adaptation. Consequently, workers are placed in circumstances of considerable stress and anxiety, for instance on so-called 'outward bound' courses, in order to enhance their ability to learn to work together and rely upon one another. Again, it is commonly argued that the experience of stress serves to tone up the immune system, and thereby to stimulate the somatic as much as the mental and social effects of training.

Thus, in the most developed industrial economies, the worker's body has once again become an important object within the purview of managerial theory and practice. However, the conceptualization of this body differs significantly from earlier understandings of the body as a source of productive energy, or as a site for the articulation of welfare politics. From the most modern view, workers' bodies provide the somatic basis for functional flexibility, making it possible for workers to assimilate and manage information, to take responsibility for a wide range of tasks, and to adapt to the changing managerial demands of modern industry. Such an understanding is entirely in keeping with new ideas about flexible production, and places the worker's body squarely in the frame of 'total quality management' and other extensions of managerial control and regulation. Within the more technically and managerially sophisticated industries, workers' bodies are more closely integrated than ever before into the organization and management of industrial production.

It is also worth noting that economic and managerial thinking has once again begun to adopt the view that industrial corporations, if not nation states, can usefully be thought of as analogous to living organisms in the way that they maintain their integrity, adapt and survive within a changing environment. The particular body of biological knowledge to which economists and managers now make reference has changed since the early twentieth century, however where physiology used to provide the favored model of organismal homeostasis, managerial and biological interests alike now incline towards the more flexible and open-ended processes of immunology. Nevertheless, the continuing exchange of ideas about biological organization and regulation on the one hand, and about industrial organization and regulation on the other, betrays an underlying synergy between the two spheres of thought.

For over a hundred years, the apparently disparate enterprises of biology and industry have frequently shared a common concern with the maintenance and reproduction of complex divisions of labor. For both enterprises, the biological organism literally embodies basic principles of good management. They may differ in their instrumental aims: for biology, it is to characterize those managerial principles in the definitive language of modern science; for industry, it is to put those same principles into practice, not least as a means of extracting the greatest possible productive value from workers' bodies. But both are animated — the one perhaps less directly, the other more so — by a prevailing concern with the bodily regulation and management of human life for the purpose of industrial production. Throughout the twentieth century, accounts of the biological body repeatedly reflected a concern with, and provided theoretical and practical tools for, the management of the industrial body.

That said, it must be reiterated that even in the late twentieth century, this concern with workers' bodies — and indeed with biological bodies more generally — was still largely restricted to particular areas of technically advanced production within the most industrially developed countries. In large areas of the global industrial economy, the existence of free labor markets, cheap labor and technically simple methods of production means that workers' bodies are no more a focus of managerial interest than they were in the earliest stages of Western industrialization. For the vast majority of the world's workers, sophisticated accounts of organic regulation have little bearing on their own bodily experiences of labor, or on the methods of management to which they are exposed. For these workers, as for their employers, the body remains little more than the means by which individuals may earn a living, and through which they experience such subjective satisfactions and hardships as industrial work may offer them.

## REFERENCES

1.  George Helms, *Die Lehre von der Energie* (1887), quoted in Anson Rabinbach, 'The Body Without Fatigue: A Nineteenth-Century Utopia,' in Seymour Drescher, David Sabean and Allan Sharlin (eds), *Political Symbolism in Modern Europe: Essays in Honor of George L. Mosse* (New Brunswick: Transaction Books, 1982), pp. 42–62, at p. 50.
2.  Mike Parker and Jane Slaughter, 'Management-by-Stress: The Team Concept in the US Auto Industry,' *Science as Culture* (1990), **8**: 27–58.

## FURTHER READING

Bartrip, P.W.J., *Workmen's Compensation in Twentieth Century Britain.* (Aldershot: Gower, 1987).
Bayer, Ronald (ed.), *The Health and Safety of Workers: Case Studies in the Politics of Professional Responsibility.* (New York/Oxford: Oxford University Press, 1988).
Cooter, Roger and Luckin, Bill (eds), *Accidents in History: Injuries, Fatalities and Social Relations.* (Amsterdam: Rodopi, 1997).
Dumett, Raymond, 'Disease and Mortality Among Gold Miners of Ghana: Colonial Government and Mining Company Attitudes and Policies, 1900–1938,' *Social Science and Medicine* (1993), **37**: 213–232.

Figlio, Karl, 'How does Illness Mediate Social Relations? Workmen's Compensation and Medico-Legal Practices, 1890–1940', in P. Wright and A. Treacher (eds), *The Problem of Medical Knowledge: Examining the Social Construction of Medicine*. (Edinburgh: Edinburgh University Press, 1982).

Fishback, Price V., 'Liability Roles and Accident Prevention in the Workplace: Empirical Evidence from the Early Twentieth Century,' *Journal of Legal Studies* (1987), **56**: 305–328.

Gillespie, Richard, 'Industrial Fatigue and the Discipline of Physiology,' in Gerald L. Geison (ed.), *Physiology in the American Context, 1850–1940*. (Bethesda, MD: American Physiological Society, 1987).

Gillespie, Richard, 'Accounting for Lead Poisoning: The Medical Politics of Occupational Health and Safety,' *Social History* (1990), **15**: 303–331.

Gray, Robert, 'Medical Men, Industrial Labour and the State in Britain, 1830–1950,' *Social History* (1991), **16**: 19–43.

Harrison, Barbara, *Not Only the 'Dangerous Trades': Women's Work and Health in Britain, 1880–1914*. (London: Taylor & Francis, 1996).

Ineson, Antonia, 'Science, Technology, Medicine, Welfare and the Labour Process: Women Munition Workers in the First World War,' University of Sussex, M. Phil. dissertation, 1981.

Jones, Helen, 'Employers' Welfare Schemes and Industrial Relations in Inter-war Britain,' *Business History* (1983), **25**: 61–75.

Kippen, Sandra, 'The Social and Political Meaning of the Silent Epidemic of Miners' Phthisis, Bendigo 1860–1960', *Social Science and Medicine* (1995), **41**: 491–499.

Labisch, Alfons, 'Doctors, Workers and the Scientific Cosmology of the Industrial World: The Social Construction of "Health" and the "Homo Hygienicus",' *Journal of Contemporary History* (1985), **20**: 599–635.

Martin, Emily, *Flexible Bodies: Tracking Immunity in American Culture — From the Days of Polio to the Age of AIDS*. (Boston: Beacon Press, 1994).

McIvor, A.J., 'Manual Work, Technology, and Industrial Health, 1918–39,' *Medical History* (1987), **31**: 160–189.

Navarro, Vicente, 'Work, Ideology, and Science: The Case of Medicine,' *Social Science and Medicine* (1980), **14**: 191–205.

Rabinbach, Anson, *The Human Motor: Energy, Fatigue, and the Origins of Modernity*. (New York: Basic Books, 1990).

Rabinbach, Anson, 'Social Knowledge, Social Risk, and the Politics of Industrial Accidents in Germany and France,' in Dietrich Rueschmeyer and Theda Skocpol (eds), *States, Social Knowledge, and the Origins of Modern Social Policies*. (Princeton, NJ: Princeton University Press, 1996).

Rosner, David and Markowitz, Gerald, *Deadly Dust: Silicosis and the Politics of Occupational Disease in Twentieth-Century America*. (Princeton: Princeton University Press, 1991).

Rosner, David and Markowitz, Gerald (eds), *Dying for Work: Workers' Safety and Health in Twentieth-Century America*. (Bloomington: Indiana University Press, 1987).

Sellers, Christopher C., *Hazards of the Job: From Industrial Disease to Environmental Health Science*. (Chapel Hill: University of North Carolina Press, 1997).

Stabile, Donald R., 'The Du Pont Experiments in Scientific Management: Efficiency and Safety, 1911–1919,' *Business History Review* (1987), **61**: 365–386.

Waldron, H.A., 'Occupational Health During the Second World War: Hope Deferred or Hope Abandoned?,' *Medical History* (1997), **41**: 197–212.

Weindling, Paul (ed.), *The Social History of Occupational Health*. (London: Croom Helm, 1985).

Wise, M. Norton and Smith, Crosbie, 'Work and Waste: Political Economy and Natural Philosophy in 19th Century Britain', parts 1–3, *History of Science* (1989), **27**: 263–301, 391–449; (1990) **28**: 221–261.

## CHAPTER 16

# The Third-World Body

### WARWICK ANDERSON

A specific 'Third-World body' does not exist; nor can we invent it. Representations of the native body or colonial body abound in popular and technical literatures of the nineteenth and early-twentieth centuries, but with formal decolonisation these bodies are necessarily, if imperfectly, disguised in an emergent discourse on global citizenship. One can find discussions of the Third-World citizen, an identity perhaps precarious and faulty, but any appearance of bodily difference in this governmental discourse implies its failure. The Third World is, in effect, a project for overcoming corporeal specificity and stigma through modernization. In providing an enunciatory position, Third-Worldism exacts a dematerialization, a transcendence of the native body — thus the Third World can afford to have a distinctive literature but not a distinctive body. And when bodily specificity resurfaces, as it does in representing famine or diseases like AIDS, it is usually taken to reveal the would-be expressive citizen as no more than a recidivist dirty native. In regaining such a body, one can lose the world.

My concern here is limited to Western biomedical representations of Asian and African bodies in the twentieth century. I will try to treat some recent work in the history of colonial medicine as though it could be read as a critical history of constitutions of the body. In so doing, I want to suggest a loose framework for understanding discourses of colonial embodiment and post-colonial citizenship. My argument is basically that colonial medicine was a socio-spatial discourse that becomes reframed as a discourse on human rights and governmentality during the twentieth century. Medical experts continued to represent African and Asian bodies as diseased, lazy, and grotesque — as symbolic inversions of a European social body — but they also began to hold out the hope that a colonial body subject to strict protocols of personal and domestic hygiene might reform itself, or rather, that an individual might use these technologies of self-care to acquire a generic citizenship. No longer just objects to provoke European self-satisfaction, the colonized were offered Western subject positions and a role in global capitalism. And yet the apparently hygienic citizens produced in these new medical discourses always teetered on the brink of atavism: they were always dressed natives, recovering natives, their full citizenship necessarily incomplete or deferred. Economic failure, incurable disease and the lack of God's grace could all mark their lasting abjection. Post-colonial identity has been produced as a bipolar disorder, with the natural repeatedly overbalancing the cultural, the savage overwhelming the civilized, the black overshadowing the white. The figure of the insubordinate native body thus keeps on staging its return with the help of the IMF, global media, and Mother Teresa.

These flexible typologies of native bodies illuminate a relentlessly dichotomizing European imagination more than they reveal the experience of any colonial body. Asians and Africans were not palimpsests awaiting European inscription; one can find as much resistance and indifference to protocols of hygiene as acceptance. The body may have been the target of colonial discourse but there is little evidence of a direct hit. Recent ethnographies of health and disease suggest that if changes in clothing, housing, diet, toilet, and manners occasionally reshaped subjectivities, they did so in ambiguous or unpredictable ways. Accordingly, I am not so concerned with the truth of these cultural inscriptions on the body as with the political effects of their supposed truth. It is the politics of colonial bodily control and discipline, and not phenomenology or biology, that interests me here. Of course the history of Asian and African bodies should be more than the history of European perception of them, or European imprinting on them, but these imperial ideologies continue to provide the more salient landmarks for that larger history.

Is there anything distinctively colonial or Third World about this story? Surely the same processes of stereotyping, the same marking and remarking of social boundaries, the same rituals of bodily purification, took place in Europe and North America during this period, the targets there women and the poor as much as other races. David Arnold, following Michel Foucault, has pointed out that there is a "sense in which all modern medicine is engaged in a colonizing process."[1] And yet, given the obvious gender and class analogies, I believe we can still detect some distinctive features of the colonial poetics of pollution. The authors of imperial medical discourses on embodiment found themselves peculiarly foreign and vulnerable, and therefore so much more anxious to assign marks of danger to others; in alien circumstances more is at stake in defining corporeal boundaries. Not surprisingly, the lines they drew, so rigid and yet so readily recast, traced more explicitly than in Europe the boundaries of race (even if this category could still presuppose a gender and a class). By the late-nineteenth century, the colonial sciences of man were thoroughly genealogical. They were also intimately connected with the expansion of the colonial state, a nexus which, as much as anything else, must have impressed on the local population the foreignness of this typologic discourse, at once more assertive than it had been domestically, and less hegemonic.

The history of a specifically colonial framing of the body is well disguised in conventional histories of twentieth-century medicine and imperialism. It is hard to detect any body in the glorious history of 'insect wars,' in tales of the triumph of germ theory in the tropics, and, more recently, in the story of Western medicine's complicity with colonial expansion. No doubt these instrumentalist histories work well in their proper context, but they tell us little or nothing about representations of European and native embodiment. There are, of course, some exceptions. Arnold regards the body (in late-nineteenth-century India) as a site of contestation between the colonized and the colonizers, and not simply a colonial construction or a biological given. In a recent series of articles, Ann Laura Stoler has examined early-twentieth-century medical inscriptions on the bodies of subordinate colonizers in Southeast Asia. Lenore Manderson and Nancy Hunt have traced the development of an interest in the reform of bodily habits of mothers and children in diverse colonial settings. In Randall Packard's account of discourses on African susceptibility to tuberculosis, we can find the construction of the body of the maladjusted, detribalized African. John and Jean Comaroff discuss the "interplay of natural facts and semantic projects,"[2] including Western medicine, in the cultural production of the African body in the early-twentieth century. Megan Vaughan has provided us with an even more detailed survey of the framing of the African social body in later biomedical discourses. All of these studies have been produced in the last decade or so; most of them are inspired by the interest of anthropologists such as Pierre Bourdieu in embodied cultural practices, and by the work of Michel Foucault on the construction of the modern biopolitical subject. In what follows, I draw principally on these texts and my own work to suggest a tentative, and perhaps provocative, framework for a history of colonial and post-colonial bodies.

## EUROPEANS, NATIVES, AND THE SOCIAL BODY

In the late-nineteenth century, colonial public health was still primarily a social-spatial discourse; it had governmental implications, but its logic was generally more repressive than disciplinary. By this I mean that colonial public health officers set out to control collectives in a pathogenic landscape; if they happened to reshape an individual's sense of self this was an unanticipated benefit.

That Europeans characterized non-Europeans as primitive, lazy, lascivious, profligate, superstitious, untrustworthy, grotesque and irresolute has become, through the work of Philip Curtin and Edward Said among others, a commonplace of colonial history. "My body was given back to me sprawled out, distorted, recolored," writes Frantz Fanon. "The negro is an animal, the negro is bad, the negro is mean, the negro is ugly...."[3] This sort of disparagement generally meant that the features assigned to native races were exactly those traits that Europeans believed they had themselves transcended: their perceptions of others described what they imagined had been expunged from their own identity. Sander Gilman has found a psychoanalytic explanation for the generation of these stereotypes; others, including Nancy Stepan, point to more obvious political and economic reasons for classifying different groups of people as inferior, even sub-human. Whatever the cause, there can be little doubt that the various classifications of races, and various orderings of these human types (always, though, with Europeans on top), informed most Western medical theory in the late-nineteenth century. Typologies of race provided Europeans with compelling generalizations to account for an otherwise bewildering array of biological and cultural differences. These ready-made categories allowed colonial emissaries to write homogeneity onto foreign populations and onto themselves. Every society, and especially their own, could be regarded as an organic whole, a social body with distinctive characteristics.

These racial types could be ambiguously gendered and sexualized. Of course, European males tended to present themselves as epitomes of self-possessed masculinity, according to the current conventions of this historically variable trait, but native races were always something else, or rather, someone else. What this was could vary by time and region. Gilman, in considering representations of Africans, argues that the black female in the nineteenth century comes to serve as the icon for her sexualized race. Other scholars have claimed that the colonized, especially Asians, are generally represented in the passive feminine; still others emphasize the popularity of tropes of perverse masculinity, applied particularly to African males and occasionally to Asian females. The common feature of all these attributions is the location in another race of abnormality, excess and danger. Boundaries between the colonizer and the colonized necessarily would be marked by hygiene and sexual control.

In attempting to define races, European scientists were at the same time structuring (and restructuring) the relations of humans to their environment and to one another. Each race was located securely in its ancestral realm and derived its distinctive biological and cultural forms from long residence in a distinctive environment. The bounding and typing of physical space thus went together with the production of definite types of racial bodies: to a great extent, then, racial determinism in the late-nineteenth century was an environmental determinism. In defining the tropical environment, for example, scientists were specifying the character of all the living organisms, including humans, that had struggled for existence there, or that God in his economic wisdom had placed there. The tropics are particularly apposite as an example. Philip Curtin and others have observed that by the eighteenth century, Europeans had created a myth of tropical redundance, contrasting a primitive exuberance with the staid gardens of Europe, and furthermore, they followed Montesquieu in suggesting an intimate relationship between this tropical vegetation, tropical bodies, and tropical mentality. In a sense, these doctrines were no more than specifications of revived Hippocratic environmentalist theory. The tropical races — improvident, relaxed, disordered — seemed to exist in the easiest of natural conditions. In a region of apparently female plenitude, no wonder that feminization of the local inhabitants was the default drive of colonial discourse, and that the torrid zones implied not just heat but passion too. Darwin and Wallace could seize on the homologies of race and environment to suggest that humans in the tropics had evaded those selection pressures that had in the distant past produced the hardier, go-ahead, European races. An over-nurturing mother nature had allowed her human charges to remain louche, irresolute and primitive. In an evolutionary schema tropical bodies bore the marks of a difference that was as much temporal as physical.

With the effort to make Europe global, the most pressing question was what would become of a race transplanted from its native soil and climate. Europeans feared they might either evolve into local types, so that acclimatization might mean pigmentation and worse, or they would degenerate and die out, like the exotic tropical organisms then languishing in chilly northern zoological gardens. The principle that a race was best fitted to resist the diseases of its ancestral realm — and, as a corollary, was especially vulnerable to ailments encountered in a foreign land — was a remarkably resilient element in late-nineteenth-century biomedical understandings of disease susceptibility. An enormous amount of colonial epidemiological research and diverse clinical experience could be built into this framework of meaning, as to a large extent it did not matter to such predispositionist theories whether the cause of the ailment was miasma or microbe. Theories of racial immunity thus constructed European imperialism as a medical conundrum: foreign places evidently could be taken as white dominions yet they were no place for a white man. During the first decades of the twentieth century, medical scientists sought first to reformulate and then to resolve this impediment to European expansion, so that responsible citizens might be projected onto any part of the globe and flourish in spite of their bodies.

Although white bodies in the colonies were deemed especially vulnerable, not all of them were degenerating or recuperating from illness, nor were all natives in robust good health. Racial bodies could be ambiguously diseased, or deemed prone to disease. While most Europeans continued to regard racial adaptation as the chief determinant of disease expression, they also appreciated the influence of other factors, including diet, character, energy, and the degree of exposure to pathogenic material. At the same time, with the consolidation of imperial control in the late-nineteenth century, and prompted by an interest in developing local labor, improved epidemiological surveillance was indicating that natives succumbed to disease at least as often as foreigners. Clearly racial resistance was less absolute than previously thought. Many public health officers were quick to attribute the newly recognized native liability to moral failings, for if the locals were acquiring diseases that their race had previously resisted, then they must surely have become very depraved indeed. After all, natives should have had a long process of adaptation on their side, unlike whites who got sick: disease among natives suggested a pathological race culture, while Europeans remained, usually, the innocent victims of migration. With germ theory, the increasingly evident disease burden of the locals, yet another reason for cultural self-satisfaction, soon also became a cause of intense somatic anxiety for Europeans.

## DIRTY NATIVES AND HYGIENIC CITIZENS

At the beginning of the twentieth century, as colonial economies became better integrated into a global economy, native bodies were increasingly recognized not simply as the body of the other, but more importantly perhaps, as the body of the worker, or the body of the future worker's mother. These were bodies to be studied, surveyed, disciplined and, when necessary, reformed to ensure their efficiency as parts of the emerging world system.

In this context, bacteriology provided a new resource and rationalization for surveillance. From the 1890s, colonial public health officers had dedicated themselves to tracking down and isolating portable microbial pathogens. The transmission of these germs could be traced ever more efficiently and persuasively through local insect and human populations, so much so that during this period we see, in effect, an anthropomorphic mobilization of pathology. Disease was more likely to derive from other bodies, less likely to emanate from environmental filth. As a result, soon after it had become common knowledge that many native bodies were manifestly diseased, colonial medical scientists were able to reveal a more widespread, and hitherto disguised, disease carriage among even apparently 'healthy natives.' In native blood they found malarial parasites; in native stools they found enteric parasites; in their sputum, the germ of tuberculosis. 'Apparently healthy' native disease carriers were blamed for outbreaks of typhoid, cholera, and even plague. Being of a tropical race no longer conferred a likely immunity to tropical disease: more often, it could be taken as complicity in the transmission of local germs. Had not native races evolved with these pathogens and so developed a symbiotic relationship, a partial immunity to them? The native body was thus represented as a special physical reservoir for local disease organisms, a container that unhygienic racial custom and habit seemed ever to be filling to the brim. Previously, medical authorities had thought that bad native habits would simply overcome the local race's supposed resistance to local disease; now it seemed likely that unhygienic behavior could also turn many locals into embodied agents of disease, while remaining meretriciously healthy. (One might argue that this is a generalization to all diseases and all locals of long-standing fears of contracting venereal disease from native women.) Physical and cultural difference was never more congruent with the threat of disease.

Colonial health authorities initially concentrated on building barriers between deceptively diseased natives and vulnerable whites. Thus after 1900 the native body was often a segregated body. Systematic racial segregation, justified on sanitary grounds, became common in settler societies such as South Africa, and remained in place so long as it was consistent with local labor arrangements. New theories of disease etiology had inflamed fears of racial contact, but these were old fears and easily fueled. In any case, racial segregation in colonies of exploitation was less consistent with economic needs and was rarely enforced with the same vigor.

Instead, the more progressive and optimistic imperial powers, such as the United States in the Philippines, increasingly emphasized education and retraining of supposedly disease-dealing natives. Where segregation was not feasible, reculturation might be tried. As an appreciation of supposedly insidious cultural practices, especially those concerning defecation and eating, began to supplement the emerging biological understanding of disease transmission, colonial medicine, long modelled on the military campaign, rapidly assumed more the character of a world-wide evangelical movement with the goal of converting local peoples to the gospel of hygiene. (This was predicated on an emerging biomedical and anthropological consensus that culture could be freed from its biological shackles and independently historicized.) Strict enforcement of the rules of personal and domestic hygiene promised multiple benefits: local populations, less manifestly unwell, would be able to work more efficiently; less likely to carry disease organisms, they would present fewer dangers to foreigners. One can argue, then, that tropical medicine was principally a localized form of industrial hygiene, first for the colonizer, and then for the laboring colonized.

Beginning in the American empire, and later generalized by the efforts of the Rockefeller Foundation and the international health organizations of the interwar period, public health authorities sought to ensure that colonial possessions were inhabited with what they regarded as propriety. Medical texts insistently contrasted the closed, ascetic body of the colonizer with the open, grotesque native body, the former typically in charge of a sterilized laboratory or clinic, the latter squatting in an unruly, promiscuous marketplace. In this medical poetics of pollution, the imagery of waste practices offered a potent means of organizing a teeming, threatening environment and society. The self-asserted bodily control of the colonizer symbolized political and social control, while the apparently 'promiscuous defecation' of the natives mocked and trangressed the firm, closed colonial boundaries.[4] In constructing these symbolic inversions of the formal European body, colonial health officers justified their power to inspect and regulate the personal conduct and social life of the colonized. Faced with all this apparent danger and promiscuity, the only responsible course was to examine systematically the colonial population, to disinfect it, and to reform its customs and habits. Public health thus produced a space for the somatic disciplining of supposedly refractory natives: the colonizing process was represented more than ever as a civilizing process. As a result, the infantilization of the native had become as significant as any gendering.

During the twentieth century there has been a massive expansion in health education and publicity projects directed at 'normal' children and adults. Health services have issued regular bulletins, cartoons, and films to instruct local populations in personal hygiene, home cleanliness, the preparation of balanced meals, and the care of the sick; they have maintained exhibitions of sanitary model houses, sanitary methods of sewage disposal, and sanitary villages; they have sent photographs, parade floats and 'healthmobiles' to fairs and fiestas in order to illustrate modern methods of hygiene; and they have issued warnings about the poisonous nature of fecal matter, the evils of handling food, the dangers of spitting. New marketplaces built with hygienic concrete came to replace the old unwholesome plazas; the promiscuous fiesta turned into the martial Clean-Up Week; and toilets sprouted everywhere, even inside houses. Through the schools, children learnt of the perils of raw vegetables, impure water, poorly ventilated houses, a sedentary way of life, and deformed posture; each child had to bathe daily, wear shoes, wash his hands before eating, and never touch the food. In the Philippines, health experts urged every seventh-grade boy to learn how to construct a toilet. Megan Vaughan has observed that in Africa from the 1930s a missionary discourse on mother and child health was secularized and applied more widely. Zimbabweans in the 1940s learnt that they required Lifebuoy soap and other cosmetic or hygienic products. Nutritional research and advice also became more common during this period, with the expectation that environmental changes could elevate, and so normalize, the race.

In a sense, colonial health officers in the twentieth century had staged a binary opposition between themselves (European or Europeanized) and the typical native, and then asked the colonized to resolve this typological difference through personal conversion, so demonstrating that their failings could be overcome, that they could, in effect, transcend tainted embodiment and primitive culture. The prevention of disease transmission was linked intimately with training in civic responsibility, with the production of self-possessed, disciplined colonial (and proto-national) subjects. From the 1930s, colonial public health is argued increasingly in terms of 'human rights,' and not just as the social control of dangerous bodies. Accordingly, histories of the international health services, which document the emergence of this discourse, can be read as disembodying modernization stories. The framing of international health promotion and the development of governmentality had come to resemble two transparencies laid over each other.

Perhaps one of the more telling examples of this superimposition is the Gandhian association of national independence with individual self-government, a "microphysics of self-discipline."[5] For Gandhi, who described the body as a bag of filth, the reform of personal hygiene was linked through the logic of modern public health to a scheme for national self-purification. Taking colonial asceticism seriously, he argued for a celibate nation of manly, self-controlled citizens with generic bodies of steel. We thus have the paradox of a decolonization, an entry into the Third World, predicated on the colonizing, or the overcoming, of one's own body.

Disciplined, purified Third-World citizens make themselves available as labor power and commodities. The rise of an international trade in organs attests as much to the cultural production of generic, interchangeable body parts as it does to advances in surgery and immunosuppression. Desperately ill members of a globalized middle class can pay for the kidneys of poor Indian villagers or choose more widely from the organs of executed Chinese prisoners. Even so, surgical purification rituals may still be subverted by the polluting agents of hepatitis and AIDS, diseases that limit participation in the global body market. Thus the return of the native body still interferes with the circulation of generic body parts. The generic body may be a global commodity, but the production of such commodities has not yet become fully standardized in the Third World.

## CONCLUSION: AIDS AND THE RETURN OF THE NATIVE

The primitive and the abject are never fully expelled from the body in this medical discourse of governmentality: the erstwhile modern citizen is represented as having constantly to abstract himself from nativism. In this sense the destabilizing tropics in the twentieth century have been internalized in all of us. Since Freud, Europeans have recognized the savage within; and since Fanon, natives have formally been given a superego. In this shift to interiority, the governmental self seems to operate as an unstable, conflicted duality of body and mind, nature and culture. If colonialism often presupposed a monist self, implicated in a racialized poetics of pollution, in the 'post-colonial' world this social dichotomy has been internalized, so that we may appear to progress, in representation if not experience, from a polarized social hybrid to an equally polarized individual hybrid, a microcosm of the political order.

But not all hybrids are equal, and not all individuals appeared equal to discipline. In particular, medical reports of the colonial civilizing process often seem no more than a litany of its failures. Randall Packard has described the invention of the problem of the "dressed native," which "placed responsibility for the apparent physical and moral failings of urban Africans, reflected in high mortality rates, alcoholism, family separations and crime, on African inexperience with the conditions of urban industrial life"[6] — a colonial version of blaming the victims. Like all transitional figures, the modernized native, as matter out of place, caused classificatory uncertainty and anxiety. Cultural reform had been linked symbiotically to bodily reform, and both were endlessly deferred, so that the colonized would remain precariously in remission rather than cured, and always on the verge of responsible self-government, yet never quite there. In the Third World, that place of liminal modernities, the primitive seemed always on the point of expunging the civilized from subjectivity. The locals were represented inseparably as both recovering natives and incipient citizens.

In accounting for disease in the Third World, first-world commentators have often summoned up these images of the scarcely civilized, recalling the atavistic passion and depravity of the native type. (Of course the real atavism is more in their own vocabulary than in any actual behavior.) The naturalization of social suffering is vividly illustrated in the standard famine-and-disease shots on television and in the newspapers. In the construction of 'African AIDS' notions of promiscuity, ignorance, superstition, flawed maternal instincts, and natural associations with monkeys, have all returned. Africans are again represented in popular texts and in medical reports as intractable primitives scattered over the sick continent. Through this discourse on the failure of governmentality, "the child-like 'primitive' is immediately identified as a sexual adult and as a sexually active child."[7] Paula Treichler has pointed out an homogenization of the grotesque and licentious in images of AIDS in Africa, which renders Africans recognizable in the West, but unfamiliar to themselves.[8] Cindy Patton also emphasizes a displacement in 'African AIDS' of the political and social onto the sexual and racial; anthropological efforts to identify distinctive African sexual practices thus have 'resexualized' African bodies. The implication, then, of much of the medical discourse on AIDS in Africa is that native sexuality "requires rapid reorganization into bourgeois families"[9] — demands, in effect, a recolonization of the continent by NGOs. At the same time, Nancy Scheper-Hughes has argued that, if anything, some natives have been regarded as rather too well dressed, too civilized, in policy discourses on AIDS in Africa. She believes that the emphasis on education and voluntarism, with an assumption of individual human rights, apparently so characteristic of the public health response to AIDS in the Third World, has put people not included in this 'androcentric' governmental discourse (such as women and children) at special risk.[10] Despite their apparent differences, all of these analyses share a conviction that the metaphors we use to explain 'African AIDS' will have material effects in Africa.

Biomedical discourses concerning the Third World continue to oscillate between these poles of representation, between the generically hygienic body of modern human rights discourse and the dangerously primitive racialized body of typological thinking, between the contained body of the responsible citizen and the excessive body of the promiscuous native, between the civilized and the sexualized, even though the site of this oscillation has moved inwards to describe a relentlessly dichotomous model of subjectivity. The safely hybrid subject is made repeatedly to enact the same old colonial encounters. And so, in the Third World, the native just keeps on returning as an excitingly assailable target of disciplinary discourses.

## REFERENCES

I would like to thank Peter Phipps for research assistance and comments on this essay. Research for this essay was supported in part by a Special Initiatives Grant of the Faculty of Arts at the University of Melbourne.

1.  David Arnold, *Colonizing the Body: State Medicine and Epidemic Disease in Nineteenth-Century India.* (Berkeley: University of California Press, 1993), p. 9.
2.  John and Jean Comaroff, *Ethnography and the Historical Imagination.* (Boulder: Westview, 1992), p. 71.
3.  Frantz Fanon, *Black Skin, White Masks*, trans. Charles Lam Markmann. (New York: Grove Press, 1967), p. 113.
4.  Warwick Anderson, 'Excremental colonialism: public health and the poetics of pollution,' *Critical Inquiry* (1995), **21**: 640–669.

5.  Joseph S. Alter, 'Gandhi's body, Gandhi's truth: non-violence and the bio-moral imperative of public health,' *Journal of Asian Studies* (1996), **55**: 301–322, p. 304.

6.  Packard Randall, 'The 'healthy reserve' and the 'dressed native': discourses on black health and the language of legitimation in South Africa,' *American Ethnologist* (1989), **16**: 686–703, p. 687.

7.  Simon Watney, 'Missionary positions: AIDS, 'Africa' and race,' in Russell Ferguson *et al.* (eds), *Out There: Marginalization and Contemporary Cultures.* (Cambridge, MA: MIT Press, 1990), pp. 89–103, p. 98.

8.  Paula Treichler, 'AIDS and HIV infection in the Third World: a First World chronicle,' in Barbara Kruger and Phil Mariani (eds), *Remaking History.* (Seattle: Bay Press, 1989), pp. 31–86.

9.  Cindy Patton, 'From nation to family: containing 'African AIDS," in Andrew Parker *et al.* (eds), *Nationalisms and Sexualities.* (New York: Routledge, 1992), pp. 218-34, p. 225.

10. Nancy Scheper-Hughes, 'AIDS and the social body,' *Social Science and Medicine* (1994), **19**: 991–1003.

## FURTHER READING

Burke, Timothy, *Lifebouy Men, Lux Women: Commodification, Consumption, and Cleanliness in Modern Zimbabwe.* (Durham NC: Duke University Press, 1996).

Butchart, Alexander, *The Anatomy of Power: European Constructions of the African Body.* (London: Zed Books, 1998).

Cooper, Frederick and Stoler, Ann Laura (eds), *Tensions of Empire: Colonial Cultures in a Bourgeois World,* (Berkeley: University of California Press, 1997).

Curtin, Philip, *The Image of Africa: British Ideas and Action, 1780–1850,* 2 vols. (Madison: University of Wisconsin Press, 1964).

Farmer, Paul, *AIDS and Accusation: Haiti and the Geography of Blame.* (Berkeley: University of California Press, 1992).

Gilman, Sander, *Difference and Pathology: Stereotypes of Sexuality, Race, and Madness.* (Ithaca: Cornell University Press, 1985).

Lambek, Michael, and Strathern, Andrew (eds), *Bodies and Persons: Comparative Perspectives from Africa and Melanesia.* (Cambridge: Cambridge University Press, 1998).

Manderson, Lenore, *Sickness and the State: Health and Illness in Colonial Malaya, 1870–1940.* (Cambridge: Cambridge University Press, 1996).

Packard, Randall, *White Plague, Black Labor: Tuberculosis and the Political Economy of Health and Disease in South Africa.* (Berkeley: University of California Press, 1989).

Radin, Margaret Jane, *Contested Commodities.* (Cambridge MA: Harvard University Press, 1996).

Stepan, Nancy, *The Idea of Race in Science: Great Britain 1800–1960.* (Hamden CT: Archon Press, 1982).

Vaughan, Megan, *Curing Their Ills: Colonial Power and African Illness.* (Stanford: Stanford University Press, 1991).

# CHAPTER 17

# The Temporal Body

DAVID ARMSTRONG

What is the relationship of the body to time? At the level of everyday experience the body exists in a context of passing time. Therefore one account of the temporal body in medicine during the twentieth century would describe the changes around the processes of birth, growth, aging and death. This would involve plotting the various manifestations of childhood, adult-hood and old age and how they have been perceived within medicine during the century. Such an account would treat time as a constant, a mere backdrop for corporal change. But time itself also changes — in terms of its periodization, its intensity, its meaning. This suggests a question prior to a description of the temporal changes inscribed on and in the body: if time itself has changed then how can its effects be independently analyzed? The solution adopted here is to be agnostic about the conceptual and methodological prioritizing of bodies and time, seeing both as artefacts.

But what would this imply for the question of agency in the account of the relationship between bodies and time? Who changes bodies and time? What interests bring about shifts in such fundamental elements of everyday life? Or perhaps the question should be reversed: how do bodies and time intersect to create identities and interests? Suffice it to say that such questions cannot be answered by the historical record inasmuch as the historical record is itself an artefact of bodies and time. Instead what seems possible is to conduct an arche-ology of knowledge, to uncover the way things have been reconstructed, but not through the eyes of individuals nor their groupings, but through the practices that enabled a reality to be forged. Thus, writing a death certificate and measuring the height of a child are, as will be shown, the sorts of events that refashioned both bodies and time in the twentieth century.

In summary, the framework of this chapter is one that does not treat time as the 'outside' medium through which the body passes during its life course, rather it describes the mutual constitution of both time and bodies. The analysis is divided into four parts that describe different facets of the relationship between time and the body. First, the temporal segmentation of the body will be described in which time invests the body, sub-dividing it, and then in a reciprocal gesture the body itself becomes a sort of clock against which time can be measured. Second, time moves from its position of bodily context in the form of natural time to become co-terminous with the body's new-found social status. Third, the new relationship between the body and time finds expression in the increasing temporalization of illness. Finally, the emphasis on a temporal dimension for health care delivery provides the space in which the body can be crystallized as a temporal object.

## THE BODY IN TIME: TEMPORAL SEGMENTATIONS

Birth and death of the body have been the traditional outer markers of the temporal space of the life span. However, the twentieth century is remarkable for the extent to which this temporal line has been remapped, its space sub-divided, scrutinized, and reconstituted as a web of temporal movements, its outer boundaries increasingly blurred. Of course, at the beginning of the twentieth century the life span was not a medically undifferentiated temporal space: the child was recognized as different from the adult, though only to a degree. But the new century saw the greater differentiation of the child into a more distinct object as well as the further medical sub-division of childhood itself. The beginnings of this segmentation of the life span occurred in the mid-nineteenth century with the analysis of the distribution of childhood deaths.

Registration of deaths began in England in 1838. In 1857, for the first time, the Registrar-General reported the total number of deaths under the age of one, and in 1877 he gave the figure formal recognition in the form of the 'infant mortality rate' statistic. The importance ascribed this latter statistic gradually increased such that by 1908, the Registrar-General could claim that "since the close of the century the subject of the waste of infant life, formerly treated with apathy, has received close and increasing attention from all classes of the community."[1] In effect, the figure of the child began to have a progenitor in the body of the infant. But where did the infant itself come from? It seemed that the temporal line could be pushed back further into the womb: at what point then did the infant's precarious life begin?

In the nineteenth century, stillbirths had seemed indistinguishable from miscarriages and abortions as all represented a non-live birth. Yet while there was no fundamental biological difference in the birth of a dead fetus at any gestational age, there was certainly a problem in distinguishing between a fetus and an infant once the latter had a defined existence. Although there was no legal requirement to do so, Medical Officers of Health began to report the occurrences of stillbirth that came to their notice early in the twentieth century. The Annual Report of the Chief Medical Officer at the newly constituted Ministry of Health (1919) drew these reports together but it was not until 1926, with the passing of the Births and Deaths Registration Act, that stillbirths were formally defined as occurring after 28 weeks of pregnancy. From that date the temporal space of infancy, which had been given an ending half a century earlier, also possessed a formal beginning.

A further strand in the elaboration and consolidation of a separate temporal space for the infant was the subdivision of the first year of life. One month, two month and three month mortality figures were variously used during the nineteenth century but with little pattern or consistency. Monthly figures were introduced with regularity in the 1905 Registrar-General's Annual Report following the mounting public concern over infant mortality. In time it was claimed that the first month of life really meant the first four weeks and, in 1938, formal recognition was accorded these deaths with the introduction of the term 'neonatal mortality' by the Registrar-General. The general use of neonatal mortality established a benchmark in the infant's first year of life: from the vantage point of four weeks it was possible to construct a period which extended to one year (post-natal mortality) and further sub-divide the first four weeks into two components and create early neonatal mortality in the first week and late neonatal in the subsequent three.

Neonatal mortality described a temporal space immediately following the birth but the birth itself no longer signified the new existence of the infant; that point came after 28 weeks gestation. Therefore, whereas in the nineteenth century stillbirths were joined to miscarriage and abortions as manifestations of fetal loss, in the inter-war years they became the natural partner of neonatal mortality, separated only by a single breath. And if there was an affinity between stillbirths and neonatal mortality, there was an even greater one between stillbirths and early neonatal mortality: a baby that survived only minutes or hours was hardly much different from a stillbirth. In the early 1950s a new statistic, the perinatal mortality rate — deaths in the first week of life plus stillbirths with a denominator of all births and stillbirths — came into general use.

It was therefore only by the mid 1950s that the sub-division of infancy took on its modern form. Stillbirths, perinatal, neonatal and infant deaths — together with their various derivative statistics — mapped out the first year of life for medicine. This segmentation of the early part of life not only established a detailed temporal trajectory, but also transformed the traditional beginning of life. Birth was no longer the beginning but just another step in temporal space. This blurring of the traditionally strongly bounded limits of the life span can also be seen at the other end of life.

Death had been a singular event: at one moment the patient was alive then the patient had died, and the clinician could examine the body to determine whether the patient had crossed the threshold. But during the early 1960s death began to be transformed into a temporal 'trajectory of dying.' Closer clinical examination of the moment of dying produced a multiplicity of different deaths. There was somatic death, organ death, molecular death, etc; indeed there were as many deaths as tissues and cells. From the early 1960s when the flat EEG reading which was held to mark brain death came to dominate analysis of the moment of death, the time of death became a matter for debate. For the 1968 International Declaration of Sydney, irreversibility of the processes leading to death was identified as the key event. In effect this meant that death and life became blurred: dying was a "long-drawn-out process that begins when life itself begins and is not completed in any given organism until the last cell ceases to convert energy."[2]

Life had been relatively undifferentiated internally yet strongly delineated externally by the traditional gateways of birth and death. The new segmentation of the body's time-line opened up a differentiated temporal space through which the trajectory of life was projected, with neither exact beginning nor exact end.

## THE BODY THROUGH TIME: TRANSCENDING NATURAL TIME

Birth and death had marked out the beginning and ending of the body; in between, life moved between these two outer markers. This temporal space between birth and death was governed by a cycle of 'natural' time represented by growth followed by degeneration and decay. But in the early twentieth century the body began to break away from this time type and became inserted into a new temporal space that was social rather than natural in character.

The introduction of death registration in 1838 had involved the completion of a death certificate which included a requirement to state a cause of death. So what could cause a death? An accident or a murder could be clearly defined as they fell within the remit of the coroner's court (and still do so) as 'unnatural' causes of death. But for the vast bulk of other deaths the idea of a cause was contingent on the classification system: it could, for example, be defined in terms of failure of a vital organ, or in terms of the weakening brought about by age, or in terms of a pathological process inserted into the body. The system adopted, following the conceptual framework of the new medicine of the Clinic that had emerged a few decades earlier, involved identifying a pathological lesion that ended life. Accordingly, during the rest of the nineteenth century the Registrar-General struggled to ensure adoption of the 'new' system against the old one which had relied heavily on the decay induced by natural time.

However, there were many older descriptions of cause of death that fell outside the Registrar-General's classification system and in these cases exhortations were made and letters were written to encourage a more precise terminology from the certifying doctor. In particular, there was a group of causes of death which, by the Registrar-General's own admission, were "of uncertain or variable seat."[3] In infants, this latter designation referred to deaths largely due to atrophy, debility, malformation and sudden causes (with the addition of premature births to debility in 1854). Significantly, atrophy, debility and sudden death were equally found as causes of death — together with 'old age' — amongst the elderly. The Registrar-General recognized this correspondence between infancy and old age in 1855 when he removed these deaths from "uncertain seat" and created a new sub-classification of "diseases of growth, nutrition and decay."[4]

Within the new category of diseases of growth, nutrition and decay there were four causes of death. Congenital malformations embraced those deaths in which the evolution of the embryo had been arrested at some earlier form; premature births and debility pointed to a birth before its natural moment or to the lack of 'vitality' in a new-born baby; atrophy referred to a wasting and loss of substance without any discernable disease and was found in both infancy and old age; finally old age itself, the result of decay, made up the fourth category in the framework.

Within this classification the body was clearly an object of natural time. It was still principally the great irreversible laws of growth and decay that governed mortality. In congenital malformations the embryo, whose evolution was under the control of nature, stopped growing. It was not that the growth was pathological — as it would be in later years — but simply that it stopped too early. Prematurity represented a similar failure of natural timing when birth took place before its proper moment and debility was a lack of that life force that made existence possible. Atrophy belonged, like deaths from 'old age,' to the natural decay of the body such that it was found in the elderly when the life force was on the wane, and also in the infant when the decay set in earlier than usual.

But gradually, during the closing years of the nineteenth century and the opening decades of the new, the body was moved from under the control of natural time. In 1866 it had been possible for the Registrar-General to note the large numbers of infants in whom the 'body wastes' and life forces fail without any apparent disease. But by 1921 this language and form of analysis had disappeared. A new classification abolished atrophy as a cause of death. The term debility still remained from the old order but it no longer referred to a temporal decline. Congenital debility decreased rapidly as the certified cause of death but remained in use, if unsatisfactorily, until 1948 when it disappeared in the 6th Revision of the International Classification of Disease.

Prematurity continued as a common cause of infant deaths until the middle of the twentieth century, sustained in part by deaths reclassified from atrophy and debility. In 1950 it disappeared with the advent of a new term, 'immaturity,' a designation of the 6th Revision of the International Classification of Disease. Immaturity was not however simply another description of one type of death. Under the heading of "Certain diseases of early infancy" — which included such items as birth injury, asphyxia and infection of the newborn — there was a place for "immaturity with mention of other subsidiary conditions" and "immaturity without mention of other subsidiary conditions."[5] In effect it was possible for the infant to be classified twice, once with a specific pathological cause and also with the label of immature. Immaturity was less a cause of death and more a context of death. As such, wrote the Registrar-General it "would be more precise if it were possible to show separately the death risks in respect of infants successfully carried to term and infants that fail to reach term as judged by a simple criterion of maturity such as the infant's birth weight, or the length of the gestations."[6] In other words, the forces embedded in natural time were still present in the health of the infant but rather than being a key determinant of life and death represented only background 'noise' in its proper measurement.

Just as the forces associated with natural time were eliminated from infant deaths, so they were challenged at the other end of life. Deaths from 'old age,' which had been relatively common up until the end of the nineteenth century, were gradually eliminated, together with their accompanying deaths from atrophy, senility, etc. Similarly there was a reaction against the established place of aging in clinical practice: "time and again older patients present with a series of symptoms often dismissed by the medical profession as 'due to age' when age has nothing to do with the problem at all."[7] Medicine was not to be bound to the natural rhythm of growth followed by decay but had to separate the aging process from pathology.

In summary, it was not until the middle of the twentieth century that the dominance of natural time in life and disease was removed. Natural time was replaced by a pathological space in which the causes of illness could be separated from the irreversible laws of nature. The body still passed through time but its markers were not the inexorable natural processes of growth and decay but the socially segmented periods that were colonized by the new medical specialties of pediatrics and geriatrics.

### TIME IN THE BODY: DEVELOPMENTAL STAGES

By the late nineteenth century, the practice of medicine, particularly in hospitals, was primarily concerned with the identification and treatment of pathological lesions. As such, clinical medicine was little concerned with the age of the body beyond the likelihood of involutionary changes aiding the progress of the disease. But the identification of diseases characteristic of particular age groups enabled a new medical classification that differed from the atemporal nosography of organ system or pathological process. Life stage could join the various symptom indicators in the differential diagnosis: as the type of pain might distinguish respiratory from cardiac pathology, so too might the age of the patient. Thus it became possible to rearrange the medical typology of disease, previously based on underlying spatial lesion, into a temporal order in which, because of their respective probabilities, diseases could be assigned to children, adults and the old.

At first such a classification device was merely heuristic: to argue that children's diseases were in any fundamental way different from adult diseases would be like claiming that the different symptomatic presentations of, say, tuberculosis, signified different diseases. In the nineteenth and early twentieth centuries physicians could claim that had their practice been solely restricted to pediatrics their knowledge of children's diseases would have been much worse. The name given to the Society for the Study of Diseases in Children (founded 1901) signified the subsidiary position of the child relative to the disease. In effect, the division of life into its consecutive stages was simply a means of acquiring a further understanding of the distribution of pathology.

However, by mid-twentieth century a new perspective on the significance of age had begun to emerge. For example, it had become the rule rather than the exception for physicians in the diseases of children to confine themselves to that speciality: this signaled the change from an emphasis on diseases *in* children to diseases *of* children. In retrospect the new pediatricians could claim that in the past, pediatric teaching had begun "with the assumption that the child is but a miniature version of the adult... his diseases were the same as in adults but less severe... his psychological make-up was similar to that of the adult but more innocent... and that his treatment is identical except that it is scaled down to size."[8] But the new pediatrics claimed that childhood could be neither understood nor taught simply by extrapolating back from adults.

Pediatrics was not based solely on the simple observation that children and adults were different: children were different precisely because childhood was a temporal space. In short, the age of the patient did matter — pediatrics was "not merely diseases of children" but embodied more positive criteria of health. A frequent claim of pediatrics was that the two basic criteria of a child's health status were first "his growth and development" and second "his behaviour as a separate, though immature member of society"; the various methods of clinical examination, the bulwark of clinical medicine were "techniques towards this end (but) they must be regarded as preliminaries."[9]

Growth and development were now the key features of childhood. It was not a case of childhood passing through time like some remote traveler, but of time investing the body of the child. On the one hand within the diseased child there was the natural inherent struggle to maintain or regain growth and on the other hand growth and development had their influence on the disease process itself. It remained for the pediatrician to decide whether the derangement from the average was of quantitative importance.

The notion of growth and development became the key idea on which the specialty of pediatrics could professionalize. The children's physician metamorphosed into a pediatrician, moved away from his specialization in organic disease in the age group of birth to puberty, as he realized the importance of development during childhood and infancy. Growth and development became the quintessence of modern pediatrics and developmental pediatrics the foundation of the discipline.

Pediatrics transformed 'atemporal' clinical medicine. No longer was disease strongly classified and static. Instead the intersection of the axes of human growth and development and of the full natural history of disease in all its manifestations provided the space in which pediatricians could use their skills. In effect, the break with the traditional clinico-pathological medicine of the nineteenth century was to replace the question: 'Has this patient a disease?' with: 'Is this child growing normally?'

Because the child's body became construed as a distinct temporal object it justified a regime of separate management. For example, whereas admission to hospital was relatively incidental for the adult, for the child it was viewed as an experience occurring during a critical period of growth which may leave a lasting mark on his or her personality. Thus in the 1960s in the UK it was necessary to point out that the failure to segregate children in Accident and Emergency Departments was not in accord with the generally accepted Report on the Welfare of Children in Hospital and remind the Faculty of Ophthalmologists that their policy of seeing children in Ophthalmology Departments contravened the Report's recommendations.

If the particular needs of children demanded separate wards and hospitals they also warranted specialist personnel. The principle of having children in hospital cared for by sick child nurses was firmly established, the British Paediatric Association having successfully resisted an attempt by the General Nursing Council to abolish the sick child nurse register in the early 1960s. The Report of the Committee on Child Health Services in 1976 (The Court Report 1976) carried the 'pediatric principle' further. It recommended special child health visitors, general practitioner pediatricians and pediatric experts in various fields of medicine. The Report reaffirmed the need for pediatric neurologists, cardiologists, nephrologists, endocrinologists, gastroenterologists, hematologists and oncologists. Allied specialists included pediatric surgeons, anesthetists, radiologists, orthopedic surgeons, ear nose and throat surgeons, ophthalmologists, dermatologists, medical geneticists, morbid anatomists, histopathologists, chemical pathologists and microbiologists. "Since paediatric specialists work and share facilities with adult specialists in the same discipline, why are they necessary? The answer is that the needs which justified the separation of paediatrics from adult medicine apply here with equal force."[10]

Whereas in pediatric medicine it was the socially contingent force of 'growth and development' that replaced the dominance of natural time, in geriatric medicine there were problems in replacing the notion of aging as a negative medical force with anything as powerful in explanatory terms. If the body was not allowed to 'wear out' its death would require a pathological cause, and more, without such a pathology the body should not die. The new underlying philosophy was given in the axiom 'old age is not a disease,' but how, without the concept of aging — and without the possibility of construing changes in terms of development — could the normal be distinguished from the pathological?

It was obvious to geriatrics that a clearer conception of what ought to be accepted as normal was a first step in the rational treatment of old people, though this was not easy as morbidity increased with age and the physiological shaded almost imperceptibly into the pathological. Moreover, not only did physiological variation pass into abnormality of function by "hardly perceptible variation (but the) variation in involution may at times be so accentuated as to become pathological and result in a state which is obviously a departure from normal old age."[11]

One attempt to solve the problem of distinguishing pathology from aging, suggested that aging, like life itself, should be divided into normal and pathological. In effect there had to be a pattern of aging that was free from all attacks of disease. The notion was developed by identifying a group of elderly individuals who seemed to be as healthy as possible and from their anatomical, physiological and biochemical attributes establish a pattern of 'normal aging.' On another occasion those same individuals might be construed as 'abnormally' healthy given their very small numbers, but in an attempt to provide a theoretical underpinning for the new geriatrics time had to be tamed.

The other strategy for temporalizing the latter end of life was to impose a developmental model articulated on death itself. The period before death — the process of dying — could be segmented and reassembled as a series of stages. Following a debate in the 1950s about whether or not to 'tell' the dying their prognosis, it came to be agreed that the patient had a 'right to know.' This 'liberating' gesture opened up dying as a process, as a temporal space that could be further analyzed and sub-divided. The process of dying, just like the growth of the child, was therefore further fragmented under the common rubric of 'stages of dying' that, from the late 1960s, individual patients were required to negotiate. Thus the customary bereavement reaction of friends and relatives was transferred to the body of the patient as they were invited to mourn their own deaths.

In summary, during the twentieth century a new temporal order became located in the body; not a natural time of growth, atrophy and decay that invested other living things, but a processual model of time, of stages, of development, that in the final analysis was not governed by nature but by the triumph of the norm.

### TIME IN ILLNESS: MONITORING THE BODY

The pathological lesion was revealed at a single point in time: the diagnosis was an event. True, the lesion had a past history and a prognosis, and the diagnosis may, for some reason, have been delayed but these temporal elements were essentially subsidiary to the immediacy of the lesion. But during the twentieth century, time became another dimension, independent of the three-dimensional corporeal localization of the lesion, which enmeshed illness.

For much of clinical practice illness became less an event and more a process whose context and essential nature was contained within a temporal trajectory. Concepts of illness changed from the triumph of the momentary revelation of the clinical examination, to the minor steps along a temporal continuum. In 1950 a survey of illness in a community had uncovered the fact that much illness went unreported to the doctor. The general practitioner (GP) researchers reported this finding "difficult to believe."[12] The discovery by medicine that illness, much of it serious, went untreated marked the beginning of a search for the path that led 'person' to become a 'patient.' Illness no longer started with the visit to the doctor but preceded that event in terms of patients' interpretations and decision-making contained in the sociological notion of "illness behaviour."[13] Illness was increasingly construed in processual terms, the process of becoming ill, or reacting to illness and to treatment, and to becoming well. The emergence of chronic illness as one of the major morbidity problems in post-war medicine marked the crystallization of both illness and time in a common space.

As illness began to be reconstructed with a temporal dimension, medical intervention aimed itself not so much at a specific lesion as at this temporal space of possibility. This new perception first manifested itself in the notion of early or presymptomatic diagnosis, particularly in the field of general practice. A key (and new) role for the GP observed a government committee set up to examine the organization of general practice, included the detection of the earliest departure from normal of the individual and families of his population. A plethora of texts were published in the 1960s on early signs of illness and early diagnosis. Indeed with a fresh look "practically everything which the general practitioner does for his patients contains an element of prevention and presymptomatic diagnosis in the widest sense."[14]

Early diagnosis was part of a preventive outlook that pushed the identification of illness or its precursors back in time. But equally, intervention at the earliest stages of illness was justified in terms of protecting the future. Thus early diagnosis and prevention merged almost imperceptibly along the temporal dimension with health education and health promotion. By, as it were, intervening in the past the future could be made secure because the past and future were directly linked: "We can see 'prevention,'" stated the working party on health and prevention in primary care, "as measuring 'care with an eye to the future' or 'anticipatory care.'"[15]

Perhaps the most salient characteristic of this new medical perceptual framework was the invention of the notion of 'risk' and 'risk factors' in the middle of the twentieth century. Medicine of the Clinic had relied on identifying signs and symptoms (together with the results of laboratory investigations) to identify the pathological lesion. But the risk factor pointed not at the hidden pathological truth of disease, but opened up a space of future illness potential.

Symptoms and signs were only important to the extent that they could be re-read as risk factors. Equally, the illness in the form of the disease or lesion that had been the end-point of clinical inference was also deciphered as a risk factor in as much as one illness became a risk factor for another. Symptom, sign, investigation and disease thereby became conflated into an infinite chain of risks. A headache may have been a risk factor for high blood pressure (hypertension), but high blood pressure was simply a risk factor for another illness (stroke). And whereas symptoms, signs and diseases were located in the body, the risk factor encompassed any state or event from which a future probability of illness could be calculated. Each illness of clinical medicine existed as the discrete endpoint in the chain of clinical discovery: in the new temporal medicine each illness was simply a nodal point in a network of health status monitoring. The problem was less illness *per se* but the semi-pathological pre-illness at-risk state.

Illness therefore came to inhabit a temporal space. Illness had a life history: from a series of minor perturbations that indicated its early presence to its 'pre-' forms, from its subtle indicators of existence to its overt clinical manifestations, from its first appearance to the medical attempts to alter its natural history. The sub-division of illness prevention into primary, secondary and tertiary forms summarized the points at which medicine could intervene in the new great cycle of illness. The clinical techniques of the hospital had invested the three-dimensional body of the patient; the new medicine analyzed a four-dimensional space in which a temporal axis was joined to the living density of corporal volume. And to map onto this temporal space of illness the new medicine deployed new techniques based around patient monitoring and surveillance of risk factors.

As the episodic nature of illness was replaced with a temporal characterization, so medical work was reconceptualized and reorganized. For example, early studies of morbidity by the Research Committee of the College of General Practitioners noted the difficulty of measuring illness episodes as the end of an episode was impossible to define. The assessment of morbidity in general practice, they concluded, depended on continuing observation. The corollary in general practice clinical work was continuity in patient management. The 'discovery' of the importance of continuity of care is, perhaps, ironic in view of the increasingly fragmented nature of care provided by GPs as they joined together into group practices. Nevertheless, in the early 1960s general practice embraced the significance of continuity for good quality care and gave its newly discovered importance a history: "Continuity in general practice is so important and so all-pervading that paradoxically it tends to be over looked."[16]

Clinical practice needed to construct a temporal trajectory for its patients. For decades general practitioners had treated patients' illnesses as they arose; some history was kept in memory, but mostly it was a case of treating the immediate problem. Care was essentially of episodic illness. But illnesses infused by time required a solution to this problem of temporal fragmentation: that solution was the medical record.

The opportunity for a record of patient illnesses to be kept in general practice had first been introduced for National Health Insurance patients: in 1920 the medical record envelope was introduced and has changed very little over the century. However, until relatively recently very few records were kept in these envelopes or, if they were, their haphazard nature undermined any claims to continuing observation. Indeed as late as 1978 an editorial in the *Journal of the Royal College of General Practitioners* confessed that "medical records are the Achilles heel of general practice and reveal the current state of disorganisation bordering in some cases on chaos."[17]

However it was not so much that records were bad than that standards by which record keeping were evaluated had been changing. One of the criteria of good practice became a record system adequately filed, every contact recorded, letters stored, summary sheets, regular up-dates, and so on: "Only systematic records can replace the series of memories in which a patient's medical history may at present reside, in greater or lesser detail."[18]

Before records, every patient, every 'contact,' was a singular event; there may have been a 'past history' in the consultation and indeed the doctor might have remembered a significant past occurrence but past and present were different domains of experience. However, with the record card, which marked the temporal relationship of events, time became concatenated. Clinical problems were not simply located in a specific and immediate lesion but in a biography in which the past informed and pervaded the present. The medical record was another device for the manipulation of time and the temporalization of illness. Together with new illness categories such as chronic illness, new strategies such as early diagnosis, the new techniques of record keeping marked the construction of illness as a temporal phenomenon.

## A TEMPORAL BODY

It has been argued that the temporal body is largely a twentieth-century phenomenon and that time has been managed in a number of different ways. One strategy has been the usurpation of the old 'natural time.' The old temporal delimiters of birth and death have become blurred and natural time has been increasingly stripped from the body and replaced with notions of development according to some socially defined norm. In that sense the defeat of natural time is the triumph of social time; if the body is a temporal object it also is a social one.

And in response to this reconfigured body — or should it be said one of the manifestations of this new object — are a series of clinical shifts as medicine struggles to bring this moving object under its clinical eye. Medicine becomes involved in the process of capturing corporal time, reconceptualizing illness, reconfiguring clinical method and reorganizing health care, each at once a means of engaging with and constituting a new temporal space of illness.

## REFERENCES

1.  Registrar-General, *Annual Report for 1906*. (London: HMSO, 1908), p. xxxvii.
2.  R.S. Monson, 'Death: process or event?' *Science* (1971), **173**: 695.
3.  Registrar-General, *Annual Report for 1850*. (London: HMSO, 1852).
4.  Registrar-General, *Annual Report for 1853*. (London: HMSO, 1855).
5.  *International Classification of Disease*, 6th Revision. (Geneva: WHO, 1948).
6.  Registrar-General, *Statistical Review for 1952*. (London: HMSO, 1954), p. 30.
7.  J. Burston, 'Clinical medicine and the elderly,' in J.T. Leeming (ed.), *Doctors and Old Age*. (British Geriatric Society, 1976), p. 10.
8.  P. Catzel, 'Paediatrics' *British Medical Journal* (1955), **ii**: 1028.
9.  N.B. Capon, 'Development and behaviour of children,' *British Medical Journal* (1950), **i**: 859.
10. Report of Committee on Child Health Services (Court Report), *Fit for the Future*. (London: HMSO, 1976), p. 27.
11. A.N. Exton-Smith, *Medical Problems of Old Age*. (Bristol: Wright, 1955).

12.  J. Horder and E. Horder, 'Illness in general practice,' *Practitioner* (1954), **173**: 184.

13.  D. Mechanic, 'The concept of illness behaviour,' *Journal of Chronic Diseases* (1962), **15**: 189–194.

14.  D.L. Crombie, 'Preventive medicine and presymptomatic diagnosis,' *Journal of the Royal College of General Practitioners* (1968), **15**: 345.

15.  Working Party of Royal College of General Practitioners, *Health and prevention in primary care*. (RCGP 1981).

16.  Editorial, 'Continuity of care,' *Journal of the Royal College of General Practitioners* (1973), **23**: 749.

17.  Editorial, 'Medical records in general practice,' *Journal of the Royal College of General Practitioners* (1978), **28**: 521.

18.  R.J.F.H. Pinsent, 'Continuing care in general practice,' *Journal of the Royal College of General Practitioners* (1969), **17**: 226.

## Further Reading

Armstrong, D., 'Child development and medical ontology,' *Social Science and Medicine* (1979), **13**: 9–12.

Armstrong, D., 'Pathological life and death,' *Social Science and Medicine* (1981), **15**: 253–57.

Armstrong, D., 'Space and time in British general practice,' *Social Science and Medicine* (1985), **20**: 659–666.

Armstrong, D., 'The invention of infant mortality,' *Sociology of Health and Illness* (1986), **8**: 211–232.

Armstrong, D., 'Silence and truth in death and dying,' *Social Science and Medicine* (1987), **24**: 651–57.

Armstrong, D., 'The rise of Surveillance Medicine,' *Sociology of Health and Illness* (1995), **17**: 393–404.

Roth, J., *Timetables*. (Indianapolis: Bobbs-Merrill, 1963).

Zerubavel, E., *Patterns of Time in Hospital Life*. Chicago University Press, 1979).

# CHAPTER 18

# The Sexual Body

## LESLEY A. HALL

Medicine and the allied sciences have studied most aspects of the human body over a period of centuries, building up coherent bodies of 'scientific' knowledge. The development and emergence of most disciplines and specialisms can be traced through changes in different editions of standard textbooks, the inception of specialist journals, and the creation of institutional centers. Sexual functioning in humans, however, forms a significant exception: its study has been and continues to be very much marginalized. The history of attempts to develop a science of sex and appropriate medical approaches to the subject has been a matter of stops and starts.

The very pervasiveness of sex militated against its readily fitting into the model of medical specialization over the last hundred years. Problems of sexual functioning fell within the purlieu of public health, forensic medicine, the gynecologist, the venereologist, the psychiatrist, and even the general practitioner, none of whom had any great desire to incorporate sex and sexuality into their territory. It is claimed that the late nineteenth century saw an increasing medicalization of sexual matters and the development of a medical sexual discourse of positively imperial ambitions, and that this persisted and increased up to the present, a view particularly associated with the French philosopher Michel Foucault's *The History of Sexuality: Volume I: Introduction* (published originally in French as *La Volonté de Savoir*, or 'The Will to Know').

Foucault made the important (though not entirely original) point that sexuality is discursively produced; that is, it is something which is formed by what people say and think about the bodily phenomena involved rather than simply emerging from a set of physical processes. However, he tended to infer a set of medical and scientific discourses becoming predominant from the late nineteenth century, far more extensive and cohesive than can altogether be substantiated, and neglected other discourses (religious, folk, popular, commercial, legal) which were at least as influential. Actual medical discourses of sexuality at the turn of the nineteenth and twentieth centuries were largely associated with a handful of rather idiosyncratic individuals with very specific agendas. Historians are still attempting to calibrate how influential even the most discussed works were.

This chapter is based very largely on the British experience, providing some contrast to a story often told from a specifically American perspective. Similar trajectories, while differing in specific details, can be discerned in Continental Europe and North America.

The way in which sexuality was discussed was undoubtedly becoming increasingly medical (instead of, for example, religious): but this relates to the growing medicalization of discourses generally, something quite distinct from actual medical discourse. Advertisements for 'quack' remedies during the later nineteenth and twentieth century based their appeal in 'modern science': a notable example was the trade in 'electrical' belts. A century later the sexologist and clinician, Professor John Bancroft would remark on the contemporary commercial exploitation of the "flashing lights and digital dials of modern technology."[1]

The tendency to privilege 'medicine' and 'science' bears an equivocal relation to what doctors and scientists may be saying or doing. The legal demarcation of the appropriate limits of sexual conduct has been rather less studied, even though legal penalization of homosexuality was a powerful force in generating such scientific investigations as there were. The regulation of conjugal sexuality in the divorce court and in actions for annulment and separation reveals competing assumptions about appropriate and permissible sexual behavior both between spouses and between judges, lawyers, and plaintiffs. The operation of the law in controlling prostitution, in setting boundaries to the use of, and dissemination of information about, contraception and abortion, and in dealing with cases of rape (and increasingly sexual harassment more generally) provides valuable insights into an array of attitudes about sexuality and gender. Medical evidence (and 'expert evidence' generally) may have become more important, but it has remained a subsidiary element within the judicial process, structured by its parameters rather than those of medicine.

Even though the historian or the sociologist of knowledge might want to deconstruct heroic narratives about medical/scientific disciplines, these can at least be constructed in most cases, describing the accumulation of knowledge, the replacement of error by truth, the emergence from ignorance towards enlightenment. Puzzles and difficulties may remain, but can readily be subsumed within a coherent trajectory of progress. It is very hard to apply such a narrative form to the study of the sexual body. As the pioneer British sexologist Havelock Ellis (1858–1939) remarked in 1899 "in no other field of human activity is so vast an amount of strenuous didactic morality founded on so slender a basis of facts… often ostentatiously second-hand, usually unreliable."[2] Nearly a hundred years later, Bancroft comments that "Human sexuality is… an enigma or a riddle," its biological substrate "ill understood except for its link with reproduction."[3]

In spite of the differences in Ellis' and Bancroft's own status (a humble Licentiate of the Society of Apothecaries, with no institutional affiliation, eking a meager living by his pen, as opposed to a clinical consultant in the Medical Research

Council Reproductive Biology Unit at the Royal Infirmary in Edinburgh) which suggest that some changes have occurred, Bancroft's account indicates how little, comparatively, matters have progressed since Ellis' day. "[O]bvious reasons for the shortage of scientific endeavour" in the field persist, given "widespread and powerful opposition to any objective enquiry" discouraging study and adversely affecting those who engage in it.[4]

An interest in sex may not be the route to the heights of professional reputation, but it can be profitable. No 'gold standard' exists whereby writings of the serious investigator can easily be differentiated from derivative catchpenny works, or tested to gauge whether the significance of commercially 'hyped' works is in their advancement of knowledge or their demonstration of the persistent saleability of sex. There has been a notable lack of criteria for evaluating work in this field and continued resistance to attempts to tear aside "the veil overhanging the mystery of sex,"[5] as Blair Bell put it in 1916, a desire that it should be left in some way sacrosanct (which in practice tends to mean a repository for unexamined assumptions). The lack of informed critique and intradisciplinary debate has been deleterious for even the most serious and well-intentioned student of the subject.

Because of this lack of a disciplinary structure, the reign of particular recognized authorities has often extended for decades. The name of William Acton, FRCS, appears coterminous with a certain set of Victorian ideas on sexual functioning, particularly the lack of female desire, because his book, *The Functions and Disorders of the Reproductive Organs,* went on being a standard (though not entirely uncontested) authority from its publication in 1857 at least until 1900 largely through lack of competition. From the turn of the century Havelock Ellis took over this somewhat ambiguous position of recognized expert.

When the medical profession did, with reluctance, engage with sexual matters, it was often in response to wider societal pressures. In the case of birth control negative pronouncements of the medical profession followed extra-medical initiatives bringing the subject to public notice. Charles Bradlaugh and Annie Besant's 1877 trial for publishing a contraceptive tract generated C.H.F. Routh's diatribe *On the Moral and Physical Evils likely to follow if practices intended to act as Checks to Population be not strongly discouraged and condemned* (1878), and a flurry of medical debate followed Marie Stopes' successful efforts to publicize contraception in the early 1920s. Attempts to define 'inversion' and deal with the problem of deviance, succeeded rather than generated legal change: the subject scarcely figured in British medical writing (except forensic texts) until Labouchère's Amendment to the 1885 Criminal Law Amendment Act made all homosexual acts illegal.

The female reproductive organs became objects of developing surgical expertise during the late nineteenth century as surgery was being transformed by anesthesia and antisepsis. The challenge presented by these organs, concealed as they were within the abdominal cavity, was at least one reason for the interest surgeons took in developing their technique in gynecological surgery. The male organs, which did not pose such a fascinating problem for heroic surgery, tended to be neglected. This imbalance, however, does reflect the tendency to consider the female as problematic and the male as representing normality.

The medical profession was hardly evolving a coherent discourse on sexuality. Though some opinions were more privileged than others, there was scarcely a congenial climate favouring the emergence of an agreed consensus. Havelock Ellis wrote in 1899 that

> any serious and precise study of the sexual instinct will not meet with general approval; [the investigator's] work will be misunderstood; his motives will be called in question; among those for whom he is chiefly working he will find indifference. Indeed, the pioneer in this field may well count himself happy if he meets with nothing worse than indifference.[6]

The first of Ellis' *Studies in Psychology of Sex, Sexual Inversion* (homosexuality), was prosecuted for obscenity in 1898. Though leading medical journals agreed that his subject fell within the medical purlieu, not a single doctor joined the campaign for the book's defense. Subsequent volumes of the *Studies* were published outside the UK, and while the medical press increasingly conceded Ellis' importance as an authority in his "peculiar field,"[7] he was very much a lone figure. Though doubtless regarded as *the* authority on sexual functioning from the 1890s to the 1950s, Ellis' actual influence on medical thinking and practice was limited; like other pioneers he was not in the mainstream of the medical profession, a marginalization not uniquely British.

Scientifically speaking, as a corollary to this state of medical neglect, the sexual body was an undiscovered country. Much significant research has occurred outside borders of medical and biological science, in social surveys, cross-cultural anthropology, or animal ethology. During a period when the other major organ systems of the body were being thoroughly investigated by physiologists the sexual organs were almost entirely ignored. F.H.A. Marshall pointed out in 1910 that "no attempt has yet been made to supply those interested in the reproductive processes with a comprehensive treatise." In textbooks of physiology the reproductive organs were mentioned if at all in, as he remarked, "a few final pages seldom free from error."[8] Major advances occurred when discoveries about the sex hormones enabled their investigation in organisms well removed from the human. The topic became even more acceptable as it became even further distant from living human bodies, a matter of biochemical analysis. Direct investigation of the actual human sexual system was not widely welcomed, even under the apparently respectable rubric of reproductive biology, in spite of its relevance to recurrent concerns over population decline. Evidence from other countries tends to tell similar tales of researchers stigmatized for studying sex, of the subject being pursued by marginal and often eccentric figures, of public furores and a lack of funding.

Sex was seldom explicitly included in the medical curriculum, even when it might have been supposed that it was unavoidable. In Britain, prior to the Royal Commission on Venereal Diseases which reported in 1916, venereology was not routinely taught at the undergraduate level (and it is not clear how far it was included subsequently) even though venereal diseases were widely regarded as a major threat to public health. Well after birth control became acceptable and even desirable it was not a subject taught in medical schools. In a 1957 survey published in *The Lancet*, Bernard Sandler found that few medical schools specifically included sex education. He deplored their "mechanistic approach" of studying anatomy and physiology divorced from psychological considerations. Students were expected to perform operations they were never likely to undertake again, but sex and marriage were treated as incidental matters, with emphasis on organ dysfunction rather than the patient as a whole.[9]

Evidence suggests that many doctors knew (and know) nothing of these subjects, and that their ignorance and embarrassment has deterred patients from taking sexual problems to them. Well after the so-called 'Sexual Revolution' Bancroft comments

> The discomfort of the clinician in talking about sexual problems and the lack of training in dealing with them is therefore a major factor in determining how these problems present or whether they are presented at all... One can only speculate on the number of patients who set out to seek advice for their sexual difficulty but fail because of the discouraging response of the clinician involved.[10]

Similar points have been made by writers on the subject throughout the twentieth century, and it would appear that open communication about sex has still not been reached. The omnipresence of sexual imagery and allusions in the media occludes the degree to which inhibition and ignorance prevail.

Medical concepts of the sexual body were not shared by most members of the profession in the same way as (for example) concepts of the bacterial transmission of disease or the efficacy of vaccination. There was not an orthodox line with a fringe of muttering dissenters. Under an assumption of common beliefs and knowledge many wild ideas flourished, such as the pervasive notion of the deleteriousness of masturbation. For decades after the microscopic examination of semen had made possible the examination of spermatozoa, many doctors were unclear about the difference between male sterility and impotence. Other reported medical misconceptions were the confusion of vasectomy with castration and a disbelief in female orgasm.

Medical attitudes to homosexuality have had less to do with deliberate stigmatization than with a willful blindness to its existence and a determination to ignore it as far as possible. Havelock Ellis commented on the "medical men of many years' general experience who have never, to their knowledge, come across a single case."[11] One of his informants reported first hearing about the subject as a medical student, "very summarily and inadequately" during a class on Medical Jurisprudence.[12] The degree of confusion which reigned on this particular subject is illustrated by the following, cited as "a mistake it is well to avoid": a police surgeon in a case of alleged sodomy examined the penis of the passive and the anus of the active agents.[13] The advent of AIDS in the 1980s saw the expression of medical views owing more to unexamined prejudice than reason or informed knowledge, described in a 1985 leader in the *British Medical Journal* entitled 'Intolerance 1980s Style.'[14]

Some of the ideas which were and are current in medical thinking about sexuality will be discussed next. It is not suggested that all doctors would have held these opinions or applied them in encounters with patients. There are two main sections: firstly the definition of the sexed body within the gender system; secondly the question of how bodies were supposed to be interacting with one another in sexual activity. A number of issues around the concept of bad sexual bodies will also be considered.

'Sex' is usually, in current debates, conveniently employed to signify actual biological differences between bodies (testicles *vs* ovaries, penis *vs* vagina, lactating *vs* non-lactating breasts), and 'gender' to signify the socially-ascribed set of values pertaining to sexual difference. However, this usage is not always used with absolute consistency. There are two main schools of thought concerning the relationship of societally-ascribed gender roles to sexual difference: the first assumes that gender roles flow naturally out of this difference, the second suggests that gender roles follow a pattern of assigning the various terms within a dualistic schema to one or other of the sexes and that there is nothing per se 'natural' about this.

Thomas Laqueur[15] proposed a major change in the perception of differences between the male and the female occurring in the later eighteenth century. He argued that the previous "one-sex" model, under which the female body was an inferior version of the male, and the female organs inside-out or interior versions of the male equivalents, transmuted into a "two-sex model" under which the two sexes were seen as opposites, completely different. A number of historians have criticized Laqueur's chronology, and certainly "two-sex" interpretations existed earlier than his model would suggest, while assumptions associated with the "one-sex" model persisted much later. Sex is notoriously a subject upon which humans tend to think less than coherently, and there must have been, and still is, a good deal of slippage between one model and the other when thinking and arguing about a range of sex and gender issues.

The scientific investigation of sexual difference in the nineteenth century was a defensive response to general feelings about the instability of society during an era of rapid social change and rising demands for female emancipation. It was not simply the expression of an unquestioningly confident patriarchal elite. The qualities of the dominant white European male were supposed to be superior to those of women, the lower classes, non-white non-European males, etc., but this could no longer be unthinkingly accepted, it had to be proved. Investigators were not looking at difference in a neutral way but establishing hierarchies reflecting those already in existence. If women were assigned superiority in anything it was usually to compensate for their inferiority in the characteristics displayed by the male, and would relate to something (such as emotionality) which was not an alpha quality like, for example, intellect and rationality. Factors other than gender, such as race and class, additionally influenced the ways in which particular bodies were sexualized.

Even when studies of sexual difference explicitly endeavor to evade this hierarchical structure, they still often assume that what is, is natural. This may be because of the unacceptability of the null hypothesis, which does not appeal to those anxious to hear confirmed facts. It is a rare writer who concludes, as Havelock Ellis did that "We have not succeeded in determining the radical and essential characters of men and women uninfluenced by external modifying conditions."

A "sufficiently wide induction of facts" sometimes differentiated the artificial from the real: in other cases, "the more complex and mobile become our results."[16] Ellis is often dismissed as 'biologizing' but in his ideas of gender difference he argued that society exaggerated slight or even non-existent biological indications. While it might be supposed that Ellis, writing in the 1890s, lacked the benefits of more recent scientific discoveries, Bancroft, in an extensive discussion of the state of current scholarship, indicates that different studies have produced very contrary findings about behavioural sex differences. Like Ellis, he comes down in the middle, suggesting that "nature and nurture are both fundamental." While controlling a child's environment may not completely shape its destiny, nonetheless the complex and sophisticated human mechanisms of learning are crucial in individual development.[17]

In the early twentieth century it was widely accepted in medical/scientific discourse that sexual difference was not the absolute that, for common social purposes, it was generally assumed to be. The presence of latent characteristics of one sex in the other was recognized. "[I]ndividuals are rarely, if ever, wholly male or wholly female," claimed Otto Weininger in Sex and Character,[18] a work now largely forgotten, but a great success and much discussed when it appeared. It gave considerable currency to the view that "Sexual differentiation, in fact, is never complete."[19] Weininger argued that all individuals were made up of differing proportions of male and female qualities, though he still divided these qualities in this gendered fashion. William Blair Bell, a British gynaecologist observed that

> some men are described as effeminate, while many a woman has the smallest possible balance of femininity in her favour.... Further evidence of bisexuality... is to be found in the embryological remains of the latent sex, which always exist.[20]

Few took up the potential social implications of this fluidity of gender. The socialist (and homosexual) Edward Carpenter suggested that there were "no limits... within which love is obliged to move,"[21] but he was a marginal and utopian thinker, though influential in left-wing and progressive circles.

Yet, given this argument for a no-man's land between the two sexes, and the existence of degrees of 'masculine' qualities in a woman or 'feminine' characteristics in a man, there was still nonetheless an assumption not only that such qualities were readily genderable, but that the 'real, manly' man and 'real, womanly' woman were readily identifiable. Blair Bell painted a picture of the normal woman, fortunate enough to have exactly the right amount of ovarian secretion:

> [She] finds pleasures in sexual intercourse… desires children, is truly feminine in all her characteristics: she menstruates freely, her breasts are well formed and her mind is feminine in its outlook and aspirations.[22]

The insufficiently productive ovaries of the "feebly menstruating" women "largely masculine in type" could be deduced from their "flat breasts and coarse skin," even without the "assertiveness and aggression of their conversation."[23] Over-productive ovaries, however, were just as bad, leading to "profuse and protracted menstruation," and "excessive sexuality, amounting perhaps to sexual insanity," resulting in masturbation or lesbian practices.[24]

Seven stages of the development of gender identity are currently defined: the chromosomes, the gonads, the hormones, the internal sexual organs, the external genitalia, secondary sexual characteristics, gender assigned at birth, and the gender identity that the individual makes for her or himself. Each of these leads on to the next stage, but problems can occur at any point, and thus (at the time of writing) chromosomal tests are being performed on Olympic athletes to determine whether they are 'really' qualified to compete as men or women. Given the deep discomfort around ambiguity of gender, when children are born with ambiguous genitalia (there is a long medical literature of this), the attending doctor may make a fairly arbitrary assignment to one or the other, and a different dominant sex may emerge at puberty.

Fears of ambiguity can also be seen in attitudes to and ideas about homosexuality. Recent studies by, for example, Simon LeVay and Chandler Burr attempt to establish inborn genetic reasons why a man becomes homosexual (though say little about female homosexuality). The desire to identify a specific 'third sex' has persisted for a long time, reflecting the wish to clearly define and demarcate such a group. However, boundaries persistently blur, with heterosexual activity by those of predominantly homosexual inclinations (Oscar Wilde himself was, after all, married with two children) and occasional homosexual activity by those defining themselves as 'normal,' perhaps under the situational pressure of a single-sex environment.

The famous American investigator Alfred Kinsey, whose monumental survey found a far greater degree of male homosexual activity in the USA than had ever been imagined, set up a classificatory 7-point scale from exclusive interest in the other sex, through slight and increasing degrees of same-sex interest, via complete bisexuality, to exclusive same-sex desire. This constituted perhaps yet another attempt to classify the fluidities of sexual desire into a system and does not take account of disjunctures between desires, activities, and sense of personal sexual identity. There have been recent advocates of establishing a specific identity as bisexual for those who find themselves equally or almost equally attracted to both sexes, which may be considered yet another endeavor to create a restricted number of particular types of sexual body.

The actual possibility of literal reshaping of the body into that of the opposite sex has only been possible for a few decades, although history has many tales of individuals 'passing' as the other gender: the reasons for so doing, however, particularly among women at periods of reduced economic opportunity for the female, may have been very different to those of late twentieth-century gender reassignment seekers and also cannot now be distinguished from the rather different phenomenon of transvestism. In some cases formation of gender identity may have gone astray at one of the stages of development, but this is not a satisfactory explanation for all of them. There is some cross-cultural evidence from societies in which such operations are available that the uptake varies greatly between different cultures both in absolute numbers and in the proportion making the change from man to woman or woman to man. The persistent gendering of specific qualities and preferences is seen at its most acute in this phenomenon of the trans-sexual.

Ideas about what the bodies of these hopefully distinct sexes should do together has varied over the course of a century. It is something of a cliché to remark that sexual mores moved from Victorian repression to liberation, with, perhaps, a proviso that the advent of AIDS has led to serious revaluation of the virtues of liberation since the early 1980s (slightly earlier moral panics around 'incurable' genital herpes and antibiotic-resistant gonorrhea have been occluded by the rise of this devastating epidemic). However, it must be said that neither Victorian repression nor 1960s liberation were ever all-pervasive.

It is sometimes supposed that much the same level and type of sexual behavior has been present throughout history. In fact both historical and cross-cultural anthropological studies suggest that there is a considerable degree of malleability in sexual behavior. For example, premarital sex may be rare or common, same-gender sexual activity may be accepted or condemned, an exclusively homosexual role may exist (even if not approved of) or not, and the prevalence of rape may vary widely. However, what also appears is a wide difference between the accepted ideology of sexual conduct and what people actually get up to: for example, even when premarital sex is condemned it seldom vanishes entirely, and societies which viciously punish the crime of sodomy fail to eradicate it.

The accepted orthodox rhetoric of sexual conduct at the end of the nineteenth century was that sexual activity should take place as little as possible, ideally only for reproductive purposes. Some authorities considered that the act was beneficial to health, and even that mutually agreeable acts cemented conjugal happiness.

The over-riding concern, however, was with the dangers of excess. Too much expenditure of semen was thought to be extremely debilitating to the male, and this applied not only to the wastage implicit in masturbation or nocturnal emissions but to over-enthusiastic 'spending' in conjugal intercourse. Nonetheless, there was a degree of tacit acceptance (the Double Moral Standard) of men's greater sexual needs, implying the necessity for prostitution, and the relatively venial nature of male sexual misconduct.

Women's antipathy to the codification of the Double Standard had been given form by the opposition to the Contagious Diseases Acts, passed in the 1860s, as a measure to improve soldiers' and sailors' health, by regulating prostitution in designated port and garrison towns. By the 1890s some women were openly arguing for the wife's right to regulate the amount of sexual intercourse within marriage, specifically to space children. Birth control was generally considered reprehensible, while many women felt that it would merely enable men to indulge their lusts unconstrained by fears of conception.

The rhetoric of marriage, however, did suggest that marital sex was meant to be agreeable for both parties. Women were not supposed to experience spontaneous sexual desire: their sexual feelings could only be engendered by carnal contact with a male (hence raped or sexually-abused women were deemed 'corrupted'). Meanwhile men were largely brought up in ignorance of the female body. In the early twentieth century writers on sex — the Swiss Auguste Forel, Iwan Bloch of Berlin, and Britain's own Havelock Ellis — deplored the current state of marriage between women who were usually uninstructed about sex and men whose sexual education, either from other men's 'smutty talk' or experience with prostitutes, was likely to have been misleading. The more popular works which proliferated during the 1920s, based on the pioneering work of these sexologists, persistently besought men not to begin marriage with a rape. The bridegroom was depicted as thoughtless and impetuous, concerned only with his own gratification and likely to traumatize his shrinking bride into prolonged frigidity, if not actual insanity, by his brutish lust.

A rather different picture was presented in volumes for the clinician on the disorders of the male encountered in the consulting room. There were far fewer of these than works on gynecology, but they demonstrate remarkable consistency in finding a wide prevalence of impotence and male sexual anxiety. 'Wedding-night impotence' was well-known: fears about their own sexual powers and concerns about hurting their wives rendered many incapable of consummating the marriage. The predominant image of male sexuality, however, was of rampant lust which it was necessary to contain.

Male sexuality was on the whole seen as far less problematic than female. The need was to educate the man as to how best arouse and satisfy the woman for mutual pleasure. A famous and influential work of marriage advice was T.H. Van de Velde's *Ideal Marriage: its physiology and technique.* Van de Velde was a Dutch gynecologist who left the Netherlands after eloping with a married patient. This work, first published in 1926 in Dutch and German, had a wide circulation throughout Europe. It was translated into English two years later, and continually republished over the next forty years. Brecher testifies to Van de Velde's popularity and influence in the United States, claiming that "He taught a generation how to copulate."[25]

Van de Velde dealt with two key issues: initiation of the virgin bride, and the maintenance of erotic freshness within the marriage. Believing in an ideal of erotic reciprocity — "equal consent and equal pleasure in sexual union"[26] — his sole concern was "normal intercourse" between

> two sexually mature individuals of opposite sexes... [It] concludes with the ejaculation — or emission — of the semen into the vagina, at the nearly simultaneous culmination of sensation — or orgasm — of both partners.[27]

Non-coital practices were defined as foreplay, and had their place, but only as preliminaries. The responsibility for achieving harmonious coitus was placed squarely on married men, "naturally educators and initiators of their wives." For a wife to be "educated to full erotic efficiency" required considerable self-control as well as technical mastery.[28] Maintaining interest in marriage demanded hard work, developing sexual skills, experimenting with different positions and caresses.

The decoupling of sex from reproduction made possible by increasingly reliable and acceptable contraception has probably constituted the most dramatic change in heterosexual relations during the twentieth century. By the middle of the century ideal sexual activity took place within marriage, was male-directed but mutually satisfying, and important for the stability of the relationship, not just reproduction. By the 1950s if not earlier, under the influence of Freudian theory (often in a watered-down and populist version), sexological theory and marriage advice increasingly differentiated the (supposedly 'mature') vaginal orgasm from the 'immature' clitoral version, though pragmatic British sexologists were rather less absolute in disdaining the clitoris than, for example, most American writers. However, many couples failed to achieve the kind of harmony hymned in works such as *Ideal Marriage*. Conversely many individuals felt that such a desirable thing need not be bound by convention, while gaining useful performance tips from these works. Sex was increasingly perceived as one of the consumer goods of society: both a concomitant of a reasonable standard of living, and something that has to be worked at.

The publication of Alfred Kinsey's monumental studies of the sex-life of Americans (1948, 1953) had an explosive effect on ideas about sexuality, revealing far greater amounts of various transgressive forms of sexual behavior than had ever been imagined by even the most paranoid moralist. He gave statistical evidence, substantiating perceptions of earlier sexologists, for the chasm between society's ideals of sexual conduct and the ways in which individuals (even decent God-fearing citizens) behaved in and out of the bedroom.

Though the subject of much criticism, Kinsey's volumes ushered in an era in which there was a move from ideals of sexual conduct to the idea of 'normal' (conforming to a statistical norm) sexual behavior. A transition can be seen from the notion prevailing in 1900 that sexual expression and activity should be controlled, to more recent beliefs that sex is good and the more of it the better.

There is little evidence that this has been any less productive of sexual anxiety, as the problems described by Bancroft reveal. Whereas in 1900 couples who were having marital intercourse once a month might have enjoyed it while also getting a virtuous glow from their 'restraint' or even feeling naughtily indulgent, in the 1990s couples who are only having sex once a month may feel that everyone else is doing it more. Advertisements directed towards the sexually anxious male used to be highly coded small ads on the back pages of 'tabloid' newspapers and in dubious magazines; they are now explicitly worded offers of assistance with impotence in the 'quality' Sunday and daily papers. This suggests not only that the problem (whether actual sexual dysfunction or the perception of it) is very persistent but that so also is the reluctance to take it to one's doctor, seeking instead 'specialist' help.

The 'second wave' of feminism which began in the late 1960s produced attacks on the phallocentric assumptions of the standard model of sexual intercourse. The 'safe sex' recommended in the AIDS era also tries to de-emphasize the penetrative paradigm. The degree to which such practices are seen as mere substitutes, and how far the idea of sexual pleasure as diverse and even polymorphous has actually made an impact, remains questionable.

There may have been changes in the idea of 'good' sex over the course of the century, from something infrequently indulged in for primarily reproductive purposes within marriage, to a mutually satisfactory erotic experience between healthy consenting adults. But sexual discourses have always been haunted by the idea of 'bad' sexual bodies. These are often conceived of as bodies which physically bear the stigmata of illicit sexual practices: for example, the assumption that the habitual masturbator shows unequivocal physical signs. The law at least often assumed that the 'common prostitute' was a readily identifiable specimen. The idea of the sexually loose woman having defining characteristics is persistent, and by no means entirely defunct in this era of 'political correctness.' *Taylor's Principles and Practice of Medical Jurisprudence* (1910) mentioned the enduring belief that "[sodomites] exhibit certain general characteristics," though adding that "some undoubtedly do not show such stigmata… [and] it is unnecessary to enumerate them."[29] Venereal diseases were similarly supposed to inhabit very specific dangerous bodies — attitudes prevalent in the days of syphilis have resurfaced in the era of AIDS.

This again exemplifies the desire to classify and define, by siphoning the bad and dangerous things associated with sex into particular recognizable bodies. The most persistent example has perhaps been the prostitute, identified with disease and sexual disorder to an extent which has almost entirely concealed the other partner in the transaction, but the male homosexual has also been a stigmatized figure and the AIDS panic has reactivated old stereotypes and paranoia. The success of the 'British system' for venereal disease treatment established in 1917 was based on its attempts (however compromised in practice) to avoid the identification of sufferers as 'bad bodies' undeserving of treatment in publicly funded institutions.

Paradoxically, fears of sexual dangers and bad bodies have often been the lever for opening up sexual discussions. Sex education originated late in the nineteenth century as a defense against venereal diseases, masturbation, illegitimacy and prostitution. AIDS is similarly changing the parameters of the mentionable with explicit discussions of safe and unsafe sexual praxis.

These days it sometimes seems that the sexual body as we know it is vanishing. There are discussions of the 'performativity' of gender: though the trangressive effect of 'queering' sexual identities requires the existence of conventional assumptions. We are offered the potential thrills of cybersex, though 'virtual reality' so far fails to live up to its promises. Individuals are reported masquerading in electronic communications not merely under a different identity but as another sex: meanwhile brutal sexual harassment over the internet is reported, suggesting that this is far from being a new innocent realm free from the gendered and sexual meanings of embodied life. Meanwhile claims for the deep biological programming of sexual behavior continue.

On the one hand we can see the persisting idea of plasticity, or the possibility of moulding sexual behavior: eg., marital intercourse limited to reproduction, objects of desire restricted to the 'right' sex, adolescent masturbation avoided — although seldom entirely successfully. On the other hand the idea of fixity, of deep biological programming, has also proved enduring, yet undercut by the ways in which sexual behaviour is fluid, not tied down to reproductive necessity, influenced by learning.

Bancroft remarks that human sexuality is "as good a model of psychosomatic relationships as one can find," but that the "complexities of mind-body interaction" create considerable "intellectual discomfort."[30] The medical profession (and the general public) are happier with things that are either definitely physical or 'all in the mind' just as clear distinctions of sex and gender and specific types of sexual bodies are felt to be reassuring. But the sexual body continues to muddle the very categories that it seems to proffer, and this perhaps accounts for the continuing sense that it is somehow enigmatic, a mystery that science may yet be on the point of solving.

REFERENCES

1.  John Bancroft, *Human Sexuality and its Problems*, (2nd edition). (London: Churchill Livingstone, 1989), p. 506.

2.  Havelock Ellis, *Studies in the Psychology of Sex Volume I: The Evolution of Modesty; The Phenomena of Sexual Periodicity; Auto-Erotism*, (first published 1899). (New York: Random House, 1937), pp. xxxiii–iv.

3.  Bancroft, *Human Sexuality*, p. 1.

4.  *Ibid*, p. 4.

5.  William Blair Bell, *The Sex Complex: A Study of the Relationships of the Internal Secretions to the Female Characteristics and Functions in Health and Disease*. (London: Bailliere, Tindal and Cox, 1916), p. 2.

6.  Ellis, *Studies... Vol I*, pp. xxiv–v.

7.  'Reviews and Notices of Books: *Studies in the Psychology of Sex*, Vol VI, *Sex in Relation to Society*,' *The Lancet* 1910, **i**: 1207.

8.  Francis H.A. Marshall, *The Physiology of Reproduction*. (London: Longmans, Green and Co., 1910), p. 1.

9.  Bernard Sandler, 'The Student and Sex Education,' *The Lancet* 1957, **i**: 832–3.

10. Bancroft, *Human Sexuality*, p. 366.

11. Havelock Ellis, *Studies in the Psychology of Sex Volume II: Sexual Inversion*, (first published 1897 as Volume I). (New York: Random House, 1937), p. v.

12. *Ibid*, p. 103.

13. F.J. Smith (ed.), *Taylor's Principles and Practice of Medical Jurisprudence*, 6th edition. (London: J. and A. Churchill, 1910), Vol. II, p. 293.

14. *British Medical Journal* 1985, **ii**: 1747.

15. Thomas Laqueur, *Making Sex: body and gender from the Greeks to Freud*. (Cambridge, Mass.: Harvard University Press, 1990).

16. Havelock Ellis, *Man and Woman: A Study of Human Secondary Sexual Characters*, (first published 1894). (London: Walter Scott Ltd, 2nd edition 1897), pp. 385–6.

17. Bancroft, *Human Sexuality*, pp. 160–1.

18. Otto Weininger, *Sex and Character*. (London: William Heinemann, 1906), p. 3.

19. *Ibid*, p. 5.

20. Blair Bell, *The Sex Complex*, p. 13.

21. Edward Carpenter, *Love's Coming of Age. A Series of Papers on the Relation of the Sexes*, (first published 1896). (London: George Allen and Unwin Ltd, 13th edition, 1930), p. 157.

22. Blair Bell, *The Sex Complex*, p. 119.

23. *Ibid*, pp. 120, 207.

24. *Ibid*, pp. 179, 204.

25. Edward M. Brecher, *The Sex Researchers*. (London: Andre Deutsch, 1970), p. 82.

26. T.H. Van de Velde, *Ideal Marriage: its physiology and technique*, (first published 1928). (London: William Heinemann, 1962), p. 151.

27. *Ibid*, pp. 126–7.

28. *Ibid*, p. 155.

29. *Taylor's Principles and Practice of Medical Jurisprudence*, Vol. II, p. 293.

30. Bancroft, *Human Sexuality*, p. 3.

FURTHER READING

Comfort, Alex, *The Anxiety Makers: some curious preoccupations of the medical profession*. (London: Nelson, 1967).

Ejlersen, Mette, *I Accuse!* (London: Tandem, 1969).

Foucault, Michel, *The History of Sexuality Volume I: An Introduction*. (Harmondsworth Middlesex: Penguin Books, 1981).

Gagnon, John H. and Simon, William, *Sexual Conduct: The Social Sources of Human Sexuality*. (Chicago: Aldine Book Co, 1973).

Hall, Lesley A., *Hidden Anxieties: Male Sexuality 1900–1950*. (Oxford: Polity Press, 1991).

Hall, Lesley A., *Sex, Gender and Social Change in Britain since 1880*. (London: Macmillan, 2000).

Irvine, Janice M., *Disorders of Desire: Sex and Gender in Modern American Sexology*. (Philadelphia: Temple University Press, 1991).

Kinsey, Alfred C., Pomeroy, Wardell B. and Martin, Clyde E., *Sexual Behaviour in the Human Male.* (Philadelphia: W.B. Saunders Co. Ltd., 1948); and Paul H. Gebhard, *Sexual Behaviour in the Human Female.* (Philadelphia: W.B. Saunders Co. Ltd., 1953).

Koedt, Anne, 'The Myth of the Vaginal Orgasm, first published in *Notes from the Second Year*, 1970, reprinted in Leslie B. Tanner (ed.), *Voices from Women's Liberation.* (New York: Signet/New American Library, 1971), pp. 158–166.

Mead, Margaret, *Male and Female: A Study of the Sexes in a Changing World*, (first published 1950). (Harmondsworth Middlesex: Penguin Books, 1962).

Moscucci, Ornella, *The Science of Woman: gynaecology and gender in England, 1800–1929.* (Cambridge: Cambridge University Press, 1990).

Porter, Roy and Hall, Lesley, *The Facts of Life: the creation of sexual knowledge in Britain 1650–1950.* (New Haven: Yale University Press, 1995).

Robinson, Paul, *The Modernization of Sex: Havelock Ellis, Alfred Kinsey, William Masters and Virginia Johnson.* (New York: Harper and Row, 1976).

Tiefer, Leonore, *Sex is not a natural act and other essays.* (Boulder, Colorado: Westview Press, 1995).

Wellings, K., Field, J., Johnson, A.M. and Wadsworth, J., *Sexual Behaviour in Britain: The National Survey of Sexual Attitudes and Lifestyles.* (Harmondsworth: Penguin Books, 1994).

# CHAPTER 19

# The Reproductive Body

## NAOMI PFEFFER

In 1866, J. Matthews Duncan, an influential English Victorian physician accoucheur, described the fecundity of the average woman "as forming a wave which, from sterility, rises gradually to its highest point, and then, more gradually, falls again to sterility."[1] That the fecundity of a woman is related to her age has been believed from the time of Matthews Duncan onwards. Yet in July 1992, at the age of 61, Liliana Cantadori gave birth to her first child, after undergoing hormone treatment to reverse her menopause and the transfer into her uterus of an embryo created by *in vitro* fertilization of an egg procured from another woman.

Matthews Duncan understood variation in women's fecundity as indicating the extent to which their conduct conformed to natural laws governing the female reproductive body. Age was considered a crucial factor; he cautioned women to marry young as a delay might bring them perilously close to the period of natural sterility. For Matthews Duncan, marriage was a necessary precondition of heterosexual intercourse which, in turn, was essential to reproduction. Liliana Cantadori exemplifies the extent to which developments in the twentieth century made this advice anachronistic. The association of marriage and heterosexual intercourse was disrupted; heterosexual intercourse came to be regarded as no longer essential in human reproduction; the apparently immutable relationship of age and fecundity was contravened. Using material drawn mainly from English sources, this chapter explores the contribution of medicine to what rightly can be called a revolution in human reproduction. During the twentieth century, doctors laid claim to the female reproductive body, extending their capacity to manage and manipulate it. The impact of the revolution on the male reproductive body however was almost negligible. The medical community which can now transform a post-menopausal woman into a mother has no remedy for an apparent diminution in sperm numbers, and cannot assuage the fear that, in the near future, many men will be incapable of fathering children.

The developments touched on in this chapter are many and complex. But this is not an exhaustive history of reproductive medicine; innovations have been selected to highlight the most significant developments. Medicine can take the credit for the discovery of relatively few of the techniques described here; most have been appropriated from such diverse sources as the pharmaceutical industry, research laboratory, farm, meatpacking industry, battlefield, and social sciences. Some of the techniques have been exploited in the management and manipulation of the reproductive body; others have been transformed into tests which have given doctors the authority to determine which bodies are capable or incapable of reproduction, and whether or not medicine should assist them in exercising or acquiring that capacity. The tests were often combined severally, hence it is inappropriate to talk about one reproductive body; many different types of reproductive body have come into existence by virtue of medicine. Female reproductive bodies have been diversified more than male ones for two reasons. First, women more than men have formed the material of science, especially in investigations of reproduction, and when the male reproductive body has been scrutinised, it has been treated gently, protectively and conservatively. Second, an important and persistent modern response to ethical, social and political concerns has been to concede to doctors the management and manipulation of the female reproductive body. (This process is sometimes called medicalization.) Because gynecology emerged as a medical specialty in its own right in the first half of the twentieth century, it has sometimes been suggested that doctors deliberately set out to capture women as patients as a means of furthering professional ends; men being ignored as irrelevant to doctors' schemes. While such tidy suggestions have appeal, they simplify and distort complex processes.

Until very recently, Liliana Candatori's body would have been incapable of reproduction. Past menopause, her body no longer produced enough of the hormones essential for a menstrual cycle, and her ovaries were depleted of potential eggs. Nonetheless, in her uterus, an embryo created by fertilization *in vitro* of egg and sperm procured from male and female reproductive bodies with the capacity of gametogenesis, was brought to term. Her body had been prepared for pregnancy and, once established, the pregnancy was sustained, by the administration of exogenous synthetic hormones.

Every aspect of Liliana Candatori's pregnancy represents a major development in reproductive medicine in the twentieth century. The developments can be grouped roughly into three overlapping stages. In the first half of the twentieth century, understandings of the female reproductive body were transformed, not least by the discovery and manipulation of hormones. From the end of the Second World War until the early 1970s, the limitation of female reproductive capacity became a governmental goal, mediated by medicine. In the inter-war period, and especially in the final quarter of the century, techniques were assembled to render fertile the bodies of women previously unable to bear children, as epitomised by the case of Liliana Candatori.

## Transforming the Reproductive Body

Victorians had not suspected that within the reproductive body, the gonads — ovaries and testes — produced substances which we now call sex hormones, or that the anterior lobe of the pituitary gland, sometimes called the 'master' gland, secreted complex protein hormones which 'orchestrate' the reproductive process in both women and men. In the closing years of the nineteenth century, hormones, defined as "chemical messengers that circulate in the blood delivering instructions to the body's tissue and organs,"[2] were first made responsible for the regulation of all bodily functions. By the 1930s, anatomists and physiologists had established that both ovaries and testes secreted hormones which were subsequently identified by biochemists as steroid chemicals. When the steroids were isolated, physical and behavioral characteristics associated with male and female reproductive bodies were attributed to them. In effect, "chemicals were sexualized:"[3] secretions of the testes were labeled 'male,' and those of the ovary 'female,' thus adding 'sex' hormones to the biological indices used by medicine to classify reproductive bodies into male or female.

'Hormonal man' and 'hormonal woman' were painstakingly pieced together in the laboratory, reaching full formation by the time the Second World War was declared. The male reproductive body led the way: in 1889, the seventy-two year old French physiologist and neurologist C.E. Brown-Sequard informed readers of the *British Medical Journal*, that he had experienced rejuvenation after injecting himself with a 'dynamogenic' substance extracted from dogs' testicles. The experiment was a logical operationalization of the then widely held belief that loss of semen diminished physical strength, and masturbation led to nervous debility. Little wonder then that Brown-Sequard postulated that testes produce a substance — a spermatogenic fluid — nutritive to nerves, and which might be extracted. Brown-Sequard extended his theory to other body tissues, explaining other physical and mental symptoms in terms of an inadequate production of internal secretions, the generic name he gave to the fluids concerned. Inspired by the marvellous results experienced from his auto-injections, he claimed many conditions could be reversed by the ingestion or injection of an appropriate fluid.

The system of therapeutics developed by Brown-Sequard was called organotherapy, a new branch of medicine using organs, tissues and fluids from living and dead, human and non-human animals (sheep, cows and pigs procured mostly from abattoirs). Although considered not really respectable in some elite medical circles, organotherapy stimulated scientific investigations into the source, role and applications of extracts of non-human and human animal materials. Through organotherapy the medical specialty of endocrinology emerged.

In the 1930s laboratory evidence came to support the benefits claimed by Brown-Sequard for injections of spermatogenic fluid. In 1931 a hormone, called androsterone, was found in men's urine. Four years later, testosterone, a closely related substance, was isolated in bulls' testicles. Both substances were deemed 'male sex' hormones because of their capacity to restore male secondary sexual character-istics to castrated non-human animals; they can, for example, stimulate the growth of a splendid comb on a caponized cock. The male reproductive body came to be defined in terms of its secondary sexual characteristics which, according to evolutionary theory, confer reproductive advantage to males over other males; the male with the most gorgeous attributes wins access to the female and succeeds in passing on his genetic material to the next generation.

A whole ton of bull's testicles was found to contain only 100 to 150 milligrams of pure 'male sex' hormone, so both research and therapeutic applications were extremely expensive. When cheaper synthetic equivalents became available, they were promoted, albeit half-heartedly, by pharmaceutical companies. The principal application was as a treatment for the so-called 'male climacteric.' Adverts some-times featured exhausted, middle-aged men, accompanied by text referring to 'the penalties of a tumultuous life,' a euphemism for impotence and flagging libido. Respectable doctors insisted they rarely saw symptoms of the male climacteric in their patients, and only reluctantly prescribed male hormone replacement therapy. By the 1950s, male sex hormones had largely been discredited as medicines; they passed into the realms of quackery.

For men, no-one tried to correlate sexual attractiveness (measured in endocrino-logical terms) with reproductive capacity (sperm counts, etc.,) perhaps because most investigations into sex hormones were carried out in research laboratories whereas the scientific scrutiny of human sperm which began in the 1930s was carried out in hospitals, using semen acquired from husbands of patients seeking help for involuntary childlessness. Moreover, sperm of hospital patients were rarely examined. Many doctors were reluctant to ask men for a semen specimen because its production required masturbation, a practice then seen as corrupting.

When a human spermatozoon had first been visualized in 1674 by Leeunwenhook, he thought it contained a homunculus, or 'little man,' that grew to maturity when implanted in the womb of the female. Procreative stories have been rewritten by science many times since then, but the homunculus still haunts ideas about male fertility. Before the 1930s, a man was judged fertile if 'living' sperm were found in his semen (criteria of life and death in sperm remain controversial). In the 1930s, when more exacting ways of testing male fertility began to be explored, three measures of sperm 'quality' were favored: morphology, motility, and numbers. Because the shape of normal human spermatozoon varies greatly, it was assumed that sperm morphology had a distinct bearing on fitness for procreation. In the 1930s for example, New York gynecologist Gerald Moench suggested that a very long, tapering and narrow sperm's "head" [sic] was "sinister" and incompatible with fertility.[4] A small percentage of abnormally formed sperm was considered normal, but if many looked misshapen then, doctors claimed, the chances of conception were diminished. Some investigators believed a rate of more than one in ten mishapen sperm made conception unlikely, others were discouraged by a rate of one in three.

The relevance of motility was based on a different idea: sperm were thought to be capable of autonomous, purposeful action, competing against each other in a race to reach the egg. Hence a sperm quick off the mark must be fertile. It became increasingly obvious however that sperm beauty was in the eye of the beholder, and sperm movement does not necessarily describe function. Although it was understood that fertilization requires only one sperm, the capacity to produce vast numbers of sperm became the pre-eminent measure of male fertility: productivity was taken as a sure sign of reproductivity. Sperm numbers as a test of male fertility has survived the passage of time despite mounting evidence of a weak relationship between sperm density and actual pregnancies.

The transformation of the female reproductive body into a biochemical factory began in 1905 when Walter Heape, a Cambridge scientist, concluded that the stimulus to the generative system during the onset of the breeding season in sheep and cows was due to a special substance in the blood, a "generative ferment" thought by him to be nutritive in nature and induced by the warmer spring and new food.[5] Heape could only speculate on the bodily source of the generative ferment. In 1917, Stockard and Papanicolaou found a correlation between sloughed — dead and shed — cells in the vaginal smear of guinea pigs and cyclic morphologic changes in ovaries and estrus behavior (receptivity toward the male). They provided the scientific community with the first reliable index of internal ovarian activity which did not necessitate cutting open the female body. Significantly, external indices of female gonadal activity were intimately concerned with processes of immediate relevance to fertility, whereas in males, as has already been pointed out, tests focused on secondary sexual characteristics.

In possession of an external index of ovarian activity, scientists embarked upon what turned out to be a massive program of research. In 1923, in the US, Allen and Doisy isolated the first ovarian hormone from sows' ovaries procured from 'waste' in stockyards. It was called 'estrus-producing' hormone because it was capable of producing signs of estrus in the vagina of female rats and mice which had had their ovaries removed before reaching sexual maturity.

Initially it was assumed that the 'estrus-producing' hormone, known nowadays as estrogen, was the 'female sex' hormone, and that it was found only in the female and affects only her sexual organs. Similarly, testosterone was assumed to be the 'male sex' hormone. In effect, the working premise of both scientists and doctors was "femininity and virility reside in the gonad."[6] Imagine the shock felt by the researchers who found both sets of active substances occurred in the gonads and body fluids of both sexes; there are testicular estrogens and ovarian androgens. By the 1930s it had been realised that it is not possible with certainty to distinguish a male from a female reproductive body by examining its secretions. The idea of maleness and femaleness as clearly defined endocrine states gradually gave way to the idea of sex as a balance of endocrine factors.

As the chemical messenger of femininity, estrogen was seized upon both to explain and to treat symptoms associated with the notoriously unstable, unreliable, female reproductive body. Therapeutic applications of female sex hormones proliferated in the 1930s when cheaper, more convenient, synthetic analogues were produced, including the now notorious diethylstilboestrol (DES). Palmlund combed issues of the prestigious *Journal of the American Medical Association* published between 1938 and 1987 and found more than eighty indications for estrogens in medical practice.[7] These included asthma, deafness, diabetes, vertigo and varicose veins, as well as menstrual disorders, breast pains, menopausal symptoms and contraception (more of this below).

In 1933, the isolation of progesterone, the steroid hormone which prepares the uterus for reception and development of the fertilized ovum, marked the final phase in the transformation of the female reproductive body. Probably the most significant event in this stage was the reconceptualization of the menstrual cycle, hitherto understood in morphological and chronological terms, as a dynamic, physiological process. Before about 1900, the menstrual cycle of female primates, including humans, had been assumed to be the same as estrus in non-human animals: both were major events in the female reproductive cycle, both were marked by bleeding. However by the end of the second decade of the twentieth century, the human cycle was acknowledged as "a clearly understandable special case of the generalised estrus cycle, from which it differs in two major points — namely, that sexual responsiveness is not limited to a sharply defined period at the time of ovulation, and that the corpus luteum phase terminates more stormily than in lower mammals, with hemorrhage from the endometrium."[8] The constituent events of the menstrual cycle were documented, including the time-relation of ovulation to menstruation, and the exact relation of the retrogression of the corpus luteum (the remains of the structure in the ovary from which the ova emerges at ovulation), to the onset of the menstrual flow. The recognition that ovulation occurred mid-cycle provided women with new 'scientific' techniques of managing their reproductive body: the Knaus-Ogino 'safe period' method of avoiding conception; and the establishment of the 'fertile' phase of women attempting to conceive a child. Both techniques leave the reproductive body unscathed, relying on the cooperation of men in the regulation of heterosexual intercourse: in the former, it is forbidden, in the latter, encouraged.

In the 1930s, when medical texts began to incorporate gonadal hormones in accounts of the structure and functions of the female reproductive body, their influence was described mostly in negative terms. "The fall in blood progesterone, which results from *regression* of the corpus luteum, *deprives* the highly developed endometrial lining of its hormonal support... *disintegration* starts, and the entire lining...begins to *slough*" [emphasis added].[9] In this typical account, menstruation is represented as a process of breakdown and deterioration. Though a plausible alternative might describe it as the first stage in a process of renewal, medical metaphors suggest menstruation is a pathological condition, perhaps because gynecologists tend to encounter deranged female reproductive bodies, and have little experience of trouble-free ones. However, despite some feminist writers' assertion to the contrary, the female reproductive body is not always healthy or tractable. Some of the developments described in this chapter have transformed the lives of women by freeing them of physical pain and discomfort, from the distress associated with conceiving 'unwanted' children, and from the anguish of involuntary childlessness. Women patients often use negative metaphors when talking about their body. Menstruation for example, represents failure to women experiencing difficulty in conceiving. Nonetheless it is also undoubtedly the case that medicine has a tendency to portray *normal* aspects of the female reproductive body as pathological, and pathological aspects of the male reproductive system as normal. Consider these chapter headings in a textbook titled *Systemic Pathology* published in 1966:

Chapter 26: The Male Reproductive System
Chapter 27: Gynecological Pathology

Both chapters discuss disease.[10]

The menopause provides another example of medicine's tendency to denigrate the female reproductive body. It is called a *deficiency disease,* as if a diminution of female sex hormones inevitably disturbs a woman's physical and mental health. Yet similar judgements have not been made of ageing men. Their pathology has been hidden. Early investigations with testosterone established that the prostate, the organ which produces the bulk of seminal fluid, enlarges 'normally,' and sometimes, pathologically, with age, as a result of diminished production of the hormone by the testes. That enlarged prostates are treated by urologists conveys the impression of a problem of urination rather than reproduction.

GOVERNMENTAL GOALS

That early research on hormones led to few applications can be explained partly by technical problems and scarcity of materials. However the pursuit of certain applications was actively discouraged, in particular those concerned with 'unwanted' pregnancies. Before the Second World War, helping women avoid unintentional conceptions was sometimes illegal and almost always considered improper.

Risking official opprobrium and legal sanction, birth control campaigners became increasingly active after the First World War. They cannot however take credit for the secular decline in the crude birth rate which, in England and Wales had fallen from 36.6 per thousand of the population in 1876 to 24 per thousand by the First World War. In the 1920s, demographers developed new 'scientific' ways of measuring the net effects of reproductive behavior which, they claimed, enabled them to predict accurately the size and composition of the future population. In the mid

1930s, it was discovered that the reproduction rate of Britain (and most industrialized countries) had fallen far below the level then considered healthy for a nation: insufficient girl babies were being born to replenish the stock of mothers presaging a fall in the overall size of the British population. Why this had happened remains controversial although most people now believe it was because conception was increasingly prevented by abstinence from heterosexual intercourse, the 'rhythm' method, 'withdrawal,' the diaphragm, or spermicidal creams and pessaries. The first three methods depend on the cooperation of men. The last two allow women to exercise some control over their reproductive body, but were not then widely available. As I point out below, a considerable number of women who were unable to prevent conception had their pregnancy terminated illegally, often paying the price in physical harm, and even death.

Concern about the political, economic and social implications of a declining population prompted investigations into why women were having fewer babies. Because the bodies of well-born women appeared to be less reproductive than those lower down the social scale, it had been assumed that wealth, education and high social status were somehow 'naturally' negatively correlated with fecundity. The phenomenon of differential fertility exercised eugenists who foreshadowed a nation 'swamped' by people of low intelligence. However investigations into women's reasons for having fewer babies revealed that the decline in the birth rate had not been confined to the better classes: many poor, ill-educated women were having fewer children. Cherished ideas about the relationship of social status and fertility began to be challenged.

To some extent, eugenic concerns informed birth control campaigners such as Marie Stopes. However they were also motivated by a mixture of paternalism, feminism, liberalism and socialism, expressed as concern for the toll taken on women's reproductive bodies by repeated pregnancy. Birth controllers succeeded in widening access to information and contraceptive technology. Very few doctors and scientists supported their program. Although sex hormones had transformed understanding of the reproductive body in the inter-war years, doctors used them only in the promotion of fertility in involuntarily childless women and men, and in the treatment of gynecological and urological complaints. Contraceptive research then was regarded as socially and politically unacceptable and "few doctors and scientists were prepared to undertake it for fear it would undermine their reputation."[11]

The end of the Second World War saw a major transformation of both geopolitics and biopolitics. Attention was diverted away from the metropolitan, industrial populations to those of the colonies now striving for independence. Censuses carried out during the 1950s revealed birth rates far higher than had previously been imagined possible. A Malthusian disaster seemed imminent. American anti-communists saw the threat of political uprisings in an over-populated Third World. In the talk of impending global overpopulation, of standing room only, every female reproductive body seemed at risk of pregnancy.

The panic about global overpopulation prompted a rethink of attitudes towards the prevention of pregnancy which coincided with the development of oral contraceptives. In 1960 the Federal Drug Administration (FDA) approved Enovid-10, the first hormonal contraceptive agent, 'the pill,' a combination of estrogen and progesterone. It promised to protect women from the perils of repeated pregnancy and childbirth, and to liberate the world from the nightmare of overpopulation. It also gave doctors and the pharmaceutical industry unprecedented influence over the female reproductive body.

'The pill' works by overriding the complex hormonal system governing the female reproductive body. Its production and packaging encouraged the notion of a universal female reproductive body. "Formulated on the basis of the hormones that all women were thought to possess, the pill was regarded as a drug which all women could consume across the world."[12] Administered in packages containing pills sufficient for a twenty-eight day cycle, it conveyed the impression that a normal menstrual cycle is of this length.

The numerous agencies set up in the 1950s to tackle the impending population crisis began to encourage women to use the pill. In many Third World countries, concern over high rates of reproduction took precedence over other health-related issues, such as water- and air-borne infections. In the developed world, doctors' reluctance to be associated with contraception was broken down. In 1974 for example, the British National Health Service assumed responsibility for providing contraceptive services to women irrespective of marital status. Hormonal contraception became the most popular method of preventing pregnancy. Provided free at the point of delivery, it was available only on a doctor's prescription.

Attitudes towards contraception may have softened in the second half of the twentieth century, but the controversy over the moral legitimacy of abortion continues to rage. Struggles in the domain of reproduction have spread the language of 'owning' or 'controlling' one's reproductive body. In the abortion battle, the territory fought over is the female reproductive body. Who has the stronger claim on ownership: the woman or the fetus? Women's title was not an issue until the nineteenth century when abortion began to be prohibited and regulated. In England, The Offences Against the Person Act 1861, made it illegal for anyone, including the woman herself, to 'procure her own miscarriage.' The 1861 Act was supplemented by the Infant Life (Preservation) Act 1929 which provided that it was an offense deliberately to cause the death of a child before it had an existence independent of its mother. The 1929 Act went on to say however, that abortion would not be an offense under the Act if such an act were done in good faith with the intention of saving the life of the mother. This clause was famously exploited in 1939 by a judge to acquit Alec Bourne, a gynecologist, who performed an abortion on a 14-year-old victim of a multiple rape. Bourne's case set an important legal precedent. It allowed an abortion to be performed where a doctor believed in good faith that it was necessary to prevent the woman from becoming a physical or mental wreck. In effect, the judgement conferred on doctors the right to evaluate a women's moral worth before agreeing to treat her.

Not every woman could find a doctor prepared to believe her story and, in desperation, might attempt to terminate the pregnancy herself or seek a 'back-street' abortionist. Syringes, fluid, knitting needles, or tubes of glass or rubber, might be pushed through the cervix into the uterus. As a result, many women suffered terribly, becoming irremediably sterile and, sometimes, dying from infection, hemorrhage or shock.

A death resulting from an abortion was registered on the birth certificate as a maternal death: the authorities insisted the woman was a mother even where she died attempting to avoid that condition. In the 1930s concern about rising rates of maternal mortality drew the public's attention to the consequences of illegal abortion. The practice seemed widespread. A report of a British Medical Association Committee published in 1936 estimated that between 16 and 20 per cent of pregnancies in England and Wales ended in abortion, but found it impossible to assess what proportion had been deliberately induced.

From the 1930s onwards, vocal and active women demanded the decriminalization of abortion and a widening of women's access to safe operations. In claiming the fetus is an unborn child, their opponents rendered invisible the pregnant reproductive body on which it is wholly dependent. The pro-abortion lobby was eventually successful. The English 1967 Abortion Act was the first in a new wave of legislation in Western countries. Following the Act, the annual number of abortions carried out in England and Wales rose rapidly, so that around one in five conceptions — the same proportion as in the 1930s — was terminated safely and legally. Between the introduction of the Act in April 1968 and the end of 1996 over 4.5 million abortions were carried out in England and Wales under the conditions of the Act. Around fifteen per cent of these have been performed on women who were not residents of England and Wales but who travelled here from countries where abortion was illegal. The 1967 Act did not however give women the legal right to choose abortion; like the judge in the Bourne case, it conferred protection on doctors who terminate a pregnancy under the conditions of the Act. Pregnancies terminated outside of the conditions of the Act are still illegal. In other countries such as France, Italy, and Canada, under certain conditions, women have the legal right to choose. For women who undergo it, an abortion is an intimate and deeply personal experience, but the decision to make it a legal or criminal act is a political one. In some instances, politicians have been motivated by a population policy, or by a sympathy to women's plight. In others they have been guided by the knowledge that election victories can depend on a candidate's stance on abortion.

## Rendering Fertile Infertile Bodies

Throughout history some married women have conceived after engaging in heterosexual intercourse with a man other than their husband. In the 1940s, a few maverick doctors admitted inseminating women married to irremediably infertile men with semen obtained from another man. They claimed artificial insemination using donated semen (AID) protected the institution of marriage: it enabled married women to conceive without committing adultery and transformed involuntarily childless women into contented wives and mothers. The donor was anonymous and had been selected for reasons of physical similarity to the woman's husband, who could 'pass' as biological father of her children, and keep hidden his shameful sterility. Their opponents were not convinced. For them, AID corrupted everyone involved in it: the semen donor because he masturbated; the women because she was reduced to the status of non-human animals (AID had recently been introduced into farming); the infertile husband because he was a cuckold; the doctors because they flouted their profession's ethical codes by being party to immoral acts.

AID was the first 'treatment' of infertility to provoke public outrage. However strictly speaking, it was not a treatment; AID bypasses the problem of male infertility, it is not a cure for it. Treatments proved elusive, perhaps because male fertility was enigmatic. A satisfactory explanation of the significance of the vast numbers of sperm in each ejaculate has still not been found. Indeed since the classic studies of Macleod in the US in the early 1950s describing average sperm density in 'normal' and subfertile men, medical authorities have regularly lowered the 'critical mass' threshold of sperm density associated with fertility.

Medical journals concerned with fertility and sterility are replete with articles condemning the reliability and validity of published results of tests of sperm density. Yet in the 1980s doctors began to claim that average sperm concentration and quantity of semen in each ejaculate had fallen dramatically over the past fifty years: men with sperm counts poised on the brink of fertility were being pushed towards infertility. Weakly estrogenic substances in the environment were — and remain — the most popular explanation of the apparent fall in sperm counts. In some quarters, their presence was explained by the vast quantities of estrogen ingested by women taking 'the pill' or hormone replacement therapy contaminating the water supply.

Paradoxically in the 1980s, the two explanations offered for the apparent increase in numbers of women seeking medical treatment for infertility made no mention of environmental pollutants or falling sperm counts. First, it was claimed, women were delaying having children until they were well past their reproductive prime. Second, involuntarily childless women had been given hope by the development of powerful interventions into the infertile female reproductive body. Medically assisted procreation, one of the terms used to describe these interventions, was made possible by three separate innovations. The first was reported in 1958 by

Gemzell, a Swedish gynecologist. As a result of experiments begun in the 1920s, control of the gonads of both women and men had been conceded to the anterior pituitary body. Two gonadotrophins — trophic means regulating, hence gonadotrophin means regulation of the gonads — found in blood and urine were traced back to the anterior pituitary body: follicle stimulating hormone (FSH), responsible for stimulating the development of both sperm and ova, and encouraging the production of estrogen and testosterone; luteinizing hormone (LH), which provokes the release of gametes. However despite demonstrating powerful effects in the laboratory, in the hospital, gonadotrophins isolated from non-human animals such as sheep, cows and pigs, were disappointing; they failed to provoke ovulation in anovular women or spermatogenesis in sterile men. A reason for this had been found in the 1940s: hormones of the anterior pituitary body are proteins and are relatively species specific: gonadotrophins isolated from non-human animals will not work in humans.

Gemzell was responsible for the first successful clinical application of same-species gonadotrophins. He had isolated crude FSH from pituitary glands procured from cadavers lying in the mortuaries of Stockholm's hospitals. Without 'Gemzell's method,' as it was sometimes called, the techniques that enabled Liliana Candatori to become a mother could not have been developed. However human gonadotrophins were scarce, expensive, powerful and unpredictable medicines. During the 1970s, they were responsible for several higher order multiple pregnancies — quins, sextuplets, septuplets, and even octuplets — which ended in tragedy and reconfirmed the controversial proclivities of reproductive medicine.

During the 1960s, in Oldham General Hospital, the gynecologist Patrick Steptoe pioneered a technique called laparoscopy, in which instruments are inserted through a small hole made in the abdominal wall into the pelvic cavity. The technique allowed him to visualize directly and explore women's reproductive organs. In 1968, Robert Edwards, a Cambridge scientist studying human ova and embryology, asked Steptoe to recover human eggs for his research into human *in vitro* fertilization. As a result of their collaboration, in 1978 Lesley Brown famously gave birth to her daughter Louise.

Louise was the product of an egg retrieved from Lesley and fertilized *in vitro* by sperm from her husband John. However the techniques developed by Steptoe and Edwards made possible third party involvement in the reproductive process to an unprecedented extent; nowadays several reproductive bodies can participate in the parenting of a single child. Motherhood, once a single role for women, has been divided into three: the genetic mother, the carrying mother, and the nurturing mother. (Liliana Candatori was once a carrying and is now a nurturing mother.) AID had already made possible similar distinctions in the male role: a man can be a genetic father or a nurturing father, or both. Put another way, 57 relationships between child and male and female reproductive bodies have been made possible through third party involvement.

## Conclusion

In alienating ova and embryo from a woman's body, the new technologies have forced the issue: what does the modern reproductive body reproduce? "The mimetic relationship implied by the modern meaning of reproduction (as implied in printing and Xeroxing, and the making of furniture in antique styles) can no longer be assumed."[13] In a majority of cases, the 'original' is the mother and father, and the 'copy' their child; however like the embryo brought to term in Liliana Candatori's uterus it can be modeled on strangers' templates.

It is not surprising then that each advance in the field of reproductive technology provokes a loud public outcry. Placatory attempts include official public enquiries, such as the British Warnock Report, legislation and regulation. The Human Fertilisation and Embryology Act 1990 allows doctors working under license to manipulate sperm, eggs and embryos. However it also perpetuates the belief that gynecologists are skilled in the estimation of women's moral worth: the Act requires them to investigate women's suitability as mothers before offering treatment. Indeed as a result of the remarkable developments touched on in this chapter, medicine is increasingly being made responsible for regulating the female reproductive body.

## References

1. J. Matthews Duncan, *Fecundity, fertility, sterility and allied topics.* (Edinburgh: A & C Black, 1866), p. 43.
2. F.G. Young, 'Ideas about animal hormones', in J. Needham (ed.), *The chemistry of life.* (Cambridge: Cambridge University Press, 1970), pp. 125–155.
3. Nelly Oudshoorn, 'On measuring sex hormones: the role of biological assays in sexualizing chemical substances, *Bulleting of the History of Medicine* (1990), **64**: 243–261.
4. G.L. Moench, 'Sperm morphology in relation to fertility', *American Journal of Obstetrics and Gynecology, American Journal of Obstetrics and Gynecology* (1931), **22**: 199–210.
5. Roy O. Greep, 'Reproductive endocrinology: concepts and perspectives, an overview', *Recent Progress in Hormone Research* (1978), **34**: 1–23.
6. Diana Long Hall, 'Biology, sex hormones and sexism in the 1920s', *Philosophy Forum* (1973/4), **55**: 81–96.
7. Ingar Palmlund, 'Risk evaluation and estrogens', *International Journal of Risk & Safety in Medicine* (1991), **2**: 321–342.
8. George W. Corner, 'Our knowledge of the menstrual cycle', *The Lancet* (April 28, 1951), 919–923.
9. Emily Martin, *The woman in the body.* (Milton Keynes: Open University Press, 1987), p. 49.
10. Naomi Pfeffer, 'The hidden pathology of the male reproductive system', in H. Homans (ed.), *The sexual politics of reproduction.* (Aldershott: Gower, 1985), pp. 30–44.
11. Lara Marks, 'A "cage" of ovulating females': the history of the early oral contraceptive pill clinical trials, 1950–59', in S. de Chadarevian, H. Kamminga (eds), *Molecularizing biology and medicine: new practices and alliances, 1910s–1970s.* (Amsterdam: Harwood Academic Publishers, 1998), pp. 221–247.
12. L. Marks, '"Andromeda freed from her chains": attitudes towards women and the oral contraceptive pill, 1950–1970', in A. Hardy and L. Conrad (eds), *Women and Medicine,* (forthcoming).
13. Ludmilla Jordanova, 'Reproduction in the eighteenth century', in Faye D. Ginsburg and Rayna Rapp (eds), *Conceiving the new world order: the global politics of reproduction.* (Berkeley: University of California Press, 1995), pp. 369–86.

## FURTHER READING

Duden, Barbara, *Disembodying women: perspectives on pregnancy and the unborn.* (Cambridge, Massachusetts: Harvard University Press, 1993).

Edwards, Robert and Steptoe, Patrick, *A matter of life: the sensational story of the world's test-tube baby.* (London: Sphere, 1981).

Ginsburg, Faye D. and Rapp, Rayna (eds), *Conceiving the new world order: the global politics of reproduction.* (Berkeley: University of California Press, 1995).

Marks, Lara, *Sexual chemistry: a history of the contraceptive pill.* (Newhaven and London: Yale University Press, forthcoming).

Moscucci, Ornella, *The science of woman: gynaecology and gender in England, 1800–1929.* (Cambridge: Cambridge University Press, 1990).

Oakley, Ann, *The captured womb: a history of the medical care of pregnant women.* (Oxford: Blackwell, 1986).

Oudshoorn, Nelly, *Beyond the natural body: an archeology of sex hormones.* (London: Routledge, 1995).

Petchesky, Rosalind, *Abortion and woman's choice.* (London: Verso, 1986).

Pfeffer, Naomi, *The stork and the syringe: a political history of reproductive medicine.* (Cambridge: Polity, 1993).

Saetnan, Ann, Oudshoorn, Nelly and Kirijczyk, Martha (eds), *Localizing and globalizing reproductive technologies.* (Columbus Ohio: Ohio State University Press, forthcoming).

Sandelowski, Margarete, *With child in mind: studies of the personal encounter with infertility.* (Philadelphia: University of Pennsylvania Press, 1993).

Stacey, Meg (ed.), *Changing human reproduction: social science perspectives.* (London: Sage, 1992).

# CHAPTER 20

# The Psychological Body

MATHEW THOMSON

By the late twentieth century we had come to occupy a 'psychological society.' Three linked developments underpin this transition: the expansion and rising prestige of psychology as a science and academic discipline; the creation of myriad applied psychologies which reach deep into the social fabric; and the popularization and internalization of psychological knowledge and practice. As a science, psychology has redefined human nature and reconstituted the body: its language of the 'conscious,' 'subconscious,' and 'unconscious,' of 'intelligence,' 'personality' and 'memory,' of 'instinct' and 'sentiment' has mapped and remapped a psychological body. Applied in schools, factories, armies, prisons, and clinics, psychology has recognized, observed, measured, classified, treated, and thus redefined the body; while embedded in advertising, marketing, the politics of the opinion poll, and the confessional chat-show, it has been a vital force in shaping the culture which in turn shapes us. And finally, internalized in the popular psyche, psychology has become intrinsic to the ways in which we imagine ourselves, our relationships to others, and our bodily as well as mental states of health.

## PSYCHOLOGY AS AN ACADEMIC DISCIPLINE: THEORISING THE PSYCHOLOGICAL BODY

The history of psychology has largely been written from the internalist perspective of the discipline itself. It has been a history of disciplinary formation, and of professional and academic consolidation and expansion, all driven forward by theoretical progress. The discipline's dominant and whiggish narrative of development has been that of a passage from philosophy and metaphysics to science. Introspective speculation about consciousness and mind would be superseded by a science of behavior; study of the unseeable and ultimately unknowable would make way for observation of the actual. Such a transition had significant implications for the psychological body. In one sense it was radically circumscribed. Nineteenth-century psychologists had regarded the territory of the 'mental' as a legitimate province. This was certainly the case as long as psychology was little more than a branch of philosophy specializing in the nature of consciousness. The situation began to shift as it turned towards the alternative model of physiology to redefine itself as an experimental science and to attract doctors who wanted to specialize in the study of the mind. In histories of the discipline, this transition — the 'birth of modern psychology' — is tied to the moment when one of these doctors, the German Wilhelm Wundt, founded what is conventionally regarded as the first psychological laboratory in 1879. Within the laboratory mental operations were brought into close scrutiny as never before. And cut off from external stimuli and social influence in this artifical environment, experimentation assumed and thereby confirmed the individual autonomy of the psychological body.

In the investigation of mental activities, such as perception, memory, and wilful inhibition, psychologists accepted the dualist nature of human existence — a mental sphere running parallel to the merely physical. The role of the will in inhibiting and controlling the functions of the physical body was at the core of this mental science and was fundamental in placing man on a different plane to beast. However, the physiological paradigm also raised the question of how brain and mind were linked. Theories of reflex arcs between brain and body, of functional specialization within areas of the brain, and of the existence of layers of evolutionary development (linking the body to the history of the race) within the brain went part of the way towards bringing the two together; though none was able to replace mind, particularly since going too far was still to risk the violent accusations of materialism which had been encountered by the phrenologists earlier in the nineteenth century.

This 'mental science' would be transformed by two divergent developments: first the emergence of psychoanalytic and psychodynamic psychologies, and secondly the emergence of behaviorism. Though the first is integral to the construction of the psychological body in the twentieth century it has been dealt with elsewhere in this volume and will consequently be passed over here more briefly than its importance merits. The roots of psychoanalysis lay in part in the late nineteenth-century search for the physical basis of the mental. However, its greatest significance would be to bring to the fore a longer tradition of thought which looked beyond consciousness to the unconscious levels of mind. As such, it confirmed psychology as a mental science, and indeed pushed it radically further into investigation of the unseeable realms of the psychological body. Behaviorism, on the other hand, would emerge out of the experimental tradition and the growing dissatisfaction with attempts to establish a science on unverifiable speculation about consciousness. The realm of investigation would now be circumscribed, from that of the mental-physical body, to the behavior of that body alone.

The shift towards a behavioral science was particularly marked in the United States, but because of the great influence and rapid development of psychology within that country it has become a defining narrative for the academic discipline as a whole. In 1913 American psychologist, John Broadus Watson, published what is seen as a manifesto for the new movement. Through study of the response to stimuli, psychology was to become an objective science of human behavior. This was ultimately to give the discipline a predictive power which would establish its utility as a discipline of social control. Human behavior, like that of Watson's rats, could be manipulated and trained through the conditioning of emotional reactions. As such, behaviorism was both progressive in its radical environmentalism which countered the prevailing hereditarian pessimism, yet potentially sinister in its denial of human autonomy and its visions of an ordered society.

By the 1930s, behaviorism dominated the discipline in the United States. However, a crude behaviorism was modified as it was recognized that the response of individuals to stimuli could not be isolated from mediating factors such as learnt behavior and social situation. Observation of psychological bodies led to the recognition of the individual differences which modified behavior. And this provided fertile ground for further expansion of the discipline as it developed techniques to measure and classify the psychological body, most notably with its focus on intelligence, attitudes and personality.

Other national contexts shaped somewhat different theoretical traditions, though the attraction of a psychology which could be applied to the ordering of society remained crucial. In the Soviet Union, physiologist I.V. Pavlov's research into conditioned behavior, most famously that of his dogs trained to salivate in response to a bell associated with the prospect of food, provided a home-grown hero for an environmentalist psychology which, in countering ideas of innate inequality and instead pointing to the vast potential for human progress through social engineering, was ideologically attractive to the communist regime. However, Soviet psychologists were readily turned upon in the 1930s when their work suggested that the psychological bodies of the Party and industry would work better if they worked less, with the discipline subsequently emasculated as it was steered back towards the philosophical to be little more than a branch of Marxist-Leninism.

In interwar Germany, the home of experimental psychology and the birth place for American psychology in the nineteenth century, the discipline diverged quite radically from its transatlantic counterpart. With psychology still dominated by philosophy within academia, and with defeat in the First World War heightening a sense of loss and disenchantment in a world dominated by materialist science, Germany saw the rejection of behaviorism as crudely mechanistic and atomising and the emergence instead of the Gestalt movement. Psychologists such as Kurt Koffka, Wolfgang Kohler and Max Wertheimer rejected the assumption that individual behavior could be viewed in isolation. In their view the whole was always more than the sum of its parts, and in turn the parts — the isolated behavior — could not be understood apart from the whole; the very act of observation, for instance, was an integral part of, and transformed, the observed. The boundaries of their psychological body were thus radically opened up: it was a body in which the physical and the mental were made one; and it was a body which was defined by its situation in the social arena and the national culture. Moreover, positioned in this field of relations, the psychological body was shaped and guided by a natural order, an order which gave form and structure to the chaos of sensationalist perception. The Gestalt effect could be demonstrated in experiments into perception, however it also rested heavily on extending the principle well beyond these activities through the power of the holistic metaphor. This philosophical holism, often veering towards an apparent mysticism, and at odds with the postivism of behaviorism, undermined the influence of the Gestalt movement beyond Germany itself. Within Germany its holism could provide scientific and ideological legitimation for nationalism, social order, and even racism: the health of the psychological body was presented as both cause and consequence of the health and unity of society, nation and race; and the latter, as a result, was presented as having an organic and spiritual basis — a (national-social-racial) psychological body — in its own right. However, in circumstances of wartime mobilization, the position of this theoretical psychology was weakened, with resources instead directed towards applied psychologies of mental testing and management.

Britain also proved less conducive to behaviorism than the United States. Here, under the influence of a powerful idealist strain within intellectual thought and political culture, psychology remained more open to an introspective methodology and assumed a particular interest in the role of instincts, their control, and their channeling into the construction of 'higher' moral and social sentiments. The British psychological body was thus approached as a purposive subject (the material for the good citizen), not simply a machine reacting to its environment. Although the trend, as elsewhere, was towards a more positivist, behaviorist, and individualist psychology, there were those who shared the German misgivings about the atomization and mechanization of the psychological body. In particular, William McDougall's theory of the 'Group Mind' suggested that the mind of the individual was linked to that of society and the nation through a combination of inherited traits, organic memories and social instincts. Though highly popular, his work found diminishing support from fellow academics, particularly the idea that there was any kind of organic basis to a group consciousness. On the other hand, an interest in the way that culture moulded individual behavior and shaped national character was widespread, and was encouraged by both the anthropological encounter with colonial psychological subjects and a need to define Britishness as a source of social-psychological meaning and values in an era of ideological and social instability.

The communist world apart, national differences were less marked after the Second World War, with American psychology increasingly dominant. Though the panorama of theoretical positions became even more complex, positivism and a modified behaviorism were still to the fore. Such an approach found a new set of metaphors and a new sophistication through the growing influence of information technology. The psychological body could be seen as an information processing machine, programmable through the expertise of the psychologist.

Cognitive science placed humans alongside machines in the same field of study, and the growing sophistication of the computer questioned the uniqueness of the (human) psychological body more acutely than ever before. The behaviorist tradition was, however, paralleled and challenged by the 'humanistic' psychology of American psychologist Carl Rogers and others, which viewed critically the control of feelings and the construction of a culture of conformity and advanced instead a psychology of self-discovery, self-expression, and authenticity. Countering behaviorist objectification, it sought to understand the psychological body in its own terms. Like behaviorism, this humanist psychology benefited from lending itself to practical application: in this case, to the rapidly expanding demand for psychotherapy.

In the last decades of the century advances in psychopharmacology, neurophysiology, and genetics, alongside the critique of behaviorism and a growing disillusionment with psychoanalysis, contributed to a revived interest in the biological basis of the psychological body. At the same time, the constitution of the psychological society and the psychological self was deconstructed and relativised within the humanities, while the study of consciousness returned to the fore and attracted interest across disciplines. For these reasons, and despite its 'century of progress,' the subject of the psychological body was fractured, contested, and not the province of the psychological discipline alone.

## APPLIED PSYCHOLOGY: CONSTRUCTING THE PSYCHOLOGICAL BODY

Although the origins of the psychological profession can be pushed back in time, its emergence as a significant force was almost wholly a twentieth-century phenomenon. Membership of the American Psychological Profession (APA), founded in 1892, rose from 393 in 1920 to 2,739 by 1940. That of the British Psychological Society (BPS), founded in 1901, would rise from 100 in 1918, to 800 in 1941. In part this reflected the establishment of an academic discipline and the progress of theory (though in Britain in 1939 there were still only 6 chairs in the subject). However, the main reason for the expansion of the discipline and the force which guided the direction of its theoretical development was its emergence and success as an applied science. In turn, these applications would have a far more tangible and direct impact than did theory in defining and reshaping the twentieth-century psychological body. The explosion in the size of the profession after the Second World War was a reflection of the growing influence of psychology as an applied discipline: by 1960 membership of the APA had shot up to over 18,000, and that of the BPS to over 2,000; and the number of doctorates in psychology within the United States had risen form 1,116 in the 1930s, to 6,412 in the 1950s.

In the first half of the century, psychology's expansion would rest on its claim to be able to measure the mental abilities of individuals, and consequently its use to classify these individuals, to define new boundaries of normality within populations, and to regulate individual adjustment to social norms. After the

Second World War, such functions would continue but they would be matched in importance by a psychology of social relations and by the use of psychology as a diagnostic and therapeutic tool. Such a shift entailed a movement from a regulated, ranked, and normalized psychological body, to one of self-realisation and of less overt and internalized control; it entailed a shift from focusing on those 'deviants' beyond the boundaries of normality who were already visible and open to regulation through their location in institutional sites, to a problematization of normality itself and a movement into the private sphere of life; and it entailed a shift from a focus on the individual psychological body, to the constitution of this body through social relations and in turn the constitution of a social body through the psychological effect of education, child-rearing, and culture on a mass of individuals.

Crucial to the emergence of psychology as an applied discipline was its development of the mental test and the fact that this coincided with the appearance of states which were more willing than ever before to intervene to maintain the health, efficiency, and order of their subject populations. Best exemplifying this conjuncture was the emergence of universalist, state education systems which made visible the backward and disruptive child and provided the perfect opportunity for the emergence and expansion of a machinery for psychological testing. Initial attempts to tackle this problem came from established and far more powerful professions: teachers ranked students according to examination results; while doctors looked for physical signs such as cranial measurements. By the first decade of the century psychology was pioneering its own technology of mental testing based on two developments: first, a statistical technique for ranking individual differences within a population, as pioneered by Francis Galton in Britain; and secondly, the construction of a series of simple exercises to test the working of the higher mental processes, as pioneered by Alfred Binet in France who had been commissioned by the government to detect children with learning difficulties. Drawing on Galton's science of individual difference, Binet could assign an age level to the passage of each exercise by ranking the performance of children against their peers and against a normal distribution curve; and he could thus assign a mental age to each child based on their performance and contrast this to their mental ages — the difference a reflection of backwardness. William Stern subsequently introduced the practice of dividing mental age by chronological age and multiplying the result by 100 to give an Intelligence Quotient (IQ). There was a widespread adoption of the Binet test in Europe and the United States in the first half of the century, often adapted to the local culture or paralleled by a panoply of similar indigenous tests. Through correlating the results of a series of tests, British psychologist Charles Spearman attempted to demonstrate that there was a general factor — 'g' — which represented intelligence. As such, not only was the psychological body made measurable and rankable, but intelligence was reified as a real, stable (and thus largely inherited) quality.

By the turn of the century concern about 'mental defectives' had become acute as influential eugenic theory suggested that they were the seeds for future generations of the unemployable, criminal, and insane. In Britain such concern fueled a movement for life-long segregation, with over 30,000 mental defectives in institutions and altogether nearly 100,000 under some kind of surveillance by the Second World War. In the United States and Canada, segregation was paralleled by immigration restrictions on those ethnic groups assumed to be of low intelligence and by sexual sterilization of the 'feeble-minded.' The first sterilization law was introduced in Indiana in 1907, and by 1932 over 12,000 had undergone the operation as it spread to other states. Such a scale was subsequently overshadowed by the eugenic policing of the mentally unfit in Nazi Germany, with the sterilization of around 360,000 and 'euthanasia' extended to mentally handicapped children. However it is important to remember that the attempt to control the breeding of those deemed mentally inferior was widespread. So, too, the neglect of the rights of the psychologically sick body, which was no less a feature of the development of modern welfare systems in liberal America and social democratic Sweden (with nearly 63,000 operations between 1935 and 1975) than it was in Hitler's Germany. Though it would be grossly unfair to claim that the technology of mental testing alone either made possible or provided the scientific justification for such eugenic excesses (for instance, mental tests could be mobilized by supporters and opponents, alike, of the innate racial inferiority of non-whites), its utility as a technology for mass regulation and its assumptions about the fixity and inequality of mental ability clearly did much to facilitate such policies.

The mass recruitment of the First World War provided a perhaps premature opportunity for psychological testing to demonstrate its importance. Because of the still very limited nature and prestige of such expertise and the mass manpower demands of industrialized warfare, the British army would pay very little attention to screening troops on the basis of mental ability. In the United States the discipline was in a considerably stronger position and a mass screening operation did take place with over a million troops tested. On the other hand, even here the military authorities took little notice of the results.

The demands of mass education systems would remain the most crucial arena for the expansion of applied psychology. In particular, the interwar period would see psychology establishing a central role in the ranking of the school child. The introduction of group tests would signficantly increase the scope of the test which would now act as a sieve, not simply to weed out the feeble-minded but to stream the normal child. British educational psychologists such as Cyril Burt believed that they could detect different aptitudes among children and thus guide them on different paths in the emerging secondary education system. Eventually such assumptions would be embedded in the tripartite system of the 1944 Education Act, with an 11+ examination to channel children according to ability (assumed to be fixed by this age) into either secondary modern schools for 'concrete' thinkers, technical schools for the 'mechanical,' or grammar schools for those with an ability to think in 'abstract' terms. Historians are divided over whether these psychometrists were acting to defend their own class interests by establishing a new elitism of intellect, or whether they had a genuinely meritocratic vision of replacing a society of inherited privilege with a society of social mobility based on a ladder of educational opportunity. What is indisputable is that in this half century the concept of intelligence was placed at the very center of the construction of the psychological body, with potentially far reaching significance for the organization of society.

The mental test encroached into further areas of interwar life. It provided a tool for assessing the child delinquent and the criminal in court and in penal institutions. It was advanced as a tool for vocational selection. In the US army, tests of aptitude and leadership qualities proved rather more successful than had intelligence tests in gaining the support of the military authorities in 1917–18. And such tests were adopted (within 'characterology') by the German military in the 1930s and by all sides in the Second World War. In fact, there was a sense that virtually any mental quality could be tested and classified against a norm. For instance, the Psycho-Galvanic Test of the flow of current in the body when answering questions offered the prospect of a scientific measure of moral ability, while the Rorschach test sought to assess and measure personality through the subject's interpretation of ink-blots.

Such mental tests can be seen as crudely reductionist in the way that they represented the psychological body in terms of numbers on a scale or as fixed personality types. However, in practice the expertise of the psychologist lay in an ability to modify and interpret the tests according to a shifting environment and to recognize the unique individuality of each psychological body. Moreover, psychologists gradually moved beyond the artificial environment of the laboratory and attempted to recreate a natural situation through observation in the workplace or the clinic playroom; as such, they aimed to go beyond objectification towards an understanding of the psychological body in its own terms. Within the workplace, for instance, industrial psychologists by the interwar period were beginning to criticise the efficiency engineering best associated with the American Frederick Winslow Taylor. Instead of focusing on arranging the working body to maximize production-line speed, psychologists such as C.S. Myers and his National Institute for Industrial Psychology, founded in Britain in 1921, shifted the focus to the psychological 'human factor.' It was recognized that Taylorist maximization of the pace of work could have a longer term deleterious effect through the resulting mental stress of the worker; that the needs and capacities of each worker were different and a reflection of psychological individuality; and that the attitude and happiness of the worker were just as important as time management in enhancing productivity. Within schools there was a similar shift towards taking into account the subjectivity of the psychological body and adapting the environment accordingly as educational psychologists advanced 'child-centred' theory and practice. The most significant influence was in the schooling of the youngest children where there was a retreat from rote learning and a recognition of the importance of play and imagination. This extended well beyond noted progressive schools, such as Summerfield in Britain and the nursery schools which adopted the psychological principles of Maria Montessori, for it was already becoming standard by the interwar period for teachers to be introduced to psychological insights in the course of their training.

It is important to recognize the limitations to the influence of psychology within each of these institutional sites before the Second World War. The new profession struggled when it infringed on the territory of better established, more powerful groups. The resistance to mental tests from the military in the US Army during the First World War has already been noted. There was a similar tension in other combattant armies over whether shell-shocked troops were suffering from a psychological condition or were simply malingerers, with the military most concerned to protect manpower resources and trained to regard the problem as one of morale rather than psychology. Studies of the education system in interwar Britain also point to the relatively limited advance of psychological as opposed to more traditional scholastic examinations. This was partly the result of lack of resources and the scarcity of psychologists, and it was partly a reflection of the caution towards the new expertise from those who administered the system. The special school system in fact expanded little beyond the scale it had already reached in 1913 — before the widespread availability of psychologists and their tests.

The difficulties were even greater when psychology attempted to move beyond these institutional sites to create its own or to establish itself within the private spaces of the community. The most successful of such ventures was the creation of the child guidance clinic. Here again the United States was far ahead, with its first clinic in 1909 and 233 by 1935; in Britain, by contrast, the first clinic was opened as late as 1929, with only a further 20 opened in the next decade. Within the clinic the psychologist often played a role in the examination of the delinquent and problem child, however therapeutic authority lay with medically-trained psychiatrists. The state was far less active in funding clinics for adults, and in the private clinics which emerged and offered a range of psychodyanamic therapies the psychologist, if present at all, was again invariably subordinate to the doctor. In sum, in terms of practical results and institutional expansion alone we should be careful not to overestimate the extent or authority of an interwar psychological complex.

The fact that such a complex seemed increasingly influential owed as much to the activities and rhetoric of pressure groups and propagandists who advanced the importance of 'mental hygiene.' Though founded by a layman, the American Clifford Beers, through his autobiographical account *A Mind that Found Itself* (1911), the mental hygiene movement provided a huge opportunity for psychologists as it turned every aspect of daily life into an economy of mental health and decentred the doctor's province of cure through a preventive paradigm. By the 1930s the movement had outposts throughout much of the world, with representatives from 41 countries attending the 1930 international congress in Washington.

The Second World War, like the First, provided an important opportunity for the advance of applied psychology. It confirmed the importance of psychology as a tool of management and selection in the armed forces, and extended this to the prevention of mental breakdown and maintenance of morale amongst a civilian population facing total war. But most importantly it provided the opportunity for psychology to advance into the field of therapy. The coincidence of an acceptance of the need for psychotherapy after the lessons of 1914–18 and the exceptional demands of the wartime situation was enough to break the medical monopoly. With demand maintained after the war, and in light of the lack of widespread psychological training among doctors, clinical psychology established an enduring foothold. For instance, in the United States a dozen states passed laws to certify psychologists as therapists, and by 1960 41 per cent of APA members devoted half of their time to psychotherapy. By the 1980s clinical psychologists were performing as much outpatient psychotherapy in the United States as were psychiatrists, outnumbering their medical counterparts by 50,000 to 28,000; and in fact this psycho-therapeutic net was spread even further by 300,000 social workers with basic psychological training. In such a society it was commonplace — no longer a sign of abnormality or illness — to have psychological problems and to turn to psychological therapists. In 1957, 4 per cent of the American population had consulted psychological experts over their problems; by 1976 the figure had risen to 14 per cent of the general population and 21 per cent of those college-educated.

The extent of this psychotherapeutic apparatus within the United States was exceptional, reflecting the affluence and thriving private medical sector, the strong psychological tradition, and perhaps also a heightened obsession with self-development in this country. In Britain, where the new National Health Service dominated health care delivery after the Second World War, plans to place mental health alongside physical in the new service were never fully realized and psychiatry remained a somewhat isolated and neglected sector. There were exceptions to this. For instance, the Tavistock Clinic, founded in the interwar period to provide free psychological therapy for both children and adults, gained prestige through the important wartime work of its members and was integrated into the NHS. And in the 1950s many general practitioners were inspired by the writing of Michael Balint to integrate a psychological perspective into their understanding of illness — to consider the patient as a whole person — seeing this approach as something which might distinguish the special nature of their expertise and elevate their positions within the profession. However, state resources, or insurance funds in a country like the United States, were focused on the technological and pharmacological advances which were transforming medicine and whose efficacy was much more easily demonstrated. Thus the vision of treating the person as a whole, involving time-consuming contact and therapy, made way to treating the psychological body like the physical through the chemistry of tranquilizers and pills.

The science of mental testing, classification, and behavioral modification continued alongside the expanding psychotherapeutic regime. This objectification and rationalization of the psychological body went further in the conformist 1950s, spurred on in the United States by the 'national security state.' By 1957, 5 per cent of the APA was employed by the military, a further 5 per cent by the Veterans' Administration, and many others indirectly by the military through research in universities and private companies. The Army, the CIA and other intelligence organizations set up the secret 'Project Camelot' in the 1960s to investigate potential political trouble spots around the world, said to be the largest social science investigation ever. In the era of total war it was just as important for psychologists on such projects to understand how to manipulate civilian populations through the new sciences of public opinion and interpersonal communications as to turn troops into effective fighting machines or to defend against 'brainwashing.' Meanwhile, psychological profiles of other countries' 'personalities' provided an 'other' for the normalization of America's own individualist creed and its defense against the enemy within of communism. In the 1960s, with race hatred, street crime, and youth and sexual deviance recognized as equally threatening to the American way of life, state funding increased further, pushing this psychology of national defense into a diagnosis of these new abnormalities and into ever more intrusive examination of relations within the private sphere.

In the 1960s there was a backlash against psychology's use as a tool of social regulation and objectification. The close involvement with the national security state left its reputation for objectivity and independence tarnished. The increasing presence of psychology within everyday life was recognized as a threat to individual liberty. And there was mounting criticism of the assumptions about normality which underpinned the power of the test, and a recognition of the discipline's role in contributing to sexual and racial inequality. This was particularly marked in the struggle which developed between defenders and opponents of intelligence testing. In Britain, the tripartite system of education was now attacked as hierarchical, inegalitarian, and class-ridden rather than meritocratic, and a comprehensive system advanced in its place. And in the United States the claims of psychologists such as Arthur Jensen that blacks were innately less intelligent provoked liberal criticism in a new era of concern for civil rights and racial equality. Doubt now arose over the scientific credibility and accuracy of a measure such as IQ. In Britain, mental testing and the theory that intelligence was inherited were further discredited in the 1970s after the death of its leading exponent, Cyril Burt, when it was claimed that he had fabricated crucial evidence. A significant proportion of psychologists, however, remained convinced, not only that intelligence was measureable, but that it was inherited to a significant degree. And in the United States political scientist Charles Murray collaborated with psychologist Richard Hernnstein in a controversial attempt to account for social problems and the existence of an underclass in terms of innate intellectual inferiority, particularly among blacks. In sum, despite all of the evidence pointing towards the complexity and environmental basis of mental ability — much of this from psychologists themselves — the reductionist belief persisted, and in the last decades of the century it was fueled by a strong revival of interest in the genetic basis of human behavior.

The scope of a psychology of individual difference, like that of therapy, would always however remain limited by resources and expertise. To understand the full impact of the discipline in shaping the psychological body in the post-war period one has to appreciate its success in transcending its own boundaries: first, by its creation of a science of social behavior which was taken up by advertisers, management consultants, and political scientists; and secondly, by its diffusion of a science of behavioral adjustment and self-management into the private sphere of life. The most powerful example of this was psychology's influence on child-rearing. The mental development of the infant and child had always been one of the central concerns of psychologists, and their work had already been hugely influential in reconceptualizing childhood as a journey of psychic development, most notably in the work of American psychologist G. Stanley Hall which helped clarify adolescence as a distinct stage in life. However, in the inter-war period the influence of Freud turned the focus away from the psychological body of the child alone to the psycho-social relations within the family. This was exemplifed in the post-war work of British psychologist John Bowlby and his emphasis on the importance of the infant's attachment to the mother for at least the first five years of life. What made such ideas so significant was that they would be diffused into the private sphere of the home through popular manuals — most notoriously those of the best-selling American psychologist Dr Benjamin Spock — to shape the psychic development of a whole generation of children and help legitimate the home-bound position of women in post-war society. A second example of this post-war diffusion was in the science of management. In the inter-war period, the psychology of work had begun as a science of regulating individual bodies. Gradually the emphasis was shifted to the psychology of social relations within the workplace, with management itself embracing a psychological perspective. Eventually the diffusion would turn full circle back to the individual employee who would be trained in psychological self-management. Ultimately, such psychological technique reached a mass audience through popular advice books on how to think, how to remember, and how to assert oneself. Ironically, therefore, it was through transcending the discipline itself and popularizing psychological knowledge that dreams of a behavioralist social order came closest to being achieved.

## POPULAR PSYCHOLOGIES: REALIZING THE PSYCHOLOGICAL BODY

To regard the construction of the psychological body simply as a disciplinary story of psychological knowledge and power inventing and subsequently controlling this new dimension of the self is to understand only half of the full picture: for, in increasingly democratic, affluent, educated, and individualist Western societies, psychological bodies were present at their own making. In the first half of the century, while the discipline in alliance with the state concentrated on objectifying and controlling the psychological bodies of that section of its population which was open to view and which could not object — the institutionalized, the deviant, and the child — a very different vision of the psychological body was emerging largely from below in which an eclectic range of psychological theories was taken up creatively to construct a primitive culture of psychotherapeutic self-realization. In the second half of the century the discipline itself moved further into this territory, overcoming its own limitations by the (mediated) internalisation of psychological knowledge, language, and technique within the popular mind and within the practices and assumptions of mass culture. It was the construction of this 'psychological society' — the product of the discipline only in part — which would be the most important influence on the way most people imagined themselves as psychological bodies.

At the turn of the century there was great popular excitement at what appeared to be remarkable breakthroughs in psychological theory. The fragmentation and fluidity of theory and the lack of authority of the nascent discipline to police eclectism meant that there was considerable scope at the popular level to construct diverse and radical visions of the psychological body. Secularization and the search for a surrogate spirituality, disenchantment with materialist science, the increasing commodification of life to embrace health and lifestyle management and the limited ability of the medical profession to meet such demand, and the need to define self in an increasingly atomized society all encouraged a turn towards the new psychology. The discovery of the unconscious along with revelations of invisible forms of energy in the physical world spurred on the investigation of psychic phenomena.

The ideas that the majority of the mind was hidden from consciousness, that there was therefore a great untapped mental power, and that thought was an energy force which could pass betweeen individuals all had radical implications for the psychological body. It was reconceptualized as multi-dimensional, potentially fragmented and not wholly rational, yet also far more powerful if the whole 'personality' could be harnessed; a body in which the energy power of thought could have a physical effect, with for instance positive thought acting to heal the body; and one which no longer represented an atomized individual but which was located in a sea of mental energy, inseparably part of a broader humanity. Such ideas were taken up by psychic researchers who were searching for a new secular spirituality and who looked to the survival of personality and mind force beyond bodily death. They also had an appeal to spiritualists, both before and after the mass bereavement of the First World War, since it provided a seemingly scientific basis for their belief in an afterlife. Christian Scientists saw the theory of mind's power over body as justification for their rejection of medicine and its attack on the physical body. More commonly, a host of alternative therapists drew on such theories to support a holistic approach to health in which mind and body were addressed in tandem. Through practical psychology magazines, advice books, correspondence courses, and classes, the individual was educated to be the manager of his or (just as frequently) her own psychological body, with auto-suggestion, physico-mental exercise, and the eating of non-polluting food integrated in a comprehensive regime which reached into every aspect of life. The reception and diffusion of Freudian ideas in the first decades of the century — which has gained much more consideration from historians, and which has emphasized the emancipatory recognition of the force of sexual instincts within the psychological body — was simply one aspect of this much broader process of reinterpretation and extrapolation of the self.

Over the next half century, the millenial 'new age' excitement and radical nature of these movements dimmed, and the space which had been opened now closed as medicine began to pay increasing attention to the psycho-somatic and as psychology established greater authority to control knowledge in the field. There was a second explosion of popular energy in the 1960s, with a counter-cultural reaction against the behaviorist psychology of adjustment which was now attacked as supporting a mind-numbing conformity. The shift to a more humanistic psychology of emotional self-exploration and the expansion of therapeutic resources provided the disillusioned and affluent with a new avenue to seek confessional attention and self-realization. Within the United States, this has been seen as playing a major role in a broader socio-cultural transformation: towards what Tom Wolfe described as the 'Me Decade' of the 1970s and what Christopher Lasch described as the 'Culture of Narcissism.'[1] Personal growth, awareness, and consciousness-raising were the new mantras, with psychology once again mobilized as a path to regain a spiritual dimension within a materialist life. Ironically, such a culture tended to foster rather than remove anxiety about the state of the psychological self. Although the culture of therapy was initially confined to the most affluent and best educated, this period would also see it infiltrate mass culture through the popular press, the psychological assumptions of cinematic language, and the confessional and therapeutic drama of the television and radio talk-show. A language of repression, coping with stress, asserting onself, and recovering from trauma became ubiquitous. The explosion of cases of recovered memory of repressed abuse and of multiple personality (a condition which had hitherto been considered extremely rare) was testament to the power of this culture and to its potential for radically transmuting the psychological body.

It is too simple, however, to see the expansion of this therapeutic culture as heralding a straightforward psychologization of body and society. Strategies of coping were now as likely to be found beyond as within the boundaries of the psychological discipline: in a profusion of unorthodox schools of psychotherapy which could only be loosely policed; in the new age therapy and spirituality which echoed the occultism of the turn of the century; in alternative and non-Western medicine; and in the increasingly assertive self-help groups of sufferers and their families. In part, this reflected the irony that ever-greater diffusion of a psychological perspective could in fact undermine rather than enforce the authority of the psychological expert. It also reflected a search for solutions which embraced the psychological but went beyond it to a more holistic vision which integrated the physical and the spiritual. Thus, the idea that traumatic memory of child abuse was merely psychological was resisted by sufferers as seeming to denying the reality of their experiences. Likewise, individuals diagnosed with a growing litany of medically inexplicable late twentieth-century conditions such as ME or chronic fatigue syndrome turned to the alternative culture for succour and struggled against the idea that it was 'all in the mind' to assert the physical reality of their illnesses. As this suggests, it would be wrong to equate this increasingly holistic therapeutic culture with a new primacy of the psychological body; in certain respects it could represent just the opposite.

## Conclusion

This chapter has presented, for the sake of convenience, three narratives of the construction of the twentieth-century psychological body. Some of the connections between the three stories should be apparent; in truth they were interwoven to an even greater extent. Together they created a psychological dimension to the body which had a reality in both theory and practice. However, the chapter has also attempted to highlight some of the obstacles, limitations and compromises which were made along the way, and as such has suggested that blanket concepts such as an onward path towards a psychologization of body and society may obscure as much as they reveal. The focus of the survey has been almost exclusively that of the Western, affluent, secular and democratic world. As such it has been a story of the reconstruction of identities in response to the emergence of this type of modern society. The dilemma of freedom, on the one hand stimulated the emergence of psychology as an applied science to rationalize society through objectifying the psychological body, and on the other propelled it into the place of religion as a secular science of the soul to anchor the dislocated individual. The histories of the psychological body outside this Western world would demand separate accounts, however it can be argued that the dominance of Western psychological theory and practice still played a crucial role: firstly, in imposing a model of difference and inferiority on the colonized psychological subject; secondly, in the powerful attraction and internalization of its individualist creed of self-development; and finally, in the fragmentation of identity which could result from the contradictions, both between these two visions, and with those of indigenous cultures of the psychological body.

## REFERENCE

1.   C. Lasch, *The Culture of Narcissism*. (Norton: New York, 1975); T. Wolfe, 'The Me Decade and the Third Great Awakening', in T. Wolfe, *Mauve Gloves and Madmen, Clutter and Vine*. (New York: Bantam Books, 1977).

## FURTHER READING

Ash, M., *Gestalt Psychology in German Culture, 1890–1967: Holism and the Quest for Objectivity*. (Cambridge: Cambridge University Press, 1995).

Danziger, K., *Constructing the Subject: Historical Origins of Psychological Research*. (Cambridge: Cambridge University Press, 1990).

Geuter, U., *The Professionalization of Psychology in Nazi Germany*. (Cambridge: Cambridge University Press, 1992).

Gould, S.J., *The Mismeasure of Man*. (London: Norton, 1981).

Grob, G., *From Asylum to Community: Mental Health Policy in Modern America*. (Princeton: Princeton University Press, 1991).

Hale, N., *Freud and the Americans*. (New York: Oxford University Press, 1991).

Hearnshaw, L., *A Short History of British Psychology 1840–1940*. (London: Methuen, 1964).

Joravsky, D., *Russian Psychology: A Critical History*. (Oxford: Basil Blackwell, 1989).

Leahey, T.H., *A History of Psychology*, 2nd ed. (New Jersey: Prentice Hall, 1987).

Pfister, J. and Schnog, N. (eds), *Inventing the Psychological: Towards a Cultural History of Emotional Life in America*. (New Haven & London: Yale, 1997).

Richards, G., *'Race,' Racism and Psychology*. (London: Routledge, 1998).

Rose, N., *Governing the Soul: The Shaping of the Private Self*. (London: Routledge, 1989).

Rose, N., *The Psychological Complex: Psychology, Politics and Society in England, 1860–1939*. (London: Routledge, 1985).

Shorter, E., *From Paralysis to Fatigue: A History of Psychosomatic Illness in the Modern Era*. (New York: Free Press, 1992).

Wooldridge, A., *Measuring the Mind: Education and Psychology in England, c. 1860–1990*. (Cambridge: Cambridge University Press, 1994).

# CHAPTER 21

# The Psychoanalytic Body

## SONU SHAMDASANI

Advocates and critics of psychoanalysis are in agreement concerning one thing — that it is today in a state of decline. Its once powerful position in American psychiatry has been eclipsed by the rise of psychotropic medications, and it increasingly finds it hard to compete with the plethora of psychotherapies, counseling services and alternative medicines. In 1914 Freud wrote:

> It may be said that by his "modification" of psychoanalysis Jung has given us a counterpart to the famous Lichtenberg knife. He has changed the hilt, and he has put a new blade into it; yet because the same name is engraved on it we are expected to regard the instrument as the original one.[1]

Extending Freud's analogy, the contemporary psychoanalytic world is a battle of Lichtenberg knives, each claiming to be the sole representative of the true psychoanalysis. Surveying the academic scene, matters become worse, as psychoanalysis appears able to take on any form that an author wishes. At every turn, one comes across the assumption that psychoanalysis is an entity that can be considered known and that it has had a huge transformative effect upon Western culture. Both are questionable. It has increasingly emerged that the official history of psychoanalysis was created through manifold acts of censorship and selective, tendentious rescripting. At the same time, an increasing amount of historical work has been conducted on non-Freudian psychologies and psychotherapies. Aside from anything else, it has emerged that many of these figures were not the fools and lunatics that Freud, Ernest Jones and other psychoanalysts portrayed them to be. In both of these directions, a watershed was Henri Ellenberger's *The Discovery of the Unconscious* (1970).

In different countries, psychoanalysis became adapted and reformulated by indigenous folk psychologies and intellectual traditions, and turned into something that has increasingly little to do with Freud's work, except in name. This problem is compounded by the interpretive bias of much existing work on the social history of psychoanalysis, namely, its Freudocentrism. Thus in Elizabeth Roudinesco's history of psychoanalysis in France, one finds non-Freudian psychologists and psychiatrists generally characterized as obscurantists who simply failed to see the radical epistemic break represented by psychoanalysis, which she takes as an axiomatic truth.

There have been many attempts to explain the rise and apparent success of psychoanalysis through appealing to supposedly widescale transformations in Western society, such as secularization, crises of authority, the family, the self, sexual conduct and so forth. Such explanations work backwards, assuming that there must have been some prior condition to which psychoanalysis was the preeminent remedy. As a result, psychoanalysis is credited with bringing about widescale transformations in twentieth-century society. Historical contingencies are converted into supposed necessities that consequently require deep-rooted explanations. Thus Nathan Hale explains the rise of psychoanalysis in the United States through positing (interlinked) crises of the somatic style in American psychiatry, and of civilized morality in the culture at large, which psychoanalysis supposedly answered. Such accounts tend to be over-explanations which provide insufficient differential criteria for the ascendence of psychoanalysis over other approaches, as Hale's first point could just as well explain the rise of any psychogenic therapy, and the latter, any variety of sexology.

There has been a pervasive failure to grasp the extent to which psychoanalysis featured as part of larger psychotherapeutic and psychogenic movements, and that by political operations which have yet to be sufficiently traced, it came to stand in for these, as if it was solely responsible for the transformations that took place. Not only Freudians accord Freud the lead role in transforming Western culture; the same view, though with the opposite conclusions, is often maintained by critics of psychoanalysis, such as Frederick Crews, for whom Freud appears as the major villain responsible for the ills of contemporary psychotherapy. Before being able to assess the wider impact of psychoanalysis on twentieth-century culture, it is necessary to reconstruct how it managed to gain more currency than contemporaneous psychotherapies.

In contrast to the market driven accounts, Frank Sulloway proposed a supply side model. Following Ellenberger, Sulloway argued that the Freudian movement erected an elaborate heroic legend around Freud which was indispensable to rise of psychoanalysis. In addition, psychoanalysis was misrepresented as a pure psychology, and its biological roots hidden. This, he claimed, had the effect of shielding psychoanalysis from the effects of the repudiation of its nineteenth-century biological sources. However it is questionable to what extent this issue substantially contributed to its success, which, broadly speaking, was most marked in the humanities, popular culture and private practice psychotherapy. The Freudian legend functioned through:

> legitimating the special and hard-wrought nature of psychoanalytic truth; by nihilating the achievements and credibility of Freud's critics; and by offering a built-in therapy to explain defections from the movement.[2]

Whilst these features are undeniable, they are insufficient to fully explain how psychoanalysis came to occupy the position which it did. The following is intended as a supplementary account.

## HYPNOTIC INFLUENCING MACHINES

The end of the nineteenth century saw the rise of hypnotic and suggestive therapies, and it was in this context that psychoanalysis arose. Hypnotic researchers generally clustered around the rival schools at the Salpêtrière in Paris under Jean-Martin Charcot, and at Nancy under Hippolyte Bernheim. Crowd psychologists undertook to apply hypnotic models to explicate the behavior of crowds and nations through hypnotic models. There was widespread public debate concerning the nature and power of suggestive influence.

It has increasingly become clear that Freud and subsequent psychoanalysts consistently downplayed the legacy of hypnosis in psychoanalysis, and were mistaken in proclaiming a grand epistemic break with the era of hypnotic and suggestive therapies. As Freud's contemporary Auguste Forel, the director of the Burghölzli asylum in Switzerland commented:

> since the introduction of the doctrine of suggestion one reads at the end of the praises of a large number of vaunted new remedies, "Suggestion is excluded." It is in just such cases that a purely suggestive action is most probable.[3]

For Charcot, the leading French neurologist, hypnosis was a pathological condition, which was only found in cases of hysteria. He claimed that *grand hypnotisme* followed three stages, each of which had distinct physiological characteristics: catalepsy, lethargy and somnambulism. Charcot used hypnosis to study the underlying architecture of hysteria; because he claimed it was a pathological state, he was not interested in its therapeutic applications. The latter were the main focus of the Nancy school, where hypnosis was deployed in a hospital and an outpatient clinic. Contrary to Charcot, Bernheim simply characterized hypnosis as a heightened state of suggestibility, akin to sleep, and claimed that anyone could be hypnotized. He championed the therapeutic application of hypnosis and suggestion, which became widely practised. The term psychotherapy came to be used interchangeably with hypnosis.

How did one gain instruction in hypnotic techniques? In 1886, Forel visited Nancy after reading Bernheim's book, *Of Suggestion*, where, he was initiated into the practice of hypnotism by Bernheim, who gave practical demonstrations. On his return, he began practising hypnosis, and introduced it into the Burghölzli. His account of his hypnotic training is mirrored by many others during the same period (including Freud). Indeed, the ease by which individuals could set up as hypnotists contributed greatly to the rapid spread of hypnotic and suggestive therapies. The open nature of instruction meant that individuals could see how particular hypnotists worked, and see the patients that they wrote about.

It is still a widespread belief that the in-depth investigation of individuals' lives, with a particular accent on sexuality, was an innovation of psychoanalysis. It is important to grasp that this was already a feature of hypnotic therapies. Forel advocated an individualizing approach:

> One must gain the full confidence of the patient by affection and intimately insinuating one's self into all sides of his mental life; one must sympathize with all his feelings, get him to relate the whole story of his life, live it all over again with him, and enter into the feelings of the patient. But one must naturally never lose sight of the sexual aspect, which differs so enormously according to the kind of person, and which may form an actual danger... It must be understood that it is not sufficient to follow the usual stereotype medical control, which consists in paying attention to the discharge of semen, or coitus, and pregnancy; but it is necessary to take into consideration carefully all the higher regions of the intellect, mood, and will, which are more or less connected with the sexual sphere. When this has been carried out, one has to map out the proper definite aim in life for the patient, and start him on his way full of energy and confidence.[4]

In situations where hypnotic suggestion ran into difficulties, Forel commented:

> As soon as I notice that a person remains uninfluenced or does not obey well any longer, I ask him, "What is it that is exciting you? Why don't you tell me what you have got on your mind?" And this question, asked in a friendly but definite tone, rarely fails to elicit a positive reply. The patient notices that I have recognised the cause of the failure at once, and almost always confesses it. I can generally reassure him thereby, and, in consequence, attain what I am aiming at.[5]

Forel's recommendation strongly resembles what Freud would later call the fundamental rule of psychoanalysis, to speak whatever came to one's mind, and the analysis of resistances. Freud was certainly familiar with this work, for he reviewed it.

Jacqueline Carroy has made the important observation that in the hypnotic literature, suggestion functioned as a heterodox, umbrella term, which, as well as imperative suggestion, included paradoxical injunctions and interpretations. Extending Carroy's observation, if one studies psychoanalytic and psychotherapeutic cases in the twentieth century, one finds that 'interpretation' functions in a similar catch all manner. Whilst the theoretical account of practises changed considerably, the same was not the case in the practises themselves. Under the rubric of interpretation in the psychoanalytic literature, it is not hard to find some of the best examples of authoritarian directives.

Freud, who had attended Charcot's lectures in the winter of 1885, was anxious to defend the objectivity of Charcot's observations, and pointed out the consequences that ensued if Bernheim's views were correct:

> If the supporters of the suggestion theory are right, all the observations made at the Salpêtrière are worthless: indeed, they become errors in observation. The hypnosis of hysterical patients would have no characteristics of its own; but every physician would be

free to produce any symptomatology that he liked in the patients he hypnotized. We should not learn from the study of major hypnotism what alterations in excitability succeed one another in the nervous system of hysterical patients in response to certain kinds of intervention; we should merely learn what intention Charcot suggested (in a manner of which he himself was unconscious) to the subjects of his experiments — a thing entirely irrelevant to our understanding alike of hypnosis and of hysteria.[6]

Freud's defense of Charcot went beyond the particular theories that the latter advanced: it was a defense of the possibility of discovering an objective symptomatology from clinical investigation, which would be independent of the situation of derivation. This epistemology, in which the clinic was supposed to function like a laboratory, was critical to his enterprise. Freud correctly pointed out the consequences which would ensue if this position was abandoned: the hypnotist could generate whatever symptomatology they liked, and the study of this process would reveal nothing other than the arbitrary process by which different nosographies or disease entities could be produced. The position Freud was at pains to ward off was precisely the conclusion made by William James. He argued that the properties attributed to the trance, such as by Charcot and Heidenhaim, were actually products of suggestion. The peculiar nature of the trance state was the manner in which it took on any properties attributed to it, varying in concert with theories about it. He trenchantly points out the pitfalls that this held, for the possibility of deriving an objective account of hypnosis:

> Any sort of personal peculiarity, any trick accidentally fallen into in the first instance by some one subject, may, by attracting attention, become stereotyped, serve as a pattern for imitation, and figure as the type of a school. The first subject trains the operator, the operator trains the succeeding subjects, all of them in perfect good faith conspiring together to evolve a perfectly arbitrary result.
>
> With the extraordinary perspicacity and subtlety of perception which subjects often display for all that concerns the operator with whom they are *en rapport*, it has hard to keep them ignorant of anything he expects. Thus it happens that one easily verifies on new subjects what one has already seen on old ones, or any desired symptom of which one may have heard or read.[7]

Similar arguments had been advanced by the Belgian philosopher-psychologist, Josef Delboeuf. He stated as well as the well-known influence of the hypnotizer on the hypnotized, the influence in the reciprocal direction was critical. The subjects, generally the first or paradigm case, trained the experimenter and influenced his methods without his realizing it. This set up a template, as the experimenter reported his results to his disciples who 'replicated' them. It was this circuit of reciprocal influence which gave rise to the hypnotic schools, each monopolizing special phenomena.[8] Delboeuf and James claimed that it was impossible for the experimenter to situate themselves outside of the field of effects of the suggestive influence they were attempting to objectively study. Their critiques suggest that the respective hypnotic schools had become veritable influencing machines for the generation of evidence. The fact that different traits could be paraded forth as constituting the essence of hypnosis and appear to gain confirmation from other practitioners indicated that the mode of institutionalization was itself subject to the effects of hypnosis and suggestion, which could not be neutralized. For Delboeuf and James, the conflicts between the various schools were insolvable, for they each could point to evidence that supported their particular theories.

It was in 1896 that Freud first put forward the term psychoanalysis in the course of his papers proposing the so-called seduction theory, which stated that every case of hysteria was caused by a seduction in early childhood. The circumstances surrounding Freud's proposal and subsequent abandonment of the seduction theory have generated a great deal of controversy, which is too extensive to review here. On the one hand, Jeffrey Masson and various feminist critics contend that Freud's seduction theory was actually correct, and that in abandoning it through cowardice, he betrayed the patients who had told him of their abuses. By contrast, other critics, such as Allen Esterson and Frederick Crews, contend that Freud had actually fabricated the evidence for his initial theory. Esterson claims that Freud's patients did not speak of infantile seductions, and that these were simply reconstructions that Freud forced on them.[9] Moving away from this dichotomy of real vs. fabricated, Mikkel Borch-Jacobsen has put forward a reading of the seduction theory which has important implications for the general understanding of the generation of evidence in psychoanalysis. Taking his cue from the contemporaneous criticisms made by Freud's hypnotist colleagues, he argues that some of Freud's patients actually 'spontaneously' told him what he wanted to hear, actively responding to his suggestions and cues. Consequently, he concludes that:

> Freud did not change his mind for lack of clinical "evidence." Quite the contrary, he had plenty of it... the "influencing machine" that he had put into motion was working all too well, so well that he could no longer believe in the stories he had extorted from his patients.[10]

The significance of this argument is that it demonstrates that Freud fell precisely into the errors that Delboeuf and James would have predicted. The problem was not the lack of evidence (or the necessity of fabricating the evidence) but a surfeit of evidence. However, whilst Freud subsequently modified his theories of hysteria and the neuroses, he (and subsequent psychoanalysts) remained committed to the view that the clinical encounter could provide an objective evidential basis for a general psychology and psychopathology. There are further implications of the perspective outlined by Delboeuf and James: their remarks suggest that the question of the rise of psychoanalysis is not to be explained by the supposed adequation of its theories to a preexisting reality (such as presupposed by sociohistorical explanations), or indeed, their plausibility; but in its capacity to create conditions which made favorable the generation of particular forms of conviction.

## INCORPORATING PSYCHOANALYSIS

It is arguable that Freud's theories would not have been any more renowned today than those of Delboeuf, had he not gathered around him a group of followers. In 1902 a small group consisting of Alfred Adler, Max Kahane, Rudolf Reitler and Wilhelm Stekel began to hold regular meetings with Freud. Others soon followed. The proceedings were not harmonious. In retrospect, Freud stated that he was unable to establish friendly relations between the group or to stifle the numerous priority disputes and that the proceedings indicated the general difficulty of giving instruction in psychoanalysis.[11] One member of this society, Fritz Wittels painted an unflattering portrait of Freud's intentions in calling these meetings:

> Freud's design in the promotion of these gatherings was to have his own thoughts passed through the filter of other trained intelligences. It did not matter if the intelligences were mediocre. Indeed, he had little desire that these associates should be persons of strong individuality, that they should be critical and ambitious collaborators. The realm of psychoanalysis was his idea and his will, and he welcomed anyone who accepted his views. What he wanted was to look into a kaleidoscope lined with mirrors that would multiply the images he introduced into it.[12]

A few years later, the situation changed. Freud heard from Eugen Bleuler, Forel's successor at the Burghölzli, that his work was being studied there. It was with the entrance of Jung and the Zürich school that the psychoanalytic movement become international. Freud later recalled that the Burghölzli was the only public clinic where one could research psychoanalysis, and it became the only place where one could learn how to practise it. Consequently, most of his followers came to him by way of Zürich. The ease with which individuals could gain instruction in psychoanalytic techniques in the Burghölzli was similar to Bernheim's clinic in Nancy, and led greatly to their dissemination. Indeed, for psychiatrists interested in psychoanalysis, Zürich, and not Vienna, was initially the instruction center of choice. A large proportion of significant figures in dynamic psychiatry and psychoanalysis either worked at or visited the Burghölzli, which played a critical role in instigating the development of a psychogenic orientation in psychiatry. This has generally been attributed solely to psychoanalysis. How this misattribution took place arguably forms a template for what subsequently occurred in other contexts.

The pivotal text in this regard was Jung's 1907 *On the Psychology of Dementia Praecox: An Attempt.*[13] This has traditionally been viewed as consisting in the first major application of psychoanalysis to the psychoses. I have argued elsewhere that Jung's approach was far more closely linked with the abnormal psychology of Pierre Janet and the subliminal psychology of Théodore Flournoy, than with psychoanalysis. It was Jung's political affiliation with psychoanalysis that led to this text being misperceived as psychoanalytic. There were numerous developments in a psychogenic direction in psychiatry and psychotherapy at this time. In the former, the Swiss Adolf Meyer, who had studied with Forel and later sent many individuals to study at the Burghölzli, played a pivotal role in the United States. It was the unique mode of organization of the psychoanalytic movement, and the professional identity that it conferred, that enabled it to stand in for these wider developments.

In the experiments on word associations at the Burghölzli, the positions of subject and experimenter were readily interchangeable. It was in this context that psychoanalytic explorations initially took place. Mutual dream analysis was frequently practised. A.A. Brill attributed the genesis of the institution of training analysis to these practices.[14]

In September 1907 a Freudian society of physicians was founded in Zürich. The following year Jung organized the first psychoanalytic conference in Salzburg. At the same time, he proposed the establishment of an international journal. His plan was to form an amalgamation with Flournoy and Claparède's *Archives de Psychologie* and Morton Prince's *Journal of Abnormal Psychology*. These initiatives would possibly have had the effect of integrating psychoanalysis with developments in abnormal psychology and subliminal psychology in America and Switzerland. It was only with the collapse of these negotiations that it was decided to found an independent psychoanalytic journal, *Jahrbuch für psychoanalytische und psychopathologische Forschungen*, with Jung and Bleuler as editors. This separation was to have important ramifications.

## PSYCHOANALYTIC MONOPOLIES

In the first decade of the twentieth century, psychoanalysis attracted increasing interest among doctors and psychiatrists. Instances where individuals partially corroborated psychoanalysis proved extremely problematic for Freud. Psychiatrists such as Ludwig Frank and Dumeng Bezzola who were associated with Forel supported Freud and Breuer's cathartic treatment against Freud's subsequent development of psychoanalysis. In 1910, Freud published a paper entitled '"Wild" psycho-analysis' which addressed this situation. He began by recounting an anecdote concerning a middle aged divorced woman suffering from anxiety who had consulted a physician unknown to Freud, who had told her that her anxiety was due to the lack of sexual satisfaction, and suggested avenues by which she could procure this. The physician attributed this advice to the theories of psychoanalysis. For his part, Freud repudiated the physician's advice as having nothing to do with psychoanalysis. Ironically, Freud had himself made the same recommendation a few years earlier in his paper 'Civilized sexual morality and nervous illness.' This suggests that what was critical was not the specific practice in question, but the fact that the physician was completely independent of Freud.

Freud contended that psychoanalytic technique could as yet not be learnt from books, but only from someone already proficient in it. He went on to state:

> Neither I myself nor my friends and co-workers find it agreeable to claim a monopoly in this way in the use of a medical technique. But in face of the dangers to patients and to the cause of psycho-analysis which are inherent in the practice that is to be foreseen

of a 'wild' psycho-analysis, we have had no other choice. In the spring of 1910 we founded an International Psycho-Analytical Association, to which its members declare their adherence by the publication of their names, in order to be able to repudiate responsibility for what is done by those who do not belong to us and yet call their medical procedure 'psycho-analysis.' For as a matter of fact 'wild' analysts of this kind do more harm to the cause of psycho-analysis than to individual patients.[15]

In this statement, Freud was militantly opposed to psychoanalysis freely entering general medical practice as an auxiliary psychotherapeutic procedure — not primarily out of a concern with safeguarding the public, but with safeguarding psychoanalysis. In 1914, Freud added that the local branches of the International Psychoanalytic Association (IPA) would be responsible for instruction in psychoanalysis and the training of doctors, and that the formation of the IPA was quite justifiable given that science had proclaimed a ban against psychoanalysis and boycotted its practice.[16]

As historians have established, the notion of a ban or boycott against psychoanalysis belongs to the heroic legend of psychoanalysis. Indeed, it was due to the increasing isolationist policy of psychoanalysis vis à vis medicine and psychiatry that Eugen Bleuler resigned from the IPA in 1911. In one incident, the psychiatrist Max Isserlin was not allowed to attend the Nuremberg congress, which Bleuler found unacceptable. Freud had also requested Bleuler to break off relations with two leading psychiatrists who were critics of psychoanalysis, Alfred Hoche, and Theodore Ziehen. Bleuler wrote to Freud:

> The "who is not for us, is against us," the "all or nothing," is in my opinion necessary for religious communities and useful for political parties. For this reason I can understand the principle as such, but I consider it harmful for science.[17]

Bleuler argued that instead of seeking contacts with other sciences, psychoanalysis had isolated itself with barbed wire. Somewhat overstatedly, though with some justice, Alexander and Selesnick argued that without Bleuler's resignation, the subsequent isolation of psychoanalysis from the universities and medical schools would never have occurred.[18]

PSYCHOANALYTIC PURIFICATIONS

In 1907, Sándor Ferenczi visited Jung at the Burghölzli. Towards the end of his life, Jung recalled that he "trained" Ferenczi in psychoanalysis, but that unfortunately, Ferenczi "remained stuck with Freud."[19] This may well have been the first explicit training analysis, and it is somewhat ironic that it was not conducted by Freud.

How did one become a psychoanalyst? In 1909, Freud replied, "By studying one's own dreams."[20] As noted above, the following year, he added that one also needed to be in contact with someone proficient in psychoanalysis. In 1912 Jung put forward the recommendation that every prospective analyst had to undergo an analysis. Jung argued that success in analysis depended upon how far the analyst had been analyzed himself: "There are doctors who believe that they can get by with a self-analysis. This is Münchausen-psychology, with which they will certainly remain stuck."[21] Ernest Jones read this passage as direct attack on the unanalysed Freud.[22] Jung's suggestion has had an overpowering effect, not only on the subsequent organization of psychoanalysis, but on modern psychotherapy as a whole. Indeed this requirement forms one of the few common denominators in the plethora of psychotherapeutic schools. His suggestion took place at a crucial juncture. On the one hand, it occurred at a time of bitter disputation in the psychoanalytic movement. The discussion of diverging theoretical perspectives had largely broken down, to be replaced by attempts at mutual diagnosis and pathologization. Secondly, Jung had resigned his post at the Burghölzli in 1909, and taken up full time private practice. Whilst his own practice appears to have thrived, the institution of training analysis became critical in providing a financial base for private practice psychoanalysis, and making it an attractive professional proposition. His suggestion was quickly seconded by Freud. Whilst claiming that psychoanalysis was a medical technique, Freud argued that it was insufficient to simply be a physician or psychiatrist: further qualification was required.[23] In terms of current practices in psychotherapy, this was a striking departure. It would have been unthinkable to have established the hypnotic treatment of the physician as an essential training requirement. Indeed, on his return from the psychoanalytic congress at Weimar in 1911, the American neurologist James Jackson Putnam stated in a talk:

> Then I learned, to my surprise and interest, that a large part of these investigators had subjected themselves, more or less systematically, to the same sort of searching character-analysis to which their patients were being subjected at their hands. It is fast getting to be felt that an initiation of this sort is an indispensable condition of good work.[24]

Freud argued that it was not enough for a prospective analyst to be "approximately normal" what was required was that one should undergo a "psycho-analytic purification" to become aware of one's own complexes.[25] It is fair to suppose that this requirement was not simply to ensure that practitioners were 'ultra-healthy,' but that their self-understanding conformed to psychoanalytic theory. The training analysis was the only means to assure the transmission of analytic knowledge, through ensuring that the 'self-knowledge' of the prospective analyst developed along proscribed lines, so that one had attested to psychoanalytic truths in one's own life and hence would be capable of 'replicating' them through the lives of others. In 1914 Freud wrote to the American psychiatrist Trigant Burrow, who had been analyzed by Jung:

> If you make it possible to come to me for analysis, you will certainly be more important to me than any patient. Every student more is to me a guarantee for the future and an assurance for my own lifetime.[26]

In the summer of 1912 Ernest Jones proposed to Freud the formation of a secret committee, to secure the future of psychoanalysis. On 30 July he wrote that Ferenczi had expressed the wish that

a small group of men could be thoroughly analysed by you, so that they could represent the pure theory unadulterated by personal complexes, and thus build an unofficial inner circle in the Verein and serve as centres where others (beginners) could come and learn the work.[27]

This group, Jones wrote, would be like the "Paladins of Charlemagne, to guard the kingdom and policy of their master."[28] Freud responded favorably to the idea, and the committee was set up. The other members were Karl Abraham, Sándor Ferenczi, Otto Rank and Hans Sachs. A significant absence was the then president of the IPA, Jung. Indeed, the secret committee played an important role in widening the split between Jung and Freud. In 1914, Jung and the Zürich school formally left the IPA. The Zürich psychoanalytic society became the association for analytical psychology, and the nucleus of Jung's own movement.

After the hiatus of the First World War, the institutionalization of the psychoanalytic movement spread place rapidly. At the Budapest congress in 1918, Herman Nunberg, who had been an assistant physician at the Burghölzli, proposed that every prospective analyst had to undergo an analysis. Nunberg's proposal was not accepted, due to the objections of Otto Rank and Victor Tausk. In the following years, the Berlin Institute, founded in 1920, began to formalize its training structure. The Berlin society had been founded by Karl Abraham, another graduate of the Burghölzli. In 1924, a training analysis of four months became a requirement, and further, the approval of the training analyst was required for the candidate to continue with the training. As Siegfried Bernfeld recalled, whilst many members felt the need for an analysis, they were reluctant to confide in a local analyst. Consequently, Sachs was invited to relocate to Berlin, and he specialized in analyzing analysts.[29] During the first two years of the Berlin institute, Sachs analysed 25 candidates, wielding considerable power.[30]

It was at the Berlin society that the triad of personal analysis, supervised analysis, and seminars was established, which became the basic template of all psychoanalytic institutes. In 1925, at the psychoanalytic congress in Bad Homburg, the stipulation the requirement that every prospective analyst had to be analyzed was passed.

The secret committee played a critical role in controlling the development of psychoanalysis. Falzeder notes that the Berlin, Budapest, London and Vienna Institutes were led by the members of the Secret Committee, who exerted not only direct influence on trainees as well as 'political' control over the movement. The purpose of the secret committee was to ensure the survival of psychoanalysis, and to protect against dissidence. In the case of departures from orthodox psychoanalytic theory, two broad patterns emerged: on the one hand, outright expulsion of dissidents, and on the other, a form of in-house crisis management, in which the new departures were sanctioned as legitimate modifications of psychoanalytic theory. What is striking is that the issue of whether a particular theoretical development was seen as a secession or as a legitimate outgrowth was not primarily dependent upon how far the ideas were from psychoanalytic theory; indeed, as the institutions became more secure, more latitude was permitted. Ironically, in many respects, the heretical positions developed in turn by Adler, Jung and Rank and others are, in many respects, more congruent with mainline analytic theory today than what was then judged to be orthodoxy. Their ideas have been recycled and reincorporated within analytic theories, without acknowledgement. It is this process that has enabled psychotherapists to continue to officially call their practices psychoanalysis, and for the profession to survive, despite the fact that Freud would have in many instances denounced them as heretics. The main vehicle by which this control was effected was the training analysis. When Otto Rank's work was judged to have departed too far from psychoanalytic orthodoxy, he was denounced as mentally disturbed by Brill, dropped from the American Psychoanalytic Association, and those he had trained had to resign or be reanalyzed by an appropriate analyst.[31]

## THE DECLINE OF PRESTIGE SUGGESTION

It was through the training enterprise that psychoanalysis prospered from the 1920s onwards. The formation of a psychoanalytic training system, detached from medicine and psychiatry was crucial to the survival of psychoanalysis, and greatly contributed to its success compared with other forms of psychotherapy, as no other school had established a comparable system. By comparison, it was a full twenty years later that formalized training in analytical psychology was established, with the formation of the Society for Analytical Psychology in London in 1945. In 1936, the British psychologist William McDougall lamented his isolation and the lack of his success of his psychology, in comparison with psychoanalysis. He attributed this to the fact that "in psychology, far more than any other field of science, the prestige and authority of a like-minded group would seem to be essential to the success of any theory or system."[32] For McDougall, the public success of psychoanalysis was not due to any inherent therapeutic or theoretical superiority — far from it — but from the particular mode of institutional organization that it adopted, and the consequent suggestive effect on the wider populace, which he called prestige suggestion. Without this, the Freudian legend would have been ineffective. It was the effectiveness of the institutional structures of psychoanalysis that gave it public visibility, such that cultural debates about the new psychology were nominally cast in the idiom of psychoanalysis. In the hypnotic period, a linkage was established between the development of therapeutic and experimental practises and widespread public debate concerning the nature of influence and the hidden reaches of the mind. In many respects, psychoanalysis simply became the new idiom under which these societal concerns were framed. This is far from saying that it inaugurated them. Thus one finds late nineteenth-century popular representations of women falling prey to the powers of nefarious hypnotists were replaced by early twentieth-century depictions of their falling prey to the wiles of psychoanalysts. In addition, the institutional prominence and public visibility of psychoanalysis led many individuals to become associated with it, who may have regarded themselves as having a different orientation, such as the Harvard psychologist and student of Jung, Henry Murray. As John Burnham accurately noted:

> In the United States Freud became the agent not so much of psychoanalysis as of other ideas current at the time. Psychoanalysis was understood as environmentalism, as sexology, as a theory of psychogenic etiology of the neuroses. Likewise when Freud's teachings gained attention and even adherents, his followers often believed not so much in his work as in evolution, in psychotherapy, and in the modern world.[33]

It is the misunderstanding of the nature of these substitutions that has led to the prevalent vastly overinflated view of the significance of psychoanalysis in twentieth-century culture.

If the establishment of the psychoanalytic training system played a crucial role in the establishment of psychoanalysis, it was also an unstable matrix, as it could easily become adapted to any theoretical model. This has indeed been the case, and hundreds of psychotherapeutic schools have adopted the same institutional structure to propagate their therapies and generate evidence for their theories. The success of these rival schools, mimicking the same institutional structures as psychoanalysis, whilst making them more accessible, has in a large measure contributed to the beleaguered state of contemporary psychoanalysis.

After Freud, there have been a plethora of theoretical developments in psychoanalysis. This account has focused on the history of psychoanalysis prior to 1930, not only for reasons of length. For by that stage, the basic template for the institutional and theoretical developments of psychoanalysis had already been established. Indeed, it may be argued that subsequent developments can be considered as a series of footnotes, expanding and filling out patterns that had already been set. The complexity and internal inconsistencies of the various stratifications of psychoanalytic theory, such as the drive theory and structural model gave ample room for subsequent theorists to selectively emphasize particular features at the expense of others, and indeed, for a new scholasticism of psychoanalytic textuality to develop in the academic world. The later is principally associated with the French psychoanalyst Jacques Lacan. Under the guise of a 'return to Freud' Lacan revamped psychoanalysis: in place of Freud's nineteenth-century biology, anthropology and positivism, he imported Hegel, Heidegger, de Saussure and Lévi-Strauss. These, he claimed, were necessary if one were to properly decipher the radicality of the Freudian innovation. Expelled from the IPA, Lacan went his own way and set up his own mirror international organization, which has recapitulated the splits and internecine quarrels of the history of psychoanalysis. Lacan has been widely influential in the academic world, through promoting a radically ahistorical manner of reading Freud. As a consequence, the extension of the term psychoanalysis seems to have no limits. One may venture to predict that the loss of prestige of psychoanalysis in the public sphere will eventually have a knock on effect in the academic world, and much that has been termed psychoanalysis will transfer to another name.

Finally, there has been a great deal of controversy concerning the evidential status of psychoanalytic theories. Some critics contend that there is simply no evidence for psychoanalytic theory, or the effectiveness of psychoanalytic therapies. However, one does not have to look far to find copious testimonies as to the efficacy of psychoanalysis, by patients, and those former patients turned analysts. The question is how one is to evaluate such testimony. On the one hand, in psychoanalysis, only the analyst's account is accorded any epistemological status. Secondly, many aspects of psychoanalytic theories have built in features which discount the possibility of taking anyone's testimony at face value — even if they speak of the benefits of psychoanalytic therapies (hence the favorite exemplar of contemporary psychoanalytic research is the infant: a subject incapable of verbal testimony and of contradicting analytic constructions). More seriously, rival psychotherapeutic schools — ranging from Jungian analysis to past-life regression therapy — also have ample 'evidence' in the form of first person testimonies, and if one accepts one form of such evidence as valid, no clear differential criteria exist by which to reject other forms. The prevalent epistemology of psychoanalytic and psychotherapeutic systems has been to assert the fundamental realism of psychological theories; though supposedly derived from the clinical encounter, they remain independent of them, and can be taken as veridical accounts of general human functioning. Far from a lack of evidence, the problem appears to be the excess of evidence — for any theory imaginable. Contemporary psychoanalytic and psychotherapeutic training institutes, as Delboeuf and James long ago demonstrated apropos hypnotic schools, appear to be machines for the generation of new forms of self-evidence. What is notable about such testimonials is that they are not simply reports by subjects of particular events befalling them, but reports in which the subjects themselves attest to having undergone a transformation. In this sense, they are akin to the reports of religious experiences, such as those studied by James.[34] One awaits an anthropology that could undertake a comparative study of these new forms of psychological experience.

## REFERENCES

I would like to thank the Wellcome Trust for funding the research on which this chapter is based. A version of this paper was presented to the Philadelphia Association, London, and I would like to thank Chris Oakley, my host on that occasion. I would also like to thank Roger Cooter for his comments. James Jackson Putnam's paper "What is psychoanalysis?" is cited with the permission of the Francis A. Countway Library of Medicine, Boston.

1.  Sigmund Freud, 'On the history of the psycho-analytic movement,' ed. & tr. James Strachey, *Standard Edition*. (London: Hogarth Press, 1953–74) (hereafter, *SE*), **14**: p. 66.
2.  Frank Sulloway, *Freud, Biologist of the Mind: Beyond the Psychoanalytic Legend*. (New York: Basic Books, 1979), p. 487.
3.  Auguste Forel, *Hypnotism or, Suggestion and psychotherapy*, tr. H. Armit. (London: Rebman, 1906), p. 314.
4.  Forel, *Hypnotism*, p. 242.
5.  *Ibid.*, p. 201.
6.  Freud, 'Preface to Bernheim,' *SE* 1., pp. 77–8.
7.  William James, *Principles of Psychology*. (London: Macmillan, 1918), Vol. 2, p. 601.
8.  Josef Delboeuf, 'De l'influence de l'education et de l'imitation dans le somnambulisme provoqué,' *Revue Philosophique* (1886), **22**: pp. 52–3.
9.  Allen Esterson, *The Seductive Mirage*. (Chicago: Open Court, 1993), pp. 28–9.
10. Borch-Jacobsen, 'Neurotica: Freud and the seduction theory,' *October* 1996, **76**: pp. 39–40.
11. Freud, 'On the history of the psycho-analytic movement,' *SE*, **14**: pp. 25–6.
12. Fritz Wittels, *Sigmund Freud: His Personality, His Teaching, & His School*, tr. E. & C. Paul. (London: George Allen & Unwin, 1924), p. 134.
13. C.G. Jung, *Collected Works* 3, tr. R.F.C. Hull (ed.), Gerhard Adler, Michael Fordham, William McGuire and Herbert Read. (London: Routledge & Kegan Paul, 1960).
14. A.A. Brill, *Freud's Contribution to Psychiatry*. (London: Chapman & Hall, 1944), p. 42.
15. Freud, ''Wild' psycho-analysis,' *SE*, **11**: pp. 226–7.
16. Freud, 'On the history of the psycho-analytic movement,' *SE*, **14**: pp. 43–4.
17. Bleuler to Freud (4 December 1911), Freud collection, Library of Congress, Washington.
18. Franz Alexander and Sheldon Selesnick, 'Freud-Bleuler Correspondence,' *Archives of General Psychiatry* (1965), **12**: pp. 1–2.
19. Jung/Jaffé protocols, Bollingen collection, Library of Congress, Washington, p. 331.
20. Freud, 'Five lectures on Psycho-analysis,' *SE*, **11**: p. 33.
21. Jung, 'Attempt at a portrayal of psychoanalytic theory,' *CW*, **4**: para 449, tr. mod.
22. Jones to Freud, 22 July 1913 (ed.), Andrew Paskauskas, *The Complete Correspondence of Sigmund Freud and Ernest Jones*. (Cambridge, MA: Harvard University Press, 1993), p. 212.
23. Freud, 'Recommendations to physicians practising psychoanalysis,' *SE* (1912) **12**: p. 116.
24. James Jackson Putnam, 'What is Psychoanalysis?' Putnam papers, Countway Library of Medicine, Boston.
25. 'Recommendations to physicians practising psycho-analysis,' p. 116.
26. Freud to Trigant Burrow, 19 June, 1914, Sigmund Freud Collection, Library of Congress.
27. Jones to Freud, 30 July 1912, *Sigmund Freud and Ernest Jones*, p. 146.
28. Jones to Freud, 7 August 1912, *Ibid.*, p. 149.
29. Siegfried Bernfeld, 'On psychoanalytic training' (1952) *Psychoanalytic Quarterly* (1962), **31**: p. 464.
30. Falzeder, 'The threads of psychoanalytic filiations or psychoanalysis taking effect,' in André Haynal and Ernst Falzeder (eds), *100 Years of Psychoanalysis: Contributions to the History of Psychoanalysis*, special issue of *Cahiers Psychiatriques Genevois* (1994), p. 175.
31. James Lieberman, *Acts of Will: the Life and Work of Otto Rank*. (New York: Free Press, 1985), p. xxxii.
32. William McDougall, *Psycho-analysis and Social Psychology*. (London: Methuen, 1936), p. v.
33. John C. Burnham, *Psychoanalysis and American Medicine, 1894–1918: Medicine, Science and Culture*. (International Universities Press, 1967), p. 214.
34. William James, *The Varieties of Religious Experience*. (London: Longmans, 1902).

## FURTHER READING

Borch-Jacobsen, Mikkel, *The Emotional Tie: Psychoanalysis, Mimesis, and Affect*. (Stanford: Stanford University Press, 1993).

Borch-Jacobsen, Mikkel, *Lacan, the Absolute Master*, tr. D. Brick. (Stanford: Stanford University Press, 1991).

Borch-Jacobsen, Mikkel, *Remembering Anna O.: A Century of Mystification*. (London: Routledge, 1996).

Carroy, Jacqueline, *Hypnose, suggestion et psychologie: l'invention de sujets.* (Paris: PUF, 1991).

Chertok, Léon and Stenghers, Isabelle, *A Critique of Psychoanalytic Reason: Hypnosis as a Scientific Problem from Lavoisier to Lacan,* tr. M.N. Evans, (Stanford: Stanford University Press, 1992).

Frederick Crews *et al.*, *The Memory Wars: Freud's Legacy in Dispute.* (New York: New York Review of Books, 1995).

Erwin, Edward, *A Final Accounting: Philosophical and Empirical Issues in Freudian Psychology.* (Cambridge: Mass, MIT Press, 1996).

Gauld, Alan, *A History of Hypnotism.* (Cambridge: Cambridge University Press, 1992).

Hale, Nathan, *Freud and the Americans: The Beginnings of Psychoanalysis in the United States, 1876–1917.* (New York: Oxford University Press, 1971).

Latour, Bruno, *Pétite réflexion sur le culte moderne des dieux faitiches.* (Le Plessis-Robinson: Les Empêcheurs de penser en rond, 1996).

Mühlleitner, Elke, *Biographisches Lexikon der Psychoanalyse: Die Mitglieder der psychologischen Mittwoch-Gesellschaft und der Wiener psychoanalytischen Vereinigung 1902–1938.* (Tübingen: Edition Diskord, 1992).

Roudinesco, Elisabeth, *La Bataille de cent ans: histoire de la psychanalyse en France.* (Paris: Seuil, 1986).

Roudinesco, Elisabeth, *Jacques Lacan & Co.: A History of Psychoanalysis in France, 1925–1985,* tr. J. Mehlman. (London: Free Associations, 1990).

Shamdasani, Sonu, *Cult Fictions: C.G. Jung and the Founding of Analytical Psychology.* (London: Routledge, 1998).

Wittenberger, Gerhard, *Das "Geheime Komitee" Sigmund Freuds: Institionalisierungsprozesse in der Psychoanalytischen Bewegung zwischen 1912 und 1927.* (Tübingen: Editions Diskord, 1995).

# CHAPTER 22

# The Psychiatric Body

MARK S. MICALE

In psychiatry, as in many other branches of medicine, the twentieth century was extraordinarily eventful. Radically new theories of the life of the mind emerged; Freudian psychoanalysis was conceived and spread culturally; a huge, diversified mental health profession came into existence; psychiatric terms and concepts penetrated everyday life; drugs for alleviating the psychotic suffering of hundreds of thousands of people were engineered; and there was an explosion of knowledge about the chemistry and physiology of the brain — an explosion powerful enough to be compared by some observers to the Darwinian and Newtonian revolutions.

Psychiatric medicine in the twentieth century also exhibited more troubling, even sinister elements. The same period that ushered in a series of important benefits has witnessed the application of sadistic medical procedures to shell-shocked soldiers during the First World War, the use of psychiatric genetics in carrying out Nazi policies of racial hygiene, the confinement of political dissidents in Soviet psychiatric hospitals, the involuntary lobotomizing of thousands of psychotic patients, the movement of masses of mentally disabled persons from hospitals onto city streets, and the emergence of entire populations dependent upon powerful, mood-altering psychochemicals.

In this chapter, I take "the psychiatric body" to mean materialist mental medicine. I use the term in two senses — to denote the behavioral aspects of the human brain as a bodily organ and to discuss the body of knowledge generated by physicians about that subject. Every theory of mental activity implies a theory of physical functioning. In fact, the story of psychiatry in the twentieth century can advantageously be viewed as a series of attempts to determine the place of the body in the sciences of the mind. Two explanatory models have competed for primacy. On the one hand, psychosocial theories portray insanity as an illness of the mind or spirit, and emphasize external factors — such as family upbringing, personal history, and environmental stress — in the individual's mental development. On the other hand, organic or somatic theories view mental derangement as a cerebral disease with physical determinants such as heredity, fetal milieu, hormonal environment, and brain anatomy, physiology, and chemistry. In past therapeutic practice, psychiatrists have often attempted simultaneously to minister to both the brain and the mind, but in the realm of theory they have tended to emphasize either psyche or soma, to the exclusion of the other category. At the end of the 1990s — dubbed 'the decade of the brain' by the United States Congress — some researchers claim to have achieved the definitive integration of mind and body in a new biochemical model. Seen by some doctors and scientists to represent the triumph of materialistic mentalism, the present moment offers an illuminating perspective from which to review the twentieth-century psychiatric body.

### Nineteenth-Century Backgrounds

Materialist theories of the mind date from the beginnings of recorded medical history. It may plausibly be argued, however, that the story of the psychiatric body in modern medicine begins with two episodes from the last quarter of the eighteenth century: Philippe Pinel introduced the nonviolent '*traitement moral*' to deal with insane patients at the Salpêtrière hospital in Paris during the French Revolution; and in 1796, in England, William Tuke and his family opened the York Retreat, providing their Quaker clients with a salutary living environment and handling them with respect, friendship, and forbearance.

The Anglo-French 'moral treatment' was intended to be a humane treatment, in contrast to the use of dungeons, chains, and whips, which increasingly were recognized as cruel. Beyond that, it implied an emotional component, later labeled psychological. Pinel and the Tukes did not dissect brains; they carefully observed and often talked to the individuals under their care in the hope of improving or curing their condition. They were rudimentary psychotherapists who attempted to learn about the mental worlds of the individuals under their charge and who took some of the first steps toward establishing doctor-patient relationships with the mentally disturbed. Scholars have disagreed on whether the moral treatment was a heroic application of Enlightenment humanitarianism, a technique for the moral and social containment of irrationality, or a strategy for professional aggrandizement. This much is clear: its practitioners sought to establish with their patients a connection based on the mind rather than the body. At its founding two centuries ago, European psychiatry ministered to suffering psyches, not diseased bodies.

Practitioners of the moral treatment contrasted their techniques against the physically-oriented therapeutics of the time, which included bleeding, purging, bodily restraint, and heavy doses of medications. Nevertheless, moral therapists continued to use those procedures occasionally, especially for cases they considered maniacal. In many instances, Pinel replaced the old iron chains with straitjackets. Furthermore, after the death of its founders, the moral treatment itself became more physicalistic: in France, Pinel's most famous follower, J.-E.-D. Esquirol, returned to ancient humoral ideas of the temperaments to explain mental illness, and during the 1800s the York Retreat increasingly administered wet packs, Turkish baths, and chloral and bromides to its growing clientele. The lay, nonmedical nature of the moral treatment became an embarrassment for asylum doctors who, in a pattern later repeated many times, embraced elements of contemporary organic medicine seemingly at random in an attempt to appear scientific.

The drive to find links between disordered behavior and abnormal brain states was manifested in other areas of medicine during the first half of the nineteenth century. Parisian physicians pioneered the study of pathological anatomy by tracing diseases to localizable lesions in the body. Using this technique in 1822, Antoine-Laurent Bayle attributed the psychiatric symptoms of general paresis (later identified as syphilis of the central nervous system) to a chronic inflammation of the meninges accompanied by spinal and cerebral lesions. Bayle was the first to establish the organicity of a psychiatric disorder, and his work spurred a generation of French physicians to search for evidence of morbidity in the brains of the insane.

The second quarter of the nineteenth century was the heyday of European and American phrenology. Based on the theories of the Viennese anatomist Franz-Joseph Gall, phrenology was the belief that the conformation of the human skull indicates mental faculties and character traits. Gall further hypothesized that mental functions could be analyzed into a number of independent faculties, each faculty seated in a particular region of the brain. Gall's adherents Johann Kaspar Spurzheim and George Combe popularized his ideas in Britain and North America, where during the 1830s and 1840s many asylum doctors and proprietors subscribed to phrenological principles. Phrenological psychiatry centered on the belief that insanity, especially 'moral insanity', stemmed from the derangement of a particular personality faculty, which could be treated by strengthening neighboring faculties and which after death could be traced to a lesion in that part of the brain. Gall's system of correspondences between cerebral regions and mental faculties was wholly conjectural, and the related medical and popular beliefs in physiognomy and craniology are now judged to be pseudo-sciences. Nonetheless, phrenological psychiatry was a physiological psychology based on a belief in the brain as the organ of the mind. It pictured the brain not as an undifferentiated mass but as a congeries of functionally discrete parts. It encouraged physicalist methods of investigation. Later in the century, French and German laboratory neuropathologists returned to the idea of functional brain localization with results that proved scientifically more durable.

German-speaking central Europe was largely divorced from these occurrences. A psychiatry of sorts emerged there during the 1820s and 1830s, but the body played little part in it. This was the hightide of Romanticism, which made itself felt in many areas of thought and culture. German *Naturphilosophie* displayed a strong interest in extreme, bizarre states of mind, and 'Romantic psychiatry' took speculative issues of the relations among body, mind, and soul as its central theme. In 1808, Johann Christian Reil coined the word 'psychiatry;' his sense of the term, however, bore little resemblance to later meanings. Such *Psychiker* as Reil, Johann Christian Heinroth, Karl Wilhelm Ideler, and Justinus Kerner wrote about dreams, the soul, and the unconscious. These men relied heavily on introspection as a source of observation, and they were as informed by the theology, mythology, and metaphysics of their day as by medicine. Theirs were literal *psycho-logias*.

By the middle decades of the 1800s, major changes were afoot. As industrialization transformed Europe materially, positivist philosophies exalted science as the most important and reliable form of knowledge. As the prestige of the sciences grew, the figure of the scientist as a technically skilled, empirically-grounded professional emerged, and as scientific knowledge accumulated, professional specialization within the sciences arose. The modern research university and the new research institute developed as the preferred institutional sites for scientific endeavors. These changes produced a congenial cultural atmosphere for a new wave of materialism in science and medicine, including in the mental sciences.

This trend was most pronounced in the Germanic medical world, where an anti-Romantic reaction encouraged the formation of new schools of materialist psychiatry. At the University of Berlin in 1865, Wilhelm Griesinger became the first Professor of Psychiatry. In his *Pathology and Therapy of Mental Diseases* (1845), Griesinger emphasized that psychiatry should be rooted in a thorough study of the structure and function of the brain. In a "physiopathological preamble" to the book, he drew on contemporary concepts of cerebral irritation and nervous reflex action to formulate a model of psychopathology. "Psychological diseases are diseases of the brain," Griesinger declared famously.[1] Despite his acknowledgment of the role of emotional disturbances in mental illness and even though he was not uninfluenced by classical German metaphysics, Griesinger's scientific legacy was one of pure medical materialism.

Griesinger inaugurated what one historian has called "the first biological psychiatry."[2] This school was overwhelmingly anatomical in orientation, and it took as its major research project the association of psychiatric symptom complexes with specific areas of the brain. In central Europe during the last third of the nineteenth century, a group of professorial academic figures working in university clinics and laboratories increasingly replaced an earlier generation of humanitarian, psychologically oriented doctors in asylums. The leading second-generation Griesingerians were Carl Westphal in Berlin, Carl Wernicke in Breslau, Theodor Meynert in Vienna, Paul Flechsig in Leipzig, and Eduard Hitzig in Halle. Drawing their models of disease from branches of medicine that commanded a more secure knowledge base, Flechsig, Hitzig, Meynert, Westphal, and Wernicke hypothesized that nervous and mental disorders were caused by undetected lesions of the nervous system, electrochemical imbalances in the brain, microscopic alterations in the spinal marrow, or anemia or hyperaemia of the cortex. They wrote extensively about cortical localization and cerebral lateralization. Meynert authored a textbook titled *Psychiatry: A Clinical Treatise on Diseases of the Fore-brain Based upon a Study of Its Structure, Functions, and Nutrition* (1890), effectively a manual of neuroanatomy. By 1900, however, the medical effort to collapse the mind into the body had failed.

Despite the rhetoric of materialism in the writings of Meynert and his colleagues, their "brain mythologies" remained entirely speculative.[3] In addition, contemporary critics claimed that these neurologist-psychiatrists were interested in their patients primarily as objects of research.

Westphal, Wernicke, Meynert, Fleschig, and Hitzig were laboratory scientists with access to university clinics. In German asylum psychiatry of this time, the leading figure was Emil Kraepelin. The greatest psychiatric clinician of the late nineteenth and early twentieth centuries, Kraepelin combined an emphasis on heredity with an interest in the classification of mental illnesses and a new longitudinal perspective on the case history. To him, more than any other physician, are owed our twentieth-century notions of the psychoses. In nine authoritative editions of his *Textbook on Psychiatry* (1883–1927), Kraepelin provided classic clinical portraits of mental illnesses, including syndromes he labeled "dementia praecox" (literally, premature dementia) and "manic-depressive insanity." He interpreted the psychoses as morbid deteriorations of the brain. Kraepelin showed little concern with the inner life of the psyche of his patients, patterning his ideas about mental illness instead on neurological diseases and organic brain syndromes, such as epilepsy, general paresis, and senile dementia. In 1911, the Swiss psychiatrist Eugen Bleuler rechristened Kraepelin's dementia praecox "schizophrenia," and more recently physicians relabeled manic-depressive psychosis "bipolar affective disorder." Late twentieth-century schemes for the classification of psychopathology are based on descriptive criteria that some call "neo-Kraepelinian."

Throughout Europe and North America, the late nineteenth century was generally a grim period for hospital psychiatry. By the 1850s, the optimism associated with Pinel and the Tukes had waned; asylums were becoming less curative sites for temporary treatment than places of long-term institutional custody for the chronically insane. A new doctrine of degeneration reinforced this outlook. Psychiatric degeneration theory originated in the 1850s writings of B.-A. Morel, who directed a large provincial asylum in eastern France. Morel believed that mental illness was the manifestation of an inherited mental defect. Writing two generations before the rediscovery of Mendelian genetics, Morel did not know exactly how these defects were conveyed from one generation to the next. He argued, however, that the family was assuredly the vector of transmission, that mental disorders had an unknown physical correlate in the nervous system, and that they were incurable. He further believed that degenerates could be recognized by physical and mental stigmata. Despite its determinism, French psychiatric hereditarianism became enormously influential in late nineteenth-century European mental medicine and, beyond that, in popular belief and cultural commentary. Degeneration theory provided a comprehensive explanatory system for psychopathology, and it rationalized therapeutic impotence among asylum doctors. In a rapidly modernizing world, it also proved useful socially and culturally. During the later 1800s in France, it was common for conservative critics to identify new social phenomena in the cities, such as prostitution, alcoholism, homosexuality, and criminality, and to stigmatize them as forms of degeneration. Likewise, Victorian Britons embraced hereditary explanations for many of the perceived social and moral problems of the day. The link between psychiatric somaticism and therapeutic pessimism before the late twentieth century (and conversely between environmentalism and optimism) is clearly illustrated by degeneration theory. Two generations later, the doctrine achieved its most poisonous application in practices of sterilization, euthanasia, and genocide carried out by the Nazis in the name of racial regeneration.

## PSYCHODYNAMIC PSYCHIATRY AND THE ECLIPSE OF THE BODY (1910–1960)

The end of the nineteenth and beginning of the twentieth century witnessed perhaps the greatest 'paradigm shift' in psychiatric history. Interestingly, this change was motivated *negatively*; that is, it resulted from a crisis of knowledge and practice reinforced by social and professional factors.

The stage was set by changes in neurology. During the 1800s, knowledge about the structure of the brain and central nervous system increased rapidly, and the medical specialty of clinical neurology emerged. During this golden age of European neurology, physicians provided basic descriptions of many neurological syndromes and traced a number of diseases to nervous system lesions. In 1861 the French surgeon Paul Broca claimed to have discovered the seat of articulate speech in the left frontal lobe, providing the first proof of the localization of brain function. One group of disorders observed by nineteenth-century neurologists resisted anatomical localization, however, and became known as the 'functional nervous disorders'. Patients in this category, who were often diagnosed with hysteria, neurasthenia, or nerve prostration, suffered from a mysterious battery of shifting complaints, such as fatigue, anxiety, nervousness, fears, and obsessions. A number of prominent neurophysicians, including Jean-Martin Charcot in France, William Gowers in Britain, and George Beard in the United States, studied these strange nervous maladies in the belief that they, too, would eventually reveal an organic substratum.

Most of the nervous types who sought out Charcot, Gowers, and Beard were part of a new population of patients. They tended to be educated, prosperous, and medically knowledgeable individuals who lived in rapidly growing cities and had the financial wherewithal to consult medical specialists. Many of the male patients worked in the competitive worlds of business and the professions, while most of the women are believed to have led unhappy, frustrated lives restricted by the social and sexual mores of the time. By the turn of the century in Europe and America, a cast of 'nerve doctors' ministered to this new and lucrative clientele, a self-help literature about nervous hygiene offered advice, and a network of spas and health retreats catered to their medical needs. Nerve specialists in late Victorian times were clinical neurologists with their own medical practices, and their therapeutics were largely somatic, including massages, medications, rest cures, protein diets, hydrotherapy, and medical electricity. Nevertheless, the category of the functional nervous disorders was a precursor to the twentieth-century concept of the neuroses. Gilded Age nerve doctors brought private-practice psychiatry into existence.

Charcot, Gowers, Beard, and their contemporaries faced a major scientific dilemma. The only techniques available for studying hysteria and neurasthenia were bedside examination and postmortem inspection of the brain. Because of the limitations of these methods, year after year passed without finding the expected correlates to these disorders in the body. Furthermore, as alleged organic diseases, the functional nervous disorders were in danger of being associated with hereditary degeneration and being tainted by its undesirable social connotations. By 1900, the crisis created by the problem of the missing lesion opened up the possibility of alternative, nonorganic conceptualizations of the mind and its maladies.

These developments resulted in the advent of a group of new, psychogenic theories and therapies that collectively came to be called the psychodynamic psychiatries. The decades on either side of 1900 witnessed a burst of psychological theorizing that sympathetic later historians heralded as the birth of modern psychiatry, the Freudian revolution, and the discovery of the unconscious. Many conflicting ideas, schools, and practices developed within the domain of psychodynamic psychiatry. Despite their differences, they all shared a belief that psychiatric materialism, as demonstrated during the preceding two generations, was a sterile and outdated model of the mind.

Between the 1890s and the First World War, Sigmund Freud constructed by far the most comprehensive psychodynamic theory, which he named 'psychoanalysis'. Trained in neurology, Freud as a young man studied the nervous system of marine animals, wrote a monograph on aphasia, and dissected children's brains in the laboratory. He became convinced that the neurosciences of his day were insufficiently developed to move forward psychiatrically, so he pursued a more mentalist model that could be elaborated through clinical observation and theorizing. Early psychoanalytic theory was, above all, an alternative to the brain psychiatry taught by Meynert, with whom Freud had studied in Vienna.

For our purposes, the coming of psychoanalysis can be viewed as a massive reassertion of the idea of the psyche, submerged in Western psychiatric medicine since the time of Pinel and the Tukes. The "psychoanalytic body" is a radically decorporealized body. For Freud, psychology was the clinical study of intrapsychic forces in continual development and conflict. The mind was governed by an unconscious, which consists of a large and powerful repository of instinctual desires, repressed ideas, and unfulfilled wishes. Conversely, the body in Freudian psychology was interesting only in so far as it was an imagined object of the psyche. Even sex was reconfigured from an object of moral contemplation or chemical-hormonal phenomenon into *psycho*sexuality. Clinically, Freud chose to study precisely those maladies — hysteria, neurasthenia, compulsive states, anxiety disorders

— that Charcot, Gowers, Beard, and Meynert had tried but failed to anchor in the body. Freud also succeeded in creating a new, wholly psychological meaning of the concept of neurosis. Previously considered to be a neurological disorder caused by an undiscovered lesion, neurosis in psychoanalytic parlance became an emotional disorder of intermediate severity triggered by psychic conflict.

The ways that biologically oriented theorists deal with emotional symptoms and psychologically inclined practitioners deal with physical symptoms are always noteworthy. Freud handled the issue skillfully. How do we get "from a mental process to a somatic innervation?" he asked in 1909.[4] With the idea of conversion, he interpreted physical symptoms as materializations of intrapsychic forces. Thus he was able to use hysteria — a disease entity that mimics organic, particularly neurological, illness — as the founding disorder of psychoanalysis. Psychoanalytic psychologists regarded the florid symptom formations of hysterical illness as somaticizations of psychic conflicts, while the body of the female hysteric became the site of projection for repressed and unresolved psychological forces. Correspondingly, Freudian therapeutics privileged mind over body. In a series of changes during the 1880s and 1890s, Freud abandoned the use of medications, hypnosis, and the temple pressure technique. He ceased in his practice to minister to — literally, to make contact with — the body; in its place, he developed "the talking cure," as his famous patient "Anna O." termed it.[5] His mature notion of analytic psychotherapy involved a long, intricate exploration of the patient's remote emotional past. In the analytic situation, the patient, or analysand, used free association to reminisce subjectively about his or her past while the analyst interpreted what the patient said.

Freud was only one of many psychological theorists working in the dynamic tradition during the early decades of the century. Janetian psychology, Jungian psychology, Adlerian psychology, Rankean psychology, the dissociative psychology of Théodore Flournoy, the Protestant pastoral psychology of Oscar Pfister, the object relations school of Melanie Klein, the phenomenological psychiatry of Eugène Minkowski and Ludwig Binswanger, the existential psychiatry of Karl Jaspers, the psychoanalytic ego psychology of Anna Freud, Heinz Hartmann, and Eric Erikson, and the Freudo-Marxism of Erich Fromm — these were important psychodynamic systems that flourished at the same time. For sectarian reasons, commentators at the time dwelled on irreconcilable differences among these approaches. In hindsight, however, their commonalities are equally striking. All so-called depth psychologists worked within a psychological paradigm. They maintained strong interests in sexuality, the instincts, familial relations, emotional development, dream life, the mental aspects of sexuality, and psychological symbolism. They posited the existence of an unconscious as a unitary, functioning entity, and they reified the psyche as a known, independent category. The conscious-unconscious duality was central to the dynamic psychiatries. Clinically, psychodynamic therapists were concerned less with the severely mentally ill in public mental hospitals than with a range of troubled but nonpsychotic individuals seeking private treatment. They practiced verbal and behavioral psychotherapies.

During the first decade and a half of the twentieth century, psychoanalysis was the preserve of a small group of avant-garde intellectuals. This changed with the coming of the First World War. The war saw the outbreak of combat-related neuroses among tens of thousands of infantrymen confronting the intolerable realities of prolonged trench warfare. More than any scientific critique, the experience of epidemic shell shock in the British, French, German, Italian, and American armies called into question nineteenth-century materialist psychiatry. War doctors could not trace these cases to physical damage to the nervous system; nor, given the huge numbers, could they attribute them to defective heredity. Eventually, they turned to psychological explanations. Moreover, shell shock seemed to illustrate graphically a number of key Freudian ideas, such as the roles of trauma, repression, defense, and dream life in psychological sickness. Most important, in many psychiatric circles the war established the value of the talking therapies. What may properly be called the Age of Freud (as contrasted to the history of psychoanalytic ideas) began with World War I. The war gave psychiatrists an expanded social role. It sparked widespread interest in the psychoneuroses and inspired the founding of psychiatric clinics devoted to psychotherapy, such as London's Tavistock Square Clinic, which opened in 1920. It also brought Freud to the attention of American physicians.

In the period after the war, psychotherapeutics were an eclectic mix of theories and techniques, but psychoanalysis dominated. During the 1930s, 1940s, and 1950s, Freud's intellectual and professional ascent continued. This was especially true in American psychiatry, where the trend was greatly reinforced by the influx of emigré analysts from central Europe during the 1930s. By the end of the Second World War, psychoanalytic training institutes flourished in many American cities. The better American medical schools included instruction in psychoanalysis. Heads of university psychiatry departments tended to be analysts, and psychiatric hospitals included analysts on their staffs. New theories that reflected American social and cultural values developed, most notably psychoanalytic ego psychology.

A burgeoning community of psychoanalysts in the United States sought to embrace the scientific and cultural prestige of medicine, which was then growing rapidly. They required a medical degree for psychoanalytic practice, and they strove to integrate psychoanalysis into clinical psychiatry, despite Freud's personal acceptance of analysis by individuals without medical training and his preference for keeping psychoanalysis an independent discipline. During the inter-war and post-war years, the number of medical residents opting for specialization in psychiatry ballooned, and psychodynamically oriented psychotherapists took over from neurologists in the treatment of neurotic disorders. Reflecting psychiatry's rise in the New World, the National Institute of Mental Health was founded in 1946, and massive governmental resources were put at its disposal.

There were many social and cultural dimensions to psychological dynamism. At the height of its influence, psychoanalytic teaching informed ancillary fields such as mental hygiene, educational psychology, psychiatric social work, and criminal psychology. Psychoanalytic studies merged with philosophy, religion, mythology, anthropology, history, and the arts, and one academic discipline after another passed through a Freudian phase. Popularizations appeared in novels, films, and the press. By 1960, trickle-down Freudianism had reached street level, as terms such as ego, superego, unconscious, narcissism, defense mechanism, and sibling rivalry infiltrated everyday speaking and thinking. Many enthusiasts regarded systematic psychological analysis as an extension of the Western classical tradition of self-knowledge and therefore as a variety of modern humanism. Freud seemed to entail an entire world view. An American sociologist wrote of "the emergence of psychological man," and a Swiss historian of medicine referred to "the psychological revolution" of the twentieth century.[6]

## HOSPITAL PSYCHIATRY, 1920–1960

During the second quarter of the twentieth century, a great cleavage developed within the Western psychiatric community. In thrall to psychoanalysis, academic physicians and psychiatrists in private practice focused on intensive psychotherapy for neurotic patients over long periods of time. The brain sciences were largely irrelevant to their vision of psychiatry. Separate from the world of psychodynamic psychotherapy were the realities of asylum psychiatry.

Throughout this period, mental hospitals remained the main settings for treating persons deemed severely mentally ill. During the 1930s, 1940s, and 1950s, there was some experimental use of psychoanalytic techniques in the treatment of the mild psychoses, particularly in private American hospitals. The results, however, were not promising. Moreover, intensive daily analysis was impractical given the enormous numbers of patients in state asylums, and analysts were drawn to lucrative office practices. In institutional psychiatry, Kraepelin's attempts to base mental medicine on germ theory-like models remained influential. But while Kraepelinian psychiatry offered new ways to name, classify, and conceptualize psychopathology, it provided little by way of treatment. As Joan Busfield notes elsewhere in this volume, "the optimism associated with the early asylums and the belief in their inherent therapeutic benefits had largely foundered, and their custodial character was less easy to ignore." There were no known effective treatments, much less cures, for any psychotic disorder. Consequently, the period that witnessed the flowering of psychodynamic psychiatry was a time of therapeutic pessimism in hospital psychiatry. The most realistic hope of relief for many patients was spontaneous recovery. Practice in mental hospitals brought little in salary or professional prestige. Increasingly, asylum psychiatry consisted of curating the chronically incapacitated. To make matters worse, this population had grown dramatically. The numbers of institutionally confined in the first half of the century doubled in England and

Wales and more than trebled in the United States, where inmate numbers in state and county asylums surpassed half a million by 1950. The majority of hospitals housed well over a thousand patients.

Against this bleak backdrop, there appeared a series of new and experimental physical procedures for treating schizophrenic, manic depressive, and acutely depressed patients. These new somatic therapies represent one of the most dramatic aspects of the history of the psychiatric body during the 1930s, 1940s, and 1950s. Unfortunately, this is also one of the most morally troubling episodes in modern psychiatric history.

Before the discovery of penicillin, a sizable percentage of patients in European and American asylums suffered from general paresis, or cerebral syphilis. In 1909, the German bacteriologist Paul Ehrlich discovered an arsenical compound that killed the syphilitic bacteria, or spirochete. Ehrlich named the drug Salvarsan. Then, in 1917, Julius von Wagner-Jauregg, Professor of Psychiatry at the University of Vienna, introduced the malarial fever cure. Wagner-Jauregg discovered that an injection of blood contaminated by malaria induced a high fever that destroyed the heat-sensitive spirochetes in the body and caused a remission of symptoms. Salvarsan had horrible side effects, and the induction of high fever associated with a life-threatening disease was obviously dangerous. Nevertheless, the draconian procedures of Ehrlich and Wagner-Jauregg contained neurosyphilitic symptoms, and they proved that chemotherapy could alleviate certain mental illnesses. In 1927, Wagner-Jauregg received a Nobel Prize for his innovation, the first psychiatrist to receive that honor.

Ehrlich and Wagner-Jauregg's work emboldened a generation of doctors to attempt other extreme, interventionist procedures. In the 1920s, there was a fad, primarily in the United States, for treating mental illnesses by removing the focal infections believed to cause them, particularly in diseased teeth and infected tonsils. In the early twenties, Jakob Klaesi, a Swiss-German physician working at the famous Burghölzli hospital in Zürich, pioneered prolonged sleep therapies. These procedures involved inducing a deep sleep with barbiturate medications which, for unknown reasons, sometimes temporarily caused psychotic symptoms to lessen. Because of high risks, including the deaths of some patients from pneumonia and circulatory collapse, physicians eventually discontinued this practice. Deep insulin coma therapy began in the early 1930s. Developed by the Austrian physician Manfred Sakel, this measure involved administering intravenously or subcutaneously large doses of insulin in order to induce a series of brief comas in schizophrenic patients. Insulin coma therapy was particularly popular in Switzerland and Britain during the 1940s. In 1934, the Hungarian psychiatrist Ladislas von Meduna introduced Cardiazol, known in the United States as Metrazol. This was a powerful medication, diluted in a solution and administered intravenously, which elicited violent epileptoid fits that were believed to cause remission of psychotic symptoms. Eventually, physicians abandoned this treatment, too, not least because of patients' fear and physical injuries such as joint and spinal fractures.

The most extreme and infamous procedure from this period was lobotomy, or surgery on the cerebral cortex. The idea of intervening surgically on the brain to treat mental illness is as old as ancient Egyptian trepanning. Twentieth-century psychosurgery was first developed in the mid-1930s by Egas Moniz, a Portuguese neurologist, who also received a Nobel Prize for his work. Two other doctors, the neurologist Walter Freeman and neurosurgeon James Watts, popularized Moniz's work in the United States and coined the term lobotomy. Psychosurgeons used two different techniques: prefrontal leucotomy, which involved boring small holes in the front of the cranium, and transorbital lobotomy, which involved approaching the brain through the roof of the orbit of the eye socket. In both procedures, a scalpel or ice pick-like object was inserted into the brain and used randomly to transect the frontal gray matter. Both measures were reported to tranquilize patients. The heyday of psychosurgery occurred in the United States during the late 1940s and early 1950s. By 1955, over 20,000 of these mutilating procedures had been performed on American mental patients. The practice declined rapidly after the late 1950s, in part because of belated recognition of the irreversible brain damage it often caused and in part because of the introduction of new chemical treatments.

Two new practices in the therapeutic arsenal of this period have been retained, in modified forms, up to the present. First, in the later 1930s Ugo Cerletti, a professor of neuropathology and psychiatry in Rome, and Lucio Bini introduced electroshock, or, as it was later relabelled, electroconvulsive therapy. Enlightenment Mesmerists and Victorian nerve doctors had applied low doses of static electricity to the skin surface. ECT, in contrast, involved the direct mechanical stimulation of the brain with electrodes placed on the temples in order to produce momentary, therapeutic convulsions. For reasons that were — and remain — unclear, shocking the brain often provides relief from major depression. The one serious side effect, doctors discovered, was selective, short-term memory loss. In the late 1940s and 1950s, ECT clinics for daily administrations of electroshock therapy to large numbers of patients were common features of British, American, and Canadian mental hospitals. In the 1970s, the psychiatric profession, responding to popular, scientific, and governmental concerns, established guidelines for the use of ECT.

A second new and promising line of treatment involved the first so-called antipsychotic medications. Doctors had used drugs to combat madness for thousands of years, and chloral and bromides were standard elements in the Victorian pharmacopoeia. The practice entered a new phase, however, during the mid-twentieth century. Most important historically was chlorpromazine, known popularly as Thorazine. Early in the 1950s, the French pharmaceutical house of Rhône-Poulenc synthesized chlorpromazine, a phenothiazine derivative synthesized initially as a centrally active antihistamine. Parisian psychiatrists first used the drug clinically, and Heinz Lehmann, a German psychiatrist working in Montreal, helped to introduce it into English-speaking countries. Chlorpromazine calmed many schizophrenic patients without sedating them. Much later, physicians discovered the possible serious aftereffects, such as involuntary grimacing and uncontrollable bodily movements.

Chlorpromazine was the first anti-psychotic compound. Increasingly during the 1960s and 1970s, hospital psychiatrists were using a number of phenothiazine derivatives to treat schizophrenia, lithium carbonate to stabilize manic patients, and imipramine to relieve psychotic depression. None of the new drug treatments addressed the underlying pathology of these disorders, and at that time there was little understanding of their mechanism of action. Nonetheless, their dramatic relief of symptoms encouraged development of an ever-broadening pharmacopeia of psychotropic drugs. The new field of psychopharmacology burst onto the scene. By the early 1970s, the production of these substances involved thousands of laboratory scientists in a dozen countries. Their marketing became an international, billion-dollar industry.

The first historical scholarship about fever therapies, barbiturate narcosis, insulin coma, Metrazol convulsion treatment, ECT, psychosurgery, and the early anti-psychotic drugs has recently appeared. Not surprisingly, scholars are sharply divided over matters of interpretation. While still controversial among the public, ECT went on to become a mainstay of psychiatric treatment for severe depression. Similarly, psychopharmacology, buttressed by advances in the understanding of its neurobiological basis, utterly transformed the practice of psychiatric medicine. Nevertheless, the great wave of physical therapies of the second quarter of the century extends well beyond these two measures. It will not do to excuse these other practices on the grounds of therapeutic desperation or historical aberrance, and the internationalism of the story prevents us from incriminating the medical community of any single nation.

News of these procedures, sometimes presented in oracular tones as major breakthroughs, spread rapidly through the medical world, and their use quickly became widespread. At the time, their scientific basis remained obscure. There were no longterm studies, and there was little knowledge of or attention to possible late side-effects. All these treatments were drastic and dangerous. Insulin treatment and psychosurgery involved the direct destruction of great numbers of nerve cells in the cerebral cortex. Medical records reveal that many practices terrified patients and were performed against the will of those forcibly interned. For years some procedures were conducted on whole categories of patients for which they subsequently turned out to be useless. These therapies were deplored by many contemporary psychiatrists, and most of the procedures were eventually discredited on scientific or ethical grounds. Furthermore, by the 1960s the radical therapeutic interventionism of this period had helped to spawn patients' rights lobbies in the UK and US as well as a powerful, international anti-psychiatry movement. It also generated sharply negative cultural representations of asylum psychiatry, which continue to influence popular thinking.

Desperation partly explains these therapeutic techniques. But this story should also be understood as an aggressive attempt by psychiatry to embrace the medical mainstream, which during the 1920s, 1930s, and 1940s was gaining new prestige with the advent of sulpha drugs and antibiotics. These practices reveal a culture of science that consistently privileged the medical model in the treatment of human suffering — hence, Nobel Prizes were awarded for malarial fever cure and psychosurgery whereas no innovation in psychotherapy has been so honored. More broadly, this episode reflected a spirit of *furor therapeuticus* in Western medical history, in which the sheer technical capacity to perform a given procedure becomes the ethical license for doing so.

## THE REVIVAL OF BIOLOGICAL PSYCHIATRY, 1960 TO THE PRESENT

Psychodynamic psychiatry, which dominated academic Euro-American psychological medicine during the middle of the twentieth century, produced an impressive constellation of ideas and observations about human mental life in health and sickness. Freud created the most influential, single-authored theory of the mind the twentieth century produced. Nevertheless, by the early 1970s, dynamic psychiatry was in serious scientific and professional trouble. This time, the psychiatric sea change was wrought by a combination of positive and negative factors.

By the 1960s, classical psychoanalytic therapy had proven too lengthy and expensive to be used widely. For acutely distressed psychiatric populations, it was largely useless. The psychoanalytic movement, moreover, was to some degree a victim of its own success: by the decade after Freud's death in 1939, psychoanalytic theory had lost its groundbreaking quality, and its specific revolutionary force had diminished. Freudian theory hardened, becoming first doctrinal, then dogmatic. Psychoanalytic training became standardized, its power institutional rather than intellectual. The movement was also beset by endless sectarianism. Perhaps most decisively, American psychoanalysis began to pay for its insistence on being part of the medical world. Critics pointed out that its methods followed none of the principles of prediction, experimentation, control, and quantification that were adhered to by the medical sciences. In the 1970s, efficacy studies failed to establish that psychoanalytic therapy was superior to shorter and cheaper treatments. Because of lack of demonstrable results, government funding for psychoanalytic research in America dwindled, and in the late 1970s and 1980s insurance funding for psychotherapy declined in view of inconclusive results. Furthermore, American psychologists, furious at being excluded from practicing analysis, developed a variety of popular alternative therapies, many based on behavioral and cognitive psychology. What Hans Eysenck, a behavioralist psychologist at the Maudsley Hospital in London, called "the decline and fall of the Freudian empire" was also cultural as well as clinical.[7] During the second half of the twentieth century, psychoanalytic theory and praxis were subjected to withering critiques by biographers, historians and philosophers of science, literary critics, academic feminists, anti-psychiatrists of various stripes, and angry ex-analysands. Many of the more far-ranging cultural applications of psychodynamic theory came to appear extravagant.

Ultimately, however, the rejection of the psychoanalytic anti-body, and the eclipse of the mentalist paradigm of which it was a part, were not brought about by critiques of Freud, no matter how vehement or voluminous. Rather, the change was caused more positively by new knowledge and the powerful professional interests brought into existence by that knowledge. At its inception, psychodynamic psychiatry defined itself against psychiatric organicism, which in the late 1800s seemed bankrupt. In the second half of the twentieth century, however, there emerged a modernized biological psychiatry that fared much better than its nineteenth-century precursor.

Neuropsychopharmacology provided the spark. The new anti-psychotic drugs were believed to establish the existence of a physical dimension to certain major mental illnesses. This discovery suggested an entire research program. What was now perceived to be necessary was a more experimental and empirically based psychiatry, much more drug research, better and statistically-based techniques for the clinical study of new medications, and an understanding of the precise mechanism of action of anti-psychotic chemicals. What is more, the success of the early anti-psychotics revealed the immense economic potential of these medications as well as the gain in scientific standing for psychiatrists who embraced medical models of theory, practice, and research.

As a consequence of these developments, the period from 1970 to the present has witnessed a tremendous resurgence of biologism, especially in the world of Anglo-American psychiatry, which has become evermore influential throughout the medical world. During the final quarter of the twentieth century, the chemistry, biology, and genetics of the brain has become the object of one of the most intensive research programs in the history of medicine. The result has been an explosion of knowledge about the human brain and the central nervous system, especially the biology of the cerebral cortex. The neuroscientific revolution has not been the work of any single, founding figure; rather, it has been the result of teams of scientific researchers working in many different institutions and countries. Furthermore, the new interest in brain and behavior has not been limited to physicians in mental hospitals; it extended to general psychiatry and the laboratory neurosciences, thereby reuniting branches of the mental sciences that were previously divided.

Late twentieth-century biological psychiatry has been physiological, chemical, and genetic in nature. If dynamic psychiatry saw the humanities as its sister disciplines, the new biological psychiatry has fed directly on the neurosciences, which consist of the overlapping subfields of neuroanatomy, neurophysiology, neuropathology, neuropharmacology, neurochemistry, neuropsychology, and neuroendocrinology. Biopsychiatry has taken as its subject the brain as the organ of mind. It has envisioned the brain as a collection of highly specialized functional units composed of billions of neurons, or nerve cells, continually engaged in complex electrical and chemical communication.

At the center of brain-behavior studies has been the phenomenon of neurotransmission. Neurotransmitters are chemicals that convey nerve impulses from one neuron to another across the synapse or gap between the neurons. Dopamine, norepinephrine, and serotonin are the chemical messengers that have received the most scientific attention, although by 1995 over 40 such chemical agents had been isolated. The newly reconstituted psychiatric body was formed from the discovery that an excess or shortage of certain chemical-transmitting substances in the central nervous system may effect mood states, including psychotic conditions. Furthermore, identification of particular brain cells and neural systems that secrete particular neurotransmitters has allowed pharmacologists to synthesize chemicals that act directly on the neuronal receptor sites. To test these new compounds, researchers in the clinic and laboratory have turned away from the old case history method that psychodynamic psychiatry relied on. Instead, they have developed a new clinical trial methodology involving intricate statistical analyses and controlled experiments with double-blind, placebo-controlled samples.

A comparative examination of Western psychiatric textbooks from the 1950s and the 1990s highlights the changing place of the body in twentieth-century psychiatry. Classical psychodynamic models of psychopathology emphasized overwhelming instinctual forces, inadequate psychological defenses, and clashes among the id, ego, and superego. In contrast, late twentieth-century organic psychiatrists have viewed mental illnesses as brain function disturbances caused by structural, biochemical, or neuroendocrinological abnormalities. These abnormalities are often grounded in defective genetic hardwiring. Biologically oriented psychiatrists have tended to pattern their models of mental and nervous disorders on the paradigmatic organic brain syndromes. They have drawn their historical inspiration from the evolutionary neurobiology of Hughlings Jackson and the clinical brain psychiatry of Kraepelin. Conversely, they have tended to ignore the psychological interpretation of mental symptoms and to accord importance to these phenomena only insofar as they may be indications of underlying biological malfunctions. Reversing the Freudian reading, they have interpreted many psychological aspects of mental diseases as epiphenomena of brain events.

A clear expression of these views is found in the *Diagnostic and Statistical Manual of Mental Disorders*, the influential reference work produced by the American Psychiatric Association, which claims to be an authoritative list of all known nervous and mental pathologies. In the Introduction to the fourth edition of the *DSM*, published in 1994, the authors reject the age-old notion of a duality between somatic and psychological causation, a distinction they regard as a meaningless and reductionistic anachronism of Cartesian philosophy. They express interest in striking the term 'mental' from the title but maintain the term for semantic continuity. They voice a faith that in time all mental disorders will be traced to biochemical bases. Future revisions of the manual, as they see it, will primarily integrate discoveries from the neural sciences.

Dramatic developments in neurodiagnostics have reinforced the return to psychiatric physicalism in the late twentieth century. The idea of creating visual images of the brain, as noted earlier, has a long and colorful history. From the 1970s onward, however, new technologies have modernized this concept. Computerized axial tomographic (CAT) scanning and magnetic resonance imaging (MRI) has allowed psychiatry to study directly and in extremely high resolution the size, density, and related structural features of the brain. Other procedures, such as cerebral blood flow (RCBF) and positron-emission tomographic (PET) scanning, have pictured living brains engaged in various tasks by displaying the activation of its parts, indicated by the volume of blood flow or of glucose metabolism in its different regions. These diagnostic methods have joined older techniques, such as postmortem brain examination and neuropsychological testing, to form the contemporary armamentarium of techniques for studying the psychiatric body.

In the final decades of the twentieth century, these theoretical, experimental, and diagnostic developments inspired a massive research campaign to determine the physical correlates of every possible form of psychopathology. Studies have cascaded from the press dealing with the neurophysiology of hysteria, brain cell loss in bipolar affective disorders, basal ganglia and limbic system dysfunction in obsessive-compulsive disorders, positron emission tomographical image measurements of borderline personality disorders, parietal glucose metabolic rate change of anorexia nervosa patients, and volumetric analyses of the brain and cerebrospinal fluid of severe depressives. Genetic studies of hysteria, agoraphobia, panic disorder, depression, and hypochondriasis have appeared. Schizophrenia is the most interpreted disease category in modern psychiatry. Organically inclined psychiatrists have variously associated schizophrenic illness with a diminution of higher cortical function, weakened left hemisphere function, hypofunction of the neurotransmitter dopamine in the prefrontal cortex, and lowered levels of blood flow in the frontal lobes. Building on nineteenth-century work on cerebral lateralization, researchers have studied differential hemispheric brain function in all the major psychiatric disorders. A new subfield, psychoneuroendocrinology, has investigated psychiatric aspects of the interaction between the body's glands — the thyroid, the adrenals, the part of the pancreas that produces insulin, and the sexual glands — on the central nervous system.

The therapeutic implications of the recorporealization of psychiatry have been no less transformative. Addressing 'the psyche,' Freud, Jung, Adler, Rank, and their followers practiced psychotherapies based on intricate verbal exploration and interpretation of an individual's emotional past. In stark contrast, descriptive biological psychiatrists of the late 1900s record symptoms, inquire about the medical history of relatives, match complaints with model symptom profiles, interpret laboratory results, and prescribe pills. As the place of the body changes within psychiatric thought, the individual seeking therapy undergoes fundamentally different experiences. Patient populations have changed, too. The discovery of a neurochemical component in human behavior applies not only to psychotics but to the operations of the normal human brain. It has opened up the possibility of chemotherapy for a wide range of nonpsychotic mental states, including the so-called neuroses, the behavioral disorders, and minor mood disturbances. In the 1960s, two new benzodiazepine compounds, known colloquially as 'tranquilizers' and commercially as Valium and Librium, became available to alleviate common anxiety and unhappiness. And by the 1990s, the tricylic antidepressants such as imipramine were supplanted by more easily tolerated medications, such as Zoloft and Prozac, for which physicians wrote millions of prescriptions yearly. By the century's end, the age of Freud had been replaced by "the antidepressant era."[8]

## FROM THE PSYCHIATRIC BODY TO SOCIAL NEUROBIOLOGY

Not surprisingly, the intellectual ascendance of the neural sciences during the last third of the twentieth century greatly enhanced the professional standing of biologically based psychiatry. In the 1970s, 1980s, and 1990s, biopsychiatrists displaced psychodynamic physicians as university professors, departmental chairs, journal editors, and organization leaders. Medical training changed as well: the number of psychiatric residents specializing in psychoanalysis dropped, and psychiatric residents received far fewer hours of training in psychotherapy than a half-century earlier. Instead, they were expected to master the latest neurosciences and psychopharmacology and to train in specialized drug management. Similarly, researchers studying disorders amenable to biomedical illumination, such as addiction, anxiety, depression, and trauma, became more likely to receive governmental funding than non-biologically oriented researchers.

The influence of biological psychiatry has extended to the social, cultural, and popular spheres, too. Like many of the most successful and wide-ranging paradigms in science history — Newtonian physics, Darwinian evolution, Freudian psychology — late twentieth-century biomedical psychiatry was much more than a technical theory for mental health specialists: it represented an entire reading of human nature. During the late 1800s, medics believed that human anatomy, particularly structural and functional differences between the sexes, was responsible for fundamental differences between the natures of men and women. A century later, neurobiology was destiny.

In the 1980s, this larger vision was conveyed to general educated readers through a series of skillful and attractive popularizations. Nancy Andreasen, a psychiatry professor at the University of Iowa, summarized for a nonmedical readership the ongoing transformation in psychiatry. Contemporary psychological medicine, Andreasen wrote in 1984, is "undergoing a revolutionary change and realigning itself with the mainstream biological traditions of medicine."[9] The author announced what she saw as the message of contemporary neuroscience for humankind:

> [w]e need not look to theoretical constructs of the 'mind' or to influences from the external environment in order to understand how people feel, why they behave as they do, or what becomes disturbed when people develop mental illness. Instead we can look directly to the brain and try to understand both normal behavior and mental illness in terms of how the brain works and how the brain breaks down.[10]

All symptoms of mental illness, Andreasen continued, "must be understood in terms of the interaction of neural systems and neural circuits." "The growth of our understanding about how the brain works," she added, "is perhaps the most exciting story in the history of science."[11]

In *Neuronal Man: The Biology of the Mind* (1983), Jean-Pierre Changeux of the Institut Pasteur in Paris shared Andreasen's exhilarated vision. Changeux suggested that chemistry and neurobiology would eventually replace the concepts, methods, and languages of the former mental sciences, including clinical psychology, and he recommended discarding altogether the terms mind and spirit. Nonmaterialist readings of human nature he labeled "spiritualist theses." "It seems quite legitimate to consider that mental states and physiological or physico-chemical states of the brain are identical," he concluded.[12]

As Andreasen and Changeux revealed, the intellectual aspirations of the new neurosciences have been stunning. Most striking, researchers in the 1990s hypothesized about many aspects of higher cerebral function that account for the most distinctively human mental activities. A raft of books, headed by Daniel Dennett's *Consciousness Explained* (1991), have explored the physical dimensions of human consciousness. These works have posited materialist, functionalist, selectionist, and dualist models to account for the subtle, continuous, and ever-shifting process of consciousness that has challenged the finest intellects of the West from Aristotle to the Romantic poets and beyond. A related area of study has focused on what the Moscow neurophysiologist Pavel Simonov has called "the emotional brain."[13] The literature on this topic has conceptualized human moods and feelings as the complex, somatopsychic interaction of brain with collateral organ systems. Still other researchers have investigated the psychobiology of cognition, memory, instinct, sexuality, and language acquisition. American psychobiologist Michael Gazzaniga used modern brain research to account for many of our personal and collective beliefs about life and society. And, retheorizing Freud, Jonathan Winson, among others, has advanced a materialist model of unconscious mental activity. The Nobel-Prize-winning British molecular biologist Francis Crick has even speculated on the implications of the latest neurosciences for consciousness, free will, and the immortality of the human soul.

Yet another indication of the field's intellectual expansiveness has been the

attempt by some exponents to synthesize the neurosciences with powerful paradigms from other branches of science. In a brilliant, far-ranging series of books
published during the late 1980s and early 1990s, Gerald Edelman probed the
theoretical interface between neurobiology and Darwinian evolution. A distinguished biochemist who directs the Department of Neurobiology at the Scripps
Research Institute, Edelman has attempted to apply his widely-discussed theory of
"neuronal cell group selection" to "diseases of consciousness," including schizophrenia, dissociative disorders, affective disorders, and obsessive-compulsive neuroses.[14] Other scientists have tried to integrate brain-based models of consciousness
with computer science theory and artificial intelligence studies.

The jump from the psychiatric body to the social body has perhaps been most
evident in contemporary work on psychiatric genetics. During the 1950s and 1960s,
a series of studies of twins, which suggested the existence of family-based patterns
of mental illness, revived scientific interest in psychiatric genetics, a field disgraced
since the Nazi era. Then, in the 1970s and 1980s, advances in molecular biology
opened up the possibility of identifying the actual gene, or chromosome, involved
in specific psychopathologies. In the genetic world view of the late twentieth
century, nature largely eclipses nurture. Psychiatric geneticists have explored
behaviors believed to be scripted directly into our biological fate regardless of
subsequent environmental variables. They have posited a primary hereditary
background for a wide span of human behaviors and personality traits, ranging
from violence, promiscuity and alcoholism to shyness, sociability and altruism.

During the 1980s and 1990s, researchers isolated genes for cystic fibrosis, muscular
dystrophy, and Huntington's Disease. In light of these discoveries, some medical
authorities believe it is only a matter of time before they lay bare the genetic
foundations of mental and nervous disorders. They see the Human Genome
Project, a worldwide research effort that seeks to isolate the genes on every
chromosome in the human body and to determine their biochemical nature, as
the sourcebook for psychiatry in the twenty-first century. Widely publicized reports
in the 1990s announced the discovery of genetic markers for schizophrenia,
depressive illness, affective disorders, and even alcoholism, drug addiction, and
child hyperactivity.

Not unexpectedly, the most attention-attracting ideas of late twentieth-century
social neurobiology centered on issues of race, gender, and sexuality. In two book-
length studies, a British neuroanatomist working in the United States claimed to
have unriddled the question of the determining cause of sexual object choice.
Simon LeVay maintained that a certain nucleus in the hypothalamus, called the
INAH-3 nucleus, is smaller in homosexual males than in heterosexual males. This
anatomical fact, LeVay argued, is determined by prenatal differentiation of the
brain under the influence of circulating sex hormones. Other researchers claimed
to have located genetic markers for female homosexuality. In a more overtly
sociological idiom, two American social scientists, Richard Herrnstein and Charles

Murray, have argued at great length and with the latest quantitative methods, that the lower intelligence test scores of African-Americans were expressions of innate brain differences.

Beyond doubt, the neuroscientific renaissance of the past quarter-century has generated a flood of information about the functioning of the human brain. Intellectually, the exploration of the chemistry, physiology, and genetics of human mentation has been an extremely exciting project. Current-day neurobiology has illuminated brain function in a way few would have dared to imagine even a generation ago. Similarly, the rise of biochemical psychopharmacology has transformed the treatment of schizophrenia, bipolar affective disorder, and severe depression. The new treatments have alleviated the suffering of hundreds of thousands of individuals. For the first time in human history, many victims of cruel and crippling mental illnesses can hope for real improvement from medicine.

At the same time, late twentieth-century biological psychiatry aroused sharp criticism from numerous quarters on a variety of grounds. Some observers pointed out recurrent difficulties of logic, reasoning, and interpretation in the new literature of neuropsychiatry and noted that many of its findings were inconsistent, inconclusive, and contradictory. Other critics warned of the danger of a kind of neurobiological reductionism. Mindful of the past, many commentators highlighted what they perceive to be the social risks involved in psychiatric genetics. Others expressed fear of the unregulated prescription of powerful mood-altering medications and the possibility of a growing culture of "cosmetic psychopharmacology."[15] On a separate issue of ethical import to an increasing number of people, brain science research required the evisceration of millions of sentient animals in laboratory experiments. Finally, some critics became troubled by the economically invested role of powerful drug companies in fueling a drive to biologize as many human behaviors as possible, behaviors which are then treated chemically. As so often in its past, psychiatry in the late twentieth century was simultaneously the site of great energy and optimism as well as much criticism and anxiety.

## CONCLUSION: HISTORY AND THE PSYCHIATRIC MIND-BODY

The historical record suggests that there exists less a psychiatric body than a psychiatric mind-body, or mind-bodies, continually reconfigured through time. The story of this hybrid creature is unstable, ever-shifting, and ideologically freighted. Each episode in its history involves a relational reconceptualization of its two constituent parts.

While past theories of the psychiatric mind-body have often been opposed to one another, they in fact share a number of features. Each change in the comparative placement of psyche and soma is labeled by sympathetic contemporaries a revolution in psychiatry. Each mind-body paradigm has philosophical implications, moving outward from a technical model of mental illness to a theory of the self. During its high, hegemonic period of influence, each model attempts to extend its interpretative powers to nonmedical domains of culture. And each claims it has been able, or will be able, to solve the Sphinx's riddle of human nature. Each reorientation in theory also declares itself to be predicated on scientific methods and the accumulation of empirical knowledge. In truth, powerful social, cultural, and professional determinants contribute to clinical and scientific considerations.

History suggests further that forms of psychiatric mentalism tend to be more accessible popularly, to have greater cultural applicability, and to be more successful at satisfying those human needs known as spiritual and metaphysical. Their humanistic content appears greater. Psychological theories, however, are typically open to sharp criticism concerning scientific status. For their part, organic models have invariably drawn their strength from neighboring sciences that boast firmer epistemological foundations. They employ a more positivist rhetoric, and they address more effectively psychiatry's longstanding "crisis of legitimacy" as a branch of medicine.[16] In the marketplace competition with other retailers of mental health, the organicist can emphasize new medical knowledge. In their pure and exclusionary forms, both positions are inherently deterministic and reductionistic.

Perhaps most striking, the intertwined histories of the psychiatric mind and body are united in their intellectual absolutism. We might have expected that the study of the psychiatric mind-body in the late twentieth century would have consisted of a synthesis of the accumulated ideas, methods, and insights of many past sciences of the mind. We might have thought that this history would produce evermore subtle and sophisticated understandings of the endless and intricate interweavings of the mental and the physical. By and large, this has not been the case. Despite a few admirable exceptions, and despite an abundance of programmatic statements about the desirability of theoretical eclecticism, the majority of twentieth-century psychiatrists have ascribed causal priority to one category or the other. Psychiatric "brainlessness" has been followed by psychiatric "mindlessness" in a continual cycle of onesidedness.[17] Each theory has strived for comprehensive explanatory power, and each has tended to suppress or supplant alternative models, rather than to view them as potentially complementary and mutually enriching.

At present, a new somatic style dominates. Biological psychiatry has altered almost beyond recognition the science and therapeutics of mental illness. It sustains an international research enterprise, and it consumes immense intellectual, professional, and governmental resources. Some participants believe it represents the definitive and presumably unchanging model of the human mind. The biopsychiatric program appears to be realizing the neophrenological dream of linking mental behaviors with events that are localizable in the brain; in its grander moments, it claims to have answered formidable metaphysical quandaries, like the mind-body problem, that have eluded the foremost thinkers of the past. Only time will test these assertions. This much, however, is certain: at the outset of the twenty-first century, the power, promise, and problems of modern psychiatry are great. For precisely this reason it is imperative to have an historically informed psychiatric profession and a biomedically enlightened public.

## REFERENCES

My thanks to Howard Kushner and Helen Longino for bibliographical guidance and to Joel Braslow, Roger Cooter, Ian Dowbiggin, Paul Lerner, Roy Porter, John Pickstone, and Andrew Scull for close, critical readings of this chapter.

1. Cited in Erwin H. Ackerknecht, *A Short History of Psychiatry*, sec. ed. trans. from the German by S. Wolff. (New York: Hafner, 1968), p. 64.
2. Edward Shorter, *A History of Psychiatry: From the Era of the Asylum to the Age of Prozac*. (New York: John Wiley & Sons, 1997), chap. 3.
3. Karl Jaspers, *Allgemeine Psychopathologie für Studierende, Ärzte und Psychologen* (1913), third edition. (Berlin: Springer, 1923), p. 13.
4. Sigmund Freud, "Notes upon a Case of Obsessional Neurosis" (1909), in James Strachey *et al.*, eds. *The Standard Edition of the Complete Psychological Works of Sigmund Freud*, 24 vols. (London: Hogarth Press, 1960), **10**: p. 157.
5. Josef Breuer and Sigmund Freud, *Studies on Hysteria* [1895], in *Standard Edition*, **2**: p. 30.
6. Philip Rieff, *Freud: The Mind of the Moralist*. (New York: Viking, 1959), chap. 10; Henri F. Ellenberger, *La psychiatrie suisse*. (Paris: L'Évolution psychiatrique, 1950), pp. 748–51.
7. Hans J. Eysenck, *The Decline and Fall of the Freudian Empire*. (New York: Viking, 1985).
8. David Healy, *The Antidepressant Era*. (Cambridge, Mass.: Harvard University Press, 1998).
9. Nancy Andreason, *The Broken Brain: The Biological Revolution in Psychiatry* (1984), p. viii.
10. *Ibid.*, p. 138.
11. *Ibid.*, p. 88.
12. Jean-Pierre Changeux, *Neuronal Man: The Biology of the Mind* [1983], trans. from the French by L. Garey. (New York: Pantheon, 1985), pp. 274, 275.
13. Pavel Simonov, *The Emotional Brain: Physiology, Neuroanatomy, Psychology, and Emotion*, trans. from the Russian by M.J. Hall. (New York: Plenum, 1986).
14. Gerald Edelman, *Neural Darwinism: The History of Neuronal Group Selection*. (New York: Basic Books, 1987); idem., *The Remembered Present: A Biological Theory of Consciousness*. (New York: Basic Books, 1989).
15. Peter D. Kramer, *Listening to Prozac: A Psychiatrist Explores Antidepressant Drugs and the Remaking of the Self*. (New York: Viking, 1993), pp. 45–46.
16. Charles Rosenberg, 'The Crisis of Psychiatric Legitimacy: Reflections on Psychiatry, Medicine, and Public Policy,' in G. Kriegman, R. Gardner and D.W. Abse (eds) *American Psychiatry: Past, Present, and Future* (Charlottesville, Virginia: University Press of Virginia, 1975), pp. 135–48.
17. Leon Eisenberg, 'Mindlessness and Brainlessness in Psychiatry,' *British Journal of Psychiatry* (1986), **148**: pp. 497–508.

## FURTHER READING

Braslow, Joel, *Mental Illnesses and Bodily Cures.* (Los Angeles: University of California Press, 1998).

Berrios, German E. and Freeman, Hugh (eds), *150 Years of British Psychiatry, 1841–1991.* (London: Gaskell, 1991).

Clarke, Andy, *Being There: Putting Brain, Body, and World Together Again.* (Cambridge, Mass.: MIT Press, 1997).

Crick, Francis, *The Astonishing Hypothesis: The Scientific Search for the Soul.* (New York: Charles Scribner's Sons, 1994).

Dahlbom, Bo (ed.), *Dennett and His Critics: Demystifying Mind.* (Oxford: Blackwell, 1993).

Dennett, Daniel, *Kinds of Minds: Towards an Understanding of Consciousness.* (New York: Basic, 1996).

Dicks, H.V., *Fifty Years of the Tavistock Clinic.* (London: Routledge, 1970).

Dowbiggin, Ian, *Keeping America Sane: Eugenics and Psychiatry in the United States and Canada, 1880–1940.* (Ithaca, New York: Cornell University Press, 1997).

Durant, John, 'Brain Research, Animal Awareness, and Human Sensibility: Scientific and Social Dislocations,' in Anne Harrington (ed.) *So Human A Brain: Knowledge and Values in the Neurosciences.* (Boston: Dibner Institute Publication, 1992), 179–92.

Ellenberger, Henri F., *The Discovery of the Unconscious: The History and Evolution of Dynamic Psychiatry.* (New York: Basic, 1970).

Endler, Norman, 'The History of ECT,' in Edler and Emmanuel Persad (eds) *Electroconvulsive Therapy: The Myths and Realities.* (Toronto: Huber, 1988), 3–30.

Freeman, Hugh and Berrios, German E. (eds), *150 Years of British Psychiatry, vol. 1, The Aftermath.* (London: Athlone, 1996).

Gay, Peter, *Freud: A Life for Our Time.* (New York: Norton, 1988).

Gazzaniga, Michael, *Nature's Mind: The Biological Roots of Thinking, Emotions, Sexuality, Language, and Intelligence.* (New York: Basic Books, 1992).

Grob, Gerald N., *Mental Illness and American Society, 1875–1940.* (Princeton: Princeton University Press, 1983).

Hale, Nathan G., *The Rise and Crisis of Psychoanalysis in the United States: Freud and the Americans, 1917– 1985.* (New York: Oxford University Press, 1983).

Henderson, David Kennedy, *The Evolution of Psychiatry in Scotland.* (Edinburgh: Livingstone, 1964).

Herrnstein, Richard J. and Murray, Charles, *The Bell Curve: Intelligence and Class Structure in American Life.* (New York: Free Press, 1994).

Horgan, John, 'Eugenics Revisited,' *Scientific American* (June, 1993), 122–28.

Johnson, F. Neil, *The History of Lithium Therapy.* (London: Macmillan, 1984).

Jones, Kathleen, *Asylums and After: A Revised History of the Mental Health Services: From the Early 18th Century to the 1990s.* (London: Athlone, 1993).

LeVay, Simon, *Queer Science: The Use and Abuse of Research into Homosexuality.* (Cambridge, Mass.: MIT Press, 1996).

Micale, Mark S., *Approaching Hysteria: Disease and Its Interpretations.* (Princeton: Princeton University Press, 1995).

Porter, Roy and Micale, Mark S., 'Reflections on Psychiatry and Its Histories,' in Micale and Porter (eds) *Discovering the History of Psychiatry.* (New York: Oxford University Press, 1994), 3–38.

Postel, Jacques and Quétel, Claude (eds) *Nouvelle histoire de la psychiatrie.* (Toulouse: Privat, 1983).

Reiser, Morton F., *Mind, Brain, Body: Toward a Convergence of Psychoanalysis and Neurobiology.* (New York: Basic Books, 1984).

Rinkel, M. and Himwich, H., *Insulin Treatment in Psychiatry.* (New York: Philosophical Library, 1959).

Scott, Alwyn, *Stairway to the Mind: The Controversial New Science of Consciousness.* (New York: Copernicus, 1995).

Scull, Andrew, 'Somatic Treatments and the Historiography of Psychiatry,' *History of Psychiatry* (1994), 5: 1–12.

Smith, Theresa C. and Oleszczuk, Thomas A., *No Asylum: State Psychiatric Repression in the Former USSR.* (New York: New York University Press, 1997).

Swazey, Judith P., *Chlorpromazine in Psychiatry: A Study of Therapeutic Innovation.* (Cambridge, Mass.: MIT Press, 1974).

Valenstein, Elliot S., *Great and Desperate Cures: The Rise and Decline of Psychosurgery and Other Radical Treatments for Mental Illness.* (New York: Basic Books, 1986).

Zilboorg, Gregory, *A History of Medical Psychology.* (New York: Norton, 1941).

# CHAPTER 23

# The Diseased Body

DAVID CANTOR

The dominant account of Western medicine's portrayal of the body and disease is that it has become increasingly fragmented and reductive in the twentieth century. Modern medicine, the story goes, tends to treat the body and disease as ontologically distinct entities. It focuses on the specific cause of disease at the expense of the body's response to it. It looks at a snapshot of disease, rather than its development over time. It draws a rigid distinction between health and disease. It centers on the parts of the body rather than their inter-relations. And it portrays the body and disease in isolation from the psychological, social and environmental factors that contribute to illness. Medicine's representation of the body and disease is, therefore, characterized by a broad set of often contradictory tendencies to divide, compartmentalize, reduce and fragment. The standard narrative suggests that it was only in the 1960s that a challenge to a reductive account of the body and disease emerged. Crudely put, there are two diseased bodies in this tale; the reductive one of modern medicine, and the holistic one of its critics.

Focusing primarily on Anglo-American clinical medicine, this chapter suggests that such a narrative is quite misleading. Firstly, as Christopher Lawrence and George Weisz (1998) have argued, this tale tends to take the distinction between holism and reductivism as unproblematic. Both terms have had many meanings, and what may be reductivist to some may be holistic to others. For example, a 'holistic' focus on the body as an isolated but internally-integrated and functioning entity may be 'reductive' to those who prefer to explore its relations with a particular physical or social environment. Secondly, the standard account is quite wrong in assuming that it was only in the 1960s that a challenge to medical reductivism emerged. 'Holistic' and 'anti-reductivist' thinking can be traced in clinical medicine throughout the nineteenth century, though the term 'holism' was only coined in 1926. Indeed, the coining of this term is suggestive, for it coincided with a revival in synthetic, integrative thinking *within* clinical medicine; this at the very time that reductive medicine is often portrayed as attaining some of its greatest achievements. Thirdly, the standard account is incorrect in assuming that holistic visions of the body and disease were the sole province of alternative medicine. They can be found in the basic biological sciences as well as in orthodox clinical medicine. This chapter traces concerns over clinical medicine's portrayal of the body and disease as reductive or fragmented.

## DISSOCIATING BODIES FROM DISEASE

The roots of the tensions between fragmented and synthetic accounts of disease and the body can be traced back to early modern medicine. In the early modern period patients and practitioners shared a common framework for understanding illness. For physicians and sufferers alike, illness was something that affected the entire individual. It was peculiar to that individual, a departure from his or her natural and moral state. Sickness followed from a combination of problems, including defects in constitution, inheritance, diet, exercise, sleep, and sexual and bowel habits. It was the result of an imbalance in the bodily humors, a change in the environment, mental illness, or spiritual or moral weakness; a sign of God's displeasure. Moral chaos often resulted from breaking the rules which governed health, as indicated by, for example, the vomiting, sweating or diarrhea that followed intoxication or promiscuity.

Since sickness was peculiar to the individual, diagnosis meant figuring out what the particular problem was from a knowledge of the sick person's life, the recent history of the sickness, and disturbances in the natural, moral and social order. Orthodox medicine had no monopoly on such diagnosis. In a competitive medical market place, and in a world where bodily disorder had powerful social, religious and moral meanings, orthodox practitioners had to pay close attention to their patient's understanding of illness. Thus diagnosis and treatment was often negotiated between doctor and patient. The signs and symptoms of the illness were written on the outside of the body, there for all to read. The inside of the body — "which God did secret make"[1] — was generally closed to view. Practitioners might claim privileged knowledge of the hidden meanings of disease, but they often had no means of enforcing such claims.

By the twentieth century the relationship of the body to disease was quite different. The meaning of illness was often located inside of the body, accessible only to those with the skills and techniques to bring them to light and name them — namely medicine. So too, individual illness increasingly had meaning for medicine only to the extent that it could be mapped onto pathological processes that were common to populations of patients. At the same time, holistic explanations of disease that treated the body as an individual, integrated entity began to give way to more reductive modes of thinking. Medical practitioners increasingly tended to reduce the body to its component parts — cells, organs, and tissues. Disease came to be defined in terms of a lesion specific to these parts or, from the late nineteenth century, in terms of the action of a specific microbe on the body. Furthermore, disease came to be something that could be reproduced outside of the human body, in experimental animals, on the petri-dish, and in tissue culture.

Cancer's grown on mice became models for human cancer. The effects of radiations or chemicals on animal cells grown in tissue culture provided models for their effects on human patients.

Such developments facilitated an increasing tendency among practitioners to dissociate disease and the body. Diseases came to be seen as entities, quite distinct from their manifestation in the individual patient, and therapeutics came to be directed towards the disease rather than the person. Thus, whereas the early modern medical practitioner tended to fit his treatment to each individual patient, his or her twentieth-century counterpart had recourse to a standard set of treatments that could be given to all patients suffering from a particular disease, and supplied by so-called 'ethical' pharmaceutical companies, or by the manufacturers of X-ray and other physical equipment such as sun lamps or electrotherapy apparatus. Patient's illnesses came to be judged in part by the extent to which they responded to a standardized dose: so many physical units of radiation, or milligrams of the active principle of a drug, for example. Older ideas of regime were increasingly standardized and rationalized. The body's dietary requirements were measured out in calories. The body itself was measured and weighed: height and weight became signs of its health or illness.

Such dissociation between body and disease was emphasized by the militaristic and colonial imagery used to describe their relations. In the medical imagination the body was engaged in a 'war,' 'struggle' or 'fight' against disease. From the late nineteenth century, bacteria and viruses were on a mission to 'attack,' 'ravage' and sometimes 'colonize' the body. The body came to be portrayed as a fortress to be protected from invisible armies of germs. It was the site of battle, a 'dugout' for microbes. To an earlier generation, medical attention might have focused on the broad environmental determinants of illness that allowed germs to attack. By the beginning of the twentieth century, practitioners tended to reduce the environment to the immediate home environment, and to focus considerable attention on defending vulnerable portals where the bugs might enter the body — the mouth, nose, anus, and other orifices, natural or not. Increasingly, practitioners saw the removal of the foci of infection as crucial to combating disease.

The body itself also came to be portrayed in dissociated terms. Practitioners often described it as a sort of machine, whose component parts could be treated individually, much as the parts of an engine might be reconditioned or replaced. If a particular part of the body went wrong, the solution was to take it out or to fix it. Instead of treating disease as something that affected the whole person, attention focused on the local phenomena of disease, or on its bacterial or viral cause. Thus, whereas cancer was often something that affected the whole body in the early modern period, by the early twentieth century the focus was on its local tumorous manifestation. The aim of surgery — and later radiotherapy (from the 1900s) and chemotherapy (1940s) — was to destroy the tumor, while inflicting minimal damage to the surrounding tissue.

If dissociated portrayals of the body focused on local structural changes, from about the 1870s they also focused on functional changes. The case of heart disease illustrates the point. Around 1900, clinicians often thought of heart disease in morbid anatomical terms — as, for example, a deformity of the valves — which could be identified by traditional clinical methods of auscultation and percussion, and from the 1890s radiography. In this respect, there was nothing special about heart disease: it was just another structural change in the body. In the first decades of this century, however, some clinicians (often with academic connections) began to utilize concepts and techniques derived from the physiological laboratory to redefine the heart as having peculiar properties such as irritability, rhythmicity and tonicity, which were the basis of normal function: the origins of cardiac disease lay in disturbances in such function. These clinicians adapted devices such as the polygraph and later the electrocardiogram to demonstrate, at the bedside, these properties of the heart. In such ways, the heart was constructed as a discrete object of attention, the focus of a new specialty of cardiology that tended to define disease in functional rather than ontological terms.

Dissociated portrayals of the body and disease can be traced in medical discourse throughout the twentieth century. On the one hand, they tended to be associated with a depiction of the body as a producer of goods and services. From this perspective, when a component of the body went wrong, the bodily mechanism became less efficient, costing industry in lost production and employees in lost wages. Collectively such inefficiency could undermine a nation's industrial com-petitiveness and military preparedness. From the late nineteenth and early twen-tieth centuries, commentators came to fear that losing the war against disease could lead to national and industrial decline. Healthy bodies meant a healthy nation: diseased bodies meant decline and degeneration; an old theme, previously present in, for example, eighteenth-century debates over animal economy. Metaphorically, the image of disease as a disruption of part of the bodily machine came to represent local disturbances that could upset the delicate mechanism of urban, industrial society. To some this analogy warned against excessive individualism and *laissez faire;* to others, it cautioned against an altruism that preserved the maladapted.

On the other hand, dissociated images also tended to be associated with the portrayal of the body as a consumer of goods and services. Images of the body as a machine (which had to be maintained through replacement of worn out parts) or a house (upon which vast sums could be lavished in maintenance) or the focus of a military campaign (which had to be supported through the purchase of a vast pharmaceutical armamentarium) evoked obvious images of consumption. Thus the public was invited to gargle with Listerine or, in the words of a more recent advertisement, to 'kill all known germs dead' with the proprietary disinfectant, Domestos. And when all that failed, the individual was to turn to his or her medical allies for help, and to the increasing array of therapeutic and prophylactic agents emerging from the laboratory in the early part of the century: tuberculin for tuberculosis, diphtheria antitoxin, Salvarsan for syphilis, and numerous gland extracts and therapeutic vaccines. Innovations in biochemistry and in nutrition science supplemented this war against invisible enemies with invisible helpers, such as vitamins, should the individual consume the right sorts of food. Individuals who failed to purchase such commodities could be portrayed as disrupting the social and economic relations which underlay their production and distribution. They also challenged attempts by pharmaceutical advertisers to equate, as Thomas Richards puts it, "the making of the self with the consumption of commodities."[2]

Despite the tendency towards reductivism, holistic, vitalistic and organic understandings of the body and disease persisted in nineteenth-century clinical medicine. Even the late nineteenth-century interest in microbial causes of disease did not shake medical beliefs in, for example, the importance of constitutional explanations of disease and illness. Thus, the discovery of the causative organism for tuberculosis in 1882 did little to undermine the medical conviction that the onset of this disease was dependent on constitution. The ubiquity of the organism appeared to many doctors to argue for the disease's dependency on a variety of predisposing factors: the bacillus seemed a necessary but insufficient cause of the disease, and it was unclear whether its eradication was the best solution. Twentieth-century opponents of the pasteurization of milk, for example, argued that some exposure to tubercle bacillus was necessary. In their view, a tuberculorized body was a healthy body, resistant to the onset of the disease.

Nevertheless, by the late nineteenth and early twentieth centuries a broad range of practitioners came to see dissociated thinking as obscuring the real nature of illness and disease. To such practitioners there were no diseases of cells, organs, or tissues, and disease processes could not be reduced to the action of a microbe on the body or a failing in one body system. Mechanistic and war-like images of the body belied its organic and integrative nature. Diseases, they argued, were little more than 'fictions,' useful means of classifying knowledge perhaps, but not to be confused with the actual manifestation of illness in the individual patient.

For some commentators, part of the reason why people tended to believe in the reality of such fictive entities lay in the fragmented nature of modern, urban society. In such a society, the argument ran, traditional ties of family, kin and neighborhood had been replaced by a sense of uncertainty, loss of direction, and a feeling that individuals were on their own. City-people lived isolated, alienated lives, and their work was often repetitive and compartmentalized. Workers devoted their lives to a particular task on the factory floor: the professional classes were increasingly divided along specialty and occupational lines. Commentators argued that the modern division of labor ensured that few were able to take a broad overall view. Most people saw little further than their own special interests: their minds were limited by the fragmented nature of their lives, and they tended to fit the world to their narrow imagination.

Criticism of fragmented portrayals of the body and disease were thus often criticisms from a broad range of groups — often from a liberal-individualist perspective — of the sort of the society that produced such images. Social fragmentation, some critics claimed, produced minds which were capable only of limited understanding, which interpreted the world from this limited perspective, and which tended to confuse mental categories with material reality. How was it possible, one British physician wondered in 1919, "to believe that there actually exist in Nature objects or things known as 'special diseases,' that attack people physically as do bolshievicks or Huns?"[3] As worrying was the suggestion that such confused and narrow outlooks helped to sustain an antagonistic world-view. In the aftermath of World War I, critics portrayed a world in which people over-identified with the limited part of the whole they knew. Nations were divided against nations, workers against their employers, men against women, Bolshievicks against fascists, and many other divisions; all fed by a 'compartmentality' that refused to rise above narrow interest and view the whole. War-like images of a body engaged in battle against disease came to symbolize anxieties about the antagonistic compartmentalism that pervaded modern society and thought.

If critics worried about the sort of society that produced fragmented visions of the body, they also worried about the ways in which such fragmentation affected medicine. For some, such thinking on disease was evidence of the increasing importance of the bureaucrat in modern medicine. To their critics, bureaucrats had a departmentalistic view of the body and disease. They never treated patients, and so never saw them as individuals. The bureaucrat tended to slot individual patients into pre-existing standardized categories of disease. He or she thus also tended to dictate to practitioners the sorts of care an individual patient might receive by determining the sorts of treatment appropriate to a particular disease. Thus critics attacked those systems in which the bureaucrat dominated, arguing that the growing involvement in medicine of the state and of the insurance industry threatened the autonomy and status of the practitioner, and so the value of care to the patient.

Practitioners also saw fragmented thinking as a product of the increasing role of laboratory scientists and of specialists within medicine. According to such criticisms, laboratory scientists rarely ventured into the wards. Like bureaucrats, they did not see patients. The diseased body for them was the section they saw down the microscope, the part of it they analyzed in the test tube, or grew in the petri dish. They had too narrow a view of disease. They were unable to take a broader view of the patient's illness, and their limited outlook was coming to dominate thinking in the medical schools. So too, such critics complained, specialists took too narrow a view of disease. They focused on a particular part of the body, a certain type of disease, or a specific technique for treating or analyzing it. They rarely looked beyond their own special interests to the broad range of factors that might affect the health of the patient. The diseased body for them was that part of the body or that particular disease they specialized in.

Finally practitioners also saw fragmented thinking on disease as evidence of the working of the mass mind in medicine. By the mass mind, commentators tended to refer to two things. On the one hand, they referred to the tendency to classify people according to the characteristics they shared with others. Thus the bureaucrat, specialist and laboratory scientist were said to exhibit the mass mind by their predilection for pigeonholing people according to pathological features common to particular populations, and so denying the individual and idiosyncratic aspects of illness. On the other hand, the mass mind also referred to the peculiar ways in which people tended to act in groups, often described as a sort of 'herd mentality' that undermined individual will and allowed baser emotions to overcome the higher faculty of reason. The modern mind was therefore characterized not only by fragmentation, but also by irrationality and credulity, which made people particularly prone to be lead. The two concepts were related because, by defining people as part of a group, bureaucrats and others encouraged people to think of themselves as part of a collective with interests quite distinct from and often antagonistic to others.

As criticisms of fragmented thinking emerged, so commentators began to revive older notions of the body and disease, and, from 1926, to label them holistic. In this vision the body was portrayed as an organic system, in precarious and dynamic equilibrium, constantly responding to changes in diet, climate, work, and regimen, all interacting with the body's constitutional make-up to maintain health. A change in any of these factors could result in ill-health, as could the onset of normal developmental changes such as teething and puberty, or menstruation and menopause in women. The body's need for food and water, the changing environment in which it existed, and the emotional and physical assaults to which it was subjected, all necessitated unending physiological adaptations which could make it susceptible to illness. Disease was thus very rarely the result of a specific cause: it was the product of a disequilibrium in the bodily system; the result of a change in the relations between the body and its environment; or the outcome of an emotional or mental upset. The diseased body was as much a product of unhealthy minds, environments and societies, as of pathological changes in its physical make-up.

If the (diseased) body was portrayed as a dynamic integrated entity, the categories used to understand it became problematic. 'Health' and 'disease' were no longer mutually exclusive categories. Instead, they ranged along a spectrum, each color shading discreetly into another. And if 'health' and 'disease' lost their distinct identity, so too did specific disease categories. The body was often portrayed as a sort of container for a shifting set of signs and symptoms that might one day configure as one disease, and later rearrange to form another or disappear altogether. Some illnesses might crystallize out with a distinct identity. Others flitted across the stage of the body like ghosts, blurring into and camouflaging one another, and leaving only the most elusive and misleading hints as to their presence or nature. It all made diagnosis and treatment a particularly tricky problem. A disease could vary from individual to individual, and change with the shifting influence of constitution, mind, and environment: childhood ailments might affect adults very differently; an illness in its early stages was often a very different entity to its later manifestations.

Such a vision of disease and the body could be found in nineteenth-century medicine. Nevertheless, a growing number of practitioners began to argue, especially after World War I, that a 'new' synthetic and dynamic conception of the body and disease was emerging. Such claims were, in part, an attempt by general clinicians to reassert their leadership in medicine over specialists, laboratory scientists and bureaucrats, all of whom had, in their view, too narrow a view of disease. From this perspective, a broad general knowledge of body and disease, combined with an intimate knowledge of the individual patient and his or her circumstances, was essential to understand all the complexities that made up human illness and to treat them. Yet, if the 'new' synthetic approach was represented as an attack on specialists, it was also taken up by many specialists, who sought to integrate generalist values in their particular area, for example by ensuring a long period of training in general medicine before embarking on specialist work. So too, during the 1920s and 1930s 'constitutional,' 'psychological' and 'social' medicine began to emerge as specialties in their own right, all taking a broadly holistic view of the body and disease, albeit emphasizing respectively the role of body, mind and environment in the onset of disease.

The 'new' synthetic account of disease was often cast as an attack on laboratory definitions of disease, but it was also facilitated by laboratory research which portrayed the body in integrative and dynamic terms, as something that responded positively to changes in its environment. Thus, although many practitioners attacked bacteriology for focusing too much attention on the microbial causes of illness, clinicians also turned to bacteriology to bolster the body's ability to fight microbial assaults and to explain the body's response to bacterial and viral infection. For example, was immunity innate or acquired, active or passive, cellular (the work of phagocytes, cells which devoured invading bacteria) or humoral (the work of antitoxins or antibodies directed to bacterial components called antigens)?

So too, clinicians also incorporated insights derived from the physiological laboratory. Thus, although many were anxious that physiological research encouraged a fragmented outlook by defining certain diseases primarily in terms of physiological function, they also welcomed its attempts to understand the functional integration and control of living organisms via a physiological system such as the vegetative, nervous or endocrine systems. Studies included research on how impulses were transmitted through the nervous system via the action of chemicals such as adrenaline; work in physiological chemistry (later biochemistry) which showed how cells were regulated by different chemical catalysts called enzymes; and investigations of how biochemical processes were regulated by internal chemical secretions (from 1905 known as hormones) released by certain organs.

Endocrinology provides an example of the complex nature of this synthetic vision. The first hormone — secretin, which regulated pancreatic enzyme secretion — was isolated in 1902 and was followed rapidly by many others. Some clinicians worried that this would eventually lead to a further fragmented vision of the body as a new range of disorders emerged defined by disturbed endocrine function. Yet they also welcomed its focus on the way the endocrine system served to integrate the body, and on the body's adaptive response to changes in its environment. Endocrinology portrayed the body as a fluid entity, constantly changing with variations in its internal chemistry. While such fluidity fitted well with dynamic visions of disease and its relations with the body and its physical or social setting, it also raised some classificatory problems. Thus in the 1920s researchers discovered that both men and women had male and female sex hormones: previously it was believed that male and female hormones were divided evenly between anatomical men and women respectively. Small changes in the balance of sex hormones could have striking anatomical results that might question the basic human categories of male and female, normal and pathological.

If the 'new' synthetic account of the body was an attempt to come to terms with the fragmented nature of modern society and thought, it also provided a role for practitioners as social commentators. Thus when practitioners claimed that modern society produced fragmented ways of thinking about the body and disease, they also argued for forms of social organization that promoted more suitable models. For a broad range of commentators this meant a return to something like the organic and harmonious forms of social organization that they believed existed prior to industrialization and urbanization, and which would in turn promote organic forms of thinking. At the same time, the 'new' account also provided an organic, vital analogy by which practitioners could conceptualize modern social and economic problems. Thus, concerns about a 'crisis' of civilization could be discussed in terms of Hippocratic notions of 'critical days,' the time when an illness — social or bodily — achieved crisis and began to move towards resolution. So too, mass unemployment, political unrest and economic troubles could be portrayed as disequilibria in societies or economies portrayed as organic entities, like the body constantly adjusting to external threats and internal disorder. Some argued that without intervention by the state such disequilibria would turn pathological. Others argued that new social or economic equilibria or health would reestablished themselves naturally without intervention.

Modern society was thus portrayed as not only mechanistic and fragmented, but also dynamic and organic, constantly responding to change. In turn commentators came to worry about the ability of the human body to adjust. For example, according to the historian T.J. Jackson Lears, the mid-nineteenth century American commodity culture had been organized around an ethos of scarcity. According to this ethos the over-stimulative character of modern, especially urban, life was a major cause of illness, epitomized by neurasthenia or nerve exhaustion, but also many somatic problems. Put briefly, the body could only take so much excitement, and illness could result if the body was overly aroused. In general, the stimulative impulses of the modern world were kept at bay by means of self-control. (Where self-control failed, the remedy was to reduce stimulation; patients being kept in rest and quiet.) But such self-control was at odds with a commodity culture that stressed personal fulfillment through the consumption of commercially-produced goods and services. Thus, during the first decades of the twentieth century the ethos of 'scarcity' eventually gave way to one organized around 'abundance'; the pursuit of emotional fulfillment and endless growth through experience. For those who stressed the value of 'abundance,' the problem of modern life was rooted in the older tendency to keep the stimulative world at bay. The body's ills were a product of the enormous effort needed to maintain self-control. The remedy was to 'open up' towards the world and make it a source of one's self-fulfillment and self-expression.

Many clinicians felt uneasy with the new ethos. In their view commercial attempts to persuade patients to open up to the outside world had enormous dangers. Many continued to argue that modern commodity culture was overly-stimulative and could lead to nervous exhaustion and other ailments, especially among women and children whose bodies were commonly seem to be particularly susceptible. All too often, they claimed, commercial culture played on the emotional vulnerability of people. Quacks, the purveyors of patent medicines, and those orthodox practitioners driven by commercial imperatives tended to promise sensational cures which medicine could not provide. The result was that many patients gave up less-sensational treatments, only to be disappointed in the long term when the promised 'miracle cure' failed to materialize. By then the damage had been done. Practitioners claimed that patients who earlier might have benefited from orthodox medicine were often left in clinically hopeless conditions. In other words, the stimulative effects of modern commodity culture were often at odds with the body's therapeutic requirements. The diseased body of the patient could not be healed unless he or she was persuaded to maintain a particular course of treatment.

Integrative accounts of the onset of illness often fluctuated between the body and environment. Some saw the problem as within the body, others saw it as within the body's physical or social setting. Constitutionalists, for example, tended to fall into the former camp. Many saw individual bodies as the carriers of the pathological histories of their race or type, such 'defects' being passed from one generation or social group to another, and tending, by their multiplication, to lead to racial degeneration. Such a perspective was in part an outgrowth of nineteenth-century concerns about degeneration, the role of heredity in spreading disease, and social Darwinist views that nations and races were entwined in a struggle in which the weakest would loose. In the twentieth century, such a view of the body informed eugenic proposals to breed-out characteristics deemed to be deficient or undesirable through marriage regulation, sequestration of the mentally deficient, sterilization of the unfit, and, in 1930s and 1940s Germany, the murder of Jews, gypsies and the mentally 'unfit'. The German example is the most notorious, but other countries also implemented some of these policies. For example, in the US fears that 'progressive races' would be overwhelmed by diseased 'stock' resulted in restrictions on immigrants with suspected hereditary diseases, such as tuberculosis or polio; the stigmatizing as carriers of infection of African-Americans and newly arrived ethic groups from Asia, Ireland and Central and Southern Europe; and the promulgation by several states of programs of enforced castration and sterilization of so-called degenerate groups such as the feebleminded.

If constitutionalists tended to see the diseased body as the product of a hereditary constitution, those advocating social medicine tended to see it as a product of their environment, susceptible to programs of preventive medicine. If nineteenth century practitioners emphasized the role of broad programs to improve the physical environment, their twentieth-century counterparts increasingly emphasized changes in social behavior: bacteriology, for example, highlighted the role of individual habits and behavior in the spread of infections. Thus, despite attempts at improving housing, air quality and factory conditions, in the first few decades of this century increasing attention came to focus on changing habits of domestic hygiene, and identifying those groups at risk both in terms of their physiological and social characteristics. The most vigorous promoters of this new perspective were public health officials — through welfare programs for infants and mothers, school children, workers, the elderly, the sick and the infirm. Such a role brought public health officials into areas clinicians previously claimed as their own, and one of the reasons why social medicine became so popular among such clinicians was in response to such 'intrusion.' More broadly, it also raised questions as to the balance between individual liberty and public health, perhaps most famously illustrated in the 1900s by the case of Mary Mallone — also known as Typhoid Mary — whom the American authorities institutionalized and demonized as a threat to health because she carried the disease.

## Biomedicine and Neo-holism

After World War II concerns about fragmented portrayals of the body and disease changed as attention focused on what came to be known as the 'biomedical model.' This formulation was in part a restatement of earlier suggestions that medical thinking was dominated by a reductive and mechanistic model of disease and the body that had first emerged with laboratory, state and technological medicine in the nineteenth-century. What was different about the 1960s was that criticisms emerged from a constellation of groups that had not been prominent before. Feminists, minority rights activists, workers organizations, consumer advocates, patient groups, and academic sociologists and social scientists increasingly argued that the biomedical model was almost inevitably political since its reductive emphasis served to divert attention from the social and economic causes and consequences of disease. Some went further, arguing that social and economic interests and values were built into biomedicine's knowledge of disease itself: diseases were 'constructed' categories which routinely incorporated such interests and agendas. It was therefore impossible to divest medical knowledge of its political content without changing the social relations in which it was embedded. In such ways criticisms of the biomedical model were part of a broader critique of power and society that emerged in the 1960s.

For many critics, the biomedical model was sustained by changes in the post-war organizational structure of medicine. The greater involvement of the state and of private insurance companies in health care raised older concerns about the dehumanizing, bureaucratization of medicine. As before the war, the fear was that such organizations would focus care on diseases rather than individual patients. In addition, commentators were also concerned that they would frame diseases in ways that worked against patients: cost-cutting, for example, might be achieved by questioning ills for which no specific biological cause could be isolated. So too, critics pointed out that the vast increase in support for basic biomedical research from government and philanthropic organizations tended to divert attention away from socio-economic causes and consequences of illness: the hope of understand-ing the molecular 'cause' of illness too often provided a justification for inaction on well-known epidemiological 'causes.' Critics thus claimed that basic research provided governments with an excuse for doing nothing on issues that might be politically difficult, and that such research was also encouraged by the tobacco, asbestos, nuclear and chemical industries in an effort to undermine health meas-ures that might harm them commercially.

Critics also linked the biomedical model to the emergence after the war of a 'medico-industrial complex,' a reference to the close inter-connections between medicine, biology and industry akin to the military-industrial complex. Such inter-connections were not new to medicine, but what characterized post-war develop-ments were their scale and complexity. The definition of disease was increasingly dependent on sophisticated, often capital-intensive, technologies and processes provided by biomedical researchers, some of whom were employees, shareholders or executives in industrial corporations. Powerful economic and financial interests were thus vested in particular definitions and treatments of disease. Moreover, the technologies used to define diseases often incorporated assumptions about the sorts of organizations (medical, industrial and financial) necessary to support them. Increasingly medical services involved a complex division of medical labor around laboratory-based and technologically intensive services located in large scale hospitals, often with associated university and industrial research depart-ments.

For many critics the centrality of the hospital to modern health care systems also helped sustain a fragmented understanding of the body and disease. Where once hospital care had focused on the poor and working class, from the 1920s and 1930s middle-class patients increasingly sought treatment in hospital rather than at home. The very groups that tended to advocate an individualist ethos were at risk of being subjected to the deindividualized forms of treatment previously the privilege of the poor. Hospital bureaucrats, their critics claimed, would extend their ability to impose disease definitions on such patients, who would also be fitted into the limited disease categories of specialists and scientists who dominated such institutions. Especially in the US, but also elsewhere, patients increasingly began to seek out specialistic care and to by-pass the general practitioner. Critics despaired that no-one was now responsible for the whole patient; care was divided between many practitioners, none of whom was fully aware of what the other was doing. The result was that patients were often given inappropriate combinations of drugs, or turned from one specialist to another whenever they got dissatisfied.

Other aspects of hospital medicine also generated concerns about fragmentation. Surgeons, to many of their critics, seemed increasingly willing to regard the body in mechanistic terms, each part substitutable if it went wrong. Hearts, lungs, kidneys and other internal organs all became replaceable, while microsurgical techniques in the 1980s allowed severed fingers, arms and other appendages to be rejoined to the body. Some of the replacement body parts came from the recently dead, but others came from living donors. In the age immediately following decolonization, the purchase by the West of human body parts from the Third World highlighted the problematic connections with former colonies. It also raised two other questions of connection. The use of artificial body parts — hips in the 1960s, hearts in the 1980s — prompted debates about the boundaries between human and machine. So too, the use of animal parts in replacement surgery generated questions about the boundaries between humans and animals, and the transfer of animal diseases to humans.

More broadly, critics felt that the prestige of post-war surgery, combined with the success of wonder drugs such as penicillin and high-tech equipment such as the cyclotron or CAT scanners had helped to undermine the sorts of integrative vision proposed by public health officials and advocates of social medicine. Biomedical scientists, for example, successfully used penicillin to argue that the decline of infectious disease was the product of high-technology, scientific medicine rather than public health measures. So too, practitioners used the success of drug and surgical interventions to assert their control over the treatment of chronic and degenerative diseases, increasingly joining acute infectious disease in public attention. For example, after World War II, chronic heart disease came to be treated by radical invasive therapy (including from the 1960s heart transplants), while chronic forms of arthritis came to be treated by the replacement of hips and other joints. Less attention, critics claimed, focused on the social or psychological conditions which gave rise to chronically diseased, disabled and degenerating bodies, or sustained their long term development.

Finally, critics also pointed to changes in the nature of basic science — notably immunology, genetics and molecular biology — as encouraging a reductive and fragmented view of the body and disease. Research in immunology was crucial to the vast expansion of organ transplantations after the war by providing solutions to problems of rejection. It also facilitated the emergence of a new class of diseases defined by disruptions in immunological function. From the early 1980s the most notable of these diseases was AIDS — Acquired Immune-Deficiency Syndrome. In 1984 French researchers showed that AIDS resulted when a virus — eventually named Human Immune-Deficiency Virus (HIV) — deactivated the immune system by destroying certain white blood cells, so making the body vulnerable to a variety of (sometimes previously rare) illnesses.

So too, new classes of genetic disease emerged in the post-war period, especially following the publication in 1953 of the double helix model of DNA, the nucleic acid of the chromosome. From the late 1950s numerous variants of the blood protein hemoglobin were described some being associated with specific diseases such as hemophilia or sickle-cell anemia. From the 1980s, methods of DNA analysis began to be applied to human diseases; the genes at fault in Duchenne muscular dystrophy, Huntington chorea, cystic fibrosis and other conditions were identified and mapped. With the creation of the Human Genome Project in the mid 1980s, which aimed to clone and sequence all the genes on the human chromosome, concern emerged about the implications of DNA testing. For some it was a neutral means of identifying and preventing disease. Others doubted the validity of attempts find the genes 'responsible' for a variety of 'diseases' such as homosexuality and criminality. Thus genetics carried with it the possibility of stigmatizing certain groups and of a return to eugenic policies. Moreover, in those conditions less controversially called 'diseases,' genetics might also divert attention from social and economic causes, while the issue of 'copyrighting' genes raised issues of corporate power in biomedicine. Finally, genetic screening feed into controversies around abortion, euthanasia and privacy. What should be done if a fetus or elderly person was diagnosed with a genetic problem, and who should know about it?

Although, criticisms of the biomedical model came from many groups outside of medicine, many clinicians were also uneasy about the continuing tendency towards reductive portrayals of the body and disease. As before the war, clinicians worried that where once they had collected information by history-taking and physical examination, they had now become (some said 'overly') reliant on diagnostic technologies to collect and measure clinical 'facts.' Diseases, clinician critics claimed, were defined by notionally objective and demonstrable changes in the body's structure or function, that could be quantified by reference to 'normal' physiological movements. Such pathological changes were portrayed as 'entities,' each with their unique identity: cause, clinical picture, results of hospital investigation, natural history, prognosis and appropriate treatment. Such entities were universal in form, progress and content. The personality, religious beliefs, culture and socio-economic status of the patient were largely irrelevant. Medicine had become unresponsive to human needs and concerns.

Clinicians also worried that post-war medicine's conception of disease was overly reductive. Physicians, they claimed, no longer saw diseases as abnormalities in the patient's clinical state, but what the Yale physician Alvan Feinstein called 'para-clinical entities.'[4] Diagnoses of such ills as fever, jaundice or chest pain had largely given way to diseases of morphological structure (coronary artery disease, carci-noma), biochemical function (diabetes mellitus, hyperthyroidism), physiological function (atrial fibrillation, malabsorption) or microbial invasion (viral infection, meningococcemia), and especially from the 1980s immunological function and genetic expression. As in the 1920s and 1930s critics argued that such definitions were a partial and misleading view of disease. Feinstein invoked older images of disease as a 'spectrum,' involving a diverse range of clinical manifestations that might or might not always occur specifically or consistently. Put simply, modern medical textbooks provided little help in distinguishing between forms of a disease that ran different courses. In such cases, clinicians might easily mistake the nature of the illness, for example when faced with the asymptomatic subset in a disease's spectrum.

The existence of such concerns begins to problematize the extent to which the post-war medical portrayal of the body and disease can be characterized as reductive. Some doctors were themselves uneasy about the reductive tendency within medi-cine, and advocated a return to more holistic and humanistic forms of medicine. For example, in the 1940s and 1950s many practitioners cautiously revived older ideas of disease as a problem of adaptation, borrowing the ideas of the Canadian pathologist Hans Selye first developed before the war. Selye argued that in adapting to stresses such as cold, fatigue, infection, starvation, or mental anxiety, protective changes occurred in many of the tissues and organs of the body. An acute attack, he claimed, could result in a temporary departure from homeostasis before a return to the previous physiological state. However, if the stress was too violent or too prolonged a shift to a new level of homeostasis could occur, a new state of adaptation that initiated a wearing down process that could result in disease.

Selye's ideas were given some prominence by the introduction of the drug cortisone in the late 1940s, so problematizing the characterization of post-war wonder-drugs as reductive. Similarly, the depiction of post-war basic research as reductive also needs qualification. For example, while critics argued that immu-nology encouraged the reductive focus of spare-parts surgery, immunologists themselves often claimed that their science reinvigorated holistic and integrative visions of the body. From the 1950s, they claimed, immunology united the humoral and cellular immune responses into a vast immune system that integrated the body alongside the endocrine and nervous systems. It also sustained notions of the uniqueness of the individual by elaborating the ways in which the immune system helped the body to differentiate self and non-self. Finally, immunologists claimed, it also encouraged an ecological view of the body and disease with its focus on unstable boundaries such as between host and parasite or tumor and carrier.

Other developments also problematize the characterization of post-war medicine's vision of the body and disease as reductive. Thus the introduction of mass screening programs for tuberculosis, cancer and other diseases tended to blur the boundary between health and disease. From this perspective, everyone was potentially ill and medical attention focused on monitoring the 'normal' population for incipient illness. Similarly, during the 1950s British general practitioners supplemented their traditional focus on treating disease, by monitoring and treating the 'normal,' as did a number of medical specialties. A new focus on the prevention of disease from its earliest stages and on continuity of care became important claims for post-war general practice. So too, pediatrics supplemented its earlier focus on diseases of children by attending to the normal child — what were normal dietary requirements, hemoglobin levels, or psychological adjustments? And geriatrics supplemented its focus on diseases of old age with attempts to define what was normal in the elderly. Indeed, the 'normal' itself became relative. Normal senescence could only be established by identifying whether changes in a patient were normal for his or her years.

The blurring of the boundary between health and disease was also evident in the use of numerical definitions of health and disease. With the vast array of diagnostic devices available after the war, health and normality were increasingly defined by reference to certain physical and biochemical parameters, such as weight, height, circumference, blood count, hemoglobin level, levels of electrolytes or hormones, blood pressure, heart rate, respiratory rate, heart size or visual acuity. For each measurement there was a numerical range within which the individual was 'normal' and 'healthy,' and outside of which was the 'abnormal,' 'unhealthy' or 'pathological.' For example, hypothyroidism and hyperthyroidism were respectively below and above the normal range of thyroid hormone. Disease was thus a deviation from normal values, accompanied by abnormalities in the structure or function of body organs or systems.

If clinical medicine and science was problematically reductive, the application of new epidemiological techniques to chronic and degenerative conditions further complicate the picture. Thus, in the 1950s the identification by epidemiologists and statisticians of an association between smoking and the increase in mortality from lung cancer challenged older models of specific causality which stated that to be considered a 'cause' a particular agent had *always* to be associated with a particular disease and proved through animal experimentation. Despite initial resistance, by the 1960s official reports in Britain and the US began to accept multi-causal models of lung cancer proved through statistical techniques. To prove a causal relationship between smoking and lung cancer one no longer had to demonstrate a consistent relationship between the habit and the disease. Such thinking eventually opened the way to the risk-factor concept of disease, which stated that persons exposed to an aetiological factor were *more likely* to develop a particular disease.

More broadly, from the 1950s and especially the 1960s, medicine's claim to have reduced infectious disease was increasingly challenged by epidemiologic and demographic studies that suggested that its contribution to mortality decline was second to improvements in the standard of living and public health measures, and that it had done little to reduce inequalities in health: the poor, women and minority groups were more prone to ill-health than the rich. As worrying was the fear that even in those areas where high-technology medicine had triumphed, the success might be short-lived. Thus although antibiotics were originally portrayed as a major triumph of high-technology scientific medicine, this triumph came to be questioned following problems of over-prescribing, the emergence of drug-resistant strains of bacteria, and the re-emergence in the 1980s of nineteenth-century killers such as tuberculosis. Increasingly, the effectiveness of such drugs was understood in ecological terms. So too, the emergence of AIDS challenged the hopes invested in curative medicine built upon the model of infectious disease. HIV attacked the body's immune system which treatments for infectious diseases tended to rely on for support. Such problems have promoted a greater emphasis on prevention and the management of AIDS as a chronic disease.

If changes in medicine challenged the dominance of the biomedical model within medicine, so too from the 1960s did the growing interest of other groups in medical issues. Sociologists argued that categories of disease were social labels which often stigmatized the ill, encouraged victim-blaming, and so constituted part of the problem of illness for the sick. Feminists highlighted the ways in which such labels reinforced sexual and gender stereotyping, while others pinpointed the assumptions about class and race built into such 'constructed' categories. Disability rights activists and patients' groups questioned the ways in which the biomedical model could explain the experiences of illness or disablement, or provide practical help in living with such conditions. Although some people found comfort in the knowledge that their conditions were not 'simply psychological,' studies showed that such beliefs did not imply that the lay public valued biomedical models of disease in the way that doctors valued them. Such public beliefs could be understood in terms of individual attempts to come to terms with the effect of (often chronic) illness or disablement in their lives, and raised important questions about the meanings of science in the lives of ordinary people.

With the recognition that diseases were labels that might stigmatize came hopes that knowledge of disease might be stripped of its political aspects. If prejudicial language were abandoned, the 'real' nature of a disease might be distinguished from the social or cultural responses to it. From the late 1960s, however, others came to argue that it was impossible to rid the biomedical model of its political content, since social, political and economic interests and agendas were an integral part of biomedical knowledge itself. If this was the case, then it was unclear to what extent biomedical accounts of disease should predominate over others. The point was emphasized by biomedicine's inability to deal adequately with chronic and degenerative conditions such as cancer, arthritis and AIDS or a variety of ills thought to characterize the late twentieth century — attention deficit disorder, hypoglycemia, anorexia nervosa, bulimia, chronic fatigue syndrome, repetitive strain injury, multiple chemical sensitivity. Concern about medicine's response to these conditions brought to public prominence a disjunction between lay and medical perspectives of disease and the body. Such a disjunction was nothing new. But such illnesses have been the focus of attempts to re-privilege lay accounts of the body and disease and so to empower patients. Whether such empowerment will result is unclear. Attempts by American religious fundamentalists to portray AIDS as a 'gay plague' and divine punishment, suggests that certain lay accounts of illness can be as stigmatizing and repressive as the allegedly neutral biomedical accounts they seek to challenge.

## REFERENCES

1.  Jonathan Sawday, *The Body Emblazoned. Dissection and the Human Body in Renaissance Culture.* (London and New York: Routledge, 1995), p. 98.

2.  Thomas Richards, *The Commodity Culture of Victorian England: Advertising and Spectacle, 1851–1914.* (London and New York: Verso, 1991), Chapter 4.

3.  F.G. Crookshank, 'The Importance of Symptoms,' *West London Medical Journal* (1919), **24**: 50–60: p. 53.

4.  Alvan R. Feinstein, 'Science, Clinical Medicine, and the Spectrum of Disease,' in Paul B. Beeson, Walsh McDermott, James P. Wyngaarden, *Cecil Textbook of Medicine*, [Fifteenth Edition]. (Philadelphia: W.B. Saunders, 1979), 3–6, p. 4; see also Alvan R. Feinstein, *Clinical Judgment.* (Baltimore: Williams & Wilkins, 1967).

## FURTHER READING

### GENERAL

Armstrong, David, *The Political Anatomy of the Body: Medical Knowledge in Britain in the Twentieth Century.* (Cambridge: Cambridge University Press, 1983).

Brandt, Allan M., 'The Cigarette, Risk and American Culture', *Daedalus* (1990), **119**: 115–76.

Bynum, W.F. and Roy Porter (eds), *Companion Encyclopedia of the History of Medicine*, (Two Volumes). (London and New York: Routledge, 1993).

Canguilhem, Georges, *The Normal and the Pathological.* (New York: Zone Books, 1989), [Originally published 1966].

Foucault, Michel, *Birth of the Clinic: An Archaeology of Medical Perception*, [trans. A.M. Sheridan Smith]. (London: Tavistock, 1973).

Helman, Cecil, *Culture, Health, and Illness: An Introduction for Health Professionals.* (Bristol and Boston: Wright-PSG, 1984).

Jewson, N.D., 'The Disappearance of the Sick-man from Medical Cosmology, 1770–1870' *Sociology* (1976), **10**: 225–244.

Kiple, Kenneth F. *et al.* (eds), *The Cambridge World History of Human Disease.* (Cambridge and New York: Cambridge University Press, 1993).

Kraut, Alan M., *Silent Travelers. Germs, Genes, and the "Immigrant Menace."* (Baltimore and London: Johns Hopkins Press, 1995), [First Published 1994].

Lawrence, Christopher, *Medicine and the Making of Modern Britain, 1700–1920.* (London: Routledge, 1994).

Lears, T.J. Jackson, 'From Salvation to Self-Realization,' in Richard Wrightman Fox and T.J. Jackson Lears (eds), *The Culture of Consumption: Critical Essays in American History, 1880–1980*. (New York: Pantheon Books, 1983), 1–38.

Oudshoorn, Nelly, *Beyond the Natural Body. An Archaeology of Sex Hormones*. (London and New York: Routledge, 1994).

Rabinbach, Anson, *The Human Motor; Energy, Fatigue, and the Origins of Modernity*. (Berkeley & London: University of California Press, 1992).

Rosenberg, Charles E., *Explaining Epidemics and Other Studies in the History of Medicine*. (Cambridge: Cambridge University Press, 1992).

Rosenberg, Charles E. and Janet Golden (eds), *Framing Disease: Studies in Cultural History*. (New Brunswick, New Jersey: Rutgers University Press, 1992).

Temkin, Owsei , 'The Scientific Approach to Disease: Specific Entity and Individual Sickness', in *The Double Face of Janus and Other Essays in the History of Medicine*. (Baltimore and London: Johns Hopkins University Press, 1977), 441–455.

Tomes, Nancy, *The Gospel of Germs. Men, Women, and the Microbe in American Life*. (Cambridge, Mass. & London: Harvard University Press, 1998).

## HOLISM AND DISEASE

Cantor, David (ed.), *Hippocrates and Modern Medicine*. (Aldershot: Ashgate, forthcoming) especially the papers by Cantor, Weisz and Timmermann.

Cross, Stephen and William R. Albury, "Walter B. Cannon, L.J. Henderson, and the Organic Analogy', *Osiris* (1987), **3**: 165–92.

Lawrence, Christopher and George Weisz (eds), *Greater than the Parts: Holism in Biomedicine, 1920–1950*. (New York & Oxford: Oxford University Press, 1998).

Porter, Dorothy, 'John Ryle: Doctor of Revolution?', in Dorothy and Roy Porter (eds), *Doctors, Politics and Society: Historical Essays*. (Amsterdam and Atlanta: Rodopi, 1993), pp. 247–74.

Tracy, Sarah, 'George Draper and American Constitutional Medicine, 1916–1946: Reinventing the Sick Man', *Bulletin of the History of Medicine* (1992), **66**: 53–89.

## SPECIFIC DISEASES

Bates, Barbara, *Bargaining for Life. A Social History of Tuberculosis, 1876–1938*. (Philadelphia: University of Pennsylvania Press, 1992).

Bliss, Michael, *The Discovery of Insulin*. (Edinburgh: Paul Harris, 1983).

Brandt, Allan M., *No Magic Bullet: A Social History of Venereal Disease in the United States since 1880*. (New York: Oxford University Press, 1985).

Brumberg, Joan Jacobs, *Fasting Girls: The Emergence of Anorexia Nervosa as a Modern Disease*. (Cambridge Mass.: Harvard University Press, 1988).

Bryder, Linda, *Below the Magic Mountain: A Social History of Tuberculosis in Twentieth Century Britain*. (Oxford: Clarendon Press, 1988).

Bynum, W.F., C. Lawrence and V. Nutton, *The Emergence of Modern Cardiology*. (*Medical History Supplement No. 5*. (London: Wellcome Institute for the History of Medicine, 1985).

Dubos, René and Jean Dubos, *The White Plague. Tuberculosis, Man and Society*. (New Brunswick, NJ: Rutgers University Press, 1987), [First Published 1952].

Fee, Elizabeth and Daniel M. Fox (eds), *AIDS: The Burdens of History*. (Berkeley and London: University of California Press, 1988).

Fee, Elizabeth and Daniel M. Fox (eds), *AIDS: The Making of a Chronic Disease*. (Berkeley: University of California Press, 1992).

Gould, Tony, *A Summer Plague: Polio and Its Survivors*. (New Haven: Yale University Press, 1995).

Leavitt, Judith Walzer, *Typhoid Mary. Captive to the Public's Health*. (Boston: Beacon Press, 1996).

Ott, Katherine, *Fevered Lives: Tuberculosis in American Culture Since 1870*. (Cambridge: Mass. & London: Harvard University Press, 1996).

Patterson, James T., *The Dread Disease: Cancer and Modern American Culture*. (Cambridge Mass: Harvard University Press, 1987).

Proctor, Robert N., *Cancer Wars: How Politics Shape What We Know and Don't Know About Cancer.* (New York: Basic Books, 1995).

Rogers, Naomi, *Dirt and Disease. Polio before FDR.* (New Brunswick, NJ.: Rutgers University Press, 1992).

Rosner, David and Gerald Markowitz, *Deadly Dust: Silicosis and the Politics of Occupational Disease in Twentieth Century America.* (Princeton: Princeton University Press, 1991).

Rothman, Sheila M., *Living in the Shadow of Death: Tuberculosis and the Social Experience of Illness in American History.* (New York: Basic Books, 1994).

Smith, F.B., *The Retreat of Tuberculosis, 1850–1950.* (London & New York: Croom Helm, 1988).

Teller, Michael, *The Tuberculosis Movement. A Public Health Campaign in the Progressive Era.* (Westport Conn: Greenwood Press, 1988).

Wailoo, Keith, *Drawing Blood. Technology and Disease Identity in Twentieth-Century America.* (Baltimore and London: Johns Hopkins Press, 1997).

## EUGENICS

Adams, Mark B. (ed.), *The Wellborn Science. Eugenics in Germany, France, Brazil and Russia.* (New York: Oxford University Press, 1989).

Barkan, Elazar, *The Retreat of Scientific Racism: Changing Concepts of Race in Britain and the United States Between the World Wars.* (Cambridge: Cambridge University Press, 1992).

Burleigh, Michael, *Death and Deliverance. "Euthanasia" In Germany c.1900–1945.* (Cambridge: Cambridge University Press, 1994).

Burleigh, Michael and Wolfgang Wippermann, *The Racial State: Germany, 1933–1945.* (Cambridge: Cambridge University Press, 1991).

Cravens, Hamilton, *The Triumph of Evolution. American Scientists and The Heredity-Environment Controversy, 1900–1940.* (Philadelphia: University of Pennsylvania Press, 1978).

Göetz, Aly, Peter Chroust and Christian Pross, *Cleansing the Fatherland. Nazi Medicine and Racial Hygiene.* (Baltimore: Johns Hopkins University Press, 1994).

Haller, Mark H., *Eugenics. Hereditarian Attitudes in American Thought.* (New Brunswick, NJ: Rutgers University Press, 1984).

Hasian, Marouf Arif Jr, *The Rhetoric of Eugenics in Anglo-American Thought.* (Athens: University of Georgia Press, 1996).

Jones, Greta, *Social Hygiene in Twentieth Century Britain.* (London and Wolfeboro, N.H.: Croom Helm, 1986).

Kevles, Daniel, *In the Name of Eugenics. Genetics and the Uses of Human Heredity.* (Cambridge: Mass. and London: Harvard University Press, 1995), [First Published 1985].

Kuhl, Stefan, *The Nazi Connection. Eugenics, American Racism, and German National Socialism.* (New York: Oxford University Press, 1994).

Kuklick, Henrika, *The Savage Within. The Social History of British Anthropology, 1885–1945.* (Cambridge: Cambridge University Press, 1995).

Larson, Edward J., *Sex, Race and Science. Eugenics in the Deep South.* (Baltimore and London: Johns Hopkins Press, 1995).

Mazumdar, Pauline M.H., *Eugenics, Human Genetics, and Human Failing: the Eugenics Society, Its Sources and Its Critics in Britain.* (London & New York: Routledge, 1992).

Pernick, Martin S., *The Black Stork: Eugenics and the Death of "Defective" Babies in American Medicine and Motion Pictures Since 1915.* (New York and Oxford: Oxford University Press, 1996).

Proctor, Robert N., *Racial Hygiene. Medicine Under the Nazis.* (Cambridge, Mass. and London: Harvard University Press, 1988).

Reilly, Philip P., *The Surgical Solution. A History of Involuntary Sterilization in the United States.* (Baltimore and London: Johns Hopkins Press, 1991).

Searle, G.R., *Eugenics and Politics in Britain, 1900–1914.* (Leyden: Noordhoff International Pub., 1976).

Stephan, Nancy, *The Idea of Race in Science. Great Britain, 1800–1960.* (London: Macmillan, 1982).

Thomson, Mathew, *The Problem of Mental Deficiency: Eugenics, Democracy, and Social Policy in Britain c.1870–1959.* (Oxford: Clarendon Press, 1998).

Weindling, Paul, *Health, Race, and German Politics between National Unification and Nazism, 1870–1945.* (Cambridge: Cambridge University Press, 1989).

# CHAPTER 24

# The Disabled Body

ROGER COOTER

The late twentieth century might easily be described as the age of disability (at least in Western nation states). Public consciousness of the rights and needs of physically and mentally handicapped persons was never greater, in part because disability rights advocates were never more outspoken on the social prejudices and economic injustices suffered by the disabled. By analogy with racism and sexism, 'disablism' was coined to summarize and subvert such discrimination. At the same time, in the same Western states, politicians and others entered into fierce and fundamental debate over welfare expenditure on a much broader category of disabled persons — the 'chronically disabled.' Included in this group were not only the victims of AIDS and sufferers from coronary, respiratory and other degenerative conditions, but also those incapacitated through afflictions commonly associated with old age, such as severe arthritis and rheumatism. Over the second half of the twentieth century the size of this disabled population grew dramatically, and since it required expensive long-term medical maintenance, politicians rightly feared its 'crippling' effects on state economies. By 1977 public expenditure on the chronically disabled in the US alone was nearly $50 billion. Contemporary advocates of the healthy body could argue that we were all doomed to this costly future for failing to take affirmative action against every conceivable risk to our health. From that perspective the disabled body in the disabled state became the fate to which we were all destined.

More awesome destinies were reflected in other contemporary discussions around the disabled body. Prominent were the ethical and religious debates over the prevention and elimination of certain disabling conditions through medical interventions, whether initiated genetically, antenatally, or postnatally. While the routine monitoring and manipulating of 'defective' genes in the parents of would-be disabled children was still some time off, the screening for and aborting of fetuses manifesting signs of potential disablement became commonplace. The 'selective management of severely disabled new-borns' became widely practiced. Although doctors did not necessarily control the decision making, in all such procedures the disabled body was posed as the rationale for intervention. The specter of disablement gave urgency to questions over the equality of fetuses, over who was responsible for making antenatal life-and-death decisions, and (in the case of deciding for the fetus) who was to be financially responsible for the maintenance of the 'disabled' humans, and on what social philosophical grounds? In such discussions (as my inverted commas are meant to reflect) social constructions of 'disability' were recognized as inseparable from the ethics, economics and politics of disablement.

Different, though no less controversial, became another consideration: the view of disability as a part of the 'postmodern condition'. The 'normal' body, some intellectuals came to argue, was increasingly prosthetic; it was tied to and dependent in all sorts of ways upon 'higher-order' cyborg technologies which threatened to radically transform the social and psychic order. Whether the 'disabled' were those wired to the new limbs of artificial intelligence and information technology or those deprived of them, was open to interpretation. The interpretation was no easy matter, however, for sophisticated prosthetic technology was also advocated by many as the solution to a wide range of physical handicaps. Behind the interpretive problem, moreover, lay the more crucial question to which disability activists increasingly drew attention: what is the 'normal' body? Even if chronic disability and/or prosthetic envelopment was not to be everyone's fate, it could be appropriate to speak of the majority of people being, at best, merely 'temporarily abled' over the course of their lives. If 'normalcy' was recast, then 'dis-ability' was removed from the pejorative category of pathology. 'Disabilism' disappears in a world of merely 'differently-abled' people.

Thus in a variety of far from trivial ways, the disabled body became central to late twentieth-century thought, as well as to formal politics and health economics. Albeit according to different definitions and understandings of 'disability,' it was a body embedded in political economy and inscribed with social, cultural, religious, moral and ideological values and uncertainties.

This chapter outlines the emergence of this body in the twentieth century. Accepting that the human body (like everything else) is what it is, and does what it does "because of the categories in which it is conceptualized,"[1] or, as Ian Hacking has put it, we "make up people"[2] by the categories we assign or invent for them, I concentrate here on the history of the categorization of disability. In particular, my focus is in relation to those persons with visible neuromuscular or orthopedic abnormality, and especially those who acquired rather than inherited such conditions, for in the course of the twentieth century, for historical reasons, it was principally they who were conventionalized as 'the disabled.' Drawing mainly on British examples, this chapter surveys the institutions and agencies that compelled or necessitated the deployment of the category, and the forces that sustained and transformed it. Central to the discussion — developed more fully in the second part of the chapter — is the role of medicine in framing the concept of disability and in socializing others into it. Medical practitioners were involved with the physically disabled for most of the twentieth century, but what that involvement consisted of in practice and whether, through it, the disabled were 'medicalized' (and what that might mean) are matters for inquiry. Such questions merit our attention, not least because for much of the second half of the twentieth century they preoccupied those involved with disability — not only sociologists and administrators of welfare services, but the disabled themselves and those who became politically active on their behalf.

## THE POLITICS OF DISABLEMENT

The poor, the maimed, the halt, and the blind may have always been with us, but 'the disabled' have not. While the cultural practice of translating physical abnormality into social inferiority (stigmatization) extends deep into the past, 'the disabled,' as a separate administrative category of state welfare, are almost wholly a creation of the twentieth century. Before the late nineteenth century there was little incentive for anyone to be labeled 'disabled.' As far as the state was concerned, persons who were physically handicapped were not unlike other sick, impotent or old persons in their dis-ableness, or inability to work or fight and, hence, crucially, in their dependence on relief. An Act of 1603 in Britain lumped together all such persons requiring 'necessary relief,' and this remained unchanged with the new Poor Law of 1834 which was to see the indigent disabled attended in workhouses by parish doctors. Although the architects of the new Poor Law had sought to construct welfare eligibility around the capacity to work, welfare continued to be dispensed according to the moral imperative of the 'deserving' (in part because 'able-bodied' was difficult to define precisely). A cripple might be more deserving than a non-cripple, but the criteria of evaluation was not around his or her disability. A physical handicap was at most a recognition of the continuation of a form of sickness; it was not a warrant for extra benefits or a recognition of special needs.

In only one respect were some physically disabled persons slightly different from other welfare recipients: the instability of their disabledness. As their bodies often wandered between degrees of impairment, improving and deteriorating, so they wandered between employment and nonemployment, the degree of impairment and the capacity for employment often being causally connected. Such persons were often problematic for purposes of welfare administration, in particular, because this 'vagrancy' of body suggested, and was strongly associated with, deception or 'cripple fraud'. The association with fraud long predated the classification of disability that came into being during the late nineteenth century and the application of those conditions to welfare eligibility criteria. It has been argued, though, that because of the close association between disability and deception, "the very category of disability was developed to incorporate a mechanism for distinguishing the genuine from the artificial,"[3] or the 'deserving' from the 'undeserving.' Thus definitions of disability and the means to determine the category became intimately linked.

One of the primary sites for the elaboration of the distinction between real and feigned disability was in the military, and it was here where disability-based exemptions were first introduced. At least since the Napoleonic wars, states have been concerned with soldiers who malingered to evade conscription, avoid action, or secure pensions. One of the main functions of the medical profession in the military was to guard against such deception, as well as to gatekeep pensions for the deserving disabled.

Appropriately, it was in reference to injured soldiers and sailors that the word 'disabled' had its main application prior to the twentieth century. The term mostly denoted honorable decrepitude often allied to old-age, as in an appeal of 1710 on behalf of 'poor disabled soldiers pensioners and out-pensioners of the Royal Hospital at Chelsea,' or as in the mariner John Griffin's *Proposals for the relief and support of maimed, aged, and disabled seamen* (1745). Outside the military the most common usage in the nineteenth century was in reference to equal rights, especially in relation to women, as in the article on "The Political Disabilities of Women" in the *Westminister Review* in 1872. On the basis of the latter usage, while it might have been anachronistic, it would not have been etymologically incorrect for late twentieth-century disability rights advocates to have campaigned against the 'disabilities of the disabled.'

Beyond the military, a social, economic or even medical concept of disability could have existed in the absence of the word. To some extent this became the case towards the end of the nineteenth century when one group — 'crippled' children — came to be socially segregated. Their segregation was largely a consequence of the education acts adopted in most Western states by the late 1870s. Certain children, overwhelmingly those from slums and suffering mostly from rickets and tuberculosis of the bones and joints, began to look conspicuous by their absence from school, and efforts were made to solicit special provision for them. However, the differentiating of these children has to be seen in the first instance in terms of the exclusion of *all* children from the labor market, rather than a categorization of the disabled per se. Through compulsory primary education all children were 'dis-abled' insofar as they were placed in positions of economic dependence. As Viviana Zelizer has phrased it, the wage-earning child of the working class was transformed into the worthless but emotionally precious middle-class child-scholar. For most children, though, this was only a temporary 'disablement;' primary education, moreover, was in part conceived as an occasion to inculcate into them the virtues of industry and discipline that would better 'enable' them for employment. The uniqueness of crippled children in this context was their enrollment as exemplars of the prevailing pedagogy and ideology. For the Charity Organization Society and similar voluntarist bodies at the turn of the century, the crippled child who could be encouraged to stand or walk without a crutch provided a model of self-help; glowing representations of crippled children triumphing over their handicaps provided an idealization of what (without state aid) individuals could do for themselves. In cripples' homes, such as that established by the carpet manufacturer Sir William Purdie Treloar at Alton in Hampshire in 1906 (expressly as a 'labor colony'), crippled children were transformed into 'useful and independent' members of society, capable of standing up to "the emery wheel of competition."[4] Cases deemed unimprovable were excluded from these homes, just as mentally handicapped children (also made more visible by universal education) were generally excluded from this kind of rhetorical exploitation. Indeed, the crippled children's movement of the late nineteenth and early twentieth-century largely succeeded in having the word 'cripple' restricted to only those children with mobility impairment.

A part of the wider context in which the 'economically worthless' crippled children of the laboring poor became 'ideologically precious' was the introduction of workmen's compensation. There is no need here to review the background to this legislation which was introduced into the same industrial states as introduced compulsory primary education, and at roughly the same time. Suffice it to say that for the first time in the sphere of industrial employment (as opposed to welfare) disability benefit became the responsibility of the state. It should be noted, however, that although accidental injury at the workplace became compensable, 'disability' under this legislation applied mainly to industrial or occupational diseases. As under National Health Insurance (NHI) in Britain (implemented in 1913) disability benefit was "the continuation of sickness benefit under another name and at a lower rate."[5]

As this suggests, disability in the context of workmen's compensation and NHI was more an administrative than a social category. Doctors were enrolled into it as certifiers of disablement and as agents for the insurers in calculating benefits in relation to degrees of inability to work. Nevertheless, as in the military, disability claims were never outside a social and disciplinary framework. Concerns over malingering or worker frauds in respect to benefits preoccupied employers and state administrators from the moment the legislation was introduced. Those concerns reached a feverish pitch just before the outbreak of World War I, to the extent that doctors themselves came under state surveillance for their supposed 'lax certification' of disability. Against this backdrop it is not difficult to further comprehend the appeal of crippled children to certain sectors of the ruling class: the alleged innocence of these children (and their practical exclusion from the labor market) served to highlight a disability that was ostensibly disconnected from deception.

The First World War added massively to the disabled population and greatly extended medical involvements. In Britain by 1918, twenty special military orthopedic centers had been established for the care and rehabilitation of the disabled (some 65 per cent of all the casualties of the war involved impairment of locomotor functions). Other hospitals were requisitioned for the treatment of non-orthopedic disabilities as well as for fitting artificial limbs. At the front, doctors were not only involved with the primary treatment of the wounded, but, more pervasively, with the detection of malingering. Yet, for all this, it is not clear that the war radically altered conceptions of disability or, for that matter, permanently changed public assumptions and attitudes. Pre-war disabled adults soon found that, with no uniform to wear, their begging bowls went empty. And once the war was over — especially when the economic recession of the early 1920s set in — disabled veterans suffered neglect, medical as much as social and political. Only in America, partly in response to the political strength of veterans, was vocational legislation introduced "to convert wounded soldiers into useful citizens."[6]

As Seth Koven has shown for Britain, it was essentially into the ideological construction of the crippled child that the disabled soldiers of World War I were cast. They were even compelled to occupy many of same institutions as crippled children. Here, ironically, they were reduced to child-like soldier boys, fitting in with a further pre-war (masculine) imaging of crippled children as 'brave little warriors' aspiring to the noblest expressions of adulthood and citizenship, to fight for their country. Moreover, because the majority of those disabled in the war suffered from locomotor injuries, they also conformed to and helped consolidate the narrow association of the word 'disabled' with mobility impairment. Significantly, the victims of shellshock and gas poisoning were initially denied this status and were forced to occupy a medical and symbolic no-man's land between woundedness and sickness, the latter being associated with effeminacy, degeneracy, and malingering. Only rarely before the 1960s did medical journals refer to the 'mentally disabled.'

Finally, although the First World War introduced a category of disabled persons who were separate from the sick, it did not redefine disablement outside the economic parameters of industrial labor. Among troops, governments, and the medical profession, disablement through military action meant the same as inability to return to full able-bodied labor. The conflation of war-disabled with labor-disabled was perhaps inevitable, for the Great War was waged overwhelmingly by civilian workers, and the experience of the war was industrial for all intents and purposes. It was highly mechanized and troops went to the front in shifts. In their diaries soldiers spoke of being engulfed by "the industrialism of war."[7] Pensions were finely graded (by a growing body of medical experts) to the veteran's degree of incapacity to compete in the labor market. Even the phenomenon of phantom limbs among those who lost arms and legs was reduced to "hallucinations brought on by the memory of physical labour,"[8] as was maintained by Jules Amar, the war-time and post-war Director of the French 'Laboratoire de prothése militaire et travail professionnel.' Such reductions of disability to this single aspect of productive capacity were to remain dominant for nearly half a century within the discourse on rehabilitation, even though, as early as the 1920s, there was often talk of restoring the disabled to participation in leisure activities and social life generally. For the socialist physician-turned-historian Henry Sigerist in the 1930s, no less than for the liberal policy maker William Beveridge in his famous *Report* of 1944, the reintegration of disabled persons into labor markets was perceived as a primary goal of modern medicine.

During the first half of the twentieth century then, the disabled body was constructed primarily in terms of the industrial body, or the productive body, or the ergonomic body. The medical profession was involved in its measure and in gatekeeping benefits, but it neither constructed the category nor controlled its social use. Predominantly, as Wilhelm Reich and others of the interwar generation believed of the human body in general, the disabled body was "shaped by the world of machinery."[9] The industrial or war-disabled body served to illustrate and epitomize this world: medical practitioners spoke of "repairing the human machine"[10] whilst replacing lost limbs with mechanical ones that literally rendered the worker a part of a machine, or adapted him (rarely her) to a particular mechanical function. Often, however, the work performed by these re-'naturalized' industrial bodies was construed not as work at all, but as therapy. In some respects (especially in some protected vocational settings) these were 'patients' not workers and, therefore not strikers, as large-scale employers of the disabled such as Henry Ford appreciated. And, of course, like crippled children before them, these reconstructed men-machines nicely served ideological as well as productive ends.

The disabled-yet-productive (or potentially-productive) body was one well suited to celebrating the moral discourse of the 'deserving.' But this was not the only way in which the disabled body was socially constructed and morally valorized. A range of non-economic factors, from aesthetics and religion to racism and sexism continued to shape the image and the experience of disablement. American feature films in the 1930s, possibly in response to the economic disablement of the state, seldom tired of rehearsing the role of these other factors, melodramatically reinforcing through them stereotypes of the disabled as persons to be both pitied and admired for their moral purity and courage. The 'good' but physically 'flawed' rise from their wheelchairs or discard their orthopedic shoes and crutches to walk, not onto the factory floor, but into romantic sunsets, accompanied by those whose enlightened gaze sees beyond mere physical stigmata. Between them, love and modern medicine conquer physical adversity, as in *Have a Heart* (MGM 1934) and *The Best Man Wins* (Columbia 1935), or in *The Healer* (Monogram 1935) where little 'soldier' Jimmy miraculously regains the use of his legs to cycle for the help that saves the day. Except when the paralysis was faked, as in *The Black Room* (Columbia 1935), which inevitably brings the malingerer to a sticky end, the role of the disabled in these films was heart-plucking. Medicine, however, did not always feature so benignly. While surgery proudly serves crippled Barbara in *Great O'Malley* (Warner 1936), wheelchaired *Winnie in City Streets* (Columbia 1938) fares poorly at the hands of a exorbitantly expensive recent European emigé surgeon. And although the main character in *The Ape* (Monogram 1940) eventually rises from his wheelchair as a result of the serum therapy administered by the sinister doctor played by Boris Karloff, the doctor must die.

The 'difference' of the physically handicapped in these representations is largely superficial; indeed, most often it is non-apparent, being signified only by a wheelchair. It is superficial, too, in that, explicitly or by inference, the disablement has been acquired through some mishap after birth and is invariably remediable under the right moral conditions. Although some congenital deformities appear in the fiction and film of the first half of the twentieth century, they are rarely aesthetically disturbing and are usually treatable, as for example, the club foot at the center of Somerset Maughan's *Of Human Bondage* (1915) which was made into a film in 1934 and again in 1946. Such representations of physical disability were at odds with the visually unpleasing depiction of 'degenerates' and the 'unfit' in American movies and the mass media of the 1910s and 1920s which, as Martin Pernick has argued, helped popularly to shape and promote the science of eugenics. By contrast, films with cripples in them celebrated inner strength, moral purity and the triumph of character. Such portrayals, however, left no room for expressions of collective 'entitlement' or of the 'rights' of the disabled in law, nor for psychologically sensitive interiorizations of disabled lives. Not until the 1960s would these constructions encroach upon Hollywood's triumphalist narratives, and upon the imperative of economic productivity that mostly conferred social legitimacy upon the disabled off-screen.

Nevertheless, the soil from out of which the seeds of these reconfigurations of the disabled would germinate was under tillage as early as mid-century. The Second World War and the decade or so of economic growth that followed rendered the category 'disabled' less politically controversial than ever before (or after). Full employment meant that many disabled persons entered the labor market for the first time. Simultaneously, governments perceived welfarism as an affordable and necessary exercise in the social incorporation of those unable to work. In Britain, the state's mobilization of human resources during the war years, the ideological marginalization of charity, and the desire of policy makers to rationalize the several existing forms of provision for the disabled led to the Disabled Persons (Employment) Act (1944) which, among other things, provided sheltered 'Remploy' factories for the severely disabled. The Second World War itself generated far fewer limbless soldiers than the First, and those who were disabled by it were better provided. Overall, they benefited from the post-war enthusiasm for medical and social rehabilitation, as expressed for example, in the hugely popular *Beveridge Report.*

By the mid-twentieth century disability was also becoming less class specific. A remaining major cause of physical disability among children, polio, was a 'classless' disease by comparison with rickets and tuberculosis — American presidents, not just paupers, were known to succumb to it. At the same time, incapacitating injuries sustained by workers in industry diminished proportionate to the population due to greater safety awareness and the protective measures urged by governments and unions. Motor vehicle and household accidents took up the slack, but these sources of disablement were not only less class specific than industrial accidents, they were also less gender specific. Reflecting these changes in the social production of disablement was the adoption in welfare policy and in society generally of the less labor-defined (and would-be less stigmatizing) label for the disabled, the 'handicapped.' In public discourse the label united the mentally with the physically disabled, at the same time as suggesting a more psychologically sensitive approach to the latter.

But already by the mid-1960s, the status and meaning of being handicapped was beginning to shift as a result of a variety of professional, economic, social, cultural and political developments. Indirectly, and then directly, cutbacks in welfare were partly responsible. In the UK in the mid-1960s the government proposal to introduce payments for drug prescriptions (hitherto free under the National Health Service) and to exempt from these charges persons who were chronically sick or disabled, led to initiatives in calculating and reclassifying the disabled. Concomitant with these efforts were new government concerns with unemployment among handicapped persons and, hence, with the level of their demands on social services. The 1971 report produced by Amelia Harris for the Office of Population Censuses and Surveys was notable, among other things, for embedding into official discourse a new three-fold classification distinguishing *impairment* from *disability* and *handicap* — a bureaucratic refinement with implications for the re-scaling of benefits. Independently, in America in 1967, emerging also from concerns over welfare costs and the organization of services, a similar classification was proposed by the applied sociologist of medicine, Saad Nagi. In 1981, in slightly modified form, these distinctions were embraced internationally in the World Health Organization's *Classification of Impairments, Disabilities and Handicaps*, prepared by the Manchester epidemiologist of disability, Philip Wood. Such labels, while reflecting changing social and cultural attitudes to the disabled, could be divisive for the disabled. For governments, however, they afforded a politically instrumental means to welfare economies. This is clear through one further change in terminology in Britain in the 1980s, from 'invalidity' to 'incapacity' benefit, a re-labeling adopted explicitly (in the interest of political capital) to rid the social security system of 'malingerers.' As a result, benefits became more difficult to obtain and those who refused to be discouraged from applying became subject to further economizing barriers.

For the sociologists and others involved in these reclassifications there were positive implications for professionalization. This was particularly so in relation to Wood's discipline of epidemiology, which prior to the 1960s was mainly disease-focused and lacklustre. The social investigation of disability helped lend new legitimacy and direction to the field, as manifested in Wood's subsequent research for the Arthritis and Rheumatism Council.

From the early 1960s various other sociologists and social psychologists became interested in disability, by which they often meant not only physical and mental handicap, but *all* illness. Erving Goffman and others began to open up a psycho-social space which dwelt on the purported alienation of physically handicapped persons resulting from their loss of ability to perform socially expected role activities. Eliot Friedson and other 'normalization' theorists began arguing that 'disability' was a socially constructed life-long status of deviance. Linked to these perceptions and nourished by the growing counter-culture of the late 1960s challenges emerged to professionalism itself. A notable contributor was Ivan Illich who proposed the mid-twentieth century as "The Age of Disabling Professions." It was an age, he submitted, "when people had 'problems,' experts had 'solutions' and scientists measured imponderables such as 'abilities' and 'needs'"[11] — an age, in other words, in which professionals 'disabled' individual expression, personal autonomy, and democratic voice. Appearing in the same volume as Illich's essay was Irving Zola's "Healthism and Disabling Medicalization" which described the medical profession's ever greater influence on and control over society.

All of this interest in disability, literal and metaphoric, helped raise the consciousness of the disabled. So, too (with public support), did the devastating realization that modern medicine was itself capable of manufacturing gross deformity. The thalidomide tragedy which unfolded in the early 1960s was the first of several such revelations marking, in retrospect, the end of a golden age of medicine in which public trust had been almost absolute. In the wake of thalidomide, and in the face of welfare cutbacks, civilian mutual support groups emerged, such as the Disablement Income Group established in Britain in 1967. From these began the 'handicapped' movement, as it might now be styled to distinguish it from the later disability rights movement into which it later merged. The handicapped movement met with both national and international success. Legislation was passed, such as the 1970 Chronically Sick and Disabled Act for England (a permissive bill for better home care and for rationalizing the existing legislation). And in 1976, the same year in which the Disabled Peoples' Movement was established, the United Nations resolved to make 1981 the International Year of Disabled People, to help "disabled people in their physical and psychological adjustment to society."[12]

By 1981, however, the UN's heart-plucking, psycho-socially integrative message was already under siege. Even before some flag-burning American disabled veterans from Vietnam added political fury to the cause of the disabled, activists were seeking to (as one slogan put it) 'piss on pity.' Spurned was the discriminatory label 'handicapped,' though some argued that its horse-racing and golf associations were "entirely appropriate to the social model of disability where 'society' plays the role of the organizers of the competition in imposing a handicap."[13] Groups such as the Union of the Physically Impaired Against Segregation (UK) and the Action Group to Defend the Rights of the Disabled (USSR) joined with others in demanding a substantially transformed material, social, and intellectual environment adapted to the needs of the disabled (or rather, 'people with disabili-ties'). As encapsulated in the title of one contemporary publication, the contest was now seen as between "Disabling Barriers [and] Enabling Environments."[14] A growing body of similar literature reflected the fact that 'disability studies,' like gender studies, had become a flourishing academic sub-specialty as well as a popular agenda. It even acquired its own publishing outlet, 'The Disability Press,' based in the School of Sociology and Social Policy at the University of Leeds.

By the end of twentieth century the question of what exactly best 'enables' was still subject to considerable debate. Among the disabled themselves views were divided: for some the emphasis was on greater rights to welfare; others stressed civil rights and recognition as a minority group; still others called for the wholesale transformation of the environment so as to reconceive the world in terms of 'differently-abled people.' Others, wary perhaps of the too-easy appropriation of the latter rhetoric into merely the provision of curb-cuts and wheelchair access, insisted on entry into the labor market as the primary goal, yet divided over the virtues of accepting the new disability technologies as the appropriate route, or as a route at all. The new technologies, some argued, assisted the entry of persons with disabilities into consumption rather than production. The industry around this technology was founded on consumption, and its markets were increasingly made available through disablement assistance schemes promoted by politicians seeking to pacify and enroll the high-profile disability lobby. Ironically, but not surprisingly in view of that lobby, it was in the world of advertising — not least for the sale of information technology products — that positive images of physically handicapped persons were sold and 'disablism' most widely contested.

## THE ROLE OF MEDICINE

Within the politics of disablement, medicine was to occupy a privileged place, though one of little honor. Disability activists came to regard medicine as central to the process of the social exclusion of the disabled through the legitimacy it gave to physical difference. Medicine's pathologization of disability, by thus occluding the social construction of the category of disability and by individualizing disable-ment, was perceived to operate against disabled persons' own self-assessment of their situation, as well as against collective action for the rights of the disabled. Some authors went so far as to claim disability wholly a 'medical construct.' Michael Oliver, for example, in *The Politics of Disablement*, whilst admitting that there have been "few attempts to discuss the medicalization of disability, either in historical or current context,"[15] embraced medicalization theory in order vigorously to attack its socio-political implications for persons with disabilities. The exclusion of the disabled from the family, the community, and the work-place, he main-tained, was connected with "the rise of capitalism" and facilitated by the medical profession.

As disabled people were part of the process of control by exclusion, the medicalising of disability was connected to the rise of the medical profession and the development of 'the germ theory of illness and disease.'[16]

Leaving aside Oliver's romantic view of the social place of the disabled in the past (with its worrying implications for a return to familial responsibilities for the disabled) and his curious historical conflation of the rise of capitalism with germ theory, his viewpoint is readily grasped. It is the well-worn critique of doctor-driven medicine: professionally monopolizing, diseased-based, clinically orientated, reductive, individualizing, and dismissive of patients' own experience of illness. As perceived by the sociologists Friedson, Illich and Zola in the 1960s and 1970s, medicine was an alienating, regulating, disciplining and social controlling enterprise, achieving social control through a pathologizing process whereby conditions morally freighted as 'bad' (such as alcoholism) were converted into conditions of 'sickness.'

Although it would be hard to argue against the pathologization of disability in the twentieth century, the question of whether this amounts to the 'medicalization' of the disabled in the above sense is open to question. Certainly, a number of objections can be raised to the implied complicity and instrumentality of the medical profession in such a process (and can be raised without re-embracing medicine's own heroic account of its role as one simply of disinterested struggle against handicap through preventive and interventive procedures). What goes against the argument, firstly, is the dearth of historical evidence of medical practitioners having had much professionalizing interest specifically in the disabled (in contrast to some epidemologists and medical sociologists). The late nineteenth-century 'discovery' of the crippled child, for instance, was not made by medical men, but by philanthropists and social investigators. The medical profession were followers, and were not especially privileged in the movement which was largely educational and occupational. Some doctors became interested in the correction of physical disability (rehabilitation) during the First World War, but the interest was not widely shared. Rehabilitation medicine, involving orthopedic surgery, prosthesis fitting and vocational training, was overwhelmingly state funded and poorly remunerated, and therefore low in the professional hierarchy. Although there was much talk after the war about developing rehabilitation medicine around the 'wounded soldiers of industry,' the project hardly got off the ground. Rehabilitation medicine fared somewhat better during World War II, but, in Britain at least, its glory was short-lived, in part because the new National Health Service left intact the old division between industrial health and the rest of medicine, and the latter became increasingly sub-divided between specialist groups with interests mostly in acute conditions. As late as 1972 the report of a sub-committee of the Department of Health and Social Security into rehabilitation lamented the lack of medical interest in the area. "[T]he medical profession must take due share of the blame"[17] for this situation, the report submitted, for many practitioners did not recognize disability as a medical problem and had little incentive to move into this area given the "low levels of remuneration" and "poor career prospects." Similar circumstances in America in 1955 led the editors of the newly-founded *Journal of Chronic Diseases* to lament that "the handicapped was truly the forgotten and neglected man … [whose condition] was deplored, but little or nothing was done about them except for an insufficient amount of charity."[18] Such statements were at the same time indicators of change, hastened in particular by fee-for-service payments from insurance companies looking for the most effective means to removing claimants from their books. It was not therefore around an interest in permanent disability that some doctors sought to mobilize, but rather, around interventions into the category of acute conditions. More generally, as reflected by the use of the word 'diseases' in the above mentioned journal title, the medical profession sought to transform chronic conditions (which may be disabling, such as multiple sclerosis) into acute curable diseases. They sought the means to stabilize conditions so as to permit enablement as, for example, by the use of drugs to allow epileptics to function 'normally'. To this end the medical profession were successful (to the delight of many patients) and in so doing continued to keep professional attention focused on acute rather than chronic impairments.

Secondly, for most of the century medical interest in the permanently disabled was demonstrably not to the exclusion of social understandings of disability. Already by 1900 almost everybody involved with the cripples movement had come to the conclusion that cripples were 'made not born,' that is, that the physically handicapped were the product of their unfortunate social circumstances, more so than the victims of stigmatizing and non-remedial congenital diseases such as syphilis. The slogan 'cripples are made not born' (with none of the eugenic associations about un-making that would be heard at the end of the century) remained dominant throughout the interwar period and beyond, among doctors as well as social welfarists. The phrase may not have pleased everyone, least of all those handicapped persons it excluded and hence further stigmatized, but as part of a combined curative and preventative discourse in medicine which exposed the interdependence of the health of individuals and communities, it appeared progressive in tone and spirit. Interwar and post-Second World War leaders in rehabilitation (which included well-intentioned lay benefactors such as President Franklin D. Roosevelt's friend, the philanthropist Bernard Baruch) did not subscribe to an individuating type medicine. From the start, those involved in rehabilitation medicine thought holistically. Working from a dynamic physiological model of the body, they consciously embraced the idea that to render the dismembered whole, one needed to assume an integrated approach not just to the body, but to patients, taking into account their social conditions, psychology, housing, employment concerns, education, and so on. In assisting this social-environmental understanding of disability, the rehabilitationists appear close to what many disability advocates later came to seek in the medical profession. And as the rehabilitationists did not conceive of patients in terms of fragmented body parts, so neither did they conceive of medical practice in that way. Rehabilitation medicine was not the preserve of one group, but rather that of an ensemble or team of several medical and para-medical groupings — physiotherapists, occupational therapists, physical medicine experts, orthopedists, psychologists, etc.

Thirdly, and finally, in connection with the implementation of the administrative categories of disability, the medical profession was more passive than active. Welfare categories were largely military and political, not medical; in America no less than in the Soviet Union, they tended to be thrust upon the medical profession. To be sure, in the drafting of workmen's compensation legislation and the like, medical advice was taken, but it was rarely crucial. After all, communities without medical experts have been able to draft laws finely calculating the relative value of severed fingers, hands, arms, etc., as the Anglo-Saxons apparently did in charging those responsible for maiming. Within the administration of disability benefits, medical practitioners were functionaries not innovators of policy. Their job was to fill in the forms which officialdom supplied. The medical profession in some cases, and doctors individually, may have *wanted* the power to decide who should receive disability benefits, but almost always they were outflanked by bureaucrats and/or insurers, and/or, in the case of National Health Insurance in Britain, the Approved Insurance Societies themselves who, by law, were "always free to grant benefit on the basis of evidence other than of medical examination."[19] As mentioned above, doctors themselves came under government scrutiny for 'lax certification' of disability benefits under the NHI, as some also had for turning a blind eye to malingerers during the Great War. In the early 1930s in Britain the government imposed a major clamp down, adding new layers of administration the more effectively to vet the certification work of general practitioners. Much the same policy was endorsed by anti-welfare governments in the 1980s and '90s, who claimed that the medical profession was incompetent or lax in its role as gatekeeper to disability benefits.

There is, moreover, little evidence of the medical profession actually *wanting* to gatekeep disability benefits — least of all in the more entrepreneurial medical market of the United States, as Deborah Stone has argued in *The Disabled State*. For example, in 1948 a Congressional Advisory Council on disability, worried over the costs of false claims, sought to obtain a reliable clinical test for disability from the medical profession. But the overwhelming majority of practitioners attempted to persuade Congressmen that "physicians could not possibly provide the kind of objective determination desired."[20] The doctors argued that the very process of labeling a person 'disabled' would weaken incentives to recovery and rehabilitation; that the adoption of the certifying role "would only create enormous tensions between doctors and their patients;"[21] and that income awards on the basis of disability would only encourage malingering. These were of course mostly politically-motivated objections, the doctors being fearful that any government disability program would lead to some kind of socialized medicine undermining lucrative private practice. But the fact remains that doctors were nowhere desperate to gatekeep disability benefits. As Stone concludes, it was the politicians, not the doctors, who forced the profession to draw up objective criteria for vetting disability claims. The doctors, she submits, were at best "reluctant imperialists."[22]

Thus evidence of the medical profession actively seeking to medicalize the disabled is scarce. This does not mean, however, that 'medicalization' has no place in the twentieth-century history of the disabled body outside the imagination (and professionalizing interests) of sociologists of disability. After all, 'reluctant imperialists' are imperialist nonetheless; the medical profession has on occasions drawn up 'objective criteria' for vetting the disabled; and almost the first port of call for material or educational aid for the handicapped is through the medical profession, whose general training is precisely to the task of individual pathologization, not social contextual appreciation or socio-psychological understanding.

What is in doubt is not medicalization per se, but rather, its vulgar sociological rendering in terms of social control models that exclude, or can be juxtaposed to, other kinds of disability narratives. By casting medicalization in this way, and styling it a "traditional narrative,"[23] disability advocates in the late twentieth century in effect did unto the medical profession what they would not have others do unto the disabled: treat as 'other.' But not only is this 'othering' and juxtaposing historically wrong (as we have seen), it is also misguided. Besides conflating pathologization with the empowering of doctors to control it, it overlooks the fact that in 'late-modern' Western society, the culture of medicine extends to the whole of culture, not just to pathologized parts. Medical discourse now reaches into the corners of everyone's social and psychological selves. 'Being' no longer hinges crucially on the ability to enter into productive labor; rather, it has become tantamount to 'well-being' which, if not always subject to professional medical management, is, consciously or unconsciously, subject to our own medicalized measurement and monitoring. In this sense we have all been medicalized. To speak of the medical profession as an external social controlling force on the disabled is therefore naive.

If we add to this that medicine as a practice increasingly intervenes in our bodies from before birth to death in order to detect and define an ever-widening compass of potentially 'disabling' conditions, it can also be said that we are now all disabilized. Increasingly the fictionalized or fantasized disabled body is the locus for the conceptualization of the body of well-being: through blood and urine tests, pap smears, X-rays, cardiograms, genetic screening and all the rest, the technologies of modern medicine measure our disablement over the course of our lives. Thus, just as the politics of disablement have helped to define our body politic in the late-twentieth century, so in a culture orientated to health, leisure, and the fantasy of perfection, it is through the potentially disabled body that we come to know ourselves. For good or ill, the 'age of disability' looks set to remain.

## REFERENCES

For valuable comments on an earlier draft of this chapter I am grateful to David Armstrong, Claudia Castaneda, Martin Pernick, John Pickstone, Nick Watson, and the Edinburgh seminar in Social Studies in Science.

1. Caroline Walker Bynum, *Fragmentation and Redemption, Essays on Gender and the Human Body in Medieval Religion.* (New York: Zone Books, 1991), p. 19.
2. Ian Hacking, 'Making Up People' in T.C. Hellier *et al.* (eds), *Reconstructing Individualism.* (Standford University Press, 1986), 222–36.
3. Deborah Stone, *The Disabled State.* (London: Macmillan, 1984), p. 32.
4. Cited in Roger Cooter, *Surgery and Society in Peace and War: Orthopaedics and the Organization of Modern Medicine, 1880–1948.* (London: Macmillan, 1993), p. 56.
5. 'Disablement Benefit Under the British Health Insurance System,' *International Labour Review* (1933), **28**: 192–213 at p. 194.
6. Claire H. Liachowitz, *Disability as a Social Construct: Legislative Roots.* (Philadelphia: University of Pennsylvania Press, 1988), p. 32.
7. Guy Chapman, *A Passionate Prodigality, Fragments of an Autobiography.* (Leatherhead: Ashford, Buchan & Enright, 1985; 1st edn. 1933), p. 80.
8. Cited in Roxanne Panchasi, 'Reconstructions: Prothetics and the Rehabilitation of the Male Body in World War I France,' *Differences: A Journal of Feminist Cultural Studies* (1996), **7**: 109–40.
9. Cited in Daniel Pick, *War Machine: The Rationalisation of Slaughter.* (New Haven and London: Yale University Press, 1993), p. 212.
10. F.G. Elton, 'Repairing the Human Machine,' *New York Journal of Medicine* (1923), **118**: p. 107.
11. Ivan Illich, 'Disabling Professions,' in Illich *et al.*, *Disabling Professions.* (London: Marion Boyars, 1977), p. 11.
12. Quoted in Gordon Campbell, *Disablement: Problems and Prospects in the United Kingdom.* (London: The Nuffield Provincial Hospitals Trust, 1981), p. 15.
13. Richard Berthoud, Jane Lakey and Stephen McKay, *The Economic Problems of Disabled People.* (London: Policy Studies Institute, 1993), p. 6.
14. John Swain, Vic Finkelstein, Sally French and Mike Oliver (eds), *Disabling Barriers — Enabling Environments.* (London: Sage and Open University, 1993).
15. Oliver, *The Politics of Disablement.* (London: Macmillan, 1990), p. 51.
16. *Ibid.*, p. 47.
17. Central Health Services Council (Department of Health, and Social Security Welsh Office), *Rehabilitation: Report of a Sub-committee of the Standing Medical Advisory Committee.* (London: HMSO, 1972), p. 21.
18. 'Introduction,' *Journal of Chronic Diseases* (1955), **1**: p. 4.
19. *Intern. Lab. Rev.* (1933), p. 199.
20. Stone, *Disabled State*, p. 80.
21. *Ibid.*, p. 112.
22. *Ibid.*, p. 112.
23. Tom Shakespeare, 'Disability, Identity and Difference' in Colin Barnes and Goef Mercer (eds), *Exploring the Divide: Illness and Disability.* (Leeds: Disability Press, 1996), 94–113 at p. 95.

## FURTHER READING

Arney, William R. and Bernard J. Bergen, 'The Anomaly, the Chronic Patient and the Play of Medical Power,' *Sociology of Health and Illness* (1983), **5**: 1–24.

Berkowitz, Edward D., *Disabled Policy: America's Programs for the Handicapped. A Twentieth Century Fund Report.* (Cambridge/New York: Cambridge University Press, 1987).

Bolderson, Helen, 'The Origins of the Disabled Persons Employment Quota and its Symbolic Significance,' *Journal of Social Policy* (1980), **9**: 169–86.

Buchanan, Allen. 'Choosing Who Will Be Disabled: Genetic Intervention and the Morality of Inclusion,' *Social Philosophy and Policy* (1996), **13**: 18–46.

Cooter, Roger, 'Malingering in Modernity' in Roger Cooter, Steve Sturdy and Mark Harrison (eds), *War, Medicine and Modernity*. (Stroud: Sutton, 1998).

Cooter, Roger and Bill Luckin (eds), *Accidents in History*. (Amsterdam: Rodopi, 1996).

Driedger, Diane, *The Last Civil Rights Movement: Disabled Peoples' International*. (London: Hurst & Co, 1989).

Field, Mark, 'Dissidence as Disability: The Medicalization of Dissidence in Soviet Russia,' in William O. McCagg and Lewis Siegelbaum (eds), *The Disabled in the Soviet Union: Past and Present, Theory and Practice*. (Pittsburgh: University of Pittsburg Press, 1989).

Fine, M. and A. Asch, 'Disability Beyond Stigma: Social Interaction, Discrimination, and Activism,' *Journal of Social Issues* (1988), **44**: 3–22.

Fox, Daniel M. and David P. Willis (eds), *Disability Policy: Restoring Socioeconomic Independence*, special issue of *The Milbank Quarterly* (1989), **67**: supplement 2.

Friedson, Eliot, 'Disability as Social Deviance,' in Marvin B. Sussman (ed.), *Sociology and Rehabilitation*. (Washington DC: American Sociological Association, 1966).

Gartner, Alan and Tom Joe (eds), *Images of the Disabled, Disabling Images*. (New York: Praeger, 1987).

Hakken, David, 'Electronic Curb Cuts: Computing and the Cultural (Re) Construction of Disability in the United States,' *Science as Culture* (1995), **4**: 502–34.

Harris, Amelia, *Handicapped and Impaired in Great Britain*. (London: HMSO, 1971).

Hevey, David, *The Creatures Time Forgot: Photography and Disability Imagery*. (London: Routledge, 1992).

Jain, Sarah, 'The Prosthetic Imagination: Enabling and Disabling the "Prosthesis" Trope,' *Science, Technology and Human Values* (1999), **24**: 31–54.

Koven, Seth, 'Remembering and Dismemberment: crippled children, wounded soldiers, and the Great War in Great Britain;' *American Historical Review* (Oct. 1994), **99**: 1167–1202.

Levidow, Les and Keven Ruben (eds), *Cyborg Worlds*. (London: FAB, 1989).

Mitchell, David and Sharon Snyder (eds), *The Body and Physical Difference: Discourses of Disability in the Humanities*. (Ann Arbor: University of Michigan Press, 1997).

Morton, Desmond and G. Wright, *Winning the Second Battle: Canadian Veterans and the Return to Civilian Life 1915–1930*. (Toronto: University of Toronto Press, 1987).

Nagi, Saad Z., *Disability and Rehabilitation: Legal, Clinical, and Self-concepts and Measurement*. (Columbus, Ohio: Ohio State University Press, 1969).

Pernick, Martin, *The Black Stork: Eugenics and the Death of 'Defective' Babies in American Medicine and Motion Pictures Since 1915*. (New York: Oxford University Press, 1996).

Tanenbaum, Sandra, *Engineering Disability: Public Policy and Compensatory Technology*. (Philadelphia: Temple University Press, 1986).

Wendell, Susan, *The Rejected Body: Feminist Philosophical Reflections on Disability*. (New York/London: Routledge, 1996).

Wood, Philip and E. Badley, 'An Epidemiological Appraisal of Disablement' in A.E. Bennett (ed.), *Recent Advances in Community Medicine*. (Edinburgh/London; Churchill Livingstone, 1978).

Zelizer, Viviana, *Pricing the Priceless Child*. (New York: Basic Books, 1985).

# CHAPTER 25

# The Defended Body

## ANNE MARIE MOULIN

I n this part of the book we follow a variety of medical approaches to try to capture the body, an object which eludes any specific science. Each one of us offers a construal of the body, elaborated on the basis of his or her scientific expertise and singular experience of life. My viewpoint on the defended body is colored by my previous work on the history of immunology and on international public health.[1]

But the defended body is not just one among many bodies waiting for analysis; it seems to offer an overarching view that articulates all the others — in "the age of immunology."[2] It links two major aspects of twentieth-century medicine: the successful fight against infectious diseases, and the scientific elaboration of a new function of the organism — immunity. Immunology, which stemmed from the germ theory of disease, has evolved to provide an encompassing view of the body which subordinates all physiological events to a common purpose: the defense and representation of the self.

Around the Mediterranean sea one sometimes finds abandoned fortresses — reminders of the lazarettos which until the beginning of the twentieth century formed the defensive line of Western Europe against epidemics from the East. Modern times have seen the transformation of the ancient order. The defensive frontier has shifted from lines in geographical space to another type of barrier — fragmented and reorganized. Individual bodies have come to be the first line of defense, prompted and trained by modern medicine. The human body is the defending body, naturally equipped to oppose attack but also integrated into a new order of equally trained bodies. The defensive attributes of the body have come into sharp focus and they seem essential for survival — for life itself. Defense is life. This centrality of the defended body has modified the language of medicine and suggested a new version of pathogenesis, prevention and cure.

Contemporary thinkers, following Michel Foucault, have stressed that the body is the site of power, but this statement, meant to recall that the body is a target for manipulation, should not make us forget that the body is also a source of power. This chapter will reflect on the dialectic between the defending (active) body and the defended (passive) body; their linkage can be construed as the articulation between public health and immunity.

The very idea of defense raises the issue of knowing what defends itself or is defended and against what? At least two branches of medical knowledge, intimately historically linked, have dealt with the question. On the one hand, a politically-oriented science — public health — has organized defense at the social level, and distributed responsibilities and duties between individuals and collective groups. On the other hand, a biologically-oriented science — immunology — has focused on the ontogeny and phylogeny of bodily defenses. These two sciences became established disciplines only in the twentieth century, but today can claim their due shares of a key development over the last hundred years — the exponential growth of world population.

The advent of bacteriology and the germ theory encouraged defensive and even offensive strategies, implemented by various international and national organizations. On the other hand, immunity, once limited to the management of infections, has evolved to be synonymous for general defense of the integrity of the organism, engendered in the entrails of life.

The theme of the defended body suggests the importance of military metaphors in contemporary medical thinking. Though this metaphor had long featured in medical literature, the germ theory of disease, in reshaping medical categories from about 1880, gave it a particular and persistent impact, both among the professionals and among lay people.

## BODILY STATISTICS

The major demographic event of the twentieth century has been the explosive increase of life-expectancy, even if the developing countries are still lagging. While the average life span had stagnated at around thirty five years almost from the Middle Ages to the mid-nineteenth century, our century has seen a dramatic decline of infantile mortality and an exponential growth in population. This improvement was mainly due to the reduction of the burden of infectious diseases; once responsible for two thirds of the mortality, their share of death in the Western world is today less than 10%.

Demographers are still disputing the interpretation of the phenomenon. The success was initially attributed to the progress of medical knowledge, and to the process later called the medicalization of society. Following the provocative book, *The Modern Rise of Population*[3] written by Thomas McKeown, historians have reconsidered the role of other factors such as nutrition, working conditions and housing, as well as 'public health' provision. More recently, some cultural determinants have also been included — such as community cohesion and strong social interactions, and the parallel between social disturbances and pathological disorders has been discussed.

The changes of mortality patterns have been marked by the elimination of smallpox and the containment of old scourges such as plague and cholera. As the year 2000 was approaching, the World Health Organization listed diphtheria, tuberculosis, poliomyelitis, meningitis, tetanus and measles as the next targets for eradication. Even if we are now led to talk about a 'return' of the infectious diseases, as we will discuss later, our simultaneous concern with world overpopulation underlines the success of defensive measures (in the broadest sense) in the dramatic decrease of infant mortality, even in countries with a low income per capita.

NATURAL RESISTANCE

Long before bacteriology presented germs as the enemy, bodily defense had been thought of as physical or mechanical 'resistance.'[4] Sticks and stones could shatter bones, knives and swords could pierce the skin; the physical body was confronted by its environment. Travellers were assaulted by the wind and piercing cold, and by beasts in the forest. Most men and women worked outdoors — the peasantry being by far the largest group in the world. Seamen were tossed on the ocean, and houses did not afford adequate protection. The era of central heating and air-conditioning had not begun. The body's resistance had its limits.

But more positively, the body was also seen as directly influenced by food and by the four elements, with humors flowing in and out. Medical care sought to optimize these exchanges, by diet and by bleeding, blistering, and cupping — the backbone of ancient medicine. The prebacteriological era even saw the reinforcement of these conceptions: in the middle of the nineteenth century, a revival of Hippocratic epidemiology fostered an array of works dedicated to the study of local constitutions and medical geography. In his impressive synthesis, *Handbuch der Geschichte und Geographie der Krankheiten*, published in Berlin in 1876, August Hirsch reviewed all possible factors involved in the genesis of diseases, with special emphasis on climate. The same prebacteriological period saw the flourishing of physical anthropology as doctors refined their classifications of races on the basis of anatomical features such as the size and shape of the skull — viewed as the shield of the brain and the adaptive faculties.

That medical nosology referred to climate as a cause of disease appears in the phrase *a frigore,* still appended to such diseases as pleurisy and palsy. The skin was not so much a barrier as a *sensorium* where microcosm and macrocosm came close to each other and interacted. The skin expressed external influences as well as internal fermentations. Smallpox, before being related to a virus, appeared as the expression of a ferment innate to the body and therefore of a universal nature.

In other words, the body has long been regarded as a microcosm reflecting the macrocosm and poised in an unstable equilibrium. Following the advent of bacteriology and the germ theory of disease at the turn of the century, the relationship between the body and nature came to be seen predominantly as an inimical relationship — a struggle. Medicine was looked to for weapons that could be used to aid the body in these hostilities.

Natural resistance had long been linked to the anatomical fabric of the body, but in the age of microscopical studies, the anatomical body of the dissection room

— hard bones and soft flesh — was displaced by other kinds of animal bodies such as the cellular body. Cells and their products would provide another kind of defense. The body was hereafter viewed as a collection of different lines of cells, bathed by humoral fluids carrying secretions.

The metaphor of fighting the enemy operated in both medical and political discourse. The new hygiene promoted by Lister and Pasteur's disciples reorganized itself as a program for drawing a line between the invisible realm of microbes and the assaulted bodies, by enrolling the community and its official tutor — the modern state.

## IMMUNE DEFENSE

Meditating on our destiny to die, the Greek philosopher Epicurus compared mankind to an open city, deprived of ramparts. Modern civilization invented fortifications of a novel kind.

With the germ theory of disease, there emerged the idea that individual bodies bore their own systems of defense, so opening the era of immunological thinking. The theory depicted germs as enemies, launching attacks against a barricaded organism. Virchow, one of the founders of the cell theory, clearly saw the alliance between the new age of nationalism and the emerging concept of the defending body — and he despised both. A champion of democracy and civil rights in a Europe of open-frontiers, he derided the vision of germs as immigrants, rejected by cells acting as guards and "escorting them to the border."[5]

The imperatives of antisepsis, and then asepsis, reformed surgical procedures in the operating room, creating a germ-free land. To combat the germs, all kinds of antiseptics were lavishly sprayed on the walls, not only of dwellings but of the patients' intestines. In France, for example, Charles Bouchard fed infected patients with various antiseptic drugs. In the first decade of the century, new hospitals embodied the conception of sanitized space and isolation of patients in rooms or pavilions. The Pasteur hospital in France (1900) and the Rockefeller hospital in New York (1906) were good examples of the new architecture — banishing non functional furniture, eradicating hiding places where microbes might lurk, creating a panopticon for the surveillance of microscopic life.

More insidiously, bacterium-oriented hygiene profoundly transformed the "social uses of the body."[6] In most Western countries, scientific hygiene was taught in elementary schools, by then open to most children under new laws on compulsory education; it transformed table manners and conviviality. Promiscuity was vigorously stigmatized as the source of sexually transmitted diseases, the sharing of spoons and domestic utensils was vilified. Historians have described the forced medicalization of manners, and the gap so created between two generations who fed themselves, cleaned themselves and made love differently.

But most attention was given to what happened in the theater of the individual body. In 1883, the Russian-born Elie Metchnikoff described phagocytosis or the way cells engulf bacteria in a organism in the same way starfish larvae incorporate thorns or unicellular protozoa ingest fungi. The body itself was reconceptualized as a battlefield, where newly-identified cells, called phagocytes, patrolled the invading bacteria and disposed of germs, along with aging or damaged cells.

The idea of phagocytosis was seized on by Louis Pasteur as he tried to interpret the defensive power of the organism. For Pasteur, Metchnikoff's theory was satisfying because it tended to equalize the forces concerned. "There is something disproportionate in a bacterium that can kill a bull";[7] one can better understand a local struggle between the leukocytes of the bull and the weakened microbes. Although Metchnikoff insisted that living phagocytes were the principal agents of immunity, one could not ignore the role of the humoral factors present in body fluids, such as antibodies or complement.

The idea of war on germs was easily accessible and resonated with the view of life as struggle which had been nurtured by the Darwinian debates. Immunology was born of early intuitions about the defense provided by phagocytosis and antibodies.

## THE EMERGENCE OF IMMUNOLOGY

The discovery of antimicrobial immunity linked the definition of the living individual to the idea of a permanent struggle against the pathogens — a struggle built into the fabric of the body, a function which had escaped scientific investigation in the past. A physiological function among others, immunity came increasingly to be seen as essential for survival. Severe congenital immunodeficiencies were recognized as incompatible with life.

Today, textbooks state that the envelope of the individual, the skin and mucosae, is the first frontier between the organism and the environment, preventing the penetration of most pathogens. They speculate that it represents the most archaic system of defense. Pathogens, throughout evolution, probably developed new strategies for adhering to the host tissues, penetrating the cells, and even invading the cellular genome. The individual would have constructed a complex array of defensive mechanisms, today described as the immune system.

This immune system is commonly defined as the sum of cellular and molecular phenomena which contribute to the physiological integrity of the individual. Although some of its components are still traced back to Metchnikoff's system of phagocytes, the full development of the idea has involved several steps, including the identification of various types of cells responsible for recognition of all kinds of antigens — no longer just bacterial components — and the demonstration of cooperation between these various cell populations and their products in the preservation of the organismic integrity.

The link between the defense of the organism against infections and the definition of the individuality was initially obscure. In the first decades of the century, natural immunity came to include a set of characters like blood groups, evidenced by serological reactions but with no known link to previous infections, and whose physiological signification was elusive.

In the 1930s, a famous Polish physician, Ludwik Hirszfeld, who had been working at Heidelberg on the hereditary transmission of blood groups, tried to conceive of immunity as a more complex dynamic than the mere management of infections. In an influential work, he mapped a grand conception of immunity as a function responsible for the outcome of all kinds of diseases, including chronic disorders and cancer. He even pointed to immune reactions as important for such apparently remote physiological phenomena as reproduction and aging. For example, he regarded the successful outcome of pregnancy as a fascinating exception to the constitutional defense-process of the mother. He described the response to infections as a mosaic of reactions, some of which were either strong or weak, not only according to the pathogen but according to the host organism. Differences in resistance to infections in human species could be hereditary (or constitutional), or acquired through personal history. The immune system displayed a variety of features pointing towards the definition of biological individuality.

Immunology, born from microbiology as the science of defense, thus came to resonate with the philosophical problem of the identity of the self. Molecules involved in defense reactions, such as antibodies, could serve the more general purpose of singling out the individual. If during the first decades of the century, the blood group antigens had been the main markers of this phenomenon, additional substances were described in the 1960s, this time borne by most of the cells of the organism and serving to define other human groups analogous to the blood-groups defined by red-cells. As these new molecules were involved in transplantation rejection, they were called histocompatibility leucocyte antigens (HLA system). They represented a gross mechanism for recognition of foreign cells. That human populations are, genetically, very varied in their HLA antigens has been seen as a result of evolutionary selection, perhaps permitting the human species to escape extinction when confronted with pathogens.

HLA molecules later came to be seen as the level at which the 'self' was recognized; it was through the workings of the HLA system that the body's own tissues were 'immune' from the defense-reaction provoked by 'non-self' materials. This role (the so-called HLA restriction) was first demonstrated by Rolf Zinkernagel and Peter Doherty (who received the Nobel Prize in 1995) in relation to antiviral cytotoxicity — where the organism destroys its own cells which are infected by a virus. The themes of defense and biological identity were thus tightly linked. Immunity conforms to a general pattern for the species, but also displays the "uniqueness of the individual,"[8] as the British immunologist Peter Medawar described it in 1960. Between herd immunity and individual immunity, between collective and individual defense, a dialectic has developed, with alternating periods of harmony and tensions between immunological knowledge and public health strategy.

## INTERNATIONAL DEFENSE

During the nineteenth century, ten international sanitary conferences had emphasized quarantines and the surveillance of travelers and goods, principally against pandemics spreading from the East — firstly cholera but also the plague and, at a later stage, yellow fever. In 1903, an international convention created a *cordon sanitaire* around Europe and America. Following the treaty of Rome in 1907, the International Office for Public Hygiene was formed in Paris to supervise the application of the conventions and to organize the exchange of diplomatic notices about epidemics. The diplomatic arrangements were defensive in essence; they tried to limit the risk that privileged nations would be contaminated.

At the end of World War I, the Rockefeller Foundation, established in 1913 to promote public sanitation throughout the world, developed ambitious programs in Europe (for tuberculosis and venereal diseases) and in America. Reformist doctors, bolstered by new scientific knowledge and committed to hopes of general peace, thought that the time was ripe for going beyond negative measures, for a more positive public health based on better nutrition, education and research. To them, the similarities of epidemiological conditions across borders argued the necessity for nations to co-ordinate their public health programs, rather than trying to exclude silent germ-carriers from their territories. The long-term consequences of the discovery of America and of the imperial scrambles into Africa and Asia were now formulated and addressed; public health reformers recognized 'the microbial unification of the world' and its corollary — the necessity of global thinking. A permanent institution was created, the League of Nations Hygiene Organization (LNHO), staffed by health professionals, to lay the foundations for scientific investigation, data-collection and preventive health-promotion as means of collective defense against diseases.

Even if quarantines were not immediately abolished (and are still sporadically enacted today), their rules of confinement not adapted to the new epidemiological knowledge, a radically new agenda was set for the protection of individual and collective bodies, irrespective of political borders. Defense against diseases referred to frontiers of a new kind, those enclosing the living individual. The new programs encouraged the self-defense of individuals and a new system of collective defense built on healthier forms of interaction (food hygiene, sex hygiene, etc.). The human organism's defenses and interactions would be monitored by governments which thus increased their grip over their citizens, claiming public health as one of their prerogatives.

Although Ludwik Rachjmann and the other experts of LNHO had neither the time nor the financial means to implement this grand policy, they paved the way to the post-World War II work of the WHO. This well-known international organization, founded in 1948, launched campaigns against infectious and parasitic diseases at the world level. The most advertised episode of this policy is of course the eradication of smallpox, considered as a model and a considerable source of pride for the institution. Although it is true that prophylaxis against smallpox has a long history in many nations, the disease had never been the object of an international program before the WHO era.

Although immunity revealed itself as a complex function influenced by many factors such as hormones or the nervous system, public health officers adopted the agenda of collective immunization in order to disrupt the transmission chain. In contrast with Pasteur's early use of anti-rabies vaccine as an individual treatment, vaccines in the twentieth century were administered to populations as a collective prophylaxis — in each recipient body, biological defenses would be created — for that body and for the collectivity.

The first modern vaccines tried on a large scale were for typhoid, in the British and the French armies during World War I. Although slower than suggested by the triumphalist announcements of pioneering microbiologists, the quest for further vaccines succeeded for tetanus (1921), diphtheria (1923), yellow fever (1932), and then after World War II, for poliomyelitis, measles, whooping cough, and hepatitis. Most of these vaccines were widely accepted and some were made compulsory at the eve of World War II, with one notorious exception — BCG. This long-awaited tuberculosis vaccine, launched in France in 1921 by Pastorians Albert Calmette and Camille Guérin, was widely tried in French colonies and made compulsory in metropolitan France in 1938, but it remained controversial and never gained the international acceptance of its predecessors.

After World War II, in order to combat the new scourge of poliomyelitis in children, two rival vaccines were produced in the United States. Jonas Salk's killed vaccine, funded by the famous March of Dimes, was rivaled by Albert Sabin's live oral vaccine. Interestingly, Salk's vaccine was tried in the United States in 1951, while trials of Sabin's vaccine took place in the Soviet Union two years later. In the context of the Cold War, prophylactic vaccines were used as defensive weapons on both sides.

In the 1970s, WHO joined UNICEF to encourage a world-wide Extended Immunization Program, including vaccines against diphtheria, tetanus, polio-myelitis, whooping-cough, and later measles. The defensive program was pursued vigorously under the banner of 'Health for All in the Year 2000,' but less impor-tance was given to such other components of immunity as adequate nutrition and improved standards of living.

The eradication of smallpox, proclaimed in 1979, was a dream come true; part of the prophecy in Pasteur's 1882 program for general immunization now seemed within reach. But the whole idea of eradicating diseases — the spearhead of WHO strategy — ground to a halt in the 1980s. Alas, the reservoirs of most diseases include hosts such as wild rodents and insects which defy human enterprise. Doomsday for germs would have to wait on means appropriate for the control of animal pests.

On the other hand, the vaccination enterprise was not without its "hazards,"[9] starting with the early disaster at Mulkowal (India) in 1902 when earth-soiled antiplague vaccine fatally infected people with tetanus. It is hard to estimate how many people have suffered from adventitious contamination, such as syphilis through arm-to-arm Jennerian vaccination or hepatitis thanks to the addition of human serum to vaccine against yellow fever (during the Second World War), but it became clear that the defensive enterprise had to balance risks to the few against protection for the many, as it had to balance the infringement of individual freedom with the public good. The administration of vaccines, even when not contaminated, sometimes triggers damaging and even fatal disorders. Although the modern state officially assumed the defensive capacity to be roughly identical in all organisms, it had to acknowledge the ethical dilemma, and in most countries it has also assumed responsibility in case of accidents.

Indeed, the study of allergy sprang from studies of the unpredictible effects of immunization. Jenner himself had admitted exceptions to the practice of vaccination, for conditions such as eczema. The same immunology which had fostered the idea of collective immunization also harbored reflections on bodily idiosyncrasies.

We do not have an international history of the antivaccinationist movement which was initiated in early nineteenth-century Britain, but we do know that state-vaccination (and other forms of immunization) have recurrently aroused anxiety among opponents of state-intrusion into civil liberties. They have seen the state trying to control "flexible bodies,"[10] they have highlighted the complexity of the scientific issues related to vaccination — effectiveness and safety, uncertainty over long-term effects on individual and collective health, and they have disputed the claims of medicine over the body. Several religious sects were active in denouncing medical infringement of civil rights, questioning the source of the healing power and the legitimacy of the medical intervention. Even now, part of the public sees illness as divine dispensation and morality as the best defense against evils of all kinds. Even the WHO was not always above moralizing (contextualising?) the preventive measures it sought to promote.

## ALTERNATIVE STYLES OF DEFENSE

Today the failures of eradication campaigns and the successes of new conceptions of the immune system are convergent in suggesting modifications of the defended body.

Bodily defense, once taken for granted, has turned out to be very complex; in the 1960s, for example, it was recognized that defensive or immune reactions can sometimes destroy the cellular components of the self. Autoimmunity was held responsible for a new, and growing, category of diseases. It can affect various organs, producing multiple sclerosis, diabetes, or lupus, and susceptibility differs from one individual to another. In a surgical context, defensive reactions seem deleterious for the organism when they target a grafted organ, coming from another individual but intended as a cure.

Autoimmunity led immunologists to reconsider their conception of the body as an organism at war against invaders. As the defense of the body was subordinated to recognition phenomena, described in terms of self and notself, paradoxes have emerged which had been touched upon but lightly at the beginning of the century: in order to defend against the outer world, the immune system must actively differentiate the self from not-self, which means that the organism has a reactivity or a sensitivity to itself. Latterly, autoimmunity has come to be seen as a phenomenon occurring within certain limits, and as normally involved in cellular interactions and communication.

The description of a great number of natural antibodies directed against constituents of the self has led to the view that the main purpose of the immune system is homeostasis (rather than defense). Cells and factors secreted by immunocompetent cells seem to play a role in regulating other biological systems of the body, such as the nervous and the endocrine systems; only in extreme cases would natural reactions to the self lead to imbalance and damage. For the proponents of this alternative view, the very successes of immunization have misled doctors into seeing the immune sustem as primarily defensive, reacting to foreign substances. By contrast, recognition of the sharing of molecules between the self and the not-self has favored the view that the outer world is mirrored in the bodily self. This has led to a more ecological view, reminiscent of the ancient solidarity between micro- and macrocosm, and newly attentive to neglected notions of commensalism and symbiosis in the "uncut self."[11]

In this perspective, new light has been shed on the graft-host relationship, and the recipient now appearing to a certain degree as a chimera — a mixture of identities. Defense then appears as a process which can be 'negotiated' for the survival of the organism. And from this angle, as we reflect back on older notions of the defending/defended body, we may see more than the work of nature. We may also see in the "metaphors of twentieth-century biology,"[12] as in a mirror, the aggressiveness of our male-dominated societies, fostering violence and obsessed by it (as Evelyn Fox-Keller pointed to in her analysis of contemporary science).

Nowhere have societal and immunological concerns been so closely interwoven as in the AIDS epidemic. This recent, startling and highly political plague did not at first view contradict the classic idea of a defending body, but it has come to illustrate the complexities of the relationship between the body and its cosmos.

## THE AIDS EPIDEMIC

In the 1980s AIDS was an immunologically-defined disease (before it became a virological disease). It seemed then to show the body as a defensive organism; the disease appeared to develop as in cities 'open to death', according to an analogy suggested by Epicurus. The virus, when identified as the cause of the disease, was supposed to stamp-out the body's defenses by attaching to the cells responsible. The fortress of the body was overcome from inside. The era of optimism was over: a modern but defenseless human being now faced disease as a naked *Homo sapiens* had once faced a den of lions.

But the knowledge of AIDS has also contributeded to a re-examination of the defending/defended body. Patients with AIDS do not die of damage directly caused by the virus itself, but usually from pathogens called 'opportunistic.' Yet for biologists, the notion of opportunistic germs is contradictory; all germs seize their opportunities whenever they can. There is no clearcut line between active and potential pathogens. As the hero of Albert Camus' *The Plague* eloquently reflected: "I know by science that everybody carries the plague in himself. Nobody is free from it… Microbe is natural."[13] Thus the notion of attack and defense becomes explicitly contextual. Even AIDS does not provide a simple example of annihilated defense: the weakening of the immune response follows a long period where the organism copes efficiently with the heavy antigenic burden resulting from the active multiplication of the virus.

The emergence of opportunistic pathogens suggests that the AIDS case, although extreme, reflects the commonplace — the permanent quest by the body of an equilibrium in a hazardous environment. A broad range of immunological situations extends from the healthy to the dying. The new status of hospitals vis-à-vis contagion illustrates the point: viewed a century ago as the first line against infectious diseases, they are now (again) targeted as the site of dangerous infections caused by multiresistant germs. Scared by the rise of nosocomial infections acquired through a period spent on the wards, surgeons have come to consider that even minor surgery is a major hazard: the operating wound challenges *ipso facto* the vital equilibrium.

## SELF-DEFENSE OF THE INDIVIDUAL

We can see now how nuanced immunological conceptions and older public health views of the body can diverge from each other. In industrialized societies, our focus in this book, the emphasis on the individual defense can be seen as an emerging feature of the post-modern regimen of thought. Immunologists point now to views which partially contradict the official creed of public health. For them, the recognition of genetic differences modulating defensive powers pleads in favor of the exquisite management of the individual. They underline the gaps in our knowledge. They address the consequences for evolution of blind spots induced by the destruction of potentially useful clones, or the artificial stimulation of others. The rise of lymphomas (tumors originating from immunocompetent cells) raises unanswered questions about the long term impact of vaccination and more generally about the 'immunomanipulation' of populations and the influence of environmental changes on disease pattern.

With the AIDS epidemic, it was argued that, whatever the antiquity of retroviruses, contemporary society had, by its various modifications in lifestyle and innovative technologies, fostered a new beast. As there were neither effective drugs or vaccines, rather than segregating the sick, the defense fell back to individuals who were encouraged to choose safe behaviors and avoid contamination. This injunction that the body must defend itself is now frequently adopted by public health experts who tend to blame the subject — who should abstain from drinking and smoking, should regularly attend the doctor for epidemiological surveillance, submit to updated vaccination schedules, avoid any risky behavior, and comply with various treatments following the detection of debilitating diseases such as hypertension or diabetes.

Public health officers, however, have not repudiated their management of collective defense on the basis of standardized individual measures. The number of compulsory vaccines has grown and a wave of protest has followed the introduction of vaccine against chicken pox in the United States or hepatitis B in France. The argument has been raised that no biological rhythm is common to all citizens and that each vaccine should be scheduled in relation to his or her age, social professional status, and style of life. This appears to be a departure from a fundamentally egalitarian democratic style of management of public health issues but it has a post modern ring to it. Family doctors join the chorus, evoking their traditional knowledge of the individual and suggesting vaccination *à la carte*.

Scientific considerations are opportunistically invoked to reinforce this shift. The eradication policy and the lavish use of antibiotics have upset the ecology of disease and may have helped to create niches for new viruses, rather in the same way that AIDS created the conditions for the "emergence"[14] of new opportunistic agents. Yet those who are anxious about the overstimulation of the immune system by multiple combined vaccines and the emergence of new viruses, are also concerned that with the disappearance of many other infectious diseases, the immune system could suffer from idleness, triggering more frequent autoimmune and allergic disorders, or even be condemned to a slow atrophy by lack of evolutionary pressure! All these arguments, even if contradictory, throw doubt on artificial defense and plead in favor of the natural acquisition of lifelong immunity. They echo Pasteur's anxious question: would artificial immunity ever equal the immunity provided by natural smallpox?

History never reproduces itself. Sketching a history of the defending/defended body over the past one hundred years reveals a persistent drive for more security and defense, but also the rise of major doubts over the the strategy for this defense — either individual or collective, national or international or even global. The emphasis shifts between the frontiers of the individual body, guarded by its own cells and their products, and the extension to social groups and populations provided with 'herd immunity.' The ideas of biological defenses are thus constantly reshaped by considerations, both political and biological, on the circulation of germs and organic fluids between bodies.

There is no doubt that the idea of a body equipped with natural defensive forces, stimulated by medical artifacts, has been an important axis of twentieth-century medicine. At the same time, the ambitious project of disease eradication, heir to the Baconian and Cartesian enterprise of radically transforming nature, has roused anxiety, fostered by the detection of new and threatening diseases for which AIDS provided a crucial model. The medical care of the individual diverges from the planned management of populations, while they seemed to stem from the same project. Death, once forgotten, demands to be reintegrated into the medical landscape as more than the mere failure of defense, natural or artificial. The prevailing conceptualization of the germ/host relationship as attack and defense may have led doctors to overlook other possibilities, morally superior and perhaps more rational. Do doctors need to depart from their traditional philosophy of battling against disease? Is the defended body on the point of becoming an archaic view? Are we on the way to a more ecological management of disease with the recognition that the body is immersed in its environment? Surely, the defended-defending body has been central to twentieth-century medicine, but its hegemony may be fading, as a more subtle (and also more ancient) model of the body-environment emerges from its successes as well as from its failures.

## REFERENCES

1. Anne Marie Moulin, 'L'actualité des maladies infectieuses: évolution ou histoire?,' *Revue d'épidémiologie et des santé publique* (1996), **6**: 519–529.
2. David Napier, *The Age of Immunology*, forthcoming.
3. (London: Arnold, 1976).
4. Anne Marie Moulin, 'Une devise pour l'organisme,' *Autrement* (March 1994), 22–36.
5. Rudolf Virchow, quoted by L Rather, 'On the source and development of metaphorical language in the history of Western medicine,' in L.G. Stevenson (ed.), *A Celebration of Medical History*. (Baltimore: Johns Hopkins University Press, 1982), p. 145.
6. Luc Boltanski, 'Les usages du corps,' *Annales ESC* (1971), **1**: 205–228.
7. E. Duclaux, *Pasteur. Histoire d'un esprit*. (Sceaux, 1896), p. 391.
8. Peter B. Medawar, *The Uniqueness of the Individual*. (London: Methuen, 1957).
9. G.S. Wilson, *The Hazards of Immunization*. (Oxford: Oxford University Press, 1967).
10. Emily Martin, *Flexible Bodies. Tracking Immunity in American Culture from the days of Polio to the Age of AIDS*. (Beacon Press: Boston, 1994).
11. Lynn Margulis, 'The Uncut Self', in A. Tauber (ed.), *Organism and the Origins of Self*. (Dordrecht: Kluwer, 1993), pp. 361–374.
12. Evelyn Fox-Keller, *Refiguring Life: Metaphors of Twentieth-Century Biology*. (Washington: Columbia University Press, 1995).
13. Albert Camus, *La peste*. (Paris: Gallimard, 1947).
14. Stephen Morse, 'Factors in the emergence of infectious diseases,' *Emerging Infectious Diseases* (1995), **1**: 7–15.

## FURTHER READING

Corbellini, Gilberto, *L'evoluzione del pensiero immunologico*. (Torino: Boringhieri, 1990).
Daëron, Marc, Fougereau, Michel, Fridman, Hermann W., Moulin, Anne Marie, Revillard, Jean-Pierre, *L'immunité, cent ans après Pasteur*. (Paris: Nathan, 1996).

Fassin, Didier, *L'espace politique de la santé.* (Paris: Presses universitaires de France, 1996).

Foucault, Michel, *La naissance de la médecine sociale,* in *Dits et Ecrits.* (Paris: Gallimard, 1994 (1977)), 207–228.

Hannaway, Caroline, *et al.* (eds), *AIDS and the Public Debate, Historical and Contemporary Perspectives.* (Washington: IOS Press, 1975).

Ludwik, Hirszfeld, *Konstitutionsserologie und Blutgruppenforschung.* (Berlin: Springer, 1928).

Lupton, D., *The Imperative of Health: Public Health and the Regulated Body.* (Newbury Park (Cal.): Sage, 1995).

Mazumdar, Pauline M.H., *Species and Specificity: an Interpretation of the History of Immunology.* (Cambridge: Cambridge University Press, 1995).

Moulin, Anne Marie, *Le dernier langage de l'immunologie, Histoire de l'immunologie de Pasteur au Sida.* (Paris: Presses universitaires de France, 1991).

Moulin, Anne Marie (ed.), *L'aventure de la vaccination.* (Paris: Fayard, 1997).

Silverstein, Arthur M., *A History of Immunology.* (San Diego: Academic Press, 1989).

Sontag, Susan, *Illness as Metaphor.* (New York: Farrar, 1978).

Tauber, Alfred, *The Immune Self, Theory or Metaphor.* (Cambridge: Cambridge University Press, 1994).

Weindling, Paul (ed.), *International Health Organizations and Movements 1918–1939.* (Cambridge: Cambridge University Press, 1995).

CHAPTER 26

# The Genetic Body

JON TURNEY AND BRIAN BALMER

On the face of it, few subjects could be more fitting for any history of the twentieth century than genetics. The subject is as old as the century. Mendel published his results in 1865, but they were ignored or misunderstood until others were ready to assimilate his statistical approach to inheritable factors, they were famously 'rediscovered' in 1900.

In some ways, there has been a steady line of progress since then. Horace Judson tells that story particularly well, pointing out that the first genetic map, showing the relative location of six fruit-fly genes in one chromosome, was published in 1913. As he also emphasizes, the dependence on (usually harmful) mutations as markers has meant that "from the start the genetic map of any species — molds or flies, maize or humans — has been primarily the map of defects."[1] Human genetics, while sharing the wider discipline's concern with similarity and difference, has from the outset also been especially concerned with difference as pathology — with the determinants of what is normal/abnormal, healthy/unhealthy.

As we approach the end of the century, researchers around the world — though mainly in the United States and Europe — are well on the way to mapping and sequencing every human gene, perhaps 50,000–100,000 of them, and their effort is accompanied by a chorus of claims that the results will transform medical practice. The pace of advance has accelerated. The nature of the genetic material remained obscure for half the century but it took just twenty years from the elucidation of the double helix in 1953 for the outlines of recombinant DNA technology to be pieced together. Since then, tools, techniques and data have been added at an ever-increasing rate. It is hard to write about the current state of the art or to make predictions, so fast is the field now moving; but it is safe to endorse Thomas Caskey's judgment in 1992, that:

> we have already attained an ability to examine the human body, from individual cells to nuclear DNA and patterns of gene expression, that would have been unthinkable only twenty years ago.[2]

It is tempting to present the growth of medical genetics in the last hundred years as a series of scientific successes, one of the twentieth century's more striking bequests to the twenty-first. And so it is. But there are several qualifications and complications to the story which make it less straightforward. We shall try and highlight four.

One is the way the early history of Mendelism was bound up with concerns which came to prominence in the last two decades of the nineteenth century, especially post-Darwinian concerns about racial degeneration, and tainted stock. With the formulation of August Weismann's notion of the germ plasm, these concerns seemed to have a close fit with contemporary cell biology, and were frequently translated into calls to emphasize the maintenance of the germ plasm rather than of individual health. This was readily combined with a simplified Mendelian framework after 1900, and helped foster the climate which led to the pre-World War II eugenic legislation of the USA, Nazi Germany and many other countries, later repudiated by the majority of human geneticists but forever influencing attitudes to their work.

A second emphasis is that the scientific story of human and medical genetics, like that of biology in general, is one of a series of reconstitutions of ideas about hereditary transmission, rather than a simple linear progression. Mendelian factors were worked up into the abstract entities of classical genetics. Then they were placed as genes on chromosomes, with a fixed chemical composition. In the last phase, with the advent of molecular genetics, the chemical structure of the genes was reconfigured as an information storage device — so that decoding all the genes is equivalent to reading the *Book of Man.*

A third point to stress is that, in spite of this series of reconceptualizations, an essentialist strand has been preserved at each stage which dates from Weismann. The germ-plasm was the sole vehicle for one generation's influence on the next. And later the heritable material, whatever it might be, was seen as that which contained the irreducible minimum specification of what one is. This feature of genetics is in tension with a growth of anti-essentialist thinking in other areas, as debates around notions like the 'gay gene' illustrate very clearly. While much opinion sees facets of identity like sexual orientation as largely, if not entirely, socially constructed, those searching for 'genes for' homosexuality take the opposite view.

Finally, in the latest phase of medical genetics, as the tools are assembled to do to the genes almost anything one wishes, how one reads this history itself becomes part of the story. In particular, views of the relations between human genetics and eugenics are newly contested in the light of debates about the social implications of the Human Genome Project. Some see the project as constructing an essentially eugenic set of technologies, which will inevitably lead to renewed efforts to improve the human gene pool. And there are new debates about the significance of genetic data for the regulation of social order. Does the focus on the genetic body necessarily mean a body redesigned to fit an engineering specification, a possibility long foreshadowed but only now apparently coming to fruition? Or does the body disappear altogether, to be replaced by a set of readouts from within the cell, dissolving into information?

## FROM MENDELISM TO MORGANISM

"The new facts are of especial interest to medical practitioners," wrote J. Arthur Thomson in the preface to his treatise on *Heredity* of 1908.[3] The new facts he had in mind were both Weismann's theory of the germ-plasm and the Mendelian laws of distribution of character. Both implied radically new ways of looking at inheritance.

In the mid-nineteenth century, evolutionary theory had drawn renewed attention to the need for an explanation of heredity, but Charles Darwin's offering, pangenesis, still assumed that all parts of the body contribute to production of particles, 'gemmules' which influence the formation of the next generation. Weismann, in contrast, reasoning from cytological observations, proposed in the 1880s that the hereditary substance was contained in the nucleus of the germ cells, and that it was this germ-plasm which passed between the generations. There were two crucial implications: that there was no way for the environment to alter the germ plasm, no mechanism, in other words, for the inheritance of acquired characteristics; and that the body played no role in the business of inheritance. "The body, or soma, was considered the temporary and mortal custodian of the continuous line of germ cells."[4]

Mendel's observations were relatively easy to read in the light of this theory, as the segregation of the chromosomes appeared to match the pattern of Mendelian factors. But Mendelism emphasized a further break with the past — it was a statistical study. Outcomes were predictable for populations, but not for individuals. This outlook, which of course was elaborated with great sophistication in evolutionary theory as it developed during the twentieth century, made problematic any direct link between the new theory and medical thinking. What were doctors, dealing with individual patients or families, to make of a set of rules for deriving probable outcomes for large breeding groups?

In consequence, when Thomson turned to the direct medical implications of the facts of heredity, in a chapter which came before his account of Mendelian theory, he had less to say than his introduction promised. He was concerned to establish a clear division between innate and acquired disease, even though this distinction "looks better on paper than by the bedside."[5] He had a list of candidates for conditions which might be inherited, including color-blindness, short-sightedness, "bleeding,"[6] inability to digest the proteids of eggs and milk, excessive freckling (leading to Kaposi's disease), alcoholism and nervous diseases. A year later, William Bateson's authoritative review of progress in human genetics stressed how much more evidence there was about "laws of descent followed by many striking peculiarities which are of the nature of deformity or disease"[7] than about normal characteristics, citing skeletal abnormalities, eye and skin diseases and

Huntington's disease. But when it came to individual clinical cases, Thompson was clear that all that could be claimed was that there were heritable "predispositions," and furthermore that "individual prediction as to the inheritance of predispositions to certain diseases is impossible."[8]

One can read in Thompson's text the beginnings of a division between hereditary disorders and those due to post-natal influences, as he tried to move beyond the common nineteenth-century medical view that 'constitutional' disorders encompassed *both* those in which a predisposition to some condition might be inherited, and those in which weakening of the constitution during a patient's life could be passed on to his or her offspring. However, at this time there was little that was lawful about outcomes in Thomson's scheme of things:

> Variability is one of the fundamental properties of the living organism, and the germ cells are potential organisms. In their relation to the body which is their mortal vehicle, and in their own history, there is ample opportunity for variation to arise, and among these variations we must rank predispositions to disease. In short, such predispositions form part of the puzzle of individuality."[9]

But Thomson, like so many others, saw implications for the health of the population in the 'new facts.' The meeting point for the statistical science of heredity and the treatment of individuals was that other statistically based enterprise, eugenics. And before leaving Thomson's 1908 text, it is instructive to note the tension in his position. He is optimistic about the problems of 'taint' in the germ plasm because;

> By the education of conscience on a scientific basis there is already arising a wholesome prejudice against the intermarriage of subjects in whom there is a strong hereditary bias to certain diseases such as epilepsy and diabetes."[10]

But what are doctors to do about the actual patients who suffer from these diseases? Natural selection, left to itself, would doubtless cleanse the 'taint': "Rotten twigs are always falling off the tree of life. There is a continual irrecoverable precipitation of incapables, who thus cease to muddy the stream."[11]

But while this may be fine for populations, doctors have real patients, and are moved to interfere with this process by the human urge to treat suffering individuals. It was a dilemma which could only be resolved by a treatment capable of affecting the genes themselves.

By the time Thomson wrote, Bateson had already coined the term 'genetics,' and Johannsen was shortly to offer the word 'gene.' The latter became the word of choice because "He had the wisdom to leave the gene undefined and to request that his simple term replace all those other terms that implied some specific structure or function."[12] Among those who adopted it was Thomas Hunt Morgan who was on the verge of making the fruit fly the model for classical genetics. Here was a rapidly reproducing organism with clearly identifiable traits which lent themselves to precise analysis. But humans were not like that. While Morgan and his disciples counted flies in bottles, drew up maps of genes, and built up the framework of classical genetics, studies of people were stronger on conviction than data. In Britain, the doctor-researcher Archibald Garrod provided a clear direction for studies of biochemical individuality with his landmark studies leading to the lectures published as *Inborn Errors of Metabolism* in 1909. But the rare disorders he discussed were of little interest to other doctors and his work was largely ignored until the microbial geneticists Beadle and Tatum established the "one gene — one enzyme hypothesis" thirty years later.[13]

However, there *were* those who took up human genetics but most of them were interested in rather more loosely defined traits, and for rather different reasons. They were, of course, the eugenists. The doctrines of eugenics, the term coined by the polymathic Francis Galton in 1883, combined a reading of the implications of Darwinian natural selection with a fear of degeneration, especially among the proliferating urban poor. After the turn of the century, both positive eugenics (improving the race) and negative eugenics (preventing deterioration) gained a large following among the professional classes of Britain, the United States, Germany and elsewhere. The historical literature on eugenics in all these countries is now very large.

Not all scientifically-inclined eugenists were Mendelians; Karl Pearson at the Galton Laboratory at University College London was a notable exception. But the vast majority of Mendelians interested in human genetics were eugenists. From laboratories like Charles B. Davenport's Eugenics Record Office at Cold Spring Harbor in the US they began compiling pedigrees of traits like feeble-mindedness, alcoholism, criminality, and others even less easy to define with any precision. All were claimed to be due to single, simple Mendelian factors, recessive or dominant, and exhibiting none of the subtleties of genotype-phenotype relations apparent in the growing body of knowledge about other organisms.

Their data was used to support eugenic policies, mostly, as it turned out policies aimed at negative eugenics. They included immigration control and compulsory sterilization in the US, and, ultimately, mass execution in Germany. This was the use of ideas about heredity to define those bodies which should either be prevented from reproducing or eliminated altogether.

## The Development of Human Genetics

Eugenic zealotry seemed scientifically unsatisfactory, as well as politically objectionable, to some of the scientists who pursued the cytological, evolutionary and, increasingly, mathematical intricacies of classical genetics. As J.B.S. Haldane put it in 1938,

> I believe that the facts concerning human heredity are far less simple than many people think them to be. And I hold that a premature application of our rather scanty knowledge will yield little result, and will merely serve to discredit the branch of science in which I am working."[14]

Haldane was correct in his judgment that knowledge was still scanty, in spite of some pioneering efforts. Lionel Penrose had already done important work in the 1930s on heredity and mental disorder. The landmark "Colchester Survey," based on patients in the Royal Eastern Counties Institution (for the mentally deficient), brought a new scientific rigor, and Penrose's anti-eugenist eye, to the origins of mental handicap. His studies identified phenylketonuria as an inborn error of metabolism, and characterized Downs' Syndrome in great detail, repudiating the racist accounts of its origins embodied in its then prevalent name — Mongolism. But he and his colleagues still had to contend with a medical profession most of whom "perceived no value in genetic knowledge for the treatment of disease; if a malady was hereditary, the prevailing medical attitude had it, it must be neither treatable nor preventable."[15]

But in spite of this, and Haldane's more general reservation, the logic of the underlying Galtonian argument — that understanding selection might lead to improvement in the human condition — was still compelling to many. Some leading geneticists, such as Haldane, Julian Huxley and, from the founding group around Morgan, Herman Muller, remained drawn to the idea — Kevles calls them reform eugenists. They wanted a eugenics free from racism and other forms of prejudice, and based on reputable science, as they saw it. On the eve of World War II, the 7th International Genetics Congress in Edinburgh received a cabled query from the editor of the US Science Service news agency; "How could world's population improve genetically?" Their reply, signed by Huxley, Haldane, Lancelot Hogben and Joseph Needham, among others, was a "Geneticists' Manifesto." Viewing a world apparently on the brink of dissolution, they nevertheless reaffirmed their faith in positive eugenics, but stressed that "the genetic improvement of mankind is dependent upon major changes in social conditions, and correlative changes in human attitudes."[16]

By the 1930s, in line with such sentiments, some geneticists were contemplating a new look at human genes. Scientifically, they wanted to keep their distance from the studies of the eugenists, but there was still little else to go on. James Neel describes the outcome of a literature search by his mentor Curt Stern at Rochester in 1939, the prelude to a seminar series on the state of the art in human genetics:

> When we moved to the specifics of human genetics, Stern had been able to locate for our consideration no more than two dozen papers dealing with specific inherited diseases that attempted to treat the inheritance of human traits with a rigor approaching that in experimental genetics."[17]

Three years later, Neel inspected the data held in the by-now defunct Eugenics Record Office, and was dismayed by what he found: "The concerns expressed by so many of my friends and advisors about the parlous intellectual state of human genetics in the United States had been fully deserved."[18] All he could rescue from the mountains of paper was a little, poor quality data on red hair-color, one of the few traits the office's workers had studied with a more or less objective definition.

Nevertheless, Neel persisted, and within a few years published an important paper using his own data to demonstrate that sickle-cell anemia — previously thought to be a dominant trait — was a simple recessive condition. Heterozygous individuals, with one copy of the altered gene, were carriers of the sickle-cell trait. People homozygous for sickle-cell had a serious condition affecting their red blood cells. His department at the University of Michigan became one of the first important centers for medical genetics in the US, and was soon joined by that of Victor McCusick at Johns Hopkins Medical School and Arno Motulsky at the University of Washington in Seattle.

However the US researchers were widely scattered and the British, especially those working alongside Haldane and Penrose in London, were the immediate post-war leaders in human genetics. Penrose was by now installed in the chair created by Galton's endowment at University College London, alongside Haldane. They were part of a core of British researchers who, along with a few American groups, renewed their commitment to pursue human genetics in a fashion rigorous enough to satisfy other scientists. Some suggest that eugenics was generally far from their concerns. It was certainly harder to argue for it explicitly once the scale of Nazi racial atrocities became widely known. Intellectuals of all persuasions in the Weimar Germany of the 1920s had enthusiastically promoted eugenic ideas, but as the political climate changed they became identified with the political Right, and eventually blended with Hitler's doctrines of racial purity, and ultimately the Nazis' project to eliminate undesirables by mass slaughter.

Kevles suggests that the consequences reinforced the movement of scientific ideas, so that after World War II:

> the revelations of the Holocaust had turned 'eugenics' into virtually a dirty word. Besides, the more that was revealed about the complexity of heredity in human beings, the less did eugenics appear defensible in principle, or even scientifically within reach.[19]

Nevertheless, there was a eugenic element to the genetic counseling clinics ('heredity clinics' as they were known in the US at the time) which doctors like Neel, who were trained in genetics, began running, even though the wariness engendered by Nazi atrocities led to an emphasis on the advice offered to couples contemplating reproductive decisions being neutral. As Neel recalls,

> Anxious to avoid the taint of eugenics, we were as non-directive as one can be in counselling situations, contenting ourselves with explaining the genetic facts as clearly and simply as possible. But it was a little difficult to stay uninvolved when, as so often happened, the patient asked: 'Doctor, what would you do if you were me?'[20]

The Michigan effort began in December 1940, five years before its head, Lee Dice, recruited Neel. Dice's philosophy was set out in his Presidential address to the three year-old American Society for Human Genetics, in 1951. Although making the obligatory declaration of repugnance toward the Nazis, he nevertheless remained sympathetic to sterilization of 'defectives' — the old eugenists' favorite target — under 'proper safeguards.' But he suggested that any program of sterilization extensive enough to eliminate any large proportion of harmful genes would infringe liberty. The alternative was to persuade people not to reproduce: "Compulsion should play no part in our programme, except only in the most extreme cases of irresponsibility."[21]

Such was the assumption underlying the advice in Dice's clinic. A similar approach was taken by John Fraser Roberts, who in 1946 set up the first genetic counseling clinic in Britain at the Great Ormond Street children's hospital. Although Roberts was a long-standing member of the British Eugenics Society, he advocated non-directive counseling based on risk estimates. Others in Britain, however, such as Cedric Carter, were more strongly eugenically minded, and saw counseling as a means to reduce the number of children born with heritable disease.

The scale of operations in this period was very small. After reviewing other clinics, Dice told the American Society that facilities then available in North America were woefully inadequate: "At less than a dozen places on the whole continent are there clinics where competent advice on all phases of human heredity is regularly offered."[22] He called for a nationwide expansion:

> The knowledge of genetics which already has been acquired through research is largely unavailable to our people... I urge, therefore, the establishment in every state of a series of heredity clinics which will cooperate closely with physicians, dentists, hospitals, schools, probate judges, welfare agencies, and others responsible for the public welfare, in order to provide dependable advice on human heredity.[23]

The genetic counseling clinics which have emerged in the decades since Dice's prescription was offered followed his approach with some fidelity. What was on offer was not treatment, but 'counseling.' And it was based on a notion, usually tacit, of 'responsible' behavior which often reduced to understanding risk estimates in the same way as the presiding physician and acting accordingly. Since the 1950s, an extensive literature has grown up on the giving and receiving of advice in counseling sessions, on communication, understanding and outcomes. But what there is to be communicated has gradually changed, both in quantity and quality. Today, it is as likely to involve information derived from a molecular genetic test as a reading of a family tree.

But for the time being it was cytogenetic advances which began to reinforce the place of genetics in broader clinical practice. The inseparability of advances in human genetics from work in other species was well illustrated by work on the rhesus blood factors by Cyril Clarke at Liverpool University Medical School, UK. Clarke was both a medical doctor and a specialist in the genetics of butterflies. He showed that the genetics of mimicry in tropical butterfly species were closely akin to the patterns of inheritance of rhesus factors, and in the 1960s this paved the way for successful prevention of rhesus haemolytic disease of the newborn.

## MOLECULAR BIOLOGY, AND MOLECULAR DISEASE

The most often-told story about human genetics after the Second World War is of the influence of the advent of molecular genetics. This was to some extent separate from the further development of clinical human genetics in the first decades after the war, although it was not long before some physicians became aware of speculations that identifying genes might lead to attempts at repairing faulty ones. But the two stories intersect at many points.

When Neel showed that sickle-cell anemia was a Mendelian trait, his data were strictly classical. He examined the behavior of the blood cells of subjects from families where the condition was found. But the new discoveries of molecular biology were quickly brought to bear on the condition as well, and sickle cell became the paradigm case of a simple genetic pathology.

Just a few months after Neel's paper appeared in *Science* in 1949, Linus Pauling and his collaborators published another article on the disease, reporting that the hemoglobin proteins of people with sickle-cell trait, sickle-cell disease and normal blood cells gave different patterns when separated by an electric field — using the new technique known as electrophoresis. This confirmed Pauling's hypothesis that this was a 'molecular disease.'

Seven years later, Vernon Ingram showed that one of the two protein chains in normal hemoglobin, the beta chain, differed by a single amino acid residue in sickle-cell hemoglobin. This was enormously significant news, for Ingram was in the midst of discussions in Cambridge over the implications of the DNA structure of 1953. Francis Crick, now deep in the puzzle of the genetic code, was convinced that a single change in the DNA would alter a single protein. With Ingram's discovery, "what was clear to us before it was done then became clear to everybody."[24]

So from its beginnings, molecular genetics was pointing the way to a fundamental understanding of some disease processes. With the elucidation of the three-dimensional structure of the hemoglobin molecule by Perutz, and the eventual ability to sequence genes and proteins, sickle-cell anemia became one of the best understood diseases, though not one of the most effectively treated. Some things did not change immediately as the idea of the gene was reconstituted in terms of codes and messages. The effect on patients of these refinements in knowledge was minimal. Those with a double dose of the gene still tended to experience recurrent crises, which sent them to hospital for relief of intense pain. With hindsight, sickle-cell was an early example of what would become a feature of the genetics of molecular medicine, the so-called diagnostic-therapeutic gap.

Meanwhile, human genetics as a clinical discipline was becoming established, in large part, separately from these developments in understanding at the molecular level. Cytogenetic advances (including the final identification of the correct human chromosome number in 1956) led to discovery of the chromosomal basis of a number of congenital abnormalities — including Down's syndrome (trisomy 21), and Klinefelter's and Turner's syndromes. New laboratory procedures made chromosomes much easier to visualize. They "gave us 'our' organ" as Victor McKusick put it.[25]

Efforts were made to determine the presence of such syndromes pre-natally. Fetal cells in the amniotic fluid were the first answer, and by the late 1960s the first abortions after mid-trimester amniocentesis and chromosome typing took place. Further technical innovations, including the widespread introduction of ultrasound and withdrawal of cells by chorionic villus sampling, were incorporated in a medical practice which placed more emphasis on surveillance of the fetus.

These techniques would also be prerequisites for the more refined diagnostic testing which later became possible using DNA technology. But in the 1960s, the realities of medical practice belied the nevertheless powerful feeling that molecular biology was laying hold of the fundamentals of inheritance and the optimism that it would eventually lay the ground for new approaches to disease.

This feeling also inspired new images of positive eugenics, based on the ability to read the genes. This would be allied with new reproductive technology to yield complete control over the product. For example, as early as 1965, the distinguished animal biologist ESE Hafez predicted in *Life* magazine that embryo freezing techniques would soon be applied to people, so that:

> A woman will be able to buy a tiny frozen embryo, take it to her doctor, have it implanted in her uterus, carry it for nine months, and then give birth to it as though it has been conceived in her own body. The embryo would, in effect, be sold with a guarantee that the resulting baby would be free from genetic defect. The purchaser would also be told in advance of the color of the baby's eyes and hair, its sex, its probable size at maturity, and its probable IQ.[26]

This is the scenario now repeated many times under the heading of the "genetic supermarket," or more recently as procuring "designer babies."[27] But in spite of all this speculation, the actual work on human traits which could be done at the time was rather more limited, mainly consisting of the gradual cataloguing of loci associated with particular, usually rare, diseases.

At the beginning of the 1980s, Yoxen described medical specialization in clinical genetics as a restricted affair, confined mainly to child health. He saw genetic disease as limited to a large number of uncommon abnormalities, dealt with by a new expert group in one field:

> it is precisely in the area of medicine where the burden of acute [ie., infectious] disease had disappeared in the post-war period, pediatrics, that an interest in a very specialised, preventive clinical genetics has appeared.[28]

A decade and a half later, the picture is quite different. There are still experts in this group, and they now have a good deal to be more expert about. The definitive catalogue of human traits, Mendelian Inheritance in Man, is now maintained on the internet, and in the Summer of 1996 had some 8,000 entries (the number was rising by around 50 a month).

There are also clinical geneticists trying to teach their colleagues in the wider profession about the relevance of genetics, in primary care for example. And there are those arguing for a wider appreciation of the relevance of the new genetics to clinical practice. But the textbooks produced by clinical specialists are still traditional in outlook, and read as sober, conservative tracts compared with the predictions of the molecular geneticists. For the limited phase Yoxen describes in the development of medical genetics was relatively short-lived. The rapid spread of the new molecular genetic techniques in biological research soon went along with a much stronger claim about the role of genes in disease.

Strohman offers the most extreme interpretation of these claims, suggesting that Crick's famous "central dogma"[29] — stating that DNA governs RNA, which governs protein production — was implicitly extended to read: DNA>RNA>protein>Everything else, including disease. According to Strohman, "by the late 1980s, the vast majority of the National Institutes of Health (NIH) research budget was going to projects reflecting this dogma."[30] Also within those budgets was a major sponsorship of the new human genome initiative.

## THE HUMAN GENOME PROJECT

Human genetics in the 1980s and 1990s has been dominated by genetic mapping and sequencing in the form of the international Human Genome Project. The Project has been hailed as the quest for the 'holy grail of human genetics' by its supporters, and as 'mediocre science, terrible science policy' by its critics. It is, to date, the largest collaborative research effort to have taken place in the life-sciences and has frequently been referred to as 'big science' for biology.

The benefits for disease diagnosis and therapy have been frequently touted as justification for public support of this effort to inventory the entire human genetic complement. Walter Gilbert describes the program in terms which come close to Strohman's characterization:

> The possession of a genetic map and the DNA sequence of a human being will transform medicine... When we have a detailed genetic map, we will be able to identify whole sets of genes that influence general aspects of how the body grows or how the body fails to function... A whole variety of human susceptibilities will be recognised as having genetic origins."[31]

In the same collection of essays, Thomas Caskey sees great days ahead:

> The diagnosis of disease-predisposing genes will alter the basic practice of medicine in the twenty-first century. Perhaps in twenty years time it will be possible to take DNA from

newborns and anlyze fifty or more genes for the allelic forms that can predispose the infant to many common diseases... For each defective gene there will be therapeutic regimens that will circumvent the limitations of the defective gene. Thus medicine will move from a reactive mode (curing patients already sick) to a preventive mode (keeping people well).[32]

What were these expectations based on? Although the explicit goal of obtaining a gene map can be traced back to the late 1950s, a number of technical developments now encouraged the belief that a full map was a realistic goal. They also signaled greater contact between studies in human genetics and molecular biology throughout the 1970s and 1980s . The discovery in the late 1970s of sequence differences between individuals, so-called restriction fragment length polymorphisms (RFLPs), with no phenotypic effect greatly expanded the available genetic markers. In addition, Sanger in Cambridge and Gilbert and Maxam at Harvard developed reliable DNA sequencing methods. The early 1980s then saw the introduction of a range of molecular biological techniques which expedited physical mapping. These included the ability to manipulate long strands of DNA, to separate large fragments of DNA from each other, and to transfer long stretches of DNA between cells.

The idea of an organized program germinated in the US during the mid-1980s and their 'Human Genome Initiative' was officially launched at the start of the 1991 financial year with a target of completion in fifteen years. This was most certainly not a simple culmination of the technical developments within molecular biology. Plans for the project were fiercely debated. There were fears surrounding the diversion of money toward what some saw as a parochial area of genetics; accusations that mapping and sequencing were handle-cranking technical exercises; discussion over whether to emphasize mapping or sequencing in the project; and struggles over who would be the lead agency.

Over the period of planning and debate in the US, the idea of a project spread to a number of other countries. In early 1991 a world-wide survey of genome mapping activities published by the UK Medical Research Council listed eight countries with established national genome projects (Denmark, France, Germany, Italy, UK, Japan, USSR and US) and a further seven which had made moves to instigate national programs (Australia, Netherlands, Canada, Chile, Sweden, Korea and New Zealand) although not all were successful . In addition, international programs had been instigated or proposed by the EC, UNESCO, Latin-America and the Nordic countries. World-wide co-ordination, but not research funding, of the initiative was undertaken by the Human Genome Organization (HUGO), established in 1988 with its headquarters in Geneva. In the absence of an overarching program, the international effort is best conceived of as a loose confederacy of programs. And the association with advances in medical understanding was reinforced by a series of discoveries of single genes, which in altered form were responsible for conditions as varied as cystic fibrosis, Huntington's disease and muscular dystrophy. Genes associated with some cases of more common conditions — breast cancer, Alzheimer's disease, diabetes and arthritis — also followed, together with claims (often subsequently retracted) to have located gene loci influencing susceptibility to schizophrenia, depression, and alcoholism. Diagnostic tests using DNA probes from these genes soon began to appear.

## TURNING THE BODY INSIDE OUT

What, then, will happen as the genome is progressively charted? An obvious consequence of locating all of the genes in the human body is that the biological map will be re-drawn. The human genome map, however, is not the only map being created by scientific endeavor. In addition, the relationship between genes, bodies and society is being reconfigured.

There is already a huge volume of commentary on the genome project, partly because of the decision in the US to earmark a small percentage of the budget for ethical, legal and social aspects of the new genetics. This, in turn, was a response to concerns about the potential consequences of a 'new genetics' which had been widely expressed since at least the mid-1960s . But the main point to stress, as the tenor of the predictions for medical impacts suggests, is that the genome project is not, or not simply, a matter of acquiring knowledge of the number, location, and ultimately DNA sequence of genes on chromosomes. It is a technological project, both in terms of the ability to detect and identify DNA sequences and, perhaps, to rewrite them. As Paul Rabinow has put it:

> Like most modern science, it is deeply imbricated with technological advances in the most literal way, in this case the confidence that qualitatively more rapid, accurate and efficient machinery will be invented if the money is made available (this is already happening). The second sense of technological is the more interesting one: the object to be known — the human genome — will be known in such a way that it can be *changed*.[33]

Although this ability to intervene promises many medical benefits, a host of concerns have also been raised by various commentators. Much of the present discussion focuses on screening tests, and the potential of genetic information to legitimize discrimination has received fresh attention. For which traits and what purposes should people be screened? Should employers and insurers have access to the results? In health care, screening also raises new problems concerning the practice and purpose of counseling, for late onset disorders such as Huntington's disease, for example, or for conditions where many genes affect outcomes, like heart disease. As screening becomes more widespread, the diagnostic-therapeutic gap is beginning to affect more people.

The potential to screen for large numbers of traits has raised additional questions over access to information. The debate over whether genetic data should be owned publicly or privately is not just about whether to treat DNA as a commodity. In the absence of regulation, it is easy to imagine that some genetic testing agencies might guarantee confidentiality, whereas others might offer cheaper testing subsidized through selling genetic information to third parties. Privacy itself becomes commodified. Charlie Davison has argued, in a similar vein, that the probabilistic nature of genetic tests means that their "essential function is the production of uncertainty."[34] It is consumption of this commodity, uncertain risk information, in a 'measure and manage culture' which increasingly defines "who we are and who we appear to be."[35]

After screening comes genetic manipulation. Some concerns are related to current research on somatic gene therapy. This work aims to remedy genetic dysfunction in the non-reproductive cells. More contentious is the possibility of germ-line manipulation, altering the genome of the reproductive cells in order to change future generations. This is plainly a technology for eugenics.

Anxiety about the consequences of inapt reductionism underlies many of these specific concerns. Sophisticated arguments against untrammeled genetic reductionism have been made by both geneticists and non-geneticists. But a number of commentators suggest that in recent biomedical discourse the genetic script is regarded as the sole basis for building bodies or guiding behavior. Lippman has launched a focused attack on this *geneticization* of medicine, the process in which "differences between individuals are reduced to their DNA codes."[36] From this perspective, maps of the human genome "objectify the body and make the genome the focus of medical attention, rather than the person."[37] The resultant 'genetic body' is described in similar terms by Gilbert who writes:

> We are what our genes tell us we are. This is a body full of potentials. It is who we are and who we might have been. This is the body where the centre of identity is within the nucleus of every somatic cell. It is the body sought by human genome project."[38]

All of these developments have been widely advertised in the mass media, where they have blended with earlier currents of gene talk. The public image of the gene in the twentieth century is a history in itself. Today, according to Dorothy Nelkin and Susan Lindee, the gene has become a modern cultural icon which perpetuates Weismann's genetic essentialism.

> Instead of a piece of hereditary information, it has become the key to human relationships and the basis of family cohesion. Instead of a string of purines and pyrimidines, it has become the essence of identity and the source of social difference. Instead of an important molecule, it has become the secular equivalent of the human soul. Narratives of genetic essentialism are omnipresent in popular culture, here explaining evil and predicting destiny, there justifying institutional decisions. They reverberate in public debates about sexuality and race, in court decisions about child custody and criminal responsibility, and in ruminations about the meaning of life.[39]

More abstractly, we can begin to identify a historical tendency for bodies to be not merely reduced to genes but displaced by them. The body is *turned inside out* as decisions once made on the basis of the inspectable surfaces of the body become the province of the (now visible) genome. There were instances of this before the advent of gene probes and DNA databases. The sexing of female athletes, for example, moved in the late 1960s from being based on a medical certificate, to a visual inspection of the athlete's body and finally to a chromosomal test. This shift took place notwithstanding several anomalous cases in the scientific literature, such as males who carry two X rather than an X and Y chromosome. Molecular genetics is accelerating the spread of this particular way of construing the body in relation to genetics.

Critiques of this tendency center on the nature and consequences of reductionism. Flower and Heath broaden the critique to look at the potential uses of reductionism in structuring and ordering society. Drawing on Foucault, they outline an emerging *micro-anatamo politics* of the human genome. They argue that the Human Genome Project is a nexus for two expressions of power, the disciplining of entire populations (*bio-politics*) and the regulation of human bodies (*anatamo-politics*). Populations will become defined by reference to the genetic body, expressed in monolithic terms as 'the' human genome. This consensus map then becomes the benchmark for defining what is 'normal' and what is 'deviant.' Individuals are judged by that standard, and their status defined accordingly as 'included' or 'marginal' in areas such as access to healthcare, insurance and employment.

The displacement of bodies by genes thus becomes, in its broadest sense, a potential solution to the problem of governance. This task has only recently been construed as a problem focusing on bodies. So, in Turner's influential theory of the body, social systems are presented with four related problems: the reproduction of populations to provide continuity over time; the restraint of internal desire; the regulation of populations in space; and the external representation of bodies. Schilling points out that these are the "minimal bodily tasks which societies must fulfil in order to reproduce themselves."[40]

We can begin to see how all of these problems can be addressed as genetic tasks. Genetic screening and counseling are centrally concerned with reproductive choices, the search for the 'gay' gene carries the potential for regulating desire at the genetic level, genetic profiles on databases provide a means of intimate surveillance by both the state and private corporations. Finally, the idea of reconfiguring the body, of producing 'designer babies,' is inherent in the promise of gene therapy. Of course, the extent to which these problems of governance are solved in a liberatory or oppressive way becomes a question of the social, technical and political network — including the regulatory system, the legal provisions, the research agendas, the markets which are envisaged — in which the new genetics is being researched and commercialized. It also, of course, depends on the evolution of health care systems around the world. But there we leave history and enter the politics of contested futures.

REFERENCES

1.  Horace Judson, 'A History of the Science and Technology behind Gene Mapping and Sequencing', in Daniel Kevles and Leroy Hood (eds), *The Code of Codes*. (Cambridge, MA: Harvard University Press, 1992).

2.  Thomas Caskey, 'DNA-Based Medicine: Prevention and Therapy', in Kevles and Hood, *ibid.*

3.  J. Arthur Thomson, *Heredity*. (London: John Murray, 1908).

4.  L. Dunn, 'Ideas About Living units, 1864–1909: a chapter in the history of genetics,' from *Perspectives in Biology and Medicine* (Spring 1965). Reprinted in E. Garber (ed.), *Genetic Perspectives in Biology and Medicine*. (Chicago and London: University of Chicago Press, 1985), pp. 5–16.

5.  Thomson, *op. cit.*

6.  Thomson, *op. cit.*

7.  William Bateson, 'Mendel's *Principles of Heredity*, Cambridge, 1909'. Quoted in David Barker, 'The Biology of Stupidity: Genetics, Eugenics and Mental Deficiency in the Inter-War Years', *British Journal for the History of Science* (1998), **22**: 347–375.

8.  Thomson, *op. cit.*

9.  *Ibid*, p. 268.

10. *Ibid.*

11. *Ibid*, p. 307.

12. Elof Carlsson, 'Defining the Gene: An Evolving Concept', *American Journal of Human Genetics* (1991), **49**: 475–487.

13. A.G. Bearn, *Archibald Garrod and the Individuality of Man*. (Oxford: Clarendon Press, 1993); A.G. Bearn and E.D. Miller, 'Archibald Garrod and the Development of the Concept of Inborn Errors of Metabolism', *Bulletin of the History of Medicine* (1979), **53**: 315–328.

14. J.B.S. Haldane, *Heredity and Politics*. (London: George Allen and Unwin, 1938), p. 10.

15. Kevles, *op. cit.*, p. 177.

16. Anon, 'Mice and Men at Edinburgh: Reports from the Genetic Congress', *Journal of Heredity* (1939), **30**: 371.

17. James Neel, *Physician to the Gene Pool: Genetic Lessons and Other Stories*. (New York: John Wiley, 1994), p. 9.

18. *Ibid*, p. 17.

19. Kevles (1992), *op. cit.*

20. Neel, *op. cit.*, p. 29. See also Paul *op. cit.*, pp. 126–128.

21. Lee Dice, 'Heredity Clinics: their value for public service and for research', *American Journal of Human Genetics* (1952), **4**: 1–13. Reprinted in C. Bajema, *Eugenics, Then and Now. Benchmark Papers in Genetics*, Vol. 5. (Dowden: Halsted Press, 1976).

22. Dice, *op. cit.*

23. Dice, *op. cit.*

24. Horace Judson, *The Eighth Day of Creation: The Makers of the Revolution in Biology*. (New York: Simon and Schuster, 1979), p. 308.

25. Victor McKusick, 'The Growth and Development of Human Genetics as a Clinical Discipline', *American Journal of Human Genetics* (1975), **27**: 261–73.

26. Anon, 'Control of Life', *Life* (September 20, 1965), **39, No 6**: 53–72.

27. The term 'genetic supermarket' was used in Robert Nozick, *Anarchy, State and Utopia*. (Oxford: Basil Blackwell, 1974), p. 315.

28. Edward Yoxen, 'Constructing Genetic Disease', in Peter Wright and Andrew Treacher (eds), *The Problem of Medical Knowledge: Examining the Social Construction of Medicine*. (Edinburgh: Edinburgh University Press, 1982).

29. Richard Strohman, 'Ancient Genomes, Wise Bodies, Unhealthy People: Limits of a Genetic Paradigm in Biology and Medicine', *Perspectives in Biology and Medicine* (Autumn 1993), **37**: 112–145.

30. Strohman, *op. cit.*

31. Walter Gilbert, 'Vision of the Grail', in Daniel Kevles and Leroy Hood (eds), *The Code of Codes: Scientific and Social Issues in the Human Genome Project*. (Cambridge, MA: Harvard University Press, 1992), p. 94.

32. Thomas Caskey, 'DNA-Based Medicine: Prevention and Therapy', in Kevles and Hood, *The Code of Codes*, *op. cit.*, pp. 112–135.

33. Paul Rabinow, 'Artificiality and Enlightenment: From Sociobiology to Biosociality', in J. Crary and S. Kwinter (eds), *Incorporations, Zone 6*. (MIT Press, 1992), p. 236.

34. Charlie Davidson, 'Predictive Genetics: The Cultural Implications of Supplying Probable Futures', in Marteau and Richards (eds), (*op. cit.*, 1996), pp. 317–330.

35. Dorothy Nelkin and Laurence Tancredi, *Dangerous Diagnostics: The Social Power of Biological Information*. (New York: Basic Books, 1989).

36. Abby Lippman, 'Led (Astray) by Genetic Maps: The Cartography of the Human Genome and Health Care', *Social Science and Medicine* (1992), **35 No. 12**: 1469–1476.

37. *Ibid.*

38. Stephen Gilbert, 'Resurrecting the Body: Has Postmodernism Had Any Effect on Biology?' *Science in Context* (1995), **8 No. 4**: 563–577, at p. 571.

39. Dorothy Nelkin and Susan Lindee, *The DNA Mystique: The Gene as a Cultural Icon*. (New York: W.H. Freeman, 1995), p. 198.

40. Chris Schilling, *The Body and Social Theory*. (London: Sage, 1993), p. 92.

## FURTHER READING

Cook-Deegan, Robert, *The Gene Wars: Science, Politics and the Human Genome*. (New York: WW Norton and Co., 1994).

Dunn, L., 'Ideas about living units, 1864–1909: A chapter in the history of genetics.' *Perspectives in Biology and Medicine*, Spring 1965. Reprinted in Garber, E., (ed.), *Genetic Perspectives in Biology and Medicine*. (Chicago: University of Chicago Press, 1985), pp. 5–16.

Judson, Horace, 'A History of the Science and Technology Behind Gene Mapping and Sequencing', in Daniel Kevles and Leroy Hood (eds), *The Code of Codes*. (Cambridge MA: Harvard University Press, 1992).

Kevles, Daniel, *In the Name of Eugenics: Genetics and the Uses of Human Heredity*. (Berkeley: University of California Press, 1986).

Keynes, Milo, *Sir Francis Galton: The Legacy of his Ideas*. (London: Macmillan, 1993).

Neel, James, *Physician to the Gene Pool: Genetic Lessons and Other Stories*. (New York: John Wiley, 1994).

Olby, Robert, *Constitutonal and Hereditary Disorders*. In William Bynum and Roy Porter (eds), *Companion Encyclopedia of the History of Medicine*. (London and New York: Routledge, 1994), Chapter 20, pp. 412–437.

Paul, Diane, *Controlling Human Heredity — 1865 to the Present*. (Atlantic Highlands: Humanities Press, 1995).

Thom, Deborah and Jennings, Mary, 'Human Pedigree and the 'Best Stock': From Eugenics to Genetics?', in Theresa Marteau and Martin Richards (eds), *The Troubled Helix: Social and Psychological Implications of the New Human Genetics*. (Cambridge: Cambridge University Press, 1996).

Yoxen, Edward, 'Constructing Genetic Disease', in Peter Wright and Andrew Treacher (eds), *The Problem of Medical Knowledge: Examining the Social Construction of Medicine*. (Edinburgh: Edinburgh University Press, 1982).

# CHAPTER 27

# The Analyzed Body

OLGA AMSTERDAMSKA AND ANJA HIDDINGA

Analysis of the body is not a twentieth-century invention but, depending on how narrowly or broadly the term is understood, a common feature of all attempts to understand disease by identifying a problem within an ill person. Clay oracles, humoral interpretations, and systems of bodily fluxes are means to analyse the body as much as HIV tests, opsonic indexes, PET scans, and DNA fingerprinting. Even if we restrict the meaning of analysis to refer only to chemical decomposition, physical dissection, and close visual inspection, the history of medical analysis would reach well into the past. This is not to deny, of course, that modes of analysis changed profoundly around 1800 when physicians began to regard the body as an objective entity operating according to universal biological laws, and came to treat disease as a localizable and definite phenomenon. This new way of understanding enabled doctors to see diseases as impairments of particular parts of the body of the individual and not of constitutions and situations. It permitted a separation between the patient as a social being and the patient as a biological organism — which is so often the crux of present day critiques of medical care. One also cannot ignore the fact that the variety, number, and complexity of contemporary modes of analysis far exceed those of the past. It has been estimated that while in 1950 some 160 different diagnostic tests could be performed in clinical laboratories in the United States, by the early 1980s more than 600 such tests were available. The numbers of tests that were actually being performed in such laboratories grew at an even faster rate: in 1971 in the US two thousand million such tests were performed; by 1976 this figure had risen to some five thousand million and it was estimated that their number would increase to 12.2 thousand million by 1986.[1]

Still, many of the new, diagnostic methods and techniques developed in the course of the twentieth century are the progeny of nineteenth-century ideas about the proper methods of analyzing the body rather than results of completely new conceptualizations of pathology and physiology. There are clear intellectual continuities linking simple dissection and gross pathology to the microscopic study of tissues and cells, nineteenth-century physiological laboratory apparatus to today's CT scans and EEGs, or nineteenth-century methods of testing albumin in urine to today's autoanalyzers which provide detailed and precise measurements of the chemical composition of bodily fluids.

### ANALYSIS IN THE CLINIC

In the course of the nineteenth century the idea of diagnosis based on the testimony of the patient and the doctor's intuition gradually gave way to the conviction that the body itself could yield data independently of what the patient thought or felt. Physical signs in the patient came to be seen as indications of underlying structural abnormalities, and careful observation as necessary to detect them. In the beginning, these careful bedside observations were made with un-aided senses, their focus being primarily anatomical, the precise localization of lesions. Soon, however, instruments were developed to reach where the eye, the ear, and the hand could not. The stethoscope, for example, extended the possibilities of auscultation and percussion when examining sounds in the chest cavity. Likewise, the ophthalmoscope, the laryngoscope, and scopes permitting the examination of stomach, bladder, rectum, and vagina extended the range of visual examination of gross anatomical changes. Reiser points out that because these instruments were developed from an anatomical perspective on diagnosis, their use contributed to an atomization of the body, partitioning medical examination and orienting it toward smaller and more precisely defined areas.

The anatomical perspective on disease remained strong throughout the century, reaching a culmination in 1896 when Wilhelm Roentgen published his research on the mysterious X-rays. Roentgen irradiation seemed to have rendered the body transparent and to have exposed the living patient's innermost organs to the doctor's eye, as if it were an autopsy on the living. The rapidity with which clinical researchers adopted this new tool for the analysis of medical conditions was unsurpassed. And although acceptance of X-ray equipment for routine analysis in the clinic proceeded at a much more moderate pace, the influence of the technology was profound. The introduction of X-ray technology is even said to mark the beginning of a new technological era in medicine. Since that time, medical practice has become increasingly dependent on technology for the analysis of bodily structures and processes. Some of the visual representations of disease produced by modern technologies, such as ultrasound echography, computed tomography (CT), magnetic resonance imaging (MRI), and positron emission tomography (PET), can be seen as direct continuations of the anatomical tradition in medicine.

Using different physical and chemical principles, all of these diagnostic techniques produce pictures of bodily structures. Echographs are images representing the changes in velocity that ultrasonic waves undergo when passing through different tissues; they show anatomical abnormalities. The apparent harmlessness of ultrasound has made this technique especially practical in obstetrics, where, particularly since the 1950s, concern for the safety of the fetus has come to limit the use of Roentgen radiation. Since the 1960s, the position, length, and anatomical abnormalities in the growing fetus have been established through ultrasonic examination of the pregnant woman. CT scans, in use since the 1970s, are made with X-rays and show computer-reconstructed images of successive cross-sections of a particular part of the body, allowing for anatomical analysis in a three-dimensional space. Computers also play an essential role in magnetic resonance imaging (MRI) developed for clinical use in the 1980s. MRI scans are computer compilations of cross-section images made not by means of X-rays but by waves of radio-frequency which are manipulated in magnetic fields. Moreover, MRI does not necessarily image anatomical structures. The resulting scan can be made to reflect one of a number of subtle, essentially chemical properties of bodily tissue, requiring highly specialized skills for their production and interpretation. This is certainly true for PET scanning, the latest diagnostic imaging technique the clinical applications of which have been explored since the late 1980s. A whole team of experts is necessary to run this diagnostic device. Because of its high initial and operating costs, it is rarely found outside major medical centers and teaching hospitals. PET scanners trace flows of chemicals through tissues and can measure, for example, metabolic activity as reconstructed by computer calculations. The quantitative recordings of such biochemical processes in functioning organs like the heart and especially the brain, are spatially organized, often by means of an X-ray or MRI image. The resulting PET scans, often reproduced in the media in bright colors, resemble familiar anatomical representations. That these pictures are created from complicated compilations of various sorts of data, suggests the dominance of visual representations in the evaluation of disease and abnormality. Because these newest techniques of analyzing the body reflect both function and structure, the traditional separation of these two modes of analysis may be dissolving.

The anatomical perspective on disease dominant in the nineteenth century did not easily allow questioning as to what had caused the observed lesions. Growing interest in the clinical applicability of physiological research in the second half of the nineteenth century introduced a new, functional perspective on disease in which questions about etiology were prominent. Processes like circulation, digestion, and respiration came to be seen as susceptible to disturbances that were invisible at first, but could produce anatomical lesions at a later stage. The hope was that if the proper signs of such disturbances were recorded early enough, the disease could be detected long before anatomical changes would occur and perhaps in time for effective treatment.

Within this functional perspective on disease an instrument like the thermometer acquired a new meaning. It had been available from as early as the eighteenth century, pioneered by Herman Boerhaave in Leiden, but its use elsewhere was very limited. Only in the second half of the nineteenth century did it achieve its place in the medical armamentarium, becoming one of the very basic analytical tools of the physician. Since Galen, an increase of 'body-heat' was considered a disease *sui generis,* but when seen from a physiological perspective it became a physical sign indicating an underlying disease process. The thermometer not only traced this sign, extending the doctor's touch as a means to gain information from the patient, but it did so in a quantitative way. The classical study of the subject was CA Wunderlich's treatise on temperature in disease published in 1868 in which he presented observations of changes in body-temparature of some 25,000 patients suffering from a variety of conditions. Other instruments, like the sphygmograph and polygraph recording the movements of the pulse, were in some respects similar to the thermometer, though based on very different physical principles. They could be used to monitor disease processes in living patients and allowed the results to be uniformly recorded. Many of these techniques produced quantitative data and represented states and processes in the body in terms of numbers or graphs. The introduction of these instruments thus resulted in new classificatory criteria for disease, while old disease categories were frequently redefined to include various new subcategories.

This process of refining and redefining concepts of disease is an inherent consequence of the adoption of each new analytical method in the clinic. In obstetrics, for example, technology to monitor the baby during labor was developed in the 1950s and '60s. Through clinical research the feasibility of continuous measurement of fetal heart-tones during labor was established, the normal rate of heart-tones was defined, and new criteria for the conceptualization of a normal delivery were created. With the availability of such measurements, the existing notion of 'fetal distress' became substantiated, changing from a subjective, personal impression to a quantitative and precise medical category requiring a doctor's intervention. Such defining of states of disease or of being at risk is by no means unproblematic. Recordings of continuous processes show no marked inherent transition points between the healthy state and the diseased. Especially when the patient is not experiencing pain or discomfort, the question of whether a measurement is indicative of risk or disease at all can be a subject of debate. As George Pickering's reflections on the concept of hypertension show, the establishment of cut-off points can be seen as the result of a negotiation process involving all sorts of assumptions, both philosophical and purely practical.

While the recordings produced by various instruments could still be seen as extensions and refinements of direct sensual perceptions, the growing influence of laboratory data in the evaluation of disease processes introduced a whole new variety of dimensions in which to conceptualize the functioning of the body. Physicians explored not only qualities like pressure, rate, or temperature, but also those that were not directly accessible to the senses. Laboratory research analyzing body functions (re)introduced categories from physics into medical thinking. Since the latter half of the nineteenth century, for example, physiologists had been studying the functioning of the nervous system through animal experiments. While some of this work (particularly in England) focused primarily on the localization of functions in the brain, other physiologists studied the electrical activity of the nervous system, prompting the idea that the electrical activity of the human brain could be used as a sign of its functioning. In 1929, the German physiologist Hans Berger published a paper on the use of an Edelman string galvanometer to record the electrical activities of the brain, essentially the same machine as the electrocardiograph developed some years earlier by the Dutch physiologist Einthoven. Berger was the first to publish the ink tracings of electrical activities in the human brain that his machine produced, but it was not until the mid-1930s that his work was picked up by the international community working on the functioning of the nervous system. Berger's publications consisted of a number of case studies. The normal 'brain wave' pattern was defined on the basis of an analysis of the brains of healthy individuals. After this norm had been set, a whole series of papers on neurological disorders was produced, in which particular deviations from this standard were reported. This work became paradigmatic. By the end of the 1930s, not only physiologists but clinicians as well had embraced Berger's electroencephalograph (EEG) as a valuable tool in the analysis of (dys)functioning of the brain. Soon most neurological disorders could be analyzed in terms of EEG recordings, and 'brain wave patterns' came to play an important and sometimes dominant role in the classification of neurological disease.

## ANALYSIS IN THE LABORATORY

The anatomical tradition, so important in the development of clinical medicine, was also of central importance in the development of analysis in the laboratory, the key site for analysts in twentieth-century medicine. Morbid anatomy originating in the autopsy room constitutes one of the sources of modern pathological understanding and techniques. In the course of the nineteenth century the pathologico-anatomical correlations, which initially focused on the gross pathology of organs, shifted to the analysis of diseased tissues, and then of cells. The developments in histology and cell-theory, the use of improved microscopes (from the 1830s), and new fixing, sectioning, and staining techniques (in the second half of the nineteenth century) promoted the observation and classification of morphological changes in ever smaller structures and in ever finer detail. As the attention of researchers shifted from organs to tissues and cells, so did the manner in which they localized, differentiated, and classified pathologies. These changes were also accompanied by the establishment of the new locations where pathological work took place: the dissecting room came to be supplemented first by the research laboratory, and then the clinical pathological laboratory.

The differentiation of tumors, for example, was one of the central foci of nineteenth-century histopathology and cellular pathology, and led researchers to classify various tumors in terms of the morphology of tissues and cells. The role of these analytical techniques in the clinical management of disease, however, continued to evolve well into the twentieth century. In the second half of the nineteenth century, the pathologist, whose activities until then focused on post mortem examination, would be requested by a surgeon to examine microscopically tissues excised during surgery. Initially, these examinations of tumors by pathologists were usually performed after surgery and, as Jacyna has shown, used more as a post facto commentary on the case than for diagnostic or prognostic purposes. Despite the fact that the frozen section technique was available since the 1870s, histopathological examination came to be used as a means of prospective diagnosis and an indicator for further treatment only in the first decades of the twentieth century, when biopsies came to be performed first during and then prior to surgical intervention. After World War II, cytological diagnostic techniques, most prominently the Pap smear for the diagnosis of cervical cancer, would be used also as a means of finding cancerous changes prior to any clinical manifestation of disease. George Papanicolaou had already observed exfoliated cancer cells in women's vaginal smears in the late 1920s, but the use of his technique for routine screening in healthy populations was a post-World War II development which involved a new (gendered) division of labor and various attempts to standardize and automate the test. Thus, although today's biopsies and cytological diagnostic techniques derive from nineteenth-century traditions of medical microscopy, they occupy quite a different place in clinical practice.

The reductionist impulse to analyze ever smaller bits of bodily structures can be traced not only in the history of pathological examinations of solid tissues, but also in the development of analytical techniques for the study of a variety of bodily fluids (including blood, urine, and sputum). Although the examination of urine for pathognomic signs is an ancient medical procedure, the technical development of many aspects of twentieth-century urinalysis grew out of nineteenth-century research. In the course of the nineteenth century, direct visual inspection of urine for color, turbidity, and sediment, reaction to litmus, and measurement of specific gravity were supplemented by both microscopic examinations for pus, casts, and crystals, and chemical analyses for traces of albumin (protein), sugar, and other substances. At the basis of these new methods of analyzing urine was the mid-nineteenth century work of Bright and his colleagues, many of them chemists, who established a relationship between kidney disease and the presence of protein in urine. New chemical tests for urinary sugar, long associated with diabetes, were developed in the same period. Microscopic examination of urinary casts associated with different types of morphological changes of the kidney served as a basis for the diagnosis and classification of different types of nephritis. In the late nineteenth and early twentieth centuries, a number of German investigators and American clinical biochemists such as Otto Folin and Stanley Benedict extended these chemical methods of urinalysis by adapting newer chemical laboratory techniques to clinical applications and by emphasizing quantitative measurements of a variety of substances (for example, urea, creatine, uric acid, ammonia, and sugar). However, as Howell shows for two American hospitals, the adoption of many of these more sophisticated chemical techniques was very gradual, even though simple urinalysis was performed routinely on almost all hospital patients. The test changed its meaning in the early decades of the twentieth century when instead of being performed only on admission it came to serve as a way to monitor the clinical course of diseases such as diabetes or nephritis.

Even though analyses of blood and its constituents also have a long tradition, both microscopic and immunological techniques of blood analysis came to be used as routine methods of clinical diagnosis somewhat later than urinalysis. Knowledge gained in pathological and physiological laboratories in the second half of the nineteenth century linked various abnormal blood conditions (red blood cell or hemoglobin deficiency in anemia, or increases in the number of leucocytes in leukemia) with specific diseases. The direct utilization of such knowledge in clinical practice was, however, a protracted process. After the decline in the practice of blood-letting, drawing sufficient amounts of blood for analysis came to be regarded as a problematic and highly invasive process. Venepuncture became an acceptable method of drawing blood for analysis only after the First World War, and in the early decades of the century substantial effort was made to develop techniques which would make it possible to perform both microscopic and chemical analyses on small quantities of blood which could be obtained by pricking a finger or an earlobe. Moreover, early microscopic techniques (such as Vierordt's blood counts introduced in 1852) required considerable skill and were much too time-consuming to be used in regular clinical practice. Measurement of red blood cells was made more clinically practicable through the use of hematocrit (measuring the volume of red blood cells, using the centrifuge to separate them) and by colorimetric analysis introduced by Gowers in the late 1870s. Around the turn of the century, the introduction of new staining techniques for white blood cells (Ehrlich) made them more easily visible under the microscope and allowed for their differentiation. As the numbers of different types of leucocytes were associated with various pathological conditions (from leukemia to inflammation), blood counts and differential counts came to be used more often for both diagnostic and prognostic purposes. By the 1920s they were routinely performed on hospital patients suffering from a variety of conditions.

Despite some earlier attempts to analyze the components of blood and to measure its reaction chemically, the development of chemical analyses of blood for clinical use is a twentieth-century development. It was closely linked to the emergence and professionalization of medically oriented biochemistry in the American medical schools. As Kohler has shown, the reform of American medical education opened up unusual opportunities for the professionalization of biochemistry while, at the same time, promoting close interaction between biochemical research and the clinic. The institutional arrangement stimulated research on the development of analytic diagnostic techniques. The chemistry of blood was believed to reflect pathological changes more accurately than urine, and the development of chemical methods for blood analysis was also easily coupled to clinical and biochemical research on such conditions as nephritis, diabetes, and other hormonal and metabolic disorders. At Harvard in 1919, Otto Folin and his student Hsien Wu presented a system of chemical microanalysis of blood adopted for clinical purposes. In 1915, Donald Van Slyke and his colleagues working on diabetic acidosis at the Rockefeller Institute Hospital published a method for estimating its severity using a volumetric apparatus to measure the $CO_2$ combining power. The use of this relatively simple apparatus was later extended to measure other gases and, indirectly, a variety of other components of blood. In the 1920s, when Van Slyke's group moved to investigations of nephritis, another series of tests was developed for the measurement of urea, urea concentration and clearance, as well as chlorides, proteins, lipids in blood plasma, and so on. Studies of the chemical changes associated with nephritis also inaugurated attempts to analyze not only changes in the chemical composition of blood and urine, but also measurements (such as blood urea clearance) designed to trace changes in the physiological functioning of the body and its organs.

The close engagement of biochemists such as Van Slyke, Folin, and Benedict in clinical research not only promoted the development of new diagnostic methods, but also led to a more thoroughly chemical understanding and classification of pathologies. Van Slyke and Peter's *Quantitative Clinical Chemistry*, published in 1931/32 and repeatedly dubbed the 'bible of modern iatro-chemists,' dealt successively with the individual chemical constituents of the body, and organized its discussion of pathologies and diagnostic methods according to chemical categories. Similarly, pathologies of the acid-base balance were differentiated and classified by Van Slyke not in terms of traditional disease concepts or of the underlying physiological mechanisms and pathological disturbances, but in terms of physico-chemical equilibria.

Since the 1950s, many of these tests in clinical chemistry have been fully standardized and automated, making them quicker to perform and less labor intensive. The first automatic analyzer, the continuous flow apparatus for blood chemistry, was developed in the early 1950s by Leonard Skaggs from the Cleveland Veterans Administration Hospital, and put on the market in 1957 by the Technicon Corporation. Other automatic instruments have been developed since then, and today almost all the chemical tests performed either in the hospital or in (often privately-owned) independent laboratories rely on the use of automated equipment.

The bacteriological revolution also brought into medicine a whole array of new means of analyzing the diseased body. Bacteriological techniques ranged from the visual, microscopic examination of stained specimens of sputum, blood, or urine to enrichment cultures and chemical analysis of bacterial products as a means of identifying the presence of pathogenic species, to the immunological methods such as agglutination or complement fixation which were developed around the turn of the century. Many of these bacteriological techniques were first developed and used by Robert Koch and his co-workers in the 1880s to identify bacterial species associated with specific infectious diseases. Koch's courses in bacteriology at his institute in Berlin played an important role in teaching these techniques to medical practitioners and researchers from around the world, and many of them were quickly adopted for clinical use (for example, the staining methods used in the isolation and identification of tubercle bacilli or the early 'gelatin stab' test for cholera bacillus cultures). Throat swabs for diphtheria and the examination of sputum for tubercle bacilli were introduced on a mass scale in the last decade of the nineteenth century. Bacteriologists were also attempting to develop rapid and relatively uncomplicated chemical methods, often selective cultivation media to which an indicator has been added, to isolate and identify pathogenic bacteria for purposes of clinical diagnosis. Such selective media were particularly important for the differentiation of enteric bacteria necessary for the identification of typhoid bacilli, and a number of them were proposed in the 1890s and in the first decade of the twentieth century (for example by Theobald Smith in the US, Ferdinand Widal and André Chantmesse in France, Drigalski and Conradi in Germany, and AJ MacConkey in England). In the late 1890s attention shifted to serological tests which were easier to perform routinely: they involved testing the patient's serum against a known pathogen (rather than the isolation of bacteria from his or her body). Agglutination tests, especially the Widal reaction for typhoid developed in the mid-1890s by the French bacteriologist Ferdinand Widal and an English researcher, HE Durham, working in Max Gruber's laboratory in Vienna, were soon incorporated into the armamentarium of the clinical pathologist/bacteriologist and into the new laboratories of public health workers. Complement fixation reaction, described in 1898 by the Belgian immunologist Jules Bordet, served as a model for August von Wasserman's work on the diagnosis of syphilis (1906). Though it was initially a delicate, uncertain, and difficult test, the Wasserman reaction became the standard widely used method for the diagnosis of syphilis. Despite radical changes in immunological theory in the twentieth century, and developments in the understanding of both the chemical and the cellular basis of immunity, the basic principles of testing for antigen-antibody reactions which underpinned these early serological tests are no different from those on which such recent tests as those for HIV infection are based.

The development of germ theory was followed not only by the development of a whole new set of diagnostic tests, but also by a new, more 'ontological' mode of understanding disease, which was seen as competing with the 'physiological' model. The identification of specific microbial species with specific diseases separated the cause of disease from the pathological changes and physiological processes in the body. Some clinicians and physiologists were reluctant to accede to this redefinition, and for many conditions, such as pneumonia and tuberculosis, much of the clinical routine (including diagnosis) remained largely unaffected by changes in the understanding of etiology until new therapies were developed in the 1930s and '40s. Nevertheless, the laboratory has gradually assumed a far more prominent place in the clinic and the definition of a number of infectious diseases has shifted accordingly.

As this brief history demonstrates, many of the features of twentieth-century analysis are direct continuations of nineteenth-century ideas and techniques. The shifts from qualitative to quantitative data and from anatomical to physiological perspectives, as well as the drive towards more reductionist (biochemical) modes of analysis all originated in nineteenth-century clinical and biological research. The newer modes of analysis have not necessarily replaced the older ones. In many ways, the history of these techniques has been one of continuous accretion: newer chemical methods have come to supplement the existing microscopic observations, and modern scans have not replaced the stethoscope. The introduction of multiple modes of analysis was accompanied by changes in the ways in which diseases have been understood and classified. And, at the same time, the purposes for which tests and techniques were used were also changing: tests used initially for purposes of research, or to confirm an earlier diagnosis, assumed an ever more prominent place in the clinic. They were used more and more routinely not only as a means to diagnose specific conditions but also for purposes of monitoring, screening, and predicting imminent disease.

Clearly, the object of much analysis in twentieth-century medicine is no longer the patient, and not even the 'body-as-a-machine,' but rather the preanalyzed and preconstructed fragments of the body which are stained, chemically treated, cultured, cloned, fixed, or imaged with the help of a variety of instruments and techniques in locations far removed from the bedside. If general practitioners might be said to analyze the patient's 'body as a machine' in order to attempt a diagnosis or monitor the course of disease and treatment, and if the specialists's analytical jurisdiction extends only to a part of fragment of the body which had to be previously analyzed and found pathological, those working in the laboratories might never even encounter the 'owners' of the bits and pieces of bodies they analyze (and even if they do encounter them, they do so only fleetingly in order to extract a sample to be analyzed or to produce an image of some fragment of a body to be interpreted in a setting in which the whole body is no longer present). In this sense, neither the patient nor his or her body is the relevant object of laboratory work. The focus is instead on the manipulation, analysis, and interpretation of tissue fragments, chemical substances or reactions, cells, genes, etc. The most distinctive feature of analysis in twentieth-century medicine is perhaps the omnipresence of this 'second order' analysis whose objects are no longer bodies, but biological fragments interpreted in a variety of biochemical, immunological, cytological, neurophysiological, endocrinological, hematological, or genetic frameworks and by practitioners working far from the bedside.

## THE SOCIAL ORGANIZATION OF ANALYSIS

These multiple modes of analysis of the twentieth-century body interact in complex ways with social and organizational differentiation and specialization in medicine. One can argue that the modes of analysis map not only the body, but also the social organization of the clinic. On the one hand, specialized settings were established and new professions assumed the responsibility for specific forms of laboratory analysis, while, on the other hand, specialization in clinical medicine produced physicians who devoted their attention to particular parts of bodies, specific organs or organ systems, or even chemical substances and cells.

Traditionally, pathologists worked in autopsy rooms, but gradually began to perform some examinations of tissues from living patients. By the mid-nineteenth century individual physicians were also likely to own some simple laboratory equipment (such as a microscope or test tubes and reagents for urinalysis) to perform tests on their patients. In the second half of the nineteenth century, medical research laboratories, either private or attached to university hospitals, began to contribute to the development and performance of diagnostic tests. In the 1880s, the first clinical laboratories were established in Germany and the US. Von Ziemssen's clinical laboratory in Munich, established in 1885, is often cited as a prototype for similar laboratories established in the 1890s, such as the William Pepper Laboratory at the University of Pennsylvania Hospital, or the pathological laboratory at the Johns Hopkins Medical School. While these laboratories were mainly established for purposes of research, they increasingly provided diagnostic services to the physicians. As the number of such tests grew, many of these laboratories specialized in performing routine testing, and new ward laboratories were established to conduct simple examinations close to the bedside. The introduction of bacteriological techniques played an important role in the expansion of clinical laboratories in hospitals as well as in the establishment of local public health laboratories.

This differentiation of settings went hand in hand with the specialization of tasks and the establishment of service specialties such as radiology and clinical pathology. As a JAMA editorial claimed in 1921,

> The old time pathologist, the prototype of the modern laboratory physician whose function in clinical diagnosis was to determine the nature of lesions from gross and microscopic examination of tissues, has undergone differentiation into clinical chemist, clinical bacteriologist, clinical serologist, clinical microscopist, and roentgenologist, and there has come forth a formerly unknown adjunct to medical practice, the laboratory technician.[2]

What was new was not so much that blood, urine, sputum and increasingly other tissues were being analyzed, though obviously they were being analyzed in more ways, more systematically, more quantitatively, and with ever more sophisticated apparatus, but that they were analyzed routinely not by the primary physicians, but, in the name of greater efficiency, rational division of labor, and special expertise, by people whose clients were not patients but (other) doctors. Professional medical journals during the first three decades of the century repeatedly discussed the negotiations and conflicts about the status of the clinical pathologist, as a technician, a 'lay' scientist, or specialist consultant. Clinicians disputed the right to proffer diagnoses on the basis of laboratory tests 'without seeing the patient.' Together with some teachers of clinical medicine, they expressed concerns about the supposedly growing inability of primary physicians to diagnose patients without the help of bacteriological, chemical, immunological, or roentgenological tests and voiced accusations that clinical laboratories were being overburdened with unnecessary routine requests for analyses. While clinicians argued that "medicine cannot be made in the laboratory alone, for it has to do with living man,"[3] laboratory workers invoked the authority of science to claim the primacy of their perspective. These conflicts and negotiations were important not only for the development of relations between clinicians and laboratory workers, or as jurisdictional battles between professional or professionalizing groups, but they also served to reorganize the social structure of the hospital and other forms of medical care creating a setting within which future innovations in analytical techniques were to be accommodated.

They also seemed to affect the notion of what it means to practice 'medicine,' which could now apparently be practiced without any contact with patients or their 'bodies.' In fact, when the AMA established its standards for an 'approved clinical laboratory' in 1926, the laboratory not only had to be staffed with a licensed physician, but was required to provide its reports and interpretations of their diagnostic significance "solely to the physician in charge of the patient," that is, not to the patient him or herself.[4]

The disputes over the place, status, jurisdiction, and the relationship of the laboratory worker to the primary physicians also played an important role in the introduction of X-ray technology. As Howell argues, despite the early acknowledgement of the utility of X-rays and the enormous publicity Roentgen's discovery received, the establishment of its routine use in the hospital had to wait for social reorganization: the settlement of the roentgenologist's status in the hospital as a consultant rather than technician, the development of a payment system for the services provided by such a consultant, and the provision of routine forms for the reporting of results. The standardization and control of testing procedures were thus accompanied by standardization of laboratories, their staffs, and their relations with other hospital workers.

Seen from the perspective of professionalization, the 'hunger for new analytical methods' or other new technology can be understood, at least in part, in terms of the direct interests of professional groups such as clinical pathologists and radiologists, whose place in medical care is defined in terms of technology, and whose status is closely bound up with control over sophisticated technology and the provision of expertise to doctors. Blume has argued that this certainly holds true for radiology, where the establishment of a special jurisdiction over the X-ray technology has been followed by attempts to extend their jurisdiction to other large diagnostic instruments such as CT scanners, MRIs, etc., even if they are based on very different principles. Blume shows that new imaging technologies underwent more orderly and successful developmental trajectories and were introduced into medical practice with relatively little difficulty when they could easily be accommodated and appropriated by the radiologists whose entire *raison d'être* depended on the control of sophisticated technology and who enjoyed firmly established positions and settled working relations within hospitals. Whether a similar pattern holds in the case of the analytical techniques used by clinical pathologists and its more recent specialized offspring remains to be investigated [see Chapter 12].

Specialization and professionalization in the laboratory settings have been paralleled by similar processes among clinicians. Clinical specialties like gastroenterology, cardiology, neurology, orthopedics, endocrinology, and clinical genetics constitute examples of the ways in which the body came to be mapped onto the organization of clinical activities. Each of these specialisms presupposes the existence not so much of an integral body-as-a-machine, but rather of a body as a congery of systems, each of which is subject to independent or at least semi-independent manipulation. Most, though not all, medical specialisms reflect such prior "dissection" of the body and each is equipped with its own, often specialized armamentarium for analyzing, visualizing, dissecting, and measuring its own fragment. Or as Atkinson puts it, "the technical division of labor in the modern clinic is, in part, a diversity of specialized means for visualizing and enumerating the fragmented body."[5] The hospital, as a central locus for all these activities, has thus become an increasingly complex organization. This complexity is reflected today even in the physical layout of the hospital and its annexes, with patients being assigned to specialty wards and a variety of laboratories located in or near the wards. When such arrangements were being established in the early decades of the twentieth century, they were often accompanied by disputes among the various specialists about the location of the particular laboratories and instruments, and the authority over them.

We still know relatively little about the processes of specialization in medicine, but the relationship between particular analytical techniques for examining the organ, system, or fragment of the body and the development of specialties is relevant. In his classical study of specialization, George Rosen lists improved technology as one of the conditions for the emergence of specialties and emphasizes the importance of the ophthalmoscope for the development of ophthalmology. However, the link between the process of specialization and authority over the use of particular analytical techniques or instruments may not be straightforward, as Howell and Lawrence argue in their studies of the history of cardiology and its ambivalent relation to the electrocardiograph. Still, the theoretical frameworks in which diseases have been defined within particular specialities might be closely linked to the techniques or instruments to which the specialist community attributes a central role, as suggested in Hiddinga's study of eclampsia and pre-eclampsia. These conditions were defined and understood by neurologists in terms of EEG patterns, whereas obstetricians preferred to define them in terms of other analytic parameters (proteinuria, high blood pressure, and edema). The EEG apparatus apparently acquired a central significance within the analytic framework of the specialty of neurology.

Clinical specialization serves as an important mechanism for alleviating potential conflicts between different analytical perspectives. As patients suffering from particular conditions are 'distributed' among the different specialties, latent inconsistencies or lack of compatibility among the frameworks for understanding these conditions are not made explicit, unless the specialty itself is internally divided (for example, between the biomedically and psychodynamically oriented psychiatrists). For example, if epidemiologists and gynecologists use different definitions of menopause, classifying it respectively in terms of hormone levels or prolonged amenorrhea, the disparity does not seem to lead to open conflict given the separation of their practices and concerns. Even significant local and national differences in diagnostic or treatment schemes do not necessarily result in explicit controversies. At the same time, specialization itself contributes to the increasing fragmentation of analytical perspectives, even if they share some of the common assumptions of the 'biomedical model' of disease. For example, a clinical geneticist's understanding of what constitutes disease includes conditions which are likely to manifest themselves as health problems only in the future and which would not be treated as disease states by other specialists.

Conflicts among researchers working in different biomedical fields are also commonly related to their reliance on distinct analytical perspectives. Thus, cellular pathologists (and clinicians) were reluctant to accept bacteriological explanations of disease; the history of cancer research is riddled with conflicts among proponents of different explanations of malignancy; and immunologists', virologists', and neuropathologists' explanations of multiple sclerosis as an auto-immune disease encountered opposition from the proponents of the vascular theory, who were specialists in underwater medicine and were alert to the similarities of this disorder to decompression sickness. Analytical frameworks offer researchers not only techniques and paradigmatic modes of understanding disease, but also specific ways of constructing analogies and developing classifications. For example, the bacterial model of infectious diseases prompted the search for analogical mechanisms in a wide variety of conditions such as beri beri or cancer. Similarly, viral, immunological, and genetic explanations of causes of disease now provide the dominant models for researchers.

It has often been said that the modern biomedical sciences are reductionistic and that the chemical understanding of physiology and pathology has become dominant in twentieth-century biomedicine. It is questionable, however, whether we can speak here of a single reductionism rather than of a variety of potentially incompatible reductionist analytical frameworks. It is one thing, for example, to reduce disease to a failure in the functioning in the immunological system, quite another to see it in terms of a vitamin or hormone deficiency, and a different one yet to understand it in terms of genetic defects. Even if each of these options can be given a biochemical interpretation, and even if each is subject to some sort of chemical analysis, the frameworks within which the chemical interpretations make sense can be seen as multiple and not always compatible ways of representing 'analyzed' bodies.

But the proliferation of ways of analyzing the body and the dispersal of analysis among laboratories and specialists also poses new organizational problems in the clinic itself. Those who criticize biomedicine for treating a patient as a body-machine divorced from his or her social environment claim that modern medicine violates the integrity of the patient as an individual. But modern modes of analysis threaten not only to dissociate the patient from his or her body, but also to dissolve the idea of a body as a physical organism to be treated as an integrated whole. In some situations, however, some reintegration of the body is necessary for the management of the problem.

Such (re)integration of the body is, on the one hand, left to the discretion of a general practitioner or an attending physician, and on the other, brought about by the collaborative work of specialists and other medical personnel in the hospital. The physician, whether the specialist in the hospital or the general practitioner, is faced with the task of interpreting and combining the results of various tests and examinations into a diagnosis and a proposed course of action. This process of constructing medical disposals involves a selection, transformation, reinterpretation, and weighing of the relevance and significance of the various bits of an often heterogenous set of data in a specific local setting governed both by routine practices and by emergent contingencies. At the same time, physicians need to bridge the gap between universalistic and analytical biomedical knowledge and the actual management of individual patients. From this perspective, the physician pieces together not only the specific laboratory data, the history of the patient, and physical examination results, but also adapts the available biomedical knowledge to each individual and often idiosyncratic case. It is also his or her job to present this information to the patient.

The 'reintegration' of the body is obviously a far more complex problem in the hospital than in more individualized primary care. Given the extensive division of labor, cooperation and collaboration become a central part of hospital routine and serve to an extent to offset the fragmentation of the body. Such collaboration can assume a variety of forms (referrals, face to face consultations, ward rounds, and clinical-pathological conferences) and involves not only doctors, but also nurses and other technical personnel. Nurses, for example, are likely to play an important role in the 'reintegration' of the various expertises through their personal contact with the patients, in coordinating ward routines, and in monitoring and maintaining patient records. Patient records not only serve as a locus where the heterogenous data are gathered together, but also constrain the type of data that is collected, its form, and the manner in which it is represented. Accordingly, they also facilitate the piecing together of the patient's body and allow for a more or less routine functioning of the collaborative practices even without direct contact between the specialists.

Despite the shared medical framework and the organizational arrangements, the process of combining information from different sources into a coherent account and course of action does not necessarily result in an integral view of the patient and his or her problem. For the patient the reconciliation of the medical analytical categories with personal experience of illness remains even more elusive.

## REFERENCES

1.  Jane Levitt, 'The growth of technology and corporate profit-making in the clinical laboratories,' *Journal of Health Politics, Policy and Law* (1984), **8**: 732–42, at p. 732.
2.  'Editorial,' *Journal of the American Medical Association* (Nov 5, 1921), **77**: 1498–99.
3.  James B. Herrick, 'The relations of the clinical laboratory to the practitioner of medicine,' *Boston Medical and Surgical Journal* (1907), **156**: 763–768, at p. 765.
4.  'Report on clinical laboratory service in the United States,' *Journal of the American Medical Association* (1926), **86**: 1065–72, at p. 1069.
5.  Paul Atkinson, *Medical Talk and Medical Work: The Liturgy of the Clinic.* (London: Sage, 1995), at p. 62.

## FURTHER READING

Amsterdamska, Olga, 'Chemistry in the clinic: The research career of D.D. Van Slyke,' in Harmke Kamminga and Soraya de Chaderevian (eds), *Molecularizing Biology and Medicine: New Practices and Alliances, 1910s–1970s.* (London: Harwood Academic Publishers, 1998), pp. 47–82.

Armstrong, David, *Political Anatomy of the Body: Medical Knowledge in Britain in the Twentieth Century.* (Cambridge: Cambridge University Press, 1983).

Atkinson, Paul, *Medical Talk and Medical Work: The Liturgy of the Clinic.* (London: Sage, 1995).

Berg, Marc, 'The construction of medical disposals. Medical sociology and medical problem solving in clinical practice,' *Sociology of Health and Illness* (1992), **14**: 151–180.

Blume, Stuart S., *Insight and Industry. On the Dynamics of Technological Change in Medicine.* (Cambridge, MA: MIT Press, 1992).

Casper, Monica J. and Clarke, Adele E., 'Making the PAP smear into the "right tool" for the job: Cervical cancer screening in the U.S., c1940–1995,' *Social Studies of Science* (1998), **28**: 255–290.

Cunningham, Andrew and Williams, Perry (eds), *The Laboratory Revolution in Medicine.* (Cambridge: Cambridge University Press, 1992).

Davis, Audrey D., *Medicine and Its Technology: An Introduction to the History of Medical Instrumentation.* (Westport, CT: Greenwood Press, 1981).

Faber, Knut, *Nosography. The Evolution of Medicine in Modern Times.* (New York: Paul Hoeber, 1930).

Fleck, Ludwik, *Genesis and Development of a Scientific Fact*, trans. Fred Bradley and Thaddeus Trenn. (Chicago: Chicago University Press, 1979); orig. 1935.

Foster, W.D., *A Short History of Clinical Pathology.* (Edinburgh: Livingstone, 1961).

Hiddinga, Anja, *Changing Normality: Pregnancy and Scientific Knowledge Claims 1920–1950, with special reference to the U.S.A.*, Ph.D. Diss. (University of Amsterdam, 1995).

Howell, Joel D., '"Soldier's Heart": The Redefinition of heart disease and specialty formation in early twentieth-century Great Britain,' *Medical History*, supp. no. 5 (1985), 34–52.

Howell, Joel, *Technology in the Hospital: Transforming Patient Care in the Early Twentieth Century*. (Baltimore: Johns Hopkins University Press, 1995).

Hunter, Kathryn, *Doctors' Stories: The Narrative Structure of Medical Knowledge*. (Princeton: Princeton University Press, 1991).

Jacyna, Stephen, 'The laboratory and the clinic: The impact of pathology on surgical diagnosis in the Glasgow Western Infirmary, 1875–1910,' *Bulletin of the History of Medicine* (1988), **62**: 384–406.

Kohler, Robert E., *From Medical Chemistry to Biochemistry: The Making of Modern Biomedical Discipline*. (Cambridge: Cambridge University Press, 1982).

Lawrence, Christopher, '"Definite and material": Coronary thrombosis and cardiologists in the 1920s' in Charles E. Rosenberg and Janet Goldin (eds), *Framing Disease: Studies in Cultural History*. (New Brunswick: Rutgers University Press, 1992), 50–82.

Nicolson, Malcolm and McLaughlin, Cathleen, 'Social constructionism and medical sociology: A study of the vascular theory of multiple sclerosis', *Sociology of Health and Illness* (1988), **10**: 234–255.

Pickering, G.W., 'The concept of essential hypertension,' in Brandon Lush (ed), *Concepts of Medicine*. (Oxford: Oxford University Press, 1960), 170–176.

Reiser, Stanley J., *Medicine and the Growth of Technology*. (New York: Cambridge University Press, 1978).

Rosen, George, *The Specialization of Medicine with Particular Reference to Ophthalmology*. (New York: Arno Press, 1972, orig. 1944).

Vogel, M.J. and Rosenberg, C.E. (eds), *The Therapeutic Revolution: Essays in the Social History of American Medicine*. (Philadelphia: University of Pennsylvania Press, 1979).

Wailoo, Keith, *Drawing Blood: Technology and Disease Identity in Twentieth Century America*. (Baltimore: Johns Hopkins University Press, 1997).

CHAPTER 28

# The Experimental Body

ILANA LÖWY

## THE 'EXPERIMENTAL BODY': BETWEEN REPRESENTATIONS AND MODELS

'Experimental bodies' are entities which can be substituted for patients'
bodies in order to investigate diseases and look for treatments. 'Experimental bodies' include laboratory animals and their organs and tissues,
but also human tissues, cells and cell-fragments, and entire human bodies. In the
latter use of the 'experimental body,' the body of an individual patient is replaced
with the 'statistical body' of all patients enrolled in a clinical trial. While the idea
that animals can be substitutes for humans in testing new medical techniques is
a very old one, at least in surgery and in the evaluation of the toxicity of drugs,
the intensive use of 'experimental bodies' as major instruments of development
and validation of medical knowledge is much more recent. It was directly linked
to the development of 'scientific medicine' in the mid-nineteenth century, then
to the expansion of biomedical research and the growth of the pharmaceutical
industry in the twentieth century. An extensive reliance on 'experimental bodies'
became one of the hallmarks of twentieth–century biomedicine. However, the
importance of the 'experimental bodies' in shaping medical knowledge and practices did not eliminate controversies over their use. The adequacy of the substitution processes by which animals, fragments of human body, or statistical entities
are made representatives of a unique suffering person were and are a frequent
subject of debate.

'Statistical bodies' excepted, 'experimental bodies' are found in specific ecological niches, the biomedical laboratories. The unique characteristics of these niches,
the philosopher and historian of medicine Georges Canguilhem explains, affect
their inhabitants: "If we may define the normal state of a living being in terms
of a normal relationship of adjustment to environments, we must not forget that
the laboratory itself constitutes *a new environment* in which life certainly establishes
norms whose extrapolation does not work without risk when removed from the
conditions to which these norms relate. For the animal or for man the laboratory
environment is one possible environment among others... It is not possible that
the ways of life in the laboratory fail to retain any specificity in their relationship
to the place and the moment of the experiment."[1]

Canguilhem aptly sums up one of the main dilemmas of the biomedical scientist: to what extent is it justified to extrapolate from studies conducted in the artificial environment of the laboratory to real-life clinical situations, and to ground the treatment of sick persons in experiments conducted in a test-tube or in an animal. This dilemma appeared relatively late in the history of 'experimental bodies.' Its history is intimately linked with that of biological laboratories which allow the reproduction of life phenomena in a controlled setting. 'Experimental bodies' are used in these laboratories in two ways. They may be employed to study the characteristics of the class of organisms to which they belong (such investigations may be named 'specific studies') or to study traits shared by larger groups of living organisms (such investigations may be named 'analogous studies'). In the first case, controlled conditions in a biological laboratory enable scientists to complete observations of a given group of living organisms, to extend them through experimentation, and to describe traits typical of this group (e.g., laboratory conditions may facilitate the detailed observation of the mating habits of a given species of insects, while experimentation may reveal elements affecting these habits, and highlight differences between the studied group and other groups). In the second case, scientists assume that observations made in the laboratory using animals of one species will reveal mechanisms shared by numerous other species, and occasionally by all living organisms. For example, the fruit fly (Drosophila) and the bacterium *Echerichia coli* were (and are) perceived as adequate representatives of fundamental genetic mechanisms shared by numerous other living organisms. In 'analogous studies,' the scientist's dilemma, outlined by Canguilhem, about the validity of the extrapolation from observations made in the artificial environment of the laboratory to the behavior of a given organism in its natural environment, is amplified by questions about the validity of extrapolation from studies made in one species to another. When the goal of 'analogous studies' is the understanding of a human disease, this interrogation can be divided into two related but not identical questions: the degree of similarity of normal phenomena and of pathological phenomena observed in different species. The second question is not identical to the first, because, e.g., inter-species differences in the structure of proteins on cell surface may have little effect on a normal function of the cell, but may play an important role in the development of a pathological condition.

The principle that laboratory investigations conducted on animals are one of the major sites of elaboration of understanding of human diseases and of development of efficient cures for these diseases was established in the nineteenth century, as an extension and codification of older medical practices. It was established in circumstances which did not favor interrogations on the validity of extrapolations from observations from animals to humans.[2] In the mid-nineteenth century, animals were used by surgeons to perfect surgical operations and by physiologists to study fundamental physiological mechanisms. In both cases, the use of animals to gain knowledge about humans took into consideration intrinsic differences between animal species, but both surgeons and physiologists assumed that the degree of anatomical and physiological similarity between animal species was directly correlated with the distance between these species on the phylogenetic ladder. This view is represented in Claude Bernard's influential *Introduction to Experimental Medicine* of 1865, a work which identified 'experimental medicine' with 'experimental physiology,' and postulated a non-problematic transition from experimental studies made in laboratory animals to the understanding of pathological states in humans.

The physiologists' claim that laboratory studies are indispensable to the understanding of human diseases was not fully accepted until the advent of bacteriology. Laboratory animals were in the very center of bacteriological research. They were used to isolate pathogenic bacteria, to study their effects, and to develop vaccines and anti-sera. Bacteriology rapidly demonstrated the importance of laboratory-produced knowledge for the prevention and cure of infectious diseases. It vindicated and enlarged earlier proposals to ground diagnosis, therapy and prevention of diseases in laboratory-based research, and firmly linked the fate of sick individuals to that of laboratory animals.[3] One of the central elements of Koch's postulates (rules which govern the definition of a pathogenic germ as an etiologic cause of a disease) was the reproduction of typical pathological manifestations of a disease in an animal. In parallel, the Pasteurian model of development of vaccines, based on the passage from a 'virus,' (a virulent germ) to a 'vaccine,' (an attenuated germ) was grounded in animal experimentation. Pasteur and his followers proposed that proof of the efficacy of a vaccine should come from laboratory studies which directly demonstrated the protective value of a vaccine in controlled conditions, rather than from attempts, viewed as less reliable, to evaluate the extent of protection of human populations by vaccination.[4]

## ANIMAL MODELS OF INFECTIOUS DISEASES: PROBLEMS WITH ALIGNMENT

The new science of bacteriology relied extensively on the use of laboratory animals; the rapid spread of bacteriological research in the late nineteenth and early twentieth centuries encouraged the use of animals to study human diseases. The bacteriologists had found, however, that it was not always easy to determine which animal should be used to investigate a given pathology. No simple correlations were found between the susceptibility or resistance to a pathogenic germ and proximity on the phylogenetic ladder. In addition, the same germs frequently induced very different pathological symptoms in closely related species and very similar symptoms in unrelated species. The observation of the variability of responses to a single germ in different animal species opened the way to debates on the conditions which justify the extrapolation of results observed in animals to humans. These debates were, however, focused on the criticism of specific experimental models and did not challenge the principle that the reproduction of an infectious disease in the laboratory is a key step in the control of this disease, or the supposition that it is possible to develop an adequate animal model of each human infectious disease.

The search for the cause of cholera, and attempts to develop anti-cholera vaccine, illustrate the difficulties of correlating the 'experimental body' studied in the bacteriology laboratory, with the bodies of sick individuals. Shortly after Koch formulated his postulates, he started a study of a disease which failed to conform to these postulates. The germ *Vibrio cholera* was linked to human cholera by numerous clinical and pathological observations, but animals fed or injected with this germ failed to produce cholera-like symptoms. The development of a laboratory model of cholera was viewed nevertheless as an indispensable step in the development of an anti-cholera vaccine. Bacteriologists who had obstinately attempted to develop such a model, discovered that their failure was due to the fact that *Vibrio cholera* was destroyed by the acidity of the stomach, and, in addition, was prevented from multiplying by the peristaltic movement of the intestine in this site. To overcome these two obstacles, peristaltic movements of the intestine of laboratory animals were paralyzed with opium; pathogenic vibrios were then introduced directly into the immobilized intestine. Animals which were infected in this way — and which survived the insertion of a tube into their intestine and did not die of opium poisoning — did develop a severe vibrio-induced diarrhea. A competing 'animal model' of cholera was based on the induction of acute peritonitis in guinea pigs following intraperitoneal injections of guinea pig-adapted strains of vibrio. Both models were used by some researchers to demonstrate the efficacy of anti-cholera vaccines, and both were contested by other researchers who argued that these models had at best distant links with human cholera, a diarrheic disease acquired through the ingestion of pathogenic vibrios. No better animal model of cholera could be found, however, and scientists continued to use the existing models to develop anti-cholera vaccines and to study therapies for this disease.

## REPRODUCIBILITY VERSUS VALIDITY: THE DILEMMAS OF THE IDEAL MODEL

While bacteriologists and immunologists elaborated animal models of infectious diseases, physiologists and biochemists continued to use animals to study general biological mechanisms. Their studies also included investigations of selected human pathologies such as deficiency diseases, metabolic diseases and hormonal deficiencies. In these studies, laboratory animals — and later cells and sub-cellular fractions — were perceived as faithfully representing a given class of general biological phenomena. The development of a successful therapy for diabetes, and the large scale production and commercialization of insulin, directly displayed a continuum between the 'animal body' (veal and pig pancreases collected in the slaughter house and used for insulin production), the 'experimental body' (dogs employed in early insulin studies), and the 'sick body' (diabetic patients treated with insulin). In the 1920s and '30s the growth of the pharmaceutical industry and the development of links between medical researchers and industrialists favored the development of laboratory investigations of physiopathological phenomena.[5] These studies were, however, based on a different principle than bacteriological studies. The bacteriologist's task was to construct the right model — one which is as close as possible to a human disease, while the physiologist's task was to select the right animal for their studies — one that is a faithful representative of a general physiological mechanism.

In the early twentieth century, scientists usually assumed that it was sufficient to use laboratory animals belonging to the same species to ensure the reproducibility of experimental results. This assumption was inded valid in some areas, such as physiology, biochemistry or bacteriology, in which it was sufficient to use animals belonging to the same species, and which were homogenized in regard to age, sex and weight to obtain comparable results. This assumption was, however, found incorrect in other domains of biomedical investigation. In specialties such as experimental oncology or transplantation studies, results were strongly affected by intra-species genetic variability of laboratory animals (two mice can look alike, but react very differently). Consequently, immunological investigations and cancer studies increasingly employed genetically uniform (inbred) animals. The use of such animals facilitated the standardization and the quantification of experimental data and the comparison between results obtained in different laboratories. It also favored the collaborations between researchers who worked in the same domains and the development of networks of laboratories. The development of such networks was accelerated in the 1920s and '30s, with the spread of laboratories linked with teaching hospitals (their diffusion often preceded the proof of their utility for diagnosis and therapy of human diseases), and with the consolidation of links between research laboratories, industrial laboratories and hospitals. The development, testing and diffusion of sulfa drugs in the 1930s made visible the multiple links between the research laboratory (where these drugs were developed and tested in mice), the production plant (which made possible mass manufacture of biologically active molecules) and the clinics (the site of clinical trials of sulpha drugs).[6]

The development (which started in the 1910s) and then the diffusion of genetically controlled laboratory animals for biomedical research (the trade in such animals started in the 1930s, and it was developed on a large scale from the 1950s) also favored the elaboration of new animal models expected to mimic human pathology more accurately. This goal was first achieved through selective breeding of naturally-occurring mutants (the increase of the scale of production of genetically-controlled animals enhanced the probability of finding 'interesting' mutants). More recently it became possible to produce genetically manipulated animals, frequently constructed according to the researchers' specifications (e.g., transgenic mice which are developed through a selective transfer of genes into the fertilized egg). Some scientists perceive such 'engineered' animals, which often contain elements of the human body (genes, cells), as an improvement over the earlier animal models of human pathologies. Other medical investigators view such highly artificial animal models of human disease as problematic. Thus for some cancer researchers a 'nude' mouse grafted with a human tumor ('nude' mice lack T-lymphocytes, a category of white blood cells which play a central role in the rejection of foreign tissue, and are therefore unable to reject grafts) is a perfect model for the testing of anti-tumor drugs, since the activity of these drugs is studied directly on human tumor cells. For other investigators, the graft of human cells into an immunologically-defective mouse is not very different from the growth of these cells in a test tube. Mice which spontaneously developed a tumor, or even mice grafted with a transplantable mouse tumor, may be seen as more faithful models of human malignancies, since they possess the physiological mechanisms which facilitate or inhibit the development of malignancies. Similar problems had arisen with 'OncoMouse®.' The OncoMouse® is a transgenic mouse engineered to be more susceptible to cancer than normal mice, and to develop a large variety of spontaneous tumors through the transfer of specific genes of suspectibility for cancer (here, the oncogene 'ras'). The oncomouse was the object of a long juridical struggle centered on the possibility of patenting a genetically modified animal. It was finally patented in the US, but scientists found that it was less useful than expected as an animal model of human cancer.[7]

### 'EXPERIMENTAL BODIES' AS MEASURING TOOLS

'Experimental bodies' have an additional use: they may become measuring tools. Organisms, especially microorganisms, may be used by chemists and biochemists as indicators of a presence of traces of a chemical substance (e.g., a substrate metabolized by a bacterium). Such traces are often difficult to detect with traditional methods of analytical chemistry. Another important use of living organisms by biomedical researchers is the quantification of biologically active substances. This use is often linked with the circulation of standardized biological reagents and with mass production of such reagents, especially those used in the therapy of human diseases. Chemical and pharmaceutical industries were the most important promoters of such uses of 'experimental bodies,' and while the first studies which used living organisms and their fragments as measuring tools were made in the nineteenth century (e.g., Pasteur used microorganisms to distinguish between optic isomers of chemical substances) the growth of the pharmaceutical industry in the twentieth century extended this use of 'experimental bodies.'

A slightly different approach measures the effects of a biologically active substance in a higher organism. An early example is the calibration and standardization of anti-diphtheric sera. The process was of key importance in the production of commercial anti-diphtheric sera. The announcement (made by Emile Roux during the International Congress of Medicine held in Budapest in 1894) of the important decrease of mortality observed in diphtheric children treated with anti-diphtheric serum was followed by rapid take-over of the production of such sera by industry. However, the results obtained when sera from different producers were used in the clinics varied greatly, and some of the commercial preparations seemed devoid of any anti-diphtheric activity. Public health authorities worried about the health hazards of inefficient drugs, while industrialists feared a global discredit of their products and the loss of a promising market. An efficient method to standardize anti-diphtheric sera which would allow quality control of industrially-produced sera could answer these preoccupations. The German chemist and bacteriologist, Paul Ehrlich (whose research was co-funded by industrialists and by the German health ministry) developed such a method in the late 1890s. Guinea pigs were injected with a fixed, fatal dose of diphtheria toxin, and then with increasing dilution of anti-diphtheric serum. The test determined the LD50 of a given serum — the dilution which prevented the death of 50% of animals — made possible the calibration of commercial sera to a pre-defined strength, and was used to control the quality of sera already on the market. Sera quantified and tested in the 'experimental bodies' of guinea pigs were then administered to the 'sick bodies' of diphtheric children.[8] In the early twentieth century Ehrlich's method became the usual way of calibrating industrially-produced antisera.

Another telling example is the use of laboratory animals to detect and quantify hormones. Before the development of chemical methods of analysis of steroid hormones, male hormones were measured through the so called 'comb test' — the increase in size of the comb in castrated roosters injected with a preparation containing human hormones — or through the increase in weight of seminal vesicles in castrated mice or rats. Female hormones were measured through the stimulation of the growth of the uterus in ovariectomized rabbits, and later by the observation of cytological changes in a vaginal smear of castrated female mice or rats treated with hormone preparations. Both methods were first used in research, and later in the calibration and quantification of industrially produced female hormones. They also play a central role in defining molecules as 'male' or 'female' entities. 'Experimental bodies' were therefore used to sexualize chemical substances, first in research laboratories and then in clinics and industrial settings (the use of female hormones to treat dysfunction of the female reproductive systems started in the 1930s). On the other hand, the use of living organisms as measuring tools led to the complexification of the initially straightforward schema. Substances defined as 'male' or 'female' hormones were found to have other biological activities as well, while some 'male' characteristics (such as the rooster's plumage) were found to be negatively controlled by female hormones (females developed male plumage after ovariotomy, while castrated males did not change plumage). The argument was then turned on its head, and characteristics which were earlier defined as 'male' were redefined as 'sex neutral' or 'feminine negative,' following a pattern established in bodies of castrated laboratory animals.[9]

## Experimental Bodies and 'Big Science'

From the late nineteenth century on, medical practices were increasingly legitimated by knowledge developed in the laboratory, while medical researchers strove to translate medical problems into biological ones. The result was not always the expected one: a successful 'translation' was closely related to the use of experimental systems and techniques of biologists and favored the solution of a biological rather than a medical problem. On the other hand, a certain number of major therapies, such as anti-diphtheric toxin, insulin or antibiotics were presented as innovations originating in the research laboratory. These therapies reinforced the conviction that laboratory studies are of central importance in developing efficient cures for major human pathologies. This conviction in turn legitimated increased interest in 'experimental bodies' (that is, in fundamental biological and biomedical research). Their success also contributed to the expansion of biomedical research — thus of studies made, mainly, with 'experimental bodies' after the Second World War.

The success of war-related research programs, in particular the production of penicillin, stimulated an important influx of public funds into biomedical research and led to the development of 'big biomedical science': large-scale programs, increases in budgets and in the numbers of researchers, the increasing role of instruments and of standardized reagents. Such 'big biomedical science' was closely associated with the clinics through an alliance between academic medicine and fundamental biological research. This alliance reinforced the position of leading medical schools and leading research centers, and marginalized the non-academic medical practitioner. The central role of scientific disciplines in the medical curriculum, in the reorganization of university and hospital departments, in the attribution of resources, and the intertwining of medical and research careers (leading academic physicians are frequently also leading medical researchers, and their ability to treat 'sick bodies' is often legitimated by their expert manipulation of 'experimental bodies') led to the transformation of laboratory research into an important organizational device in medicine. The growing importance of laboratory research in medicine strengthened the pre-war tendency to identify the 'experimental body' with the 'molecularized body,' that is, the conviction that biological questions — and medical problems — should be analyzed and solved on the molecular level. From the 1970s, the rise of molecular biology and the development of techniques of genetical engineering led to a shift from an 'enzymatic body' studied with biochemical methods, to a 'genetic body' studied with computers and statistical approaches (the genome project), and from the investigation of dysfunctions which are already present, to attempts to evaluate the probability of future dysfunctions.

The expansion of biomedical research had an additional consequence — the growing homogenization of medical knowledge and medical practices. Sick bodies are infinitely variable. They combine the endless variety of normal human bodies (a combination of unique genetic patrimony and unique biological history) with the infinite variety of reactions to pathological stimuli. Moreover, cultural, societal and political attitudes towards disease are far from being uniform. Twentieth-century Western biomedicine is nevertheless a remarkably homogenous enterprise. This uniformity was generated, among other things, through the standardization of elements of 'experimental bodies' (easier to control than 'native bodies') through the circulation of these standardized elements (such as genetically-controlled animals, homogenized cell-lines, tumors, anti sera, and other biological reagents), and through the development of medical practices based on their use.

## CLINICAL TRIALS AND 'STATISTICAL BODIES'

The expansion of biomedical research — that is, of the uses of 'experimental bodies' in the laboratory — was accompanied by a new phenomenon: the codification of experimentation on patients through the development of controlled clinical trials. This codification was linked to changes of scale in medical activities in the post-war era: the increased importance of hospital-based medicine, of collective activity in biomedical research, and of governmental funding of both. Clinical trials may be seen as the substitution of a 'statistical body' — that is, an abstract mathematical entity — for the concrete, and suffering body of the patient. Thus clinical trials organized in parallel by the Public Health Administration (US) and the Medical Research Council (UK) in the aftermath of Second World War to test the efficacy of streptomycin to cure tuberculosis, relied exclusively on the probabilistic reasoning of statisticians and disregarded the clinical judgment of physicians. The statisticians then explained that in order to obtain valid results it is necessary to randomize the attribution of patients to streptomycin-treated or control group, and to replace the doctor's evaluation of the patients' clinical status by an impersonal judgement of clinical progress — in this case, by a 'blind' reading of the patients X-ray films by radiologists.[10]

Doctors resisted the use of statistics and did not always welcome the surrendering to statisticians of their role in evaluation of therapies. This resistance was rooted in doctors' reluctance to give part of their power to statisticians and to surrender privileges linked to their individualized and embodied expertise (they claimed that an experienced doctor, familiar with the disease and personally acquainted with the patient, is a much better judge of the efficacy of a therapy than statisticians who analyze anonymous results of 'objective tests'). In addition, physicians tend to privilege therapies that *should* work because they are the logical answer to a given physiological problem, and are often slow to check if such 'logical' treatments do indeed work in a clinical setting.[11] Resistance to controlled clinical trials was, however, counterbalanced by the importance of such trials as an organizational device. The rise of 'big medicine,' and the increased intervention of the state in the organization of health care also increased the public scrutiny of medical activities. Tax payers — and their political representatives — wanted to ascertain that public funds dedicated to health care were employed in the most efficient way, were not wasted, and did not serve the personal enrichment of doctors and health administrators. Clinical trials, presented as a scientific method to evaluate therapies, have became an efficient means to deflect accusations of incompetence or the suspicion of conflict of interests (e.g., that doctors have a financial interest in promoting specific therapies). Their importance increased in the late twentieth century when budgetary restrictions increased the pressure on health professionals to prove that they make the best use of public money (resulting in the vogue for 'evidence-based medicine'). The diffusion of clinical trials after World War II has also been boosted by legislation which makes such trials obligatory before obtaining a marketing permit for a new drug — hence the scarcity of clinical trials of established therapies and of new therapies (e.g., surgical treatments) which do not need a marketing permit.

### Cancer Chemotherapy as an Illustration of the Advantages and the Limits of 'Experimental Bodies'

Clinical trials of cancer chemotherapy exemplify the central importance of use of laboratory animals and cell cultures in the development of new areas of medicine, but also the difficulty of linking pre-clinical research with clinical data and of articulating the 'experimental body' of the laboratory with the concrete body of a cancer patient. The chemotherapy program of the NCI (National Cancer Institute, USA) organized in the 1950s by the Cancer Chemotherapy National Service Center (CCNSC), assumed — on the basis of principles that guided the search for new antibiotics — that initial screening of a very large number of molecules is the best way to find new anti-cancer drugs. The screening panel of CCNSC selected three mouse tumors (a sarcoma, S-180, a carcinoma, Ca 755 and a leukemia, L-1012) as 'universal screens,' and promoted a mass-production of tumor-carrying mice to allow the rapid screening of a large number of chemical compounds. Chemical substances which were found promising in the initial screening were sent to the pharmacological panel to be evaluated by pharmacologists for toxicity, and then transferred to the clinical trials panel which coordinated their testing in patients. The NCI chemotherapy program was thus based on large-scale use of the 'experimental body' (of laboratory mice) and then a large-scale use of the 'statistical body' (of patients enrolled in clinical trials). The enlargement of scale of experimentation, and the administrative and organizational innovations linked with this enlargement, were presented as the preconditions for the success of the screening enterprise.

The NCI program failed to uncover new anti-tumor drugs. The chemotherapeutic drugs developed in the 1950s and '60s, were the by-product of programs which did not initially aim to develop a cure for cancer. Alkylating agents were developed in the framework of research on war gases, actinomycin-D was first studied for its antibiotic properties, and antagonists of folic acid were described during studies on nutrition. The chemotherapy program was criticized in the early 1960s for the absence of scientific guidelines — it was nicknamed: the 'nothing too dumb to test' program — and for the too narrow selection of experimental models of cancer (three mouse tumors were not perceived to be adequate representatives of all the existing human malignancies). Consequently, the program was modified in 1961: the principle of screening anti-tumor substances in tumor-bearing animals was not questioned, but the number of tested substances was reduced, while the number of malignancies and of animal species used to test these substances was increased. The new program rated better with the cancer experts, but was no more successful in developing efficient therapies for human malignancies.

The NCI chemotherapy program was not perceived as a clinical success, but it was nevertheless viewed as an important organizational success. It established institutional patterns of large-scale production of standardized animals and tumors, and for the organization of well-controlled multicenter clinical trials of cancer therapies. Chemotherapy of malignant tumors displays the intrinsic tension between the construction of standardized animal models of a human disease which can be easily transported into different settings and which yield reproducible results, and the necessity to relate the results obtained in these models to a highly heterogeneous human pathology. These tensions were never resolved: critiques of animal models of human malignancies continued in the 1970s, 80s and 90s, but these models maintained their central role in experimental cancer studies and in the development of new therapies against this disease.[12]

## WHAT IS THE FUTURE OF 'EXPERIMENTAL BODIES'?

As the century ends, the development of new techniques of biological research opens new avenues to the investigation of human pathologies through direct studies of biological parameters in patients, thus through a partial fusion between the 'experimental body' and the 'analyzed body.' AIDS research may illustrate these new possibilities. No universally accepted 'animal model' of AIDS was developed in the first fifteen years of the epidemic. The HIV virus does not infect small laboratory rodents. It does infect monkeys, but even the expensive monkey model is not viewed as perfectly reflecting the intrinsic complexities of the human disease. Similarly, 'humanized' mice (immunologically depressed mice grafted with human lymphatic cells) were not seen as a fully adequate model for AIDS: the researchers argued that an immunologically defective mouse is not a perfect tool to study how a virus inactivates the immune system. The HIV itself can be maintained in cell culture and studied in the laboratory, but investigations centered on the interactions between HIV and human cells in the test tube did not lead to the development of an efficient therapy for AIDS.

In parallel, the direct intervention of HIV infected persons in the definition of rules of clinical trials of anti-AIDS compounds changed these rules. For example, AIDS activists strongly objected to clinical trials of anti-AIDS drugs which included placebo-treated control groups because, they claimed, it is immoral to deny a person suffering from a lethal disease the access to a potentially efficient drug in the name of an abstract collective good. Under their pressure, investigators agreed to shift from testing against placebo to the use of 'surrogate markers' — biological parameters, measured in the laboratory, which are assumed to faithfully reflect the progress of HIV infection in a treated patient. It was found, however, that changes in 'surrogate markers' (such as the number of CD4+ lymphocytes or the concentration of HIV antigens {p-120, p-24} in the blood) were imperfect indicators of the evolution of a clinical disease, especially in patients treated with anti-retroviral compounds, such as AZT. The absence of animal models of AIDS, coupled with difficulties in studying biological effects of drugs in humans, led to a temporary standstill. This difficulty was partly overcome by the development of direct methods (quantitative polymerase chain reaction, branched DNA test) which allow the quantification of viral charge in the serum and in tissues, and the direct observation of the effect of antiretroviral drugs on the amount of virus present in the body. In the mid-1990s, an HIV-infected individual was thus found to be the best available 'experimental body' for the testing of anti-AIDS drugs.

Another example which points up the blurring of limits between the 'experimental body' and the 'analyzed body' is the use of the fluorescein-activated cell sorter (FACS). FACS is an instrument which automatically analyses molecules at the surface of cells (usually, blood cells). The FACS was developed as a research tool, and was at first used (mainly by immunologists) to analyze white blood cells of laboratory animals. Rapidly, however, the new instrument was adapted to clinical investigations and introduced to research on human pathologies, and then to semi-routine investigations of these pathologies. FACS was thus used in the study of blood disorders, in particular leukemias and lymphomas, and then in the investigation of clinical status of individuals infected with the HIV virus. The latter use became especially important when the administrative definition of passage from 'pre-AIDS' to full blown AIDS was linked to the qualification of the number of CD4+ lymphocytes of HIV-infected individuals, made with FACS (HIV infected individuals who have less that 200 CD4+ cells/ml were defined as AIDS patients, a status which, in the USA, gave them access to free health care). The extended use of FACS in the clinics (on 'normal bodies' and on 'sick bodies') rapidly eclipsed its use in the research laboratory and its application to 'experimental bodies' of laboratory animals. Doctors and researchers accumulated much more data on humans than they ever had on mice (the animal most frequently used in immunology laboratory). By consequence, immunological standards changed: while in the 1960s and 70s, data were extrapolated from mice to humans, in the 1980s and 90s, immunologists attempted to repeat in mice observations first made in humans, while standards (e.g., the classification of proteins on the surface of white blood cells) first elaborated in the clinics were transferred into research laboratories.[13]

The development of new analytic techniques points thus to a new possibility of overcoming the difficulties of extrapolation from the 'experimental body' to the 'native body': the extension of the 'analyzed body' (and, more specifically, the 'analyzed sick body') into an entity which incorporates elements of the 'experimental body.' One may suppose, however, that the increased use of patients' bodies in medical research will not put an end to the use of non-human 'experimental bodies' in biomedical research. Their use may continue for economical reasons: for the moment at least, it is cheaper to screen active molecules in cell cultures and in laboratory animals. It may continue for ethical reasons: the limits of experimentation on human bodies are narrower than those on non-human ones. Finally it may continue for organizational reasons: there are strong material and institutional incentives for the continuation of close association between research laboratory, the clinics and industry. The intrinsic imperfection of 'animal models of human diseases' favors such collaboration.

The concept of an 'animal model' of a human disease (first developed to study infectious diseases, and later extended to the investigation of other pathologies) is underdetermined, because the very notion of a 'model' presupposes representation, not identity. The degree of similitude between a human disease and its experimental model is, we have seen, negotiated between scientists who study laboratory animals and clinicians who observe patients. Such negotiation may — and often does — change both the laboratory model and the understanding of a given human disease. The mutual adaptation of laboratory models and medical practices was frequently a complicated process. Controversies on the validity of disease models reflected the difficulty of aligning the clinicians' and the scientists' points of view. However, while the absence of agreement makes collaboration between laboratory and clinic difficult, an imperfect correspondence between a human disease and a laboratory model of this disease may sometimes become an advantage. Practice-oriented biomedical research is conducted by heterogeneous professional groups — biologists, physicians, and industrialists. A loosely determined experimental model of a given human pathology may facilitate interactions between these professional groups. An 'experimental body' may allow the bridging of differences through the development of open-ended, 'boundary' concepts which may have one meaning in their common use by several professional groups, and another when used by each specific group.[14] It may also favor the development of shared practices and techniques (such as the use of inbred strains of animals and the development of transgenic animals) and favors the establishment of shared zones of activity (e.g., medical bacteriology, immunology, experimental cancer research, pharmacology). The important role of 'experimental bodies' in the promotion of efficient articulations between the laboratory, the clinic and the production plant, is probably sufficient to ensure their survival in the twenty-first century.

## REFERENCES

1.  Georges Canguilhem, *The Normal and the Pathological*, (transl. Carolyn R. Fawcett) (New York: Zone Books, 1991), 148–149. Italics in the text.
2.  See e.g., John Harley Warner, 'Science, healing and the physician's identity', *Clio Medica* (1991), **22**: 65–88, and on resistances to the central place of laboratory in medicine, Gerald L. Geison, 'Divided we stand: Physiologists and clinicians in the American context', in Morris J. Vogel and Charles E. Rosenberg (eds), *The Therapeutic Revolution*, (Philadelphia: University of Pennsylvania Press, 1979), 67–90; Christopher Lawrence, 'Incommunicable knowledge: Science, technology and the clinical art in Britain, 1850–1914', *Journal of Contemporary History* (1985), **20**: 503–520.
3.  Bruno Latour, *The Pasteurization of France*, (transl. Allan Sheridan and John Law). (Cambridge, Mass.: Harvard University Press, 1988).
4.  Statistical rules of evaluation of efficacy of vaccines started to be elaborated only in the 1910s. Donald MacKenzie, *Statistics in Britain, 1895–1930: The Social Construction of a Scientific Knowledge.* (Edinburgh: Edinburgh University Press, 1981).
5.  John P. Swann, *Academic Scientists and the Pharmaceutical Industry: Cooperative Research in Twentieth Century America.* (Baltimore and London: The Johns Hopkins University Press, 1988).
6.  Charles Rosenberg, 'Looking backwards, thinking forward: The roots of hospital crisis', *Transactions and Studies of the College of Physicians of Philadelphia* (1990), **12(2)**: 127–150.
7.  Daniel Kevles, 'The political economy of patenting life: Law, morals and interests in United States and Europe', in press.
8.  Jonathan Liebenau, 'Paul Ehrlich as a commercial scientist and research administrator', *Medical History* (1990), **34**: 5–78; Paul Weindling, 'From medical research to clinical practice: Serum therapy for diphtheria in the 1890s', in John V. Pickstone (ed.), *Medical Innovations in Historical Perspective.* (Houndsmills, Basingstoke: Macmillan, 1992), 72–83.
9.  Nelly Oudshoorn, 'On measuring sex hormones: The role of biological essays in sexualizing chemical substances', *Bulletin of the History of Medicine* (1990), **64**: 243–261.
10. Harry Marks, 'Notes from the underground: The social organization of therapeutic research', in Russel C. Maulitz and Diana E. Long (eds), *Grand Rounds: One Hundred Years of Internal Medicine.* (Philadelphia: University of Pennsylvania Press, 1987), 297–335.
11. Bernard S. Bloom, 'Controlled studies in measuring the efficacy of medical care: A historical perspective', *International Journal of Technology Assessment in Health Care* (1986), **2**: 299–310.
12. Jean Paul Gaudillière and Ilana Löwy, 'Disciplining cancer: Mice and the practice of genetic purity', in J.P. Gaudillière and I. Löwy (eds), *The Invisible Industrialist: Manufactures and the Production of Scientific Knowledge.* (Macmillan, 1998).
13. Peter Keating and Alberto Cambrosio, 'Interlaboratory life: Regulating flow cytometry' in J.P. Gaudillière and I. Löwy, *The Invisible Industrialist, Manufactures and the Production of Scientific Knowledge.* (Macmillan, 1998).
14. Susan Leigh Star and James R. Griesemer, 'Institutional ecology, 'translations', and 'boundary objects': Amateurs and professionals in Berkeley's Museum of Vertebrate Zoology', *Social Studies of Science* (1988), **19**: 387–420.

## FURTHER READING

Austoker, Joan, *A History of the Imperial Cancer Research Fund, 1902–1986.* (Oxford: Oxford University Press, 1988).

Bernard, Claude, *Introduction à la medecine expérimentale.* (Delgrave, Paris, 1865).

Bynum, William F., ' 'C'est un malade': Animal models and concepts of human disease,' *The Journal of the History of Medicine and Allied Sciences* (1990), **45**: 397–413.

Cunningham, Andrew and Williams, Perry (eds), *The Laboratory Revolution in Medicine.* (Cambridge: Cambridge University Press, 1992).

Canguilhem, Georges, *The Normal and the Pathological*, (transl. Carolyn R. Fawcett). (New York: Zone Books, 1991 (1966)).

Clarke, Adele and Fujimira Joan (eds), *The Right Tools for the Job: Materials, Techniques and Work Organization in Twentieth-Century Life Sciences.* (Princeton: Princeton University Press, 1992).

De Kruif, Paul, *The Microbe Hunters*. (New York: Harcourts and Brace, 1926).

Feinstein, Alvan R., 'The intellectual crisis in clinical science: Medaled models and muddled mettle,' *Perspectives in Biology and Medicine* (1987), **30**: 215–229.

Fox, Renée, *Experiment Perilous: Physicians and Patients Facing the Unknown*. (Philadelphia: University of Pennsylvania Press, 1974).

Geison, Gerald L., 'Divided we stand: Physiologists and clinicians in the American context,' in Charles Rosenberg and Morris J. Vogel (eds), *The Therapeutic Revolution*. (Philadelphia: University of Pennsylvania Press, 1979), 67–90.

Keating, Peter and Cambrosio, Alberto, 'Interlaboratory life: Regulating flow cytometry', in Jean Paul Gaudillière and Ilana, Löwy (eds), *The Invisible Industrialist: Manufactures and the Production of Scientific Knowledge*. (London: Macmillan, 1998), 250–295.

Lawrence, Christopher, 'Incommunicable knowledge: Science, technology and the clinical art in Britain, 1850–1914,' *Journal of Contemporary History* (1985), **20**: 503–520.

Marks, Harry, *The Progress of Experiment: Science and Therapeutic Reform in the United States, 1900–1990*. (Cambridge: Cambridge University Press, 1997).

Maulitz, Russel A., 'Physician versus bacteriologist: The ideology of science in clinical medicine', in Charles Rosenberg & Morris A. Vogel (eds), *The Therapeutic Revolution*. (Philadelphia: University of Pennsylvania Press, 1979), 91–108.

Oudshoorn, Nelly, *Beyond the Natural Body: An Archeology of Sex Hormones*. (London: Routledge, 1995).

Patton, William, *Man and Mouse*. (Oxford: Oxford University Presss, 1984).

Swann, John P., *Academic Scientists and the Pharmaceutical Industry: Cooperative Research in Twentieth Century America*. (Baltimore and London: The John Hopkins University Press, 1988).

Warner, John Harley, *The Therapeutic Perspective: Medical Practice, Knowledge and Identity in America*. (Cambridge, Mass.: Harvard University Press, 1986).

CHAPTER 29

# The Ethical Body

ROGER COOTER

Like most of the 'bodies' in this volume, 'the ethical' is not to be found as such in medical textbooks. Nor is it a body that constitutes the object of a medical gaze in the manner of the 'diseased body' or the 'dead body.' On the contrary, contemporary medical ethics gazes critically *at* medicine. And although modern medical ethics is now pursued academically and practiced in the laboratory as well as at the bedside (ostensibly), it does not refer to a specific physical site or geographical space in the manner of the 'industrial body' or the 'Third World body.' Nor, if reckoned as a body of knowledge, is it one of stunning intellectual coherence. Current textbooks of medical ethics reveal a compound of different and distinct moral conundrums, such as those over abortion and reproductive technology, sex selection, eugenics, genetic engineering and cloning, anomalous forms of procreation, human experimentation, the rights of patients and embryos, informed consent, the use of placebos and drugs, privacy and confidentiality, euthanasia, the selling of body parts, and the allocation of scarce resources in health care. Divergent constituencies are involved: philosophers, humanists, theologians, doctors, lawyers, feminists, politicians, sociologists, and social policy analysts, to name but a few. Indeed, the elaboration of medical ethics extends well beyond the community of academic commentators to include patients as well, and all *potential* patients. Some would also add the unborn, along with the 'dead,' or those on respirators.

Yet, insofar as all these voices amplify moral responses to medical and bio-medical practices, modern medical ethics can be understood as a culturally bounded 'body' of discourse. Why else should it be considered one of the most engaging concerns of our times? Why else are we subjected to a relentless torrent of documentaries, movies, talk shows and news items on medical-ethical issues? Why else does hardly a day pass without some disputed medical practice being brought to light, or some new ethical quandary or litigation captured in headlines? That many of those headlines dredge up practices from the past is indicative of the retrospective operation of values which hitherto were not so dominant, or at least were not so widely shared, deeply felt, and keen to be exercised. That the academic study of medical ethics now flourishes can also be attributed to this change. According to the philosopher Stephen Toulmin, medicine saved the life of ethics, restoring to it "a seriousness and human relevance" which it had almost completely lost during the inter-war years.[1] Philosophy in general, through the medical ethical reprocessing of such mentors as Kant and J.S. Mill, and philosophy departments in particular, through greater student numbers, have gained enormously through the limelighting of the medical ethical body. So, too, have departments of law and medical sociology, to say nothing of the territory of some of the limelighters themselves, in medical journalism. Even the business world has sought to cash in on the discourse in its efforts to "bridge the integrity gap,"[2] while certain market-wise pharmaceutical companies have established their own 'advisory councils on bioethics.' Little wonder that some in the medical profession, at the receiving end of much of this outpouring, and at the receiving end of increasing litigation for 'unethical' practices, have spoken cynically of a "burgeoning ethics industry."[3]

It is, moreover, largely through our bodies that the discourse of medical ethics has come to operate. Our bodies have become the primary site through which we navigate, negotiate and render tangible ethics in general. Historical studies reflect this quite as much as other academic domains: as Jenner and Taithe note in their contribution to this volume, many historians now routinely follow Foucault and others in perceiving the body as the primary locus upon which power has been inscribed. It has not always been so. At end of the nineteenth century Herbert Spencer outlined the 'Data of Ethics' as essentially the external social and political agencies that acted upon the welfare of self and others. By the end of the twentieth century, however, it was the individualized body — especially in its medical context — that was the referent point for the explication and contestation of right and wrong, good and bad. As reinforced popularly through films such as *Whose Life Is It Anyway?* (1979), the body became the medium of the modern moral maze, the stage whereon not only the power of medicine and its social relations were acted out, but power relations in general. At a popular level, even the authority of the academics engaged in medical ethics became contestable. To the public at large medical ethics is attractive because it does not have to be philosophical; it touches chords of sentiment and feeling which transcend the logical rigor and mystifications of philosophy. For many people "ethics is an integral part of religious belief;"[4] for others, deliberations on medico-ethical issues constitute a secular alternative to religion — a forum for the personal exploration of the human condition, a platform for defending human values.

This chapter seeks to account for this phenomena as manifested over the last three or four decades of the twentieth century. In view of the importance now attached to medical ethics in academic, legal, and medical circles, and the social pervasiveness of the ethical contemplation of bio-medical practices, no history of medicine in the twentieth century would be complete without its inclusion. Crucial decisions in therapeutics, jurisprudence, medical research and the political economy of health care frequently depend upon the outcome of medical ethical exercises. Life and death, literally, can hang upon such decisions, many of which are manifestly in the public realm and influenced by public opinion.

Unfortunately, however, there are few studies to help us make general sense of the phenomena. Where historically-informed writing on modern medical ethics has not focused narrowly on ethical codes, it has tended to concentrate on the parts rather than the whole — on the history of abortion, euthanasia, embryo research, human experimentation, informed consent, the trade in body organs and so on. Much of the discussion, moreover, has been by and for contemporary philosophy, law, sociology and politics. With the partial exception of David Rothman's study of the rise of bioethics in the US, *Strangers at the Bedside* (1991), which will be discussed below, no attempt has been made at a history of modern medical ethics in which the growth of the interest in the subject is seen as the problem demanding contextual explanation. At best, commentators within the field of medical ethics acknowledge "strong outside forces" and the importance of "the entire social context."[5] Even Rothman's study refers more to developments within medicine than to those in society and culture as a whole. Trans-national comparisons meanwhile remain largely unexplored.

## THE BIOETHICISTS' TALE

In the absence of any such history, it has been the practitioners themselves who have scripted historical accounts, whether intentionally or not. Often believing themselves to traffic only in moral truths, contemporary medical ethicists or bioethicists implicitly parade a positivist narrative of 'moral progress' comparable to the tale of 'scientific progress' imbibed and issued by the scientific and medical community. Inimical to this endeavor is any recognition of socio-economic or political determinacy either in asking the 'right' medical ethical questions, or in arriving at the 'right' answers. Indeed, a claim to ethical correctness that admitted such contextual determinacy — that confessed in other words to the historical transience of moral truths — would command little authority. Although 'an ethic for our time' might be convincingly argued for, it is rarely attempted. The tendency of medical ethics, rather, is to the de-contextualization of the ethical in medicine, be it the family that surrounds the life-support patient (as opposed to the decision to pull or not to pull the plug), or the social welfare ideology enveloping the single mother seeking in-vitro fertilization (as opposed to the ethics of the technology involved). Such de-contextualization contributes to the impression of medico-ethical arguments as essentially free from social or ideological prejudice, and as usable in a value-free manner (despite the allegiances of ethicists to utilitarian or other philosophical positions). Thus it is lamented by bioethicists that their arguments are too frequently 'abused' or put "to political and self-interested use."[6] In deploying this use/abuse model, medical ethicists can be seen as striving for the same would-be value-transcendent status of scientists.

Like the controversial issues over which medical ethicists debate, their own professional enterprise cannot be reckoned outside of, or above, the parameters of politics and society. It follows that their endeavors can be treated in much the same way as historians and social analysts have long studied the medical profession, namely, as a part of the institutionalization and exercise of professional power. One might in fact subject the business of modern medical ethics to the same sort of political 'unmasking' that the legally-trained medical ethicist Ian Kennedy performed on medicine as a whole in his 1980 Reith lectures. But this task runs the risk of ascribing to medical ethicists a status and authority they only aspire to. Moreover, it can lull us into thinking of bioethicists as themselves the primary agents behind the cultural elevation of medical ethics — as the legitimate inventors, as it were, of their own history. Such, indeed, is the interpretative tendency of Rothman's *Strangers at the Bedside: a history of how law and bioethics transformed medical decision-making.*

Rothman argues that the estrangement of doctors at the bedside was the crucial precondition for the ascension of bioethical and legal decision-making. Partly as a result of the vast expansion of research-based laboratory medicine during and after World War II, and of the attitudes and practices that went with it, the social distance between practitioners and patients widened. At the same time, post-war work among America medical scientists estranged general practitioners from the cutting edge of medicine, so that the latter's practical wisdom (accumulated over years of clinical experience) came increasingly to seem "less impressive and relevant than the wisdom that the philosopher or lawyer had accumulated through the study of first principles."[7] Over the same period, Rothman submits, the social distance between hospitals and communities also widened. Thus bedside ethics gave way to bioethics as medical decision-making fell to 'outsiders' in the course of doctors becoming 'strangers.'

Rothman sees the decisive act in this tidy estrangement process as occurring in June 1966 when Henry Beecher, Dorr Professor of Research in Anesthesia at the Harvard Medical School, blew the whistle on human experimentation in medicine in his paper 'Ethics and Clinical Research' published in the *New England Journal of Medicine.* Although Rothman offers no explanation for Beecher's sudden prick of conscience, other than to say that he had a strong "commitment to good science,"[8] everything in his account is designed, ultimately, to heighten the unique significance of Beecher's 1966 performance. Beecher is thereby transformed into an honorary 'outsider' whose act of whistle blowing cleaves a sharp divide between medical ethics past and present. The very use of the word 'bioethics' in Rothman's subtitle contributes to this demarcation. As fostered by the American doyen of medical ethics, Robert Veatch, 'bioethics' was intended to indicate a medical ethics which was "not the same as the past ethics of physicians."[9] Thus any effort such as Rothman's to historicize 'bioethics' implicitly legitimates the bioethicists' claim to authority over the medical profession in ethical decision-making. *Strangers at the*

*Bedside*, though a sophisticated work of historical analysis, is nevertheless a defense of the professional claims of American bioethicists. If only inadvertently, it contributes to what it embraces: the bioethicsts' own construction of a self-serving historical narrative — "the bioethicists' tale."[10]

Paradoxically, this interpretative tendency of the book — what might be regarded as its critical weakness — serves to highlight the value of its account of the American medical profession's disempowerment and the bioethicists' empowerment. For above all it reveals that modern medical ethics *is* about power, or struggles for authority in medical decision-making. This can be illustrated in a number of different ways, as will be seen below. But it can also be demonstrated though what is necessary to address first: the contention that underlies Rothman's study, that medical ethics past and present can be sharply divided, and that the division hinges historically on the agency of the bioethicists.

## CONTINUITIES AND DISCONTINUITIES

While it would be difficult to deny that medical ethics today is differently constituted than in the past, it would be wrong to suppose that medical ethicists themselves transformed and/or capitalized upon medical decision-making to anything like the extent that Rothman suggests. In Britain, the main point of comparison for this chapter, medical ethics is barely recognized as an independent professional field, yet medical ethical consciousness is very much in evidence in society generally. British medical ethicists have preferred to stay within the disciplines of philosophy, theology, sociology and law. Centers for the study of medical ethics have emerged in British universities, but there has been little development of a recognizable career structure within a self-styled professional field of 'bioethics' (a term that British ethicists tend to regard as an Americanism). In large part this difference between the two countries hinges on the different structures of medicine involved. The state controlled National Health Service in Britain contrasts with the predominantly open medical market in the US which is governed by insurance schemes and private practice. In America, bioethicists are frequently consulted to deliberate on morally contentious hospital practices and procedures which might otherwise (at great expense) be forced to be decided in the courts. The decision to turn off a respirator is but one example of such consultation. But in Britain there has been much less demand for this kind of intervention. Comparable ethical issues tend to be reduced by hospital consultants to matters of 'risk calculation' (for example, the chances of a patient's survival if 'x' or 'y' technique is used, *versus* benefit to a similar patient), or they are simply deferred to the courts, which traditionally have been far less generous than in America in meting out financial settlements. Ethical committees exist in British hospitals, but they review proposed research, not patient care. Thus in Britain there has been little market incentive to professionalize in medical ethics. Typically, British medical ethicists frown upon the priest-like role assumed by American bioethicists.

Nor, for historical reasons to do with the structure of the medical profession in Britain, has there been any tradition of medical ethical codes issued by the profession in their own self-interest. Protectionist medico-ethical societies were established in some British cities in the nineteenth century, but it was not until 1980 that the British Medical Association issued its first book exclusively on medical ethics. The General Medical Council, created by the Medical Act of 1858, has primarily concerned itself with disciplining doctors for gross medical misconduct and with legally protecting the profession, rather than with issuing ethical legislation. Not until 1995, in *Good Medical Practice*, did the GMC feel compelled to set out the ethical responsibilities of doctors. In the absence of such advice, legislation, and codes, it has been much more difficult than in America for outsiders to pit themselves against the medical profession's putative monopoly over what constitutes ethical medical practice. Only gradually, with greater commercialization of British medicine, did the space open for more American-like contestations. Government initiatives in the 1980s to break old medical elites and foster more fluid wealth-based social structures lay behind this change. It was also furthered by increased effort on the part of the legal profession to seek out cases for medical litigation. Overall, the effect of greater commercialism, consumerism and litigation was to undercut the sovereignty of the state in British medicine, thus enabling the market to enter more freely into the relationship between doctors and patients.

As it would be wrong to suppose that medical ethicists themselves were responsible for raising ethical consciousness, so it would be mistaken to assume that the type of issues of concern to medical ethicists were unheard of before Henry Beecher's 1966 publication. One has only to recall George Bernard Shaw's *The Doctor's Dilemma* (1906) to appreciate that, within and without medicine, medico-ethical anxieties have a long ancestry. The dilemma faced by Shaw's medical characters was that of deciding between providing a scarce life-saving resource to a poor, undistinguished, elderly fellow practitioner, or providing it for a young gifted but 'immoral' artist. In this fictional setting at least the dilemma facing the doctors was about more than merely protecting medical professional interests. Recent historical studies also confirm that what came to be styled 'medical ethics' in the late eighteenth- and early nineteenth-century publications of medical practitioners like Thomas Percival and William Gregory did not neglect issues such as the sanctity of life, patient confidentiality and autonomy, or 'proper' doctor-patient relations. 'Informed consent,' perceived by many ethicists since the 1970s as at the very heart of modern medical ethics, but as having "no historical roots in medical practice,"[11] can in fact be traced in Anglo-American medicine and law as far back as the early-nineteenth century (though admittedly we know little about the concept's diffusion within medicine or within the wider community). Historically-minded medical sociologists in the mid-1970s often insisted that doctors in the past were solely concerned with 'etiquette' or with the protection of intra-professional relations, rather than with the 'real' ethics of doctor/patient relations and patient autonomy. 'Traditional' medical ethics was thus narrowly defined by these sociologists. But being informed by the then current critique of medicine's paternalistic authoritarianism and market monopoly (notably by Ivan Illich's influential *Medical Nemesis* [1975]), they read the past anachronistically. Although they provided useful material for the historical analysis of medical ethics, they also contributed (in the manner of Rothman after them) to the bioethicists' tale.

## POLITICS BY OTHER MEANS

If the historical sociologists of the 1970s had ventured into the history of medical ethics in the twentieth century they might have discovered not only that their so-called 'real ethics' of doctor-patient relations were on the agenda of medicine long before the rise of bioethics, but also, that that agenda-setting could often be a part of a politically explicit strategy on the part of the medical profession. Since the late-nineteenth century, doctors in America, Britain and other European countries responded to real or perceived threats to their autonomy from the state and from the laity by invoking rhetoric on the morally sacred nature of the doctor-patient relationship. In many ways the language of doctor-patient relations was their invention, not that of 1970s sociologists. It was born of political necessity. As one doctor anticipated in the 1880s, a medical ethics that enshrined doctor-patient relations could be a defense "against anarchy and communism."[12] A 1927 American edition of Thomas Percival's *Medical Ethics* was justified on the grounds that it would fortify the profession against "group practice, health insurance, and state medicine."[13] In Britain, doctors espoused similar rhetoric in the face of incursions by the state, especially after the passage of the National Health Insurance Act in 1911, and after being compelled to work for the military during the First World War. General practitioners, fearful of the loss of their market-sovereign autonomy, came to extol the sanctity of voluntary relations with patients, even upholding them as "the primary reason for the doctor's being."[14] The consultant elite did likewise in their defense of professional freedom, often (as in Henry Brackenbury's *Patient and Doctor* [1935]), idealizing the relationship within an allegedly 'time-honoured' holistic neo-Hippocratic humanism. Such was the language invoked by doctors in the House of Lords in 1936 during the debate over euthanasia. The "special doctor patient relationship"[15] was seen by the medical lords as sufficient to render unnecessary any state legislation for medically-assisted euthanasia. Although this kind of anti-state medical paternalism was muted in Britain after the introduction of the National Health Service in 1948, it could still be heard in domains where clinical autonomy was perceived as under threat. In the 1960s, for instance, the *British Medical Journal* argued against claims for 'abortion on demand' on the grounds that "the object of medical ethics is to protect not the profession but the public."[16] In America the anti-statist rhetoric remained strong within textbooks of medical ethics (most of which were written by Roman Catholic doctors). Offered were dire warnings of "moral enslavement" through the "totalitarian plans" for "physicians, — hospitals, medical schools and patients."[17]

In some ways the pre-World War II medical deployment of the doctor-patient relationship as ethically 'sacred' was comparable to the deployment of the concept of 'informed consent' by physicians in the 1960s and 1970s. It is surely no coincidence that the celebration of the concept by Beecher in the US, and by the Harley Street physician and medical coach, Maurice Pappworth in Britain, began at a time when the medical profession was coming under new public and political scrutiny. The costs of medical care were soaring, partly as a result of expensive new techniques and procedures such as organ transplants. Especially in the US, tensions mounted in the profession over public and private medicine and between generalists and specialists — tensions exacerbated by the implementation of Medicare and Medicaid in the mid-1960s, and by the unprecedented "national chauvinism and ... ego epidemic"[18] of transplant surgeons. Medicare and Medicaid meant that charity cases were funded by the Federal government, the administration of which wrought new tiers of non-medical management in hospitals. Managers, not bioethicists, it might be argued changed the ethical face of medicine by routinizing, if not alienating clinicians. In any case, many of these clinicians (not just the general practitioners that Rothman refers to) felt marginalized by the growing importance and prestige of bio-medical researchers and the consequent effects of this on clinical encounters with patients. Pappworth 'blew his whistle' after he heard stories from his students of how at the new Hammersmith Post-Graduate Medical School in London the clinical encounter with patients had been transformed into something akin to a research experiment. Beecher, as an anesthetist, must have witnessed some of this first hand at the Harvard Medical School. In Pappworth's case personal circumstances may perhaps have compounded a sense of clinical marginalization, for his own application for a professorship at the Hammersmith had been rejected.

At the same time, outside medicine, for contextual reasons that will be discussed below, the bubble of post-war optimism was bursting. In 1962, the year that Pappworth's first article on the experimental use of humans in medicine was published, the thalidomide scandal broke. Within a decade several high-profile exposés of medical 'inhumanity' also hit the headlines. In 1966 it was revealed that researchers at the Sloan-Kettering Cancer Foundation had injected live cancer cells into un-informed geriatric patients at the Jewish Hospital Medical School in Brooklyn. In 1972 experiments came to light charting the progress of untreated syphilis in the black population in Tuskegee. Around the same time it emerged that an American virologist had exposed severely retarded children to the hepatitis virus without sufficiently informing their parents or guardians of the nature of his experiments. Public outrage combined with fiscal concerns led to increased political scrutiny and to demands for greater public accountability in the funding of medical research, especially in the US where most of the soaring costs of this research was tax-payer funded. In the mid-1970s the US Congress created the National Commission for the Protection of Human Subjects of Biomedical and Behavioral Research which was instructed to "identify the ethical principles that should govern such research, [and] to make recommendations regarding the ethical circumstances under which the federal government could support research."[19] In Britain the bulk of research funding was directly or indirectly from the pharmaceutical industry which was far less open to public scrutiny. For the most part, the norm in the UK has been to voluntary self-policing, such as the code of practice issued by the British Paediatric Association in 1983.

Although the scandals of the 1960s and 1970s were not exposed by the medical profession, their efforts to contain them through assertions of professional ethics or in-house avowals of ethical reform illustrate how, within the profession, medical ethics continued to serve as a form of politics by other means. It is, in fact, hard to see how the advocacy of medical ethics could ever be otherwise. Arbitrating the good and the bad in medicine (as in society) is necessarily about commanding authority. For the most part, professional claims to the ethical high ground in medicine have either been attempts at empowerment, such as those by American bioethicists, or attempts at defending vested power, such as those by doctors. For the most part, medical ethics during the second half of the twentieth century was structured by the dialectic between these two rival claims to authority.

Any such view is at odds with conventional thinking which typically juxtaposes the 'ethical' to the 'political.' Nowhere has this opposition been more insisted upon than in connection with the alleged moment of the birth of modern medical ethics, the Nuremberg trials. As consolidated in the Nuremberg Code and in the American Medical Association's code of 1946 (guarding against unwarranted experiments on human subjects), modern medical ethics is often seen as wholly rooted in a "great revolution of sensibility ... and deeper awareness of our moral responsiblities toward our fellow beings" that emerged from the "enormities of inhumanity that accompanied or preceded World War II."[20] But such a view is historically slipshod. It forgets that Nuremberg was a show trial concerned with creating an image of medicine as ideologically pristine and uniquely orientated to the defense of humanitarianism — an image in stark contrast to that on trial. It also forgets what was glossed over at the trials: first, that some of the medical research conducted by the Nazi doctors in the 1930s (such as by Josef Mengele) had been supported by American research funding bodies such as Rockefeller and the Loeb Foundations; and second, that subsequently the research findings of the Nazi experimenters were keenly sought by medical researchers elsewhere. "I hope those notes aren't lost," remarked one American researcher when told about the experiments conducted at the Buchenwald death camp, "they ought to prove invaluable to future research."[21] The Japanese medical experimenters were granted pardons from prosecution in exchange for their research notes.

The exposé of the Nazi medical experiments, and to a lesser extent those of the Japanese, created a caricature of the dehumanized 'mad doctor.' This extreme caricature enabled medical researchers elsewhere to carry on with their work — no matter how mindless — confident that they were acting rationally in the best interest of humanity. Such a belief was not difficult to sustain in a context in which penicillin and various other therapeutic breakthroughs were contributing to a view of medicine as nothing less than miraculous and as wholly incapable of doing harm in and of itself. Discredited in this context were formerly popular alternative images of medical practice, such as that of the misguided Dr. Moreau in H.G. Wells' novel of 1896, or the "old stories" that George Orwell recollected about "doctors cutting you open out of sheer curiosity or thinking it funny to start operating on you before you were properly 'under.'"[22] The worry expressed by Churchill's doctor, Lord Moran, that the effect of the Nuremberg trials might lead the British public to question British medical research, was largely unfounded. Post-penicillin, pre-thalidomide (to conjure history pharmaceutically), the effect of the Nuremberg trials was more a numbing than a sharpening of ethical awareness in medicine or in culture generally. Indeed, not until the 1970s would the sterilization of mentally 'defective' Scandinavians come to an end. The least that can be said is that if the Second World War was good for medical ethics, it took an unconscionable amount of time for it to be realized.

## GOD, THE MARKET, AND OTHER SOCIO-POLITICAL FIELDS OF FORCE

If modern medical ethics was not in any effective sense born at Nuremberg, when, where and how was it born? As suggested at the outset there can be no easy answer to this question, though the contrary is often conveyed in popular literature on medical ethics. While it may be that in American medicine the pre- and post-World War II estrangement of general practitioners from the bedside links causally to the rise of bioethics, neither in America nor elsewhere can the general rise of the modern discourse of medical ethics, or the legal, academic and journalistic industry around it, be so neatly or narrowly understood. (In major British and Continental hospitals patients and practitioners have always been 'estranged.') Nor can the phenomena be comprehended only in terms of legal reflexes to abuses of professional power, or to new medical technologies and procedures. Issues high on the medical ethical agenda, such as abortion and euthanasia, often have little to do with new technology, while outrage at the organ transplant industry rotates less around the procedures than the rank commercialization of body parts. More apparent in the rise of medical ethical consciousness since the 1960s has been the existence of a political and cultural context in which the desire to expose medical 'abuse' and challenge its perceived social authority has gained legitimacy. To comprehend this it is necessary to take cognizance not only of events in medicine, but of the operation of social and political forces outside it.

Among these forces, obvious at the time but now largely forgotten in the narrative of the origins of modern medical ethics, is that of religion, and of

Catholicism (and the reactions to it) in particular. As noted above, the American discourse on medical ethics was largely dominated by Roman Catholic doctors before mid-century. As the psychologist Karl Menninger remarked in his preface to the Protestant theologian Joseph Fletcher's *Morals and Medicine* (1954), Catholic moralists were "the one stellar exception" to the "strange blindspot about the ethics of health and medicine in almost all ethical literature."[23] Fletcher's book, a bestseller, was a revision of the lectures he delivered at Harvard in 1949, and it owed much to the polemic, *American Freedom and Catholic Power*, written by the journalist Paul Blanshard two years previously. Fletcher's particular preoccupation was with the stranglehold of prohibitory Catholic medical injunctions prevailing in Catholic general hospitals. This was of considerable concern to Americans, since there were then 692 such hospitals in the US treating over three million patients annually, most of whom were non-Catholics. Particularly oppressive and subversive of human dignity, Fletcher felt, were Catholic prohibitions on 'advances' in medicine in the areas of contraception, artificial insemination, sterilization and euthanasia — issues exacerbated in any case by the post-war trend to hospital care over home care. Surrounded by one's peers, doctors were less at liberty to carry out such procedures. Fletcher's argument thus amounted to an assault on the barriers to professional practice and autonomy in American medicine imposed by the Catholic Church. Whether the medical profession responded to Fletcher's work in this light is unclear. The important point here is that his book was issued for other reasons, independent of the profession's interests. It is also significant that it was published in Britain by the socialist firm of Victor Gollancz, the same who later commissioned (though did not publish) Pappworth's *Human Guinea Pigs*. Gollancz was among those active in the humanitarian movement of the 1930s, a movement whose roots ran deep into the nineteenth century and, within which, before Nuremberg, the medical profession occupied no privileged position.

Catholicism and the reactions to it have borne importantly on medical ethics throughout the second half of the twentieth century. Whether or not any store can be placed in the allegation that Ivan Illich, in writing *Medical Nemesis*, "had his own hidden, traditional Catholic 'reactionary' agenda,"[24] there can be no denying that the Catholic Church was at the back of a great deal of contemporary medico-ethical controversy. The story of the cell of Catholic doctors and their wives who mobilized against the legalization of abortion in the State of California in the early 1960s has become familiar through several recent historical studies. Less well known is, for example, the marker status (among ethicists) of the 1958 letter of Pope Pius XII on the ethics of removing life-support from patients whose consciousness would never return. It is also worthy of note that the major centers for the study of medical ethics in America and Continental Europe have been on Catholic campuses, even if most of the ethical agendas pursued in these places have not been narrowly sectarian. Other religious denominations have played a far less conspicuous part in the history of medical ethics or in raising medico-ethical consciousness, although in the case of the Jehovah's Witnesses the practice of refusing blood transfusions has led to some interesting ethical discussions as well as enhancing the sect's legitimacy as a result of new medical and political concern over the impurity of blood supplies.

Another impetus to the rise of modern medical ethics — again, hardly mentioned in technologically-fixated popular accounts — lies in the history of mental care. In the absence of systematic study of the popular impact of exposés of practices such as lobotomies and shock therapy it remains difficult precisely to measure this impetus. It is noteworthy, however, that both Fletcher and Pappworth paid particular attention to such practices. Fletcher may have been influenced by the late 1940s critique of American mental asylums by the socialist practitioner and activist, Albert Deutsch. Pappworth was doubtless influenced by his own consultancy in an asylum in south London, as well as by the UK's National Council for Civil Liberties which, as early as 1951, published on cases of wrongful detention in mental institutions — a civil libertarian issue in Britain stretching back to the eighteenth century. In the course of the emergence of the intellectual 'anti-psychiatry' movement in the 1960s and 1970s, and the turning into popular films of novels such as Ken Kesey's *One Flew Over the Cuckoo's Nest* (1973), the National Association for Mental Health (MIND) became active in publicizing many aspects of psychiatric abuse, neglect and injustice. In the early 1970s, under its campaign director, David Ennals (subsequently Minister of Health in the Labour government of 1974–79), MIND decided that safeguarding the rights of mental patients should be its first priority. In so doing it was following the lead of the New York Civil Liberties Union, which in 1968 began a vast program of court actions "to protect and expand the rights of mental patients."[25]

Organizations such as MIND and the NYCLU were themselves the outgrowth of broader civil rights movements, the concerns and vocabularies of which, from the late 1960s, were crucial to the consciousness of medical ethics at both popular and academic levels. Indeed, without the civil rights movement it is doubtful if modern medical ethics as a cultural force would have emerged when it did, or would have been so concerned with the protection and empowerment of patient groups against medical abuse and authority. In the nineteenth century the medical profession had been implicated in the abuse of individual rights by campaigners against compulsory vaccination for smallpox and the compulsory medical inspection of prostitutes. But in those cases the profession had acted more as a self-serving auxiliary to the state than as the principal culprit. To a degree, by the late 1930s, medical professional groups had exonerated themselves. The British Medical Association's first ever pamphlet on medical ethics was issued in 1939 specifically in connection with defending the civil liberties of Jewish refugee doctors.

The Tuskegee exposure of 1972 did much to forge a connection between civil rights for black Americans and the issue of patients' rights. 'Tuskegee' was to enter popular rhetoric as synonymous with the involvement of black and impoverished peoples in medical experiments, especially those conducted by pharmaceutical companies. But by the time Tuskegee hit the headlines another powerful dissident voice had been added to the chorus — the feminist movement. Women, even more than blacks, were concerned with the combined exercise of commercial and medical control over their bodies, and were no less strident in their demands for liberation. Although the pervasive cultural fall-out from the women's struggle of the late 1960s and 1970s now makes it difficult to be precise about its effects on ethics in medicine, it is clear that without that struggle medico-ethical consciousness would have been far less robust. Linked to the civil rights movement, the women's movement, with its marches, protests and demonstrations, constituted a part of the counter-culture of the same decades. Inseparable from Illich-like attacks on the social power of medicine in general was its critique of male patriarchal medical authority in particular, as captured in the titles alone of such popular works as *Our Bodies Ourselves* (1973) issued by the Boston Women's Health Book Collective, or *For Her Own Good: 150 years of the experts' advice to women* (1978) by Barbara Ehrenreich and Deirdre English. Perceiving that childbirth, obstetric techniques, fetal monitoring, pain-killing drugs, and so on had estranged them from their own bodies and reproductive lives, women fought back to regain control, including control over the medical metaphors that alienated them from themselves. As in the late-nineteenth century, analogies were drawn between the plight of women and that of animals at the hands of medical science, although the specific links between the women's liberation movement and that for the rights and liberation of animals (and the broader ecology movement) remain to be explored.

Around one area of medical ethical debate in particular — abortion — the women's movement was to serve as a major force in raising political consciousness. Among American commentators it is now widely recognized that "the abortion issue ... brought crucial questions about entitlement and the politics of the law to the attention of more United States citizens than any issue since civil rights."[26] But care must be taken not to read history backwards. As Kristin Luker pointed out in 1984 (*Abortion and the Politics of Motherhood*), the involvement of the women's movement in the abortion issue followed upon, rather than preceded, the legalization of abortion. In fact little public controversy surrounded abortion when it was legalized in America and Britain in the late 1960s. The legislation for it was introduced by junior politicians who were primarily concerned with preventing the evils of back-street abortionists, and with legally safeguarding the therapeutic abortions that doctors were already performing. The legislation harmonized with the sexual liberation of the times (including, ironically, the introduction of 'the pill'), as well as with the mounting concern over global population explosion. Outside some Catholic circles and certain sections of the medical profession, abortion only became controversial after the grass-roots feminist movement challenged the medical professions' right to gatekeep and control the procedure. 'Abortion upon demand' as a woman's 'right' then became the issue, and the medical profession's authority to decide on procedures for controlling birth was effectively challenged.

Like many of the medical issues of concern to Catholic moralists, the politics of abortion in the 1960s and 1970s touched fundamentally on attitudes to sexuality and reproduction. Prior to the 1960s the medical profession had mostly shared with Catholics and other religious bodies the social norms regulating sexual behavior. In the course of the 1960s and 1970s, however, partly as a result of the changes in the law around abortion, but more generally in response to the counter-culture, the medical profession drifted away from the role it had assumed as one of the guardians of conventional sexual morality. Catholics were thus left exposed as the main defenders of 'traditional' medical ethics in this area. But not for long; within a decade their 'default' position had turned proactive as other religious and secular groups sought a return to traditional values. By then the moral authority of the medical profession in this area, as in others, had been sapped largely as a result of the challenges to its autonomy over the previous decades from civil rights and feminist activists, as well as from other anti-authoritarian forces. In turn, as the power of the latter groups also diminished, a space was opened for the assertion of a new (essentially amoral) authority in medicine and society generally — the consumerist ethics of 'choice' in the free (deregulated) market — to which its advocates on the political right sought to ally 'traditional' moral values.

Whereas in the 1970s a slogan such as "Dignity starts with a patient's choice" (uttered by the paralyzed hero in *Whose Life Is It Anyway?*) signified political challenge to the perceived paternalistic authority of the medical profession, by the 1980s 'choice' was conforming more to the 'free-market' rhetoric of Reganomics. "Choice is the essence of ethics,"[27] declared Margaret Thatcher, around the same time that she fostered the managerial and financial mechanisms that lead to the introduction of internal markets in the National Health Service. In Britain, as in America, politicians recognized the economic expediency of displacing welfarist notions of 'rights to health' with those of 'healthism' (self-maintenance of healthy living) and of encouraging 'choice' among middle-class health consumers with disposable incomes. Medical ethicists, on the whole, embraced the new rhetoric, if sometimes attenuating it by reference to *social* choice — their rationalist deliberations over particular issues purporting to guide the laity in making and implementing such decisions. Despite the recognition among many in society that such 'choice' in medical delivery was a fallacy, and despite the move among some contemporary makers of health policy to 'collective rights' in the face of arguments about scare health resources, the power of an ethics of choice in medicine was difficult to dislodge. Indeed, it became pervasive, in part because it so easily appropriated the language of civil rights and patients' rights, exchanging sociopolitical vocabularies for those of individualist consumption. Around abortion, for instance, not only was the language of civil rights and liberation displaced by the 'rights' of putative individuals (fetuses), but the practice (where not simply outlawed) was re-cast in terms of the consumerist rhetoric of individual 'choice' — choice within political contexts where actual choice had become increasingly restricted for many women. Economically privileged health consumers came to demand their 'right' to shop in the 'supermarkets of life' where everything was to be available at a price. Perhaps inevitably — if ironically — consumerist lobby groups stepped into the boots once occupied by black activists and feminists. In the exposure of "Tuskegee Part II"[28] (the use of pregnant women in Africa, Thailand and the Caribbean as unprotected controls in HIV experiments), a consumer advocacy organization, 'Public Citizen,' was to play the leading role.

## CONCLUSION

Clearly, by the turn of the twenty-first century modern medical ethics had outgrown its origins in the civil rights movement, the women's movement, and the counter-culture of the 1960s and 1970s. No less obvious, however, is its continuing social and cultural resonance. There is little indication that the 'body' of medical ethical discourse has become slim-lined or has lost, or is losing, its cultural legitimacy. Within the consumerist parameters of 'choice,' no less than within the unblurred political framework of 'rights,' medical ethics continues to thrive at popular and academic levels. In fact, consumerism, including the increased public willingness (or legal encouragement) to take to the courts, has greatly broadened the social base for medical ethical thought, rhetoric, and action. Claims for legal redress for unethical medical procedures, and demands for statutory regulations to protect against further unethical practices has never been greater. At the same time, while the ethical leverage exerted by religious groups, animal rights advocates, women's groups, and ethnic and other minorities continues, popular hospital soap-operas and 'all-hang-out' TV confessionals and web-sites have come to provide a forum both for exposing the latest perils of bio-medicine and technology and for their ethical debate. For the most part, vicariously, with popcorn in hand, do the majority of people entertain and get entertained by the moral dilemmas raised by modern medicine. From being counter-cultural, medical ethical consciousness has become conventional, even banal. Meanwhile, within the medical profession, anything and everything has become subject for ethical review, from the individual and collective behavior of doctors, researchers and hospitals, to the use of "evidence-based frameworks for decision-making."[29]

In that ethical dilemmas in medicine arise out of the conflict between interest groups, there is every reason to suppose that ethical controversy will continue to flourish. With the sundering in the 1970s and 1980s of the autonomous power of the medical profession and the gradual withdrawal of the state's compliance in the profession's own ethical governance, a multitude of new interest groups have emerged in the medical arena. In today's medical market, health consumers, lobby groups, bio-scientists, technology and pharmaceutical companies, the state, and a more fractionated medical profession, are all in varying degrees of conflict or potential conflict. Fundamental tensions have opened out as a result. On the one hand medicine is expected to protect the public from 'the unwanted' (be it through abortion, vaccines, or genetic manipulation); on the other, it is perceived as itself a threat (be it through the dispensing of dangerous drugs, administering unnecessary vaccines, or by conducting bad surgery). While consumers demand unfettered freedom to buy, or have access to, reproductive technologies, kidneys, hearts, cloning, assisted suicide and so on, they also expect the state to protect them from the hazards of a commercially-minded medicine that might be tempted too far into 'mercy killing,' the harvesting of organs from the still living, and genetic engineering. The 'public' itself is deeply divided and confused; as old certainties about human life and its biological boundaries have broken down, so too have conventional sources of moral authority. Priests, philosophers, academics and politicians scarcely have greater credibility than a television presenter (very likely they have less). Moral legitimacy is up for grabs. 'Dolly,' a cloned lamb with a tart's name, serves perhaps as a meaningful symbol of the uncertain, ambivalent moral precipice on which we now stand.

Given the compass of these divisions, doubts, ambiguities, tensions, and searchings, the prospects for the discipline of medical ethics look bright. Gone are the days when it could be content with deliberating the difference of interests between doctors and patients. But as this chapter has sought to show, medical ethical arbitration at any location can never be outside the social, political and ideological context in which it is conducted. Nor can its putative arbiters. Like 'nature,' the 'ethical' is what society and culture attribute to it at any particular historical moment. Whether pursued in medicine, parliament, the courts, the academy, or the soaps, it is an ideological construct and resource, a means to social authority. The question for the future of medicine is who among the contending voices and arenas of interest can achieve that authority.

## REFERENCES

This chapter profited from stimulating discussions at King's College, London, and at the London School of Hygiene and Tropical Medicine. I am also grateful to the late Margot Jefferys, and to Susan Lederer and John Pickstone for incisive comments and helpful suggestions.

1. Stephen Toulmin, 'How Medicine Saved the Life of Ethics,' *Perspectives in Biology and Medicine* (1981–82), **25**: 736–50.

2. 'Ethics Codes Required to Bridge the Integrity Gap,' 'Inside Business,' *Independent on Sunday* 18 July 1993, p. 24.

3. 'The Ethics Industry,' *Lancet* (27 Sept. 1997), **350**: p. 897.

4. Roger L. Shinn, 'The Moral Arguments and the Traditions of Religious Ethics,' *Annals of the New York Academy of Sciences* (29 Dec. 1989), **577**: p. 40.

5. Bradford Gray and M. Osterweis, 'Ethical Isues in a Social Context' in William G. Rothstein (ed.), *Readings in American Health Care.* (Madison: University of Wisconsin Press, 1995), p. 403.

6. Daniel Callahan, 'Ethics without abstraction: squaring the circle,' *Journal of Medical Ethics* (1966), **22**: 69–71.

7. David Rothman, *Strangers at the Bedside.* (New York: Basic Books, 1991), p. 11.

8. *Ibid.*, p. 71.

9. Robert Veatch, *The Patient-Physician Relation.* (Bloomington: Indiana University Press, 1991), p. 1. On the origins of 'bioethics,' see W.T. Reich, 'The Word "Bioethics": The Struggle Over Its Earliest Meanings,' *Kennedy Institute of Ethics Journal* (1995), **5**: 19–34.

10. Roger Cooter, 'The Resistible Rise of Medical Ethics,' *Social History of Medicine* (1995), **8**: p. 269.

11. Jay Katz, 'Disclosure and Consent in Psychiatric Practice: Mission Impossible?' in Charles K. Hofling (ed.), *Law and Ethics in the Practice of Psychiatry.* (New York: Brunner/Mazel, 1980), p. 98, quoted in the excellent critique of this view by Martin S. Pernick, 'The Patient's Role in Medical Decision-making: a social history of informed consent in medical therapy' in The President's Commission for the Study of Ethical Problems in Medicine and Biomedical Research, *Making Health Care Decisions.* (Washington, DC: US Government Printing Office, 1982), vol. 3, 1–35, at p. 2.

12. 'The Codes of Medical Ethics,' *Ephemeris* (1883), **1**: p. 195.

13. Thomas Percival, *Medical Ethics*, edited by Chaucey D. Leake (1927), pp. viii–ix.

14. R.C. Buist, 'Medical Etiquette, Ethics, and Politics,' *British Medical Journal* (21 March 1914), p. 641.

15. *Hansard Parliamentary Debates (House of Lords)* (1936), **103**: 465–506.

16. 'The Abortion Act (1967),' *British Medical Journal* (30 May 1970), p. 535.

17. Bernard J. Ficarra, *Newer Ethical Problems in Medicine and Surgery.* (Westminster, Maryland: Newman Press, 1951), pp. 110–11.

18. Francis D. Moore, *A Miracle and a Privilege: recounting a half a century of surgical advance.* (Washington: Joseph Henry Press, 1995), p. 201.

19. Gray and Osterweis, *op. cit,* p. 394.

20. Sir Peter Medawar, 'On the Use of Animals in Research,' *Medical and Health Annual.* (Chicago: Encyclopedia Britannica Inc., 1984), p. 6.

21. Quoted in Albert Deutsch, 'Wartime Influences on Health and Welfare Institutions in the United States,' *Journal of the History of Medicine and Allied Sciences* (1946), **1**: p. 318.

22. George Orwell, 'How the Poor Die [1946],' in *The Collected Essays, Journalism and Letters,* vol. 4: *In Front of Your Nose, 1945–1950.* (Penguin, 1970), p. 269.

23. J. Fletcher, *Morals and Medicine: the moral problems of the patient's right to know the truth, contraception, artificial insemination, sterilization, euthanasia.* (Princeton University Press, 1954), p. viii.

24. Petr Skrabanek, *The Death of Humane Medicine.* (Bury St Edmunds: The Social Affairs Unit, 1994), p. 12.

25. Quoted in Peter Sedgwick, *Psycho Politics.* (London: Pluto Press, 1982), p. 215.

26. Mary Poovey, 'The Abortion Question and the Death of Man,' in Judith Butler and Joan W. Scott (eds), *Feminists Theorize the Political.* (New York and London: Routledge, 1992), p. 254.

27. Quoted in Hugo Young, *One of Us: a biography of Margaret Thatcher.* ('Final edn.,' London, 1993), p. 123.

28. Jon Cohen, 'Ethics of AZT Studies in Poorer Countries Attacked,' *Science* (16 May 1997), **276**: p. 1022.

29. Larry Culpepper and T.T. Gilbert, 'Evidence and ethics,' *Lancet* (6 March 1999), **353**: p. 829.

## FURTHER READING

Annas, George and Grodin, M.A. (eds), *The Nazi Doctors and the Nuremberg Code: Human Rights in Human Experimentation.* (New York: Oxford University Press, 1992).

Baker, Robert, 'The History of Medical Ethics,' in W.F. Bynum and Roy Porter (eds), *Companion Encyclopedia of the History of Medicine.* (London: Routledge, 1993), 852–87.

Brookes, Barbara, *Abortion in England, 1900–67.* (London: Croom Helm, 1988).

Burleigh, Michael, *Death and Deliverance: 'Euthanasia' in Germany, 1900–45.* (Cambridge University Press, 1994).

Chadwick, Ruth (ed.), *Ethics, Reproduction and Genetic Control.* (London: Routledge, 1992).

Faden, Ruth and Beauchamp, Tom, *A History and Theory of Informed Consent.* (Oxford University Press, 1986).

Fennell, Phil, *Treatment Without Consent: Law, Psychiatry and the Treatment of Mentally Disordered People Since 1945.* (London: Routledge, 1996).

Jones, James H., *Bad Blood: The Tuskegee Syphilis Experiment.* (New York: Free Press, 1981).

Jonsen, Albert, *The Birth of Bioethics*. (New York: Oxford University Press, 1998).

Keown, John, *Abortion, Doctors and the Law*. (Cambridge University Press, 1988).

King, David, 'The Limits of Bioethics,' *Science as Culture* (1995), **5**: 303–13.

Lederer, Susan, *Subjected to Science: Human Experimentation Before the Second World War*. (Baltimore: Johns Hopkins, 1994).

Reich, T. (ed.), *Encyclopedia of Bioethics*, 4 vols. (New York: revised edn, 1995).

Reiser, S.J., Dyck, A.J. and Curran, W.J. (eds), *Ethics in Medicine: Historical Perspectives and Current Concerns*. (Cambridge, MA: MIT Press, 1977).

Rodwin, Marc A., *Medicine, Money and Morals: Physicians' conflict of interest*. (New York: Oxford University Press, 1993).

Weisz, George (ed.), *Social Science Perspectives on Medical Ethics*. (Philadelphia: University of Pennsylvania Press, 1990).

# CHAPTER 30

# The Dead Body

ROGER COOTER

Paradoxically, the non-living body has undergone more change in the twentieth century than almost any other. Whether viewed from the perspective of commerce, politics and law, or ethics, epidemiology, and education, the dead body's social and cultural status has altered fundamentally. Indeed, along with 'death' and 'dying,' the dead body has, in some respects, been transformed out of existence. It's not just that, off camera — outside the emergency department soaps, documentaries and violent feature films — corpses and cadavers are rarely to be seen. Rather, old-fashioned 'clinical' death, one of life's few certainties, has slipped from its moorings. Once momentous and revelatory, or at least terminal, the *moment* of death is no longer necessarily absolute. It has been turned into a *process* to be managed; its time regarded as "arbitrary rather than actual."[1] Depending partly on which country your mortal coil decides to slip, you may be dead (but not deprived of life) when your heart stops, or when your brain cortex shows no signs of electric life, or merely when your body's switchboard (the brain-stem) goes down. While the commonest marker of death remains cardiac arrest confirmed by ausculation, increasingly this indicator has been deemed insufficient. In cases of apparent death through barbiturate intoxication, for example — a considerable cause of concern after the widespread marketing of sleeping pills in the 1960s — simple ausculation with a stethoscope is now regarded as inadequate as the once-prized 'life-tests' of feeling for the pulse, pupillary reaction, or feathers and mirrors to the mouth.

While old definitions of death have come unstuck, new ones have become more open to interpretation. In part this is because the meaning of *life* in relation to death has also become a problem. In law, the commencement of human life is now pitched at between 26 and 28 weeks of fetal development. At this point a fetus is said to be 'viable' because it can be self-sustained outside the womb. Following this logic, death has been proposed as 'life that can no longer be self-sustained' — in effect, an application to life itself of the Victorian ethic of self-sufficiency. Some biologists drive this logic beyond measures of conscious life to cellular viability. Others reduce life and death still further, to genetic encoding; death is perceived as 'programmed' and, as such, potentially manipulable in the hands of the new eugenists. However these arguments go, one thing is clear: death is a far more extended and more inclusive category than it was in the past. Its epistemological status has been destabilized.

In other ways, too, death became one of the preoccupations of the late twentieth century. Concerns over abortion, selective feticide, terminal care, brain death, transplantation, resuscitation, perinatal salvage, persistent vegetative state, withdrawal of treatment, euthanasia, doctor-assisted suicide and bereavement filled ever increasing columns of type in the popular and medical press. The same issues, along with others such as *post-mortem* pregnancies from the sperms of dead partners, sustained the enterprises of medical ethicists, journalists and news broadcasters. The mysteries of 'Sudden Infant Death Syndrome,' or 'cot death,' not only instilled fear in the minds of new parents and pediatricians, but came to preoccupy mattress manufacturers and legislators.

Death was further made prominent by anti-smoking campaigns, environmental pollution, publicity over AIDS and HIV, dire warnings about bad diet, loose sex, and lack of exercise. In most of these areas the moral power of the grim reaper's scythe was still considered a stimulus to self-reform, despite the neo-fatalism inherent in the idea of our hour of death being governed genetically. Death also surfaced, gruesomely, but in culturally interesting ways, in the sensational return and media coverage of capital punishment. In places such as Missouri's Potosi Correctional Center and Georgia's 'Diagnostic and Classification Center' murderers were transformed into 'patients' for medicalized killing, a procedure undertaken to relieve the pain or 'close the wounds' of the families of the murdered victims. Thus killing the 'patient' came to constitute a part of an alleged healing process. At the same time as this new twist was added to the medical use of dead criminals an old one threatened to become unstuck, some lobbyists contending that criminals for execution ought not to be allowed to donate their organs lest their genetically encoded and cloneable parts entered into future life. Somehow (more so than semen of old, it seems) medical knowledges and practices that appeared to potentialize new human life from 'corrupted' old body parts profoundly threatened to release the moral disorder contained on death row.

Meanwhile, as movie-goers found fascination in images of Nazi death camps, news of ethnic 'cleansings,' religious 'purges' and tribal butcheries became all too familiar. And as Russians debated the fate Lenin's embalmed remains and re-interred the remains of the Romanovs, the Anglo-American demand for popular texts such as Sherwin B. Nuland's *How We Die* (1994) and Cedric Mims' *When We Die* (1998) went unabated. Commentators on late twentieth-century American culture spoke of death as "one of the liveliest growth industries,"[2] and of a nation "obsessed with a world that lurks beyond life as we know it."[3] Little wonder that death studies took hold among historians, sociologists, anthropologists and psychologists. A bibliography on *Dying, Death and Grief* lists some 1700 books published between 1979–86 alone. Many more volumes have been published since then, to say nothing of the flood of learned articles and conference proceedings.

Explanations for this phenomenon necessarily transcend mere morbid fascination. At least in part, some of the interest can be attributed to the "burgeoning ethics industry,"[4] though medical ethicists themselves put it down to a new felt need to control our destinies, our bodies, and our self-identity in the face of "modernization."[5] Other analysts attribute the obsession, more credibly, to technological advancements in bio-medicine that have "blurred the boundaries between life and death allowing concerns with death to freely enter the realm of the living."[6]

As for the dead themselves, their world has been turned upside down and inside out: dead bodies now have living parts, and living bodies have parts from the dead. 'Desacralized' hardly suffices to capture so fundamental a transgression of hitherto widespread and deep-seated taboos about dead bodies and their mutilation. The valuation of body parts by commercial 'organ vendors' compounds the violation, trivializing the wildest dreams of nineteenth-century secularists and Gothic fantasy writers. Indeed, the transplantation enterprise of modern medicine puts at stake the entire concept of individuality. Biologically and philosophically, 'Who am I?' has taken on a whole new meaning.

Thus the subject of the dead body now encompasses virtually every aspect of medicine and culture from before the cradle to beyond the grave. To cover it all would be impossible. Nor, given both the proximity and the profundity of these changes is it possible to make full historical sense of them. What is attempted here is merely an overview and explanation for some of major forces for change in the medical perception and regard of the dead body in the twentieth century. As will be illustrated mainly through a focus on Britain and America, the medical profession's studied interest in death and dying has been checkered and uneven. At one and the same time the dead body has been medically valued and devalued, exploited and degraded, commodified and psychologized, trivialized and sacralized. But it should not be assumed that the dead body has come simply to be ruled over and revalued by medicine and biotechnology alone. As will also be seen, the medical management and disposal of dead bodies has never been free from social, economic and demographic contingencies, nor independent of deep-seated social and cultural values which have endorsed, as well as contested medical interest in the dead and dying.

## DEATH'S MEDICAL DISCOURSES

Current controversy over death and its meaning is widely perceived as stemming from greater medical and medico-technological involvement in the process of dying. The idea of the 'good' or 'natural' death, with the doctor hardly in view, persists as an image of how things were before the intrusion of intensive care units and the growth of trade in cadaver parts. In reality, though, the dying and the dead have been enveloped in different kinds of medical discourse and practice throughout the twentieth century. Broadly speaking, what changed over the course of the century were the dominant forms of medical control over, and medical conceptions of, the dying and the dead.

It is true that until well into the century the role of the doctor at the death-side was restricted to predicting or fixing its moment, and to administering relief to its pain. More heroic interventions with death as 'the enemy to be conquered' came later. Yet less visible spheres of medical involvement were in operation, some of them reaching back centuries. Since antiquity dead bodies have been quarried for medical educational purposes — the rise of anatomy was founded on them — and since the eighteenth century the dead have been central to study of the morbid pathology of lesions and, hence, to the modern medical gaze on the living. The evolution of much of the bureaucratic superstructure still in evidence can be traced to the late eighteenth and early nineteenth century: death certificates, *post-mortem* (or autopsy) reports, and various other medico-legal rituals. By the late nineteenth century most Western countries had passed legislation making it compulsory for death and its cause to be registered. Forensic pathology to interpret wounds and other unnatural processes that may have caused or contributed to death, and forensic odontology in the identification of decomposed or skeletal remains, were both well established. So, too, was toxicology in the identification of poisonous substances in the tissues of the dead. Reading the signs of death was still regarded as an uncertain business, however, as illustrated by the long lists of publications on 'premature burial' and on 'sudden death' in end-of-the-century medical bibliographies. The hope expressed by the authors of *Death and Sudden Death* (1902), for instance, that "the uncertainties which sometimes arise at the moment of death, and in the hours which directly follow, may be removed by the physician," reflects ongoing professional anxieties in this area which were closely bound to longstanding public unease.[7] For reasons we will come to, the anxieties and the unease were slow to fade, and then only temporarily.

Also in evidence by the late nineteenth century was the medical study of death, as distinct from the study of the dead. Extending from Pasteur's work, death came to be seen in medical research as the consequence, not of the privation of life, but of its microscopic profusion. Life was in death, or at least in the dead. Subsequent studies of cellular destruction through putrefaction in the gut or auto-intoxication, stressed 'death in life,' a concept elaborated in connection with the use of antitoxins in the arrest or destruction of specific micro-organisms in the body and popularized through the removal of infection-producing organs such as the appendix.

The microbic study of death in life and life in death was not unrelated to the most pervasive medical discourse around the dead by 1900, that of public health. Although for centuries the bodies of plague victims had been subject to emergency disposal measures, supposedly to protect the living from contamination, only with the rise of public health movements in the nineteenth century did all dead bodies come under close sanitary control. The dead body, previously under regimes of religious practice, entered regimes of hygiene and was "transformed into a possibly dangerous object" to be rid of.[8] In England, corpse disposal came under the law of public nuisances; dead bodies in private homes (especially in the crowded unsanitary dwellings of the poor) came under the same rubric as public middens and the domestic keeping of pigs. For this reason public mortuaries were advocated from the 1840s, though the popular distrust of such places because of their association with the dissection of the dead taken from poor houses held back their development as free-standing institutions separate from hospitals. To miasmatic rationales for such measures, late nineteenth-century germ theory added rhetorical strength. By the 1900s laws were in force in most Western countries compelling the interment of the dead within days of death.

Linked to sanitary preoccupations with the decomposition of dead bodies as "destructive of public decency, utterly indefensible, and seriously and increasingly injurious to public health"[9] was the growth of the cremation movement from the 1870s. In Britain a cremation society was formed in 1874 with, as elsewhere in Europe, strong support from the medical profession — Ernest Hart, for example, the editor of the *British Medical Journal* was one of its spokesmen. In the wake of bacteriological evidence on the longevity in rotting corpses of some deadly germs and spores (such as anthrax), the idea of cremation as a 'disinfecting process' gained ground, especially in Germany. Fittingly, Robert Koch, the hero of hygiene and bacteriology, was cremated in 1910 before being laid to rest in a mausoleum in his former institute in Berlin. Increasingly, concerns with efficiency and waste in relation to the disposal of dead bodies added force to the hygienic arguments for crematoria, particularly among sanitary-minded engineers like Henry Simon, the German emigré who presided over the movement for the Manchester Crematorium in the early 1890s (along with the medical author of *Modern Cremation* and 45 other German emigrés). In England, thirteen crematoria were in operation by 1907, the first municipally operated one opening in Hull in 1901 (a year prior to the passage of the Cremation Act).

## SOCIAL INTERACTIONS

It is obvious, however, that reasons other than those narrowly defined as public health contributed to the sanitizing the dead. The social control of the poor and their 'offensive smells' could be one reason; religion, notably Levitican rationales, could be another. And aesthetic-cum-commercial interests could also be involved, as when American morticians in the early twentieth century began to undertake embalming on a regular basis. Around cremation, in particular, a variety of non-public health motives can be discerned, not least in Germany where metaphors of fire fused with those of purity and salvation to drive the movement forward. As among some seventeenth-century radicals, the advocacy of cremation was seldom divorced from religious dissent, or secularism, or materialism. In part, this explains why many persons opposed cremation as an affront to human dignity.

But as with the advocacy, so with the opposition, the motives could be multiple. In Paris the municipal crematorium built at the famous Père Lachaise cemetery in 1887 became decidedly unpopular as knowledge spread of the incineration there not only of victims of contagious diseases, unclaimed bodies from hospitals, and the remains of dissected bodies, but also, thousands of fetuses. In England, the force of custom (blended with popular distrust of the medical profession) meant that cremation was little practiced even after its legal status had been clarified in the mid-1880s, and after various technical problems were overcome (the furnaces in the 1870s took as long as two hours to reduce a body to five percent of its initial weight). Before the Second World War, only 3.8 percent of English funerals involved cremation. By 1945 this figure had risen to 7.8 percent, but not until 1967 did the number of cremations exceed burials. By 1991, 70 percent of funerals involved cremation, a reflection of yet other non-medical considerations: cost and convenience (behind which, of course, stands the secular culture in which these criteria can legitimately be applied to the disposal of the dead). As to why, in popular consciousness (as opposed to recent holocaust studies) no significant connection appears to have been made between cremation and the Nazi death camp ovens remains an open question.

Cremation and other new customs and behaviors around death and dead bodies in the late-Victorian period tended to be taken up first by the socially better off. For reasons not entirely clear, but which probably have as much to do with morality and bourgeois notions of private property as medically policed rules of hygiene, the domestic display of dead bodies to family and friends came to be regarded as undignified and distastefully morbid. Even royalty had their coffins screwed shut. Like public executions (perceived by polite society as "odious, sickening and repulsive spectacle[s]" by the time they were outlawed in England in 1868 and confined to prisons),[10] the business of death and dead bodies became a more private matter. In coroners courts, too, the dead body disappeared from public gaze, and eventually even from the inspection of the jury (through the 1926 Coroner's Amendment Act in England and Wales). To make a spectacle of the dead came to be regarded as ill-mannered, comparable to the invasion of privacy in observing a person at sleep. And, increasingly, the dead were 'at sleep.' Thus instead of being laid out for display and dwelt upon, corpses began to be removed to 'chapels of rest' — unconsecrated warehouses run by professional undertakers where the dead were stored and 'dealt with' before being transported to the place of funeral. Chapels of rest, akin to present-day 'funeral homes' in North America, were first established in Britain in the fashionable Kensington area of London in the 1890s. In terms of the disposal of corpses, the chapels of rest functioned for the rich in essentially the same way as public mortuaries did for the less well off or for those dying in hospital, except that the chapels were used by choice, while public mortuaries never were. The latter, which existed in most municipalities by the 1910s, were legislated repositories for bodies between the time of death and funeral, and were publicly perceived as extending government control over the body.

Working-class attitudes to dead bodies were generally more resistant to change, in part because of long-standing and wholly justified fears of the medical abuse of the bodies of the poor. By 1900, bitter memories of illegal acts and legal enactments to alleviate the shortage of bodies for medical dissection had not faded. The public still regarded dissection as a fate worse than death, and the poor in particular continued in the tradition of their Victorian forbears in taking every precaution to guard against it. In Britain, just before the century opened, the issue of the confiscation of the institutionalized dead resurfaced as a matter of political contention. Democratically elected local authorities, who came to control the supply of dead bodies, were sensitive to the class nature of the existing legislation and refused to consign the dead to medical schools for dissection. It was a widely held view that the poor had grief enough in their lives without this addition, and that instead of confiscating the bodies of the poor, doctors ought to bequeath their own bodies for dissection. Failure to do so was taken as a sign of professional hypocrisy. By 1921 there were "deplorable shortages" in anatomy schools all over Britain.[11] Mental asylums became one of the few source of corpses, and when even these were denied, the profession was driven to appeal for public generosity. Ultimately, honesty and openness with the public, rather than secrecy and hypocrisy, proved a better means to procuring cadavers. In Britain, bequests for dissection rose from 3 percent of all bodies dissected in 1934 to between 70 and 100 percent of bodies in the 1960s. By the 1980s, in both Britain and America more bodies were offered for dissection than required. Again, cost-cutting in respect to burials can be invoked in part explanation, along with degrees of humanitarianism on the one hand, and revulsion at racketeering in the undertaking trade on the other. Transformations in health and welfare provision during the second half of the twentieth century also bore upon this change; during its 'golden age,' up to the late 1960s, medicine was held to be beneficent and worthy of favors in return. Finally, attitudes and behavior have been influenced by changing patterns of mortality which, in turn, have affected the extent of actual contact with the dead and dying.

MORTALITY PATTERNS AND THE WITNESSING OF DEATH

Before the Second World War the living were less alienated from the dead and the dying. Their witnessing of death was not routine, but neither was it remote. Most dying, including sudden and premature death, still took place at home. With infant mortality in 1900 as high as 163 per 1000 live births in some of the poorer areas of Britain, the chances of not beholding such a corpse were slim. And in these same localities many also experienced the sight of adolescents dying of pneumonia, scarlet fever, diphtheria, whooping cough, and measles (the latter three not declining significantly in England and Wales before the Second World

War). Maternal mortality was also shockingly high well into the interwar period; in 1920 the national average for England and Wales, France and the US per 10,000 births was 43.3, 66.4 and 79.9 respectively. The rate in 1930 in the industrial town of Rochdale, in the north of England, was as high as 90 per 10,000 births. Tuberculosis, diminishing but still widely prevalent, had no cure.

By the mid-twentieth century, however, mortality from all such sources was drastically reduced, and hence the actual witnessing of death and dying in families and communities was far less commonplace, independent of the fact that more dying now took place in hospital. The death rate was in decline everywhere in the West, relative to the size of populations. The diseases that formerly ravaged infant life were mitigated; stillbirths and maternal mortality declined radically; antibiotics staved off a number of other killers such as pneumonia and bronchitis; and tuberculosis submitted to streptomycin. Infant mortality in the UK in 1950–52 stood at 30 per 1,000 live births, in 1994 it was 6. Overwhelmingly, by the 1950s, the leading cause of death among the age group 1-to-44 in the Western world was not from the old (or new) infectious diseases, but from accidents, especially those involving motor vehicles. In the UK, deaths from this source peaked in 1970 at around 8,000, falling back by 1992 to half that figure. Death on the roads, besides cutting across conventional social, occupational, age and gender mortality patterns, and bearing a different cultural meaning than, say, infant mortality, also severed completely the domestic experience of death (or the process of dying) from family and community. More recently, deaths from AIDS have outstripped those from motor vehicle accidents; some 12,000 persons dying from AIDS in the UK between 1982 and 1995, the majority young adult males. It is too soon to tell what the full cultural effects of this form of premature death might be, but to judge from mass support for candle-lit memorial processions and the media coverage of such events, another significant turning (or returning) has been made in society's collective regard for, and experiencing, of death and grieving. What is undeniable is that the social and cultural impact of death during the twentieth century has shifted as much as dominant mortality trends have, and directly in relation to one another.

## DEATH IN HOSPITAL

Accompanying the institutionalization of death in hospitals in the twentieth century were changes both in mortality patterns and in the alienation of the dead from the living. In general, corpses followed the dying in moving out of the home. Like giving birth, dying in hospital was a trend manifested earlier in America than in Britain. In England and Wales, whereas in 1897 only 13 percent of all deaths were in hospitals and medical institutions, by 1967 this figured had more than quadrupled (58 percent).[12] In part, this largely post-World War II trend can be seen as an extension of a public-health perspective on hospitals as healthy, hygienic spaces, rather than, ironically, dreaded 'gateways to death,' as in the past. But political and social factors are not separable here. In Britain, the municipalization of the Poor Law infirmaries in 1929 and the upgrading of the care they could offer, served to destigmatize them and render more attractive. The National Health Services furthered this process, as well as instilling community pride in 'the people's hospitals.' In part, too, the trend towards the hospitalization of dying was a consequence of chronic and degenerative conditions overtaking the number of terminal cases of infectious diseases; home care for the victims of cancer and heart disease, for instance, was increasingly perceived as undesirable or impossible. Whereas in Britain in 1913, 10.3 percent of all deaths were from heart disease and 7.6 from cancer, by 1945 these causes were 26.5 percent and 15.1 percent. Like the intensive care available in hospitals for the victims of accidents, the expensive specialized equipment for the management of the terminally ill was largely unavailable outside of hospitals, and faith in the efficacy of the ever-more-sophisticated gadgetry and pharmaceutical concoctions was seldom questioned before the late 1960s.

One did not of course have to die in hospital to end up there. Since the late nineteenth century, those killed by accidents in industry or on the streets and highways have been transported to hospitals to receive their final pronouncement. And autopsies in hospital mortuaries could be required by law on those who died at home or in public places if the circumstances were sudden, suspicious, or obscure, or if a doctor had not been in recent attendance. In England and Wales by the 1960s *post-mortems* were carried out on more than 27 percent of dead bodies. It is also worth noting that by the 1930s it was hospital consultants in forensic pathology who were regarded as the best experts to call for evidence in the courts, whereas formerly general practitioners had sufficed.

While the rituals surrounding death became more private and personal in the twentieth century, dying in hospital became more impersonal and open to medical scrutiny. Among other things, the medical 'assisting of death' became far less possible in contexts where the management of the dying could be the work of many hands. As with abortions, once they came to be conducted in hospitals, peer group monitoring increased — and increased still further in the 1960s and 1970s when medical ethics became a lay enterprise bound to the courts, legislatures and the popular press. Until the last third of the twentieth century the death scene in hospital was deemed suitable only for medical witnesses. Family and friends were excluded, partly on grounds public health, partly on grounds of inconvenience (death usually transpiring during the early hours of the morning, as observed statistically since the 1840s), and partly on grounds of the propriety of an emotion-free medico-scientific environment. Not until the 1970s did these rationales begin seriously to be eroded, at which time the importance of witnessing death became a plank in the argument for the psychological health of the bereaving. But with this change, as we shall see later, there was no diminution in the medical control over dying and death in hospital.

LIFE VERSUS DEATH IN MEDICINE

As the place of death has changed during the twentieth century, so too has the value of the dead to the living. For at least 300 years before Dr Thomas Southwood Smith delivered his famous oration 'On the Use of the Dead to the Living' over the corpse of Jeremy Bentham in 1832, the dissection of the dead had been regarded as crucial to the advancement of the art of healing. In medical education, dissection permitted the opportunity to understand, learn, and experience at first hand the architecture of the body and to develop manual technique in the use of scalpel, saw and other surgical tools. Exploration and experimentation on the dead also permitted improvements in diagnosis and operative procedures. And, not least, the dissecting room taught clinical detachment toward the body — what the famous eighteenth century anatomist William Hunter deemed "necessary Inhumanity."[13]

Many of these practices on the dead were eroded and their rationales undermined during the second half of the twentieth century. During the first half, they simply stagnated. To a considerable extent dead bodies ceased to be medically interesting or to serve as resources for novelty. In biological understanding, death became essentially a footnote to life, rather than something integral to it. Early twentieth-century physiology and, more especially, embryology and endocrinology, opened up exciting frontiers within the *living body*. The physiological effects of shock, the function of the adrenal glands, the operation of the lymphatic system, the role of hormones, vitamins and diet management, the nature of the immune system, the growth of cancer cells, the effect of drugs, and the consequences of a variety of surgical, electrical and pharmaceutical operations on the brain, all required bodies alive. The new medical discourses around these projects increasingly separated the living from the dead, devaluing the study of the latter. Previous medical interest in, for example, the gasses generated by dead bodies, or the microbiology of putrefaction, fell to the wayside. Pathological anatomy (the study of tissues), vibrant since the early eighteenth century, was perceived as an exhausted field by the early twentieth. Fame in pathology was now to be acquired only at the popular level of murder mystery solving, as in the publications of the forensic pathologists Sir Bernard Spilsbury (*The Famous Cases of*, 1936) and Sir Sydney Smith (*Mostly Murder*, 1955). Within medicine, death was inert, its study intellectually moribund. In medical textbooks death and dying hardly got a look-in. Editions of the catalogue of *Lewis's Lending Library* — a standard port of call for British and Commonwealth medical students and practitioners — reveal that for the first half of the century there were few books on death that could in any way be regarded as 'scientific.' In their stead were popular works such as R.W. MacKenna's *Adventure of Death* (1916), T.B. Scott's, *Why Do We Die* (1921), and *The Mysteries of Life and Death* (1936).

As in history and sociology, so in medicine, the study of death and dying, if not the dead, was manifestly unanimated. Looking into this matter as late as 1973, the cell biologist-turned philosopher, Rupert Sheldrake asserted unequivocally, "Death is out of fashion."[14] Surveying patterns of thought within modern biology, Sheldrake noted that they were all essentially mechanistic, with the cell and the organism being seen in a steady state unless change was imposed from without. "Within this framework of thinking," he concluded, "ageing and death are very difficult to explain. Indeed they are not explained. They are ignored as much as possible; they are hardly mentioned in most biology textbooks." Newer DNA theories about death were hardly corrective in this respect, Sheldrake contended, for not only were they extensions of biological mechanistic thinking (mere reductions of death to the molecular level), but they lead many to conclude that the problem of death had been solved "at least to the extent that no serious thought need be given to it by most biologists."

There is as yet little evidence that anyone in contemporary bio-medical science has seriously heeded Sheldrake's call for a non-mechanistic understanding of death-in-relation-to-life. But it is no longer the case that "death is out of fashion" among biologists. In fact, death has never been more *in* fashion. 'Apoptosis,' the term for genetically programmed cell death or cell suicide (as distinct from necrotic cell death from oxygen deprivation or other causes) is now one of the most popular areas of research in biology. Whereas only six publications on apoptosis appeared in 1981, 6,000 had appeared by 1997. In part this explosion of interest in death reflects the belief among biologists that the mystery of life has been solved through its reduction to DNA. Apoptosis is the equivalent quest for the genetic program for death. As a branch of the study of 'biological death,' apoptosis research threatens further to challenge the old notion of 'clinical death' (and possibly the profession in charge of it), but whether it has the potential to eliminate senescence and death so as to render life never-ending is another matter. The production of an anti-death pill is not currently on the agenda; cell death occurs naturally in a variety of body tissues and understanding the process is seen as a means to arresting diseases in those tissues.

## DISAPPEARING CORPSES IN MEDICAL EDUCATION

Ironically, during the last third of the twentieth century, as the public came to accept and favor the educative use of their bodies after death, medicine's interest in dead bodies for such purposes diminished. Within ever-more crowded curriculums the 'luxury' of spending hours scraping back fatty tissue and viscera to reveal significant organs and learn anatomy came to be regarded by students and medical deans alike as time poorly spent. Interactive CD-ROMs could bring the dead not just to life but into virtual reality, and were held to be more efficient and cheaper than corpses, as well as more sanitary and odour-free. Further undermining the value of the dead to the living in medical education was the advent of scopes and probes inserted into *living* bodies to provide screenfuls of information and sample tissues (biopsy). In only one respect — in relation to

William Hunter's 'necessary Inhumanity' — was the dead body still held to be of use, at least in some American medical schools. There the handling of corpses came to be advocated, not as a means to inculcating the repression of humane feelings in the assault on human flesh, but, on the contrary, as an essential rite of passage in rendering doctors psychologically healthy. Hands-on engagement with dead bodies is perceived as a means to the overt understanding and training of emotions, or of coping with feelings of transgression, guilt, unease, indeed, as "a laboratory for self-discovery about death and dying."[15] Some of these same ends are now sought in British medical education through the 'follow-through' of cases of dying, although by this type of training the corpse itself is further marginalized.

The dead body is still exploited in the learning of new techniques. The pioneer in *in vitro* fertilization, Patrick Steptoe, for example, spent his lunch breaks in the morgue of the Oldham General Infirmary mastering the use of the laparoscope to facilitate the removal of ova. Others, in taking up such techniques, also rely on corpses for part of their training. And doing 'sections,' if not always any more dissections, remains a required part of medical school education. Nevertheless, the cadaver is under threat, not least by the CD-ROM human analogue of the 'normal' body (generated from a single set of very fresh male and female cadavers). It is also noteworthy that the type of practicing on the dead, such as undertaken by Steptoe, is done alone, independent of medical schools and teachers. And as the pathology of the living (or the 'virtually' alive) has come to replace the pathology of the dead, departments of anatomy in medical schools have been restructured and realigned. For example, the anatomy department of University College London, which became internationally famous after World War I under the presiding genius of Grafton Elliot Smith and with the funding of the Rockefeller Foundation, exists today as part of a department of developmental biology.

The need for autopsies has also been undermined. The more accurate diagnoses and prognoses facilitated by biopsies has rendered the dying body legible before death, so that necroscopic examinations have become less essential. That a patient's diagnosis and course of treatment might be found to have been mistaken through autopsy has further hastened the demise of the procedure for fear of litigation, especially in the US. Already by the 1970s, throughout the West, the trend of the first half of the century to ever more autopsies (on ever-older patients) was in noticeable decline, its rationale beleaguered by cries of "scientific folly" and "old relic."[16] Once a "temple of truth,"[17] the autopsy came further under siege by the growing realization from the 1950s that the pathological signs of death, such as cardiac arrest, did not necessarily constitute the 'cause' of death. The mental state of a person before death might more accurately represent the cause of death — a realization that called into question both death certificates and autopsies. By the 1990s, the Institute of Pathological Anatomy in Trieste, which managed to sustain a steady level of 60 percent of deaths autopsied, was being regarded as internationally unique. (Why this particular Institute should have been different requires further research.)

## COMMERCIALIZATION

But if the educative value of the dead body was radically attenuated by the late twentieth century, its commercial value was not. Although whole-body procurement by medical schools became increasingly a thing of the past, bodies that could be labelled 'dead' and quarried for their spare parts came into great demand. Indeed, the 'value' of the dead to *some* of the living became untold, thanks to the rise of the transplant industry. Transplantation was barely heard of before the 1950s, at which time the number of donation of organs made for transplantation was zero. In the 1980s, however, more than 400,000 transplants were performed in the US; in the UK 5,200 were performed in 1992 alone. Not all of these operations depended upon parts from fresh cadavers, but that was decidedly the trend by the 1960s, especially after 1967 when the first successful human heart transplant created unlimited demand for more. Hitherto, as in the pioneering work on kidney transplant (1954, and routinized by the mid-1960s), *living* donors had been required, initially members of the same family. By 1960, however, the use of 'foreign' dead body parts was sufficient to warrant legislation. The UK Human Tissue Act, for example (1961, and still in force) permitted the medical removal of cadaver tissue not only from those who had expressed a wish for this during their lifetime, but also from those who had never expressed any objection during their lifetime and whose surviving relatives made no such objection. The Act affirms that "the person lawfully in possession of the body after death" and able legally to authorize the removal of tissues is the local Health Authority "or one of their servants, including consultants"[18] — a statement on the place of the dead body in our culture surely meriting further study. Worthy of exploration, too, is why the question over the corpse ("Whose body is it anyway?")[19] took so long to emerge, relative to the debates over 'who own's the embryo?,' and 'whose life is it anyway?'

Legislation like the Human Tissue Act was not centrally concerned with protecting the still-living from premature 'harvesting' by zealous transplant teams, nor with medical definitions of death that might encourage such acts. These issues only became central after the possibilities for an industry in heart transplants became apparent; the earliest re-defining of 'dead' — the Harvard criteria of 'brain death' — emerging only in 1968. Two years later the state of Kansas enacted the first brain death law, and within a decade all but 16 American States had passed such laws. In Europe, Finland led the way with legislation in 1971. By 1983, when the British neurologist Christopher Pallis penned the *ABC of Brain Death*, new medical definitions of bodily conditions, such as 'persistent vegetative state' (introduced in 1972) were facilitating ever more scope for the transplant industry. The criteria used for defining brain death were themselves widened (both brain 'stem' and brain 'cortex,' for example, being included) and while some institutions and/or States were insisting on flat EEG readings, others (such as the UK) were not. A survey in 1984 of American neurosurgeons and neurologists revealed that one-third did not use EEG as a criterion of brain death, and neither did they support the case for national standards.[20] The guidelines on death's definition, so far as they exist, and the non-legally binding 'codes of practice' in this area of medicine continue to be stretched, bent or abandoned. Although the gift relationship still animates much dead-body donation, literary and cinematic depictions of the exploitation of comatosed bodies by spare parts entrepreneurs, such as in Robin Cook's *Coma* (1977, and an MGM film in 1978), give warning of practices perilously close to reality. As the integrity of the dead body has given way to its post-modern fragmentation into potentially commercial parts, so, to a degree, "the fear of premature burial has given way to premature dismemberment."[21] As testified though Renée Fox's courageous exposé of the "cannibalism" that goes on in certain hospitals in Pittsburgh under the guise of "planned terminal management", the commercial incentive for organ 'donation' all too easily slides into committing inhumane and irreverent deaths.[22] That the public is confused about the medical meaning of 'dead,' and only half convinced of the need for an expanded transplant industry seems hardly surprising. Too evidently in this area of medicine, humane metaphors and values give way to those of the automobile repair shop, if not the car factory or automotive industry itself.

### Psychologization and Palliative Care

Running alongside the commercial and therapeutic revaluation of the dead body have been two other closely linked forums for its revaluation: the growth of psychological studies of dying and bereavement, and the development of the hospice movement for the terminally ill. Though both have profited from humanitarian impulses, neither can be considered apart from, or counter to, the medicalization of death. The psychology of bereavement (the analytical fruits of the interrogation of death's survivors) occurred at the same time as those dying in hospital also came under psychological scrutiny — initially in North America. In 1968, a year after the launch of *Omega: journal of death and dying*, the pioneering work *On Death and Dying* by the psychiatrist Dr Elisabeth Kübler-Ross was published, mapping the emotional stages of response to death among the terminally ill. Subsequent 'stages-of-dying' studies (and subsequent medical journals for their publication, such as *Death Education*, 1976) further submitted the subjectivities of the dying to the analytical discourses of medicine. In Britain, by 1984, only four medical schools were *not* providing formal teaching on death and dying.[23] All of which supports the contention of some medical sociologists that Kübler-Ross's work signifies the emergence of a new and increasingly pervasive paradigm in medical understanding — one reaching beyond the *visible* physical lesion for its analysis to the *audible* psycho-social. The dying body, arguably, has replaced the corpse as the means to the medical interrogation of the living.

The hospice movement, which in Britain developed in the 1960s and 1970s independent of the National Health Service was, as Caroline Murphy indicated, the means of putting the care of the dying firmly back on to the clinical agenda. Proposals for such places at the end of the nineteenth century ('Friedenheims') were abandoned in the early twentieth as support for clinical laboratory research into cancer was given priority. Crucial to the reinvention of the hospice were two realization: first, that however many laboratories were endowed, cancer was not to be 'conquered' in the manner of some other diseases and, second, that hospital medicine had become so accustomed to thinking in terms of the maintenance of life that it could only shun death as 'failure.' The hospice movement in Britain, under the inspired guidance of Cicely Saunders, succeeded in restoring some dignity to the dying of the terminally ill. At its heart, however, was the *medical* management of pain. Saunders, an opponent of 'active' euthanasia, was both a qualified nurse and a doctor; her intention and her accomplishment "was to lay the foundations of terminal care and in so doing make the care of the dying *medically* respectable."[24] She succeeded admirably. In 1967 she established St. Christopher's Hospice in London as the first research and teaching hospice, thereby effectively laying the foundations for the now thriving discipline of palliative medicine. Since then, hospices have been founded on every continent, and the World Health Organization has taken a leading role in advocating pain relief and palliative care for all who need them.

Thus, from being an absent or 'non-subject' in health care, dying emerged as a medical interest in its own right. But like other areas of medicine where new boundaries are staked and careers made, the 'object' of the exercise — the dying patient — is sometimes in danger of being lost sight of. 'Terminal vision' risks becoming clouded midst the competing teams of specialist pain managers and psychologists crowding round the bedside.

## DEATH'S FUTURE?

Further transformations in the social values and medical practices surrounding death and its interpretation, and continuing moral controversy seem likely, but more specific predictions are difficult. As in the 1970s, when over-optimistic hopes of widely available heart transplants floundered on curbs to health sector spending, so more recent hopes for xenotransplantation, the use of animal tissues for transplants into people, have struck the shoals of cross-species viral infection (zoonosis). Dreams such as that of "only 100 breeding sows to negate the entire UK kidney shortfall"[25] have shattered. Indeed, as a result of a variety of sensational revelations of pollutions in the animal-to-human food chain, researchers and the public alike have glimpsed some of the mortality that may be strewn along this particular pathway to death's would-be abatement — yet another of the ironies in the history of the dead body in the twentieth century. Doubtless organizations such as the 'Natural Death Centre' (London), the international Hemlock Society, the 'Right to Die' lobby, and the movement for 'green burial' will continue to flourish, partly in response to the 'unnatural' technological impositions upon the dying, just as 'death supermarkets' for do-it-yourself funerals should thrive in the face of new commercial trends in undertaking, such as the privatization of British crematoria since the late 1980s. On the other hand, fresh corpse quick-freeze (cryogenics) will probably remain a tempting option for the mindlessly rich and self-important. As for the dead… who knows? In a real sense, perhaps they have never have been with us, and it may be that in the future the very idea of a dead body will be wholly anachronistic. Certainly, an end to death is more conceivable than when the century began; like the 'industrial body' it may be that, historically speaking, its time is nearly past. For the foreseeable future, however, the medical management of the dead and dying will doubtless continue to be fashioned as it has throughout the twentieth century: in relation to the possibilities and constraints of scientific, professional, commercial, political, legal, religious and social interests and cultural norms — in a deeply furrowed dialectic between that which is possible and that which appalls.

## REFERENCES

This chapter owes enormous debts to Ruth Richardson with whom it was begun. I am also grateful to Roberta Bivins, Brian Hurwitz and Pedro Lowenstein for crucial assistance.

1.  B. Jennett, 'Brain Death and the Vegetative State' in D.J. Weatherall *et al.* (eds), *Oxford Textbook of Medicine.* (3rd edn., Oxford University Press, 1966), vol. 3, p. 3933.

2.  Ian Kennedy, *The Unmasking of Medicine.* (London: Allen & Unwin, 1982), chapter 7: 'The Last Taboo', p. 154.

3.  Karen Cerulo and J.M. Ruane, 'Death Comes Alive: Technology and the Re-conception of Death', *Science as Culture* (1997), **6**: 444–66.

4.  'The Ethics Industry' (editorial), *Lancet* (27 Sept. 1997), **350**: p. 897.

5.  Daniel Callahan, 'Our Fear of Dying', *Newsweek* (4 Oct. 1993), p. 67; idem, *The Troubled Dream of Life: Living with Mortality.* (New York: Simon and Schuster, 1993).

6.  Cerulo and Ruane, 'Death Comes Alive', p. 447.

7.  P. Brouardel (Dean of the Faculty of Medicine in Paris) and F. Lucas Benham, *Death and Sudden Death.* (2nd edn; London, 1902), p. ix. See also the editorial, 'The Bogey of Premature Burial', *Lancet* (19 March 1910), pp. 803–4.

8.  David Armstrong, 'Public Health Spaces and the Fabrication of Identity', *Sociology* (1993), **27**: p. 399.

9.  Henry Simon, *Cremation* (1893), quoted in Brian Simon, *In Search of a Grandfather: Henry Simon of Manchester, 1835–1899.* (Leicester: Pendene Press, 1997), p. 119.

10. V.A.C. Gatrell, *The Hanging Tree: Execution and the English People 1700–1868.* (Oxford University Press, 1996), p. 600.

11. Ruth Richardson, *Death, Dissection and the Destitute.* (London: Routledge, 1987), p. 256.

12. Home Office, *Report of the Committee an Death Certification and Coroners.* (London: HMSO, 1971), p. 1.

13. Quoted and discussed in Richardson, *Death, Dissection and the Destitute*, p. 31ff.

14. Rupert Sheldrake, 'Death', *Theoria to Theory* (1973), **7**: 31–8.

15. S.L. Bertman and S.C. Marks Jr., 'The Dissection Experience as a Laboratory for Self-discovery about Death and Dying: another side of clinical anatomy', *Clinical Anatomy* (1989), **2**: 103–13. See also F.W. Hafferty, *Into the Valley: Death and the Socialization of Medical Students.* (New Haven: Yale University Press, 1991).

16. S. Burrows, 'The Post-mortem Examination: scientific necessity or folly?', *Journal of the American Medical Association* (1975), **233**, 441–3; S.J. Peacock *et al.*, 'The Autopsy: a useful tool or an old relic?', *Journal of Pathology* (1988), **156**: 9–14.

17. David Armstrong, 'Silence and Truth in Death and Dying', *Social Science and Medicine* (1987), **24**: 651–7; idem, 'A Social Role for Technology: making the body legible' in Ian Robinson (ed.), *Life and Death Under High Technology Medicine*. (Manchester University Press, 1994).

18. B. Knight, 'Forensic Medicine' in D.J. Weatherall *et al.* (eds), *Oxford Textbook of Medicine*. (3rd edn, Oxford Univeristy Press, 1966), vol. 3, p. 4311.

19. Lori Andrews and Dorothy Nelkin, 'Whose Body Is It Anyway? Disputes over body tissue in a biotechnology age', *Lancet* (3 Jan. 1998), **351**: 53–60.

20. Jennett, 'Brain Death and the Vegetative State', p. 3933.

21. W.R. Albury, 'Ideas of Life and Death' in W.F. Bynum and Roy Porter (eds), *Companion Encyclopedia of the History of Medicine*. (London: Routledge, 1993), p. 272.

22. Renée Fox, '"An Ignoble Form of Cannibalism": Reflections on the Pittsburgh Protocol for Procuring Organs from Non-Heart-Beating Cadavers', *Kennedy Institute of Ethics Journal* (1993), **3**: 231–39.

23. D. Field, 'Formal Instruction in United Kingdom Medical Schools About Death and Dying', *Medical Education* (1984), **18**: 429–34.

24. Caroline Murphy, 'From Friedenheim to Hospice: a century of cancer hospitals', in Lindsay Granshaw and Roy Porter (eds), *The Hospital in History*. (London: Routledge, 1989), p. 236 (my emphasis).

25. Sara Abdulla, 'Xenotransplantation Debate Boils On', *Lancet* (20 Sept. 1997), **350**: p. 868.

## FURTHER READING

Alter, George C. and Carmichael A.G. (eds), 'Classification of Causes of Death', Special Issue of *Continuity and Change* (1997), **12**: 169–265.

Arney, William Ray and Bergen, B.J., *Medicine and the Management of Living*. (Chicago University Press, 1982).

Burney, Ian A., 'Viewing Bodies: Medicine, Public Order, and English Inquest Practice', *Configurations* (1994), **1**: 33–46.

Clark, David (ed.), *The Sociology of Death*. (Oxford: Blackwell, 1993).

Cooter, Roger and Luckin, Bill (eds), *Accidents in History: Injuries, Fatalities and Social Relations*. (Amsterdam: Rodopi, 1997).

Elliot, Gil, *Twentieth Century Book of the Dead*. (London: Allen Lane, 1972).

Jupp, Peter and G. Howarth (eds), *The Changing Face of Death*. (London: Macmillan, 1997).

President's Commission for the Studies of Ethical Problems in Medicine, 'Guidelines for the Determination of Death', *Journal of the American Medical Association* (1981), **246**: 2184–6.

Prior, Lindsay, 'Making Sense of Mortality', *Sociology of Health and Illness* (1985), **7**: 167–90.

Rothman, David, 'Life Through Death' in his *Strangers at the Bedside*. (New York: Basic Books, 1991).

Simpson, M., *Dying, Death and Grief: a critical bibliography*. (Berkeley: University of California Press, 1987).

Southard, S., *Death and Dying: a bibliographical survey*. (New York: Greenwood Press, 1991).

Stark, Tony, *Knife to the Heart: the story of transplant surgery*. (London: Macmillan, 1996).

Stroebe, W. and M., *Bereavement and Health*. (Cambridge University Press, 1987).

Swinburne-Hanham, J.C., 'Cremation,' *Encyclopedia Britannica, 11th edn* (1910–11), **7**: p. 403–7.

Veatch, Robert, *Death, Dying and the Biological Revolution: Our Last Quest for Responsibility*. (London: Yale University Press, 1989).

Vovle, M., 'Rediscovery of Death Since 1960', in Renée Fox (ed.), *The Social Meaning of Death, Annals of the American Academy of Political and Social Science* (1980), **447**: 89–99.

Weindling, Paul, *Epidemics and Genocide in Eastern Europe, 1890–1945*. (Oxford University Press, 2000).

Youngner, Stuart J., Fox, Renée and O'Connell, L.J. (eds), *Organ Transplantation: Meanings and Realities*. (Madison, Wisconsin University Press, 1996).

# CHAPTER 31

# Media

## SUSAN E. LEDERER AND NAOMI ROGERS

In the twentieth century the experiences and expectations that patients brought
to their encounters with the medical profession and medical institutions were
profoundly shaped by their exposure to newspapers, magazines, novels, and,
above all, cinema and television. The mass media made familiar the image of the
white-coated male physician, stethoscope in hand, and the worlds of the hospital,
laboratory, and waiting room. Through film and television, the iconic technologies
of modern medicine — test-tubes, injections, scalpels, and drips — became both
powerful and naturalized.

Some features of the complex relationship between medicine and media deserve
special note. Initially wary of close interactions with what physician William Osler
labeled in 1897 "the Delilah of the press,"[1] physicians and medical organizations
had by the 1920s realized the power of the media to influence lay attitudes and
attract patients. Over the course of several decades, organizations like the American Medical Association took an active role in producing their own popular media
— lay magazines and radio programs — and attempting to influence the production of others. Concerned about negative portrayals of physicians, for example,
leaders of the organized American medical profession lobbied film producers for
changes in scripts and screen characterizations, in some cases seeking to suppress
altogether what they perceived as 'damaging' to their profession. Working with
government and industry film censors, physicians attempted to present the public
a sympathetic portrait of the medical profession in a variety of medicalized settings.
With the advent of television, such proactive behavior intensified. Since 1978, for
example, the *British Medical Journal* has published an ongoing column on 'Medicine and the Media.' Medical schools and professional societies routinely offer
media-preparation training for their members.

Another significant feature of the relationship between media and medicine is
the fluid boundary between genres of popular culture. Film makers eager for new
material cannibalized medical novels and non-fiction books for screen material;
images from these movies subsequently appeared on book jackets. The success
of a film characterization of physicians in turn prompted 'novelization' of its
screenplay. This blurring of genre contributed to greater integration of both

characters and images into popular culture. Both medical and media professionals (scriptwriters, producers, and reporters) participated in dissolving the boundaries between entertainment and education. Fictionalized depictions of medicine and medical encounters have been used to teach medical knowledge to lay audiences, to inculcate rules of healthy living, and to present a model of patient and practitioner behavior. In turn, documentary programs on American cable networks in the 1990s televising actual operations — caesarean section, hip replacement, and other surgeries — are intended to entertain as well as instruct audiences.

## EARLY IMAGES

In the early twentieth century, the medical profession often served as a target of satire and caricature in popular media. In Britain, playwright and critic George Bernard Shaw radically dissected the medical profession in *The Doctor's Dilemma* (1906), in which a physician must choose between saving the life of a dissolute artistic genius and an unimaginative, if well-intentioned doctor.[2] Hostile to both vaccination and vivisection, Shaw attacked the business ethic of the medical profession, excoriating physicians for their pretensions at infallibility and omniscience. In the United States, doctors and medical faddism appeared as a frequent foil in *Life*, one of the most popular comic weeklies of the era. John Ames Mitchell, editor of the magazine, devoted many pages to cartoons and written satires of medical men (with names like Dr. Futyll Werk and Slasher Quick, M.D.), reflecting his own aversion to compulsory vaccination and vivisection.

In the waning years of the nineteenth century, a new medium that would come to dominate twentieth-century popular culture made its early, faltering debut. In the work of pioneering French cinematographer Georges Méliès, the doctor as character appeared on screen in several short, silent films. Méliès' cinematic doctors included an American surgeon and the physicians from Molière's *Le Malade Imaginaire*, who know everything about a disease except how to cure it. Long before sheriffs chased outlaws and policemen arrested gangsters, doctors in both dramatic and comic films were busy chasing patients and seducing nurses. The doctor, surgeon or dentist, as historian Michael Shortland has observed, was "the first recognizable professional in the picture palace."[3] One should add the nurse to this description; the female nurse performed a variety of cinematic functions, serving as both an object of lust and as submissive handmaiden to male medical activity.

The silent films of the early twentieth century frequently portrayed physicians and surgeons. In the years between 1911 and 1920, American studios released 123 feature films in which physicians and surgeons figured prominently, and 219 in which they appeared as minor characters. In many of these films and in those of the 1920s, physicians and surgeons played comic figures or villains. In *The Monster* (1925), American actor Lon Chaney played an insane physician who lured unsuspecting motorists to his isolated sanitarium, where he used them as laboratory subjects. In *A Blind Bargain* (1927) Chaney appeared as both the scientifically ambitious Dr. Lamb and his hunchbacked simian assistant, who assists the doctor with his surgical experiments on both human beings and animals.

## POPULAR MEDIA AS EDUCATIONAL VEHICLES

Health officials and reformers in the early twentieth century quickly seized the opportunity to adapt new forms of popular media, especially film, to sell medicine and public health to the public. Their faith in the technological expertise exemplified in the new sciences of bacteriology and immunology was mirrored by their faith in the ability of film to educate lay audiences and inspire them to change both their behavior and their attitudes. The form and structure of health propaganda in the first three decades of the twentieth century drew on the emerging technology of film, radio, and professional advertising, as well as older traditions established by nineteenth-century patent medicine makers, who used almanacs, posters, advertising cards, calendars, and the spectacle of the medicine show to market their merchandise. Health departments in major urban centers in the United States began to feature health education as a prominent part of their commitment to the New Public Health.

Films and slide shows were particularly powerful vehicles for transmitting the lessons of public health. Among the early productions of the Edison Studios, established by American inventor Thomas Edison, were health films for the National Association for the Study and Prevention of Tuberculosis (a voluntary organization founded in 1904). Edison films like *Hope* (1912) and *The Temple of Moloch* (1914) visually conveyed the strategic use of scientifically-directed public health and the efforts of public health experts. Historian Martin Pernick has estimated that in the years between 1905 and 1927 film makers, such as Edison, produced more than 1000 health-related films.[4]

The public health films of the 1910s and 1920s, with a running time of 11 to 14 minutes, were silent and were screened not only in theaters, but on the walls of churches, factories, schools, and tenement buildings. While these films sought to reach an audience diverse in class, race, and gender, much of their content reflected the cultural stereotyping and ethnocentrism of their makers. In *The Temple of Moloch*, for example, a Swedish factory worker initially rejects the advice of the public health physician, but reforms after his children succumb to tuberculosis. In *Helping Negroes to Become Better Farmers and Homemakers*, a 1921 film produced by the United States Department of Agriculture, black tenant farmers, able to live and to work productively through the efforts of the federal government's Farm Extension Service, celebrate by eating watermelon and dancing to the strains of "Swanee River." Some of these films dealt with controversial issues of the day, including birth control, eugenics, and euthanasia. The melodrama *The Black Stork* (1917), loosely based on a case in which a physician permitted a 'defective' newborn to die, was shown in commercial theaters from 1917 through the 1920s.[5]

American entry into the First World War intensified the commitment to using popular media as an educational vehicle. The United States Army produced a series of sexual hygiene films for American soldiers, which were later shown to civilian men and women in sexually-segregated audiences. *Fit to Fight* (1918) featured the dramatic stories of five draftees who risk the dangers of venereal disease by consorting with prostitutes. The film, which included graphic images of syphilitic lesions, was reissued after the war as *Fit to Win* (1919). Intended for female audiences, *The End of the Road* (1919) emphasized the need for childhood instruction about venereal diseases. The effectiveness of these films and others devoted to social hygiene received extraordinary scrutiny in the 1920s from Johns Hopkins University psychologists Karl Lashley and John B. Watson, who, with funds from the United States Interdepartmental Social Hygiene Board, exhibited the films to some 5,000 Americans in order to investigate the "informational and educative effects of certain motion-picture films used as propaganda against venereal disease."[6] From their study of the responses of a variety of groups (including medical professionals, business executives, members of a literary club, motormen and railway conductors, merchant sailors, soldiers, and mixed audiences), Lashley and Watson concluded that their subjects received general impressions rather than accurate knowledge of details relating to venereal disease, its spread and treatment, and the films did not lead to a lasting change in the behavior of viewers.

After the war, organizations such as the Child Health Organization (founded in 1918) and the American Child Health Association (founded in 1923) turned to film as a means to inspire civic responsibility for the well-being of children. The ACHA hired professional advertisers, who designed explicitly modernistic health campaigns featuring updated fairy tales and folk songs, as well as the vernacular of the Jazz Age. Schools and colleges incorporated the new media into their curricula. In a 1920s community health project in North Dakota, sponsored by the Commonwealth Fund, elementary school boys developed their own 'health movie' on a home-made projector. At the high school level, the National Tuberculosis Association organized health play-writing contests for students.

Health film making burgeoned in the 1920s, becoming the focus not only of small-for-profit specialty companies, but also a critical wing of health departments and philanthropic health groups. Commercial organizations, such as the United States National Dairy Council, increasingly exploited the power of the media in the production of health-related films. Agencies of the American government expanded their film offerings. The United States Public Health Service, for example, produced and distributed numerous films on the dangers of spitting, flies, mosquitoes, hookworm disease, and the communal drinking cup. Organized medicine similarly embraced film making. By the 1930s and 1940s films had become an integral part of medicine. Hospitals, philanthropic organizations, and medical groups all produced films to educate and entertain students, patients, and the lay public. The American Medical Association's popular health magazine

*Hygeia*, begun in 1923, devoted coverage to popular films and radio progams featuring doctors and medicine.

From the 1920s to the 1960s — before a majority of households in western nations had televisions — radio was a crucial source of information and entertainment. Considered "of first importance in the control of the attitudes and opinions of the general public,"[7] radio exploited the growing social prestige of physicians, even as it undermined it by providing airtime for both alternative medical practitioners and makers of patent medicines. In the United States, such critics of organized medicine as Kansas fundamentalist Gerald B. Winrod used radio in the 1950s both to broadcast a new cancer cure, Gyloxylide, and to attack the Food and Drug Administration for persecuting its discoverers. Hospitals and doctors' offices provided the setting for many radio commercials in which physicians, both real and imaginary, extolled everything from soda to cigarettes. Weekly medical advice programs, often sponsored by a medical society or a life-insurance company, habituated listeners to the sounds, if not the sights, of modern medicine. Advertisers of food, drugs, and cleaning products adapted parts of the public health message to sell their products, familiarizing consumers not only with brand names — 'Post Bran Flakes promote health and regularity' — but cultural conceptions of the healthy and diseased body.

Like advertisers, public health officials sought to influence behavior using radio. During epidemics, for example, officials provided information to help the public identify suspicious symptoms. More controversial were the efforts by public health workers to use radio in campaigns against venereal disease. In 1934, just before a scheduled radio address on the future of public health, New York State Health Commissioner Thomas Parran was told by the Columbia Broadcasting Company that he could not mention syphilis or gonorrhea by name on the air. Angry at this censorship, Parran cancelled his talk, prompting the network to substitute piano melodies for the public health message.

By the 1930s, the physician and the nurse were readily identifiable in mass culture. Through health films, radio programs, and commercial advertisements in popular magazines, the lay public learned the new language and images of bacteriological science. Doctors in white coats signifying the modern hospital and the laboratory appeared in numerous advertisements warning about the dangers of germs and extolling the virtues of products that could protect the body. Advertising copy familiarized audiences with the equipment — the microscope, the petri dish, and the x-ray — and the concepts — germs, viruses, cells — of the modern laboratory and the clinic.

## HOLLYWOOD AND THE DOCTORS

In October 1927 the advent of sound technology transformed the Hollywood film industry, further revolutionizing the possibilities of representation and profoundly affecting patterns of thinking. The popularity of the 1931 screen adaptation of

American novelist Sinclair Lewis' novel *Arrowsmith*, the story of a crusading medical researcher, signaled the beginning of a golden age for American medicine on screen. During the 1930s and 1940s Hollywood studios released hundreds of films featuring doctors, nurses, and hospitals. "The dramatization of medicine on the stage and screen was a response to popular tastes already apparent," argued historian Richard Shryock. The popularity of such films as *Men in White, Women in White, The White Parade,* and *The White Angel* made it seem, Shryock noted, "as though anything 'in white' was good for box-office returns."[8]

Medicine enjoyed a high profile in the popular culture of the 1930s. A number of books highlighting medical themes — both fiction and non-fiction — attracted wide readership during the decade. Among the best-selling books in the United States were Lloyd C. Douglas' *Green Light* (1935), French surgeon Alexis Carrel's *Man the Unknown* (1936), Victor Heiser's *An American Doctor's Odyssey* (1936), *The Citadel* by British physician-author A.J. Cronin (1937), Eve Curie's biography of her mother *Madame Curie* (1937), and Arthur Hertzler's, *The Horse and Buggy Doctor* (1938). The 1930s also witnessed the introduction of the enormously popular and enduring Doctor Kildare character first introduced by novelist Max Brand in a short story in 1936.

The most influential popular text of the 1920s and 1930s, however, was medical journalist Paul de Kruif's *Microbe Hunters*. Published in 1926, the book, containing twelve vignettes of bacteriological discovery written in romantic and rhapsodic prose, was spectacularly successful. Even before *Microbe Hunters*, de Kruif's collaboration with Sinclair Lewis helped make *Arrowsmith* a success. The box-office success of the 1931 film version of the novel and the audience's "intense interest in the plague scenes"[9] encouraged playwright Sidney Howard (who had adapted *Arrowsmith* for the screen) to collaborate with de Kruif on a play about American army surgeon Walter Reed and the 1900 yellow fever expedition, which had also been featured in *Microbe Hunters. Yellow Jack* opened on Broadway in 1934, and in 1938, Metro-Goldwyn-Mayer Studios, which had purchased the film rights to the play, released the screen version. The success of *Microbe Hunters* also inspired feature-length film biographies, known in the industry as bio-pics, of both French chemist Louis Pasteur and Nobel Prize-winning scientist Paul Ehrlich. In addition to these films, touted for their historical accuracy, fictionalized treatments of bacteriological discovery, such as *Green Light* (1937) which depicted the search for the organism that caused Rocky Mountain Spotted Fever, capitalized on the exploits of real microbe hunters. The success of these films in turn influenced sales of de Kruif's books. When Pocket Books issued its first paperback version of *Microbe Hunters* in 1940, both the title and the cover art reflected the Hollywood version. The publishers retitled the book *Dr. Ehrlich's Magic Bullet and the Discoveries of Eleven Other Microbe Hunters* and featured actor Edward G. Robinson as Doctor Ehrlich on the cover.[10]

Most of the films of the 1930s and 1940s portrayed physicians and surgeons in a positive light. As they had in the silent film era, film makers turned to books and short stories as sources for screen depictions of doctors and nurses, including the enormously popular fiction of Unitarian minister Lloyd Douglas. In such novels as *Magnificent Obsession* (1929) and *Green Light* (1935), Douglas employed physicians as redemptive figures, Christ-like in their devotion to curing the sick and healing souls at the same time. Such films as *A Man to Remember* (1938), earned praise from medical reviewers for the "accurate picture of the life of the family doctor with all its devotions and services to mankind."[11]

Not all films in these decades cast the medical profession in the same rosy light. Challenging the emergent stereotype of the self-sacrificing physician or surgeon, these films explored issues about the exploitation of patients, the greed of some physicians, and even the dangers of incompetent doctors. During the worldwide economic depression of the 1930s, access to medical and hospital care prompted renewed calls for socialized medicine, a move strenuously resisted in the United States by the American Medical Association. Not surprisingly the AMA objected to the 1938 film version of *The Citadel*, a story of an idealistic doctor in a Welsh mining village who takes on the medical establishment. Although the film makers opened with the film with the disclaimer "This motion picture is a story of individual characterizations and is in no way intended as a reflection on the great medical profession which has done so much towards beating back those forces of nature that retard the physical progress of the human race,"[12] the organized medical profession condemned the film as propaganda. Disapproval from the AMA did not deter American audiences from seeing the film, which was named one of the ten best pictures of the year by the *New York Times* and nominated for several Academy Awards.

Just as they had in the silent film era, physicians and surgeons continued to appear as characters in horror films of the 1930s and 1940s. In many of these films, innovative film makers incorporated the latest medical technologies as reported in the popular press, thus lending verisimilitude to their productions and spreading images of advanced medical technology to larger audiences. The 1935 Universal Studios' release *Bride of Frankenstein*, sequel to the enormously successful *Frankenstein*, included scenes of an external heart pace-maker, first announced in the early 1930s. The 1939 Columbia Pictures film, *The Man They Could Not Hang*, starring Boris Karloff as Dr. Savaard, featured the 'glass heart' introduced in 1935 by American aviator Charles Lindbergh and French surgeon Alexis Carrel, as well as a revivification procedure developed by American chemist Robert Cornish.

In the years between 1930 and 1960, the vast majority of screen doctors were male, their patients and nurses female. Although women had appeared occasionally as doctors since the early days of silent film, such portrayals remained rare. In the 1930s, for example, five feature films used women doctors as major characters; women doctors appeared as lesser characters in four other films of that decade. As patients, attractive women offered film makers the opportunity to display undraped or semi-clothed female bodies, and play on the double entendre of 'bedside manners.' Intimate relationships between men and women were replicated in screen surgeries in which a male surgeon operated, in the words of one contemporary reviewer, "on the unconscious and presumably expiring form of his sweetheart."[13] As nurses, women offered similar possibilities for romance and sexual encounters on screen. One significant exception to this was the 1946 RKO film *Sister Kenny*, based on the true story of an Australian nurse (played by Rosalind Russell) who, practicing in the bush, developed a method to help children paralyzed with polio regain the use of their muscles.[14]

During these decades, few men or women of color appeared as physicians or surgeons in Hollywood films. One notable exception was *Arrowsmith*, which included the portrayal of a dedicated and self-sacrificing black physician, Oliver Marchand, played by Clarence Brooks. In the late 1940s, several Hollywood 'social document' films emphasized the problems encountered by black professionals. Based on the actual experiences of light-complexioned Dr. Albert Johnson who practiced medicine for twenty years 'passing' as white, *Lost Boundaries* (1949) featured actor Mel Ferrer as a "Negro doctor forced to renounce his race to follow his career."[15] The 1950 film *No Way Out* offered a similar sympathetic portrayal of the race prejudices encountered by Negro doctors.

## SCREENING MEDICINE

Before 1960, in response to organized medicine's lobbying, censors in both Britain and Hollywood actively dictated the ways medicine and medical procedures were presented on screen. Like lawyers and the clergy, physicians benefited from special protection by the censors, pledged to maintain public faith in the learned professions. In the 1930s British censors banned five films, including a proposed film of George Bernard Shaw's *The Doctor's Dilemma*, on the grounds that they would "shake the confidence of the nation in the medical profession."[16] In many other films, British censors required extensive deletions. Sensitive to the highly controversial issue of animal vivisection, for example, British film censors demanded that scenes involving animal experiments be eliminated from films. The British censors similarly decided "to reduce to an absolute minimum all scenes taking place inside an operating theatre, and to object to the showing of surgical instruments in use or about to be used."[17] Because American studios relied heavily on international markets for their films, such decisions on the part of the British film censors influenced the production of Hollywood films. In the United States, the staff of the Production Code Administration, a film industry institution dedicated to maintaining standards of decency in films from major Hollywood studios, compelled American film makers to follow the British guidelines in order to avoid numerous deletions or 'mutilations' so that their films could be screened in Britain and elsewhere. During the filming in 1939 of Lloyd Douglas' *Disputed Passage*, for example, censors from the Production Code Administration warned film makers from Paramount Studios that scenes portraying operations would be cut by both British and American censors, who would also require deletion of scenes showing the actual insertion of hypodermic needles, the administration of chloroform, and the use of instruments on a patient.

In addition to graphic depictions of surgical and medical practice, censors challenged the portrayal of such volatile moral issues as abortion and euthanasia. American censors routinely insisted that all references to abortion be excised from Hollywood films. In the case of euthanasia, censors worked closely with film makers to insure that representations of mercy-killing on screen did not offend both professional and lay audiences. In 1935, for example, following extensive press coverage of the "right-to-die" campaign led by "one of Britain's most distinguished surgeons,"[18] the Twentieth-Century Fox Studio proposed a film about a mercy-killing. The head of the Production Code Administration warned film producers that their plans to exploit such a sensational issue were not acceptable. After protracted negotiations between the producers and the censors over presenting the moral issue of euthanasia as dramatic entertainment, the studio released *The Crime of Doctor Forbes* in 1936. Although the original screenplay featured a doctor who administers an opiate overdose to a badly injured colleague who begs for help to die, in the film version the doctor merely confesses to mercy-killing in order to save the reputation of his colleague who, in fact, has committed suicide.

Responsive to censorship and industry pressure, film makers worked closely with medical professionals in order to achieve 'realism' on screen. Some studios maintained research departments to insure the accuracy of details in their films. The research department at Warner Brothers Studio, for example, did extensive inquiries to insure the accuracy of medical and historical detail in the 1940 film *Dr. Ehrlich's Magic Bullet*, including obtaining advice from two medical consultants from the American Medical Association. In 1955, deluged with requests for medical consultants by film and television production companies, the AMA established a committee to standardize media medical images and behavior. The Physicians' Advisory Committee on Television, Radio and Motion Pictures reviewed in an average year some 500 scripts and script rewrites featuring physicians and hospitals. Although committee members remained dissatisfied with accuracy in media representations of medicine, citing among things one television actor who refused to wear a mask in a surgical scene because he didn't want to disguise his face and the frequent and torrid love scenes between nurses and residents, they nonetheless believed that their ability to transmit to millions of viewers the knowledge that certain diseases, like breast cancer, could be cured with early detection was a valuable public service.

## RESISTING IMAGES

During the 1930s and 1940s, the cultural prestige of American medicine was reinforced and sustained by the image of medicine in popular media, especially film. Perceiving the power of the cinema to affect public attitudes and concerned about the low status of his specialty, a leading anesthesiologist urged his colleagues to adopt a media campaign in 1940, because, as he explained, he was tired of seeing movies with dramatic operating scenes in which heroic surgeons dominated the action but relegated anesthesiologists to filling rubber bags and jiggling valves.[19]

In the 1940s, however, the prestige of organized medicine suffered a series of blows. In 1943 the United States Supreme Court upheld the fine against the American Medical Association, which promoted itself as the 'voice of American medicine,' for conspiring to coerce and restrain physicians from engaging in prepaid group practice. Amid both Presidential and popular support in the 1940s for a national health insurance plan, physicians organized a media campaign to oppose this intrusion of 'socialized medicine.' The National Physicians' Committee spent close to a million dollars on pamphlets, radio talks, and leaflets, one of which featured a reproduction of the 1891 painting "The Doctor" by English painter Sir Luke Fildes.

The Fildes painting depicted an older, white-haired physician hunched over the bedside of a sick child whose grief-stricken mother and bereft father await the doctor's prognosis. The value of this painting to the medical profession had long been recognized; shortly after Fildes unveiled the work, a leader of the British medical profession informed his students: "A library of books written in your honour would not do what this picture has done and will do for the medical profession in making the hearts of our fellow men warm to us with confidence and affection."[20] In the United States "The Doctor" also proved enormously popular. The subject of a 1911 Edison film, the painting was exhibited by the Petrolagar Laboratories at Chicago's Century of Progress Exposition in 1933; this exhibit which featured "The Doctor" traveled to 18 American cities where an estimated five million people viewed the symbol "of the importance of the family physician."[21] In 1947 the United States Postal Service selected the image for the stamp commemorating the one-hundredth anniversary of the founding of the American Medical Association. When the AMA took up the battle against national health insurance in 1949, the organization billed each of its members $25 to hire the public relations firm of Whitaker and Baxter, which mounted the most expensive lobbying campaign in American history. In addition to pamphlets and AMA-sponsored radio documentaries, Whitaker and Baxter revived the use of the Fildes painting. Distributed as a poster for display in the waiting rooms of some 625,000 physicians, a gigantic banner with a reproduction of "The Doctor," with its implicit attack on the third-party intrusion into the doctor-patient relationship, appeared prominently at AMA meetings. In 1981 the AMA was still receiving two or three requests a year for the painting.

The power of oil paintings to communicate meaning about the medical and pharmaceutical professions was not lost on drug companies. In the 1930s and 1940s the Philadelphia-based John Wyeth and Brother drug company sponsored a series of paintings, whose subjects included William Osler, Army surgeon William Beaumont, and Walter Reed. On a much grander scale, the Parke, Davis and Company in the 1950s and 1960s featured oil paintings of what they christened "Great Moments in Medicine" in their corporate magazine. The company received thousands of requests from physicians, educators, and others for copies of the paintings suitable for framing. Recognizing the value of this public relations device, the firm provided sets of the eighty-five paintings. Widely displayed in doctors' offices and pharmacies throughout the United States and Canada, these images of Hippocrates, Galen, and other great men provided both professionals and the lay public with access to a past seldom captured visually. Mass produced for advertising, these illustrations "may have had a far-reaching impact on the conceptual outlook of a generation."[22]

Cinematic representations of medical practitioners and medical institutions continued to exert a powerful influence after the Second World War. Three years after the publication of her expose of American hospitals for the mentally ill, Twentieth-Century Fox Studios purchased the film rights to Mary Jane Ward's book *Snake Pit*. Starring Olivia de Havilland as a young woman incarcerated in a mental hospital, the 1948 film version of *The Snake Pit* excited controversy in both America, where it was banned in several states, and in Britain, where the film's harrowing images of insane patients and graphic portrayals of shock therapies, 'wet packs,' and straitjackets prompted considerable discussion of the potentially dangerous impact of the film on viewers. After cutting nearly 1,000 feet of the film, British film censors approved the movie for viewers over the age of sixteen. Within a week of the film's opening in Britain came news that *The Snake Pit* had driven a Luton woman insane, leading to her voluntary commitment in a mental hospital. As historian Michael Shortland points out, such a response today would seem disproportionate to the film's impact, but audiences in the 1940s and 1950s identified with both actors and movies to a much greater degree than is true in the 1990s.[23]

One reassuring feature of *The Snake Pit* was the portrayal of the psychiatrist who leads the de Havilland character out of the darkness of mental illness. Screen images of the psychiatric profession became increasingly common in the 1950s, presenting a profession distinguished by compassionate and effective care for the mentally ill. This conception was increasingly challenged in the 1960s and 1970s when psychiatry, like other medical specialties and medicine in general, experienced considerable public skepticism. Films like *King of Hearts* (1968) and *One Flew Over the Cuckoo's Nest* (1975) not only depicted psychiatrists in a less than flattering light, but they questioned the very existence of the category of mental illness. The diagnosis of mental illness, these films implied, functioned as a type of cultural straitjacket for rebellious free-spirits, non-conformists, and iconoclasts who did not fit neatly into middle-class society.

Assessing the impact of movie images of both psychiatrists and their patients remains problematic. Many people continue to believe in the power of visual media

— movies and television — to shape public perceptions of the mentally ill and to stigmatize patients with mental illness. In light of this power, some psychiatrists and mental health advocacy groups have urged both careful monitoring of the portrayal of mental illness in movies and television and letter-writing campaigns to film producers and to newspapers and magazines that advertise films which stigmatize the mentally ill. In 1990, for example, patient advocacy groups in the United States mounted a letter-writing campaign against the film comedy *Crazy People* (1990), although the influence of this effort on the film, which performed badly at the box office, is difficult to gauge.

## DOMESTICATING MEDICINE: TELEVISION AND THE 'DOCTOR SHOWS'

In the 1950s the explosive spread of the new medium of television did much to domesticate doctors and medicine. A hospital or doctor's office proved a flexible setting for both a recurring stable of characters and occasional guest stars. Television producers initially turned to familiar names and situations. Doctor Kildare first appeared on screen in the 1937 Paramount film *Internes Can't Take Money*, starring Joel McCrea and Barbara Stanwyck. Over the next thirty years, fifteen films, seven books, one radio program, and two television shows featured the Doctor Kildare character.

In the 1950s and 1960s, television presented a largely uncritical picture of health professionals and medicine, rarely addressing controversial medical issues like abortion or incompetent physicians. A major incentive for such positive images was financial. Medical organizations offered budget-strapped television producers access to operating rooms and doctors' offices, making the building of studio sets unnecessary. In return, the medical society demanded control over the accuracy of medical scripts. In the case of the 1950s television series *Medic*, the agreement between writer James Moser and the Los Angeles County Medical Association required that each script undergo rigorous review for medical accuracy. Members of the review committee from the medical society, moreover, insisted that physicians be portrayed as 'proper professionals,' necessitating changes and alterations in many of the *Medic* scripts. External pressures also contributed to a more sedate image of medicine on television. When *Medic* producers planned to show a caesarean birth, complete with incision, on their television show, intervention by Timothy Flynn, the Roman Catholic archbishop of New York, led the network to remove the offending episode from the air. When the producers of *Medic* proposed an episode focusing on a black physician, a number of Southern affiliated television stations refused to air the program, and the network, faced with a loss of revenue, insisted that the episode be pulled from the series. These continuing controversies over the series led producers to cancel the program after two years.

In the 1960s the enormously popular television programs, *Dr. Kildare* (1961–1966) and *Ben Casey* (1961–1966), continued the tradition of relying on medical consultants to achieve realism in their programs. Like the Los Angeles County Medical Society, the American Medical Association's Advisory Committee for Television and Motion Pictures, established in 1955, not only monitored accuracy but insisted on appropriate medical behavior. The Advisory Committee, for example, did not permit images of physicians smoking in the presence of their patients or sitting on the edge of a patient's bed. Pleased by the public relations potential of these programs, the committee did sometimes approve scripts with minor inaccuracies and even some professionally controversial issues as malpractice and incompetent doctors in the interests of maintaining good relations with the television producers. The popularity of these television series prompted a variety of products which insured that the images of Drs. Kildare and Casey reached even broader audiences. In addition to clothing and jewelry, marketers developed children's games and toys, comic books, newspaper comic strips, and paperback books all tied to the television programs. In the late 1960s a new image of the American family physician displaced both Kildare and Casey. Played by mature actor Robert Young, his face familiar to viewers of the popular situation comedy *Father Knows Best, Marcus Welby, M.D.* became the most successful program in the history of the American Broadcasting Company. In the course of the series' eight-year run, Young received tens of thousands of letters from viewers seeking medical advice. Medical and nursing organizations around the country honored both Young and actress Elena Verdugo, who played Welby's loyal nurse.

During the 1970s the Welby image of competent, compassionate family physician was challenged by more biting portrayals of physicians and surgeons. Based on the Robert Altman film M*A*S*H, the series of the same name debuted on American television in 1972. Using its setting in the Korean conflict to criticize American involvement in Vietnam, the series which ran until 1982 depicted surgeons using comedy to deflect the numbing realities of performing countless surgical procedures on wounded soldiers and civilians. The technically superb, if morally flawed, male surgeons on M*A*S*H offered audiences multidimensional characterizations of physicians. Despite the feminist health movement of the 1970s, however, the series, like American television in general, continued to stereotype the female nursing staff as either sexual objects or as viragos, as in the character of Chief Nurse Major Margaret "Hot Lips" Houlihan.

Comic portrayals of physicians and nurses were not in themselves novel. American television writers and producers drew on English films and television programs set in hospitals. In the years between 1958 and 1972, the *Carry on* series of films in "the British music hall tradition of exuberant zaniness, punctuated freely by vulgar dialogue, toilet humor, and visual effects" influenced some American writers even though the double entendres and sexual situations in these films were considered too extreme for American audiences.[24]

In the 1980s the prime-time television series *St. Elsewhere* (1982–1988) set the stage for a new and gritty portrayal of physicians struggling to cope with overlapping personal and professional problems. Although initially slow to gain an audience, the series drew large numbers of women and found a following among young, urban professionals. In the 1990s, the series *ER*, created by physician-novelist Michael Crichton, became one of the most popular programs of the decade attracting more than 24 million American viewers each week. Set in a chronically underfunded hospital emergency room, the series features graphic images of badly injured patients and high-tech medical and surgical interventions offered by a culturally and ethnically diverse staff, including a HIV-positive physician-assistant who continues to provide care after her condition is diagnosed and a physically-disabled physician who runs the ER. In light of patient reports that they obtain most of their medical information from popular media, the series, along with other medical dramas, has been scrutinized for accuracy in its portrayal of medical treatments. In 1996 a leading American medical journal published an analysis of the frequency of successful cardiopulmonary resuscitation on *ER* and two other programs (*Chicago Hope*, a medical drama, and *Rescue 911*, a program combining both 'actual photography' and simulated rescue scenes). They concluded that survival rates were significantly higher than in the medical literature, providing viewers with an "unrealistic impression"[25] of these resuscitation techniques. Because the attraction of these programs rests in their graphic 'realism,' the physicians assumed that many Americans would not be able to distinguish medical fact from the fictional presentation, and advised that physicians should both be aware of the images of CPR on television and be prepared to discuss these with their patients in order to promote well-informed decisions about resuscitation.

The distinction between factual and fictional presentations of medicine becomes even more problematic with the rise of such medical documentary programs as "The Operation," a widely-accessible prime-time American cable program. Hosted by a woman surgeon, the program presents each week an actual surgical procedure performed on camera on an actual patient. To prepare viewers for graphic images of blood and surgical incisions, audiences receive the advance warning "What you are about to see is a real operation. This kind of program is not for everyone."[26] Of course, a 'real operation' does not take place in front of a large television audience, nor is it edited to fit the conventions of television (commercial interruptions, one-hour time limit, good outcome for patient and surgeon). The problem of factual accuracy also arises in another technology currently shaping patient access to medical knowledge, the Internet. Through the World Wide Web, patients and consumers have increasing access to massive and largely unfiltered amounts of medical information.

## SCHOLARSHIP

Given the power of the mass media to shape attitudes and behavior, there has been surprisingly little systematic attention to the impact, influence, and especially production of films, television programs, magazine articles, novels, advertisements and newspaper stories. Although some authors have sketched the broad contours of media and medicine, this work remains mostly descriptive. Only a handful of scholars (notably Michael Shortland, Anne Karpf, Martin Pernick, and Joseph Turow) have produced thoughtful and insightful analyses of some dimensions of the intersections of medicine and twentieth-century media. Over the past few decades, a growing body of feminist scholarship has begun serious examination of women and medical images, encompassing both old and new medical imaging technologies as well as popular film. As this essay suggests, medicine's relationship with the media is complex, multi-faceted and crucial. More attention to the production, reception, censorship and import of medical media and media medicine is essential to understanding this most significant feature of twentieth-century society.

## REFERENCES

1. William Osler, *Aequanimitas*. (Philadelphia: Blakiston, 1932), p. 144.
2. Roger Boxill, *Shaw and the Doctors*. (New York: Basic Books, 1969), p. 101.
3. Michael Shortland, *Medicine and Film: A Checklist, Survey and Research Resource*, Research Publication Number IX. (Oxford: Wellcome Unit for the History of Medicine, 1989), p. 1.
4. Martin S. Pernick, 'Thomas Edison's tuberculosis films: mass media and health propaganda,' *Hastings Center Reports* (1978), **8**: 21–27.
5. Martin S. Pernick, *The Black Stork: Eugenics and the Death of 'Defective' Babies in American Medicine and Motion Pictures Since 1915*. (New York: Oxford University Press, 1996).
6. Karl S. Lashley and John B. Watson, *A Psychological Study of Motion Pictures in Relation to Venereal Disease Campaigns*. (Washington: United States Interdepartmental Social Hygiene Board, 1922), p. 3.
7. Gertrude Duncan and Frederick H. Lund, 'The validity of health information gained through radio advertising,' *Research Quarterly* (1945), **16**: 102–5, at p. 102.
8. Richard H. Shryock, *American Medical Research: Past and Present*. (New York: Commonwealth Fund, 1947), p. 243.
9. Sidney Howard to John Moran, 22 Dec. 1931, Philip S. Hench Collection, box 32, Claude Moore Health Sciences Library, University of Virginia.
10. Susan E. Lederer and John Parascandola, 'Screening syphilis: *Dr. Ehrlich's Magic Bullet* meets the Public Health Service,' *Journal of the History of Medicine* (1998), **53**: 345–70.
11. 'Medicine in the movies,' *Hygeia* (1939), **17**: 486–89, at p. 488.
12. 'The Citadel,' *The American Film Institute Catalog of Motion Pictures Produced in the United States, Feature Films, 1931–1940*, Patricia King Hanson (ed.). (Berkeley: University of California Press, 1993), 2526.
13. Susan E. Lederer, 'Repellent subjects: Hollywood censorship and surgical images in the 1930s,' *Literature and Medicine* (1998), **17**: 91–113.
14. Naomi Rogers, 'Sister Kenny,' *Isis* (1993), **84**: pp. 772–74.
15. 'Superior Documentary,' *Newsweek* (1949), **85**: p. 72.
16. Jeffrey Richards, *The Age of the Dream Palace: Cinema and Society in Britain 1930–1939*. (Routledge: New York, 1984), p. 118.
17. Derek Mayne to Albert Deane, 7 May 1937, 'The Story of Louis Pasteur,' Production Code Administration files, Margaret Herrick Library, Academy of Motion Pictures Arts and Sciences, Beverly Hills, California.
18. Susan E. Lederer, 'Medical ethics and the media: oaths, codes and popular culture,' in Robert Baker, Stephen Latham, Arthur Caplan and Linda Emanuel (eds), *The American Medical Ethics Revolution*. (Baltimore: Johns Hopkins University Press, forthcoming).
19. Rosemary Stevens, *In Sickness and In Wealth: American Hospitals in the Twentieth Century*. (New York: Basic Books, 1989), p. 181.
20. L.V. Fildes, *Luke Fildes, R.A.: A Victorian Painter*. (London: Michael Joseph, 1968), p. 118.

21.  'Sculpticolor of Fildes's masterpiece 'The Doctor' goes to Rosenwald Museum,' *New England Journal of Medicine* (1938), **218**: p. 1116.

22.  Jacalyn Duffin and Alison Li, 'Great moments: Parke, Davis and Company and the creation of medical art,' *Isis* (1995), **86**: 1–29.

23.  Michael Shortland, 'Screen memories: towards a history of psychiatry and psychoanalysis in the movies,' *British Journal for the History of Science* (1987), **20**: 421–52.

24.  Joseph Turow, *Playing Doctor: Television, Storytelling and Medical Power.* (New York: Oxford University Press, 1989), p. 202.

25.  Susan J. Diem, John D. Landaus and James A. Tulsky, 'Cardiopulmonary resuscitation on television: miracles and misinformation,' *New England Journal of Medicine* (1996), **334**: 1578–82. See rejoinder by series co-producer, Neal Baer, M.D., 'Cardiopulmonary resuscitation on television: exaggerations and accusations,' *ibid.*, 1604–05.

26.  Catherine Belling, 'Reading 'The Operation': television, realism and the possession of medical knowledge,' *Literature and Medicine* (1998), **17**: 1–23.

## FURTHER READING

Apple, Rima D. and Apple, Michael W., 'Special section on history of science in film: Screening science,' *Isis* (1993), **84**: 750–74.

Boon, Timothy M., 'The smoke menace: Cinema, sponsorship and the social relations of science in 1937,' in Michael Shortland (ed.), *Science and Nature*, British Society for the History of Science, Monograph 8. (Oxford: British Society for the History of Science, 1993), 57–88.

Duffin, Jacalyn and Li, Alison, 'Great moments: Parke, Davis and Company and the creation of medical art,' *Isis* (1995), **86**: 1–29.

Gabbard, Krin and Gabbard, Glen O., *Psychiatry and the Cinema.* (Chicago: The University of Chicago Press, 1987).

Jones, Anne Hudson, 'Medicine and the physician in popular culture,' in M. Thomas Inge (ed.), *The Handbook of American Popular Culture*, Volume III. (Westport, CT: Greenwood Press, 1981), 183–203.

Kalisch, Philip A. and Beatrice J. Kalisch, 'When Americans called for Dr. Kildare: Images of physicians and nurses in the Dr. Kildare and Dr. Gillespie movies, 1937–1947,' *Medical Heritage* (1985), **1**: 348–63.

Karpf, Anne, *Doctoring the Media: The Reporting of Health and Medicine.* (London: Routledge, 1988).

Lederer, Susan E., 'Repellent subjects: Hollywood censorship and surgical images in the 1930s,' *Literature and Medicine* (1998), **17**: 91–113.

Lederer, Susan E. and Parascandola, John, 'Screening syphilis: *Dr. Ehrlich's Magic Bullet* meets the Public Health Service,' *Journal of the History of Medicine* (1998), **53**: 345–70.

Pernick, Martin S., *The Black Stork: Eugenics and the Death of "Defective" Babies in American Medicine and Motion Pictures Since 1915.* (New York: Oxford University Press, 1996).

Shortland, Michael, *Medicine and Film: A Checklist, Survey and Research Resource*, Research Publications Number IX. (Oxford: Wellcome Unit for the History of Medicine, 1989).

Shortland, Michael, 'Screen memories: Towards a history of psychiatry and psychoanalysis in the movies,' *British Journal for the History of Science* (1987), **20**: 421–52.

Turow, Joseph, *Playing Doctor: Television, Storytelling and Medical Power.* (New York: Oxford University Press, 1989).

White, Suzanne, '*Mom and Dad* (1944): Venereal disease "exploitation,"' *Bulletin of the History of Medicine* (1988), **62**: 252–70.

# CHAPTER 32

# Hospitals

JOEL D. HOWELL

Early in 1900, a carpenter who we shall call John Smith, having newly moved from a rural area into a large US city, was crossing the street on his way home from a long day's work when he found himself directly in the path of an onrushing horse-drawn carriage. Although attempting valiantly to get out of the way, he was struck a glancing blow by the lead horse and sent tumbling to the ground. On arising he found it impossible to walk on account of severe pain in his left leg. A passerby sent word to the nearby general hospital, which sent out a horse-drawn ambulance to take him in. Carpenter Smith was to stay in that general hospital for some time. His visit will serve as an exemplar for our thoughts about the patient's experience in the hospital of the early twentieth century, and as a touchstone against which we shall measure the hospital of later years.

The hospital that housed Carpenter Smith was marginal to the US health care system. This has changed, and near the end of the twentieth century the hospital has assumed a shape and form that places it at or near the center of health care delivery. But this transition was far from inevitable. As this chapter will demonstrate, the places that we call 'hospitals' have no obvious, natural form. Instead, they have always been defined by the particular social, political and economic context in which they happen to exist. This chapter will focus primarily on hospitals in the context of England and the United States, but will also touch on experiences in some other countries and areas. Space constraints as well as the availability of secondary sources do not permit a systematic survey. The chapter will try to quote patients' experiences whenever possible, but most patients, particularly in the earlier periods of the twentieth century, were unlikely to create a direct record of their care, and discussions of their hospital experience must of necessity be largely inferential.

Soon after Mr Smith was taken to the hospital a house doctor diagnosed his broken leg based solely on direct physical examination of the injured limb, notably without reference to (or likely any thought of) the brand-new X-ray machine that sat only a few dozen meters away in the hospital's equipment room. One feature of Mr Smith's experience that would be striking for the late-twentieth century reader was the almost total dependence of Mr Smith's caregivers on direct observation, unmediated by tests or images. Someone might have looked at his urine on admission, once, but laboratory tests such as blood tests were to play little or no role in Smith's care during the two months that he was confined to the hospital. Nor was such a length of stay unusual. Over half the patients admitted to US or English hospitals with a broken leg stayed in the hospital wards over a month.

Even though there was little to be done for him save immobilize his leg and let it heal, going home was hardly an option for Mr Smith, who in healthier days shared his boarding house room with three other single, male laborers, who could hardly be expected to forfeit their employment (and their salary) in order to stay home and care for him. So, Mr Smith spent his days in a hospital ward, daydreaming, gazing out the window and, once he became a bit more mobile, helping to clean the hospital ward and caring for those more ill than he. In these latter activities he was functioning as a nurse, for a trained nursing staff was not to be found in many turn-of-the-century hospitals in the United States.

## LIFE ON THE WARDS

Mr Smith likely spent his days and nights with about 20 other men in what was termed a 'Nightingale Ward,' an arrangement of beds and windows advocated by the English nursing pioneer Florence Nightingale, who based her theories of hospital design on the idea that diseases spread through the air in a sort of 'miasma,' and thus that the hospital ward should allow enough space so that air should never stagnate around a patient. Because of the emphasis on air, wards based on her designs were said to have embodied "an edifice built up out of pure air."[1]

The arrangements allowed patients to enjoy each others' company. There was usually a space down the middle of the ward — a place for tables, chairs, an occasional piano for Sunday services, and often flowers. The whole design was intended to allow patients such as Mr Smith the brightest possible space for recuperation, with brilliant sunlight whenever outside conditions permitted. Along with these inspirational and recreational touches came the military efficiency of the tightly-made up beds, reflecting Nightingale's extensive military experience. All patients could be seen from a single vantage point, thus making it easier for the charge nurse to supervise the unit.

The hospital design inspired by Florence Nightingale was amazingly resilient. Before too many decades of the century had passed, urban hospital designers shared in the invention of skyscrapers, creating tall hospitals to make more effective use of the increasingly-limited space available in urban environments. Although utilizing the latest in construction technology, as well as inventions such as elevators, many of these hospitals were still based on some version of the Nightingale Ward. Indeed, this design remained dominant in many English and American hospitals well past the midpoint of the twentieth century. As we near the end of the century, most people's perceptions of the Nightingale Wards have changed, from something fresh and modern and scientific to something old-fashioned, quaint and somewhat disreputable. But some recent historians claim that those critics, who have "seen only the last decrepit descendants of this ward in state institutions for the most decrepit patients, cannot possibly imagine how cheerful, sunny, and almost enticing a multiple-bed ward can be. A happy hum rises from these extraordinarily well-run wards. It must be heard to be believed."[2]

Mr Smith spent his days in a large, open, very public ward. For some years before his 1900 admission there had been a few alternative, private places set aside in hospitals. Such rooms were usually either for the very infectious or the very wealthy. Those of the latter status hardly wished to share their space with the itinerant or the servant. "When I return, put me in a closet rather than in the ward!" complained a distressed patient to the superintendent of the Presbyterian Hospital of Chicago.[3] Private rooms were created for such patients, rooms that emulated the hotels where the well-to-do, in better health, would have paid for a bed. In private rooms patients need not tolerate their neighbor's noise. They could keep the temperature where they wanted it, and even entertain visitors at what would otherwise be forbidden hours. In times of pain and suffering they need not witness their neighbor's distress nor be assailed by the unwanted sounds or odors of other patients. Even as hospitals became more generally acceptable to the well-to-do, the idea of more special places for those able to pay more has persisted late into the century. Some private rooms still resemble a high-class hotel, as a recent room for VIP's that "was carpeted and had upholstered furniture … burgundy and pink sofas and chairs and oriental tchotchkes on the coffee table. It was equipped with a television, a VCR, a radio, and a tape player. It could have been a hotel suite if it weren't for the hospital bed and examining lights occupying one corner."[4]

In the 1910s and 1920s increasing numbers of middle-income patients entered the hospitals. Unlike those patients who entered the hospital in the nineteenth century precisely (and only) because they could not care for themselves, these patients could have paid for care at home, but they believed that newly-scientific hospitals offered a better chance for cure or relief. Unlike the wealthy patients who could afford an expensive private room, middle-income patients needed a middle ground, a semiprivate environment, with perhaps 2–4 other patients. This space was not as isolated (or as expensive) as a completely private room, but had less hustle and bustle than a large, 15–20 (or more) bed ward. In the US a rapid shift came with the great depression, as "Almost overnight … the country was flooded with semiprivate accommodations."[5] The historian Rosemary Stevens has pointed out that this designation was a curious one, revealing something that was not a "public" accommodation, with all of the negative connotations from the earlier, nineteenth century, dependent model, but was not quite a private room.

## TECHNOLOGY, SURGERY, AND TEACHING IN THE HOSPITAL

During much of the nineteenth century, most patients who entered the hospital were poor; a person of means would never dream of entering a hospital for care, even for the most serious injuries or for a surgical procedure. But in the United States around the turn of the twentieth century increasing numbers of paying patients wished to enter the hospital. For Mr Smith, inability to obtain care at home was a major determinant of his decision to enter the hospital. For other people who became ill in the 1910s and 1920s, even those who might have easily been cared for by family members at home, hospital care offered the allure of burgeoning medical technology such as X-ray machines. Rapidly familiar to the lay public after Roentgen's 1895 invention, these machines were both fascinating and frightening. Having an X-ray examination was a dramatic (and sometimes dangerous) experience in which the patient would descend to the bowels of the hospital, where in the dimly-lit basement a large X-ray apparatus with sparks flying would allow a doctor to peer deep within the person's body. Such examinations were infrequent for the first decade or so after the machine's invention, but changes in hospital organization made the institution a more hospitable place for X-ray examinations by the 1920s. Not all of the new technologies were so dramatic or so obvious. The urine analysis served as the precursor of a whole panoply of laboratory tests, yet patients probably noticed little whether their urine was poured into the sewer or sent to a laboratory for analysis. Having blood drawn for analysis involved some measure of discomfort, and though such tests have now become routine and are less likely to be noticed by those who study the process of health care, they were (and continue to be) important events in the life of a patient lying in a hospital bed.

An even more significant event for most patients — surgery — was also a major element in both increasing the prestige of hospitals and drawing into the hospital people who had the means to pay for a good part of their care. Major surgery was always conspicuous, but until the late-nineteenth century it was rare. The early twentieth century saw a rapid increase in both major and minor surgery and was the 'golden age of surgery.' Hospitals became the preferred site for the rich as well as the poor, if not yet for monarchs. Perhaps the most notable operation of the early-twentieth century took place in June 1902, in London, when only two days before his expected coronation, Edward VII had an appendiceal abscess surgically drained, an operation that did much to encourage the acceptance of abdominal surgery as a routine event. Edward VII had his operation done at Buckingham Palace, but that venue was not readily available for most other people. In earlier years some might have had the operation done in a much smaller and less commodious home, but within a short period after Edward's medical success most people would have wanted an operation for similar circumstances, and the home was no longer to be preferred over the hospital.

In the mid-nineteenth century, some operations in hospitals took place in operating rooms, but many went on in the middle of the ward for all to see and hear — those yet to be operated on would anticipate their own screams to come, those recovering would have their rest impeded by the pain of others. By the turn of the twentieth century, more and more special places were being set aside for operations, elaborate rooms in which the surgeon would ply her or (more often) his trade. Those rooms were often among the first to boast the accoutrements of the modern environment in the form of brilliant electrical light or telephonic communication with the rest of the hospital. The First World War did nothing to dampen the enthusiasm for the surgeon's standing. The speed and intensity of surgical care increased still more with the popularization of a theory that a wide variety of ailments could be traced to a localized (or focal) area of infection. That area was often held to be the tonsils, and in quest of better health countless children had their tonsils removed. The dramatic increase in the numbers of patients admitted to hospital for operations made the hospital seem almost like a factory. Not that being called 'factory-like' would have been a pejorative term in the 1910s and 1920s, particularly in the United States where the assembly line seemed the logical culmination of a quest for perfectibility.

Patients have always entered hospitals in search of medical attention. For patients who entered teaching hospitals, the presence of trainee doctors shaped the experience of being a patient. Although in many European countries and in England medical schools had long been associated with hospitals, early in the twentieth century United States medical training was only starting to move into the hospital. US medical schools found it important to have access to a hospital; conversely, hospitals found a medical school affiliation prestigious and potentially useful for patient care. This affiliation at times was realized by the creation of new affiliations between old organizations, and at times by universities creating their own hospitals. Some patients may have found attention from students flattering, as in the (difficult to believe) 1902 French image of a male patient with a dramatic anal fistula being examined by a group of surgeons. Perhaps the delight is as a result of believing that with so many people attending to his needs he is more likely to receive the best possible treatment. Or perhaps he does not realize that those who are looking at him may have little to do with his care. Such was the case later in the century for an oft-examined, noted American writer with a neurological problem who underwent "muscle tests ... by ... my own physicians, visiting physicians from other parts of the hospital who dropped by just out of curiosity, residents on training duty in other areas who were coming to look, professors from the medical school with their pupils, other specialists with residents to whose training they were contributing. Sometime no more than ten minutes would elapse between [tests] by people I might not see more than that single time. It did not occur to me to say no. I did not know that often these strangers had nothing to do with my care."[6]

One might expect that entering a teaching hospital would always involve some tension for alert patients. They may hope that in such hospitals a patient would get the very best medical care that can be offered. On the other hand, there is the fear that the patient will be the 'first' person upon whom some inexperienced trainee does a particular procedure. Not always disaggregated in the patient's mind is a different concern of the later-twentieth century, the fear of being the subject of medical experimentation. Such fears have been only slightly lessened by recent increases in formal reviews of experimental protocols.

Though teaching hospitals comprise only a small proportion of the total number of hospitals, they exert a disproportionate influence on patients' experiences — even on the majority of patients who are hospitalized elsewhere — partly because care givers who will later go into the community hospitals learn patterns of behavior at teaching hospitals. Also, large, academic institutions serve as exemplars in genre fiction and popular television shows, and thus condition patient expectations for what is at least initially a voyage into unfamiliar territory.

In that territory, there has always been some pattern in which caregivers interact with patients, a pattern that does much to define hospital life for patients, a system that has during the twentieth century usually gone by the name of 'rounds' — some sort of systematic survey of patients in a particular unit. Rounds may serve a teaching purpose or a clinical one. Rounds may or may not involve care givers actually going to see patients, and when they do not the patient is usually unaware of the activity. During rounds at the bedside care givers often spend very little time with each patient, but the interaction may have an impact disproportionate to the number of minutes, for those rounds may be the only face-to-face interaction of the day between patient and doctor. Whereas doctors view the rounds as a necessary but small part of their job, patients may view those rounds as specific visits to them, and often judge doctors harshly for what they consider to be inappropriate or condescending behavior. Rounds often highlight a gap between two groups of people. The doctor may be "amazingly ignorant" of the world of the patient. Conversely, patients are unaware of what doctors do when they are not at the bedside, and may wonder whether they are off playing golf or involved in other recreational activity.[7] Rounds are scheduled for the convenience of the care giver, not the patient, and as the hospital day has become increasingly packed, not in small part as the result of medical technology and surgery, the initial morning rounds extend earlier and earlier into the pre-dawn hours, with physicians or other staff awakening the patient as early as 5AM for a perfunctory examination, urine sample, or dressing change.

## HOSPITALS TAKE CENTER STAGE

By the 1920s, most people had come to see hospitals as central for health care. Private patients came in with some regularity. With increasing urbanization, more people lived close to hospitals. New technologies were important as well. Telephones enabled people to locate health care providers more easily. Improved means of transportation in the form of automobiles and ambulance services capable of rapidly moving injured people to hospital emergency rooms increasingly made the hospital the focus of health care.

Hospitals were important not only in urban settings. More hospitals were created in medium-sized and small communities; in England they were known from the mid-nineteenth century as 'cottage hospitals', and were usually run by general practitioners rather than consultants; most patients were expected to pay for some part of their care. In the US they were often refurbished homes run by all manner of doctors; they opened and closed frequently, making it hard to trace their history. But community hospitals were often a source of local pride; their existence provided evidence that a community had achieved some sort of standing, stability, and foresight. Having a hospital nearby also enabled patients more easily to maintain ties with their social support network when hospitalized. Even later in the century, well educated patients often choose to stay in their own community. As one reflected, "Maybe I should have gone to the larger St. Luke's or Cleveland Clinic where they do a dozen of [these procedures] a day ... But I opted to stay here, close to home, where it would be easier for my family to visit me."[8]

From the middle of the twentieth century the hospital seemed to be a never-ending source of high-technological wonder. Older technologies such as the X-ray machine saw expanded uses, although doctors were no longer the primary operators of these imaging devices. Dramatic new machines entered as well. The Drinker respirator — later called the iron lung — was used for patients who could not breathe, most commonly on account of polio. First widely used in the 1930s, it was a rigid cylinder into which a patient was placed, and positive and negative pressure applied at regular intervals. The device enabled patients who would otherwise have died to live for long periods of time. Some of these patients spent many years in the hospital, dependent — always — minute by minute — on the iron lung that sustained their respiration, and dependent at somewhat greater remove for the nursing staff for their every personal need. Life inside of an iron lung had its own set of unique circumstances, watching the world through a mirror over your head, wanting (yet fearing) eventual 'weaning' and release from the device. The wards of patients on iron lungs developed a social structure of their own, with rumors passed along with a speed "like a small town."[9] Following the introduction of polio vaccine and the development of other forms of respirators the iron lung gradually disappeared, but in its place patients shared other forms of technology.

Different countries have had different styles of medical care throughout the twentieth century. In the United States, a salient tension has been the conflict between hospitals as necessary social organizations and as symbols of the power of technology and medicine. In Britain there has been far less emphasis on medical technology than in the United States, and far more of an attempt to portray the hospital as a place where warm-hearted human beings come together, whether or not they are eventually cured. The superintendent of the large Charing Cross Hospital in London wrote widely-published tear-jerking stories of life in the 1920s hospital, which he insisted was "not the sordid and sickly place many people imagine it to be. Bruised, broken and battered men and women are found within its doors, it is true, but for everyone who succumbs at least fifty are restored. And life is often all the sweeter after having passed by the gateway of death."[10] In these stories couples are reconciled, Harley Street surgeons befriend Bolsheviks, and Englishmen and Germans share a common goal in a unifying therapeutic community. Even near the end of the century it is common in an English hospital to see ambulatory patients moving about the ward, "distributing early morning tea and during the rest of the day chatting about each other's affairs, medical and domestic."[11]

## THE HOSPITAL AS A SOCIAL INSTITUTION

Hospitals always exist in relation to a society's larger social system. The social relationships that exist outside of its walls do not disappear when patients are admitted, and patients who do not die will eventually leave the institution. Social stratification that exists outside the hospital may be reflected within by having different hospitals that serve different groups of people; public vs private, urban vs suburban, cancer hospitals, hospitals for incurables (now hospices). Within the hospital, stratification exists in part by the fact that different people get different types of accommodations (private vs ward).

Segregation by race has been (and continues to be) an unfortunate reality for many African Americans. Well into the twentieth century, many African Americans perished because they were deprived of care at a hospital, either because the hospital was all-white or because the few beds available for 'colored patients' happened to be full when they arrived. In the United States, the 1946 passage of the Hospital Survey and Construction law, popularly known as the Hill-Burton Act, mandated that all Americans should be provided with access to equal quality health care. Although the Act helped open up hospitals to people of diverse races, it continued to allow the possibility of continued segregation, often segregation of hospitals by rooms. The 1964 Civil Rights Act and a 1964 federal court decision that institutions receiving Hill-Burton funds could not discriminate helped push forward the desegregation of hospitals in the 1960s.

Most patients have families, and when those families were forced to stay outside of the hospital walls they still sought to be aware of and at times influence the care of their loved ones. In some instances they could play a more active role. Even as hospitals became more scientifically-centered palaces of healing early in the twentieth century, many families continued to be omnipresent, mediating food and bedding choices, even observing procedures carried out within the operating room. However, as the organization of the hospital became more complex, families left, and parts of the hospital were created to fulfill some of the same teaching roles that families had previously played. Once, a woman would have learned how to breast feed her newborn child from her mother, her aunt, her sister. Now, women who enter the hospital for childbirth are offered formal classes and instruction, covering such very basic topics as how to breast feed their child, how to bathe her, how to put her to sleep, and burp her. In some hospitals in the 1980s and 1990s, rooms for childbirth have started to be designed to bring families back into the hospital, with not only spouses but also children and other families encouraged to be present throughout the birth process. When children become patients, their families are now encouraged to be present as much as they like, where once they were relegated to being present for only the formal (and infrequent) visiting hours.

Traditional medical models have viewed disease as intimately related to the external environment. Thus, it is probably no coincidence that at precisely the time and place when the major changes in medical thinking were of precise, scientific, inward-looking technological models, the first US hospital social work department was created in an attempt to extend the hospitals' 'efficient' reach outside the wards. The Massachusetts General Hospital employed a social worker in 1905 to go out into the urban community and address the root causes of disease. The official recognition of this department followed in 1919. In England, the almoner (often the 'lady almoner') was created early in the century, both to understand the social setting of the patient and to invite the patient to contribute payment for her or his hospitalization. The role of the almoner was gone by the 1960s, at least in name, replaced by the 'Medical Social Worker.' Although the idea of social work has survived, in most hospitals the department and its practitioners remain marginal; hospitals are most concerned with life within their walls. The almoner (or social worker) was seen by the 1960s as being someone to take care of matters for which the consultant had no time: "Let the almoner deal with him — a consultant has no time for extra-mural comforting."[12]

## LIFE AS A PATIENT

It is easy to be nostalgic for a less technical past, for hospitals that were part of the community rather than "repair shops." Hospitals have always involved alienation, as patients moved into a strange environment where they had little control. But from about 1950, the alien nature of hospital wards became a frequent cause of complaint. As services grew more technical and more kinds of workers were involved, and as the economic gap between doctors and patients grew wider, patients worried that they were becoming anonymous. 'Mr Smith' too often became 'the fracture in (room) 304.'

In hospital, patients are no longer in control of their daily life. Even quite minute levels of detail — what the patient can wear, what he can eat, when he must get up — are decided by someone else. This loss of control over almost every aspect of a daily routine is consistently described as an alienating and frightening experience. Staff may at times disappear, sometimes leaving a patient "literally in midair in a lift to go on a coffee break."[13] Social boundaries, professional boundaries, personal boundaries are repeatedly subject to thoughtless violation. "Doctors walked into the bathroom to examine me on the commode... Maintenance staff were there to greet me when I walked out of the shower."[14] For patients who might be able to watch and listen but not move, even as seemingly simple a task as controlling the VCR may be beyond their reach, and they may find the machine shut off 15 minutes before the end of a movie by a staff member who never even looks at the patient, committing such a thoughtless act perhaps without even thinking about it. As in many institutional settings, patients in the hospital may feel better when they are allowed some token of their life outside, be it a favorite article of clothing, food cooked at home or according to their religious beliefs (as kosher food for a Jewish patient), or when they have a modicum of control over their daily routine.

Patients may find the experience of having to accommodate to the loss of personal privacy profoundly disquieting. A male patient may move from a world in which women have very little say in decision-making to a world in which women, women doctors or nurses, sometimes young women, are asking (and sometimes telling) him what to do. For some male patients (perhaps especially older ones), this new role may be profoundly disturbing to their sense of modesty and to their beliefs about the proper roles of men and women. Women may find personal questions and physical examinations by men a source of great discomfort. Staff attention to concerns about modesty and privacy will go far to make patients feel more at ease.

## DEVELOPING COUNTRIES

Hospitals in parts of the world other than the United States and Western Europe have presented a very different picture during the twentieth century, both to the outside observer and to the patients within. In some instances a Western medical system was imported first to care for the colonizers and only somewhat later to care for the indigenous population of the country. In India, hospitals based on explicitly British models served as vehicles for colonization and as a means of spreading Western medicine both within and outside of the urban centers.[15] Western medicine was not always used in constructive and benevolent ways. Some doctors served as allies of the colonial capitalists who used hospitals to enforce continued segregation of the native population, as was the case in parts of Africa. In other instances, hospitals took resources away from preventive health needs.

Many hospitals modeled on Western institutions offered a much more diverse range of therapeutic options than would at first meet the eye. Sometimes native healing practices accompanied Western medicine, occasionally without the senior medical staff knowing that this was going on. At other times ideas about the hospital were incorporated into the existing model of health; the hospital might be seen as a 'no go' area for the spirits that caused disease, but then the disease might well recur once a patient left the institution. Increasing globalization combined with the plight of refugees means that many patients in the US and England may elect to practice native healing practices while housed in modern hospitals.

Understanding this clash of cultures requires considerable work on the part of the care-givers, patients, and members of the community.[16]

Hospitals are different in areas that were not colonized. In post-revolutionary China, hospital organization has come to be based on the 'danwei,' or 'work unit.' Patients are referred to the hospital from their work unit, and the hospital provides housing for most members of the staff. All staff members wear the same type of coat, and the egalitarian dress means that one cannot easily distinguish different occupations from each other. The situation in China differs markedly from that in the neighboring, formerly colonial country of Vietnam, in which there are clear status codes associated with the clothing worn by hospital staff. The lack of overt hierarchy in China extends even to the discussion of a patient's case. Whereas in many Western hospitals the concept of privacy is held to be extremely important, in the Chinese hospital there are often no curtains between the beds. Patients make no attempt to conceal their interest in what's going on with the person next door; when one patient's case is being discussed at the bedside other patients may feel free to join the circle of people considering the diagnosis.

Patients in developing countries may have more access to their personal possessions, friends, relatives, and food, but they have distinctly less access to the sort of high technology that has come to characterize many Western hospitals. Hospital patients in China and Vietnam experience blood drawing or X-rays much less than those in the US; in Vietnamese hospitals in the 1960s intravenous infusions were taken out every afternoon because there was no one to watch over the patients through the evening. The reasons are in part economic — such technology is expensive, and if there is little money for health care, it may (appropriately) be spent not on fancy machines, but on sanitation and clean water. The reason may also be cultural, the belief that excellence in health care is machine-dependent may be less important in some parts of the world.

The boundaries around the hospital world are more permeable in some developing countries. For example, in the 1970s at a teaching hospital in India stray dogs and goats were said to wander around the wards, often carrying off fruit or other food that had been intended for patients. Patients' families frequently bring cooking utensils onto the ward and cook for their relatives in the hospital itself. The primary mission of a hospital often reflects specific local environment. In some parts of India the most notable need of a hospital is for the treatment of snake bites. A hospital always reflects the larger world. There is no single model of what an idealized hospital will be, nor is there any clear path that hospital change will follow in different countries or in different environments.

## RECENT CHANGES

The Second World War had a dramatic impact on health care in general, and on hospitals in particular. In England in the late 1930s, the Ministry of Health, expecting massive casualties in the coming war, paid hospitals to set aside beds to be used by injured soldiers and civilians, thus leading hospitals to start to count on regular government payments. Increasing attention to the relationship between city and country hospitals set the stage for the restructuring of the health system that was to follow the end of the war. But general and specialty hospitals (run by consultants) became remote from ambulatory care (provided by general practitioners). In the mid-1960s Rosemary Stevens saw the separation of the hospitals from the rest of the British system as a major problem and suggested that the hospital ought to be brought more into the center of the organization.

Over the past century hospitals have become much more dependent on the use of medical machines, in part as the result of technologies that simply were not available in 1900 such as CAT and MRI scanners. Different countries have coped with the new technologies differently. The US is clearly at one extreme in the use (and overuse) of medical technology, often to no apparent good end. Other countries have displayed more restraint. For example, the MRI (Magnetic Resonance Imaging) scanner is a sophisticated and expensive device for taking pictures from within the human body; in 1995 there were more scanners in prosperous Orange County, California, with its 2.4 million people, than in the entire country of Canada, with 27 million people.[17]

The hospital's place in the medical care system is also changing. Starting in the mid-1970s the per capita use of hospitals in the US started to decline. That fall continued during the late 1970s and the 1980s, a period that preceded the widespread implementation of prospective payment, and thus a period in which most payment systems continued to reward hospitals and physicians for increased utilization of hospital care. The reasons for this fall in the use of hospitals remain as yet unclear. Some have suggested that increased attention to ambulatory medicine among both administrators and patients (who may have correctly realized that hospitals had become inhospitable places to receive ambulatory care) may have played an important role, as well as perhaps increased autonomy among women who rejected the notion that childbirth required extended hospitalization. Another important factor was doubtless a feeling that the cost of health care was increasing too rapidly, and that hospitals (and the high technology they contain) were the cause of much of that increasing cost. On the other hand, although the initial cost of hospitalization may be considerable, the presence of excess capacity may mean that the true incremental costs of providing care in hospitals may not be all that high.[18] Day hospitals in the UK may contribute to a decrease in utilization of general hospitals.

For whatever reasons, recent years have seen a drastic shortening of the length of stay for people in the hospital. When the US president Dwight Eisenhower suffered a myocardial infarction ('heart attack') in 1955 he was confined to bed for three weeks to recuperate. Now he would be out of the hospital in about 6 days. One of the most contentious issues in the US has had to do with the usually much less morbid process of childbirth. At the start of the twentieth century women were encouraged to come into the hospital to deliver children; at the end of the century they are being pushed out of the door as fast as possible, so called 'drive-by deliveries.' In response, federal legislation has mandated insurance companies to cover minimum lengths of stay after childbirth; it is unlikely that many other conditions will result in this sort of legislative action. Many common operations such as hernia repairs and cataract extractions that once required a hospital stay of several days are now done without overnight admission. Of course, patients recovering from surgery must still be cared for, only now the work is done by family rather than by hospital staff. Were Carpenter Smith to be taken to a hospital today, his leg more likely broken by a car than a horse, he would probably not even spend the night in the hospital. In fact, he might well find himself seen and treated at a separate location, perhaps one carrying the name of the hospital but located dozens of kilometers away, a reflection of the diffuse nature of the health care system at the end of the twentieth century.

Another major, recent change in hospitals has reflected a wider belief in the value of patients' feelings and beliefs. Who gets to decide what a hospital should be like? Partly in reaction against 'technocracy,' and partly in response to a new 'market sensitivity,' patients are being asked about their preferences for hospital accommodation. The results have been surprisingly mixed. Some patients want privacy and are willing to pay for it. Other patients seem not to care, and a considerable proportion of patients would rather have a companion than be left alone for most of their waking hours; patients who suffer from vision problems tend to want companionship more than others. But there is more to the desirability of a hospital room than simply how many bodies are placed within. Patients pay a lot of attention to their hospital room — after all, they have plenty of time to look at it. Windows are important, making patients feel less imprisoned in their rooms. Patients like scenic views; they also seem to like even views of demolition and construction work, perhaps because it gives them something to watch as the days pass. Recent studies suggest that following surgery, patients with more scenic views require less medication for relief of pain. Modern hospitals are increasingly being built so that patients can see outside, even from their beds.

There are cultural differences in hospital design involving the nursing staff. In Britain, perhaps because of the influence of Florence Nightingale, there is less interest in private rooms and more emphasis on the need for supervision. Nurses wish to be able directly to see — or at least to hear — all of the patients on their ward. If there are to be areas that cannot be seen by the nursing staff some form of communication becomes essential, be it a call buzzer, an intercom, or a telephone. But during the day such systems are used far more often by staff than by patients, far too often in an attempt to locate staff, a kind of 'paging' system that irritates far more than it succeeds. In the evening the calls tended to be more often from patients seeking assistance.

This end-of-the-century emphasis on patients' autonomy is changing, yet again, the experience of hospitals. Were he to be admitted today, Carpenter Smith might well have been asked to weigh in with an opinion on the type of care he would receive. Patients have to pay more attention to what is going on, but this attention may not always make patients any happier. As one recalled when a spinal tap was discussed, "It did little to lower my anxiety when [the physician] explained the details of this to me ... a collapse might occur, which would then cause my rapid death. I had no idea such possibilities were even in the air, and the explanation gave me some uneasy hours. It was apparent that [the physician] was not particularly sensitive to the need for acting reassuringly..."[19] In 1900, Mr Smith probably would not have thought of reading his case record; many late-twentieth century patients not only would ask for it, but would be allowed access to their record in detail without such a request being seen as unusual.

Once community hospitals were seen as great sources of pride. That may still be the case, but pride has its costs. In the US, many smaller hospitals sit with the majority of their beds unoccupied, the victims of better means of transportation and communication that lead to local patients going elsewhere for care, often leaving small-town hospitals the victims of integrated and overtly profit-oriented systems that see consolidation of regional care as more consistent with a market-oriented structure. Many hospitals in small towns have closed and many more are at risk. The role of the public hospital in the US seems also to be in jeopardy. One in five public hospitals closed between 1979 and 1996, leaving many to question whether the goals of the public hospital could (or would) be adequately met through other sources of health care.

Experiences in hospitals are not confined to patients. Health care consumes an ever-increasing portion of the economy, and more and more people are involved in hospitals, either as direct providers of care to patients (physicians, nurses, social workers, technicians, etc.) or as part of the support staff that enables the large and complex institution to continue to function. The National Health Service is the largest employer in the United Kingdom. In the US, hospitals have created elaborate catering services, incorporating on their grounds fast food providers, more sedate restaurants, newsstands, and even substantial shopping precincts. Moreover, as hospitals shorten their length of stay and join forces with providers of outpatient care, the 'hospital' is frequently being renamed the 'medical center,' co-ordinating many kinds and sites of caring. The meaning of 'hospital' is changing fast.

In a sense, this encyclopedia chapter, completed in the middle of 1997, is being written at the wrong time. Hospitals are under increasing pressure to modify their patterns of care, to move patients such as Carpenter Smith in and out of the hospital not in weeks to months but in hours to days. Yet late twentieth-century hospitals continue to evoke a sense of wonder. They are seen as performing life-saving work; they are seen as a place where elite physicians practice. Despite the recent US enthusiasm for primary care, many Americans continue to believe that optimum health care is carried out by a specialist, usually one associated with a hospital. During the century, many meanings have defined the institution known as the hospital. It is unclear what the future will bring, what the twenty-first century will hold for hospitals around the globe. Yet it seems likely that the meaning of a 'hospital' will continue to change in ways that reflect the many social environments in which such institutions are and will be created.

## REFERENCES

I wish to thank Carl Schneider for allowing me to consult his incomparable collection of patients' accounts of their illness. This work was suppported by a Robert Wood Johnson Foundation Investigator Award in Health Policy Research and by a Burroughs Wellcome Fund Award in the History of Medicine.

1. John D. Thompson and Grace Goldin, *The Hospital: A Social and Architectural History.* (New Haven: Yale University Press, 1975), p. 159.
2. Grace Goldin, *Work of Mercy: A Picture History of Hospitals.* (Ontario: Boston Mills Press, 1994), p. 188.
3. Asa S. Bacon, 'Efficient Hospitals,' *Journal of the American Medical Association* (1920), **74**: 123–126.
4. Gilda Radner, *It's Always Something.* (New York: Avon Books, 1989), p. 70.
5. Thompson and Goldin, *The Hospital*, p. 216.
6. Joseph Heller and Speed Vogel, *No Laughing Matter.* (New York: G.P. Putnam's Sons, 1986), p. 84.
7. Cecilia M. Roberts, *Doctor and Patient in the Teaching Hospital: A Tale of Two Life-Worlds.* (Lexington Massachusetts: Lexington Books, 1977), pp. 51–65.
8. James L. Johnson, *Coming Back.* (Springhouse Publishing, 1979), p. 12.
9. William F. Sayers, *Don't Die on My Shift.* (Canoga Park, California: Major Books, 1977), p. 65.
10. Philip Inman, *The Human Touch.* (London: Geoffrey, 1927), p. 105.
11. Margot Jefferys, 'Britain's National Health Service in 1986: Comments From a Native User,' in Marilynn M. Rosenthal and Marcel Frenkel (eds), *Health Care Systems and Their Patients: An International Perspective.* (Boulder, Colorado: Westview Press, 1992), pp. 240–241.
12. G.L. Cohen, *What's Wrong With Hospitals?* (iii, 57, 1964), quoted in the Oxford English Dictionary, 2nd ed., under 'extramural.'
13. Arnold R. Beisse, *Flying Without Wings.* (New York: Doubleday, 1989), p. 35.
14. Judith Alexander Brice, 'Ulcerative Colitis and Avascular Necrosis of Hips,' in Harvey Mandell and Howard Spiro (eds), *When Doctors Get Sick.* (New York: Plenum Medical, 1988), 171–192, at p. 179.
15. David Arnold, 'The Rise of Western Medicine in India,' *Lancet* (1996), **348**: 1075–1078.
16. Anne Fadiman, *The Spirit Catches You and You Fall Down, A Hmong Child, Her American Doctors, and the Collision of Two Cultures.* (New York: Noonday Press, 1997).
17. Steven A. Schroeder, 'Cost Containment in U.S. Health Care,' *Academic Medicine* (1995), **70**: 861–866.
18. Uwe E. Rienhardt, 'Spending More Through "Cost Control:" Our Obsessive Quest to Gut the Hospital,' *Health Affairs* (Summer, 1996), **15**: 145–154.
19. Ernest A. Hirsch, *Starting Over.* (North Quincy, Mass: Christopher Publishing House, 1977), pp. 24–25.

## FURTHER READING

Abel-Smith, Brian, *The Hospitals, 1880–1948: A Study in Social Administration in England and Wales.* (Cambridge, Mass.: Harvard University Press, 1964).
Feierman, Steven and Janzen, John M., *The Social Basis of Health and Healing in Africa.* (Berkeley: University of California Press, 1992).
Freidson, Eliot (ed.), *The Hospital in Modern Society.* (New York: Free Press, 1963).
Gamble, Vanessa Northington, *Making a Place for Ourselves: The Black Hospital Movement, 1920–1945.* (New York: Oxford University Press, 1995).
Granshaw, Lindsay and Porter, Roy (eds), *The Hospital in History.* (London: Routledge, 1989).
Long, Diana Elizabeth and Golden, Janet (eds), *The American General Hospital: Communities and Social Contexts.* (Ithaca: Cornell University Press, 1989).

Henderson, Gail, *The Chinese Hospital: A Socialist Work Unit.* (New Haven: Yale University Press, 1984).

Howell, Joel D., *Technology in the Hospital: Transforming Patient Care in the Early Twentieth Century.* (Baltimore: Johns Hopkins University Press, 1995).

Pickstone, John V., *Medicine and Industrial Society: A History of Hospital Development in Manchester and Its Region, 1752–1946.* (Manchester: Manchester University Press, 1985).

Risse, Guenter B., *Mending Bodies, Saving Souls: A History of Hospitals.* (New York: Oxford University Press, 1999).

Rosenberg, Charles E., *The Care of Strangers: The Rise of America's Hospital System.* (New York: Basic Books, 1987).

Rosenthal, Marilynn M. and Frenkel, Marcel (eds), *Health Care Systems and Their Patients: An International Perspective.* (Boulder, Colorado: Westview Press, 1992).

Rosner, David, *A Once Charitable Enterprise: Hospitals and Health Care in Brooklyn and New York, 1885–1915.* (Cambridge: Cambridge University Press, 1982).

Stevens, Rosemary, *Medical Practice in Modern England: The Impact of Specialization and State Medicine.* (New Haven: Yale University Press, 1966).

Stevens, Rosemary, *In Sickness and In Wealth: American Hospitals in the Twentieth Century.* (New York: Basic Books, 1989).

Terry, Susan, *House of Love: Life in A Vietnamese Hospital.* (London: Newnes, 1966).

Vogel, Morris, *The Invention of the Modern Hospital: Boston 1870–1930.* (Chicago: University of Chicago Press, 1980).

# Chapter 33

# Nurses

## Anne Marie Rafferty

The history of nursing in the twentieth century is the history of tensions and colliding contradictions. While the image of the nurse as angel in white dominates the public perception of nursing, the experience of nursing revolves around these tensions. This chapter considers a typology of tensions and their ordering around a series of dichotomies including: occupation/profession, unionized labour/profession, doctor/nurse, civil/military, matron/rank and file, amateur/professional, art/craft/science, apprenticeship/higher education, task/research based-activity, regional/national, qualified/unqualified, immigrant/indigenous, government/professional autonomy, central/local relations, male/female, community/hospital, public/private, proximity/distance, and generalist/specialist. A second related theme tracked here is the mythical imagery of uniformity in the profession as 'general' nursing. Behind the image lurk many identities and specialist nurses working in a range of social and geographical settings: mental, mental deficiency, district/community, industrial, school, tuberculosis, pediatric, orthopedic, and professionally-driven/managed care. This chapter concentrates upon the UK and US, but material and examples will be 'imported' from other areas as appropriate. Central to the discussion is how these dichotomies and tensions arose and how they were transformed over the twentieth century. There is no single totalizing experience or explanation of nursing within this period. There exists only the manner and means by which the social and political tensions traverse and translate across time and space throughout the century.

### REFRAMING THE IMAGE

Nursing reinvents itself when the political and ideological tide turns. Reports of striking nurses in South Africa in 1996 shocked our cultural expectations and offended our moral sensibilities of what we assumed the ethical basis of a nurse's conduct ought to be. Extreme economic pressure and the complex and competing demands on resources and health care have contributed to a crisis of caring and a massive challenge to governments and nursing organizations worldwide. But strike action by nurses is not new; it can be dated to the turn of the century when female nurses lead one of the earliest industrial protests in nursing at the Radcliffeon-Soar Asylum near Nottingham. Salutary and shocking lessons lie in nursing's historical store. Nursing in Nazi Germany, for example, entailed rationalizations of the pernicious practice of easing to death those in 'care.' There can be few more poignant and sinister examples than this of the way in which the political context shapes the content of nursing practice, and of the profound contradiction it raises with the image of nurses as 'angels.' The contradistinction between the nurse as nasty, nefarious neer-do-well, and the innocent, irridescent angel shows how strong and stable our stereotypes are and how difficult they are to subvert and shake off. However, the written history of nursing in the twentieth century has been dominated by the history of professionalization. Partly this is a result of the overlapping role of nurse leaders as historians, and the opportunistic symbiosis that has emerged between the historical and leadership agendas. Inevitably, this history has privileged the view from the top and high politics. Thus the aims, ambitions and strategies of the leadership are much better known than those of the clinical nurses and, least of all, patients. Moreoever the dominant reference point for the history of nursing remains that of general hospital nursing. Hidden from history has been the domiciliary nurse and her fellow workers, along with mental nurses, learning disabilities nurses, fever and children's nurses. Health visitors, nurses in different specialisms, tuberculosis, and orthopedic nurses have all been obscured from view. Part of this double marginalization may be due to erratic preservation policies. Certain groups of nurses have been harder to reach, especially if not associated with those institutions which are all too self-consciously aware of their own role in history. Training and educational programs have been designed to provide safeguards in the form of acceptable and desirable standards of behavior and practice. Yet fear of nurses' authority and the potential to exploit opportunities for self advancement at the expense of vulnerable patients is a recurring anxiety which runs through the early fictional portraits of nurses and nursing history. Not surprisingly therefore the emphasis in recruitment and training has tended to stress moral purity and the provision of a social insurance system against mishap and misdemeanor. Hence the qualifications of nurses, in contrast to doctors, came to be defined in terms of character rather than intellect. Nurses tended to be portrayed by reformers as agents of socialization and 'civilization,' a tradition in which the European nurse excelled and provided a model for emulation.

Exchanges of expertise presuppose some common standards of qualification and reciprocity of registration across national jurisdictions. From the early part of the century international meetings provided an important channel through which ideas on nurses' registration and organization were disseminated. Like many women's international organizations formed before World War I, the International Council of Nurses (ICN) was a communication and support network for national nurse leaders who subscribed to a common set of values. It also operated as a pressure group whose political ethos revolved around a shared commitment to improving the economic and social status of nurses and women. This commitment translated into state registration plus the provision of nationally-determined standards of nursing education. Together these two variables were to define what it meant to be a trained nurse.

## COLONIAL CARE

Throughout the twentieth century organisations such as the Colonial Nursing Association (CNA) promised travel and travail to candidates keen to cut their clinical teeth in the colonies: "Join the Colonial Nursing Association and see the world ... you too can become one of the women pioneers ... blazing civilisation's trail in far corners of the world." This jaunty exhortation, published in *Good Housekeeping* in 1949, was one of many used to market the Association to potential recruits. Throughout the twentieth century the CNA recruited nurses to work in different parts of the British Empire. 'Skilled' nursing, by which was meant European nursing, was unobtainable in many isolated parts of the Empire. British officials, settlers and their families were thought to suffer excessive ill-health and hardship as a consequence. Doctors, in particular, were thought to be compromised in what they could achieve, and inconvenienced by having to act as nurses themselves! Nursing was therefore seized upon as an adjunct to the Colonial Medical Service and as crucial to the success of government hospitals throughout the 'Empire.'

The role of nursing and health care in imperial practice forces us to confront the ways in which cultural power is mediated through clinical practices and ideologies, and how these collide and coalesce in the process of cultural reconnaissance. Barbara Brush has pointed to the long term consequences of American attempts to introduce public health nursing in the Phillippines during the interwar period. This, she argued, introduced a pipeline of labor ready to replenish the registered nursing workforce in the US as American hospitals expanded in the post-Second World War period. A similar argument can be applied to nursing in Britain in the 1950s and '60s where the training schools in the colonies were recruiting grounds for hard-pressed matrons in search of a ready-made supply of subordinate labor.

## WARRING FACTIONS

All this came to be challenged by the outbreak of World War I. The effort to provide an adequate supply of nurses in the war effort brought about the 'birth' in Britain of the Voluntary Aid Detachment (VADs). The VAD's shorter form of training filled the purists of nursing reform with anxiety. The war exerted considerable effect upon public attitudes towards women in general and nurses in particular. But the flood of volunteers coupled with the redistribution of nurses between hospitals and sectors, and the return of nurses to civilian employment stretched administrators to achieve an appropriate structure for grading staff and for matching skills to needs.

The end of World War I also witnessed a wave of industrial assertiveness which induced some general nurses to unionize. Women workers had become increasingly assertive in their demands for improved pay and conditions. Female membership of unions had risen from 183,000 in 1910 to 1,086,000 by the end of 1918. The Asylum Workers' Association had been formed as an alternative to the Royal British Nurses Association (RBNA) by doctors prominent in the Royal Medico-Psychological Association (RMPA), but it eschewed any connection with trade unionism. Ten years later it was eclipsed in membership strength by the National Asylum Workers' Union (NAWU) and it was finally superseded by the latter in 1919. By 1920, membership of NAWU stood at 16,000 of which 7,000 were women. The Poor Law Workers' Trade Union was also established in 1918, and its officer counterpart, the National Poor Law Officers' Association became increasingly assertive in the aftermath of the war. Significantly, the nursing press contained extensive comment on the question of unionization in nursing but remained divided in its support.

Meanwhile the movement for nurses' registration became split between those who favored a less stringent market-oriented approach, backed by the College of Nursing, established in 1916, and those who advocated a levelling up of standards regardless of employers' needs. The introduction of a government Bill for nurse registration at the end of war has been traditionally explained in terms of the combined outcome of the occupation's unity in the face of potential dilution from an influx of VADs, and a movement of public and political sympathy towards measures which enhanced the status of women, as reflected in the extension of the franchise in 1918. But government intervention in Britain was only forthcoming when it became complementary to the establishment of the Ministry of Health in 1918 and the centralization of administrative arrangements for health policy after the war. Registration provided the means of promoting industrial stability simultaneously with regulating the conduct of nurse training and discipline.

## UNITY AND DISUNITY

One issue which remained unresolved by registration and proved a constant scourge throughout the inter-war period was the place of specialist groups within the 'new' profession that would be created by registration. A 'caste' system existed in nursing according to which midwives, mental, male, fever and children's nurses were regarded as inferior due to their shorter training. Specialists allegedly lacked the all-round competence of the general nurse at a time when specialism was denigrated rather than lauded. Thus specialist nurses were to be relegated to a supplementary (peripheral), rather than general (central) part, of the register in the various Bills put forward to Parliament. One of the chief arguments against separate and specialist qualifications was that they provided a 'back door' into the profession for 'inferior' practitioners. Nurses who qualified for entry on the supplementary register (mental nurses, male nurses, childrens' and fever nurses) were branded as semi-educated.

Throughout the 1930s the General Nursing Council (GNC), which had been set up by the Nurses' Registration Act in 1919, was forced to respond to the intensifying demographic pressures which threatened to reduce the supply of nursing labor. In the course of its work as a validation body for training institutions and as a gatekeeper to entry into the occupation, the Council was forced to confront the interdependence of the service and the educational implications of its work. State sponsorship of nursing through registration proved to be a blunt instrument with which to regulate the supply of nursing labor. Little changed for the rank and file. High levels of wastage and poor conditions persisted, old and new tensions arose in the form of bureaucratic control versus professional power. Complications associated with competing certifications combined with sectional disputes between specialists and generalists-unions and professions continued to structure the politics of nursing, leaving power vested in the hands of the metropolitan elite. The dispersed and divided nature of nursing's power base left it too weak to resist the incursions of the state. Furthermore the voluntary hospital sector continued to act as a drag on reform. Economic retrenchment and the political economy of welfare ensured that depressed levels of remuneration fomented frustration, demonstrating that demoralization was never far from the surface.

Before 1937, the Trades Union Council (TUC) paid little attention to nursing. However, by the end of the year it had convened a 'Joint Advisory Council for the Nursing Profession' to consider improvements in organisation. A 'Draft Charter for the Nursing Profession' was drawn up containing eleven demands related to conditions of service and training, but rival charters were produced by different union organizations in competition with each other as well as with the College. This fragmentation of effort weakened overall union effectiveness. The Royal College of Nursing (RCN) fought a determined rearguard action to wrest the political advantage from the TUC, but it was hampered in its endeavors by its apolitical stance.

## WAR AND WELFARE

The outbreak of the Second World War precipitated a crisis in nurse staffing as preparations for receiving casualties began to be undertaken. Expanding the quality, quantity and distribution of nursing and hospital services presupposed a sound basis for planning. At the beginning of hostilities this was not available. Officials had little appreciation of the variable standard of hospital accommodation. As the Director General of the Emergency Medical Service (EMS) remarked in 1939 "even those institutions that want to be regarded as the centres of enlightenment and teaching in our large cities are with few exceptions structurally unsafe or antiquated." In establishing the EMS the Ministry of Health had to weld together the facilities of a disparate range of resources, standards, value systems and heritages.

But standards in some institutions had deteriorated to such an extent that they were regarded as contributors to the rise of mortality from dysentery and TB. Short and longer-term strategies were adopted to boost the supply of nursing labor. Remedying the maldistribution of the nursing workforce implied rationalizing payments to nurses of different grades.

Intelligence tests were seized upon as a solution to selection and recruitment. Their apparent capacity to discriminate between innate talent and educational background was considered especially useful in selecting recruits of poor educational attainment but with intellectual promise. Yet, in nursing circles and in government, conflicting views were held on the need for nurses to be intelligent. Curricular discussions revealed a degree of anti-intellectualism which assumed that intelligence and practical skill in nurses were incompatible. Like teachers, some argued, the best scholars did not always make the best practitioners.

The wartime emergency health services had a number of important consequences for nurses. One was the acceptance by all political parties that there could be no return to the pre-war heterogeneity of health care. The state had not only come to assume financial responsibility for health services, but also to be a major co-ordinating force in the health service, including the direction and control of labor. Job analysis was considered crucial to determining training needs and selecting personnel by policy makers. Demographic data on sources of recruitment, social composition of the workforce, educational history and pre-nursing education, were all identified as appropriate for investigation. Comparative studies of different training methods such as the 'block' versus the 'sandwich' systems were also to be considered. Morale was a priority issue and its relationship to the quality of leadership in institutions examined. Social relationships between different levels of the nursing hierarchy were to be scrutinized. Discipline, the use (and abuse) of authority, and opportunities for nurses to lead 'normal' lives were regarded as particularly important. All of these recommendations were contained in the post-war investigation, the Working Party on the Recruitment and Training of Nurses, which was unique in its endeavor to draw comparisons between countries such as the US, Finland, and selected Commonwealth countries. Nevertheless, it was in this context that one of the most radical critiques of nurse recruitment and education emanated from a psychologist and civil servant, Dr John Cohen. This Minority Report, signed by Cohen and Geoffrey Pyke in 1948, was an emphatically personal document recording the authors' commitment to the integration of health care within the wider socio-political and economic context. It denounced the 'muddling through' approach to policy-making and presented a plea for the rational organization of nursing and health services within a planned economy. Cohen, in particular, used nursing to publicize his views on the methodological weaknesses in health-service planning more generally. Indeed debates about nursing in the early health service prefigured many of the planning problems which were to plague generations of NHS policy-makers. Nursing problems, Cohen asserted, could only ever be amenable to solution if examined in the context of wider health service developments. An integrated and comprehensive approach to health service, attentive to social and economic planning, was fundamental to the optimum use of man and woman-power. Health was to be co-ordinated within the master plan of the national economy.

## ENGINEERING EFFICIENCY

Cohen was also convinced that an understanding of the emotional and social factors in human behavior was crucial to understanding the dynamics of change more generally. Cohen's theorising on productivity in nursing reflected the wider research tradition of industrial psychology, especially in America. Improving human relations in hospitals, it was hoped, would enhance productivity in the same way as it had in factories. Training effectiveness and retention of staff could therefore be improved by enriching training and reshaping the division of labor. Underlying Cohen's contentions was a faith in scientific management as the key to efficiency. Scientific management could simultaneously justify the adoption or eradication of 'functional' or task allocation. It could imply greater control and autonomy over nursing work and was therefore imbued with a strong emancipatory appeal to those committed to professionalism. The efficiency movement, which had infiltrated American nursing by the late 1940s, legitimized the authority of psychologists to measure, design and determine nursing work. A leaner but intellectually more demanding form of training and work organization promised greater satisfaction for rank and file nurses.

But a thoroughgoing analysis of nursing work was deferred until the Nuffield Provincial Hospital Trust seized the initiative by funding a large-scale study in the early 1950s. This was the first full-blown attempt to quantify and qualify the scope and so-called 'proper' sphere of nursing work. One of the acknowledged drawbacks of the 'time and motion' approach to nursing care was the difficulty of capturing the social and psychological aspects of care. It was noted that factors such as 'mental worry' could impede a patient's recovery and researchers were somewhat surprised to find the small amount of time spent in personal conversation with patients. While some nurses rejected the division between the physical, medical and emotional as artificial, the fear of being admonished for wasting time was given as one reason for not doing so. The possibility that emotional care was incorporated within the physical signalled a contradiction in care that remained an enduring part of the nursing work ethic.

## MANAGING TO CARE

Techniques of work study and those derived from industrial psychology attempted to compute the calculus of nursing care prior to ascertaining an appropriate division of labor both within nursing, and between nursing and other health care workers. Underlying such a project was the notion that streamlining labour was the key to efficiency and economy in the management of a crucial health service resource. Several strategies have been employed in different health systems to contain expenditure, ranging from rationing or removing services, imposing charges and cost-shifting to incomes policies, and finally management. Lack of success in containing expenditure by direct central government means led policy makers in the 1960s and 1970s to look to management for other ways of extracting efficiency. It was against this background that the Salmon Committee proposals on the Structure of Senior Nurse Staffing in the UK were introduced into nursing, enabling nurses to take their place within the management fashion of the time — consensus management. The Senior Nurse Staffing Committee reported in 1966 that, as a step towards modernizing nurse management, nurses adapt to the new environments of the recently launched Hospital Building Plan. For the first time nurses had management structures that could give them parity with other professional workers — an important step towards consensus management.

Consensus management reached its hey-day in the 1970s. By the 1980s the tide of managerial opinion changed from professional consortia working towards agreed objectives, to a rejection of this on the grounds that it led to conservative and inefficient outputs (while featherbedding both managers and workers at the expense of consumers). Just as British industry and services were to become more market-oriented, if they were to become internationally competitive, so nurses were to be prepared to give people what they wanted rather than what producers provided. This led to a new management philosophy in which speed, cost and decisiveness, rather than consensus, were to the fore. Within the new system faster responses to changing market conditions were required to overcome the cumbersome processes that consensus management could achieve. The critique of professionalism wrought by the new managerialism was one in which peer patrol merely induced professional profligacy. The extravagance of professional expertise was to be replaced by a spectrum of review techniques ranging from quality assurance, clinical audit, and performance indicators in various forms and guises. Much of this scrutiny was external and seen as a direct attack upon clinical autonomy, against which certain groups, such as doctors and less successful nurses, fought a rearguard action. Caught in the anti-professional fervour of Thatcherism, nursing saw its influence in policy circles dismantled, delayered and downsized.

## HIGHER ASPIRATIONS

In the 1980s nursing came under increasing scrutiny from social scientists keen to explore the psycho-social dynamics of nursing care, its different organizational forms and its effects on outcomes such as productivity, patient recovery, staff turnover and morale. In Britain, the lack of a well-developed research infrastructure and a robust higher education system for nurses, led to models of care organization being imported from the US. The development of university programs for nursing in the UK, of which the first was located at Edinburgh University, were heavily influenced by American intellectual leadership mediated through the Rockefeller Foundation (RF). The RF sponsored travel fellowships, provided seed-corn funding for the department and helped to create the networks through which innovations and ideas could flow across the Atlantic. The location of the Edinburgh department within a social science faculty laid down an intellectual legacy that was to exert significant influence upon the disciplinary development of nursing in Britain.

The halting history of the development of higher education for nurses in the UK only shifted seismically when nursing became one of the largest beneficiaries of, and contributors to, its 'massification' in the 1990s. It remains to be seen however, how enduring such potential benefits might be in the face of health reforms driven by increasing pressure for cost-containment, local pay bargaining, and reductions in junior hospital doctors' hours. All of these have generated major stresses and strains for nurses as the front-line workers, and increased the complexity of nursing work whose boundaries are in flux both at the top and tail ends of the nursing division of labour.

## 'No Good Lines'

It has taken more than 40 years for the image of nursing as a career requiring intelligence to find its way into official recruitment material. Nurse Ratchet, so vividly portrayed in Ken Kesey's *One Flew Over the Cuckoo's Nest*, has given way to Michael Crichton's science-smart-looking and talking nurses in the popular television program *ER*. However, nurses in celluloid still tend to be peripheral characters performing supporting roles, literally. Rarely are they given the good lines unless they are breaking the mould. The Puerto Rican male nurse in Tony Kushner's epic dramatization of the AIDS epidemic, *Angels in America*, is one such case. Kushner's nurse combines the qualities of acerbic and astringent wit with intelligence, compassion, camp competence and caring. Perhaps it is noteworthy that Kushner's nurse is also male.

As the sociology of the professions takes gender into its analysis, our understanding of nursing as adjunct medical labor is beginning to emerge. The shape and form of nursing in the next millennium not only depends upon medicine, but also, upon the funding and organization of health care. Symbiosis and reciprocity between different health care workers are likely to become an increasing part of future health-care systems. But nothing is fixed or predictable. In Romania, for example, Caecescu abolished nurse training for the decade preceding his own demise. After the revolution, nursing in Rumania is in the process of rapid reinvention and looking towards Europe and the US for models of practice to adopt and emulate.

Similarly the urgency and complexity of South Africa's historical legacy is in the process of unravelling. Some public hospitals have been plunged into crisis wrought by the need to expand access to services without concomitant increase in resources.

The crisis has stimulated a stream of strikes and press reports suggesting that conditions in some public hospitals have deteriorated to an all-time moral(e) and economic low. Such catastrophes of care have taken place in a context of intensifying pressure on services and overstretched and underpaid staff. They symbolize the stress and tinder box conditions under which nurses are required to work and patients are expected to be nursed. Investment in infrastructure, training, education and management practices, especially in more remote and rural areas, is urgently required.

## CONCLUSION

At the end of the twentieth century nurses in industrialized countries are caught in a web of contradictions. As emotional laborers in the vineyard of health care they titrate the tension between the ideology of intimacy advocated by nurse leaders and the increasingly impersonal nature of services occasioned by the intensification of care. Attempts to 'scientize' and 'sanitize' nursing knowledge by placing it upon a rational footing continue apace. Indeed, direct continuity exists between the rationale underpinning the introduction and importation from the US in the 1970s of care planning via the nursing process, and the 'evidence-based' movement in health care of the 1980s and '90s. Thus, where the nursing process sought to inject a scientific and systematic ethos and approach into patient care, in doing so it drew attention to gaps in knowledge which could well have provided the basis for a research agenda for nursing. No such initiative, however, was taken forward. Instead, the magnetic managerial qualities of the nursing process converted it into a tool for enhancing professional accountability. The promise of the nursing process was never fulfilled, since it presupposed a high concentration of graduates, capable of articulating the content and context of care operating ideally within an academically-supported clinical career structure. Management's hegemony continues through 'managed care,' a phrase that perhaps embodies the ultimate contradiction. Process reingineering and multi-professional education seem set to further blur the boundaries between nursing and other groups. Whatever, as health care reform in 1990s America demonstrates, doctors will not give up their power easily to any breed of nurse without a fight, no matter how superlative in substitutive capacity. Similarly, if the traditional professional paradigm shifts into multi-professionalism(s), so too will our conception of nursing history. Those groups hitherto hidden may well turn out to be nursing's greatest assets in the much vaunted shift to community-based care. But above all nursing needs to strengthen its kinship connections with advocacy, consumer, and care groups. Is the consumer role the latest stage in the 'career' of the patient? What will this mean in the context of a multi-professional agenda? Will the nurse of the past become an anachronism, a figment of the future? Historical and cultural comparisons reminds us that a nurse is and is not a nurse. There is no stable or single historical image or category of 'nurse'. Riven with rivalries and famously fragmented, nursing is subject to the structural inequalities of race, class and gender, deriving in part from nursing's colonial legacy and own historical processes of internal stratification. Whatever agenda emerges for health care in the twenty-first century, the most poignant paradox would be that we look back wistfully to a legacy that was lost with the eradication of Dickins' Mrs Gamp. Was it not the unregulated and disparaged Gamp of the pre-reform era who exercised a level of autonomy to which the professionalizers of nursing have come to aspire? The irony might be that history proves Mrs Gamp to be the most enduring nursing model of all.

## FURTHER READING

Abel-Smith, B., *A History of the Nursing Profession.* (London: Heinemann, 1960).

Dingwall, R., Rafferty, A.M. and Webster, C., *An Introduction to the Social History of Nursing.* (London: Routledge, 1988).

Fairman, J. and Lynaugh, J., *Critical Care Nursing: A History.* (Philadelphia: University of Pennsylvania Press, 1998).

Hart, C., *Behind the Mask: Nurses, Their Unions and Nursing Policy.* (London: Balliere Tindall, 1994).

Lewenson, S., *Taking Charge: Nursing, Suffrage and Feminism, 1873–1929.* (New York: Garland Press, 1993).

Marks, S., *Divided Sisterhood: Race, Class and Gender in the South African Nursing Profession.* (London: Macmillan, 1994).

MacPherson, K., *Bedside Matters: The Transformation of Canadian Nursing, 1900–1990.* (Toronto: Oxford University Press, 1998).

Melosh, B., *The Physician's Hand: Work and Culture in American Nursing.* (Philadelphia: Temple University Press, 1984).

Reverby, S., *Ordered to Care: The Dilemma of American Nursing.* (Cambridge: Cambridge University Press, 1987).

Rafferty, A.M., *The Politics of Nursing Knowledge.* (London: Routledge, 1996).

Rafferty, A.M., Robinson, J. and Elkan, R. (eds). *Nursing, Women's History and the Politics of Welfare.* (London: Routledge, 1997).

Strachan, G., *Labour of Love: The History of the Nurse's Association in Queensland 1860–1950.* (Sydney: Allen and Unwin, 1996).

Summers, A., *Angels and Citizens: British Women as Military Nurses 1854–1914.* (London: Routledge, 1988).

Webster, C., *The Politics of the National Health Service.* (Oxford: Oxford University Press, 1998).

White, R., *The Effect of the National Health Service upon the Nursing Profession.* (Oxford: Oxford University Press, 1988).

# CHAPTER 34

# Health Workers

GERRY LARKIN

Medicine in the twentieth century is characterized by its ever-growing workforce and by an increase in the number of types of health worker. At the beginning of the century the division of labor was limited in range; one profession, that of doctors, was recognized and a few other occupations such as nursing and midwifery were beginning to consolidate the formal patterns of training and qualifications characteristic of modern professions. This is not to deny that nineteenth-century formal health care held its own complexities, involving other personnel such as pharmacists, administrators and hospital staff of various kinds in addition to doctors and nurses. However, this earlier complexity still stands in contrast to the proliferation of the many types of health worker during the twentieth century.

The term 'health worker' cuts across the many differences in status found in health care employment, but cannot cover every occupation required, for example, to run a modern hospital, from surgeons to plumbers. If we confine the definition to workers immediately involved in the treatment of patients, we still exclude groups such as managers who are increasingly influencing the shape and direction of health care in many countries. Nonetheless, this narrower definition will be used here.

The division of labor immediately surrounding the treatment of patients has been profoundly influenced in modern times by the expansion and accumulation of medical knowledge. Towards the end of the nineteenth century, medicine experienced a number of major innovations, which promoted new specialities and more effective interventions. The discovery of the principles of asepsis, of the medical uses of X-rays, of new drug applications in anesthesia and treatment, and the growing knowledge of the micro processes of human physiology and biochemistry, all helped to diversify medical work and to stimulate the emergence of twentieth-century specialties in medical and surgical practice. As Stevens points out, by 1900, most large hospitals in England had departments for obstetrics, children, skin diseases, electricity, radiography, otolaryngology, ophthalmology, anesthesiology and orthopedics. Specialization, however, although gathering force at this time was still on the fringe of medical practice, and its practitioners were subject to opposition from generalists in medicine and surgery. In the ensuing decades, however, specialization became the norm in hospital medicine. The precise numbers of specialties found depend on definition, country in question and year of measurement, but by way of illustration, by the 1980s Britain's National Health Service classified hospital medical staff into fifty-four categories. By this point, pathology alone had become sub-divided into practitioners specializing in general pathology, blood transfusion, chemical pathology, hematology, histopathology, immune-pathology, medical microbiology, virology and neuropathology.

Specialization within medicine was matched by specialization between a number of emergent paramedical health professions. Indeed, specialization within the medical profession would not have been possible without specialization between medicine and other health care occupations. This link has been central to the formation, identity and everyday experience of the health care workforce. Before examining this relationship, however, the scale of complexity in this second zone of specialization can be illustrated, again by NHS statistics which group paramedical professions and occupations into forty categories (excluding nurses and midwives), ranging from chiropodists to medical physicists. As in the case of medical specialization, paramedical occupations vary across countries, in terms of occupational boundaries and of work-specifications. Nonetheless, in the overall picture of paramedical complexity Britain is typical of all advanced health care systems. By the late 1970s, for example, the American Medical Association and the American Hospital Association were involved through their Allied Health Accreditation program in the recognition of twenty-three allied health professions. The American Society of Allied Health Professions in the same period counted 139 occupational categories in its inventory of recognized collegiate training programs. Indeed the steady growth in the numbers of occupations has led governments into reviewing their licensing or state registration procedures. For example, in the mid 1980s the Canadian province of Ontario completed a review and reform of its historical pattern of health professional legislation, granting new or continued recognition to twenty-five out of the seventy-five occupations which had requested official licensed status. In 1995 the UK's Department of Health commissioned a review of its legislation affecting professions supplementary to medicine in part under similar pressures to those in Ontario.

Governments and related agencies have been forced into reviewing the divisions of health care labor, not least because the pattern of growth has continued into the second half of the twentieth century. In the US for example, the increase in the total health workforce has been described as staggering: from 345,000 in 1900 to 2 million in 1960 and 4.3 million in 1970. Equally notable have been the accompanying changes in the nature and composition of the workforce, such that from the handful of occupations recognised by 1900, at least twenty-seven new occupations, including dental hygienist, dietician, occupational therapist, physical therapist, speech pathologist, radiologic technologist and medical technologist, were established between the turn of the century and 1940. From 1940 onwards many other occupations came into being, from respiratory therapists to physician assistants, and indeed a third phase of specialization has begun in recent decades through the arrival of technicians and assistants to the older health occupations which had themselves been seen as helpers to the medical profession. This growth not only expanded overall numbers, but further emphasized the minority status of doctors, who in 1900 formed approximately a third of the formally trained health workforce in America. By 1960 the ratio of doctors to other health workers was only one in ten, and by 1970 they were just one in thirteen of the workforce. These changing ratios also characterize the British case, where according to the NHS Manpower statistics for the 1970s, doctors again represented only one in thirteen of the total numbers employed in health care.

This continuous expansion of paramedical groups described above challenged the role of the medical profession in the regulation of other health care occupations, who increasingly sought recognition in their own right, free of any taint of subordination. The accumulating costs and complexity of the labor force also brought governments into the regulation of this area, particularly, but not exclusively, in the second half of the century. In America, the Allied Health Professions Personnel Training Act was passed in 1966, in part to regulate and improve the training of the new occupations. In Britain, the Professions Supplementary to Medicine Act had been passed in 1960, with the same broad aims. Governments were being drawn into an arena which historically had been managed by the organized medical profession and the newer professions themselves, often in ways which had come to seem archaic. In the United States in 1967 the American Society of Allied Health Professions was founded to promote the status and education of practitioners, reflecting their growing sense of maturity and autonomy. In the UK, likewise, many health professions had pressed for reforms in their status and their links with the medical profession.

As previously emphasized, there are no entirely 'separate' histories of medical and paramedical occupations; they are all interconnected, although each group of health workers has features unique to its history. Moreover, the histories vary both between and within countries, particularly in North America where states and provinces have differed in licensing practices and policies. Nonetheless it is still possible to identify some broad types of health worker and by choosing examples within these categories to illustrate some common formative experiences and themes.

Firstly, some occupations have a pre-twentieth century history and to some degree may be seen to have 'negotiated' a relationship with modern medicine, within which they offer their services directly and autonomously to the public as separate practitioners in the market place. Examples here include pharmacists, dentists, podiatrists and optometrists (chiropodists and opthalmic opticians in UK terminology). These groups work relatively autonomously within carefully demarcated body sites or specific professional functions. Typically the vast majority of such practitioners work outside of hospital medicine, whether in solo or small group practices of their own, or as employees of major pharmaceutical and retail organizations.

A second broad group of occupations is specifically linked to scientific diagnosis and to the hospital focus of much of modern medicine. They implement the technologies of investigation and measurement required for medicine's scientific practices. Typical examples include technicians in radiography and laboratory science, who work closely with the doctors involved in radiology and pathology. As treatment, as well as diagnosis, has come to draw on complex technologies, this group has further expanded its range to include scientists such as hospital physicists. With the incorporation of computer science into medicine, the expansion will probably continue through further developments in diagnosis and treatment.

A third group, often called 'therapists,' are part of the 'therapeutic' expansion of modern medicine but not immediately linked to any specific technology or scientific innovation. Practitioners in this third category developed in response to emergent treatment needs, for example for rehabilitation after trauma or surgery; but they also reflect a continuing development of basic concepts of health care, expanding over the century from pharmaceutical and surgical intervention to broader concepts of rehabilitation, and more recently and more broadly still to life-style regulation. Examples from the earlier stage include physiotherapists, speech therapists and occupational therapists, whilst dieticians, psychologists and counsellors of various kinds have more recently come to the fore. Outside of the conventional medical umbrella are numerous alternative therapists who to some degree compete with this third group of regular health care workers as well as directly with medical practitioners. Alternative therapists, by definition, are health workers, and in some instances they have acquired some measure of conventional medical status, for example osteopaths gained state registration in the UK in 1993. But historically they form a fourth category not to be considered here of workers whose philosophies, treatments and concepts of health and illness were at variance with mainstream medical science. By contrast, the first three groups have shared the regular medical knowledge paradigm. The remainder of this chapter will review the histories of these three groups using particular examples in each category.

## INDEPENDENT HEALTH WORKERS

By the turn of the century, dentists and pharmacists had stabilized their relationships with the medical profession. Each had their own internal occupational problems with competition from untrained competitors, or more precisely, practitioners without the formal qualifications preferred by the elite; but their professional identity and respectability were not in question. By contrast, in both the UK and the US, optometry has struggled through this century to secure practice rights and recognition. Although the pace of development has differed between the two countries, the fundamental issues have been similar; whereas most doctors were happy to leave tooth-work to dentists, they did not wish to relinquish their work on eyes.

It is worth considering this case in more detail. Optometrists have a long history and a claim to a knowledge base independent of medicine. Spectacle-makers may be traced back to the late medieval guilds found in the major cities, and in 1629 the Worshipful Company of Spectacle Makers received a royal charter. Thereafter it tried to regulate standards of spectacle making and the training of apprentices, but had difficulty in enforcing its mandate outside the City of London. In the nineteenth century, a number of scientific innovations enhanced the optician's knowledge and craft, including the studies of astigmatism by Thomas Young (1773–1829) and Sir George Biddell Airey (1801–1892). But perhaps the major innovation, for spectacle makers (and for medical ophthalmology) was Herman von Helmholtz's (1821–1894) invention of the ophthalmoscope in 1851, which allowed inspection of the retina and the tracing of light through the refracting media of the eye. Two years later von Helmholtz invented an ophthalmometer to measure the curvature of the eye surface and lens, which led to Frans Donders' pioneering work of 1864 'on the Anomalies of Accommodation and Refraction of the Eye.' Donders is described by Hirsch and Wick in their review of optical history as the true founder of clinical optometry and scientific measurement of refraction. So armed, opticians claimed that defects of refraction were different from visual deficiencies caused by disease. Medical ophthalmologists and general practitioners in turn claimed an overlap between the two, which only those with a medical training were equipped to separate.

The introduction of mass-manufactured lenses in the late 1890s created a mass market for spectacles and sharpened competition. Previously lenses had been ground by hand, so enhancing the craftsman's monopoly at least in the supply of spectacles, but now they became available in bulk for direct sale, and not just by opticians. The picture was complicated at this point because opticians themselves also worked as jewellers, watchmakers or instrument-makers, and spectacles were supplied by itinerant peddlers and sold in chemists' shops. In these changing conditions, the more ambitious opticians in both Britain and America began to offer eye examinations to assist customers in their choice of spectacles. To identify this expanded work domain and to distinguish themselves from the 'mere' lens-grinders of the past, the new class of refractionist selected the name 'optometrist.'

The American Optometric Association was founded in 1896, and the earliest university program was established at Columbia University in 1908, based on two years of preparation, (rising to four years training by the mid-century). After 1900 a number of legislative and court battles to define optometry began in New York and subsequently spread through the country, and by 1925 all the states of America had passed optometry licensing laws despite sustained medical opposition. The hostility between the two professions continued for decades. Up to 1950, the

American Medical Association still banned medical ophthalmologists from any formal participation in the training of optometrists, and subsequently opposed their reimbursement for services through Medicare and Medicaid schemes. Controversies continued through the 1970s and 1980s over the authority of optometrists to treat diseases of the eye, exclusive of surgery. In Britain, medical opposition was even more successful; the recognition gained by American optometrists in the first decades of the century was not matched in Britain until the 1958 Optician's Act.

The British Optical Association had been founded in 1895 by the new class of refractionist opticians, dissatisfied with the Worshipful Company of Spectacle Makers and its links with the hand manufacture and craft side of the trade. Early attempts to gain recognition, for example, a parliamentary bill of 1906 and a request for a royal charter, were hampered by internecine disputes between these two rival organisations who faced united opposition from the medical profession. Although the first post-graduate diploma in medical ophthalmology only began at Oxford University in 1907, and the subject received scant attention in medical training, the General Medical Council was clear in its opposition. Up to the 1920s it impugned the integrity and status of optometrists and argued that optical defects could only be corrected after a medical practitioner had excluded disease as their cause. In practice the ambitious opticians of the period were aided by the shortage of properly trained medical specialists, and by an ever-growing demand for their services. As the 1910 Enquiry into Unqualified Practice in the UK noted, people were turning to the better class of optician because of difficulties in obtaining expert advice from registered medical practitioners. The British Medical Association subsequently recommended that the diagnosis and treatment of diseases of the eye, including the estimation of refractive errors and retinoscopy should be compulsory elements in every medical curriculum. Medical expertise, however, ran behind popular need throughout the ensuing decades.

Controversies between the two professions continued through the 1920s and 1930s, occasionally breaking into public arenas through draft bills and committees of enquiry set up by the Ministry of Health. Opthalmic opticians managed to bring their two organizations under a joint council, and by 1936 the premier organizations were recognized through the National Insurance Act as the qualifying agencies for reputable opticians. Medical opposition now focused on the need for medical control of 'dispensing opticians,' but it was proving hard to demonstrate that unsupervised opticians were overlooking eye disease, as rival doctors had claimed. By 1949 the Crook Report concluded that opthalmic opticians, although hampered in training by exclusion from hospital eye departments, were competent refractionists and were able to 'suspect' disease and thus refer patients for specialized medical treatment. This verbal formula — that opticians could suspect but only doctors confirm — finally satisfied both professions and was greeted in the medical press as bowing to the inevitable. It led on to the 1958 Opticians' Act which set up a General Optical Council with medical professional representation to oversee the training, practice and registration requirements of practitioners. Thus, after a half-century of rivalry, an accommodation was reached which defined the respective spheres of responsibility. In fact, it confirmed the custom and practice through the century, leaving medical specialists in the hospitals and opticians in the commercial outlets.

The development of podiatry/chiropody has also taken a somewhat different course in the United States and Britain. In the former case federal and state laws classify podiatrists, with optometrists, pharmacists and dentists as separate from allied health personnel, thereby recognising a greater autonomy in their practice. The starting points were similar — the American National Association of Chiropodists was founded in 1911 and the British Society in 1912 — but again, in Britain, extensive medical opposition postponed state registration or licensing until 1960. This delay meant that chiropody came to be defined as a profession supplementary to medicine rather than as an autonomous profession. British chiropodists are more restricted in their range of surgery, anesthesia and drug treatments than their American counterparts, and from the inter-war years they have been more subject to medical control. This subordination to the British Medical Association, with tacit government support, followed a number of failures to secure the more autonomous recognition of their American colleagues, whose stratagems and professional definitions they studied. The relatively close relationship between the British medical profession and a single Ministry of Health, uncomplicated by federal and state governments, may in part explain these national differences in professional outcomes. British chiropodists now practice as independent but comparatively restricted practitioners; they continue to press for fewer restrictions on their own work and for the legal prohibition of their unqualified competitors.

TECHNICAL HEALTH WORKERS

For the occupations most closely associated with the diagnostic progress and the hospital focus of modern medicine, developments in Britain and North America have been rather similar, particularly in radiology and pathology. In 1895 Wilhelm Roentgen, a physicist at the University of Wurzburg, discovered the penetrative properties of X-rays. From remarkable pictures of bone structures further medical applications quickly developed. In 1904 bismuth was first used as a contrast medium and the new science moved on beyond the initial imaging of fractures and bone malformations. In Britain the Roentgen Society was formed in 1897, and included physicists and engineers as well as interested doctors; but by 1903 complaints began to appear in the medical press about 'lay involvement.' The *British Medical Journal* argued that laymen should confine themselves to the more mechanical act of producing a picture and abstain from assuming a scientific knowledge of the bearings of radiographs on diagnosis or prognosis. Medical radiologists were beginning to define their territory, but for at least twenty more years the situation was confused.

Various categories of worker — specialist doctors and general practitioners, physicists, photographers, engineers, and 'radiographers' — all produced and interpreted X-ray plates without any finalised demarcation of responsibilities between them.

During the 1914–18 war the situation became further confused as numerous doctors and orderlies underwent emergency training in the new technology. By 1917 a purely medical society was formed, the British Association for the Advancement of Radiology and Physiotherapy, and a Cambridge University Diploma in Medical Radiology and Electrology was proposed by this group. Medical radiologists seeking to define their new speciality were often seen by their own medical colleagues as 'mere photographers'; they felt a corresponding need to stress the *special medical* expertise that distinguished them from others involved in the process. As Stevens points out, the central question of the time — which was to be raised again in specialties such as anesthesiology, pathology and physical medicine — was whether the radiologist was to be regarded a full medical consultant or as a mere technician. A closely associated problem was whether radiographers might make diagnostic reports directly to other clinical staff or whether they always had to work through a medical radiologist. Through the 1920s, especially in the US, medical radiologists were accorded faint respect by fellow physicians in other specialities. Hospitals did not routinely employ radiologists, but rather 'non-professional' technicians who both produced X-ray plates and interpreted them.

Radiographers were also combining to develop their interests, founding in 1920 both the British Society of Radiographers and the American Society of Radiologic Technicians. British radiographers then came under pressure from radiologists, supported by the General Medical Council, who wanted to restrict their code of ethics and professional development. By the mid-1920s radiographers were forbidden to comment on or interpret X-ray plates, except to 'describe their appearances' to any non-comprehending doctor in the absence of a radiologist. Henceforth radiographers were to specialize in the technology of production, not the art and science of interpretation. The American Society was similarly subordinated by the Radiological Society of North America, which inspected and approved the Schools of X-ray technology until 1944, when it passed this function to the American Medical Association's Council for Accreditation in 1944. Trainee radiographers were told the position of the X-ray technician was quite similar, in many respects, to that of the trained nurse. They should all work only under the direct supervision of a properly qualified radiologist, physician, surgeon or dentist. The X-ray technician was not to express an opinion or enter into a discussion regarding interpretation diagnosis or therapy but only to work in the capacity of an assistant to the medical profession.

In both Britain and America radiography subsequently became principally a female profession. A similar process of demarcating a subordinate role also characterized laboratory science. In Britain, as the very terms of their very title suggest, the 'Pathological and Bacteriological Assistants Association' (1912) had to acknowledge a subservience to medical pathologists. In the late-nineteenth century, most laboratory procedures had involved no more than a doctor with a microscope and slides, but by the early-twentieth century both the number of tests and the complexity of equipment were growing rapidly. As Starr points out, American doctors wanted to maintain a monopoly of competence and control of their new laboratories, without themselves becoming hospital employees. The solution to this problem — how to maintain autonomy, yet not lose control — had three elements: first, to use trainee doctors (interns and residents) in the operation of hospitals; second, to encourage responsible professionalism among the higher ranks of subordinate health workers; and third, to employ women who, though professionally trained, would not challenge the authority or economic position of the doctor. In 1929 the recently formed American Society of Clinical Pathologists began a system for certifying laboratory personnel, with a code of ethics prohibiting any diagnostic activity or reporting on specimens. The pathologists in effect controlled the labor market on terms similar to those of other medical specialties. Laboratory workers in the following decades were to refine their skills in processing and producing results rather than interpreting them.

## THERAPEUTIC HEALTH WORKERS

Of the workers associated with the therapeutic expansion of model medicine, physiotherapists form one of the first and most established segments. In Britain they may be traced back to the Society of Trained Masseuses founded in 1895, in part by nurses specializing in techniques described as 'medical rubbing' and influenced by the graduates from the Central Institute of Stockholm with its tradition of education in massage and medical gymnastics. From the outset, unlike the cases described above, this was a female occupation, and (in line with its early links with nursing) many masseuses worked strictly under terms of medical professional authority and referral. They deliberately sought and accepted medical patronage, but physical medicine itself in Britain was not one of the growing scientific-medical specialties. Many doctors thought that its treatments by heat and electricity were part of the paraphernalia of charlatans, and the techniques of massage and manipulation were associated with cults such as osteopathy and chiropractic which began to cross the Atlantic, especially after the First World War. But despite these suspicions, that war had a dramatic effect on the status of and demand for physiotherapy in both Britain and the United States. The daughter of the Commander-in-Chief of the British Expeditionary Force in 1914, Lady Essex French, was a trained masseuse. She founded the Almeric Paget Massage Corps, and the demand by orthopedic surgeons for assistance with the maimed and wounded began to expand dramatically. Prominent doctors with high-class connections joined the council of the Society of Trained Masseuses despite the relatively low repute accorded the area by some of their colleagues. By 1920, through exploiting these connections and the respectability of its wartime efforts, the Society obtained a royal charter.

In America, the First World War saw the start rather than the consolidation of organized physiotherapy. Prior to that point, a few orthopedic surgeons in private practice had employed women with some instruction in massage and corrective exercise, and some medical electrotherapeutists also employed lay assistants. During the war, many of these women were recruited as 'Reconstruction Aides' and approximately eight hundred were trained on military short-courses. After the war Dr Harold Corbusier, a member of the American Association of Electro-Therapeutics and Radiology, used military contacts to launch a national association in collaboration with Mary McMillan, a leading aide. The American Women's Physical Therapy Association was founded in 1921; nurtured within a military tradition, it accepted a clear subordination to doctors. As Gritzer points out, Corbusier envisaged using aides as part of the physical-therapy physician's crusade for legitimacy. The development of a subordinate group of workers to do the laying on of hands would permit physicians to concentrate on the more esoteric tasks such as research, teaching and refining clinical diagnostic skills. As Stevens notes, physical medicine was then hardly an independent specialty; it included a range of treatments such as balneology, actinotherapy electrology and massage; but demand for these services grew, and during the 1920s and 1930s both the British and American Medical Associations were concerned to keep physiotherapists under their tutelage, chiefly by controlling the certification of training courses.

In the years before and after the Great War, the cachet of medical approval was thought valuable by a number of aspiring professions, despite its subordinating character. Occupational therapists, like physiotherapists, were boosted by war-time conditions, especially in America. Their active national organization began after 1918, culminating in 1931 when the American Occupational Therapy Association requested the American Medical Association to inspect its various Schools. However, for several aspiring professional organizations the acceptance of subordination was in part a stratagem in the pursuit of further recognition. In Britain, physiotherapists joined the British Medical Association's Board of Medical Auxiliaries, but in 1944 they were amongst the first groups to withdraw their affiliation, marking the early stages of a more autonomous phase of development.

The advent of the National Health Service, when the British government in effect became the employer of all health workers, quickly brought a review. The BMA wanted to carry forward its inter-war system of accreditation, but this was rejected after years of controversy which ended in the 1960 Professions Supplementary to Medicine Act. The seven professions thereby gaining power of self-regulation included chiropodists, dieticians, occupational therapists, orthoptists, physiotherapists, radiographers and medical laboratory scientists. For all of these the legally recognized roles and identities were those previously established in their contests with the medical profession.

CONCLUSION

Before mid-century the broad story was relatively clear — continuing medical specialization, the emergence of a group of autonomous health professionals and of two broad classes of groups more subordinate to medicine. But since the 1950s, the historical patterns of subordination in the latter two areas have been increasingly challenged and the situation has become less clear. Occupational identities are always in process of formation and reformation, but perhaps especially so where the professional autonomy granted to some health occupations has set a model for the less privileged. By the early 1970s the American Society of Medical Technologists were in legal conflict with the American Medical Association over training and authority within their work. Therapists of various kinds began to see patients without medical referral, in effect joining the first group of practitioners. Physiotherapists, for example, are now in this position in Britain and in many American states.

There are many pressures from within and outside medicine which ensure continuing change in the division of labor. Scientific and technological developments continually re-shape patterns of work between professionals. Imaging modalities in radiology, for example, have multiplied to include ultrasonic and magnetic resonance imaging, so rendering somewhat archaic the traditional division between doctor and technician. Such developments create additional complexities, but may also reduce and redefine previous activities, breaking down previously clear distinctions between medical and 'lay' sciences. Changes within medicine, however, are not limited to physical techniques; for example, a shift within psychiatry to various forms of psychotherapy has created many new occupational frontiers, negotiated between doctors, therapists, nurses, social workers and other groups, who have also reformed their roles and skills. As the knowledge base changes, the division of labor will be further reshaped, often in new ways.

These internal dynamics interact with many and varied changes in the external context of health care. One key factor here is gender. In the first half of the century women health workers had to contend with notions of male authority and female subordination; more recently, gender hierarchies have been attacked, if not always changed. A second external factor relates to the spread of university education, from the beginning of the twentieth century, when only doctors were university graduates, to the present abundance of graduates in all the health professions of the developed world. A third factor is the increasing role of governments in regulating health care as its costs and political significance have grown through the century. Professional proliferation, once thought a desirable part of progress, may not be so well regarded at the century's end, as the paymasters look for cost reductions. Developing countries in particular cannot afford — and indeed now question — health services based on complex occupational structures.

In summary, the internal and external dynamics of health care seem likely to produce an expansion of the first occupational category and to reduce the degrees of historical subordination within the second two groups of health worker. If so, then authority within the division of labor will become ever more distributed, and the co-ordination of health care will constitute one of the major management and policy challenges of the twenty-first century.

## Further Reading

Begun, J.W. and Lippincott, R.C., 'The Politics of Professional Control,' in J.H. Roth (ed.), *Research in the Sociology of Health Care*. (Connecticut: JAI Press Inc., Vol 1, 1982).

British Medical Association, *Complementary Medicine*. (Oxford University Press, 1993).

Brown, C.A. 'The Division of Labourers, Allied Health Professions,' *International Journal of Health Services* 1973, **3**(3): 435–44.

Gritzer, G. 'Occupational Specialisation in Medicine,' in J.H. Roth (ed.), *Research in the Sociology of Health Care*. (Connecticut: JAI Press Inc., Vol 2, 1982).

Hirsch, M.J. and Wick, R.E., *The Optometric Profession*. (New York: Chilton Book Co, 1968).

Holder, L. 'Allied Health Perspectives in the 1980's,' *Journal of Allied Health* (Feb 1981), 5–14.

Jerman, E.C., *The Modern X-ray Technician*. (Minneapolis: Bruce Publishing Co, 1928).

Larkin, G. *Occupational Monopoly and Modern Medicine*. (London: Tavistock Pubs Ltd, 1983).

Levitt, R. *The Reorganised National Health Service*. (London: Croom Helm, 1976).

National Commission on Allied Health Education, *The Future of Allied Health Education*. (California: Jossey-Bass Inc, 1980).

Starr, P. *The Social Transformation of American Medicine*. (New York: Basic Books, 1982).

Stevens, R. *Medical Practice in Modern England*. (Yale University Press, 1966).

Wicksteed, J.M. *The Growth of a Profession*. (London: Edward Arnold & Co, 1948).

# CHAPTER 35

# Going to the Doctor

JULIAN TUDOR HART

I n this chapter, I try to recover the experiences of patients and of general
practitioners (especially in Britain), and place them within changing society.
Going to the doctor is a common experience, and one which has a history.

By the end of the nineteenth century a social agenda for medicine had been
clearly defined as a progress away from private trade toward a state-organized cash-
free economy addressing human needs rather than market demand. By the end
of the twentieth century, that definition seemed to be falling apart, with this
concept of progress not only questioned but often contemptuously dismissed.

By the eve of World War I, hammering at the gates had spurred sufficient social
conscience to make medical care accessible to most of the population through
services organised and funded by the state, a process completed soon after World
War II in all developed economies except the United States. Since the collapse
of the USSR and rebirth of mass unemployment in developed economies, this
hammering has subsided. The unregulated global market rules, and states are
increasingly under pressure to abdicate their responsibilities for social care to
corporate players in the most rapidly growing and potentially profitable market
of all time — multinational trade not only in health care but in life itself. Yet
medicine still seems for the most part to believe in itself, to retain public confidence, to prefer human needs to market demands, and to require locality, continuity, and personality.

Despite its increasing industrialization, late twentieth-century medicine increasingly seeks to transcend its original paternalism. Over the final third of this century,
a more generous theory of medical science, the biopsychosocial model, has evolved,
particularly at the leading edge of primary care. This is as yet incompletely accepted or applied in practice, but if social stability were to reappear as a major
political objective, it could provide a new agenda sufficient to engage the next
century. Medical schools the world over are at last preparing to redefine their task
in terms of this model, and clinicians are beginning to address the real obstacles
to more democratic concepts of accountability.

## GOING TO THE DOCTOR'S SHOP

For the first half of this century, patients' experiences were recorded mainly by the educated upper middle class, paying customers in a buyers' market, whose doctors could make time to give visible value for their fees. Rich patients had rich doctors, poor patients had poor doctors, but all doctors did their best to look rich. Medical poverty, well described by Bernard Shaw in *The Doctor's Dilemma*, diminished rapidly after the Lloyd George Insurance Act of 1911, and disappeared after 1948 with the National Health Service (NHS). Few doctors in Britain were women, fewer still in North America, and even today, despite a slight majority of female medical students, only about 25% of British general practitioners (GPs) are women.

British patients would usually see the doctor either in their own home, or the doctor's front parlor. There they would be shown in by his wife doubling as receptionist, and offered a seat in the waiting room to one side of the entrance hall. This would have a polished table piled with old copies of *Punch* and *The Tatler*, reassuring patients that their doctor never failed to do anything that everyone else did, nor dared to do anything that everyone else did not do, thus meeting Shaw's criteria for the English medical conscience.

When your turn came, you crossed the hall to the parlor, where your doctor rose to greet you from behind a large desk, and invited you to sit down. Behind him was a glazed white metal cabinet, in which instruments of torture lay on glass shelves. The room smelled of phenol, reminding you that surgery lay at the heart of good general practice. As late as 1938–39, British GPs were performing an average of three operations each week, mostly in cottage hospitals. In most of the United States, GP surgery persisted into the 1970s.

Your GP provided a folding screen behind which you took off your clothes, and an examination couch covered in permanently cold dark green American cloth. He wore a wing collar, and whatever his age, did his best to look ancient. If you were a child, almost all his questions were addressed to your accompanying parent. There was a struggle over relaxing your tummy when he poked his claws into it in search of grumbling appendix or floating kidneys, but you could usually win this one. He got his own back by thrusting a metal tongue depressor down your throat, to see if he could take your tonsils out, as they seemed worth more to him than to you. Even by the 1950s, when most thoughtful doctors were beginning to doubt that more or less routine tonsillectomy had any rational basis, the catarrhal children of affluent Boxhill were still 27 times more likely to lose their tonsils than the snotnoses of impoverished Birkenhead.

By 1980, tonsillectomies in Britain had fallen to 26 per 1000 population, 16 times less than the Netherlands, 10 times less than Ireland, 9 times less than Denmark, 8 times less than the US, about a quarter the rate in Australia or Canada, and about half that in Sweden, Japan or Switzerland. There are similar consistent and substantial differences for most other clinical interventions, including prescribing. During the second half of the twentieth century, British doctors became sceptics;

still perhaps too credulous to be good scientists, but not credulous enough to remain good salesmen. The reasons for this are complex, cultural as well as economic, but early dominance of prepaid care of registered lists by GPs, rather than fees for items of service in a free market, surely had something to do with it. Transition from shopkeeping to science is the real, still unfinished, story of British general practice through the twentieth century.

## MASS CARE

Historians in search of scientific practice have understandably looked first to genteel private care for the middle class rather than mass care for industrial workers. To the most progressive, socially conscious leaders of the profession like Sir Clifford Albutt, Lloyd George's Insurance Act threatened the tender shoots of innovative fee-paid clinical medicine by nationalizing cheap and nasty prepaid club medicine developed in the nineteenth century. It would, Sir Clifford said, provide "perfunctory care by perfunctory men."[1] The process began in 1912, when most employed workers came into prepaid care, and was completed in 1948, when the NHS extended this to the entire population.

The NHS also deepened the divide between community-based generalists and hospital-based specialists, fuelling fears that general practice was just inferior medicine. "Murder at the crossroads," fulminated Erich Geiringer,[2] "the decapitation of general practice." Contemporary evidence showed that at mid-century, GPs in the US and Canada were just as isolated from good clinical medicine as Collings[3] had shown their UK colleagues to be. The argument was not about how bad they were, but how to make them better. In North America and Sweden they were 'improved' by assimilation to hospital specialism, creating a new category of specialoids ('specialists' accessible directly to self-referred patients, as in the USSR). In the UK the clinical quality of GPs was simply ignored until the foundation of the Royal College of General Practitioners in 1952, but by then the specialoid option was already closed. The NHS expelled the last GP surgeons and physicians from their cottage hospitals, completing the division of British medicine begun at the turn of the century, when as Rosemary Stevens put it, specialists got the hospitals but let the GPs have the patients, with a strictly regulated referral system between them. To GPs, the immediate effect was catastrophic; they were cut off from the apparent growing point of medical science. The ultimate effect was to compel GPs to redefine their work, to develop their share in the referral system as something more than a signpost, and thus to allow rational and therefore economic use of technology, changes now pursued everywhere and recognized as essential to efficient and effective practice.

For patients, particularly of the lower middle class, the NHS was deliverance from their biggest single cause of personal bankruptcy. Before 1948, every potentially catastrophic illness threatened to incur equally catastrophic costs. This is still the situation in the US, where one study showed that more than half the families of 2,600 seriously ill patients suffered severe financial or care-giving burdens, one third lost most of their savings or major source of income, and one fifth had to make major changes in family plans to meet costs of illness such as moving home or school or delayed treatment for illness in another member of the family; almost all these families had hospitalization insurance.

However, to most contemporary observers, the least credible basis for medical science was mass prepaid care of the sort represented by 'sixpenny doctors', prepaid club practice for industrial workers. This was nationalized by the Lloyd George Insurance Act of 1911 (the panel), and extended by the NHS to everyone in 1948. This reminds us how wrong respected contemporary observers can be, and how the first requirement for solving public health problems is simply to include the whole population, because those excluded always have the biggest problems of every kind, including health problems. As most fee-earning doctors work hard, it is difficult for them to understand that in any fee-paid service, public needs are greater than presented personal demands. In 1995, when the State of Oregon made limited primary medical care available to all citizens for the first time, planners anticipated 13,100 new registrations in the first two months. In fact there were 25,000 in the first two weeks.[4] Unsung and unresourced, British GPs got through this stage 40 years earlier.

## CONSTRAINTS OF MASS PRACTICE

Common to all state funded systems for prepaid mass care, and to the prepaid small business systems which mostly preceded them, were squalid buildings, rapid throughput, and prescription of money (access to state insurance benefits) as an often higher perceived priority than clinical decisions. People had to have something to live on when they were sick, and this inevitably took precedence over

TABLE 1: EXAMPLES OF AVERAGE TIME AVAILABLE FOR EACH VISIT IN PREPAID GENERAL PRACTICE

| Year | Place | Minutes per patient |
|------|-------|---------------------|
| 1949 | 'bad' English industrial | 1.25 |
| 1949 | 'good' English industrial | 3.6–6.0 |
| 1970 | Scottish urban | 5.0 |
| 1981 | English urban | 7.0 |
| 1985 | Quebec | 15.0 |
| 1986 | BMA-sampled UK practices | 8.2 |
| 1987 | Finnish health centers | 12.0–13.0 |
| 1988 | Swedish health centers | 21.0 |
| 1989 | Spanish urban | 5.2 |
| 1989 | Spanish urban | 6.7 |
| 1990 | Hong Kong government clinics | 3.0–4.0 |

anything else that industrial GPs did, or pretended to do, to change the course of illness.

Time is the real currency of general practice; long hours for doctors, short minutes for patients. Rich patients have rich doctors who can afford to work slowly, and therefore to work as they were taught; poor patients have poor doctors, who can survive only by discovering their own short cuts, with much even of these few minutes wasted on administrative decisions about access to benefits rather than clinical decisions about health. Table 1 offers a selection of statistics on average time per visit for GP/patient encounters.

Finland, Quebec and Sweden provide the only examples of adequate consultation time. All these use salaried GPs, but so do those giving miserably brief consultations in Madrid; people get what their governments pay for. Table 2 shows the usually (but not always) longer average consultation times given by fee-paid GPs.

## Doctors Going to Patients

Home visits were the cutting edge of medical trade in 1900. Though by the 1970s they had virtually disappeared from North American practice, in Belgium over half of all GP contacts with patients were still in their homes even in 1985. This seems to have been a product of intense fee-competition with specialists. With fewer than 600 patients per GP, they saw on average only 11 patients a day despite working long hours. Readiness to do home visits seems to have been their main competitive asset.

Before World War I, the Lloyd George Insurance Act, and tacit agreement by specialists to see patients only by referral, British GPs courted patients in much the same way. Dr Harry Roberts, running a huge practice among the poor in Hackney in London's East End in the winter of 1908, was collected at 11.00 by a cab driver each morning after his first office session, to visit over 80 patients before 18.30, when his evening session began. Home visits never exceeded office attendance, but at 6 pence for patients coming to the GP and 12 pence for the GP going to the patients, house calls were more profitable. Virtually all the male patients in this practice joined the Lloyd George 'panel' after the 1911 Insurance Act.

TABLE 2: EXAMPLES OF AVERAGE TIME AVAILABLE FOR EACH VISIT IN FEE-PAID GENERAL PRACTICE

| Year | Place | Minutes per Patient |
|------|-------|---------------------|
| 1979 | France | 14.0 |
| 1981 | Germany | 9.0 |
| 1985 | US | 14.0 |
| 1985 | Netherlands | 5.0 |

All of these except the US included their whole national populations.

In 1949, in the first year of the NHS, Collings found GPs seeing 30–50 patients at their offices in the morning, another 30–50 in the evening, but still fitting in 38 home visits as well as time for lunch between 11.00 and 16.30, in an industrial practice with a good reputation among local consultants. By the 1970s, home visits had dropped to around 8–15 daily per GP in almost all practices.

Though Hackney's Dr Roberts was proud of his radical views, like other GPs he wore a top hat for these visits. It maintained his authority, promoting the placebo effect on which he mostly depended.

> They all had the same routine: the silk hat, walking cane, white gloves and a Gladstone bag, in which they had their stethoscope and other items. The usual formula when my father was ill was that the doctor would be shown into the parlour, the best room of the house, and the first thing he would do would be to take one glove off, then the other glove off, put them both on the table, then put the walking stick on the table, then the top hat and then go upstairs and see the patient.[5]

In my own time, from the 1950s to the 1990s, GPs serving industrial workers had undisputed right of entry to their homes, if only because workload precluded standing at the front door waiting for housewives to make themselves presentable. We ran bag in hand to the kitchen door, gave it two or three bangs, shouted 'Doctor!,' and strode into our shared territory. As a rule, the patient would be in bed, upstairs for an acute illness, in the parlor for terminal care. The doctor sat on the left side of the bed (to examine the patient from the right), his right foot often striking a chamber pot, ringing a cheerful note to start the consultation. The style was frankly paternal, but was at least a human relationship. Except in rural areas with long journeys between patients, civilized practice was just possible at a rate of about four home visits an hour, five or six in epidemics.

The human relationships of home visits were different from office visits; doctors were smaller, patients were bigger, and their families could participate in consultation, as they rarely did otherwise. The only technology was what the GP could carry, and decisions were surrounded by visible evidence of the material constraints within which they had to be applied.

Today, doctors everywhere are reducing home visits. By the early 1980s, about 17% of GPs in Manchester were doing less than one a day, and an equal proportion five or more. Home visits were less than 2% of the work of some GPs, over 25% for others. The downward trend has continued since, and some doctors now entering general practice deny their value in any circumstances. As predictable death at home rather than hospital continues to be preferred by most patients, terminal care is still accepted by most GPs as a major responsibility, and acute emergencies requiring immediate treatment (such as coronary thrombosis or acute left ventricular failure) still occur, it is difficult to understand how home visits could be eliminated without loss of quality. By 1987, Cartwright found a large decline in home visiting by GPs even during the year preceding patients' deaths, and reluctance or failure to visit was the main criticism of GPs by their patients.

## THE CONSULTATION PROCESS

Consultations (US = visits) remain the basic units of production in clinical medicine, from which all else flows. The technical processes of examination and investigation, though outwardly impressive and often necessary, are almost always less important than mutual exchange of information, questioning, listening, and explaining in both directions. Though almost all the evidence on this was collected in the second half of the century, there are no reasons to doubt that most of it would have applied as well in 1900 as it does now and will into the foreseeable future.

The predominant role of bilateral questioning and listening was verified by two similar studies in North America and Britain, both on hospital out-patients, but their similar results probably apply as much if not more to primary care. The following data come from the British study.[6] 86 patients referred to a general internist went through three standard stages of clinical consultation: first, listening to and asking questions about patients' stories; then examining them; and finally studying routine laboratory and x-ray investigations. At the end of each stage, participating doctors made a tentative diagnosis. Three months later, a final diagnosis was made using all this and subsequent evidence, including the course of the illness. 85% of all final diagnoses were reached simply by listening to patients' stories. Physical examination added another 7%, and laboratory or x-ray investigations (chosen from indications in the first two stages) added a final 8%. Diagnosis, even in these entirely doctor-centered terms, depended overwhelmingly on verbal exchange.

So does treatment. Outside hospitals, where nurses put pills into patients whether they like it or not, continued treatment depends on patients' compliance, which in turn depends on their agreement with professionals on the nature of their problems, and if they agree, on their understanding. Medication compliance for patients followed up by specialists in hospital-based studies is consistently lower than by GPs who know them and the social context within which their problems must be solved. However, knowing patients is time consuming, and hard to reconcile with rapid throughput.

The majority of serious errors in medicine occur because of deficiencies in behavior rather than in knowledge or skill. The most powerful single predictor of successful outcome in consultations (measured as patient satisfaction) is agreement between both partners, patients and professionals, on the nature of the main problems to be addressed. Studies in the 1980s showed this agreement was achieved in only about half of all consultations. Even for those involving bodily complaints there was agreement in only about 75% of consultations, and for those mainly concerning the mind, agreement fell to 6%.[7] Studies in Canada found 54% of patients' complaints and 45% of their concerns were not identified.[8] This is unsurprising in view of other studies showing that doctors gave patients an average 18 seconds, virtually never more than 2 minutes, to tell their story in their own words, before interrupting and diverting them to doctor-based topics,[9] though a study in Yugoslavia found that letting patients talk as long as they liked made virtually no difference to overall length of consultations.

All these data come from studies in the second half of this century, most from the last 20 years, but all the evidence we have suggests that earlier consultations were even more doctor-centered, and their dependence on inputs from patients was even more systematically ignored. Patients have always had their own priorities, above all to understand what is happening to them, and what can be done about it. Studies in North American primary care clinics in the early 1980s showed that in both new and return visits, patients valued explanations twice as much as tests and 50% more than treatment.

All this shows that the underlying productive process in GP consultations can only be a mutual exchange of information to define and understand patients' problems, and thus to agree on rational solutions. For this to become explicit, patients must act as co-producers rather than consumers. This reality was, and for the most part still is, subordinated to and concealed by an entirely different, grossly unequal relationship, in which patients appear to consume a set of commodities produced entirely by their doctors. From this angle, the twentieth century has been an accelerating progression from virtual denial of any active and intelligent role for patients in decisions on either diagnosis or treatment, to their acceptance either as critical and potentially adversarial consumers of medical care as a commodity, or as respected co-producers of social values, (diverging alternatives the choice of which will be critical for the future of clinical practice). An important factor in this transition has been the shift from mainly placebo treatment at the start of the century, entailing uncritical submission of patients to medical authority, to a general availability of effective weapons against disease, requiring rational relationships between both players. This transition will advance further as knowledge of the human genome expands, and is either profitably marketed or rationally applied.

THE DOCTOR'S WORKSHOP

Within the constraints of their 3 to 15 minute consultations, what actually happened to patients who went to their GPs?

Throughout the world, local medical centers reflect who pays the doctor and how. With a few outstanding exceptions in Scandinavia, Holland, and Spain, government clinics have mostly been Spartan, concrete buildings designed for cheap construction and maintenance, with large waiting areas and bench seating. Consulting rooms have been designed with little or no regard to confidentiality. Health posters were usually their only decoration, but these were often colorful, and if locally produced, imaginative (the best examples were in the former USSR). Consulting rooms were often used by successive doctors on three or four two-hour shifts (as in the Spanish *ambulatoria* established by Franco in 1940 and by most similar clinics in Latin America) and therefore lacked individuality, despite the often vivid personalities who worked in them.

Similar to these, but less well designed, more crowded, and often dirtier, were the buildings used by private GPs serving the poor. Prepaid care, with the state paying a small fixed capitation, guaranteed that primary medical care would not only be cheap, but also as nasty as local custom would tolerate. As late as 1969, only 17% of British general practice was conducted from purpose-built premises, 22% had no suturing equipment, 31% had no typewriter, 32% had no vaginal speculum, and 90% had no ECG (EKG) machine.

Until 1967, most British industrial general practice was conducted from converted shops, usually with a plate glass front painted inside to above eye level. These shops were generally shabby, and no business other than general medical practice could have been conducted from them. The front part would be a waiting room, often too small for the patients, who would then queue outside in the street, often in rain. In group practices which could afford to pay a receptionist, she would sit behind a counter, removing and refiling patients' charts (government A6 medical records were introduced in 1920, and over 90% of GPs in England and Wales still use this, though well over half their always more progressive Scottish colleagues have replaced these with A4 records similar to those used in hospitals. Since 1948, all citizens have had such records, providing a cumulative history of care both by GPs and hospital specialists. When patients move to a new doctor, this record follows them). In industrial practice, at least up to the late 1960s, receptionists were often responsible for most repeat prescribing (on the edge of the law), and for much of the apparently straightforward certification of unfitness for work (well beyond the edge of the law).

Appointment systems were rare in industrial practice before the late 1960s. For a session beginning at 09.00, patients would start queuing outside at 08.00. The receptionist or caretaker would open up at 08.45, and the waiting room would then be heaving for the next two or three hours, providing an audible hum to remind the doctor to work as fast as possible.

A notice outside displayed office hours, usually 08.00 to 10.00 in the morning and 17.00–19.00 in the evening. In both cases, the end times represented not when work finished, but when the door could be locked to stop more patients getting in. In Glyncorrwg, my predecessor performed the 'ceremony of the keys.' Promptly at 10.00, he stopped whatever he was doing, stalked out into the waiting room, cast a vigilant eye round it, and then locked the door. If anyone managed to get in after this, he made them climb out of the small waiting room window.

By the 1960s, virtually all GPs had running water in their consulting rooms, and most, though not all, gave their patients access to a toilet. The industrial GP's consulting room would generally contain a large desk almost covered with piles of paper weighed down by promotional knickknacks from drug salesmen. There would usually be an examination couch with a screen, or in purpose built premises there might be a small adjoining examination room. How often the couch was used was indicated by the objects accumulated upon it; in the worst cases, stacks of unopened medical journals.

Before World War II, panel (state insurance) patients had no chair, and had to stand throughout the consultation. I saw this in Spain at an otherwise excellent, innovative health center in 1985. Self-employed doctors for poor people must aim at small profits with large turnover, and letting them sit may seriously impede production. Here is a report from a small US town in the 1970s:

> Dr Rea has four examining rooms in his suite of offices... "I have only one sit-down desk in the three rooms, because when you sit down you double the office call length. You get someone sitting on their backside; they talk longer than when they're standing." Doesn't he find people are more relaxed if they are sitting down? "If I want them to relax I'll sit them down. That sounds cruel maybe. But I'm here predominantly as a medical man, and if people are waiting I don't think they would appreciate me sitting here talking about something other than medicine."[10]

Dr Rea's arrangement was a central aisle, with 6 to 10 cubicles opening off it, each with its own examination couch, so that examinations could proceed rapidly without any delays for preparation by nurses or getting clothes on and off. This was common throughout North America, and in European countries like Germany, where fees for service similarly maximized emphasis on diagnostic and treatment procedures rather than talking and listening.

One of the most telling changes in British general practice in the 1970s was a fairly general shift of patients' chairs from across the desk, with the doctor at a safe social distance, to beside the desk, where doctors and patients could come close enough to recognize their often desperate need to talk about "something other than medicine." When this need is not recognized, there may be colossal waste through inappropriate referral and use of technology.

## SHIFTING CLINICAL CONTENT AND DEFINITIONS OF PROFESSIONAL RESPONSIBILITY

Throughout the twentieth century, doctors of first contact accessible to all of the people have had to deliver clinical science on the run. For most, their only means of escape from time pressures was to the equally damaging but entirely different pressures of fee-earning. For British GPs this alternative largely closed in 1948.

It is important to recognize that specialists directly accessible to the public without referral inevitably lose contact with the ambiguous border between what is or is not within the scope of medicine. This spares them from very difficult decisions, but these decisions still have to be made without skilled assistance. A patient who consults her gynecologist, dermatologist, or psychiatrist has already excluded a huge range of other possible ways of labeling her problems, and narrowed the range of solutions for them. The specialoid of her choice has large incentives to agree. Between one third and one half of all patients referred by GPs for further investigation by hospital-based internists have no detectable organic disease, an order of magnitude found in every country and care system sufficiently advanced to study the subject, and probably no smaller at the start of this century than at its close.

These patients are either told there is nothing wrong with them (which, if they feel ill, they find hard to believe) or are offered a somatic label in current fashion. In my lifetime, hysterical paralysis became chronic postviral fatigue, and ill-defined abdominal pains without positive findings from barium meals and enemas, ultrasound scans, or endoscopies from both ends, were consecutively labeled grumbling appendix, spastic colon, chronic cholecystitis or irritable bowel syndrome; treated respectively by appendectomy, low-fiber diet, cholecystectomy and high-fiber diet.

Alternatively, especially in prepaid insurance or NHS care in which somatization ceased to be a source of fees, they may be labeled as hypochondriacs, hysterics, neurasthenics, neurotics, or (the latest) heartsink patients. So far as these symptoms usually originate from the mind and its experiences, including behavior learned from parents and horrific childhood secrets like sexual abuse, these psychological labels may seem more rational, but the outcome for patients will not improve unless these labels lead to appropriate action, entailing time-consuming talking and listening rather than indiscriminate prescription of psychotropic drugs.

It is hard for later generations to appreciate the hostility of almost all British GPs in the first two thirds of this century to any psychiatric diagnoses other than the gross institutionalized end-stage psychoses they had seen as students. This is still obvious in countries which have more recently turned toward clinically autonomous primary care, for example in Southern Europe and the former Soviet bloc. Dr Arthur Watts was a pioneer of GP psychiatry, with formal training in mental hospitals before he went into practice in the 1940s. He was a kind, thoughtful, and exceptionally honest man, as the following passage reveals:

> In those days I had a complete blind spot as regards depression. I had heard about melancholia, and Hector McPhail had showed us cases of a woman who could not stop weeping, and an old man verging on a stupor. When a man came to see me complaining of constipation I gave him a good physical examination: I even referred him for a bowel x-ray, which was negative. Once I had the hospital report I saw my patient, and gave him a clean bill of health and told him he had nothing to worry about. He went straight home and put his head in a gas oven. Even when I heard the news, it never dawned on me I had missed a classic case of depression; indeed, I felt rather indignant that he hadn't believed me.[11]

This pervasive blindness to the unity of mind and body came to an end for British general practice when Michael Balint's book *The Doctor, his Patient, and the Illness* provided the basic text for the pioneering generation which founded the Royal College of General Practitioners in 1952. But imaginative application of this perception to most patients depended on investments in staff time which many practices have yet to make. Labels and treatments changed, but underlying causes remained unsought or avoided. Both doctors and patients preferred problems with mechanistic solutions, appropriate to existing medical skills, referable to specialists, or treatable within minutes rather than hours, and casting patients as passive consumers. Surgical intervention rates for procedures known to provide illusory solutions to somatized psychosocial problems are systematically lower in Britain than the United States, or other countries where fees encourage persistence of a transactional, provider-consumer relationship between GPs and patients (though other cultural determinants make this issue far more complex than this crude analysis may seem to suggest).

Most British GPs continue to prescribe pills for non-psychotic forms of unhappiness, frankly accepting causes as unchangeable but hoping to give symptomatic relief. All too often, treatments promoted to relieve the mind impede mental function, the principal means through which any solution must eventually be found. The list of panaceas starts with alcohol, opiates and cocaine, through chloral, bromides, barbiturates, phenothiazines, and benzodiazepines, and now fluoxetine (Prozac) and methylphenidate (Ritalin), but no end is in sight. All these drugs were introduced with blind optimism, all ended with new problems and a more drug-dependent society. However, slowly but surely, both GPs and their patients seem to be growing less credulous, despite promotional pressures from the pharmaceutical multinationals, which recognize and deplore the longstanding and increasing sales-resistance of UK prescribers. In 1989/90, UK prescription items per head were 47% less than in Germany, 49% less than in Spain, 62% less than in Italy, and 80% less than in France.[12] Between 1975 and 1987, UK sales of 'new' chemical entities introduced within the last five years fell from 10% to just over 3% of all prescriptions, compared with 13% in France, 17% in Germany, 19% in Spain, 22% in the US, 26% in Japan, and 29% in Italy.

### APPROACHING THE MILLENNIUM

By 1986 many practices were greatly improved, having invested in better premises, nursing staff, ECG machines, and information technology. Most of this change was in affluent areas with growing populations and employment. This trend has accelerated since managed competition in an internal NHS market was imposed in 1989/90.

This has had a huge and complex effect on general practices, most obviously in a rapid expansion of employed nursing and administrative staff, and the delegation of clinical tasks to them. The expansion in recorded information demanded by managed care led to administrative use of on-site computers in almost 90% of all NHS practices by 1995; 55% of practices also used computers during consultations. This puts Britain ahead of all other countries in the extent to which computers are used for processes of patient care, as opposed to billing. Computer-assisted consultations last 48–54 seconds longer, doctor-initiated and medical content tend to increase, and patient-initiated social content falls.[13]

For the first time, most hospital specialists have become interested in the opinions of GPs and patients about the services they provide for referred patients, a new experience which has offset, for both GPs and patients, many of the worst effects of competition.

As this chapter is written (in 1997) British GPs remain self-employed entrepreneurs, private providers of public service. There was no need to privatize, as GPs had never been made fully accountable either to administration, or to the neighborhoods they served. They are no more likely than other small businessmen to invest in the areas of social decline which present our most serious and intractable health problems. Though some British GPs enjoy being businessmen, a large majority still seem to prefer clinical medicine and public service. This seems to be at least as true of newly qualified entrants as of older GPs, who have opted massively for early retirement since the new contract. It probably underlies the rapid recent decline in recruitment to general practice, reversing previous trends, leading to the collapse of trainee schemes in areas of high morbidity and workload, and more recently to serious difficulties in maintaining a GP workforce.

As the century approaches its end, both GPs and patients face fundamental choices. Private practice is now the main source of income (but not of work) for many NHS consultants, though their expertise could not survive without their NHS base. This is not true of GPs, for whom private practice is rarely a serious option. However, most GPs are likely to remain private purveyors of public service as long as governments continue to accept the inefficiencies inherent in an essentially unplanned service of extremely uneven quality, in which GPs can define their work to suit themselves so far as their patients will let them.

Few critics of the old NHS seem to have noticed that new outpatient referrals per GP have fallen much faster than average list sizes ever since 1949. British GPs have moved slowly but steadily toward greater acceptance of responsibility for long-term management of chronic disease, and less responsibility for diagnosis of acute conditions such as fractures or injuries, a rational division of labor with hospital specialists. However, they are probably moving more slowly than NHS administrators would like. Resources, for staff and for team development, were and still are the rate limiting factor; for example, to shift responsibility for long term care of non-insulin dependent diabetes from hospital out-patient departments to GPs would, on the evidence we have, be dangerous without a major investment program to improve organization and teamwork in primary care.

Sentimental rhetoric about family doctors won't wash with today's public; there is little evidence that British or any other GPs ever gave the priority to continuity of care or knowledge of families which provided their defensive rhetoric over the last hundred years. In 1995 they rejected the 24-hours a day, 365 days a year responsibility for their patients on which, more than anything else, their moral claim to independent contractor status depended. Starting in inner-cities like London or areas of post-industrial collapse like the South Wales valleys, a salaried option must emerge if rational primary care services are to be developed or maintained. This has now been conceded by the latest package of Government options for the future of general practice, allowing virtually any administrative body, public, private, or corporate, to employ staff to provide primary care, *except* NHS Health Authorities (which alone have, or could most easily acquire, the skills needed to assess local health needs). As the vain search for a formula to make doctors businesslike without being businessmen continues, the quasi-market gets ever quasier. Anything goes, so long as responsibility for decisions can still be attributed to the market rather than agencies of elected government.

For more than 40 years, British doctors and their patients enjoyed freedom to do the best they could without worrying about fees. GPs enjoyed their right to work more or less as they pleased, with erratic quality of service and poorly developed teamwork. Administration of a public service for private gain seemed an anomalous survival from the eighteenth century, but now, on a corporate scale, it is offered as a serious option for the twenty-first century.

Looking to this future, veteran US health economist Rashi Fein posed fundamental questions which all GPs and all patients will sooner or later have to face:

> The world will be different, but whether it will be bad is up to us. We can choose our fate. What are our choices? Not the presence of controls or their absence, but the form of the controls and who will impose them ... Do we prefer market competition as the control mechanism that tells us how far to cut costs, or do we prefer government?[14]

Elected governments are fallible, but at least they still claim to pursue human ends through human judgements; markets pursue only the bottom line. For medical care to be more than a byproduct of greed, some other way must be found.

## REFERENCES

Colleagues in many countries sent material for this chapter, but space allowed me to use little of it. I am particularly grateful to Dr Ekke Kuenssberg for advice, and to the late Dr Arthur Watts for permission to quote his work. The following books offer useful further reading on what actually happened to patients and what GPs actually did, to supplement more doctor-centered histories.

1.  C. Albutt, 'The Act and the future of medicine,' Letter to *The Times*, (3 January, 1912).
2.  E. Geiringer, 'Murder at the crossroads: or the decapitation of general practice,' *Lancet* (1959), i: 1039–45.
3.  J.S. Collings, 'General practice in England today,' *Lancet* (1950), i: 555–585.
4.  J. Roberts, 'Oregon overwhelmed in its first three weeks,' *British Medical Journal* (1994), **308**: 618.
5.  Hackney Workers' Educational Association, *The Threepenny Doctor: Dr. Jelley of Hackney.* (London: Hackney WEA & Centreprise Publishing, 1974).
6.  J.R. Hampton, M.J.G. Harrison, J.R.A. Mitchell, J.S. Prichard, C. Seymour, 'Relative contributions of history-taking, physical examination, and laboratory investigation to diagnosis and management of medical outpatients.' *British Medical Journal* (1975), **ii**: 486–9.
7.  R.C. Burack and R.R. Carpenter, 'The predictive value of the presenting complaint,' *Journal of Family Practice* (1983), **16**: 749–54.
8.  M.A. Stewart, I.R. McWhinney and C.W. Buck, 'The doctor/patient relationship and its effect upon outcome,' *Journal of the Royal College of General Practitioners* (1979), **29**: 77–82.

9.  H.B. Beckman and R.M. Frankel, 'The effect of physician behaviour on the collection of data,' *Annals of Internal Medicine* (1984), **101**: 692–6.

10. J. Turner, 'The American dream,' *General Practitioner* (14 October 1977).

11. A. Watts. 'Looking back at psychiatry in general practice,' *Bulletin of the Royal College of Psychiatrists* (July 1986), **10**: 162–5.

12. J.P. Griffin and T.D. Griffin. 'The economic implications of therapeutic conservatism,' In G.T. Smith (ed.), *Innovative Competition in Medicine: a Schumpeterian Analysis of the Pharmaceutical Industry and the NHS.* (London: Office of Health Economics, 1992), pp. 85–96.

13. F. Sullivan and E. Mitchell, 'Has general practice computing made a difference to patient care? A systematic review of published reports,' *British Medical Journal* (1995), **311**: 848–52.

14. R. Fein, 'Choosing the arbiter: the market or the government,' *New England Journal of Medicine* (1985), **313**: 113–5.

## FURTHER READING

Balint, M., Hunt, J., Joyce, D., Marinker, M. and Woodcock, J., *Treatment or Diagnosis: A Study of Repeat Prescriptions in General Practice.* (London: Tavistock Publications, 1970).

Byrne, P. and Long, B., *Doctors Talking to Patients: A Study of the Verbal Behaviour of General Practitioners Consulting in their Surgeries.* (London: HMSO, 1976).

Cartwright, A., *Patients and their Doctors: A Study of General Practice.* (London: Routledge & Kegan Paul, 1967).

Cartwright, A., Hockey, L., Anderson, J.L., *Life Before Death.* (London: Routledge & Kegan Paul 1973).

Cartwright, A., *General Practice Revisited: A Second Study of Patients and their Doctors.* (London: Tavistock Publications, 1981).

Hart, J.T., *A New Kind of Doctor: The General Practitioner's Part in the Health of the Community.* (London: Merlin Press 1988).

Honigsbaum, F., *Division in British Medicine: A History of the Separation of General Practice from Hospital Care 1911–1968.* (New York: St. Martin's Press, 1979).

Huygen, F.J.A., *Family Medicine: The Medical Life History of Families.* (Nijmegen: Dekker & Van De Vegt, 1970).

Kleinman, A., *The Illness Narratives: Suffering, Healing and the Human Condition.* (New York: Basic Books, 1988).

Konner, M., *The Trouble with Medicine.* (London: BBC Books, 1993).

Smith, F.M., *The Surgery at Aberffrwd,* Crofton, D.H. (ed.). (Hythe, Kent: Volturna Press 1981).

Stevens, R., *Medical Practice in Modern England.* (New Haven: Yale University Press, 1966).

Taylor, S., *Good General Practice: A Report of a Survey.* (London: Oxford University Press, 1954).

Tuckett, D., Boulton, M., Olson, C., Williams, A., *Meetings Between Experts: An Approach to Sharing Ideas in Medical Consultations.* (London: Tavistock Publications, 1985).

Wilkin, D., Hallam, L., Leavey, R. and Metcalfe, D., *Anatomy of Urban General Practice.* (London: Tavistock, 1987).

# CHAPTER 36

# Childbirth and Maternity

### HILARY MARLAND

T he summer and early autumn months of 1996 were marked by a childbirth
story of *fin de siècle* proportions, as in Britain, and elsewhere, the future
of Mandy Allwood's eight fetuses, gestating in a flurry of publicity, was
discussed and debated. In a drama which absorbed press, public and medical
profession, a private dilemma passed rapidly into the public domain, the claims
of 'public interest' becoming paramount, the ethics surrounding reproductive
technology the subject matter of breakfast table, office and pub. The media had
a field day, particularly when the *News of the World* reputedly offered financial
support to Ms Allwood if she went ahead with the pregnancy. Health authorities
quibbled over the costs of embarking on a foolhardy and very costly obstetric trial.
Ms Allwood, though warned of the risk to her babies of carrying on with an octuple
pregnancy and the potential danger to her own health, decided to go ahead and
not take the option of selective abortion.

Public opinion was divided, medical opinion less so given that this was an
experiment which could end only in disaster, although some doctors reminded
us that the patient's right to choose should be respected under all circumstances,
even the extreme and highly unusual. 'Life,' the Roman Catholic organization
dedicated to opposing abortion as part of its advocacy of motherhood, supported
Ms Allwood's choice, applauding her decision to 'protect' *all* her babies, and
depicting her as a moral stalwart with true maternal feelings in an age where
termination is all too easily carried out on medical, social or financial grounds.
Ms Allwood's decision was regarded by many as rash, even immoral; if any of the
fetuses did reach viability, they were likely to be terribly handicapped. The issue
was resolved in a tragic but anticipated way in late September 1996 when all eight
babies, three girls and five boys, were stillborn over a period of two days. The
London hospital where the saga reached its sad end issued a statement expressing
deep regret, which overrode any disapprobation of Ms Allwood's actions. The
nation, still divided on the issues, but steered by the tabloids, 'mourned' with
Mandy Allwood.

Ms Allwood's experience is at the time of writing unique, but it highlights
many of the issues dominating childbirth at the close of the twentieth century.

It publicized the current pinnacle of obstetric possibilities, of conceiving eight babies, and was testimony to the high standards and effectiveness of obstetric care and technology, given that Ms Allwood carried the babies for some 19 weeks without apparent harm to herself. The case turned on the issue of risk to mother and babies, an issue which has prevailed since early in the century but under the rubrics of danger or fear of death or debility rather than risk. It focused attention too on the 'morality' of opting for selective abortion, on fetal rights, privacy and the protection of life in the 'maternal ecosystem.' The question of the appropriateness of fertility treatments on offer, which often give rise to multiple pregnancies, came to the fore. This linked with the issue of the discretion of obstetricians in assisting women — including single, widowed and gay women — to conceive, the quality and depth of backup and counseling services, and the role of professionals and hospitals in providing and shaping maternity care in more general terms. Choice and individual rights were set against professional and moral concerns, and were seen not always to be compatible. The case highlighted the problems of funding and cost. It was also testimony to apparently endless public interest in unusual obstetric occurrences.

All women have been affected by the enormous changes in childbirth practice and the management of birth during the twentieth century. The changes have been revolutionary, many beneficial, some questionable, and a few disturbing. Giving birth is one of the most fundamental of female activities, and such changes touch vast numbers of women and their families. Perhaps this, more than other forms of contact with medicine, has shaped attitudes and expectations of medicine and ideas of 'medical progress' and the 'power' of technology. Many women have applauded and demanded 'progress' in obstetrics through the twentieth century, the majority appear to have accepted it. But there has also been a constant stream of opposition by those deploring and resisting it, questioning whether the stepping up of technology, monitoring and birth management through drugs and machines can be termed 'progress.'

Many will be unaware of the depth of change, but overall public interest, particularly women's interest, in birthing practices and outcomes has grown enormously. Women have also gradually become much better informed, particularly as publishers and the media have shown great interest in childbirth issues. At the beginning of the century concern with childbirth, as a medical event and demographic phenomenon, was the preserve of politicians and doctors. Other interest groups, midwives, mothers and their families, were largely excluded. However, the more active representatives of these groups began to organize and campaign, largely for improved maternity services, through a variety of professional, voluntary and political organizations: in Britain organizations as varied as the Women's Cooperative Guild, the National Council for Maternity and Child Welfare, the Labour Party Women's Organization, the Eugenics Society, the National Birthday Trust Fund, and many more. Massive structural changes occurred in the organization of childbirth services, a move from home to hospital births, particularly after the 1930s, with the associated intrusions of birthing technology. This shift, and the stepping up of attendance by doctors as obstetrics developed as a speciality (with, in Britain, its own Royal College of Obstetricians and Gynae-cologists being founded in 1929), on the whole went unchallenged because such changes were associated with progress and the implementation of 'better' services.

Other major themes have been played out during the century within Western Europe and North America, which will surface in this chapter, alongside the tripartite shift in place, intervention and attendance at birth. The first of these is the diminishing danger of childbirth for mothers and their babies. Public involvement, particularly on the part of mothers, in demanding improvements in services and treatment during pregnancy and delivery, was stepped up after the 1950s, linking with increased knowledge and expectations about how childbirth should proceed, and reaching a high point towards the end of the century. The century has been marked too by raised levels of childbirth consumerism, not only in terms of the consumption of products, but also in the sense of women seeing themselves very much as consumers of a service, who are able to demand specific things of the services and make choices. These demands, however, are not always met, and choices in practice can be very limited.

The relative importance of mothers and babies in the maternity equation has shifted dramatically since 1900. At the beginning of the century antenatal care did not exist, nor did maternity grants or the concept of maternity leave. In the early 1900s motherhood was dominated by debates on race and eugenics and by poli-ticians' concern with falling birth rates, nationhood, supremacy and 'keeping up the reinforcements' in a period where war or the threat of war was rarely absent. In the last quarter of the nineteenth century fewer babies were born, and, while general mortality was declining, more children were dying at a very early age. Infants perished in alarming numbers: in 1876 146 out of every 1,000 babies born in England and Wales died before their first birthday, and this rate rose to 156 by the end of the century. The Boer War (1889–1902) and First World War (1914–18) — when a third of potential recruits were rejected as unfit — brought anxieties not just about numbers but also physical status to a head, and further stimulated the nascent infant welfare movement. The movement concentrated on correcting mothers, re-educating them in their duties, though some nations invested substan-tially in services and benefits too. It was made concrete by establishing infant welfare centres (well-baby clinics), schools for mothers and mothercraft courses, where they were taught proper hygienic and childrearing practices. Mothers were urged to breast feed their babies, thus diminishing the danger of death from diarrhea and giving the child a proper start in life. The golden rule was to 'Feed with the mother's milk... If you really love your child and would do the best for it, *feed it at the breast*.'[1] The early decades of the century also saw the expansion of health visiting, and campaigns to make the notification of births compulsory throughout Europe and North America.

Pro-natalist movements used a variety of tactics to stimulate mothers to have more babies. Motherhood was glorified as being women's natural duty and their greatest source of fulfilment, while at the same time mothers were criticized and vilified as being neglectful of this duty, either because they were inept and allowed their babies lives to be forfeited, or because they were evasive, and, wickedly, through the practices of birth control and abortion, destroyed lives they were meant to nurture. The number of abortions carried out in Germany, for example, grew from 250,000 a year in the early 1920s to one million in the last years of the Weimar Republic, when they exceeded the annual number of births. Maternalist policies were far-reaching in some countries, and included the provision of maternity benefits and state assistance, and, by the 1930s and 1940s, family allowances. France, where the birth-rate dipped below the death rate in 1938, with a population decline of 35,000 per annum, stimulated motherhood in a big way, discouraging the employment of women, introducing harsh penalties for abortion, and rewarding mothers who had big families not only with cash benefits — paid maternity leave (1928), family allowances (1932), payments to mothers who nursed their own children (1935) and first-birth premiums (1939) — but also medals, a bronze for five living children, silver for mothers of eight, and a 'gold' medal for women with ten children. Pro-natalism, with its cruel twists of policies for 'race regeneration' and sterilization, reached its apogee in Nazi Germany with the motto 'not only quantity but quality,' urged by expectations of large families of healthy Volkish children to populate the New Europe. The 'eugenic movement,' concerned with heredity and population decline amongst the 'fit,' was a powerful force across the Western World. The sterilization of the unfit was activated in other nations, including Scandinavia and the United States, where 'defective' infants were also allowed to die by doctors in their effort to eliminate the 'unfit,' but never with the intent, force, extent and viciousness of Nazi Germany.

It could be argued that perceptions of the well-being of mothers has shifted thrice during this century, although not in any neat or decisive way, centering early in the century on their actual survival, then on their health and welfare, and during the last few decades, on their satisfaction with the process of birthing and experience of maternity. In the early twentieth century maternal mortality deeply concerned doctors and midwives, politicians and policy makers, and particularly mothers who regarded birth with dread, fearing injury, incapacity or death. Alice Gregory, one of the founders of the reforming Midwives' Institute and author of a textbook on midwifery, wrote in 1923 of the tragedy of the death of a woman in childbirth:

> I have twice seen the desolation of a working-man's home when the mother is suddenly taken from her young children, and I never want to see it again. She went up to her room in apparently good health perhaps twelve hours before, and she will never come down again until her body is carried to the grave...[2]

Few women had any form of antenatal care. Many doctors and midwives had a cavalier attitude to performing check ups unless the woman was visibly ailing, and even well-to-do women would rarely see their attendant until confinement. By the 1940s, however, antenatal care was increasing, with a steady growth in antenatal clinics (an afterthought of the infant welfare movement), and stepped up monitoring of pregnant women: blood and urine tests, blood pressure measurement, weighing and abdominal examinations.

Maternal mortality rates, in contrast to the steady decline in mortality in general, remained unremittingly high; in the decade 1920–29 25,000 women in Britain and at least a quarter of a million in the US died from childbirth-related causes, the most common being puerperal infection, toxemia (blood poisoning), and hemorrhage. Rates varied dramatically from nation to nation and from region to region. Social and economic considerations and the general level of maternity services helped determine the safe delivery of mothers, but perhaps most significant until the mid-1930s was the quality of care offered.

Maternal death or harm was linked to a lack of experience or mismanagement of the delivery by the obstetrician, general practitioner or midwife, to infection resulting from excessive interference, 'failed forceps' or simple neglect. Some general practitioners used forceps and anesthesia as routine, rushing the delivery through, without taking proper antiseptic precautions. Standards of practice on the part of midwives and their untrained contemporaries, the handywomen — who continued to work in large numbers across Europe and North America until the 1930s and 1940s — also varied greatly. Accusations of unhygienic practice, neglect, lack of skill and roughness abound, but so does praise of experience and inordinate skill and kindness, such of that of Mrs Quinton in Flora Thompson's *Lark Rise to Candleford*, "a decent, intelligent old body, clean in her person and methods and very kind," or Martha, "one of the good old midwives and it was only a few shillings for a confinement."[3]

Comparatively low national rates of maternal mortality in Scandinavia and the Netherlands by the 1920s (around 25 deaths per 10,000 births) reflected the quality of midwife training in these countries. In the US a shocking rate of almost 80 deaths per 10,000 deliveries was a result largely of low standards of obstetric education, a rapid forcing out of midwives from practice, condemnation of home births and the move to often inappropriate hospital environments, and an 'orgy of interference' by doctors. Within countries rates also varied considerably. In 1930 Rochdale, a cotton town in industrial Lancashire, ranked as the most dangerous place in Britain for mothers to give birth, with just under 90 deaths per 10,000 deliveries.

The poor health and miserable lives of childbearing women early this century is demonstrated nowhere better than in the 'amazing' letters written by members of the Women's Cooperative Guild, published in 1915. The letters testify to the weariness, discomfort and despair women felt during pregnancy and after giving birth; they suffered from backache, varicose veins, sickness, swellings, tearings and prolapsed wombs; many had experienced several miscarriages and terrible births; they objected to having to continue with their heavy domestic duties until they delivered and almost immediately after, to the lack of government support, poor standards of obstetric care, and the dearth of birth control advice, for many saw family limitation as the best way of improving their lot.

> Three months before the baby came, I was practically an invalid... Of course, I had chloroform; indeed I had it with all my seven children, except two, as I have always such long and terrible labours,... I am never able to get up under three weeks after confinement, as I always start to flood directly I make any movement,... I always have terribly sore breasts,... to me [childbirth] is a time of horror from beginning to end.[4]

Many of these women expressed a wish to have their babies in hospital, where they anticipated good care, rest and peace. They began to perceive the hospital as being the safe and proper place to give birth, where skilled attendance, emergency cover and pain relief would be close to hand.

As childbirth has become synonymous with the hospital, so too has hospital birth with 'safe' birth. More than anything this has provided the justification for the move to hospital. Yet there is little evidence that giving birth in hospital makes a contribution to safe childbirth. Though data on maternal and perinatal deaths are difficult to analyze, especially cross-nationally, it is argued in some interpretations of the statistics that mothers and their babies are at least as safe, perhaps safer, at home. Recent outbreaks of infection caused by virulent strains of hospital bacteria confirm that maternity wards are far from being sterile havens.

In 1900 the vast majority of births would be attended at home by a midwife, in the 1930s birth at home with a GP or midwife was still standard, but by the 1950s the trend towards the hospital had set in. A recent book on midwives, midwifery and women in Britain, which explores the 'social meaning' of midwifery, starts with the premise — it could hardly do otherwise — that "the site of the labour process... is that of a hospital labour ward, and this is, of course, the overwhelmingly common experience of birth for both 'labouring' women and practising midwives in Britain today."[5]

The shift to hospital births, at first slow, has been sustained; it has proved to be a one-way street. The US led the way to the hospital, chronologically and in terms of the rapidity of change. By 1935 37 per cent of births in the US took place in hospital, by 1960 96 per cent. While in 1960 some 33 per cent of women in England and Wales still gave birth at home the rate had dropped to 13 per cent in 1970. In 1992, in the US and Britain, only one per cent of women gave birth outside the hospital, and in the US this one per cent included deliveries at short-stay birth centres. The timing of this relocation of birth has varied from country to country depending on socio-cultural and economic factors, geography, the organization of services, and the accessibility of midwives, doctors and hospitals. Sweden was one of the first countries in Western Europe to see hospital and clinic births replace home deliveries, with the turning point occurring as early as the 1920s and 1930s; by the end of the Second World War only 27 per cent of Swedish women gave birth at home. Radical social and economic changes in Sweden stimulated enthusiasm for hospital culture and the new ideals of modernity, hygiene, science, and technology. Only in the Netherlands was the pattern broken or at least skewed, for while hospital births did rise, especially in the 1970s, from 47 per cent in 1970 to 65 per cent in 1980, in the 1990s over 30 per cent of Dutch women still give birth at home. They are urged to do this by their midwives, who prefer to assist women at home and who work autonomously. Dutch midwives are supported by and large by obstetricians and a government which encourages home birth because its sees no reason why it should do otherwise: obstetric services function well and home birth is comparatively cheap. Dutch women are also encouraged to stay at home because a rich birthing culture has survived — some families still place a model of a stork, the traditional bringer of babies, outside their houses after the birth of a baby. The *kraambezoek*, lying-in visit, is a serious neighbourly obligation, colleagues and friends are treated to cakes and biscuits. The lying-in woman is assisted for several days after the delivery by a maternity nurse (paid through the health insurance schemes to which everyone belongs) who cares for the mother and baby and helps with the housework.

Elsewhere the culture of home births has taken a serious knock. Hospital delivery has been consistently mooted as safer (without proof of this), and as qualitatively better. By the 1920s and 1930s private nursing homes had become popular with the well-to-do, who saw them as offering higher standards and status. To give birth at home, especially with a midwife, was not the done thing. Many poor women, meanwhile, were eager to give birth in hospital where they also expected better care and a break from domestic work. In a study of working-class women in northern England, based largely on interviews, Elizabeth Roberts recorded the survival of fatalism, shame, stoicism, and traditionalism into the interwar period. Yet increasing numbers of these women also expected more and better professional help, whether in the form of a doctor or qualified midwife, and they began to demand pain relief and a hospital bed 'in case something should go wrong.' Their expectations were all too often not realized. Hospital birth could be miserable, the maternity ward far from restful. The eminent obstetrician Sir George Pinker, reflected that at the end of the 1940s:

> the labour ward and delivery room were archaic. The instruments were still boiled in a fish kettle, and the approach to patients was, frankly, dictatorial. Husbands weren't allowed in, and visitors were deterred. The delivery of a baby was carried out almost mechanically, and pain-relief was minimal.[6]

Women's recollections describe the loneliness and sense of abandonment of a hospital delivery. Women would be left to labour alone, with a midwife popping in from time to time to do internal examinations and check on the dilation of the cervix. The delivery room resembled an operating theatre. Birth took place lying down, often with feet in stirrups. Women lost privacy and dignity and this was not substituted by quality care, but by the rigors of ward routine, including four-hourly feeds and obsessive hygiene. Though hospital regimes have changed immensely, the temptation to use the gadgetry — after all it is there — to induce and monitor progress, and to ensure routines are kept is still strong; many women feel intimidated and powerless. After 1970, following the unequivocal findings of the Peel Report which declared the hospital as the proper place to give birth, home births were officially frowned upon in Britain. Around the same time, however, women became increasingly assertive in campaigning for the option of a more 'natural' and woman-centred birth, and prepared to insist on their right to a home delivery.

From the mid-nineteenth century and the first use of anesthesia in obstetrics, women and their attendants have sought smooth, quick and painless childbirth; it is one area in particular where women have been insistent in their demands for medical intervention. Women welcomed chloroform. It was one reason why women chose, if they could afford it, to have a doctor attend them rather than a midwife. The move to hospital was linked inextricably to a stepping up of surgical procedures, and the increased use of analgesics and anesthetics. By the early twentieth century, women had heightened expectations about the possibility of a painless delivery, and doctors too commonly accepted the use of pain relief. It made their job easier. The search for a perfect solution to pain in childbirth was on. The setting up of the National Birthday Trust Fund in Britain in 1928 by a group of upper-class philanthropists was stimulated by a report on maternal mortality by Dr Janet Campbell of the Ministry of Health. Aiming at 'safer motherhood' through better maternity services, the NBTF first promoted anesthesia in maternity hospitals, but later shifted their concern to midwife training and equipping midwives with methods of analgesia at home.

Chloroform remained the predominant form of analgesia up until the Second World War, often administered by a GP at home. But the quest for the perfect solution to pain reached its apogee, not in terms of levels of usage but certainly in extremes of misguidedness, in the US and a number of European countries in the 1920s, with the introduction of scopolamine. Scopolamine obliterated memory rather than pain, with confinements being 'dropped out' of women's lives. What became known as 'Twilight Sleep' demanded rigorous supervision; the mothers, in considerable danger of self-injury as they thrashed about during delivery, were strapped down in special crib beds. The technique was regarded as dubious by many, and it proved to be dangerous, making the newborn lethargic and resulting in the death of Twilight Sleep mothers. Yet so eager were women to have access to this form of amnesia that they campaigned vigorously for it, some even making the journey from America to Germany, where the method was better established, to ensure that they could have a Twilight Sleep birth.

The Twilight Sleep phenomenon is interesting because it shows that demand for intervention did not necessarily come from doctors, but could result from the vigorous campaigns of women's groups. Debate has continued about the pros and cons of pain relief, and particularly its effect on the baby. Changes in usage of obstetric analgesia have not always safe-guarded the fetus. In Britain the safe but not completely effective painkiller nitrous oxide was replaced in the 1940s by the more powerful analgesic, pethidine, a synthetic narcotic, which had a depressant effect on the respiration of the fetus. The introduction of the Apgar score to assess new-born babies' functions has been associated with advances in obstetric anesthesia, but the very fact of its introduction reflects the concern of mothers, doctors and midwives about the doping of babies during labour.

The introduction of pain relief has also taken its toll on midwives' work and status. In the mid-1930s, in England and Wales midwives still carried out 60 to 70 per cent of deliveries, mostly at home. They were not allowed to give chloroform, though after 1936 they could use 'gas and air.' As the demand for pain relief grew and new methods developed — particularly spinal anesthesia, which could only be administered in the hospital environment and often by an anesthetist rather than birth attendant — the midwife's role was further undermined.

As the century progressed, the idea of birth as a natural process where problems would be met if and when they arose was replaced by a more interventionalist model. Birth was seen increasingly as pathological and obstetrics as preventive. It is a phenomenon which is hard to date, and there was great variation from country to country. Again, the US took the lead. Joseph B. DeLee of Chicago recommended the routine use of forceps and episiotomy (incision to enlarge the birth passage around the vagina to avoid tearing) in *all* births, with mothers being heavily sedated, ether administered when the baby entered the birth canal, and ergot being given to speed the delivery of the placenta. DeLee was highly influential, and, by the 1930s, coincident with the massive shift to the hospital, prophylactic obstetrics had become the norm in the US. Midwives, who DeLee campaigned to eliminate, were not of course permitted to perform these procedures. Again, where America led, Europe followed, but never in such a drastic way. DeLee's work also led to increased concern with the well-being of the fetus. Perinatology, the care of the infant in late pregnancy and the first week after birth, became a new sub-specialty, and led to a whole range of medical interventions: induction of labor, monitoring of the fetal heartbeat, episiotomy, the use of instruments and Cesarean section.

In one country in particular, the Netherlands, obstetricians have been wary of embracing the new technologies, and the use of instruments and pain relief have been kept, if not at a minimum, then at least at a low level. Cesarean sections, for example, were carried out in 8 per cent of deliveries during the 1990s, compared with 25 per cent in many other developed countries, and peaks of up to 60 per cent in some US hospitals. Pain relief is rarely administered in the Netherlands even today. Rather it is argued that women must be supported emotionally through birth and offered reassurance and encouragement instead of drugs. In Greece, to take a counter example, the idea of home birth is unthinkable, amongst the medical profession and women. Medical students are taught to do three scans per normal pregnancy, partly in response to women's requests to 'see the baby,' hospital birth includes routine shaving, enemas, intravenous drips, pitocin to augment labour, electronic fetal monitors, episiotomies, the lithotomy position with arms and legs strapped to the delivery table, and cesarean birth for about one-third of women.

One influential British woman journalist recently depicted advocates of natural childbirth, who have existed in some form or another from the 1940s onwards, as lentil-eating earth mothers, and those who would prefer epidurals as the silent majority. It is true that expectations about birth have dovetailed to a great extent; mothers often want, more or less, what is on offer. But it is also true that the 'choices' offered by standard hospital midwifery are limited ones and deeply embedded in the system.

Arising out of the rush to the hospital in the 1950s was the first 'counter-movement' in midwifery care. One of the pioneers of a new attitude to childbirth was Grantly Dick-Read, obstetrician and pioneer of natural childbirth. In what has become a well-known story, Dick-Read related how when attending a woman at the birth of her first child in a slum in Whitechapel, shortly after he became a medical student at the London Hospital in 1911, she refused chloroform. The baby was born without 'fuss or noise,' and when Dick-Read was preparing to leave the woman turned to him to explain why she refused assistance: "It didn't hurt. It wasn't meant to, was it doctor?"[7] Dick-Read crystallized his ideas on childbirth into the 'fear-tension-pain' syndrome. If women knew more about what was happening to their bodies during pregnancy and birth and could be shown how to relax, pain relief would not be necessary, and if women felt pain it would not be sufficient to need drugs. This flew in the face of convention in post-war obstetrics when women were poorly informed about pregnancy and birth. In 1950 the *Sunday Express Baby Book* gave few details of the actual delivery: "Do not be alarmed by the appearance of the labour ward, which will look rather like an operating theatre, … with cases of instruments and so on. These do not mean a thing…."[8] Dick-Read's books, particularly *Childbirth Without Fear* (also published as *Revelation of Childbirth*, 1942), became best sellers and Dick-Read the acknowledged leader of the natural childbirth movement. But others were also offering less publicized 'alternative' birthing regimes. Sir Dugald Baird, practising in Scotland in the 1930s, described how he:

> was doing what young women are advocating now — natural childbirth… They could get up and walk around if they wanted to. Then I used to say to them, now what do you want to do? Do you want to push it out yourself, or have it taken out for you?… What you did depended on what the patient was like.[9]

In recent decades the National Childbirth Trust has encouraged awareness of pregnancy and birth and taught relaxation methods as a route to a more natural birth. Childbirth gurus, particularly Ferdinand Lamaze, Frederique Leboyer and Michel Odent, and in Britain Sheila Kitzinger, have advocated an active role for women in birth, pain relief through breathing and relaxing, and concern that the child too experiences a gentle birth.

In 1985 the Wendy Savage case provoked intense public interest, and highlighted again the question of individual choice. Wendy Savage, an obstetrician working in a London hospital, was suspended for allowing women to undergo a 'trial of labour' rather than opt directly for a cesarean section when there were strong indications that this would be necessary. Savage was reinstated after a public enquiry during which she won massive support from her patients, GPs, midwives and the general public. Radical midwives organizations campaign with similar goals in mind: the possibility of a natural, possibly home, birth, as an 'alternative' to doctor-centered, service-directed births.

For midwives, the twentieth century has brought mixed blessings. Expectations were varied at the beginning of the century, but in many Western countries midwives had high hopes. They were after all still the usual childbirth attendants, even in the US where they delivered around half of all births. Midwives sought to recreate themselves, to acquire the trappings of professional authority, to improve their training, and to brush off their associations with their traditional counterparts, the 'Gamps' and the handywomen said to have 'graveyard luck,' who saved the mother but lost the child. The 'new' midwife wished to present another image as she competed for clients — ladylike, modern, professional and hygienic. Midwives organized locally, nationally and internationally, through professional societies and journals, seeking increased recognition, a larger role in public health work, disassociating themselves in a highly unsympathetic climate from fertility control and abortion. They sought to position themselves correctly in the brave new world of preventive medicine. For some politicians and reformers the midwife was the solution and she was recruited in the drive to improve health education and encourage hygienic practices, especially proper infant rearing, but for others she was the problem and liable to be an object of cleansing or removal exercises herself.

The dawn of hospital obstetrics, the increased participation of doctors, and the stepping up of public concern and institutional provision for mothers and babies, did not necessarily anticipate midwives' demise, but in many countries their role changed out of all recognition. In the US they fared worse than anywhere else. The specialist obstetrician, with his armamentarium of instruments and analgesics — playing on the notion that twentieth-century women were more feeble than their mothers and grandmothers and ill-equipped to withstand the rigors of birth — moved forcefully into a maturing and increasingly lucrative discipline. In a campaign dating from early in the twentieth century, the American midwife was diminished, vilified, almost eliminated. The well-documented 'debate' on the future of the midwife in the US was largely an attempt to challenge and undermine her position. The attacks of the medical profession were unrelenting and vitriolic, the typical midwife being declared as a drag on the progress of obstetrics and 'un-American,' "filthy, ignorant, not far removed from the jungles of Africa, typically old, gin-fingering and guzzling, periferous and vicious."[10] Some discordant voices were heard, who sought improved training and licensing based on European models, but the overwhelmingly successful line was to force the midwife out, and put doctors trained in obstetrics in her place. This has resulted in a deep crisis today for American obstetrics. As insurance coverage to protect doctors from being sued for obstetric malpractice and negligence has shot up, GPs have withdrawn from midwifery, leaving large swathes of rural America without birth attendants. Meanwhile, in neighbouring Canada, the midwife is enjoying a revival. Direct-entry midwifery has been legalized and given government support in several provinces in the 1990s, and there has been a rush to enter the midwife training schools and great demand for midwives as birth attendants.

Towards the end of the century, midwife organizations are seeking not only a reversal but also a reassessment of the main premises of childbirth practice. In America where the law is the problem as much as the resistance of the medical profession, Raymond DeVries points to the power of the established system of obstetric care, even in the face of soaring costs, a severe shortage of midwifery practitioners in some regions, a service crippled by fear of litigation and one which in terms of perinatal mortality and maternal well-being is far from successful. The account he relates is both absurd and poignant, seeming to fly in the face of the evidence, and representing a clinging to the established ways, with failure being seen as not embedded in the shortcomings of the system of obstetric care, but in it not being implemented in a rigorous enough way:

> In 1995 a team of investigative reporters for the *New York Times*, looking to explain poor perinatal outcomes in New York City, turned their gaze to that which seemed out of place in American medicine: midwives... the authors maligned midwives and the insufficient use of obstetric technology as the culprits for poor obstetric results... The solution must be more technology, more intervention. Following this logic, the authors faulted the midwives for their low rate of Cesarean sections, 12.9 per cent, and asked why it was not closer to the city average of 23.1 per cent.[11]

Whatever the differences in timing and extent of change, by the close of the twentieth century the vast majority of women in the Western World give birth in hospital; in doing this, the majority are now following in the footsteps of their mothers and grandmothers. A new 'tradition' has grown up over the century. For many women, childbirth is the only point of contact with a hospital; it has come to equal the hospital, and at the same time in the last few decades the hospital has become a more comfortable and relaxed place to give birth, with birth partners being encouraged, bathing, music and birth menus on offer. Yet there is little which points to the superiority of hospital birth in terms of standards of care, results or, in many cases, satisfaction.

Childbirth has undoubtedly become, despite national differences, more uniform and safe. Maternal deaths began a steep decline after 1940 which has continued to the present, a result of improved standards of maternal care, the introduction of sulphonomides in 1936–37, which effectively treated puerperal fever, the use of ergometrine which prevents bleeding after birth, the introduction of blood transfusion services, and improved nutrition and general health. In the last quarter of the century, it has become rare for women in prosperous countries to die as a result of childbirth (usually less than 0.10 per 1,000 births). However, in poor countries women run 100 to 200 times the risk of dying in pregnancy or birth. In the 1980s about half a million maternal deaths occurred each year, and 99 per cent of these were in developing countries.

The nature of fear surrounding birth has changed, but for some women is still part of giving birth. Few women nowadays anticipate death or harm in childbirth. Yet there is still dread of feeling pain or anxiety about not 'coping' properly during delivery. But most fear focuses on the unborn baby. The notion that birth is only normal in retrospect has become commonplace amongst obstetricians, and many women would support this view, and approve their pregnancies being closely monitored and supervised, intervention is generally early and effective, and 'abnormalities' quickly identified. Ideas of what constitutes a 'normal' birth are slippery, but it is reasonable to say that, during the twentieth century, birth has been increasingly seen as potentially abnormal and pathological, and, while support for natural birthing practices and a return to home birth has gained momentum, this trend continues. As one recent account of the effects of fetal diagnosis explained, the question 'Is the baby all right' is likely to be posed, and efforts made to answer it, ever earlier in pregnancy, instead of at the traditional moment of birth. During the last few decades a whole range of genetic and technological developments have increased possibilities of monitoring and checking on progress or for 'faults.' The results of tests such as amniocentesis are vague, and point to increased risk rather than definite disability; the tests themselves can endanger the fetus, and are psychologically devastating for the mother. Our grandmothers and great-grandmothers may have been weary and fearful about pain or injury at birth, but did they face the same forms of anxiety which many women now feel throughout pregnancy, as a range of potential medical defects is unfolded before them?

At the outset of the twenty-first century women are healthier in general, their nutritional status improved, and their pregnancies and births are in many ways — though perhaps not all — easier than those of their predecessors. What is shocking is that, while health in general has improved, many women still give birth and bring up their children in extreme poverty, and not just in the developing countries. The timely appearance of *Mother Courage*, a volume of letters published in 1997 as a sequel to *Maternity*, collated by the Women's Cooperative Guild in 1915, shows that, while we have moved on in some ways, much that we might have expected to change has not changed. The Maternity Alliance, set up in 1980, campaigns for the rights of women to choose where and how to give birth, and, just as the Women's Cooperative Guild did at the beginning of the century, to ensure that no woman faces maternity in poverty. Fewer of the mothers writing in the 1990s complained of serious health problems associated with childbirth, though pain, breast and bleeding problems, tiredness and depression were recorded. Complaints about standards of obstetric care were more subdued by the 1990s, but many mothers recorded struggling on in poverty and were frustrated by the government's neglect of their plight. Figures show that in the 1990s nearly one baby in every three is born into a family living on means-tested benefits in Britain, and low birthweight babies (and subsequent deaths) are more likely to be born in families with fathers in manual occupations and to lone mothers.

This is made all the worse by the high standards set by those eager to enjoy the good birth experience to the full, reflected in regular visits to antenatal clinics, attendance at parenting classes, 'menus' to select analgesics and delivery options, diet and vitamin supplements, exercise classes, the purchase of fashionable maternity clothes. There is nothing new about expenditure on babies being encouraged, but the expansion of necessary items from the simple layette of the 1920 and 1930s, with families scrimping and saving to pay for doctors' or midwives' bills, milk and a cot (poor parents were urged to make these of orange boxes) to the designer baby kit of the 1990s has been nothing short of phenomenal. There is an intensely 'right(eous)' path to the good birth. It is rigorous and those who want to do 'best' invest much time, trouble and expense in preparation. For the poor birth has always been a risky financial undertaking, a crippling burden on family budgets, but the costs of parenting have soared at the end of the century, linked to a vast industry in books and magazines on pregnancy, birth and parentcraft, baby items, toys, and clothing.

Governments and mothers at the end of the twentieth century are no longer absorbed with the demands of nationhood and eugenic considerations, although such influences have not disappeared entirely. Whereas the *bête noire* of those seeking to reform maternity services early in the twentieth century was the woman who claimed to know about childbearing and childrearing because she had 'born 12 and buried 8,' towards the end of the century this has become the single 'welfare mother,' depicted by the media as immoral, a poor citizen and a major drain on resources. Families have changed: they are much smaller than at the beginning of the century and more births occur outside of marriage (almost 34 per cent in England and Wales in 1995). The advent of the lone parent can be lain alongside concerns that materially better off, highly educated, double-income couples are less likely to have families. A number of European countries have responded to this, improving maternity benefits and conditions for maternity leave, indicating continued anxieties about the quantity and quality of national populations. Yet at the same time many parts of the Western World have shown little commitment to improving the conditions of women giving birth in poverty without proper state back up and assistance. While base level needs remain untackled, anxieties about the impact of genetic research, even cloning, for those planning families, the ever more extensive possibilities for fertility control and enhancement, and sharpening notions about the status of the fetus, promise that childbirth and maternity will continue to occupy a shifting space between public and private concern.

## REFERENCES

1.  Annual Report of the Medical Officer of Health, Huddersfield, 1905, pp. 20, 22. Cited in Hilary Marland, 'A pioneer in infant welfare: The Huddersfield Scheme 1903–1920,' *Social History of Medicine* (1993), **6**: 25–50, at p. 39.
2.  Alice Gregory (ed.), *The Midwife: Her Book.* (London: Frowde & Hodder, 1923), p. 135.
3.  Flora Thompson, *Lark Rise to Candleford.* (Harmondsworth: Penguin edn, 1978), pp. 135–6; Elizabeth Roberts, *A Woman's Place. An Oral History of Working-Class Women 1890–1940.* (Oxford: Basil Blackwell, 1984), p. 106.
4.  Margaret Llewelyn Davies (ed.), *Maternity. Letters from Working Women.* (London: G. Bell & Sons, 1915; Virago edn, 1978), letter 48, pp. 74–6.
5.  Sheila Hunt and Anthea Symonds, *The Social Meaning of Midwifery.* (London: Macmillan, 1995), pp. xv, 1.
6.  Cited Johanna Moorhead, *New Generations. 40 Years of Birth in Britain.* (London: HMSO in collaboration with the National Childbirth Trust, 1996), p. 17.
7.  Mary Thomas (ed.), *Post-war Mothers. Childbirth Letters to Grantly Dick-Read, 1946–1956.* (Rochester, NY: University of Rochester Press, 1997), p. 9.
8.  Cited in Moorhead, *New Generations*, p. 17.
9.  Interview with Sir Dugald Baird, Edinburgh 1983. Cited in Jenny Carter and Thérèse Duriez, *With Child. Birth Through the Ages.* (Edinburgh: Mainstream, 1986), p. 156.
10. Irvine Loudon, 'Childbirth,' in *idem* (ed.), *Western Medicine. An Illustrated History.* (Oxford and New York: Oxford University Press, 1997), p. 218.
11. Raymond DeVries, *Making Midwives Legal. Childbirth, Medicine, and the Law*, 2nd edn. (Columbus: Ohio State University Press, 1996), p. xv.

## FURTHER READING

Abraham-van der Mark, Eva (ed.), *Successful Home Birth and Midwifery. The Dutch Model.* (Westport, CT and London: Bergin & Garvey, 1993).

Carter, Jenny and Duriez, Thérèse, *With Child. Birth through the Ages.* (Edinburgh: Mainstream, 1986).

DeVries, Raymond, *Making Midwives Legal. Childbirth, Medicine, and the Law*, 2nd edn. (Columbus: Ohio State University Press, 1996).

Donnison, Jean, *Midwives and Medical Men. A History of the Struggle for the Control of Childbirth.* (Historical Publications: New Barnet, Herts., 1988).

Davis-Floyd, Robbie E. and Sargent, Carolyn F. (eds), *Childbirth and Authoritative Knowledge. Cross-Cultural Perspectives.* (Berkeley and Los Angeles: University of Los Angeles Press, 1997).

Davies, Margaret Llewelyn (ed.), *Maternity. Letters from Working Women.* (London: G. Bell & Sons, 1915; Virago edn, 1978).

Garcia, Jo, Kilpatrick, Robert and Richards, Martin (eds), *The Politics of Maternity Care. Services for Childbearing Women in Twentieth-Century Britain.* (Oxford: Clarendon Press, 1990).

Gowdridge, Christine, Williams, A. Susan and Wynn, Margaret (eds), *Mother Courage. Letters from Mothers in Poverty at the End of the Century.* (Harmondsworth: Penguin in association with The Maternity Alliance, 1997).

Leap, Nicky and Hunter, Billie, *The Midwife's Tale. An Oral History from Handywoman to Professional Midwife.* (London: Scarlet Press, 1993).

Leavitt, Judith Walzer, *Brought to Bed. Childbearing in America, 1750–1950.* (New York and Oxford: Oxford University Press, 1986).

Lewis, Jane, *The Politics of Motherhood. Child and Maternal Welfare in England, 1900–1939.* (London: Croom Helm, 1980).

Loudon, Irvine, *Death in Childbirth. An International Study of Maternal Care and Maternal Mortality 1800–1950.* (Oxford: Clarendon Press, 1992).

Marland, Hilary and Rafferty, Anne Marie (eds), *Midwives, Society and Childbirth. Debates and Controversies in the Modern Period.* (London and New York: Routledge, 1997).

Oakley, Ann, *The Captured Womb. A History of the Medical Care of Pregnant Women.* (Oxford: Basil Blackwell, 1984).

Rothman, Barbara Katz, *Recreating Motherhood. Ideology and Technology in a Patriarchal Society.* (New York and London: W.W. Norton, 1989).

Tew, Marjorie, *Safer Childbirth? A Critical History of Maternity Care.* (London: Chapman and Hall, 1990).

Towler, Jean and Bramall, Joan, *Midwives in History and Society.* (London and New York: Croom Helm, 1986).

Williams, A. Susan, *Women and Childbirth in the Twentieth Century. A History of the National Birthday Trust Fund 1928–93.* (Stroud: Sutton Publishing, 1997).

# CHAPTER 37

# Children's Experiences of Illness

RUSSELL VINER AND JANET GOLDEN

D o we really know anything about children's experiences of illness and health-care? Children in the late twentieth century experience the full gamut of available medical and surgical procedures and treatments, from neonatal intensive care intended to keep alive babies at the lower extremities of viability, through the most complex heart or liver transplants in infancy, to hormone treatments in adolescence using recombinant genetic material to facilitate development. The links between child and adult health have been made even more compelling in recent decades with the rise of genetics and of programming theories linking neonatal life with later adult disease. Yet, as Western medicine presses forward to reach new scientific, clinical, and therapeutic frontiers, the question of experience remains largely unexplored and both intellectually and practically compelling.

The tableau of distressed parents seeking treatment for their sick child is one of the most potent and recurring images of modern medicine. The social, emotional, and political power of this image has driven the development of modern health and welfare systems and the disciplines of pediatrics and public health. The care and nurturing of future citizens is a public enterprise, rewarding the nation-state with future soldiers and mothers. As such, child health efforts express the interests of modern capitalism and those who would reform it, so that measures of infant mortality rates, childhood immunization rates, and occupational injuries to children become critical indices of social well being. Starting from this understanding, historians have explored the ideologies, demographics, and social ecologies of child health as well as the ways in which children and parents utilize medical services and the types of treatment given. But they have not viewed the medical enterprise through the eyes of its child-participants.

## NEEDS AND OPPORTUNITIES

Awaiting exploration are issues of children's consent or assent to treatment, their experience of pain and its relief, their understanding of their illness, and their perceptions of their relations with parents, doctors, and other health-care workers. Additionally, we must ask how children's experiences of care and treatment, and their lives and deaths, have changed the practice of medicine. If children were written into the experience of patienthood we could better understand how experience with illness shapes culture. All societies seek to insure the survival of their youngest and most vulnerable members in order to maintain themselves. The particular way in which the care of sick children is organized thus reflects social structures, cultural values, and the interests and actions of the sick and their closest kin.

A second task is seeing how children's experiences shape medical practice. Historically, contradictory and unsupported assumptions have underpinned adult perceptions of children's responses to pain, suffering, and illness. While, on the one hand, the suffering of children has drawn a strong emotional response from most adults and been deployed by those in power to gain support for new programs and institutions, on the other hand, it has had little effect on the practice of medicine. Until recently, physicians assumed children do not feel pain as adults do. Their illiteracy, innumeracy and dependency implied a lack of nervous sensation and, following this reasoning, physicians denied young infants anesthesia and analgesics. Even premature baby nurseries, commonly seen as a triumph of modern humanitarian medicine, were almost completely devoid of any methods of pain relief before the 1990s.

Recent studies by psychologists and anthropologists working from modern theories of socialization, have begun to redress our ignorance of children's experiences of illness and health care. They have examined how children and adolescents often express unhappiness and emotional distress through withdrawal or acting out rather than through verbal communication. They have challenged dominant notions of the inability of children to give informed consent to medical treatments, suggesting that children as young as four or five often have well-established systems of beliefs about their illness that should be taken into consideration when planning treatment. And finally, they have looked at the ways in which children come to know they are dying and how they convey or conceal this knowledge when dealing with parents and health-care workers. In this way, modern scholars have written children into late twentieth-century medicine, helping to change the contours of practice.

It remains for historians to excavate the historical experiences of children's encounters with illness and suffering. And while this task poses particular methodological and theoretical challenges, it can no longer be ignored. Such investigations promise to yield not only a deeper understanding of how children experience illness, but to enrich our knowledge of what Roy Porter has called, "sufferers' history"[1] in which experience is primary, in which non professionals are understood as the primary agents of care, and in which the intellectual agenda encompasses beliefs and conditions that medical historians have traditionally overlooked. Consider for example what can be gleaned from the July 5, 1836 diary entry of Emily Shore, the sixteen year old daughter of an English minister.

Dr. Clark examined me most minutely, tapped me, and tried his stethoscope on my chest, neck, back, side, shoulder. He said nothing about the result of his observations, but retired with Mamma to another private conference. I, in the mean time, was left in a state of anxiety amounting almost to agony. I could by no means compose myself; the doctor's tapping had given me pain of the left side of my chest, and I had no small reason to apprehend the pulmonary disease had already begun.[2]

Why did the physician leave her to consult with her mother? What kinds of medications was she given for her pain? Did the physician understand, as she did, that her life would soon end? And how did the collective suffering of adolescents with tuberculosis shape the practice of medicine and the research agenda? Shore's diary is a valuable source, for she continued to record her suffering from tuberculosis until her life ended three years later. More critically, her diary reminds us of the power of children's voices, and the reasons sources such as these must be sought, investigated, and incorporated into our histories.

METHODOLOGICAL ISSUES

The neglect of children's voices is of course partly due to a lack of such sources as Emily Shore's diary; children's voices are infrequently recorded because of their lack of literacy. Yet there are diaries, letters, memoirs and other materials that demand examination. And, although we cannot recover many aspects of children's experiences in medicine, we can use these sources to reconstruct an external picture of the child in medical situations, studying the demographics of practice, the social geography of medical interactions, and the types of procedures children experienced or were denied. We can also draw conclusions about the social relations of children with their parents and doctors in both illness and health, and map how physicians redrew the child's body and life, bringing it under increasingly closer scrutiny.

Biographers and cultural historians have made use of first-hand accounts of illness. Biographers of American President Theodore Roosevelt have examined his adolescent diaries to describe his terrible suffering from bronchial asthma, his treatment, which was often provided by family members, and the probably psychosomatic elements of the disease, which attacked almost always on a Sunday. One diary entry reads "I sat up for 4 successive hours and Papa made me smoke a cigar,"[3] another simply recorded "I was very sick on the sofa and lay in bed all day,"[4] a third "I was sick and did not go out at all except for my Russian bath."[5] The diaries of twentieth-century American girls have been examined to assess the changing meaning of adolescence, and to explore in depth such commonplace events as menstruation, acne, and dieting. Letters sent to magazines can be revealing, such as one from a girl who wrote "I am fourteen and have not as yet begun to menstruate, which worries me considerably. Since I am nearly fifteen, I often wonder if I am abnormal."[6] She was referred to a gynecologist.

Historians have also charted the sales of new products, such as sanitary napkins, and the rise of new medical treatments — such as X-rays for acne — as well as how adolescents shaped medical practice in areas such as dermatology. As this work suggests, in addition to first-hand accounts, historical sources — from advertising and sales data for patent medicine to instrument catalogs showing devices developed for treating small patients — offer important pieces of evidence about children's experiences of health and illness and their very definitions of those terms. Further, we can examine fictional and artistic representations of remembered encounters with sickness, as well as photographs and other visual materials and more traditional materials such as the casebooks of medical practitioners, hospital records, accounts from institutions involved with caring for sick children, and the visiting logs of reformers.

The testimony of family members is also a crucial source. We need to ask how adults acted on behalf of sick children — seeking advice, purchasing treatments, applying healing techniques based on local customs and folk practices. From such sources we can tease out the concerns and treatments parents and physicians brought to the bedside and, when matched with first-person accounts, the effects of these remedies on the bodies and psyches of the children treated.

All of these sources must be treated with caution. First-hand accounts from children are likely to be incomplete, poorly contextualized, and inarticulate. Furthermore, first-person accounts are likely come from only a small, well-off group of youngsters. Doctors' casebooks and publications often illustrate the disease rather than the patient. Adult recollections of childhood illness are flawed by selective recall. Other sources too are tainted by their intended use. Child-health reformers used vignettes of suffering children to advance their own purposes in ways that may have disguised the experiences of those they portrayed. In a picture of children at a so-called Adenoid Party held by the New York Bureau of Child Hygiene in 1908, we see happy children meeting together before their operations, being introduced to the kindly doctors and nurses who would relieve their suffering. Undoubtedly, like modern pre-hospital introductory programs, these parties served to make the medical experience more acceptable and less painful for children and parents alike. But can we really believe children happily looked forward to this painful surgical procedure?

A second limitation is theoretical. The voices and perceptions of children have had no champion. Children have not been seen as historical actors but as subjects, largely because their choices and actions were highly constrained by their dependency, particularly in the case of infants and young children. However, recent work in women's history and the history of slavery have shown that apparent dependency, powerlessness, and illiteracy need not remove individuals from consideration as historical actors. But while historians of women and slavery can chart the collective actions of their subjects, historians of children must probe more deeply into the individual lives of their subjects, even while placing them in context.

A third limitation is variation in children's experiences according to their race, class, and gender, their cultural, religious, geographic and national diversity, across time, and by diagnosis. The experience of a Russian Jewish immigrant child at the Adenoid Party in New York differed significantly from that of a child disabled with polio in a chronic disease hospital and again from that of the British middle-class school child having his chest percussed by the doctor. Despite these differences, fundamental changes occurred in the twentieth century that in turn transformed all children's experiences with medicine. These changes were in part quantitative: the number of contacts between children and health workers increased dramatically in the early decades of the century. They were also qualitative: medicine changed the way children experienced their lives — at home, at school, in their bodies, in their minds, in sickness, and in health. The medical sphere of influence expanded to incorporate large portions of children's lives, making experiences once outside the world of medicine central to the work of the profession. In the following pages we will briefly review what we know about children's medicine in the twentieth century for the consideration of children's experiences with illness. We need to begin with the nineteenth century, however, for it was towards the end of it that middle-class children began to be sentimentalized and removed from the marketplace, while working class children began to receive new protections from the state.

## The Nineteenth Century

Many of the interactions between children and doctors in the mid-nineteenth century would be easily recognizable today. Parents took children to doctors when they were feverish or irritable and doctors in turn treated common ailments such as sore throats, diarrhea, measles, chicken-pox, and mumps. What differed were the treatments. After examining their young patients, physicians prescribed and sometimes concocted remedies to reduce their fevers, pacify them, and remove the cause of their ailments. For sore throats they prescribed iron or bismuth, for croup alum or emetics, and for diarrhea, alcohol or opiates. Although leeching and bleeding began to fall out of favor, lancing the gums remained a popular treatment as many physicians considered teething to be the cause of many ailments.

When the doctor came, he (rarely she) would try to pacify the young child, perhaps with a sweet or candy, assess the child's temperament and color, and feel its pulse. To assess the temperature the doctor applied his hand, as mercury thermometers were rare until late in the century. He might, if well educated, count the child's breathing with his watch. Although some of the more scientific doctors used stethoscopes to listen to the child's heart and chest, this clinical skill was rarely applied to children until very late in the century.

Although children made up around one-third of the clientele of the average general practitioner, many youngsters never saw a regular doctor and instead received treatment from alternative practitioners of myriad different sects, such as homeopathic, botanic or eclectic doctors. The unpleasant side effects of drugs used by regular physicians, such as calomel (mercury), opium and digitalis, led many parents to use milder homeopathic or botanic remedies for their children while consulting a regular doctor for the adults of the household. In response, regular physicians sometimes provided only small sweetened doses and mild treatments for children in an effort to compete with the alternative practitioners.

The most common attendant in illness was, of course, the mother, and probably the second most common was the local wise-woman. Poverty and geographic isolation obstructed most medical consultations, but there were cultural reasons why families eschewed medical visits. Immigrants in the United States, for example, customarily preferred folk remedies and practitioners from the homeland. Nevertheless, children, especially in urban areas, probably received a mix of folk, alternative, and regular medical treatments, and in the absence of economic impediments, cultural and religious practices likely determined which treatments and practitioners were chosen. For croup or other breathing difficulties a doctor might be called; for fevers and teething traditional remedies, consultations with local women often sufficed.

Sick children, rich or poor, received medical care in their own bed in their own home. Doctors called on children in wealthy families as often as required, sometimes staying overnight for severe cases. Poor children obtained care from a charitable dispensary and, if extremely ill, might receive a home visit from a dispensary physician. Volunteers from charities that specialized in visiting the poor also arranged for home medical visits and in these instances the sick child might receive food, tea, Bible tracts and prayers, as well as medicines.

European countries began establishing hospitals for sick children in the early nineteenth century, with many created after the 1850s. In a curious juxtaposition, sick children were thought particularly vulnerable to moral contamination from mixing with the adult poor, while adult hospitals shunned young patients because they were perceived to pose a risk of infection. Isolation thus constituted the primary ingredient in the children's hospital regime. Reformers conceived of these institutions as refuges, places in which poor sick children could received treatment and recover from illness away from the filth, poverty and immorality that characterized their homes and presumably caused or contributed to their ill-health. Not surprisingly then, the hospitals strictly regulated the behavior of patients, confining them (often literally), enforcing good Christian conduct (including regular prayers) and demanding respectful subservience to doctors and nurses. Typically the institutions forbade visits from parents.

Nineteenth-century medicine focused on the individual sick child; the needs of well children received little considered. By the last third of the century children in many Western nations needed a certificate guaranteeing their vaccination against smallpox in order to attend school, but only the richest schools had either nursing or medical attendants. Similarly, children's physical environments remained free of medical oversight. Public health measures to improve school buildings, play-grounds, and streets and to prevent contagious diseases began only in the 1890s. Children's private space was likewise devoid of medical scrutiny; few doctors thought to enter the child's internal psychological world until after the mental hygiene movement and studies of delinquency spawned child guidance clinics in the 1920s.

## THE TWENTIETH CENTURY

The concept of child health, until the twentieth century, was defined simply the absence of discernible disease. However, as children came to be sentimentalized — valued as individuals, rather than judged by their earnings potential — an interest developed in protecting and promoting their health. In the nineteenth century children had significant economic value to the family, while babies, par-ticularly given the lack of effective contraceptives, were in oversupply and almost economically worthless. By the early twentieth century this paradigm began to shift, as middle-class children were removed from the marketplace and became economically worthless while emotionally beyond price.

Historians disagree about the reasons for the rise of the sentimentalized middle-class family, advancing competing demographic, economic, and cultural explana-tions. Demographic factors cited include the reduction in infant mortality and the fall in average family size, which together with structural changes in employment, a rising standard of living and the improved status of women, allowed middle-class parents to focus their child-raising efforts on fewer longer-surviving offspring. While the transformation of childhood may rest on this economic and demo-graphic foundation, socio-cultural ideals proved critical to the expression of modern notions of childhood. They also spawned the creation of new institutions and laws aimed at promoting the well being of children. Middle-class reformers, for exam-ple, promoted libraries, baths, and youth clubs for working-class youngsters and crusaded for laws prohibiting child labor. In many cases working-class families resisted these efforts on behalf of their children, as they continued to rely on the earnings of all family members.

Child health became invested with a high social value in many twentieth-century nation-states as it was understood that high rates of ill health among the young put the nation at risk. Thus, the medicalization of childhood in the twentieth century was driven neither by scientific advances in medicine nor by the realization that children were a neglected group in health care. Nor did it only reflect hege-monic professional action by doctors and other health workers. Rather, it expressed the increased cultural valuation of children, which in turn reflected the rise of the bourgeois family, imperial rivalries in Europe, and concern over the effects of immigration in the United States. Also important to the rise of new child-health measures were the growing critiques of classical political economy and hereditarian concerns over the deterioration of national races. In this context, medical examination became an almost universal experience for twentieth-century children.

Doctors entered New York City schools in 1897 (and nurses in 1902), inspecting those reported as unhealthy by teachers. Beginning in 1905, children received a medical examination of sorts, walking past a seated physician who would pull down eye-lids, open mouths, inspect hands and, in the case of girls, check their hair, in a quick assessment of health. The doctor judged their mental state by general observation. Those deemed infective or diseased received further examination. Similar medical examinations were conducted on children accompanying parents immigrating into countries such as Australia, New Zealand, Canada, and the United States.

Medical examinations also became necessary for children under sixteen years to gain employment. Since the early nineteenth century opponents of child labor claimed it undermined health and, in the case of factory and mine work, morality. Thin, poorly grown children appeared in exposés of the condition of the poor. By the twentieth century, reformers in the United States had made some progress in their crusade and child workers required a doctor's certificate stating that they were over fourteen years and of sufficient bodily development so as not to be harmed by labor. When reformers learned such certificates could be easily obtained from corrupt doctors, they turned to positive methods of determining fitness, such as skeletal X-rays and the assessment of height and weight for age. As a result, the concept of bone age replaced chronological age in assessing fitness for labor and military service. And, through the roentgenogram (X-ray) machine that recorded their bone age, children began to encounter the new technologies of health that characterized much of twentieth-century medicine.

Other new technologies included the weighing chair and the stadiometer (an instrument for measuring height) as physicians began to assess the development of normal children. Since the late nineteenth century, isolated doctors had measured groups of children in order to compare racial and socio-economic groups. By the second decade of the twentieth century, however, all American and many British children were routinely weighed on scales and measured against wall-mounted tape-measures. The results were plotted onto charts that related their growth to previously measured groups of children. The impetus for this standardization was the belief that poorly grown and under-nourished children could be identified and aided before they became sick and, concomitantly, that without such assessments and the interventions they provoked, these youngsters would later be unfit for work or for military service in the case of boys, and for motherhood, in the case of girls.

By the mid-twentieth century, weighing and measuring had become a ritual in both the maternal and child health centers that developed in many countries and in private medical practice. Normal growth was no longer defined by the simple comparison of a child with its peers. Instead it came to be determined by statistical patterns the doctor or nurse read from the centile chart that averaged the growth patterns of large populations of children. Other efforts to quantify development soon followed, as physicians began to plot the milestones signaling that appropriate intellectual coordinates had been reached, that appropriate emotional growth was occurring and that traits such as physical coordination had been achieved. Although not as pervasive as the assessment of physical growth, these measures did represent the extension of medical supervision into new areas of childhood, the redefinition of normality in statistical and clinical terms, and a shifting locus of judgment from family and peers to clinicians.

Judgements begin early. The well-baby examination is the first of a series of medical rituals through which twentieth-century children had to pass to be certain of having a normal childhood. Today, most infants encounter a pediatrician within their first three days of life, whether within an incubator in a highly specialized special care nursery, or as part of the routine well-baby examination designed to certify the normality of all new-born children. For boys in America, the well-baby check almost always concludes with a routine neonatal circumcision. Other body parts allegedly made redundant by evolution — tonsils, adenoids and appendix — were routinely extracted throughout much of the twentieth century. Today the well-baby check is followed by the six-week check, and this leads to subsequent visits for vaccinations and examinations. Painful experiences with needles have become a necessary part of modern childhood, gladly exchanged by parents seeking to spare their children diphtheria, tetanus, mumps, rubella, chicken-pox and more generally an early death. And it was this, the prevention of death, that gave medicine for children the power to reach into new venues and to assert more control over old ones, among them the schoolroom, the hospital, and the nursery.

## SCHOOLROOM MEDICINE

The schoolroom became a new site for medical practice in the twentieth century. School nurses attended to children with minor problems. For lice, the hair was washed with an equal mix of kerosene and sweet oil; those with ringworm were washed with Green Soap and had their lesions covered with Flexible Collodion; those with conjunctivitis received irrigation of the eyes with a saturated solution of boric acid. Moreover, schools served as sites of clinical investigation, as medical personnel conducted large-scale experiments in standardizing and improving children's health and in so doing transformed children into research subjects. School milk, school meals, school vaccinations, and routine health checks contributed to improving the health of many children.

The school health clinics and doctors' surgeries that measured and classified children were part of a wider network of public health supervision that characterized early twentieth-century progressivism. In many Western nations, baby milk stations, settlement houses, health visitors, visiting nurses and midwives, child welfare clinics, child guidance and psychopathic clinics, travelling vaccination clinics, school dentistry, social work and other services provided a patchwork system of health care for poor children. They also served as a means for the state to observe the health and development of children. And the question of who would lead these programs of surveillance and care — government officials, private health professionals, welfare advocates, or volunteers — provoked a number of professional rivalries and ultimately helped spur the development of pediatrics as a medical specialty.

## PEDIATRICIANS AND CHILDREN'S HOSPITALS IN THE TWENTIETH CENTURY

Increasingly in both the United States and much of Europe, doctors specifically trained in medicine for children began to assume responsibility for the health supervision of sick and well children. Few doctors practiced exclusively with children until the early decades of the twentieth century. The United States had about twenty or thirty children's specialists practicing in large cities at the turn of the century, with similar numbers found in France and Germany. In Britain, exclusive practice with children involved only two or three members of the Royal College of Physicians until the 1920s, and pediatricians became common only after the advent of the National Health Service in the late 1940s. Most pediatricians were men, replacing the female doctors predominant in the public health services for children since the late-nineteenth century. With this shift in gender came a shift in location, as contacts between doctors and children moved from mother and child clinics to clinics for children alone. The new pediatric medicine challenged many of the traditional bonds between mother and child, conceptualizing the child as an independent medical object rather than as an indivisible part of a mother-child unit and transforming the role of the mother from family healer to thera-peutic attendant to the expert physician.

In many countries, the early twentieth century saw an explosive growth in the number of children's hospitals and children's wards in general hospitals. No longer the refuge only of the very poor and no longer custodial, hospitals began to offer advanced treatment and therefore attracted large numbers of middle and upper-class children. By the 1950s in Britain, the United States, and Australia, the hospital was the preferred site of care for very sick children, and parents were banished from the wards except during the strictly limited visiting hours.

Pediatricians also found a growing place in maternity units, supervising nurs-eries and in particular, supervising the care of babies born prematurely. Active efforts to save early and tiny babies were not new; attempts to resuscitate new-born children by blowing into their lungs had been common since the eighteenth century, although what might be termed formal interest in neonatal medicine did not begin until the late-nineteenth century. The first effort to institute systematic medical control over premature infants occurred in France in the early 1870s, with the invention of the infant incubator by Pierre Budin and Etienne Tarnier.

For Budin and Tarnier, saving premature babies was a means of increasing the French population, thus avenging the military humiliations of the 1870 Franco-Prussian War. The belief that the care of a nation's babies was intimately linked to the military strength of a nation was widespread by first decade of the twentieth century, and for many in Britain, Germany and America, saving premature and weak babies became a piece of a broader program to improve the racial stock of these competing empires. In this imperial competition, babies in their incubator cages were star exhibits in early twentieth-century celebrations of national technological advancement. The incubators themselves were more symbol than substance. There were few incubator nurseries and most were confined only to large hospitals in big cities until the 1940s.

By the second half of the twentieth century, however, incubators were widespread in developed nations. Their dissemination reflected no significant changes in technology (indeed, the modern incubator closely resembled its nineteenth-century prototype) but rather the growing influence of the pediatricians who operated them, particularly in the case of the new National Health Service in Britain. Through the 1960s and 1970s, neonatal nurseries became a central feature of even the smallest general hospital, and pediatricians developed new techniques of intensive care to save ever more premature and tiny infants. Today, approximately five percent of newborns in the developed world spend their first hours and days cocooned within one of the most technologically advanced environments known to humanity, their tiny bodies invaded by intra-arterial lines, endotracheal tubes, intercostal catheters and complex, computerized monitoring equipment.

In addition to assessing infants in the first hours of life, pediatricians have now become partly responsible for managing the transition to adulthood by guiding them through the stormy years of adolescence. Historians disagree about whether a period of adolescence existed before the late nineteenth century. Although an extended period of dependence and education after physical maturity is identifiable for many young people from at least the seventeenth century, some argue that a defined period of adolescence is an artefact of modern industrial society. Regardless of the economic and cultural origins of their status, twentieth-century teenagers became object of investigation and management for physicians. In child guidance clinics established from the 1920s, primarily in America, adolescents and younger children encountered doctors intent on helping them through the period of life newly understood as psychologically and physically stressful. Later elaborations of the physiological experience followed from developments in hormonal research in the 1930s and 1940s which shed light on the processes of puberty.

In their continuing zeal to quantify, physicians constructed charts of normal sexual development as they had for other milestones of growth. Using orphanages and children's homes as large scale laboratories (as their predecessors had used schools) James M. Tanner and his colleagues developed five Tanner stages through which adolescents progressed to sexual maturity. Appropriate Tanner staging became a necessary medical task, and the divulging of intimate details of sexual development became a standard part of the interaction between teenage patients and their physicians.

## THE NEW DISEASES AND THE OLD

Central to the experience of medical supervision and treatment for children in the developed world has been a dramatic shift in the diseases children suffer and die from, and in the way doctors and families understand the diseases of childhood. Improved nutrition and sanitation, together with immunization and antibiotics have removed infectious diseases as the major foes of children in the developed world. Many of the great killers of the nineteenth century — diphtheria, whooping cough, scarlatina, malaria and small-pox — are now largely abolished. Other feared diseases, such as gastroenteritis, polio and measles, also now hold little fear for children or their attendants. Instead, the position once held by infectious disease is now occupied by the new mortalities — diseases with social and environmental causes. Overall childhood mortality has diminished dramatically over the twentieth century, and accidents and injuries at home and on the roads, congenital illnesses, and cancer now account for most childhood deaths. However, among adolescents there has been no change in overall mortality rates in the last fifty years, as deaths from social disorders such as drug abuse, accidents, suicide and homicide balance the reduction in infectious disease mortality.

Despite (or even because of) the eclipse of infectious disease, the medicalization of childhood continues unabated. With the change in mortality patterns has come the formulation of elements of the child's social world as medical disorders which are brought under medical surveillance and treatment. Conditions such as conduct disorder, oppositional disorder, learning difficulties, and hyperactivity and attention-deficit disorder pathologize the child's behavior in their social world, and extend the hegemony of the experience of medicine into all areas of the child's life.

## CONCLUSION

In the twentieth century, children's experience of medicine was transformed from the symptoms of infectious diseases treated by the individual doctor to the focus of a pervasive system of medical examination, certification and bio-medical and psychosomatic treatment aimed at controlling the biological, social and psychological pathologies understood to threaten healthy childhood and healthy society. This system was unique to childhood — an age range that was extended to the earliest hours of life and into the delayed adolescence of modern youth. While all of the twentieth-century advances in medicine — intensive surgical and medical treatments, antiviral and genetic therapies — developed for adults were also available to children, the experience of medicine for children and adolescents in the twentieth-century was characterized by repeated investigations of normality involving assessment against population norms combined with recurrent rituals of examination and vaccination in a way that it was not for adults.

We began this chapter by questioning whether we really know anything about children's experiences of illness and health-care. It is clear that we know a great deal about what children underwent in twentieth-century medicine — the examinations and consultations, the technological interventions, and the psychosomatic surveillance. However, the task remains to incorporate children's experiences into the history of medicine and in so doing rewrite that history to see how children's illnesses and deaths, treatments and recoveries as well as their responses to physicians, nurses, hospitals, public health officials and family members have individually and collectively endowed the medical system we operate with today. We stand to gain not only a richer understanding of the historical experience and meaning of medicine and of childhood, but to make modern medicine more sensitive to the needs of children.

## REFERENCES

1. Roy Porter, 'The Patient's View: Doing Medical History from Below,' *Theory and Society* (1985), **14**: 167–74.
2. Margaret Emily Shore, *Journal of Emily Shore.* (London, 1891) excerpted in Erna Olafson Hellerstein, Leslie Parker Hume and Karen M. Offen (eds), *Victorian Women: A Documentary Account of Women's Lives in Nineteenth-Century England, France, and the United States.* (Stanford, CA: Stanford University Press, 1981), p. 114.
3. Cited in David McCullough, *Mornings on Horseback.* (New York: Touchstone, 1981), p. 95.
4. *Ibid*, p. 101.
5. *Ibid*, p. 103.
6. Cited in Joan Jacobs Brumberg, *The Body Project: An Intimate History of American Girls.* (New York: Random House, 1997), p. 48.

## FURTHER READING

Aries, Philippe, *Centuries of Childhood.* (Harmondsworth: Penguin, 1979).

Bluebond-Langner, Myra, *The Private World of Dying Children.* (Princeton: Princeton University Press, 1978).

Brumberg, Joan Jacobs, *The Body Project: An Intimate History of American Girls.* (New York: Random House, 1997).

Cone, Jr., Thomas E., *History of American Pediatrics.* (Boston: Little Brown, 1979).

Cooter, Roger, (ed.), *In the Name of the Child: Health and Welfare, 1880–1940.* (London: Routledge, 1992).

Dwork, Deborah, *War is Good for Babies and Other Young Children: A History of the Infant and Child Welfare Movement in England, 1898–1918.* (London: Tavistock, 1987).

Harris, Bernard, *The Health of the Schoolchild: A History of the School Medical Service in England and Wales.* (Buckingham: Open University Press, 1995).

Graff, Harvey J., *Conflicting Paths: Growing Up in America.* (Cambridge, MA: Harvard University Press, 1995).

Hendrick, Harry, *Children, Childhood, and English Society, 1880–1990.* (Cambridge: Cambridge University Press, 1997).

Meckel, Richard A., *Save the Babies: American Public Health Reform and the Prevention of Infant Mortality, 1850–1929.* (Baltimore: Johns Hopkins University Press, 1990).

Porter, Roy, 'The Patient's View: Doing Medical History from Below,' *Theory and Society* (1985), **14**: 167–174.

Tanner, James M., *A History of the Study of Human Growth.* (Cambridge: Cambridge University Press, 1981).

# CHAPTER 38

# Wartime

JOANNA BOURKE

Modern warfare may be represented either as antithetical to the healing profession, or its fulfilment. Second only to the armed forces, the knowledges, disciplines, and rituals of medicine exerted unprecedented power over men's lives during periods of war. In the twentieth century, military needs exposed and exacerbated an inherent tension: at the institutional level, medicine was unequivocally dedicated to corporeal health, yet it claimed a seat at the center of a state apparatus bent on human destruction. During wartime, physicians forged an alliance with an institution immeasurably more powerful than equivalent allies within schools, factories, and local authorities and, as a consequence, they shifted their attention from infants, young children, and the poor towards healthy, young men of every social class. Medical officers in the army, navy, and air-force confronted a huge and dependant population of men who were at immediate risk of disease and disablement: yet, the 'clients' were not these men but their military superiors. In the wars prior to 1914, this emphasis was rarely questioned. During periods of 'total' war, volunteer and conscripted servicemen thought differently. In this chapter, the subjective experiences of these men is given equal weight to that of medical officers. Military medicine also affected men, women, and children far from any war zone. No single trend can be identified: the experience of medicine during modern military conflicts was diverse and contradictory, but always fundamental to individual well-being.

The twentieth century has been characterized as a century of bloody armed conflict. Leaving aside military confrontations involving a small number of nations, the two 'world' wars resulted in a staggering number of casualties. During the Great War, 780,000 men from the British and Dominion armies were killed or 'missing' and over two million were wounded. The Second World War saw a further 357,000 people killed and 369,000 wounded (excluding the victims of the Holocaust). Until the first of these 'world' wars, medical services remained peripheral to the armed forces: in most countries, medical service corps had only recently been established and they tended to be poorly funded. Although the Japanese (during their 1904–05 conflict with China) was the first army to bestow full military rank and status on medical officers and to require that all combat operations provided medical support, nevertheless, the status of physicians within the armed forces remained extremely low until the Great War. The conscription of medical personnel, the wholesale devastation wrought by modern weapons of war, and the exigency of 'world' war provided the political and cultural space for the rise of military medicine.

The scale of modern warfare was daunting to any medical administration. To cope with the high levels of wounding at the front, and in recognition of the diagnostic, therapeutic, and psychological benefits of rapid treatment, carefully delineated 'routes' of medical help had to be formalized. Regimental medical officers accompanied the fighters. They were followed by Field Ambulances, then by Casualty Clearing Stations, and finally by General Hospitals at some distance from the fighting. Although these 'routes' varied according to the army described and became more flexible from 1939, this general protocol remained throughout the century.

In other areas, dramatic changes occurred. The Boer War saw the first use of medicalized field dressings and the appointment of the first dentist to the British army. X-rays, invented by Wilhelm Roentgen in 1895, came to be used by military doctors to locate bullets without disturbing wounds during the conflicts at the turn of the century (albeit at some distance from the fighting until the lighter x-ray equipment of the Great War). The increasing mechanization of medicine provides us with some of the most enduring images of war: motorized vehicles picked up the wounded during the Great War; aeroplanes evacuated men from the Second World War; helicopters dominated the scene in Korea and Vietnam. Movable laboratories able to conduct diagnostic bacteriology near the front lines (from the Great War), roaming surgical teams which meant that over three-fifths of men could be operated on within twelve hours of being wounded (from the Second World War), and Mobile Army Surgical Hospital units or MASH (from the Korean War) dramatically improved survival rates. During the Great War, intravenous saline transfusions were introduced and the first field blood transfusion teams were appointed to deal with shock. The Spanish Civil War and the Second World War saw the large scale use of tetanus vaccines, sulfanamides, penicillin, and blood transfusions. During the Korean War, vascular repair significantly reduced the need to amputate limbs, and the provision of blood transfusions lowered mortality rates. Throughout, plastic surgery generated an immense amount of research, enabling men who had suffered severe facial injuries to live their lives openly rather than behind painted masks.

In some areas, the remedial systems and knowledges triggered by military requirements fundamentally altered the entire world of medicine. For instance, in Britain during the Boer War, the panic resulting from the realization that the majority of young men suffered from appallingly bad health provided the impetus (through the medium of the 1904 report of the Select Committee on Physical Deterioration) for wide-ranging sociological classification of civilians according to medical criteria, and led directly to medical intervention into the lives of thousands of people, especially infants, school children, and mothers. Preventive medicine was part of this new agenda, and received additional encouragement by the recognition that disease (rather than wounding) was decimating armies. For instance, during the Spanish American War of 1898, 968 men died in battle compared with 5,438 who died of infectious diseases. During the Boer War, twenty times more soldiers were admitted to hospital for disease than for wounds. Governments proved willing to invest capital in preventive medicine in order to reduce such 'wastage,' both in the army and in the workplace.

Another area where war medicine significantly affected wider medical practices concerns serious injuries to limbs. From 1914, this was a major type of injury for both servicemen and (due to bombing raids) civilians. As a consequence, there was a massive expansion of orthopedics as a powerful specialism within military medicine, and (after the wars) within civilian medical practices. Disabled civilians who in the early decades of the century would have been treated by general practitioners, by medical officers in 'casualty' departments of hospitals, or by house surgeons on the wards, now found themselves in specialist 'fracture clinics.' As the historian, Roger Cooter, put it: "In this new environment, patients no longer had their fractures merely reduced and splinted before being sent home; instead, they were subjected to a specially organized routine involving systematic case-recording at reception, x-ray examination, plaster-of-paris bandaging by a specially trained nurse, after-care physiotherapy, and post-operative monitoring — all under the careful watch of a fracture surgeon-in-charge."[1] Military requirements did not 'create' this specialism, but provided a new and powerful impetus for its influence.

It is important not to exaggerate the impact of military medicine on civilian practice. In Britain, the creation of the Ministry of Health after the First World War and the National Health Service after the Second World War owed as much to pre-war politics as to any military crisis. Most of the techniques and methodologies developed within military contexts were specific to war. Improvization was unnecessary in most civilian practices. After all, what post-war doctor would need to use his front-line experience in amputating limbs with an axe? Grenades were not thrown at people in peacetime (except in Northern Ireland); gas poisoning rarely disabled civilians; trench-foot was unknown. Doctors in the busiest emergency departments in inner-city hospitals rarely if ever had to face the immense influx of severely wounded men that was common within battle hospitals. The need to 'compromise' the treatment of individual patients was alien to civilian practice. Civilian doctors were also seldom required to make split second decisions affecting life or death. The comment of one doctor is instructive of the unique decisions medical officers were often forced to make during wartime. Ian Samuel recalled being faced with a wounded officer during the evacuation at Dunkirk:

> He had no lower jaw, no lower lip or anything and looking at him one looked straight at his palate — the tongue had gone. But the horrible thing about it was he was still alive. Of course he couldn't speak — he had nothing to speak with. His eyes looked at me and

moved and he moved his arms. I knew that (1) nothing could be done for him surgically and that (2) we would probably be moving quite soon, but I had to do something for him... I gave this casualty a large dose of morphia and was relieved to see him become unconscious very quickly and in twenty minutes time he died... Some of my medical colleagues to whom I tell this story ask me how much morphia I gave him and I give you the same answer that I gave to them — "I cannot remember."[2]

The practice of medicine within the military was difficult for other reasons. The temporary, 'for the duration of the war' alliance between military and medical institutions meant that medical, surgical, and psychiatric lessons learnt in one conflict had to be rediscovered in the next. Medicine's integration into the war machine was bought at a cost to diagnostic independence. As psychiatrists came to be regarded as crucial in promoting troop morale, their duties became more narrowly tied to military ends. 'Morale' was medicine's primary goal. Company commanders with no medical training revised prescriptions and proscribed treatments. As the medical officer, Captain J. H. Dible, fumed in 1915:

> One cannot say "Look here, who is best able to judge of this man's condition: I, who have had him under observation for a week, or you, who blew in suddenly like a breath of foul air from the sewerage-farm across the way?" One cannot ask such pertinent questions, because the grey haired dodderer is a colonel and you happen to be a subaltern.[3]

Military medicine could also be extremely alienating for the patient. Increased medical specialization during wartime (made possible by the size of the population at risk of disablement and disease, and by large-scale state investment in medical research) dramatically reduced long-term care and attention to individual needs. Physicians were rarely able to follow through their treatments: they were unaware of their successes or failures. Modern management techniques (such as the use of record cards and the establishment of rigid hierarchies of medical personnel) further distanced the individual patient from the individual doctor. In the words of the historian, Robert Weldon Whalen, referring to wounded Germans:

> Through this complex system, the injured man was shipped, examined, tagged, loaded on to hospital trains and unloaded into ambulances, all the while unconscious or semi-conscious, and in every case unable to control what was happening to him.... He was wheeled here, shipped there, bandaged and unbandaged, dressed and undressed, cut open and sewn back together, and through it all, he was, unavoidably, an object.[4]

The longer military conflict was prolonged, the more 'militaristic' hospitals became: mechanical precision and rapidity replaced personal attention. The supremacy of the group over individual medical needs was explicit military ideology. It reached its logical conclusion with the elaboration of 'triage' in which the most seriously wounded men would be labeled 'expectant' (that is, expected to die) and set aside while men who might be rapidly returned to battle were treated. Sick and wounded servicemen became 'ineffectives' who required 'salvaging.'

The role of medical officers in the armed services was also inextricably linked with military administration. At one level, this simply meant holding medical parades, completing forms accurately, examining feet, and inspecting sanitary facilities. However, physicians were also crucial to the entire system of discipline: their primary function was to return men to their military duties. Most medical men had little difficulty embracing their disciplinary functions. After all, it was a role they were familiar with in civilian practice, albeit at a lower level of intensity. They rationalized the extension of their power during wartime by arguing that they formed a buffer between servicemen and the harsher forms of military justice. In addition (as with other military officers), physicians feared the consequences of indiscipline. Thus, the Australian medical officer, Charles Huxtable, reflecting on his service during both the world wars, mused: "Sometimes, I have pangs of remorse, but it doesn't do to dwell on past mistakes. If you relax and give favours to one man, there may be a flood of others."[5] Medical officers tended not to question the right of their military superiors to command the men as they saw fit.

The attitude of doctors within the armed forces, however, led to great resentment amongst the Other Ranks. The Royal Army Medical Corps (RAMC), for instance, never managed to shrug off the title, 'Rob All My Comrades' corps. Bitterness was widespread. As an Australian private told his family on 15 December 1916:

> I wouldn't advise my worst enemy to enlist... they are dying everyday nearly & you cant get any attention, there was a man in the 13th Batt. he was sick & went to the doctor, who said oh a few days of Physcyhal Jerks will do you good, two days after he was in his grave peunimo this is true Lil, one of our chaps broke a rib coming over on the boat, the doctor on board Ship said he would have to go under an operation in England, he went to the doctor here yesterday & he told him Physical Jerks for a day or two would fix him up. what do you think of that. the hospital here is a bonzer they sleep on the floor, & if you dont die quick enough you get into a decent hospital but they usually die quick.[6]

The poor reputation of medical officers amongst the other ranks was not wholly avoidable. Merely to diagnose a man as suffering from venereal disease was to ensure that he was punished. Senior servicemen might resent any show of sympathy concerning their mental state: was the doctor implying that he was incompetent? Battle-weary doctors and patients could easily misunderstand each other's intentions.

Furthermore, certain medical personnel were exempted from sweeping accusations of harshness. Nurses (who were important auxiliary workers throughout the century and constituted 40% of medical personnel serving during the Gulf War) often provided crucial physical and emotional sustenance for exhausted servicemen. In addition, stretcher bearers were not only admired for risking their lives to save the wounded, they were also adored for mothering injured or sick men. Many medical personnel found ways to mitigate the harsher side to their job. They might be persuaded to commit dissenters (such as Siegfried Sassoon in Britain or Ernst Toller in German) to insane asylums or mental hospitals in order to protect them from being court martialled. Although gonorrhea was a punishable offense, non-specific urethritis was not: medical personnel might secretly give men sulfa drugs, enabling them to treat themselves effectively. They lied to military authorities. M. Ralph Kaufman, for example, was the consultant psychiatrist in the South Pacific during the Second World War. His commanding officer was notoriously brutal towards officers suffering from neuropsychiatric disorders. Kaufman responded by diagnosing all distressed officers as suffering from organic disorders. Physicians turned many blind eyes to military offenders.

However, there was a limit to the extent to which medical officers could act kindly. As Sigmund Freud put it: "The physicians [during the war] had to play a role somewhat like that of a machine gun behind the front line, that of driving back those who fled. Certainly, this was the intent of the war administration."[7] Consequently, like other servicemen, they were subjected to disciplinary action if they were thought to be 'lax.' For instance, when Lieutenant G. N. Kirkwood, medical officer to the 11th Border Regiment 97th Infantry Battalion during the Great War, supported the men in his battalion when they claimed that they were too emotional and physically exhausted to carry out a raid, he was rebuked, disgraced, and dismissed from the service. In the words of the commander of the 32nd Division: "Sympathy for sick and wounded men under his treatment is a good attribute for a doctor but it is not for an M.O. [medical officer] to inform a C.O. [commanding officer] that his men are not in a fit state to carry out a military operation. The men being in the front line should be proof that they are fit for any duty called for."[8]

As the last two examples suggest, the relationship between military needs and medical diagnosis was most tense in the case of psychiatric breakdown (known variously as shell shock, battle fatigue, combat exhaustion, and post-traumatic stress disorder). The extent and nature of psychological problems of war varied by conflict, unit, and theater of war. During the Great War 25% of all discharges were neuropsychiatric casualties; estimates during the Second World War ranged from 20% to 50%; and during the Vietnam War it was generally thought that half of men who saw combat suffered post-traumatic stress. Of the first 1,500 Israeli Defence Force casualties during the Yom Kippur War in 1977, 900 were diagnosed as suffering from 'battle fatigue.' Medical attention shifted during the course of the Great War from organic explanations to psychological ones and remedies involved a mixture of punitive regimes, rest, occupational therapy, and hypnosis. Second World War medical officers placed greater stress on exhaustion as a cause. From the end of the Second World War, but especially during the Vietnam War, treatment was summed up in terms of three principles: immediate treatment, continued proximity to the battle, and constant reassurance of healing. From the

Second World War, drugs were widely employed. Despite the greater sympathy accorded to these men by medical officers, within the military context mental illness never shed the stigma of cowardice. Men were expected to give their 'nerves' for their country with the same unconditional obedience as they gave their limbs and lives.

There was another tension inherent in the conjunction of medicine and the military. Medical officers could not avoid acknowledging that their role was to aid in the killing process. This reached its lowest level within the Third Reich where physicians and nurses participated in schemes of mass murder, supervised death camps, 'selected' prisoners for death or forced labor, carried out experiments, tortured, and medicalized the entire killing process. As the nurse, Pauline Kneissler, wrote in 1947: "At the bed of a patient, there is a doctor who is superior to the nurse. It's his decision whether or not to prescribe a chest compress, an enema, heart medication, or a sleeping pill. In this case it was mercy killing. I never understood mercy killing as murder."[9]

Even the more routine duties of medical officers involved destroying human life, or facilitating its destruction. Medical personnel were responsible for developing gas and biological weapons of war. Without the help of scientists and physicians, the devastation caused by the atomic bomb explosions at Hiroshima and Nagasaki would not have been possible. Although technically non-combatants, doctors were often anxious to carry arms and were sensitive to hints that they were allocated a lowly status because they did not possess weapons. In the words of Ralph H. Covernton (a volunteer in the RAMC during the Boer War), his non-combatant status left him with an enduring "inferiority complex."[10] Medical officers resented and resisted the introduction of conscientious objectors into their ranks.

Within the armed services, doctors were taught to kill with their hands and with small arms. As one Welsh medical officer in 1941 recalled, he was taught "how to kill a man in seconds bare-handed, and how to blind a man with forefinger and middle finger outstretched. So that I, having spent my adult life in learning how to preserve life and health, now knew how to kill."[11] Furthermore, from the Second World War, and in some theaters of conflict throughout the century, medical personnel were forced to fight. Thus, in the war in Malaya, J. Thompson Rowling recalled firing into bushes in an attempt to 'flush out' bandits. He reflected on the 'natural perversity' of being a combatant surgeon in war in which he might be called upon to operate on a man he shot:

> I considered from time to time the ethics of killing communists. The RAMC was, I suppose, a non-combatant unit, but I felt no reluctance to fight the bandits. There seemed three good reasons for so doing. The first was that they were the King's enemies. The second was that I wore the King's uniform and my duty constrained me so to act. And thirdly, and perhaps more pressingly, an encounter with a man who has every intention of killing you inclines you to try to kill him first.[12]

The question of one Canadian medical officer was echoed by many others: "What am I, a doctor or a killer?"[13]

Combative servicemen experienced war, and military medicine, from a different standpoint. For them, medical officers were an integral part of an institution which might provide them with exhilarating adventures, but which often humiliated, frightened, and pained them. Doctors on Medical Boards stripped and prodded their bodies to facilitate 'grading.' No matter how kindly medical personnel treated them, or how clean the hospital bed, mutilation and disease reduced any sense of human dignity. In the words of an unnamed soldier describing a hospital during the Great War: "The wounded were often perfectly silent. But more often they would groan or wail or shout. Sometimes they would all howl in chorus like cats on a roof."[14] For combat serviceman, the experience or expectation of suffering was fundamental to their experience of war and military medicine. The nature of the suffering varied according to the technology of the particular combat (gas and flame throwers during the Great War and dive bombers and atomic bombs during the Second World War raised levels of fear) and the medical processes available to relieve pain. Equally, the expectation of suffering varied according to an individual's age, sex, and class position. There was no unified 'human nature' through which people experienced medicine during periods of war.

As argued earlier, faced with the combined strength of the military and medical institutions, the individual serviceman felt powerless. This sense of impotence was exacerbated by the (usually unjustified) suspicion that they were being used as experimental subjects. For men accustomed to receiving medical help from poor law institutions or charities, this was not a new fear. During the 'mass' wars of the twentieth century, medical officers openly relished the opportunities provided by the provision of a huge, dependant population of potential patients. At times, and in all countries, the extent of experimentation could be extremely large, as in the research establishments at Porton Down (Britain), Camp Detrick (USA), Suffield (Canada), Luneburger Heide (Germany), and Pingfan (Japan). In the words of a wounded medical student, Wilfred Willett: "You'd have thought the war was being fought just to give [surgeons] healthy specimens. Once up in the theatre they didn't care a bit about the case. Electric stimuli ligatures, anything; like frogs in the phys. lab."[15]

Experimentation was rare in comparison to the other disciplinary functions of military medical officers. The chief of these was the policing of shirkers and malingerers. During wartime, men had the strongest of motives for exaggerating fear and ill-health. For the unwilling serviceman, there were only a few routes to freedom: "pull[ing] it on" medical officers "toot sweet" was one of the most promising.[16] 'Mateship' included sharing typhoid samples, or providing soap with which to feign epileptic fits. Madness was frequently attested to. Servicemen imbued drugs such as digitalis, belladonna, and thyroid extract to produce circulatory disturbances. They pricked their tonsils in order to cough up blood. Epistaxis was provoked by self-induced injuries to the nose. Albuminuria was feigned by the addition of egg-albumen to urine. A deliberately fractured arm would delay mobilization. Glasses and dental plates were 'lost.' Petrol, paraffin, or turpentine could be injected into the body to induce abscesses. Conjunctival lesions (which could be passed off as trachoma) were simulated by the insertion of tobacco ash, soap or other irritant inside the eye lids. When chewed, a stick of cordite, extracted from a .303 rifle cartridge, would cause a high temperature and symptoms of an erratic heart condition. Lumbago could attack any man. From the Second World War, men could refuse to take their malaria pill. While on leave, venereal disease could be deliberately sought. Self-inflicted wounds were a desperate method and, ironically, these men were at a greater risk of dying from their wounds than their comrades who were 'legitimately' injured.

The extent of malingering within the army is impossible to determine with any accuracy for two reasons. Firstly, it was difficult to police effectively. In the words of a British expert on malingering, Sir John Collie, a soldier did not have to shoot off his own fingers because "by holding his hand up he can get the enemy to do it for him."[17] Secondly, it is clear that many more men attempted to malinger than actually succeeded. Thus, sick parades would lengthen with the arrival of a new doctor and shorten if he proved as astute as his predecessor. As doctors and patients testified, however, malingering was ubiquitous, and it encouraged medical officers to suspect that every serviceman who reported sick as being a 'skrimshanker.' As an anonymous diarist suffering severe dysentery in Mesopotamia complained in his diary of 18 May 1916:

> I am still hanging on, very weak, but unless you have a temperature of about 150 [degrees], or half your head blown off the *Dear* Doctor says there is nothing the matter with you and you are loafing. Our Doctor is sick himself. I hope he doesn't die, that would be too easy. I only hope he is ill about a year, so we don't see him again and so he will have time to think of the way he has treated sick men here. I heard him tell a youngster who said he was run down and could not do his duty: "Oh, I've nothing to give you. A lot of you have got to die yet."[18]

Military medical officers were responsible for policing malingering, and they developed an almost obsessive fascination with techniques of detection. As one British army doctor responded when asked if he was a medical officer: "No... I am a detective."[19] Or, as C. P. Blacker noted: "It is a crime in the army to report sick for inadequate cause."[20] Medical journals and textbooks devoted much space to discussing the signs by which the malingerer could be distinguished, and the means with which they could be 'persuaded' to give up the pretence. In this latter category was included a range of techniques, from trickery and threats, to the use of drugs such as barbiturate narcosis (from the Second World War), to subjecting suspects to painful or humiliating rituals. Managerial techniques were also regarded as indispensable in the fight against malingering. For instance, sick parade was generally set for the early morning in order to discourage attempts to malinger since anyone attending sick parade would end up with a cold breakfast, if he did not miss it altogether. Record cards were introduced to ensure that 'unwilling soldiers' did not spend their service between hospitals and convalescent camps. Medical information was closely guarded lest soldiers use this knowledge to convince less wary medical officers of the veracity of their incapacity.

The malingerer also had to be punished. The most common form of punishment for minor types of malingering was 'jankers' or confinement to barracks for a few days and being made to perform the most odious jobs (such as emptying urinal tubs). Extensive use was made of imprisonment and Field Punishment Number One (that is, lashing a man to a gun wheel by his wrists and ankles for a period of time). Malingerers sentenced to a period of imprisonment frequently found their sentences commuted to Field Punishment to ensure that they returned to duty as soon as possible: after all, imprisonment gave malingerers what they wanted, that is, to be moved away from the front lines. Other coercive measures included denying separation allowances to the widows, wives, and mothers of deviants. Pay was forfeited by men in hospitals accused of inflicting their own injuries and, in serious cases, they were removed from the army without pensions.

During times of war, medical power came to be controlled by an establishment devoted wholly to victory in the field of battle. On the one hand, the integration of medicine within the military required its subordination to the larger and more powerful institution. On the other hand, medicine was empowered to intervene into people's lives to an extent rarely regarded as appropriate in peacetime. The kindly and constructive labor performed by most medical officers could never distract them from the coercive, disciplinary role they were required to embrace. At the end of each of the wars, the experience of military medicine held few attractions for medical personnel or patients. The benefits bestowed by medical 'advances' resulting directly from military requirements have been exaggerated, and the impetus provided by the wartime centralized medical service for socialized medicine after the wars ignores basic differences between military and civilian contexts. Twentieth-century military conflict was increasingly bloody and progressively 'total' in its range and nature: in consequence, while people's relationship to military medicine became more desperate, their experience of it became increasingly ambivalent. The knowledges, disciplines, and rituals of medicine responded to the needs of the military establishment, and were fundamentally altered in the process. The patient became of secondary importance to the group; medicine was subsumed under the military.

### References

1. Roger Cooter, 'The Politics of a Spatial Innovation: Fracture Clinics in Inter-War Britain', in John V. Pickstone (ed.), *Medical Innovations in Historical Perspective.* (London: Macmillan, 1992), p. 146.
2. Ian Samuel, *Doctor at Dunkirk with the 6th Field Ambulance at War.* (London: Autolycus Pubs., 1985), p. 26.

3.    James Henry Dible, 'Diary and Account', entry for 6 February 1915, 65–66, Imperial War Museum.

4.    Robert Weldon Whalen, *Bitter Wounds. German Victims of the Great War, 1914–1939*. (Ithaca: Cornell University Press, 1984), pp. 53–4.

5.    Charles Huxtable, *From the Somme to Singapore*. (London: Costello, 1987), pp. 29–30.

6.    Hubert P. Demasson, *To All My Dear People. The Diary and Letters*. (Fremantle: Fremantle Arts Centre Press, 1988), pp. 101–2. Spelling and punctuation as in original.

7.    K.R. Eissler, *Freud as an Expert Witness: the Discussion of War Neuroses Between Frued and Wagner-Jaugegg*, translated by C. Trollope (Madison, Connecticut: International Universities Press, Inc., 1986), pp. 60–1.

8.    'Shell Shock', July 1915, in Sir Charles Burtchaell, 'Papers and Reports', The Wellcome Contemporary Medical Archives Center.

9.    Quoted in Hilde Steepe, 'Nursing in the Third Reich', *History of Nursing Society Journal* (1991), **3**: p. 30.

10.   Captain Ralph H. Covernton, 'Fifty Odd Years of Memoirs', p. 25, Liddle Hart Centre.

11.   Gerald F. Petty, *Mad Gerry*. (Risca: The Starling Press, 1982), p. 28.

12.   J. Thompson Rowling, *A Time to Kill and a Time to Heal*. (London: Excalibur Press, 1991), pp. 45–6.

13.   Quoted in Barry Broadfoot, *Six War Years 1939–1945*. (Don Mills: Paper Jacks, 1974), p. 41.

14.   'F.A.V.', *Combed Out*. (London: Sworthmore Press, 1920), p. 56.

15.   Wilfred Willett, 'Memoirs', p. 104, Imperial War Museum.

16.   Letter from Private William Thomas Naughton instructing his brother how to fool the doctors, p. 29 April 1917, Australian War Memorial.

17.   Sir John Collie, *Malingering and Feigned Sickness*, second edition (London: Edward Arnold, 1917), p. 368.

18.   Anonymous diary, 'Mesopotamian Diary', *The Great War. The Illustrated Journal of First World War History* (November 1990), **3**: part 6, p. 29.

19.   William Wallace, 'The Vision of the Soldier', *Journal of the Royal Army Medical Corps* (July 1921), **xxxvii**: p. 43.

20.   C.P. Blacker, *Notes for the R.M.O. [Regimental Medical Officer] of an Infantry Unit*. (Oxford: Oxford University Press, 1943), p. 20.

## FURTHER READING

Bourke, Joanna, *Dismembering the Male: Men's Bodies, Britain and the Great War*. (Chicago and London: University of Chicago Press and Reaktion, 1996).

Bourke, Joanna, *An Intimate History of Killing: Face-to-Face Killing in Twentieth-Century History*. (London: Granta, 1998).

Cooter, Roger, 'The Politics of a Spatial Innovation: Fracture Clinics in Inter-War Britain' in John V. Pickstone (ed.), *Medical Innovations in Historical Perspective*. (London: Macmillan, 1992).

Cooter, Roger, *Surgery and Society in Peace and War*. (London: Macmillan, 1993).

Cooter, Roger, 'War and Modern Medicine' in W.F. Bynum and Roy Porter (eds), *Companion Encyclopedia of the History of Medicine*, volume 2. (London: Routledge, 1993), 1536–73.

Cooter, Roger, et al (eds), *War, Medicine and Modernity*. (Stroud: Sutton, 1998).

Cooter, Roger, et al (eds), *Medicine and Modern Warfare*. (Amsterdam: Rodopi, 1999).

Copp, Terry and McAndrew, Bill, *Battle Exhaustion*. (Montreal: McGill-Queen's University Press, 1990).

Cowdrey, Albert E., *The Medics' War. United States Army in the Korean War*. (Washington, D.C.: Centre of Military History, United States Army, 1987).

Gabriel, Richard A. and Metz, Karen S., *A History of Military Medicine. Volume III. From the Renaissance Through Modern Times*. (New York: Greenwood Press, 1992).

Kaufman, Ralph M. and Beaton, Lindsay E. , 'South Pacific Area' in Lieutenant General Hal B. Jennings (ed), *Neuropsychiatry in World War II. Volume II. Overseas Theatres*. (Washington: Office of the Surgeon General, 1973), 461.

MacNalty, Arthur S. (ed.), *History of the Second World War. United Kingdom Medical Services*, 21 volumes. (London: HMSO, 1952–72).

Macpherson, W.G. (ed.), *History of the Great War Medical Services*, 12 volumes. (London: HMSO, 1923–31).

O'Keefe, Brendan G. (with F.B. Smith), *Medicine at War. Medical Aspects of Australia's Involvement in Southeast Asia 1950–1972*. (St. Leonards: Allen and Unwin, 1994).

Rees, John Rowlings, *The Shaping of Psychiatry by War*. (London: Chapman and Hall, 1945).

Stone, Martin, 'Shellshock and the Psychologists' in W.F. Bynum, Roy Porter and Michael Shepherd (eds), *The Anatomy of Madness. Essays in the History of Psychiatry. Vol. II. Institutions and Society*. (London: Tavistock Pubs., 1985).

Whalen, Robert Weldon, *Bitter Wounds. German Victims of the Great War, 1914–1939*. (Ithaca: Cornell University Press, 1984), 53–4.

CHAPTER 39

# Supported Lives

## JENNIFER STANTON

We all led supported lives once: before we were born. And we are familiar with images of supported lives in science fiction and actuality. From Jules Vernes' characters 20,000 leagues under the sea, to Apollo space-men hovering over their controls, explorers in extreme alien environments depend on their womb-capsules for survival. Reading of fictional, or watching factual, re-entry to the 'normal' world, the spectator experiences vicarious anxiety — and excitement — with fatal outcomes always in mind.

Just as there were precursors in nineteenth-century literature for whole life-support systems, there were at the same time life-restoring systems in operation. Indeed, there were organized movements for the resuscitation of the newborn, the drowned, or other prematurely dead. Artificial respiration and/or restoration of the heart's action can be traced from the later eighteenth century through to present-day intensive care, and to the almost ubiquitous 'cardiac arrest,' which is one source of patients for the intensive care unit (ICU). We can ask at what point, and to what extent, there has been anything new or characteristically twentieth-century in this line of supported lives.

The movement in nineteenth-century Germany which built massive mortuaries, where the dead could lie unburied in case signs of life returned, clearly drew on anxieties surrounding premature burial and the dread of waking in a sealed tomb. Is it the converse case, or a complementary one, when the image of an Iron Lung in the mid-twentieth century conjures anxieties about a living death? Earlier systems aimed to produce a relatively modest reversal of temporary dysfunction: they supported lives that would otherwise be lost, bringing the sufferer a rebirth to normal life. But technical developments have increasingly allowed a 'supported life' to continue indefinitely, with irreversible organ failure compensated by the machine. So, one new feature has been chronic rather than (or additional to) acute support.

Another thread appeared in science fiction and fantasy, reflecting anxieties about pushing back the boundaries of control over our bodies. We might argue that the twentieth century witnessed a growing realization of the 'brave new world' of technical substitutes for 'natural' processes; and that the response — in fiction as in life — was divided between astonished admiration on the one hand, and revulsion on the other. H.G. Wells' nightmare of animal-human transplant in *The Island of Dr Moreau* was echoed in Lindsay Anderson's film satire on later twentieth-century Britain (*O Lucky Man!*), while organ harvesting from lower social strata to produce patchwork immortality for the rich was projected in one of our futures by Marge Piercy in *Woman on the Edge of Time*. Yet Piercy also adapted Aldous Huxley's model of the surrogate womb, from a negative to a positive role: whereas baby-bottling in Huxley's brave new world was an agent of social differentiation and control, for Piercy it liberated women from childbirth to facilitate a genuinely equalizing mix of gender roles. Examples multiply: the bionic 'good guy' of Robocop films in the 1980s can be viewed as a questionable reflection of JBS Haldane's *Daedalus* of 1929, and so on. Used for repair or perfectibility, technology and borrowed organs disturb our notions of what it is to be human.

As the century progressed, more people with organ failure could depend on a machine, an artificial or transplanted organ, or a chemical substitute. But such dependency introduced a range of issues around body image and disability, with implications varying over type and time. External, visible supports obviously impacted on the popular imagination more dramatically than internal, invisible ones, but they did so in a range of ways. While the Iron Lung echoed a coffin or tomb, its successor, in the form of internal positive pressure ventilation (IPPV), hooked the patient to a machine via tubes that entered the airway, preventing speech and thus removing the final mainstay of autonomy. Tubes entering the body for ventilation or nutrition were frightening enough, a sort of assault: more so tubes taking a vital substance — blood — out of the body for extracorporeal circulation or hemodialysis. Here, and to a lesser extent with removal of bodily waste via tubes, there may often have been a sense of things which ought to be hidden being made visible.

Injections, the daily injections of insulin by diabetics or the intermittent injections of Factor VIII by hemophiliacs, were another assault on the body, a penetration of its interface with the outer world; but they were more contained, or containable, than ventilators and dialysis machines. Attitudes to injection, oral medication, and use of suppositories are notoriously culture-bound, but taking medicines by mouth has generally been seen as more 'natural,' on the analogy of healthy ingestion of food. Injecting of medicines has usually been done privately, with something of an air of shame attached, enhanced by the parallel with illicit drug taking.

Internal supports — transplanted organs, pacemakers — have not carried the same connotations of assault, despite the complex surgery involved. Of course there was another kind of 'unnaturalness' in one body incorporating parts of another. However blood transfusions, which became routine in surgical practice during the Second World War, have familiarized us with the notion of transfer of vital tissues from one body to another; they have appeared in a positive light in everyday medical contexts, despite the enduring fascination of Dracula imagery.

The connotations of assault and unnaturalness borne by these technologies have elicited both sympathy and repulsion from the public towards patients. Living with insulin injections, a ventilator, or a dialysis machine, has more recently been formulated as a disability, for which a late twentieth-century 'rights' approach demands social support; thus the problem of the machine or the illness can be redefined as a problem of society's response to disability. The technical response has been to reduce the obtrusiveness of the support. But technical sophistication, and apparently increasing patient control over treatment, have to some extent been countered by a proliferation of medical and non-medical systems and staff with which the patient has to contend. Where there is poor coordination (perhaps in the majority of late twentieth-century health services) patients have had to work hard to manage the people who help to service their condition. The technical side of supported lives may have become smoother, while the human resources may have become more problematic.

This chapter will focus on the experiences and meaning of supported lives for patients and practitioners, via five case studies: insulin therapy for diabetes, kidney dialysis, ventilators, intensive care units and transplants. There is overlap with work on medical technologies more generally, but here we will be looking at technologies that replace the function of bodily organs, either temporarily or permanently. The chapter will employ the work of historians where possible, but also the writings of those involved, and studies from other disciplines such as sociology.

## INSULIN

Insulin, first used in 1921, was one of the first great 'triumphs' of twentieth-century scientific medicine. It was arguably the greatest input from science to medicine in the first half of the century, between the germ theory and antibiotics. In administering an extract from calves' pancreas to diabetics, Fred Banting and Charles Best (with Prof. J. Macleod and James Collip) of the University of Toronto, Canada, replaced the function of the diabetic's pancreas. Diabetics had previously been treated by strict diet, but were liable nevertheless to degenerate to an early death; now they were offered a return to near-normal life. When patients were revived from a diabetic coma that would previously have resulted in certain death, witnesses drew parallels to resurrection.

After Banting and Best's initial trials, the University of Toronto's Connaught Laboratory could not meet the demand, and the American pharmaceutical company Eli Lilly was given the right to manufacture insulin under an exclusive license for one year. There was still a shortage of insulin in the first year or two; the price was high, and impurities often led to abcesses at the injection sites. In Britain, the Medical Research Council took control over the introduction of insulin and insisted on greater purity before allowing wider access to the drug, which was made by appointed firms. This delayed its introduction in the UK but by late 1923 large quantities of pure, locally manufactured and lower-price insulin came on-stream.

Standardization was an issue from the beginning, with the first international standard set in 1925.

Though insulin-dependent diabetics could now expect to live far longer, their condition was not completely rectified by artificial insulin, and complications (from foot disorders to loss of sight or kidney failure) often followed later in life. Problems of dosage and side-effects continued to haunt patients for decades, until more sensitive means of assay and synthetic insulins apparently offered solutions. Most promisingly, the pen-injectors of the 1980s used genetically engineered human insulin, combining ease of application with more compatible molecules. However, by 1992 an investigation was underway into claims that human insulin caused hypoglycemic (low blood sugar) symptoms to occur in low-level forms that were hard to detect.

It was predicted that the introduction of insulin would lead to an increase in the numbers of diabetics in the general population, as those who would have died young lived to pass on the diabetic gene. The fulfilment of this prediction is one reason for the keen commercial interest in producing both better insulins and better appliances for administration: diabetics form a vast and always expanding market. However, their health and survival have probably depended as much on the services available as on better techniques. In Leicester (UK) in the 1950s, the combination of an outpatient clinic with home visiting and consistent record-keeping enabled patients to maintain diets and medication, and thus avoid crises; such services improved the health and quality of life of diabetics. Looking at the US, Chris Feudtner argues that, from the patient's perspective, living with diabetes "has involved unremitting effort and work," within the frame of a disciplined, measured life that "often became a point of pride or rebellion."[1] We should look at this sort of supported life not as technological high drama, but as a conglomeration of routine tasks involving relationships with family, employer and health workers.

## KIDNEY DIALYSIS

Dialysis for *acute* renal failure preceded dialysis for chronic conditions. The essential preconditions developed during the 1930s were heparin (an effective anticoagulant) and cellophane sausage skins which were used in most of the early devices. Willem Kolff, a Dutch physician, evolved the first successful artificial kidney during the Second World War, subsequently developing his machines in the US. Early Kolff artificial kidneys were given to centers in London, New York and Montreal; alternative designs rapidly appeared in Sweden, Canada and the US. The air forces adopted some of the first dialysis machines, following wartime observation of pilots suffering acute renal failure after crashes; but there was little military need so they mainly served the civilian population during the 1950s, saving the lives of a few car crash victims and attempted suicides. Longer term dialysis was precluded because a new vein and artery had to be used each time the patient was connected to the machine, limiting the number of sessions to about eight.

In 1960 a Seattle physician, Belding Scribner, devised a shunt which allowed repeated dialysis by creating a lasting artificial bridge between a vein and an artery, usually in the wrist. Using non-stick teflon, a spin-off from the space program, the Scribner shunt could stay in place for months, until the site became infected or clotting ruined the vessels. At each dialysis, the shunt was opened and the patient was connected up to an artificial kidney, which in the early days was one of various gargantuan models that had to be dismantled, cleaned and reassembled after every session.

There are many parallels between the experiences around long-term hemodialysis and those described for insulin. With terminal kidney failure, as with diabetes, doctors saw (and were often distressed by) patients in terminal coma — in renal failure, the skin became coated with white crystals of urea salts. In each case the innovation promised life to those apparently condemned to die, and demand soon led to drastic shortages: the 'insulin famine' of 1921–2, and the more prolonged shortfall of dialysis from 1960 until 1973 in the US, when Congress enacted provision for almost universal financing of dialysis. The shortage persisted in other countries. As with many innovations, there was initial scepticism from some practitioners, and queries over whether the treatment had to be given in hospital, or whether patients might learn to administer it themselves at home. There was a tendency to treat preferentially 'sensible' patients, who would manage the regime better. Gradually a transition occurred from an experimental to a routine order, with more standardized procedures, and technologies that were easier to use. Meanwhile clinics or units multiplied and divisions of labor around the supported life grew more complex. Short and long term side-effects haunted both treatments, and there were special difficulties in extending them to children.

In the mid-1960s, dialysis units were established in America, Canada and Europe, with physicians and nurses visiting the Seattle center to learn the technique, and subsequently developing and publishing their own variants. Availability of dialysis for the few created a lack for the many. Calculations of how many patients could benefit from dialysis were uncertain, and constantly revised upwards, from 30 new patients per million per year in the 1960s, to 40 in the 1970s, to 80 in the 1990s. In the early phase in Seattle, a mixed lay/clinical selection committee weighed up potential patients in terms of social and psychological factors as well as clinical considerations. An article in *Life Magazine* dubbed this the "God Committee," and led to much criticism of the Seattle selection process.[2] Outside the US there was little public discussion of selection of dialysis candidates, but covert rationing undoubtedly occurred. Only patients otherwise in good health would be considered; children under fifteen, people over fifty, diabetics or patients with heart disease were told they were not suitable for dialysis.

A partial solution to the problem of shortage was to enable patients to dialyse at home. Stanley Shaldon of the Royal Free Hospital in London, John P. Merrill in Boston, and Scribner in Seattle, started home dialysis programs in 1964. The unblocking of hospital beds made this a compelling alternative. Though more expensive in terms of capital outlay, home dialysis greatly reduced running costs because few paid staff were required. Here, compared with hospital dialysis, selection often took greater account of patients' supposed level of intelligence and ability to organize their homes and lives to accommodate the dialysis routine. A supportive spouse, to assist with the shunt connections and preferably with cleaning and reassembling the machine, was seen almost as a necessity. Personal accounts of living with dialysis often contain episodes of home dialysis, with a partner (usually a wife) playing a strong role — so much so that male patients tend to complain of role reversal, of wives going out to earn a living and taking over decision-making in the home. On the other hand, helping with the management of the machine, plus all the other demands arising from the partner's illness, could be almost too great a burden for the healthy partner. An intermediary solution was provided with the establishment of 'satellite' dialysis centers, less expensive than hospital units, and aimed at reasonably fit patients who preferred not to dialyze at home.

Two technical (as opposed to organizational) innovations are cited by many patients and renal staff as having a major impact on the experience of dialysis. One was a surgical means of connecting vein to artery, known as the Cimino shunt, which was introduced in 1966. By 1975, over 80% of patients on hemodialysis used this method rather than the Scribner shunt. Since it involved connection by hollow needles inserted into the vein at each dialysis, it enabled patients to perform dialysis single-handedly (in a way, analogous to diabetics self-injecting insulin). Some adept patients could now dialyze at home without a partner; those with partners could maintain greater independence.

Another key innovation grew from peritoneal dialysis, a means of dialyzing in emergencies that had been tried with varying degrees of success from the 1920s. In this method, dialysis fluid is poured into the patient's peritoneal cavity through a needle or tube in the abdomen; the membranes lining the cavity allow waste products in the bloodstream to pass through by osmosis, and the fluid is removed and replaced either continuously or intermittently. The weak point in this method was the insertion of a needle or tube bringing a high risk of peritonitis. As with the Scribner shunt, new materials changed the picture and in 1978 a Canadian team devised a permanent indwelling cannula, inserted in the wall of the abdomen below the navel, which allowed fairly safe repeated dialysis — 'repeated' here meaning every six hours. This process, known as Continuous Ambulatory Peritoneal Dialysis (CAPD) took off as a serious alternative to hemodialysis from about 1980. Some patients objected to having a tube protruding from their bellies, while others preferred this method because it allowed greater freedom of diet and fluid intake than hemodialysis. The varying extent of uptake of CAPD in different countries was largely, however, a matter of macro-policy. The US, with its generous funding for dialysis, retained a high level of hemodialysis; the UK, which had one of the lowest levels of provision in Western Europe in the 1970s, aimed to increase coverage while keeping costs down, and so used more CAPD than most other European countries.

## VENTILATORS

It might be convenient to talk of three stages in the history of artificial respiration. During the nineteenth century (and earlier), devices were invented to assist the respiration of persons whose breathing had ceased through poisoning, drowning or paralysis. None gained general use, and rival methods of manual artificial respiration — by pressing on the chest or moving the arms — gained wider circulation. The second phase was long-term negative pressure ventilation (reducing air pressure around the patient's chest to draw breath out) which included various 'cuirass' machines, but really became established with the development of the Drinker tank respirator in 1928. This was the machine popularly known as the 'Iron Lung,' designed by Philip Drinker, an engineer at Harvard School of Public Health. The demand for a more effective ventilator was especially urgent during outbreaks of infantile poliomyelitis, in which a proportion of the child victims died slowly as their respiratory muscles became paralyzed. The third phase is also connected with a polio epidemic, that in Copenhagen in 1952, when a different sort of polio led to patients dying in the iron lung. As an alternative, air was pushed into the trachea via tubes: internal positive pressure ventilation (IPPV).

The iron lung has served as the focus for a debate in the literature on medical technology, an important debate in terms of policy but also in terms of historical interpretation. It was one of the technologies cited in 1971 by Lewis Thomas, eminent American physician and 'biology-watcher,' as a 'half-way technology' offering a technical fix for a disease or condition that could not be cured.[3] Such technologies, according to Thomas, tended to be expensive, in contrast with truly effective 'definitive technologies,' which arose from basic research that revealed the inner working of the disease. In the case of polio, the definitive technology was the Salk vaccine. James Maxwell, of the Massachusetts Institute of Technology, challenged this view in 1986, claiming the iron lung "as an intermediate step in the evolution of modern-day respiratory equipment."[4] At the core of this debate is a disagreement over the centrality of basic research, with Maxwell holding that most advances arise from empirical investigation, often made possible by technologies crafted to meet emergencies, while Thomas holds to the superiority of science-based solutions. There are serious implications for resource allocation. However, both agree on the life-saving role played by the iron lung in the exigencies of mid-twentieth century polio outbreaks.

Tony Gould has recorded the stories of British and American polio victims in his book on polio. Part of his own account was written four years after the events and vividly captures the experience of being confined in an iron lung. Gould was stricken with polio in 1959, when he was twenty, in Hong Kong doing National Service:

> I was struggling for breath, my head going from side to side like a metronome ... They lay me down between the jaws of a yawning box which had appeared from nowhere ... Suddenly it came to me that they had made a terrible mistake, that this was a coffin and they were burying me alive.[5]

In contrast to the trauma of first contact, there followed the tedium of lying in the ventilator for days and nights on end. Gould described a routine swabbing just before dawn, when the sister and an orderly had opened the box and the patient was breathing unaided for a few moments:

> The sister lifted one heel and rubbed it with surgical spirit, which stung the raw flesh but eased away the ache ... Before they clamped the iron lung shut again, they adjusted all the supporting pads, and replaced the wads of cottonwool around my neck to keep it airtight. This was the moment I both longed for and dreaded; comfortable again, I would have to stay in this position for hours, since I could hardly ask the sister to open up the lung again for anything so trivial as an itch that I couldn't reach ... The orderly went out. "Please leave the door open," I called after him. "Then I can see when it's dawn."[6]

Even this part of his experience conferred special status, which Gould contrasted with the mundanity of months at a rehabilitation center in England where he learned to walk again. But his true rehabilitation began when he made a new life without full physical power (he was left with a limp): his life changed so much that he divided his life into BP and AP, before and after polio.

Every history of ventilators states that the iron lung was definitively superceded by IPPV during the Copenhagen polio epidemic of 1952. It is retrospectively assumed that it was logical to summon an anesthetist. Anesthetists had developed positive pressure ventilation to support patients undergoing surgery, especially on the chest, when spontaneous breathing ceased; it had become more widespread following the introduction of curare to paralyze patients during surgery. Ger Wackers has challenged this *post hoc* wisdom, pointing out that infectious disease specialists in Copenhagen thought that their patients with bulbar polio were dying in the iron lungs because of neurological damage, not inadequate ventilation. The freelance anesthetist who was called in, Bjørn Ibsen, battled to convince the experts that carbon dioxide build-up was the main cause of death, and that tracheostomy and IPPV was the answer. In the case of the first polio patient he was asked to treat, a twelve-year-old girl in extreme respiratory distress, Ibsen demonstrated how effective ventilation affected not only oxygen and carbon dioxide levels in the girl's blood, but also her temperature and blood pressure. Just as the saving of one patient's life convinced doctors in Copenhagen that IPPV was worth trying, many physicians around the world were persuaded to follow this method by the reduction of weekly mortality in the Copenhagen epidemic. In many places, the success of an initial local case was perhaps almost as crucial as in Copenhagen. For instance in Oxford, UK, the recovery of a young girl on an improvised machine in 1953 was "the decisive case" that guaranteed the continuing use of IPPV for respiratory failure, and helped support the establishment of a respiration unit.[7]

The design of better tank ventilators which allowed patients more comfort and nurses readier access, was now paralleled in the development of IPPV with better pumps incorporating more sensitive monitoring devices. Any 'mechanical student' tended to be less sensitive to the needs of the patient than the relays of medical students who kept patients alive in the Copenhagen epidemic; constant personal observation had to be replaced by automated monitoring devices. Provision of ventilators and monitors, skilled nurses, and anesthetists with specialist skills in helping maintain a patient's vital functions, can be seen as the beginning of intensive care.

## INTENSIVE CARE UNITS

The origin of intensive care units (ICUs, also known as intensive therapy units, ITUs) outlined above emphasizes the role of respiratory technologies. Other interpretations see intensive care closely linked with postoperative recovery rooms and monitoring technologies; or as providing a means of dealing with the most serious cases admitted to accident and emergency departments. An alternative view focuses on the rationalization of 'special' nursing that was taking place in many wards of the hospital during the 1950s. Such nursing involved ventilators in some cases, especially post-operative chest patients, but also such skills as continuous (visual and mechanical) monitoring. The first intensive care units were established in American hospitals in the 1950s, with subsequent growth unevenly spread. By 1990, according to one estimate, about 5% of beds in American hospitals were intensive care beds, compared with 1–2% in Europe, with the UK having one of the lowest rates.[8]

Physicians writing about intensive care often focus on ethical issues: how to choose which patients to admit, and how to decide when treatment should be stopped. Admission choice need not be a problem, some argue, if there were more intensive care beds and nurses, but one cannot avoid the perennial and universal problem of allowing people to die. As one patient recalled being told in an intensive care unit: "The ITU is one place where it is not so easy to die. We have ways of keeping you alive."[9] Intensive care is one of the areas of medicine that since the 1960s have brought puzzles of life, death and patients' rights that are perceived as quite different from anything that has gone before, though this view is open to challenge as unhistorical. Ethically thorny zones surround creation of life by artificial means, destruction of fetuses, manipulation of genes, 'heroic' multi-organ transplants, and euthanasia. This last — often in the modified form of not intervening further — is the main issue at stake in intensive care.

Intensive care is expensive care. A large floor-space is required to allow machines to be wheeled up to each patient's bedside at a moment's notice. The machines — ventilators, dialysis machines, monitors — are sophisticated and costly, as are many of the drugs. Ideally there is one nurse to each patient all round the clock, that is three per patient per day; and these must be highly trained specialist nurses. It is difficult to generalize about costs and 'success' rates. Many studies have shown costs to be much higher for non-survivors as more resources are applied to them for longer, compared with those who recover. Overall costs have spiraled with the growth of ICUs, to perhaps one-fifth of all hospital costs in the US.[10] Survival in the ICU, in hospital, and after discharge varies enormously, but those who do survive show good recovery in terms of quality of life. Do we define the technologies used in intensive care as 'half-way technologies' or essential treatments, and how does our definition impact on debates over allocation of resources? And how do such technologies affect medical and nursing care? In an intensive study of intensive nursing in The Netherlands, Marjan Groen showed that nurses felt their mastery of technology did not necessarily distance them from patients; they relied strongly on their own sense of the patient's physical state, treating each sophisticated monitor as another tool rather than an oracle. However, it might be argued that the special training, high status, and technical competence of ICU nurses has made them more like doctors, thereby increasing the likelihood of distance from patients.

Most patients are in ICU for less than 24 hours, and most are unconscious during their stay, or heavily sedated. This in itself obviously reduces interaction between staff and patients. But a patient may appear insensible, and yet be aware: one patient described lying immobile in ICU after a road accident, unable to move or see or speak, thinking she was dead, as staff talked around but not to her. Only after a friend had persistently requested admission (usually allowed only for relatives) and explained the situation to her while holding her hand, did this woman feel she might live.[11] A few patients who were in ICU for longer periods, conscious for part of the time, have recorded their experiences. One remarked on the constant noise in the unit: "The nurses attached to the ITU were a special breed — the elite corps among the nursing profession — but to my extreme surprise, I found them to be the noisiest lot."[12] Another patient described as "torture" the ministrations of physiotherapists who tipped and thumped him to drain fluids from his lungs.[13] Above all, the lack of explanation of what was happening seems to have induced fear.

In intensive care units, patients lead supported lives almost like babies, reflected in language such as 'weaning off' the ventilator. But there has always been a tension over including children alongside adults in ICUs. Increasingly, younger children and newborn babies needing special care have been allocated separate intensive care spaces: pediatric and neonatal intensive care units (PIC and NIC units). The earlier history of the artificial womb, the incubator, was chequered, with notable national differences: French obstetricians favored simpler incubators, concentrating on warmth; American pediatricians sought complete life-support systems and more quickly rejected the technology. Both came to rely on the mother to save the child, with nurses entering the equation as intermediaries: "The tension between the machine and the mother was eventually reconciled by introducing the professional nurse."[14] In Groen's present day study, she found that:

> In the interviews with PIC/NIC nurses the patient is viewed as consisting of a child and parents: a trinity. In this perception the parents need almost as much support as the child … The child itself is regarded as a patient who does not fret and worry, but who lets you know when it is happy or sad, and it allows you to comfort it.[15]

So the infant is inside a glass womb that allows hands as well as machines to reach in to offer support. Its prognosis in the late twentieth century is probably better than that of adults in ICUs, on average, but statistics vary widely.

## TRANSPLANTS

Organ transplants are partly a matter of fancy needlework, which could be learned by plenty of surgeons; partly a matter of persuading the recipient's body that this foreign object is acceptable. Even after differences in blood groups were worked out, making blood transfusion safer, experiments in organ transplantation failed because of rejection. In the 1950s, the growing science of immunology offered new understandings of rejection, while new drugs — steroids — dampened the immune response. The first successful kidney transplant in 1954, in the US (on identical twins), was followed by escalating numbers of transplants of kidneys, livers and hearts around the world: the first heart transplant, in South Africa in 1967, attracted more publicity than any of the others.

But the great transplant boom really took off after the 1983 'advent' of cyclosporine, the anti-rejection wonder drug. Renée Fox, an American sociology professor, and her collaborator Judith Swazey, who have worked for forty years in the field of dialysis and transplantation, recently analyzed the changing mood of reports on cyclosporine in the medical literature: from gung-ho optimism in the early 1980s, to deepening concern over side-effects by the early 1990s. Fox and Swazey became increasingly critical towards the culture of transplantation during the 1980s, while they were observing an experimental artificial heart program that eventually was subject to a moratorium. Their growing unease was also provoked by the explosion of multi-organ transplants — an apparent competition between transplant surgeons to be first to replace every organ in the human body.

Besides the indignities and suffering of patients, who accepted surgery at the experimental stage as their only alternative to death, the procurement of organs for transplantation was another cause for concern. Scandals in the British press revealed that fears of 'organs for sale' were based on actuality, as surgeons in a London private hospital purchased kidneys from desperate Turkish men. Worse stories emerged from other countries, with suggestions of mentally-ill patients 'disappearing.' The historian Ruth Richardson compares the modern underground trade in organs with 'body-snatching' in the nineteenth century — in both cases, the procurers start with dead bodies, but in their greed they might proceed to dismember the living.

Besides this dark margin, there are intractable socio-cultural problems in obtaining sufficient donated organs. Fox and Swazey have long argued that insufficient attention was paid to the cultural meanings of the 'gift' of donated organs. Right through the 1970s and 1980s, Elizabeth Ward of the British Kidney Patients Association campaigned for a change in British law, to allow organs to be removed at death as a rule, with an opt-out option. Repeatedly when the question was raised in Parliament, the health minister would reply that public opinion did not favour such a scheme. It has also been argued that many more organs would be forthcoming if there were more positive procedures in ICUs for requesting relatives of brain-dead patients to agree to organ donation. Many transplant doctors, and patients needing transplants, feel that ICU staff are over-cautious about approaching relatives, who might derive comfort from granting such a request. At times discussion focuses on the definition of brain death, and on the public's lack of understanding of this definition, so finely portrayed in the video-within-a-film in Pedro Almodovar's *The Flower of My Secret* (1995).

Britain has had a higher rate of kidney transplantation than many other countries, and has led the field in setting up a centralized system of allocating available organs; many countries have developed similar systems. Among transplant teams and potential patients, discussion has continued to focus on the need to increase the supply of organs. But such discussions generally regard people's reluctance to give organs as irrational, and fail to recognise the full range of cultural reasons for such behaviour. The relatively high rate of kidney transplants in the UK compared with other European countries shows the importance of economic factors — the low level of funding for dialysis in the UK — which in this case have counterbalanced cultural resistance.

## CONCLUSION

The number of patients living 'supported lives' is relatively small, but the impact of such lives on our perceptions of medicine in the twentieth century has been enormous. The introduction to this chapter remarked on our mixed response, between technophilia and technophobia; ambiguous attitudes towards technologies in general have been especially apparent in relation to life-prolonging technologies which risk trapping an active mind in an immobile body. The five examples surveyed here varied widely: from low-technology insulin therapy for diabetics, to high-technology intensive care. Locations ranged from home to hospital, clinic to out-patient facility. Professionals involved in the early stages were variously physicians, engineers, technicians, physiologists and nurses; over time a cluster of para-professions developed in each area. Insulin, dialysis for renal failure, and organ

TABLE 1: TIMELINES FOR 'SUPPORTED LIVES' CHAPTER

| | Insulin | Dialysis | Ventilators | ICUs | Transplants |
|---|---|---|---|---|---|
| 1900 | | | [Resuscitation contd from C19] | | |
| | [relevant animal experimentation contributing to all areas continued] | | | | |
| 1910 | | | | | |
| 1920 | 1921: insulin (Canada) | | 1928: Drinker 'iron lung' (US) | | |
| 1930 | | | 1937: 'Both' respirator (UK) | | |
| 1940 | | 1942: Kolff hemodialysis (Holland) | | | |
| 1950 | 1955: sulfonamide treatment | | 1952: IPPV for polio (Denmark) | ICUs/resp units (US, Can, UK, Sw) | 1954: 1st successful twin tr (US) |
| 1960 | Synthetic insulin | 1960: Scribner shunt > repeated dialysis (US) | Expansion in use of automated IPPV (for ICU not polio) | Electronic monitors | 1967: 1st heart tr (SA) |
| 1970 | | 1973: US funds 1978: CAPD (Can) | | Expansion incl PIC/NIC | |
| 1980 | Gen.eng. insulin/ pen inj | | | | Cyclosporine > 'heroic' multi-organ transplants |
| 1990 | Nos of patients involved in 'supported lives' mid-1990s: | | | | |
| | 1 in 100 | 80 per mill (UK target) | Mainstay of ICUs | 10–15% hosp beds in US: 1–3% Europe | 1000s in US & Europe |
| 2000 | | | | | |

transplants have turned terminal illness into chronic supported lives, with unavoidable side-effects. Ventilators and intensive care were usually applied over a limited span, with the aim of returning the patient to a normal life; but they carried the fearful connotation of maintaining life beyond the point of viability, as in brain death.

At the stage of innovation, while their application could fairly be described as experimental, these life-supporting technologies each met with opposition. In overcoming the doubts of conservative practitioners, 'pioneers' gained notoriety and eventually won accolades. What had been audacious became routine, what had seemed to provide a miracle cure proved to have serious drawbacks; further innovations were introduced. Meanwhile the smaller details of administering these technologies and maintaining patients' lives in a reasonable state of physiological and psychological equilibrium fell to a large number of helpers with complementary skills — including the patients themselves and their families.

The more a life-supporting technology came to be seen as acceptable, widely available and routine, the less acclaim and status accrued to the associated professionals, for example the doctor and home-visiting nurses of the Leicester diabetic clinic. By contrast, the more controversial, constrained and experimental the procedure — such as a novel transplant — the greater the publicity and reward commonly accorded to the practitioner. But there have also been questioning voices, not necessarily saying these things should not be done at all, but querying the timing. Supported lives have raised key questions of wider social responsibility — for financing expensive therapies, and deciding who receives them. Where the voice of the patient can be heard, recounting the experience of a supported life, different decisions have appeared: whether illness and technology determine one's life, or how to live despite them.

## REFERENCES

The author is a member of the 'Science speaks to Policy' History Programme supported by the Wellcome Trust, at the London School of Hygiene and Tropical Medicine.

1.  Chris Feudtner, 'Getting the point: medical management and the daily work of diabetes during the twentieth century,' in *Abstracts*, American Association for the History of Medicine 68th Annual Meeting, 1995.
2.  Renée Fox and Judith Swazey, *The Courage to Fail: A Social View of Organ Transplantation and Dialysis*. (Chicago: University of Chicago Press, 1974), pp. 240–79.
3.  Lewis Thomas, 'Notes of a biology-watcher: the technology of medicine,' *New England Journal of Medicine* (1971), **285**: 1366–8.
4.  James Maxwell, 'The iron lung: halfway technology or necessary step?,' *Milbank Quarterly* (1986), **64**: 3–29, at 16.
5.  Tony Gould, *A Summer Plague: Polio and its Survivors*. (New Haven and London: Yale University Press, 1995), pp. 309–10.
6.  *Ibid*, p. 311.
7.  Jennifer Beinart [Stanton], *A History of the Nuffield Department of Anaesthetics, Oxford, 1937–1987*. (Oxford: Oxford University Press, 1987), p. 114.
8.  Simon L. Cohen, *Whose Life is it Anyhow?* (London: Robson Books, 1993), p. 11.

9.  Pittu Laungani, *It Shouldn't Happen to a Patient. A Survivor's Guide to Fighting Life-threatening Illness.* (London: Whiting and Birch, 1992), p. 72.

10. Lis Dragsted and Jesper Qvist, 'Epidemiology of intensive care,' *International Journal of Technology Assessment in Health Care* (1992), **8**: 395–407, at 405.

11. Personal communication.

12. Laungani, *It Shouldn't Happen*, p. 73.

13. W.L.C. Chilver, 'On being a patient in an intensive care unit,' *Nursing Mirror* (6 April 1978), 33–5.

14. Jeffrey P. Baker, *The Machine in the Nursery: Incubator Technology and the Origins of Newborn Intensive Care.* (Baltimore and London: Johns Hopkins University Press, 1996), p. 179.

15. Marjan Groen, *Technology, Work and Organisation: A Study of the Nursing Process in Intensive Care Units.* (Maastrict, The Netherlands: University of Limburg Dissertation no. 95–29, 1995), pp. 76–7.

## FURTHER READING

Bliss, Michael, *The Discovery of Insulin.* (Chicago: University of Chicago Press, 1982).

Drukker, W., 'Haemodialysis: a historical review,' in W. Drukker, J.F. Maher and F.M. Parsons (eds), *Replacement of Renal Function by Dialysis.* (The Hague, Boston, London: Martinus Nijhoff, 1978), pp. 3–37.

Fairman, Julie, 'Watchful vigilance: nursing care, technology and the development of intensive care nursing units,' *Nursing Research* (1992), **41**: 56–60.

Feudtner, Chris, 'The want of control: ideas, innovations, and ideals in the modern management of diabetes mellitus,' *Bulletin of the History of Medicine* (1995), **69**: 66–90.

Fox, Renée, and Swazey, Judith, *Spare Parts; Organ Replacement in American Society.* (New York and Oxford: Oxford University Press, 1992).

Gallagher, Eugene, 'Home dialysis and sociomedical policy,' in M. Stacey *et al.* (eds), *Health and the Division of Labour.* (London: Croom Helm, 1977), pp. 63–85.

Halper, Thomas, *The Misfortunes of Others. End-stage Renal Disease in the United Kingdom.* (Cambridge: Cambridge University Press, 1989).

Hilberman, M., 'The evolution of intensive care units,' *Critical Care Medicine* (1975), **3**: 159–65.

Limb, Mike, *A Patient's View of Renal Failure and Dialysis.* (London: Dulwich Kidney Patients' Association, 1991).

Marks, Harry, 'Medical technologies: social contexts and consequences,' in W. F. Bynum and R. Porter (eds), *Companion Encyclopaedia of the History of Medicine.* (New York: Routledge, 1993), Vol. 2, pp. 1592–1618.

Moulin, Anne Marie, 'The ethical crisis of organ transplants — in search of cultural "compatibility,"' *Diogenes* (1995), **172**: 73–92.

Pernick, Martin S., 'Back from the grave: recurring controversies over defining and diagnosing death in history,' in R. Zaner (ed.), *Death: Beyond Whole-brain Criteria.* (Dordrecht: Kluwer, 1988), pp. 17–74.

Reiser, Stanley J., 'The intensive care unit: the unfolding and ambiguities of survival therapy,' *International Journal of Technology Assessment in Health Care* (1992), **8**: 382–94.

Richardson, Ruth, 'Fearful symmetry: corpses for anatomy, organs for transplantation,' in Stuart J. Younger, Renée Fox and Laurence J. O'Connell (eds), *Organ Transplantation: Meanings and Realities.* (Madison: Wisconsin University Press, 1996).

Wackers, Ger, 'Innovation in artificial respiration: how the "iron lung" became a museum piece,' in Ghislaine Lawrence (ed.), *Technologies of Modern Medicine.* (London: Science Museum, 1994), pp. 40–57.

Walker, Joan B., *Chronicle of a Diabetic Service.* (London: British Diabetic Association, 1989).

# CHAPTER 40

# Old Age

PAT THANE

The experiences of 'old people' throughout the twentieth century, and indeed for very much longer, have been more extreme than those of other age groups. 'Old age' embraces significant numbers of people who are highly, if not perfectly, fit, and people in states of severe physical and/or mental deterioration; the very rich and the desperately poor; the most powerless and the most powerful. Contemplate the advanced age of many world leaders through the century. Stalin, Mao Tse Tung, Tito, Churchill, Margaret Thatcher matched none of the conventional sterotypes of old age even when they were past the customary age barrier. Contemplate also the very many active older people in any community. Yet the stereotype of old age as a phase of dismal decrepitude survives. Popular discourse contrives to overlook the many visible exceptions. It is, surely, a discourse profoundly influenced by our own fears of those later years of unpredictable length and unknowable condition, expressing these terrors more accurately than it expresses what is known of the experience of old age.

In the twentieth century, for the first time in history, it became normal to grow old. Throughout all previous centuries, so far as can be traced, those who survived the hazards of infancy had a reasonable though uncertain chance of reaching old age. People over 65 accounted for between 8 and 10% of the English population between the sixteenth and eighteenth centuries, falling to 5% in the nineteenth century. The surprisingly widespread belief that in 'the past' most people died at around age 35 is due to confusing life expectancy at birth, in the high infant mortality regimes which characterized most societies up to the early-twentieth century, with the life expectancy of those who survived early life.

Something that has not changed is that old age is especially a female experience. At the dawn of the twenty-first century more women survive to later ages than men in all but a cluster of South Asian societies; this gender gap is stable or slightly widening. It is sometimes thought that this is a twentieth-century phenomenon, but it has been evident in England and Wales since official registration of births, marriages and deaths began in 1837. Throughout Europe since medieval times commentators have expressed surprise that, despite the 'natural' greater longevity of the male, *per accidens* females lived longer. There is no convincing evidence that males have ever consistently had longer life expectancies than females. The common belief that death in childbirth removed the female advantage is greatly to overestimate maternal mortality in the past.

Women outlive men, but all too often to experience poverty, due to their lesser capacity to amass assets over their lifetimes. Partly in consequence old women suffer worse health than old men.

### THE AGEING OF TWENTIETH–CENTURY SOCIETIES

The decline of infant and later mortality in the twentieth century combined with lower birth rates has increased the proportion of older people in all developed and many less developed societies.

Some see this as cause for alarm. They suggest that as old people lose their rarity value they will be less respected than before. The belief that older people are less respected than they used to be has regularly been expressed, and contradicted, at least since Plato incorporated a discourse on the theme in *The Republic*. Anthropologists report that it is hard to find any society in which people are respected simply for being old. To gain respect older people must hold wealth or power or credit for past achievements. Medieval European folklore constantly warned old people of the danger of passing their wealth or power to the young; the outcome they might expect was most sublimely portrayed in *King Lear*. Where older people are customarily housed with their families, as in many Asian societies in the twentieth century, they were not necessarily respected.

Most people are now living into old age and more are living to the oldest ages, eighty and beyond. This too is sometimes seen as cause for gloom. It is assumed that if people live longer they will be sick and dependent for a longer period before death. But this is to forget that one reason for longer lives is that people are living more healthily throughout life. To project the health conditions of the 1990s onto octogenarians of future generations is to overlook the massive changes in lifetime experience over the twentieth century and their complex, barely understood, effects upon health. There are indications that disabling conditions are striking people at later ages and are not disabling for longer periods than in the past. It must also be remembered that most people do not experience a long period of serious dependency and ill-health before death. This is another stereotype perhaps induced by private fears.

The social and economic implications of the ageing of modern societies are equally controversial. More often than not they are discussed pessimistically, surprisingly since this change is the outcome of improvements in health and living standards of which people have dreamed over the centuries.

### HOW OLD IS OLD?

But does 'old age' mean the same thing in the twentieth as in earlier centuries? Did people grow older, physiologically, at earlier ages in the past? The twentieth century has seen the formal stratification of society by age as never before. In the age of form-filling, knowing one's age is a constant bureaucratic requirement. Fixed ages of schooling and payment of pensions have constructed the schoolchild and the old age pensioner as social categories defined by age. The first British state pensions, introduced in 1908 were paid at age 70, but this was an economy measure which went against the popular belief that most people were old enough to need them at 60 or 65. The British pensionable age was reduced to 65 in 1925 and for women to 60 in 1940. All modern states have introduced state pensions at some time since the 1880s at ages ranging upwards from 55.

Yet in medieval Europe, and even in the ancient world, laws prescribed upper age limits for work, military or other public service and these were normally fixed at 60 or above. In all periods in which it can be traced the popular perception was that old age, in the sense of declining capacities, began somewhere in the fifties, as it remains. There is striking continuity in official and popular definitions of old age over time. It is in the twentieth century, at the same time that they have been still more firmly inscribed in law, that they have become increasingly detached from the experiences of older people. Now, in developed countries, it is normal to remain fit until one's mid-70s. The raising or abolition of the pensionable age, the official definition of the onset of old age, is being implemented and discussed in countries such as Sweden, Japan, the US, Australia. It may be that at the outset of twenty-first century the barriers between age-groups are being dismantled. Certainly we should be wary of generalizing about the experiences of a vast and growing age group ranging from the age of around 60 to over 100.

### RETIREMENT

Along with the introduction of pensions came the expectation of a period of 'retirement' from paid work, a time of ease before the onset of debility. For wealthy older people this has always been an option, though one they have often been unwilling to take. Politicians for example have not observed the retirement ages they have decreed for others. Retirement at about 60 or 65 was gradually introduced in the first half of the century for white collar workers (mainly male) in Britain and elsewhere. Retirement at about the age of 65 became a mass experience for manual workers only from the later 1940s, due partly to improvements in state pensions. Large-scale unemployment in European countries in the 1980s and 1990s brought, most acutely first to France, then elsewhere a reduction in the 'retirement' age, not always voluntarily, to white as well as blue-collar workers. In the mid-1990s the median retirement age in Britain was 57 for men and 59 for women.

### THE MEDICINE OF OLD AGE

One response to the growing proportion of older people in twentieth-century societies has been the gradually greater attention paid to their health. Medical interest in old age is at least as old as recorded time. Hippocrates and Galen discussed the causes of bodily ageing and whether it could be slowed; whether old age was itself a disease or an unalterable natural condition. These debates continued through the centuries, and understanding of the physiology of ageing increased, though until the twentieth century as little could be done for disease in old age as for younger ages.

A specialized medicine of old age emerged strongly in France in the nineteenth century along with the falling birth-rate and ageing of French society, which occurred earlier than in comparable countries. It was in the US around the time of the First World War that a specialism named 'geriatrics' emerged, guided by an Austrian-born immigrant Ignatz Nascher (1863–1945). Nascher was concerned above all to redress the neglect of older patients by the medical profession, who thought them uninteresting and unworthy of the effort of treatment. This view was slow to change, if indeed it ever has. The practice of geriatric medicine spread slowly in the USA, Germany, USSR, Britain and elsewhere in the middle years of the twentieth century. Diagnosis and treatment improved, for example for heart conditions, hypertension and some cancers. We can illustrate the wider story by surveying the experience and treatment of older people in poor health in Britain.

## GERIATRICS IN BRITAIN

Conventionally the development of modern British geriatrics is traced to 1935 when Dr Marjorie Warren became deputy medical director of a poor law infirmary which had been taken over by the West Middlesex Hospital. This was an outcome of the Local Government Act 1929 which transferred poor law institutions into the control of local authorities in the hope of reducing the stigma attached to poor relief and improving conditions in the institutions.

Both district hospitals, such as the West Middlesex, and voluntary teaching hospitals generally specialized in acute medicine, treating the more 'interesting' and supposedly more curable patient; the chronically, supposedly incurably, ill, very many of them aged, were relegated to poor law infirmaries unless they could afford better. Doctors in training had no contact with such patients. A rationing system, providing inferior medical care for most older patients was firmly in place.

For the first time at the West Middlesex highly trained staff were exposed to conditions in the chronic wards. Warren was appalled to find that she was responsible for about 700 mostly bedbound old people, in large, dismal wards. They were kept clean and fed but given little further care or hope of recovery whatever the cause of their condition. Nurses on these wards had inferior training to those on surgical and medical wards.

Warren had the wards painted in attractive colors, with improved lighting, individual lockers, day rooms and activities, so there was an incentive for patients to get out of bed. She introduced serious diagnosis of the patients'conditions in place of the previous, largely silent because taken for granted, assumption that whatever the precipitating cause of hospitalization, older people were close to death; that illness was an unavoidable correlate of ageing and it was hardly worth seeking to improve or cure their conditions. Warren discovered that cure, or at least considerable improvement, was possible but often more difficult than in younger people. Older people were more likely to suffer from multiple conditions and it was even more difficult than in younger people to disentangle the physical, mental and social components of their problems. Some did not improve because they were depressed and lonely with little to look forward to if they left the institution. A succession of surveys indicated that long-stay patients were highly likely to lack close relatives or friends.

Warren promoted physiotherapy and other forms of rehabilitation, inventing exercises to encourage movement in the previously bedridden. A high proportion of the patients were stroke victims whose paralysis was assumed to be irreversible. Doctors had been trained to confine them to bed to avoid the danger of another stroke. After rehabilitation 200 of the initial patients were able to leave hospital to live with their relatives or in residential homes, after Warren had interviewed family and friends.

Warren's innovative work came about partly due to institutional change following the 1929 Act. But the situation she described of so many bedbound old people was also new. Until the interwar years few had long survived acute illness. They died relatively quickly from infection or pneumonia. Improvements in workhouse hospitals since the First World War, especially in standards of nursing and the treatment of infection, meant that more older people survived strokes and other acute episodes, but no-one then knew what to do with them other than to leave them in bed. The introduction of sulphonomide drugs from 1935 held out the prospect that still more would survive. Warren was tackling a new and extensive problem.

Others in the 1930s were increasingly concerned with the health of old people in England and in Scotland, especially in Glasgow where public health clinics had an active role in ensuring that old people in need had speedy access to care, including referral to hospital, though conditions after referral were variable. In Glasgow the closer association between teaching hospitals and old poor law hospitals revealed to appalled consultants conditions as bad as those discovered by Warren.

## THE SECOND WORLD WAR

At the beginning of the Second World War the Emergency Medical Service was established to co-ordinate health institutions, public and private, nationwide under official control to ensure efficient provision for the victims of the expected bombing and other casualties. On the outbreak of war 140,000 patients, mostly aged and chronically sick, were discharged from hospital in just two days, some to unsuitable private homes and others to distant public assistance institutions, to make room for the expected war casualties. Others who needed hospital treatment were removed from waiting lists. The majority of the beds thus freed remained empty for at least the next nine months and, throughout the war, the need never matched the initial estimates. Nevertheless, this prioritization of what the Ministry of Health called 'potential effectives' over old people continued throughout the war and in 1946 old people often still could not secure necessary medical treatment and care. Mortality rose, particularly of old people in institutions.

A few were fortunate and the upheaval drew the attention of sympathetic doctors to their problems. For example L.Z. Cosin was Medical Superintendant at Orsett Lodge Hospital in Essex when a number of old people were transferred from London. In response to this unexpected challenge he began to use exercise and massage to help the bedridden to walk. He was among the leading figures in post-war geriatrics.

But few benefitted from such work. In 1942 the National Council of Social Service reported that: "it is felt generally that many pensioners go without medical assistance or do not ask for it soon enough."[1] Old people, and many younger ones, often had as low expectations of their health as did the professionals. An official investigation of the condition of a sample of pensioners receiving Public Assistance in 1944 rated 39 of them as in 'good health.' These included individuals suffering from:

> Rheumatoid arthritis and is almost helpless.
> Had a stroke six years ago and another eighteen months back. She is very frail.
> Owing to septic foot has been forced to give up work. Daughter and hospital cannot do anything for him.
> Failing eyesight caused by sugar diabetes. Daily injections and special diet.
> Had to give up work owing to bronchitis and myocardial degeneration.
> Much crippled by rheumatism (hospital treatment).
> Suffering from anaemia and a cancer growth.

And many more.[2] To be classified as in 'poor' health required the pensioner to be bedridden.

The chief source of medical care for older working-class people under the National Insurance system was from overworked 'panel' doctors. One London doctor was reported to be dealing with 30 to 40 cases an hour, another with 60. A third had spent two hours in surgery, the first dealing with 25 panel patients, the second with six private cases. Those who were not covered by National Insurance, which included most women, were only entitled to worse treatment under the Poor Law, unless they could afford to pay for a doctor. Those who could not would buy patent or herbal medicines or frequently neglect serious problems.

That the needs of older people took lower priority than those of the young was taken for granted. Even the Beveridge Report of 1942, the blueprint for the post-war Welfare State, asserted: "It is *dangerous* to be in any way lavish to old age until adequate provision has been assured for all other vital needs, such as the prevention of disease and the adequate nutrition of the young."[3] (my emphasis).

## 'NORMAL' AGING

At this point almost all of the limited number of studies of the (ill)-health of older people were of those already receiving medical treatment. Almost nothing was known of the 'normal' health potential of older people; to what degree and in what ways, if at all, old age was unavoidably associated with ill-health. Nor was there any clear picture of how much ill-health among older people went undetected and unreported.

The Nuffield Foundation funded a survey in 1945–7 by Dr J.H. Sheldon of a sample of older people in Wolverhampton, a town of average size, with a mixed economy. In a sensitive and thoughtful survey, by the standard of the time, Sheldon was impressed by the generally good health and level of activity of the old people he interviewed and observed (but did not examine) in contrast with those he had encountered during twenty years of medical practice, though it has to be said that his expectations were low.

Sheldon found to his surprise that only 2.5% were confined to bed, 8.5% to their houses, 22.5% to the immediate neighborhood. The numbers who were confined increased with age, being rare before age seventy. Many had little contact with doctors. He concluded that old age in the ordinary sense of the phrase begins to show itself "in most cases at about the age of 70 and thereafter becomes increasingly frequent."[4] Before age 70 ailments seemed much the same as afflicted the remainder of the adult population, thereafter what Sheldon described as "specific problems of old age emerged, e.g. weakness, vertigo, spondylitis, difficulty with traffic and loss of confidence,"[5] a list which suggests the blend of psychological, social and medical conditions which characterized the experience of old age and its medical discussion.

Women exhibited poorer health than men although they lived longer. They were often suffering the legacy of childbirth in poor conditions, but they were less likely than men to be confined to bed with minor ailments, and they were more lively and vigorous. Sheldon concluded that this was because women did not 'retire' but carried on with housework, rarely thinking of giving up before their late seventies at least. Sheldon commented "up to the age of seventy-five at least, women give the community more than they take in the matter of domestic responsibility,"[6] including nursing other older and younger people.

An important finding was that very many people were seriously disabled or disadvantaged not by major illnesses but by problems which were, in principle, minor and curable: bad feet, defective vision and hearing, incontinence. Too many people had poor eyesight but no spectacles of their own due to cost. Sheldon noted "ignorance of the individual nature of spectacles — no less than ten per cent obtain them in haphazard ways-as by a gift or after the decease of a relative."[7] Or they were bought cheaply in chain stores, without adequate testing or awareness about how the eyes might change over time. One person commented: "The glasses are all right; it's my eyes that have gone weak — I've got too old for glasses."[8]

Hearing aids were rare and the quality available to poor people was inadequate. Sheldon found the mental health of the old people much better than he was accustomed to encounter in institutions. He concluded that when old people seemed depressed or apathetic it was due to loneliness, economic anxieties, poor health or limited mobility and that, again, in principle, it was curable. He was well aware of the limitations of his study and of the need for more investigation of 'normal' old age. He was also convinced of the importance of enabling people to live in their accustomed homes for as long as possible. Even when they lived alone few that he interviewed claimed to be 'lonely' or neglected by relatives.

## THE NATIONAL HEALTH SERVICE

Sheldon's survey was published in 1948 on the eve of the inauguration of the National Health Service (NHS). At that time the chronically sick, most of them old people, occupied some 70,000 hospital beds. There were great variations in periods of stay in hospital. In Birmingham the mean duration of stay for female chronic patients was 37 months. The national average was 260 days. At the Orsett Lodge Hospital, Cosin had the figure down to 52 days.

The British Geriatrics Society (BGS) was formed in 1948 and was supported by the British Medical Association. It worked to promote improved medical services for old people, research, and training of medical professionals to care for them. The existence of a separate specialism of geriatrics remained controversial. The geriatricians insisted that without it old people would continue to be at the end of the queue for medical care.

## GERIATRICS IN SCOTLAND

Geriatrics was somewhat more readily accepted in Scotland and clinical posts sooner established. Because of the lesser separation between teaching and 'chronic' hospitals, Scottish medical students were more likely to encounter geriatric patients. Its further development in the 1950s and 1960s owed much to the work of Ferguson Anderson who had experienced the shock of the condition of the chronically sick in the pre-war Poor Law hospitals of Glasgow. He found that conditions had worsened with the coming of the NHS. The public health clinics had been closed. More hospitals had become acute hospitals and were reluctant to take old people. They always gave preference to admitting younger patients. Anderson resisted the assumption that the needs of the young were 'naturally' greater than those of older people.

He was inspired by a visit to Marjorie Warren, who was still working at the West Middlesex, commenting that "she wasn't well regarded in her own hospital because they hadn't the insight to see what a brilliant woman this was."[9] Gradually he established small units for the diagnosis of older people in the Glasgow General hospitals, because such facilities were lacking in the old poor law institutions where sick old people were still mainly kept. From 1953 he worked with Dr Nairn Cowan at the Rutherglen Centre of Older People examining people over age 55 referred by their GPs with minor complaints, seeking to understand 'normal' aging. They discovered above all how much investigation was needed to establish the medical needs of older people: "the symptoms are much more insidious... the older people tend to have more than one thing wrong with them, so one gets interwoven with the other."[10]

Anderson encouraged younger doctors to attend the clinics to help them to build up knowledge of "the clinical picture of an active healthy, elderly person." He became convinced that "chronological age is almost meaningless and many individuals are extremely fit until over ninety."[11]

Anderson and Cowan published a string of research papers defining the characteristics of old age and forms of treatment, emphasizing the interaction of the medical and the social and the importance of treating apparently mundane conditions such as bad feet in order to improve the lives of older people and reduce their demands on medical services. Anderson gave the example of a woman who was bedridden, apparently deaf and thought to be suffering from mild dementia. Once her severe corns were treated, the impacted wax removed from her ears and her severe constipation dealt with she was active again. He was convinced that much illness and disability in old age was remediable and that active life could be prolonged.

Anderson concluded that certain principles should guide geriatric medicine and that the needs of old people were specific enough to merit specialist treatment: Older people are happier and healthier in their own homes if they are fit enough to be there and so desire.

> They are ill not due to advancing age but due to illness.
> They have an altered physiology which may render the presentation of disease atypical. Pathology when it occurs is commonly multiple.
> Older people have an immense potential for recovery.
> Their altered physiology might lead to impaired hearing, diminishing sensations of pain and perception of temperature
> There were real physiological differences in old people. The two greatest changes were loss of elasticity in skin, bone, arteries, lungs, brain and loss of reserve function in heart, liver, lungs, kidneys, brain.
> Presenting symptoms altered making accurate diagnosis difficult.
> It was necessary to assess the home environment.[12]

It was important to examine the apparently healthy in order to catch disease in its early stages. Regular check-ups were more important in the old than the young and middle-aged. Depression might present as insomnia or constipation. Multiple diseases might lead doctors to prescribe too many harmfully inter-acting drugs, and often to compound the harm by prescribing them for too long.

In the early 1960s Anderson was still concerned that it was not yet possible to reach an accurate and complete diagnosis of cerebro-vascular disease and that numerous neurological disorders of older people were still undefined. Too many not very elderly patients were "labelled on very flimsy clinical evidence."[13] Apparently minor symptoms which could warn of the possibility of a stroke were often overlooked.

Anderson achieved much needed and important advances in Glasgow. A national survey in 1956 concluded that "by and large the older age groups were currently receiving a lower standard of service than the main body of consumers and that there were substantial areas of unmet need among the elderly."[14] They found that provision was best where an individual took the initiative. The problems to be overcome were still immense. Their extent was vividly expressed by one of Anderson's young assistants, later a very eminent geriatrician, as he described his first encounter with the chronic wards of what had once been a poor law hospital in Glasgow as late as 1958.

I stood in the dayroom of Ward C8 in utter disbelief at the sight. I was overwhelmed with horror, numbed with sorrow. Tears rose to my eyes. I had not expected to see a cheerful picture here, but the mass of misery and degradation which greeted me lay far beyond expectation, outside the realm of my previous experience, at a level of irresponsibility, disorganization, neglect and humiliation I had not dreamed existed in a democratic egalitarian society... The dayroom was not a large room, perhaps six metres square. Its main item of furniture was a great grimy black stove, which stood in the centre of the room. It emitted very little heat, but evil smelling wisps of smoke escaped from cracks and seams in its structure, blackened the walls and ceiling and set the inhabitants of the room coughing and spluttering.

Bunched around this stove, sitting on ricketty wooden kitchen chairs were some thirty or forty old men of terrifying appearance. Their countenances espressed a kind of dying rage, a wrath that had been replaced by despair, now become lifeless, unmoving, as though carved out cold, grey stone.

The bunch of crouched, unmoving bodies, silent apart from the occasional wracking cough or the switch of spittle into the stove... were dressed in what answered for blue jackets and blue trousers. The clothes had suffered from the ravages of ageing as bitterly as had the old men whose feeble bodies they now covered; or, more correctly left uncovered. The jackets were shrunken, crumpled, shapeless, devoid of all buttons, thickly stained with dried soup, saliva, caked tobacco. The trousers, unsupported by belt or braces, devoid of all fly buttons, remained in position only by virtue of a chance fit between the circumference of the garment and that of the wearer's waist. This piece of good fortune was rare. In most cases the trousers had shrunk even more than the patient. With difficulty they covered the upper half of the wearer's legs, in monstrous imitation of Bermuda shorts; but they abandoned all effort to conceal his abdomen and his genitals were exposed for all to see. The more slender patients wore trousers which were many sizes too large and which fell to the floor if they attempted to stand.

The blue jacket and trousers were virtually all that the patients wore. There were no vests, no shirts, no ties, no underpants, no pullovers and cardigans.

Thus 'dressed' the old men queued out-of-doors in all weathers for their unappetizing meals. The remainder of their experience in the institution was as degrading as this description suggests. The women, who were in separate acommodation, fared no better, though they did not have to stand outdoors before their meals. The condition of the bedbound was worst of all:

> Most were appallingly malnourished and emaciated. Many lay in urine and faeces, waiting to be cleaned up. Pressure sores were numerous, many of them deep and gangrenous.

He found that the General Hospitals still routinely refused to admit old people, though GPs could persuade them to take their better-off older patients.[15]

His fellow medical practitioners were convinced that the problem of geriatrics was caused by neglectful families, feather-bedded by the welfare state. Home visits taught him a more complex story. Old people who were ill-treated had often ill-treated their children. Many lived contentedly with adult children: "In between the extremes was a range of interpersonal reactions which reflected a lifetime of relationships."[16] As a Consultant from 1961–4 he was, with difficulty, able to make some improvements, for example in the clothing of the old men, but the conditions remained appalling. Around the same time Peter Townsend found similar misery in Old People's Homes, the "last refuges," also often former workhouses.[17]

In Britain in 1962–3 around 900,000 old people were bedridden or unable to walk unaided outside their place of residence; 140,000 were in institutions, 750,000 in private households. There were still high rates of unreported illness. Doctors continued to attribute symptoms to ageing rather than to disease, leaving many treatable conditions undiagnosed. Old people complained that their GPs never examined them. Most doctors still assumed that past age 70 most people had only inactive lives ahead.

This is not surprising when we examine the textbooks available to them. The widely used *Our Advancing Years, An Essay on Modern Problems of Old Age* (1953) by Trevor Howell, one of the progressive pioneers of British geriatrics, declared:

> Of course the basic fact is that old people consume more of our national wealth then they produce... in fact from the economic point of view most old people are parasites.[18]

Whilst encouraging improved prevention, rehabilitation and care, Howell commented on the need to be aware of old peoples' "lack of response to logical reasoning,"[19] the mental processes of later life are so strongly colored by past experience, by suspicion, by previous modes of thought and by subconscious dread of the future, that rational trains of thought are almost impossible... old people are naturally suspicious. This may explain why it in the 1960s and 1970s medical students became *less* sympathetic to geriatric patients in the course of their training. The development of geriatrics as a specialism may have had ambiguous effects. It has enhanced the care of older patients, but it has encouraged some doctors to take even less interest in them, consigning them to the geriatricians.

Psychological theory was no more positive. Cumming and Henry's influential *Growing Old. The Process of Disengagement* (1961) erected into a general theory the observation that many older people withdrew from social engagement. This they concluded was the normal and necessary process of adjustment to ageing. It came to be questioned whether 'disengagement' was not rather a response to rejection by younger people and whether it indeed characterized a high proportion of 'normal' older people. In the 1970s it was challenged by the more optimistic activity theory that the majority of older persons maintain fairly constant amounts of activity or social participation, the amount depending more upon past life style and socio-economic forces than upon age itself.

In 1964 Ferguson Anderson was internationally a leading geriatrician and became Britain's first professor of geriatrics, at Glasgow. He increased the amount of geriatric training which was obligatory for medical students in Glasgow. Only in 1976 did the British Medical Association urge such training in all medical schools, as the World Health Organization had done two years previously. The number of posts grew and by the 1970s there were hospital based geriatric units in all health districts in England and Wales, but still sometimes in outdated buildings and understaffed.

## COMMUNITY CARE

One cause which united the Scottish and English geriatricians and NHS administrators was the desirability of keeping older people at home for as long as possible and an awareness of the extent of support provided by families. This can be interpreted as a search for cheaper services and as placing the burden of care on the family, especially on women rather than the state. This was not the intention of the geriatricians, or of the social researchers who argued that families needed social service support for this work, yet district nurses, health visitors, deliveries of hot meals, home helps, were all slow to be made available even for older people living alone. None of them doubted that the surest guarantee of a fit, active, happy old age was to retain independence for as long as possible, echoing folk wisdom through the ages. They emphasized that old people were not necessarily a burden on their relatives and friends, but were active contributors to their families and communities, except for a minority of unfortunate cases or for a short period of decline before death.

The need for support in the community for those with and without supportive relatives was made clear by a survey in 1951 of 39 old people admitted to a Liverpool hospital suffering from malnutrition. Not illness or inability to manage were responsible for their condition but poverty, poor living conditions and inadequate cooking facilities. At least 15 of 31 patients were trying to manage on just the very inadequate Old Age Pension. All but three were anemic due to lack of protein; nineteen had scurvy, in all but two cases because they could not afford fresh fruit and vegetables. Another had false dementia due to Vitamin B deficiency.

A number suffered from false incontinence which cleared up when they were given adequate food. A very few, not included in the survey, were suffering from 'extreme starvation' and died within a few days of admission. Half of the patients were discharged to the same unsatisfactory diets and living conditions that had caused their admission, with no official attempt to help them. There were similar discoveries in Edinburgh and London.

Improved community care services for old people became part of the electoral armory of both Labour and Conservative parties from the mid 1950s, supported by official reports of the 1950s. Action lagged behind the rhetoric, underpinned by largely unspoken scepticism about whether the costs of prevention, rehabilitation, community support and treatment of old people would extend their active lives to a worthwhile extent in national cost-benefit terms. No-one knew, but uninformed prejudice ruled. There were more explicit assertions that helping old people too much would encourage filial irresponsibility, despite abundant evidence that expansion of services reinforced rather than undermined family care. A survey of services published in 1976 concluded:

> If the elderly person is living with relatives, especially children, the service is withheld on the assumption that the family will provide needed care. In other situations it would seem that even when family members cannot or will not provide care, the service is refused on the basis that they should do so.[20]

This was still the case in the 1990s. There was pessimism, as there appears to have been throughout history, that family responsibility for old people was declining. It was attributed to geographical mobility, falling family size, increasing numbers of married daughters in paid work, divorce and separation, increasing numbers of old (and young) people living alone. But most striking was international evidence of the resilience of family cohesion and the mutual support of old and young. Often the generations remained in close contact, enhanced if anything by modern communications technology (motor vehicles, airplanes, telephones). If women bore fewer children at the end of the century, more of them gave birth. Women still combined paid work and care of older relatives as poorer women always had. Divorce and separation tended to strengthen intergenerational ties as lateral ties weakened. New partnerships and step-relatives added to, rather than reduced, resources of family support. Old people expressed their pleasure that they could afford to live alone, in contact with their relatives, rather than in enforced co-habitation, with the tensions that could result.

### MEDICAL

In Britain the medical needs of older people were best provided for when they were shared with younger people. Spectacles, dentures and dental care were available as never before; chiropody was not. From 1951 charges were gradually introduced and increased for the new services. By the 1960s there were still old people with poor eyesight but no spectacles, or wearing those fitted for someone else. Few of those investigated in one survey had hearing aids, many needed but still did not get chiropody treatment.

And yet medical research increasingly made breakthroughs, most notably the use of cardiac pacemakers from the 1960s, kidney dialysis from the late 1960s, coronary artery surgery from the 1970s, also cataract, hip and organ replacement surgery. Except for the birth control pill, all of the major breakthroughs in medical technology since the 1950s had their most widespread impact on people past their fifties and the further past their fifties they were, the greater the impact. The growth of various forms of state subsidy for health services in many countries after World War II have made these advances widely available. However, from the 1970s economic recession in many countries, combined with increased demand due to increased awareness among old people of the treatments available and belief in their right to receive them, together with the potential growth in demand due to the growing numbers of older people, again raised publicly, at least in Britain, the question of age-based rationing of treatment. Whether rationing indeed become more prevalent or never went away is a secret domain. Greater publicity may be a response to greater assertivenes on the part of older people and their friends and relatives.

Despite fears about the growing costs of increasingly high-tech medicine, reductions in some causes of death in older age groups, above all a drop in cardiovascular disorders from the late 1960s, owed hardly anything to medical advance, but rather to improved exercise and diet. Hypertension has been shown to respond to low-cost techniques and sometimes very ancient therapies, such as yoga, which induce relaxation and control over mind and body. At the other extreme, are developments in medical technology to a point at which people can be kept technically 'alive', but hardly meaningfully functioning, apparently indefinitely. Such developments now pose medicine with one of its greatest ethical dilemmas.

The improvements in mortality rates from some of the killer diseases at later ages, such as heart disease and strokes, are highly variable among similarly developed countries (Britain has performed poorly in most of them) which suggests scope for further international improvement.

Awareness of the interaction of physical and mental illness with the environment has grown. Poverty, bereavement, lack of status and disability can lead to depression, which in Britain it is known to afflict between 10 and 30% of the older population. Yet counseling for older people is not readily available. Both outpatient and institutional services for older people with psychiatric or neurological disorders, though less appalling than before World War II, remain in most countries markedly inferior to other health care services, though it is one of the health care sectors in which demand is growing fastest.

By the end of the twentieth century, then, there was the simultaneous emergence of the largest proportion of fit older people ever known and the largest number of chronically ill elderly people ever known. Older people may now recover from acute medical problems which would have killed them in the past only to succumb to sometimes complex sets of chronic non-lethal disorders for which relatively little can be done (e.g., Alzheimer's disease) other than to be kept alive with diminishing functional capacity.

An irony of modern medicine is that the least valued medical specialism takes up most of general practitioners' time and fills most hospital beds (though only 2.5% of old people are in hospital at any one time) and funding is relatively sparse for research into the unglamorous conditions which fill them. Health professionals, social workers and social researchers who experience mainly the tragedies and miseries of old age are especially prone to pessimism about old age in the twenty-first century. In reality we can no more predict the experience of old age in the next century than could an observer in 1900 have forseen the extraordinary changes of the twentieth century.

REFERENCES

1. J. Fogerty, *Growing Old in England 1878–1948*, Ph.D. thesis. (Australian National University, 1992), p. 148.
2. *Ibid*, p. 157–9.
3. HMSO Cmd 6404 1942, *Social Insurance and Allied Services*, p. 92.
4. J.H. Sheldon, *The Social Medicine of Old Age*. (Oxford University Press for the Nuffield Foundation, 1948).
5. *Ibid*, p. 74.
6. *Ibid*, p. 141.
7. *Ibid*, p. 85.
8. *Ibid*, p. 85.
9. W. Ferguson Anderson, interview with the author 1992, in the possession of the author and Wellcome Institute for the History of Medicine, University of Glasgow.
10. *Ibid*.
11. W. Ferguson Anderson 'Life's Equities after 65' in *Transactions and Studies of the College of Physicians of Philadelphia*, series 5, vol. 6, np. 4 (1984), p. 266.
12. Sir Ferguson Anderson 'An historical overview of geriatric medicine' in M.S.J. Pathy (ed.), *Principles and Practice of Geriatric Medicine*. (John Wiley & Sons Ltd, 1985), pp. 8–9.
13. W.F. Anderson 'Memorandum on the need for a research unit in geriatric medicine,' 1963. (Glasgow University Archives).
14. Ministry of Health Report of the Committee of Enquiry into the Cost of the National Health Service (Guillebaud Report) HMSO 1956, p. 40.
15. The above description and quotations from 'Extracts from the Memoirs of Bernard Isaacs', prepared 1994, Ms Greater Glasgow Health Board Archives, University of Glasgow.
16. *Ibid*.
17. P. Townsend, *The Last Refuge*. (London: Routledge, 1962).
18. T. Howell, *Our Advancing Years. An Essay on the Modern Problems of Old Age*. (London: Phoenix House, 1953), p. 13.
19. *Ibid*.
20. R. Moroney, *The Family and the State: Considerations for Social Policy*, (London), quoted in R. Means and R. Smith, *The Development of Welfare Services for Elderly People*. (London: Croom Helm, 1985), p. 294.

## FURTHER READING

Amoss, P. and Harrell, S. (eds), *Other Ways of Growing Old. Anthropological Perspectives.* (Stanford University Press, 1981).

Anderson, Sir Ferguson, 'Geriatrics' in G. McLachlan (ed.), *Improving the Common Weal. Aspects of the Scottish Health Services, 1900–1984.* (Edinburgh University Press, 1986).

Avorn, L., 'Medicine: the life and death of Oliver Shay' in A. Pifer and L. Bronte, *Our Ageing Society.* (London and New York: W.W. Norton, 1986).

Hannah, L., *Inventing Retirement.* (Cambridge University Press, 1986).

Trevor Howell, *Our Advancing Years. An Essay on Modern Problems of Old Age.* (London: Phoenix House, 1953), p. 137.

Shahar, Shulamith, *Growing Old in the Middle Ages.* (London: Routledge, 1997).

Thane, P., 'Old Age: Burden or Benefit?' in H. Joshi (ed.), *The Changing Population of Britain.* (Oxford: Blackwell, 1989).

Thane, P., 'Geriatrics,' in W. Bynum and R. Porter, *Companion Encyclopaedia to the History of Medicine.* (London: Routledge, 1993).

Thane, P. (ed.), *Origins of British Social Policy.* (London: Croom Helm, 1978).

Thane, P., *Foundations of the Welfare State.* (London: Longmans, 1982, second edition, 1996).

Tout, K., *Aging in Developing Countries.* (Oxford University Press, 1989).

Townsend, P. and Wedderburn, D. *The Aged in the Welfare State.* (London: Bell and Co. 1965).

Townsend, P., *The Family Life of Old People.* (London: Routledge, 1957).

Webster, Charles, 'The elderly and the early National Health Service' in R. Smith and M. Pelling, *Life, Death and the Elderly. Historical Perspectives.* (London: Routledge, 1991).

Wrigley, E.A. and Schofield, R., *The Population History of England 1541–1871.* (Cambridge University Press, 1989).

# CHAPTER 41

# Mental Illness

## JOAN BUSFIELD

Psychiatry — the medical speciality which deals with mental illness — has been the most controversial field of medical practice during the twentieth century. The legal powers of compulsory detention which have been applied to many psychiatric in-patients throughout the century, the desperate and sometimes dangerous treatments that have been used, notably ECT (electro-convulsive therapy) and psychosurgery, and the willingness of many psychiatrists to regard what patients say and do merely as symptoms of their illness and largely to ignore their experiences and deny them any voice, have all generated forceful criticisms of psychiatrists and psychiatric practice from academics, professionals and patients — criticisms that reached their peak in the anti-psychiatry movement in Britain and the United States in the 1960s. Indeed, though medicine's interest in diseases of the mind is long-standing, from its inception as a distinctive speciality in the mid-nineteenth century, psychiatry's position has never been entirely secure and its territory never clearly demarcated. On the one hand, critics have questioned both the assumption that there is a distinctive group of illnesses of the mind, and the relevance of medical expertise, with its focus on the body, to the understanding and treatment of mental illnesses. On the other hand, they have questioned the use and abuse, witting and unwitting, of psychiatrists' power over their patients and the role they have been called on to play as healers and custodians of the difficult, disturbed and unwanted.

The history of twentieth-century psychiatry cannot be accurately portrayed as a clear, linear picture of scientific progress from ignorance, harshness and repression to humanity and scientific understanding. Rather what we find is a complex picture with some continuities over time and some similarities between countries, alongside some significant transformations in psychiatric ideas and practices, yet little in the way of undisputed, linear progress.

Twentieth-century continuities in psychiatric ideas and practice largely reside in the character of the ongoing struggles and conflicts both within and outside the profession. Two have been of central importance and have directly affected patients' experiences of mental illness. The first is the tension between custody and control on the one hand — represented most strikingly by compulsory detention — and care and treatment on the other. The second is the tension between a focus on the body in contrast to a focus on the mind, consciousness and experience. These two areas of struggle permeate and underpin some of the major changes in psychiatry, and consequently the experience of mental illness, during the twentieth century.

In order to explore the experience of mental illness in this period I want to highlight three areas of transformation: the locus of treatment, the framing of mental illness, and types of treatment. All three have affected patients' experiences of mental illness, as well as that of their families, friends and the wider society.

### THE LOCUS OF TREATMENT

The major, and certainly the most visible, transformation in psychiatry during the twentieth century has been in the locus of medical treatment for the mentally ill: a shift from the asylum to the 'community' — a shift associated with significant changes in the types of mental illness with which psychiatry has dealt, in the role and power of psychiatrists and in forms of treatment.

At the beginning of the twentieth century the asylum was the dominant locus of medical activity vis-à-vis the mentally ill across Europe and the US and it provided the standard model of mental-health care which spread widely under the impact of colonial ideas. Asylums, mostly established in the nineteenth century, had served as the domain in which the new specialism of psychiatry could take root and flourish. Developed initially on progressive models informed by a strong environmentalism which put faith in the healing power of a well-ordered institution for the care and treatment of insanity, by the end of the nineteenth century they were usually large-scale, regimented, custodial, poorly resourced institutions, whose inmates were detained on a compulsory basis. They catered for lunatics, persons whose behavior was identified as dangerous, disruptive, or a threat to the moral order of society and considered the product of some disturbance of mind, itself increasingly viewed within medicine as the result of some inherited defect, and as unlikely to be amenable to much in the way of active treatment. While some small private institutions survived from the earlier private madhouses for the rich, providing a suitably leisured but confined life for their inmates, the large-scale public asylums, along with workhouses, mainly detained those from the lower classes where often no clear distinction was made between dangerous, disturbed *individuals* and dangerous *classes*. Difficult, dangerous behavior in both private and public institutions was controlled by physical and chemical means, including straitjackets, solitary confinement or sedatives.

Inmates, whether rich or poor, dangerous or harmless, had to be 'certified' insane on admission, a procedure designed to protect the public against the fear of wrongful detention. Yet processes of certification, whether medical or judicial, have, despite their bureaucratic complexity, never been sufficiently stringent to prevent wrongful detention of unwanted persons by the well-meaning or malevolent, not least because the criteria of lunacy and mental illness embedded in the various legal processes of detention, as elsewhere, inevitably lack precision. Whilst whole-scale political abuse of the system has been relatively rare, with the post Second World War Soviet abuses against political dissidents the most notorious example, there are many instances where social wrongdoing has mistakenly occasioned the questioning of a person's sanity — the detention in asylums earlier in the century of women who bore illegitimate children is but one example. Montagu Lomax, writing in 1921, contrasted psychiatric theory and practice, examining one psychiatric text and comparing it with his own experiences as a doctor working in an asylum during the First World War:

> Dr Mercier speaks of the "fitness for such patients to be detained in an asylum" as proved by the fact that "the necessary legal formalities have been complied with." I maintain, on the contrary, that as regards the justice in the continued detention in asylums of many of the so-called insane, the compliance, with the "necessary legal formalities" is often no safeguard, and that many paupers are not only sent to asylums, but are also detained in them, who ought never to have been so sent or detained.[1]

Moreover, there is considerable evidence that those belonging to more marginal groups within society, especially those belonging to the lowest social class or disadvantaged ethnic groups, have been over-represented in asylum populations, often on a compulsory basis. Whilst informal admissions are now common, and rights to contest compulsory detention have generally been strengthened during the century, nonetheless the shadow cast by the threat of compulsory detention remains, and the legitimate exercise of legal constraints is still a significant problem for psychiatry. Notwithstanding 1960s' critics, it is hard to see how compulsory powers could be abandoned entirely, yet they sit very uneasily within any area of medical practice.

The absolute numbers confined in madhouses and asylums by the beginning of the twentieth century were already surprisingly large. In England and Wales, at a time when the total population was only some 32 million, there were nearly 100,000 persons identified as insane in madhouses, asylums and workhouses (of whom 74,000 were in county asylums whose average size was close on one thousand inmates). In the United States, where the development of asylums began somewhat later, the number of lunatics in institutions was almost 200,000 in 1904 in a population of around 80 million — a lower proportion than in Britain — and institutions were on average a little smaller at this time. Long-stay inmates filled the bulk of the places in both countries, but a significant proportion remained in the institution for a shorter period — perhaps three to six months. Moreover, the numbers confined increased rapidly during the first half of the century, doubling in England and Wales and more than trebling in the United States, where inmate numbers in state asylums had reached more than half a million by 1950. Consequently, many individuals had experience of lunacy, either as inmates themselves, or as a relative, friend or acquaintance of an inmate, or because they knew someone who worked at the local asylum.

Madness in the family was invariably experienced as shameful and stigmatizing. Admission to a public asylum typically involved a dual stigma: the stigma of compulsory detention, with the attendant process of certification, and the stigma of pauperization; consequently the experience was very distressing for those admitted and for their families and friends. Certification not only signaled inmates' loss of freedom but imposed a clear and apparently definitive label of insanity, with its connotations not only of irrationality and loss of reason, threatening enough in themselves because of the importance attached to reason and rationality, but also of dangerousness and violence. In this respect the siting of asylums outside towns and cities, with the aim of providing clean, healthy air for inmates in a period when dirt and pollution were endemic in urban areas, almost certainly added to the view that lunatics belonged to the outcasts of society. So, too, did the fact that then as today, criminal lunatics — people accused of some crime of violence, often against the person — provided the most powerful public images of insanity. Criminals, if found insane, a process in which medical experts played a key role, often disagreeing amongst themselves in their expert testimony, were usually sent to special institutions for criminal lunatics (in England, Broadmoor had opened in 1863).

Asylums continued to provide the dominant locus for the specialist treatment of mental illness well into the second half of the twentieth century, and numerous narrative accounts (fictional and non-fictional) reveal that the experience of asylum life for inmates was often demoralizing and unpleasant. Antonia White's autobiographical narrative of her descent into madness in the early 1920s, *Beyond the Glass*, conveys the agony of becoming mad, and the bleakness and terror she experienced when placed in a padded cell on admission to contain her violence:

> Months, perhaps years, later, she woke up in a small bare cell. The walls were whitewashed and dirty, and she was lying on a mattress on the floor, without sheets, with only rough, red-striped blankets over her. She was wearing a linen gown, like an old-fashioned night-shirt, and she was bitterly cold. In front of her was the blank yellow face of a heavy door without a handle of any kind. Going over to the door, she tried frantically to push it open. It was locked. She began to call out in panic and to beat on the door till her hands were red and swollen. She had forgotten her name. She did not know whether she were very young or very old. Had she died that night in Nell's studio? She could remember Nell and Richard, yet she knew that her memory of them was not quite right. Was this place a prison? If only, only her name would come back to her.[2]

Physical conditions and standards of care varied considerably between institutions. However, as Erving Goffman argued so effectively, asylums, like other total institutions — places where people work, sleep and play — have certain characteristics in common, including the techniques staff use to control inmates, which affect inmates' experiences. These techniques include the 'mortification of self' generated by a range of indignities, less common in the outside world, to which the individual is often exposed. The bare mattress and the cold in Antonia White's account of her experience are examples, as are the loss of personal possessions, lack of privacy, the requirements to reveal personal information, the compulsion often involved in admission, and direct physical constraints such as straightjackets. Goffman quotes an example from another study of the use of privileges and punishments to control inmates in one asylum:

> The privileges consist of having the best job, better rooms and beds, minor luxuries like coffee on the ward, a little more privacy than the average patient, going outside the ward without supervision, having more access than the average patient to the attendant's companionship or to professional personnel like the physicians, and enjoying such intangible but vital things as being treated with personal kindness and respect.

> The punishments which can be applied by the ward attendants are suspension of all privileges, psychological mistreatment, such as ridicule, vicious ribbing, moderate and sometimes severe corporal punishment, or the threat of such punishment, locking up the patient in an isolated room, denial or distortion of access to the professional personnel, threatening to put, or putting, the patient on the list for electro-shock therapy, transfer of the patient to undesirable wards, and regular assignment of the patient to unpleasant tasks such as cleaning up after the soilers.[3]

Ken Kesey's novel, *One Flew Over the Cuckoo's Nest*, published in 1961 and produced as a film in 1975, gave popular currency to such practices and to inmates' experiences. The precise list of privileges and punishments may vary, including the level of harshness and brutality, yet the exercise of power by staff by some such means does not, and people admitted to asylums have often, by virtue of their mental state, been particularly vulnerable to them.

Individuals do, of course, usually adjust to life in an institution; Goffman lists four types of adaptation: "situational withdrawal;" the "intransigent line;" "colonization," where "a stable, relatively contented existence is built up out of the maximum satisfaction procurable within the institution;" and conversion where "the inmate appears to take over the official view of himself and tries to act out the perfect inmate."[4] Certainly for many long-stay inmates, the experience of asylum life became as much one of dependence and attachment as of terror, fear and anxiety. Though there is plenty of evidence of harshness and brutality, including sexual abuse, physical violence and theft from patients, and of the ongoing power of staff over inmates, there is also evidence of kindness, support and a sense of community in some institutions. For many the asylum became their home — a place where compliance with routines was rewarded with some freedoms, even luxuries, and an inmate culture developed, often grounded in forms of resistance to those in authority. The asylum's grounds, for those considered trustworthy, were often large and attractive; work, though often monotonous, was provided for many;

the daily routines and inmate and staff contact gave a sense of security (albeit for some whose admission might have been inappropriate); and inmates developed close, personal friendships. Yet these forms of adaptation, though essential to individuals' survival, represented in themselves a process of institutionalization marked by the individual's dependence on the institution, which became one of the focal points for criticism of asylums particularly in the period following the Second World War.

The twentieth-century shift from asylum to community as the locus for the care and treatment of mental illness in the second half of the century in many Western countries has its foundations in developments both inside and outside the asylum. On the one hand, the optimism associated with the early asylums and the belief in their inherent therapeutic benefits had largely foundered, and their custodial character was less easy to ignore. (One response to this was frequent calls to transform the institutions from asylums into hospitals, which led, for example, to the introduction of voluntary admission for some patients). On the other hand, new services were increasingly developed outside asylums. For those with chronic problems, these included half-way houses, training centers and after-care facilities, and policies of discharging such patients into alternative facilities was the initial dominant meaning of the term community care. For those in the acute stages of illness, or with less severe problems, the new services included acute psychiatric units in general hospitals, out-patient clinics, and office-based practice, services which in catering for less severe disorders often attracted more middle-class pa-tients and a higher percentage of women. Such people, if they had the necessary resources, had long sought help from specialist private physicians outside the confines of the asylum. But from the 1920s and 1930s, access to specialists outside the asylums began to increase in Britain, even for those who could not afford private care. New out-patient psychiatric clinics were set up, often attached to general hospitals (given some impetus by the 1930 Mental Treatment Act which gave powers to local authorities to fund such clinics). Access to primary care also improved through the development of state insurance-based health schemes. In addition, psychiatric wards for people in the acute stages of illness began to be opened in general hospitals, and offered an alternative model of in-patient care.

This diversification of institutional locations for the care of mental illness and improved access to many types of medical services in itself meant some shift in the balance of mental health services, in the range of mental health professionals, and in the social composition of patients. But it still left the asylum at the center of provision, surrounded by a more diverse range of additional services. From the Second World War, however, new models of service organization began to emerge. In Britain, there was increasing emphasis on the advantages of acute psychiatric units attached to general hospitals, on the value of therapeutic communities, and on more active treatment regimes for those with chronic problems. In the US, the new model of service organization placed the community mental health center

(CMHC) at the nub of the mental health services — a model that was subsequently very influential in Europe. The CMHC was to be a centrally-located, multi-purpose unit staffed by a range of professionals — psychiatrists, psychologists, social workers and nurses — and providing a range of services, including drop-in, emergency and out-patient services as well as acute beds. However there was no provision for long-stay patients — long the stumbling block to more active, therapeutic models of care. Existing long-stay patients were to be cared for in the community and either sent to boarding houses, nursing homes, or half-way houses, or returned to their families, and a new wave of therapeutic optimism encouraged a belief that there would be no new long-stay patients.

In the US, the implementation of these policies was rapid. From a peak of state and county asylum inmates of 559,000 in 1955, the number had already halved by 1972 and halved again by 1980. In Britain implementation was slower, delayed by the costs of creating new publicly-funded alternatives to the asylum, and in-patient numbers had only fallen from 143,000 to 103,000 by 1970. However the pace of implementation accelerated in the 1980s and 1990s with the New Right policy agenda with its emphasis on private provision, and an increasing number of asylums closed down with psychiatric in-patients reduced to below 50,000 by 1994. Elsewhere in Europe the precise policy details and the pace of change varied, with Italy noteworthy for its relatively late but very marked deinstitutionalization from 1978 onwards.

Andrew Scull, in his forceful analysis of this process of 'decarceration,' described vividly the experience of community care for those with chronic problems turned out of the old asylums who often found little support in the community, and were left either to fend for themselves on the street or in hostels for the homeless, or else ended up in other institutions for the unwanted and dependent:

> Clearly a certain proportion of the released inmates are able to blend unobtrusively back into the community from whence they came… But for many other ex-inmates and potential inmates, the alternative to the institution has been to be herded into newly emerging 'deviant ghettoes,' sewers of human misery and what is conventionally defined as social pathology within which (largely hidden from outside inspection or even notice) society's refuse may be repressively tolerated. Many become lost in the interstices of social life, and turn into drifting inhabitants of those traditional resorts of the down and out, Salvation Army hostels, settlement houses, and so on. Others are grist for new, privately-run, profit-oriented mills for the disposal of the unwanted — old-age homes, halfway houses, and the like. And yet more exist by preying on the less agile and wary, whether these be 'ordinary' people trapped by poverty and circumstance in the inner city, or their fellow decarcerated deviants.[5]

For many, the experience was in fact of moving from one institution into another — a process of transinstitutionalization not deinstitutionalization, with former asylum inmates often ending up in nursing homes or boarding houses with poorer facilities and less support.

Whilst the idea of community care is attractive, the reality frequently differs markedly from the ideal. In particular the problem of providing suitable care for those with long-term mental health problems remains. These include the increasing numbers of those with some form of senile dementia, such as Alzheimer's disease, a condition whose prevalence has increased with greater longevity. Yet the shift to community care, alongside public expenditure anxieties and policy commitments to privatization, has meant a growing unwillingness to provide public facilities or financial support for long-stay patients and a growing reliance on the poorly regulated private sector, including nursing homes and care homes, where staff are often inadequately trained. Moreover, public provision for those with acute or less severe problems is all too often under-resourced, and publicly-funded services are increasingly directed solely at those whose problems are very severe, especially if they appear dangerous or threatening.

## THE FRAMING OF MENTAL ILLNESS

The way in which an individual's psychological problems and difficulties are given expression varies between cultures, as do the understandings of these problems and the precise way in which the boundaries of mental illness are set. The forms disturbance takes are partly shaped by the wider culture and in part by medical ideas about the nature and causes of mental disorder.

A central feature of specialist medical activity in relation to mental illness over the last two centuries has been the development of new categories of mental illness — categories that in Charles Rosenberg's terms 'frame' disease.[6] Categories of mental disorder contribute to the intellectual foundations on which psychiatric practice is based and help to order an apparently inchoate world, as well as helping to provide and legitimate the profession's claims to specialist knowledge and expertise in the care and treatment of mental disorder. Developed by the profession in response to the problems with which it is called upon to deal, the categories also frame lay constructions of mental illness. They are the currency in which both professionals and the lay public commonly think about mental illness.

During the twentieth century there have been marked changes in the framing of mental illness, not least in the broadening of the boundaries of professional, psychiatric interest from the narrow category of lunacy to a wider terrain of mental illness. At the beginning of the century efforts to develop and enhance the classification of types of lunacy found in asylums dominated psychiatry as a scientific endeavor. Indeed, the final decades of the nineteenth century have often been termed the era of classification, and are associated with radical transformations in the framing of psychiatric disease. The best-known of the late nineteenth-century psychiatric nosologists was the German, Emil Kraepelin, whose key psychiatric text, first published in 1883, went through nine editions under various titles. Kraepelin followed Wilhelm Griesinger in viewing mental diseases as discrete entities to be differentiated in terms of their etiology, course and outcome — a framework that has continued to be influential. Equally influential was the distinction he introduced between two major types of psychosis, the medical label for what in lay terms was regarded as 'real madness' on which asylum doctors focused, in contrast to the wider territory of less severe mental problems which played little part in their professional practice in asylums. Kraepelin's two types were manic-depressive psychosis (now bi-polar depression) and dementia praecox, both of which, under somewhat different guises, still feature predominantly in current classifications. Manic-depressive psychosis brought mania and melancholia, the two disorders which had dominated the psychiatric lexicon in the eighteenth and nineteenth centuries, into a single group. Dementia praecox, renamed schizophrenia by the Swiss psychiatrist Eugen Bleuler in 1911, became the archetypal mental illness in twentieth-century Western psychiatry, and the focus of much (mostly unsuccessful) explanatory endeavor. However, the term schizophrenia was adopted quite slowly within psychiatry and did not feature much, even in psychiatric texts, until the late 1920s. In lay contexts, the term tended to suggest a split mind and found popular representation in films and novels as in the film *The Three Faces of Eve* (1957).

As a psychosis involving what psychiatrists have often described as a 'loss of contact with reality,' schizophrenia was described in official classifications as characterised by symptoms such as hallucinations, delusions, thought disorder and inappropriate affect — thought and behavior that in Karl Jaspers's term is "ununderstandable", difficult to comprehend.[7] Kraepelin followed the dominant ideas of the time, which emphasized heredity as the major cause of madness, and viewed it as an endogenous (inherited) illness that involved inevitable and irreversible deterioration (unlike manic-depressive psychosis). Diagnosis of schizophrenia, as of other conditions according to the Kraepelinian model, required attention not only to immediate symptoms but to the history and course of the illness. Consequently clinical examination and the taking of a case history became standard features of Kraepelinian psychiatry. Critics such as R.D. Laing have emphasized the degrading character of the clinical examination, arguing that patients are required to produce their symptoms, which are treated as objective indicators of illness, whilst the intrinsic value of their feelings and experiences are ignored as is the content of their ideas.

Numerous accounts have been provided by patients of the subjective experience of the symptoms of schizophrenia which illuminate the way in which thoughts, feelings and perceptions become distorted. This is an extract from an anonymous patient's narrative, first published in 1951:

> Unreality finally reached such a point that Mama herself [her analyst] would no longer make contact between us. For some time I had been complaining bitterly how things were tricking me and how I suffered because of it.

As a matter of fact, these 'things' weren't doing anything special; they didn't speak nor attack me directly. It was their very presence that made me complain. I saw things, smooth as metal, so cut off, so detached from each other, so illuminated and tense that they filled me with terror. When, for example, I looked at a chair or a jug, I thought not of their use or function — a jug not as something to hold water and milk, a chair not as something to sit in — but as having lost their names, their functions and meaning; they became 'things' and began to take on life, to exist.

This existence accounted for my great fear. In the unreal scene, in the murky quiet of my perception, suddenly the 'thing' sprang up. The stone jar, decorated with blue flowers, was there facing me, defying me with its presence, with its existence.[8]

Another described the experience of:

my body breaking up into bits. I get all mixed up so that I don't know myself. I feel like more than one person when this happens. I'm falling apart into bits ... I'm frightened to say a word in case everything goes fleeing from me so that there's nothing in my mind. It puts me into a trance that's worse than death. There's a kind of hypnotism going on.[9]

R.D. Laing's account of schizophrenia in *The Divided Self* offers an analysis of such narratives in terms of 'ontological insecurity' which is characterized by feelings of engulfment, implosion and petrification — an account which has resonated with the experiences of many patients.

The impact of Freudian ideas was of even greater significance to the transformations that have occurred in the framing of mental illness during the twentieth century. Freud's focus was on trying to understand the causes of mental illness — particularly of less severe mental illnesses which did not require treatment in asylums and were the focus of his private practice in Vienna. He introduced the term psycho-neurosis, to describe disorders which, unlike actual neuroses (that is, disorders of the nervous system), he believed had psychological causes. Psycho-neuroses involved an 'exaggerated response to reality' and were contrasted with the psychoses with which psychiatry, founded on asylum-based practice, had been primarily concerned. They included hysteria, phobias and obsessions (Freud regarded neurasthenia and anxiety states as actual neuroses and he paid little attention to neurotic/reactive depression though he discussed melancholia). His etiology of the psycho-neuroses attributed central importance to the mind rather than the body and in particular to unconscious psychological processes — symptoms were the expression of an underlying psychological conflict, such as the repression of unacceptable desires. Consequently, in contrast to Kraepelin, the content of the patients' ideas and their utterances in the clinical encounter became all important, though not to be treated at face value.

Freud illustrated his theories by describing some of his cases in detail — cases which have become hotly contested narratives around which debates about the validity of Freudian ideas have often been played out. The case of 'Dora' described as a case of hysteria, was drafted following *The Interpretation of Dreams* and published in 1905. Dora, described by Freud as 'unmistakably neurotic' with coughing attacks and voice loss as key symptoms, began her treatment with Freud at the age of 18, brought by her father who had had a series of severe illnesses, including TB, throughout much of her childhood.[10] Dora had received sexual advances from Herr K, a close friend of the family. However, Freud did not regard his initial traumatic theory of the psycho-neuroses as adequate and focused not on these events but on Dora's love for her father (and for Herr K) even though her father was having an affair with Herr K's wife, Frau K, which Dora felt encouraged him to ignore Herr K's behavior towards her. The following passage reveals Freud's argument:

> Let us now apply our theory to the instance provided by Dora's case. We will begin with the first hypothesis, namely, that her preoccupation with her father's relations to Frau K. owed its obsessive character to the fact that its root was unknown to her and lay in the unconscious. It is not difficult to divine the nature of that root from her circumstances and her conduct. Her behaviour obviously went far beyond what would have been appropriate to filial concern. She felt and acted more like a jealous wife — in a way which would have been comprehensible in her mother. By her ultimatum to her father ('either her or me'), by the scenes she used to make, by the suicidal intentions she allowed to transpire, — by all this she was clearly putting herself in her mother's place. If we have rightly guessed the nature of the imaginary sexual situation which underlay her cough, in that phantasy she must have been putting herself in Frau K.'s place. She was therefore identifying herself both with the woman her father had once loved and with the woman he loved now. The inference is obvious that her affection for her father was a much stronger one than she knew or than she would have cared to admit: in fact, that she was in love with him.[11]

Freud's etological shift from traumatic events to unconscious processes and phantasy led him largely to ignore the reality of external events (such as sexual abuse) and to pathologize the individual — a shift for which he has been strongly attacked by feminist critics amongst others.

The direct impact of Freud's framing of disease was considerable. His ideas and treatments began to flourish in the context of private practice outside the asylum. They had less direct impact on psychiatric practice in public asylums which dealt primarily with those with psychotic or organic disorders. But the indirect impact on psychiatry was profound, as was the impact on lay ideas about mental disorder. His ideas contributed to the growing interest in the psycho-neuroses so visible in Europe and the United States in the second half of the twentieth century, and to what has been called the psychiatrization or psychologization of everyday life — a process in which psychiatrists and a range of other mental health professionals, such as psychologists, psychotherapists, psychiatric social workers, psychiatric nurses and a broad range of counsellors, are called on to participate in, and pronounce on, all aspects of people's everyday lives. In this process not only are psychiatric ideas widely diffused and extended to new areas, but so too is the activity of new groups of professionals — professionals who compete with, as well as complement, the work of psychiatrists. At the same time, psychodynamic ideas had a major impact on lay understandings and representations of psychological problems, drawing attention to unconscious psychological processes, to the importance of childhood psychological experiences, and to sexuality — ideas which permeated literature, films and art across the Western world and were, in the process, adapted and transformed.

Whilst it is hard to detect any single revolutionary transformation in the framing of psychiatric disease since the Second World War, two features merit attention. First, the strengthening of the imperative to standardize and formalize psychiatric classifications and psychiatric diagnosis. This is most evident in the American Psychiatric Association's work on its *Diagnostic and Statistical Manual* (DSM), now in its fourth edition, and has been associated with a shift from etiology as a basis for classification, since it is invariably contested, to symptomatology. The second, contradictory, tendency has been the continuing change in the categories of mental disorder and their importance — sometimes in response to developments in psychopharmacology. Hysteria, a condition strongly identified with women, has followed melancholia in almost disappearing from the formal psychiatric lexicon (but not lay thinking), whilst new conditions such as pre-menstrual disorder and hyperactivity emerge, and others like anorexia nervosa and various types of depression receive increasing attention. The growing importance of eating disorders (almost unknown outside materially affluent societies and especially associated with women) is one of the striking features of the mental health terrain in recent years, and indicates the importance of social and cultural factors in the shaping, expression and experience of psychological problems. Anorexia nervosa and bulimia are conditions which have captured the popular imagination and are widely discussed in popular magazines and newspapers.

## TREATMENT

At the beginning of the twentieth century treatment had a relatively small place within psychiatry. The influence of hereditarian ideas and assumptions of mental degeneration encouraged a focus on custody and care rather than treatment. In large-scale asylums routinization and containment had usurped the earlier principles of moral treatment in which care within a well-ordered institution was itself viewed as intrinsically therapeutic. For long-stay inmates no longer considered dangerous, work was seen as having some value in maintaining a person in a stable, calm state, though not in curing them. Drugs such as opiates were given to some patients to control symptoms, hydrotherapy was quite common and electrical treatments were also used to stimulate various parts of the body. Overall, however, within the confines of the asylum, medical interventions were relatively limited.

Outside the asylum other treatments were in vogue amongst those specializing in mental illness. Hypnosis and electrical treatments were fashionable and the rest cure, first introduced in the US in the 1870s, was also used. The experience of such a cure is beautifully evoked in Charlotte Perkins Gilman's autobiographical novella, *The Yellow Wallpaper*, first published in 1896, in which she describes the regime of rest imposed by her husband, a doctor:

> He is very careful and loving, and hardly lets me stir without special direction.
>
> I have a schedule prescription for each hour in the day; he takes all care from me, and so I feel basically ungrateful not to value it more.
>
> He said we came here solely on my account, that I was to have perfect rest and all the air I could get.

And later:

> I think sometimes that if I were only well enough to write a little it would relieve the press of ideas and rest me.
>
> But I find I get pretty tired when I try.
>
> It is so discouraging not to have any advice and companionship about my work. When I get really well, John says we will ask Cousin Henry and Julia down for a long visit; but he says he would as soon put fireworks in my pillow-case as to let me have those stimulating people about now.[12]

The enforced passivity of the rest cure, based on principles first developed by Weir Mitchell in the US to deal with soldiers suffering from fatigue during the Civil War, did not long survive Freud's 'talking cure' with its focus on unconscious processes. Freud did not himself regard psychoanalysis as a distinctively medical therapy and various forms of psychoanalysis and psychotherapy — usually less frequent and shorter lasting — were used by a range of professionals. Significantly the cases of shell-shock identified in the First World War encouraged wider use of psychoanalytic ideas in treatment. Seigfried Sassoon described his experience of being treated by W.H. Rivers on his arrival at Craiglockhart Hospital:

> Readers of my previous volumes will be aware that I am no exception to the rule that most people enjoy talking about themselves to a sympathetic listener. Next morning I went to Rivers' room as one of his patients. In an hour's talk I told him as much as I could about my perplexities. Forgetting that he was a doctor and I was an 'interesting case,' I answered his quiet impartial questions as clearly as I could, with a comfortable feeling that he understood me better than I understood myself.[13]

Not all accounts were so favorable, but treatments based on Freudian ideas which allowed patients to describe their experiences often had a more positive reception than the physical treatments developed in the 1930s which concentrated on patients' bodies rather more than their minds.

The introduction of shock therapies in the 1930s — insulin therapy, ECT (in which electrodes are applied to the head), and psychosurgery — and then chemically synthesized psychotropic drugs in the 1950s, represented major transformations in the treatment of mental illness. ECT and psychosurgery in particular came to symbolize the harshness and brutality of psychiatric treatment, perhaps because of the direct mechanical action on the brain of patients whose life was not threatened — procedures that can conjure up terrifying, powerful images.

ECT, whose precise mode of operation on brain processes is still unclear, was initially used quite widely and frequently for a range of mental illnesses, including schizophrenia; later it was considered primarily of value for endogenous depression, and better anesthetics and chemical relaxants made the treatments somewhat less terrifying. Since the 1970s, it has been used less extensively but still regularly. Its use has always been highly controversial and patients' descriptions, reveal clearly the fear and hostility it has often invoked. Sylvia Plath's fictionalized account in *The Bell Jar*, published in 1961, provides one vivid portrayal:

'Don't worry,' the nurse grinned down at me. 'Their first time everybody's scared to death'

I tried to smile, but my skin had gone stiff, like parchment.

Doctor Gordon was fitting two metal plates on either side of my head He buckled them into place with a strap that dented my forehead, and gave me a wire to bite.

I shut my eyes.

There was a brief silence, like an indrawn breath.

Then something bent down and took hold of me like the end of the world. Whee-ee-ee-ee-ee, it shrilled, through an air crackling with blue light, and with each flash a great jolt drubbed me till I thought my bones would break and the sap fly out of me like a split plant.[14]

A course of treatment usually involved repeated ECTs and this tended to increase patients' fear. An anonymous patient who had sixteen ECTs in the 1950s conveys the horror of waiting for each treatment:

... Despite all my pleadings, the treatments were continued.

I hated every moment of them. The waking in the morning with the consciousness that I would be one of those on the doctor's list for treatment that day. The sister in charge of the ward read the names in a stentorian voice when the breakfast trolley arrived. Those due for treatment were allowed only one cup of tea and a piece of bread and butter. Then came the wait for treatment, which was carried out reasonably early in the morning, but for which the waiting nevertheless seemed long. A kind of sleeping tablet was given to each patient about half-an hour beforehand, and then, stripped of such metal things as hair-grips or rings and teeth, we were led to the waiting room which adjoined the theatre to await our turn to be 'shocked.'

To my dying day I will remember these waits, the black marble lino on the floor, the deathly quiet of the room, and the red, serpent-eye of the light which showed the current was 'on' and the job in progress in the adjoining room. Occasionally one heard the muffled shout of the 'victim' as she went 'out.'[15]

That fear is also described in Janet Frame's autobiographical account of waiting for ECT in *Faces in the Water*, first published in 1961:

> I was cold. I tried to find a pair of long woolen ward socks to keep my feet warm in order that I should not die under the new treatment, electric shock therapy, and have my body sneaked out the back way to the mortuary. Every morning I woke in dread, waiting for the day nurse to go on her rounds and announce from the list of names in her hand whether or not I was for shock treatment, the new and fashionable means of quieting people and of making them realise that orders are to be obeyed and floors are to be polished without anyone protesting and faces are made to be fixed into smiles and weeping is a crime. Waiting in the early morning, in the black-capped frosted hours, was like waiting for the pronouncement of a death sentence.[16]

Other accounts, however, including reports from psychiatrists, mention the demand for ECT from some patients and the benefits patients experienced, and there can be no doubt that for some a course of ECT did reduce the level of depression and the treatment seemed worthwhile. The use of psychosurgery, which involved cutting the frontal lobes of brain, on patients with long-term problems was even more controversial, though it was used less widely than ECT. Its use increased in the 1950s and 1960s and then declined, though modified techniques in the 1980s led to some renewed interest.

The introduction of chemically synthesized psychotropic drugs in the 1950s has produced the most significant transformation in the treatment of mental illness this century — significant less because of any power to cure (though drugs do frequently control symptoms) than because of their pervasive use and because of their impact on psychiatric practice itself. Since the 1950s almost all patients treated for mental health problems have been prescribed some psychotropic medication and for many it is the only specific form of treatment provided. Consequently developments in drug treatments have strengthened and further legitimated the biological orientation of psychiatry over recent decades. The first chemically-synthesized drug to be introduced in the 1950s was chlorpromazine. Initially developed as a possible treatment for morning sickness during pregnancy, its potential as an anti-psychotic was soon recognized. Since then an enormous range of psychotropic drugs have been synthesized. From the early 1960s tranquilizers such as Valium and Librium were introduced and were very widely used across the Western world in the treatment of anxiety and depression, initially with little attention to the dependency they could generate. At present Prozac, a treatment for less severe forms of depression, has already replaced them as the most widely used psychotropic medication.

Drug treatments in psychiatry raise a range of issues. In the first place the side effects of drugs used to treat the more severe mental illnesses tend to be very marked. Whilst psychiatric symptoms may be brought under control by anti-psychotic medication, patients complain of dryness in their throat, uncontrollable bodily movements and feelings of being drugged and zombie-like. A psychiatrist,

Kay Jamison, describes the experience of taking lithium, which is particularly used in the treatment of manic-depression, like this:

> There was never any question that lithium worked very well for me — my form of manic-depressive illness is a textbook case of the clinical features related to good lithium response: I have grandiose and expansive manias, a strong family history of manic-depressive illness, and my manias precede my depressions, rather than the other way round — but the drug strongly affected my mental life. I found myself beholden to medication that also caused severe nausea and vomiting many times a month — I often slept on my bathroom floor with a pillow under my head and my warm, woolen St. Andrews gown tucked over me — when, because of changes in salt levels, diet, exercise, or hormones, my lithium level would get too high... When I got particularly toxic I would start trembling, become ataxic and walk into walls, and my speech would become slurred...[17]

Valium and Librium had fewer clearly visible side effects, but they proved to be addictive. Prozac, though it has advantages over other drugs and is often viewed very positively by patients, still has some side effects, and because it lifts mood may be psychologically if not physically addictive. Indeed, the major problem with psychotropic drugs is ensuring that they are not used excessively, inappropriately and unnecessarily. Inevitably they are often used by doctors on a trial and error basis across a wide range of patients in an effort to control symptoms and, once used, doctors can be reluctant to discontinue them or to reduce dose levels if they appear to have a positive impact. This can mean long-term or even life-time medication and it is often difficult if not impossible to determine whether continuing medication is necessary. It also too frequently means a blindness to the individuals' feelings and social circumstances. Drugs become the 'solution' even if the problem is known to have psycho-social origins.

## CONCLUSION

There have been major changes in psychiatric ideas and practice during the twentieth century. These include the shift from psychiatry centered on the asylum providing custody and care for lunatics to a psychiatry spread across a range of locations offering care and therapy for a broader terrain of mental illness; the formulation of new categories of illness; and the development of new treatments both psychological and physical. These changes have been associated with profound changes in the way individuals think about mental disorder, and in the language and concepts they employ, changes which have been shaped both by psychiatric ideas and practice and by wider social and cultural changes.

All these changes have had a significant effect on the specificities of the experience of mental illness for all concerned: patients, friends, staff and the wider community. Yet beneath the surface the experience of mental illness has probably changed rather less than might appear at first sight. We can see this more clearly if we consider the experiences of three main groups of patients. First, there are persons who manifest dangerous (to themselves or others) or disruptive behavior apparently linked to some disturbance of mind, who often receive a psychotic diagnosis. Care and control of such persons has been, and continues to be, central to psychiatric practice. The means of control and coercion have changed over time — straitjackets, solitary confinement, locked doors and sedatives have increasingly been replaced by medication, particularly anti-psychotics, and by special observation of highly disturbed patients, and no doubt these changes affect elements of the experience of detained patients. Certainly drugs, by controlling symptoms, may reduce the length of stay in hospital (though a common pattern is of discharge followed by later readmission). However in the acute stages of the illness physical and social coercion and control remain dominant (drugs have been widely described as providing a chemical straitjacket), including continuing legal powers of detention. For the individual patient and their family the experience of in-patient treatment is still one of loss of freedom and of repression, albeit that drugs may quickly dull the patient's senses and hospital stays may be much shorter on average than they were at the beginning of the century.

Second, there are those with chronic, long-term complaints whose psychological functioning is in some way impaired, including those with some form of senile dementia, but where aggression is less of a problem and compliance has become more routine. Here compulsory detention under legal powers is rarely necessary and is now little used. But the picture is in some respects hardly more optimistic now than it was at the beginning of the century. Arguably because of the benefits of psychotropic medication, proportionately fewer people with psychotic disorders now face chronic mental ill-health, or their condition is less impaired than it might have been a century ago. And fewer are to be found in large-scale institutions. Moreover, the material conditions in institutions catering for the mentally ill have improved in many cases (though there are some countries where conditions in mental hospitals are routinely harsh and cruel and some institutions where abuses occur). Yet the majority of those with long-term complaints, even if they are no longer found in large-scale asylums, still usually end up in some institution — a nursing home, old persons' home, half-way house or some other type of residential home, or else some impersonal boarding house or, failing that, even the streets. Many live on benefits and have limited material resources, spend much of their day sitting around with little to do, watching television or gazing blankly. Many, too, are on long-term anti-psychotic medication with marked side effects that may dull pain and suffering but also makes life less varied and interesting, and has unpleasant side effects especially if used long-term. The result is a life that is still materially and socially impoverished and the experience, even if the individuals escape harshness and cruelty, is still likely to be one of routine and boredom.

Finally, there are those with less severe problems, the troubled in mind, who now tend to receive diagnoses of depression or anxiety. Such people, even those with little money, have during the century been increasingly brought into the formal terrain of psychiatry and the mental health services. They now have far greater access to professional support than at the beginning of the century, though this support is often provided by a psychiatric nurse or psychologist rather than a psychiatrist, and far more resources are now invested in this type of work. Many receive care and treatment in a primary care setting from a general practitioner or, if they are more affluent, from a psychotherapist or psychodynamic counsellor. Psychological and social accounts of these conditions have shaped lay understandings of them and the way psychological difficulties are expressed. Yet frequently all that is offered is the palliative of some psychotropic medication which may well reduce pain and suffering (which is clearly desirable) but does not provide much in the way of cure, and improvement is dependent on continuing medication.

What of the future? Undoubtedly there will be major advances in the neurosciences and in understanding the brain chemistry underpinning mental states, and new 'designer' drugs will be developed to control and suppress symptoms. Equally advances in genetics will facilitate genetic counseling and the development of new gene therapies. Whilst these new developments will probably be enough to sustain and to continue to legitimate psychiatric work in the field of mental health (though they may lead to the secession of some territory to neurology), and may permit psychiatry to extend or consolidate some of its disputed boundaries, they will not make it safe from the competition of more psychologically and socially-oriented mental health professionals. Whilst new drugs may, for example, slow or even prevent the brain deterioration of Alzheimer's disease in the future, examination of the physical changes that are a concomitant of the disease may prove to have little relevance to understanding why some people and not others develop Alzheimer's. Genetic factors may well be implicated sometimes but are unlikely to provide the whole story and attention will also need to be paid psychological and social factors. Many would argue the need for more holistic models of mental ill-health, as of ill-health more generally, in which primacy is not accorded by fiat to the body but due weight is given to the interaction of biological, psychological and social processes. To focus exclusively on controlling the mind via the body as psychiatry often does is to simplify and distort the complexity of human experience.

## REFERENCES

1.  Montagu Lomax, *The Experiences of an Asylum Doctor.* (London: George Allen and Unwin, 1924), pp. 11–12.
2.  Anthonia White, *Beyond the Glass,* in *Frost in May,* Vol. 2. (London: Fontana, 1982 [1954]), p. 430.
3.  Ivan Belknap (1956) in Erving Goffman, *Asylums.* (Harmondsworth: Penguin, 1961), p. 54.
4.  Erving Goffman, *ibid,* pp. 61–3.
5.  Andrew Scull, *Decarceration.* (2nd edn., New Brunswick, NJ: Rutgers, 1984), pp. 152–3.
6.  Charles E. Rosenberg, 'Introduction to Framing Disease, Illness, Society and History,' in C.E. Rosenberg and J. Golden (eds) *Framing Diseases, Studies on Cultural History.* (New Brunswick: Rutgers University Press, 1992).
7.  Karl Jaspers, *General Psychopathology.* (London: Manchester University Press, 1963), p. 577.
8.  Marguerite Sechehaye, *Autobiography of a Schizophrenic Girl.* (New York: Grune and Stratton, 1951), p. 40.

9.   Quoted in Louis A. Sass, *Madness and Modernism, Insanity in the Light of Modern Art, Literature and Thought.* (Cambridge, Mass: Harvard University Press, 1994), p. 229.

10.  Sigmund Freud, 'Fragment of an analysis of a case of hysteria' in *Case Histories, I, 'Dora' and 'Little Hans'.* (Harmondsworth: Penguin, 1977 [1905]), p. 49.

11.  Sigmund Freud, *ibid,* p. 90.

12.  Charlotte Perkins Gilman, *The Yellow Wallpaper.* (London: Virago, 1981), pp. 12, 16.

13.  Seigfried Sassoon, *The Complete Memoirs of George Sherston.* (London: Faber and Faber, 1937), pp. 517–8.

14.  Sylvia Plath, *The Bell Jar.* (London: Faber and Faber, 1963), p. 151.

15.  'Strange Therapeutics' in D. McI. Johnson and N. Dodds (eds) *The Plea for the Silent.* (London: Christopher Johnson, 1957), p. 77.

16.  Janet Frame, *Faces in the Water.* (London: Women's Press, 1980 [1961]), p. 15.

17.  Kay Redfield Jamison, *An Unquiet Mind: A Memoir of Moods and Madness.* (London: Picador, 1997), p. 93.

## FURTHER READING

Brown, Phil, *The Transfer of Care, Psychiatric Deinstitutionalization and its Aftermath.* (London: Routledge and Kegan Paul, 1985).

Busfield, Joan, *Men, Women and Madness: Understanding Gender and Mental Disorder.* (London: Macmillan, 1996).

Clark, David, H., *The Story of a Mental Hospital: Fulbourn 1858–1983.* (London: Process Press, 1996).

Dorn, M.J. and Wolch, J.R., *Landscapes of Despair: From Deinstitutionalization to Homelessness.* (Cambridge, Polity, 1987).

Fernando, Suman, *Mental Health, Race and Culture.* (London: Macmillan, 1991).

Geller, J.L. and Harris, M., *Women of the Asylum: Voices from Behind the Walls, 1940–1945.* (New York: Doubleday, 1994).

Gittins, Diana, *Madness in its Place: Narratives from Severalls Hospital.* (London: Routledge, 1998).

Goodwin, Simon, *Comparative Mental Health Policy: From Institutional to Community Care.* (London: Sage, 1997).

Grob, Gerald, *Mental Illness and American Society, 1875–1940.* (Princeton: Princeton University Press, 1983).

Lunbeck, Elizabeth, *The Psychiatric Persuasion: Knowledge, Gender and Power in Modern America.* (Princeton: Princeton University Press, 1995).

Porter, Roy, *A Social History of Madness: Stories of the Insane.* (Weidenfeld and Nicholson, 1987).

Prior, Lindsay, *The Social Organisation of Mental Illness.* (London: Sage, 1993).

Rogers, Anne, Pilgrim, David and Lacey, Ron, *Experiencing Psychiatry: Users' Views of Services.* (London: Macmillan, 1993).

Shorter, Edward, *A History of Psychiatry: From the Era of the Asylum to the Age of Prozac.* (New York: John Wiley, 1997).

Valenstein, Elliot S., *Great and Desperate Cures: The Rise and Decline of Psychosurgery and Other Radical Treatments for Mental Illness.* (New York: Basic Books, 1986).

# CHAPTER 42

# Surgeons

## CHRISTOPHER LAWRENCE AND TOM TREASURE

On 2 July 1900, one of America's most promising young surgeons, the thirty-one year old Harvey Cushing, disembarked from the transatlantic liner *Servia* at Liverpool, England. He had left his position as resident surgeon at the prestigious Johns Hopkins Hospital, Baltimore, to expand his surgical experience, to meet eminent medical men and to see Europe. Cushing was to become one of the most distinguished surgeons of the twentieth century and a creator of a new speciality — neurosurgery. Shortly before Cushing arrived in England, a British surgeon, Wilfred Grenfell, crossed the Atlantic in the other direction to set up a medical mission in Labrador. In their lifetimes Grenfell was undoubtedly more famous than Cushing and was best known for exploits other than his surgical ones. The careers of these figures characterize the extremes of surgical experience in the twentieth century. Much of Cushing's life was lived within university hospitals where he shaped surgery to such an extent that some of the academic and technical experiences of surgeons later in the century were possible only because of Cushing's work. For Grenfell on the other hand surgery was a means to achieve other things. His life probably had no influence on the technical experiences of other surgeons but, as a heroic figure, Grenfell no doubt shaped the lives of many aspiring practitioners. Surgery too enabled Grenfell to change the lives of the Labrador poor. Thus surgery in the twentieth century has been a discipline which surgeons have changed and a resource they have used to change the world at large. These categories of course overlap considerably.

It is not easy to distil into generalizations accounts of the experiences of surgeons in the twentieth century. One is that it has been an overwhelmingly male experience. The surgeons discussed here are mostly British and American, often with academic connections, but we have tried to go beyond the lives of Cushing and those like him. Another generalization about the experience of being a surgeon in the twentieth century is that, at the beginning of the century, surgical experience was diverse and that, at the end, experiences were more uniform. By the end of the century most surgeons in the Western world practised in hospitals whereas at the beginning many worked in private houses or nursing homes. Yet the years before the First World War and those after the Second had things more in common with each other than they did with the intervening age. In both periods surgeons considered themselves about to transform their discipline and, indeed, in many instances they went on to do so, entering organs and cavities that were previously taboo. Around 1900 surgeons began to work in the abdomen and the cranium, and after the Second World War the heart was the object of surgical expansion. Both of these eras were characterized by confidence in reductionist approaches to disease and mechanistic solutions. In the inter-war years medicine in general showed greater concern for the whole individual and interest in functional rather than structural questions and surgery had a rather more business-as-usual feel to it. Uniting all periods, however, has been the high esteem in which surgeons have been held by the public although the form of that esteem has varied. Around 1900, in an era of imperialism and westward expansion in America, surgeons were heroes, likened to frontiersmen and explorers. Later, with the rise of Hollywood, surgery was pictured as romantic and glamorous.

As the new century began, many doctors and lay people considered that the problems of disease would soon be conquered by technical expertise based on new laboratory sciences such as bacteriology and physiology. Surgery in particular was invested with much of this optimism, for by this time it had been transformed from what many called a craft into what was now deemed an art based upon scientific principles. Comparable with their expanding practical skills, the social and professional status of surgeons had risen. In Britain, Joseph Lister had been made a Baron and in America surgeons viewed themselves as embodying the virtues of modernity: independence, individuality and courage. In 1905 an American professor of surgery proclaimed:

> There is no science that calls for greater fearlessness, courage, and nerve than that of surgery, none that demands more of self-reliance, principle, independence and the determination in the man... it is these old-time Puritan qualities... which have passed into surgeons of America, giving them boldness in their art, and enabling them to win that success in surgery, which now commands the admiration of the civilized world.[1]

The public seemed to endorse this self confidence, if books of the time with such titles as *Surgeons and their Wonderful Discoveries* are anything to go by.

Harvey Cushing was born in Cleveland, Ohio, in 1869 and entered Yale in 1887 where he studied classics and science. Yale at this time was developing a distinguished scientific school and it was physiological chemistry that fired Cushing with the desire to pursue a medical career. In 1891 he entered Harvard Medical School and at the Massachusetts General Hospital (MGH) Cushing gave ether at operations, washed instruments and assisted the surgeons. In 1893 he recorded such experiences as "Etherized for Dr Warren... Carcinoma of the breast" and "Saw M.H. Richardson perform oesophagotomy and remove a teaspoon from the oesophagus of a crazy woman." He also recorded "Strangulated hernia case–woman died on table."[2] In his fourth year Cushing was doing experimental surgical work on dogs and when he graduated in 1895 he stayed on at MGH as an intern where he helped inaugurate the use of X-rays.

An institution that, in many eyes, embodied twentieth-century surgical excellence was the Johns Hopkins Hospital, the clinical wing of the Johns Hopkins medical school that had opened in 1893. In August 1895 Cushing visited Hopkins and met William Halsted, professor of surgery, and "became enamoured of the place."[3] He angled for a position and Halsted advised him to study in Germany, then seen as the home of scientific medicine. Cushing shelved these plans when, in 1896, Halsted found him a place as an assistant. Halsted, a former cocaine addict, appeared infrequently and Cushing worked hard. Cushing had, he recalled, "to make all the clinical, bacteriological and pathological studies for every patient."[4] He also introduced X-rays to the surgical department. He learned of the new syndrome of inflamed appendix and the operation for the vestige's removal and in 1897 he diagnosed the condition in himself and implored his chief to operate, which he did. At about the same time he began experimenting on patients, infiltrating nerve trunks with cocaine for procedures such as amputation. In 1898 he had his first experience of war surgery; soldiers injured in the Spanish American conflict. He saw wounded men and typhoid perforation of the gut (for which he operated) and among the troops in Huntsville, "such terrible specimens of humanity... Filth, disease, rags."[5]

Thus it was an already experienced and successful Harvey Cushing who arrived in England in 1900 and who traveled to London to breakfast with the aggressive, dogmatic Victor Horsley, acclaimed as a pioneer neurosurgeon. Horsley was a man twelve years Cushing's senior and, like Cushing, was devoted to experimental science in medicine. Cushing related how

> They drove off the next morning in Horsley's cab, after sterilizing the instruments in H.'s house and, packing them in a towel, went to a well-appointed West End mansion. Horsley dashed upstairs, had his patient under ether in five minutes, and was operating fifteen minutes after he entered the house; made a great hole in the woman's skull, pushed up the temporal lobe — blood everywhere, gauze packed into the middle fossa, the ganglion cut, the wound closed, and he was out of the house less than an hour after he had entered it.[6]

Cushing abandoned his plan to study with Horsley. In London, thanks to the distinguished Hopkins medical professor William Osler, Cushing rubbed shoulders with the British medical elite, attended lectures and ate at convivial dinners. He left England and visited hospitals in France and French Switzerland. Cushing found French surgical practice casual and careless and he recorded seeing a surgeon who "slapped a patient and did not seem to know his business."[7] He spent ten days in Lausanne at the clinic of Cesar Roux and watched admiringly as Roux performed gastro-enterostomy procedures and goitre operations, the latter with no anesthetic. At Berne he spent time at Theodor Kocher's clinic, regarded by some as the surgical capital of Europe. Here he could have learned, as he realized, surgical arrogance.

Back at Hopkins, Cushing pursued his career by publishing, experimenting on animals and patients and devising new operations and techniques. For example, he introduced blood pressure measurements for monitoring surgical patients. In 1903 he established the Hunterian Laboratory for the study of experimental surgery. Cushing was becoming a well known figure in the medical world traveling North America and Europe, learning and teaching.

That surgery at the dawn of the twentieth century was in a position to expand further both in terms of technical achievement and social status was, as it turned out, not simply an empty boast. Cushing was far from being the first 'brain surgeon' but the facilities of American clinics offered him almost unrivaled possibilities for developing the subject. At Hopkins, Cushing began to accumulate neurological cases with surgical potential and in the years before the First World War he made himself into the world authority on neurosurgery. He developed a particular interest in diseases of the pituitary (endocrinology was then fast becoming a major field of pathological and physiological enquiry). Cushing developed an operation for removal of pituitary tumors and in turn taught others so that, in time, it became a routine procedure.

By 1912, aged forty one, Cushing was at the peak of his profession and he was inundated with invitations to accept surgical chairs. He was also in a position to dictate his own terms and in May 1912 he was appointed to the senior chair of surgery at Harvard and as surgeon-in-chief to the Peter Brent Brigham Hospital. Such appointments provided the opportunity for yet another form of surgical experience: the politics of academic surgery. Cushing negotiated with the hospital Trustees to have paying patients admitted and organized clinical services, directing the labors of pathologists, chemists and photographers. In London in 1913, he delivered an address attacking the standards of British hospitals and medical training upsetting many of his transatlantic colleagues. The following year he became deeply embroiled in the proposal to introduce full-time clinical profes-sorships at Harvard in line with the recommendations of the General Education Board. Cushing even tendered his own resignation over this issue.

At just this moment in Cushing's career world events offered yet further new experiences: war had broken out in Europe. By the end of 1914 Cushing was organizing a Harvard unit to serve the military hospital organized by American residents of Paris. Seventeen of Harvard's medical personnel composed the unit. Cushing was one of the six senior staff. The hospital was a converted lycée with 164 beds. Cushing's first case was a French soldier, shot in the back with a French bullet. Cushing saw many "dreadful deformities... broken jaws, and twisted scarred faces." He spent hours inspecting and was shocked by the way the wounded were moved, recording the case of "one English officer who had been six days in transport... with a musket for a splint tied to a compound fracture of the femur, no dressing whatsoever almost no food or drink, he was in delirium." After the battle of the Marne the operating room was in "continuous performance."[8]

Cushing went back to Boston in 1915 and in 1917 returned to Europe with a unit of nearly 300. He operated "almost incessantly," carefully recording cases of soldiers with head wounds. His technical publications on these patients enhanced his reputation as the world's leading neurosurgeon. After the war Cushing further cemented the formation of a new speciality by founding The Society of Neurological Surgeons. By the twenties, Cushing was one of the most distinguished medical men in the world. He worked hard, traveled, published and had numerous honors bestowed on him. His reputation was further enhanced by his widely acclaimed, massive biography of William Osler of 1925. He died in 1939.

The sum total of Cushing's experiences were hardly typical of an early twentieth-century surgeon but many surgeons pursuing an academic career then and later would have had many experiences in common with him; for example: innovating, publishing in professional journals, traveling, experimenting, reading, and cultivating those with power to appoint to positions in university hospitals. In addition trying to make enough money in private practice to lead a life style commensurate with a high social status. Some surgeons of course did these things with more success than others. Cushing was an extreme example.

Few things in surgery could have been further from an academic career than the life of Wilfred Grenfell. Grenfell was born in England in 1865. At school at Marlborough he internalized the Victorian cult of manliness which valued moral and physical strength and abstemiousness. He entered the London Hospital Medical College in 1883. British medical education at this time was known for its practical emphasis and this was the bias which appealed to Grenfell. He shared with his surgical teacher, Frederick Treves, a love of athletics and the Christian faith. As a student Grenfell boxed, played football, taught Christianity to the East end poor in London, reclaimed (or tried to reclaim) the local drunks and qualified with the relatively lowly conjoint diploma in 1888.

The challenge of being a physician with the Mission to Deep Sea Fishermen was perfect for Grenfell. It required an intensely practical surgeon of an evangelical turn of mind. Beating about the North Sea, living in a cold cabin with the nauseous fumes of a paraffin stove, Grenfell stitched up injured sailors and preached the evils of both drink and pornography. Grenfell had found his vocation and in 1892 he arrived at the burning town of St John's Newfoundland to save the souls and the emaciated bodies of the fisherfolk living there. The first decade of the twentieth century saw Grenfell make himself the hero of Newfoundland and Labrador. He divided his life between fund raising in North America and working on his mission vessel, the *Strathcona*, kitted out as church and hospital. By 1904, publicising the plight of the Labrador and Newfoundland poor had enabled the mission to raise sufficient funds to run three hospitals ashore. Nearly 3,000 patients a year were treated.

Grenfell had a flair for attracting both the money and admiration of philanthropists. The word 'heroic' clung to him. The frozen north and the heroic Grenfell were widely circulated images in North America. When he piloted the *Strathcona* into some isolated harbor, small boats flocked to it and the sick and poor came aboard in large numbers. Grenfell, like Cushing, also made his name through publishing. In Grenfell's case, however, it was not technical surgical monographs but more than thirty books about Labrador, Jesus and himself. Honors and acclaim were showered on him. In 1907 Oxford conferred on him its first ever honorary medical doctorate. Schemes for transforming Labrador were started and money raised. In the midst of all this, Grenfell was at work, operating in the hospital or miles up country treating cases too sick to travel. Spectacularly, in 1908, he set off with his dogs and sled to operate on a young man 50 miles from base. The following day he was reported marooned with the dogs, on a large flat 'pan' of ice. Darkness prevented rescue. The following day, he was nearly in the open sea, dressed only in "knee-length football shorts, Richmond socks, a flannel shirt and a sweater vest" and with all his supplies sunk.[9] He drifted. After a night to which the word terrible scarcely does justice, his rescuers were unsure whether he was alive or dead. Grenfell soon became almost a synonym for hero in every home in the northern hemisphere that took an English language newspaper. He was far from shy of contributing to this process. His own *Adrift on an Icepan* appeared in 1909. Now an international figure, Grenfell traveled, raised funds, wrote, preached and operated. The Great War, not surprisingly, saw him at the front, operating, organizing and writing. By the 1920s he was living out his own reputation, lecturing, fundraising, getting involved in Canadian politics and upsetting not a few people. Others, however, saw in him the selfless idealist who stood against everything the inter-war years seemed to deliver: materialism, industrialism, mass consumption and death of the spirit.

If Cushing's was an extreme example of a career in which surgery was an end in itself and Grenfell's one in which surgery was a means to promote other things, in other lives surgery and wider political ends seem more densely mixed, attempts to further the one being entwined with efforts to advance the other. In this sense the everyday business of surgery was itself experienced as a political activity, something which was probably not the case for Cushing or Grenfell, except, perhaps, in the extreme case of war.

Daniel Hale Williams was born in Pennsylvania 1856. His parents were of very mixed racial background and Daniel showed faint signs of African ancestry. He trained as a barber in Wisconsin and at the same time began to educate himself. He went to Chicago Medical College in 1880 and in 1883 graduated MD. He practised indiscriminately among white and black, operating in patient's homes and at the South Side Dispensary in Chicago. Williams, who identified strongly with negro causes, encountered little prejudice himself, except when he tried to marry a white woman. Galvanized by lack of opportunity for black nurses and doctors, however, Williams organized the local community to found the Provident Hospital. It took patients from all backgrounds but had only black staff. Williams carried out many operations there and famously in 1893 opened the chest and sutured the pericardium after a stab wound. Shortly after this he was appointed surgeon to Freedman's Hospital for blacks in Washington. It was underfunded, badly administered and had a high mortality. Williams reorganized it, appointed white doctors alongside black and established Freedman's as an institution for the postgraduate education of black physicians. Besides his routine operating Williams developed a reputation for heroic, but necessary intervention, notably in obstructed labor. Apparently his successes were discussed at the District Medical Society from which, because of his racial background, he was barred.

Williams left Freedman's after local politics got the better of him in 1898 and returned to Chicago. The new century saw him building his private practice, practising charitably among the black poor, attempting to reinstate himself at the Provident and championing the role of the laboratory in surgical diagnosis. He published and crossed swords with local surgeons on matters of technique. Williams operated on negroes who traveled from the south to consult him and urged the need for a special hospital for them in the South. He began to travel to Nashville each year for ten days as advisory professor of clinical surgery at the black Meharry Medical College. He campaigned for hospitals and training schools in the South for negroes. Soon he was traveling all over the United States, operating and teaching, usually at small hospital or medical schools for blacks. He often encountered prejudice and refused to operate at all-white hospitals. Williams became increasingly involved in the local black politics of Chicago and was eventually forced out of the Provident. He had a professional and political feud with George Hall, a black surgeon at Provident, also deeply involved with local humanitarian projects and black medical education. Ironically, William's light skin was probably contributory to his local downfall, it having made it easier for him to mix in white company to the chagrin of some of his black colleagues. Nationally, however, he continued to lecture and practice and in 1913 he was the sole non-white installed as charter member of the American College of Surgeons. He died in 1931.

Williams' story is that of an individual promoting both surgery and the cause of an oppressed minority, the two things being entwined in complex ways. His surgical operations were themselves direct interventions into the sufferings of people who were the victims of prejudice and in many instances the same operation was an expansion of surgical boundaries. Williams simultaneously used his skill and profile as a surgeon to raise the status of the black surgeon. Williams also exploited his white skin to further his own career and in turn those of others. It cut both ways, however, for as both a citizen and a surgeon he experienced the prejudice of both black and white communities.

There are great similarities here with the career of British surgeon, Louisa Martindale. Like Williams, Martindale came from a group experiencing discrimination, in this instance on the grounds of gender. But Martindale had rather more resources than Williams which she could exploit to offset overt political disadvantage. Money, education and connections went a long way. Martindale was born in England in 1872 into a comfortably-off, liberal Nonconformist family, a background which furnished significant psychological resources: a sense of independence and a determination to succeed. Aged 19, Martindale entered the London (Royal Free Hospital) School of Medicine for women. She qualified in 1899 whereupon she toured the world with her mother and sister. She attended obstetric clinics in Vienna, hospitals in India and Australia and saw the famous gynecologist Howard Kelly operate at Johns Hopkins Hospital. After a spell of general practice in England she visited Berlin for post-graduate study at Robert Olshausen's gynecological clinic (presumably an experience made possible by private means and determination). She returned to London and proceeded MD in 1907. She then settled in general practice in Brighton where she helped form the local women's suffrage society. Martindale was no ordinary practitioner. She was well connected, frequently meeting distinguished London doctors and spending time in Freiburg, a recognized center for pursuing gynecology.

In Brighton she bought X-ray apparatus for the radiation therapy of gynecological disorders. She developed a reputation as a radiation therapist and began to be sent cases from outside the area. She began to publish on both medical and women's issues, notably prostitution. Her pamphlet on the latter subject, *Under The Surface*, being called obscene in House of Commons. Excluded from the staff of the Sussex County Hospital on the grounds of gender she and several other local folk opened a small hospital in 1913, soon to be called the New Sussex Hospital, staffed only by women. Fund raising took a great deal of her time as the hospital expanded and flourished. In her autobiography, Martindale proudly remembered "it was the first [hospital] in Sussex to provide single private wards for women of the professional classes who cannot afford a nursing home."[10] Martindale operated on all manner of women's disorders at the hospital and used X-rays extensively after mastectomy. As her surgical career blossomed so did her political life. She became extremely influential locally, as a Justice of the Peace for example. The First World War was spent mainly in Brighton but also as a surgeon in the Scottish Women's Hospital in Royaumont, France. Her days being filled, she remembered, with "hundreds of dressings, operating and taking notes."[11]

After the war Martindale increasingly began to make trips to London to consult and operate and in the early 1920s she moved to a large house in London where she continued her X-ray therapy. In London as in Brighton she was instrumental in founding a hospital for women and by the 1930s she was deeply involved in radium therapy for cancer of the cervix. Surgical and social success went hand in hand. She moved in literary circles and gave lavish parties, with servants and chauffeurs facilitating her schedule. Gender boundaries notwithstanding, Martindale spent the inter-war years as a medical celebrity speaking at medical and women's societies all over the world. She was committed to medical women's politics, campaigning for equality of opportunity. Martindale's experience of being a surgeon was inextricably entwined with her political experience of being a woman. Surgery made it possible to help (as she saw it) suffering women and women in the medical profession. Conversely her own status as a middle class women coupled with her determination and character made it possible for her to have an extraordinarily successful and, presumably, satisfying surgical career.

Martindale's surgical experiences, unusual though they were in many respects, had much in common with those of many inter-war surgeons. In this period hospital practice became more common but lots of operations were still done in patient's houses or nursing homes. Like the vast majority of her contemporaries, she pursued her career almost entirely outside the walls of academia. For the generation that followed Martindale the possibilities of an academic life became increasingly real and a career pattern like Cushing's with lots of practical surgery initially and medical politics and administration later were fairly common. Claude E. Welch, born in 1906, arrived at Harvard Medical School in 1928. Taught by Harvey Cushing he graduated in 1932 and practised as a surgical intern at MGH. Many operations at the hospital were performed by visiting surgeons who had lucrative private practices in the city. They constituted an elite and as Welch recalled "Their staff room was fitted with leather chairs; ours had wooden benches."[12] The role of heroic, individualist, masculine surgeon could easily accommodate petulance and contempt for juniors. Welch testified:

> Somewhat annoyed because a nurse was not on hand to grant his every wish, one of these men calmly crossed to the instrument table and pulled off the sheet. All of the instruments fell with a great clatter on the tiled floor. So great was the commotion that everyone in the operating suite ran to find out what catastrophe had occurred. To the multitude he said quietly, "May I have a mosquito snap, please?" (This is the tiniest instrument on the operating table).[13]

Many interns, Welch regretted, not only learned surgery from these men, but also how a surgeon could behave.

Welch also learned his surgery from men emboldened by experiences in the Great War. He assisted at total gastrectomies, hepatic lobectomies and entered the chest to perform pericardectomies and pulmonary lobectomies. Nonetheless these were not radical deviations from pre-war practices. Operative technology still remained at a minimum. Orthopedic wards were filled with iron lungs and patients with fractured necks of the femurs lay in traction for long periods. Daily life revolved around dressings, draining abscesses, and giving transfusions. There was no remuneration. The sense of operating in a team, however, developed in this period as, for example, specialist anesthetists appeared. Welch stayed on at MGH climbing the surgical ladder until, once again, the outside world took a major role in shaping the experience of surgeons.

The United States entered the Second World War in 1942. Unlike the First World War, when it was possible to endure the whole conflict in a single hospital behind a motionless front, the Second World War was usually spent on the move. Welch first drilled in the heat and humidity of Florida and in January 1943, in the snow, he arrived in New Jersey for embarkation for Casablanca. There, a former school was converted to a hospital and casualties from the North African conflict began to pour in. He remembered for several months the forty male captains and lieutenants were quartered in one large dormitory with no privacy and one busy latrine at the end.

> The traffic to the latrine was unbelievable and sleep impossible… The armed forces radio played music continuously, repeating the usual jingles (including 'The Little Brown Jug') over and over. Arabs ran up and down the street early in the morning selling their wares, and shouting *"huitres et vieux habits"* ('oysters and old clothes').[14]

Daily surgical life centred on amputations, laparotomies and the removal of shell fragments. The Italian campaign followed and a spell in a general hospital close to the front. Chest wounds, which had been rare in Casablanca, were common and, like many surgeons who were to practice thoracic surgery after the war, Welch got his experience in action. Besides practical surgery, Welch experienced "Strong bonds of fellowship." Such ties led after the war to "mutual respect and patient referrals."[15] He arrived home in October 1945 and, like Cushing before him, Welch's mature years were spent writing, teaching, traveling, administering, organizing and being celebrated.

Welch's slightly younger British contemporary, Reginald Murley, had a similar career. He was born in 1916, and entered St Bartholomew's medical college in 1934. As a student Murley was attached to the surgical professorial unit. That is, he was taught by a full-time professor of which there were very few at this time. He brought his own simple instruments which he had to boil before each dressing he carried out. In 1936 he traveled to Vienna to watch the accident surgeon Lorenz Böhler at work. Böhler, Murley considered, had little respect for his patients. He nailed fractured necks of femurs under local anesthetic. In one operation when a woman screamed with pain, "Böhler promptly shouted, *'Haben sie keine stolz?'* ('Have you no pride?')."[16] Murley graduated in May 1939 and by the next January he had embarked for Dunkirk, entrained for Marseilles, and steamed to Haifa. The months following saw no action, only visiting cards, reading and bed bugs. A move to the Sudan ensued. Here Murley saw action at first hand when his own dressing station was bombed in spite of the red crosses on the tents. Casualties accumulated rapidly after this and Murley learned a great deal about orthopedics and plastic work including treating a German soldier whose whole jaw had been blown away and who confessed, after Murley had saved his life, he did not know whether to say "Heil Hitler or God Save the King!"[17] Like Welch, Murley encountered what, to many, *being* a surgeon meant. In Cairo, the surgeon Michael Oldfield was performing a nephrectomy when he said,

> "From where did that drainage tube come?," "Out of the emergency drainage tube jar, sir," replied Miss White. "And how was it sterilized?" asked Michael. "In carbolic solution, Major Oldfield," said Miss White. Without another word Oldfield turned to the trolley, grasped the towel on which the instruments lay, and pulled everything on to the floor. He then calmly sat on a theatre stool, "And now, Miss White" he said, just boil those up for 20 minutes."[18]

Wartime experience and a newly acquired Fellowship of the Royal College of Surgeons saw Bart's welcome back Murley as chief assistant. Post-war reconstruction in medicine as in anything else offered opportunities for the ambitious and Murley was at the head of affairs at an angry meeting at the Royal College of Surgeons in 1948 where the young Turks felt their views had not been taken into account as their elders took them into the National Health Service (NHS). Ironically it was after the introduction of the NHS that Murley got his early experience of private practice, renting rooms in Harley Street. He climbed to the top of his profession eventually becoming President of the College.

The extraordinary career and experiences of Joshua Horn exemplify many of the points made so far, yet his life was quite unlike any of those already discussed in that it was a theorized and practical fusion of surgery and politics. A poor boy born in 1914, Horn studied medicine, by way of a scholarship, at University College, London where he joined the Socialist Medical Association. His first clinical experiences were treating the blisters of hunger marchers. He qualified in 1936 and signed on as a ship's surgeon bound for China. He wrote vividly in later years of the poverty and prostitution he saw in Shanghai. He returned to England and when war broke out worked as a surgeon at the London docks and abroad. After the war he was appointed consultant surgeon in Birmingham, England.

In 1954 the most fascinating part of his career began. In that year, a committed Communist and disciple of Mao Tse Tung, he returned to China to help build a socialist state. Horn spent fifteen years in China, practising as an accident surgeon both in Beijing and in the countryside. In addition to treating recent injuries (Horn pioneered the reattachment of severed limbs) he attended to sufferers from the pre-Communist regime. He recorded treating "a youth whose penis had been chopped off by a landlord because his father couldn't pay the rent" and a Tibetan serf whose hamstrings had been slashed by a nobleman as punishment for running away.[19]

For Horn the organisation and practice of surgery were explicitly political activities which meant reading Mao, discussing the text with colleagues and endeavoring to "Weld hospital workers of all grades into a team." Horn perceived all of medicine in this way. The claimed control of VD in China he saw as owing to "social and political factors... as opposed to a purely technical medical or legislative approach."[20] Horn returned to England in 1969 where he taught anatomy.

He went back to Beijing in 1975 where he died. If all experience is ultimately political, Horn lived out the view that politics must be explicitly theorized and used to shape experience and action. Surgical experiences for Horn, at one level, had much in common with those of Cushing, yet, at another, they could not have been further apart.

Edward D. Churchill, who had been Welch's teacher at MGH and, during the war, 'Consultant to the Mediterranean Theatre,' returned to the United States in 1945 but left behind, in the US Military Hospital in Cirencester, the 35 year old Dwight Emary Harken as the Consultant for Thoracic Surgery. Harken was the son of an Iowa general practitioner and surgeon. This was a not an uncommon combination at the beginning of the century, but improbable at its end, when specialization had become the norm. Harken was a Harvard graduate who had worked for two years in London's Brompton Hospital (1939–1940) under Arthur Tudor Edwards before returning to work in the Boston City Hospital (1940–1942). He was called to army service after the bombing of Pearl Harbour, and returned to England.

The war gave surgeons great opportunities for innovation and the expression of self confidence. Most of them would have been familiar with the view of Stephen Paget, expressed in 1896, that, "Surgery of the heart has probably reached the limits set by Nature to all surgery: no new method, and no new discovery, can overcome the natural difficulties that attend a wound of the heart."[21] In all probability, Harken and others would have seen such a sentiment as a challenge rather than an admonition. Surgeons knew that suturing the heart was at least possible, although they were also aware of the high mortality that followed attempts at cardiac operations in the 1920s and 1930s. At Cirencester, Harken operated to remove bullets and shrapnel fragments from around the heart and great vessels of soldiers, despite the discouragement of his surgical mentor, Churchill. His innovation, however, seems to have been approved of by Tudor Edwards, and also by Elliot Cutler who was Chief of Personnel for the American Surgical Forces. Harken recorded removing bullets and other metal from in and around the hearts of 134 soldiers, within a period of 10 months. He presented this record to the Association of Surgeons of Great Britain and Ireland on 2 May 1945, and reported that all of the patients survived. The surgical confidence which he gained, and the credibility which he achieved, he took back to Boston where he turned his attention to mitral stenosis, a condition in which a heart valve is narrowed, obstructing the flow of blood. This disorder was common and chronically debilitating and several writers around the turn of the century had postulated that the narrowing might be surgically relieved. Indeed Cushing had studied the problem in dogs. There had, however, been a movement away from mechanistic solutions to heart disease in the inter-war years. By the time of the war it was held that such operations were not only dangerous, but futile.

It was in such a hostile climate that Harken had gone to war but he returned to a different one. Following World War Two it was increasingly held that mechanistic solutions to structural problems were appropriate. There had also been a move towards specialization and teamwork and away from the surgical generalism that was characteristic of the early part of the century. This was in keeping with post-war reductionist approaches which saw a massive economic and political investment in laboratory medicine; a form of optimism sustained by the triumphs of specific therapeutic agents such as penicillin and streptomycin. Harken's surgical intervention into mitral stenosis did not meet with immediate success, but he was encouraged to persist and when he had his first survivor in 16 June 1948 he was able to command space for an article in the world's most prestigious medical journal, the *New England Journal of Medicine.*

Harken was not alone in testing therapeutic possibilities. Medical optimism had encouraged surgeons in public competition for 'firsts.' Indeed on 10 June 1948 the Philadelphia surgeon, Charles Bailey, had successfully performed a mitral valve operation upstaging Harken by a week. Bailey in marked contrast to Harken turned to the public rather than the profession for applause and featured on the front of *Time Magazine.* Bailey had that fearless, almost reckless approach to operations, that is frequently venerated in surgical hagiography. He had a series of deaths — four in his attempts to operate on this condition — and had lost his operating rights, or at least was restricted, at one hospital after another. Immediately after a patient died on the operating table at Philadelphia General Hospital on the morning of 10 June, he went to the Episcopal Hospital to operate on another in the afternoon. This was his first survivor of the mitral stenosis operation. He followed it by taking the patient on a 1,000 mile train journey, eight days later, to show to colleagues at a conference.

At the same time, in England, Russell Brock was a well established thoracic surgeon at Guy's Hospital, London. He had worked in America from 1929–1930 and had been appointed a hospital consultant at the young age of 33. In 1947 he obtained the agreement of the Guy's Medical Committee to form a Thoracic Surgical Unit. His physician colleague, Maurice Campbell, volunteered to give up his position as a Full Physician to become 'Cardiologist' to the Unit; a move away from generalism that ran the risk of diminished status and income. The Committee also formalized arrangements for consultant exchanges between Guy's surgeons and Johns Hopkins, following Brock's exchange with his opposite number Alfred Blalock. In early 1948 Brock formed the Peacock Club, an internal group devoted to surgical aspects of heart disease. With this combination of internal and international networks and a specialist team, Brock began his work on mitral stenosis.

Harken and Bailey, educated within the marked individualist ethos of American surgery, had published single cases as their 'first' successes. Although Brock shared a flair for the dramatic with these two, his approach was different. Brock devised a series of operations for mitral stenosis, planned the operations with a team and carried them out in one hospital without publicity. When he published, it was an account of six survivors of eight operations. It was a sign of a difference between practitioners on opposite sides of the Atlantic but also of changing sense of the possible or desirable. After the Second World War there were increasing constraints, informal then formal, on experiments on patients and pressure to restrain surgical flamboyance.

A colleague of Brock's in Guy's, who also had a distinguished career was Hedley Atkins. In 1948, while Brock was performing his first mitral valve operations, Atkins was engaged in a series of major operations for hypertension in which the sympathetic nervous system was ablated by wide exposure of the thoracic and lumbar spine. The operation was deemed effective but developments in pharmacology replaced it. At the time, however, it appeared an exciting innovation. In other words surgeons in this period were innovating in all sorts of areas, many in ways that are lost to the historical record. Atkin's view of what was needed in a good surgeon was recorded in his later years in his *The Surgeon's Craft*. He wrote that the surgeon should possess "a rather more than normal degree of common-sense" and have "a natural liking for his fellow men." "The surgeon's training" he declared "must teach him to resist the temptation to 'show off.'"[22] Significantly, perhaps, Atkins devoted his last researches to the treatment of breast cancer, a common disease, managed by virtually every general surgeon, in every country, and not surrounded by the sort of drama that has been created around heart surgery.

A popular book *The Way of a Surgeon* which was first published in 1949 and then as a paperback in 1959 recounted case histories and depicted the surgeon as a hero — an amalgamation of technician, scientist, and a human face. A case of appendicitis resulting in peritonitis, successfully treated by surgery and antibiotics, was related. The family seemed more inclined to "Thank God" than the surgeon. The author, a surgeon, observed, "If you wish to thank God, don't do so for any special intervention on your son's behalf, thank Him, rather, for inspiring surgeons all over the world to find new and better ways of fighting peritonitis. Thank Him also for leading scientists to the discovery of the sulfa drugs — what you know, I expect, as M&B — and penicillin."[23] Public endorsement of surgical optimism can be seen in the review of the book by the *Manchester Evening News*, "If every man and woman read this book a large part of the doctor's battle against disease would be won."[24]

The quest for surgical firsts was not confined to North America and Britain. In 1951 an Argentinean surgeon, F.E. Tricerri reported in his national medical journal his first dozen mitral operations with the claim *ninguna muerte* (none died), giving credit to the work of Bailey and Harken. In 1954 he published a series of 300 operations on cardiovascular disease, which included a 100 mitral valve operations, 88 operations for hypertension, and hundred or so other operations, mirroring the case mix of Brock and Atkins at Guy's.

The Brompton Hospital in London was a major site for thoracic surgery. Harken had visited it in the early 1940s followed by Denton Cooley in 1949–50. Cooley was a trainee surgeon under Blalock at Johns Hopkins and Brock had met him there when he exchanged in 1947. Cooley epitomizes the glamorous surgeon: technically brilliant, elegant, and highly successful as a doctor, lecturer and writer. He built around himself a very large practice and from an institution styled by him, 'The Texas Heart Institute,' he led a surgical industry — a production line, performing thousands of heart operations each year, done to a protocol and refined to maximum efficiency. In partnership with manufacturers he gave his name to a series of products promoting both himself and the item.

Cooley presided over an organization that foreshadowed the immediate future. Large scale production-line surgery, minimizing costs and maximizing efficiency and, arguably, quality, has become the environment which currently shapes surgical experience. Surgeons are consumers and users of expensive high technology. The surgeon is not just purchaser but also the joint developer and promoter, along with industrial partners. Every day experience for the successful surgeon at a major institution includes such things as accessing computer based waiting lists, negotiating contracts, receiving referrals by 'fax', and it may include negotiating the retrieval and transport of a donor organ from another city or even another country. In many instances diagnosis, decision making, and post operative care are in the hands of others. But what of operating? This is still central to the surgeon's experience, but has now often become a more limited, technical exercise with the surgeon carrying out a smaller range of procedures than earlier in the century. Surgeons are more likely to see themselves, and to be seen, as technicians. The pluripotent, at times omnipotent, surgeon is gone.

As the century closed, 200,000 heart operations were being performed each year in the United States alone and on more than 500 per million of the population in all the developed world. Most Third World countries have sophisticated, if lower volume, heart surgery. Neurosurgery, a rarity when Cushing aimed to establish it as a speciality, is now routine and commonplace. As the century began neither neurosurgery or cardiac surgery existed. The surgeon worked on the abdomen, set fractures, and dealt with conditions such as tumors and abscesses almost wherever they occurred in the body. Many surgeons, like Harken's father, were also running a general practice. In major Western institutions, this sort of surgeon disappeared in the face of increasing specialization. Today, within surgical disciplines, there are specialists; for example, in orthopedics there are surgeons for the spine or the knees alone. Urologists now take surgical care of the kidneys, the prostate, and the bladder, which were once a major part of the work of general surgery. Surgery of the ear nose and throat, blood vessels, head and neck, eye and chest are all in the hands of highly specialized groups. These developments are endorsed by the surgical profession and by the political establishment. In England, the Royal College of Surgeons has published recommendations for the size and staffing of hospitals. This is a professional view, driven by surgeons themselves and one endorsed by the political establishment. In parallel there are similar pressures for maximizing efficiency from 'health care providers' who are not the surgeons, but executives and managers of multimillion dollar institutions.

Cushing failed to help his first ten brain tumor cases. Bailey had a succession of deaths on the operating table, but his personal standing or security were not in question. At the end of the century, the results of surgery are widely publicized and carefully scrutinized. In New York State the mortality figures by units and by surgeons are published. In the United Kingdom, the 'Confidential Enquiry into Perioperative Deaths' identifies areas where mortality is out of line with what is expected. Those surgeons found to have unexpectedly low results are the subject of public enquiry and where they have persisted in the face of poor performance they have received attention from the General Medical Council. There is also an increasing risk of civil litigation. Surgeons feel under threat, their anxiety fuelled by malpractice insurance; which can be in excess of $100,000 per annum each in the USA.

The surgeon is now in the public domain but not just as a heroic figure. In 1996 the London *Times* ran an article headlined "Why did they allow so many to die?" in which William Rees-Mogg criticized two named surgeons for continuing to operate on children when it was public knowledge that the mortality was conspicuously higher than in other hospitals. Bernard Levin in the same paper attacked surgeons for their research, for contemplating surgery not yet attempted, and ridiculing the suggestion that the hearts of genetically altered pigs might be used for transplants.

Not only have surgeons been challenged on their results, but on whether they should interfere at all. Ivan Illich, the leader of a wave of anti-medical iconoclasm argued that many interventions were unnecessary, pointing to a range of common operations such as those on tonsils, adenoids, and hernia, performed with very variable frequency. The incidence of cholecystectomy and hysterectomy, he noted, varied by factors of 4–6, depending not on the incidence of disease, but the number of surgeons in a geographical area wanting work to do and on the repayment mechanism. This suspicion about the appropriateness of surgery and other aspects of medicine is embodied in the title of the monthly magazine *What Doctors Don't Tell You*.

The historian's dilemma is the resolution of the contradictions of continuity and change. In the instance of surgery it would be possible to render current practice as radically different from that at the beginning of the century. How unlike, after all, are the present high technology transplant and the former kitchen table tonsillectomy. Yet there are obvious continuities; not least in the presence of an operator who, in various combinations, joins, divides, removes and adds to parts of a patient's body. But in this instance the historian has the evidence of the material world to substantiate the case for continuity. Different though they may be, there are surgical texts, instruments and operating tables from 1900 and the present day which point to a continuous tradition. But to the lived experience of the past surgeon (as opposed to the reported one), however, the historian has no access, any more than a museum visitor has access to, say, the 'Blitz experience' when visiting an exhibition of that name. Naively one might postulate that certain surgical experiences are unchanging, but whether flesh and blood felt precisely the same to the surgeon in 1900 as they do to the operator today is arguable. After all, do they feel the same to a member of the public assisting at an operation (as happens occasionally) as they do to a surgeon? Surgical feeling is educated feeling, and surgical education and expectations are different now. Indeed, for many surgeons even this once essential feature of surgical continuity is no longer present. Direct surgical experience of the body is now often highly mediated. Surgeons who use lasers and 'keyhole' techniques manipulate technologies to the exclusion of fleshly contact and view the body's cavities on monitors not by direct vision.

The history of the experience of the surgeon is not unlike that of people in many other occupations in the twentieth century, which is hardly surprising given that the same broad social, political and economic forces have been at work. Aviation, which is practically contemporary with modern surgery, began as relatively single-handed practice, using fairly simple technologies. It was an unregulated occupation, dangerous to pilot and passenger alike. Daring and courage were numbered among the aviator's virtues and their demonstration passed into common parlance: 'Flying by the seat of one's pants.' Pilots were heroes. Today aviation is big business, a very high-tech enterprise to which team work is crucial. It is relatively safe and surrounded by a labyrinth of legalities. Pilots (principally male), however, retain their glamour. The comparisons with surgery scarcely need elucidating. The point, however, is that the experiences specific to surgery in the twentieth century were grounded in more general experiences of living in modern Western industrial society.

## REFERENCES

1.  Cited in Christopher Lawrence, 'Divine, Democratic and Heroic: The History and Historiography of Surgery' in Christopher Lawrence (ed.) *Medical Theory, Surgical Practice: Studies in the History and Historiography of Surgery*. (London and New York: Routledge, 1992), pp. 1–48.
2.  John F. Fulton, *Harvey Cushing. A Biography*. (Springfield, Illinois: Charles C. Thomas, 1946), p. 69.
3.  *Ibid.*, p. 101.
4.  *Ibid.*, p. 121.
5.  *Ibid.*, p. 147.
6.  *Ibid.*, p. 163.
7.  *Ibid.*, p. 171, 393, 395.
8.  *Ibid.*, pp. 393, 395.
9.  Ronald Rompkey, *Grenfell of Labrador. A Biography*. (Toronto: University of Toronto Press, 1991), p. 144.
10. L. Martindale, *A Woman Surgeon*. (London: Victor Gollanz Ltd., 1951), p. 132.
11. *Ibid.*, p. 168.
12. Claude E. Welch, *A Twentieth-century Surgeon. My Life in the Massachusetts General Hospital*. (Boston, Massachusetts: Massachusetts General Hospital, 1992), p. 63.
13. *Ibid.*
14. *Ibid.*, pp. 100–101.

15. *Ibid.*, pp. 110, 118.
16. Reginald Murley, *Surgical Roots and Branches.* (London: The British Medical Journal, 1990), p. 33.
17. *Ibid.*, p. 87.
18. *Ibid.*, p. 91.
19. J. S. Horn, *'Away with all pests...' An English Surgeon in People's China.* (London: Paul Hamlyn, 1963), pp. 30, 36.
20. *Ibid.*, pp. 58, 87.
21. Stephen Paget, *The Surgery of the Chest.* (Bristol: John Wright & Co., 1896.), p. 121.
22. Hedley Atkins, *The Surgeon's Craft.* (Manchester University Press, 1965).
23. George Sava, *The Way of a Surgeon.* (London: Great Pan 1959 [Faber and Faber Ltd, 1949]), p. 61.
24. *Ibid.*, cited on back cover.

## FURTHER READING

Buckler, Helen, *Daniel Hale Williams: Negro Surgeon.* (New York: Pitman Publishing Corporation, 1968).

Cooter, Roger, *Surgery and Society in Peace and War. Orthopaedics and the Organization of Modern Medicine.* (London: Macmillan, 1993).

'In Memoriam. Dwight Emary Harken, MD. 1910–1993,' *Circulation* (1993), **88**: 2985–6.

Holmes, F.M., *Surgeons and their Wonderful Discoveries.* (London: S.W. Partridge and Co., ND).

Illich, Ivan, *Limits to Medicine. Medical Nemesis: The Expropriation of Health.* (London: Marion Boyars Publishers Limited, 1976).

Levin, Bernard, 'Making pigs of ourselves,' *The Times.* August 4, 1988.

Minetree, Harry, *Cooley: The Amazing Career of the World's Greatest Surgeon.* (New York: Harper's Magazine Press, 1973).

Rees-Mogg, William, 'Why did they allow so many to die?,' *The Times* (April 1, 1996).

*TIME The Weekly Newsmagazine*, Vol. LXIX, no. 12, (March 5, 1957).

Treasure, Tom and Hollman, Arthur, 'The Surgery of Mitral Stenosis 1898–1948: Why Did it Take 50 Years to Establish Mitral Valvotomy?' *Ann. Roy. Coll. Surg.* (1995), **77**: 145–151.

Wangensteen, Owen H. and Wangensteen, Sarah D., *The Rise of Surgery. From Empiric Craft to Scientific Discipline.* (Minneapolis: University of Minnesota Press, 1978).

*The Provision of Emergency Surgical Services. An Organisational Framework.* (London: The Royal College of Surgeons of England, 1997).

# CHAPTER 43

# Cancer

## PATRICE PINELL

Cancer nowadays eclipses the great epidemics of the past — syphilis and tuberculosis — in the collective representations of the social world. It is perceived as the major 'scourge' of our times, and the most terrifying of diseases, even more than AIDS. Cancer represents one of the most concrete forms which misfortune can take, since it affects the individual's life *and* the equilibrium of the community. It is the "dread disease";[1] in contrast to the relatively 'happy' death by heart failure, commonly seen as quick and painless, death by cancer seems horrible. The cancerous death is evocative of the most horrible end. Its presence is inscribed on the body of the sick mainly through the effects of treatments. On the other hand, cancer is the paradigmatic illness of contemporary civilization, closely related to our daily practices and common behaviors, environmental problems, bad working conditions, and so on — it appears to be a consequence of modern life. In this sense biological cancerous disorders are the 'incarnation,' at an individual level, of all kinds of social disorders.

The metaphorical use of the word is characteristic of this close relationship with social disorder. During the twentieth century cancer has become a metaphor, representing the political enemies of the nation, and also such catastrophic socio-economic events as unemployment and inflation. Cancer is at one and the same time a sickness of society and a metaphorical expression of a 'sick' society, unable to control its development. These links between social and biological disorders and the bad death *par excellence* of our "necrophobic societies,"[2] constitute the basic schemes of perception of this disease as a scourge of modern times. The paradox is that cancer has all the attributes of modernity, although it was first described and named many centuries before by doctors of the Hippocratic school, and was always associated with horror, pain and death. Cancer has a long history. But this history has been erased from our 'collective' memory during the twentieth century as if the disease had to appear 'modern,' *ie.*, pastless. In fact, the 'old disease' turned into a new object at the beginning of the century. Its social status changed: cancer became a medical, social, economical and political issue. A new field of practice was constituted, shaped by new institutions, specialists, activists and public policies — at national and international levels. But the pace of change, and the configurations varied from one country to another. The political, social and 'medical' history of each nation-state gave it a relatively 'local' specificity, but the paucity of national 'case studies' restricts comparative historical analysis. That this chapter concentrates on the first half of the twentieth century is a deliberate choice.

## AN INSTITUTIONAL AND CULTURAL REVIVAL

Cancer was such a disappointing disease to treat that for a long time only a few physicians were interested in its study. No particular medical institutions were founded to take care of the patients, despite the fact that most hospitals refused to treat them once they were declared 'incurable.' England was a notable exception, with some early cancer hospitals opened in London: the Middlesex hospital in 1792 and the London Cancer Hospital in 1851, later named the Royal Marsden Hospital. There were also cancer hospitals in Leeds, Liverpool, Glasgow and Manchester by the 1880s. These philanthropic institutions were not only asylums for the incurable; some of them were also places devoted to medical science and therapeutics. In the late nineteenth and early-twentieth centuries the situation changed dramatically. Scientific societies and medical institutes devoted to cancer appeared in Europe, the US and Japan; authorized voices began to speak of the danger of cancer for a modern society, laying the foundations for the creation of the anti-cancer movement. Why this dramatic development of interest? The answer is not immediately obvious.

Compared to the other diseases usually regarded as 'scourges,' cancer was very different. As far as medical authorities knew, it was not an epidemic disease, and the possibility of contagion was not evident. Its onset did not appear to be related to slackening moral standards or to disorderly behaviors. Finally, it hardly impacted upon children and young people, but mostly affected middle-aged adults and senior citizens. For a pathology with such characteristics to be perceived as a threat to the social balance, several conditions had to be fulfilled. An objectifying explanation, based on epidemiological arguments was not enough. The combination of an increased life-expectancy, the birth-rate decreasing and the rate of deaths through infectious diseases declining, accounted for the increasing rate of deaths due to cancer, both in relative and absolute terms. But such a phenomenon has no evident social visibility. To be perceived, those changes in mortality must be objectified and turned into statistical tables, and the demography analyzed: the results being translated into political discourse. It is only under these conditions that the dominant groups within an 'aging' society can internalize the idea of aging and appreciate the hidden growth of a disease like cancer. In other words, acknowledging cancer's social dimension presupposes modern states with sophisticated statistic-recording institutions. There is, however, no mechanical relationship between the production of data recording cancer-related death rates and the emergence of social concerns relating to this disease. Cancer became a problem for society because it was also identified by very different groups as an interesting subject for investigation.

In the field of biological sciences, the status of the cell as an elementary, organizing structure and the development of disciplines studying it (*eg.*, histopathology) gave rise to the cellular theory of cancer. In return, since cancer pathology was defined as a basic disorder of the cell, affecting the mechanisms which control its reproduction, the study of cancer became a major scientific challenge. At the same time, although the disease was then considered incurable, the first therapeutic successes were achieved — directly related to the 'revolution' in surgical practices following the introduction of antisepsis and asepsis. Excision techniques for malignant tumors were first codified in the late nineteenth century, and cancer became a field in which a new generation of surgeons could start making a name for themselves. The first figures for 'recoveries' were released without well-defined, established criteria, or any consensus on what life expectancy meant after exeresis. Although these positive results were far from being the rule, they were sufficient to substantiate the notion that cancer could be considered as curable when certain conditions were met; basically if the tumor was surgically removed at an evolutionary stage when it was still locally contained. Hence the basic axiom which supported the cancer-fighting strategy thereafter: cancer is an initially localized disease with later generalization; it is curable if treatment is applied in a timely fashion.

Successes achieved by surgery undermined the dogma of cancer being incurable, while the revolution in physics, with the discovery of X-rays (1895), radioactivity (1896), and radium (1898), provided unexpected therapeutic tools which proved useful against cancer. This time, by a stroke of good fortune, the acute responsiveness of certain skin cancers to X-rays gave credibility to the potential efficacy of 'radiotherapy' despite the rudimentary nature of this technology. Thor Stenbeck, a Swedish physician, published in 1899 the first case of recovery from 'cancroid' skin cancer after treatment with X-rays. That same year, Tage Sjögren confirmed these results. Radiation therapy was supported by its recognized efficacy in dermatology, even though, apart from skin cancers, the results were far from convincing. The complexity of questions raised through the use of X-rays and radium was revealed when attempts were made to extend cancer treatment from superficial to deeper tissues. As a result, a research field dedicated to studying the biological effects of radiation was created.

The revival of scientific, clinical and therapeutic interest in cancer had various forms of institutional expression before the First World War. At the initiation of Professor Bouchard from the Paris Faculty of Medicine, and Professor Leyden from Berlin, an International Union of People against Cancer was created in Berlin. Its objective was to organize international conferences on cancer for physicians, surgeons and experimental researchers. The first of these conferences was held in Heidelberg, Germany, in 1906; the second in Paris in 1910; the third in Brussels in 1913. However, the onset of war put an end to the organization. During the same period, learned societies, often supported by cancer research centers, were created in various countries. Germany was first, with the Deutsches Komitee für Krebsforschung in 1900, and later with privately funded research institutes in Berlin (associated with Leyden's Charity Hospital medical clinic), Heidelberg (run by Professor Czerny) and Frankfurt (at Professor Ehrlich's Experimental Pathology Institute). The UK followed, with the Cancer Investigation Committee at the Middlesex Hospital and later, in 1902, with the Imperial Cancer Research Fund whose initial objective was to finance the creation of a London-based research laboratory headed by Dr. Basford. Then came Hungary (Cancer Study Committee in Budapest), France (Association Française pour l'Étude du Cancer, 1906), the United States (the Roswell Park Research Institute and the American Association of Cancer Research, 1907), Japan (Japanese Foundation for Cancer Research, 1908), Ukraine (the Kiev Cancer Society, 1908), Sweden (the Swedish Cancer Society, 1910) and the Netherlands (the Netherlands Cancer Institute, 1913).

From the 1890s onwards, facilities for cancer patients were being created in many countries. At least three new hospitals were set up in the UK (Manchester in 1892, Bradford and Glasgow in 1893), one in Ireland (in Cork); several specialized departments or hospitals in Germany (in Berlin, Heidelberg, Hanover, Munster, Bremen, Munich and Ludgwigsburg) and in the US (General Memorial Hospital for the Treatment of Cancer in New York, Oncological Hospital in Philadelphia and Hospital for Cancer and Skin Diseases in Saint Louis); one hospital in Moscow (1903); one center in Stockholm (the Radium Hemmet, 1911); and one center in the Netherlands (Netherlands Cancer Institute, 1913). These developments mostly involved collaboration between surgeons and radiologists/ radiotherapists. In France, although the process of medical specialization was already quite advanced, no cancer facility was created before the First World War, due to a lack of collaboration between surgeons and radiotherapists. Cooperation was hindered by the institutional and social gap separating hospital clinicians from physicians working in laboratory disciplines, as most radiotherapists originally were. This obstacle was removed only by the large-scale experience gained from multidisciplinary practices imposed by war surgery during the First World War.

The most meaningful indication of the change in representation of cancer is indisputably the emergence of non-profit making organizations whose primary target was to fight the disease on both scientific and social fronts. Cancer was labeled as a national enemy against which social forces would be mobilized, and consequently these institutions played a major role in the social construction of cancer as a 'curse.' The American Association for the Control of Cancer (created in 1913) and the Ligue Franco-Anglo-Américaine de Lutte contre le Cancer (created in 1918) were the first organizations of this type to be founded. They multiplied during the inter-war years and united in 1934 to form the International Union Against Cancer. Thirty-four countries were represented, and conferences were regularly held. Another indication of the international recognition of the social and political magnitude of the disease was the creation in 1925 of a Cancer Commission within the League of Nations. This Commission took the initiative to draw up comparative tables on cancer mortality in each country, and established the basis for evaluative approaches to therapeutic strategies used in specific localizations of cancer, (*eg.*, cervical cancer). On the eve of World War Two, cancer was well-established as a social curse alongside, competing with, and about to replace tuberculosis and syphilis.

The organized fight against cancer originated from these specialized scientific societies and research or treatment centers. It reflected the convergence of the medical profession's various interests in cancer, a convergence which helped to relate the social dimension of the disease (as evident from statistical surveys objectifying its impact on the population) and the relevant scientific and therapeutic challenges. But, as long as the fight remained the concern of medical professionals only, it could not find an effective form of realization outside the medical field. This situation changed when ties were established between cancer 'specialists' and other groups of agents from what we will call, following Pierre Bourdieu, "the "field of power."[3] These ties were formalized through the creation of cancer-fighting organizations as separate from scientific societies. While little research has been carried out on the sociology of these organizations at a national level, the available data point to local specificities. The American Society for the Control of Cancer, for instance, was initially based on an alliance between professional associations of doctors, with surgeons playing a leading role, along with representatives of insurance companies. In the second phase the Association created a 'Women's Field Army.' Trained by physicians, these non-professional female volunteers were given the responsibility of intensifying nationwide propaganda and public education. Here the 'cancer fight' had a close relationship with American feminist, literary, sports and religious groups (*eg.*, General Federation of Women's Club, Chicago Women's Club, Nebraska Women's Club, National Women's Christian Temperance Union, National Council of Jewish Women). In France, the Ligue contre le Cancer was created within the context of the First World War, from the social network of the Secrétariat d'état au service de santé des Armées. The association integrated a wide variety of social components, which the war effort and military alliances had already forced to collaborate on health issues. Unlike the American Society for the Control of Cancer, the French Ligue's membership did not include *ex officio* representatives from professional associations of doctors, and the relative weight of the radiation specialists was much greater. Claudius Regaud, the manager of the biological section at Institut du Radium and Fondation Curie, played a pivotal role in this organization. Justin Godart, the president of the organization, a member of the French Parliament and several times Minister of Health Affairs during the inter-war period, made Regaud's positions known to the government. This personal involvement of a number of politicians and of several wives of Ministers and Prime Ministers was another difference from the

American association. Deploying intense international efforts, the French Ligue was used as a model in creating cancer-fighting organizations in several other European countries (Poland, Spain, Portugal and Belgium) and in South America (Argentine, Uruguay).

The involvement of representatives from the ruling classes was a critical move. The purpose of their mobilization was to ensure that cancer was regarded as a new public health concern, and integrated into the political and philanthropic culture, along with tuberculosis, syphilis and alcoholism. However, instead of duplicating the organizational and interventional models implemented against other social problems, the fight against cancer drew its strength and energy from its specific features. At a time when major scourges were perceived as being caused by poverty, cancer was the first 'social danger' indiscriminately affecting the whole population: it threatened the upper and middle, as well as the lower classes. In these conditions, philanthropic involvement could not be limited to its 'usual' social targets but had to control the disease in the very social classes the involvement stemmed from.

While controlling infectious pathologies and alcoholism was first and foremost a matter of prophylaxis and prevention, controlling cancer was based on finding therapies. Cancer policy was thus the first public health policy exclusively based on obtaining recovery: no prevention based policy was in sight. Hence the two strategic orientations which defined it as unique. The first one, dubbed 'scientific,' aimed at advancing therapies and creating the material and institutional conditions to allow adequate treatment for patients. The second one, *ie.*, the social fight against cancer, aimed at creating conditions favoring early diagnosis since, in order to be curable, cancer had to be localized in its development; a spreading, or worse, metastasized tumor was beyond treatment. Attached to these two main orientations were the issues of 'quackery', of the organization of the work between specialized doctors and general practitioners and of the care given to incurable patients.

## THE 'SCIENTIFIC' FIGHT AGAINST CANCER

Since therapeutical efficacy was the prerequisite for 'controlling' cancer, the development of scientific and technological research became a central concern for anti-cancer organizations and an important issue for governments. This research was multilayered: examining the causes and mechanisms of the pathogeny, studying the biological impact of radiation, developing therapeutic protocols in clinical research and designing more powerful roentgen and radium therapy devices. The growing interest in cancer among the biological sciences went hand in hand with their development and disciplinary differentiation. The result was a great diversity of approaches, with each discipline establishing a different 'cancer object,' based on its own paradigms. Underlying the construction of these various cancers (immunological, endocrinological, virological, genetic cancer, *etc.*), were *ad hoc* theories, since this dynamic was fed partly by the fact that studying cancer was turning out to be a valuable source of private and public funding.

One aim of cancer research during the inter-war years was to attract the attention of governments as well as encouraging more donations from patrons. Governments tended to intervene by financing research projects and/or supporting the creation of institutes with laboratories from several disciplines. The diverse ways in which governments intervened depended on the various national contexts. In the UK for instance, government intervention was implemented through the Medical Research Council, an organization founded before the First World War to support the development of the various fields of medical research. In 1937, the United States Congress voted to create an organization dedicated to cancer research, the National Cancer Institute, which had its own laboratories but also funded outside research. In France, the role played by the poorly funded Fond National pour la Recherche Scientifique remained nominal, but government involvement was realized through significant efforts to help cancer research. The Institut du Cancer, opened in 1935, associated with the Paris Faculty of Medicine and the Villejuif Cancer Center, appears to be the first major organization in biomedical research to be created by the French government. But, as important and meaningful as the development of research on etiology and pathogeny may have been, its importance remained limited compared to the influence of radiation medicine during the inter-war years. In the early 1920s, radiotherapy treatment techniques saw various breakthroughs, increasing their efficiency. Radiumpuncture was improved through the improved design of needles containing radium, which allowed the irradiation source to be introduced into tumoral tissues (while filtering out unwanted radiation and only allowing gamma rays to pass). Penetrating roentgen therapy, the principle of which was invented by Perthes in 1903, became possible only because industrialists began to manufacture machines capable of generating continuous currents of high voltage. Because the credibility of the fight against cancer depended on treatment efficacy, equipping hospitals with radium and penetrating roentgen therapy devices became crucial.

In the hospital world, where treatment costs were normally only a small fraction of the expenses for accommodation and nursing staff, the funding needed to equip a cancer department or center raised a new and drastic problem. The outrageous market prices for radium and the cost of a penetrating roentgen therapy device allowed only a limited number of patients to be treated. In addition, equipment maintenance and repair required a physics laboratory, run by technically qualified personnel. This 'business' aspect raised various issues. Private hospitals could pass these investment costs to their 'paying' patients, but this would result in selection, since treatment would be unaffordable to many middle and lower-class patients. For public hospitals caring for lower-class patients, the problem was acutely political. Acknowledging cancer as a social problem meant that lower-class patients, who were in the majority, could not be excluded from treatment. Since local and/or national authorities were directly responsible for these people's access to hospitals, a nationwide network of specialized facilities was established to answer to their needs, based on the principle of social profitability. Investing in appropriate treatment for destitute cancer patients was justified by calculating the savings made by preserving the lives of these individuals, whose social value was still significant in terms of industrial, business or home productivity. The objective was therefore to treat only those destitute cancer patients who had a chance of recovery. There was no room for incurable patients in these specialized facilities.

Yet, despite these limitations, the number of cancer facilities grew significantly. In the early thirties, there were twelve cancer hospitals and sixty-eight general hospitals with a cancer department (equipped with specific instrumentation) in the US, eighteen hospitals or approved cancer centers in the UK, six public cancer departments, the Fondation Curie and the Villejuif center in Paris, and thirteen government approved centers in the French Provinces. The target of cancer-fighting policies, as developed in the early twenties, was to cover a country's needs gradually, in terms of specialized facilities — their type depending on the currently prevailing, which specified centers with an average capacity of eg one hundred beds, equipped with three to four penetrating roentgen therapy stations stocked up and which stocked up to one or two grams of radium, divided up in minute quantities for Radiumpuncture. Financial investment from the government was gradual, especially in terms of radium allocation to centers; the allocation grew yearly, and was occasionally supplemented at a given center by donations in kind from a local patron. But this long-term political strategy of capital spending based on the advancement of radiotherapy techniques in the early twenties implied that these techniques were stable. The innovative development of the 'telecurietherapy,' or teleradiumtherapy, at the Paris-based Fondation Curie in 1925, changed the problem.

This new technique, based on radium's properties for remote irradiation, used a radium 'bomb' containing between four and five grams of radioactive product, *ie.*, one unit contained the equivalent of more than a third of the radium allocation for all the recently established cancer centers in France. Over the years following the introduction of 'telecurietherapy,' X-ray therapy was in turn similarly transformed with the invention in the United States of 'highly penetrating radiotherapy.' This technique used ultra-high voltage power generators (800,000 volts) and radiotherapy tubes capable of generating over 600,000 volts. The equipment (very large tubes weighing up to two tons) required complex facilities in special premises (an elevator to move the tube or a mobile floor to move patients). In the thirties, the 'big medicine' era started. It generated new conditions for practising medicine, in many aspects contradicting the current organization of health systems. While equipping cancer centers had raised new problems from the outset, the radium 'bomb' and highly penetrating radiotherapy gave this issue new scope as they questioned government, private medicine and philanthropy concerning their capacity to financially support the modernization of cancer research and treatment, during a period marked by an acute economic crisis.

Responses varied a great deal from one country to another. In France, the proximity of the issues raised by these new therapies had an obvious impact on governmental policy. The invention of 'telecurietherapy' owed nothing to public funding and everything to the *Fondation Curie.* Claudius Regaud grasped the importance of this, and the implications of this technical innovation. He was able to convince the Cancer commission to adopt a selective policy. The French government decided to focus its investment efforts on a very limited number of centers and to equip them with state-of-the-art machinery, albeit at the expense of major regional disparities. The British government was led to implement a different policy as the level of institutionalization of basic research was much higher than in France. The MRC's Radiology Committee, which was in charge of coordinating and financing radiotherapy research, was confronted with a conflict between research laboratories and hospitals as to how radium therapy investigations should be conducted. The creation of the Radium Trust, from a donation by King George V, temporarily put an end to this conflict because the Trust's assigned task was to regulate radium allocation to medical centers. In the US, the fact that surgeons dominated both hospitals and the American Society for the Control of Cancer prevented radiotherapy from becoming more than a mere supplement to surgery. In the mid-thirties, only the Chicago Mercy Hospital had a giant tube for highly penetrating radiotherapy, capable of generating 800,000 volts and built by General Electric. It was only after the National Cancer Institute was created that a large amount of money was invested in radium 'bombs' and in financing research on the cyclotron, the new post-war stage into modernizing radiotherapy.

While radiotherapy capital spending was a problem for governments, it was even more difficult for private medicine institutions to overcome this obstacle. These institutions could not pass on this technological progress to their customers nor, therefore, offer 'leading edge' treatments. And, in the few instances where this was possible, the cost to the patient was astronomical. This situation raised the issue of the relationship between public and private medicine and led, notably in France, to a questioning of the existing balance. The principle of non-competition between public hospitals (reserved for the destitute) and private medicine (which had a monopoly on 'paying' customers) proved more and more difficult to comply with, since it prevented the middle and upper classes from having access to the most modern and efficient therapies. Through its very development process, the scientific fight against cancer made it necessary to review the position of public hospitals within the health system, so that they could be open to all classes.

While the growing efficacy of treatment was a pillar of the cancer fight, and legitimized governmental involvement in the building of high-tech centers, the growing specialization of therapeutic practices favored an increased division of medical work. When, in order to be properly applied, treatments started to call for increasingly specialized expertise, cancer specialists — surgeons and radiotherapists — vigorously pleaded for an organized division of labor. The idea was to assign the role of 'diagnoser/referrer' to 'general' practitioners (and, more generally, to all doctors without specialized expertise in cancer therapy). Hence a dual-purpose intervention occurred within the medical profession, supported by cancer-fighting organizations: to train 'ordinary' practitioners in early cancer screening — since their lack of training was dangerously apparent — and to convince them to delegate to others their responsibility for treating patients. The propaganda was organized by medical authorities and channeled to the population through the anti-cancer organizations. It stressed the lethal danger for patients of improperly conducted therapies — radium-based treatments especially — and treatments which did not meet the scientific criteria accepted by specialists. The problem was difficult to resolve due to popular acclaim for radium, seen as a 'magic bullet.' Since it was not possible to legally prevent cancer patients from being treated by non-specialists, the tactic was to present those doctors involved as dishonest practitioners and charlatans, or even push victims and their families to file complaints in court against them. In France, the Ligue contre le Cancer denounced these practitioners in campaigns, presenting them as more dangerous than mere 'quack' doctors, and joined the chorus demanding the creation of a national Medical Association to regulate and control medical practice. But that warnings against medical charlatanism were repeated throughout the inter-war period demonstrates how difficult it was for 'official' oncology to impose its views.

## THE CAMPAIGNS FOR EARLY DIAGNOSIS AND THE INVENTION OF THE SENTRY PATIENT

"It may be said that an accessible cancer, diagnosed right at the start, is a disease which medicine can most certainly cure."[4] The belief that therapies were increasingly efficient gave the cancer propaganda from the twenties a resolutely optimistic tone. It was later tempered by the awareness of a significant obstacle: for most of the patients admitted for treatment, the cancer was too advanced for therapy to be efficient. Private practitioners were partly responsible for this situation, having a poor knowledge of cancer's clinical signs in its early stage of development. Whilst training doctors was a necessary condition for establishing early diagnosis, it was far from sufficient since patients still had to seek a consultation in time. "We are confronted with the paradoxical situation where the general population is the first and foremost guardian of its own safety and where it must learn to be concerned by signs which are neither painful nor typical nor even worrisome,"[5] explained the Secretary of the Ligue Française contre le Cancer. From a social point of view, the implementation of early cancer diagnosis therefore set itself an extremely far-reaching objective. It was to ensure through educational propaganda, that each individual (as a potential cancer patient) completely changed the way he/she perceived his/her own body, in order to acquire the ability to discriminate as 'signs,' symptoms previously considered innocuous, and to become capable of interpreting them as an indication or non-indication of incipient cancer, *ie.*, a threat to his/her life. This dramatization of cancer as a deceitful, 'insidious,' 'perverse' disease supported demands for actively providing medical care to the population. The dramatization of body symptoms which were previously perceived as harmless was part of the growing process of controlling individuals though medical knowledge — urging people to consult a doctor is only a secondary component. Designed to educate through salutary fear, the propaganda for early screening aimed to medicalize our relationships to our own bodies and to turn these bodies into 'sentry patients.' Potential patients had to be 'front-line' agents in the diagnostic process.

This medicalization was deeply rooted in the long philosophical tradition of 'self-care' which demanded from 'men of means' that they control their urges, and avoid all excesses. But the 'self-doctor' ideal referred to a prescientific conception of medicine preceding the radical transformation analyzed by Michel Foucault in *Naissance de la clinique.* By contrast the 'sentry patient' is a subject of modern medicine. This potential cancer patient is to act as a medical auxiliary with minimal qualification. His/her task is to exercise a certain type of clinical expertise, gained through educational propaganda, in a specific field (his/her own body) while respecting organizational and hierarchical rules. When identifying suspect signs, he/she is to consult a doctor whose own responsibility is to formulate a diagnosis and, in turn, refer the patient to a specialist. Based on the intrinsically human ability to distance one's self from one's body, this duty required the individual to be responsible for monitoring his health, and imposed a scientific self-objectification, *ie.*, the capacity to consider one's body non-subjectively for it to become a clinically decipherable object.

This new form of medicalization is part of the social dynamic analyzed by Norbert Elias as the "civilizing process."[6] Here, the civilizing pressure was exercised by institutions involved in the campaign for early screening, their primary targets being the 'milieu' of their own volunteers, the upper and middle classes. Only in a second phase, by using social workers, the mainstream press, and the generalization of radio broadcasting, was educational action extended to the lower classes. These campaigns were first orchestrated in 1935 by the *Union Internationale de Lutte contre le Cancer* and included organizing International Cancer Weeks. Their efficiency was primarily symbolic since they managed to substantiate the illusion that the population was made up of individuals who were capable of monitoring their bodies and turning them into clinical objects. As part of this illusion, clinical practice exercises were reduced to knowledge-related issues (the early signs of cancer) and know-how issues (*eg.*, breast self-palpation), and the social and emotional distance between doctors and patients — the primary condition for objectification — was simply ignored. It may be said that, in a context marked by the impossibility of implementing a mass screening strategy, cancer-fighting policies could develop only by this social illusion, which was shared by all agents involved in implementing these policies. It did not matter therefore that the actual impact of the campaigns for early diagnosis was very limited (it started being criticized in the fifties). The important thing was that this impact made the fight against cancer credible. While the fear of cancer partly explains why 'potential patients' subscribed to this illusion, the massive manifestations of 'cancerphobia' noted by doctors following action-weeks reflected the price to be paid for this illusion. According to doctors who complained about this behavior, which was overhastily described as 'irrational,' the sentry patient was a poor medical auxiliary who, more often that not, consulted a physician out of anxiety about symptoms unrelated to signs of early cancer.

## THE PROBLEM OF CANCER'S MISFITS: FROM THE NOTION OF INCURABILITY TO THE IDEA OF REMISSION

In terms of the two major axes of cancer policies — the scientific fight against cancer and the campaigns for early diagnosis — support for 'incurable' cancer patients appeared to be a secondary concern, leading to no special social policy, despite the efforts of the NGO movements. The report on medical and social aid to cancer patients presented to the second conference of the Union Internationale contre le Cancer in 1936 blamed this failure on governments as well as medical institutions. Apart from a minority of patients who were wealthy enough to be able to afford treatment by a doctor or private clinic, the vast majority of 'incurable' patients were abandoned. No plans were made for them and hospitals refused to accept them, or got rid of them based on the argument that these people would take up the beds of curable patients. Facilities for 'chronic' patients often opposed the presence of the incurable, arguing that it was not their responsibility to treat these people due to the evolutive nature of their pathologies, and because their facilities were not suitably equipped. A few hospital department heads, out of charity, set up beds or a room to accommodate these patients. In effect only charitable organizations offered them any institutional solution, but these organizations were scarce, and the number of beds available was grossly insufficient. Cancer organizations, in charge of the social monitoring of patients, and responsible for the institutional hospitalization of destitute incurable patients, were moved by the situation. Eventually, confronted with indifference from doctors and public services, they became indignant and started campaigning for change. But by the start of the Second World War, attempts at raising public awareness about the unfairness to incurable patients had had little success in terms of practical solutions.

Only after the war, when the Nazis treatment of incurable patients was exposed, was the 'incurability' issue politically addressed again as a general category of social and medical classification (this category included the mentally ill or handicapped, the chronically ill and people with cancer). Although they were unsuccessful, campaigns to muster medical support for incurable cancer patients did have some impact. On the one hand, a reformistic project was formalized, redefining the responsibilities of hospitals by giving them a central role in implementing palliative therapies. This project resulted from questioning the 'curable vs. incurable patient' dichotomy, and examining how it was used by medical and governmental authorities to exclude incurable cancer patients from treatment institutions. A so-called 'incurable' cancer is not essentially a specific disease, it is simply a pathology with irreversible lesions. Its progressive and unpredictable nature manifests itself through diverse disorders, which are common to many other pathologies and about which medicine can and should always do something. Patients suffering from cancer are therefore perfectly entitled to hospital treatment. On the other hand — and the report to the *Union Internationale contre le Cancer*[7] insisted on this point — the 'curable vs. incurable patient' dichotomy was created at a time when cancer therapies were still mostly surgical treatments and when 'curable' actually meant 'operable.' Now, because of the tremendous progress in radiotherapy techniques, the 'local-stage cancer → operable tumor → curable patient vs. spreading cancer → inoperable tumor → incurable patient' opposition system no longer reflected the reality, which had become much more complex. The advances in radiotherapy, coupled with those in surgery, not only pushed the limits of therapeutic efficacy, but also created new situations where patients, without permanently recovering from cancer, still saw their lives prolonged for variable periods of time.

While the support for 'incurable' patients did not change much during the inter-war years, an evolution in outlooks began to replace previous binary thought patterns with a new, gradual vision. As the notion of remission developed and emphasized the great number of intermediate stages between 'curable' and 'incurable' cases, therapeutic breakthroughs made it necessary to refine the classification system of cancer evolution phases. The distinction between localized and generalized cancer was no longer operative when it came to assessing new treatments and establishing prognoses. It was replaced by a model giving each type of cancer a series of stages, each reflecting the degree of regional extension of the tumor, ganglionic invasiveness and the existence or non-existence of metastases. This model led to the first international cancer nomenclature after World War Two. Since this type of therapeutic assessment revealed variable survival rates for a given treatment — rates for a given treatment depending on the 'stages,' — the conditions were there for a complex, problematic vision for 'chances' of recovery.

## CANCER AFTER WORLD WAR TWO

Post-war anti-cancer policies built on those of the inter-war period. With cyclotrons, the perfecting of chemotherapy, the invention of immunotherapy, and the use of more sophisticated and expensive molecules, oncology was established as a paradigm of 'Big Biomedicine.' Cancer research followed in these footsteps. First, in the thirties, temples to worship 'Scientific Medicine' were erected — the anti-cancer centers with their 'marvelous' radium and X-rays machines — as celebrated grounds for hope. Forty years later, their position was occupied by the cancer research laboratories. Nevertheless, despite advances, the notion of therapeutic treatment was showing limitations, and cancer was still perceived as an unrivaled scourge in the field of public health. Hope was displaced, and turned to focus on solving the mystery of cancerization, as the best way to find a cure. The development of research, however basic, became a popular concern and the hunt for private funding elicited support from large sections of the population, in all developed countries. Anti-cancer associations assumed the mantle of fund-raisers, collecting enough money to have the authority to join scientists and public authorities in defining research policy orientations and priorities.

However, a succession of disappointing results challenged the belief that the enigma of cancer could be solved as a matter of investment. Unraveling the mysteries of cancer could not be politically planned, as if arranging the conquest of the moon. President Richard Nixon's crusade was a failure, in as much as finding a cure for cancer was the purpose. But the National Cancer Act of 1971 allowed for tremendous development in large sectors of biological research, primarily in financing their implication in cancer programs, such as the virus and cancer program. Through cancer research, biomedical sciences developed and grew in stature, based on the conglomeration of networks, tying together medical wards, research laboratories, philanthropic associations and different industrialist groups. The search for the 'magic bullet' now seems a utopia belonging to the past, and it has become a matter of consensus that each kind of cancer is specific and needs to be treated specifically. Advances in therapeutics in recent decades are real, but are still ineffective when applied to certain cancers or situations — spectacular results in the case of child acute lymphoblastic leukemia, for instance, but poor when attempting to combat lung cancers. The result for most cancers is an improved utilization of drugs (new drugs and/or new combinations of drugs). This improvement is in many cases organized on an international scale — the strategies of treatment being decided, applied and evaluated by networks of clinical wards belonging to different countries (such networks giving the opportunity to gather sufficient patients to constitute an adequate sample for clinical trials).

The internationalization of the division of medical work in the struggle against cancer is a reality in progress. But another reality is the increasing role played by patients in this same division of labor. By introducing the sentry patient, the campaign for early diagnosis inaugurated a series of current issues raised by patients in their role as medical auxiliaries. With different changes affecting the efficiency of treatments, first with radiotherapy, then with chemotherapy, cancer patients are more involved in the daily organization of their therapeutical strategy, mainly because this strategy has planned large sequences of medical activities outside hospital, ie., far from the oncologist's glance. Once he/she has been diagnosed, the patient is then (more or less) educated to become an accomplished assistant in the medical follow up. This new patient's position is a phenomenon characteristic of contemporary medicine, and a result of the gain in life-expectancy related to progress in palliative treatments. In the case of cancer patients, such a position is illustrated through the generalization of the concept of remission to almost all the situations, from cases near to recovery (but can recovery ever become a certitude?) to remission following a relapse (and proceeding another one?). The inclusion in the team work, with its contradictions (the unskilled assistant is in the meantime a patient whose life is in danger) and the reconceptualization of his/her life as someone living in the suspended time of remission, are the two major structuring dimensions of the patients' daily experience. With them come questions about doctors'/patients' power relationships, and about the right to choose a time for dying. With that too, comes a rise in cancer self-help patients' organizations.

The very novelty in the history of post-World War Two cancer is perhaps the epidemiological dimension of the disease. The problem of carcinogens is an old story, since Percival Pott's identification of scrotal cancer among chimneysweeps in 1775. Coal distillates, petroleum products, and then X-rays were identified as capable of causing cancer under certain conditions. By the middle of the twentieth century, a list of hundreds of chemical carcinogens had been established. But in spite of this evidence the prophylactic perspective was still absent from anti-cancer policies, mainly because a complex coalition of interests refused to consider that industrial carcinogenic waste posed a real danger to the population's health. The turning point was the epidemiological demonstration that smoking tobacco correlated with lung cancer and was responsible for its expanding incidence. As cancer epidemiology developed, the number of specific practices accused of causing cancer increased. The problems of occupational and pollution related cancers turned into an important debate, resulting in controversial discussions, with various national responses, in terms of methods to protect the exposed population. This differing epidemiological evidence has social consequences. The range of daily behaviors deemed to be self-controlled (or legally prohibited under certain conditions, like smoking) increased. Workers' protection measures were increased, and ecological concerns were developed. Finally, the attitude that life is a risky game arose, whereby a lot of (pleasant) habits and behaviors must be avoided, or strictly kept under control due to their 'carcinogenic' nature; but, however vigilant, one can still become the victim of the uncontrolled 'cancerogenous' society's practices.

## REFERENCES

1. J.T. Patterson, *The Dread Disease*. (Cambridge, MA: Harvard University Press, 1987).
2. L.V. Thomas, 'Mort découverte, mort escamotée,' in *La mort aujourd'hui*. (Marseille: Rivages, 1982).
3. P. Bourdieu and M. Saint-Martin, 'Le champ des grandes Écoles et le champ du pouvoir,' *Actes de la recherche en sciences sociales* (1987), **69**: 250.
4. C. Regaud, 'Le role du medecin sans specialité dans le diagnostic du cancer,' *La Lutte contre le cancer*, 1925, **10**: 112.

5.    R. Le Bret, 'Rapport devant l'Assemblée générale du 7 Avril 1927,' *La Lutte contre le cancer* 1927, **16**: 220.
6.    Norbert Elias, *The Civilizing Process: The History of Manners*. (Oxford: Blackwell, 1978).
7.    R. Le Bret, 'L'aide médico-sociale aux incurables, Rapport présenté au Congrès international de lutte scientifique et sociale contre le cancer, Bruxelles, Septembre 1936,' *La Lutte contre le cancer* (1937), **55**: 20–30.

## FURTHER READING

Aiach, P., 'Peurs et images de la maladie: l'opposition cancer/maladies cardiaques,' *Cancer Bulletin* (1980), **67(2)**: 183–190.

Austoker, J., *A History of Imperial Cancer Research Fund, 1902–1980*. (Oxford: Oxford University Press, 1988).

Brunning, D.A. and Dukes, C.E., 'The origin and early history of the institute of cancer research of the Royal Cancer Hospital,' *Proceedings of the Royal Society of Medicine* (1965), **58**: 33–36.

Cantor, D., 'The MRC's support for experimental radiology during the interwar years,' in J. Austoker and L. Bryder (eds), *Historical Perspectives of the Role of MRC*. (Oxford: Oxford University Press, 1989), pp. 181–204.

Darmon, P., *Les cellules folles: L'homme face au cancer, de l'antiquité à nos jours*. (Paris: Plon, 1993).

Foucault, Michel, 'Technologies of the self,' in P.H. Hutton, H. Gutman and L.M. Martin, *Technologies of the Self. A Seminar with Michel Foucault*. (Amherst: The University of Massachusetts Press, 1988), pp.16–49.

Foucault, Michel, *Naissance de la clinique*. (Paris: PUF, 1963).

Gaudillière, J.P., 'NCI and the spreading genes: About the production of mice, viruses and cancer,' in E. Mendelsohn (ed.), *Human Genetics*. (Dordrecht: Kluwer, 1993).

Löwy, I., *Between Bench and Bedside*. (Cambridge Massachusetts, London: Harvard University Press, 1996).

Pickstone, J.V., *Medicine and Industrial Society*. (Manchester: Manchester University Press, 1985).

Pinell, P., 'How do cancer patients express their points of view,' *Sociology of Health and Illness* (1987), **9(1)**: 244.

Pinell, P., 'Cancer policy and the health system in France: 'Big Medicine' challenges the conception and organization of medical practice,' *Social History of Medicine* (1991), **4(1)**: 75–101.

Pinell, P., *Naissance d'un fléau*. (Paris: Éditions Métailié, 1992).

Rettig, R.A., *Cancer Crusade: The Story of the National Cancer Act of 1971*. (Princeton, NJ: Princeton University Press, 1977).

Schlanger, J., *Les métaphores de l'organisme*. (Paris: Vrin, 1971).

Waro, N., 'A Pilgrim's Progress,' *Cancer Research* (1974), **34**: 1667–1674.

Yarmechuk, William A., 'The origins of the National Cancer Institute,' *Journal of the NCI* (1977), **59**: 551–558.

CHAPTER 44

# AIDS and Patient-Support Groups

VIRGINIA BERRIDGE

## AN HEROIC STORY?

By comparison with diseases such as cancer and TB which are also represented in this volume, AIDS is still relatively new in its impact on health policy and welfare. But the relative newness of the syndrome has not prevented the emergence of what I have termed the 'official history' of AIDS.[1] By the term 'official history,' I mean that representations of 'the AIDS story' have become formalized. This 'formal story' always includes the initial role of the CDSC in Atlanta in tracing the outbreak, the role of Gay Men's Health Crisis (GMHC) in New York, the Gallo/Montagnier controversy over the virus, together with a selection of other developments. Key actors have taken a role in the formalization of the AIDS history, and leading participants have 'told their story' in public, often several times over; so creating an 'official record' which is often significantly different from the picture revealed by non-oral sources. This process of formalization has also been aided by the high profile of AIDS in the media, where 'instant history' and TV documentaries have been a feature from quite early on. It can also be related to the high policy profile of AIDS and its controversial nature; key participants wanted their versions of history on the record.[2]

Much of this 'formal history' has been structured by an agenda of 'conspiracy and delay,' round the argument that governments were slow to respond to AIDS primarily because it was a syndrome which affected gay men and did not appear to impact on the population at large. Homophobia, it is argued, dictated policy responses. Such interpretations have an element of truth, but they are by no means the whole story. Government responses were underpinned by a whole host of other operative factors. 'Government as villain' history is a tempting and easy framework; but it cannot adequately represent the complex interactions which in reality go to make policy.

Where governments were villains, gay men were heroes. The heroic story goes roughly as follows. Government inaction and delay was met by an upsurge of voluntary activity in a number of different countries. Gay men formed organizations, set up support networks and organized the funding of research to impact on policy, to stir a more effective response. Subsequently, gay input focused specifically on treatment and trials and, in countries at the cutting edge of such research, gay men obtained an oversight and an input into the conduct of both which was quite unprecedented and perhaps a model for 'consumer involvement' in other health conditions and diseases. 'AIDS today, breast cancer tomorrow' runs the argument.

Such is the heroic history of the patient support group for AIDS. What is my attitude to it in this chapter, which focusses on experiences of AIDS? Like most historians, I am wary of stories written in terms of 'inevitable progress' and of moral absolutes; they invite questioning and assessment. But it is not my purpose to denigrate. The experience of AIDS on individuals has been conveyed eloquently elsewhere.[3] This chapter will focus on the experience of organization building, of the initial directions and of change in the groups that responded to AIDS. It will critically assess the early history of gay voluntarism and its cross-national variation; focussing on the impact on AIDS policy, and especially on research and treatment policies. But voluntarism was not set in stone. Time moved on; different organizations and relationships emerged and initial responses were modified. I go on to discuss the changing history of gay voluntarism.

But there are also other experiences and histories which do not figure at all in the 'official' accounts. Here the chapter will take account of voluntarism in other affected groups — hemophiliacs, women, drug users. Different 'risk' locations are important. So, too, are geographic differences, especially those between First and Third World countries. The history of AIDS and support groups has been very different in developing countries; that history, which has barely been written, must also be included.

## GAY SELF-HELP IN THE 1980S: ORIGINS

The early history of the gay response has been described in a number of different countries. In the United States, what Fox, Day and Klein have called "the crisis of authority in health affairs in the early 1980s" and the concern about AIDS among gay men, who were often politically sophisticated, permitted new players to have influence on health policy.[4] The construction of this influence was voluntaristic and self-helping. The formation of GMHC in New York in the early 1980s encapsulates this early self-help ethos. Small groups of gay men met in writer Larry Kramer's apartment to hear a doctor talking about a disease spreading like an epidemic among gay men in New York City. Funds were collected for research on 'gay cancer.' A few months later, a smaller number of men met again to continue the fund raising on a regular basis, with the formal title of Gay Men's Health Crisis.[5] They worked on a number of fronts — pushing for action from the city politicians, detailing gaps in service provision, providing advice through a hotline and a variety of counseling and direct services to persons affected with AIDS. By the end of the 1980s, GMHC had recruited over 8,000 volunteers, working with over 9,000 clients, serving up to one third of people with AIDS living in New York City.[6]

Prior to the advent of AIDS, the political influence of gay men in New York City had not been impressive. But in San Francisco gay men were the most important voting bloc in the city and held considerable power within city government as a result of gay immigration in the 1970s.[7] Two in five adult males were openly gay, which strongly conditioned the city's response to AIDS. The closing of the gay bath houses as a public health measure was vigorously resisted as homophobic and a denial of the advances of gay liberation. But San Francisco also developed its own network of services; the community care program in the city organized by the Shanti Project later became a model for other countries, not least Britain, looking for flexible and lower cost means of dealing with the syndrome. These developments arose from a combination of the political power of the gay lobby and several years of budgetary surplus.

In Britain, the gay response looked in some respects to this American model. The early days were a period of 'unambiguous voluntarism,' where, despite the gloomy and threatening nature of the new syndrome, there was also an intense interest and excitement as the following quotation from a volunteer indicates:

> Everyone was in constant communication, it was mad, it was hectic … fund raising, visiting, a little bit of social life … Everything was HIV and AIDS, your whole life was taken over. All that incredible energy, just like gay lib and we were all contributing and feeding off it.[8]

In London, the gay response grew out of a gay self-help group established in the 1970s, the Gay and Lesbian Switchboard. Switchboard organized the first public conference in the UK on AIDS in May 1983, opening up a special helpline after a BBC Horizon program, 'Killer in the Village,' was broadcast that April. The Horizon program and the May conference also led to the refounding of the Terrence Higgins Trust (THT), which was to become the leading AIDS voluntary sector organization. The Trust had its origins in an earlier organization founded by the friends of Terry (not Terrence, as later) Higgins, who had died of AIDS in 1982. In this earlier incarnation it had a working-class image, and connections with gay leather and biking clubs; its activity was focused on pub benefits and fundraising for research. Its relaunch in 1983 brought the support of a raft of middle class gay men with political experience, and it refocused its activities on health education, educating the gay community about the danger it faced, but also with a concern to influence government policy. Other national organizations such as Body Positive were established, although on a different basis to that of the Trust. The response was also a strongly local one, with local groups in Cardiff, Bristol, Cambridge, Brighton, Exeter and elsewhere establishing helplines, calling meetings, and trying to obtain funding.[9]

The London based response was influenced by the US in two ways — through the initial notion of AIDS as a disease of American gay men, and also through adaptation of US voluntary responses to the British situation. Gay men later recalled how Mel Rosen, Director of GMHC, spoke at the Conway Hall meeting.

"There's a train coming down the track, and it's heading at you" were his prophetic words. But a similar pattern of gay self organization can also be seen in other countries. In Germany, the AIDS-Hilfe movement joined with Federal health officials in March 1985 to explore possibilities of cooperation over AIDS. The Deutsche AIDS-Hilfe developed as the national coordinating tier, with regional and local variants; the Berlin AIDS-Hilfe represented the most active of the city-focused organisations.[10,11] France did not have a gay movement of the size and strength of that in Germany. Gay self-organisation around AIDS grew in France from the personal initiative of Daniel Defert, the former lover of the philosopher Michel Foucault. But Defert's AIDES organization explicitly rejected a focus on gay men as too marginal and gay social identity, based only on sexual liberty, as too fragile. Its initiative was more wide ranging and political. Initially it focused on improving conditions around acute medical care in hospitals. It rapidly became a pressure group urging voluntary, free test facilities and preventive measures such as publicity for condoms and the open sale of syringes.[12-14] So this was the overall initial model in a number of Western, or Western influenced countries, such as Australia.[15] Such was its power and influence that similar organizations were later developed in Eastern Europe where there was no indigenous gay movement and where countries had only recently acknowledged the presence of AIDS.[16]

## THE WIDER CONTEXTS OF SELF-HELP

Accounts of the origin of these self-help organizations tend to be AIDS specific and to locate their initial activities in the need to respond swiftly to the new syndrome. But there was also a broader context. AIDS organizations grew out of two earlier tendencies: the doctor/patient revolution of the 1960s and '70s; and the decade of organization building round gay health issues in the 1970s. For the 'gay community,' AIDS intersected with the 1960s and '70s agenda of gay liberation and the demedicalization of gay sexuality, and the growing importance of health issues for gay men in the 1970s and '80s.[17] The defeat of the disease model of male homosexuality had, ironically, been paralleled by the rise of health as a matter of concern in gay groups and as a specific concern of self-helping organizations. In the UK, organizations like Switchboard and Gay Friend had developed a clear health dimension to their advisory and counseling activities. Self-help groups, such as Group B for gay carriers of the hepatitis B virus, had come into existence; and gay men were increasingly using Genito-urinary medicine (GUM) clinics for non judgemental primary health care, informed by informal networks of information and advice about which offered the best service. The response to AIDS thus fitted into pre-existing gay medical and health paradigms, drawing on gay 'consumerism' in health. A broader context was the 'rise of the patient' since the 1960s, a movement which the present chapter has no space to discuss in depth.[18] Drawing also on the self-help ethos, it found expression, for example, through the movement to reclaim control of childbirth from high technology and medical control.

Concerns for self-help, lay knowledge and patient input were clearly important as formative influences for the generation to be subsequently most affected by AIDS.

Accounts of the origin of these groups often fail to acknowledge the intense disagreements over strategy and orientation which were part of the initial organizational experience. The tendency has been to draw on a myth of a 'golden past' in particular after the rise of the 're-gaying of AIDS,' which is discussed below. Yet clearly, there were enormous tensions in the early days, in particular between those suspicious of incorporation and those seeing it as the way forward. Such debates related to the earlier history of gay demedicalization in the 1970s.[19]

## THE INITIAL IMPACTS OF SELF-HELP

What was the impact of this voluntary organization and mutual self-help? This must be looked at on a number of different levels and in different national settings. As Blaxter notes, the relationship between private and public responsibility for health and the participatory traditions of different countries, have been crucial issues in varying policy development.[20] In a sense, culture and history have determined responses as much as the objective realities of the syndrome. At one extreme is the US, where public health has been held to be primarily a local and state concern; the strong tradition of voluntary organizations and mutual support groups has been evident in the field of AIDS, as in other areas of health. By contrast, the policies of many European countries have been shaped by the dominant position of the national state in health and social welfare. Voluntary organizations have helped form policy in, for example, the UK, Switzerland and the Netherlands but have had little influence in France or Italy and none until recently in Eastern Europe. But within policy, we need to consider at least three separate areas of influence: overall government policy making and the general direction of policy; policy on treatment and trials; and the development of service provision.

In Britain, activists in the THT initially stressed the threat to the heterosexual population. In so doing, they were part of an emergent 'policy community' which included clinicians, scientists, and civil servants from within the Department of Health. That group reached the pinnacle of its policy influence in the autumn of 1986 when central government adopted a high level crisis response to AIDS which involved greatly increased public funding for research and services, together with a national mass media prevention campaign.[21] In the US, such direct political influence occurred more at the local level, and gay influence was directed in more defensive routes — resisting the closure of the bath houses for example, or the testing of blood donors.[22] In Australia, AIDS Councils, initially gay-focused, and the Australian federation of AIDS Organisations (AFAO) ensured community participation in HIV policy making and opposition to 'medicalization' and the bringing of AIDS policies into the mainstream of public health responses.[23] AIDS was defined as an issue of individual human rights rather than one of infection control as a result of these activities.

As general policies developed in different ways in different nations, self-help groups came to focus more specifically on issues of treatment and trials. Here there were some ironic developments. Gay men had rejected the 'medical model' of homosexuality in the 1970s, and in the early 1980s many in gay circles had rejected warnings about the spread of 'gay cancer' out of a feeling that homosexuality could thereby be 'remedicalized.'[24] Yet the bulk of activist input eventually focused on just these medical issues. Gay men in Western countries spent much effort in becoming 'lay scientists,' in developing expertise about CD4 levels, about T-cell counts and combination therapies. Some gay men accepted the ultimate rationale of the need to 'trial' new drugs, or combinations, but sought to influence and inform how those trials were conducted. In both Britain and the US, activist input became axiomatic on trial committess and other groups considering treatment issues.[25] As Edgar and Rothman point out, gay men argued that "the system of testing should not deny individuals the right to choose their own therapeutic options simply because scientists need controls in order to determine by their own canons of evidence what works best."[26] As a result, the design of the randomized controlled trial, the 'gold standard' of scientific objectivity in the post-war period, was modified. Some trials ended early, most notably the US trial of AZT in early treatment.[27] In Britain and elsewhere, the design of trials was modified to take account of activist objections to 'unethical' placebos. The Alpha trial of DDI, for example, offered an arm of the trial which simply randomized between high and low dose options, rather than high dose, low dose and placebo, as originally intended. Some critics argued that the subsequent results meant little, if anything, in terms of demonstrated efficacy. In the US, such pressure also brought considerable changes in the regulatory structures established by the Food and Drug Administration. The 'pharmacological Calvinism' enshrined so that drugs like thalidomide would be kept off the market went into reverse under the impact of AIDS activism. As Edgar and Rothman wryly note, "large parts of the AIDS advocates' critique of the FDA could have been scripted by the Pharmaceutical Manufacturers Association."

There were other strands to this 'treatment activism.' Some sought to provide alternative information to support patient self-help and autonomy, or mounted direct action in opposition to the pharmaceutical hegemony over the development of new drugs. Yet others became absorbed in rooting out fraud and 'unofficial medicine' in opposition to orthodox science. Some opposed orthodox medicine, other sought to influence it; for all, medicine and treatment was central.

Involvement in trials and treatment brought dilemmas; and so, too, did the involvement of support groups in services. Early AIDS organizations had developed their own networks of services for lack of any others. GMHC in New York and the THT in London were among the best known. But they were soon joined by a raft of others. Groups such as Crusaid, for example, established in 1986 to help, fund, support and care for people with AIDS and HIV, drew on the support of gay men who were not activist in any directly political sense but who had equally developed a sense of community. This was self-help and 'unambiguous voluntarism' at its best. But such developments also had inherent dangers. Larry Kramer, one of the original founders of GMHC, criticised the service delivery ethic for taking resources and energy away from activism and relieving the government of service responsibility.[28] In Britain, Tony Whitehead of THT made much the same points in a speech in 1988:

> Instead of getting up and banging the table at those meetings as we should have done, instead of pulling the rug from under the government, we said, 'Yes, we must do something. We must strengthen the voluntary sector. Yes, we will do all we can to work with you.' … The work that the gay community has done in fighting section 28 of the 1988 Local Government Act has not been paralleled by any kind of direct challenge to the inadequacies of AIDS funding and government policies … Our immediate response to the tragedy of AIDS has been to rush off to hold people's hands at bedsides. We have not taken our fight out onto the streets as has happened in the United States …[29]

Such dilemmas were an inescapable part of all voluntary activity, not just that for AIDS. There was a classic tension between social-movement activism and institutional involvement. But for AIDS support organizations, these dilemmas were compounded by a further raft of issues. In Britain, these were highlighted in 1991 by the collapse of Frontliners, a self-help organization for people with AIDS, established in 1986 as an offshoot of the THT. A Department of Health report on the collapse instanced three key factors in the closure — a lack of relevant management experience; the rapid expansion of the organization; and its transition from self-help to service provision. But there were other issues which made AIDS organizations different. Here the report touched on the periods of illness suffered by leading voluntary personnel, the networks of sexual relationships between participants, and the gay liberation agenda. With all this, the organization had been forced to rush headlong through several stages of organizational growth, from 'birth' to 'maturity,' missing out 'childhood' and 'adolescence' altogether.[30] Frontliners provided an extreme example of more general dilemmas for AIDS support organizations.

### TIME MOVES ON; GAY SELF-HELP AFTER THE FIRST DECADE

Nor were these dilemmas static; time moved on and relationships were redefined. The classic early history of gay self-help and voluntarism underwent significant change towards the end of the 1980s and in the first half of the 1990s. The formalization of government policies on AIDS in the second half of the 1980s ended the unusual period of direct input to policy making. In Britain, inner circles of policy making developed which 'mainstreamed' AIDS, a deliberate strategy on the part of some leading civil servants who felt they had been 'duped' by a 'homosexual conspiracy' in 1986–7. Inner circles focused more on general issues of sexual health, a tendency reinforced by the government's 'Health of the Nation' policy document in 1992.[31]

Support group responses were also redefined at a number of different levels. Activism revived. ACT-UP was the most visible, and cross national early manifestation of this. Originating in the US in 1987, it gained widespread initial support there with well publicized 'zaps' on the National Institutes of Health, the FDA, and CDC, and with its slogan 'Silence = Death.' Its arrival on the UK scene in 1990 was marked by a well publicized intervention at the annual meeting of the Wellcome Foundation, where activists sought a reduction in the price of AZT. But the 'National AIDS Manual' argued that an American style ACT-UP would be out of place in Britain because of very different political structures and styles of campaigning.[32] ACT-UP sponsored notable annual (later biannual) international conferences on AIDS, but by the time of the 1996 conference in Vancouver, the protests had an almost ritual air with little political or scientific excitement: "It's become part of the conference program. In the old days, when they had a lot less power and less control over their lives, these things were real. But this is theater" commented a Toronto physician.[33]

The "old days" were also the animating force behind other activist developments. Initially gay men had adopted the 'national threat' strategy as a means of deflecting an anti-gay backlash. By the 1990s there was a feeling that non-discrimination had gone too far; gay men were, so it was argued, in danger of being forgotten in the rush to warn others. In Britain, these struggles came to a head in 1992 over the issue of health education. 'Gay Men Fighting AIDS' had been formed out of the gay men's health education group of the THT, which had been advising the Health Education Authority about the tone and content of a gay-focused campaign in pubs and clubs. They wanted a new agenda for AIDS education, one which returned to the previously despised 'risk group' focus:

> The needs of gay men have been neglected ... The tragic irony is that contrary to public opinion, there hasn't been a 'gay lobby' during the AIDS crisis. Instead there has been an AIDS establishment which has sought to heterosexualize itself. After five years of 'de-gaying' of AIDS organizations and 'de-AIDSing' of gay politics, it is not surprising that less than 10 per cent of health authorities do adequate HIV education work aimed at gay men. Once again, as in the early 1980s, safer-sex educators are coming to the conclusion that the only people who can be trusted to look after gay men's interests in the AIDS crisis are gay men ourselves ...[34]

Subsequently, this strategy impacted on the London health regions through the 'Stop AIDS London' project. But it was also a movement with international ramifications. Both Dennis Altman, a gay Australian sociologist who had written one of the earliest histories of the epidemic, and Simon Watney, a commentator on the British scene, drew attention in major conference presentations in 1993 to the need to refocus on gay men. Altman in particular stressed the need to recognize the 'expertise' of those who 'know' AIDS rather than relying on 'scientific' authority.[35,36]

The emergence of these arguments and strategic disagreements in a sense marked the 'end of war' so far as AIDS was concerned. Despite the evocation of the early period of struggle and self-organization in the 're-gaying' movement, different strategies came to operate among different groups and many found themselves locked into a bureaucratic and service provision role, operating as arms of the state. Altman cited the example of the Australian AIDS Councils which, as they became larger and better funded, became more and more like 'mini-health departments,' with professional staff monopolizing decision making: a "very sophisticated and incestuous world of AIDS leaders ... This group — of which I am a member — sits on proliferating government and non-government committees, which fly us around the country at an expanding rate, while rarely demanding that we account in any real way to the people for whom we allegedly speak."[37] Almost all AIDS specific organizations had come to reflect the dominant bureaucratic structures of the state in which they operated.

The dilemmas this could present were underlined by the impact in Britain both of the gradual withdrawal of special factor funding for AIDS services in the 1990s, and by the impact of the NHS and Community Care Act of 1990, which emphasized the provision of community care through a 'mixed economy' of services. Like many other voluntary groups, AIDS service organizations such as THT were faced with making a multiplicity of applications to different purchasers, and so were locked into a dependent role far from the original activist self-helping ethos. Tensions between voluntarism and professionalism had marked the internal histories of many AIDS organizations. In the 1990s, the debate between 'altruism and expertise' entered a further stage as external forces impacted on the nature of the relationship between voluntarism and the state.[38]

Time was moving on so far as the AIDS voluntary sector was concerned. It was also moving on in the area where gay activism was considered to have had greatest impact, that of clinical trials. Activist input had initially modified trial design and led to the earlier release of drugs which appeared to be promising. But in Britain, the Concorde results of 1993 and the results of the Alpha trial of DDI brought a change of activist stance. For Alpha, the original proposal had been for a three arm trial — of high dose, low dose and placebo, in the absence of any data to indicate whether the drug did any good at all. The MRC in consultation with activist groups had changed the design of the trial; there was randomization to high dose/low dose or to high dose/low dose/placebo arms and most participants chose the first option. But the results showed no difference in mortality between the different dosages. The imprecision of the Alpha results led to a swing back to methods which had operated before AIDS: even ACT-UP argued the necessity for placebo controls. The Concorde results, which showed the advantages of results obtained over a longer time scale, also reaffirmed the medical rather than the activist model of trials.[39]

## OTHER EXPERIENCES; DIFFERENT MODELS OF VOLUNTARISM

By the mid 1990s, the 'heroic' early roles of the AIDS patient support groups had changed considerably but there were also other models in operation, whose circumstances were also changing. The final section of this chapter will outline the collective experiences of hemophiliacs, women and drug users in relation to AIDS. It will also look to the developing world to touch on a rather different history of patient support groups and voluntary input.

The gay organizations such as THT and GMHC constituted a new voluntary sector specifically focused round AIDS and its ramifications but they also intersected with other and older models of voluntarism. When AIDS and blood products became an issue in some countries around 1983, hemophiliac groups were brought into the picture. Likewise, the possible spread of AIDS into the general population through injecting drug users and their sexual contacts, an issue which came onto the agenda around 1985, involved the drug voluntary sector. In Britain, the Haemophilia Society, the main voluntary organization, reacted with ambivalence. It had been set up in 1950, had a paid secretary since the 1970s and appointed a paid AIDS coordinator in 1987. But its ethos of voluntarism was quite different from the activism of some of the early gay organizations: the AIDS obituaries in the organization's newsletter sat oddly beside the reports of very traditional fund-raising activity in the localities. Members originally asked for information about AIDS to be given separately from general information about hemophilia, and the Society published 'Haemofacts' from 1984 to 1987. Its campaign for compensation achieved a success of sorts in 1990, when agreement with government was finally reached.[40] The hemophilia compensation case was a very traditional British single issue campaign, conducted by a traditional British charity. The Society, as one member commented was "not a voluntary organization"; there was only one volunteer at headquarters, although there were volunteers in plenty out in the local groups. In general, the society was anxious to leave the compensation battle, which had been divisive, and get back to questions of health care for hemophiliacs. By the mid 1990s, AIDS figured little if at all in the society's newsletter and new issues such as hepatitis C were center stage.

A different political culture treated the issue of blood products very differently. In France, the car belonging to the head of the national blood transfusion service was fire-bombed by hemophilia activists. Medicine and the health service were 'on trial.' As Ann Marie Moulin has described, four senior figures from the blood transfusion service were charged with failing to withdraw infected blood from the market; and jail sentences were initially imposed.[41–43]

For illicit drug users as for hemophiliacs, there were already established voluntary organizations. In Britain the voluntary sector had played a major role in the provision of treatment since the late nineteenth century and had been increasingly drawn into policy circles since the 1970s. There was already a coordinating network organisation, the Standing Conference on Drug Abuse (SCODA), established in the early 1970s. Like the Haemophilia Society, it had its established parliamentary and lobbying links. Just as AIDS had forced some harsh reappraisals on the gay community, so it did for the drug voluntary sector, where harm minimization strategies and the possibilities of accepting and modifying injecting drug use, forced reassessments of the abstentionist policies of the drug rehabilitation establishments. But harm minimization strategies had also emerged from grass-roots initiatives in the drug-related voluntary sector. In that sense, AIDS exposed existing divisions as it added new complications. Several of the 'new' AIDS organizations, THT for example, took on drugs-related support work, which caused some problems with the older drugs organizations. There were complaints that the AIDS machinery in the Department of Health responded more to the 'new' organizations and their drug offshoots than did the drugs section of the Department. How such tensions operated in different countries is impossible to analyze, given the dearth of research on drugs voluntarism. But in general, drugs, like hemophilia, was an area of 'surrogate voluntarism,' where activism was the province of paid workers. Though many drugs workers were ex-users, the type of activism which had marked the early gay organizations was largely absent from the drugs area. Drug users themselves had few traditions of self-organization.[44]

Among the new support organizations which AIDS brought into existence, some related specifically to women. Positively Women, a new AIDS charity, began in a classic self-help way in 1986 when two seropositive women put stickers in phone boxes asking others to contact them. Like other new organizations, Positively Women underwent rapid expansion as funding came on stream from 1988 onward. A member of the management committee recounted the problems which this brought for a fledgling organization:

> We've had massive change and expansion — a staff of ten now and rising. We've got huge premises and a vast number of different funders. We've had all the problems of fast expanding organisations, chickens before eggs, salaries paid before pay scales, a lack of policies and the management committee lagging behind developments.[45]

Such stories were common currency for many of the new AIDS organizations, as the earlier story of Frontliners demonstrated. They were reflected in the often painful shift from early self-help to professionalization and bureaucratic procedures. The problem for many was how to combine altruism and professionalism, with all the tensions inherent in that relationship.

## DEVELOPING COUNTRIES

For developing countries, the issues which AIDS presented for patient support and for voluntarism were rather different. Traditions of voluntary activity were less firmly entrenched and were complicated by patterns of international aid, which was increasingly channeled through non-governmental organizations (NGOs). As in the West, there were early AIDS organizations such as TASO (The AIDS Support Organisation) in Kampala, Uganda, which grew rapidly from a small group focused on services to families to a national network with branches across Uganda. In Manila, 'Reach Out' started by teaching HIV prevention to mainly middle-class gay men, but later operated a wider range of programs, including those aimed at women and young people.[46] But in general, the patterns of development were again dependent on marginalized groups with traditions of political self-organization. Funding complicated matters. In 1987, the US government launched the largest donor driven AIDS program in the world, aiming to channel funds through NGOs in almost every sector and country; "Indeed," as O'Malley et al remark, "some have sought to secure their won funding base or legitimacy through AIDS activities." In the 1990s a greater internationalism brought these organizations together through networks such as the UK NGO Consortium on AIDS and the International Council of AIDS Service Organisations (ICASO).

But the issues for some of these countries remained different. Take clinical trials, for example, where AIDS groups had much less success in moulding research policy, nor was it even clear that they wished to do so. Groups in West Africa remained silent about a large trial of AZT versus placebo in pregnant African women which counterparts in Europe and America found objectionable; the African groups did not have the same access to the policy making process. Africans were not involved in protocol development, although, as one researcher put it: "we try to make it convenient for them."[47] Trials were seen rather as means of obtaining drugs which might not otherwise be available; it was for this reason that the notion of the placebo was discounted.

## CONCLUSION

To look back from the beginning of the twenty-first century at two decades of AIDS is to be struck by the diversity of responses, not just at the level of governments but among the self-help organizations and other charities. In different countries and at different times the epidemiology and clinical manifestations of AIDS have been markedly different, but even where patterns of incidence have been comparable, the patterns of response have been shaped by the political and social histories of the different countries and regions. Like other epidemics studied by historians, AIDS has highlighted pre-existent cultural differences. If AIDS has sometimes served as a model of self-help and political activism among sufferers and those at special risk, it was largely because of the political organization and skills already commanded by gay men in the metropolitan centers of the West. For other groups affected — in the West and the Third World — advocacy was often left to traditional 'expert charities' (eg., for British hemophiliacs) or to medical workers (eg., Third-World specialists in sexually transmitted diseases).

But, for the West at least, we can perhaps see some common features in the response to AIDS. It was usually seen as a medical emergency in countries that had become unaccustomed to the possibility of new and lethal infectious diseases. The initial responses were often dominated by grass-roots organizations, self-help and political activism — only later would the disease be slotted into the 'normal' concerns of health bureaucracies. AIDS organizations offer case studies in rapid political evolution, as new patients' organizations interacted with established charities and the organs of the state, and as all these components evolved, along with the epidemiology, public perceptions, medical understandings and forms of treatment. The seeming immediacy and novelty of the threat, and the political influence of some affected groups, meant that AIDS often unleashed special funds — from state medical systems or as foreign aid to Third World countries. Such funds brought opportunities for influence and action but also posed new challenges. And in Western countries, these complex debates were usually played out under intense media coverage. The speed, global span and visual emphasis of the late twentieth century media are constitutive of this history.

AIDS is no simple story. Collective experiences have been shaped by many other histories, to which AIDS has also contributed. AIDS may have served gay politics as legitimization through disaster as Altmann suggested but the history of the support groups has proved far from a linear progress.[48] Nor has it been the history of only one type of organization or grouping. Generally, it would seem, AIDS has become a government responsibility but the responses are uncertain and the story is only just begun.

REFERENCES

1.  V. Berridge, 'Researching contemporary history: AIDS', *History Workshop Journal* (1994), **38**: 227–234.
2.  It could be argued that these processes are common to all historical story making. Here are also parallels to the construction of particular mythologies after periods of national crisis, the Second World War providing a comparison point with AIDS in this respect. There is no time to explore these issues in the current article, but the issues can be approached through R. Samuel and P. Thompson (eds), *The Myths We Live By*. (London: Routledge, 1990).
3.  See, for example, the interviews carried out by Simon Garfield in *The End of Innocence. Britain in the Time of AIDS*. (London: Faber and Faber, 1994); the weekly column written by Oscar Moore in the *Guardian* until his death in 1996; and for visual and verbal experience, S. Mayes and L. Stein, *Positive Lives. Responses to HIV — a Photodocumentary*. (London: Cassell, 1993).
4.  D.M. Fox, P. Day and R. Klein, 'The Power of Professionalism: Policies for AIDS in Britain, Sweden and the United States' in S.R. Graubard (ed.), *Living With AIDS*. (Cambridge, Mass: MIT Press, 1990), pp. 309–328.
5.  S.C.O. Kobasa, 'AIDS Volunteering: Links to the Past and Future Prospects' in D. Nelkin, D.P. Willis and S.V. Parris (eds), *A Disease of Society. Cultural and Institutional Responses to AIDS*. (Cambridge: Cambridge University Press, 1991), pp. 172–188.
6.  See also the account in R. Shilts, *And the Band Played On. Politics, People and the AIDS Epidemic*. (London: Penguin, 1987).
7.  Ibid, p. 13.
8.  Gay volunteer, quoted in V. Berridge 'Unambiguous Voluntarism? AIDS and the Voluntary Sector in the United Kingdom' in C. Hannaway, V.A. Harden and J. Parascandola (eds), *AIDS and the Public Debate. Historical and Contemporary Perspectives*. (Amsterdam: IOS Press, 1995), pp. 153–169.

9.  V. Berridge, *AIDS in the U.K.: the Making of Policy, 1981–1994*. (Oxford: Oxford University Press, 1996).

10. R. Freeman, 'The Politics of AIDS in Britain and Germany' in P. Aggleton, P. Davies and G. Hart (eds), *AIDS. Rights, Risk and Reason*. (London: Falmer Press, 1992), pp. 53–67.

11. M. Pollak, 'AIDS in West Germany: Coordinating Policy in a Federal System' in B.A. Misztal and D. Moss (eds), *Action on AIDS. National Policies in Comparative Perspective*. (New York: Greenwood Press, 1990), pp. 121–134.

12. M. Steffen, 'AIDS Policies in France' in V. Berridge and P. Strong (eds), *AIDS and Contemporary History*. (Cambridge: Cambridge University Press, 1993), pp. 240–264.

13. M. Steffen, *Les Politiques Publiques face au defi du SIDA. Comparison Internationale dans Quatre Pays Europeens: France, Grande Bretagne, Allemagne, Italie*. (Grenoble: CERAT, 1995).

14. M. Pollak, 'AIDS Policy in France: Biomedical Leadership and Preventive Impotence' in B.A. Misztal and D. Moss (eds), *Action on AIDS*, pp. 79–100.

15. B.A. Misztal, 'AIDS in Australia: Diffusion of Power and Making of Policy' in B.A. Misztal and D. Moss (eds), *Action on AIDS*, pp. 189–215.

16. C. Williams, *AIDS in Post-Communist Russia and its Successor States*. (Aldershot: Avebury, 1995).

17. For gay liberation, see J. Weeks, *Coming Out. Homosexual Politics in Britain from the Nineteenth Century to the Present*. (London: Quartet Books, 1977).

18. For a general account, see V. Berridge and C. Webster, 'The Crisis of Welfare, 1974 to the 1990s' in C. Webster (ed.), *Caring for Health: History and Diversity*. (Milton Keynes: Open University Press, 1993).

19. For a fuller discussion of these issues, see V. Berridge, '"Unambiguous Voluntarism?": AIDS and the Voluntary Sector in the UK, 1981–1992' in C. Hannaway, V. Harden and J. Parascandola (eds), *AIDS and the Public Debate: Historical and Contemporary Perspectives*. (Washington: IOS Press, 1995).

20. M. Blaxter, *AIDS: Worldwide Policies and Problems*. (London: Office of Health Economics, 1991).

21. A detailed analysis of these events is given in V. Berridge, *AIDS in the U.K.: the Making of Policy, 1981–1994*. (Oxford: Oxford University Press, 1996).

22. R. Bayer and D.L. Kirp, 'The United States: At the Center of the Storm' in D.L. Kirp and R. Bayer (eds), *AIDS in the Industrialized Democracies. Passions, Politics and Policies*. (Rutgers: University Press, 1992), pp. 7–48.

23. J. Ballard, 'Australia: Participation and Innovation in a Federal System' in D.L. Kirp and R. Bayer (eds), *AIDS in the Industrialized Democracies*.

24. Discussed in V. Berridge, *AIDS in the U.K.*

25. V. Berridge, *AIDS in the U.K.*, p. 268.

26. H. Edgar and D.J. Rothman, 'New Rules for New Drugs: The Challenge of AIDS to the Regulatory Process' in D. Nelkin, D.P. Willis and S.V. Parris (eds), *A Disease of Society*. (Cambridge: Cambridge University Press, 1991), pp. 84–115.

27. V. Berridge, *AIDS in the U.K.*, p. 187.

28. Kobasa, *op. cit.*, p. 184.

29. Quoted in V. Berridge, *AIDS in the U.K.*, p. 165.

30. L. Mortland and S. Legg, *Managing and Funding AIDS Organisations: Experience from the Closure of Frontliners*. (London: Department of Health, 1991).

31. V. Berridge, *AIDS in the U.K.*

32. See F. Beckett, 'Protest Politics', *AIDS Matters* (1992), **8**: 5; and *National AIDS Manual*, pp. 3–20.

33. Quoted in the *Vancouver Sun* (9 July, 1996).

34. *Guardian* (25 June, 1992).

35. D. Altman, 'Expertise, Legitimacy and the Centrality of Community' in P. Aggleton, P. Davies and G. Hart (eds), *AIDS: Facing the Second Decade*. (London: Falmer Press, 1993), pp. 1–12.

36. For developments on the US gay scene, see R.A. Padgug and G.M. Oppenheimer, 'Riding the Tiger: AIDS and the Gay Community' in E. Fee and D.M. Fox (eds), *AIDS. The Making of a Chronic Disease*. (Berkeley: University of California Press, 1992), pp. 245–278.

37. Altman, 'Expertise, Legitimacy ...', p. 9.

38. The phrase was originally Jeffrey Weeks' in J. Weeks, 'AIDS, Altruism and the New Right' in E. Carter and S. Watney (eds), *Taking Liberties: AIDS and Cultural Politics*. (London: Serpents Tail, 1989).

39. This is discussed in the US context by D.J. Rothman and H. Edgar, 'Scientific Rigor and Medical Realities: Placebo Trials in Cancer and AIDS Research' in E. Fee and D.M. Fox (eds), *AIDS. The Making of a Chronic Disease.* (Berkeley: University of California Press, 1992), pp. 194–206.

40. See V. Berridge, *AIDS in the U.K.*, pp. 233–6 for details of the compensation campaign.

41. A.M. Moulin, 'Reversible History: Blood Transfusion and the Spread of AIDS in France' in C. Hannaway, V.A. Harden and J. Parascandola (eds), *AIDS and the Public Debate*, pp. 170–186.

42. See also M. Steffen, *Les Politiques publiques face au defi du SIDA.* (Grenoble: CERAT, 1995).

43. For a general review of the state of play in the blood area in different countries in the 1990s, see N. Gilmore, 'Blood and Blood Product Safety' in J.M. Mann and D.J.M. Tarantola (eds), *AIDS in the World II. Global Dimensions, Social Roots and Responses. The Global AIDS Policy Coalition.* (New York: Oxford University Press, 1996), pp. 287–301.

44. This point is also made by Don Des Jarlais et al. in a study of AIDS among drug users in New York; little has been written from the perspective of drug users themselves. See D.C. Des Jarlais, S.R. Friedman and J.L. Sotheran, 'The First City: HIV among Intravenous Drug Users in New York City' in E. Fee and D.M. Fox (eds), *AIDS. The Making of a Chronic Disease.* (Berkeley: University of California Press, 1992), pp. 279–295.

45. Interview by author with member of management committee, Positively Women (March 1992).

46. See J. O'Malley, V.K. Nguyen, and S. Lee, 'Nongovernmental Organisations' in J.M. Mann and D.J.M. Tarantola (eds), *AIDS in the World II. Global Dimensions, Social Roots and Responses. The Global AIDS Policy Coalition.* (New York: Oxford University Press, 1996), pp. 341–361.

47. Comment from researcher on AIDS in Africa, London School of Hygiene (September, 1996).

48. D. Altman, 'Legitimation through Disaster: AIDS and the Gay Movement' in E. Fee and D.M. Fox (eds), *AIDS. The Burdens of History.* (Berkeley: University of California Press, 1988), pp. 301–315.

## FURTHER READING

Aggleton, P., Davies, P. and Hart, G. (eds), *AIDS: Facing the Second Decade.* (London: Falmer Press, 1993).

Berridge, V., *AIDS in the U.K.: The Making of Policy, 1981–1994.* (Oxford: Oxford University Press, 1996).

Berridge, V. and Strong, P. (eds), *AIDS and Contemporary History.* (Cambridge: Cambridge University Press, 1993).

Fee, E. and Fox, D.M. (eds), *AIDS. The Burdens of History.* (Berkeley: University of California Press, 1988).

Fee, E. and Fox, D.M. (eds), *AIDS. The Making of a Chronic Disease.* (Berkeley: University of California Press, 1992).

Foster, J. *AIDS Archives in the U.K.* (London: London School of Hygiene and Tropical Medicine, 1990).

Graubard, S.R. (ed.), *Living with AIDS.* (Cambridge, Mass.: MIT Press, 1990).

Grmek, M.D. *History of AIDS. Emergence and Origin of a Modern Pandemic.* Translated by Russell Maulitz and Jacalyn Duffin. (Princeton, N.J., Princeton University Press, 1990).

Hannaway, C., Harden, V.A. and Parascandola, J. (eds), *AIDS and the Public Debate. Historical and Contemporary Perspectives.* (Amsterdam: IOS Press, 1995).

Herdt, G. and Lindenbaum, S. (eds), *The Time of AIDS. Social Analysis, Theory and Method.* (Newbury Park, Ca.: Sage, 1992).

Kirp, D.L. and Bayer, R. (eds), *AIDS in the Industrialized Democracies. Passions, Politics and Policies.* (Rutgers: University Press, 1992).

Mann, J.M. and Tarantola, D.J.M. (eds), *AIDS in the World, II. Global Dimensions, Social Roots and Responses. The Global AIDS Policy Coalition.* (New York: Oxford University Press, 1996).

Mizstal, B.A. and Moss, D. (eds), *Action on AIDS. National Policies in Comparative Perspective.* (New York: Greenwood Press, 1990).

Nelkin, D., Willis, D.P. and Parris, S.V. (eds), *A Disease of Society. Cultural and Institutional Responses to AIDS.* (Cambridge: Cambridge University Press, 1991).

# CHAPTER 45

# Malaria

LYN SCHUMAKER

At the time in question I was suffering from a sharp attack of intermittent fever, and every day during the cold and succeeding hot fits had to lie down for several hours, during which time I had nothing to do but to think over any subjects then particularly interesting me. One day something brought to my recollection Malthus's 'Principles of Population'... The more I thought over it the more I became convinced that I had at length found the long-sought-for law of nature that solved the problem of the origin of species... I waited anxiously for the termination of my fit so that I might at once make notes for a paper on the subject.[1]

This was how Alfred Russel Wallace described the attack of malaria that purportedly led to his discovery of the law of natural selection in 1858. His ruminations over Malthus ran the gamut of life and death, fitness and unfitness, and differences between the savage and the civilized in the struggle for existence, and lurking in the deeper background may have been memories of his brother's death, by a different kind of fever, on the coast of South America the year before. Fitter than his brother, Wallace survived his fever, which also survives in the footnotes of every book on evolution, testimony to our continuing belief in the link between fever and creative imagination.

In the past, the *experience* of disease — the physical, emotional, intellectual and spiritual experiences that ordinary individuals, communities and even nations suffer and survive if they are lucky — has figured as a backdrop in histories of medical responses to disease. More recently, these experiences themselves are becoming the subject of historical analysis. But why should we be interested? Because understanding the experience of disease at every level offers insight into the emergence of those metaphors and practices that scientists and the public use to frame disease and that ultimately come to constitute both popular and medical/scientific knowledge. Furthermore, most histories of malaria still focus primarily on the researchers' and doctors' side of the story. A focus on experience has the potential to equalize the stories of the scientist and the sufferer of this disease in our historiography.

Wallace's experience of 'intermittent fever,' as malarious fevers were also known in the mid-nineteenth century, came on the cusp of major changes in medical perceptions of fever, which would result in the definition of malaria as a parasitical disease rather than one that derived from bad air — mal'aria. This shift from miasmatic disease to tropical disease was by no means fore-ordained. Scientists entertained many and various theories of malarial etiology in the period from 1850 to 1879 when Adolphe Laveran discovered the *Plasmodium* parasite, including both old-fashioned miasmic etiologies and trendy new bacterial theories that proposed the existence of a *Bacillus malariae*. Even after Laveran discovered the parasite, Patrick Manson and Ronald Ross for a long time fixed their attention on possible etiologies involving soil, water and air transmission in combination with the mosquito.

The miasma metaphor was not easily shaken off, for intermittent fever had been the quintessential miasmatic illness. Nevertheless, by the turn of the twentieth century, malaria had become the quintessential tropical disease and the revelation of its etiology the chief triumph of the new discipline of tropical medicine. This chapter will try to capture the effects of that medical scientific triumph in the twentieth century and its subsequent unraveling. It will also deal with other equally compelling experiences — from the parasitical to the personal and cultural. The emerging history of the experience of malaria in the developing countries will be considered here, as well as the more thoroughly understood experience of Western explorers, colonizers, tourists and scientists.

And to begin, what about the least understood experience of all, that of the parasite?

## A PARASITICAL POINT OF VIEW

Historians have paid little attention to *Plasmodium*'s side of the story, and those who know it best are the researchers attempting to run the creature to ground with anti-malarial drugs and vaccines. The parasite's experience, as well as the experience of these scientists, must be distilled from the scientists' own overviews of recent research, though nothing short of a laboratory ethnography could fully capture this rapidly evolving contemporary history.

The complexity of the life cycle of *Plasmodium* is matched only by the difficulty of uncovering its evolutionary history and its protean responses to the challenge of new anti-malarial drugs. According to current scientific understanding, when *Anopheles* mosquitoes feed on humans or animals, sporozoites of *Plasmodium* reach the blood through the mosquitoes' saliva. They then invade the liver and develop over a week or more into a mature parasite called a 'schizont.' The schizont bursts, releasing merozoites that develop to a mature stage in the blood, invading the red blood cells. In the resulting 'erythrocytic,' or blood-stage, schizonts can release more merozoites in subsequent cycles that cause the periodic fevers characteristic of the disease. After one or more of these cycles, a new stage begins in some of the schizonts, producing sexually differentiated forms. When the infected blood is consumed by a mosquito, the sexual stage schizonts release male and female gametes. Together inside a mosquito, they form zygotes and eventually more sporozoites. What we popularly recognize as the disease occurs during the erythrocytic stage, when the parasites are reproducing in the blood and producing toxins — which on the microscopic scale of blood cells is a process reminiscent of the invaded bodies and bursting pods of low-grade science fiction movies.

*Plasmodium* originated in Africa and/or Southeast Asia and spread during the Pleistocene with its human and mosquito hosts wherever they found a mutually agreeable environment. Thus, malaria probably reached large parts of Asia and the Middle East before it spread significantly in Europe, where Ice Age temperatures were too low for the parasites and their most efficient mosquito vectors. Of the four *Plasmodium* species that infect humans — *P. vivax, malariae, ovale* and *faliciparum* — *falciparum* is the most virulent and most recently evolved.

Through most of *Plasmodium*'s history, it has had little to fear from its human hosts, who have been able to do nothing to destroy the parasite itself short of swatting the mosquitoes they infested. The human body developed ways to live with the parasite, however, and some species of the parasite may have become less virulent and less likely to kill their hosts. Both sickle cell anemia and thalassemia may have developed in populations long exposed to malaria, especially the *P. falciparum* variety, because of the slight survival advantage they conferred (see below.)

Eventually, humans developed indigenous medicines of various kinds to use against the fever — though historical writers have focused almost exclusively on the tale of cinchona bark and its successful refinement into a wide array of drugs, beginning with quinine, for preventing and treating malaria among Western travelers, explorers and armies. Quinine's efficacy took ages to establish, and side effects still accompany its use and that of most of its successors. For example, soldiers in World War I resisted taking quinine because they feared it caused impotence, and similar fears made soldiers in World War II sometimes avoid Mepacrine, which also turned the skin yellow. After the war, the parasiticide pharmacopoeia blossomed, again sometimes prompted by the needs of war, as when scientists tested mefloquine on American soldiers in Vietnam. Nevertheless, as this Western tale of triumph has been eroded by the emergence of resistance to drugs — quinine-based or otherwise — in certain strains of *Plasmodium*, the newest round of anti-malarials has been developed out of another herbal medicine, *qinghaosu*, derived from the plant, *Artemisia annua*, long used in China to suppress fevers.

But some mutant strains of *Plasmodium* may now be pre-adapted to resist any newly developed anti-malarial drugs. One popular writer provides a breathless description of scientific discoveries pointing to a drug-gulping pump used by *P. falciparum* to remove unwanted chemicals before they can cause damage, a pump easily adapted to each new drug as it arrives in the parasite's environment. Although frightening, this image has a tantalizing simplicity, dramatically different from the image of *Plasmodium* portrayed by those who write about efforts to develop a vaccine. In these latter writings, *Plasmodium*'s life cycle is presented as both demonically complex and potentially vulnerable in all of its multiple stages.

Vaccine researchers have been focusing on vaccines that can attack the parasites in each of the three stages of the life cycle because the parasite changes its coat proteins at each stage, an adaptive trait which also makes it difficult for the infected body to build a strong natural immunity. This situation is complicated further by the existence of multiple strains of each species of *Plasmodium*, not all likely to be sensitive to the same vaccine at any particular stage. Even a thoroughly effective single-stage vaccine is unlikely to be enough, and the ultimate goal is to produce a "multivalent, multi-immune response" vaccine — or a "vaccine cocktail," as one author puts it.[2]

The picture becomes even more complex when one considers at what level protection should be provided, for vaccines could be developed to protect individuals or to protect communities; the former vaccines would have to prevent the illness from occurring, while the latter would prevent death but not disease. Researchers fear that prevention of illness may not be sustainable and that short periods of freedom from infection will cause populations to lose the semi-immunity that humans develop in endemic malarial regions. The result could be devastating epidemics, similar to those that have occurred in the recent past when malaria control programs have broken down, leaving newly non-immune populations vulnerable. Scientists' response to this may be to focus on producing an 'anti-disease' vaccine — one that prevents the symptoms without killing the parasite — an outcome *Plasmodium* might applaud.

Even if immunization resulted in sustainable immunity of populations, some researchers question how much good it might do. Will it save children — who are malaria's chief victims — only to have them die from other diseases rife in those poor populations that suffer the most from malaria? And if they do live to adulthood, what will be the consequences of the increase in population of the developing world? One wonders if these questions would be asked at all if the disease affected the population of the developed countries. But all of these questions are overshadowed by a larger question — will the developed countries provide the funding to produce an effective vaccine in the first place, considering that such a vaccine will largely benefit the developing world, and the occasional unlucky tourist?

SEX, GENES AND ANOPHELINES

In the human history of malaria, the mosquitoes have gotten greater attention than the parasites because of their more obvious and irritating role in the disease. To add insult to injury, *Anopheles* mosquitoes do not suffer the disease themselves, though other mosquitoes that do not ordinarily transmit malaria might be killed by *Plasmodium* if they unwittingly feed on an infected human. Easily recognizable because they tilt their bodies at a 45 degree angle when resting on a surface, anophelines have captured the popular imagination, appearing in tropical 'fear flicks' as giant-sized flying hypodermic needles, as in the recent Robin Williams film, *Jumanji*. The myriad species of *Anopheles* that transmit *Plasmodium* also figure in the public health imagination, being the chief target of malaria eradication campaigns ever since "Mosquito Ross" confirmed their role as vectors on "Mosquito Day" — 20 August 1897.[3]

In the first half of the twentieth century, *Anopheles* may have experienced a shrinking of its geographical domain, partly due to control measures, but more importantly caused by a long-term shift in mosquito species competition due to changes in human settlement patterns. In some places, massive DDT spraying and other control measures took a temporary toll on mosquito numbers before mosquitoes with insecticide resistance evolved, while in a few places, like Sardinia, Cyprus and Greece, malaria was completely eliminated. More important for the nature of mosquito habitats in Europe and North America were changes associated with agricultural development. Drainage, new agricultural methods, shifts in housing styles and greater separation of animals from humans led to the dominance of species of *Anopheles* less efficient at transmitting *Plasmodium* and/or more likely to prefer the blood of pigs and cattle. The phenomenon of "anophelism without malaria" — the presence of anopheles mosquitoes in malaria-free regions — was at first taken as a disturbing anomaly for the mosquito theory of transmission, but by the 1930s it became the foundation of a new approach to malaria control — that of "species sanitation," i.e., ecological interventions designed to promote the dominance of harmless species of *Anopheles*.[4]

Development — including environmental changes brought about by economic, political and social factors — has had contradictory consequences, however, leading to reduction of mosquitoes in some parts of the world and their proliferation in others. Colonial and post-colonial development projects — damming of rivers, irrigation projects and plantation agriculture — have increased the habitat of *Anopheles*. At the same time forced relocation of human populations and circular migration of laborers from previously malaria-free regions have exposed non-immune people — and previously *Plasmodium*-free anophelines — to infection. These factors increase malaria transmission and can lead to epidemics even in places where mosquitoes have not evolved DDT-resistance. Development that causes climate change may also enlarge mosquito habitat and bring malaria to places previously untouched, like the highlands of Africa. Indeed, malaria may return to the marshes of south-eastern England — which are well-stocked with anophelines — according to some global warming scenarios.

The historical focus on the mosquito has largely been a product of the sources of funding for the prevention programs that spawned large-scale anti-malaria campaigns beginning in the 1920s. Nevertheless, these campaigns followed a model established in previous control efforts that had depended on the availability of cheap colonial labor, such as in Ross' mosquito brigades, to pursue this visible and vulnerable enemy. The British and the Americans tended to see malaria control as dependent on control of the mosquito, whereas the French and Germans attempted to destroy the parasite itself through use of quinine. Funding from the Rockefeller Foundation gave the Anglo-American approach the advantage, and the development of DDT in the 1940s contributed to mosquitoes being the chief target of the World Health Organization's global eradication campaign, announced in 1957.

Preoccupation with the mosquito resulted in an enormous amount of mosquito-oriented research, though historians have primarily focused on Ross and the other pioneers of tropical medicine who studied the life-cycle of *Plasmodium* in the mosquito. Ross, for example, found the small anophelines he worked with inconvenient experimental animals, difficult to breed or get to bite, difficult to infect and given to dying young — though this latter may have been due to his originally not allowing them to feed more than once. Part of the problem was that the experimental animal was really a composite one — the human/mosquito nexus — and humans could be even less co-operative than mosquitoes. Thus, he found the disease much easier to research in its bird form, using pigeons and a different species of anopheline, and feeling free to infect or dissect either party whenever the pursuit of science commanded.

Other types of research led to other kinds of practices, none particularly pleasant for the mosquitoes. Favorites included studies of different species' flying distances, important for judging how wide an area to cover in malaria control efforts in any particular locality. Researchers captured mosquitoes, tagged them with fluorescent dusts, released and recaptured them sometimes miles away, with native assistants — 'mosquito boys' — doing most of the legwork. Native assistants, organized in 'mosquito brigades,' also did most of the work involved in the early control campaigns on the model advocated by Ross, oiling ponds and irrigation ditches, sweeping or filling puddles and cleaning up discarded bottles and other trash in which water might collect and provide breeding sites. In some control efforts 'larvivorous' fish could be used instead of oil, especially when dealing with mosquito larvae in wells used for drinking water. Later Rockefeller-financed research and eradication efforts focused on mosquitoes, attacking their larvae with poisons like Paris Green, rather than oil, and later the adult mosquitoes with DDT. Many of these studies examined mosquito behavior, habitats and speciation in great detail, before DDT convinced many that complexity could be ignored.

Since the World Health Organization recognized the failure of world-wide eradication in 1969, complexity is back on the agenda of both research and control efforts. Researchers now pay attention to a wide range of factors, including drug prophylaxis and treatment; drug distribution factors; mosquito sex and feeding habits; their odor, color and temperature preferences; large-scale environmental factors, such as irrigation projects; small-scale environmental factors, such as house ecology and daily human patterns of movement; drug resistance and even economic factors and poverty. Those who advocate control programs nearly always recommend a combination of approaches including treatment, spraying and changes in human behavior. A good example of this new approach is the enormous amount of attention that has been focused on insecticide-impregnated bednets.

The mosquito net has a long cultural and social history little explored by scholars. First used to reduce the nuisance of mosquitoes at night rather than to prevent malaria, bednets initially replaced 'turtling,' as it is called in Jamaica where today it is still practiced — sleeping with one's head under the covers to avoid bites. Now associated with tropical elegance, they appear in films about Africa or India, wafting in the breeze of punkahs and suffused with colonial nostalgia. Since the 1980s, however, bednets have been increasingly suffused with insecticides. Ordinary nets, for all their elegance, do little to prevent malaria unless used under the strictest regime of tucking, folding and mending. Indeed, mosquitoes have often found them convenient perches from which to probe for an exposed hand or foot touching the net. Pyrethroids, which have low mammalian toxicity but are deadly to insects, prevent them from perching and sometimes drive them from the room altogether.

Nevertheless, the chief benefit even of insecticide-impregnated nets may be in reducing mortality rather than eliminating infection — at least according to some studies of children sleeping under them — by allowing immunity to gradually build while preventing overwhelming illness. Cultural variation also complicates the picture, and the acceptance and successful use of bednets depend on myriad factors. In developing countries, people go out to work before dawn and return at dusk, placing them outdoors rather than under bednets at the mosquitoes' favorite feeding times. Most important is whether people see the nets as conducive to health, a reduction of mosquito nuisance or improving personal privacy, or whether they see them as an expensive, suffocating, smelly nuisance themselves. And then there is the little matter of impregnating them with the insecticide, which must be done correctly and at regular intervals — and which is undone by washing. Getting around these obstacles promises much work for researchers in designing more acceptable nets, as well as for crusading armies of development workers to convince people to buy and use them.

Appropriate technology solutions, like impregnated bednets, are not the only ones on today's scientific agenda, however. Researchers are also pursuing high-tech biotechnology studies focusing on anophelines, their genes and their sexual behavior. The problem of determining generally whether mosquitoes are monogamous plagued early sex behavior research, with the answer being no. Neither are they territorial — no alpha males driving away the beta males as among baboons — though the swarming varieties of mosquito do favor particular bushes for their sexual activities.

Scientists have also begun promising studies of *Anopheles* and *Plasmodium* genetics, the latter the subject of a 'malaria genome project' that may solve the problem of drug resistance and/or make the parasite more vulnerable to future vaccines. Mosquito genetic studies involve the development of 'lethal genes' that could tip the balance of survival in some mosquito populations. For example, a researcher has discovered an inherited mechanism that causes partial sterility, so that a breeding population flooded with genetically engineered mosquitoes might be suppressed or even die out. Artificial sterilization has been used successfully to eradicate the Mediterranean fruit fly from Mexico and northern Guatemala, and it is proposed that a similar process for anophelines might be used to eradicate mosquitoes like *Anopheles stephensi*, which clusters in urban areas in India and would not be able to renew its numbers from wild rural populations. Unlike the Med fly, however, *Anopheles stephensi* is protected by a commercially based distribution of resources that supplies money for eradicating crop destroying insects but not for attacking malaria in the developing world. Which brings us to the human side of the story.

## THE HUMAN EXPERIENCE

Historically, malaria is one of the most widely experienced diseases of the human race. It plagued our hominid ancestors, and even when the written record fails to mention it, malaria has left its traces: in his history of *Ancient Egyptian Medicine*, John F. Nunn reports that though he found no overt references to malaria, tests for antigen to *Plasmodium falciparum* were positive in mummies from all dynasties. Throughout history, the majority of people living in tropical regions of the world — and in temperate regions until recently — have experienced malaria. Today the disease has become a nearly ubiquitous feature of poverty in developing countries and, only occasionally, an experience of Western tourists, the price paid for a holiday in the sun. Most of its victims are children who have not yet developed resistance. The disease also causes premature and stillbirths, and its debilitating consequences may be a factor complicating other illnesses. It kills between one and three million each year and infects hundreds of millions more, primarily in Africa. Despite its having one of the highest morbidity and mortality rates in the world, however, malaria is today one of the most easily ignored diseases because of its unequal distribution between rich and poor nations. And this is despite — or partly because of — past eradication campaigns that did not seriously address its political, social and economic 'epidemiology.'

Precisely this type of epidemiology is the concern of some recent historical work on malaria. Although it does not deal with the twentieth century, Mary Dobson's analysis of malaria in England from the sixteenth to the nineteenth centuries is a remarkably thorough example of this approach. She describes a cycle of economic exploitation, social ostracism, endemic disease and death — possibly triggered and certainly worsened by the 'ague' — that created an entire population in the Kentish marshes labeled as degenerate. Numerous scholars have also looked at the work of J.W.W. Stephens' and S.R. Christophers and their labeling of another population — African children — as a reservoir of infection that endangered a more 'civilized' and therefore more vulnerable population — European colonial settlers. Debates continue over the degree to which the resulting strengthening of segregatory practices was a recognition of the limits of public health measures to help indigenous people or a racist 'writing off' of a health problem partly created by colonialism itself.

Also relevant to malaria's use as a label for human populations is Keith Wailoo's history of technologies of blood in the United States. A chapter on the framing of sickle cell anemia reveals how this disease could be racialized in contrasting ways that responded to both the politics of the larger context and to the politics of medicine and its subspecialties. Physicians acting as 'race detectives' saw sickling as evidence of 'Negro blood,' in a climate of fears of miscegenation in the period between 1910 and the 1940s. In the 1950s and 1960s climate of anti-racism, however, molecular biologists and molecular hematologists reconstructed the disease, seeing it as a marker of an adaptive human genetic diversity, the occasional ill effects of which could potentially be eradicated through molecular engineering. Despite its political interpretations, however, sickle cell trait's protective effects are so slight that they only become significant in survival differences between large populations over long periods of time.

The more direct effects of malaria — the symptoms and consequences of the disease — have received the least historical attention. Chills, fever, vomiting, diarrhea, headache, lassitude and other symptoms alternate with symptom-free periods. Untreated malaria often recurs once or several times, and babies of mothers suffering with malaria can be born with the disease, if they survive the greater risk of dying before birth. Malaria can lead to severe anemia in mothers and children and depresses the immune system in all of its victims.

The experience of the symptoms of the disease has shaped literary conventions, as well as medical cures. Malaria has long contributed to the European cultural representation of fevers, as in the literary trope of the 'fevered imagination.' In fiction, Europeans come down with fever almost immediately on arrival in Africa or India, more likely victims of a tropical trope than the real disease. For example, one of Elspeth Huxley's heroines, in *Murder at Government House*, wanders the African bush delirious with a malarial fever only two days after arrival, scarcely time for the parasite to move from the liver to the blood. Certain psychiatrists in the 1930s found fevers useful, however, and employed malaria's often very high fevers to treat syphilitics suffering from madness — a delirium used to cure a dementia — though whether the fever is the true mechanism of cure is still unknown.

Part of the cultural side of the human experience of malaria has been explored in histories of tropical hygiene. Tropical hygiene focused its defenses on small European populations in the colonies and on imperial armies that often suffered greater casualties from disease than from warfare. Hygiene touched every aspect of colonial Europeans' lives, from the clothes they wore to the organization of the cities they lived in or their choice of camping sites when on safari. Gin helped the 'bwanas' or 'sahibs' and 'memsahibs' to get down their quinine-dosed tonic water each day and led to the tradition of 'sundowners,' drinking sessions at dusk which, ironically, may have caused colonial gentlemen to linger on the veranda during the prime anopheline biting times. Never mind — hygiene also recommended donning long-sleeved shirts and high-topped mosquito boots to protect vulnerable parts. Repellents of various kinds could take care of any remaining exposed skin. If one stayed outdoors to sleep, mosquito nets could be draped over a camp bed in a big cottage tent. However, the experienced colonial administrator on tour amongst his subjects preferred sleeping in the open, depending on light breezes to drive away mosquitoes that might otherwise shelter in the corners of a tent waiting to bite. Ceiling fans performed a similar function in houses, not merely driving away heat but also mosquitoes.

Tropical architects experimented with numerous house styles designed, at first, to reduce general miasmatic influences and, later, to discourage mosquitoes. Entire colonial cities were designed on hygienic lines that corresponded with race, with indigenous women and children kept at the greatest possible distance from the homes of Europeans. Hygienic city planning also reinforced the European preference for the higher, drier and breezier areas long recommended by miasma and climatological theories.

These individual and community experiences were shaped by larger national contexts, as well. State governments and nationalist movements have historically asserted their identity in campaigns to eradicate disease and reverse national degeneration. In Italy, for example, malaria control caught the imagination of Mussolini, for its potential to create a more efficient and competitive population. The Germans hoped that Mepacrine — which they had developed in the 1930s — would help them win in the tropical theaters of the Second World War.

Imperial ambitions also found expression in malaria control. In British India, Ross pointed to malaria rather than irreversible racial degeneration as the chief cause of the Indian people's weak and exhausted nature. In this he reflected a late-nineteenth–century shift in imperial medical interests in India, from a focus on the health of the army to a concern for the health and efficiency of the indigenous labor force. For different reasons, middle-class Indian nationalists took up malaria control as an essential aim in the project of regenerating, modernizing and freeing the nation from the ill effects of colonial economic exploitation. In contrast, in colonial Zimbabwe in the 1950s progressive Africans used malaria in arguments protesting the loss of their agricultural lands to Europeans and displacement into forested frontier areas. They depicted these areas as rife with disease, savagery and superstition and lacking in the essential medical facilities they associated with modernity — characterizing them as places they were being sent to die.

In the twentieth century nations have also experienced malaria as an aspect of their competition with other nations, both in the initial scramble to understand the etiology of the disease and in the subsequent campaigns for control and eradication. The rivalry between the Italian scientist, Grassi, and the British scientist, Ross, has figured at some point in most histories of malaria. Ross, characterized by one writer as "a genius, of course, but also a dickhead,"[5] eagerly engaged in quarrels much closer to home as well, judging from the literature on his disputes with Manson. The bacteriologist, Robert Koch, also lent his scientific weight to what became an international dispute, that between the Germans, French and Italians, and the British and Americans, over the best way to pursue malaria control — through attacking the mosquito or attacking the parasite.

Important to recent scholarship is the connection between wars against malaria and wars among nations. The disease presented enormous problems to armies fighting in malarious regions during both world wars, and scholars have debated the importance of the role of medical officers and the control of malaria in determining the course of the wars. Less debatable is the influence of the military experience with malaria on the initial anti-malaria campaigns following the discovery of the role of the mosquito and, especially, on the major eradication campaigns that followed World War II. Military and former military men, including Ross and Manson, may have comprised the largest single professional grouping among malaria researchers and members of control campaigns. Their experiences of anti-mosquito campaigns in a military or quasi-military setting (as in the Panama Canal Zone) helped to develop a culture of ideas and practices that would shape civilian malaria control campaigns. The successful completion of the Panama Canal, for example, was hailed as a vindication of the type of control program promoted by Ross and earlier tested by William Crawford Gorgas in his fight against the yellow fever mosquito in Havana after American troops occupied the city in 1899.

Moreover, during the Second World War, DDT spraying proved its effectiveness. After the war this experience gave both policy makers and the public reason to believe that they could rely on that one weapon to win the war on the disease. Portrayed as the "atomic bomb of the insect world," DDT formed the backbone of major eradication campaigns in the United States and elsewhere, though in the US it only hastened the demise of a disease that was already nearly eradicated. As in other settings, however, DDT was welcomed because it promised a solution to the problem of malaria that did not require policy makers to deal with its context — the "intractable problem of poverty."[6]

Which brings us to the politics of international health. Conflicts over different approaches have shaped the response of the international community to malaria. The chief debate has been over the importance of socio-economic factors in rendering populations vulnerable to the disease: to put it simplistically, does poverty cause malaria or malaria cause poverty? Although poverty and the disease are mutually reinforcing, the choice of focus is crucial for determining strategy.

Does one focus energy and resources on attacking the disease or attempt a broader strategy that includes addressing issues of a population's political and economic marginality? This debate had already emerged in the 1920s in the conflict between the Malaria Commission of the League of Nations (which supported a broad approach focusing on socio-economic development and general improvement of health services) and Ross and the American malariologists (who focused on vector control).

The failure of the World Health Organization's malaria eradication campaign clearly showed that the latter approach, even with the help of DDT, could not break the cycle of disease and poverty, particularly given the radical changes in population movement in the postcolonial developing world. Wars and refugee movements, environmental degradation, resettlement and labour migration due to development itself, often reversed any progress made in local or even national campaigns. The most important obstacle to malaria control, however, is the uneven distribution of resources across the globe. Despite its listing of malaria as a top priority, the World Health Organization can do little to fight the disease given the developed nations', and particularly the United States', failure to provide the United Nations with adequate funding.

Moreover, colonial and military models have continued to dominate anti-malarial interventions when they occur, often criticized as 'top-down' and imposed by experts from the developed world upon the most powerless people within the developing world. The World Health Organization and other agencies involved in health interventions now advocate a 'participatory model' that attempts to involve local people in their own development. But how can participatory practices succeed if the local people's ideas about malaria and the history of their own encounters with the disease are still largely unknown? In moving away from triumphalist histories of the discovery of malaria's etiology and early control efforts, the literature on malaria has become increasingly critical. Yet despite its critical nature, recent scholarship still follows a pattern set by the earlier hagiographic scholarship, asymmetrically focusing on Western ideas and campaigns while neglecting the ideas and initiatives of the people most affected by the disease. A literature on this very subject, however, exists outside the boundaries of historical scholarship — the literature of medical anthropology. Although medical anthropology's approach usually fails to address the historical context of disease, its close attention to the details of people's cultural and bodily experiences has the potential to enrich our historical perspective.

## CONCLUSION: PARASITES AND POSTMODERNISM

What is largely absent from the historical scholarship on malaria in the twentieth century is history from below — history from the perspective of the sufferers themselves. Malaria's history is mainly focused on scientists and control or eradication campaigns, and on histories of medical specialties and public health reforms, though scholars no longer write in an uncritical, triumphalist mode. This is a disease history that is in need of reframing in order to capture a wider range of experience and understanding. Medical anthropology, on the other hand, focuses on the experience of the sufferers and can provide accounts of current ethnomedical understandings of fevers and/or malaria. Malariologists, as well as historians, could profit from this deep local knowledge. For example, studies of the use (or non-use) of bednets in China or Guatemala say a great deal about people's understanding of the connection between mosquitoes and malaria, their uses of space within and outside their homes and how their sleeping patterns differ by age and sex. Or, to take another example, ethnomedical studies in Africa and Asia have delved thoroughly into local categories of fever and local health-seeking strategies, and have especially attempted to answer the questions of when and why people choose 'traditional' or Western medicine or various combinations of possible treatments.

This ethnomedical literature, however, is limited in its historical reach and could benefit from broader contextualization. Moreover, both medical anthropology and the history of malaria have much to gain from oral historical approaches that seek out past experiences in particular settings, revealing the very different histories told by local people compared to those told by the scientists, the malaria control experts and the archives.

To return to the theme raised at the beginning of this chapter, understanding the experience of disease may be not only the best way to track the emergence of those metaphors that scientists and the public use to frame disease and which ultimately constitute popular and medical scientific knowledge. It may also suggest alternative metaphors, discourses and practices. For example, the 'mosquito discourse' that through most of the century dominated many scientists' understanding of malaria and motivated the eradication campaigns is an example of the dominance of a certain kind of frame that allowed the neglect of socio-economic factors.

Today, the 'insecticide-impregnated bednet discourse' is one example of a new kind of framing, with elements that can also be found in representations of vaccine research and other current work on malaria control. In the attention this kind of discourse gives to a wide range of local environmental factors it signals a return to an ecological perspective. Along with this local sensitivity, however, comes a disturbing fragmentation and privatization of interventions, hitched to the infrastructure of international development and its questionable practices, hierarchies, priorities, and tendency to depoliticize every problem. In the impregnated bednet discourse, as well as in the discourses of complexity surrounding vaccine research and accelerating parasite resistance, we see an emerging story of postmodern complexity and fragmentation. This story also supports a professional strategy of scientists, seeking to colonize new research sites — for both proper bednet use and appropriate vaccine cocktails, every locality demands research — a fragmentation and proliferation of research which, perhaps once again, allows policy makers to focus on technical questions and avoid the intractable problem of poverty and its necessarily political solutions.

A small number of scholars are now not only providing critical histories of the scientific and technocratic experience of malaria and its framing of the disease, but are also beginning to construct alternative histories. What they explore in these histories are experiences situated in other cultural, social and political contexts — the experiences of the majority of those who have historically suffered and combated this disease. Examples include Arnold's discussion of Indian nationalists' views of malaria and racial degeneration and Ranger and McGregor's discussion of progressive Africans' views of the disease in the context of forced resettlement in colonial Zimbabwe (see above). Similarly, K.T. Silva's account of malaria eradication efforts in colonial Sri Lanka attempts to capture local people's divergent views of the disease and its meaning. Often these local accounts focus on political solutions or play crucial roles in the imagining of a people's identity, in contrast to the scientists' and policy makers' focus on technical solutions that avoid the necessity of political analysis or imagination. Thus, these local histories can make it possible for historians to dislodge scientific discourses from their privileged position in the history of malaria and provide alternative and, ideally, useful, understandings of the disease.

The most imaginative moves in this direction, however, must be reserved for fiction, though fiction can also be a great stimulus to the historical imagination. In *The Calcutta Chromosome: A Novel of Fevers, Delirium & Discovery*, Amitav Ghosh provides a counter-history of the discovery of malaria, adventurously reading against the grain of the standard accounts dominated by Ross' scientific heroism and the Western meaning of the disease. In Ghosh's alternative account, the main actors are the marginalized and subordinated Indians who suffer the disease, the impoverished sweepers and dung-gatherers whom Ross uses as his assistants and the subjects of his experiments. In the end they use Ross to accomplish their own very different and more profound goals — and they use malaria itself to transcend the experience of disease, poverty and powerlessness.

REFERENCES

1.  Alfred Russel Wallace, *My Life: A Record of Events and Opinions*, Vol. 1, (London: Chapman & Hall, 1905), pp. 361–363.
2.  Hoffman and Miller, in Stephen L. Hoffman, (ed.), *Malaria Vaccine Development*. (Washington, DC: American Society for Microbiology, 1996), p. 11, and Brian Greenwood, 'What Can Be Expected from Malaria Vaccines?', in Hoffman, (ed.), 1996, p. 284.
3.  W.F. Bynum, 'An Experiment that Failed: Malaria Control at Mian Mir,' *Parassitologia* (1994), **36**: 107–120, p. 107.
4.  B. Fantini, 'Anophelism without Malaria: An Ecological and Epidemiological Puzzle,' *Parassitologia* (1994), **36(1–2)**: 83–106.
5.  Amitav Ghosh, *The Calcutta Chromosome*. (London: Picador, 1996); p. 51.
6.  Margaret Humphreys, 'Kicking a Dying Dog: DDT and the Demise of Malaria in the American South, 1942–1950,' *Isis* (1996), **87(1)**: 1–17.

## FURTHER READING

Bruce-Chwatt, L.J. and Zulueta, J. de, *The Rise and Fall of Malaria in Europe: A Historico-Epidemiological Study*. (Oxford: Oxford University Press [on behalf of the] Regional Office for Europe of the WHO, 1980).

Bynum, W.F. and Fantini, B., 'Malaria and Ecosystems: Historical Aspects, Proceedings of a Rockefeller Foundation conference, Bellagio, 18–22 October 1993', *Parassitologia* (1994), **36**: (1–2).

Curtin, Philip, *Death by Migration: Europe's Encounter with the Tropical World in the Nineteenth Century*. (Cambridge and New York: Cambridge University Press, 1989).

Desowitz, Robert S., *The Malaria Capers*. (New York: W.W. Norton & Company, 1991).

Ghosh, Amitav, *The Calcutta Chromosome: A Novel of Fevers, Delirium & Discovery*. (Picador, 1996).

Hackett, L.W., *Malaria in Europe*. (Oxford: Oxford University Press, 1944).

Harrison, Gordon, *Mosquitoes, Malaria & Man: A History of the Hostilities Since 1880*. (London: John Murray, 1978).

Harrison, Mark, *Public Health in British India: Anglo-Indian Preventive Medicine, 1859–1914*. (Cambridge: Cambridge University Press, 1994).

Hoffman, Stephen L., (ed.), *Malaria Vaccine Development*. (Washington, DC: American Society for Microbiology, 1996).

Jarcho, Saul, *Quinine's Predecessor: Francesco Torti and the Early History of Cinchona*. (Baltimore: Johns Hopkins University Press, 1993).

Jones, J. Colvard, 'Are Mosquitoes Monogamous?', *Nature* (March 30, 1973), **242**: 343–4.

Targett, G.A.T., (ed.), *Malaria: Waiting for the Vaccine*, London School of Hygiene and Tropical Medicine First Annual Public Health Forum. (Chichester: John Wiley & Sons, 1991).

Wailoo, Keith, *Drawing Blood: Technology and Disease Identity in Twentieth-Century America*. (Johns Hopkins University Press: Baltimore and London, 1997).

Worboys, Michael, 'Manson, Ross, and Colonial Medical Policy: Tropical Medicine in London and Liverpool, 1899–1914' in R. McLeod and M. Lewis (eds), *Disease, Medicine, and Empire: Perspectives on Western Medicine and the Experience of European Expansion*. (London: Routledge, 1988), pp. 21–37.

# CHAPTER 46

# The Chinese Experience

FRANCESCA BRAY

I n 1900 China was known as 'the sick man of Asia.' Racked by foreign predations and civil rebellions, the weakened Qing dynasty was ailing and so too were its subjects. The diseases of poverty were rife throughout the cities and villages of China. People lived debilitated by chronic complaints and in constant fear of sickness and death. One newborn in five died; life expectancy was thirty-five years. Western medical services were available only in a few missionary clinics in the cities; few people could afford the services of Chinese-style physicians; and when illness struck, the poor and uneducated saw little reason to prefer either system of formal medicine to prayers and rituals.

Since 1949 China's health experience has been transformed. Primary health care systems pioneered in a few rural regions under the Republican government in the 1930s were revived by the Communist state as the basis of a nation-wide network integrating local basic health care and preventive medical services into an urban grid of modern hospitals and other specialist centers. Life expectancy has risen to seventy years (comparable to the UK and the US, though still less than in Japan) and infant mortality has officially fallen to under thirty-five per thousand live births (Tables 1, 3). Today the most common causes of death in China are diseases of the elderly like strokes and cancer (Table 2); when a child dies it is an unexpected tragedy. The Chinese nowadays consider that their main health challenges are the 'diseases of modernization.' Many medical specialists believe that the most promising avenue for future medical progress is the development of an 'integrated' medicine combining biomedicine and Traditional Chinese Medicine (TCM), but many ordinary people simply prefer TCM.

## TRADITION, SCIENCE AND PATRIOTISM

A thumbnail sketch of the historical formation of TCM will clarify its changing fortunes and nature in the course of this century, and its shifting relations with biomedicine.

The founding works of China's indigenous medical tradition, such as the *Yellow Emperor's Classic of Internal Medicine* and the *Treatise on Cold Damage Disorders*, date back about two thousand years. These classical works remained the touchstone of

TABLE 1: HEALTH FACILITIES IN CHINA

|  | 1937 | 1949 | 1957 | 1970 | 1980 | 1992 |
|---|---|---|---|---|---|---|
| Pop (mi) |  | 560 | 633 | 820 | 983 | 1,183 |
| Mortality/oo |  | 20 | 10.8 | 7.64 | 6.34 | 6.64 |
| Life expectancy |  | 35 | 57 | 68 | 68 | 70 |
| County hospitals | 181 | 1,392 | 2,078 | n/a | 2,078 | n/a |
| Hospital beds |  |  |  |  | 1,982,000 | 2,744,000 |
| State-employed W doctors (full med. graduates) | 5,400 | 41,000 [15,000] | 74,500 | 150,000 | 447,000 | 1,327,875 |
| Intermed W. med graduates |  | 107,000 | 302,000 | 400,000 | 444,000 | 422,352 |
| TCM doctors employed by state |  | n/a | 487,000 | n/a | 262,000 | 243,502 |
| Paramedics, Barefoot Doctors, Country Doctors |  |  | 261,000 | 1,000,000 | 1,600,000 | 1,269,000 |
| Midwives and sparetime PH workers |  |  |  |  | 3,800,000 | 58,397 |
| W nurses |  |  |  |  | 466,000 | 974,541 |

This table was compiled using figures from Judith Banister, *China's Changing Population* (Stanford, Stanford University Press, 1987); the papers in 'Aspects of the medical care system in the People's Republic of China,' special issue of *Social Science and Medicine* 41, 8 (1995); and the *Human Development Report 1995* (United Nations Development Programme, Oxford: Oxford University Press, 1995).

The population figure for 1949 is a reconstruction (Banister Table 2.7). There were no censuses between 1851 and 1953; the population in 1851 was estimated at 430 million.

The *mortality figures* are almost all significant underestimates, as are the infant mortality figures in Table 3 (see discussion below).

County hospitals: the total number of counties in the PRC is 2182.

The fluctuations and inconsistencies in the figures for different categories of medical personnel reflect inconsistencies in the categorizations used in different surveys, and the potential confusion over personnel employed by the state and those in private practice. Between about 1957 and 1979, there were theoretically no private medical practitioners in China. Since 1979, not only has private practice been allowed, but also numerous state employees combine their official jobs with private practice. If figures were available recording the medical personnel in private practice in 1992, the rapid expansion of medical services that has occurred over the last ten years would be more clearly visible.

TABLE 2: LEADING CAUSES OF DEATH

| 1929–31[a] | 1957 (urban)[b] | 1973–75[c] | 1987[b] urban | 1987[b] rural | 1992[c] urban | 1992[c] rural |
|---|---|---|---|---|---|---|
| Dysentery 216 | Respiratory 17% | Circulatory 155 [21%] | cancer 21.6% | respiratory 20.8% | cancer 126 [21.7%] | respiratory 168 [26.6%] |
| Smallpox 207 | Infectious 8% | Respiratory 95 [13%] | cerebro-vascular 20.6% | heart 18% | cerebro-vascular 123 [21.2%] | cerebro-vascular 104 [16.4%] |
| Typhoid 196 | TB 7.5% | Cancer 74 [10%] | heart 15% | cerebro-vascular 14.8% | respiratory 98 [16.8%] | cancer 103 [16.2%] |
| TB 181 | Digestive 7.3% | Accidents, injury 57 [7.8%] | trauma 7.6% | cancer 14.2% | heart 85 [14.7%] | injury & intoxication 69 [10.9%] |
| Cholera 164 | Heart 6.6% | Digestive 54 [7.4%] | digestive 4.5% | trauma 10.3% | injury & intoxication 40 [7%] | heart 65 [10.2%] |
| Measles 122 | Cerebro-vascular 5.5% | Infectious 51 [7.0%] | | digestive 5% | | |
| Diphtheria 65 | Cancer 5.2% | Perinatal 37 [5.1%] | | TB 2.9% | | |
| Pneumonia 40 | nervous system 4.1% | TB 35 [4.8%] | TB 1.6% | | | |

[a]: per hundred thousand population
[b]: percentage of total deaths
[c]: per hundred thousand [percentage of total deaths]

Figures are taken from Banister 1987: 51, 111; Wenbo Xu, 'Flourishing health work in China', *Social Science and Medicine* 41, 8 (1995); and William C.L. Hsiao, 'The Chinese health care system: lessons for other nations', (*ibid*). Some figures for 1987 are missing because Hsiao's table compares death rates from the main diseases in 1957 and does not list the eight main causes of death, urban or rural, in 1985. Xu's figures for 1992 give only the five leading causes of death, urban and rural.

The main points to note are the following. The figures for 1929–31 reflect a very high prevalence of infectious diseases. Parasitic diseases were also very common in Republican China, though they were seldom the primary cause of death. The early years of the PRC saw large-scale campaigns to eliminate flies, paddy snails, mosquitoes and other transmitters of disease, improvements in sanitation and nutrition, and systematic vaccination programs. The necessary emphasis during this period on preventive medicine explains the marked reduction in deaths from infectious diseases seen in the figures for 1957. From the 1960s the investment in local basic medical services and the development of more sophisticated central hospitals allowed curative medicine to play a greater role, and by the late 1980s the health profile of the PRC approaches that of the advanced industrial nations.

learned medical debate throughout the imperial era (which lasted altogether from 221 BC to AD 1911), and they still form the core of the Chinese medical curriculum as taught in medical schools today.

The first centuries of the imperial era saw the elaboration of models of physiological process and of categorizations of disease, and the compilation of the first great compendia of *materia medica*. The Song state (960–1279) established an imperial medical college, sponsored the compilation and printing of medical works, and set up dispensaries to aid victims of epidemics. The Yuan dynasty (1279–1368) was famous for the sophisticated theories of physiological process developed by a group of medical scholars to one or the other of whom most later physicians traced their allegiance. During the later part of the Ming dynasty (1368–1644) state participation in medical education and the provision of health services declined, to be replaced (at least in prosperous regions like the Lower Yangzi provinces) by private sponsorship and a thriving market for medical services and publications. The resulting intellectual ferment lasted well into the Qing dynasty (1644–1911). Medical thinkers sought new explanations of epidemics and contagion and devised new forms of therapy; the vigor of medical debate even produced a form of medical journal at the end of the eighteenth century.

Confucian ethics held that learning should be put at the service of one's family and of the state, and as a well-known saying had it, if one could not become a good minister then one might try to be a good doctor. Many physicians were scholars and philosophers for whom the chief source of knowledge was the medical classics. But there was another famous saying, that one should only consult a doctor whose father and grandfather had been doctors before him. There were also many physicians who depended much less on books but learned their craft from their fathers (some families were famous for secret remedies passed down from generation to generation), or by apprenticing themselves to a sequence of experienced doctors.

It was generally held that an ethical physician should treat poor patients without charge. But although free medical services were sometimes offered to poor people by the state or by gentry organizations, and though medical biographies suggest that many physicians did treat poor patients for nothing, such charity was at best a drop in the ocean. Furthermore learned Chinese medicine used 'explanatory models'[1] that were alien to the majority of the population.

In very early times shamans and diviners were the principal healers, but learned Chinese medicine avoided supernatural explanations of disease, concentrating instead on cosmological reasoning according to which health depended on the balance of *yin* (female, cool, damp, condensed) and *yang* (male, warm, dry, dispersed) principles, and the proper circulation of *qi* (vital energy) through the tracts and organs of the body. Physicians examined their patients by pulse-taking, observation and questioning, and treated them with subtle combinations of drugs in which the well-known general formulae appropriate to a broad category of disorder were modulated to match an individual patient's particular manifestation of that disorder. Medicine applied secular cosmological principles to the microcosm of the human body, and viewed illnesses as the natural outcome of internal imbalances triggered by environmental or behavioral factors. But most people continued to believe that illness was also caused by fate or pernicious spirits. People who could afford to consult a learned physician hedged their bets by also calling in priests or shamans, not to mention rival physicians. But the majority could at best afford a few fire-crackers or incense sticks to exorcise the evil spirits of sickness, like C.C. Chen's family in the remote city of Chengdu:

> As a child in the city of Chengdu in the early 1900s, I often heard people striking gongs in our neighborhood. Sometimes I would go to take a look, finding that someone was ill, usually lying in bed. The sound of gongs, together with the smell of burning incense, was supposed to drive away ghosts believed to be haunting the sick. I dimly remember that this kind of incantation has been rendered in our home — consisting of three dark rooms — during my mother's final illness. What that ritual was all about, I had no idea. I only knew that it had not saved my mother, and that she had died of some unknown disease.[2]

Physicians in imperial China frequently complained of the ignorance that led the families of sick people to call in a priest or a 'quack' rather than a proper physician. By the beginning of the twentieth century Chinese learned medicine faced an even more dangerous threat than superstition and poverty. Starting with the first Opium War of 1840, the incursions of the Western imperial powers had brought the Qing state to its knees; the ease with which China was defeated and the stunning technological superiority of Western gunboats and industrial plants convinced many politically-active intellectuals that traditional Chinese learning was not only worthless but pernicious. Only 'Mr Science and Mr Democracy' could save China and make it into a modern, independent nation. Chinese medicine was not only failing to cure China, argued the young patriots, it was making China sick. It should be banned in favor of scientific medicine.

Most ordinary Chinese still distrusted the foreign 'missionary medicine.' The treaties of the nineteenth century had obliged the Chinese government to allow entry to Christian missionaries, most of whom offered basic medical services in the hope of attracting converts. In the first few decades of the missionaries' presence, Western medicine offered few advantages over Chinese. Cataract surgery and the virtues of soap were regarded with some dubiety by locals. Some thought Christian medicine only worked for Christians, others believed the missionaries boiled down human eyes to turn them into silver. In nineteenth-century Japan a strong government was able to enforce general vaccination against smallpox, with such spectacular results that the population at large was convinced of the superiority of Western medicine, and the state was able to impose a national system of Western medical training and services. In China no such enforcement was possible and missionaries made little headway against the Smallpox Deity.

However, by the beginning of the century Western biomedicine was widely considered by educated people, at least on its home ground, to have outstripped all traditional medicines in therapeutic efficacy. The belief in the superiority of biomedicine was closely connected to its claims to apply science to the problems of health. Doctors took quantitative measurements of their patients' vital signs. Anesthesia allowed surgeons to make full use of their anatomical knowledge, asepsis and sterilization gave patients a better chance of recovery; bacteria were isolated and antitoxins and vaccines developed for several of the common diseases. For those around the world who became acquainted with the germ theory of disease, the power of modern drugs, and the principles of hygiene, modern medicine seemed a tool with almost miraculous powers to control health, combat sickness and death, and improve society. Young people eager to change the world scientifically or politically threw themselves into medicine.

C.C. Chen, who played a distinguished role in the development of public health services in the 1930s and in the 1980s, lost all his close relatives except his father and uncle to illness while he was still a child. His mother, stepmother, brother, sister and aunt all died; in retrospect he was able to diagnose TB and typhoid as the cause of death in some cases; others remained mysterious. "Because of this child-hood experience with suffering, disease, and death," he tells us, "from an early age I was determined to find another, better system of medicine and to make that medicine available throughout urban and rural China."[3] In 1917 Chen accompanied his dying stepmother to the French consulate in Chengdu where a physician examined her using a thermometer, stethoscope and sphygmomometer. Although the French doctor was unable to cure his stepmother's terminal TB, Chen "was impressed by the status and prestige the physician seemed to enjoy, and more so by the scientific instruments at his disposal. Then and there, I determined to become a modern physician myself."[4]

The Qing dynasty fell in 1911. At first the new Republican government showed no particular eagerness to support medical reform; however an epidemic of plague in Manchuria marked a turning-point in official attitudes. In the first months of the epidemic, in 1910 and 1911, the plague took 60,000 lives. Wu Liande (1879–1960), who had studied medicine at Cambridge, managed to bring the epidemic under control by means of a massive immunization campaign combined with strict quarantine measures. Wu's dramatic success in curbing an epidemic against which Chinese medicine had proved helpless convinced some officials as well as members of the public that Western scientific medicine had its advantages. Official blessing was given to the establishment of medical schools and societies.

The most famous was the Peking Union Medical College, funded by the Rockefeller Foundation and equipped to the highest international standards for teaching, treatment and research. C.C. Chen enrolled in the PUMC in 1921, one of a cohort of young Chinese who studied medicine as a patriotic commitment to curing the sick man of Asia. Some went abroad, to Japan (like Lu Xun, the famous writer, and Guo Moro, who served as Minister of Culture under Mao) or to the West (Sun Yatsen, the revolutionary founder of the Guomintang party, and the first president of the Chinese republic, studied medicine in Hong Kong and Hawaii); some, like Chen, studied in China. In 1915 there were enough practitioners to form a National Medical Association; in 1919 a missionary report calculated that there were about 600 foreign physicians in China, and 900 Chinese physicians trained in Western medicine, and China had several minor medical colleges as well as the flagship PUMC.

Conventional modernizers felt that well-equipped hospitals should form the nucleus of a new health system for China. But others like Wu and Chen believed that the first priority was the provision of basic public health and preventive medical services at village level. It was important not only to provide health care services but also to educate ordinary people to stop thinking of Western medicine as 'foreign' and to start thinking of it as 'scientific'. This populist perspective on China's needs was not confined to young firebrands at the PUMC, nor to the domain of medicine, but was shared by a number of activists who argued that China could never achieve stability until the poverty, poor health, ignorance and political apathy of the peasantry were overcome. A key figure was James Y.C. Yen, who was educated at Yale and worked with the Chinese contract workers recruited to France during the First World War. On his return to China Yen helped organize a Mass Education Movement which started in the cities but in the mid-1920s managed to start up a pioneer project in a barren rural district called Dingxian, not far from Beijing and with a population of just under half a million. The MEM was premised on self-help; its goals were to teach basic literacy skills; to alleviate poverty by teaching improved farming methods; to combat disease by introducing scientific medical knowledge and public health measures; and to reform local political structures so as to foster an ethos of public service. The project was supported by sympathetic local officials, gentry and intellectuals, as well as funding from foundations and from Yen's personal contacts abroad.

The first Director of Rural Health was appointed at Dingxian in 1928 and oversaw the construction of a small hospital with American funds. C.C. Chen took over the position in 1932, and served in Dingxian until 1937 when the Japanese advance made the MEM position untenable. During his time in Dingxian, Chen and his colleagues pioneered a system of local public health education and services that rapidly reduced mortality rates and improved health levels. The pyramidal structure of the rural health organization at Dingxian, with its emphasis on the training of paramedics, provided an almost exact model for the health-care institutions of the People's Republic. The provisions differed signally, however, in that Dingxian offered only 'scientific' medicine and medical ideas. As far as Chen was concerned, TCM was exclusively curative in its approach and therefore had no role to play in the program of health maintenance and disease prevention that he and his colleagues designed for Dingxian.

Chen however was moderate in his attitude towards TCM compared with many of his pro-science contemporaries, who called for the official banning of Chinese medicine. Given the weakness of the state, these attacks did not destroy Chinese medicine but prompted practitioners to join forces to justify their discipline. There was a variety of responses to the accusations that Chinese medicine was unscientific, incoherent and inefficacious. They included a flurry of laboratory investigations of the chemical qualities of traditional drugs, the founding of journals and associations, and attempts to professionalize traditional medical training by establishing formal colleges and curricula, by standardizing texts, case-records, and so on. Some strove to make Chinese medicine more like Western medicine, making translations between Chinese and Western terminology that suggested the scientific nature of TCM. Others emphasized the incommensurability of the two underlying philosophies, and stressed the contrasts between Western and Chinese diagnosis and therapy.

Throughout the imperial period classical medical theories had continually been reinterpreted and reassessed, while the institutional and intellectual contexts in which medicine was practised changed repeatedly. Confronted with the powerful threat of Western knowledge, not a few educated Chinese started to conceive of Chinese medicine as representing the essence of Chinese natural wisdom and social ethics. As well as embodying a distinctively Chinese cosmology in its conceptions of bodily processes and interactions with the environment, the importance of history in Chinese medical theory and practice was inescapable: a diagnosis always involved reference to the classical works and their later interpretations, a prescription was a variation on a drug combination that was perhaps invented by a famous physician eight hundred years ago, its modifications and improvements over the centuries recorded and drawn upon by the physician prescribing for his patient in 1925 (or in 1997). To practise or to consume Chinese medicine was consciously to partake of a historical tradition. In Republican China both biomedical and traditional physicians claimed the patriotic high ground, the former in the name of social progress, the latter in the name of cultural identity.

## STANDING ON TWO LEGS: SOCIALIST MEDICINE AND THE WISDOM OF THE MASSES

In 1949 the People's Republic of China was established; after decades of civil war and the ravages of the Japanese invasion, the unity of the Chinese state was restored. Socialist principles required the Chinese Communist Party to provide health services for the entire population, but it had few obvious resources at its disposal. The number of scientifically-trained doctors and of Western-style clinics was small (many doctors like other professionals had either fled the civil war or chose to leave China at the Communist victory). The Chinese state had few funds of its own and few sources of outside support. The answer, declared Mao Zedong, Chairman of the CCP, was for China to 'stand on two legs.' This meant making optimal use of both biomedical and TCM personnel and facilities.

The most urgent medical priority for the Communist government was the provision of basic health care throughout rural China. The collectivization of rural production (first as cooperatives, then from 1959 as People's Communes — large administrative units that included as many as 50,000 people) provided the fiscal and administrative infrastructure for the development first, in the 1950s, of county hospitals and clinics, and then, in the 1960s, of a coordinated public health system very similar in structure to the model pioneered in Dingxian. A fundamental difference was that traditional Chinese healing methods were an integral part of the pyramid of services provided.

Biomedicine is in general much more expensive than traditional medicines, if only because sophisticated technical equipment is required for much diagnosis, treatment and research. The three-level health system developed by the Chinese state reduced costs by centralizing expensive biomedical services at the tertiary level of care, in provincial hospitals with attached medical schools; the majority of doctors working in such hospitals had a full MD. At the secondary level of county clinics, which were equipped at a much more basic level, many of the junior biomedical personnel had only an intermediary qualification, while primary level services were provided largely by paramedics with only a rudimentary training in biomedicine. A system of referral offered access to sophisticated treatment to anyone who was seriously ill, but filtered out patients with minor problems at the primary and secondary level, thus avoiding the overloading of tertiary facilities.

In the thirty years between the founding of the PRC and the collapse of the people's communes, socialized medicine and public health produced a transformation of Chinese health (Tables 1, 2). This was achieved at extraordinarily low costs (an average of US$5 per capita per annum for the period 1952 to 1982), although the state was never able to provide free health for all, and inevitably the system proved less than totally fair. Hospital running costs and the salaries of medical workers at the secondary and tertiary levels were paid for directly by the state. At the primary level, the paramedics known as 'Barefoot Doctors' were paid by the collective at the same work-point rates as other members. Communal medicine (the Cooperative Medical System) was available to all collective members and their dependants for a small fee; a patient who was referred to a medical school hospital in the provincial capital would have to pay her expenses on leaving the hospital, but would be able to reclaim a percentage from her collective afterwards. However while urban industrial collectives were often able to reimburse their members at almost the full rate, rural collectives might only be able to manage 70 or 60%, and rural incomes in China in the 1970s were roughly one-third of urban incomes. Although a number of diseases endemic to rural China, including malaria and schistosomiasis, were treated free, if a peasant required hospital treatment in a tertiary-level facility the family might have to pay more than half a year's income. Doctors in the infectious diseases unit of the Hubei Provincial

Medical College Second Attached Hospital in Wuhan, one of China's main cities, said this meant they had to think carefully about costs when prescribing medication for rural patients; they were also likely to recommend an earlier discharge for patients without insurance.

One remarkable aspect of this system, which still forms the backbone of the Chinese health system today, is the symbiosis between biomedicine and TCM. At the secondary and tertiary levels patients are offered a choice of biomedical or TCM clinics or wards; but flexibility is not limited to the level of patient choice. Biomedical physicians are required to take basic courses in Chinese medicine as part of their training, while the curriculum in the numerous official colleges of TCM established since 1959 includes courses in anatomy, physiology and pharmacology. During the ten years of the Great Proletarian Cultural Revolution (1966–76) many doctors and medical students who were 'sent down' to work in villages acquired interests and skills in TCM or folk techniques. So in China it is quite routine for a doctor on a biomedical ward to call in a TCM colleague for an opinion or to prescribe TCM treatment as part of the therapy — as an example, a patient in the infectious diseases ward of a teaching hospital, suffering from hemmorhagic fever, was prescribed acupuncture to control a severe case of hiccups that was exhausting him.[5] Perhaps the most famous combination of biomedical and 'traditional' Chinese medical technology is acupuncture anesthesia — for the roughly 70% of patients who are receptive, this procedure avoids the dangers and side-effects of a total anesthetic. Some surgeons routinely recommend traditional Chinese tonic drugs to aid in recuperation after surgery.

This flexibility on the part of biomedical doctors probably appears more remarkable to the reader than the fact that many TCM physicians today include temperature and blood counts in their diagnosis rather than relying exclusively on qualitative signs, or that they refer their patients to a surgeon if they suspect appendicitis. That a 'traditional' medicine should borrow from 'real' medicine seems obvious in a country like Britain where non-biomedical treatments are at best tolerated by the medical establishment as eccentric alternatives. But in China economic and political exigencies have steadily blurred the boundaries between the two conceptual systems of biomedicine and TCM, permitting a growing therapeutic complementarity and conceptual convergence.

Let us take drugs as an example. In the 1950s the Chinese government lacked hard currency to purchase proprietary biomedical drugs from abroad, so it urged researchers to develop substitutes made from local products wherever possible. At the same time it encouraged research into the chemical properties of Chinese drugs and prescriptions, as part of a drive to provide scientific validation for traditional medicine. Today traditional explanations of drug action are still given in terms of TCM physiology, for example ginseng builds up *yang* energy, angelica nourishes blood. Chinese prescriptions target the disorder categories of traditional medicine, which seldom correspond exactly to biomedical disease categories. But chemical analysis of their properties permits the action of Chinese drugs to be translated into biomedical terms, and they can then be prescribed for biomedically defined problems. This not only bolsters the scientific claims of TCM as it is practised today but can extend these claims into the past. To give an extreme example, it has been discovered that dried sea-horse, first mentioned in *materia medica* many centuries ago as a tonic of vital energies, has positive effects on the auto-immune system; from there to headlines declaring "Ancient Chinese had cure for AIDS" is but a step.[6] More seriously, Chinese pharmaceutical research has produced many low-cost substitutes not only for Western proprietary drugs but also for rare and costly ingredients such as rhinoceros horn that are much favored in Chinese medicine.

As well as becoming steadily more 'scientific', TCM also became markedly more popular, both for institutional and political reasons. The famous Barefoot Doctors who were trained in their hundreds of thousands in the 1950s and 1960s to provide basic health services at the level of the work-brigade (or village) were local people with some previous medical experience. This experience, obviously, was seldom biomedical. Some had been midwives, some herbalists, acupuncturists or bonesetters. Doctor Shen of Longbow Village, the central figure in the film "To Taste a Hundred Herbs," worked as his father's apprentice and started practising traditional medicine (specializing in 'nervous' problems) at the age of seventeen. Very few of the Barefoot Doctors had any formal qualifications. When they were recruited they were given three to six months' training (followed up at intervals by further training courses) in the basic concepts of hygiene, anatomy and physiology, and TCM. They were taught to recognize common ailments, biomedical or traditional, to give basic therapy in the form of first-aid, acupuncture, and simple prescriptions (again these might be biomedical or traditional). Aided by village health workers, the Barefoot Doctors educated villagers in hygiene and nutrition; they organized sanitation and the eradication of pests such as malarial mosquitoes or the schistosomiasis-carrying snails that lived in the rice paddies; and they immunized children. Roughly a third of Barefoot Doctors were women; every brigade had either a female Barefoot Doctor or a midwife who was responsible for giving birth-control advice and helping with delivery in normal births. When Barefoot Doctors encountered cases more serious than they could deal with, they referred patients up the system.

Many Barefoot Doctors were at best 'quacks' by traditional standards, and their incorporation into the medical establishment produced some interesting modifications in TCM. The first decades of the PRC, and in particular the ten years of the Cultural Revolution, turned all the intellectual snobberies of earlier eras upside down. Abstract scholarship was denigrated, the empirical knowledge accumulated over the centuries by the Chinese working masses extolled. Medicine was an ideal field for recovering and developing popular knowledge that was unmistakably Chinese. Acupuncture is a good example. First used in very ancient times, for the last few centuries it had been neglected by learned physicians in favor of herbal prescriptions; during the Qing dynasty acupuncturists were regarded as vulgar healers. But acupuncture is an extremely cheap form of therapy and much easier to learn than herbal prescription; it was revived to great effect as part of the training program for the Barefoot Doctors. The 1960s saw a torrent of publications on new acupuncture techniques contributed by health workers on the ground, though it was usually left to research scientists or textual scholars to provide theoretical explanations of how these new acupuncture treatments worked. The period also saw the publication of numerous collections of folk remedies, whose editors often had to work hard to provide justifications that were convincing whether in terms of TCM or of biomedicine, and to exclude the elements of sympathetic magic or other forms of 'superstition' that were anathema to the Communist Party.

The most striking effects of China's rural health care system depended on biomedical knowledge: sanitation measures, education in hygiene and nutrition, sterilized blades for cutting the umbilical cord, birth control, and immunization. But the paramedical personnel who did so much to transform the health profile of rural China had really only the thinnest veneer of biomedical training. In cultural terms, one might say that the establishment of primary healthcare in the PRC had exactly the opposite effect from what C.C. Chen and his colleagues strove for in Dingxian. When Chen first went to work in Dingxian, 220 out of the 472 villages had no medical facilities of any kind; by the mid-1960s, they all had a Barefoot Doctor. A greater proportion of the population than ever before became familiar with the concepts and therapies of TCM, while knowledge of biomedicine remained largely superficial. Urban Chinese might say that Chinese medicine works well for chronic complaints while 'Western' medicine is best for acute problems; rural Chinese were more likely to opine that Western medicine deals only with symptoms, while Chinese medicine gets to the root of the matter.

## "BLACK CAT, WHITE CAT": MEDICINE IN THE MARKET-PLACE

In 1976 Mao died. After the apogee of socialism exemplified by the People's Communes and the Cultural Revolution, a new era began. The new Chinese leadership decided that revolutionary fervor and material self-denial had reached the limits of their potential. The time had come to increase standards of living, and to modernize China's economy so that it could join the ranks of the developed nations by the year 2000. Formal education (disrupted between 1966 and 1976) was reinstated, research in science and technology encouraged, and in 1979 the state endorsed a range of New Economic Policies, under which the collectivist organization of production was disbanded and households were encouraged to strive for socialist prosperity as independent units — as Deng Xiaoping put it, "What does it matter if a cat is black or white as long as it catches mice?" All these measures had repercussions in the domain of medicine and health.

One domain in which the new emphasis on modernization and economic growth produced dramatic changes was family planning. In the early years of the PRC, population was viewed as a resource in its own right and couples were not discouraged from having children. However as part of the program to improve rural health, in the 1950s and 1960s birth control methods were made available to rural couples, who were encouraged to space their families for the sake of both mother and children's health. The contraceptive technique of choice was usually IUDs for women. Though Chinese researchers investigated several promising drugs for controlling male fertility, men in China as elsewhere were fearful that drugs or sterilization would damage their health and virility, so the burden of birth control fell almost entirely on women. At that time most women welcomed having the technological means to avoid frequent pregnancies. Meanwhile improved standards of health and medical care meant that fewer infants and children died, and adults lived longer, so even thought the fertility rates of the sixties were much lower than before, they nevertheless contributed to an inexorable swelling of the population.

From 1971 to 1978 the state encouraged a 'later-longer-fewer' policy: couples should marry later, leave longer gaps between pregnancies, and have fewer children. Peasant couples were allowed three children in the early years of the policy, only two from 1977. Collective organization of production and administration made it relatively easy for the state to control reproductive behaviour, refusing permission to under-age couples to marry or imposing heavy fines on those who exceeded the norms of childbearing. Fertility fell dramatically in the course of the campaign, from six to just under three children per woman (Table 3). Even so China's population grew from 540 million in 1949 to around a billion in 1979 — a tribute to improvements in living standards and health care, but a serious challenge to matching population and resources.

The One-Child Family Policy was imposed in 1979, limiting each couple to a single child, whatever its sex. Certain exceptions were allowed: members of ethnic minorities, couples whose child died or was born deformed or otherwise defective. All other couples had a constitutional duty to practise contraception, and any woman who became pregnant in infringement of the rules was to undergo an abortion, however far advanced the pregnancy. The One-Child Family Policy has worked rather well in the towns. Even under the New Economic Policies many urban people are still employed by large work units that are able to offer medical care and pensions after retirement, and employment opportunities for urban women are good. But in the countryside families need more children, and especially more sons, if they are to prosper under the competitive system of household production units. After an initial phase of draconian enforcement most rural family planning committees now operate to more lenient and flexible standards.

The end of the Maoist era also marked a dramatic change in attitudes towards formal qualifications and learning. During the Cultural Revolution more weight

TABLE 3: FERTILITY TRENDS

| | 1929–31 | 1949 | 1957 | 1973 | 1975 | 1980 | 1992 |
|---|---|---|---|---|---|---|---|
| Female fertility | 5.5 | 6.1 | 6.4 | 4.5 | 3.6 | 2.2 | 2.0 |
| Contraceptive rates (married women) | | | 2.2 | | | | 83 |
| Av. age of women at first marriage | 17.5 | 18.7 | 19.2 | 21.0 | 21.7 | 23 | n/a |
| Infant mortality | 300 | n/a | 150 | 59 | 59 | 35 [40][1] | 34.7 [44][2] |

Figures are drawn from the same sources as Table 1.

The figures for 1929–31 are based on a survey of 46,601 rural families and are considered by demographers to be reasonably representative of the period; the figures for infant mortality are estimated (Banister 1987: 5 ff).

The contraceptive figure for 1957 is the proportion of the married population that available contraceptive stocks were considered sufficient to supply (Banister 1987: 91). The state invested in contraceptive research and the development of contraceptive factories in the course of the 1960s, and by the early 1970s was in a position to offer free contraception through local family planning associations to almost all its citizens. During the periods of strict family planning that ensued it has been in women's interest to declare that they are using contraception even when they are not; unfortunately for the 1970s and 1980s available figures are in terms of methods used rather than overall rates, but the figure of 83% estimated for 1986–93 is undoubtedly much too high (see Banister 1987; Susan Greenhalgh, 'Controlling births and bodies in village China,' *American Ethnologist* 21, 1 (1994): 3–30).

Female fertility rates and infant mortality rates are underestimated. Children may simply not be registered at birth (in the hope that the policies on the number of children allowed will eventually become less restrictive), or unwanted children (usually girls) may be killed at birth (see the discussion of sex ratios in Banister 220 ff). We can expect an additional official bias in the production of infant mortality statistics, given the importance of infant mortality figures as an indicator of human development. The infant mortality figures for 1957 are a rough estimate agreed upon by outside demographers (Banister 1987: 83; UNDP 1995). Those for 1975–75 are indirectly derived from the National Cancer Epidemiology Survey, and are therefore likely to be reasonably accurate. Those for 1980 and 1992 vary greatly from source to source; Hsiao estimates that among the poorest 15% of China's population the average infant mortality rate exceeds 75 per thousand (Hsiao 1995: 1048), whereas Xu claims that it is as low as 14.5 per thousand in the cities and 23 per thousand in rural areas — and then arrives at an overall average of 34 per thousand (Xu 1995: 1043).

Age at marriage may be calculated either Western style or according to the Chinese reckoning of one's year of life, whereby a child enters its first year at birth and its second at the New Year. A child born on 31st December 1995 is thus two on 1st January 1996 according to Chinese reckoning. Although PRC marriage laws presume Western age in prescribing lower limits, officials have often allowed couples to take advantage of the discrepancy to give their age in Chinese reckoning and marry younger. In Western terms, therefore, the figures given here are overestimates.

[1]: The lower figure is quoted in Banister (1987: 116), the higher is the estimate given in Hsiao 1995.

[2]: The lower figure is given by Xu 1995; the higher by UNDP 1995.

had been placed on practical experience in the service of the people than on formal education or laboratory research. Universities, including medical schools, were closed; academics and students were sent down to the countryside to learn from the masses. People from low down the conventional hierarchies of qualification were given unprecedented opportunities for advancement — for example a talented (and confident) nurse might move from handing the scalpel to performing surgery herself, or might take charge of diagnosing and prescribing for patients on her ward. In the post-Mao drive to modernization, formal education and qualifications were reinstated. Millions of students competed for places in the universities as soon as they were re-opened, and from 1979 the number of qualified doctors began to increase rapidly (Table 1). At the secondary and tertiary levels of health-care, the policy has been not to dismiss medical personnel who lacked formal qualifications, but to give them opportunities and encouragement to study further and to take formal qualifying examinations; unqualified staff are seldom promoted.

At the village level a new category of physicians has been created, the 'Country Doctor'. Barefoot Doctors can now take a formal examination that places them midway between the rank of Barefoot Doctor and that of a regular medical school graduate. As C.C. Chen points out, most of the Country Doctors offer TCM rather than biomedical services.

The salaries paid to state medical personnel have been kept low. This, together with cuts in state support of health insurance, has allowed the state to keep down the proportion of GNP spent on health services (3.6% in 1990 compared to 6% in Denmark and over 11% in the United States) — although this equilibrium is threatened by the impact on state insurance disbursements of steep rises in drug prices. The state hospital system is also in danger of losing its best-qualified doctors to the better rewarded private sector. In order to encourage private investment in health facilities the government has allowed private hospitals to open, many of them funded by foreign joint-venture companies and charging rates that are sometimes ten to twenty times those charged in public hospitals. They also pay higher salaries. Until the reforms people were not able to change jobs or residence at will; now medical markets and the increased mobility allowed by the reforms encourage qualified biomedical physicians to move from the countryside to the cities, and from the public to the private sector.

The reforms left the secondary and tertiary level of state health services in place, but their state funding has been reduced. The state continues to pay the salaries of personnel in state hospitals and township health centers, as well as covering the cost of new capital investments, but these institutions now have to fund roughly two-thirds of their costs from user fees. Almost all medical fees in state institutions are set by the government at less than cost. In 1984 an appendectomy in a county hospital cost 30 yuan (roughly US $5) to perform and the charge to the patient was 12.60 yuan; an outpatient visit at a town clinic cost 0.80 yuan and the patient was charged 0.10 yuan. Hospitals are now allowed to charge new high-technology services at profit-making levels, and to mark up Western drugs by 13–15% over wholesale prices, Chinese drugs by 25%. Not surprisingly, hospitals today carry out more high-tech diagnostics and prescribe more drugs than formerly. In the hard-pressed county hospitals, the proportion of income derived from sales of medicine increased from 45% in 1980 to 54% in 1990, while state support dropped from 13.6% to 4.4% of their spending budget.

At the village level, the disbanding of the communes quickly brought about the collapse of the former Cooperative Medical System, to be replaced by a largely private fee-for-service system. Since communes no longer paid Barefoot Doctors a regular salary, many of them preferred to retire (between 1978 and 1985 numbers fell from 1.8 to 1.3 million). Others qualified as Country Doctors and set up privately: in 1982 only 5% of village health posts were private practices, but by end of 1980s this had increased to about 48%. The main source of income for village doctors, as for urban hospitals, is the sale of drugs. 1985 saw the deregulation of drug production and distribution, which had previously been strictly controlled through state farms, laboratories and dispensaries. Village doctors, like urban hospitals, now make most of their profits by selling drugs; this is good news for hereditary doctors still in possession of time-honored family recipes, like Dr Shen of Longbow Village who finds eager clients for his Nerve Tonic Number One and Number Two.

Unfortunately the new fee-for-service system in the villages operates against the efficient provision of public health and prevention services. While charges for a diagnosis are typically 0.70 yuan, or 0.50 yuan for an injection, the fee for a vaccination is only 0.10 yuan, of which the physician returns 0.07 yuan to the state and keeps a mere 0.03 yuan. Dr Shen of Longbow complains that the hygienic disposal of manure has become difficult to organize now that animals are owned and stabled by individual families rather than the collective, and checking-up on compliance with the rules is not feasible now that the village no longer provides him with health aides. Since village doctors have to compete for profits and are minimally supervised, observers fear that the way is open for all kinds of abuse as well as neglect of basic preventive and diagnostic health care. However so far there is no evidence of a decline in health status.

There is evidence, however, of growing disparities in access to health care. In 1986 a senior official complained that an appendectomy cost no more than a pound of cucumbers. To try to reduce expenditure as well as the pressure on higher-level facilities, the government has introduced a series of changes in the insurance system since 1979. China's population is still 70% rural; until the end of the 1970s the majority (80–90%) had automatic if not full health coverage as members of rural communes. But now most rural families have to buy their own insurance if they want any; only about 20% currently have any protection from state or work-place medical care schemes; the proportion of the urban population covered by such schemes is higher because many of them work either for the government or for large industrial enterprises.

The urban-rural ratio of expenditure per capita on health was 3:1 in 1981 but is currently 5:1. Because they have little health insurance, peasants try to reduce medical costs wherever possible; for instance their average hospital stay is significantly shorter than that of town-dwellers with insurance. But the costs are still often beyond their means. In a survey of over a thousand poor households, almost half said debts incurred by illness had tumbled them into poverty. Rises in the fees of village doctors and in the cost of drugs also affect poor people disproportionately. Meanwhile the disbanding of the communes means that the biomedical services offered at the village or township level are not likely to improve, especially in poor or remote regions: in 1985 a national survey showed that 22% of village health stations did not have a blood-pressure cuff, 28% had no sterilizing machine.

The response of the government to the growing imbalance between urban and rural health services was to attempt to establish a specialized public TCM hospital in every county. Officials felt that this would provide a relatively cheap form of medicine that was readily acceptable to the rural population. By 1992, out of altogether 61,532 public hospitals (most of which already offered TCM in parallel to biomedical services) 2269 were devoted exclusively to TCM; the state employed 243,502 TCM physicians, compared to 1,327,875 biomedical doctors. Meanwhile private TCM clinics and practices have sprung up everywhere, including of course those of the 1.3 million former Barefoot Doctors who have retrained as Country Doctors.

It seems true that despite better education, exposure to biomedical ideas at school and in clinics, and enthusiasm for the general idea of science and technology, the concepts of TCM have rooted more deeply than those of biomedicine in the minds of most rural Chinese — and not a few urban Chinese too. In 1979 C.C. Chen noted rural patients' preference for Chinese medicine in a commune health center in Sichuan. The TCM clinic was bustling, with a dozen physicians prescribing drugs; a few streets away the modern Western-style clinic was almost empty. Judith Farquhar observed the same thing in Zouping, a county town in Shandong province, in 1993, where some 40 small private TCM clinics were thriving while the state clinics languished. Patients were said to prefer the private clinics to public health services because they were more conveniently located, required less paperwork and charged less — even though they were allowed to charge as much as a 30% mark-up on drugs.

Part of the explanation for popular preferences for TCM may be epidemiological. The Chinese population is ageing and degenerative diseases have become more common. Among the younger population, biomedicine's success in bringing acute diseases under control has opened the way for a greater preoccupation with allergies and chronic diseases. Because of its emphasis on organic processes and on the specific characteristics of individual patients, TCM has a long tradition of dealing with 'difficult problems,' and it is said by medical scientists to achieve good results in the prevention and treatment of cardio-cerebro-vascular diseases and malignant tumors (now among the leading causes of death), as well as arthritis, immunological diseases and skin disorders. Much medical research in the PRC now aims to 'integrate' the best features of biomedical and TCM therapies.

TCM is currently favored in Britain and the United States as an alternative by people who think of biomedicine as 'reductive' and prefer the 'holism' they see in Chinese medicine. Holism is a term that can be interpreted in several ways. If it is taken to mean a philosophy that conceptualizes the body and its workings as a microcosm of a grand, somehow spiritual cosmos, then we must remember that in TCM the spiritual and cosmic element often plays a very minor role in the reasoning of classically-trained physicians, while patients are frequently quite ignorant of the underlying cosmological principles. If holism is taken to imply an organic approach to the body, in which the treatment of any part is considered to affect the whole, then TCM is undoubtedly holistic. Finally, if holism means that no distinction is drawn between mind and body as objects of healing, then once again TCM can be considered holistic, for it regularly treats what we would regard as mental disorders as part of a broader, physiologically-based syndrome — often with great success.

The organic and emotional holism of Chinese medicine aspect is appreciated in China too, where it is commonly said that biomedicine treats symptoms while TCM treats the fundamental causes of a person's sickness. Yet the 'cosmological', mystical, or religious elements that many anti-modernist Westerners hanker after hardly feature at all in the classical texts of TCM as they have reached us today after centuries of systematic secularization, and since 1949 all officially-endorsed research and writing has insisted on the scientific, materialistic nature of Chinese models of the body. Even so it seems that admitting folk healing into the fold of TCM in the 1950s and 1960s has opened up the way for many ideas and practices that are a long way from conventional science. One good example is *qigong*, 'working with *qi* energy.' *Qigong* experts used *qi* in a variety of ways, from circus feats like having a steamroller run over your chest, to healing by laying on hands. TCM is centrally concerned with ensuring the healthy circulation and equilibrium of *qi*, but this is achieved within the patient's body through acupuncture or prescription. TCM theory offers no explanation for the mobilization of *qi* typical of *qigong*. Until a few years ago *qigong* was condemned by the government as 'superstition.' Recently the medical establishment has been showing interest in the processes of *qigong* healing and how they might be incorporated into TCM, and although their relation with the state is still uneasy, the number and popularity of *qigong* healers has been growing steadily.

Furthermore, as Judith Farquhar remarks, by emphasizing the importance of the individual and their personal circumstances in diagnosis and therapy, TCM "valorizes the personal"[7] in a way that appeals to many Chinese exhausted by decades of suppressing their individual identities in favour of the interests of the collective. In the 1960s medical publications glorified the collective production of knowledge by the masses, but in the 1980s the cult of the master doctor was revived in the TCM colleges. Such masters gather around them a band of disciple-pupils, who revere them for their learning and expertise; as their published cases show, they diagnose and prescribe in a dialogue with ancient physicians, confirming their authority by tying themselves into a lineage of erudition that stretches back for centuries. Similarly we might cite the huge current popularity of 'secret prescriptions' that have been handed down in physician families for generations. Another dimension of the revival of the personal is shown in the case Farquhar describes of a small-town doctor who has built up a successful practice diagnosing and treating "difficult and doubtful diseases" with the help of cosmological analysis based on the patient's horoscope.[8] Maybe the widespread preference for TCM also signals a renewed attachment to that which is distinctively Chinese, arising this time not from the fear of succumbing to Western imperialism, but rather from confidence that China can forge its own path to a bright future.

The Chinese experience of medicine in the course of the twentieth century offers a curious paradox: the introduction and consolidation of biomedical science and institutions has reinvigorated TCM. During the turmoil and crisis of the Republican period, from 1911 to 1949, most Chinese reformers believed that TCM should be abandoned in favor of 'scientific' medicine. As Marxists, the Communist leaders who established the PRC in 1949 were firm believers in the need to replace superstition with science, but political circumstances as well as the lack of economic resources led them to promote the 'scientization' of TCM, and to develop a health service in which biomedical and TCM facilities were given equal support. In the post-Maoist era marked by the inauguration of the New Economic Policies in 1979, public medical facilities are obliged to operate in competition with private doctors and clinics, and this seems to promise a further enracination of faith in TCM in rural areas, while in the cities both the public and medical practitioners are largely committed to a fusion of TCM and biomedical therapy. While TCM remains a dubious 'alternative' in the West, in China it is well on the way to remoulding the science of medicine.

REFERENCES

1. Arthur Kleinman, *Patients and Healers in the Context of Culture: an Exploration of the Borderland between Anthropology, Medicine and Psychiatry.* (Berkeley: University of California Press, 1980), 71–118.
2. C.C. Chen (in collaboration with Frederica M. Bunge), *Medicine in Rural China: a Personal Account.* (Berkeley: University of California Press, 1989), p. 9.
3. C.C. Chen, (1989), p. 23.
4. *Ibid.*
5. Gail E. Henderson and Myron S. Cohen, *The Chinese Hospital: a Socialist Work Unit.* (New Haven: Yale University Press, 1984), p. 63.
6. 'East cures West', *Far Eastern Economic Review* (21 October 1993), pp. 36–41.
7. Judity Farquhar, 'Market magic: getting rich and getting personal in medicine after Mao,' *American Ethnologist* (1996), **23, 2**: 257.

8.   Farquhar (1996), **240**: 247–50.
9.   Lu and Needham, p. 165.
10.  *Barefoot Doctor's Manual*: p. 127.

## FURTHER READINGS

*A Barefoot Doctor's Manual: the American Translation of the Official Chinese Paramedical Manual.* (Philadelphia: Running Press, 1977).

Croizier, Ralph, *Traditional Medicine in Chinese Society: Science, Nationalism, and the Tensions of Cultural Change.* (Harvard University Press, 1968).

Farquhar, Judith, *Knowing Practice: the Clinical Encounter of Chinese Medicine.* (Boulder, Co.: Westview, 1994).

Hinton, Carma and Richard Gordon (dirs), *To Taste a Hundred Herbs: Gods, Ancestors and Medicine in a Chinese Village.* (New York: Longbow Group, 1988).

Hsu, Elisabeth, *The Transmission of Chinese Medicine.* (Cambridge: Cambridge University Press, 1999).

Kaptchuk, Ted J., *The Web that has no Weaver: Understanding Chinese Medicine.* (New York: Congdon and Weed, 1983).

Leslie, Charles and Allan Young (eds), *Paths to Asian Medical Knowledge.* (Berkeley: University of California Press, 1992).

Lock, Margaret, *East Asian Medicine in Urban Japan: Varieties of Medical Experience.* (Berkeley: University of California Press, 1980).

Lu, Gwei-Djen and Joseph Needham, *Celestial Lancets: a History and Rationale of Acupuncture and Moxa.* (Cambridge: Cambridge University Press, 1980).

Lucas, AnElissa, *Chinese Medical Modernization: Comparative Policy Continuities, 1930s–1980s.* (New York: Praeger, 1982).

Ohnuki-Tierney, Emiko, *Illness and Culture in Contemporary Japan.* (Cambridge: Cambridge University Press, 1984).

Sivin, Nathan, *Traditional Medicine in Contemporary China.* (Ann Arbor: University of Michigan Press, 1988).

Unschuld, Paul, *Medicine in China: a History of Ideas.* (Berkeley: University of California Press, 1985).

Unschuld, Paul, *Medicine in China: Nan-ching, the Classic of Difficult Issues.* (Berkeley: University of California Press, 1986).

*The Yellow Emperor's Classic of Internal Medicine* (tr. Ilsa Veith). (Berkeley: University of California Press, 1987).

# Index

Tranquilizers, 340
Transgenic mice, 439
Transplant surgery, 458, 481
Transvestism, 269
Treponema, 23
Tropical medicine and hygiene, 70, 98
Tuberculosis (TB), 13, 24, 44, 47, 78, 91, 102, 147, 351, 374, 387, 443
Turner's syndrome, 407
Tuskegee, 462–463
Tumor differentiation, 421–422
Typhoid Mary, *see* Mary Mallone
Typhus, 52, 74, 147, 392

Ultrasound, 178, 408, 418
UNICEF, 98, 103
Union Carbide, 177
Union of Medical Workers, 63
Union of the Physically Impaired Against Segregation, 376
United States Operations Mission (USOM), 101
Upjohn, 150
Urinalysis, 422–423

Vaccine, 24, 47, 392
Vaillery-Radot, Pasteur, 76
Valium, 148, 340, 647, 648
Van de Velde, T.H., 270–271
Vascular repair, 590
Vasectomy, 265
Venepuncture, 422
Venereal disease, 265, 272, 490, 663
Veratrine, 141
Vietnam War, 376
Viswanathan, A., 101
Vitamins, 48, 145
Vivisection, 118
Voluntary Aid Detachment (VAD), 521

Wagner-Jauregg, Julius von, 333
Wagner-Murray-Dingell Bill, 137
Waksman, Selman, 24, 147
Waksman Institute of Microbiology, 147
Warren, Marjorie, 620
Wartime, 589–600
  biological weapons, 595
  blood transfusion, 590
  doctors taught to kill, 595
  Boer War, 590
  casualty clearing stations, 590
  dentistry, 533–534, 590
  experimentation, 596
  field ambulances, 590
  field dressings, 590
  malingering, 596–598
  Medical Boards, 596
  medical officers, 589
  nursing, 593
  orthopedics, 591
  psychiatric breakdown, 594
  stretcher bearers, 593
  triage, 592
  venereal disease, 593, 594
  Vietnam, 376
  WWI (World War I), 196, 223, 371, 378, 490, 521, 561, 589, 656–657
  WWII (World War II), 374, 513, 523–525, 589, 621–622, 662, 713
  X-rays, 590
Wasserman reaction, 425
Water cure, 115
Watson, John Broadus, 292
Weider, Jo, 211
Weimar constitution, 42
Weininger, Otto, 86
Welch, Claude E., 661–662
Welch, William H., 26
Welfare State, 155–170
  aging populations, 163
  Counter-Reformation, 159, 160
  fiscal stress, 159
  globalization, 163
  Gross Domestic Product (GDP), 157
  oil price rise, 158
  proposition, 13, 158
  public expenditure, 157
  single currency, 163
    1930–1970, 125–140
    consolidation, 129–132
    convergence, 126–127
    divergence, 127–128, 134–138
    doctors, 128–129
    golden age of welfare 1945–1975, 132–134
Wellcome Trust UK, 26, 27
Well Women's Clinic, 118
Wertheimer, Max, 293
Whooping cough, 392
Williams, Daniel Hale, 658–659